한 권으로 끝내는

해커스 토익 600+

LC + RC + VOCA

실시간 토익시험 정답확인&해설강의
Hackers.co.kr

한 권으로 끝내는 해커스 토익 600+ LC+RC+VOCA

토익,
한 권으로
목표 달성하세요.

취업, 졸업, 공무원 시험, 승진…

여러분의 멋진 꿈을 향해 가는 길에 토익 점수가 걸림돌이 되어서는 안 되겠죠?
《해커스 토익 600+》는 여러분이 다른 중요한 일들에 더 집중할 수 있도록,
꼭 필요한 내용만으로 토익 목표 점수를 빠르게 달성할 수 있게 구성되었습니다.

CONTENTS

책의 특징과 구성   6
토익 소개   8
파트별 출제 유형 및 전략   10
600+ 정복 학습 플랜   20

LC

LC 기초 다지기   24

PART 1

DAY 01	사람 중심 사진	30
DAY 02	사물/풍경 중심 사진	36

PART 2

DAY 03	의문사 의문문: Who, What/Which	44
DAY 04	의문사 의문문: Where, When	50
DAY 05	의문사 의문문: Why, How	56
DAY 06	일반 의문문 및 선택 의문문	62
DAY 07	부정 의문문 및 부가 의문문	68
DAY 08	제안/제공/요청 의문문 및 평서문	74

PART 3

DAY 09	전체 대화 관련 문제	82
DAY 10	세부 사항 관련 문제	88
DAY 11	회사 업무 및 사무기기 관련 대화	96
DAY 12	인사 및 사내 행사 관련 대화	100
DAY 13	마케팅/판매/재무 관련 대화	104
DAY 14	일상생활 관련 대화	108
DAY 15	여행 및 여가 관련 대화	112

PART 4

DAY 16	음성 메시지 및 회의 발췌	118
DAY 17	공지 및 관광 안내	124
DAY 18	연설 및 강연	130
DAY 19	방송 및 보도	136
DAY 20	광고 및 소개	142

RC

RC 기초 다지기   150

PART 5

DAY 01	명사	빈출 어휘 명사 1	156
DAY 02	대명사	빈출 어휘 명사 2	164
DAY 03	형용사와 부사	빈출 어휘 명사 3	172
DAY 04	전치사	빈출 어휘 명사 4	180
DAY 05	동사의 형태와 수일치	빈출 어휘 동사 1	188
DAY 06	동사의 종류와 태	빈출 어휘 동사 2	196
DAY 07	동사의 시제	빈출 어휘 동사 3	204
DAY 08	to 부정사와 동명사	빈출 어휘 형용사 1	212
DAY 09	분사	빈출 어휘 형용사 2	220
DAY 10	등위/상관접속사와 관계절	빈출 어휘 부사 1	228
DAY 11	부사절과 명사절	빈출 어휘 부사 2	236
DAY 12	비교 구문	빈출 어휘 어구	246

PART 6

DAY 13	문맥 파악 문제: 문법	256
DAY 14	문맥 파악 문제: 어휘	262
DAY 15	문맥 파악 문제: 문장	268

PART 7

DAY 16	이메일/편지 및 메시지 대화문	276
DAY 17	양식 및 광고	286
DAY 18	기사 및 안내문	296
DAY 19	공고 및 회람	306
DAY 20	다중 지문	316

시험장에도 들고 가는 토익 기출 VOCA [별책]

DAY 01 PART 1 기출 어휘	DAY 11 PART 5&6 기출 어휘
DAY 02 PART 1 기출 어휘	DAY 12 PART 5&6 기출 어휘
DAY 03 PART 2 기출 어휘	DAY 13 PART 5&6 기출 어휘
DAY 04 PART 2 기출 어휘	DAY 14 PART 5&6 기출 어휘
DAY 05 PART 3 기출 어휘	DAY 15 PART 5&6 기출 어휘
DAY 06 PART 3 기출 어휘	DAY 16 PART 5&6 기출 어휘
DAY 07 PART 3 기출 어휘	DAY 17 PART 5&6 기출 어휘
DAY 08 PART 4 기출 어휘	DAY 18 PART 7 기출 어휘
DAY 09 PART 4 기출 어휘	DAY 19 PART 7 기출 어휘
DAY 10 PART 4 기출 어휘	DAY 20 PART 7 기출 어휘

| 실전모의고사 [별책]
| 온라인 실전모의고사 [Hackers.co.kr]
| 해설집 정답·해석·해설 [책 속의 책]

책의 특징과 구성

01 LC, RC, VOCA를 한 권으로 완성!

LC

RC
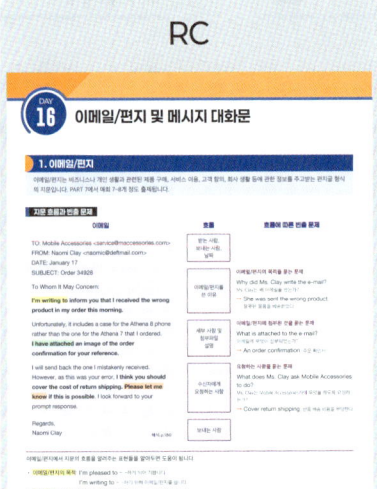

VOCA

02 토익 최신 출제 경향 완벽 반영!

최신 경향 및 전략

3초컷 정답 공식
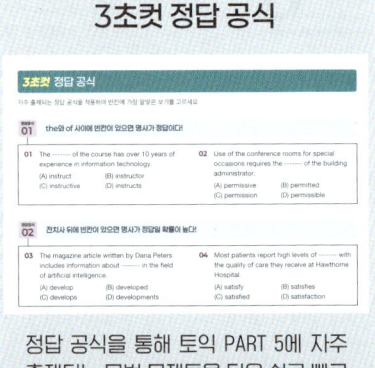

빈출 어휘
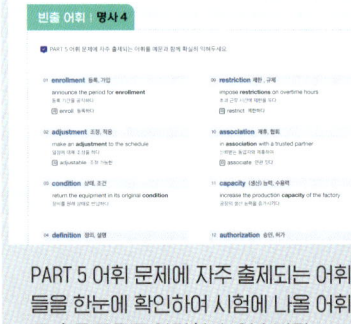

최신 토익 출제 경향을 파악하고, 이를 바탕으로 목표 점수를 효과적으로 달성할 수 있는 전략을 익힐 수 있습니다.

정답 공식을 통해 토익 PART 5에 자주 출제되는 문법 문제들을 더욱 쉽고 빠르게 풀 수 있습니다.

PART 5 어휘 문제에 자주 출제되는 어휘들을 한눈에 확인하여 시험에 나올 어휘를 효율적으로 암기할 수 있습니다.

한 권으로 끝내는 해커스 토익 600+ LC+RC+VOCA

03 기초부터 실전까지 함께 학습하여 빠르게 목표 달성!

기초 다지기

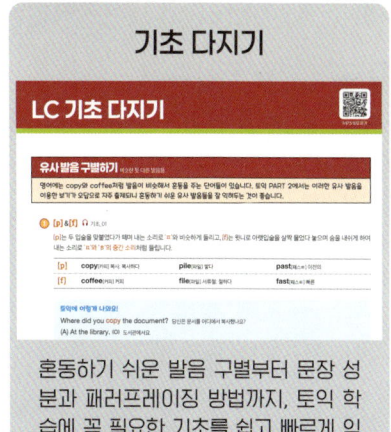

혼동하기 쉬운 발음 구별부터 문장 성분과 패러프레이징 방법까지, 토익 학습에 꼭 필요한 기초를 쉽고 빠르게 익힐 수 있습니다.

HACKERS PRACTICE / HACKERS TEST

각 유형별로 학습한 기출 포인트와 전략을 연습 문제에 바로 적용한 후, 실전 문제를 통해 한 번 더 점검하면 실전 토익에 필요한 실력을 다질 수 있습니다.

실전모의고사

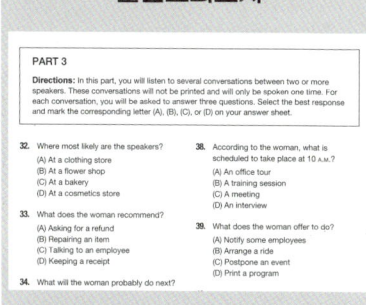

토익 경향이 완벽하게 반영된 실전모의고사를 통해 실전 감각을 한층 더 키울 수 있습니다.

04 다양한 부가 학습자료와 상세한 해설로 확실하게 복습!

단어암기장

핵심 어휘를 정리한 단어암기장과 MP3로, 이동할 때나 자투리 시간에 효율적으로 단어를 암기할 수 있습니다.

받아쓰기 & 쉐도잉 워크북

교재에 수록된 핵심 문장을 복습할 수 있는 받아쓰기 & 쉐도잉 워크북으로, 토익 리스닝에 필요한 기초 실력을 쌓을 수 있습니다.

해설집

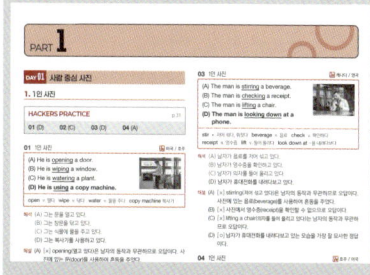

정확한 해석과 해설로 문제를 확실하게 이해할 수 있습니다. 오답에 대한 상세한 설명을 통해 틀렸던 문제의 원인을 파악하고 보완할 수 있습니다.

책의 특징과 구성 7

토익 소개

■ 토익이란 무엇인가?

TOEIC은 Test of English for International Communication의 약자로 영어가 모국어가 아닌 사람들을 대상으로 언어 본래의 기능인 '커뮤니케이션' 능력에 중점을 두고 일상생활 또는 국제 업무 등에 필요한 실용영어 능력을 평가하는 시험입니다. 토익은 일상생활 및 비즈니스 현장에서 필요로 하는 내용을 평가하기 위해 개발되었으며, 다음과 같은 실용적인 주제들을 주로 다루고 있습니다.

- 협력 개발: 연구, 제품 개발
- 재무 회계: 대출, 투자, 세금, 회계, 은행 업무
- 일반 업무: 계약, 협상, 마케팅, 판매
- 기술 영역: 전기, 공업 기술, 컴퓨터, 실험실
- 사무 영역: 회의, 서류 업무
- 물품 구입: 쇼핑, 물건 주문, 대금 지불
- 식사: 레스토랑, 회식, 만찬
- 문화: 극장, 스포츠, 피크닉
- 건강: 의료 보험, 병원 진료, 치과
- 제조: 생산 조립 라인, 공장 경영
- 직원: 채용, 은퇴, 급여, 진급, 고용 기회
- 주택: 부동산, 이사, 기업 부지

■ 토익 시험의 구성

구성	내용	문항 수	시간	배점
Listening Test	PART 1 | 사진 묘사 PART 2 | 질의 응답 PART 3 | 짧은 대화 PART 4 | 짧은 담화	6문항(1번-6번) 25문항(7번-31번) 39문항, 13지문(32번-70번) 30문항, 10지문(71번-100번)	45분	495점

Reading Test	PART 5 | 단문 빈칸 채우기(문법/어휘)
	PART 6 | 장문 빈칸 채우기(문법/어휘/문장 고르기)
	PART 7 | 지문 읽고 문제 풀기(독해)
	    - 단일 지문(Single Passage)
	    - 이중 지문(Double Passages)
	    - 삼중 지문(Triple Passages)
		30문항(101번-130번)
		16문항, 4지문(131번-146번)
		54문항, 15지문(147번-200번)
		- 29문항, 10지문(147번-175번)
		- 10문항, 2세트(176번-185번)
		- 15문항, 3세트(186번-200번)
			75분	495점

Total	7 PARTS	200문항	120분	990점

■ 토익, 접수부터 성적 확인까지!

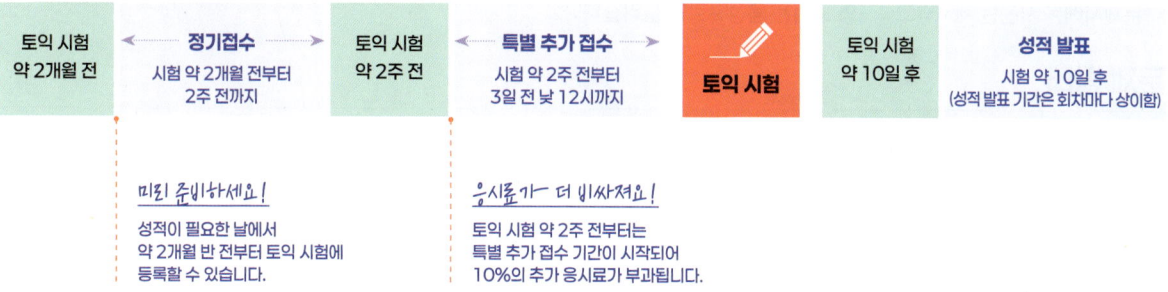

1. 토익 접수
- 인터넷 접수 기간을 TOEIC위원회 인터넷 사이트(www.toeic.co.kr), 혹은 공식 애플리케이션에서 확인하세요. 정기 토익은 시험 약 2개월 전부터 접수가 가능하며, 특별 추가 접수 기간에는 정기접수 기간 응시료에서 10%가 추가된 응시료로 접수할 수 있습니다.
- 추가 토익 시험은 2월과 8월에 있으며 이외에도 연중 상시로 시행되니 인터넷으로 확인하고 접수해야 합니다.
- 접수 시, jpg 형식의 사진 파일이 필요하므로 미리 준비해야 합니다.

2. 토익 응시
- 토익 응시일 이전에 시험 장소 및 수험번호를 미리 확인합니다.
- 시험 당일 신분증이 없으면 시험에 응시할 수 없으므로, 반드시 ETS에서 요구하는 신분증(주민등록증, 운전면허증, 공무원증 등)을 지참해야 합니다. ETS에서 인정하는 신분증 종류는 TOEIC위원회 인터넷 사이트(www.toeic.co.kr)에서 확인 가능합니다.

3. 성적 확인

성적 발표일	시험일로부터 약 10일 이후 (성적 발표 기간은 회차마다 상이함)
성적 확인 방법	TOEIC위원회 인터넷 사이트(www.toeic.co.kr) 혹은 공식 애플리케이션
성적표 수령 방법	우편 수령 또는 온라인 출력 (시험 접수 시 선택) *온라인 출력은 성적 발표 즉시 발급 가능하나, 우편 수령은 약 7일가량의 발송 기간이 소요될 수 있음

파트별 출제 유형 및 전략

PART 1 (6문제)

- PART 1은 주어진 4개의 보기 중에서 사진의 상황을 가장 잘 묘사한 보기를 선택하는 파트입니다.
- 문제지에는 사진만 제시되고 4개의 보기는 음성으로만 들려줍니다.

문제 형태

[문제지]
1.

[음성]
Number 1.
Look at the picture marked number 1 in your test book.

(A) A woman is serving a meal.
(B) A woman is washing a bowl.
(C) A woman is drinking from a bottle.
(D) A woman is preparing some food.

출제 경향 및 대비 전략

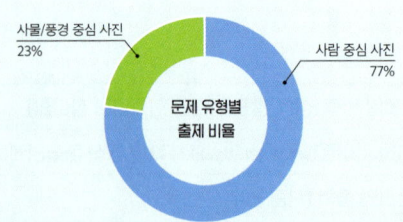

사람 중심 사진이 평균 4~5문제로 가장 많이 출제되며, 사물/풍경 중심 사진은 주로 후반에 평균 1~2문제 출제됩니다.

핵심 대비 전략

보기를 듣기 전에 사진 유형을 확인하고 관련 표현을 미리 연상합니다.
보기를 듣기 전에 사람의 유무 및 수에 따라 사진 유형을 확인하고, 사람의 동작/상태 또는 사물의 상태/위치와 관련된 표현들을 미리 연상하면 보기를 훨씬 명확하게 들을 수 있어 정답 선택이 쉬워집니다.

PART 2 (25문제)

- PART 2는 주어진 질문이나 진술에 가장 적절한 응답을 선택하는 파트입니다.
- 질문과 3개의 보기는 문제지에 제시되지 않고 음성으로만 들려줍니다.

문제 형태

[문제지]	[음성]
7. Mark your answer on the answer sheet.	Number 7. Where is the nearest park? **(A) There's one on Lincoln Avenue.** (B) No, I don't drive. (C) I'm nearly finished.

출제 경향 및 대비 전략

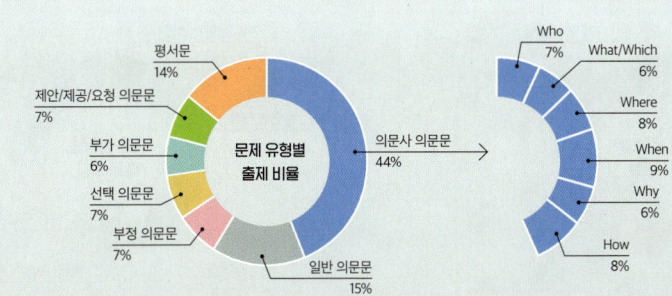

의문사 의문문이 평균 11문제로 가장 많이 출제되며, 일반 의문문이 평균 4문제로 그다음으로 많이 출제됩니다.

핵심 대비 전략

질문의 첫 단어는 절대 놓치지 않고 듣습니다.
PART 2에서 평균 11문제 정도 출제되는 의문사 의문문은 첫 단어인 의문사만 들어도 대부분 정답을 선택할 수 있습니다. 단, 부가 의문문은 평서문 뒤에 덧붙여진 'isn't it'이나 'right', 선택 의문문은 질문 중간에 접속사 'or'를 듣고 그 유형을 파악해야 합니다.

파트별 출제 유형 및 전략

PART 3 (39문제)

- PART 3는 2~3명의 대화를 듣고 이와 관련된 3개의 문제의 가장 적절한 답을 선택하는 파트로 13개의 대화가 출제됩니다.
- 문제지에는 각 문제의 질문과 4개의 보기가 제시되며, 일부 문제는 시각 자료가 함께 제시됩니다.
  음성으로는 각 대화와 이에 대한 3개의 문제의 질문을 들려줍니다.

문제 형태

[문제지]

32. What did the woman do during lunchtime?

　　(A) Spoke with a supervisor
　　(B) Called an important client
　　(C) Visited another company
　　(D) Finished a report

[음성]

Questions 32 through 34 refer to the following conversation.

W: I'm sorry I couldn't make it for lunch today. Our CEO wanted to talk to me about the advertising campaign for Sorel Incorporated. This is a big project, and I'm a little nervous about it.
M: Don't worry. Our clients are always happy with your work. I can help you come up with some ideas.
W: That would be great. I could really use some help.

Number 32.
What did the woman do during lunchtime?

출제 경향 및 대비 전략

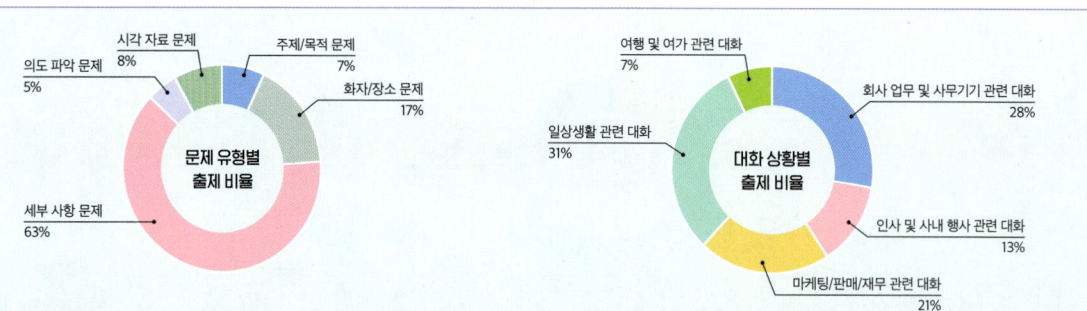

세부 사항을 묻는 문제가 가장 많이 출제되며, 주제/목적 및 화자/장소 문제도 꾸준히 높은 비율로 출제됩니다. 대화 상황은 회사 업무 및 사무기기 관련 대화와 일상생활 관련 대화가 가장 많이 출제됩니다.

핵심 대비 전략

대화를 듣기 전에 반드시 문제를 먼저 읽어야 합니다.
질문의 핵심 어구를 미리 읽으면 대화의 어느 부분을 중점적으로 들어야 할지 전략을 세울 수 있습니다. 시각 자료가 제시된 문제라면, 문제와 시각 자료를 함께 파악합니다.

대화의 초반은 반드시 들어야 합니다.
PART 3에서는 대화의 초반에 언급된 내용 중 80% 이상이 문제로 출제되며, 특히 주제/목적 문제나 화자/장소 문제처럼 전체 대화 관련 문제에 대한 정답의 단서는 대부분 대화의 초반에 언급됩니다.

PART 4 (30문제)

- PART 4는 1명의 담화를 듣고 이와 관련된 3개의 문제의 가장 적절한 답을 선택하는 파트로 10개의 담화가 출제됩니다.
- 문제지에는 각 문제의 질문과 4개의 보기가 제시되며, 일부 문제는 시각 자료가 함께 제시됩니다.
  음성으로는 각 담화와 이에 대한 3개의 문제의 질문을 들려줍니다.

문제 형태

[문제지]

71. What did the speaker do yesterday?

   (A) Raised dish prices
   (B) Attended a staff gathering
   (C) Met with customers
   (D) **Sent menu information**

[음성]

Questions 71 through 73 refer to the following talk.

As many of you already know, our restaurant's menu will be updated soon. I sent everyone an e-mail with the details yesterday, but I I'll quickly go over the main changes now. First, the prices of our dinner menu items have been reduced by 10 percent to attract more evening customers. Some new dishes will be offered as well. I will now pass around a list of these dishes and the ingredients they will contain.

Number 71.
What did the speaker do yesterday?

출제 경향 및 대비 전략

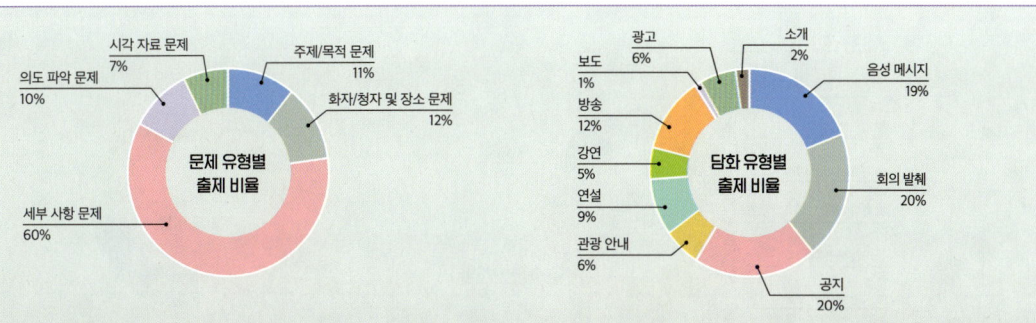

PART 4는 PART 3와 문제 유형이 거의 동일하며, 세부 사항을 묻는 문제가 가장 많이 출제됩니다. 담화는 유형별로 골고루 등장하지만, 음성 메시지, 회의 발췌, 공지가 꾸준히 가장 많이 출제됩니다.

핵심 대비 전략

담화를 듣기 전에 반드시 문제를 먼저 읽어야 합니다.
질문의 핵심 어구를 미리 읽으면 담화의 어느 부분을 중점적으로 들어야 할지 전략을 세울 수 있습니다. 시각 자료가 제시된 문제라면, 문제와 시각 자료를 함께 파악합니다.

담화의 초반은 반드시 들어야 합니다.
PART 4에서도 담화의 초반에 언급된 내용 중 80% 이상이 문제로 출제되며, 특히 주제/목적 문제나 화자/청자 및 장소 문제처럼 전체 담화 관련 문제에 대한 정답의 단서는 대부분 담화의 초반에 언급됩니다.

파트별 출제 유형 및 전략

PART 5 (30문제)

- PART 5는 한 문장의 빈칸에 알맞은 문법 사항이나 어휘를 골라 채우는 파트입니다.
- PART 7 문제 풀이에 시간이 모자라지 않으려면 각 문제를 20~22초 내로, 총 30문제를 약 11분 내에 풀어야 합니다.

문제 형태

1. 문법

> 101. Amy Wilson is a recent graduate who ------- a month ago to help the marketing team with graphic design.
> (A) hired
> (B) hiring
> **(C) was hired**
> (D) is hiring

2. 어휘

> 102. In spite of the traffic delays, Mr. Cho showed up ------- for his coworker's retirement party.
> (A) gradually
> (B) intensely
> (C) considerably
> **(D) punctually**

출제 경향 및 대비 전략

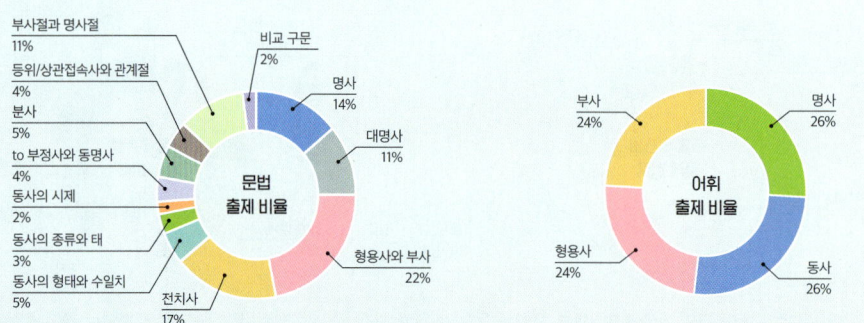

문법 문제가 평균 20개, 어휘 문제가 평균 10개 출제됩니다. 문법 문제에서는 전치사 문제가 매회 3~4개, 접속사 문제가 매회 1~3개씩 꾸준히 출제되고, 어휘 문제에서는 명사, 동사, 형용사, 부사가 거의 비슷한 비율로 출제됩니다.

핵심 대비 전략

보기를 보고 문법 문제인지, 어휘 문제인지를 파악합니다.
보기가 어근은 같지만 형태가 다른 단어들로 구성되어 있다면 문법 문제, 같은 품사의 어휘들로 구성되어 있으면 어휘 문제입니다.

자주 출제되는 빈출 어휘를 미리 암기합니다.
PART 5에 특히 자주 출제되는 최신 기출 어휘를 암기해 두어야 합니다. PART 5에 자주 출제되는 어휘는 RC DAY 01~12의 빈출 어휘 리스트와 VOCA (시험장에도 들고 가는 토익 기출 VOCA) DAY 11~17에서 학습할 수 있습니다.

PART 6 (16문제)

- PART 6는 한 지문 내 4개의 빈칸에 알맞은 문법 사항이나 어휘, 또는 문장을 골라 채우는 파트로 4지문이 출제됩니다.
- PART 7 문제 풀이에 시간이 모자라지 않으려면 각 문제를 25~30초 내로, 총 16문제를 약 8분 내에 풀어야 합니다.

문제 형태

Questions 131-134 refer to the following e-mail.

Dear Ms. Swerter,

It was a treat to see your group ------- its music at the community event in Morristown. Do you think you could do the same for us at a private gathering next month? My company ------- a welcoming celebration for some clients. -------.
We are planning a special dinner and are hoping your group can provide the accompanying entertainment. We'd also like to book the dancers who were with you at the concert. Their performance was quite ------- to watch. Our guests would surely enjoy seeing both acts together. Please let me know.

Shannon Lemmick

131. (A) act
 (B) explain
 (C) perform
 (D) observe

132. **(A) will be hosting**
 (B) hosted
 (C) hosts

133. (A) I'd like to buy tickets for the afternoon show.
 (B) You may request their services for an additional charge.
 (C) It will be their first time meeting with my company's staff.
 (D) We approve of the schedule you have proposed.

134. (A) tough

출제 경향 및 대비 전략

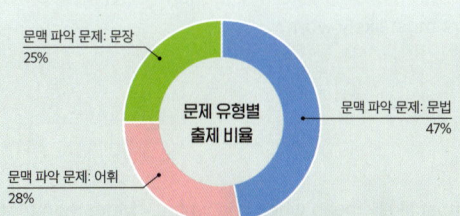

문법 문제가 평균 7~8문제, 어휘 문제가 평균 4~5문제, 문장 고르기 문제가 4문제 출제됩니다. 문법 문제와 어휘 문제 중 평균 6~7문제는 앞뒤 문장이나 전체 지문의 문맥 파악이 추가로 필요한 문제들입니다.

핵심 대비 전략

문법 문제로만 출제되는 문법과 어휘를 익혀둡니다.
PART 6의 문맥 파악이 필요한 문법 문제로는 주로 시제, 대명사, 접속부사가 출제되고, 어휘 문제로는 명사 어휘가 자주 출제됩니다. 따라서 이 유형들을 확실히 학습해 두면 문맥 문제 풀이가 쉬워집니다. PART 6에 자주 출제되는 어휘는 VOCA(시험장에도 들고 가는 토익 기출 VOCA) DAY 11~17에서 학습할 수 있습니다.

문맥에 알맞은 문장을 고르는 방법을 익혀둡니다.
빈칸 바로 앞뒤의 내용을 확인하는 전형적인 풀이 방법 외에도, 보기 안의 대명사 또는 연결어를 활용하여 문제를 풀이하는 방법을 익혀둡니다.

파트별 출제 유형 및 전략

PART 7 (54문제)

- PART 7은 제시된 지문을 읽고 이와 관련된 2~5개의 문제의 가장 적절한 답을 선택하는 파트입니다.
- PART 7은 단일 지문(Single Passage), 이중 지문(Double Passages), 삼중 지문(Triple Passages)으로 나뉘며, 단일 지문 10개에서 29문제, 이중 지문 2세트에서 10문제, 삼중 지문 3세트에서 15문제가 출제됩니다.
- PART 7의 모든 문제를 제한 시간 내에 풀려면 한 문제를 약 1분 내에 풀어야 합니다.

문제 형태

1. 단일 지문(Single Passage)

Questions 149-150 refer to the following text-message chain.

Natasha Lee 4:08 P.M.
Robert, about the sponsorship packages for the Shoreland Music Festival, do you want to go for the Platinum package? It allows us to broadcast commercials during the event.

Robert Brown 4:09 P.M.
That would give us good exposure. Plus, we can put up company banners at the venue.

Natasha Lee 4:10 P.M.
That's right. So, should I go ahead and sign us up? The deadline is this Friday.

Robert Brown 4:10 P.M.
Well, we can't spend any more than $6,000 on this. How much is it?

Natasha Lee 4:12 P.M.
More than that. How about the Gold sponsorship package then? It costs $5,250, and festival announcers will mention our company over the loudspeakers throughout the day.

Robert Brown 4:13 P.M.
That sounds OK to me. Send me all the details once you're done.

149. In which department do the writers most likely work?

(A) Accounting
(B) Marketing
(C) Customer service
(D) Human resources

150. At 4:12 P.M., what does Ms. Lee most likely mean when she writes, "More than that"?

(A) She believes that registering after the deadline is acceptable.
(B) She acknowledges that a cost exceeds a budgeted amount.
(C) She would like to receive some additional sponsorship benefits.
(D) She doubts that $6,000 is their maximum spending allowance.

2. 이중 지문(Double Passages)

Questions 176-180 refer to the following e-mails.

To: Natalie Mercer <n.mercer@silverfield.com>
From: Robert Altieri <r.altieri@silverfield.com>
Subject: Digital Creators Conference (DCC)
Date: October 9
Attachment: DCC passes

Natalie,

I have attached four passes for you and your team to the upcoming DCC in San Francisco and would now like to go ahead and book your accommodations there. I know you stayed at the Gordon Suites and the Grand Burgess Hotel in previous years, but I think I have found some better options. Please indicate which of the following hotels you wish to stay at in response to this e-mail.

The Bismarck Hotel is close to the convention center but unfortunately does not offer access to Wi-Fi. Those who need to work from the hotel may thus be interested in the Newburg Plaza, which provides free Internet use. However, staying at this location would require the reservation of a car service, as it is a 20-minute drive from the conference venue.

Let me know which one you prefer when you have a moment. Also, please note that the passes I have attached allow entry to the event halls on all four days. Meals are not included, but there are places to purchase food at nearby restaurants. Thank you.

Robert

To: Robert Altieri <r.altieri@silverfield.com>
From: Natalie Mercer <n.mercer@silverfield.com>
Subject: Re: Digital Creators Conference (DCC)
Date: October 9

Robert,

I think it's best for us to have access to the Internet at the hotel. Some of my team members will be convening on evenings following the conference events and may want to reference information online. As for the car service, I believe we can have expenses reimbursed for that. Everyone agrees that a 20-minute ride doesn't sound like a major inconvenience.

But before you make the reservation, could you check what the rates are for parking at the hotel? Francine will be taking her own vehicle to San Francisco and will need to leave it in a lot for the duration of the conference. Thanks in advance.

Natalie

---

176. Why did Mr. Altieri write the e-mail?

(A) To invite a guest to speak at a conference
(B) To ask about a preference for a trip
(C) To explain a travel expense policy
(D) To ask for airline recommendations

177. What is NOT mentioned about the Digital Creators Conference?

(A) It lasts for four days.
(B) It is a short drive from the airport.
(C) It is close to dining establishments.
(D) It is being held in San Francisco.

178. In the second e-mail, the word "reference" in paragraph 1, line 2, is closest in meaning to

179. Which hotel will Mr. Altieri most likely book?

(A) The Gordon Suites
(B) The Grand Burgess Hotel
(C) The Bismarck Hotel
(D) The Newburg Plaza

180. What is indicated about Ms. Mercer?

(A) She has a team member who will bring her own car.
(B) She might change her mind about attending the DCC.
(C) She has an issue with Mr. Altieri's proposals.
(D) She is busy preparing for a series of presentations.

파트별 출제 유형 및 전략

3. 삼중 지문(Triple Passages)

Questions 186-190 refer to the following e-mail, schedule, and article.

TO: Ben Finch <ben.finch@mymail.com>
FROM: Taylor Gray <t.gray@streetmag.com>
SUBJECT: Welcome to *Street Magazine*
DATE: June 12

Hi Ben,

Congratulations on being selected as an intern for *Street Magazine*. For 25 years, the citizens of Seattle have looked to us weekly for the latest fashion, art, and music news.

Your internship will be from July 1 to December 31. You will report to me five days a week from 9:00 A.M. to 6:00 P.M. As an intern, you will not be a salaried employee, but we will provide an allowance for some expenses. If you do well, there may be a place for you here after your internship ends.

Please note that although you will have to do office work for various departments as the need arises, your responsibilities will be to research, take notes, and fact check content for me.

Taylor Gray

Personal Work Schedule: Taylor Gray
Thursday, August 7

Time	Activities	To do
09:30	Discuss budget with Mr. Robinson	
11:30	Leave for lunch appointment with photographer Stacy Larson	
13:00	Review photo submissions for "People" section	
14:30	Proofread articles for print version of lifestyle section	Send final list to Ms. McKee
16:00	Cover photo shoot at West Town Music Club	Assign to Ryan Oakley
16:30	Fact check music section for Web site	
17:30	Pick up laundry at Van's Cleaners	
18:00	Interview owner of Contempo Art Space	

Street Magazine

"Fusion In Fusion"
Opening Reception, Contempo Art Space
Thursday, August 7, 6:00 P.M. – 8:00 P.M.

This exhibit of artwork expresses an appreciation for all creative art forms, such as visual art, music, dance, film, and more. Works are representational or abstract, in 2D or 3D. All pieces exhibited in the main gallery will be for sale. This exhibit will be on display until November 6. For details, please contact gallery owner Mischa Michaels at 555-3941.

186. What is NOT true about the internship position at *Street Magazine*?

    (A) It does not pay a regular salary.
    (B) It involves working with different departments.
    (C) It can lead to offers of a permanent job.
    (D) It is available only during the summer.

187. What is suggested about *Street Magazine* in the e-mail?

    (A) It is planning to relocate its office.
    (B) It is published on a weekly basis.
    (C) It is mainly devoted to fashion news.
    (D) It has subscribers in many cities.

188. What task will Mr. Finch most likely be assigned on August 7?

    (A) Proofreading lifestyle section material
    (B) Collecting items from a laundry facility
    (C) Reviewing photographic submissions
    (D) Fact checking music section content

189. What can be inferred about Ms. Gray?

    (A) She will be interviewing Ms. Michaels.
    (B) She is unable to make her lunch appointment.
    (C) She will be supervising a photo shoot.
    (D) She is responsible for approving a budget.

190. What is mentioned about the exhibit at Contempo Art Space?

    (A) It is a collection of past works by a group.
    (B) Some of the artworks may be purchased on-site.
    (C) It will run in conjunction with another event.
    (D) Most of the participants are known artists.

출제 경향 및 대비 전략

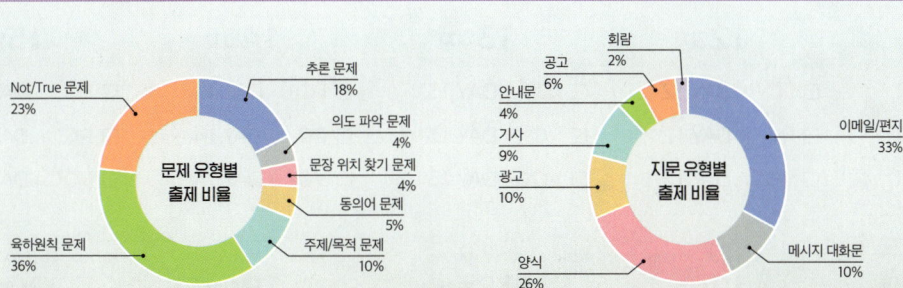

육하원칙 문제가 가장 높은 비율로 출제되며, Not/True 문제가 그다음으로 많이 출제됩니다. 지문은 이메일/편지가 가장 높은 비율로 출제됩니다.

핵심 대비 전략

지문의 종류나 글의 제목을 먼저 확인하여 지문의 개괄적인 내용을 추측해야 합니다.
지문 위의 디렉션 문장을 보고 지문의 종류를 확인하거나 글의 제목을 읽어서 지문이 어떤 내용을 담고 있을지 추측하며 문제를 풀도록 합니다.

시간 관리 능력을 키워야 합니다.
지문의 일부만 보고도 비교적 빠르게 풀이할 수 있는 육하원칙 문제와 같은 세부 사항 관련 문제에서 시간을 절약하고, 지문의 전체 내용을 확인해야 하는 Not/True 문제나 지문에 직접적으로 언급되지 않은 내용을 유추해야 하는 추론 문제에 시간을 투자하는 방식으로 효율적으로 시간을 관리해야 합니다.

600+ 정복 학습 플랜

20일 완성

매일 LC, RC, VOCA의 한 개 DAY를 학습함으로써, 더욱 확실하게 목표 점수를 취득하길 원하는 학습자에게 추천합니다.

1일차	2일차	3일차	4일차	5일차
☐ LC 기초 다지기	☐ LC DAY 02	☐ LC DAY 03	☐ LC DAY 04	☐ LC DAY 05
☐ LC DAY 01	☐ RC DAY 02	☐ RC DAY 03	☐ RC DAY 04	☐ RC DAY 05
☐ RC 기초 다지기	☐ VOCA DAY 02	☐ VOCA DAY 03	☐ VOCA DAY 04	☐ VOCA DAY 05
☐ RC DAY 01				
☐ VOCA DAY 01				

6일차	7일차	8일차	9일차	10일차
☐ LC DAY 06	☐ LC DAY 07	☐ LC DAY 08	☐ LC DAY 09	☐ LC DAY 10
☐ RC DAY 06	☐ RC DAY 07	☐ RC DAY 08	☐ RC DAY 09	☐ RC DAY 10
☐ VOCA DAY 06	☐ VOCA DAY 07	☐ VOCA DAY 08	☐ VOCA DAY 09	☐ VOCA DAY 10

11일차	12일차	13일차	14일차	15일차
☐ LC DAY 11	☐ LC DAY 12	☐ LC DAY 13	☐ LC DAY 14	☐ LC DAY 15
☐ RC DAY 11	☐ RC DAY 12	☐ RC DAY 13	☐ RC DAY 14	☐ RC DAY 15
☐ VOCA DAY 11	☐ VOCA DAY 12	☐ VOCA DAY 13	☐ VOCA DAY 14	☐ VOCA DAY 15

16일차	17일차	18일차	19일차	20일차
☐ LC DAY 16	☐ LC DAY 17	☐ LC DAY 18	☐ LC DAY 19	☐ LC DAY 20
☐ RC DAY 16	☐ RC DAY 17	☐ RC DAY 18	☐ RC DAY 19	☐ RC DAY 20
☐ VOCA DAY 16	☐ VOCA DAY 17	☐ VOCA DAY 18	☐ VOCA DAY 19	☐ VOCA DAY 20
				☐ 실전모의고사

*학습이 완료된 DAY의 상자에 체크(√) 표시를 하세요.

한 권으로 끝내는 해커스 토익 600+ LC+RC+VOCA

> 빠르게

10일 완성

점수가 쉽게 오르는 LC부터 집중 공략해서, 더욱 빠르게 목표 점수를 취득하길 원하는 학습자에게 추천합니다.

1일차	**2일차**	**3일차**	**4일차**	**5일차**
☐ LC 기초 다지기	☐ LC DAY 06-10	☐ LC DAY 11-15	☐ LC DAY 16-20	☐ RC 기초 다지기
☐ LC DAY 01-05	☐ VOCA DAY 04-06	☐ VOCA DAY 07-08	☐ VOCA DAY 09-10	☐ RC DAY 01-03
☐ VOCA DAY 01-03				☐ VOCA DAY 11-12
6일차	**7일차**	**8일차**	**9일차**	**10일차**
☐ RC DAY 04-06	☐ RC DAY 07-09	☐ RC DAY 10-14	☐ RC DAY 15-18	☐ RC DAY 19-20
☐ VOCA DAY 13-14	☐ VOCA DAY 15-16	☐ VOCA DAY 17-18	☐ VOCA DAY 19	☐ VOCA DAY 20
				☐ 실전모의고사

*학습이 완료된 DAY의 상자에 체크(√) 표시를 하세요.

600+ 정복 학습 플랜

한 권으로 끝내는 해커스 토익 600+ LC+RC+VOCA

실시간 토익시험 정답확인 & 해설강의
Hackers.co.kr

LC 기초 다지기

PART 1
PART 2
PART 3
PART 4

 ◀ MP3 바로 듣기

교재에 수록된 모든 MP3를 무료로 다운받거나 바로 스트리밍하여 더욱 편리하게 이용해 보세요.
고속 버전 MP3도 구매하여 학습하면 실전에 더욱 완벽하게 대비할 수 있습니다.

LC 기초 다지기

유사 발음 구별하기 비슷한 듯 다른 발음들

영어에는 copy와 coffee처럼 발음이 비슷해서 혼동을 주는 단어들이 있습니다. 토익 PART 2에서는 이러한 유사 발음을 이용한 보기가 오답으로 자주 출제되니 혼동하기 쉬운 유사 발음들을 잘 익혀두는 것이 좋습니다.

1 [p] & [f] 🎧 기초_01

[p]는 두 입술을 맞붙였다가 떼며 내는 소리로 'ㅍ'와 비슷하게 들리고, [f]는 윗니로 아랫입술을 살짝 물었다 놓으며 숨을 내쉬게 하여 내는 소리로 'ㅍ'와 'ㅎ'의 중간 소리처럼 들립니다.

[p]	**copy**[카피] 복사; 복사하다	**pile**[파일] 쌓다	**past**[패스트] 이전의
[f]	**coffee**[커피] 커피	**file**[파일] 서류철; 철하다	**fast**[패스트] 빠른

토익에 이렇게 나와요!

Where did you copy the document? 당신은 문서를 어디에서 복사했나요?
(A) At the library. (O) 도서관에서요.
(B) I need some coffee. (X) 저는 커피가 좀 필요해요.
→ (B)는 질문에서 사용된 copy와 발음이 유사한 coffee를 사용하여 혼동을 주는 오답입니다.

2 [b] & [v] 🎧 기초_02

[b]는 두 입술을 맞붙였다가 떼며 내는 소리로 'ㅂ'과 비슷하게 들리고, [v]는 윗니로 아랫입술을 살짝 물었다 놓으며 내는 소리로 'ㅂ' 보다 바람 새는 소리가 더 들립니다.

[b]	**boat**[보우트] 배	**base**[베이스] 기초, 기반	**best**[베스트] 최고의
[v]	**vote**[보우트] 투표하다	**vase**[베이스] 꽃병	**vest**[베스트] 조끼

토익에 이렇게 나와요!

How can I travel by boat? 제가 배로 이동하려면 어떻게 해야 하나요?
(A) Buy a ticket at the dock. (O) 선착장에서 표를 사세요.
(B) I will vote next week. (X) 저는 다음 주에 투표할 거예요.
→ (B)는 질문에서 사용된 boat와 발음이 유사한 vote를 사용하여 혼동을 주는 오답입니다.

③ [l] & [r] 🎧 기초_03

[l]은 혀끝을 앞니 뒤에 댔다가 떼며 내는 소리로 '(을)르'와 비슷하게 들리고, [r]은 입술을 둥글게 해서 혀를 입천장 가까이 가져가며 내는 소리로 '(우)르'와 비슷하게 들립니다.

[l]	**load**[(을)로드] (짐을) 싣다	**light**[(을)라잇ㅌ] 가벼운	**lead**[(을)리드] 이끌다
[r]	**road**[(우)로드] 도로	**right**[(우)라잇ㅌ] 옳은	**read**[(우)리드] 읽다

> **토익에 이렇게 나와요!**
>
> Who will **lead** the project? 누가 그 프로젝트를 이끌 건가요?
> (A) I usually **read** during lunch. (X) 저는 보통 점심시간 동안에 독서해요.
> (B) Ms. Chen is in charge. (O) Ms. Chen이 담당하고 있어요.
> → (A)는 질문에서 사용된 lead와 발음이 유사한 read를 사용하여 혼동을 주는 오답입니다.

④ [i] & [iː] 🎧 기초_04

[i]는 짧게 끊어서 내는 소리로 '이'처럼 들리고, [iː]는 입술을 옆으로 크게 벌리고 길게 내는 소리로 '이-'와 비슷하게 들립니다.

[i]	**fill**[필] 채우다	**live**[(을)리브] 살다	**hit**[힛ㅌ] 치다
[iː]	**feel**[피일] 느끼다	**leave**[(을)리이브] 떠나다	**heat**[히잇ㅌ] 열

> **토익에 이렇게 나와요!**
>
> Should I **fill** the tank before returning the car? 제가 차를 반납하기 전에 연료통을 채워야 하나요?
> (A) Yes, it needs to be full. (O) 네, 그것은 가득 차 있어야 해요.
> (B) I **feel** tired. (X) 저는 피곤해요.
> → (B)는 질문에서 사용된 fill과 발음이 유사한 feel을 사용하여 혼동을 주는 오답입니다.

⑤ [ou] & [ɔː] 🎧 기초_05

[ou]는 입을 동그랗게 해서 내는 소리로 '오우'와 비슷하게 들리고, [ɔː]는 입을 동그랗게 한 채 발음하는 소리로 '오'와 '아'의 중간 소리처럼 들립니다.

[ou]	**low**[(을)로우] 낮은	**cold**[코울드] 차가운	**hold**[호울드] 잡다
[ɔː]	**law**[(을)러어] 법	**called**[커얼드] 전화했다(call의 과거형)	**hall**[허얼] 홀, 복도

> **토익에 이렇게 나와요!**
>
> Will it be **cold** tomorrow? 내일 추울까요?
> (A) Yes, bring a jacket. (O) 네, 재킷을 가져오세요.
> (B) I **called** her this morning. (X) 저는 오늘 아침에 그녀에게 전화했어요.
> → (B)는 질문에서 사용된 cold와 발음이 유사한 called를 사용하여 혼동을 주는 오답입니다.

연음 듣기 단어들이 이어지면서 나는 소리

연음이란 단어들이 이어지면서 나는 소리를 말합니다. 토익의 대화와 담화에 나오는 긴 문장들을 정확히 듣고 이해하기 위해서는 연음으로 인한 발음의 변화를 알아두는 것이 좋습니다.

① 똑같거나 비슷한 자음이 연이어 나오면 한 번만 들립니다. 🎧 기초_06

send documents에서 같은 자음인 d[드]가 겹치므로, 뒤의 d만 읽습니다. 따라서 [센드도큐먼츠]가 아닌 [센도큐먼츠]로 들립니다.

토익에 이렇게 나와요!

1. I saw her waiting at the bus stop. 저는 그녀가 버스 정류장에서 기다리는 것을 봤어요.
2. Let's try again next time. 다음번에 다시 시도해 봐요.
3. We need to finish this today. 우리는 이것을 오늘 끝내야 해요.

② 앞 단어의 끝 자음과 뒤 단어의 첫 모음은 이어져서 들립니다. 🎧 기초_07

log in에서 앞 단어의 끝 자음 g[그]와 뒤 단어의 첫 모음 i[이]가 이어져 [로그인]이 아닌 [로긴]으로 들립니다.

토익에 이렇게 나와요!

1. You need to fill out the application. 당신은 신청서를 작성해야 해요.
2. When can I pick up my order? 제가 주문을 언제 찾을 수 있나요?
3. How long does it take to get there? 거기까지 가는 데 얼마나 걸리나요?

미국식·영국식 발음 차이 같은 생김새, 다른 발음

토익에서는 미국식 발음뿐만 아니라 우리에게 다소 낯선 영국, 캐나다, 호주식 발음도 사용됩니다. 캐나다 발음은 미국과 비슷하고, 호주 발음은 영국과 비슷하므로, 대표적인 미국식 발음과 영국식 발음의 차이를 알아두는 것이 좋습니다.

🎧 기초_08

[r]

미국식 영어에서는 단어 끝의 r을 혀를 굴려 [ㄹ]로 발음하지만, 영국식 영어에서는 r을 발음하지 않습니다.

	car	wear	hour	door
🇺🇸	[카아ㄹ]	[웨어ㄹ]	[아우어ㄹ]	[도어ㄹ]
🇬🇧	[카아]	[웨어]	[아우어]	[도어]

[t]

미국식 영어에서는 모음 사이에 있는 t를 [ㄹ]로, 영국식 영어에서는 정확히 [ㅌ]으로 발음합니다.

	computer	meeting	item	data
🇺🇸	[컴퓨우러ㄹ]	[미이링]	[아이럼]	[데이러]
🇬🇧	[컴퓨우터]	[미이팅]	[아이텀]	[데이터]

[a]

미국식 영어에서는 [애]에 가깝게, 영국식 영어에서는 [아]에 가깝게 발음합니다.

	ask	pass	answer	last
🇺🇸	[애스크]	[패쓰]	[앤써ㄹ]	[래스트]
🇬🇧	[아스크]	[파아쓰]	[안써]	[라아스트]

[o]

미국식 영어에서는 [아]에 가깝게, 영국식 영어에서는 [오]에 가깝게 발음합니다.

	topic	copy	option	job
🇺🇸	[타픽]	[카피]	[압션]	[잡]
🇬🇧	[토픽]	[코피]	[옵션]	[좁]

한 권으로 끝내는 해커스 토익 600+ LC+RC+VOCA

PART 1

DAY 01 사람 중심 사진
DAY 02 사물/풍경 중심 사진

◀ MP3 바로 듣기

교재에 수록된 모든 MP3를 무료로 다운받거나 바로 스트리밍하여 더욱 편리하게 이용해 보세요.
고속 버전 MP3도 구매하여 학습하면 실전에 더욱 완벽하게 대비할 수 있습니다.

PART 1 알아보기

PART 1은 1번부터 6번까지 총 6문제로, 사람이나 사물 또는 풍경이 등장하는 사진을 보고 4개의 보기를 들은 후, 사진을 가장 잘 묘사한 보기를 선택하는 파트입니다. 문제지에는 사진만 제시되고, 4개의 보기는 음성으로만 들려줍니다.

PART 1 미리 보기

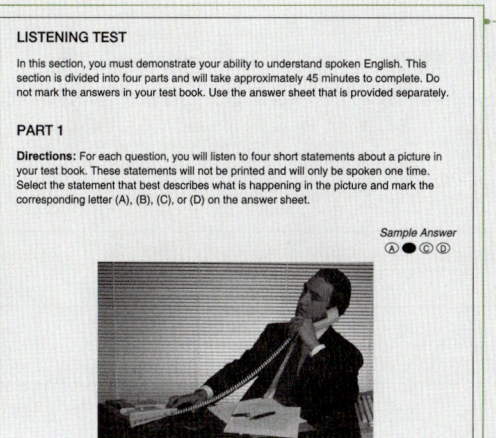

리스닝 영역과 PART 1을 소개하는 디렉션입니다. 리스닝 영역은 4개의 파트로 구성되어 있고 45분이 주어집니다.

각 문제의 보기를 다음과 같이 들려줍니다.

Number 1.
Look at the picture marked number 1 in your test book.

(A) She is writing with a pen.
(B) She is holding a document.
(C) She is facing a window.
(D) She is typing on a laptop.

PART 1 학습 전략

- **사진 유형별 최신 경향 및 전략 익히기**
  사람 중심 사진은 등장인물의 동작에서, 사물/풍경 중심 사진은 사물의 상태나 위치에서 정답 여부가 주로 결정됩니다. 이러한 경향과 사진 유형별 전략을 익혀두면 정답 보기를 빠르게 판단할 수 있습니다.

- **PART 1에 자주 나오는 사진 상황별 표현 익히기**
  보기의 내용을 정확히 파악하여 정답을 고르기 위해 PART 1에 출제되는 사진의 상황별로 자주 나오는 표현을 익혀두어야 합니다.

DAY 01 사람 중심 사진

MP3 바로듣기

1. 1인 사진

1인 사진은 한 명의 사람이 중심이 되는 사진입니다. 한 사람이 사무실에서 일하고 있는 사진이나 한 사람의 주변에 물건이 쌓여 있는 사진이 자주 출제됩니다. PART 1 전체 6문제 중 매회 2~3문제 정도 출제됩니다.

최신 경향 및 전략

1. 보기의 주어로 사람을 나타내는 표현(He, She, A man, A woman 등)이 주로 사용됩니다.
2. 보기에는 '~하고 있는' 사람의 동작이나 상태를 묘사하기 위해 현재 진행형(is + -ing) 동사가 주로 사용됩니다.
3. 사람의 동작이나 자세와 무관한 동사를 사용한 오답, 동작 또는 시선의 대상이 되는 사물을 잘못 언급한 오답, 사람의 옷차림을 잘못 묘사한 오답에 유의하며 듣습니다.

자주 나오는 표현 🎧 D01_1_표현

동작/자세	use v. 사용하다	climb v. 오르다, 기어오르다
	kneel v. 무릎을 꿇다	reach for ~을 향해 손을 뻗다
시선	examine v. 자세히 살펴보다	inspect v. 살펴보다, 점검하다
	look down 내려다보다	look at ~을 보다, 살피다
옷차림	wear v. 입고 있다	put on ~을 입다
	try on ~을 입어 보다	take off ~을 벗다

Example 🎧 D01_2_예제

(A) (B) (C) (D)

🇦🇺 호주
(A) A man is painting a fence.
(B) A man is climbing a ladder.
(C) A man is repairing a car.
(D) A man is sitting on a porch.

해설   **정답 (B)**
(A) [×] painting(페인트칠하고 있다)은 남자의 동작과 무관하므로 오답입니다.
(B) [○] 남자가 사다리를 오르고 있는 모습을 가장 잘 묘사한 정답입니다.
(C) [×] 사진에 자동차(car)가 없으므로 오답입니다.
(D) [×] sitting(앉아 있다)은 남자의 동작과 무관하므로 오답입니다.

해석
(A) 남자가 울타리를 페인트칠하고 있다.
(B) 남자가 사다리를 오르고 있다.
(C) 남자가 자동차를 수리하고 있다.
(D) 남자가 현관에 앉아 있다.

어휘
paint v. 페인트칠하다 fence n. 울타리 ladder n. 사다리
porch n. 현관

HACKERS PRACTICE

음성을 들으며 사진을 가장 알맞게 묘사한 보기를 고르고, 빈칸에 들어갈 내용을 받아쓰세요. (음성은 두 번 들려줍니다.) 🎧 D01_3_Practice

01

(A) (B) (C) (D)

(A) He is _____ a door.
(B) He is _____ a window.
(C) He is _____ a plant.
(D) He is _____ a copy machine.

02

(A) (B) (C) (D)

(A) Some furniture is _____.
(B) A woman is _____ a purchase.
(C) A woman is _____ an item.
(D) Some clothing is _____.

03

(A) (B) (C) (D)

(A) The man is _____ a beverage.
(B) The man is _____ a receipt.
(C) The man is _____ a chair.
(D) The man is _____ at a phone.

04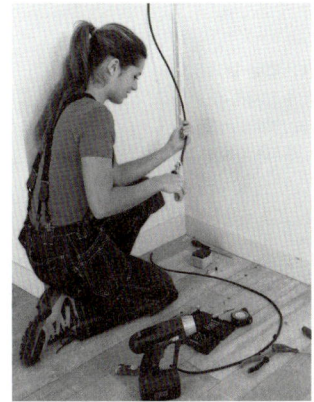

(A) (B) (C) (D)

(A) The woman is _____ to work with a wire.
(B) The woman is _____ a tool.
(C) The woman is _____ supplies into boxes.
(D) The woman is _____ the floor.

2. 2인 이상 사진

2인 이상 사진은 두 명 이상의 사람들이 등장하는 사진입니다. 여러 사람들이 회의를 하는 사진, 야외에서 물건을 구경하거나 식당에서 주문하는 사진이 자주 출제됩니다. PART 1 전체 6문제 중 매회 2~3문제 정도 출제됩니다.

최신 경향 및 전략

1. 보기의 주어로 여러 사람을 나타내는 표현(They, People, Some people 등)이나 한 사람을 나타내는 표현(One of the men, One of the women, One of the people 등)이 주로 사용됩니다.
2. 보기에는 사람의 동작이나 상태를 묘사하기 위해 현재 진행형(is/are + -ing) 동사가 자주 사용되고, 사물의 상태를 묘사하기 위해 수동형(is/are + p.p., is/are + being + p.p., has/have + been + p.p.) 동사가 사용되기도 합니다.
3. 개별적인 동작을 공통적인 것처럼 묘사하는 오답이나 서로의 동작을 바꾸어 묘사하는 오답, 사물의 상태를 잘못 묘사하는 오답이나 사람의 동작과 무관한 사물을 언급한 오답에 유의하며 듣습니다.

자주 나오는 표현 🎧 D01_4_표현

공통 동작	perform v. 공연하다, 연주하다	greet v. 인사하다
	attend v. 참석하다	shake hands 악수하다
	discuss v. 토론하다, 의논하다	wait in a line 한 줄로 기다리다
	talk to ~에게 말하다	walk together 함께 걷다
	have a conversation 대화를 나누다	face each other 서로 마주 보다
	watch a presentation 발표를 보다	look in the same direction 같은 방향을 쳐다보다
공통 상태	be gathered 모여 있다	be seated side by side 나란히 앉아 있다

Example 🎧 D01_5_예제

(A)   (B)   (C)   (D)

🎙 영국

(A) One of the women is holding a cup.
(B) One of the women is washing some dishes.
(C) Some people are standing at a counter.
(D) Some people are preparing food.

해설   정답 (C)

(A) [×] 사진에 컵을 들고 있는(holding a cup) 여자가 없으므로 오답입니다.
(B) [×] 사진에 접시를 씻고 있는(washing some dishes) 여자가 없으므로 오답입니다.
(C) [o] 몇몇 사람들이 계산대에 서 있는 모습을 가장 잘 묘사한 정답입니다.
(D) [×] preparing food(음식을 준비하고 있다)는 사람들의 동작과 무관하므로 오답입니다.

해석

(A) 여자들 중 한 명이 컵을 들고 있다.
(B) 여자들 중 한 명이 접시를 씻고 있다.
(C) 몇몇 사람들이 계산대에 서 있다.
(D) 몇몇 사람들이 음식을 준비하고 있다.

어휘

wash v. 씻다   dish n. 접시   counter n. 계산대, 판매대
prepare v. 준비하다

HACKERS PRACTICE

음성을 들으며 사진을 가장 알맞게 묘사한 보기를 고르고, 빈칸에 들어갈 내용을 받아쓰세요. (음성은 두 번 들려줍니다.) 🎧 D01_6_Practice

01

(A)   (B)   (C)   (D)

(A) They are _____ a building.
(B) A man is _____ a window.
(C) A woman is _____ a handrail.
(D) They are _____ some stairs.

02

(A)   (B)   (C)   (D)

(A) One of the men is _____ a computer.
(B) Some people are _____ a presentation.
(C) One of the men is _____ a whiteboard.
(D) Some people are _____ a monitor.

03

(A)   (B)   (C)   (D)

(A) A cashier is _____ fruit in a bag.
(B) A customer is _____ an item to a cashier.
(C) A customer is _____ a credit card.
(D) A cashier is _____ some beverages.

04

(A)   (B)   (C)   (D)

(A) A cabinet is _____ with containers.
(B) The woman is _____ a cup on a shelf.
(C) The man is _____ over a table.
(D) Some dishes have been _____ in a sink.

정답·해석·해설 p.2

HACKERS TEST

음성을 들으며 사진을 가장 알맞게 묘사한 보기를 고르세요. 🎧 D01_7_Test

01

(A)　(B)　(C)　(D)

02

(A)　(B)　(C)　(D)

03

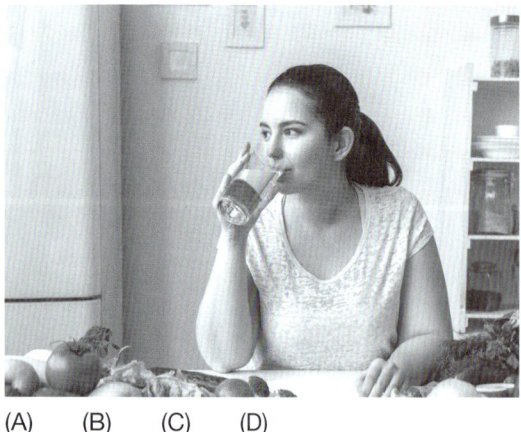

(A)　(B)　(C)　(D)

04

(A)　(B)　(C)　(D)

05

(A)　(B)　(C)　(D)

06

(A)　(B)　(C)　(D)

07

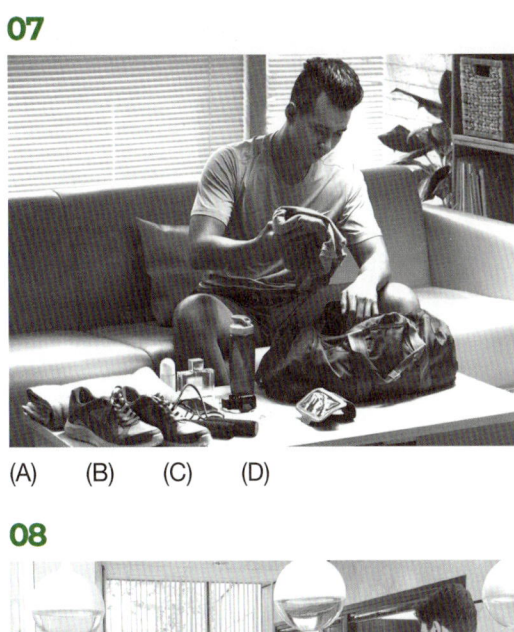

(A)　　(B)　　(C)　　(D)

10

(A)　　(B)　　(C)　　(D)

08

(A)　　(B)　　(C)　　(D)

11

(A)　　(B)　　(C)　　(D)

09

(A)　　(B)　　(C)　　(D)

12

(A)　　(B)　　(C)　　(D)

DAY 02 사물/풍경 중심 사진

MP3 바로 듣기

1. 실내 사진

실내 사진은 실내 공간의 사물이 중심이 되는 사진입니다. 여러 물건이 놓인 사무실이나 제품이 진열된 상점 또는 가구가 배치된 거실 사진이 자주 출제됩니다. PART 1 전체 6문제 중 매회 1~2문제 정도 출제됩니다.

최신 경향 및 전략

1. 보기에는 사물의 상태를 묘사하기 위해 'There is/are', 'is/are + -ing', 'is/are + p.p.' 또는 'has/have + been + p.p.' 동사가 주로 사용됩니다.
2. 보기에는 사물의 위치를 나타내기 위해 'is/are + 전치사구' 형태의 문장도 사용되며, on(~ 위에), underneath(~ 아래에), by(~ 옆에) 등의 전치사가 주로 사용됩니다.
3. 사람이 나오지 않은 실내 사진에서 주어가 사람인 오답에 유의하며 듣습니다.

자주 나오는 표현 🎧 D02_1_표현

사물의 상태	be placed on ~에 놓여 있다	be arranged in ~에 배치되어 있다
	be stacked on ~에 쌓여 있다	be displayed on ~에 진열되어 있다
	be hanging from ~에 매달려 있다	be mounted on ~에 고정되어 있다
사물의 위치	on a table 탁자 위에	underneath a sofa 소파 아래에
	by a window 창문 옆에	between two chairs 두 의자 사이에
	under a lamp 전등 아래에	beside a monitor 모니터 옆에

Example 🎧 D02_2_예제

(A) (B) (C) (D)

🎤 캐나다
(A) Coffee cups have been placed on a table.
(B) A napkin is being folded.
(C) A pot is being refilled with water.
(D) Plates have been stacked on a tray.

해설 　　　　　　　　　　　　　　　**정답 (A)**
(A) [○] 커피잔들이 탁자 위에 놓여 있는 모습을 가장 잘 묘사한 정답입니다.
(B) [×] 냅킨이 접히고 있지(being folded) 않으므로 오답입니다.
(C) [×] 주전자가 물로 다시 채워지고 있지(being refilled with water) 않으므로 오답입니다.
(D) [×] 접시들이 쟁반(tray) 위가 아니라 탁자 위에 쌓여 있으므로 오답입니다.

해석
(A) 커피잔들이 탁자 위에 놓여 있다.
(B) 냅킨이 접히고 있다.
(C) 주전자가 물로 다시 채워지고 있다.
(D) 접시들이 쟁반 위에 쌓여 있다.

어휘
fold v. 접다　pot n. 주전자, 포트　refill v. 다시 채우다
plate n. 접시　stack v. 쌓다　tray n. 쟁반

HACKERS PRACTICE

음성을 들으며 사진을 가장 알맞게 묘사한 보기를 고르고, 빈칸에 들어갈 내용을 받아쓰세요. (음성은 두 번 들려줍니다.) 🎧 D02_3_Practice

01

(A)　(B)　(C)　(D)

(A) The floor is _____.
(B) Sofas have been _____ for display.
(C) There is a lamp _____.
(D) There are some pillows _____.

02

(A)　(B)　(C)　(D)

(A) Some light fixtures are _____ the ceiling.
(B) Some chairs are _____ against a wall.
(C) There are _____ on a table.
(D) There is a _____ in front of a window.

03

(A)　(B)　(C)　(D)

(A) A decoration is _____ on a windowsill.
(B) Magazines have been _____ on the floor.
(C) Books have been _____ on shelves.
(D) A worker is _____ next to a bookcase.

04

(A)　(B)　(C)　(D)

(A) Plants are _____ onto a balcony.
(B) Some rolling chairs are _____.
(C) A room is _____ for a meeting.
(D) A screen has been _____ on a wall.

정답·해석·해설 p.6

2. 야외 사진

야외 사진은 야외 공간의 풍경이 중심이 되는 사진입니다. 야외 식사 공간이나 항구, 주차장, 도로 주변, 공원, 건물 외부 등의 사진이 자주 출제됩니다. PART 1 전체 6문제 중 매회 1~2문제 정도 출제됩니다.

최신 경향 및 전략

1. 보기에는 풍경과 사물의 상태를 표현하기 위해 현재 시제 동사, 'is/are + -ing', 'is/are + p.p.' 또는 'has/have + been + p.p.' 동사가 자주 사용됩니다.
2. 보기에는 사물의 위치를 나타내기 위해 next to(~ 옆에), near(~ 근처에), along(~을 따라서), in front of(~ 앞에) 등의 부사나 전치사들이 자주 사용됩니다.
3. 동작이 이미 완료된 상태인데, 'is/are + being + p.p.' 동사를 사용하여 동작이 현재 진행 중인 상태로 묘사하는 오답에 유의하며 듣습니다.

자주 나오는 표현 D02_4_표현

풍경	overlook v. 내려다보다	run v. (도로 등이) 이어지다, 뻗다
	flow v. (운하 등이) 흐르다	border v. 둘러싸다, ~의 경계를 이루다
사물의 상태	be unoccupied 비어 있다	be positioned on ~에 위치해 있다
	be stopped at ~에 멈춰 있다	be parked in ~에 주차되어 있다
	be surrounded by ~에 둘러싸여 있다	be covered by ~에 의해 덮여 있다
사물의 위치	next to a building 건물 옆에	near the waterfront 물가 근처에
	along the shore 해안을 따라	in front of a vehicle 차량 앞에

Example D02_5_예제

미국
(A) Some umbrellas have been left closed.
(B) Some chairs are arranged in a circle.
(C) A sign is attached to a railing.
(D) A dining area is unoccupied.

(A) (B) (C) (D)

해설 정답 (D)
(A) [×] 파라솔들(umbrellas)이 접혀 있지 않고 펼쳐져 있으므로 오답입니다.
(B) [×] 의자들이 원형으로 배치되어 있지(are arranged in a circle) 않으므로 오답입니다.
(C) [×] 사진에 표지판(sign)이 없으므로 오답입니다.
(D) [○] 식사 공간이 비어 있는 모습을 가장 잘 묘사한 정답입니다.

해석
(A) 몇몇 파라솔들이 접힌 채로 있다.
(B) 몇몇 의자들이 원형으로 배치되어 있다.
(C) 표지판이 난간에 부착되어 있다.
(D) 식사 공간이 비어 있다.

어휘
umbrella n. 파라솔, 우산 in a circle 원형으로 railing n. 난간
dining area 식사 공간 unoccupied adj. 비어 있는, 사용되지 않는

HACKERS PRACTICE

음성을 들으며 사진을 가장 알맞게 묘사한 보기를 고르고, 빈칸에 들어갈 내용을 받아쓰세요. (음성은 두 번 들려줍니다.) 🎧 D02_6_Practice

01

(A)　(B)　(C)　(D)

(A) A bicycle is _____ with water.
(B) Signs have been _____ on a wall.
(C) A car is _____ .
(D) Bikes have been _____ on a rack.

02

(A)　(B)　(C)　(D)

(A) A truck is _____ in a tunnel.
(B) A pedestrian is _____ a street.
(C) Traffic cones are _____ on a road.
(D) Vehicles are _____ in a row.

03

(A)　(B)　(C)　(D)

(A) There are picnic tables _____ by roofs.
(B) Diners are _____ a meal.
(C) There are leaves _____ in a field.
(D) Trees _____ shade on a patio.

04

(A)　(B)　(C)　(D)

(A) A ship is _____ under a bridge.
(B) Buildings are _____ the coastline.
(C) A motorcycle is _____ near the waterfront.
(D) People are _____ along the shore.

HACKERS TEST

음성을 들으며 사진을 가장 알맞게 묘사한 보기를 고르세요. 🎧 D02_7_Test

01

(A) (B) (C) (D)

02

(A) (B) (C) (D)

03

(A) (B) (C) (D)

04

(A) (B) (C) (D)

05

(A) (B) (C) (D)

06

(A) (B) (C) (D)

07

(A) (B) (C) (D)

08

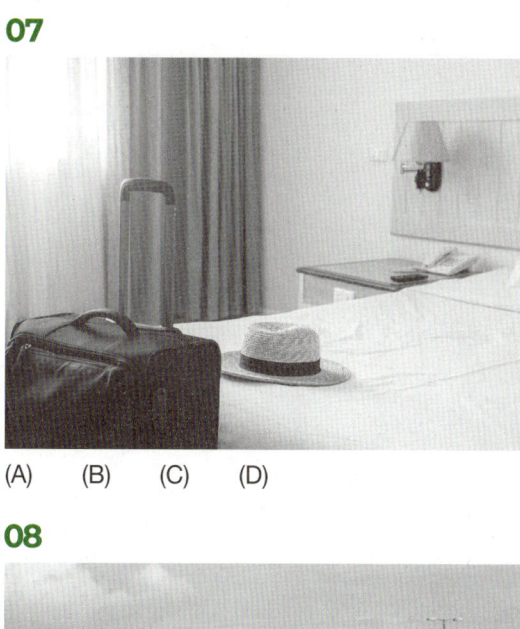

(A) (B) (C) (D)

09

(A) (B) (C) (D)

10

(A) (B) (C) (D)

11

(A) (B) (C) (D)

12

(A) (B) (C) (D)

한 권으로 끝내는 해커스 토익 600+ LC+RC+VOCA

PART 2

- **DAY 03** 의문사 의문문: Who, What/Which
- **DAY 04** 의문사 의문문: Where, When
- **DAY 05** 의문사 의문문: Why, How
- **DAY 06** 일반 의문문 및 선택 의문문
- **DAY 07** 부정 의문문 및 부가 의문문
- **DAY 08** 제안/제공/요청 의문문 및 평서문

◀ MP3 바로 듣기

교재에 수록된 모든 MP3를 무료로 다운받거나 바로 스트리밍하여 더욱 편리하게 이용해 보세요.
고속 버전 MP3도 구매하여 학습하면 실전에 더욱 완벽하게 대비할 수 있습니다.

PART 2 알아보기

PART 2는 7번부터 31번까지 총 25문제로, 1개의 질문과 3개의 응답을 듣고 질문에 가장 적절하게 응답한 보기를 선택하는 파트입니다. 질문과 3개의 보기는 문제지에 제시되지 않고 음성으로만 들려줍니다.

PART 2 미리 보기

PART 2

Directions: For each question, you will listen to a statement or question followed by three possible responses spoken in English. They will not be printed and will only be spoken one time. Select the best response and mark the corresponding letter (A), (B), or (C) on your answer sheet.

7. Mark your answer on the answer sheet.
8. Mark your answer on the answer sheet.
9. Mark your answer on the answer sheet.
10. Mark your answer on the answer sheet.
11. Mark your answer on the answer sheet.
12. Mark your answer on the answer sheet.
13. Mark your answer on the answer sheet.
14. Mark your answer on the answer sheet.
15. Mark your answer on the answer sheet.
16. Mark your answer on the answer sheet.
17. Mark your answer on the answer sheet.
18. Mark your answer on the answer sheet.
19. Mark your answer on the answer sheet.
20. Mark your answer on the answer sheet.
21. Mark your answer on the answer sheet.
22. Mark your answer on the answer sheet.
23. Mark your answer on the answer sheet.
24. Mark your answer on the answer sheet.
25. Mark your answer on the answer sheet.
26. Mark your answer on the answer sheet.
27. Mark your answer on the answer sheet.
28. Mark your answer on the answer sheet.
29. Mark your answer on the answer sheet.
30. Mark your answer on the answer sheet.
31. Mark your answer on the answer sheet.

> PART 2를 소개하는 디렉션입니다.

> 각 문제의 질문과 보기를 다음과 같이 들려줍니다.
>
> Number 7.
> Where is the nearest park?
>
> **(A) There's one on Lincoln Avenue.**
> (B) No, I don't drive.
> (C) I'm nearly finished.

PART 2 학습 전략

- **빈출 질문과 응답 익히기**
  질문 유형에 따라 자주 출제되는 질문과 응답 패턴이 있으므로 이를 익혀두면 실전 시험에서도 PART 2를 쉽게 공략할 수 있습니다.

- **PART 2에 자주 나오는 간접적인 응답 익히기**
  PART 2에는 간접적인 응답이 자주 출제되므로 빈출 간접 응답을 꼭 학습해야 합니다.

DAY 03 의문사 의문문: Who, What/Which

MP3 바로듣기

1. Who 의문문

Who 의문문은 의문사 who(누가)를 사용하여 특정 행동의 주체나 업무의 담당자를 묻는 의문문입니다. PART 2 전체 25문제 중 매회 2~3문제 정도 출제됩니다.

빈출 질문과 응답 🎧 D03_1_예문

사람 이름, 부서명, 직책명, 인칭대명사를 사용한 응답이 정답으로 자주 출제됩니다.

Q **Who** is organizing the conference?
누가 컨퍼런스를 준비하고 있나요?

A I think **Ms. Johnson** is. [사람 이름]
제가 생각하기에는 Ms. Johnson이요.

A The **marketing department**. [부서명]
마케팅 부서요.

A The **sales manager**. [직책명]
영업부 관리자요.

A **I'm in charge of that.** [인칭대명사]
제가 그것을 담당하고 있어요.

Example 🎧 D03_2_예제

(A)	(B)	(C)

🔊 캐나다 → 영국
Who visited your office this morning?
(A) The new intern.
(B) They were first in line.
(C) Yes, at eight o'clock.

해설   **정답 (A)**
(A) [O] 새로운 인턴사원이라며 사무실을 방문한 사람을 언급했으므로 정답입니다.
(B) [X] 누가 사무실을 방문했는지를 물었는데, 이와 관련이 없는 그들이 줄의 맨 앞에 있었다는 말로 응답했으므로 오답입니다.
(C) [X] 의문사 의문문에 Yes로 응답했으므로 오답입니다.

해석
누가 오늘 아침에 당신의 사무실을 방문했나요?
(A) 새로운 인턴사원이요.
(B) 그들은 줄의 맨 앞에 있었어요.
(C) 네, 8시에요.

어휘
office n. 사무실   intern n. 인턴사원

HACKERS PRACTICE

음성을 들으며 질문에 가장 알맞은 응답을 고르고, 빈칸에 들어갈 내용을 받아쓰세요. (음성은 두 번 들려줍니다.) 🎧 D03_3_Practice

01 (A) (B) (C)

_____ on the _____?
(A) A couple of _____.
(B) Because _____ was rejected.
(C) Someone from the _____.

02 (A) (B) (C)

_____'s going to _____ to the movie?
(A) Paul will _____.
(B) It's a _____.
(C) She failed her _____.

03 (A) (B) (C)

_____ should I _____ about the deadline?
(A) After you _____.
(B) One of _____.
(C) _____ too.

04 (A) (B) (C)

_____ the press release?
(A) I'm _____ than before.
(B) Susan _____.
(C) The _____.

05 (A) (B) (C)

_____ this photo for the article?
(A) I'll take _____ for you.
(B) My _____.
(C) *The Daily Business News* _____.

06 (A) (B) (C)

_____ is Juan _____ Spain with?
(A) We're _____.
(B) _____ just landed.
(C) No, an _____.

2. What/Which 의문문

What/Which 의문문은 의문사 what(무엇)이나 which(어느)를 사용하여 시각, 비용, 의견, 방법, 종류 등 다양한 정보를 묻는 의문문입니다. PART 2 전체 25문제 중 매회 1~2문제 정도 출제됩니다.

빈출 질문과 응답   🎧 D03_4_예문

What/Which 뒤에 나오는 명사나 동사에 따라 묻는 내용이 달라지며 질문에서 요청하는 정보를 직접적으로 언급하는 응답뿐만 아니라 간접 응답도 정답으로 자주 출제됩니다.

Q **What time** does the store open? [시각]
가게는 몇 시에 여나요?

A It opens at **10 A.M.**
오전 10시에 열어요.

Q **What's** the **charge for** parking? [비용]
주차 요금은 얼마인가요?

A It's **10 dollars** per hour.
한 시간에 10달러예요.

Q **What** do you **think of** the new software? [의견]
새로운 소프트웨어에 대해 어떻게 생각하나요?

A It seems **user-friendly**.
사용하기 쉬운 것 같아요.

Q **What's** the **best way to** reach support? [방법]
고객 지원 센터에 연락하는 가장 좋은 방법은 무엇인가요?

A **Call the hotline.**
상담 서비스에 전화하세요.

Q **Which cake** do you recommend? [종류]
어느 케이크를 추천하나요?

A **The one** with strawberries. [The one으로 응답]
딸기가 있는 것이요.

A **I'll bring you a sample if you'd like.**
[간접적인 응답]
원하시면 제가 샘플을 드릴게요.

Example   🎧 D03_5_예제

(A)   (B)   (C)

🔊 영국 → 호주
What's the cost of sending this package?
(A) No, in 30 minutes.
(B) Around 15 dollars.
(C) Oh, it was delivered yesterday.

해설   **정답** (B)
(A) [×] 의문사 의문문에 No로 응답했으므로 오답입니다.
(B) [o] 약 15달러라는 비용을 언급했으므로 정답입니다.
(C) [×] 질문의 package(소포)와 관련 있는 delivered(배송되다)를 사용하여 혼동을 준 오답입니다.

해석
이 소포를 보내는 데 드는 비용은 얼마인가요?
(A) 아니요, 30분 후예요.
(B) 약 15달러요.
(C) 아, 그것은 어제 배송되었어요.

어휘
cost n. 비용   package n. 소포   deliver v. 배송하다

HACKERS PRACTICE

음성을 들으며 질문에 가장 알맞은 응답을 고르고, 빈칸에 들어갈 내용을 받아쓰세요. (음성은 두 번 들려줍니다.) 🎧 D03_6_Practice

01 (A)　(B)　(C)

_____ of that kitchen knife?
(A) _____ was remodeled.
(B) It's _____.
(C) With a _____.

02 (A)　(B)　(C)

_____ do you generally take _____?
(A) I'll have _____, thanks.
(B) At _____.
(C) For _____.

03 (A)　(B)　(C)

_____ is the engineering team on?
(A) They're _____.
(B) The _____.
(C) Yes, _____ is complete.

04 (A)　(B)　(C)

_____ should I do to _____ my overall health?
(A) It's quite _____.
(B) During my _____.
(C) You could start with _____.

05 (A)　(B)　(C)

_____ of food should we order for _____?
(A) The _____ to arrive.
(B) Thanks for _____.
(C) I enjoy _____.

06 (A)　(B)　(C)

_____ of the upcoming _____?
(A) At the _____.
(B) _____, I believe.
(C) It'll be _____.

정답·해석·해설 p.11

HACKERS TEST

음성을 들으며 질문에 가장 알맞은 응답을 고르세요. 🎧 D03_7_Test

01	Mark your answer on the answer sheet.	(A)	(B)	(C)
02	Mark your answer on the answer sheet.	(A)	(B)	(C)
03	Mark your answer on the answer sheet.	(A)	(B)	(C)
04	Mark your answer on the answer sheet.	(A)	(B)	(C)
05	Mark your answer on the answer sheet.	(A)	(B)	(C)
06	Mark your answer on the answer sheet.	(A)	(B)	(C)
07	Mark your answer on the answer sheet.	(A)	(B)	(C)
08	Mark your answer on the answer sheet.	(A)	(B)	(C)
09	Mark your answer on the answer sheet.	(A)	(B)	(C)
10	Mark your answer on the answer sheet.	(A)	(B)	(C)
11	Mark your answer on the answer sheet.	(A)	(B)	(C)
12	Mark your answer on the answer sheet.	(A)	(B)	(C)
13	Mark your answer on the answer sheet.	(A)	(B)	(C)

14 Mark your answer on the answer sheet.   (A) (B) (C)

15 Mark your answer on the answer sheet.   (A) (B) (C)

16 Mark your answer on the answer sheet.   (A) (B) (C)

17 Mark your answer on the answer sheet.   (A) (B) (C)

18 Mark your answer on the answer sheet.   (A) (B) (C)

19 Mark your answer on the answer sheet.   (A) (B) (C)

20 Mark your answer on the answer sheet.   (A) (B) (C)

21 Mark your answer on the answer sheet.   (A) (B) (C)

22 Mark your answer on the answer sheet.   (A) (B) (C)

23 Mark your answer on the answer sheet.   (A) (B) (C)

24 Mark your answer on the answer sheet.   (A) (B) (C)

25 Mark your answer on the answer sheet.   (A) (B) (C)

DAY 04 의문사 의문문: Where, When

MP3 바로듣기

1. Where 의문문

Where 의문문은 의문사 where(어디)를 사용하여 사물이나 건물의 위치 및 장소, 물건이나 정보의 출처를 묻는 의문문입니다. PART 2 전체 25문제 중 매회 1~2문제 정도 출제됩니다.

빈출 질문과 응답 🎧 D04_1_예문

위치, 장소, 출처를 나타내는 표현을 사용한 응답이나 사람 이름을 포함한 응답이 정답으로 자주 출제되며, 간접적인 응답도 출제됩니다.

Q **Where** were the fabric samples delivered?
원단 견본들은 어디로 배송되었나요?

A At the **reception desk**. [위치/장소]
접수처에요.

A **Ms. Park** received them. [사람]
Ms. Park이 그것들을 받았어요.

Q **Where** did you get the registration form?
등록 양식을 어디에서 받으셨나요?

A From a **Web site**. [출처]
웹사이트에서요.

A **I'm still looking for it.** [간접적인 응답]
저는 아직 그걸 찾고 있어요.

Example 🎧 D04_2_예제

(A)   (B)   (C)

3인 미국 → 호주
Where's the new company van?
(A) I don't think so.
(B) A driver's license.
(C) Behind the warehouse.

| 해설 | 정답 (C) |

(A) [×] 회사 승합차가 어디에 있는지를 물었는데, 이와 관련이 없는 그렇게 생각하지 않는다고 응답했으므로 오답입니다.
(B) [×] 질문의 van(승합차)에서 연상할 수 있는 driver's license(운전면허증)를 사용하여 혼동을 준 오답입니다.
(C) [○] 창고 뒤라며 회사 승합차가 있는 위치를 언급했으므로 정답입니다.

해석
새로운 회사 승합차는 어디에 있나요?
(A) 저는 그렇게 생각하지 않아요.
(B) 운전면허증이요.
(C) 창고 뒤에요.

어휘
van n. 승합차 license n. 면허(증) warehouse n. 창고

HACKERS PRACTICE

음성을 들으며 질문에 가장 알맞은 응답을 고르고, 빈칸에 들어갈 내용을 받아쓰세요. (음성은 두 번 들려줍니다.) 🎧 D04_3_Practice

01 (A) (B) (C)

_____ can I get a resident _____?
(A) To pay a _____.
(B) About _____ per month.
(C) From the _____.

02 (A) (B) (C)

_____ will the _____ be held?
(A) We are _____.
(B) _____, I believe.
(C) About _____.

03 (A) (B) (C)

_____ did you get the _____?
(A) Jane had an _____.
(B) To the _____.
(C) _____ immediately.

04 (A) (B) (C)

_____ is the revised copy of the partnership _____?
(A) Please make _____.
(B) Our lawyer is _____.
(C) It is _____.

05 (A) (B) (C)

_____ is the information center _____?
(A) A lot of _____.
(B) The _____ was empty today.
(C) To the left of the _____.

06 (A) (B) (C)

_____ can I _____ a colorful scarf like yours?
(A) I prefer the _____.
(B) Make sure to _____.
(C) It was a _____.

정답·해석·해설 p.16

DAY 04 의문사 의문문: Where, When 51

2. When 의문문

When 의문문은 의문사 when(언제)을 사용하여 어떤 행동이나 업무가 이루어지는 시점을 묻는 의문문입니다. PART 2 전체 25문제 중 매회 2~3문제 정도 출제됩니다.

빈출 질문과 응답 🎧 D04_4_예문

시간, 날짜, 요일 또는 불확실한 시점을 사용한 응답이 정답으로 자주 출제되며, 간접적인 응답도 출제됩니다.

Q When is the factory tour for staff?
직원들을 위한 공장 투어는 언제인가요?

A In an hour. [시간]
한 시간 후에요.

A On April 3. [날짜]
4월 3일에요.

A This Wednesday. [요일]
이번 주 수요일에요.

A Sometime next week. [불확실한 시점]
다음 주 언젠가요.

A It has been canceled due to safety concerns.
[간접적인 응답]
안전 문제로 취소되었어요.

Example 🎧 D04_5_예제

(A) (B) (C)	영국 → 캐나다 When did you complete the annual sales summary? (A) In October. (B) An increase in sales. (C) Yes, once every year.
해설 정답 (A) (A) [o] 10월에라며 연간 판매 개요서를 완성한 시점을 언급했으므로 정답입니다. (B) [×] 질문의 sales를 반복 사용하여 혼동을 준 오답입니다. (C) [×] 의문사 의문문에 Yes로 응답했으므로 오답입니다.	**해석** 당신은 연간 판매 개요서를 언제 완성했나요? (A) 10월에요. (B) 판매량 증가요. (C) 네, 일 년에 한 번이요. **어휘** annual adj. 연간의 summary n. 개요서 increase n. 증가

HACKERS PRACTICE

음성을 들으며 질문에 가장 알맞은 응답을 고르고, 빈칸에 들어갈 내용을 받아쓰세요. (음성은 두 번 들려줍니다.) 🎧 D04_6_Practice

01 (A) (B) (C)

_____ is the performance _____?
(A) About the _____.
(B) To the _____.
(C) By _____.

02 (A) (B) (C)

_____ is a good time to _____?
(A) In _____.
(B) At the _____, maybe.
(C) _____ was great.

03 (A) (B) (C)

_____ will the orientation for new staff _____?
(A) Tomorrow _____.
(B) To _____.
(C) Several _____.

04 (A) (B) (C)

_____ did you do the _____?
(A) No. We're _____.
(B) On _____.
(C) _____ across the street.

05 (A) (B) (C)

_____ do you plan to _____ the dry cleaning?
(A) Please _____ from the airport.
(B) I _____ at 4 P.M. today.
(C) We should _____ soon.

06 (A) (B) (C)

_____ can we _____ the office?
(A) Once the _____ are complete.
(B) That's _____.
(C) Come in and sit wherever _____.

정답·해석·해설 p.17

HACKERS TEST

음성을 들으며 질문에 가장 알맞은 응답을 고르세요. 🎧 D04_7_Test

01 Mark your answer on the answer sheet. (A) (B) (C)

02 Mark your answer on the answer sheet. (A) (B) (C)

03 Mark your answer on the answer sheet. (A) (B) (C)

04 Mark your answer on the answer sheet. (A) (B) (C)

05 Mark your answer on the answer sheet. (A) (B) (C)

06 Mark your answer on the answer sheet. (A) (B) (C)

07 Mark your answer on the answer sheet. (A) (B) (C)

08 Mark your answer on the answer sheet. (A) (B) (C)

09 Mark your answer on the answer sheet. (A) (B) (C)

10 Mark your answer on the answer sheet. (A) (B) (C)

11 Mark your answer on the answer sheet. (A) (B) (C)

12 Mark your answer on the answer sheet. (A) (B) (C)

13 Mark your answer on the answer sheet. (A) (B) (C)

14 Mark your answer on the answer sheet.   (A) (B) (C)

15 Mark your answer on the answer sheet.   (A) (B) (C)

16 Mark your answer on the answer sheet.   (A) (B) (C)

17 Mark your answer on the answer sheet.   (A) (B) (C)

18 Mark your answer on the answer sheet.   (A) (B) (C)

19 Mark your answer on the answer sheet.   (A) (B) (C)

20 Mark your answer on the answer sheet.   (A) (B) (C)

21 Mark your answer on the answer sheet.   (A) (B) (C)

22 Mark your answer on the answer sheet.   (A) (B) (C)

23 Mark your answer on the answer sheet.   (A) (B) (C)

24 Mark your answer on the answer sheet.   (A) (B) (C)

25 Mark your answer on the answer sheet.   (A) (B) (C)

DAY 05 의문사 의문문: Why, How

MP3 바로듣기

1. Why 의문문

Why 의문문은 의문사 why(왜)를 사용하여 어떤 일의 이유나 원인, 목적을 묻는 의문문입니다. PART 2 전체 25문제 중 매회 1~2문제 정도 출제됩니다.

빈출 질문과 응답   🎧 D05_1_예문

'~ 때문에'라는 의미의 because (of)로 시작하거나 이를 생략하고 바로 이유나 목적을 설명하는 응답이 정답으로 자주 출제되며, 간접적인 응답도 출제됩니다.

Q Why are you leaving early today?
오늘 왜 일찍 가시나요?

A Because of a family event. [Because of 사용]
가족 행사 때문에요.

A Because I have a doctor's appointment. [Because 사용]
진료 예약이 있어서요.

Q Why did the technician come this morning?
오늘 아침에 기술자가 왜 왔나요?

A A part needed to be replaced. [Because 생략]
부품이 교체되어야 했어요.

A I'll ask the building manager. [간접적인 응답]
제가 건물 관리자에게 물어볼게요.

Example   🎧 D05_2_예제

(A)   (B)   (C)

🔊 캐나다 → 영국
Why did Mr. Lyons leave the presentation early?
(A) Because he has an urgent meeting.
(B) No, this morning.
(C) With a job applicant.

해설   정답 (A)
(A) [○] 긴급한 회의가 있기 때문이라는 말로 Mr. Lyons가 발표를 일찍 떠난 이유를 언급했으므로 정답입니다.
(B) [×] 의문사 의문문에 No로 응답했으므로 오답입니다.
(C) [×] Mr. Lyons가 왜 발표를 일찍 떠났는지를 물었는데, 이와 관련이 없는 사람으로 응답했으므로 오답입니다.

해석
Mr. Lyons는 왜 발표를 일찍 떠났나요?
(A) 그가 긴급한 회의가 있기 때문이에요.
(B) 아니요, 오늘 아침이요.
(C) 취업 지원자와 함께요.

어휘
urgent adj. 긴급한, 시급한   job applicant 취업 지원자

HACKERS PRACTICE

음성을 들으며 질문에 가장 알맞은 응답을 고르고, 빈칸에 들어갈 내용을 받아쓰세요. (음성은 두 번 들려줍니다.) 🎧 D05_3_Practice

01 (A)　(B)　(C)

Why did the server _____?
(A) I'll treat you to _____.
(B) Can I _____?
(C) He gave me the _____.

02 (A)　(B)　(C)

_____ is the furnace not _____?
(A) I'll call a _____.
(B) Sure, I'll _____.
(C) Yes. In the _____.

03 (A)　(B)　(C)

_____ hasn't the _____ been replaced yet?
(A) It's a _____.
(B) I need to _____.
(C) Because the new one _____ yet.

04 (A)　(B)　(C)

_____ did Ms. Peters _____ Chicago this week?
(A) She'll _____.
(B) I found the _____.
(C) There is a _____.

05 (A)　(B)　(C)

_____ is the product _____?
(A) I can't _____.
(B) Because of _____.
(C) It's one of the _____.

06 (A)　(B)　(C)

_____ hasn't the _____ been updated?
(A) You should not _____.
(B) I had a problem with _____.
(C) It took _____.

정답·해석·해설 p.22

2. How 의문문

How 의문문은 의문사 how(어떻게/얼마나)를 사용하여 방법, 상태, 기간, 수량, 가격 등에 대해 묻는 의문문입니다. PART 2 전체 25문제 중 매회 2~3문제 정도 출제됩니다.

빈출 질문과 응답   🎧 D05_4_예문

How 뒤에 나오는 동사, 형용사, 부사에 따라 묻는 내용이 달라지며, 질문에서 요청하는 정보를 담은 응답이 정답으로 자주 출제됩니다.

Q **How** do I adjust the volume? [방법]
음량은 어떻게 조절하나요?

A **Turn this dial.**
이 다이얼을 돌리세요.

Q **How is** the budget review **going**? [상태]
예산 검토는 어떻게 되고 있나요?

A Everything is **going well**.
모든 것이 잘 진행되고 있어요.

Q **How long** will the construction continue? [기간]
공사가 얼마나 오래 지속되나요?

A For at least **six months**.
최소 6개월 동안이요.

Q **How many** customers visited today? [수량]
오늘 몇 명의 고객이 방문했나요?

A Just **over 30**.
30명이 좀 넘었어요.

Q **How much** will the repairs cost? [가격]
수리 비용이 얼마나 드나요?

A Approximately **500 dollars**.
500달러 정도요.

Example   🎧 D05_5_예제

(A)   (B)   (C)

🔊 미국 → 캐나다
How long did you stay in Japan?
(A) The hotel was very clean.
(B) Only a week.
(C) I forgot to bring my passport.

해설   **정답 (B)**
(A) [×] 질문의 stay(머무르다)와 관련 있는 hotel(호텔)을 사용하여 혼동을 준 오답입니다.
(B) [o] 고작 일주일이라며 일본에서 머문 기간을 언급했으므로 정답입니다.
(C) [×] 질문의 stay in Japan(일본에서 머물다)에서 연상할 수 있는 passport(여권)를 사용하여 혼동을 준 오답입니다.

해석
당신은 일본에서 얼마나 머물렀나요?
(A) 호텔은 매우 깨끗했어요.
(B) 고작 일주일이요.
(C) 제가 여권을 가져오는 것을 깜빡했어요.

어휘
stay v. 머무르다

HACKERS PRACTICE

음성을 들으며 질문에 가장 알맞은 응답을 고르고, 빈칸에 들어갈 내용을 받아쓰세요. (음성은 두 번 들려줍니다.) 🎧 D05_6_Practice

01 (A) (B) (C)

_____ you the photographs?
(A) By _____.
(B) _____, please.
(C) Yes. I _____ yesterday.

02 (A) (B) (C)

_____ hats are on _____?
(A) Yes, I helped _____.
(B) It _____ on you.
(C) There are six on the _____.

03 (A) (B) (C)

_____ can we _____ a booth at the trade show?
(A) The _____ was canceled.
(B) Over 300 _____.
(C) By _____.

04 (A) (B) (C)

_____ the Westwood branch of our store _____?
(A) _____ has a large parking lot.
(B) _____ lately.
(C) A _____ recently opened.

05 (A) (B) (C)

_____ to get to Bryce Park?
(A) It's 30 _____.
(B) _____ a soccer game.
(C) _____ by car.

06 (A) (B) (C)

_____ will the folding tables _____?
(A) We'll go for _____.
(B) _____ the sweater neatly.
(C) At least _____.

정답·해석·해설 p.23

HACKERS TEST

음성을 들으며 질문에 가장 알맞은 응답을 고르세요. 🎧 D05_7_Test

01 Mark your answer on the answer sheet. (A) (B) (C)

02 Mark your answer on the answer sheet. (A) (B) (C)

03 Mark your answer on the answer sheet. (A) (B) (C)

04 Mark your answer on the answer sheet. (A) (B) (C)

05 Mark your answer on the answer sheet. (A) (B) (C)

06 Mark your answer on the answer sheet. (A) (B) (C)

07 Mark your answer on the answer sheet. (A) (B) (C)

08 Mark your answer on the answer sheet. (A) (B) (C)

09 Mark your answer on the answer sheet. (A) (B) (C)

10 Mark your answer on the answer sheet. (A) (B) (C)

11 Mark your answer on the answer sheet. (A) (B) (C)

12 Mark your answer on the answer sheet. (A) (B) (C)

13 Mark your answer on the answer sheet. (A) (B) (C)

14. Mark your answer on the answer sheet. (A) (B) (C)

15. Mark your answer on the answer sheet. (A) (B) (C)

16. Mark your answer on the answer sheet. (A) (B) (C)

17. Mark your answer on the answer sheet. (A) (B) (C)

18. Mark your answer on the answer sheet. (A) (B) (C)

19. Mark your answer on the answer sheet. (A) (B) (C)

20. Mark your answer on the answer sheet. (A) (B) (C)

21. Mark your answer on the answer sheet. (A) (B) (C)

22. Mark your answer on the answer sheet. (A) (B) (C)

23. Mark your answer on the answer sheet. (A) (B) (C)

24. Mark your answer on the answer sheet. (A) (B) (C)

25. Mark your answer on the answer sheet. (A) (B) (C)

정답·해석·해설 p.24

DAY 06 일반 의문문 및 선택 의문문

MP3 바로듣기

1. 일반 의문문

일반 의문문은 Be동사(Is, Are 등) 또는 조동사(Can, Do, Have, Should 등)를 사용하여 사실을 확인하거나 의견을 묻는 의문문입니다. PART 2 전체 25문제 중 매회 4~5문제 정도 출제됩니다.

빈출 질문과 응답 🎧 D06_1_예문

Yes/No를 사용한 후 적절한 부연 설명을 덧붙인 응답이나 Yes/No를 생략한 응답이 정답으로 자주 출제되며, 간접적인 응답도 출제됩니다.

Q **Can** you finish the report today?
오늘 보고서를 끝낼 수 있나요?

A **Yes.** I'm almost done. [Yes 사용]
네. 저는 거의 끝났어요.

A **No.** I'm still working on it. [No 사용]
아니요. 저는 아직 작성 중이에요.

Q **Is** the meeting room available now?
지금 회의실을 사용할 수 있나요?

A **It's currently being used for another meeting.** [No 생략]
(아니요.) 그곳은 현재 다른 회의를 위해 사용 중이에요.

A **Are you asking about the room on the third floor?** [간접적인 응답]
3층에 있는 회의실에 대해 물어보시는 건가요?

Example 🎧 D06_2_예제

(A)　　(B)　　(C)	영국 → 캐나다 Is there a photocopier in the library? (A) I need another copy. (B) Yes. On the second floor. (C) The library opens at 10.
해설　　　　　　　　　　　　　　**정답** (B) (A) [×] 질문의 photocopier(복사기)와 관련 있는 copy(사본)를 사용하여 혼동을 준 오답입니다. (B) [○] Yes로 도서관에 복사기가 있음을 전달한 후, 2층에 있다는 부연 설명을 했으므로 정답입니다. (C) [×] 질문의 library를 반복 사용하여 혼동을 준 오답입니다.	**해석** 도서관에 복사기가 있나요? (A) 저는 다른 사본이 필요해요. (B) 네. 2층에 있어요. (C) 도서관은 10시에 문 열어요. **어휘** photocopier n. 복사기　copy n. 사본　floor n. 층, 바닥

HACKERS PRACTICE

음성을 들으며 질문에 가장 알맞은 응답을 고르고, 빈칸에 들어갈 내용을 받아쓰세요. (음성은 두 번 들려줍니다.) 🎧 D06_3_Practice

01 (A) (B) (C)

_____ that our branch in Portland closed?
(A) The _____.
(B) No. I _____ of that.
(C) I've only _____ once.

02 (A) (B) (C)

_____ the company workshop?
(A) Yes. _____.
(B) _____ I do.
(C) On _____ strategies.

03 (A) (B) (C)

Is Sarah _____ a part-time job?
(A) I work at a _____.
(B) No. She _____ right now.
(C) Fill out this _____.

04 (A) (B) (C)

_____ a color for the carpet?
(A) My car is _____.
(B) I was hoping _____ me.
(C) Oh, _____ really suits you.

05 (A) (B) (C)

_____ of taking a course abroad?
(A) It's somewhere _____.
(B) A _____, please.
(C) I _____ to.

06 (A) (B) (C)

_____ the agreement before we sign it?
(A) _____ it.
(B) Oh, _____ is lovely.
(C) It is the _____ he's written.

정답·해석·해설 p.28

2. 선택 의문문

선택 의문문은 두 가지 선택 사항을 or로 연결한 'A or B(A 또는 B)' 형태를 사용하여 둘 중 하나를 선택하도록 요구하는 의문문입니다. PART 2 전체 25문제 중 매회 1~2문제 정도 출제됩니다.

빈출 질문과 응답 ∩ D06_4_예문

두 가지 선택 사항 중 하나를 선택하는 응답, 둘 다 선택하거나 둘 다 선택하지 않는 응답, 제3의 선택을 하는 응답이 정답으로 자주 출제되며, 간접적인 응답도 출제됩니다.

Q Would you like **a window seat or an aisle seat**?
창가 좌석을 원하시나요, 아니면 통로 좌석을 원하시나요?

A I prefer the **aisle**. [둘 중 하나를 선택]
저는 통로 쪽을 선호합니다.

A **Either** is fine. [둘 다 선택]
어느 쪽이든 괜찮아요.

Q Should we discuss the plan **now or at lunch**?
그 계획을 지금 논의할까요, 아니면 점심시간에 논의할까요?

A **Tomorrow** would be better. [제3의 선택]
내일이 더 나을 것 같아요.

A **How long will it take?** [간접적인 응답]
얼마나 걸릴 것 같아요?

Example ∩ D06_5_예제

(A) (B) (C)	캐나다 → 미국 Do you prefer to walk or take the subway? (A) She prefers to walk. (B) For about an hour. (C) Let's ride the subway.
해설 　　　　　　　　　　　　　　　**정답** (C) (A) [×] 질문의 prefer를 반복 사용하여 혼동을 준 오답입니다. (B) [×] 걷는 것을 선호하는지 지하철을 타는 것을 선호하는지를 물었는데, 이와 관련이 없는 시간으로 응답했으므로 오답입니다. (C) [○] 지하철을 타자는 말로, 지하철을 타는 것을 선택했으므로 정답입니다.	**해석** 당신은 걷는 것을 선호하나요, 아니면 지하철을 타는 것을 선호하나요? (A) 그녀는 걷는 것을 선호해요. (B) 약 한 시간 동안이요. (C) 지하철을 탑시다. **어휘** prefer v. 선호하다　subway n. 지하철

HACKERS PRACTICE

음성을 들으며 질문에 가장 알맞은 응답을 고르고, 빈칸에 들어갈 내용을 받아쓰세요. (음성은 두 번 들려줍니다.) 🎧 D06_6_Practice

01 (A) (B) (C)

_____ inside the café or on the patio?
(A) I'm fine _____.
(B) How about ordering _____?
(C) _____ was really long.

02 (A) (B) (C)

_____, or should I?
(A) Let's _____.
(B) A _____ of 15 dollars.
(C) Ask the _____ about that.

03 (A) (B) (C)

Should we _____ on Thursday or Friday?
(A) We need to _____.
(B) Yes, that sounds _____.
(C) Do you need my _____?

04 (A) (B) (C)

Is the _____ today or tomorrow?
(A) Pass me the _____.
(B) It'll be done _____.
(C) It's really _____ this summer.

05 (A) (B) (C)

Do you want to go _____ this weekend?
(A) I'd like to _____.
(B) _____ up over there.
(C) The _____ is two kilometers long.

06 (A) (B) (C)

Should I buy _____ or a _____?
(A) I downloaded _____.
(B) I already have _____.
(C) It depends on the _____.

정답·해석·해설 p.29

HACKERS TEST

음성을 들으며 질문에 가장 알맞은 응답을 고르세요. 🎧 D06_7_Test

01 Mark your answer on the answer sheet. (A) (B) (C)

02 Mark your answer on the answer sheet. (A) (B) (C)

03 Mark your answer on the answer sheet. (A) (B) (C)

04 Mark your answer on the answer sheet. (A) (B) (C)

05 Mark your answer on the answer sheet. (A) (B) (C)

06 Mark your answer on the answer sheet. (A) (B) (C)

07 Mark your answer on the answer sheet. (A) (B) (C)

08 Mark your answer on the answer sheet. (A) (B) (C)

09 Mark your answer on the answer sheet. (A) (B) (C)

10 Mark your answer on the answer sheet. (A) (B) (C)

11 Mark your answer on the answer sheet. (A) (B) (C)

12 Mark your answer on the answer sheet. (A) (B) (C)

13 Mark your answer on the answer sheet. (A) (B) (C)

14. Mark your answer on the answer sheet.   (A)   (B)   (C)

15. Mark your answer on the answer sheet.   (A)   (B)   (C)

16. Mark your answer on the answer sheet.   (A)   (B)   (C)

17. Mark your answer on the answer sheet.   (A)   (B)   (C)

18. Mark your answer on the answer sheet.   (A)   (B)   (C)

19. Mark your answer on the answer sheet.   (A)   (B)   (C)

20. Mark your answer on the answer sheet.   (A)   (B)   (C)

21. Mark your answer on the answer sheet.   (A)   (B)   (C)

22. Mark your answer on the answer sheet.   (A)   (B)   (C)

23. Mark your answer on the answer sheet.   (A)   (B)   (C)

24. Mark your answer on the answer sheet.   (A)   (B)   (C)

25. Mark your answer on the answer sheet.   (A)   (B)   (C)

DAY 07 부정 의문문 및 부가 의문문

MP3 바로 듣기

1. 부정 의문문

부정 의문문은 Be동사 또는 조동사를 not과 함께 사용하여(Isn't, Don't 등) 사실의 진위를 확인하거나 자신의 의견에 동의를 구하는 의문문입니다. PART 2 전체 25문제 중 매회 1~2문제 정도 출제됩니다.

빈출 질문과 응답 🎧 D07_1_예문

확인하고자 하는 사실이 맞는 말이거나 의견에 동의하면 Yes, 사실을 부인하거나 의견에 반대하면 No라고 한 후 부연 설명을 추가한 응답이 정답으로 자주 출제됩니다. Yes/No를 생략한 응답도 정답이 될 수 있으며, 간접적인 응답도 출제됩니다.

Q **Isn't** the conference room already reserved?
회의실이 이미 예약되어 있지 않나요?

A **Yes**, for the marketing team. [Yes 사용]
네, 마케팅팀으로요.

A **No.** I just canceled it. [No 사용]
아니요. 제가 방금 취소했어요.

Q **Shouldn't** we renovate the break room?
휴게실을 개조해야 하지 않을까요?

A **It looks fine** to me. [No 생략]
저한테는 괜찮아 보여요.

A **Let's check the budget first.** [간접적인 응답]
먼저 예산을 확인해 봅시다.

Example 🎧 D07_2_예제

(A)   (B)   (C)

🌐 미국 → 호주
Aren't you coming to the workshop next week?
(A) She was busy last week.
(B) About the guest speaker.
(C) No. I'll be on a business trip.

해설 　　　　　　　　　　　　　　　　　　　　정답 (C)
(A) [x] 질문의 week를 반복 사용하여 혼동을 준 오답입니다.
(B) [x] 질문의 workshop(워크숍)에서 연상할 수 있는 guest speaker(초청 연사)를 사용하여 혼동을 준 오답입니다.
(C) [o] No로 워크숍에 오지 않을 것임을 전달한 후, 출장 중일 거라는 부연 설명을 했으므로 정답입니다.

해석
당신은 다음 주 워크숍에 오지 않나요?
(A) 그녀는 지난주에 바빴어요.
(B) 초청 연사에 대해서요.
(C) 아니요. 저는 출장 중일 거예요.

어휘
guest speaker 연사　business trip 출장

HACKERS PRACTICE

음성을 들으며 질문에 가장 알맞은 응답을 고르고, 빈칸에 들어갈 내용을 받아쓰세요. (음성은 두 번 들려줍니다.) 🎧 D07_3_Practice

01 (A) (B) (C)

Doesn't the company have a _____?
(A) At the _____ department.
(B) Yes, up to _____.
(C) To discuss the new _____.

02 (A) (B) (C)

Didn't the manager _____?
(A) Thanks, I _____ on my desk.
(B) _____ is on Elm Street.
(C) Yes. I'll _____ now.

03 (A) (B) (C)

Wasn't our _____ today?
(A) I'm glad you could _____.
(B) Take a look at _____.
(C) Are you _____ using it?

04 (A) (B) (C)

Haven't we hired _____?
(A) No. We need _____.
(B) _____ over there.
(C) I already _____.

05 (A) (B) (C)

Shouldn't employees _____?
(A) The most _____.
(B) No. We don't _____.
(C) Yes. It's a _____.

06 (A) (B) (C)

Aren't there more _____?
(A) I haven't _____.
(B) _____ in the warehouse.
(C) To buy some _____.

2. 부가 의문문

부가 의문문은 평서문 뒤에 꼬리말(didn't you, is it, right 등)을 덧붙여 사실을 확인하거나 의견에 동의를 구하는 의문문입니다. PART 2 전체 25문제 중 매회 2~3문제 정도 출제됩니다.

빈출 질문과 응답 🎧 D07_4_예문

꼬리말 앞의 내용이 맞는 말이거나 그 내용에 동의하면 Yes, 틀린 말이거나 그 내용에 반대하면 No라고 한 후 부연 설명을 추가한 응답이 정답으로 자주 출제됩니다. Yes/No를 생략한 응답도 정답이 될 수 있으며, 간접적인 응답도 출제됩니다.

Q This restaurant serves seafood, **doesn't it**?
이 식당은 해산물을 제공하죠, 그렇지 않나요?

A **Yes.** It's known for its grilled salmon. [Yes 사용]
네. 그곳은 연어구이로 유명해요.

A **No.** It only has vegetarian dishes. [No 사용]
아니요. 채식 요리만 있어요.

Q The interns aren't fully trained, **are they**?
인턴들은 완전히 교육받지 않았죠, 그렇죠?

A **They still need some guidance.** [Yes 생략]
그들은 아직 지도가 좀 필요해요.

A **I'm not sure about that.** [간접적인 응답]
저는 그건 잘 모르겠어요.

Example 🎧 D07_5_예제

(A)	(B)	(C)

🎙 영국 → 캐나다
New inventory is arriving this week, isn't it?
(A) I like the other one better.
(B) That item is currently on sale.
(C) Yes. By Wednesday at the latest.

해설 정답 (C)
(A) [×] 질문의 inventory(재고품)를 나타낼 수 있는 one을 사용하여 혼동을 준 오답입니다.
(B) [×] 질문의 inventory(재고품)에서 연상할 수 있는 item(품목)을 사용하여 혼동을 준 오답입니다.
(C) [o] Yes로 새 재고품이 이번 주에 도착할 것이라고 전달한 후, 늦어도 수요일까지라는 부연 설명을 했으므로 정답입니다.

해석
새 재고품이 이번 주에 도착하죠, 그렇지 않나요?
(A) 저는 다른 것이 더 좋아요.
(B) 그 품목은 현재 할인 중이에요.
(C) 네. 늦어도 수요일까지요.

어휘
inventory n. 재고품, 물품 목록   currently adv. 현재
on sale 할인 중인   at the latest 늦어도

HACKERS PRACTICE

음성을 들으며 질문에 가장 알맞은 응답을 고르고, 빈칸에 들어갈 내용을 받아쓰세요. (음성은 두 번 들려줍니다.) 🎧 D07_6_Practice

01 (A) (B) (C)

_____ we ordered _____, has it?
(A) No. _____.
(B) Yes. Let's _____.
(C) I _____.

02 (A) (B) (C)

There's a _____ on this floor, right?
(A) Yes. It's _____.
(B) _____ was just waxed.
(C) No, I left it in _____.

03 (A) (B) (C)

Ms. Lee will be _____, won't she?
(A) Let me _____.
(B) Submit a _____.
(C) I'd prefer to _____.

04 (A) (B) (C)

The _____, doesn't it?
(A) I enjoyed _____.
(B) Because he's my _____.
(C) No. The _____.

05 (A) (B) (C)

There's a _____, isn't there?
(A) _____ overlooks the ocean.
(B) Near the _____.
(C) You must _____ by noon.

06 (A) (B) (C)

Our client _____, didn't he?
(A) He still has _____.
(B) By improving _____.
(C) I'll read _____ soon.

정답·해석·해설 p.35

HACKERS TEST

음성을 들으며 질문에 가장 알맞은 응답을 고르세요. 🎧 D07_7_Test

01 Mark your answer on the answer sheet.   (A)   (B)   (C)

02 Mark your answer on the answer sheet.   (A)   (B)   (C)

03 Mark your answer on the answer sheet.   (A)   (B)   (C)

04 Mark your answer on the answer sheet.   (A)   (B)   (C)

05 Mark your answer on the answer sheet.   (A)   (B)   (C)

06 Mark your answer on the answer sheet.   (A)   (B)   (C)

07 Mark your answer on the answer sheet.   (A)   (B)   (C)

08 Mark your answer on the answer sheet.   (A)   (B)   (C)

09 Mark your answer on the answer sheet.   (A)   (B)   (C)

10 Mark your answer on the answer sheet.   (A)   (B)   (C)

11 Mark your answer on the answer sheet.   (A)   (B)   (C)

12 Mark your answer on the answer sheet.   (A)   (B)   (C)

13 Mark your answer on the answer sheet.   (A)   (B)   (C)

14 Mark your answer on the answer sheet.   (A)   (B)   (C)

15 Mark your answer on the answer sheet.   (A)   (B)   (C)

16 Mark your answer on the answer sheet.   (A)   (B)   (C)

17 Mark your answer on the answer sheet.   (A)   (B)   (C)

18 Mark your answer on the answer sheet.   (A)   (B)   (C)

19 Mark your answer on the answer sheet.   (A)   (B)   (C)

20 Mark your answer on the answer sheet.   (A)   (B)   (C)

21 Mark your answer on the answer sheet.   (A)   (B)   (C)

22 Mark your answer on the answer sheet.   (A)   (B)   (C)

23 Mark your answer on the answer sheet.   (A)   (B)   (C)

24 Mark your answer on the answer sheet.   (A)   (B)   (C)

25 Mark your answer on the answer sheet.   (A)   (B)   (C)

정답·해석·해설 p.36

DAY 08 제안/제공/요청 의문문 및 평서문

MP3 바로 듣기

1. 제안/제공/요청 의문문

제안/제공/요청 의문문은 Why don't we ~?(우리 ~하는 것이 어때요?), Would you like me to ~?(제가 ~해 드릴까요?), Could you ~? (~해 주시겠어요?) 등의 표현을 사용하여 상대방에게 제안이나 제공, 요청을 하는 의문문입니다. PART 2 전체 25문제 중 매회 1~2문제 정도 출제됩니다.

빈출 질문과 응답 🎧 D08_1_예문

제안/제공/요청하는 내용에 대해 수락하거나 거절하는 응답이 정답으로 자주 출제되며, 간접적인 응답도 출제됩니다. Sure(물론이죠), That's a good idea(좋은 생각이에요), No problem(문제 없어요)과 같이 제안을 수락하는 전형적인 표현도 정답으로 자주 출제됨을 알아 둡니다.

- Q **Why don't we** go for a walk? [제안]
  우리 산책하러 가는 것이 어때요?
- A **Yes**, that sounds like a great idea. [수락]
  네, 그거 정말 좋은 생각이에요.

- Q **Would you like me to** print the draft? [제공]
  제가 초안을 출력해 드릴까요?
- A **No.** I can check it online. [거절]
  아니요. 제가 온라인으로 확인하면 돼요.

- Q **Could you** pick up some coffee? [요청]
  커피를 사다 주시겠어요?
- A **Sure**, I'll grab some. [수락]
  물론이죠, 제가 사 올게요.

- Q **Do you mind** covering my shift tomorrow? [요청]
  내일 제 근무를 대신해 주시겠어요?
- A **Sorry.** I have other plans. [거절]
  미안해요. 저는 다른 계획이 있어요.

- Q **Can you** send me the files by e-mail? [요청]
  파일을 이메일로 보내주실 수 있나요?
- A **I'm about to board the plane.** [간접적인 응답]
  저는 막 비행기를 타려던 참이에요.

Example 🎧 D08_2_예제

(A)   (B)   (C)

🔊 영국 → 호주
Could you give this folder to Mr. Glenn?
(A) Documents for the Brenner project.
(B) I'll bring it to him shortly.
(C) Fold them all in half.

해설   정답 (B)
(A) [×] 질문의 folder(폴더)와 관련 있는 Documents(문서들)를 사용하여 혼동을 준 오답입니다.
(B) [○] 그에게 가져다주겠다는 말로, 폴더를 Mr. Glenn에게 주라는 요청을 수락한 정답입니다.
(C) [×] folder - Fold의 유사 발음 어휘를 사용하여 혼동을 준 오답입니다.

해석
이 폴더를 Mr. Glenn에게 주시겠어요?
(A) Brenner 프로젝트를 위한 문서들이요.
(B) 제가 바로 그것을 그에게 가져다줄게요.
(C) 그것들을 모두 반으로 접으세요.

어휘
bring v. 가져다주다, 가져오다   shortly adv. 바로, 곧   fold v. 접다

HACKERS PRACTICE

음성을 들으며 질문에 가장 알맞은 응답을 고르고, 빈칸에 들어갈 내용을 받아쓰세요. (음성은 두 번 들려줍니다.) 🎧 D08_3_Practice

01 (A) (B) (C)

Why don't we hire a _____?
(A) I really _____.
(B) Yes. _____ these days.
(C) Who did you _____?

02 (A) (B) (C)

Could you help me _____?
(A) I _____ years ago.
(B) Sure, you can _____.
(C) What will it be _____?

03 (A) (B) (C)

How about _____ I made?
(A) We have some _____.
(B) No, thanks. I have a _____.
(C) You should _____.

04 (A) (B) (C)

Do you want me to _____?
(A) A part of the _____.
(B) Inside _____.
(C) If you _____.

05 (A) (B) (C)

Can you take some time to _____?
(A) It's just a _____.
(B) _____ to me after lunch.
(C) Yes, it has a _____.

06 (A) (B) (C)

Would you _____ before the presentation?
(A) I already had some _____.
(B) Well, the presentation _____.
(C) Yes, please turn on the _____.

2. 평서문

평서문은 의문문이 아닌 형태로 제안이나 요청, 정보 제공, 의견 전달을 하며 상대의 응답을 요구하는 진술문입니다. PART 2 전체 25문제 중 매회 4~5문제 정도 출제됩니다.

빈출 질문과 응답 🎧 D08_4_예문

평서문의 의도에 따라 동의나 반대, 추가 정보 제공, 해결책을 제시하는 응답이 정답으로 자주 출제되며, 의문문을 사용하여 추가 정보를 요구하는 응답도 출제됩니다.

Q **Let's** meet in the lobby at 2 P.M. [제안]
오후 2시에 로비에서 만납시다.

A **Sure.** I'll see you then. [동의]
물론이죠. 그때 뵐게요.

A **Sorry.** I'll be out of the office. [반대]
죄송해요. 저는 사무실에 없을 거예요.

Q We **received the new ID badges**. [정보 제공]
우리는 새로운 사원증을 받았어요.

A **I'll distribute them** to everyone. [추가 정보 제공]
제가 그것들을 모두에게 나눠줄게요.

Q It's getting **too hot in the office**. [의견 전달]
사무실 안이 너무 더워지고 있어요.

A **I'll turn on the air conditioner**. [해결책 제시]
제가 에어컨을 켤게요.

Q We're **planning a company retreat**. [정보 제공]
우리는 회사 야유회를 계획 중이에요.

A **When will it be held?** [추가 정보 요구]
언제 열리나요?

Example 🎧 D08_5_예제

(A) (B) (C)	🎙 호주 → 미국 The storeroom is really messy. (A) We need to organize it soon. (B) The store is closed already. (C) I cleaned the hallway.
해설　　　　　　　　　　　　　　　　　　　　**정답** (A) (A) [o] 우리가 곧 정리해야겠다는 말로, 문제점에 대한 해결책을 제시했으므로 정답입니다. (B) [×] storeroom – store의 유사 발음 어휘를 사용하여 혼동을 준 오답입니다. (C) [×] 질문의 messy(지저분한)에서 연상할 수 있는 cleaned(청소했다)를 사용하여 혼동을 준 오답입니다.	**해석** 창고가 정말 지저분해요. (A) 우리가 곧 정리해야겠어요. (B) 가게는 이미 닫았어요. (C) 저는 복도를 청소했어요. **어휘** **storeroom** n. 창고　**messy** adj. 지저분한, 어수선한 **organize** v. 정리하다　**hallway** n. 복도

HACKERS PRACTICE

음성을 들으며 질문에 가장 알맞은 응답을 고르고, 빈칸에 들어갈 내용을 받아쓰세요. (음성은 두 번 들려줍니다.) 🎧 D08_6_Practice

01 (A) (B) (C)

The marketing budget _____.
(A) It _____ 3,000 dollars.
(B) We don't _____.
(C) It's a good _____.

02 (A) (B) (C)

We've been asked to revise the _____.
(A) It's an _____.
(B) Really? When is it _____?
(C) It's _____.

03 (A) (B) (C)

It's quite _____ today.
(A) Right. I'll wear a _____.
(B) The hourly _____.
(C) Who _____ for me?

04 (A) (B) (C)

Please _____ of the television.
(A) Sure. Let me _____.
(B) Change the _____.
(C) It's a new _____.

05 (A) (B) (C)

I _____ in my apartment.
(A) On the _____.
(B) You can _____.
(C) Don't forget to _____.

06 (A) (B) (C)

The company's sales _____ this year.
(A) Our employees have _____.
(B) Well, within the _____.
(C) Ms. Henry will _____ you.

정답·해석·해설 p.41

HACKERS TEST

음성을 들으며 질문에 가장 알맞은 응답을 고르세요. 🎧 D08_7_Test

01 Mark your answer on the answer sheet.　　　　(A)　(B)　(C)

02 Mark your answer on the answer sheet.　　　　(A)　(B)　(C)

03 Mark your answer on the answer sheet.　　　　(A)　(B)　(C)

04 Mark your answer on the answer sheet.　　　　(A)　(B)　(C)

05 Mark your answer on the answer sheet.　　　　(A)　(B)　(C)

06 Mark your answer on the answer sheet.　　　　(A)　(B)　(C)

07 Mark your answer on the answer sheet.　　　　(A)　(B)　(C)

08 Mark your answer on the answer sheet.　　　　(A)　(B)　(C)

09 Mark your answer on the answer sheet.　　　　(A)　(B)　(C)

10 Mark your answer on the answer sheet.　　　　(A)　(B)　(C)

11 Mark your answer on the answer sheet.　　　　(A)　(B)　(C)

12 Mark your answer on the answer sheet.　　　　(A)　(B)　(C)

13 Mark your answer on the answer sheet.　　　　(A)　(B)　(C)

14 Mark your answer on the answer sheet.   (A)   (B)   (C)

15 Mark your answer on the answer sheet.   (A)   (B)   (C)

16 Mark your answer on the answer sheet.   (A)   (B)   (C)

17 Mark your answer on the answer sheet.   (A)   (B)   (C)

18 Mark your answer on the answer sheet.   (A)   (B)   (C)

19 Mark your answer on the answer sheet.   (A)   (B)   (C)

20 Mark your answer on the answer sheet.   (A)   (B)   (C)

21 Mark your answer on the answer sheet.   (A)   (B)   (C)

22 Mark your answer on the answer sheet.   (A)   (B)   (C)

23 Mark your answer on the answer sheet.   (A)   (B)   (C)

24 Mark your answer on the answer sheet.   (A)   (B)   (C)

25 Mark your answer on the answer sheet.   (A)   (B)   (C)

한 권으로 끝내는 해커스 토익 600+ LC+RC+VOCA

PART 3

DAY 09 전체 대화 관련 문제
DAY 10 세부 사항 관련 문제
DAY 11 회사 업무 및 사무기기 관련 대화
DAY 12 인사 및 사내 행사 관련 대화
DAY 13 마케팅/판매/재무 관련 대화
DAY 14 일상생활 관련 대화
DAY 15 여행 및 여가 관련 대화

◀ MP3 바로 듣기

교재에 수록된 모든 MP3를 무료로 다운받거나 바로 스트리밍하여 더욱 편리하게 이용해 보세요.
고속 버전 MP3도 구매하여 학습하면 실전에 더욱 완벽하게 대비할 수 있습니다.

PART 3 알아보기

PART 3는 32번부터 70번까지 총 39문제로, 회사 생활 또는 일상생활에서 일어나는 2~3명의 대화를 듣고 그와 관련된 3개의 문제를 푸는 파트입니다. 문제지에 각 문제의 질문과 4개의 보기가 제시되고, 음성으로 각 대화와 이에 대한 3개의 문제의 질문을 들려줍니다.

PART 3 미리 보기

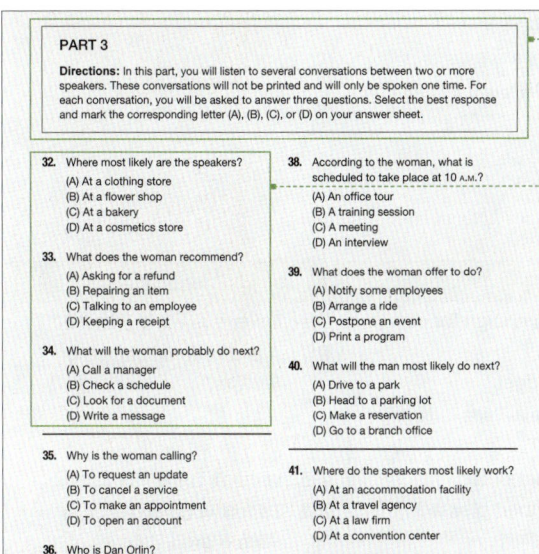

PART 3를 소개하는 디렉션입니다.

대화와 각 문제의 질문을 다음과 같이 들려줍니다.

Questions 32 through 34 refer to the following conversation.

M: Hi. I received this sweater as a birthday gift, but it's too small. Could I exchange it for a larger one? I have the receipt right here.

W: OK. Those are located in the menswear section. If you need help finding them, just talk to one of our staff members.

M: Thanks. Should I leave this item here while I look around?

W: Yes. I'll put a note on it now so that the other cashiers know why it's here.

Number 32.
Where most likely are the speakers?

Number 33.
What does the woman recommend?

Number 34.
What will the woman probably do next?

PART 3 학습 전략

- **문제 유형별 정답을 알려주는 표현 익히기**
  PART 3는 문제 유형별로 정답 단서로 자주 나오는 표현이 있습니다. 이러한 표현들을 익혀두면 실전 시험에서도 PART 3를 쉽게 공략할 수 있습니다.

- **대화 상황별 자주 나오는 표현 익히기**
  대화 내용을 정확히 듣고 의미를 파악할 수 있도록 대화 상황별로 자주 나오는 표현들을 익혀두어야 합니다.

DAY 09 전체 대화 관련 문제

MP3 바로듣기

1. 주제/목적 문제

주제/목적 문제는 화자들이 이야기하고 있는 중심 내용을 묻는 문제입니다. PART 3 전체 39문제 중 매회 2~3문제 정도 출제됩니다.

최신 경향 및 전략

1. 대화의 주제나 목적을 나타내는 내용은 주로 대화의 초반에 언급되므로 대화의 초반을 주의 깊게 들어야 합니다.
2. 주로 다음과 같은 질문을 사용하여 대화의 주제나 목적을 묻습니다.

   주제 **What** are the speakers **mainly discussing**? 화자들은 주로 무엇에 대해 이야기하고 있는가?

   What is the conversation **mainly about**? 대화는 주로 무엇에 관한 것인가?

   목적 **Why** is the man **calling**? 남자는 왜 전화를 하고 있는가?

   What is the **purpose** of the call? 전화의 목적은 무엇인가?

정답을 알려주는 표현 🎧 D09_1_표현

표현	대화 내 정답 단서	질문 및 정답
I'd like to ~ ~하고 싶습니다	W: **I'd like to** plan a promotional campaign for our store's anniversary. M: Great idea. Let's discuss the budget. 여: 저는 우리 매장의 기념일을 위한 홍보 캠페인을 계획하고 싶습니다. 남: 좋은 생각이에요. 예산에 대해 논의해 봅시다.	질문 대화는 주로 무엇에 관한 것인가? 정답 A promotional campaign 홍보 캠페인
I'm calling to ~ ~하기 위해 전화드립니다	M: **I'm calling to** check on my recent order. W: Sure. Can I have your order number, please? 남: 제 최근 주문에 대해 확인하기 위해 전화드립니다. 여: 물론입니다. 주문 번호를 알려주시겠어요?	질문 남자는 왜 전화를 하고 있는가? 정답 To follow up on an order 주문을 확인하기 위해

Example 🎧 D09_2_예제

01 What is the conversation mainly about?
(A) A work seminar
(B) A printing machine
(C) A product advertisement
(D) A software purchase

해석
01 대화는 주로 무엇에 관한 것인가?
(A) 업무 세미나
(B) 인쇄 기기
(C) 제품 광고
(D) 소프트웨어 구입

🎧 호주 → 미국
Question 01 refers to the following conversation.

M: Helen, **have you seen the sample print advertisement I designed for our client's new product? I'd like to get your feedback on it.**
W: Yes. It looks good. But I think it would be more appealing if you used brighter colors.
M: I'll use an image-editing program to make some adjustments.

01번은 다음 대화에 관한 문제입니다.
남: Helen, 제가 고객의 신제품을 위해 디자인한 인쇄 광고 샘플을 보셨나요? 그것에 대해 당신의 의견을 구하고 싶어요.
여: 네. 좋아 보여요. 그런데 더 밝은 색상을 사용한다면 더욱 매력적일 것 같아요.
남: 이미지 편집 프로그램을 사용해서 몇 가지 수정을 해볼게요.

정답 (C)

해설
대화의 주제를 묻는 문제입니다. 남자가 "have you seen the sample print advertisement ~? I'd like to get your feedback on it."이라며 인쇄 광고 샘플을 봤는지 물으며 의견을 받고 싶다고 한 후, 제품 광고에 대한 내용으로 대화가 이어지고 있습니다. 따라서 정답은 (C) A product advertisement입니다.

어휘
appealing adj. 매력적인, 호감을 사는   adjustment n. 수정, 조정

HACKERS PRACTICE

대화를 들으며 주어진 질문에 가장 알맞은 보기를 고르고, 빈칸에 들어갈 내용을 받아쓰세요. (음성은 두 번 들려줍니다.) 🎧 D09_3_Practice

01 Why is the woman calling?

(A) To provide a reminder
(B) To offer an upgrade
(C) To ask for a refund
(D) To explain a malfunction

W: This is Theresa from Appliance Mart. I'm calling to _____ about the appointment to _____ _____ this Saturday.
M: Oh, no. I got the dates confused, and I have _____ _____ downtown in the morning. Is it possible for the repair crew to come over after 2 P.M.?
W: Certainly. Our crew will arrive at around 5 P.M. The _____ will only last about 45 minutes.

02 What are the speakers mainly discussing?

(A) Finishing a summary
(B) Printing a receipt
(C) Confirming an order
(D) Picking up luggage

W: Hi, Michael. I need to _____ _____ for last month. Can you give me the receipts from your trip to St. Paul?
M: Unfortunately, the _____ at home. When's the summary due?
W: Mr. Brown is expecting it tomorrow afternoon.
M: I will _____ and give them to you first thing in the morning.

03 What is the purpose of the call?

(A) To inquire about buyers' interest
(B) To negotiate a price
(C) To confirm a date
(D) To provide instructions

M: Hello, Ms. Florence. I was wondering if _____ _____ about the retail space I put on the market.
W: I've shown it to a few people so far, but no one has been _____. I think it's because of the high price.
M: I see. I'm going to check the _____ _____ in the area and then call you back.

정답·해석·해설 p.47

DAY 09 전체 대화 관련 문제 **83**

2. 화자/장소 문제

화자/장소 문제는 화자들의 신분이나 직업, 그리고 대화가 이루어지고 있는 장소를 묻는 문제입니다. PART 3 전체 39문제 중 매회 6~7문제 정도 출제됩니다.

최신 경향 및 전략

1. 화자 및 장소와 관련된 내용은 주로 대화의 초반에 언급되므로 대화의 초반을 주의 깊게 들어야 합니다.
2. 주로 다음과 같은 질문을 사용하여 화자나 대화가 이루어지는 장소를 묻습니다.

   화자　**Who** most likely is **the man/woman**? 남자/여자는 누구인 것 같은가?
   　　　Who are **the speakers**? 화자들은 누구인가?
   　　　Where do **the speakers** most likely **work**? 화자들은 어디에서 일하는 것 같은가?
   　　　What field/department does **the man/woman work in**? 남자/여자는 어느 분야/부서에서 일하는가?
   장소　**Where** most likely are **the speakers**? 화자들은 어디에 있는 것 같은가?
   　　　Where does the **conversation** (probably) **take place**? 이 대화는 어디에서 일어나는가?

정답을 알려주는 표현　🎧 D09_4_표현

직업 및 장소	대화에 등장하는 단서 표현			
real estate agent 부동산 중개인	property 부동산	rent 임대료	tenant 세입자	landlord 집주인
sales representative 영업 사원	new product 신제품	sales strategy 판매 전략	promotional material 홍보 자료	
hair salon 미용실	haircut 머리 깎기	dye 염색하다	treatment 트리트먼트	perm 파마

Example 🎧 D09_5_예제

01 Where do the speakers most likely work?
  (A) At a health spa
  (B) At a restaurant
  (C) At a hair salon
  (D) At a supermarket

영국 → 캐나다
Question 01 refers to the following conversation.

W: Thanks for coming in on your day off, Ali. Due to a mix-up, **there are more clients scheduled for haircuts today than usual**.
M: No problem. Where do you want me to start?
W: Help me dye this client's hair. Make sure to put the same amount in all places.
M: Got it. I'll be careful.

해석
01 화자들은 어디에서 일하는 것 같은가?
  (A) 건강관리 시설에서
  (B) 식당에서
  (C) 미용실에서
  (D) 슈퍼마켓에서

01번은 다음 대화에 관한 문제입니다.

여: 쉬는 날에 와줘서 고마워요, Ali. 착오로 인해, 오늘 평소보다 더 많은 고객들이 이발 일정을 잡았어요.
남: 괜찮아요. 제가 어디서부터 시작하면 될까요?
여: 이 고객의 머리를 염색하는 것을 도와주세요. 꼭 모든 곳에 같은 양을 사용하도록 해주세요.
남: 알겠어요. 조심할게요.

해설　　　**정답** (C)
화자들의 신분을 묻는 문제입니다. 여자가 "there are more clients scheduled for haircuts today than usual"이라며 오늘 평소보다 더 많은 고객이 이발 일정을 잡았다고 한 말을 통해 화자들이 미용실에서 일한다는 것을 알 수 있습니다. 따라서 정답은 (C) At a hair salon입니다.

어휘
day off (근무·일을) 쉬는 날　mix-up n. 착오, 혼동　client n. 고객　dye v. 염색하다

HACKERS PRACTICE

대화를 들으며 주어진 질문에 가장 알맞은 보기를 고르고, 빈칸에 들어갈 내용을 받아쓰세요. (음성은 두 번 들려줍니다.) 🎧 D09_6_Practice

01 Where does this conversation take place?

(A) In a library
(B) In a gallery
(C) In a theater
(D) In a park

M: Hi, Beth. Have you had a chance to _____ _____ in the reference section?
W: Not yet. I was putting up some signs with information about _____ for local children.
M: I see. You seem really busy these days. I'll help you _____.

02 Who most likely is the man?

(A) A secretary
(B) An applicant
(C) An executive
(D) A presenter

M: Good morning. My name is Kevin Gould. I have an appointment with Ms. Brent, the regional director. I'm _____ for the market researcher job.
W: Oh, Ms. Brent is currently in a _____, and it's taking longer than expected. Do you mind waiting until she's finished?
M: No. I can wait here _____.

03 Where most likely do the speakers work?

(A) At a shipping firm
(B) At a publishing company
(C) At a law office
(D) At a real estate agency

W: Did the ink cartridges arrive yet?
M: Unfortunately, no. They were _____ this morning, but I was notified that they won't get here until tomorrow.
W: That's a problem. I have a meeting at 10 to go over some _____ for an upcoming court case.
M: Just put the files on a USB drive. I'll take it to the _____.

HACKERS TEST

대화를 들으며 주어진 질문에 가장 알맞은 보기를 고르세요. 🎧 D09_7_Test

01 Where does this conversation most likely take place?

(A) At an advertising agency
(B) At an electronics company
(C) At an architectural firm
(D) At a financial institution

02 Why does the woman need to access a file?

(A) To perform an evaluation
(B) To look over a proposal
(C) To apply for a position
(D) To prepare for a meeting

03 What does the woman request?

(A) An instruction manual
(B) A replacement device
(C) A software upgrade
(D) An account password

04 Which industry does the man most likely work in?

(A) Journalism
(B) Software
(C) Fashion
(D) Finance

05 What will probably take place in the afternoon?

(A) A sports game
(B) A fundraiser
(C) A press conference
(D) A photo shoot

06 What does the woman suggest that the man do?

(A) Leave an area
(B) Buy a ticket
(C) Wear a badge
(D) Check a bag

07 Where most likely are the speakers?

(A) In a furniture store
(B) In a medical clinic
(C) In a tailor's shop
(D) In a fitness center

08 Why does the man think a schedule should be changed?

(A) To avoid overbooking
(B) To reduce safety risks
(C) To qualify for a discount
(D) To receive a free session

09 What does the man request?

(A) Advance payment
(B) An account number
(C) Contact information
(D) A business invoice

10 What is the conversation mainly about?

(A) Determining a guest list
(B) Reserving an event venue
(C) Renting equipment
(D) Setting up furniture

11 What problem does the woman mention?

(A) Spaces are unavailable.
(B) Fees have not been paid.
(C) Prices have been increased.
(D) Preparations were not made.

12 What does the man say about the banquet?

(A) It will be catered.
(B) It can be expanded.
(C) It can be postponed.
(D) It will be inexpensive.

13 Where does the woman work?
(A) At a photography studio
(B) At a department store
(C) At a laundry facility
(D) At a delivery company

14 What does the man say about an item?
(A) It has not been used before.
(B) It is needed for a company event.
(C) It was purchased online.
(D) It is not currently available.

15 What will the man do in 20 minutes?
(A) Attend a party
(B) Create an account
(C) Place a call
(D) Visit a business

16 What is the conversation mainly about?
(A) A video conference
(B) A job interview
(C) A product launch
(D) A training session

17 Which department do the speakers most likely work in?
(A) Marketing
(B) Research
(C) Personnel
(D) Accounting

18 What did Tanya recently do?
(A) She met with a client.
(B) She talked to a manager.
(C) She purchased a device.
(D) She made a booking.

19 Why is the woman calling?
(A) To change a schedule
(B) To apologize for an error
(C) To advertise an event
(D) To provide a reminder

20 What did the woman e-mail to the man?
(A) Instructions for a test
(B) Medical records
(C) Examination results
(D) Directions to a clinic

21 What does the woman ask the man to do?
(A) Download an application
(B) Call a doctor
(C) Mail a document
(D) Bring a card

22 Who most likely is the woman?
(A) An instructor
(B) An official
(C) A programmer
(D) A researcher

23 According to the woman, what will a grant be used for?
(A) Expanding a facility
(B) Repairing a device
(C) Hiring an employee
(D) Launching a campaign

24 What will happen on May 10?
(A) A project will be completed.
(B) A document will be published.
(C) A team will be reassigned.
(D) An inspection will be performed.

DAY 10 세부 사항 관련 문제

MP3 바로듣기

1. 세부 사항 문제

세부 사항 문제는 화자가 다음에 할 일, 제안/요청하는 사항, 대화에 언급된 이유, 문제점, 장소 및 시간 등 대화에서 언급된 다양한 세부 정보를 묻는 문제입니다. PART 3 전체 39문제 중 매회 28~29문제 정도 출제됩니다.

최신 경향 및 전략

1. 화자 중 한 명, 즉 남자 또는 여자가 질문에 자주 언급되므로 질문에 언급된 화자의 말에서 정답의 단서를 파악해야 합니다.
2. 다음에 할 일, 이유, 제안, 문제점 등이 질문에 자주 언급되며, 주로 다음과 같은 질문을 사용하여 세부 사항을 묻습니다.

다음에 할 일	**What** will the woman probably **do next**? 여자는 다음에 무엇을 할 것 같은가?
이유	**Why** did the man contact the woman? 남자는 왜 여자에게 연락했는가?
제안	**What** does the man **suggest** the woman do? 남자는 여자에게 무엇을 하라고 제안하는가?
문제점	What is the **problem**? 문제는 무엇인가?
특정 세부 사항	**What** will **happen** next week? 다음 주에 무슨 일이 일어날 것인가?

정답을 알려주는 표현 🎧 D10_1_표현

표현	대화 내 정답 단서	질문 및 정답
Why don't we ~? 우리 ~하는 게 어떨까요?	W: We need a strategy to attract new customers. M: **Why don't we** offer a discount to first-time customers? 여: 우리는 신규 고객을 유치할 전략이 필요합니다. 남: 우리가 첫 구매 고객에게 할인 혜택을 제공하는 게 어떨까요?	질문 남자는 무엇을 할 것을 제안하는가? 정답 Providing a discount 할인 제공하기
I'm concerned/ worried about ~ 저는 ~에 대해 걱정입니다	W: **I'm concerned about** the low attendance at the seminar. M: Do you think we should try promoting it more next time? 여: 저는 저조한 세미나 참석률에 대해 걱정입니다. 남: 다음번에는 홍보를 좀 더 해야 할까요?	질문 문제는 무엇인가? 정답 Low participation in an event 행사의 저조한 참여율

Example 🎧 D10_2_예제

01 What does the man suggest doing?
 (A) Hiring an assistant
 (B) Giving a raise
 (C) Changing a schedule
 (D) Providing company phones

🔊 영국 → 호주
Question 01 refers to the following conversation.
W: Andy, my assistant said you want to talk to me. What's up?
M: Yeah. Some of our staff members have complained about clients calling them on weekends. **Why don't we give our employees company phones to use for work-related matters?**
W: I need to discuss this with the CEO. I'll get back to you later.

해석
01 남자가 무엇을 할 것을 제안하는가?
 (A) 조수를 고용하기
 (B) 임금을 인상하기
 (C) 일정을 변경하기
 (D) 회사 휴대전화를 제공하기

01번은 다음 대화에 관한 문제입니다.
여: Andy, 제 조수가 당신이 저와 이야기하고 싶어 한다고 하더군요. 무슨 일이신가요?
남: 네. 일부 직원들이 주말에 고객이 전화를 하는 것에 대해 불만을 제기했어요. 업무와 관련된 일에 사용할 수 있도록 직원들에게 회사 휴대전화를 주는 게 어떨까요?
여: 최고 경영자와 이것을 논의해 봐요. 나중에 다시 알려드릴게요.

정답 (D)

해설
남자가 제안하는 것을 묻는 문제입니다. 남자가 여자에게 "Why don't we give our employees company phones ~?"라며 직원들에게 회사 휴대전화를 주는 게 어떠냐고 제안하였습니다. 따라서 정답은 (D) Providing company phones입니다.

어휘
assistant n. 조수　raise n. 임금 인상　complain v. 불만을 제기하다, 불평하다　work-related adj. 일과 관련된　matter n. 일, 사안

HACKERS PRACTICE

대화를 들으며 주어진 질문에 가장 알맞은 보기를 고르고, 빈칸에 들어갈 내용을 받아쓰세요. (음성은 두 번 들려줍니다.) 🎧 D10_3_Practice

01 What will the man most likely do next?
(A) Examine a product
(B) Describe some furnishings
(C) Calculate some expenses
(D) Make an appointment

M: Hello. I need to _____ for my house. Can you make some recommendations?
W: I'm happy to help you. What is _____?
M: I don't have a specific budget. But I want something that will match the décor of _____.
W: I see. Could you tell me about the _____?

02 Why is the man traveling to Chicago?
(A) He wants to visit some relatives.
(B) He has to speak at a gathering.
(C) He needs to conduct research.
(D) He has to meet with clients.

M: Are you busy, Leena? I'm wondering if you could make arrangements for my upcoming trip. I have to _____ from August 8 to 12 in Chicago.
W: Of course, Mr. Sanders. Is there a _____ that you'd like to stay at in Chicago?
M: Anywhere downtown is fine. Please _____ later this afternoon. Thanks in advance!

03 What is the man concerned about?
(A) He will not learn sales techniques.
(B) He is unable to travel to Denver.
(C) He forgot to bring his materials.
(D) He cannot find a speaker for an event.

W: Hey, Mike. I heard that our sales seminar has been _____. The speaker was suddenly called away on an urgent business trip.
M: Really? I'm just worried because I was hoping to _____ to sell products before the trade show in Denver.
W: Well, maybe you can _____ he left behind.
M: I suppose I could. Besides, there are a number of Web sites on the topic, too.

2. 의도 파악 문제

의도 파악 문제는 대화에서 언급된 특정 문장이나 어구에 담긴 화자의 의도나 뜻을 묻는 문제입니다. PART 3 전체 39문제 중 매회 2문제 출제됩니다.

최신 경향 및 전략

1. 정답의 단서는 질문의 인용어구 주변에서 자주 언급되므로, 해당 인용어구의 앞뒤를 주의 깊게 듣습니다.
2. 주로 다음과 같은 질문을 사용하여 언급된 말의 의도를 묻습니다.

Why does the man **say**, "**Let me check with my supervisor**"? 남자는 왜 "제 상사에게 확인해 볼게요"라고 말하는가?
What does the woman **imply/mean** when she **says**, "**I've dealt with similar situations before**"?
여자는 "이전에 비슷한 상황들을 다뤄본 적이 있어요"라고 말할 때 무엇을 의도하는가?

자주 나오는 인용어구와 정답 보기 🎧 D10_4_표현

대화	질문 및 정답
M: The shipment just arrived. Could you help me move the equipment? W: I have to submit a report in the afternoon. 남: 배송품이 방금 도착했어요. 장비 옮기는 걸 도와주실 수 있나요? 여: 저는 오후에 보고서를 제출해야 해요.	질문 여자는 왜 "저는 오후에 보고서를 제출해야 해요"라고 말하는가? 정답 To decline a request 부탁을 거절하기 위해
W: Should we set up the outdoor market tomorrow as planned? M: It's going to rain tomorrow. Let's do it next week instead. 여: 내일 계획대로 야외 시장을 설치할까요? 남: 내일 비가 올 거예요. 대신 다음 주에 하죠.	질문 남자는 "내일 비가 올 거예요"라고 말할 때 무엇을 의도하는가? 정답 The schedule should be changed. 일정이 변경되어야 한다.

Example 🎧 D10_5_예제

01 What does the man imply when he says, "I've been working in the field for over 10 years"?

(A) He wants to change careers.
(B) He will meet a deadline.
(C) He has finished a project.
(D) He is focused on training.

해석
01 남자는 "저는 이 분야에서 10년 넘게 일해 왔어요"라고 말할 때 무엇을 의도하는가?
(A) 그는 직업을 바꾸고 싶어 한다.
(B) 그는 기한을 맞출 것이다.
(C) 그는 프로젝트를 완료했다.
(D) 그는 훈련에 집중하고 있다.

3㎡ 미국 → 호주
Question 01 refers to the following conversation.

W: Hi, Michael. How is the AI project for TechInnovate coming along?
M: My team is making good progress. I'm sure the client will be happy with the chatbot we're developing.
W: **Our board is concerned about the timeline. Can we deliver on schedule?**
M: **I've been working in the field for over 10 years. I know exactly what needs to be done.**

01번은 다음 대화에 관한 문제입니다.
여: 안녕하세요, Michael. TechInnovate사를 위한 AI 프로젝트는 어떻게 진행되고 있나요?
남: 우리 팀이 좋은 진전을 보이고 있어요. 고객이 우리가 개발 중인 챗봇에 만족할 거라고 확신해요.
여: 우리 이사회는 일정에 대해 우려하고 있어요. 예정대로 내놓을 수 있을까요?
남: 저는 이 분야에서 10년 넘게 일해 왔어요. 무엇이 필요한지 정확히 알고 있어요.

해설 정답 (B)
남자가 하는 말(I've been working in the field for over 10 years)의 의도를 묻는 문제입니다. 여자가 "Our board is concerned about the timeline. Can we deliver on schedule?"이라며 우리 이사회는 일정에 대해 우려하고 있다고 한 후, 예정대로 내놓을 수 있을지 묻자, 남자가 "I know exactly what needs to be done."이라며 무엇이 필요한지 정확히 알고 있다고 한 것을 통해 남자는 기한을 맞출 것이라고 의도한 것임을 알 수 있습니다. 따라서 정답은 (B) He will meet a deadline입니다.

어휘
make progress 진전을 보이다   board n. 이사회   deliver v. (사람들의 기대대로 결과를) 내놓다   on schedule 예정대로   field n. 분야

HACKERS PRACTICE

대화를 들으며 주어진 질문에 가장 알맞은 보기를 고르고, 빈칸에 들어갈 내용을 받아쓰세요. (음성은 두 번 들려줍니다.) 🎧 D10_6_Practice

01 Why does the woman say, "That might be best for you"?

(A) To advise the man to get in line
(B) To indicate that an application can be completed now
(C) To suggest the man should return later
(D) To agree with the man's suggestion

M: Hello. I'm here to take the written exam to _____.
W: OK. Just note that many people are _____.
M: Oh . . . When do you think I'll be able to take the test? I _____ at 4 P.M.
W: I doubt you'll be finished by then. We are _____ _____, though. That might be best for you.

02 What does the man mean when he says, "our company president will be attending"?

(A) An executive should be contacted.
(B) Some assistance will be given.
(C) A presentation has been delayed.
(D) An assignment is important.

W: Kyle, it's Lisa Griggs from accounting. I just want to remind you that we're _____ _____ next Friday. We should probably _____ for it soon.
M: I agree. After all, our company president will be attending. Why don't we start sometime today? When are you free?
W: Now is a good time. I won't be _____ in the afternoon because I have a meeting.

03 Why does the man say, "We don't want to look like we are copying them"?

(A) To decline an invitation
(B) To make a change to a plan
(C) To show support for a decision
(D) To praise an online campaign

M: How's your team doing with developing the _____, Denise? Our CEO wants us to start promoting our products on social media soon.
W: We're going to need more time. Our main competitor just _____ that are very similar to ours. So I decided that my team should _____.
M: We don't want to look like we are copying them. Don't worry. I'll _____ to our CEO.

정답·해석·해설 p.54

3. 시각 자료 문제

시각 자료 문제는 대화에서 언급된 내용 중 질문과 함께 제시된 표나 그래프, 지도, 쿠폰 등과 관련된 사항을 묻는 문제입니다. PART 3 전체 39문제 중 매회 3문제 출제됩니다.

최신 경향 및 전략

1. 정답의 단서는 대화에서 변동 사항, 최고/최저 항목 등의 특이 사항이 언급되는 부분에서 주로 등장하므로 해당 부분을 놓치지 않도록 주의합니다.
2. 주로 다음과 같은 질문을 사용하여 시각 자료와 관련된 내용을 묻습니다.
   Look at the **graphic**. **Which figure** does the woman **focus on**? 시각 자료를 보아라. 여자는 어떤 수치에 중점을 두는가?
   Look at the **graphic**. **Where** is the business **located**? 시각 자료를 보아라. 업체는 어디에 위치해 있는가?

자주 나오는 표현 🎧 D10_7_표현

표	the most expensive 가장 비싼	no more than 150 dollars 150달러 이하의
그래프	rank second 2위를 차지하다	the lowest earnings 가장 낮은 실적
지도	between ~ 사이에	next to ~의 옆에
	in front of ~의 앞에	toward ~쪽으로

Example 🎧 D10_8_예제

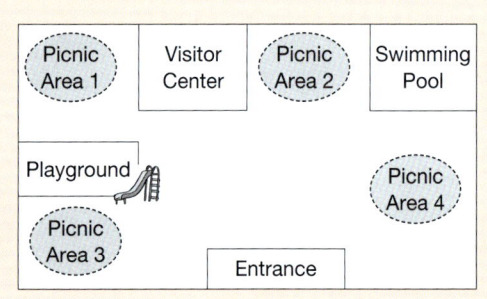

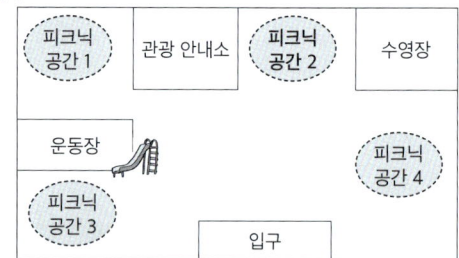

해석

01 Look at the graphic. Where will the gathering be held?
(A) In Picnic Area 1
(B) In Picnic Area 2
(C) In Picnic Area 3
(D) In Picnic Area 4

01 시각 자료를 보아라. 모임은 어디에서 열릴 것인가?
(A) 피크닉 공간 1에서
(B) 피크닉 공간 2에서
(C) 피크닉 공간 3에서
(D) 피크닉 공간 4에서

3️⃣ 캐나다 → 영국

Question 01 refers to the following conversation and map.

M: Good morning. My hiking club will be holding its monthly gathering next weekend. Can I book a group picnic area for Saturday?
W: What time would you like to use it?
M: From 10 A.M. to 1 P.M. would be perfect.
W: Let me check . . . **The picnic area between the visitor center and the swimming pool is free at that time.** Please fill out this form.

01번은 다음 대화와 지도에 관한 문제입니다.

남: 안녕하세요. 제 하이킹 클럽이 다음 주 주말에 월간 모임을 열 것인데요. 토요일에 단체 피크닉 공간을 예약할 수 있을까요?
여: 몇 시에 그것을 사용하고 싶으신가요?
남: 오전 10시부터 오후 1시면 완벽할 거예요.
여: 확인해 보겠습니다... 그 시간에는 관광 안내소와 수영장 사이의 피크닉 공간이 사용 가능해요. 이 양식을 작성해 주세요.

해설
정답 (B)

모임이 열리는 장소를 묻는 문제입니다. 여자가 "The picnic area between the visitor center and the swimming pool is free at that time."이라며 그 시간에는 관광 안내소와 수영장 사이의 피크닉 공간이 사용 가능하다고 하였으므로, 모임이 열릴 장소는 피크닉 공간 2임을 지도에서 알 수 있습니다. 따라서 정답은 (B) In Picnic Area 2입니다.

어휘
monthly adj. 월간(의)   book v. 예약하다   visitor center 관광 안내소   fill out 작성하다, 채우다

HACKERS PRACTICE

대화를 들으며 주어진 질문에 가장 알맞은 보기를 고르고, 빈칸에 들어갈 내용을 받아쓰세요. (음성은 두 번 들려줍니다.) 🎧 D10_9_Practice

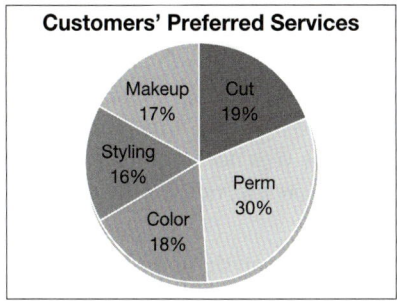

01 Look at the graphic. What service will be 50 percent off?

(A) Makeup
(B) Cut
(C) Perm
(D) Styling

W: Isaac, can you explain the details of our hair salon's plan to _____ in March?
M: We're going to _____ by up to 50 percent for the month.
W: Which services are going to be featured?
M: All of them, but we've chosen to give the _____ _____ to the service preferred by _____ _____ of our customers. It has the highest profit margin.

Product	Price
Wooden bench	$2,000
Short sofa	$1,200
Lounge chair	$250
Coffee table	$350

02 Look at the graphic. Which product will not be purchased?

(A) Wooden bench
(B) Short sofa
(C) Lounge chair
(D) Coffee table

M: Could you go over this _____ for our new lounge? Here you go.
W: These are good choices. However, I'm not sure we _____ all of them.
M: In that case, I suggest not buying the 250-dollars piece since we _____.
W: OK, good. I'm _____ with that.

Department	Extension
Sales	310
Market Research	455
Security	562
Product Design	640

03 Look at the graphic. Which extension will the woman dial?

(A) 310
(B) 455
(C) 562
(D) 640

M: My sales presentations for the clients in Berlin didn't go well. Most of them _____ that are similar to the ones we sell.
W: That's unfortunate. It seems our competitor, SecureForce, has _____ in Europe. We need to rethink our _____.
M: Absolutely. I'm going to bring this up at our meeting this Wednesday.
W: Good idea. Also, I'll call our _____ to request a report on our European competition.

정답·해석·해설 p.55

HACKERS TEST

대화를 들으며 주어진 질문에 가장 알맞은 보기를 고르세요. 🎧 D10_10_Test

01 Where most likely are the speakers?
(A) At a supermarket
(B) At a bakery
(C) At a restaurant
(D) At a café

02 Why did the man visit a Web site?
(A) To get a coupon
(B) To place an order
(C) To check a price
(D) To change a password

03 What is required to get an additional discount?
(A) A completed survey
(B) A membership card
(C) A shopping bag
(D) A sales receipt

04 What did the woman already do?
(A) She purchased a light.
(B) She sent an e-mail.
(C) She received a delivery.
(D) She browsed an online store.

05 What does the store provide this month?
(A) An extended warranty
(B) Expedited shipping
(C) Free installation
(D) A gift certificate

06 Why does the woman plan to visit another store?
(A) To request a refund
(B) To compare prices
(C) To get samples
(D) To make a complaint

07 What problem is mentioned?
(A) A deadline has been missed.
(B) A property has been damaged.
(C) A device was not working properly.
(D) A decision was not approved.

08 What will the man do at 4 P.M.?
(A) Show a property
(B) Lead a workshop
(C) Read some documents
(D) Print some blueprints

09 What does Ann offer to do for the man?
(A) Move some furniture
(B) Replace some equipment
(C) Reserve a meeting room
(D) Contact a staff member

10 Where does the man most likely work?
(A) At a gardening supply store
(B) At an architectural firm
(C) At a real estate agency
(D) At a landscaping company

11 How did the woman learn about the business?
(A) By searching on the Internet
(B) By speaking to a colleague
(C) By listening to the radio
(D) By asking a neighbor

12 What problem does the man mention?
(A) An appointment must be rescheduled.
(B) A service was recently discontinued.
(C) A project cannot begin for a month.
(D) A decision has not been made.

13. What does the man want to do?
    (A) Send some museum passes
    (B) Use an online service
    (C) Register for a tour
    (D) Display some sculptures

14. Why does the woman say, "I'm teaching classes on the weekends"?
    (A) To confirm a schedule
    (B) To indicate a problem
    (C) To explain a delay
    (D) To make a demand

15. What will happen on Thursday?
    (A) Paintings will be sold.
    (B) A prize will be given out.
    (C) Items will be moved.
    (D) An announcement will be made.

16. What industry does the woman most likely work in?
    (A) Insurance
    (B) Marketing
    (C) Transportation
    (D) Software

17. According to the man, what do all conference participants receive?
    (A) A form
    (B) A name tag
    (C) A brochure
    (D) A device

18. What does the man tell the woman to do?
    (A) Confirm a policy
    (B) Speak with a receptionist
    (C) Install an application
    (D) Print a timetable

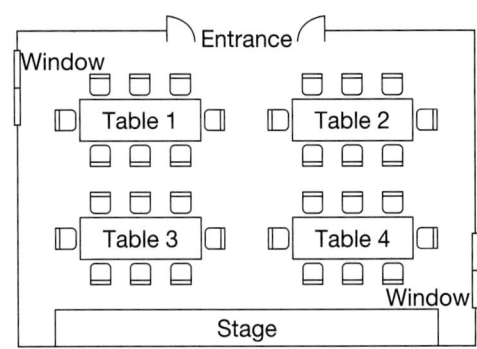

19. Who is the man?
    (A) A training coordinator
    (B) A seminar presenter
    (C) A student intern
    (D) A new employee

20. Look at the graphic. Which table has the man been assigned to?
    (A) Table 1
    (B) Table 2
    (C) Table 3
    (D) Table 4

21. What will the man most likely do next?
    (A) Listen to a speech
    (B) Watch a demonstration
    (C) Form a line
    (D) Read a handout

DAY 11 회사 업무 및 사무기기 관련 대화

MP3 바로 듣기

회사 업무 및 사무기기 관련 대화는 회의, 문서 작성, 사무기기 수리 등 회사에서 일반적으로 접하는 상황에 관한 대화입니다. PART 3 전체 13개 대화 중 매회 4~5개 정도 출제됩니다.

최신 경향 및 전략

1. 다음과 같은 상황이 자주 출제됩니다.
   · 회의 및 발표 일정, 문서 제출 기한, 파일 정리 등 기본적인 업무에 관한 대화
   · 사무기기 오작동 및 수리, 사무용품 주문 등 사무기기 및 사무용품에 관한 대화
2. 회의, 문서 작성, 사무기기 및 사무용품과 관련된 표현들을 알아두면 도움이 됩니다.

자주 나오는 표현 🎧 D11_1_표현

회의	presentation n. 발표	meeting notes 회의록
	material n. 자료, 재료	client n. 고객, 의뢰인
문서 작성	paperwork n. 문서 작업	draft n. 초안, 원고
	description n. 설명, 기술	contract n. 계약서
사무기기 및 사무용품	office supplies 사무용품	fix v. 수리하다
	malfunction v. 제대로 작동하지 않다; n. 고장	break down 고장 나다

Example 🎧 D11_2_예제

01 Why does the woman say, "A part must be ordered"?
(A) To justify an expense
(B) To request a delivery
(C) To explain a delay
(D) To make a complaint

🗣 호주 → 미국

Question 01 refers to the following conversation.

M: Hi, Alice. This is Tim from the warehouse. The air conditioner isn't working properly, and it's getting pretty warm in here. Can you send someone to fix it?
W: **A technician came by yesterday. He said he can't repair it until next week.** A part must be ordered.
M: I see . . . Well, I'll look for some fans in the meantime.

해석
01 여자는 왜 "부품이 주문되어야 해요"라고 말하는가?
(A) 비용을 정당화하기 위해
(B) 배송을 요청하기 위해
(C) 지연을 설명하기 위해
(D) 불만을 제기하기 위해

01번은 다음 대화에 관한 문제입니다.

남: 안녕하세요, Alice. 저는 창고에서 근무하는 Tim입니다. 에어컨이 제대로 작동하지 않고 있어서, 이곳이 꽤 더워지고 있어요. 수리하러 누군가를 보내주실 수 있나요?
여: 기술자가 어제 방문했어요. 그는 다음 주는 되어야 수리할 수 있다고 했어요. 부품이 주문되어야 해요.
남: 알겠어요... 음, 그동안에 선풍기를 몇 개 찾아볼게요.

정답 (C)

해설
여자가 하는 말(A part must be ordered)의 의도를 묻는 문제입니다. 에어컨을 수리하러 누군가를 보내줄 수 있는지 묻는 남자에게 여자가 "A technician came by yesterday. He said he can't repair it until next week."라며 기술자가 어제 방문했는데 다음 주는 되어야 수리할 수 있다고 한 말을 통해 지연의 이유를 설명하려는 의도임을 알 수 있습니다. 따라서 정답은 (C) To explain a delay입니다.

어휘
warehouse n. 창고 technician n. 기술자 repair v. 수리하다 part n. 부품 in the meantime 그동안에, 한편

HACKERS PRACTICE

대화를 들으며 주어진 질문에 가장 알맞은 보기를 고르고, 빈칸에 들어갈 내용을 받아쓰세요. (음성은 두 번 들려줍니다.) 🎧 D11_3_Practice

[01-02]

01 What does the woman ask the man to do?

(A) Update a client record
(B) Review a legal agreement
(C) Interview an applicant
(D) Travel to another country

02 What will the man most likely do next?

(A) Call a coworker
(B) Copy a document
(C) Write a report
(D) Research a case

W: Sanjiv, I need you to help Johanna _____ _____ for one of our clients.
M: Sure, I can do that. I've worked with her on some _____ in the past, and we seem to make a good team.
W: I know. Johanna asked to work with you specifically. As you have experience with _____ _____, she thought you'd be helpful.
M: No problem. I'll _____ right now.

[03-04]

03 What problem does the man mention?

(A) He is late for a meeting.
(B) He damaged some equipment.
(C) He is unaware of a policy.
(D) He lost some information.

04 What does the woman say about Mr. Richards?

(A) He purchased some office furniture.
(B) He called to request assistance.
(C) He is at a manufacturing facility.
(D) He is waiting for some clients.

M: Hi, Edna. It's Aaron. I'm at the furniture store looking for a new desk for Mr. Richards, but I _____ _____ with his office measurements. I've been trying to contact him, but there's _____. Do you know where he is?
W: Mr. Richards is showing some clients around the _____.
M: Will that take long?
W: Oh, if you wait just a few minutes, I will go into his office and measure it for you.

HACKERS TEST

대화를 들으며 주어진 질문에 가장 알맞은 보기를 고르세요. 🎧 D11_4_Test

01 What did the woman tell the man to do?
(A) Finish some blueprints
(B) Contact some clients
(C) Send some documents
(D) Update some records

02 Why did Mr. Carter contact the man?
(A) To order equipment for a project
(B) To request changes to a plan
(C) To check the cost of supplies
(D) To describe an issue with a schedule

03 What does the man say he did this morning?
(A) Downloaded some files
(B) Transferred some funds
(C) Made some revisions
(D) Took some measurements

04 What is the woman concerned about?
(A) The appearance of an area
(B) The size of a building
(C) The location of a display
(D) The color of a logo

05 What do the men want to change?
(A) Decorations
(B) Furniture
(C) Equipment
(D) Plants

06 What does the woman offer to do?
(A) Discuss a budget with clients
(B) Work an additional shift
(C) Collect some tools
(D) Search for some items

07 What is the man's problem?
(A) He cannot find a survey form.
(B) He forgot to place an order.
(C) He cannot print some documents.
(D) He lost a delivery invoice.

08 Where is the woman going this afternoon?
(A) To a copy center
(B) To a supply shop
(C) To a dining establishment
(D) To a storage facility

09 What will the man most likely send the woman?
(A) A link to a Web site
(B) A billing statement
(C) A product number
(D) A list of items

10 What industry do the speakers most likely work in?
(A) Architecture
(B) Publishing
(C) Education
(D) Electronics

11 What does the man mean when he says, "I've got a meeting with a client"?
(A) He needs time to prepare.
(B) He is unable to help.
(C) He changed an appointment.
(D) He is unwilling to wait.

12 What will the woman most likely do next?
(A) Speak with a coworker
(B) Prepare a receipt
(C) Evaluate some plans
(D) Sign a contract

13 Who most likely is the man?

(A) A realtor
(B) An inspector
(C) A designer
(D) An investor

14 What is mentioned about the light fixture?

(A) It was purchased nearby.
(B) It comes in multiple sizes.
(C) It is located on the second floor.
(D) It was recalled by a manufacturer.

15 Why will the man return next week?

(A) To deliver more supplies
(B) To remove some old wiring
(C) To meet with a city official
(D) To check on a problem

16 What are the speakers mainly discussing?

(A) A business trip
(B) An investment strategy
(C) Some presentation materials
(D) Some customer feedback

17 What is mentioned about the Bendale office?

(A) It will host an event.
(B) It has been understaffed.
(C) It might be expanded.
(D) It might be closing.

18 What will the woman probably do next?

(A) Book a conference room
(B) Change an appointment time
(C) Contact a store manager
(D) Adjust a timetable

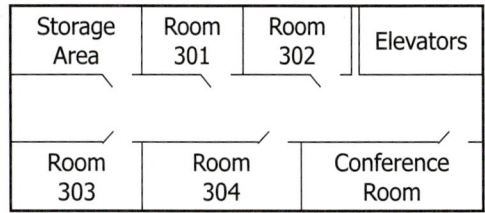

19 What will most likely happen next week?

(A) A workspace will be repainted.
(B) A storage area will be cleaned.
(C) Some equipment will be installed.
(D) Some computers will be updated.

20 Look at the graphic. Which room will the woman use on Monday?

(A) Room 301
(B) Room 302
(C) Room 303
(D) Room 304

21 What is mentioned about Mr. Hobbs?

(A) He joined another firm.
(B) He decided to take a vacation.
(C) He arranged a client meeting.
(D) He transferred to a different branch.

DAY 12 인사 및 사내 행사 관련 대화

인사 및 사내 행사 관련 대화는 채용, 인사 이동, 급여, 포상, 직원 교육, 행사 등에 관한 대화입니다. PART 3 전체 13개 대화 중 매회 1~2개 정도 출제됩니다.

최신 경향 및 전략

1. 다음과 같은 상황이 자주 출제됩니다.
   - 채용, 퇴임, 업무 평가, 승진, 전근, 급여, 포상, 출장, 휴가 등 인사에 관한 대화
   - 직원 연수, 직원 교육, 컨퍼런스, 송별회, 환영회 등 사내 행사에 관한 대화
2. 직책 및 부서, 인사, 사내 행사와 관련된 표현들을 알아두면 도움이 됩니다.

자주 나오는 표현 🎧 D12_1_표현

직책 및 부서	director n. 임원, 관리자	supervisor n. 감독관, 관리자
	human resources department 인사부	marketing department 마케팅부
인사	promote v. 승진시키다	retire v. 은퇴하다, 퇴직하다
	evaluate v. 평가하다	understaffed adj. 인원이 부족한
사내 행사	organize v. 준비하다, 조직하다	celebrate v. 기념하다
	train v. 교육하다	set up 설치하다, 준비하다

Example 🎧 D12_2_예제

01 Why is the man calling?
(A) To announce a hiring decision
(B) To confirm a meeting time
(C) To schedule a job interview
(D) To report a technical issue

해석
01 남자는 왜 전화하고 있는가?
(A) 채용 결정을 알리기 위해
(B) 회의 시간을 확인하기 위해
(C) 면접 일정을 잡기 위해
(D) 기술적인 문제를 보고하기 위해

🎧 캐나다 → 영국
Question 01 refers to the following conversation.

M: Hi, I'm calling from BrightEdge Solutions. **I'm pleased to let you know that you've been selected to join us.** Congratulations.
W: Thanks! I'm really looking forward to working at your company. When will I start?
M: Your three-day orientation will begin on May 15. It will give you the chance to learn about our policies and work processes.

01번은 다음 대화에 관한 문제입니다.

남: 안녕하세요, BrightEdge Solutions사에서 전화드립니다. 저희 회사에 합류하도록 선발되셨다는 것을 알려드리게 되어 기쁩니다. 축하합니다.
여: 감사합니다! 귀사에서 일하게 되어 정말 기대됩니다. 언제부터 일할 수 있을까요?
남: 3일간의 오리엔테이션은 5월 15일에 시작됩니다. 정책과 업무 프로세스에 대해 배울 수 있는 기회를 제공할 것입니다.

해설 정답 (A)
대화의 목적을 묻는 문제입니다. 남자가 "I'm pleased to let you know that you've been selected to join us[BrightEdge Solutions]."라며 BrightEdge Solutions사에 합류하도록 선발된 것을 알려주게 되어 기쁘다고 한 것을 통해 남자가 채용 결정을 알리기 위해 전화한 것임을 알 수 있습니다. 따라서 정답은 (A) To announce a hiring decision입니다.

어휘
technical adj. 기술적인 select v. 선발하다, 선정하다 join v. 합류하다, 결합하다 look forward to ~을 기대하다 orientation n. 예비 교육

HACKERS PRACTICE

대화를 들으며 주어진 질문에 가장 알맞은 보기를 고르고, 빈칸에 들어갈 내용을 받아쓰세요. (음성은 두 번 들려줍니다.) 🎧 D12_3_Practice

[01-02]

01 Who is the woman?

(A) A personal assistant
(B) A travel agent
(C) A corporate consultant
(D) A department head

02 Why is Janice Light traveling to France?

(A) To lead an organization
(B) To conduct some research
(C) To offer some training
(D) To interview for a position

M: Ms. Whittier, I noticed that I have to lead a lot of _____ next month. Since you're the head of the _____, I'd like to discuss this with you.
W: Well, Janice Light will be flying to France to _____ _____ to overseas staff. That means someone else needs to lead her sessions.
M: Right, but both of her _____ to me. Can I ask another staff member to cover one?
W: OK. I'm fine with that.

[03-04]

03 What type of event is being planned?

(A) An award ceremony
(B) A retirement party
(C) A musical performance
(D) A business conference

04 What will be available at no additional charge?

(A) A customized menu
(B) A valet service
(C) An audio system
(D) A professional photographer

W: Good afternoon. One of our senior managers is retiring, and I am _____ for him. Does your hotel have a reception hall big enough for 120 people?
M: Definitely. Just last weekend, we _____ _____ with 150 people.
W: Let's go ahead and _____, then. Oh, before I forget . . . Could you set up a microphone and speaker for us?
M: No problem. And there will be _____ _____ for the audio system.

HACKERS TEST

대화를 들으며 주어진 질문에 가장 알맞은 보기를 고르세요. 🎧 D12_4_Test

01 Where is the conversation taking place?
(A) At a publishing company
(B) At a financial institution
(C) At a government office
(D) At an accommodation facility

02 What position is the man applying for?
(A) Consultant
(B) Salesperson
(C) Accountant
(D) Technician

03 What does the woman emphasize about the position?
(A) It was recently created.
(B) It requires occasional travel.
(C) It is a management role.
(D) It will involve working from home.

04 What is the topic of the seminar?
(A) Finance
(B) Tourism
(C) Transportation
(D) Health care

05 How is Mr. Nelson traveling to Seattle?
(A) By train
(B) By car
(C) By bus
(D) By plane

06 What will the woman most likely do next?
(A) Call a driver
(B) Visit a hotel
(C) Attend a seminar
(D) Confirm a reservation

07 What is the conversation mainly about?
(A) Conducting a survey
(B) Improving a software program
(C) Promoting an employee
(D) Selecting a candidate

08 What is mentioned about Mike Dunlop?
(A) He received some instructions.
(B) He pushed back an interview.
(C) He majored in language studies.
(D) He developed an application.

09 What will the man do in the afternoon?
(A) Talk with a customer
(B) Install a program
(C) Revise a contract
(D) Speak to a colleague

10 Who is Mr. Henderson?
(A) A company president
(B) A restaurant owner
(C) A personal secretary
(D) A newspaper journalist

11 What are the women concerned about?
(A) A review
(B) A menu
(C) A booking
(D) A payment

12 What does the man suggest?
(A) Choosing another venue
(B) Updating party invitations
(C) Postponing a celebration
(D) Asking about a discount

13 According to the woman, what was the announcement about?

(A) A performance evaluation
(B) A project deadline
(C) A company's expansion
(D) A colleague's promotion

14 Which department do the speakers work in?

(A) Marketing
(B) Sales
(C) Legal
(D) Personnel

15 What does the man imply when he says, "The two teams need to work together"?

(A) The woman should schedule a meeting.
(B) The woman should revise a campaign plan.
(C) The company should promote senior staff.
(D) The woman should give a presentation.

---

16 What does the man suggest doing?

(A) Delaying a training session
(B) Relocating a company event
(C) Reassigning a team leader
(D) Confirming a project budget

17 What problem does the woman mention?

(A) A process will be difficult.
(B) A destination is far.
(C) A cost will be high.
(D) A policy is unfair.

18 According to the man, what can be found on a Web site?

(A) Prices for accommodations
(B) Reviews of services
(C) Directions to a venue
(D) Details about activities

Time	Talk	Speaker
10:30 A.M.	Staffing Innovations	Margot Hatch
11:30 A.M.	Global Expansion	Cynthia Bloom
12:15 P.M.	Lunch Break	
1:30 P.M.	Financial Forecasts	Gerald Fines
2:45 P.M.	Domestic Markets	Pete Strass

19 Look at the graphic. Which talk will be replaced?

(A) Staffing Innovations
(B) Global Expansion
(C) Financial Forecasts
(D) Domestic Markets

20 What does the man recommend?

(A) Adjusting a time slot
(B) Inviting another speaker
(C) Showing a video
(D) Notifying attendees

21 What will the woman print?

(A) Guest nametags
(B) Corporate brochures
(C) Seating charts
(D) Meeting programs

DAY 13 마케팅/판매/재무 관련 대화

MP3 바로 듣기

마케팅/판매/재무 관련 대화는 마케팅, 광고, 매출, 회사 재정 등과 같이 회사의 각 부서별 업무에 관한 대화입니다. PART 3 전체 13개 대화 중 매회 2~3개 정도 출제됩니다.

최신 경향 및 전략

1. 다음과 같은 상황이 자주 출제됩니다.
   - 상품 마케팅 전략, 제품 홍보, 광고 등 마케팅 업무에 관한 대화
   - 매출 증가 및 감소, 계약 성사, 생산 증진 등 판매 업무에 관한 대화
   - 예산 분배, 비용 절감, 자금 조달, 합병 및 인수 성사 등 회사 재무에 관한 대화
2. 마케팅 전략 및 홍보 수단, 매출 증가 및 감소, 경비 및 자금과 관련된 표현들을 알아두면 도움이 됩니다.

자주 나오는 표현 🎧 D13_1_표현

마케팅 전략 및 홍보 수단	advertisement n. 광고	distribute v. 배포하다, 나눠주다
	demonstrate v. 시연하다	selling point (판매 시) 상품의 강조점
매출 증가 및 감소	profit n. 수익, 이익	revenue n. 수익, 수입
	increase v. 증가하다; n. 증가	decline v. 감소하다; n. 감소
경비 및 자금	cost n. 비용; v. (값·비용이) 들다	budget n. 예산
	expense n. 비용, 경비	fund n. 기금, 돈; v. 자금을 대다

Example 🎧 D13_2_예제

01 What does the man want to buy?
(A) Display shelves
(B) Picture frames
(C) Store furniture
(D) Light fixtures

호주 → 미국
Question 01 refers to the following conversation.

M: Hi. **I'd like to buy some lights for my store's display shelves.** I'm updating the front section this weekend.
W: I'll be happy to help you out. I'm one of the sales representatives here at Global Lighting.
M: I need something stylish and bright enough to highlight the products.
W: Based on what you're looking for, I'll prepare a few recommendations for you.

해석
01 남자는 무엇을 사고 싶어 하는가?
(A) 진열 선반
(B) 그림 액자
(C) 매장 가구
(D) 조명 기구

01번은 다음 대화에 관한 문제입니다.

남: 안녕하세요. 제 가게의 진열 선반을 위한 조명을 사고 싶어요. 이번 주말에 전면 구역을 새로 단장할 예정이에요.
여: 도와드릴 수 있게 되어 기쁩니다. 저는 이곳 Global 조명사의 영업 담당자 중 한 명입니다.
남: 저는 제품을 돋보이게 할 만큼 충분히 세련되고 밝은 것이 필요해요.
여: 고객님이 찾고 계신 것을 바탕으로, 몇 가지 추천안을 준비해 드리겠습니다.

정답 (D)

해설
남자가 사고 싶어 하는 것을 묻는 문제입니다. 남자가 "I'd like to buy some lights for my store's display shelves."라며 가게의 진열 선반을 위한 조명을 사고 싶다고 하였습니다. 따라서 정답은 (D) Light fixtures입니다.

어휘
front section 전면 구역   sales representative 영업 담당자   highlight v. 돋보이게 하다, 강조하다   recommendation n. 추천(안)

HACKERS PRACTICE

대화를 들으며 주어진 질문에 가장 알맞은 보기를 고르고, 빈칸에 들어갈 내용을 받아쓰세요. (음성은 두 번 들려줍니다.) 🎧 D13_3_Practice

[01-02]

01 Why is the man visiting the woman?

(A) To discuss a partnership
(B) To perform an interview
(C) To negotiate a contract
(D) To introduce a product

02 What does the man say that his company provides?

(A) An annual membership
(B) A complimentary accessory
(C) A software upgrade
(D) An extended warranty

M: Thanks for meeting with us, Ms. Davidson. We appreciate the _____ how our company's newest face-toning device works.
W: No problem. This is exactly the kind of _____ that customers at my stores are interested in. Oh, it's much smaller than I expected.
M: That's actually one of its selling points. And I want to point out that we offer a five-year _____. This shows our confidence in the product.

[03-04]

03 According to the woman, what will happen tomorrow?

(A) A street will close.
(B) A product will launch.
(C) A store will relocate.
(D) A promotion will begin.

04 What does the man recommend?

(A) Arranging products
(B) Posting a notice
(C) Cleaning windows
(D) Visiting a shop

W: Jake, would you mind helping me put up the _____? Our clothing boutique's _____ starts tomorrow. We need to get everything ready for the customers.
M: Sure. And once we are done, maybe we should _____ in the front window. That way, everyone who walks by will know that we are having a sale.
W: I was thinking the same thing.

HACKERS TEST

대화를 들으며 주어진 질문에 가장 알맞은 보기를 고르세요. 🎧 D13_4_Test

01 What is the problem?
(A) A boutique is not currently open.
(B) A clothing line is not selling well.
(C) A dress cannot be exchanged.
(D) A purchase cannot be refunded.

02 What does the woman propose doing?
(A) Advertising online
(B) Offering a discount
(C) Hiring staff
(D) Enlarging a space

03 What does the man ask the woman to do?
(A) Help a customer
(B) Create a design
(C) Make a list
(D) Process a transaction

04 What type of business does the woman work at?
(A) A construction company
(B) A landscaping service
(C) An interior design firm
(D) A real estate agency

05 What does the man say is surprising about a product?
(A) Its durability
(B) Its appearance
(C) Its weight
(D) Its price

06 What will the woman receive for placing a large order?
(A) A special gift
(B) A gift certificate
(C) A membership upgrade
(D) A free service

07 What are the speakers mainly discussing?
(A) Rent increases
(B) Tenant notices
(C) Security equipment
(D) Online data

08 What is the woman in charge of doing?
(A) Communicating with residents
(B) Overseeing a budget
(C) Assigning tasks to workers
(D) Installing machinery

09 What does the man say he will do this afternoon?
(A) Contact businesses
(B) Read a user manual
(C) Install a software program
(D) Advertise services

10 Where most likely are the speakers?
(A) In a hair salon
(B) In a grocery store
(C) In a print shop
(D) In a health spa

11 Why does the woman say, "I've been considering that for a while"?
(A) To express agreement with a proposal
(B) To indicate uncertainty about an option
(C) To introduce a solution to a problem
(D) To ask for help with an assignment

12 What does the man offer to do?
(A) Create a design
(B) Buy some materials
(C) Hand out some flyers
(D) Meet with a customer

13. Why do the women want to borrow money?
    (A) To upgrade a facility
    (B) To purchase a vehicle
    (C) To expand a business
    (D) To develop a product

14. How did the women learn about a service?
    (A) By reading a pamphlet
    (B) By talking to a colleague
    (C) By calling a branch
    (D) By accessing a Web site

15. What will the man send in an e-mail?
    (A) A payment schedule
    (B) An operating license
    (C) A financial record
    (D) An application form

16. What does the woman want to do?
    (A) Repair some screens
    (B) Purchase office equipment
    (C) Open an account
    (D) Get a cost estimate

17. What does the woman say about her company?
    (A) It received damaged items.
    (B) It qualifies for a lower price.
    (C) It places weekly orders.
    (D) It ordered the wrong model.

18. What does the man say he will do?
    (A) Contact the warehouse
    (B) Expedite an order
    (C) Charge an account
    (D) Install a computer

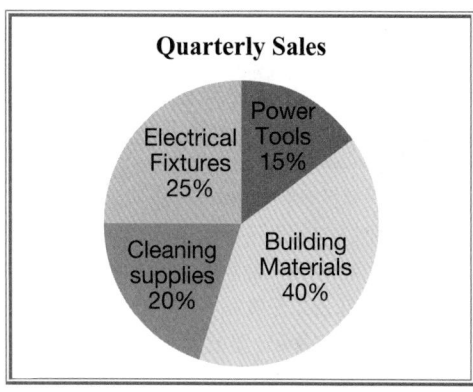

19. Who most likely is the woman?
    (A) A branch supervisor
    (B) A store clerk
    (C) A business consultant
    (D) A sales representative

20. Look at the graphic. Which product category surprised the man?
    (A) Power Tools
    (B) Building Materials
    (C) Cleaning Supplies
    (D) Electrical Fixtures

21. What does the woman offer to give the man?
    (A) A résumé
    (B) An invoice
    (C) A photograph
    (D) A summary

DAY 14 일상생활 관련 대화

MP3 바로 듣기

일상생활 관련 대화는 쇼핑, 교통수단 이용, 외식, 병원 이용, 이사 등 평범한 일상생활에 관한 대화입니다. PART 3 전체 13개 대화 중 매회 3~4개 정도 출제됩니다.

최신 경향 및 전략

1. 다음과 같은 상황이 자주 출제됩니다.
   - 상점에서의 물건 구매, 환불 등 쇼핑에 관한 대화
   - 대중교통 및 주차장 이용, 외식, 병원, 은행, 우체국, 도서관, 미용실 등 교통수단 및 편의 시설에 관한 대화
   - 이사, 가구, 집 구매 등 주거에 관한 대화
2. 물건 구매, 교통수단 및 편의 시설 이용, 부동산 매매와 관련된 표현들을 알아두면 도움이 됩니다.

자주 나오는 표현 🎧 D14_1_표현

물건 구매	carry v. (가게에서 품목을) 취급하다	sold out 매진된, 품절된
	custom adj. 맞춤의	expedited adj. 더 신속히 처리된, 촉진된
교통수단 및 편의 시설 이용	transportation n. 운송, 수송	board v. 승차하다
	parking area 주차장	facility n. 시설
부동산 매매	property n. 건물, 부동산	rent v. 세내다, 세놓다
	tenant n. 세입자	lease n. 임대차 계약

Example 🎧 D14_2_예제

01 What will Kevin most likely do next?
(A) Explain warranty terms
(B) Show some products
(C) Check the inventory
(D) Cancel a previous order

해석
01 Kevin은 다음에 무엇을 할 것 같은가?
(A) 보증 조건을 설명한다.
(B) 몇몇 제품을 보여준다.
(C) 재고를 확인한다.
(D) 이전 주문을 취소한다.

🎙 캐나다 → 영국 → 호주

Question 01 refers to the following conversation with three speakers.

M1: Pardon me. I'm looking for a swimsuit for my upcoming vacation.
W: We carry several popular brands, and many are on sale now.
M1: Great. I need to buy one today, as my friends and I leave tomorrow morning.
W: One moment, please. **Kevin, could you show this customer our men's swimwear?**
M2: **Certainly. This way, sir.** They are located on the second floor.

01번은 다음 세 명의 대화에 관한 문제입니다.

남1: 실례합니다. 다가오는 휴가를 위한 수영복을 찾고 있어요.
여: 저희는 여러 인기 브랜드를 취급하고 있고, 많은 제품이 지금 할인 중입니다.
남1: 좋네요. 제 친구들과 제가 내일 아침에 떠나기 때문에, 오늘 하나를 사야 해요.
여: 잠시만 기다려주세요. Kevin, 이 고객님께 남성용 수영복을 보여주실래요?
남2: 물론이죠. 이쪽입니다, 손님. 남성용 수영복은 2층에 위치해 있습니다.

정답 (B)

해설
Kevin이 다음에 할 일을 묻는 문제입니다. 여자가 남자2[Kevin]에게 "Kevin, could you show this customer our men's swimwear?"라며 고객에게 남성용 수영복을 보여주라고 요청하자, 남자2[Kevin]가 "Certainly. This way, sir."라며 물론이라며 남자1에게 이쪽으로 오라고 하였습니다. 따라서 정답은 (B) Show some products입니다.

어휘
swimsuit n. 수영복 upcoming adj. 다가오는 on sale 할인 중인

HACKERS PRACTICE

대화를 들으며 주어진 질문에 가장 알맞은 보기를 고르고, 빈칸에 들어갈 내용을 받아쓰세요. (음성은 두 번 들려줍니다.) 🎧 D14_3_Practice

[01-02]

01 Why does the man need assistance?

(A) He is uncertain about what to order.
(B) He wants to check some ingredients.
(C) He received the wrong order.
(D) He did not get a meal.

02 What will the man most likely do next?

(A) Ask about today's special
(B) Request a dinner order
(C) Review a menu again
(D) Wait for his food to arrive

W: Do you know what you would like to order today?
M: Actually, do you have _____?
I can't decide what to get.
W: You should try the cheese pizza. It has a delicious crust, a savory sauce, and three different types of cheese. It is one of our _____.
M: That sounds perfect. But please give me a few more minutes to _____. I need to select a beverage.

[03-04]

03 Where most likely are the speakers?

(A) At a store
(B) At a residence
(C) At an office
(D) At a factory

04 What will the man probably do next?

(A) Order a product
(B) Move an appliance
(C) Make a repair
(D) Call a technician

M: Hello, Ms. Glenn. Now that I have _____, _____, what seems to be wrong with your dishwasher?
W: Water leaks from it while it's running. I'm worried that the water will _____.
M: I see. This DryMore 3XC model has a weak bottom seal. Fortunately, that's _____. It shouldn't take me more than an hour.
W: Oh, great.

HACKERS TEST

대화를 들으며 주어진 질문에 가장 알맞은 보기를 고르세요. 🎧 D14_4_Test

01 Where most likely does the man work?
(A) At a school office
(B) At an advertising agency
(C) At a convention center
(D) At an art gallery

02 What does the man say about Ms. Wells?
(A) She registered for a class.
(B) She is currently unavailable.
(C) She is a well-known painter.
(D) She interviewed for a job.

03 Why does the woman need to leave by 1:30?
(A) To prepare for a workshop
(B) To submit an assignment
(C) To give a presentation
(D) To meet with a customer

04 Why is a discount being offered?
(A) To recognize a holiday
(B) To promote an event
(C) To celebrate an anniversary
(D) To commemorate a product launch

05 What does the woman say she brought with her?
(A) A credit card
(B) Some equipment
(C) Some food
(D) A season pass

06 What will the woman probably do next?
(A) Download an app
(B) Meet an instructor
(C) Fill out some paperwork
(D) Check a map

07 Who most likely is the man?
(A) A carpenter
(B) A plumber
(C) A cleaner
(D) An electrician

08 What does the man mean when he says, "I don't have any appointments this afternoon"?
(A) He will perform a task.
(B) He will check with a client.
(C) He will return at a later time.
(D) He will wait for a colleague.

09 What does the woman ask for?
(A) A price estimate
(B) A component list
(C) A business contract
(D) A project schedule

10 What did the woman do yesterday?
(A) She dropped off some items.
(B) She purchased some clothes.
(C) She called a business.
(D) She worked from home.

11 What does the man ask the woman about?
(A) What service she received
(B) Whether she made a request
(C) Where she currently lives
(D) When she submitted a payment

12 What does the man tell the woman to do?
(A) Pay an additional fee
(B) Inspect some garments
(C) Check online
(D) Return later

13 What did the speakers do?
(A) They watched a film.
(B) They attended a concert.
(C) They viewed an exhibition.
(D) They went to a museum.

14 What does the man suggest?
(A) Visiting an establishment
(B) Waiting for the bus
(C) Asking for directions
(D) Reading some reviews

15 What will the speakers probably do next?
(A) Place an order
(B) Take a taxi
(C) Purchase a ticket
(D) Walk to a station

16 What department does the man most likely work in?
(A) Accounting
(B) Marketing
(C) Customer service
(D) Human resources

17 What information does the man ask for?
(A) A school name
(B) A date of birth
(C) A transaction amount
(D) An account number

18 What does the man instruct the woman to do?
(A) Change a password
(B) Reply to an e-mail
(C) Download a file
(D) Go to a branch

19 Where most likely are the speakers?
(A) In a grocery store
(B) In a restaurant
(C) In a stadium
(D) In a community center

20 What does the man apologize for?
(A) Canceling an appointment
(B) Forgetting an event
(C) Misplacing an item
(D) Missing a practice

21 Look at the graphic. Which option does the woman prefer?
(A) Option 1
(B) Option 2
(C) Option 3
(D) Option 4

DAY 15 여행 및 여가 관련 대화

MP3 바로 듣기

여행 및 여가 관련 대화는 항공편 및 숙박 예약, 여행 일정, 공항, 호텔, 공연 및 전시회 관람 등 다양한 여가 생활에 관한 대화입니다. PART 3 전체 13개 대화 중 매회 1~2개 정도 출제됩니다.

최신 경향 및 전략

1. 다음과 같은 상황이 자주 출제됩니다.
   - 교통편 및 숙박 예약, 계획된 여행 일정, 공항, 기내, 호텔 등 여행에 관한 대화
   - 공연 관람, 영화 관람, 전시회 관람, 박물관 방문 등 문화 생활에 관한 대화
   - 파티 참석, 축제 참가 등 일상 여가 생활에 관한 대화
2. 교통편, 숙박 시설, 여가 생활과 관련된 표현들을 알아두면 도움이 됩니다.

자주 나오는 표현 🎧 D15_1_표현

교통편	ticket n. 표	seat n. 좌석
	car rental 자동차 대여	depart v. 출발하다
숙박 시설	accommodation n. 숙소	inn n. 여관, 호텔
	cabin n. 객실	available adj. 이용 가능한
여가 생활	museum n. 박물관	theater n. 극장
	performance n. 공연	festival n. 축제

Example 🎧 D15_2_예제

01 Why is the woman calling?
(A) To complain about a flight delay
(B) To report some lost items
(C) To change a travel plan
(D) To inquire about baggage fees

[3📢] 캐나다 → 미국
Question 01 refers to the following conversation.

M: Hispana Air. How can I assist you today?
W: Hello. My name is Karen Brewster, and **I'd like to change the date of my return flight**.
M: Sure, Ms. Brewster. However, please note that there's a 100-dollar fee for this service. If that's OK, may I have your flight number? It's on the top of your ticket.

해석
01 여자는 왜 전화하고 있는가?
(A) 항공편 지연에 대해 항의하기 위해
(B) 분실물을 신고하기 위해
(C) 여행 계획을 변경하기 위해
(D) 수하물 요금을 문의하기 위해

01번은 다음 대화에 관한 문제입니다.

남: Hispana 항공입니다. 오늘 어떻게 도와드릴까요?
여: 안녕하세요. 제 이름은 Karen Brewster이고, **저의 돌아오는 항공편의 날짜를 변경하고 싶어요**.
남: 물론입니다, Ms. Brewster. 하지만, 이 서비스에는 100달러의 요금이 있다는 점을 유의해 주시기 바랍니다. 괜찮으시다면, 항공편 번호를 알려주시겠습니까? 그것은 티켓의 상단에 있습니다.

정답 (C)

해설
전화의 목적을 묻는 문제입니다. 여자가 "I'd like to change the date of my return flight"라며 돌아오는 항공편의 날짜를 변경하고 싶다고 한 뒤, 남자가 항공편 날짜 변경에 관해 안내하는 내용으로 대화가 이어지고 있습니다. 따라서 (C) To change a travel plan이 정답입니다.

어휘
assist v. 돕다 flight n. 항공편 note v. 유의하다, 주목하다 fee n. 수수료, 요금

HACKERS PRACTICE

대화를 들으며 주어진 질문에 가장 알맞은 보기를 고르고, 빈칸에 들어갈 내용을 받아쓰세요. (음성은 두 번 들려줍니다.) 🎧 D15_3_Practice

[01-02]

01 What does the woman request?
(A) A delivery
(B) A discount
(C) A receipt
(D) A refund

02 What will the man most likely do next?
(A) Issue a card
(B) Pay a fare
(C) Upgrade a seat
(D) Check a schedule

W: Hi, I'd like to buy a train ticket to Bellingham. I think I can _____ if I pay with this credit card. Could you check for me?
M: Unfortunately, that _____ last month. But if you purchase a ticket for a standard seat, I can _____ at no additional charge.
W: That would be great. Please _____ for the 10 A.M. train.

[03-04]

03 Where most likely are the speakers?
(A) At a workshop
(B) At a party
(C) At a contest
(D) At a festival

04 What is mentioned about Kenta Yamada?
(A) He is well-known.
(B) He arrived late.
(C) He has a busy schedule.
(D) He organized an event.

M: How are you enjoying the _____ so far?
W: It's great. There are so many different types of desserts, and everything looks delicious.
M: Look over there. That booth is run by the _____ _____ Kenta Yamada. Why don't we go try his tarts? I heard they're amazing.
W: That sounds like a great idea. I've always wanted to _____. Let's go!

HACKERS TEST

대화를 들으며 주어진 질문에 가장 알맞은 보기를 고르세요. 🎧 D15_4_Test

01 What is the woman planning to do during her vacation?
(A) Go to a concert
(B) Tour a museum
(C) Attend an expo
(D) Visit a gallery

02 What does the man say about San Diego?
(A) It hosts a lot of family events.
(B) It includes many attractions.
(C) It has a good climate.
(D) It has affordable hotels.

03 What did the woman change about her travel plan?
(A) The type of accommodations
(B) The form of transportation
(C) The length of stay
(D) The date of departure

04 What is the woman doing?
(A) Purchasing tickets
(B) Upgrading seats
(C) Downloading an app
(D) Checking a schedule

05 Why has an event attracted much interest?
(A) It is free for local residents.
(B) It was promoted on a Web site.
(C) It will feature a famous athlete.
(D) It includes a musical performance.

06 What will the woman do next?
(A) Watch a game
(B) Cancel a booking
(C) Contact a friend
(D) Enter a password

07 What activity did the woman originally plan to do today?
(A) Exercising
(B) Studying
(C) Sightseeing
(D) Cleaning

08 What does the woman say about the museum?
(A) It does not have parking facilities.
(B) It was featured on a television program.
(C) It recently underwent an expansion.
(D) It is not open to visitors today.

09 How did the man learn about the displays?
(A) From a colleague
(B) On a radio program
(C) In a newspaper article
(D) Through a museum newsletter

10 Why is the man calling?
(A) To make a reservation
(B) To extend a rental period
(C) To request a discount
(D) To change a payment method

11 What will the man do in the morning?
(A) Log in to an account
(B) Sign a contract
(C) Choose a vehicle
(D) Meet with a client

12 What does Danielle remind the man about?
(A) A drop-off location
(B) An appointment time
(C) An on-site inspection
(D) A branch closure

13 What is the conversation mainly about?
(A) A performance
(B) A workshop
(C) A seminar
(D) A fundraiser

14 What bothered the woman?
(A) The location of a venue
(B) The length of an event
(C) The cost of an item
(D) The size of a facility

15 Why does the man say, "Check your e-mail"?
(A) To imply that feedback is requested
(B) To suggest that information is inaccurate
(C) To stress that permission is necessary
(D) To indicate that reimbursement is possible

16 Where most likely are the speakers?
(A) At a bus terminal
(B) At a subway station
(C) At an airport
(D) At a taxi stand

17 Why is the man traveling to Harrisburg?
(A) To participate in a concert
(B) To take part in an interview
(C) To join a wedding
(D) To attend a conference

18 What problem does the woman mention?
(A) A bag has been misplaced.
(B) Tickets have been sold out.
(C) A vehicle has malfunctioned.
(D) Passengers have arrived late.

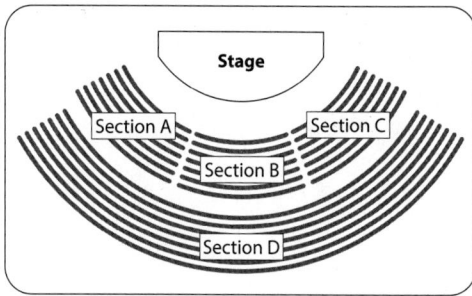

19 What type of event does the man want a ticket for?
(A) A play
(B) A music festival
(C) An awards ceremony
(D) A screening

20 Look at the graphic. Which section does the man want to sit in?
(A) Section A
(B) Section B
(C) Section C
(D) Section D

21 What does the woman suggest?
(A) Saving a payment receipt
(B) Paying for an upgrade
(C) Arriving at a venue early
(D) Reading an online review

한 권으로 끝내는 해커스 토익 600+ LC+RC+VOCA

PART 4

- **DAY 16** 음성 메시지 및 회의 발췌
- **DAY 17** 공지 및 관광 안내
- **DAY 18** 연설 및 강연
- **DAY 19** 방송 및 보도
- **DAY 20** 광고 및 소개

◀ MP3 바로 듣기

교재에 수록된 모든 MP3를 무료로 다운받거나 바로 스트리밍하여 더욱 편리하게 이용해 보세요.
고속 버전 MP3도 구매하여 학습하면 실전에 더욱 완벽하게 대비할 수 있습니다.

PART 4 알아보기

PART 4는 71번부터 100번까지 총 30문제로, 1명이 이야기하는 음성 메시지나 공지, 연설, 방송 등의 담화를 듣고 그와 관련된 3개의 문제를 푸는 파트입니다. 문제지에 각 문제의 질문과 4개의 보기가 제시되고, 음성으로 각 담화와 이에 대한 3개의 문제의 질문을 들려줍니다.

PART 4 미리 보기

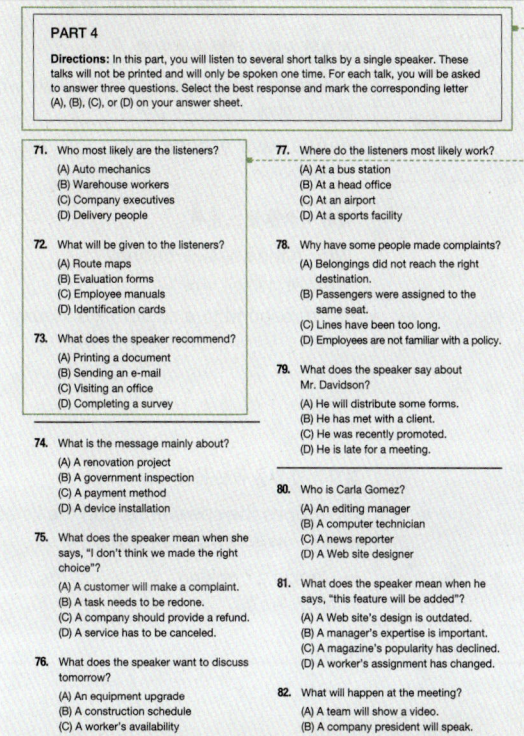

PART 4를 소개하는 디렉션입니다.

담화와 각 문제의 질문을 다음과 같이 들려줍니다.

Questions 71 through 73 refer to the following announcement.

Before you start today's shift, I have an announcement. As most of you know, Dennis Lyon left the company. Until we find a replacement delivery truck driver, you will all have a heavier workload than usual. In a few moments, I'll give everyone an updated route map with the additional areas you will need to cover. If anything about your new route is unclear, I encourage you to stop by my office and discuss it with me.

Number 71.
Who most likely are the listeners?
Number 72.
What will be given to the listeners?
Number 73.
What does the speaker recommend?

PART 4 학습 전략

- **담화 유형별로 자주 나오는 담화 흐름과 빈출 문제 익히기**
  PART 4는 담화 유형에 따른 전형적인 흐름이 있으며, 자주 출제되는 문제 유형 또한 정해진 편입니다. 실제 시험에서 더욱 쉽게 담화의 내용을 파악하여 정확하게 문제를 풀 수 있도록, 담화별 흐름과 빈출 문제를 꼭 학습해야 합니다.

- **담화 상황별 자주 나오는 표현 익히기**
  담화 내용을 정확히 듣고 의미를 파악할 수 있도록 담화의 흐름을 알려주는 표현을 익혀두어야 합니다.

DAY 16 음성 메시지 및 회의 발췌

1. 음성 메시지

음성 메시지는 예약 시간, 면접 일정, 주문 및 배송 상황 등의 정보를 제공하는 메시지 또는 기관에서 남긴 자동 응답 메시지 형식의 담화입니다. PART 4 전체 10개 지문 중 매회 1~2개 정도 출제됩니다.

담화 흐름과 빈출 문제 🎧 D16_1_예제

음성 메시지	흐름	흐름에 따른 빈출 문제
Hello. Mr. Kim. **This is** Renaldo Rolenti **calling from** GlobalTrip.	인사말 및 전화한 사람 소개	**전화한 사람에 관해 묻는 문제** Where does the speaker most likely work? 화자는 어디에서 일하는 것 같은가? → At a travel agency 여행사에서
I'd like to answer your inquiry about the discount for your tour package. I see that you booked it on our Web site, but this promotion is only available if you book it through our smartphone application. Just install the application and enter the promotion code to save 15 percent off the regular price. You will receive a confirmation e-mail afterward.	전화를 한 이유	**전화 목적을 묻는 문제** Why is the speaker calling? 화자는 왜 전화하고 있는가? → To respond to a customer's inquiry 고객의 문의에 답변하기 위해
Don't forget to cancel your previous booking. That way, you won't be double-charged. Let me know if you have any questions. 해석 p.88	청자에게 요청 및 당부하는 사항	**청자가 할 일을 묻는 문제** What does the speaker remind the listener to do? 화자는 청자에게 무엇을 하라고 상기시키는가? → Cancel a booking 예약을 취소한다.

음성 메시지에서 담화의 흐름을 알려주는 표현들을 알아두면 도움이 됩니다.

- **화자(전화한 사람) 소개**: This is 이름 (calling) from ~ 저는 ~에서 근무하는 [이름]입니다
- **전화 목적**: I'd like to answer ~ ~에 답변하고 싶습니다
  I'm calling to/about ~ ~하려고 전화했습니다
- **청자가 할 일**: Don't forget to ~ ~하는 것을 잊지 마세요
  Please contact me at ~ 제게 ~으로 연락해 주세요

HACKERS PRACTICE

담화를 들으며 주어진 질문에 가장 알맞은 보기를 고르고, 빈칸에 들어갈 내용을 받아쓰세요. (음성은 두 번 들려줍니다.) 🎧 D16_2_Practice

[01-02]

01 Why is the speaker calling?
(A) To explain a refund process
(B) To confirm a delivery address
(C) To provide an order update
(D) To describe a special offer

02 What should the listener do at the customer service desk?
(A) Fill out a form
(B) Examine an item
(C) Make a payment
(D) Present a receipt

I'm calling from Pearson's to let you know that the _____ _____ at our store tomorrow morning. You can pick up your new guitar from our shop at any time during our _____.
Make sure to _____ when you do this.
Just _____ at our customer service desk, and they will get your item for you. Thank you.

[03-04]

03 Where does the speaker work?
(A) At a travel agency
(B) At an office tower
(C) At a residential building
(D) At a shipping company

04 What does the speaker ask the listener to do?
(A) Settle a charge
(B) Provide notification
(C) Confirm attendance
(D) Review a manual

Good morning. This is Daniel at the _____.
A large package has just been delivered for you. You may pick it up before 6 P.M., or have a member of the staff bring it _____. After 6 P.M., it will be _____. We usually only keep large items for up to 15 days. Please _____ if you'd like us to keep it for longer.
Thank you.

2. 회의 발췌

회의 발췌는 회의에서 직원들에게 업무 진행 상황, 프로젝트 계획, 회사의 방침 변경 등에 관한 내용을 전달하는 담화입니다. PART 4 전체 10개 지문 중 매회 2~3개 정도 출제됩니다.

담화 흐름과 빈출 문제 🎧 D16_3_예제

회의 발췌

Good morning. **I called this meeting because** a group of officials from the Ministry of Technology will be touring our research facility today.

When they visit your section of the laboratory, **please take the time** to explain what you are working on. It is crucial that they understand the research we are doing here and why it is significant. Keep in mind that we need to create a good impression on our visitors. As you know, **most of our funding comes from the government**.

해석 p.89

흐름

- 회의를 소집한 목적
- 세부 내용 및 청자들에게 요청하는 사항

흐름에 따른 빈출 문제

주제를 묻는 문제
What is the speaker discussing?
화자는 무엇에 대해 이야기하고 있는가?
→ A tour of a facility
　시설 시찰

요청 사항을 묻는 문제
What are the listeners asked to do?
청자들은 무엇을 하도록 요청받는가?
→ Explain some work
　업무를 설명한다.

특정 어구의 의도를 묻는 문제
Why does the speaker say, "most of our funding comes from the government"?
화자는 왜 "우리 기금의 대부분은 정부로부터 나옵니다"라고 말하는가?
→ To provide a reason for a claim
　주장에 대한 이유를 제시하기 위해

회의 발췌에서 담화의 흐름을 알려주는 표현들을 알아두면 도움이 됩니다.

- **주제 및 목적**: I called the/this meeting because ~ 저는 ~ 때문에 회의를 소집했습니다
  　　　　　　　 I will give an update on ~ 제가 ~에 대한 최근 소식을 알려줄 것입니다
- **요청 사항**: Please take the time ~ 시간을 내서 ~해 주시기 바랍니다
  　　　　　　 I need you all to ~ 여러분 모두 ~해야 합니다

HACKERS PRACTICE

담화를 들으며 주어진 질문에 가장 알맞은 보기를 고르고, 빈칸에 들어갈 내용을 받아쓰세요. (음성은 두 번 들려줍니다.) 🎧 D16_4_Practice

[01-02]

01 What is the speaker mainly discussing?

(A) Improving a product
(B) Reviewing staff performance
(C) Creating an advertisement
(D) Conducting a survey

02 What are the listeners asked to do?

(A) Read some materials
(B) Develop a sample
(C) Go to a meeting
(D) Correct some errors

I called this meeting to start our _____ _____ for our company's newest camera model. Before we get started, though, I'd like you to learn more about our _____. We need to clearly _____ the two products in our advertisement. I'll give each of you a brochure about that device. Please _____ _____, and we will discuss it next week.

[03-04]

03 What industry does the speaker most likely work in?

(A) Investment
(B) Transportation
(C) Accommodation
(D) Entertainment

04 What does the man mean when he says, "I have one concern"?

(A) A job is too demanding.
(B) A schedule is tight.
(C) An applicant is unsuitable.
(D) A facility is understaffed.

Summer will be here soon, and that means we're about to get _____. Before this happens, we need to hire several front desk clerks. The goal is to have them _____ on May 20. I have one concern, though. That does not give us much _____ _____. So if you know of someone with relevant experience who is looking for a job, please _____.

HACKERS TEST

담화를 들으며 주어진 질문에 가장 알맞은 보기를 고르세요. 🎧 D16_5_Test

01 Who most likely are the listeners?
(A) Cleaning staff
(B) Delivery drivers
(C) Store clerks
(D) Security personnel

02 What will be provided to the listeners?
(A) A name tag
(B) An employee manual
(C) A clothing item
(D) A gift card

03 What will most likely be discussed next?
(A) An interview process
(B) A seasonal promotion
(C) A customer survey
(D) A team-building exercise

04 Where does the speaker work?
(A) At an insurance office
(B) At a bank
(C) At a pharmacy
(D) At a medical center

05 What does the speaker mention about the online account?
(A) It includes a scheduling function.
(B) It provides test results.
(C) It allows for bill payments.
(D) It features a chat program.

06 Why would the listener most likely return a call?
(A) To book an appointment
(B) To correct information
(C) To ask for a password
(D) To request assistance

07 Why does the speaker want to make a change?
(A) Employees have too many assignments.
(B) A software program is causing problems.
(C) A department head is considering resigning.
(D) Technicians recommend an upgrade.

08 What will happen next week?
(A) Electronic devices will be replaced.
(B) Training sessions will be held.
(C) Additional employees will be hired.
(D) Staff evaluations will be conducted.

09 How will Ms. Lauren share a schedule?
(A) By posting a notice
(B) By making a call
(C) By holding a meeting
(D) By sending an e-mail

10 According to the speaker, what will be changed?
(A) A return policy
(B) A service fee
(C) A production contract
(D) A phone number

11 What does the speaker mean when he says, "challenges are expected"?
(A) More staff are required.
(B) Customers may complain.
(C) Extra time is needed.
(D) Expenses might increase.

12 What are the listeners asked to do?
(A) Review documents
(B) Contact a director
(C) Transfer calls
(D) Promote a subscription

13 What type of business does the speaker work for?

(A) A design firm
(B) An amusement park
(C) A shopping complex
(D) A film production studio

14 According to the speaker, what will be renovated?

(A) A parking garage
(B) A movie theater
(C) A gift shop
(D) A clothing boutique

15 What does the speaker suggest?

(A) Buying tickets in advance
(B) Visiting on a certain day
(C) Signing up for a loyalty club
(D) Avoiding a specific lot

16 Who most likely is the listener?

(A) A safety inspector
(B) A business owner
(C) A Web designer
(D) A financial consultant

17 What is the listener required to do?

(A) Visit an office
(B) Confirm a decision
(C) Send a notification
(D) Make an appointment

18 According to the speaker, what will take one month to complete?

(A) A safety inspection
(B) A cost estimate
(C) A construction project
(D) An application review

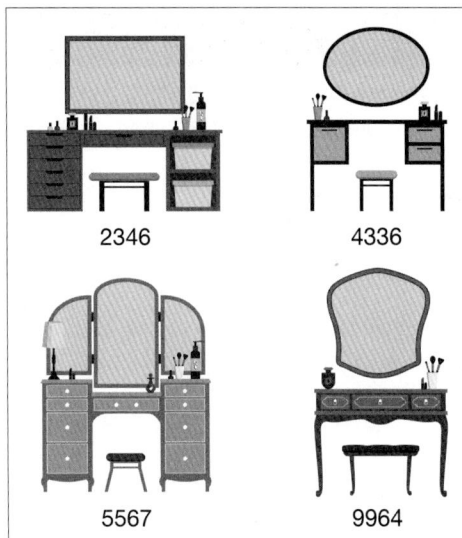

19 What is the speaker mainly discussing?

(A) Feedback from a focus group
(B) Inquiries from customers
(C) Sales of a product line
(D) Improvements to designs

20 Look at the graphic. Which model will likely be reduced in price?

(A) 2346
(B) 4336
(C) 5567
(D) 9964

21 What is the speaker concerned about?

(A) Packaging materials
(B) Delivery schedules
(C) Production costs
(D) Marketing methods

DAY 17 공지 및 관광 안내

MP3 바로 듣기

1. 공지

공지는 청자들에게 교통수단 및 시설물 관련 안내, 사내 행사 및 시설 점검 일정 등에 관한 새로운 사실이나 변경사항을 알리는 담화입니다. PART 4 전체 10개 지문 중 매회 1~2개 정도 출제됩니다.

담화 흐름과 빈출 문제 🎧 D17_1_예제

공지	흐름	흐름에 따른 빈출 문제
Attention, shoppers. Thank you for coming to Fresh Mart.	인사말 및 장소 언급	**공지가 이루어지는 장소를 묻는 문제** Where is the announcement being made? 공지는 어디에서 이루어지고 있는가? → At a grocery store 　식료품점에서
I'd like to announce that the store will be closed from May 13 to 16 for renovations.	공지를 하는 목적	**공지의 목적을 묻는 문제** What is the purpose of the announcement? 공지의 목적은 무엇인가? → To inform customers about renovations 　고객들에게 수리를 알리기 위해
We will be installing a deli near the produce section. We apologize for the inconvenience and hope that the change to the store will result in an improved shopping experience for all our customers. To celebrate the deli opening on May 17, we're giving away free samples and a coupon to use on your next visit. Please ask one of our staff at the customer service desk for your coupon. 해석 p.94	청자들에게 요청 및 당부하는 사항	**요청 사항을 묻는 문제** What are the listeners encouraged to do? 청자들은 무엇을 하도록 권장되는가? → Speak to an employee 　직원에게 이야기한다.

공지에서 담화의 흐름을 알려주는 표현들을 알아두면 도움이 됩니다.

- **공지가 이루어지는 장소**: Thank you for coming to ~   ~에 와 주셔서 감사합니다
- **공지의 목적**: I'd like to announce that ~   ~을 알려드리고자 합니다
  　　　　　　We have some reminders about ~   ~에 대해 상기시켜 드릴 것이 있습니다
- **요청 사항**: Please ask 사람/부서 for ~   [사람/부서]에게 ~을 요청해 주세요
  　　　　　You should ~   ~해야만 해요
  　　　　　Don't forget to ~   ~하는 것을 잊지 마세요

HACKERS PRACTICE

담화를 들으며 주어진 질문에 가장 알맞은 보기를 고르고, 빈칸에 들어갈 내용을 받아쓰세요. (음성은 두 번 들려줍니다.) 🎧 D17_2_Practice

[01-02]

01 Where is the announcement being made?

(A) At a train station
(B) At an airport
(C) At a hotel
(D) At a shopping center

02 What will the listeners most likely do next?

(A) Collect a complimentary item
(B) Make a payment
(C) Speak to a staff member
(D) Go to a different location

Attention _____ 813 to Toronto. Due to a technical problem, your _____ _____. You will now be boarding at Gate 26 instead of Gate 18. If you have any questions, _____ to assist you. Please _____ immediately, as boarding will begin in just a few minutes. Thank you for _____.

[03-04]

03 What is the purpose of the announcement?

(A) To present a recruitment plan
(B) To describe a customer service system
(C) To introduce an incentive program
(D) To announce a company expansion

04 What concern does the speaker mention?

(A) A sales strategy is ineffective.
(B) A commercial received negative feedback.
(C) A business has attracted few customers.
(D) A bonus payment will be delayed.

I'd like to announce that a new _____ _____ at our auto dealership. Each time one of you sells a vehicle, you will receive a 1,000-dollar payment from the company. I know some of you are concerned about the _____ _____ these days. But the company is planning to run several _____ soon. These will likely lead to an _____ at our branch.

정답·해석·해설 p.94

2. 관광 안내

관광 안내는 관광지 투어, 미술관이나 박물관 관람, 공장 견학 시 주의사항이나 진행 순서 및 일정에 관한 정보를 전달하는 담화입니다. PART 4 전체 10개 지문 중 매회 1개 정도 출제됩니다.

담화 흐름과 빈출 문제   🎧 D17_3_예제

관광 안내	흐름	흐름에 따른 빈출 문제
Hello, everyone. **I'll be your guide this afternoon. Welcome to** the Arvada Wax Museum, one of Glendale's most visited sites.	화자 소개 및 관광할 장소 언급	**관광 안내가 이루어지는 장소를 묻는 문제** Where does the talk take place? 담화는 어디에서 일어나는가? → At a museum 박물관에서
Arvada has about 100 statues of famous people from around the world. The figures are able to move and are equipped with computerized technology that makes them speak. The clothes worn by the statues are special because they have been provided by the actual people the statues represent.	장소 및 일정과 관련된 세부 내용	**전시품에 대해 언급된 내용을 묻는 문제** What does the speaker say about the clothing? 화자는 옷에 대해 무엇이라고 말하는가? → It was donated. 기증되었다.
Before we begin our tour, I need to remind everyone that food and beverages are not allowed inside the museum. **Also, do not** touch any of the items on display.	청자들에게 요청 및 당부하는 사항	**주의 사항을 묻는 문제** According to the speaker, what are the listeners not allowed to do? 화자에 따르면, 청자들은 무엇을 하는 것이 허용되지 않는가? → Touch items 물품들을 만진다.
All right, if you'll follow me, we shall start in Exhibit Hall A.	다음에 이동할 곳 안내	

해석 p.95

관광 안내에서 담화의 흐름을 알려주는 표현들을 알아두면 도움이 됩니다.

- **관광 안내가 이루어지는 장소**: Welcome to ~ ~에 오신 것을 환영합니다
  Thank you for coming to ~ ~에 와 주셔서 감사합니다
- **주의 사항**: Do not ~ ~하지 마십시오
  Please feel free to ~ 자유롭게 ~해 주세요
  I recommend that ~ ~을 권합니다

HACKERS PRACTICE

담화를 들으며 주어진 질문에 가장 알맞은 보기를 고르고, 빈칸에 들어갈 내용을 받아쓰세요. (음성은 두 번 들려줍니다.) 🎧 D17_4_Practice

[01-02]

01 Who most likely is the speaker?

(A) A mining engineer
(B) A tour guide
(C) A shop clerk
(D) A gemstone analyst

02 What does the speaker say visitors can do?

(A) Access a restricted area
(B) Listen to a short presentation
(C) Observe stones being cut
(D) Examine items closely

Welcome to the Gemstone Center. Today, I will be _____ of mineral specimens at this facility. You will _____ such as rubies and sapphires from all over the world. And we have set up the displays so that you can _____ _____. This makes it easier to see all of their _____.

[03-04]

03 Where are the listeners?

(A) At a public park
(B) At a theater
(C) At a library
(D) At an art gallery

04 What does the speaker tell the listeners not to do?

(A) Speak too loudly
(B) Take photographs
(C) Enter certain areas
(D) Block an entrance

I hope all of you have enjoyed the tour so far. We've now arrived at _____, Porec Studio. Paintings and sculptures by some of the country's most _____ here. Please note that the facility is currently undergoing renovations, so some rooms are _____ _____. For your safety, please _____ _____. Remember to stay with the group at all times as well.

HACKERS TEST

담화를 들으며 주어진 질문에 가장 알맞은 보기를 고르세요. 🎧 D17_5_Test

01 According to the speaker, what happened this month?
(A) Safety inspections
(B) Equipment malfunctions
(C) Staff meetings
(D) Worker accidents

02 What did the human resources team recently do?
(A) It revised a manual.
(B) It changed a policy.
(C) It produced a video.
(D) It updated a schedule.

03 What will happen on Friday afternoon?
(A) A board meeting
(B) A training session
(C) A facility renovation
(D) A factory tour

04 Who most likely are the listeners?
(A) Restaurant customers
(B) Event attendees
(C) Airline passengers
(D) Resort guests

05 What is located on the second floor?
(A) A dining facility
(B) A rental shop
(C) A ticket booth
(D) A lounge area

06 What is the owner of a lost item asked to do?
(A) Provide contact information
(B) Give a description
(C) Submit a receipt
(D) Show photo identification

07 What does the speaker say about the exhibit?
(A) It is located on the main floor.
(B) It includes rare fossils.
(C) It will be completed soon.
(D) It is about new technology.

08 What does the speaker imply when he says, "Today's tour has attracted a lot of interest"?
(A) An activity will be delayed.
(B) A special event is planned.
(C) A tour will be repeated.
(D) A space will be crowded.

09 According to the speaker, what is not allowed?
(A) Touching the displays
(B) Taking photographs
(C) Eating near the exhibits
(D) Bringing backpacks

10 What does the speaker say about the pass?
(A) It provides tax benefits.
(B) It renews automatically.
(C) It can be used on all transit systems.
(D) It must be shown to station staff.

11 What can the listeners receive if they make a purchase this month?
(A) A one-day pass
(B) A transit map
(C) An additional discount
(D) A facility membership

12 How can listeners buy a pass?
(A) By installing an application
(B) By visiting a ticket counter
(C) By calling a hotline
(D) By downloading a form

13 What is the main purpose of the talk?

(A) To give details on a delay
(B) To promote a special event
(C) To provide route information
(D) To announce future services

14 According to the speaker, what will be added to the upgraded ships?

(A) Concert halls
(B) Equipment for sports activities
(C) Children's playgrounds
(D) Devices for observing the sky

15 What information can be found online?

(A) Departure dates
(B) Restaurant menus
(C) Ticket prices
(D) Job listings

16 What is the announcement mainly about?

(A) A company retreat
(B) A community festival
(C) A grand opening
(D) A charity fundraiser

17 Why does the speaker tell the listeners to dress comfortably?

(A) They will be competing in a race.
(B) They will be visiting construction sites.
(C) They will be cleaning a park.
(D) They will be going for a walk.

18 What will the listeners do after some speeches?

(A) Take a lunch break
(B) Break up into groups
(C) Return to a workplace
(D) Meet some organizers

Bezel Drone Factory Tour Schedule	
Assembly area	1:30 P.M.
Testing area	2:00 P.M.
Packaging area	2:30 P.M.
Shipping area	3:00 P.M.

19 What does the speaker ask the listeners to do?

(A) Report injuries
(B) Fill out a form
(C) Wear an ID badge
(D) Put on safety gear

20 Look at the graphic. When will the listeners meet Mr. Walton?

(A) At 1:30 P.M.
(B) At 2:00 P.M.
(C) At 2:30 P.M.
(D) At 3:00 P.M.

21 What will the speaker give the listeners?

(A) A voucher
(B) A sample
(C) A catalog
(D) A map

DAY 18 연설 및 강연

MP3 바로 듣기

1. 연설

연설은 워크숍 및 직원 교육에서의 정보 전달이나 시상식 및 퇴임식에서의 인물 소개와 같이 모임이나 행사장에서 지식이나 인물에 관한 내용을 전달하는 담화입니다. PART 4 전체 10개 지문 중 매회 1개 정도 출제됩니다.

담화 흐름과 빈출 문제   D18_1_예제

연설	흐름	흐름에 따른 빈출 문제
Welcome, everyone. As part of your orientation today, I'll be giving you a tour of our ice cream factory to show you the different stages of production. But first, **I'd like to talk about some important principles that must be followed when making ice cream.** We follow the processing guidelines of the Food Safety Administration to ensure the safety and quality of our finished products. In this regard, the equipment used, including the storage containers and freezers, should be sanitized. **Now, I will** show you around the factory. 해석 p.100	인사말	
	연설의 주제 및 목적	**연설의 목적을 묻는 문제** What is the purpose of the talk? 담화의 목적은 무엇인가? → To explain key production principles 주요 제조 원칙을 설명하기 위해
	세부 내용	**연설에 언급된 세부 내용을 묻는 문제** According to the speaker, how can workers ensure the safety of products? 화자에 따르면, 작업자들은 어떻게 제품의 안전을 보장할 수 있는가? → By keeping machines clean 기계들을 깨끗하게 유지함으로써
	다음에 있을 일 안내	**다음에 있을 일을 묻는 문제** What will most likely happen next? 다음에 무슨 일이 일어날 것 같은가? → The group will tour the factory. 단체가 공장을 견학할 것이다.

연설에서 담화의 흐름을 알려주는 표현들을 알아두면 도움이 됩니다.

- **주제 및 목적**: I'd like to talk about ~ 저는 ~에 대해 이야기하고자 합니다
  I'd like to introduce you to ~ 저는 여러분에게 ~를 소개하고자 합니다
- **다음에 있을 일**: Now, I will ~ 이제, 제가 ~하겠습니다
  I invite everyone to ~ 모두 ~하시길 권합니다

HACKERS PRACTICE

담화를 들으며 주어진 질문에 가장 알맞은 보기를 고르고, 빈칸에 들어갈 내용을 받아쓰세요. (음성은 두 번 들려줍니다.) 🎧 D18_2_Practice

[01-02]

01 What is the purpose of the event?
(A) To train new employees
(B) To launch a new hotel branch
(C) To celebrate the company's success
(D) To announce a staff promotion

02 What will Clara Snow most likely do next?
(A) Make a speech
(B) Give a demonstration
(C) Announce a winner
(D) Set up a device

_____ for this party tonight. It has been _____ for Grandforth Hotels. Occupancy rates are up 20 percent from last year. Not to mention, our Havana branch, which just opened this spring, has received over 1,000 positive reviews. I especially want to _____ _____ of our head of marketing, Clara Snow. She will now _____.

[03-04]

03 Where most likely are the listeners?
(A) At an awards ceremony
(B) At a retirement party
(C) At an employee orientation
(D) At a board meeting

04 Why will the speaker pass out a form?
(A) To confirm attendance
(B) To gather feedback
(C) To create memberships
(D) To schedule appointments

I'd like to welcome you to Rosewood Corporation's _____. This morning, we are going to hear _____ _____ from our department heads. Also, next month will be our staff awards dinner, and I'd like to find out which of you will be attending. I am going to pass out a form for you to _____. OK, let's _____ on the Berlin Towers project from Sue Ling.

2. 강연

강연은 전문가의 설명, 사내 업무 처리 방법이나 시설 이용 절차 등 다양한 주제에 관한 지식을 전달하는 담화입니다. PART 4 전체 10개 지문 중 매회 1개 정도 출제됩니다.

담화 흐름과 빈출 문제 🎧 D18_3_예제

강연

Good afternoon. **We just changed the process for requesting leave here at our investment firm, so I'm going to explain** what you need to do.

You should no longer send an e-mail to your direct supervisor asking for a day off. Instead, use the company's intranet system to fill out an online request form. **This will be reviewed by the head of HR, David Reynolds, before being approved or rejected.** A decision will be made within two business days.

If you have any issues submitting a request, **please** check the employee manual for guidance.

해석 p.101

흐름

- 강연 주제 언급
- 세부 내용
- 청자들에게 요청 및 당부하는 사항

흐름에 따른 빈출 문제

강연의 주제를 묻는 문제
What is the talk mainly about?
담화는 주로 무엇에 관한 것인가?
→ An updated process
최신화된 절차

특정 인물에 대해 묻는 문제
Who is David Reynolds?
David Reynolds는 누구인가?
→ A department manager
부서장

문의사항 및 문제점에 대한 대처 방법을 묻는 문제
What should the listeners do if they have problems?
청자들은 문제가 있으면 무엇을 해야 하는가?
→ Refer to a handbook
안내서를 참고한다

강연에서 담화의 흐름을 알려주는 표현들을 알아두면 도움이 됩니다.

- **주제 및 목적**: I'm going to explain ~ 저는 ~에 대해 설명하고자 합니다
  I'd like to go over ~ 저는 ~에 대해 살펴보고자 합니다
- **문의사항 및 문제점에 대한 대처 방법**: If you have any ~, please … ~이 있다면, …해 주세요
  Refer to ~ for further details 더 자세한 정보는 ~을 참고하세요

HACKERS PRACTICE

담화를 들으며 주어진 질문에 가장 알맞은 보기를 고르고, 빈칸에 들어갈 내용을 받아쓰세요. (음성은 두 번 들려줍니다.) 🎧 D18_4_Practice

[01-02]

01 What kind of photograph is the speaker talking about?

(A) Portraits
(B) Food
(C) Landscapes
(D) Travel

02 What should the listeners do if they want feedback?

(A) Print their photos
(B) Join a class
(C) Use a mobile app
(D) Call the speaker

Today, I'll show you how to _____ _____. It's best to take them near a window where there's _____. Avoid using a flash, as it can change the food's color. If you send me your photos afterward, I'll give you _____ on how to take better ones next time. You can do this _____ we used last week. I look forward to seeing your work.

[03-04]

03 What is mainly being discussed?

(A) Documenting a process
(B) Training employees
(C) Scheduling production
(D) Relocating a factory

04 What can listeners learn by looking at a screen?

(A) The goals of a company
(B) The steps of a procedure
(C) The timelines of group projects
(D) The assignments of team members

In order to identify areas for improvement, we need to document every step of our _____. The goal is to improve efficiency and _____ _____. We will need to gather and analyze lots of data, both manually and through the use of cameras. I've broken the project down into different _____ _____ to individual members of the team. You'll see this information now if you _____ _____.

HACKERS TEST

담화를 들으며 주어진 질문에 가장 알맞은 보기를 고르세요. 🎧 D18_5_Test

01 In which department do the listeners most likely work?
(A) Legal
(B) Finance
(C) Sales
(D) Human resources

02 What does the speaker mention about the bonuses?
(A) They are paid once a year.
(B) They are based on seniority.
(C) They are available to all staff.
(D) They are a new type of benefit.

03 What does the speaker ask the listeners to do by Monday?
(A) Review a manual
(B) Select an option
(C) Form a team
(D) Contact a manager

04 What is the focus of the conference?
(A) Online advertising
(B) Workplace safety
(C) Web site design
(D) Personnel management

05 How is this year's conference different from previous ones?
(A) It involves more speakers.
(B) It features international researchers.
(C) It will include longer lectures.
(D) It is being held at a different venue.

06 Why was the closing ceremony relocated?
(A) A room has not been cleaned.
(B) An activity has been changed.
(C) A machine has malfunctioned.
(D) A facility has not opened.

07 What is the company going to do?
(A) Hold a conference in the city
(B) Organize a fundraiser
(C) Meet with hospital officials
(D) Launch a new product

08 What are the listeners asked to do?
(A) Come up with product ideas
(B) Donate used books and toys
(C) Prepare homemade foods
(D) Volunteer at a play area

09 What will the speaker include in an e-mail?
(A) A schedule for volunteers
(B) A renovation timetable
(C) A request form for equipment
(D) A list of project goals

10 Who is the speaker?
(A) A marketing specialist
(B) A product designer
(C) A news reporter
(D) A maintenance manager

11 Why does the speaker say, "I'm already using one at home"?
(A) To indicate the affordability of an item
(B) To show the convenience of a service
(C) To stress the advantages of a model
(D) To explain the functions of a device

12 What will the assistant do next?
(A) Demonstrate a device
(B) Lead visitors to a laboratory
(C) Hand out free samples
(D) Describe upcoming products

13 What is the topic of the talk?

(A) Budget reductions
(B) Performance evaluations
(C) Interviewing methods
(D) Overtime hours

14 Who most likely are the listeners?

(A) Customer service agents
(B) Human resources staff
(C) Training specialists
(D) Business consultants

15 Why does the speaker want the listeners to find a partner?

(A) To complete a questionnaire
(B) To discuss a candidate
(C) To participate in an exercise
(D) To prepare a presentation

16 Who most likely is Adrian Miller?

(A) An event host
(B) A famous researcher
(C) A school founder
(D) A corporate leader

17 What does the speaker say about BioPro?

(A) It uses minimal packaging.
(B) It makes natural products.
(C) It offers excellent service.
(D) It sponsors environmental groups.

18 According to the speaker, what is BioPro's goal?

(A) Expanding overseas
(B) Reducing costs
(C) Improving efficiency
(D) Hiring staff

Step 1	Step 2	Step 3	Step 4
Gather Data	Determine Priority	Assign Resources	Identify Problems

19 What is the speaker mainly discussing?

(A) Recruitment
(B) Production
(C) Accounting
(D) Marketing

20 Look at the graphic. Which step will be discussed today?

(A) Step 1
(B) Step 2
(C) Step 3
(D) Step 4

21 What will most likely happen next?

(A) A demonstration will be given.
(B) A question will be answered.
(C) An assistant will be introduced.
(D) A document will be distributed.

DAY 19 방송 및 보도

MP3 바로 듣기

1. 방송

방송은 라디오나 TV, 팟캐스트에서 나올 법한 교통방송, 일기예보, 인터뷰 등의 형식으로, 도로 상황 및 우회도로 안내, 날씨 정보 및 대비책, 초대 손님 소개 등의 내용을 다루는 담화입니다. PART 4 전체 10개 지문 중 매회 1개 정도 출제됩니다.

담화 흐름과 빈출 문제 D19_1_예제

방송	흐름	흐름에 따른 빈출 문제
You're listening to Ricky Doyle on COOL 105.1, one of Chicago's top radio stations.	프로그램 및 화자 소개	
It's time for an update on the weather conditions in the region.	방송 주제 언급	**방송의 주제를 묻는 문제** What is the broadcast mainly about? 방송은 주로 무엇에 관한 것인가? → Local weather 지역 날씨
A major blizzard is making its way toward the city and is expected to hit around 8 P.M. As much as 10 inches of snow could accumulate overnight. **Make sure to be careful tomorrow if you are driving, as roads will be slippery.** By this weekend, we should have clear skies once again.	세부 내용	**주의해야 할 세부 내용을 묻는 문제** What are the listeners warned about? 청자들은 무엇에 관해 주의를 받는가? → Dangerous driving conditions 위험한 운전 조건
Stay tuned for a review of the hit film *In His Way* coming up next!	다음에 이어질 방송 언급	**다음에 들을 내용을 묻는 문제** What will the listeners hear next? 청자들은 다음에 무엇을 들을 것인가? → A review 비평

해석 p.106

방송에서 담화의 흐름을 알려주는 표현들을 알아두면 도움이 됩니다.

- **프로그램 및 화자 소개**: You're listening to ~ 여러분은 ~을 듣고 계십니다
  - Welcome to ~ ~에 오신 것을 환영합니다
  - I'm your host ~ 저는 여러분의 진행자 ~입니다
- **주제**: It's time for ~ ~할 시간입니다
- **다음에 들을 내용**: Stay tuned for ~ coming up next 다음에 이어질 ~을 위해 채널을 고정하세요
  - Next up is ~ 다음으로는 ~입니다

HACKERS PRACTICE

담화를 들으며 주어진 질문에 가장 알맞은 보기를 고르고, 빈칸에 들어갈 내용을 받아쓰세요. (음성은 두 번 들려줍니다.) 🎧 D19_2_Practice

[01-02]

01 Who most likely is Jane Kearney?
(A) A film director
(B) A city official
(C) A personnel manager
(D) A real estate agent

02 What will the listeners most likely hear next?
(A) An advertisement
(B) A musical performance
(C) A weather update
(D) A traffic report

You're listening to Westville's own WGGT 97.3 radio. I'm your host, Harold LaRoche. Today, I'll be interviewing our city's newly hired parks and _____
_____
_____, Jane Kearney. Ms. Kearney will discuss plans for several _____
_____, including the summer arts festival and the regional tennis competition. And after that, our listeners are encouraged to _____
_____ and ask questions directly to Ms. Kearney. Now, let's _____
_____.

[03-04]

Northern Arc - Concert Dates	
Seattle	August 10
Olympia	August 13
Portland	August 15
Vancouver	August 18

03 What is the purpose of the broadcast?
(A) To announce the release of an album
(B) To review a recent concert
(C) To celebrate a band's anniversary
(D) To describe a musician's career

04 Look at the graphic. When will Janice Polson perform with Northern Arc?
(A) On August 10
(B) On August 13
(C) On August 15
(D) On August 18

In entertainment news, the popular band Northern Arc has _____. Titled *Out of the Wind*, it features 15 new songs. It is _____
_____ and can also be ordered from the band's Web site. To promote the album, Northern Arc will launch a four-city tour in August. And the show in Olympia will _____
Janice Polson as a special guest. Tickets for these concerts will go _____.

2. 보도

보도는 업계 매출이나 수익, 기업 합병, 지역 사회 소식, 도심 환경 개선 등 경제, 비즈니스, 교육, 환경, 건강에 관한 소식을 전하는 담화입니다. PART 4 전체 10개 지문 중 가끔 1개 정도 출제됩니다.

담화 흐름과 빈출 문제 🎧 D19_3_예제

보도	흐름	흐름에 따른 빈출 문제
Lanton Electronics has reported a strong increase in sales this quarter.	보도 주제 언급	**보도의 주제를 묻는 문제** What did Lanton Electronics announce? Lanton Electronics사는 무엇을 발표했는가? → An increase in sales 매출 증가
The company's newest wireless headphones, which feature advanced noise-canceling technology, have been especially popular with customers. **In an interview, CEO Alan Park said** he wants to thank the members of the research and development team for their efforts. He stated that their dedication to innovation has played a key role in the company's success. He also mentioned that the company plans to expand its product line next year. **Experts predict that** Lanton Electronics will continue to see steady growth in the coming months. 해석 p.107	세부 내용	**인터뷰 내용에 대해 묻는 문제** Who did Alan Park express appreciation for? Alan Park는 누구에게 감사를 표현했는가? → The research and development team 연구개발팀 **전문가들의 예측에 대해 묻는 문제** What do experts expect for Lanton Electronics? 전문가들은 Lanton Electronics사에 대해 무엇을 예측하는가? → Future growth 향후 성장

보도에서 담화의 흐름을 알려주는 표현들을 알아두면 도움이 됩니다.

- **주제 및 목적**: 회사/기업 has reported ~ [회사/기업]이 ~을 발표했습니다
- **인터뷰 내용**: In an interview, 사람 said/stated ~ 인터뷰에서, [사람]이 ~이라고 말했습니다
- **전문가들의 예측**: Experts predict that ~ 전문가들은 ~이라고 예측합니다

HACKERS PRACTICE

담화를 들으며 주어진 질문에 가장 알맞은 보기를 고르고, 빈칸에 들어갈 내용을 받아쓰세요. (음성은 두 번 들려줍니다.) 🎧 D19_4_Practice

[01-02]

01 What is the report mainly about?

(A) A product launch
(B) A factory expansion
(C) Customer complaints
(D) Pricing strategies

02 Who is Sarah Mitchell?

(A) A sales associate
(B) A public relations representative
(C) A maintenance manager
(D) A customer service agent

Now, here's the business news. Carwin Electronics has _____ about its newest electric fan. Users have noted that the product occasionally _____ _____, especially when used for long periods. Sarah Mitchell from the company's _____ _____ stated that the sound does not indicate a safety issue or a problem with the fan's performance. She added that the product remains popular because it's both _____.

[03-04]

03 What is the purpose of the report?

(A) To discuss a change to a city policy
(B) To explain delays in importing goods
(C) To introduce a business owner
(D) To announce the construction of a port

04 What problem did Martin Blake mention in the interview?

(A) A facility is not large enough.
(B) Workers are not available.
(C) A location is inaccessible.
(D) Imports are too costly.

Here's today's local news update. The city of Harrisburg is _____ to speed up the delivery of goods. The project is expected to _____ _____ more efficiently when it opens next year. In an interview, Martin Blake, the owner of a seafood import company, explained that the _____ _____, and this often causes delays. The new port will have _____ and better equipment for loading and unloading cargo.

HACKERS TEST

담화를 들으며 주어진 질문에 가장 알맞은 보기를 고르세요. 🎧 D19_5_Test

01 What is the report mainly about?
(A) A program launch
(B) A headquarters relocation
(C) A company expansion
(D) An industry trend

02 What problem did Fresh Fabric encounter?
(A) Insufficient staff training
(B) Increased competition
(C) High rental fees
(D) Reduced profits

03 Who most likely is Leanne Wilson?
(A) A business founder
(B) A property owner
(C) A financial consultant
(D) A journalist

04 Why did Norton Pharmaceuticals hold a press conference?
(A) To address a complaint
(B) To introduce a spokesperson
(C) To describe a partnership
(D) To announce a product

05 What is mentioned about the Clearwater Medical Center?
(A) It expanded a laboratory.
(B) It hired some researchers.
(C) It conducted some tests.
(D) It developed a treatment.

06 What will be discussed in the press conference on June 20?
(A) Pricing
(B) Marketing
(C) Sales
(D) Distribution

07 What is the topic of this week's podcast?
(A) Retirement planning
(B) Job interview skills
(C) Hiring procedures
(D) Employee training methods

08 Why does the speaker say, "He usually declines these requests"?
(A) To suggest that a guest is very busy
(B) To specify that an interview was canceled
(C) To indicate that a mistake was made
(D) To show that an applicant is qualified

09 What will the speaker do next month?
(A) Return calls from the listeners
(B) Host a live broadcast
(C) Receive an award
(D) Upload previous episodes

10 What type of event is the speaker mainly discussing?
(A) An exhibit
(B) A play
(C) A class
(D) A festival

11 What does the speaker say about Maxwell Hall?
(A) It is very spacious.
(B) It is near an entrance.
(C) It will be renovated.
(D) It will be sold.

12 How can some listeners get free tickets to the event?
(A) By visiting a Web site
(B) By sending a text message
(C) By replying to an e-mail
(D) By making a call

13 What is the focus of the speaker's podcast?

(A) How to share materials
(B) How to tidy a house
(C) How to reduce costs
(D) How to publish a book

14 What does the speaker emphasize?

(A) Paying for a service
(B) Making a list
(C) Using a coupon
(D) Watching a video

15 How can the listeners receive a free e-book?

(A) By visiting a Web site
(B) By downloading an application
(C) By sending an e-mail
(D) By completing a survey

---

16 What was announced this afternoon?

(A) A contract extension
(B) A business merger
(C) A facility construction
(D) A fundraising result

17 According to the speaker, how will the project affect the community?

(A) It will attract more tourists.
(B) It will lower taxes.
(C) It will lead to traffic jams.
(D) It will create more jobs.

18 What will most likely happen next year?

(A) Residents will take a vote.
(B) A sports team will use a new arena.
(C) A company will open a local branch.
(D) Architects will complete a plan.

Tuesday	☀
Wednesday	☁
Thursday	☂
Friday	☀

19 Look at the graphic. On which day will the event be held?

(A) Tuesday
(B) Wednesday
(C) Thursday
(D) Friday

20 According to the speaker, what is included on a poster?

(A) A map of a venue
(B) A list of participants
(C) A menu of a restaurant
(D) A schedule of events

21 Why do the organizers need volunteers?

(A) To direct traffic
(B) To collect tickets
(C) To prepare dishes
(D) To arrange booths

DAY 20 광고 및 소개

MP3 바로듣기

1. 광고

광고는 신제품 출시나 할인 혜택, 보상 및 보험 제도, 수리 및 공사 등과 관련된 제품이나 서비스, 또는 사업체를 홍보하는 담화입니다. PART 4 전체 10개 지문 중 매회 1개 정도 출제됩니다.

담화 흐름과 빈출 문제 🎧 D20_1_예제

광고	흐름	흐름에 따른 빈출 문제
At Baroness Hotels, we understand the needs of today's business travelers.	호기심 유발	
Operating hotels in over 40 cities around the world, the Baroness Hotel chain is famous for excellent service and attention to detail.	광고되고 있는 상품 소개	**광고 상품을 묻는 문제** What type of business is being advertised? 어떤 종류의 업체가 광고되고 있는가? → A hotel chain 호텔 체인
And now, we've added business centers to all our locations worldwide. These provide access to free Internet, conference and meeting rooms, and photocopiers. In addition, frequent guests can take advantage of our loyalty program to earn points toward room upgrades and car rentals.	상품의 특징 설명	**상품에 대한 세부 사항을 묻는 문제** What has the company added to its locations? 회사는 지점들에 무엇을 추가했는가? → Business facilities 비즈니스 시설
To learn more about Baroness Hotels or make a reservation, **visit** our Web site at www.baronesshotels.com.	상품과 관련된 추가 정보 안내	**추가 정보를 얻는 방법을 묻는 문제** What should the listeners do to learn more about the company? 청자들은 회사에 관해 더 알기 위해 무엇을 해야 하는가? → Access a Web page 웹페이지에 접속한다.

해석 p.112

광고에서 담화의 흐름을 알려주는 표현들을 알아두면 도움이 됩니다.

- **광고 상품**: 회사/제품 is famous for ~ [회사/제품]은 ~으로 유명합니다
  　　　　제품/서비스 is perfect for ~ [제품/서비스]는 ~에게 제격입니다
- **추가 정보를 얻는 방법**: To learn more about 회사/제품/서비스, visit ~ [회사/제품/서비스]에 관해 더 알고 싶으시면, ~을 방문해 주세요
  　　　　　　　　　Check ~ for more information 더 자세한 정보는 ~을 확인하세요

HACKERS PRACTICE

담화를 들으며 주어진 질문에 가장 알맞은 보기를 고르고, 빈칸에 들어갈 내용을 받아쓰세요. (음성은 두 번 들려줍니다.) 🎧 D20_2_Practice

[01-02]

01 What is a feature of the program?
(A) It connects to an online database.
(B) It functions on mobile devices.
(C) It receives monthly updates.
(D) It includes a chat program.

02 What will Crevice Industries do on February 15?
(A) Improve a service
(B) Complete a trial
(C) Release a product
(D) Increase a price

Do you wish doing accounting work were easier? If so, you need the FinancePro software from Crevice Industries. This program makes it easy to _____ _____. Also, it includes many innovative features, such as _____ with each other through an instant messaging system. Buy this software before February 15 to take advantage of the 55-dollar _____ by Crevice Industries. Otherwise, you will _____ 65 dollars.

[03-04]

03 What is being advertised?
(A) A recycling service
(B) A security system
(C) A software program
(D) A consulting business

04 Why should the listeners call a company right away?
(A) To receive a free service
(B) To get a special discount
(C) To purchase a product
(D) To find a location

Looking for a way to protect your home or office? LokTek Industries can help! Our innovative A800 package is perfect for _____.
It uses advanced sensors to monitor cameras and alarms, and it _____ if an unauthorized person enters the building. To get a _____ _____, call 555-2020 now. You can also _____ in Bentley Plaza if you want to learn more about our new system.

정답·해석·해설 p.113

2. 소개

소개는 시상식이나 기업체의 인사이동과 같은 특정 인물이나 행사에 관한 정보를 전달하는 담화입니다. PART 4 전체 10개 지문 중 가끔 1개 정도 출제됩니다.

담화 흐름과 빈출 문제 🎧 D20_3_예제

소개	흐름	흐름에 따른 빈출 문제
I appreciate you all coming today. Starting this month, **we will be holding a series of workshops on team development.**	행사 소개	**담화의 주된 내용을 묻는 문제** What is the topic of the workshop? 워크숍의 주제는 무엇인가? → Team development 팀 발전
Our facilitator for this morning is Shamara Wymer. **She has worked for over 15 years as a consultant** on organizational psychology. Ms. Wymer **is an expert in** this field, and I'm sure you will learn a lot from her.	인물 소개	**인물에 대해 묻는 문제** Who is Shamara Wymer? Shamara Wymer는 누구인가? → A consultant 상담가
In today's workshop, she will be discussing team commitment and individual accountability. You will learn about the importance of communication among team members.	세부 내용	
At the end of the session, each of you will receive a copy of her recently published book, _Building Effective Teams_. Thank you so much for coming today, Ms. Wymer.	다음에 있을 일 안내	**다음에 있을 일을 묻는 문제** What will the listeners most likely do at the end of the workshop? 청자들은 워크숍이 끝날 때 무엇을 할 것 같은가? → Receive a copy of a book 책 한 권을 받는다.

해석 p.114

소개에서 담화의 흐름을 알려주는 표현들을 알아두면 도움이 됩니다.

- **인물 소개**: 사람 has worked as ~ [사람]은 ~으로서 일해왔습니다
  사람 is an expert in ~ [사람]은 ~에 있어서 전문가입니다
  사람 is famous for ~ [사람]은 ~으로 유명합니다
  사람 has contributed to ~ [사람]은 ~에 기여해왔습니다

HACKERS PRACTICE

담화를 들으며 주어진 질문에 가장 알맞은 보기를 고르고, 빈칸에 들어갈 내용을 받아쓰세요. (음성은 두 번 들려줍니다.) 🎧 D20_4_Practice

[01-02]

01 Where is the talk taking place?

(A) At a fitness center
(B) At a hospital
(C) At a university
(D) At a library

02 According to the speaker, what is the topic of the event?

(A) Safety
(B) Nutrition
(C) Cooking
(D) Exercise

Greenhill Library is once again hosting a series of _____ this year. Because of the strong interest, we had to _____ to a larger room. Today's event is the first workshop in the series, and the _____ _____. We invited a registered dietitian to share practical tips on healthy eating and _____ _____. We're excited to begin the program and hope you learn a lot.

[03-04]

03 Who is Devon Baker?

(A) A consultant
(B) A professor
(C) A footwear designer
(D) A fashion journalist

04 What most likely will the listeners do next?

(A) Look at some designs
(B) Watch a company video
(C) Listen to a presentation
(D) Fill out a questionnaire

Our next speaker for today's seminar needs no introduction. Devon Baker has worked at Floppy Basics as a _____ for over a decade. The company is known for its casual footwear with _____ _____. Today, she will talk to you about _____. Before we begin, please take a few minutes to _____ _____ some of her shoe designs, which are on display at the back of the room.

HACKERS TEST

담화를 들으며 주어진 질문에 가장 알맞은 보기를 고르세요. 🎧 D20_5_Test

01 Where most likely are the listeners?
(A) At a bakery
(B) At a grocery store
(C) At a dining establishment
(D) At a catering company

02 What did Maria Lopez do in London?
(A) She toured a facility.
(B) She managed a business.
(C) She founded a company.
(D) She earned a degree.

03 What will the listeners do next week?
(A) Visit an establishment
(B) Participate in a luncheon
(C) Review some contracts
(D) Receive some training

04 What type of business is being advertised?
(A) A property management agency
(B) A landscaping company
(C) A cleaning service
(D) An interior design firm

05 What will first-time customers receive?
(A) A trial membership
(B) A gift certificate
(C) An informational brochure
(D) A free consultation

06 What does the speaker suggest?
(A) Reading a review
(B) Upgrading a package
(C) Visiting an office
(D) Installing an app

07 Who most likely is the speaker?
(A) A business owner
(B) A university student
(C) An award recipient
(D) An event organizer

08 According to the speaker, what was just announced?
(A) A research proposal
(B) Government funding
(C) An employment offer
(D) Industry regulation

09 What does the speaker remind the listeners about?
(A) A schedule has been changed.
(B) A presentation has been canceled.
(C) A Web site will be updated.
(D) A conference will be extended.

10 What is the topic of the convention?
(A) Financial management
(B) Corporate branding
(C) Renewable energy
(D) Architectural design

11 What is mentioned about Morgan O'Malley?
(A) He was involved in a construction project.
(B) He has developed a new device.
(C) He led a government program.
(D) He organized an industry event.

12 What does the speaker mean when he says, "Each speaker has only 30 minutes"?
(A) A schedule must be revised.
(B) Questions should be avoided.
(C) Topics will be changed.
(D) A task cannot be completed.

13 What type of business is being advertised?

(A) A gardening shop
(B) A sporting goods store
(C) A supermarket
(D) A clothing retailer

14 What is mentioned about the business?

(A) It has several branches.
(B) It plans to relocate.
(C) It has new inventory.
(D) It hires temporary workers.

15 How can customers receive a free item?

(A) By entering a drawing
(B) By making a minimum purchase
(C) By completing a feedback form
(D) By arriving at a business early

16 Why has Paula Pine been invited to the factory?

(A) To edit a manual
(B) To deliver some products
(C) To discuss some equipment
(D) To conduct an inspection

17 What does the speaker ask the listeners to do?

(A) Assemble a machine
(B) Practice for a presentation
(C) Sign up for a seminar
(D) Pay close attention

18 According to the speaker, what will be covered first?

(A) Device designs
(B) Safety measures
(C) Project details
(D) Deadline dates

Swift Corporation Product List			
Model #	Features		
	Heating Function	Custom Patterns	Voice Commands
XR485	✓		
SC837		✓	
VP938	✓	✓	
WS127	✓	✓	✓

19 What did Swift Corporation do last year?

(A) It collected feedback.
(B) It hired a designer.
(C) It launched an app.
(D) It increased production.

20 Look at the graphic. Which model is being promoted?

(A) XR485
(B) SC837
(C) VP938
(D) WS127

21 How can the listeners qualify for a discount?

(A) By upgrading an account
(B) By creating a membership
(C) By completing a survey
(D) By reviewing a product

한 권으로 끝내는 해커스 토익 600+ LC+RC+VOCA

실시간 토익시험 정답확인 & 해설강의
Hackers.co.kr

RC 기초 다지기

PART 5

PART 6

PART 7

RC 기초 다지기

8품사 영어 단어의 8가지 종류

영어 단어는 각각의 의미와 역할에 따라 8가지 종류로 분류할 수 있는데, 이를 8품사라고 합니다.

① 이름을 나타내는 명사

book	hope
(책)	(희망)

모든 사람에게는 이름이 있죠? 이와 같이 **명사**는 우리 주위에 있는 모든 것이 갖고 있는 이름이에요. 여러분의 이름, 지금 보고 있는 'book(책)' 뿐만 아니라 눈에 보이지 않는 'hope(희망)'까지 모두 명사예요.

② 명사를 대신하는 대명사

she	it
(그녀)	(그것)

'나는 샌드위치를 먹었는데, 그거 정말 맛있었어.'에서 '그거'는 앞에 쓰인 명사 '샌드위치'를 대신합니다. 이처럼 **대명사**는 같은 명사를 반복하지 않기 위해 대신해서 쓰는 말입니다. 사람을 가리키는 'she(그녀)'부터 사물을 나타내는 'it(그것)'까지 모두 대명사입니다.

③ 움직임이나 상태를 나타내는 동사

run	talk
(뛰다)	(말하다)

친구에게 '나는 …'이라고 말하면 나에 대해 정확히 무엇을 말하려 하는지 모르겠죠? **동사**는 '누가 ~이다.' 또는 '누가 무엇을 ~하다.'에서 '~이다/~하다'에 해당하는 말입니다. 즉, 동사는 문장에서 없어서는 안 될 역할로, 사람이나 사물의 동작, 상태를 나타냅니다.

④ 명사를 꾸며주는 형용사

같은 사람이라도 입는 옷에 따라 분위기가 달라 보일 때가 있습니다. 이처럼 명사도 어떤 **형용사**와 함께 쓰이는지에 따라 상태나 성질이 달라집니다. 예를 들어, 색에 'dark(어두운)'를 붙이면 '어두운 색'이 되고, 'light(밝은)'를 붙이면 '밝은 색'이 됩니다.

⑤ 꾸미기를 좋아하는 부사

'그는 조심스레 문을 닫았다.'에서 '조심스레'가 동사 '닫았다'를 꾸며주고 있습니다. 이처럼 **부사**는 여러 단어를 꾸며주어 의미를 더욱 풍부하게 합니다. 앞서 배운 형용사는 명사만 꾸며주지만, 부사는 동사, 형용사, 또 다른 부사, 그리고 문장 전체까지도 꾸밀 수 있습니다.

⑥ 명사 앞에 오는 전치사

'정오에'를 표현하기 위해서는 'noon(정오)' 앞에 'at'이라는 **전치사**를 써서 'at noon'이라고 합니다. 이처럼 전치사는 명사나 대명사 앞에 와서 시간, 장소, 방향, 이유, 목적 등의 여러 가지 뜻을 나타냅니다.

⑦ 말을 연결해주는 접속사

and	or
(그리고)	(또는)

'민호는 성실하다. 그리고 책임감이 강하다.'에서 두 문장을 '그리고'가 연결해주고 있습니다. 이처럼 두 문장을 연결하기 위해 사용한 '그리고(and)'와 같은 것을 **접속사**라고 합니다. 접속사는 문장과 문장뿐만 아니라 단어와 단어, 구와 구, 절과 절을 연결할 수도 있습니다.

⑧ 감정을 표현하는 감탄사

Wow!	Oh!
(와!)	(오!)

'와!'처럼 기쁨, 놀람, 슬픔과 같은 여러 감정을 자연스럽게 표현하는 말을 **감탄사**라고 합니다. 영어에서도 'Wow!(와!)', 'Oh!(오!)'와 같은 감탄사가 있습니다.

문장 성분 영어 문장을 만드는 재료

영어에서 문장을 만드는 여러 요소들을 문장 성분이라고 합니다. 앞서 배운 품사는 각 단어의 의미와 역할로 구별되지만, 문장 성분은 문장 안에서의 역할에 따라 구분된다는 차이점을 꼭 알아두세요.

주어와 동사

I work. 나는 일한다.
주어 동사

하나의 문장을 만들기 위해서는 '주어'(나는)와 '동사'(일한다)가 꼭 필요합니다. '누가 ~하다/~이다'에서 '누가'에 해당하는 말이 **주어**이고, '~하다/~이다'에 해당되어 주어의 동작이나 상태를 나타내는 말이 **동사**입니다.

목적어

I ate an apple. 나는 사과를 먹었다.
목적어

'나는 먹었다.'라는 문장은 '주어'(나는)와 '동사'(먹었다)가 모두 있지만 대상이 무엇인지 알 수 없기 때문에 완전한 문장이 아닙니다. '내'가 먹은 대상에 해당하는 '사과를'이라는 목적어를 넣으면 문장이 완전해지겠죠? 이처럼 **목적어**는 '누가 무엇을 ~하다'에서 '무엇을'에 해당하는 말입니다.

보어

She is sad. 그녀는 슬프다.
주어 주격 보어

The news made her sad.
목적어 목적격 보어
그 소식은 그녀를 슬프게 만들었다.

'그녀는 슬프다.'에서 '슬프다'는 주어인 '그녀'의 상태를 설명하고 있습니다. 또, '그 소식은 그녀를 슬프게 만들었다.'에서 '슬프게'는 목적어인 '그녀를'의 상태를 설명하고 있습니다. 이처럼 **보어**는 주어나 목적어의 성질이나 상태를 보충 설명합니다.

수식어

They arrived at the office early.
수식어
그들은 사무실에 일찍 도착했다.

'그들은 사무실에 일찍 도착했다.'라는 문장에서 '일찍'은 그들이 사무실에 도착한 시점을 더 자세하게 설명하고 있습니다. 이처럼 **수식어**는 문장에서 반드시 필요하지는 않지만 다양한 위치에서 문장에 여러 의미를 더해주는 역할을 합니다.

문장의 5형식 영어 문장의 5가지 형태

앞에서 배운 문장을 만드는 요소들을 이용해서 5가지 형식의 문장들을 만들 수 있습니다. 영어에서는 어떤 필수 성분을 쓰는지에 따라 문장의 형식이 정해집니다.

1형식

주어 + 동사

1형식은 <주어 + 동사>만으로도 완전한 의미를 갖는 문장입니다. 동사 뒤에 수식어가 길게 오더라도, 이를 보어나 목적어로 혼동하면 안 됩니다. 'study(공부하다)', 'sleep(자다)', 'travel(여행하다)'과 같은 동사들이 주로 1형식 문장을 만듭니다.

We study. 우리는 공부한다.
주어 동사

2형식

주어 + 동사 + 보어

2형식은 <주어 + 동사> 뒤에 보어가 오는 문장입니다. 주로 'become(~이 되다)', 'remain(여전히 ~이다)', 'seem(~인 것 같다)'과 같은 동사들이 2형식 문장을 만듭니다.

He became famous. 그는 유명해졌다.
주어 동사 보어

3형식

주어 + 동사 + 목적어

3형식은 <주어 + 동사> 뒤에 목적어가 오는 문장입니다. 주로 'buy(구매하다)', 'like(~을 좋아하다)', 'meet(~을 만나다)'과 같은 동사들이 3형식 문장을 만듭니다.

I bought a camera. 나는 카메라를 샀다.
주어 동사 목적어

4형식

주어 + 동사 + 목적어 + 목적어

4형식은 <주어 + 동사> 뒤에 우리말 '~에게'에 해당하는 간접 목적어와 우리말 '~을/를'에 해당하는 직접 목적어가 오는 문장입니다. 주로 'teach(~에게 …을 가르치다)', 'offer(~에게 …을 제공하다)'와 같은 동사들이 4형식 문장을 만듭니다.

He taught me English. 그는 나에게 영어를 가르쳤다.
주어 동사 간접목적어 직접목적어

5형식

주어 + 동사 + 목적어 + 보어

5형식은 <주어 + 동사> 뒤에 목적어와 보어가 오는 문장입니다. 주로 'find(~이 …라는 것을 알게 되다)', 'make(~을 …로 만들다)'와 같은 동사들이 5형식 문장을 만듭니다.

I found the task difficult. 나는 그 일이 어렵다는 것을 알게 되었다.
주어 동사 목적어 목적격 보어

구와 절 말 덩어리

두 개 이상의 단어가 모인 덩어리를 구 또는 절이라고 합니다. 'in the park(공원에서)'처럼 주어와 동사가 없으면 구, because you helped(네가 도와줬기 때문에)처럼 주어와 동사가 있으면 절이라고 합니다.

구 I study **at night**. 나는 밤에 공부한다.	'at night(밤에)'처럼 둘 이상의 단어로 이루어진 말 덩어리에 <주어 + 동사>가 없을 경우 구라고 합니다.
절 I feel happy **when I travel**. 나는 여행할 때 행복함을 느낀다.	'when I travel(나는 여행할 때)'처럼 <주어 + 동사>가 포함되어 있을 경우 절이라고 합니다.

PART 7을 위한 패러프레이징 바꾸어 표현하기

패러프레이징이란 어떤 말이나 글을 같은 의미의 다른 표현으로 바꾸어 전달하는 것입니다. 보통 토익 PART 7에서 지문의 내용을 패러프레이징한 보기들이 나오므로, 알맞은 정답을 고르기 위해서는 패러프레이징을 꼭 학습해야 합니다.

① 다른 표현으로 바꾸기

특정 단어나 구, 절과 비슷한 의미의 표현을 사용하는 방법입니다.

I tried to **complete** the task. 나는 그 과제를 끝내려고 노력했다.
= I tried to **finish** the task. 나는 그 과제를 끝내려고 노력했다.

→ complete(끝내다)를 같은 의미의 단어인 finish(끝내다)로 패러프레이징했습니다.

② 일반화하기

특정 단어나 구를 더 폭넓은 범주의 표현으로 일반화하는 방법이에요.

You can take **a bus or a subway** to the hotel. 당신은 호텔로 버스 또는 지하철을 타고 갈 수 있다.
= You can take **public transportation** to the hotel. 당신은 호텔로 대중교통을 타고 갈 수 있다.

→ a bus or a subway(버스 또는 지하철)의 더 넓은 범주인 public transportation(대중교통)으로 패러프레이징했습니다.

③ 요약하기

한 개 이상의 절이나 문장을 하나의 문장으로 간략하게 요약하는 방법이에요.

I **bought bananas and oranges, but** only bananas were fresh. 나는 바나나와 오렌지를 샀는데, 바나나만 신선했다.
= **Oranges were not fresh.** 오렌지가 신선하지 않았다.

→ 바나나와 오렌지를 샀는데 바나나만 신선했다는 문장을, 오렌지가 신선하지 않았다는 내용으로 요약한 패러프레이징입니다.

한 권으로 끝내는 해커스 토익 600+ LC+RC+VOCA

PART 5

DAY 01	명사		**DAY 07**	동사의 시제
DAY 02	대명사		**DAY 08**	to 부정사와 동명사
DAY 03	형용사와 부사		**DAY 09**	분사
DAY 04	전치사		**DAY 10**	등위/상관접속사와 관계절
DAY 05	동사의 형태와 수일치		**DAY 11**	부사절과 명사절
DAY 06	동사의 종류와 태		**DAY 12**	비교 구문

PART 5 알아보기

PART 5는 101번부터 130번까지 총 30문제로, 문장의 빈칸에 알맞은 문법 사항이나 어휘를 4개의 보기 중에서 골라 채우는 파트입니다. 30문제 중 문법 문제가 평균 20개, 어휘 문제가 평균 10개 출제됩니다.

PART 5 미리 보기

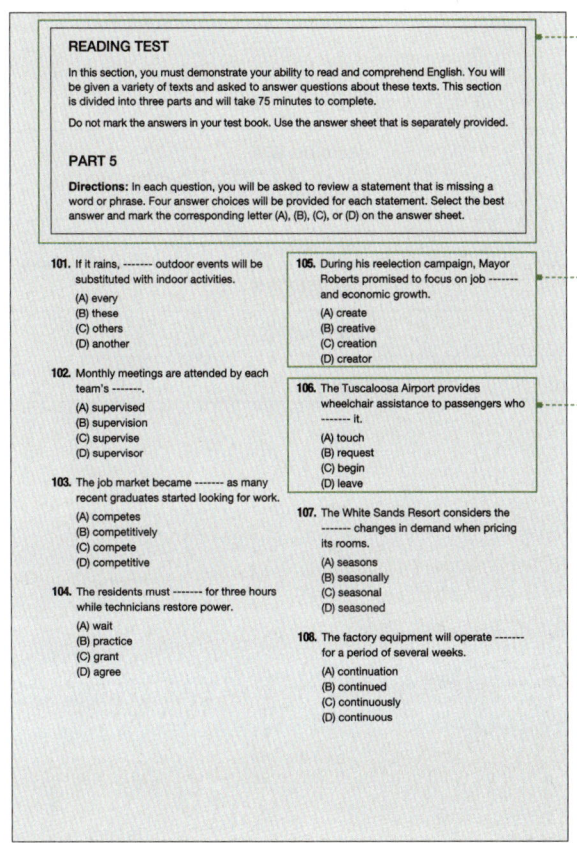

리딩 영역과 PART 5를 소개하는 디렉션입니다. 리딩 영역은 3개의 파트로 구성되며 75분이 주어집니다.

영어의 문장 구조 및 여러 문법 사항을 묻는 문제가 출제됩니다.

문장 전체의 의미에 적합한 어휘나, 빈칸 주변의 단어와 함께 어구를 이루는 어휘를 고르는 문제가 출제됩니다.

PART 5 학습 전략

- **PART 5에 자주 나오는 문법 개념과 기출 포인트 학습하기**
  PART 5에는 자주 출제되는 특정 문법 포인트가 있습니다. 따라서 가장 자주 출제되면서 필수적인 문법 개념과 정답 공식을 익혀두면 문법 문제의 정답을 빠르게 찾을 수 있습니다.

- **PART 5에 자주 출제되는 품사별 빈출 어휘 익히기**
  어휘 문제는 문장을 해석한 뒤 문맥상 가장 알맞은 의미의 보기를 정답으로 골라야 하므로, 품사별 빈출 어휘의 뜻과 쓰임을 정확히 익혀두어야 합니다.

DAY 01 명사

매회 2~3문제 출제

나의 언니는 병원에서 근무한다.
　　명사　　명사

'언니', '병원'처럼 사람, 사물 등을 가리키는 것을 **명사**라고 합니다.

기출 포인트 01 명사의 형태

● 명사는 주로 -tion/-sion, -ment, -ance/-ence, -ty, -al, -er/-or과 같은 꼬리말로 끝납니다.

-tion/-sion	contribu**tion** 기여	deci**sion** 결정
-ment	assign**ment** 과제	involve**ment** 관여
-ance/-ence	appear**ance** 겉모습	experi**ence** 경험
-ty	productivi**ty** 생산성	reliabili**ty** 신뢰도
-al	approv**al** 승인	propos**al** 제안
-er/-or	suppli**er** 공급회사	spons**or** 후원자

기출 포인트 02 명사가 오는 자리

● 명사는 문장에서 주어, 목적어, 보어 자리에 옵니다.

주어 자리　**Employment** has risen in recent years. 고용은 최근 몇 년 동안 증가했다.

목적어 자리　We received an **invitation** to the conference. 우리는 컨퍼런스에 대한 초대장을 받았다.

보어 자리　Mason Grant became a **doctor**. Mason Grant는 의사가 되었다.

● 명사는 주로 관사나 소유격, 형용사 뒤에 옵니다.

관사 뒤　　We need a̲n̲ **extension** for this project. 우리는 이 프로젝트에 대한 기간 연장이 필요하다.
　　　　　　　　관사

소유격 뒤　They accepted o̲u̲r̲ **proposal**. 그들은 우리의 제안을 수락했다.
　　　　　　　　　소유격

형용사 뒤　The marketing team showed r̲e̲m̲a̲r̲k̲a̲b̲l̲e̲ **performance**. 마케팅팀은 놀라운 성과를 보여주었다.
　　　　　　　　　　　　　　　　　형용사

실전 Check-up

01 People may indicate their ------- of participating in the event by adding their names to this list.

(A) intend　　　　(B) intention

02 A ------- should be made before the 15th of each month to avoid late fees.

(A) payment　　　(B) paid

정답·해석·해설 p.120

기출 포인트 03 셀 수 있는 명사와 셀 수 없는 명사

● 명사에는 셀 수 있는 명사(= 가산 명사)와 셀 수 없는 명사(= 불가산 명사)가 있습니다. 가산 명사는 단수일 때 명사 앞에 관사 a(n)를 쓰고, 복수일 때는 명사 뒤에 -(e)s를 붙여야 합니다. 불가산 명사는 셀 수 없는 명사이므로 앞에 관사 a(n)를 쓰거나, 뒤에 -(e)s를 붙이면 안 됩니다.

가산 명사 The company ordered (~~computer~~, **a computer**, **computers**) for the new office.
회사가 새 사무실용 컴퓨터를 주문했다.

불가산 명사 We received valuable (~~a feedback~~, ~~feedbacks~~, **feedback**) from clients.
우리는 고객들로부터 매우 유용한 의견을 받았다.

● 셀 수 없는 것처럼 보이는 가산 명사와 셀 수 있는 것처럼 보이는 불가산 명사를 잘 구별해야 합니다.

가산 명사		불가산 명사	
audition 오디션	price 가격	access 접근, 출입	furniture 가구
discount 할인	refund 환불	advice 충고, 조언	information 정보
employee 직원	responsibility 책임	assembly 조립	luggage 수하물
manufacturer 제조사	result 결과	baggage 수하물	merchandise 상품
option 선택(권)	subject 과목	consent 동의	news 뉴스
photograph 사진	tip 조언	equipment 장비	stationery 문구류

기출 포인트 04 명사 앞의 수량 표현

● 가산/불가산 명사와 함께 쓰는 수량 표현과, 단수/복수 명사와 함께 쓰는 수량 표현을 구분해서 알아두어야 합니다.

가산 명사 앞		불가산 명사 앞	가산 · 불가산 명사 모두의 앞	
단수 명사	복수 명사			
one 하나의 each 각각의	a few 몇 개의 few 거의 없는	(a) little 적은	no 어떤 ~도 ~ 아니다	all 모든
every 모든	fewer 더 적은 many 많은	less 더 적은	more 더 많은	most 대부분의
	several 몇몇의 both 둘 다의	much 많은	some 몇몇의, 어떤	any 어떤
	various 여러, 많은 a variety of 다양한			
	a number of 많은			

There were (~~much~~, **many**) <u>visitors</u> at the gallery. 미술관에 많은 방문객들이 있었다.
　　　　　　　　　　　복수 가산 명사

This report provides (~~fewer~~, **less**) <u>information</u> than the previous one. 이 보고서는 이전의 것보다 더 적은 정보를 제공한다.
　　　　　　　　　　　　　　　　불가산 명사

실전 Check-up

01 Riverside Theater Company is holding ------- for its upcoming summer production next weekend.

(A) audition　　　(B) auditions

02 The company will conduct an evaluation of each ------- twice a year.

(A) workers　　　(B) worker

정답·해석·해설 p.120

기출 포인트 05 사람명사 vs. 사물/추상명사

● 사람명사와 사물/추상명사는 모두 명사 자리에 올 수 있는데, 이 중 문장 안에서 자연스러운 의미를 만드는 명사가 와야 합니다.

사람명사	사물/추상명사	사람명사	사물/추상명사
applicant 지원자	application 지원, 신청서	inquirer 문의자	inquiry 문의
architect 건축가	architecture 건축(술)	licensor 검열관	license 면허, 자격증
assistant 조수	assistance 원조, 보조	manufacturer 제조자	manufacture 제조
attendee 참석자	attention 주의 attendance 출석	occupant 입주자	occupancy 수용 능력, 점유 occupation 직업
beneficiary 수혜자	benefit 이익	negotiator 협상가	negotiation 협상
collaborator 협력자	collaboration 협력	participant 참가자	participation 참여, 참가
complainer 투덜대는 사람	complaint 불평	partner 동업자	partnership 협력, 제휴
contestant 경쟁자	contest 대회	performer 연주자	performance 연주, 실적, 성과
contractor 계약자	contract 계약(서)	producer 생산자	production 생산 product 생산품
contributor 공헌자	contribution 공헌	regulator 규제 담당자	regulation 규제
developer 개발자	development 개발	reporter 기자	report 보도
distributor 분배자	distribution 분배	researcher 연구원	research 연구
donor 기증자	donation 기증	resident 거주자	residence 거주
installer 설치하는 사람	installation 설치	reviewer 검토자, 비평가	review 검토, 평론
instructor 강사	instruction 지시	subscriber 구독자	subscription 구독, 가입
investor 투자자	investment 투자	traveler 여행자	travel 여행

The company recognized Ms. Wilson's (~~contributor~~, **contribution**) to business growth.
회사는 사업 성장에 대한 Ms. Wilson의 공헌을 인정했다.

→ '사업 성장에 대한 공헌을 인정했다'라는 의미가 되어야 하므로, '공헌자'라는 의미의 사람명사(contributor)가 아닌, '공헌'이라는 의미의 추상명사(contribution)가 와야 합니다.

The (~~performance~~, **performer**) walked onto the stage. 그 연주자가 무대로 걸어 나왔다.

→ '연주자가 무대로 걸어 나왔다'라는 의미가 되어야 하므로, '연주, 실적, 성과'라는 의미의 추상명사(performance)가 아닌, '연주자'라는 의미의 사람명사(performer)가 와야 합니다.

실전 Check-up

01 The main ------- about this Web site is its poor display on smartphones.

(A) complainer   (B) complaint

02 She has worked as an ------- to the marketing director for three years.

(A) assistance   (B) assistant

3초컷 정답 공식

자주 출제되는 정답 공식을 적용하여 빈칸에 가장 알맞은 보기를 고르세요.

정답공식 01 the와 of 사이에 빈칸이 있으면 명사가 정답이다!

01 The ------- of the course has over 10 years of experience in information technology.
(A) instruct (B) instructor
(C) instructive (D) instructs

02 Use of the conference rooms for special occasions requires the ------- of the building administrator.
(A) permissive (B) permitted
(C) permission (D) permissible

정답공식 02 전치사 뒤에 빈칸이 있으면 명사가 정답일 확률이 높다!

03 The magazine article written by Dana Peters includes information about ------- in the field of artificial intelligence.
(A) develop (B) developed
(C) develops (D) developments

04 Most patients report high levels of ------- with the quality of care they receive at Hawthorne Hospital.
(A) satisfy (B) satisfies
(C) satisfied (D) satisfaction

정답공식 03 a variety/number of 뒤 빈칸에는 복수 명사가 와야 한다!

05 Huntington Hotel organizes a variety of ------- for its guests, including water sports and sightseeing tours.
(A) activity (B) active
(C) actively (D) activities

06 According to the survey, a number of ------- prefer working remotely rather than coming to the office.
(A) employee (B) employment
(C) employ (D) employees

정답공식 04 빈칸 뒤 동사가 be + p.p. 형태면 사물/추상명사가 정답일 확률이 높다!

07 To assess productivity, a ------- will be conducted.
(A) review (B) reviewer
(C) to review (D) reviewed

08 Active ------- is recommended for all staff during the company's strategic planning sessions.
(A) participant (B) participation
(C) participate (D) participated

정답·해석·해설 p.120

HACKERS TEST

빈칸에 가장 알맞은 보기를 고르세요.

01 Young people are drawn to big cities by ------- and opportunity.
(A) excite
(B) excited
(C) excitement
(D) excitable

02 The auditorium has a maximum ------- of 300 people.
(A) occupied
(B) occupy
(C) occupancy
(D) occupant

03 Mr. Louis is a competent employee with a strong ------- in marketing.
(A) interested
(B) interests
(C) interest
(D) will interest

04 Thurmond Rail was able to raise enough capital for the ------- of its services.
(A) expand
(B) expanded
(C) expandable
(D) expansion

05 All e-mail ------- are reviewed by customer service agents and sent to the appropriate department.
(A) inquired
(B) inquirers
(C) to inquire
(D) inquiries

06 Milkins Corporation will negotiate a two-year ------- with the former vice president of BG Holdings.
(A) contract
(B) contractible
(C) contracted
(D) contractor

07 Passengers will proceed through customs and immigration upon ------- at Changi International Airport.
(A) arrive
(B) arrived
(C) arrives
(D) arrival

08 While the CEO is away at the conference in Santiago, his assistant, Mr. Hale, will handle all official ------- on his behalf.
(A) communicate
(B) communicates
(C) communicative
(D) communications

09 The director liked the initial proposal but made a few ------- to improve it.
(A) suggests
(B) suggestion
(C) suggestions
(D) suggested

10 More than 50 young artists will be participating in a painting ------- sponsored by the Museum of Contemporary Art.
(A) contestant
(B) contestable
(C) contest
(D) contested

11 By the end of the writing workshop, participants will have gained a thorough ------- of grammar.
(A) comprehend
(B) comprehension
(C) comprehensively
(D) comprehends

12 The Vector Historical Foundation puts ------- on establishing close partnerships with other similar institutions.
(A) emphasis
(B) emphasize
(C) emphasized
(D) emphatically

13 Pillows and blankets can be provided by flight attendants to ------- requesting them.

(A) will travel
(B) traveled
(C) travels
(D) travelers

14 Many ------- by Julia Sacks inspired today's top fiction writers.

(A) works
(B) worked
(C) work
(D) to work

15 If the customers need additional ------- about our product features, they can call our toll-free hotline.

(A) inform
(B) informs
(C) information
(D) informed

16 Reviews of Alpine Footwear's hiking boots stress the ------- of these products compared to those of other companies.

(A) durable
(B) durably
(C) durability
(D) more durable

17 Government officials hope to increase ------- within the region's business community.

(A) collaboration
(B) collaborative
(C) collaborator
(D) collaborate

18 The ------- of Mr. Johnson include overseeing the marketing department and developing new business strategies.

(A) responsibility
(B) responsibilities
(C) responsibly
(D) responsible

19 According to the technician, the ------- of the office network could take up to three days to complete.

(A) install
(B) installed
(C) installer
(D) installation

20 The board of directors will evaluate investment ------- to determine which are most profitable in the current economy.

(A) option
(B) options
(C) optionally
(D) optional

21 Sales staff will spend next week offering customers ------- to our latest magazine.

(A) subscribes
(B) subscribed
(C) subscribers
(D) subscriptions

22 A number of ------- have complained about the long wait times at the entrance.

(A) visitor
(B) visitors
(C) visiting
(D) visit

23 ------- into the Velmora Association is only possible for business owners.

(A) Accept
(B) Acceptance
(C) Accepted
(D) Acceptably

24 The retail chain has contracts with several toy ------- in South America and West Africa.

(A) manufacturer
(B) manufacturers
(C) manufactured
(D) manufacture

빈출 어휘 | 명사 1

PART 5 어휘 문제에 자주 출제되는 어휘를 예문과 함께 확실히 익혀두세요.

01 proposal 제안(서), 제의
submit the **proposal** to the client
고객에게 제안서를 제출하다
파 propose 제안하다

02 location 위치, 장소
hold an event at a convenient **location**
편리한 위치에서 행사를 열다
파 locate 위치시키다

03 initiative 계획, 주도권
a new **initiative** for the community
지역사회를 위한 새로운 계획
파 initiate 시작하다

04 expense 비용, 경비
eliminate an unnecessary **expense**
불필요한 비용을 없애다
동 cost 비용

05 durability 내구성, 지속성
the **durability** of the new material
새로운 소재의 내구성
파 durable 내구성 있는

06 position 직책, 일자리
apply for a **position** through the Web site
웹사이트를 통해 직책에 지원하다

07 description 설명, 묘사
read the job **description** in the posting
공고에 있는 직무 설명을 읽다
파 describe 묘사하다

08 opportunity 기회
provide an **opportunity** for advancement
승진을 위한 기회를 제공하다
동 chance 기회, 가능성

09 committee 위원회
form a **committee** within the organization
조직 내에 위원회를 구성하다
파 commit 위임하다

10 regulation 규정, 규칙
comply with all safety **regulations**
모든 안전 규정을 준수하다
파 regulate 규제하다

11 deadline 마감 기한
meet the **deadline** for the report
보고서의 마감 기한을 지키다

12 decline 감소, 하락
prevent a **decline** in sales this quarter
이번 분기에 매출 감소를 방지하다
동 drop 감소, 하락 반 increase 증가, 상승

13 registration 등록, 신청
confirm **registration** for the seminar
세미나 등록을 확인하다
파 register 등록하다

14 priority 우선순위
list the tasks in order of **priority**
작업들을 우선순위 순으로 나열하다
파 prioritize 우선순위를 매기다

15 phase 단계, 국면
the initial **phase** of product design
제품 설계의 초기 단계

16 presence 참석, 존재(감)
request all employees' **presence** at the workshop
모든 직원들의 워크숍 참석을 요청하다
파 present 제시하다

17 policy 정책, 방침
a new **policy** regarding work hours
근무 시간에 관한 새로운 정책

18 feedback 의견, 피드백
receive **feedback** from department managers
부서 관리자들로부터 의견을 받다

19 branch 지점, 지사
visit every **branch** by the end of the month
월말까지 모든 지점을 방문하다

20 consultation 상담, 협의
schedule a **consultation** with an expert
전문가와의 상담 일정을 잡다

파 consult 상담하다

토익 실전문제

01 The Westfield Bank will open a new ------- in downtown Hartford next month.
(A) decline (B) aspect
(C) branch (D) regulation

02 The product ------- on the Web site does not match the actual merchandise we received.
(A) description (B) committee
(C) ticket (D) volume

03 Parkwell Industries has a vacant ------- in the marketing department that needs to be filled immediately.
(A) registration (B) assignment
(C) nomination (D) position

04 Although November 3 is the ------- for the team's research project, additional time may be required.
(A) report (B) decision
(C) deadline (D) outline

05 The owners hired a real estate agent to find a suitable ------- for their yoga studio.
(A) contract (B) transaction
(C) itinerary (D) location

06 The software product is in the final ------- of development.
(A) scene (B) phase
(C) result (D) issue

07 Deerwood Laboratories will gather its employees' ------- on the proposed changes to the pension plan.
(A) practice (B) effort
(C) feedback (D) admission

08 The board of directors will review Ms. Jensen's ------- for expanding operations into Asian markets next week.
(A) proposal (B) episode
(C) technique (D) presence

정답·해석·해설 p.123

DAY 02 대명사

매회 1~2문제 출제

나는 남동생이 있다. 그는 나와 닮았다.
　　　　　　　　대명사(= 남동생)

'남동생'이라는 명사를 다시 쓰지 않기 위해 '그'라는 표현을 썼습니다. 이처럼 앞에 쓴 명사의 반복을 피하기 위해 해당 명사를 대신해서 쓰는 말을 **대명사**라고 합니다.

기출포인트 01 인칭대명사

- 인칭대명사는 '그', '그녀', '그것'처럼 사람이나 사물을 가리키는 대명사로 인칭, 성, 수, 격에 따라 형태가 달라집니다. 그리고 인칭대명사에는 '소유격 + 명사'를 대신하는 소유대명사도 있습니다.

인칭/성/수			주격 (~은/는, ~이/가)	목적격 (~을/를, ~에게)	소유격 (~의)	소유대명사 (~의 것)
1인칭	단수(나)		I	me	my	mine
	복수(우리)		we	us	our	ours
2인칭	단수(당신)		you	you	your	yours
	복수(당신들)		you	you	your	yours
3인칭	단수	남성(그)	he	him	his	his
		여성(그녀)	she	her	her	hers
		사물(그것)	it	it	its	-
	복수(그들, 그것들)		they	them	their	theirs

- 인칭대명사의 주격은 주어 자리, 목적격은 목적어 자리, 소유격은 명사 앞에 오고, '~의 것'으로 해석하는 소유대명사는 주어, 목적어, 보어 자리에 옵니다.

　주격　　　**She** works in the accounting department. 그녀는 회계 부서에서 일한다.

　목적격　　The chef taught **me** the recipe. 요리사가 나에게 그 요리법을 가르쳤다.

　소유격　　The manager left **his** <u>document</u> on the desk. 관리자는 그의 서류를 책상 위에 뒀다.
　　　　　　　　　　　　　　　　명사

　소유대명사　Make sure the umbrella is **yours** before leaving the office. 사무실을 나가기 전에 그 우산이 당신의 것인지 꼭 확인하세요.
　　　　　　　　　　　　　　　　　　보어 자리

실전 Check-up

01 Ms. Breen will provide an update on the project when ------ comes back from the job site this afternoon.

(A) she　　　　　　(B) her

02 Ms. Patel interviewed Mr. Cho and decided to hire ------ for the open position.

(A) him　　　　　　(B) his

정답·해석·해설 p.124

기출포인트 02 재귀대명사

● 재귀대명사는 -self(-selves)가 붙은 형태로, '~ 자신'이라는 뜻을 가집니다.

단수	myself	yourself	himself, herself, itself
복수	ourselves	yourselves	themselves

The engineers blamed **themselves** for the mistake. 기술자들은 실수에 대해 자신들을 탓했다.
(= The engineers)

● 재귀대명사는 주어와 목적어가 같은 대상일 때 목적어 자리에 옵니다. 주어나 목적어를 강조하기 위해서 강조하고자 하는 말 바로 뒤나 문장 맨 뒤에 재귀대명사를 쓰기도 하는데, 이때 재귀대명사는 생략할 수 있습니다.

주어 = 목적어 Ms. Kim introduced **herself** at the morning meeting. Ms. Kim은 아침 회의에서 자신을 소개했다.
      주어   목적어(= Ms. Kim)

강조   The employees **themselves** developed the new system. 직원들 자신들이 새로운 시스템을 개발했다.
     주어   주어 강조

기출포인트 03 지시대명사

● 지시대명사는 '이것', '저것'처럼 대상을 가리킬 때 쓰는 대명사입니다. 가까이 있는 사물이나 사람을 가리킬 때는 this/these, 멀리 있는 사물이나 사람을 가리킬 때는 that/those를 씁니다.

This is my car, and **that** is Mr. Taylor's. 이것은 내 차이고, 저것은 Mr. Taylor의 차이다.

● 지시대명사 that과 those는 멀리 있는 사물이나 사람을 가리키는 것 외에도, 두 대상을 비교할 때 비교 대상이 되는 명사의 반복을 피하기 위해 씁니다. 이때, 비교 대상이 단수 명사나 셀 수 없는 명사이면 that, 복수 명사이면 those를 써야 합니다.

that Our service is better than **that** of our competitor. 우리의 서비스가 경쟁업체의 것보다 더 좋다.
          (= service)

those This quarter's sales are higher than **those** of last quarter. 이번 분기의 판매량이 지난 분기의 것들보다 더 높다.
            (= sales)

● this/these는 '이 ~', that/those는 '저 ~'라는 의미로 명사 앞에서 명사를 꾸며주는 지시형용사로도 쓰입니다. 단수 명사 앞에는 this/that이, 복수 명사 앞에는 these/those가 옵니다.

this/that **This** request requires approval from the department head. 이 신청은 부서장의 승인이 필요하다.
     단수 명사

these/those **Those** products sell well overseas. 저 제품들은 해외에서 잘 팔린다.
      복수 명사

● those는 관계절, 분사, 전치사구의 꾸밈을 받아 '~한 사람들'이라는 의미로 쓰이며, 복수 취급합니다.

those **Those** who arrive late may not be allowed to enter the seminar. 늦게 도착하는 사람들은 세미나에 입장하지 못할 수도 있다.
     관계절

실전 Check-up

01 The manager of the warehouse ------- called to apologize for the delay in shipping.
(A) he (B) himself

02 The products on this shelf are cheaper than ------- on the other shelves.
(A) those (B) that

정답·해석·해설 p.124

기출 포인트 04 부정대명사

● 부정대명사는 '어떤 사람', '어떤 것'처럼 정확한 수나 양을 알 수 없어서 막연하게 말할 때 쓰는 대명사입니다. 이러한 부정대명사는 뒤에 나온 명사를 수식하는 부정형용사로도 사용할 수 있습니다.

부정대명사 We ordered 100 brochures, but only **several** arrived. 우리는 책자를 100개 주문했지만, 일부만 도착했다.

부정형용사 **Several** documents are missing from the file. 몇몇 문서가 파일에서 빠져 있다.

● some과 any는 모두 '몇몇(의), 약간(의)'이라는 의미로 쓰이지만, some은 주로 긍정문에 쓰이고, any는 부정문, 의문문, 조건문에 쓰입니다.

긍정문 The apples at the supermarket looked delicious, so we bought **some**.
그 슈퍼마켓에 있는 사과들이 맛있어 보여서, 우리는 몇 개를 샀다.

부정문 She has not visited **any** of the museums in the city. 그녀는 도시의 박물관들 중 어느 곳도 방문하지 않았다.

● 사람이나 사물이 둘이 있을 경우 그 중 하나는 one으로, 나머지 하나는 the other로 나타냅니다. 사람이나 사물이 셋 이상이 있을 경우 그 중 하나는 one, 또 다른 하나는 another, 그 중 다른 몇 개는 others, 나머지 전부는 the others로 나타냅니다.

We have five branches. **One** is in New York, **another** is in Chicago, and **the others** are in smaller cities.
　　　　　　　　　　　　어떤 하나(= one branch)　또 다른 하나(= another branch)　　나머지 전부(= the other branches)
우리는 다섯 개의 지점이 있다. 하나는 뉴욕에 있고, 또 다른 하나는 시카고에 있고, 나머지 전부는 작은 도시들에 있다.

실전 Check-up

01 Most customers were satisfied with the service, but ------- complained about the delivery time.

(A) some　　　　　　(B) any

02 They ordered two types of fabric, one for the chairs and the ------- for the curtains.

(A) each　　　　　　(B) other

3초컷 정답 공식

자주 출제되는 정답 공식을 적용하여 빈칸에 가장 알맞은 보기를 고르세요.

정답공식 01 명사 앞에 빈칸이 있으면 소유격 인칭대명사가 정답일 확률이 높다!

01 We would like to confirm ------- attendance at the meeting next month.
(A) your (B) you
(C) yours (D) yourself

02 Ms. Lee's financial advice is based on ------- experience as an investor.
(A) she (B) her
(C) herself (D) hers

정답공식 02 'a(n) + 명사 + of' 뒤의 빈칸에는 소유대명사가 정답이다!

03 A colleague of ------- was recently promoted to manager at the international branch.
(A) my (B) mine
(C) me (D) myself

04 A representative of ------- will contact you about the shipping details next week.
(A) our (B) us
(C) ours (D) ourselves

정답공식 03 familiarize와 with 사이에 빈칸이 있으면 재귀대명사를 정답으로 고른다!

05 Health-care professionals must familiarize ------- with the latest guidelines in the field.
(A) them (B) their
(C) theirs (D) themselves

06 We should familiarize ------- with local customs and traditions before traveling abroad for business.
(A) ourselves (B) us
(C) our (D) we

정답공식 04 빈칸 뒤에 who가 있으면 'those who(~한 사람들)'를 이루는 those가 정답이다!

07 The town of Colville offers guided tours for ------- who want to learn more about this community's rich history.
(A) that (B) those
(C) someone (D) anybody

08 Only ------- who have a valid ticket will be allowed entry.
(A) that (B) them
(C) these (D) those

정답·해석·해설 p.124

HACKERS TEST

빈칸에 가장 알맞은 보기를 고르세요.

01 The event hall will be decorated by ------- expert event planners.
(A) us
(B) we
(C) ourselves
(D) our

02 Mr. Adams ------- volunteered to assist Calterna Technology's representatives from Korea.
(A) he
(B) him
(C) his
(D) himself

03 Keynote speaker Melanie Allen will send the draft of ------- speech to the events committee on Thursday.
(A) she
(B) hers
(C) her
(D) herself

04 ------- who register early for the conference will receive a 15 percent discount on accommodation.
(A) Them
(B) Their
(C) Those
(D) That

05 If ------- are interested in joining the tour, sign up at the information desk.
(A) your
(B) you
(C) yours
(D) yourself

06 The opinions given by Mr. Tolentino differed from ------- of the accounting department's other staff.
(A) those
(B) they
(C) this
(D) their

07 The supervisor called an assistant of ------- to help with the inventory count.
(A) hers
(B) her
(C) she
(D) herself

08 As several Greenville city buses were in bad condition, the mayor decided to purchase ------- from Trek Transportation.
(A) other
(B) some
(C) every
(D) couple

09 Marina practiced some ballet steps by ------- rather than with her classmates.
(A) she
(B) her
(C) herself
(D) hers

10 Mr. Tang left ------- vehicle in the airport's long-term parking facility before traveling to Hong Kong.
(A) his
(B) himself
(C) he
(D) him

11 We are expecting ------- deliveries of products from the supplier this week.
(A) any
(B) several
(C) this
(D) one

12 Jackson City has transformed ------- into a vibrant city by investing more in recreational facilities.
(A) it
(B) themselves
(C) itself
(D) their

13 Before he left for Florida, Coach Anderson told his players that ------- should carry on with the usual practice.
(A) them
(B) their
(C) theirs
(D) they

14 The quality of the new software is much better than ------- of the previous version.
(A) those
(B) that
(C) these
(D) they

15 Unable to attract any investors, Mr. Meyers chose to finance the new business by -------.
(A) he
(B) him
(C) his
(D) himself

16 The successful ------- between the two research institutions has led to breakthroughs in medical science.
(A) partnership
(B) partner
(C) partnered
(D) to partner

17 Only ------- of the five candidates will be selected for the position.
(A) each
(B) every
(C) one
(D) another

18 We need to review ------- documents for the client meeting tomorrow.
(A) this
(B) that
(C) it
(D) these

19 Ms. Lewis received a performance bonus this quarter because ------- completed the project ahead of schedule.
(A) her
(B) hers
(C) herself
(D) she

20 Management is planning a ------- of Hollman Realty's 10th year in business this April.
(A) celebrate
(B) celebrates
(C) celebrated
(D) celebration

21 The event organizer will provide special assistance to ------- who require wheelchair access.
(A) either
(B) them
(C) those
(D) it

22 The store sells two models of the device, one of which is lightweight while ------- is more durable.
(A) another
(B) others
(C) other
(D) the other

23 The marketing team members must familiarize ------- with the new product features before the launch event.
(A) theirs
(B) themselves
(C) their
(D) they

24 Some guests prefer a window seat, while ------- choose to sit near the aisle.
(A) other
(B) others
(C) another
(D) the other

빈출 어휘 | 명사 2

✅ PART 5 어휘 문제에 자주 출제되는 어휘를 예문과 함께 확실히 익혀두세요.

01 **inventory** 재고, 목록
check the **inventory** before ordering
주문하기 전에 재고를 확인하다

02 **selection** 선별된 것, 선정
a wide **selection** of travel-related books
다양하게 선별된 여행 관련 도서들
[파] select 선정하다

03 **overview** 개요, 개관
an **overview** of the marketing strategy
마케팅 전략에 대한 개요

04 **lack** 부족, 결핍
a **lack** of practical experience in finance
재무 분야의 실무 경험 부족
[동] shortage 부족

05 **statement** 성명, 명세서
issue an official **statement** to the press
언론에 공식 성명을 발표하다
[파] state 진술하다

06 **promotion** 홍보, 승진
launch a **promotion** for the new product
새로운 제품을 위한 홍보를 시작하다
[파] promote 홍보하다, 승진시키다

07 **replacement** 대체품, 교체
a **replacement** for the defective item
불량품에 대한 대체품
[파] replace 교체하다

08 **merger** 합병, 통합
negotiate the terms of the **merger**
합병의 조건을 협상하다
[파] merge 합병하다

09 **majority** 과반수, 대다수
secure the **majority** of votes in the election
선거에서 과반수의 표를 확보하다
[파] major 주요한

10 **expertise** 전문 지식, 전문 기술
demonstrate **expertise** in graphic design
그래픽 디자인 분야의 전문 지식을 보여주다
[파] expert 전문가

11 **profitability** 수익성
the **profitability** of the business unit
사업 부문의 수익성
[파] profitable 수익성 있는

12 **collaboration** 협업, 협력
a **collaboration** between several departments
여러 부서 간의 협업
[파] collaborate 협력하다

13 **installation** 설치, 시설
complete the **installation** of the equipment
장비의 설치를 완료하다
[파] install 설치하다

14 **certainty** 확신, 확실성
answer the investors' questions with **certainty**
투자자들의 질문에 확신을 가지고 대답하다
[파] certain 확실한

15 **dedication** 헌신, 전념
recognize the **dedication** of employees
직원들의 헌신을 인정하다
[파] dedicate 헌신하다

16 **consideration** 고려, 배려
after careful **consideration** of all factors
모든 요소에 대한 신중한 고려 후에
[파] consider 고려하다

17 organization 단체, 조직

join an **organization** for volunteer work
자원봉사를 위한 단체에 가입하다

파 organize 조직하다

18 conservation 보호, 보존

conservation measures to protect wildlife
야생 동물을 보호하기 위한 보호 대책

파 conserve 보존하다

19 guarantee 보장, 보증

offer a **guarantee** for on-time delivery
정시 배송에 대한 보장을 제공하다

20 basis 단위, 기초

pay bonuses on an annual **basis**
일 년 단위로 상여금을 지급하다

파 basic 기본적인

토익 실전문제

01 Customers should request a written ------- if they are concerned about the durability of a product.

(A) guarantee (B) margin
(C) decline (D) certainty

02 The policy cannot be implemented unless a ------- of board members agree.

(A) regulation (B) majority
(C) statement (D) procedure

03 The CEO praised the team's ------- to completing the challenging project ahead of schedule.

(A) profitability (B) investment
(C) basis (D) dedication

04 Successful product development requires close ------- between design and engineering teams.

(A) collaboration (B) strategy
(C) organization (D) enrollment

05 During the presentation, Mr. Park will provide a brief ------- of the research findings.

(A) performance (B) recommendation
(C) overview (D) promotion

06 Dr. Carter's ------- in renewable energy technology has made him a sought-after industry consultant.

(A) expertise (B) response
(C) delivery (D) allocation

07 Please categorize each ------- accurately so we can process your reimbursement quickly.

(A) event (B) inventory
(C) expense (D) description

08 Although the computers have been delivered, the ------- of the software is expected to take two more days.

(A) association (B) installation
(C) phase (D) foundation

정답·해석·해설 p.127

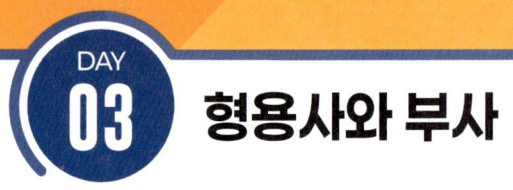

DAY 03 형용사와 부사

매회 4~5문제 출제

나는 맛있는 음식을 만족스럽게 먹었다.
　　　형용사　　　　　부사

'맛있는'처럼 명사의 성질이나 모양, 상태 등을 설명해주는 것을 **형용사**라고 하고, '만족스럽게'처럼 동사나 형용사 등을 꾸며 의미를 강조하거나 풍부하게 하는 것을 **부사**라고 합니다.

기출포인트 01 형용사의 형태

● 형용사는 주로 -ous, -tic, -y, -able/-ible, -tive/-sive와 같은 꼬리말로 끝납니다.

-ous	fam**ous** 유명한	gener**ous** 관대한
-tic	authen**tic** 진정한	automa**tic** 자동의
-y	heav**y** 무거운	risk**y** 위험한
-able/-ible	suit**able** 알맞은	access**ible** 접근 가능한
-tive/-sive	attrac**tive** 매력적인	exten**sive** 광범위한

기출포인트 02 형용사가 오는 자리

● 형용사는 주로 명사 앞이나 보어 자리에 옵니다.

명사 앞　Mr. Kim is a **famous** actor. Mr. Kim은 유명한 배우이다.
　　　　　　　　　　　　　　명사

보어 자리　The technique suggested by the expert was **effective**. 전문가에 의해 제안된 기법은 효과적이었다.
　　　　　　　　　　　　　　　　　　　　　　　　주격 보어

　　　　　Rachel thought the investment **risky**. Rachel은 그 투자가 위험하다고 생각했다.
　　　　　　　　　　　　　　　　목적격 보어

기출포인트 03 토익에 잘 나오는 'be + 형용사' 표현

● 'be + 형용사' 형태로 자주 쓰이는 표현들을 알아두면 도움이 됩니다.

be acceptable to + 명사 ~에게 수용 가능하다　　be eligible for ~에 대한 자격이 있다　　be available for ~이 가능하다
be familiar with ~에 익숙하다　　　　　　　　　be aware of ~을 알고 있다　　　　　　　be available to do ~할 수 있다
be critical of ~에 대해 비판적이다　　　　　　　be skilled in/at ~에 능력이 있다　　　　　be responsible for ~에 책임이 있다

The new development plans **are acceptable to** the local residents. 새로운 개발 계획들은 지역 주민들에게 수용 가능하다.

실전 Check-up

01 Products are not ------ after a period of 30 days from the date of purchase.

(A) refundable　　(B) refunds

02 The business development manager is ------ for identifying new business opportunities.

(A) responsibility　　(B) responsible

정답·해석·해설 p.128

기출포인트 04 부사의 형태

● 부사는 보통 형용사에 꼬리말 -ly를 붙인 형태입니다.

| briefly 간단히 | carefully 신중하게 | conveniently 간편히 | widely 널리, 폭넓게 | quickly 빨리 |

* costly(값비싼), friendly(친절한)와 같이 -ly로 끝나는 형용사도 있으므로, 이 형용사를 부사로 혼동하지 않도록 해야 합니다.

● 형용사 뒤에 -ly를 붙인 형태가 아닌 부사들도 있습니다.

| very 매우 | too 너무 | also 또한 | just 막, 방금 | even 심지어 |

기출포인트 05 부사가 오는 자리

● 부사는 주로 부사가 꾸며주는 동사, 형용사, 부사 또는 문장의 앞에 옵니다. 단, 동사를 꾸밀 때는 동사 뒤에 올 수도 있습니다.

동사 앞	Mr. Cohan **carefully** <u>reviewed</u> the contract. Mr. Cohan은 신중하게 계약서를 검토했다. 동사
동사 뒤	The technology <u>advances</u> **rapidly**. 기술은 빠르게 발전한다. 동사
형용사 앞	The jacket is **too** <u>small</u> for him. 이 재킷은 그에게 너무 작다. 형용사
부사 앞	The package was delivered **unexpectedly** <u>quickly</u>. 소포가 예상 외로 빨리 배달되었다. 부사
문장 앞	**Fortunately**, <u>I discovered the solution easily</u>. 다행히도, 나는 해결책을 쉽게 찾아냈다. 문장

기출포인트 06 토익에 잘 나오는 부사

● 시간이나 시점을 나타내는 부사가 토익에 자주 나옵니다.

| already 이미 | still 여전히, 아직 | yet 아직 |
| soon 곧 | ago ~ 전에 | once 한때, 이전에 |

He left an hour **ago**, but he's **still** not home. 그는 한 시간 전에 떠났지만, 아직 집에 있지 않다.

● 얼마나 자주 일이 발생하는지를 나타내는 빈도 부사가 토익에 자주 나옵니다.

| always 항상 | almost 거의 | often 자주 | frequently 종종 |
| usually 보통 | sometimes 때때로 | seldom 거의 ~않다 | never 결코 ~않다 |

Sometimes, traffic is worse in the evening than in the morning. 때때로, 아침보다 저녁에 교통 체증이 더 심하다.

● 숫자 표현과 함께 쓰이는 부사가 토익에 자주 나옵니다.

| roughly/approximately/about 대략 | only/just 오직 | nearly/almost 거의 |

The renovation took **roughly** <u>two weeks</u> longer than originally expected. 수리는 원래 예상했던 것보다 대략 2주 더 걸렸다.

실전 Check-up

01 Mr. Chase ------- declined the invitation to lead the workshop and suggested an alternative.

(A) kind   (B) kindly

02 The marketing team has ------- completed the budget report for this quarter.

(A) already   (B) soon

정답·해석·해설 p.128

기출포인트 07 혼동하기 쉬운 형용사/부사

● 형태가 비슷하지만 의미가 달라 혼동하기 쉬운 형용사들을 알아두면 도움이 됩니다.

considerate 사려 깊은	considerable 상당한	personal 개인적인	personable 매력적인
diagnostic 진단의	diagnosable 진단할 수 있는	profitable 유리한, 이익이 있는	proficient 능숙한
distinguishable 구별할 수 있는	distinguished 뛰어난	respectful 정중한	respective 각각의
economic 경제의	economical 절약하는	responsible 책임이 있는	responsive 민감하게 반응하는
favorite 가장 좋아하는	favorable 호의적인	seasonal 계절적인	seasoned 경험이 많은
forgetful 잘 잊어버리는	forgettable 잊혀지기 쉬운	successful 성공적인	successive 연속적인

The event attracted (~~considerate~~, **considerable**) attention from the media. 그 행사는 언론으로부터 상당한 관심을 끌었다.
→ '상당한 관심'이라는 의미이므로, considerate(사려 깊은)가 아닌 considerable(상당한)이 와야 합니다.

You should keep your (~~personable~~, **personal**) belongings in a locker. 개인 소지품은 사물함에 보관해야 합니다.
→ '개인 소지품'이라는 의미이므로, personable(매력적인)이 아닌 personal(개인적인)이 와야 합니다.

● 형태가 비슷하지만 의미가 달라 혼동하기 쉬운 부사들을 알아두면 도움이 됩니다.

close 가까이에	closely 면밀히, 자세히	late 늦게	lately 최근에
hard 힘들게, 열심히	hardly 거의 ~않다	most 매우, 가장	mostly 대부분, 주로
high 높게	highly 매우, 대단히	near 가까이에	nearly 거의

The new electric vehicle model is (~~high~~, **highly**) popular among consumers.
새로운 전기차 모델은 소비자들 사이에서 매우 인기 있다.
→ '매우 인기 있다'라는 의미가 되어야 하므로 high(높게)가 아니라 highly(매우, 대단히)가 와야 합니다.

The stores stay open (~~lately~~, **late**) during the holiday season. 상점들은 휴가철 동안 늦게까지 열려 있다.
→ '늦게까지 열려 있다'라는 의미가 되어야 하므로 lately(최근에)가 아니라 late(늦게)가 와야 합니다.

실전 Check-up

01 After several attempts, the researchers finally conducted a ------- experiment.
(A) successful (B) successive

02 The committee ------- reviewed the proposal before making a decision.
(A) close (B) closely

정답·해석·해설 p.128

3초컷 정답 공식

자주 출제되는 정답 공식을 적용하여 빈칸에 가장 알맞은 보기를 고르세요.

정답공식 01 a(n)/the와 명사 사이에 빈칸이 있으면 형용사가 정답이다!

01 Ms. Davis gave an ------- lecture about the impact of global warming on the world's ecosystems.
(A) instructs (B) instructionally
(C) instruct   (D) instructive

02 The ------- regulations will be implemented next month to improve workplace safety.
(A) strict   (B) strictly
(C) strictness (D) stricture

정답공식 02 'make/keep + 목적어' 뒤에 빈칸이 있으면 형용사가 정답일 확률이 높다!

03 The policy made employees' schedules much more -------, allowing them to balance their professional and personal lives more effectively.
(A) flexibility (B) flexibly
(C) flexible   (D) flex

04 It is the company's responsibility to keep customer information ------- from unauthorized access.
(A) secure   (B) security
(C) securely (D) securing

정답공식 03 be동사/have동사와 p.p. 사이에 빈칸이 있으면 부사가 정답이다!

05 The Web site will be ------- closed for system maintenance from 2 A.M. to 4 A.M.
(A) briefs (B) briefing
(C) brief   (D) briefly

06 The company has ------- opened a branch office in the business district.
(A) conveniently (B) convenient
(C) conveniences (D) convenience

정답공식 04 문장에 although나 despite가 있으면 still을 정답으로 고른다!

07 Despite the advancement of digital payment methods, some consumers ------- prefer using cash.
(A) still (B) once
(C) soon   (D) ago

08 Although the restaurant was renovated last year, it ------- needs further upgrades to meet new regulations.
(A) nearly (B) very
(C) still (D) much

HACKERS TEST

빈칸에 가장 알맞은 보기를 고르세요.

01 The planning committee representatives made a ------- decision to postpone the event until the end of the month.
(A) collects
(B) collection
(C) collective
(D) collectively

02 The smart watch is manufactured ------- for athletes and has many specialized functions.
(A) excluding
(B) exclusive
(C) exclusively
(D) exclusion

03 The additional funding from the government will make the research project -------.
(A) possible
(B) possibly
(C) possibility
(D) possibilities

04 The government has made ------- progress in expanding access to education in rural areas.
(A) considers
(B) to consider
(C) considerate
(D) considerable

05 Our customer service department is ------- ready to assist you with any questions about your purchase.
(A) always
(B) formerly
(C) shortly
(D) early

06 As part of their ------- routine, the technicians conduct maintenance inspections on factory equipment.
(A) normality
(B) normally
(C) normal
(D) normalize

07 The Bloomfield Science Library in Texas is ------- prepared to host the academic conference next month.
(A) completely
(B) complete
(C) completed
(D) completion

08 Following a schedule can keep employees involved in group projects -------.
(A) productive
(B) productivity
(C) produce
(D) produces

09 For this position, we need a ------- qualified professional with at least five years of relevant industry experience.
(A) higher
(B) high
(C) highly
(D) highest

10 The movie reviewer is known for being ------- of popular Hollywood productions in his weekly column.
(A) criticize
(B) criticism
(C) critically
(D) critical

11 *Millions of Viewers* will return ------- for a new season with exciting episodes.
(A) usually
(B) so
(C) soon
(D) almost

12 Employees are required to update their ------- information in the company database before the end of the year.
(A) persons
(B) personal
(C) personable
(D) personality

13. Mayor Linford ------- developed the plan to reduce traffic congestion in the downtown area.
    (A) he
    (B) his
    (C) him
    (D) himself

14. After analyzing market trends, the company found that expanding into new regions would be -------.
    (A) proficient
    (B) profits
    (C) profitable
    (D) proficiently

15. Sales of luxury vehicles fell ------- during the fourth quarter of last year due to a reduction in consumer spending.
    (A) signifying
    (B) signifies
    (C) significant
    (D) significantly

16. It is ------- that patients follow their doctor's recommendations if they want to maintain their health.
    (A) essence
    (B) essential
    (C) essentials
    (D) essentially

17. Despite the recent economic downturn, TechNova Corporation ------- maintains a strong position in the international market.
    (A) still
    (B) due to
    (C) seldom
    (D) too

18. The shipping manager believes that the Destinations software application would be ------- for tracking customers' packages.
    (A) use
    (B) useful
    (C) using
    (D) user

19. The Elmsborough town council announced a plan to build a park at a site that was ------- an industrial area.
    (A) ago
    (B) here
    (C) approximately
    (D) once

20. The ------- of the furniture was easy thanks to the detailed instructions.
    (A) assembly
    (B) assemblies
    (C) assemble
    (D) assembler

21. The construction of the new office building is ------- complete, with only the interior finishing work remaining.
    (A) near
    (B) nearly
    (C) nearer
    (D) nearest

22. The final agreement must be ------- to both parties before they can proceed with signing the contract.
    (A) accept
    (B) accepts
    (C) acceptable
    (D) acceptance

23. Many mechanics recommend using Haskell's motor oil over any other brand to help car engines run more -------.
    (A) smoothed
    (B) smoother
    (C) smoothly
    (D) smoothest

24. The elevator repair work is ------- 90 percent complete and should be finished by next week.
    (A) almost
    (B) seldom
    (C) frequently
    (D) ago

빈출 어휘 | 명사 3

☑ PART 5 어휘 문제에 자주 출제되는 어휘를 예문과 함께 확실히 익혀두세요.

01 **provision** 규정, 조항
a **provision** for early termination
조기 해지에 관한 규정

02 **assembly** 조립, 집회
complete the **assembly** of the furniture
가구 조립을 완료하다
[파] **assemble** 조립하다

03 **responsibility** 책임, 책무
take **responsibility** for dealing with the issue
문제를 처리하는 것에 대해 책임을 지다
[파] **responsible** 책임 있는

04 **permission** 허락, 승인
ask for **permission** before using the facility
시설을 사용하기 전에 허락을 구하다
[파] **permit** 허락하다

05 **addition** 추가, 덧붙임
the **addition** of a lounge to the lobby
로비에 휴게 공간 추가
[파] **additional** 추가적인

06 **direction** 지시, 방향
under the **direction** of the supervisor
상사의 지시 하에
[파] **direct** 지시하다

07 **cargo** 화물, 적재물
transport the **cargo** to the distribution center
화물을 배송 센터로 운송하다

08 **capability** 역량, 능력
build the **capability** to detect security threats
보안 위협을 감지할 수 있는 역량을 구축하다
[파] **capable** 능력 있는 [동] **ability** 능력

09 **assignment** 배정, 과제
receive a challenging work **assignment**
도전적인 업무 배정을 받다
[파] **assign** 할당하다

10 **status** 상태, 지위
check the **status** of your order online
주문 상태를 온라인으로 확인하다

11 **reminder** 알림, 상기시키는 것
send a **reminder** about the upcoming meeting
다가오는 회의에 대한 알림을 보내다
[파] **remind** 상기시키다

12 **treatment** 대우, 치료
provide fair **treatment** to employees
직원들에게 공정한 대우를 하다
[파] **treat** 대우하다, 치료하다

13 **creation** 창작(물)
the **creation** of a new logo for the company
회사를 위한 새로운 로고의 창작
[파] **create** 창조하다

14 **practitioner** 전문가, 개업의
consult legal **practitioners** about the issue
그 주제에 관해 법률 전문가들과 상담하다

15 **operation** 작동, 운영
the packaging machine in **operation**
작동 중인 포장 기계
[파] **operate** 작동하다

16 **longevity** 수명, 장수
ensure the **longevity** of the product
제품의 수명을 보장하다

17 **material** 재료, 자료

buy the raw **material** from local suppliers
지역 공급업체들로부터 원재료를 구입하다

18 **cooperation** 협력, 협동

strengthen **cooperation** with overseas partners
해외 동업자들과의 협력을 강화하다
파 cooperate 협력하다

19 **credentials** 자격 증명, 신임장

verify the **credentials** of all applicants
모든 지원자의 자격 증명을 확인하다

20 **reservation** 예약, 보류

cancel the **reservation** for the banquet hall
연회장 예약을 취소하다
파 reserve 예약하다

토익 실전문제

01 Ms. Takahashi made a last-minute ------- at the Arden Heights Hotel for the visiting executives.

(A) requirement
(B) reservation
(C) treatment
(D) accommodation

02 The software enhances our ------- to analyze large volumes of customer data quickly.

(A) capability
(B) longevity
(C) resolution
(D) deadline

03 Due to a technical issue, the machine's ------- had to be paused until the repair crew arrived.

(A) location
(B) status
(C) operation
(D) break

04 The company will run a special ------- during the holiday season to boost sales of its smartphone.

(A) statement
(B) creation
(C) conservation
(D) promotion

05 Job applicants must submit their educational ------- before the interview.

(A) instructions
(B) reactions
(C) credentials
(D) registrations

06 The newly hired employees must be trained to handle their professional ------- effectively.

(A) talks
(B) components
(C) reminders
(D) responsibilities

07 The furniture retailer provides detailed manuals to help customers with ------- of its products.

(A) direction
(B) contact
(C) assembly
(D) coverage

08 Several ------- in the rental contract specify the tenant's duties for maintaining the property in good condition.

(A) provisions
(B) characteristics
(C) priorities
(D) recommendations

정답·해석·해설 p.131

DAY 04 전치사

매회 3~4문제 출제

on the desk 책상 위에
전치사

under the desk 책상 아래에
전치사

'on the desk'와 'under the desk'에서 단어 하나로 사과의 위치가 달라집니다. 이와 같이 명사나 대명사 앞에서 시간, 위치, 방향 등을 나타내는 것을 **전치사**라고 합니다.

기출 포인트 01 전치사가 오는 자리

● 전치사는 명사나 대명사, 동명사와 같은 명사 역할을 하는 것 앞에 옵니다.

명사 앞	Please place the signed form **on** the <u>table</u>. 서명한 양식을 탁자 위에 놓아 주세요. 　　　　　　　　　　　　　　　　　명사	
대명사 앞	A discussion was held **about** <u>it</u>. 토론이 그것에 대해 진행되었다. 　　　　　　　　　　　　　대명사	
동명사 앞	She met the deadline **by** <u>working</u> late. 그녀는 야근을 함으로써 마감 기한을 맞췄다. 　　　　　　　　　　　　동명사	

● '전치사 + 명사/대명사' 형태의 말 덩어리인 전치사구는 문장에서 수식어 역할을 하여 문장 앞, 중간, 뒤에 올 수 있습니다.

문장 앞	**For decades**, he has served as CEO of Norview Technologies. 　전치사구 수십 년 동안, 그는 Norview Technologies사의 최고 경영자로 근무해 왔다.	
문장 중간	The computer **near the window** is broken. 창문 근처에 있는 컴퓨터는 고장 났다. 　　　　　　　전치사구	
문장 뒤	Some candidates were nervous **during the interview**. 일부 지원자들은 면접 중에 긴장했다. 　　　　　　　　　　　　　　　　전치사구	

실전 Check-up

01 The sales team will travel ------- Seoul for an important meeting next week.

　(A) to　　　　　　　(B) last

02 The doctor has appointments with patients ------- 4 P.M. today.

　(A) still　　　　　　(B) until

정답·해석·해설 p.132

기출 포인트 02 시간 전치사

● 전치사 at, on, in은 모두 '~(때)에'로 해석되지만, at은 시각 앞에, on은 날짜나 요일 앞에, in은 연도·월·계절 등의 앞에 옵니다.

in	연도·월·계절· 오전/오후/저녁 앞	**in** 2023 2023년에 **in** winter 겨울에	**in** October 10월에 **in** the morning/afternoon/evening 오전/오후/저녁에
on	날짜·요일·특정한 날 앞	**on** April 18 4월 18일에 **on** Monday morning 월요일 아침에	**on** Friday 금요일에 **on** Christmas Day 크리스마스에
at	시각·시점 앞	**at** 3 o'clock 3시 정각에 **at** the beginning/end of the month 월초/월말에	**at** noon/night/midnight 정오/밤/자정에

● 시점을 나타내는 전치사는 특정 시점을 나타내는 표현 앞에 옵니다.

before/prior to ~ 전에		
after ~ 후에		
since ~ 이래로	+	시점 표현 (tomorrow, 5 P.M. 등)
by/until ~까지		
from ~부터		

Mr. Thompson should finish the project **before** September. Mr. Thompson은 9월 전에 프로젝트를 끝내야 한다.

Golden Harvest Foods has expanded **since** 2022. Golden Harvest Foods사는 2022년 이래로 확장해왔다.

● 기간을 나타내는 전치사는 기간을 나타내는 표현 앞에 옵니다.

within ~ 이내에		
for/during ~ 동안	+	기간 표현 (the vacation, three weeks 등)
over/throughout ~ 동안, ~하는 내내		

* for는 숫자를 포함한 기간 표현 앞에 와서 '얼마나 오랫동안 지속되는지'를, during은 명사 앞에 와서 '언제 일어나는지'를 나타냅니다.

All complaints need to be resolved **within** 24 hours. 모든 불만 사항은 24시간 이내에 해결되어야 한다.

Sales have steadily increased **over** the past five years. 매출은 지난 5년 동안 꾸준히 증가해 왔다.

실전 Check-up

01 The air-conditioning system can be put in sleep mode ------- night.

(A) at (B) on

02 Coster Securities does not permit the use of phones for personal reasons ------- working hours.

(A) during (B) without

기출포인트 03 장소·위치·방향 전치사

● 장소, 위치, 방향을 나타내는 전치사들의 의미를 구분하여 알아두면 도움이 됩니다.

장소	in + 큰 공간 내 장소 ~에	on + 표면 위, 층, 거리 ~에	at + 지점, 번지 ~에
위치	between (둘) 사이에 inside ~ 안에 behind ~ 뒤에	among (셋 이상) 사이에 within ~ 내에 beside ~ 옆에	outside ~ 밖에 above ~ 위에 near ~ 가까이, ~ 근처에
방향	to ~으로, ~ 쪽으로 along ~을 따라	toward ~ 쪽으로, ~을 향하여 across ~을 가로질러	from ~에서, ~으로부터 through ~을 통과하여, ~을 통해

The fashion show will be held **in** Mexico City next month. 패션쇼는 다음 달에 멕시코시티에서 열릴 것이다.

The ancient artifact is displayed **inside** a protective glass case. 고대 유물이 보호용 유리 케이스 안에 전시되어 있다.

The bridge stretches **across** the river, connecting the two cities. 다리는 두 도시를 연결하며, 강을 가로질러 뻗어 있다.

기출포인트 04 토익에 잘 나오는 전치사

● 이유, 양보, 목적, 제외, 부가 등을 나타내는 다양한 전치사들을 의미와 함께 알아두면 도움이 됩니다.

이유	due to ~ 때문에, ~으로 인해 because of ~ 때문에	**due to** bad weather 악천후로 인해 **because of** delivery delays 배송 지연 때문에
양보	despite ~에도 불구하고 in spite of ~에도 불구하고	**despite** the higher price 더 높은 가격에도 불구하고 **in spite of** the difficulty 어려움에도 불구하고
목적	for ~을 위해	**for** your safety 여러분의 안전을 위해
제외	except (for) ~을 제외하고는 without ~ 없이	**except (for)** holidays 휴일을 제외하고는 **without** additional information 추가적인 정보 없이
부가	in addition to ~에 더하여 besides ~ 외에도	**in addition to** the recommendation 추천서에 더하여 **besides** managers 관리자들 외에도
기타	about ~에 관한, ~에 대한 by ~함으로써, ~에 의해 with ~을 가지고, ~와 함께 according to ~에 따라 following ~에 이어 as ~로서 such as ~과 같은 against ~에 반대하여, ~에 기대어	**about** the new policy 새 정책에 관한 **by** reducing costs 비용을 줄임으로써 **with** a valid ID 유효한 신분증을 가지고 **according to** the contract 계약에 따라 **following** the presentation 발표에 이어 **as** a team leader 팀장으로서 **such as** laptops and tablets 노트북과 태블릿과 같은 **against** the proposal 제안에 반대하여

실전 Check-up

01 The client is flying ------ Manila to the company's main office in Tokyo for the conference.

(A) by (B) from

02 A workshop ------ time management will be held in Room 3.

(A) about (B) following

3초컷 정답 공식

자주 출제되는 정답 공식을 적용하여 빈칸에 가장 알맞은 보기를 고르세요.

정답공식 01 빈칸 뒤에 셋 이상을 뜻하는 복수 명사가 있으면 among이 정답일 확률이 높다!

01 There is growing competition ------- smartphone brands in the global market.
(A) within (B) from
(C) among   (D) over

02 The charity distributed food supplies ------- the families affected by the flood.
(A) between (B) among
(C) toward   (D) despite

정답공식 02 시제가 '과거부터 ~해왔다'라는 의미의 현재완료(have p.p.)이면 since가 정답이다!

03 The IT department has not received any system error reports ------- the latest software update.
(A) since   (B) outside
(C) to   (D) throughout

04 Ms. Park has worked as the marketing director at Greenest Organics ------- its founding in 2020.
(A) along   (B) until
(C) before (D) since

정답공식 03 빈칸 뒤에 '시간 to 시간'이 있으면 from, '시간 and 시간'이 있으면 between이 정답이다!

05 The Ferndale Diner's popular lunch special is only available ------- 12 to 1 P.M. on weekdays.
(A) from   (B) with
(C) between (D) for

06 The training session will be held ------- 9 A.M. and 4 P.M., with a one-hour lunch break.
(A) to   (B) over
(C) between (D) like

정답공식 04 'business hours' 앞에는 during, 'business days' 앞에는 within을 정답으로 고른다!

07 The support team is available ------- business hours to assist you with any issues.
(A) during   (B) toward
(C) against (D) by

08 The refund will be processed and sent to your account ------- five business days.
(A) into   (B) within
(C) across   (D) between

정답·해석·해설 p.133

HACKERS TEST

빈칸에 가장 알맞은 보기를 고르세요.

01 To apply for a library card, please proceed to the service desk ------- the second floor.
(A) on
(B) as
(C) at
(D) against

02 Free copies of Richard Lucas's new book, *Lens Explorer*, will be handed out to guests ------- his photo exhibit at El Patio Museum.
(A) toward
(B) between
(C) since
(D) during

03 Bobby Ortega was chosen to be the plant supervisor ------- his excellent leadership and organizational skills.
(A) due to
(B) despite
(C) except
(D) against

04 ------- full transportation and accommodations, the tour package includes two daily meals.
(A) Prior to
(B) In spite of
(C) In addition to
(D) According to

05 The maintenance team is scheduled to complete all repairs ------- business hours today.
(A) through
(B) until
(C) along
(D) during

06 Few people know ------- the city government's decision to increase fines for illegal parking.
(A) about
(B) at
(C) with
(D) toward

07 Running daily ------- 1 P.M. to 4 P.M., Urban Travel's guided tour of Greenwich Village is popular with visitors.
(A) until
(B) before
(C) by
(D) from

08 The airport is ------- the city center, making it easy for travelers to reach their flights quickly.
(A) near
(B) for
(C) following
(D) outside

09 Riverpoint Logistics' stock price increased significantly ------- the announcement of positive quarterly results.
(A) from
(B) after
(C) about
(D) despite

10 The ingredients are listed ------- the nutritional information on the back of the package.
(A) above
(B) into
(C) out
(D) until

11 Financial experts have not seen ------- indications that the global economy has come out of the recession.
(A) firm
(B) firmly
(C) firms
(D) firmness

12 Pullman Design has hired over 20 new employees ------- the move to its new office last summer.
(A) by
(B) since
(C) with
(D) outside

13 Vendors are permitted to set up stalls ------- either side of the lane but must leave the middle open for pedestrians.
(A) along
(B) below
(C) toward
(D) over

14 Visitors to the Coleman Gallery were instructed to park ------- the building while the main parking lot was being repaved.
(A) between
(B) through
(C) among
(D) behind

15 Housing prices in this neighborhood have increased by 30 percent ------- the last five years.
(A) about
(B) over
(C) into
(D) until

16 The only replaceable components ------- the laptop are the battery and hard drive.
(A) between
(B) above
(C) inside
(D) after

17 Please make sure to return all rental equipment ------- 5 P.M. on the day of use.
(A) in
(B) by
(C) to
(D) within

18 Ms. Safi will be unavailable to meet with clients this afternoon ------- her dental appointment.
(A) because of
(B) according to
(C) such as
(D) in spite of

19 Mr. Dreyfuss remains ------- active at tourism industry events even though he has retired.
(A) notice
(B) noticed
(C) noticeable
(D) noticeably

20 ------- her busy schedule, Ms. Harris has agreed to be the keynote speaker at next month's bioengineering conference.
(A) Despite
(B) Across
(C) Above
(D) Between

21 The homeowner approved of all aspects of the renovation plan ------- the choice of tiles for the floor.
(A) according to
(B) near
(C) against
(D) except for

22 Charlie Curran is ------- the business leaders selected to participate in this Friday's panel talk.
(A) onto
(B) through
(C) among
(D) for

23 ------- three business days of receiving your application, our team will contact you to schedule an interview.
(A) Within
(B) Besides
(C) Over
(D) Behind

24 The market was too challenging for Quantanet, so the business failed ------- the owner's efforts to increase profits.
(A) due to
(B) except for
(C) in spite of
(D) in addition to

빈출 어휘 | 명사 4

✅ PART 5 어휘 문제에 자주 출제되는 어휘를 예문과 함께 확실히 익혀두세요.

01 **enrollment** 등록, 가입
announce the period for **enrollment**
등록 기간을 공지하다
[파] enroll 등록하다

02 **adjustment** 조정, 적응
make an **adjustment** to the schedule
일정에 대해 조정을 하다
[파] adjustable 조정 가능한

03 **condition** 상태, 조건
return the equipment in its original **condition**
장비를 원래 상태로 반납하다

04 **definition** 정의, 설명
provide a clear and concise **definition**
명확하고 간결한 정의를 제공하다
[파] define 정의하다

05 **opposition** 반대, 대립
public **opposition** to the policy
정책에 대한 대중의 반대
[파] oppose 반대하다

06 **circumstance** 상황, 환경
adapt to changing **circumstances** in the market
시장의 변화하는 상황에 적응하다
[동] situation 상황

07 **membership** 회원 자격, 회원(권)
renew your gym **membership** for another year
헬스장 회원 자격을 일 년 더 갱신하다

08 **specifications** 명세서, 사양
check the product **specifications** before purchase
구매 전에 제품 명세서를 확인하다
[파] specify 명시하다

09 **restriction** 제한, 규제
impose **restrictions** on overtime hours
초과 근무 시간에 제한을 두다
[파] restrict 제한하다

10 **association** 제휴, 협회
in **association** with a trusted partner
신뢰받는 동업자와 제휴하여
[파] associate 연관 짓다

11 **capacity** (생산) 능력, 수용력
increase the production **capacity** of the factory
공장의 생산 능력을 증가시키다

12 **authorization** 승인, 허가
obtain **authorization** to access secure files
보안 파일에 접근할 수 있는 승인을 받다
[파] authorize 승인하다

13 **formula** 제조법, 공식
develop a **formula** for an eco-friendly cleaner
친환경 세정제의 제조법을 개발하다

14 **revenue** 수입, 매출
additional **revenue** from a new market
새로운 시장으로부터의 추가 수입
[동] income 수입

15 **accomplishment** 성과, 업적
celebrate the great **accomplishment** of the team
팀의 훌륭한 성과를 축하하다
[파] accomplish 성취하다 [동] achievement 업적

16 **mission** 임무, 사명
fulfill the **mission** of the organization
조직의 임무를 수행하다

17 warranty 보증(서)

extend the **warranty** on electronic products
전자 제품에 대한 보증을 연장하다

18 reentry 재입장, 복귀

allow **reentry** into the exhibition hall
전시회장에 재입장을 허용하다

19 explanation 설명, 해명

a detailed **explanation** of roles and responsibilities
역할과 책임에 대한 상세한 설명

[파] explain 설명하다

20 distribution 유통, 배포

manage the **distribution** process
유통 과정을 관리하다

[파] distribute 유통시키다, 배포하다

토익 실전문제

01 The new airport security measures include additional ------- on carry-on luggage.
(A) options (B) reentries
(C) restrictions (D) preparations

02 Dr. Patel is a respected healthcare ------- specializing in preventive medicine.
(A) practitioner (B) proficiency
(C) association (D) position

03 The power plant operates at full ------- during periods of peak energy demand.
(A) capacity (B) warranty
(C) adjustment (D) resistance

04 Oakwood Golf Club offers corporate ------- packages for businesses in the area.
(A) authorization (B) membership
(C) formula (D) disclosure

05 The quarterly financial report shows that ------- has increased by 15 percent compared to last year.
(A) specification (B) circumstance
(C) feedback (D) revenue

06 The ------- of our company is to develop sustainable products for the automotive industry.
(A) application (B) evaluation
(C) mission (D) approval

07 The CEO recognized Ms. Garcia's significant ------- in expanding the company's global reach.
(A) guide (B) accomplishment
(C) payment (D) criticism

08 Despite strong ------- from local residents, the city council approved the construction project.
(A) opportunity (B) usage
(C) enrollment (D) opposition

정답·해석·해설 p.136

DAY 05 동사의 형태와 수일치

매회 0~1문제 출제

A penguin stands.
　단수 주어　단수 동사

Penguins stand.
　복수 주어　복수 동사

주어가 단수인 A penguin일 때는 단수 동사 stands를 쓰고, 주어가 복수인 Penguins 일 때는 복수 동사 stand를 씁니다.
'stand, stands'처럼 **동사의 형태**를 바꾸어 나타낼 수 있으며, 주어의 수에 따라 동사 의 수를 일치시키는 것을 **수일치**라고 합니다.

기출포인트 01 동사의 형태

- 조동사(will, can, should 등) 바로 뒤나 3인칭 단수를 제외한 주어(I, you, we, they) 뒤에서 동사가 현재를 나타낼 때는 동사원형이 옵니다. 또한, 주어 없이 동사로 시작되는 명령문의 동사 자리에 동사원형이 옵니다.

  We will travel next summer. 우리는 다음 여름에 여행할 것이다.
  　　조동사
  Submit your résumé by March 15. 3월 15일까지 귀하의 이력서를 제출해 주십시오.

- 3인칭 주어(he, she, it) 뒤에서 동사가 현재를 나타낼 때는 3인칭 단수형(동사원형 + -(e)s)이 옵니다.

  It rains a lot in this region. 이 지역에서는 비가 많이 온다.
  3인칭 단수 주어

- 주어와 상관없이 동사가 과거를 나타낼 때는 동사의 과거형(동사원형 + ed)이 옵니다.

  Ms. Russell accepted the job offer last month. Ms. Russell은 지난달에 구직 제안을 수락했다.

- be동사 뒤에는 동사의 현재분사형(동사원형 + -ing)/과거분사형(동사원형 + -ed/불규칙 변화)이 오고, have동사 뒤에는 과거분사형이 옵니다.

  The sales team is preparing for the annual trade show. 영업팀은 연례 무역 박람회를 준비하고 있다.
  　　　　　　be동사　현재분사형
  The CEO has asked the staff to reduce expenses. 최고 경영자는 직원들에게 비용을 줄이도록 요청했다.
  　　　have동사 과거분사형

실전 Check-up

01 Visitors can ------- the art gallery for free on the first Sunday of every month.

　(A) enter　　　　　(B) enters

02 The marketing director has ------- the company's quarterly report.

　(A) present　　　　(B) presented

정답·해석·해설 p.136

기출포인트 02 단수 동사와 복수 동사

● 단수 동사는 단수 주어가 나올 때 쓰는 동사로 3인칭 단수형을 쓰고, 복수 동사는 복수 주어가 나올 때 쓰는 동사로 동사원형을 그대로 씁니다. 그러나 단수 동사와 복수 동사의 구분은 현재형일 때에만 해당되고, 과거형일 때는 동일합니다.

The machine **operates** smoothly. 그 기계는 부드럽게 작동한다.
_{단수 주어 / 단수 동사}

Many students **use** the library. 많은 학생이 그 도서관을 이용한다.
_{복수 주어 / 복수 동사}

기출포인트 03 단수 주어와 단수 동사의 수일치

● 단수 가산 명사와 불가산 명사는 단수 주어로 취급되어 뒤에 단수 동사가 와야 합니다.

The brochure **describes** several tourist attractions. 그 안내 책자는 여러 관광지를 설명한다.
_{단수 가산 명사 / 단수 동사}

Your feedback **helps** improve our service. 당신의 의견은 저희 서비스를 개선하는 데 도움이 됩니다.
_{불가산 명사 / 단수 동사}

● '~하는 것'으로 해석되는 긴 말 덩어리(동명사구, to 부정사, 명사절)는 단수 주어로 취급되어 뒤에 단수 동사가 와야 합니다.

Traveling abroad **broadens** my perspective. 해외여행을 하는 것은 나의 시야를 넓힌다.
_{동명사구 / 단수 동사}

● 'each/every + 단수 명사'는 단수 주어로 취급되어 뒤에 단수 동사가 와야 합니다.

Each room **has** a window. 각 방에는 창문이 있다.
_{each + 단수 명사 / 단수 동사}

Every guest **receives** a welcome gift. 모든 손님은 환영 선물을 받는다.
_{every + 단수 명사 / 단수 동사}

기출포인트 04 복수 주어와 복수 동사의 수일치

● 복수 가산 명사는 복수 주어이므로 뒤에 복수 동사가 와야 합니다.

The athletes **train** every morning. 그 운동선수들은 매일 아침에 훈련한다.
_{복수 주어 / 복수 동사}

● 'several/many/a few + 복수 명사'는 복수 주어로 취급되어 뒤에 복수 동사가 와야 합니다.

Several cars **are parked** in the garage. 몇 대의 자동차가 차고에 주차되어 있다.
_{several + 복수 명사 / 복수 동사}

Many tourists **visit** this city every year. 많은 관광객이 매년 이 도시를 방문한다.
_{many + 복수 명사 / 복수 동사}

A few volunteers **are helping** with the cleanup. 몇몇 자원봉사자들이 청소를 돕고 있다.
_{a few + 복수 명사 / 복수 동사}

실전 Check-up

01 Each proposal ------- approval from both the department manager and the executive committee.

(A) needs (B) need

02 The current catalogs ------- available for online viewing on our company's Web site.

(A) are (B) is

정답·해석·해설 p.136

기출포인트 05 주의해야 할 주어와 동사의 수일치

- 'the number of + 복수 명사(~의 수)'는 단수 주어로 취급되어 뒤에 단수 동사가 오고, 'a number of + 복수 명사(많은 ~)'는 복수 주어로 취급되어 뒤에 복수 동사가 와야 합니다.

    The number of tourists (~~decrease~~, **decreases**) during winter. 관광객들의 수는 겨울 동안 감소한다.
    _{the number of + 복수 명사   복수(X)   단수(O)}

    A number of changes (~~was~~, **were**) made to the original design. 원래 디자인에 많은 변경사항들이 이루어졌다.
    _{a number of + 복수 명사   단수(X) 복수(O)}

- 'most/all/some/half/the rest + of 명사'가 주어로 오면 of 뒤의 명사에 동사를 수일치합니다.

    | most/all/some/half/the rest | + of + | 단수/불가산 명사 + 단수 동사 |
    | | | 복수 명사 + 복수 동사 |

    Some of the information (~~include~~, **includes**) errors. 일부 정보에 오류가 포함되어 있다.
    _{some + of + 불가산 명사   복수(X)   단수(O)}

    Most of the books (~~contains~~, **contain**) pictures. 그 책들 대부분에는 그림이 들어 있다.
    _{most + of + 복수 명사   단수(X)   복수(O)}

- 주어와 동사 사이에 수식어가 온 경우 수식어는 주어와 동사의 수일치에 전혀 영향을 주지 않으므로 주의합니다.

    The employees in the office (~~handles~~, **handle**) customer inquiries. 사무실에 있는 직원들은 고객 문의를 처리한다.
    _{복수   수식어   단수(X)   복수(O)}

실전 Check-up

01 A number of musicians ------- regularly at the downtown jazz club on weekend evenings.

(A) performs　　　　(B) perform

02 Some of the restaurants ------- delivery services through the new mobile app.

(A) offer　　　　(B) offers

3초컷 정답 공식

자주 출제되는 정답 공식을 적용하여 빈칸에 가장 알맞은 보기를 고르세요.

정답공식 01 조동사 will/may/should/can 뒤의 빈칸에는 동사원형이 들어가야 한다!

01 The new policy will ------- all employees starting next month.
(A) affecting   (B) affects
(C) affected   (D) affect

02 Staff members should ------- their ID cards at all times while in the office.
(A) wears   (B) wearing
(C) wear   (D) worn

정답공식 02 주어 없이 동사로 시작하는 명령문의 동사 자리에는 동사원형을 정답으로 고른다!

03 To assemble the product properly, ------- the instructions carefully.
(A) read   (B) reading
(C) reads   (D) to read

04 Please ------- your dietary restrictions when making a reservation.
(A) specifies   (B) specify
(C) specifying   (D) specification

정답공식 03 사람 이름이나 회사명과 같은 고유명사가 주어로 오면 단수 동사가 정답이다!

05 Architect Jennifer Wu ------- sustainable building designs for urban development projects worldwide.
(A) creates   (B) create
(C) have created (D) creation

06 Melodify Tech ------- a three-month free trial period for its streaming music service.
(A) granting   (B) are granting
(C) grants   (D) grant

정답공식 04 'those/복수 명사 + who' 뒤에 빈칸이 나오면 복수 동사를 정답으로 고른다!

07 Museum patrons who ------- to participate in the tour should register at the information desk.
(A) wish   (B) is wishing
(C) to wish   (D) wishes

08 Those who ------- licensed versions of the software are automatically qualified to upgrade to the latest one for free.
(A) owns   (B) own
(C) owning   (D) has owned

HACKERS TEST

빈칸에 가장 알맞은 보기를 고르세요.

01 The Grand Azure Hotel will ------- a free shuttle service for guests staying more than three nights.
(A) provides
(B) providing
(C) provide
(D) provided

02 The CEO is ------- expanding operations in the Asian market next year.
(A) consider
(B) considers
(C) consideration
(D) considering

03 Greenleaf Organic Food ------- locally sourced products to health-conscious consumers nationwide.
(A) distributes
(B) distribute
(C) distributing
(D) have distributed

04 Please ------- the Web site to sign up for the upcoming webinar and secure your spot.
(A) visit
(B) visits
(C) visiting
(D) visited

05 Several users ------- constantly about the new online payment system.
(A) complains
(B) complain
(C) has complained
(D) complaining

06 Ms. Lindstrom's blog serves as a useful ------- for gardeners who have little experience caring for plants.
(A) guide
(B) guider
(C) guided
(D) to guide

07 The customer satisfaction survey ------- to show that improved service response times are needed.
(A) to appear
(B) appears
(C) appearing
(D) appearance

08 We ------- that visitors use the designated parking areas during busy hours.
(A) recommend
(B) recommends
(C) recommending
(D) recommendation

09 Passengers who ------- to check additional luggage will be charged an extra fee.
(A) choose
(B) chooses
(C) choosing
(D) has chosen

10 The candidates ------- impressive educational backgrounds and relevant experience.
(A) has been
(B) has
(C) having
(D) have

11 The cultural festival ------- traditional performances from 20 different countries.
(A) featuring
(B) feature
(C) features
(D) being featured

12 The notice regarding updated safety procedures ------- in all workshop areas.
(A) has been posted
(B) were posted
(C) posting
(D) post

13 Patrons of the museum are not permitted to take photographs ------- special permission from the curator.

(A) across
(B) without
(C) over
(D) within

14 Later models of the vehicle ------- to have better fuel efficiency than the earlier ones.

(A) tend
(B) tends
(C) has tended
(D) to tend

15 The June issue of *Business Monthly* ------- an interview with the CEO of NexTech Solutions, James Wilson.

(A) includes
(B) include
(C) including
(D) to be included

16 Temperature records ------- that March was unusually warm this year.

(A) indication
(B) indicates
(C) indicating
(D) indicate

17 David Clark ------- international economics to graduate students every semester.

(A) to teach
(B) teach
(C) teaching
(D) teaches

18 All of the performers ------- additional rehearsals before the play's opening night.

(A) demands
(B) demand
(C) demanding
(D) is demanding

19 Every department ------- to submit monthly reports by the end of this week.

(A) require
(B) requiring
(C) is required
(D) are required

20 Spart-Gym has ------- its upcoming event to attract more members.

(A) publicity
(B) publicizing
(C) public
(D) publicized

21 A few technicians ------- remotely to maintain system stability during off-hours.

(A) works
(B) has been worked
(C) is working
(D) work

22 Those who ------- their expense reports late will not be reimbursed until the following month.

(A) submit
(B) submits
(C) submitting
(D) is submitted

23 The members of the Help-A-Neighbor Organization ------- a variety of local charitable groups.

(A) supportive
(B) supports
(C) supporting
(D) support

24 The increasing number of international tourists ------- the country's global reputation.

(A) reflects
(B) reflect
(C) reflecting
(D) are reflecting

빈출 어휘 | 동사 1

PART 5 어휘 문제에 자주 출제되는 어휘를 예문과 함께 확실히 익혀두세요.

01 **provide** 제공하다
provide sufficient information to investors
투자자들에게 충분한 정보를 제공하다

02 **submit** 제출하다
submit an evaluation of the new employee
신입 직원의 평가를 제출하다
[파] submission 제출, 항복 [동] hand in 제출하다

03 **announce** 발표하다
announce a final decision about the merger
합병에 대한 최종 결정을 발표하다
[파] announcement 발표, 공지

04 **acquire** 취득하다, 얻다
acquire land to build a residential complex
주거 단지를 짓기 위해 토지를 취득하다
[파] acquisition 취득, 획득 [동] obtain 획득하다, 얻다

05 **protect** 보호하다
protect sensitive customer information
민감한 고객 정보를 보호하다
[파] protection 보호

06 **ensure** 보장하다
ensure that data is saved automatically
데이터가 자동으로 저장되는 것을 보장하다

07 **reschedule** 일정을 변경하다
reschedule the interview
면접 일정을 변경하다

08 **feature** 특징으로 삼다, 특별히 포함하다
feature the latest technology
최신 기술을 특징으로 삼다

09 **expand** 확장하다
expand operations into foreign countries
외국으로 운영을 확장하다
[파] expansion 확장, 확대

10 **secure** 확보하다, 보증하다
secure funding for the research project
연구 프로젝트를 위한 자금을 확보하다
[파] security 보안, 보장

11 **recruit** 모집하다
recruit skilled workers for the factory
공장을 위해 숙련된 근로자들을 모집하다
[파] recruitment 모집 [동] hire 고용하다

12 **absorb** 흡수하다
absorb excess moisture in the box
상자 안의 과도한 습기를 흡수하다

13 **determine** 알아내다, 결정하다
determine the cause of the malfunction
오작동의 원인을 알아내다
[파] determination 결정, 결단

14 **balance** 균형을 맞추다
balance work and personal life
일과 개인 생활의 균형을 맞추다

15 **commence** 시작하다
commence construction of the headquarters
본사의 건설을 시작하다
[파] commencement 시작 [동] begin 시작하다

16 **address** 연설하다, 다루다
address the residents in the main square
중앙 광장에서 주민들에게 연설하다
[동] speak to 연설하다, 말하다

17 notify 통지하다

notify participants of the venue change
참가자들에게 장소 변경을 통지하다

파 notification 통지 동 inform 통지하다, 알리다

18 encourage 격려하다

encourage staff to share innovative ideas
직원들이 혁신적인 아이디어를 공유하도록 격려하다

동 motivate 격려하다, 동기를 부여하다

19 outline 개요를 말하다

outline the project plan in the meeting
회의에서 프로젝트 계획의 개요를 말하다

20 predict 예측하다

predict sales trends for the next quarter
다음 분기의 판매 동향을 예측하다

파 prediction 예측 동 forecast 예측하다, 예보하다

토익 실전문제

01 The appointment with the interior decorator had to be ------- to Wednesday morning.
(A) expanded   (B) canceled
(C) admitted   (D) rescheduled

02 Novoris Enterprises is presently ------- engineers for a new mining project in Chile.
(A) insisting   (B) recruiting
(C) submitting   (D) composing

03 The wall panels used throughout the theater are designed to ------- excessive noise.
(A) press   (B) absorb
(C) wrap   (D) protect

04 Instructors at the Nolan Academy take steps to ------- that students learn to operate vehicles safely.
(A) ensure   (B) achieve
(C) predict   (D) assign

05 The gallery exhibit will ------- works by several promising young artists from across the country.
(A) occupy   (B) feature
(C) transfer   (D) organize

06 Ms. Porter will ------- the city council on May 11 to request funds for cleaning the polluted river.
(A) address   (B) present
(C) outline   (D) declare

07 To avoid becoming too stressed, Ms. Gomez makes a constant effort to ------- her personal and professional life.
(A) determine   (B) balance
(C) involve   (D) collect

08 Over 30 teams will compete in the three-day Bermuda Sailboat Race, which will ------- on May 25.
(A) monitor   (B) announce
(C) commence   (D) disclose

정답·해석·해설 p.140

DAY 06 동사의 종류와 태

매회 0~1문제 출제

나는 그림을 <u>그렸다</u>.
　　　　　　능동태

그림이 나에 의해 <u>그려졌다</u>.
　　　　　　　　수동태

'나는 그림을 그렸다'처럼 주어가 행위의 주체가 되는 것을 **능동태**라고 하고, '그림이 나에 의해 그려졌다'처럼 주어가 행위의 대상이 되는 것을 **수동태**라고 합니다.

동사에는 목적어를 필요로 하지 않는 **자동사**와 목적어가 필요한 **타동사**가 있는데, 능동태 문장의 목적어가 수동태 문장의 주어가 되므로 목적어를 가지는 타동사만 수동태가 될 수 있습니다.

기출포인트 01 자동사와 타동사

- 동사에는 목적어를 필요로 하지 않는 자동사와 목적어가 필요한 타동사가 있습니다.

  She **laughed**. 그녀가 웃었다.
  　　자동사

  John **plays tennis**. John은 테니스를 친다.
  　　타동사　목적어

- 자동사가 목적어를 취하기 위해서는 전치사가 필요합니다. 우리말 의미로는 전치사가 필요 없는 타동사 같지만 전치사와 함께 뒤에 목적어를 취하는 자동사들을 알아 둡니다.

account for ~에 대해 설명하다	depend on ~에 의지하다	participate in ~에 참가하다, ~에 참여하다
agree to/with/on ~에 동의하다	differ from ~과 다르다	react to ~에 반응하다
care for ~을 돌보다	listen to ~을 듣다	speak to ~에게 말하다
deal with ~을 처리하다, ~을 다루다	object to ~에 반대하다	talk about ~에 대해 이야기하다

  He (~~participated~~, **participated in**) a marathon. 그는 마라톤에 참가했다.

- 타동사가 목적어를 취하기 위해서는 전치사가 필요하지 않습니다. 우리말 의미로는 전치사가 필요한 자동사 같지만 뒤에 전치사를 쓰지 않는 타동사들을 알아 둡니다.

access ~에 접근하다	discuss ~에 대해 논의하다, 토론하다	accompany ~와 동반하다
emphasize ~에 대해 강조하다	approach ~에 다가가다	explain ~을 설명하다
approve ~을 승인하다	interview ~와 면접하다	check ~을 확인하다
oppose ~에 반대하다	contact ~와 연락하다	reach ~에 도착하다

  We (~~discussed about~~, **discussed**) the project deadline. 우리는 프로젝트 마감일에 대해 논의했다.

실전 Check-up

01 The quality-control team must ------ each product before it can be shipped to customers.

　　(A) agree　　　　　　(B) approve

02 Many local residents ------ to the construction of the new highway near the residential area.

　　(A) oppose　　　　　(B) object

정답·해석·해설 p.140

기출 포인트 02 능동태와 수동태

- 능동태는 '주어가 ~하다'라는 의미로, 주어가 행위의 주체일 때 씁니다. 수동태는 '주어가 ~되다/당하다'라는 의미로, 주어가 행위의 대상이 될 때 씁니다.

  Tom **cleaned** the house. Tom은 집을 청소했다.
  　　능동태

  The house **was cleaned** by Tom. 집이 Tom에 의해 청소되었다.
  　　　　　수동태

- 수동태의 기본 형태는 'be동사 + p.p.(과거분사)'입니다. 여기서 be동사는 주어의 수와 시제에 따라 형태가 달라집니다.

현재 수동형 과거 수동형 미래 수동형	am/is/are + p.p. was/were + p.p. will be + p.p.	is constructed 건설되다 was constructed 건설되었다 will be constructed 건설될 것이다
현재진행 수동형 과거진행 수동형	am/is/are + being + p.p. was/were + being + p.p.	is being renovated 개조되는 중이다 was being renovated 개조되는 중이었다
현재완료 수동형 과거완료 수동형 미래완료 수동형	have/has + been + p.p. had + been + p.p. will have been + p.p.	have been published 출판되었다 had been published 출판되었었다 will have been published 출판될 것이다

- 능동태 문장의 목적어는 수동태 문장에서 주어가 되고, 능동태 문장의 주어는 수동태 문장에서 보통 'by + 목적격'으로 바뀝니다.

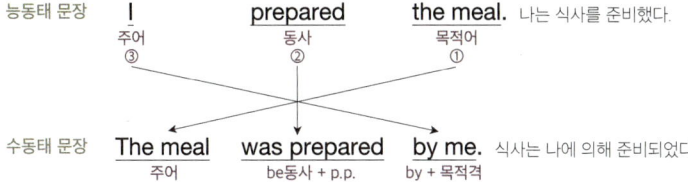

능동태 문장: I(주어③) prepared(동사②) the meal(목적어①). 나는 식사를 준비했다.

수동태 문장: The meal(주어) was prepared(be동사 + p.p.) by me(by + 목적격). 식사는 나에 의해 준비되었다.

① 목적어 the meal이 주어 자리로 온다.
② 동사 prepared를 주어의 수와 시제에 맞게 was prepared로 바꾼다.
③ 주어 I를 'by + 목적격'인 by me로 바꾼다.

실전 Check-up

01 The technician carefully ------- the equipment to ensure it was functioning properly.

(A) inspected　　　　(B) was inspected

02 Passengers ------- to check their surroundings for any items they may have left behind.

(A) remind　　　　(B) are reminded

정답·해석·해설 p.140

기출포인트 03 능동태와 수동태의 구별

● 동사 자리에 능동태가 오는지 수동태가 오는지는 동사 뒤의 목적어 유무에 따라 결정됩니다. 동사 뒤에 목적어가 있으면 능동태, 동사 뒤에 목적어가 없으면 수동태가 옵니다.

능동태   The company (was hired, **hired**) new employees.   그 회사는 새로운 직원들을 고용했다.
                        수동태(X)   능동태(O)   목적어

수동태   The budget (approved, **was approved**) by the manager.   예산은 관리자에 의해 승인되었다.
                      능동태(X)   수동태(O)

● 능동태 문장의 목적어가 수동태 문장의 주어가 되므로, 반드시 목적어를 가지는 타동사만 수동태가 될 수 있습니다. arrive(도착하다), occur(발생하다), rise(오르다)와 같은 자동사는 목적어를 갖지 않기 때문에 수동태가 될 수 없습니다.

The flight from Paris (was arrived, **arrived**) two hours late.   파리에서 출발한 비행기가 두 시간 늦게 도착했다.
→ 자동사(arrive)는 목적어를 갖지 않기 때문에 수동태가 될 수 없습니다.

기출포인트 04 토익에 잘 나오는 수동태 표현

● '수동태 동사 + 전치사' 표현

be engaged in ~에 종사하다, 관여하다	be interested in ~에 관심이 있다	be involved in ~에 관련되다
be dedicated/devoted to ~에 전념하다	be exposed to ~에 노출되다	be related to ~과 관계가 있다
be surprised at ~에 놀라다	be shocked at ~에 충격을 받다	be frightened at ~에 놀라다
be (dis)satisfied with ~에 (불)만족하다	be pleased with ~에 기뻐하다	be equipped with ~을 갖추고 있다

Ms. Garcia **is engaged in** social welfare research.   Ms. Garcia는 사회 복지 연구에 종사한다.
The dormitory **is equipped with** a comfortable study area.   기숙사는 편안한 학습 공간을 갖추고 있다.

● '수동태 동사 + to 부정사' 표현

be required to ~하도록 요구받다	be invited to ~할 것을 요청받다	be scheduled to ~할 예정이다
be allowed to ~하도록 허가받다	be expected to ~할 것으로 기대되다	be advised to ~할 것을 권고받다

Employees **are required to** wear safety gear in the factory.   직원들은 공장에서 안전 장비를 착용하도록 요구받는다.
She **was invited to** attend the international conference.   그녀는 국제 컨퍼런스에 참석할 것을 요청받았다.

실전 Check-up

01 The government inspector will be ------- through the research facility by the head of operations.

(A) escorted   (B) escorting

02 The supervisor was ------- with the performance of most of the trainees.

(A) satisfied   (B) satisfying

3초컷 정답 공식

자주 출제되는 정답 공식을 적용하여 빈칸에 가장 알맞은 보기를 고르세요.

정답공식 01
be동사와 by 사이에 빈칸이 있으면 수동태를 만드는 p.p.가 정답이다!

01 Several historical buildings were ------- by the hurricane that hit the coastal area.
(A) damaging (B) damaged
(C) damage   (D) damages

02 The ancient manuscript was ------- by archaeologists in an underground chamber.
(A) discovered (B) discovering
(C) discover   (D) to discover

정답공식 02
encourage/consider가 보기에 있으면 수동태가 정답일 확률이 높다!

03 Participants ------- to arrive at least 15 minutes early for the orientation session.
(A) encouraging   (B) encourage
(C) are encouraged (D) are encouraging

04 This performance review is ------- confidential and should not be shared with unauthorized personnel.
(A) considered   (B) consideration
(C) considering (D) considerable

정답공식 03
빈칸 뒤에 'as + 명사'가 있으면 수동태가 정답일 확률이 높다!

05 Ms. Tanaka ------- as the project leader of the international expansion team.
(A) was appointed (B) appointed
(C) appointing   (D) appoints

06 The medieval castle ------- as a treasure due to its unique architectural features and historical significance.
(A) to be regarded (B) regarding
(C) regards   (D) is regarded

정답공식 04
'~에 위치시키다'라는 의미를 가지는 동사가 보기에 있으면 수동태가 정답이다!

07 The luxury resort ------- on a private island with spectacular ocean views.
(A) situates   (B) is situating
(C) is situated (D) to situate

08 The main office of the company ------- in downtown Tokyo, close to several transportation facilities.
(A) have located   (B) locates
(C) to be located (D) is located

HACKERS TEST

빈칸에 가장 알맞은 보기를 고르세요.

01 The human resources department ------- approval from management before initiating the hiring process.
(A) to obtain (B) obtains
(C) is obtained (D) obtaining

02 All visitors seeking access to the research facility must be ------- by security personnel upon arrival.
(A) check (B) checks
(C) checking (D) checked

03 The Summit View Restaurant owner ------- as the head of the community business association.
(A) electing (B) was elected
(C) elects (D) elected

04 The admission fee of the amusement park ------- unlimited access to rides for a period of 14 hours.
(A) inclusive (B) including
(C) is included (D) includes

05 Vendors participating in the Midlands Craft Festival have been ------- to clearly display the prices of all items.
(A) instruct (B) instructs
(C) instructed (D) instructive

06 Volunteers in the clinical trial ------- to avoid eating for 12 hours before the medical test.
(A) are required (B) are requiring
(C) require (D) required

07 The materials for tomorrow's job fair ------- to the venue already.
(A) transporting (B) were transported
(C) will transport (D) had transported

08 The information desk ------- in the center of the shopping mall for easy access.
(A) will locate (B) locates
(C) is located (D) is locating

09 The committee is ------- an international trade forum that will take place in September.
(A) organize (B) organizes
(C) organized (D) organizing

10 Shutting down Web servers for ------- maintenance is vital as it can prevent system errors.
(A) periods (B) periodic
(C) periodically (D) periodicals

11 Due to inflation, the cost of living has been ------- steadily throughout this year.
(A) rise (B) rose
(C) rising (D) risen

12 Your reimbursement request ------- valid only if all required receipts are attached.
(A) considers (B) will consider
(C) is considering (D) will be considered

13 If you ------- with our products, you may return them within 30 days for a full refund.
(A) dissatisfying
(B) dissatisfy
(C) are dissatisfied
(D) dissatisfaction

14 Our recruitment team is currently ------- potential candidates for several IT department openings.
(A) interviewing
(B) interviews
(C) interviewed
(D) interview

15 The company's main production facilities ------- in industrial zones outside major metropolitan areas.
(A) situate
(B) are situated
(C) are situating
(D) will situate

16 Horizon BioTech Laboratory is ------- with advanced microscopes for detailed specimen analysis.
(A) equipped
(B) equips
(C) equipping
(D) equip

17 The winner of this raffle ------- a one-year membership package from Serenity Spa.
(A) receive
(B) receives
(C) receiving
(D) to receive

18 Travelers may be ------- at the sudden changes in weather conditions in this mountainous region.
(A) frighten
(B) frightens
(C) frightened
(D) frightening

19 Distinguished speakers from various industries ------- to share their expertise at the conference.
(A) invited
(B) were invited
(C) inviting
(D) were inviting

20 Mr. Powell is out of the office today, but he ------- on his mobile phone for any emergencies.
(A) reached
(B) may reach
(C) reaches
(D) can be reached

21 Customers are ------- to provide feedback about their shopping experience to help improve our services.
(A) encouraged
(B) encourage
(C) encouraging
(D) encouragement

22 Residents ------- large pieces of furniture to the city's waste disposal center on weekends only.
(A) bringing
(B) can be brought
(C) are brought
(D) can bring

23 Innovative Solutions Inc. ------- in various community outreach programs to support local businesses.
(A) is involved
(B) to involve
(C) involves
(D) involvement

24 The barriers preventing vehicles from accessing the Georgetown Bridge ------- as repairs to the structure were complete.
(A) removing
(B) removed
(C) were removing
(D) were removed

빈출 어휘 | 동사 2

PART 5 어휘 문제에 자주 출제되는 어휘를 예문과 함께 확실히 익혀두세요.

01 showcase 선보이다
showcase famous works of art
유명한 예술 작품들을 선보이다

02 offer 제공하다
offer technical support at no additional charge
추가 요금 없이 기술 지원을 제공하다

03 donate 기부하다
donate proceeds to charitable organizations
수익금을 자선단체에 기부하다
[파] **donation** 기부

04 confirm 확인하다
confirm that the order is correct
주문이 올바르다는 것을 확인하다
[파] **confirmation** 확인 [동] **verify** 확인하다, 검증하다

05 postpone 연기하다
postpone the introduction of a new system
새로운 시스템의 도입을 연기하다
[동] **delay** 연기하다

06 reduce 줄이다
reduce maintenance costs by 10 percent
유지보수 비용을 10퍼센트 줄이다
[파] **reduction** 감소

07 undergo 받다, 겪다
undergo major repairs due to water damage
누수 피해로 인해 대대적인 수리를 받다

08 depart 출발하다, 떠나다
depart from the hotel to the airport
호텔에서 공항으로 출발하다
[파] **departure** 출발 [동] **leave** 떠나다

09 approve 승인하다
approve the budget for the campaign
캠페인을 위한 예산을 승인하다
[파] **approval** 승인 [동] **authorize** 승인하다, 허가하다

10 lease 임대하다
lease office space near the financial district
금융 지구 근처에 사무실 공간을 임대하다

11 access 접근하다
access the database through secure servers
보안 서버를 통해 데이터베이스에 접근하다

12 analyze 분석하다
analyze sales records from previous quarters
이전 분기의 판매 기록을 분석하다
[파] **analyst** 분석가

13 divide 나누다
divide the project into three phases
프로젝트를 세 단계로 나누다
[파] **division** 분할, 구분 [반] **combine** 합치다

14 demonstrate 보여주다
demonstrate how to handle the device
기기를 다루는 방법을 보여주다
[파] **demonstration** 시연, 설명

15 signal 신호를 보내다
signal with a beep when there is an error
오류가 있으면 삐 소리로 신호를 보내다

16 maximize 최대화하다
maximize profits through efficient operations
효율적인 운영을 통해 이익을 최대화하다
[파] **maximization** 최대화 [반] **minimize** 최소화하다

17 **qualify** 자격을 갖추다

qualify for the extended warranty
연장된 보증을 위한 자격을 갖추다
[파] qualification 자격   [반] disqualify 자격을 박탈하다

18 **transform** 변화시키다, 변형시키다

transform beginners into skilled experts
초보자를 숙련된 전문가로 변화시키다
[파] transformation 변화, 변형

19 **compensate** 보상하다

compensate employees for relocation expenses
직원들에게 이전 비용을 보상하다
[파] compensation 보상

20 **soar** (가치·물가 등이) 급증하다, 치솟다

soar due to rising fuel prices
상승하는 연료비로 인해 급증하다
[파] soaring 급상승하는, 치솟은

토익 실전문제

01 Any changes to the marketing plan must be ------- by Mr. Osborne at the head office.
(A) donated   (B) responded
(C) approved   (D) elected

02 The new messaging app promises to ------- users' personal communications.
(A) showcase   (B) protect
(C) lease   (D) return

03 Please ------- that the caterer will provide vegetarian options for our guests.
(A) regard   (B) confirm
(C) demonstrate   (D) transfer

04 The town of Bradford ------- many amenities for residents, including a library and a large recreation center.
(A) advises   (B) continues
(C) offers   (D) transforms

05 It took researchers several weeks to ------- the results of the experiment.
(A) postpone   (B) relieve
(C) analyze   (D) admire

06 The workout program aims to ------- people's risk of developing weight-related diseases.
(A) omit   (B) reduce
(C) compensate   (D) ignore

07 The servers receive tips and ------- them among themselves after each shift.
(A) divide   (B) access
(C) concentrate   (D) convince

08 Using an open floor plan will allow us to ------- the limited space we have in the office.
(A) undergo   (B) devise
(C) conduct   (D) maximize

정답·해석·해설 p.144

동사의 시제

자전거를 <u>탄다</u>.
　　　　동사(현재)

자전거를 <u>탔다</u>.
　　　　동사(과거)

자전거를 <u>탈 것이다</u>.
　　　　　동사(미래)

동사 '타다'는 '탄다', '탔다', '탈 것이다' 등 시간의 변화에 따라 다양하게 나타낼 수 있습니다. 이처럼 동사의 형태를 바꾸어 어떤 행동이나 사건을 시간의 흐름에 따라 표현할 수 있는데, 이를 **시제**라고 합니다.

기출포인트 01 현재/과거/미래

● 현재 시제(동사/동사 + -(e)s)는 일반적인 사실이나 일상적으로 반복되는 동작을 나타냅니다. 특히 아래와 같은 표현들이 현재 시제와 함께 자주 쓰입니다.

| usually 보통 | often 자주, 종종 | every 매 ~, ~마다 | these days 요즘 |

The team **holds** meetings <u>every</u> week to discuss projects. 그 팀은 프로젝트를 논의하기 위해 매주 회의를 연다.

<u>These days</u>, people **communicate** through social media. 요즘, 사람들은 소셜 미디어를 통해 소통한다.

● 과거 시제(동사 + -ed/불규칙 동사)는 과거에 이미 끝난 동작이나 상태를 나타냅니다. 특히 아래와 같은 표현들이 과거 시제와 함께 자주 쓰입니다.

| yesterday 어제 | ago ~ 전에 | last 지난 ~ | in + 과거 연도 ~년에 |

John **bought** a new laptop <u>yesterday</u>. John은 어제 새 노트북을 구매했다.

The startup **launched** its first product <u>last month</u>. 그 스타트업은 지난달에 첫 제품을 출시했다.

● 미래 시제(will + 동사원형)는 미래 상황에 대한 예상이나 말하는 사람의 의지를 나타냅니다. 특히 아래와 같은 표현들이 미래 시제와 함께 자주 쓰입니다.

| tomorrow 내일 | next 다음 ~ | by/until + 미래 시간 표현 ~까지 |

We **will attend** the international conference <u>tomorrow</u>. 우리는 내일 국제 컨퍼런스에 참석할 것이다.

Mia **will travel** to Europe <u>next year</u>. Mia는 내년에 유럽으로 여행을 갈 것이다.

실전 Check-up

01 She often ------- her bicycle to work when the weather is nice.

　(A) rode　　(B) rides

02 The event organizers ------- all the invitations by the end of this month.

　(A) will send　　(B) sent

정답·해석·해설 p.144

기출포인트 02 현재진행/과거진행/미래진행

● 현재진행 시제(am/are/is + -ing)는 현재 시점에 진행되고 있는 일을 나타내며, 특히 아래와 같은 표현들이 현재진행 시제와 함께 자주 쓰입니다. 현재진행 시제는 예정된 일이나 곧 일어나려고 하는 일을 표현하여 미래를 나타낼 수도 있습니다.

| currently 현재, 지금 | at present 현재 | (right) now (바로) 지금 |

Mr. Lee **is** currently **managing** a team of five international researchers.
Mr. Lee는 현재 다섯 명의 국제 연구원 팀을 관리하고 있다. (현재 진행)

We **are having** a team lunch tomorrow at noon. 우리는 내일 정오에 팀 점심 식사를 할 것이다. (미래)

● 과거진행 시제(was/were + -ing)는 과거 특정 시점에 진행되고 있던 일을 나타냅니다.

We **were entering** the building <u>when it started to rain</u>. 비가 오기 시작했을 때 우리는 건물에 들어가고 있었다.
　　　　　　　　　　　　　　　　과거의 특정 시점

Mr. Owen **was cooking** dinner in the kitchen <u>at 7 o'clock last Sunday</u>.
　　　　　　　　　　　　　　　　　　　　　　　과거의 특정 시점
Mr. Owen은 지난 일요일 7시에 부엌에서 저녁을 요리하고 있었다.

● 미래진행 시제(will be + -ing)는 미래 특정 시점에 진행되고 있을 일을 나타냅니다.

Ms. Parker **will be meeting** with a new client <u>at this time tomorrow</u>.
　　　　　　　　　　　　　　　　　　　　　　미래의 특정 시점
Ms. Parker는 내일 이 시간에 새로운 고객과 만나고 있을 것이다.

She **will be attending** a business conference <u>next Monday</u>.
　　　　　　　　　　　　　　　　　　　　　미래의 특정 시점
그녀는 다음 주 월요일에 비즈니스 회의에 참석하고 있을 것이다.

실전 Check-up

01 Right now, the department manager ------- a workshop for his project managers.

(A) conducted (B) is conducting

02 She ------- a presentation to the board when the projector stopped working.

(A) was giving (B) is giving

정답·해석·해설 p.144

기출 포인트 03 현재완료/과거완료/미래완료

- 현재완료 시제(have/has + p.p.)는 과거에 시작된 일이 현재 시점까지 계속되고 있는 것을 나타냅니다. 특히 아래와 같은 표현들이 현재완료 시제와 함께 자주 쓰입니다.

    since + 과거 시간 표현 ~ 이래로   for + 기간 ~ 동안
    since + 주어 + 과거 시제 ~한 이래로   over the last/past + 기간 지난 ~ 동안

    Ms. Brown **has lived** in Austin <u>since 2020</u>. Ms. Brown은 2020년 이래로 오스틴에 살아 왔다.

    Orionix Technologies **has produced** high-quality electronics <u>for nearly two decades</u>.
    Orionix Technologies사는 거의 20년 동안 고품질의 전자 제품을 생산해 왔다.

- 과거완료 시제(had + p.p.)는 과거의 특정 시점을 기준으로 그보다 더 이전에 일어난 일을 나타냅니다. 특히 아래와 같은 표현들이 과거완료 시제와 함께 자주 쓰입니다.

    by the time + 주어 + 과거 시제 ~했을 즈음에   before + 주어 + 과거 시제 ~하기 전에   when + 주어 + 과거 시제 ~했을 때

    Ms. Clara **had** carefully **reviewed** the documents <u>before she signed the contract</u>.
    　　　　　　　　　　　　　　　　　　　　　　　　　　과거의 특정 시점
    Ms. Clara는 계약서에 서명하기 전에 문서들을 꼼꼼히 검토했었다.

    <u>When the police came</u>, the thieves **had** already **escaped**. 경찰이 왔을 때, 도둑들은 이미 도망갔었다.
    　　과거의 특정 시점

- 미래완료 시제(will have + p.p.)는 현재나 과거에 발생한 동작이 미래의 특정 시점에 완료될 것임을 나타냅니다. 특히 아래와 같은 표현들이 미래완료 시제와 함께 자주 쓰입니다.

    by the time + 주어 + 현재 시제 ~할 즈음에   by + 미래 시간 표현 ~ 즈음에   by the end of + 미래 시간 표현 ~ 말까지

    <u>By the time she arrives</u> at the airport, the plane **will have** already **taken** off.
    　　미래의 특정 시점
    그녀가 공항에 도착할 즈음에, 비행기는 이미 이륙하게 될 것이다.

    Sarah **will have completed** her master's degree <u>by next month</u>. Sarah는 다음 달 즈음에 석사 학위를 마치게 될 것이다.
    　　　　　　　　　　　　　　　　　　　　　　　　　　　미래의 특정 시점

실전 Check-up

01 Many customers ------- for our online service since it launched last month.

　(A) were registering　(B) have registered

02 By the time Ms. Aydin arrived at the conference venue, the keynote speaker ------- his presentation already.

　(A) finished　(B) had finished

정답·해석·해설 p.145

3초컷 정답 공식

자주 출제되는 정답 공식을 적용하여 빈칸에 가장 알맞은 보기를 고르세요.

정답공식 01 문장에 next가 있으면 미래 시제나 미래를 나타내는 현재진행 시제가 정답이다!

01. According to the itinerary, the group ------- some of the historic sites in Istanbul next Sunday.
    (A) has toured   (B) will tour
    (C) toured   (D) touring

02. The Fifth Street Fitness Center ------- much of its equipment next month.
    (A) is replacing   (B) had replaced
    (C) has replaced   (D) replaced

정답공식 02 while 뒤에 있는 빈칸에는 진행 시제가 정답이다!

03. Please do not enter the laboratory area while chemical tests ------- conducted by the research staff.
    (A) were   (B) have been
    (C) are being   (D) had been

04. The power suddenly failed while the technicians ------- the new equipment.
    (A) were installing (B) will install
    (C) have installed (D) install

정답공식 03 문장에 since가 있으면 현재완료 시제가 정답일 확률이 높다!

05. The support team ------- over 5,000 inquiries since the beginning of the year.
    (A) handled   (B) handles
    (C) has handled   (D) is handling

06. Since it first opened three months ago, Nelson Bookstore ------- the size of its customer base.
    (A) to have increased (B) has increased
    (C) was increased   (D) will be increasing

정답공식 04 주절이 과거 시제이고 after 다음에 빈칸이 있으면 과거 시제나 과거완료 시제를 정답으로 고른다!

07. The agreement was terminated after the supplier ------- multiple deadlines.
    (A) missed   (B) is missing
    (C) has missed   (D) would miss

08. After the employees ------- the new safety procedures, workplace accidents decreased.
    (A) have learned   (B) are learning
    (C) learn   (D) had learned

HACKERS TEST

빈칸에 가장 알맞은 보기를 고르세요.

01 Every day, chefs at La Mirina ------- traditional recipes passed down for generations.
(A) follow
(B) follower
(C) to follow
(D) will have followed

02 Marvin Gray ------- his new novel next Friday before starting his nationwide tour.
(A) releasing
(B) released
(C) has released
(D) is releasing

03 The security guard ------- the premises when he noticed suspicious activity near the warehouse.
(A) was patrolling
(B) to be patrolled
(C) has patrolled
(D) patrols

04 Until next week, parking fees ------- for participating vendors.
(A) waived
(B) had been waived
(C) will be waived
(D) have waived

05 While the construction ------- place in the east wing, all employees are asked to use the west entrance.
(A) is taking
(B) had taken
(C) took
(D) has taken

06 Mr. Yilmaz ------- as the financial director of Global Financial Partners for six years.
(A) works
(B) has worked
(C) working
(D) was worked

07 SkyWave Airlines changed its boarding procedures after passengers ------- numerous complaints.
(A) are filing
(B) files
(C) has filed
(D) filed

08 Currently, Veltrix Solutions ------- applications for the marketing position.
(A) is accepting
(B) had accepted
(C) accepted
(D) has accepted

09 The product launch was delayed because market researchers ------- negative consumer feedback.
(A) reported
(B) will be reporting
(C) report
(D) will report

10 The firm's stock price ------- by 30 percent since the CEO announced the merger.
(A) to increase
(B) increases
(C) has increased
(D) is increasing

11 By next year, Veridian Innovations ------- 20 retail stores throughout Europe.
(A) opens
(B) opened
(C) will have opened
(D) has opened

12 Over the past few months, Ms. Saer ------- colleagues with her deep knowledge of computer engineering.
(A) impresses
(B) impressing
(C) impressive
(D) has impressed

13 The fire alarm went off as the scientists ------- the new chemical compound.
(A) were testing
(B) tests
(C) have tested
(D) test

14 Mr. Moore has been talking with the staff and ------- a number of issues that need to be addressed at the next meeting.
(A) identifies
(B) was identified
(C) has identified
(D) being identified

15 In one month, Jensen Sportswear ------- its line of shorts and swimsuits for the summer season.
(A) launchable
(B) launching
(C) was launching
(D) will launch

16 At present, our branch office in Singapore ------- a major renovation.
(A) is undergoing
(B) will undergo
(C) underwent
(D) had undergone

17 Once viewers ------- about a lack of original content, the Spotlight Network introduced new programs that fall.
(A) complain
(B) complained
(C) complaining
(D) having complained

18 At 10 P.M. tonight, the factory workers ------- night shift production.
(A) to start
(B) are started
(C) will be starting
(D) have started

19 Mr. Davis ------- full price for his tickets before YHW Rails announced its special half-price offer.
(A) is paying
(B) had paid
(C) was paid
(D) has paid

20 Ms. Lewis revealed yesterday that ------- will be transferring to the head office at the end of May.
(A) her
(B) hers
(C) herself
(D) she

21 A Web developer ------- the social networking site 10 years ago to help people stay in touch with friends online.
(A) created
(B) creates
(C) was created
(D) to create

22 After the architect ------- the building plans, construction began immediately.
(A) has finalized
(B) is finalizing
(C) had finalized
(D) finalizes

23 From this coming June to August, the IT department ------- the company's entire network infrastructure.
(A) has been upgraded
(B) upgrading
(C) upgrades
(D) will be upgrading

24 The investors withdrew their support while the company ------- through a major restructuring.
(A) was going
(B) had gone
(C) has gone
(D) goes

빈출 어휘 | 동사 3

✓ PART 5 어휘 문제에 자주 출제되는 어휘를 예문과 함께 확실히 익혀두세요.

01 **pledge** 약속하다
pledge to support local communities
지역 사회를 지원하기로 약속하다
[동] promise 약속하다

02 **implement** 시행하다
implement safety measures at the construction site
공사 현장에서 안전 조치를 시행하다

03 **preserve** 보존하다
preserve historical documents in the library
도서관에 역사적 문서를 보존하다
[파] preservation 보존

04 **supply** 공급하다
supply raw materials to the factory
공장에 원자재를 공급하다
[파] supplier 공급자, 공급업체

05 **finalize** 마무리하다
finalize the contract with the client
고객과의 계약을 마무리하다
[동] complete 마무리하다, 완료하다

06 **rank** 순위를 매기다
rank products according to quality
품질에 따라 제품들의 순위를 매기다

07 **neglect** 소홀히 하다, 무시하다
neglect important safety procedures
중요한 안전 절차를 소홀히 하다
[동] ignore 무시하다

08 **evaluate** 평가하다
evaluate the company's assets
회사의 자산을 평가하다
[파] evaluation 평가 [동] assess 평가하다

09 **possess** 갖추다, 소유하다
possess the qualifications required for the job
그 직업에 요구되는 자격 요건을 갖추다
[파] possession 소유

10 **stimulate** 활발하게 하다, 자극하다
stimulate the economy by lowering taxes
세금을 낮춤으로써 경제를 활발하게 하다
[파] stimulation 자극

11 **attract** 끌어들이다
attract a substantial number of customers
상당한 수의 고객들을 끌어들이다
[파] attraction 매력, 유인 [동] draw 끌어들이다

12 **occupy** 차지하다, 채우다
occupy all the available seats
모든 이용 가능한 좌석을 차지하다
[파] occupation 점유, 직업

13 **improve** 향상시키다
improve staff performance through training
교육을 통해 직원들의 성과를 향상시키다
[파] improvement 향상 [동] enhance 향상시키다

14 **boost** 높이다, 북돋우다
boost production without extra resources
추가 자원 없이 생산량을 높이다

15 **relocate** 이전하다
relocate the warehouse to a suburban area
창고를 교외 지역으로 이전하다
[파] relocation 이전

16 **waive** 면제하다
waive the registration fee for early applicants
조기 지원자들에게 등록비를 면제하다
[파] waiver 면제, 포기

17 observe 관찰하다, 지켜보다

observe market trends
시장 추세를 관찰하다

파 observation 관찰

18 revolutionize 혁신을 일으키다

revolutionize the banking sector
금융 분야에 혁신을 일으키다

파 revolution 혁명

19 honor 경의를 표하다, 존경하다

honor Ms. Lena for her dedication
그녀의 헌신을 기려 Ms. Lena에게 경의를 표하다

파 honorable 명예로운

20 estimate 추정하다

estimate that the cost will be 500 dollars
비용이 500달러일 것으로 추정하다

파 estimation 추정

토익 실전문제

01 The faculty head will ------- how the new instructors manage their classes.
(A) stimulate (B) obey
(C) observe (D) claim

02 The transportation department ------- the new regulations to protect pedestrians and motorists from road accidents at night.
(A) implemented (B) supplied
(C) gathered (D) neglected

03 Ms. Tanner has not yet ------- her travel plans for the trip to Boston for the trade show.
(A) ranked (B) finalized
(C) maximized (D) regulated

04 The government plans to ------- some taxes for foreign firms that make large investments.
(A) acquire (B) possess
(C) waive (D) wield

05 The first 20 rows will be ------- by the graduating class, with parents and guests behind.
(A) represented (B) evaluated
(C) screened (D) occupied

06 Brightland Bakery has ------- to donate 100 boxes of donuts for this weekend's charity event.
(A) relocated (B) supported
(C) pledged (D) encouraged

07 Hyman Pharmaceuticals' sales in the Asian market ------- last year, resulting in a significant boost in profits.
(A) estimated (B) soared
(C) surfaced (D) rescheduled

08 The mayor created a task force dedicated to ------- buildings of historical value throughout the city.
(A) preserving (B) attracting
(C) revising (D) postponing

정답·해석·해설 p.148

DAY 08 to 부정사와 동명사

매회 0~1문제 출제

나는 사진을 찍기 위해 카메라를 샀다.
　　　　　　부사 역할

나는 사진 찍는 것을 좋아한다.
　　　　　명사 역할

동사 '찍다'가 '찍기 위해', '찍는 것'으로 형태가 바뀌어 동사가 아닌 다른 품사의 역할을 하고 있습니다. 영어에서도 동사 앞에 to가 붙은 **to 부정사**와 동사 뒤에 ing가 붙은 **동명사**가 문장 속에서 여러 역할을 할 수 있습니다.

기출포인트 01 to 부정사의 형태

- to 부정사의 형태는 'to + 동사원형'입니다.

    Employees are required (~~to attending~~, **to attend**) safety training. 직원들은 안전 교육에 참석하는 것이 요구된다.

기출포인트 02 to 부정사의 역할과 자리

- to 부정사는 명사 역할을 하여 문장의 주어, 목적어, 보어 자리에 오며, '~하는 것, ~하기'로 해석합니다.

    주어 자리　**To complete this project** will take three months. 이 프로젝트를 완료하는 것은 3개월이 걸릴 것이다.

    목적어 자리　Olivia hesitated **to accept the promotion**. Olivia는 승진을 수락하기를 망설였다.

    보어 자리　His goal is **to become a professional musician**. 그의 목표는 전문 음악가가 되는 것이다.
    　　　　　　　　　　　　　　주격 보어

    　　　　　The coach encouraged the players **to practice harder**. 코치는 선수들에게 더 열심히 연습하기를 격려했다.
    　　　　　　　　　　　　　　　　　　　　　　목적격 보어

- to 부정사는 형용사 역할을 하여 명사 뒤에서 명사를 꾸며주며, '~할, ~하는'으로 해석합니다.

    We need a volunteer **to organize the community event**. 우리는 지역 행사를 조직할 자원봉사자가 필요하다.
    　　　　　　명사

- to 부정사는 부사처럼 문장 앞뒤나 동사 뒤에서 문장이나 동사를 꾸며주며, 행위의 목적을 나타내어 '~하기 위해'로 해석합니다. 이때, to 부정사의 to는 in order to로 바꿔 쓸 수 있습니다.

    To meet seasonal demand, the factory will increase production. 계절적 수요를 충족하기 위해, 그 공장은 생산을 늘릴 것이다.
    = In order to meet seasonal demand

실전 Check-up

01 Ms. Turner is the first person ------- at the annual retreat.

(A) was arrived　　(B) to arrive

02 ------- funds for community groups, the Mayville branch of Doyle Bank often hosts special events.

(A) To raise　　(B) Raise

정답·해석·해설 p.148

기출포인트 03 동명사의 형태

- 동명사의 형태는 '동사원형 + -ing'입니다.

    (~~Take~~, **Taking**) photographs inside the museum is prohibited. 박물관 내부에서 사진을 찍는 것은 금지되어 있다.

기출포인트 04 동명사의 역할과 자리

- 동명사는 명사 역할을 하여 문장의 주어, 목적어, 보어 자리에 오며, '~하는 것, ~하기'로 해석합니다.

    주어 자리　**Renting a car** requires a valid driver's license. 차를 빌리는 것은 유효한 운전면허증을 필요로 한다.

    목적어 자리　The company considered **expanding its business in Asia**. 그 회사는 아시아에서 사업을 확장하는 것을 고려했다.
    　　　　　　　　　　　　　　동사의 목적어

    　　　　　　By **offering discounts**, the retailer attracted more customers.
    　　　　　　　　전치사의 목적어
    　　　　　　할인을 제공함으로써, 그 소매업체는 더 많은 고객을 유치했다.

    보어 자리　Her job is **managing the sales team efficiently**. 그녀의 업무는 영업팀을 효율적으로 관리하는 것이다.

기출포인트 05 동명사와 명사 구별

- 동명사는 목적어를 가질 수 있지만, 명사는 목적어를 가질 수 없습니다.

    After (~~completion~~, **completing**) <u>the form</u>, please return it to the front desk.
    　　　　　　　　　　　　　　　　목적어
    양식 작성하는 것을 마친 후, 안내 데스크에 제출해 주세요.

- 동명사 앞에는 부정관사(a(n))를 쓸 수 없지만, 단수 가산 명사 앞에는 부정관사를 쓸 수 있습니다.

    He gave <u>a</u> (~~presenting~~, **presentation**) about market trends. 그는 시장 동향에 대한 발표를 했다.
    　　　　부정관사

실전 Check-up

01 ------- a balanced diet is essential for maintaining optimal health.

(A) Following　　(B) Follow

02 The instructor insisted on ------- the correct way to use the equipment.

(A) demonstrating　　(B) demonstration

정답·해석·해설 p.148

기출포인트 06 to 부정사를 취하는 동사·명사

- '동사 + to 부정사'의 형태로, to 부정사를 목적어로 취하는 동사들은 다음과 같습니다.

want to ~하길 원하다	hope to ~하길 희망하다	agree to ~하기로 동의하다	decide to ~하기로 결정하다
expect to ~하길 기대하다	choose to ~하기로 결정하다	offer to ~할 것을 제안하다	wish to ~하길 소망하다
plan to ~할 것을 계획하다	need to ~해야 한다	promise to ~하기로 약속하다	tend to ~하는 경향이 있다
aim to ~할 것을 목표로 하다	try to ~하려고 노력하다	would like to ~하길 원하다	fail to ~하기를 실패하다

The manager decided **to hire** three new employees for the project.
관리자는 그 프로젝트를 위해 세 명의 신규 직원을 고용하기로 결정했다.

- '동사 + 목적어 + to 부정사'의 형태로, to 부정사를 목적격 보어로 취하는 동사들은 다음과 같습니다.

ask 목 to ~하라고 요청하다	want 목 to ~하길 원하다	allow 목 to ~하도록 허가하다
advise 목 to ~하도록 권고하다	expect 목 to ~하는 것을 기대하다	persuade 목 to ~하도록 설득하다
encourage 목 to ~하도록 권고하다	enable 목 to ~할 수 있게 하다	invite 목 to ~하라고 요청하다

The software enables users **to edit** videos easily. 그 소프트웨어는 사용자들이 쉽게 영상을 편집할 수 있게 한다.

- to 부정사와 함께 자주 출제되는 명사들은 다음과 같습니다.

| ability to ~하는 능력 | plan to ~하려는 계획 | opportunity to ~할 기회 |

Your ability **to analyze** data will be essential for this position. 당신의 데이터를 분석하는 능력이 이 직책에 필수적일 것이다.

기출포인트 07 동명사를 목적어로 취하는 동사

- '동사 + 동명사'의 형태로, 동명사를 목적어로 취하는 동사들은 다음과 같습니다.

| enjoy -ing ~하는 것을 즐기다 | keep -ing ~하는 것을 계속하다 | avoid -ing ~하는 것을 피하다 | consider -ing ~하는 것을 고려하다 |
| deny -ing ~한 것을 부인하다 | finish -ing ~하는 것을 끝내다 | suggest -ing ~할 것을 제안하다 | recommend -ing ~하는 것을 추천하다 |

The doctor recommended **exercising** for at least 30 minutes every day. 의사는 매일 최소 30분 동안 운동하는 것을 추천했다.

- 자주 출제되는 동명사 관용 표현들은 다음과 같습니다.

| by -ing ~함으로써 | be committed to -ing ~에 전념하다 | be dedicated/devoted to -ing ~에 헌신적이다 |

BlueCore is dedicated **to preserving** marine life in coastal waters. BlueCore는 연안 해역의 해양 생물을 보호하는 데 헌신적이다.

실전 Check-up

01 Sunrise Tower is adopting electronic invoicing, allowing residents ------ their utility bills online.
   (A) paying   (B) to pay

02 The travel agent suggested ------ during the off-season to save money.
   (A) traveling   (B) to travel

정답·해석·해설 p.149

3초컷 정답 공식

자주 출제되는 정답 공식을 적용하여 빈칸에 가장 알맞은 보기를 고르세요.

정답공식 01 결정이나 계획, 희망을 나타내는 동사(decide, plan, hope, want) 뒤에는 to 부정사가 정답이다!

01 Pinnacle Technologies plans ------- a new training center in Chicago next year.
(A) opens (B) open
(C) to open (D) opening

02 We want ------- our customers with the highest-quality service.
(A) providing (B) to provide
(C) provided (D) provision

정답공식 02 빈칸 앞에 too가 있으면 to 부정사를 정답으로 고른다!

03 The historical documents were too deteriorated ------- without special equipment.
(A) to read (B) will read
(C) read (D) reads

04 The mountain trail is too dangerous ------- during the rainy season.
(A) hiking (B) hiked
(C) hikes (D) to hike

정답공식 03 빈칸이 전치사와 a(n)/the/소유격 사이에 있으면 동명사가 정답일 확률이 높다!

05 She apologized for ------- a serious mistake in her calculations.
(A) making (B) makes
(C) make (D) to make

06 The employees were warned against ------- the details of the upcoming merger with outsiders.
(A) to discuss (B) should discuss
(C) discussing (D) discusses

정답공식 04 by와 명사 사이에 빈칸이 있으면 동명사가 정답이다!

07 Chef Martinez creates unique dishes by ------- techniques from both traditional and modern cuisine.
(A) combine (B) combined
(C) combines (D) combining

08 The engineers reduced noise by ------- materials that block sounds from outside.
(A) to use (B) uses
(C) used (D) using

정답·해석·해설 p.149

HACKERS TEST

빈칸에 가장 알맞은 보기를 고르세요.

01 The Vellonix computer is equipped with powerful chips ------- the rapid processing of large video files.
(A) enable
(B) enables
(C) to enable
(D) enabled

02 Additional funding is required to achieve our goal of ------- the medical causes of these conditions.
(A) determination
(B) determined
(C) determining
(D) determines

03 The advanced physics textbook is too technical and complex ------- without prior knowledge.
(A) understanding
(B) understood
(C) to understand
(D) understands

04 The city council announced a five-year plan ------- public transportation.
(A) will improve
(B) improves
(C) improved
(D) to improve

05 The presenter engaged the audience by ------- questions throughout the session.
(A) ask
(B) asks
(C) asked
(D) asking

06 The company invited employees to ------- in a seminar organized by Nina Chou to help improve their presentation skills.
(A) participating
(B) participation
(C) participates
(D) participate

07 It took several attempts, but Mr. Phelps succeeded in ------- management of the need to hire additional staff.
(A) convincing
(B) convince
(C) convinced
(D) to convince

08 ------- distractions, Janzyll Incorporated discourages the personal use of telephones and the Internet while on duty.
(A) Minimizes
(B) Minimize
(C) To minimize
(D) Has minimized

09 The marketing department will keep ------- promotional e-mails to customers who have subscribed to our newsletter.
(A) send
(B) sending
(C) sent
(D) sends

10 The employee denied ------- any confidential data from the company's internal database with external vendors.
(A) to share
(B) shared
(C) share
(D) sharing

11 Power tools should be handled ------- to minimize the risk of serious injury.
(A) cautious
(B) caution
(C) cautiously
(D) more cautious

12 Novexia Industries decided ------- a new flagship store in downtown Toronto.
(A) building
(B) to build
(C) build
(D) having built

13 Many graduates consider ------- abroad to gain international experience and improve their career prospects.
(A) move
(B) moves
(C) moving
(D) to move

14 Consumers are encouraged ------- with a medical professional prior to taking an herbal supplement.
(A) consultation
(B) to consult
(C) consulting
(D) consult

15 Drivers are advised to avoid ------- Brookdale Avenue during rush hour.
(A) enter
(B) entering
(C) to be entered
(D) enters

16 After the natural disaster, the community members hope ------- their homes with government assistance.
(A) to rebuild
(B) rebuilding
(C) rebuild
(D) rebuilds

17 Customers are reminded to check the address they provide ------- prevent delays with their shipment.
(A) instead of
(B) except for
(C) apart from
(D) in order to

18 Environmental scientists warn that ------- plastic waste improperly affects marine ecosystems.
(A) discarding
(B) discardable
(C) discarded
(D) discarder

19 The committee emphasized the importance of ------- the safety manual to ensure a safer work environment.
(A) revise
(B) revises
(C) revised
(D) revising

20 Once you finish ------- out the application form, please submit it to the HR department.
(A) fill
(B) filling
(C) filled
(D) fills

21 Lara Karowski's chances of winning last year's badminton finals ------- when she injured her knee badly.
(A) diminish
(B) diminished
(C) diminishingly
(D) will diminish

22 The orchestra members mentioned that they were searching for talented musicians ------- them for the upcoming season.
(A) to join
(B) join
(C) have joined
(D) joins

23 Students are encouraged to participate in sports because they offer a ------- from the everyday stress of schoolwork.
(A) releasable
(B) released
(C) releasing
(D) release

24 Due to the unexpected storm, the event organizers decided ------- the outdoor concert.
(A) to reschedule
(B) rescheduling
(C) reschedule
(D) reschedules

빈출 어휘 | 형용사 1

PART 5 어휘 문제에 자주 출제되는 어휘를 예문과 함께 확실히 익혀두세요.

01 available 이용 가능한, 구할 수 있는
make the manual **available** online
설명서를 온라인에서 이용 가능하게 하다
파 availability 이용 가능성 반 unavailable 이용 불가능한

02 popular 인기 있는, 대중적인
restock **popular** products regularly
인기 있는 제품들을 정기적으로 재입고하다
파 popularity 인기 반 unpopular 인기 없는

03 mandatory 의무적인, 필수적인
implement **mandatory** training sessions
의무적인 교육 과정을 시행하다
반 optional 선택적인

04 accurate 정확한
find **accurate** information about return policies
반품 정책에 관한 정확한 정보를 찾다
파 accuracy 정확성 반 inaccurate 부정확한

05 limited 제한된
offer services for a **limited** time only
제한된 시간 동안에만 서비스를 제공하다
파 limitation 제한 반 unlimited 무제한의

06 extensive 폭넓은, 광범위한
gain **extensive** experience through internships
인턴 근무를 통해 폭넓은 경험을 쌓다
파 extent 범위, 정도

07 motivated 의욕적인, 동기 부여된
recruit **motivated** individuals for the company
회사를 위해 의욕적인 사람들을 모집하다
파 motivation 동기 부여

08 exceptional 뛰어난, 예외적인
maintain an **exceptional** level of quality
뛰어난 수준의 품질을 유지하다
파 exception 예외

09 favorable 호의적인, 유리한
receive **favorable** reviews from critics
평론가들로부터 호의적인 평가를 받다
파 favor 호의 반 unfavorable 불리한

10 distinct 독특한, 별개의
feature a **distinct** architectural style
독특한 건축 양식을 특징으로 하다
파 distinction 차이, 구별 동 unique 독특한

11 impressive 인상적인
report **impressive** growth in the last quarter
지난 분기에 인상적인 성장을 보고하다
파 impression 인상

12 leading 선도적인
become the **leading** retailer in the country
국내에서 선도적인 소매업체가 되다
파 leader 지도자, 리더

13 knowledgeable 지식이 풍부한
select a **knowledgeable** candidate
지식이 풍부한 후보를 선발하다
파 knowledge 지식

14 exclusive 전용의, 독점적인
provide **exclusive** benefits to all members
모든 회원에게 전용 혜택을 제공하다
파 exclude 제외하다 반 inclusive 포괄적인

15 valuable 가치 있는, 귀중한
share **valuable** insights with the audience
가치 있는 통찰을 청중과 공유하다
파 value 가치

16 advanced 선진의, 고급의
utilize **advanced** technology for design
설계를 위해 선진 기술을 활용하다

17 permanent 상설의, 영구적인
set up a **permanent** display near the entrance
입구 근처에 상설 전시를 설치하다
파 permanence 영구성

18 innovative 혁신적인
present an **innovative** idea on sustainability
지속 가능성에 대한 혁신적인 아이디어를 제시하다
파 innovation 혁신

19 official 공식적인
obtain **official** approval from the government
정부로부터 공식적인 승인을 받다
반 unofficial 비공식적인

20 rigorous 엄격한, 철저한
maintain **rigorous** quality standards
엄격한 품질 기준을 유지하다
동 strict 엄격한

토익 실전문제

01 The design team had a highly ------- discussion that produced many useful ideas.
(A) vague (B) valuable
(C) redundant (D) available

02 Madison Incorporated is thought to be extremely ------- due to the market-changing service it has developed.
(A) innovative (B) conditional
(C) permanent (D) restricted

03 The staff have had ------- opportunities to attend training courses because of the high volume of work.
(A) advanced (B) exact
(C) limited (D) tense

04 Mr. Achebe published a best-selling book using material gathered from his ------- weekly newsletter.
(A) certain (B) delicate
(C) popular (D) mandatory

05 Following a successful trial run, the company changed its ------- policy to allow remote work.
(A) distant (B) official
(C) exclusive (D) noble

06 Vertex Solutions conducted ------- research to evaluate the environmental impact of the construction.
(A) fragile (B) knowledgeable
(C) potential (D) extensive

07 The warehouse manager verified that the inventory records were ------- before placing a new order.
(A) vacant (B) deliberate
(C) accurate (D) leading

08 The project manager separated the staff into five ------- teams, and each team handled one phase.
(A) distinct (B) rigorous
(C) frequent (D) terminal

정답·해석·해설 p.151

DAY 09 분사

매회 0~1문제 출제

흐르는 강물
형용사 역할

'흐르는'은 강물이 흐르고 있다는 동작의 의미를 담고 있습니다. 이와 같이 동사의 성격을 가지고 있으면서 명사를 수식하는 형용사 역할을 하는 것을 **분사**라고 합니다.

기출포인트 01 분사의 형태

- 분사에는 '동사원형 + -ing' 형태의 현재분사와 '동사원형 + -ed' 형태의 과거분사가 있습니다. 현재분사는 '~한, ~하는'이라는 능동의 의미를, 과거분사는 '~된'이라는 수동의 의미를 나타냅니다.

The man **painting** the wall is my neighbor. 벽을 칠하는 남자는 내 이웃이다.
　　　↑현재분사

The **repaired** machine was back in operation within an hour. 수리된 기계는 한 시간 내에 다시 작동되었다.
　　과거분사↑

기출포인트 02 분사의 역할과 자리

- 분사는 형용사 역할을 하여, 명사 앞이나 뒤에서 명사를 수식하거나 보어 자리에 옵니다.

명사 앞　　The **donated** supplies will be distributed to local shelters. 기부된 물품들은 지역 쉼터에 배포될 것이다.
　　　　　　　　　↑명사

명사 뒤　　People **attending** the product launch received gift bags. 제품 출시 행사에 참석한 사람들은 선물 가방을 받았다.
　　　　　명사↑

보어 자리　The document remains **unfinished** on my desk. 그 문서는 내 책상 위에 미완성된 채로 남아 있다.
　　　　　　　　　주격 보어

　　　　　I saw him **running** towards the bus stop. 나는 그가 버스 정류장을 향해 달리는 것을 보았다.
　　　　　　　목적격 보어

실전 Check-up

01 The recruiters will contact applicants ------- the necessary qualifications for the position.

(A) demonstrating　　(B) demonstrate

02 Residents of the Wiltshire Apartment Complex are asked to park only in their ------- spots.

(A) assigns　　(B) assigned

정답·해석·해설 p.152

기출 포인트 03 현재분사와 과거분사

● 꾸밈을 받는 명사와 분사가 '~한, ~하는, ~하고 있는'이라고 해석되는 능동 관계이면 현재분사를 쓰고, '~된, ~되는, ~되어 있는'이라고 해석되는 수동 관계이면 과거분사를 씁니다.

The person (~~carried~~, **carrying**) the box is Ms. Carol. 상자를 운반하는 사람은 Ms. Carol이다.
　　　　　　과거분사(X)　현재분사(O)
→ 꾸밈을 받는 명사(The person)와 분사가 '상자를 운반하는 사람'이라는 의미의 능동 관계이기 때문에 현재분사가 와야 합니다.

The paintings (~~displaying~~, **displayed**) in the gallery were created by local artists.
　　　　　　　현재분사(X)　과거분사(O)
미술관에 전시된 그림들은 지역 예술가들에 의해 제작되었다.
→ 꾸밈을 받는 명사(The paintings)와 분사가 '미술관에 전시된 그림들'이라는 의미의 수동 관계이기 때문에 과거분사가 와야 합니다.

기출 포인트 04 감정을 나타내는 분사

● 분사가 꾸며주거나 보충하여 설명하는 대상이 감정을 일으키는 원인이면 현재분사를, 감정을 느끼는 주체이면 과거분사를 씁니다.

The price increase was **frustrating** for regular customers. 가격 인상은 단골 고객들에게 좌절감을 주었다.
→ '가격 인상'은 좌절감을 일으키는 원인이므로 현재분사 frustrating을 씁니다.

The **satisfied** customers wrote positive reviews after the workshop. 만족한 고객들은 워크숍 후에 긍정적인 후기를 작성했다.
→ '고객들'은 만족을 느끼는 주체이므로 과거분사 satisfied를 씁니다.

● 감정을 나타내는 분사를 의미와 함께 구별해서 알아두면 문맥에 맞는 분사를 더욱 쉽게 고를 수 있습니다.

현재분사	과거분사	현재분사	과거분사
interesting 흥미롭게 하는	interested 흥미로워하는	disappointing 실망스럽게 하는	disappointed 실망스러워하는
pleasing 기쁘게 하는	pleased 기뻐하는	satisfying 만족스럽게 하는	satisfied 만족스러워하는
surprising 놀라게 하는	surprised 놀란	embarrassing 당황스럽게 하는	embarrassed 당황해하는

The **surprising** news spread quickly. 그 놀라게 하는 소식은 빠르게 퍼졌다.
→ '뉴스'는 놀라움을 일으키는 원인이므로 현재분사 surprising을 씁니다.

He was **surprised** by the unexpected announcement. 그는 예상치 못한 발표에 의해 놀랐다.
→ '그'는 놀라움을 느끼는 주체이므로 과거분사 surprised를 씁니다.

실전 Check-up

01 The antique shop displays many ------- items from the Victorian era.

(A) charmed　　(B) charming

02 The salesperson felt ------- when he realized he hadn't brought any business cards to the meeting.

(A) embarrassed　　(B) embarrassing

정답·해석·해설 p.152

기출 포인트 05 토익에 잘 나오는 '분사 + 명사' 표현

● 토익에 잘 나오는 '현재분사 + 명사' 표현과 '과거분사 + 명사' 표현을 구별하여 알아두면 도움이 됩니다.

현재분사 + 명사	과거분사 + 명사
leading expert 선도적인 전문가	preferred method 선호되는 방법
opening ceremony 개회식	proposed schedule 제안된 일정
promising technique 유망한 기술	experienced specialist 숙련된 전문가
existing policy 기존 정책	detailed report 자세한 보고서
lasting impression 오래 지속되는 인상	limited resources 제한된 자원
improving performance 향상되는 성과	attached file 첨부된 파일
missing document 누락된 서류	damaged item 손상된 물품

Dr. Park introduced a (~~promised~~, **promising**) technique during the seminar. Dr. Park은 세미나 동안 유망한 기술을 소개했다.

기출 포인트 06 분사구문

● 분사를 이용해서 부사절을 간단한 구로 만든 것을 분사구문이라고 합니다. 분사구문은 '부사구'의 역할을 하며 문장의 앞이나 뒤에 옵니다.

<u>Founded in 2020</u>, the company has grown into a global brand. 2020년에 설립된 후, 그 회사는 글로벌 브랜드로 성장했다.
　분사구문

● 분사구문은 '부사절 접속사 + 주어 + 동사 ~'로 되어 있는 부사절을 축약하여 '(접속사 +) 분사'의 형태로 바꾼 것입니다.

While I cleaned the room, I listened to music. 내가 방을 청소하는 동안, 나는 음악을 들었다.

~~While~~ I cleaned the room, I listened to music.
부사절 접속사 While 생략 (접속사를 생략하여 의미가 모호해질 경우, 생략하지 않는다.)

~~While I~~ cleaned the room, I listened to music.
부사절 주어 I 생략 (주절의 주어와 같은 경우에만 생략한다.)

Cleaning the room, I listened to music.
부사절 동사를 분사로 교체

실전 Check-up

01 The customer requested a refund for the ------- item she received last week.

(A) damaging　　(B) damaged

02 ------- by the customer's feedback, the team made several improvements to the product.

(A) Inspired　　(B) Inspiring

정답·해석·해설 p.153

3초컷 정답 공식

자주 출제되는 정답 공식을 적용하여 빈칸에 가장 알맞은 보기를 고르세요.

정답공식 01 빈칸 뒤에 사람을 가리키는 명사가 있으면 experienced나 leading이 정답이다!

01 We are looking for ------- engineers to join the new project team.
(A) experience (B) experiencing
(C) experiences (D) experienced

02 She is a ------- expert in the field of artificial intelligence.
(A) leads (B) led
(C) leading (D) leader

정답공식 02 빈칸 뒤에 시간과 관련된 명사(hour, time)가 있으면 limited가 정답이다!

03 Due to the ongoing renovation, the library will be open with ------- hours this month.
(A) limited (B) limiting
(C) limit (D) limits

04 TechVista Solutions is offering free trials for a ------- time to new subscribers.
(A) limiting (B) limits
(C) limited (D) to limit

정답공식 03 보기에 remain이 있으면 과거분사가 아닌 현재분사를 정답으로 고른다!

05 The ------- items on the agenda will be discussed in the next meeting.
(A) remaining (B) remains
(C) remained (D) remain

06 The ------- changes to the schedule will be communicated to all employees by e-mail.
(A) remains (B) remainder
(C) remained (D) remaining

정답공식 04 빈칸 뒤에 by가 있으면 과거분사를 정답으로 고른다!

07 Lectures ------- by international experts will be translated into three languages.
(A) conducted (B) conducts
(C) conduct (D) conducting

08 Company revenue increased by 15 percent this quarter, according to data ------- by the finance department.
(A) collects (B) collecting
(C) collected (D) collective

HACKERS TEST

빈칸에 가장 알맞은 보기를 고르세요.

01 The company has invited ------- professionals to share their knowledge at the conference.
(A) leader (B) leads
(C) leading (D) led

02 The school board approved the proposal for an ------- school day starting next semester.
(A) extend (B) extended
(C) extender (D) extension

03 Attracting new customers costs more than retaining ------- ones.
(A) existing (B) existed
(C) exist (D) existence

04 Lakeside Bistro's seasonal menu will be available for a ------- time during summer.
(A) limited (B) limit
(C) limiting (D) limitation

05 A special award was presented to Dane Evans, ------- him for his many years of service on the police force.
(A) honorable (B) honored
(C) honors (D) honoring

06 Westbrook Industries' first quarter results were quite ------- compared to earlier projections.
(A) disappoint (B) disappointed
(C) disappointing (D) disappointment

07 An electric vehicle charging station is located ------- the main entrance of the building's parking lot.
(A) from (B) beside
(C) throughout (D) down

08 ------- exceptional talent in mathematics, Lisa was offered a scholarship to a prestigious university.
(A) Displaying (B) Display
(C) Displays (D) Displayer

09 The research facility is located in a ------- area of the island, six hours from the nearest town by boat.
(A) seclude (B) secluded
(C) secluding (D) to seclude

10 ------- in handcrafted furniture, the local artisan studio has gained recognition for the exceptional quality of its products.
(A) Specialize (B) Specializes
(C) Specializing (D) Specialization

11 Membership in the dental association is limited strictly to ------- dentists with at least three years of professional practice.
(A) license (B) licensed
(C) licensing (D) licenses

12 The stagnant economy of the country has made it hard for people to find jobs, ------- in more of its citizens looking for work overseas.
(A) result (B) resulting
(C) resulted (D) results

13 Decisions ------- large sums of money must be discussed at a formal meeting with all the partners.
(A) involve
(B) involving
(C) will involve
(D) have involved

14 Our project will be guided by a team of ------- specialists in environmental sustainability.
(A) experiencing
(B) experience
(C) experienced
(D) experiences

15 The investors were ------- that quarterly profits increased by 15 percent despite the industry downturn.
(A) surprise
(B) surprised
(C) surprising
(D) surprisingly

16 The tower, ------- by a renowned architect Jonathan Green, has become a landmark in the city.
(A) designs
(B) designing
(C) designed
(D) designable

17 Ms. Goodman drove to Pasadena ------- visit the store where she purchased the blender.
(A) by
(B) to
(C) on
(D) due to

18 Guests ------- the fundraising banquet should arrive at least 30 minutes early for registration and seating.
(A) attend
(B) attends
(C) attendance
(D) attending

19 Our customer service department is open for ------- hours due to the national holiday.
(A) limited
(B) limit
(C) limiting
(D) limitation

20 There is enough food ------- in the pantry to last through the weekend.
(A) has remained
(B) remainder
(C) remained
(D) remaining

21 The team was ------- that the final design met all of their requirements.
(A) satisfying
(B) satisfied
(C) satisfy
(D) satisfies

22 The law banning the use of cell phones while driving is intended to reduce accidents involving ------- drivers.
(A) distract
(B) distracted
(C) distraction
(D) distracts

23 The ------- analysts asked detailed questions about the company's five-year financial projection.
(A) interestingly
(B) interested
(C) interest
(D) interests

24 Instructions on how to install the software are included in the ------- file.
(A) attaches
(B) attaching
(C) attach
(D) attached

빈출 어휘 | 형용사 2

✔ PART 5 어휘 문제에 자주 출제되는 어휘를 예문과 함께 확실히 익혀두세요.

01 **confidential** 기밀의
treat **confidential** information carefully
기밀 정보를 주의 깊게 취급하다

02 **supplemental** 보충하는, 추가의
submit **supplemental** documents for approval
승인을 위한 보충 서류를 제출하다
[파] supplement 보충하다

03 **comfortable** 편안한
design a **comfortable** waiting area
편안한 대기 공간을 설계하다
[파] comfort 편안하게 하다 [반] uncomfortable 불편한

04 **adequate** 충분한, 적절한
ensure **adequate** time for discussion
토론을 위한 충분한 시간을 확보하다
[반] inadequate 불충분한

05 **potential** 잠재적인
send brochures to **potential** clients
잠재적인 고객들에게 소책자를 보내다

06 **ongoing** 지속적인, 진행 중인
provide **ongoing** support for staff
직원을 위한 지속적인 지원을 제공하다
[동] continuous 지속적인

07 **compelling** 설득력 있는
offer **compelling** reasons for the policy change
정책 변경에 대해 설득력 있는 이유를 제시하다
[파] compel 강요하다

08 **commercial** 영리적인, 상업의
hire a **commercial** agency for advertising
광고를 위해 영리 대행사를 고용하다
[파] commerce 상업

09 **complicated** 복잡한
simplify **complicated** processes for convenience
편의를 위해 복잡한 절차를 간소화하다
[반] simple 단순한

10 **authentic** 진품의, 진짜의
display **authentic** works of the artist
화가의 진품들을 전시하다
[동] genuine 진짜의 [반] fake 가짜의

11 **conflicting** 상충하는
address **conflicting** opinions on the issue
이슈에 대한 상충하는 의견들을 다루다
[파] conflict 충돌하다

12 **excessive** 과도한
limit **excessive** use of paper
과도한 종이 사용을 제한하다
[파] exceed 초과하다

13 **original** 원래의, 독창적인
preserve the **original** features of the building
건물의 원래의 특징을 보존하다
[파] originate 기원하다, 시작되다

14 **adaptable** 적응성 있는, 적응할 수 있는
sell **adaptable** clothing for outdoor use
야외 사용을 위한 적응형 의류를 판매하다
[파] adapt 적응하다

15 **impartial** 공정한
conduct **impartial** interviews with applicants
지원자들과 공정한 면접을 진행하다

16 **absolute** 완전한, 절대적인
gain **absolute** control over the budget
예산에 대한 완전한 통제권을 얻다

17 ambitious 야심 찬

reveal **ambitious** plans for expansion
확장을 위한 야심 찬 계획을 드러내다

[파] ambition 야망

18 persuasive 설득력 있는

deliver **persuasive** presentations to investors
투자자들에게 설득력 있는 발표를 하다

[파] persuade 설득하다

19 outstanding 뛰어난, 두드러진, 미결제의

demonstrate **outstanding** leadership
뛰어난 리더십을 보여주다

20 extended 연장된

take **extended** leave for personal reasons
개인적인 이유로 연장된 휴가를 받다

[파] extension 연장

토익 실전문제

01 The architect said that the issue with the tower's design is not a very ------- problem to solve.

(A) complicated (B) adequate
(C) distributed (D) popular

02 The added legroom offered in business class made the long flight more -------.

(A) humble (B) clever
(C) adaptable (D) comfortable

03 The two groups have ------- demands that cannot be resolved without a compromise.

(A) crowded (B) anonymous
(C) absorbed (D) conflicting

04 Kiva Telecom's goal of obtaining a 25 percent market share this year seems ------- to most investors.

(A) ambitious (B) extensive
(C) absolute (D) mutual

05 The construction of the manufacturing plant will create many jobs and have a ------- effect on the local economy.

(A) respectful (B) mandatory
(C) favorable (D) voluntary

06 Our sales team's demonstration was ------- enough to convince many trade show attendees to order the company's product.

(A) certified (B) persuasive
(C) durable (D) predictable

07 Glasgow Antiques is known for being able to restore old and damaged items to their ------- condition.

(A) extra (B) impartial
(C) original (D) bright

08 The store's manager is unhappy with the ------- amount of time it takes to unload deliveries.

(A) confidential (B) excessive
(C) dynamic (D) advanced

정답·해석·해설 p.156

DAY 10 등위/상관접속사와 관계절

매회 0~1문제 출제

나는 농구를 좋아한다. 그리고 나는 축구를 좋아한다.
　　　　　　　　　　　 등위접속사

내가 좋아하는 운동은 농구와 축구이다.
　관계절　　　명사

첫 번째 문장에서 '나는 농구를 좋아한다'와 '나는 축구를 좋아한다'가 '그리고'로 연결되어 있습니다. 이처럼 단어, 구, 절을 대등하게 연결해 주는 접속사에는 **등위/상관접속사**가 있습니다.

두 번째 문장에서 '내가 좋아하는'이 명사인 '운동'을 꾸며주고 있습니다. 이처럼 명사를 꾸미는 형용사 역할을 하는 절을 **관계절**이라고 합니다.

기출포인트 01 등위/상관접속사

- 등위접속사는 단어, 구, 절을 대등하게 이어주는 접속사로, 문맥에 알맞은 것을 써야 합니다.

  and 그리고　　or 또는　　but 그러나, 하지만　　yet 그러나　　so 그래서, 그러므로　　for 왜냐하면

  * so와 for는 절과 절만 연결할 수 있으며, 단어나 구는 연결하지 못합니다.

  Daniel speaks English (~~but~~, **and**) French fluently. Daniel은 영어와 프랑스어를 유창하게 말한다.
  → 영어, 그리고 프랑스어를 유창하게 말한다는 의미이므로 but(그러나)이 아닌 and(그리고)를 써야 합니다.

  She didn't bring her access card, (~~yet~~, **so**) she couldn't enter the building.
  그녀는 출입카드를 안 가져와서, 건물에 들어갈 수 없었다.
  → 출입카드를 안 가져와서 건물에 들어갈 수 없었다는 의미이므로 yet(그러나)이 아닌 so(그래서)를 써야 합니다.

- 상관접속사는 단어, 구, 절을 대등하게 이어주는 접속사로, 서로 짝을 이루어 쓰이므로 알맞은 짝을 골라야 합니다.

  both A and B A와 B 둘 다　　　　　　　　not A but B A가 아니라 B
  either A or B A 또는 B 중 하나　　　　　 not only A but (also) B A뿐만 아니라 B도
  neither A nor B A도 B도 아닌　　　　　　A as well as B B뿐만 아니라 A도

  Neither the restaurant (~~or~~, **nor**) the café was open on Sunday. 식당도 카페도 일요일에는 열지 않았다.
  → 상관접속사 neither는 nor와 서로 짝이 맞으므로 or가 아닌 nor를 써야 합니다.

  The movie is not only entertaining (~~and~~, **but also**) educational. 그 영화는 재미있을 뿐만 아니라 교육적이기도 하다.
  → 상관접속사 not only는 but also와 서로 짝이 맞으므로 and가 아닌 but also를 써야 합니다.

실전 Check-up

01 Mr. Anders ------- his associates will be attending the Continental Book Fair in Berlin on May 15.

(A) and　　　　　　(B) but

02 Registered users are able to download research articles in ------- print and audio form.

(A) both　　　　　　(B) either

정답·해석·해설 p.156

기출포인트 02 관계절의 형태와 자리

- 관계절의 형태는 '관계대명사 + (주어) + 동사 ~'입니다. 이것은 두 문장에서 공통되는 명사 중 하나를 관계대명사로 바꿔 한 문장으로 만든 것입니다.

    I bought a book. + It is about Korean history. 나는 책을 샀다. + 그것은 한국 역사에 관한 것이다.
    (두 문장에서 book과 It은 같은 대상이다.)

    I bought a book **that is about Korean history**. 나는 한국 역사에 관한 책을 샀다.
    　　　　　　　　관계절(관계대명사 (+ 주어) + 동사 ~)
    (두 문장을 연결하면서 대명사 It을 대신하는 관계대명사로 바꾼다.)

- 관계절은 문장에서 형용사 역할을 하며, 꾸며주는 명사 뒤에 옵니다. 이때 관계절의 꾸밈을 받는 명사를 선행사라고 합니다.

    The client **who requested a meeting** is here. 회의를 요청한 고객이 여기에 와 있다.
    선행사　　　　　　관계절

- 관계절을 이끄는 관계대명사 자리에 대명사는 올 수 없습니다.

    The CEO thanked the manager (~~she~~, **who**) secured the major contract.
    최고 경영자는 주요 계약을 얻어낸 관리자에게 감사를 표했다.
    → manager를 꾸며주기 위한 관계절을 이끄는 자리이므로 대명사(she)가 아닌 관계대명사(who)가 와야 합니다.

기출포인트 03 관계대명사의 종류

- 앞에 나온 명사(선행사)가 사람인지 사물인지, 그리고 관계절 내에서 주격, 목적격, 소유격으로 쓰이는지에 따라 각각 다른 관계대명사가 쓰입니다.

선행사 \ 격	주격	목적격	소유격
사람	who	who, whom	whose
사물·동물	which	which	whose
사람·사물·동물	that	that	-

She is the teacher **whom** all the students respect. 그녀는 모든 학생이 존경하는 선생님이다.
　　　　　사람

The computer **which** was purchased last month has stopped working. 지난달에 구매한 컴퓨터가 작동을 멈췄다.
　　사물

실전 Check-up

01 The furniture ------ arrived yesterday needs to be assembled before use.

(A) which　　　　(B) who

02 Several artists ------ the gallery featured in the exhibition have gained international recognition.

(A) which　　　　(B) whom

정답·해석·해설 p.157

기출포인트 04 관계대명사의 격 구별

● 관계절 안에 주어가 없으면 주격 관계대명사 who/which/that을 씁니다.

Customers who spend over 100 dollars are eligible for free shipping. 100달러 넘게 지출하는 고객들은 무료 배송을 받을 수 있다.
→ 관계절 내에 주어가 없으므로 주격 관계대명사 who를 써야 합니다.

● 관계절 안에 목적어가 없으면 목적격 관계대명사 who(m)/which/that을 쓰며, 이때 목적격 관계대명사는 생략 가능합니다.

The doctor **(whom)** I consulted yesterday gave me useful advice. 내가 어제 상담한 의사는 나에게 유용한 조언을 해주었다.
→ 관계절 내에 목적어가 없으므로 목적격 관계대명사 whom을 써야 합니다.

The house **(which)** I bought recently is very spacious. 내가 최근 구입한 집은 매우 넓다.
→ 관계절 내에 목적어가 없으므로 목적격 관계대명사 which를 써야 합니다.

● 바로 뒤에 명사가 오고 '(선행사)의'로 해석되면 소유격 관계대명사 whose를 씁니다.

They found a painting **whose** value was estimated at millions of dollars. 그들은 가치가 수백만 달러로 추정되는 그림을 발견했다.
→ 관계대명사 바로 뒤에 명사 value가 왔고 관계대명사가 관계절 안에서 '~의'로 해석되므로 소유격 관계대명사 whose가 왔습니다.

실전 Check-up

01 The apartments ------- overlook the park are more expensive than the others.

(A) that (B) whom

02 A Paris-based company, ------- headquarters is located in the city, is opening a branch in New York.

(A) who (B) whose

정답·해석·해설 p.157

3초컷 정답 공식

자주 출제되는 정답 공식을 적용하여 빈칸에 가장 알맞은 보기를 고르세요.

정답공식 01 앞뒤에 연결된 절 중 부정문이 있으면 but이 정답일 확률이 높다!

01 The machine is not powerful enough to handle large volumes, ------- it works well for smaller tasks.
(A) to (B) but
(C) between (D) or

02 Main Avenue is not crowded at the moment, ------- it will be busy later today.
(A) nor (B) with
(C) but (D) by

정답공식 02 빈칸 앞에 사람을 가리키는 명사가 있고, 뒤에 동사가 바로 이어지면 who나 that이 정답이다!

03 All employees ------- participate in the training program will receive a certificate of completion.
(A) who (B) whom
(C) whose (D) which

04 The client ------- requested the design change has agreed to cover additional costs.
(A) whom (B) that
(C) which (D) whose

정답공식 03 빈칸이 선행사와 명사 사이에 있고, 빈칸 뒤에 완전한 문장이 오면 whose가 정답이다!

05 Nova University will provide grants to departments ------- research projects focus on sustainability.
(A) whose (B) those
(C) that (D) which

06 Our warranty covers products ------- serial numbers have been registered online.
(A) even (B) whose
(C) that (D) whom

정답공식 04 빈칸 앞에 콤마가 있으면 that을 정답으로 고르면 안 된다!

07 The CEO unveiled the company's new product line at the conference, ------- was attended by over 500 industry professionals.
(A) that (B) which
(C) whose (D) himself

08 Professor Kim, ------- has been teaching economics for over 20 years, published a new textbook last month.
(A) who (B) which
(C) that (D) whose

HACKERS TEST

빈칸에 가장 알맞은 보기를 고르세요.

01 The Lakeford branch will be closed on Monday, ------- customers are asked to visit nearby locations.
(A) so
(B) about
(C) or
(D) even

02 Passengers can ------- check in at the self-service kiosk or use the airline's mobile app.
(A) neither
(B) either
(C) nor
(D) both

03 Several crates of fruit were donated by Ms. Ku, ------- family owns a farm outside of town.
(A) some
(B) these
(C) whose
(D) most

04 All visitors to the Kentworth Plant are required to sign in at the security office ------- pick up a guest pass.
(A) and
(B) yet
(C) in
(D) which

05 Customers will receive points for every purchase they make, ------- they can use to buy other products sold in the store.
(A) what
(B) which
(C) these
(D) that

06 Tim Kelly evaluates consumer appliances in both his social media feed ------- his magazine articles.
(A) so
(B) and
(C) not
(D) than

07 Gift certificates will be given to those ------- complete Oriang Health Spa's survey by July 18.
(A) who
(B) they
(C) what
(D) theirs

08 The sales team did an excellent job promoting the product, ------- the device was not popular due to technical issues.
(A) and
(B) but
(C) so
(D) with

09 The intern ------- assisted with the project was offered a full-time job.
(A) who
(B) which
(C) whose
(D) this

10 ------- current and prospective investors are invited to attend the shareholders' meeting on March 15.
(A) Both
(B) Each
(C) Either
(D) This

11 All technicians are working to fix the problems ------- were reported last week.
(A) who
(B) whose
(C) that
(D) ahead

12 The company representatives ------- we met at the trade show offered valuable partnership opportunities.
(A) them
(B) whom
(C) which
(D) whose

13 The photographer ------- image is selected for this year's magazine cover will be given a cash prize of 10,000 dollars.

(A) that
(B) as
(C) whose
(D) even

14 Neither the restaurant manager ------- the owner was notified about the fire safety inspection scheduled for tomorrow.

(A) of
(B) both
(C) and
(D) nor

15 The organization announced a new benefits package, ------- was well received by employees.

(A) that
(B) which
(C) what
(D) one

16 Job candidates ------- want to apply for different jobs from the one advertised must submit separate applications.

(A) who
(B) which
(C) whom
(D) whose

17 For their five-year service anniversary, employees may select a wristwatch, fountain pen, ------- premium leather wallet as a gift.

(A) or
(B) but
(C) so
(D) nor

18 SkyNet Television announced that ------- prestigious summer film festival will be broadcast live from Los Angeles next month.

(A) it
(B) whose
(C) they
(D) its

19 It is widely recognized that adults who engage in sports ------- social activities experience less stress.

(A) within
(B) as well as
(C) accordingly
(D) ever

20 Ms. Dawson is part of the group ------- is organizing the annual office party this year.

(A) here
(B) whose
(C) that
(D) they

21 Those who ------- for remote work report higher job satisfaction in recent studies.

(A) opts
(B) opt
(C) opting
(D) to opt

22 Manufacturers are looking for ways to ------- lower operating costs.

(A) considering
(B) considerate
(C) considerable
(D) considerably

23 The equipment ------- was ordered last month has finally arrived at the warehouse.

(A) who
(B) whom
(C) which
(D) what

24 Contract terms are ------- negotiable nor adjustable after the signing date.

(A) both
(B) either
(C) often
(D) neither

빈출 어휘 | 부사 1

✅ PART 5 어휘 문제에 자주 출제되는 어휘를 예문과 함께 확실히 익혀두세요.

01 currently 현재, 지금

review **currently** available resources
현재 이용 가능한 자원을 검토하다

파 current 현재의

02 temporarily 일시적으로

close **temporarily** for renovations
보수 공사를 위해 일시적으로 문을 닫다

파 temporary 일시적인

03 completely 완전히

completely change the event schedule
행사 일정을 완전히 변경하다

파 complete 완전한

04 frequently 자주, 빈번히

update the security software **frequently**
보안 소프트웨어를 자주 업데이트하다

파 frequent 빈번한

05 significantly 상당히, 현저하게

significantly increase sales through marketing
마케팅을 통해 매출을 상당히 증가시키다

파 significant 상당한

06 evenly 고르게, 균등하게

distribute the workload **evenly** among team members
팀원들 간에 업무량을 고르게 분배하다

파 even 고른 반 unevenly 고르지 않게

07 immediately 즉시, 바로 가까이에

respond **immediately** to customer inquiries
고객 문의에 즉시 응답하다

파 immediate 즉각적인

08 diligently 부지런히

work **diligently** to meet the tight deadline
빠듯한 마감 기한을 맞추기 위해 부지런히 일하다

파 diligent 부지런한

09 thoroughly 철저히

inspect the equipment **thoroughly**
장비를 철저히 점검하다

파 thorough 철저한

10 elsewhere 다른 곳에서

look for a suitable apartment **elsewhere**
다른 곳에서 적합한 아파트를 찾다

11 conveniently 편리하게

be **conveniently** located near a subway station
지하철역 근처에 편리하게 위치하다

파 convenient 편리한 반 inconveniently 불편하게

12 closely 면밀히, 긴밀히

read the employment contract **closely**
고용 계약서를 면밀히 읽다

파 close 가까운

13 promptly 신속히

promptly deliver all documents to the lawyer
모든 서류를 변호사에게 신속히 전달하다

파 prompt 신속한

14 directly 직접, 곧장

contact the store manager **directly**
매장 관리자에게 직접 연락하다

파 direct 직접적인 반 indirectly 간접적으로

15 entirely 전적으로, 완전히

entirely agree with the revised proposal
수정된 제안에 전적으로 동의하다

파 entire 전체의

16 independently 독립적으로

carry out the project **independently**
프로젝트를 독립적으로 수행하다

파 independent 독립적인

17 **unexpectedly** 뜻밖에, 예상치 않게

unexpectedly discover a solution
뜻밖에 해결책을 발견하다
파 **unexpected** 예상치 못한

18 **precisely** 정확히

describe the current situation **precisely**
현재 상황을 정확히 설명하다
파 **precise** 정확한

19 **considerably** 상당히

expand our market share **considerably**
우리의 시장 점유율을 상당히 확대하다
파 **considerable** 상당한

20 **previously** 이전에

previously worked in the sales department
이전에 영업부에서 일했다
파 **previous** 이전의

토익 실전문제

01 A developer built townhouses on the lot ------- occupied by the shopping center.
(A) seriously (B) gradually
(C) particularly (D) previously

02 Arqua Inc. advised users to install a security update ------- to prevent potential attacks.
(A) justly (B) promptly
(C) evenly (D) abundantly

03 The one-day workshop will start ------- at 10 A.M., so participants are recommended not to be late.
(A) closely (B) smoothly
(C) precisely (D) confidentially

04 The championship basketball game has attracted a great deal of public attention, so tickets are ------- sold out.
(A) regularly (B) directly
(C) completely (D) generally

05 Any changes to the plan must be ------- discussed with the client before they are applied.
(A) seemingly (B) independently
(C) easily (D) thoroughly

06 Ms. Roberts worked ------- on the marketing report to complete it by the deadline.
(A) diligently (B) obviously
(C) clearly (D) distinctly

07 Fast-fashion companies introduce new clothing items ------- to maintain the interest of consumers.
(A) frequently (B) accidentally
(C) unexpectedly (D) nearly

08 The cost of many food products is ------- lower now that the free trade agreement has been implemented.
(A) extensively (B) considerably
(C) attentively (D) elsewhere

정답·해석·해설 p.160

DAY 11 부사절과 명사절

매회 2~3문제 출제

<u>날씨가 흐렸기 때문에</u>, 나는 우산을 챙겼다.
　　　부사절

기상 캐스터는 <u>오늘 날씨가 흐릴 예정이라는 것</u>을 보도했다.
　　　　　　　　　　　　　명사절

첫 번째 문장에서 주절은 '나는 우산을 챙겼다'이고, 앞에 있는 '날씨가 흐렸기 때문에'는 우산을 챙긴 이유를 나타내는 종속절입니다. 이처럼 주절을 수식하여 시간, 조건, 이유 등의 부가적인 정보를 제공하는 절을 **부사절**이라고 합니다.

두 번째 문장에서 '오늘 날씨가 흐릴 예정이라는 것'이라는 절이 '기상 캐스터는 보도했다'라는 문장에 포함되어 목적어 자리에 왔습니다. 이처럼 명사가 오는 자리에 와서 명사 역할을 하는 절을 **명사절**이라고 합니다.

기출포인트 01 부사절의 형태와 자리

- 부사절의 형태는 '부사절 접속사 + 주어 + 동사 ~'입니다.

    She stayed home **because** she felt sick. 그녀는 아팠기 때문에 집에 머물렀다.
    　　　　　　　　부사절 접속사(because) + 주어(she) + 동사(felt) ~

- 부사절은 문장에서 주절의 앞이나 뒤에 옵니다. 주절의 앞에 올 때는 부사절 뒤에 쉼표(,)를 반드시 붙여야 합니다.

    주절 앞　**Unless you leave now**, you will miss the last train. 만약 지금 출발하는 게 아니라면, 너는 마지막 기차를 놓칠 것이다.

    주절 뒤　Ms. Holly always drinks a cup of tea **before she starts working**.
    　　　　Ms. Holly는 일을 시작하기 전에 항상 차 한 잔을 마신다.

- 부사절 접속사는 동사가 있는 절 앞에 오고, 전치사는 동사가 없는 구 앞에 옵니다.

부사절 접속사	전치사
while ~하는 동안	during, for ~ 동안
although, even though 비록 ~이지만	in spite of, despite ~에도 불구하고
because, since ~이기 때문에	because of, due to ~ 때문에

　The phone rang (~~during~~, **while**) everyone was sleeping. 모두가 자고 있는 동안 전화벨이 울렸다.
　　　　　　　　　전치사(X)　부사절 접속사(O)

　(~~Although~~, **Despite**) the economic downturn, the company reported record profits.
　부사절 접속사(X) 전치사 (O)
　경기 침체에도 불구하고, 회사는 기록적인 이익을 발표했다.

실전 Check-up

01　------ the snowstorm will make traveling to the office difficult, the manager has decided to let everyone work remotely tomorrow.

　(A) Due to　　　　(B) Since

02　The crowd cheered loudly ------- the members of the national soccer team were entering the stadium.

　(A) while　　　　(B) during

정답·해석·해설 p.161

기출 포인트 02 부사절 접속사

● 부사절이 '~할 때/~할 때까지'와 같이 시간의 의미를 나타낼 때, 다음의 시간 접속사를 씁니다.

| when ~할 때 | while ~하는 동안 | since ~한 이래로 | as soon as ~하자마자 |
| before ~하기 전에 | after ~한 후에 | until ~할 때까지 | once ~하는 대로 |

I'll call you **as soon as** I arrive at the airport. 저는 공항에 도착하자마자 전화할게요.

● 부사절이 '만약 ~이라면/~이 아니라면'과 같이 조건의 의미를 나타낼 때, 다음의 조건 접속사를 씁니다.

| if 만약 ~이라면 | unless 만약 ~이 아니라면 | as long as ~하는 한 | in case ~에 대비하여, ~의 경우 |

They will cancel the event **if** it rains. 만약 비가 온다면 그들은 행사를 취소할 것이다.

● 부사절이 '~하기 때문에/~이므로'와 같이 이유의 의미를 나타낼 때, 다음의 이유 접속사를 씁니다.

| since/as/because ~하기 때문에 | now that ~이므로, ~이니까 |

Since the traffic was heavy, we were late for the meeting. 교통이 혼잡했기 때문에, 우리는 회의에 늦었다.

● 부사절이 '비록 ~이지만/~한 반면에'와 같이 주절과 상반된 의미를 나타낼 때, 다음의 양보 접속사를 씁니다.

| although/(even) though/even if 비록 ~이지만, ~일지라도 | while/whereas ~한 반면에 |

Although the exam was difficult, most students passed it. 비록 시험이 어려웠지만, 대부분의 학생들이 통과했다.

● 부사절이 '~할 수 있도록/매우 ~해서 -하다'와 같이 목적과 결과의 의미를 나타낼 때, 다음의 목적 및 결과 접속사를 씁니다.

| so that ~할 수 있도록 | so ~ that - 매우 ~해서 -하다 |

I'm saving money **so that** I can buy a new car. 나는 새 차를 살 수 있도록 돈을 모으고 있다.

실전 Check-up

01 A children's reading room will open in the Griswold Public Library ------- the third-floor renovations are finished.

(A) once (B) so that

02 ------- the latest version of the NX smartphone includes many features, it is less popular than its predecessor.

(A) Although (B) Until

정답·해석·해설 p.161

기출포인트 03 명사절의 형태와 자리

- 명사절의 형태는 '명사절 접속사 + 주어 + 동사 ~'입니다.

    Please tell me **whether** you can attend the seminar. 당신이 세미나에 참석할 수 있는지 제게 알려주세요.
    명사절 접속사(whether) + 주어(you) + 동사(can attend) ~

- 명사절은 문장에서 명사 역할을 하므로 명사처럼 주어, 목적어, 보어 자리에 옵니다.

    주어 자리　　**That** Mr. Moresby won the competition surprised everyone.
    　　　　　　Mr. Moresby가 대회에서 이겼다는 것이 모두를 놀라게 했다.

    목적어 자리　I wonder **if** she will accept our offer. 나는 그녀가 우리의 제안을 수락할지 궁금하다.
    　　　　　　　　　　동사의 목적어

    　　　　　　We talked about **whether** we should move. 우리는 우리가 이사해야 할지에 대해 이야기했다.
    　　　　　　　　　　　　　전치사의 목적어

    보어 자리　　My concern is **how** the project will be funded. 나의 걱정은 프로젝트가 어떻게 자금을 조달할 것인가이다.

기출포인트 04 명사절 접속사: that

- 명사절 접속사 that이 이끄는 명사절은 '~라는 것'을 의미하며, 문장에서 주어, 동사의 목적어, 보어로 쓰입니다.

    주어　　　　　**That** she speaks five languages impressed the interviewers.
    　　　　　　그녀가 다섯 개의 언어를 구사한다는 것은 면접관들에게 깊은 인상을 주었다.

    동사의 목적어　They reported **that** the mission was successful. 그들은 임무가 성공적이었다는 것을 보고했다.

    보어　　　　　His suggestion was **that** we should postpone the meeting. 그의 제안은 우리가 회의를 연기해야 한다는 것이었다.

실전 Check-up

01 ------ customers prefer online shopping or in-store experiences is crucial information for retailers.

　　(A) Whether　　　　(B) While

02 Recent market research suggests ------ consumer preferences are shifting toward more eco-friendly products.

　　(A) though　　　　(B) that

정답·해석·해설 p.161

기출포인트 05 명사절 접속사: whether, if

- whether가 이끄는 명사절은 '~인지 아닌지'를 의미하며, 문장에서 주어, 목적어, 보어로 쓰입니다.

주어	**Whether** we should postpone the event needs discussion.	우리가 행사를 연기해야 할지 아닌지는 논의가 필요하다.
동사의 목적어	They confirmed **whether** the hotel reservation was made.	그들은 호텔 예약이 되었는지 아닌지 확인했다.
전치사의 목적어	The decision depends on **whether** the budget is approved.	그 결정은 예산이 승인되는지 아닌지에 달려 있다.
보어	The issue is **whether** the company should invest in the project. 문제는 회사가 그 프로젝트에 투자해야 하는지 아닌지이다.	

- whether는 'whether A or B', 'whether or not'으로 자주 쓰입니다.

We don't know **whether** the training is optional **or** mandatory. 우리는 교육이 선택인지 필수인지 모른다.

The board is debating **whether or not** the company should proceed with the merger.
이사회는 회사가 합병을 진행해야 할지 아닌지 토론 중이다.

- if가 이끄는 명사절도 '~인지 아닌지'를 의미하는데, whether가 이끄는 명사절과는 달리 문장에서 동사의 목적어와 보어로만 쓰입니다.

동사의 목적어	The manager asked **if** we had enough stock to fulfill the orders. 관리자는 우리가 주문들을 충족시킬 만큼 충분한 재고가 있는지 아닌지 물었다.
보어	The issue is **if** the government will approve the new regulations. 쟁점은 정부가 새로운 규제를 승인할지 아닌지이다.

실전 Check-up

01 The city council will determine ------- it will provide funding for the new community center.

(A) whether (B) as long as

02 Her only concern was ------- the contract would be renewed for another year.

(A) unless (B) if

정답·해석·해설 p.162

기출포인트 06 명사절 접속사: 의문사

- who, whom, whose, what, which는 의문대명사로 명사절을 이끌며, 명사절 내에서 주어, 목적어, 보어 역할을 합니다. 따라서 뒤에 주어나 목적어, 보어가 없는 불완전한 절이 옵니다.

    I don't know **who** wrote this report. 나는 누가 이 보고서를 작성했는지 모른다.
    　　　　　　　목적어

- whose, what, which는 의문형용사로 뒤에 나온 명사를 꾸미면서 명사절을 이끌며, '의문형용사 + 명사'가 명사절 내에서 주어, 목적어, 보어 역할을 합니다. 따라서 뒤에 주어나 목적어, 보어가 없는 불완전한 절이 옵니다.

    Which backpack she buys will be determined by its style. 그녀가 어느 배낭을 살지는 그것의 스타일에 의해 결정될 것이다.
    　　주어

- when, where, how, why는 의문부사로 명사절을 이끌며, 뒤에 빠지는 것 없는 완전한 절이 옵니다.

    When the contract expires is clearly stated in the document. 계약이 언제 만료되는지는 문서에 명확히 명시되어 있다.
    　　주어

- '의문사 + to 부정사'가 명사절을 이끌기도 합니다.

    | what + to 부정사 무엇을 ~할지 | which + to 부정사 어떤 것을 ~할지 | when + to 부정사 언제 ~할지 |
    | who(m) + to 부정사 누구를 ~할지 | where + to 부정사 어디에(서) ~할지 | how + to 부정사 어떻게 ~할지 |

    He explained **how to solve** the problem step by step. 그는 그 문제를 어떻게 해결할지를 단계별로 설명했다.

- '의문사 + ever'는 복합관계대명사로 명사절을 이끌며, 문장에서 주어와 목적어 역할을 합니다.

    who(m)ever 누구든 간에　　　whatever 무엇이든 간에　　　whichever 어느 것이든 간에, 어느 사람이든 간에

    Whoever wants to join the trip must sign up by Friday. 여행에 참가하고 싶은 사람은 누구든 간에 금요일까지 신청해야 한다.

    I will accept **whichever** the committee recommends. 나는 위원회가 추천하는 것은 어느 것이든 간에 받아들일 것이다.

실전 Check-up

01 The survey asked consumers about ------- features they consider most important when purchasing a television.
(A) which　　(B) that

02 ------- is submitted by a writer must be reviewed by the magazine's editor prior to publication.
(A) Another　　(B) Whatever

3초컷 정답 공식

자주 출제되는 정답 공식을 적용하여 빈칸에 가장 알맞은 보기를 고르세요.

정답공식 01 문장에 현재완료 시제가 있으면 since를 정답으로 고른다!

01 Our international client base has expanded rapidly ------- we opened branch offices in Europe.
(A) between (B) with
(C) since   (D) from

02 It has been six months ------- the company's restructuring policies were implemented.
(A) before (B) until
(C) while   (D) since

정답공식 02 빈칸 뒤에 can/could가 있다면 so that이 정답이다!

03 All guests must check out by 12 P.M. ------- housekeeping can clean up the rooms before new guests arrive.
(A) even   (B) so that
(C) as if   (D) otherwise

04 The event was moved to a larger convention center ------- it could accommodate more people.
(A) if   (B) when
(C) instead of (D) so that

정답공식 03 빈칸 뒤에 진행 시제가 있으면 while이 정답일 확률이 높다!

05 The restaurant will be closed on Friday evening ------- the kitchen renovation is taking place.
(A) until   (B) away
(C) though (D) while

06 The passengers remained calm ------- the airplane was experiencing turbulence.
(A) while (B) so
(C) until (D) still

정답공식 04 state/inform/suggest/report/confident 뒤에 '빈칸 + 주어 + 동사'가 있다면 that이 정답이다!

07 The contract explicitly states ------- payment must be made within 30 days of receiving an invoice.
(A) what (B) so
(C) that (D) for

08 Before we departed for the mountain trail, our tour guide suggested ------- we bring water for the hiking trip.
(A) with (B) which
(C) on   (D) that

정답·해석·해설 p.162

HACKERS TEST

빈칸에 가장 알맞은 보기를 고르세요.

01 The presentation will finish ahead of schedule ------- people have a lot of questions.
(A) besides (B) despite
(C) once (D) unless

02 The report indicates ------- the company should focus its marketing efforts next quarter.
(A) where (B) which
(C) what (D) who

03 Our company's online presence has improved dramatically ------- we hired the new social media manager last spring.
(A) because of (B) since
(C) until (D) during

04 The salon's supplier asked for payment for the hair products in full, ------- they cannot be shipped until next week.
(A) even though (B) apart from
(C) as soon as (D) due to

05 Trains bound for Wesleyville will not be stopping at Jaspers ------- the station there is being renovated.
(A) while (B) aboard
(C) then (D) until

06 The manager wants to know ------- might be willing to work over the weekend.
(A) who (B) why
(C) how (D) those

07 The gift card may be used ------- the cardholder activates it online.
(A) later (B) after
(C) while (D) sometimes

08 The chef will show the cooking class participants ------- to prepare authentic Italian dishes.
(A) what (B) how
(C) which (D) whom

09 Please inform the residents ------- a test of the building's fire alarm will take place on Saturday at 8 A.M.
(A) each (B) too
(C) that (D) which

10 All players ------- in the National Tennis Tournament are required to register for the event by June 3 at the latest.
(A) competing (B) competes
(C) competed (D) has been competing

11 ------- Paskow Foods should reduce the size of its workforce is being considered.
(A) Upon (B) Often
(C) Whether (D) If

12 Owner Sylvia Aspen decided to hire more servers for her café ------- the increasing number of customers.
(A) whereas (B) so that
(C) due to (D) because

13 Fast Mail returns packages and documents to senders ------- it fails to deliver the items to their intended recipients.
(A) still
(B) where
(C) or
(D) when

14 With the advent of social networking sites, most companies made changes in ------- they advertise.
(A) about
(B) so
(C) thus
(D) how

15 The country's stock market achieved gains, ------- other nations suffered losses.
(A) thus
(B) besides
(C) whereas
(D) concerning

16 The national news agency reported ------- unemployment rates have fallen to the lowest level in five years.
(A) which
(B) that
(C) what
(D) about

17 No payments can be made to the insurance subscriber ------- the claim has been examined by the department.
(A) otherwise
(B) besides
(C) until
(D) despite

18 The inventory manager needs to determine ------- items should be restocked first based on consumer demand.
(A) whoever
(B) which
(C) who
(D) these

19 A copy of the employee manual has been posted online ------- people want to review it.
(A) even if
(B) in case
(C) on behalf of
(D) aside from

20 Beaton Dairy's annual company picnic will take place on Saturday in Maple Park ------- it does not rain that day.
(A) as long as
(B) whereas
(C) especially
(D) as well as

21 Please fill out the enclosed customer data sheet ------- we can let you know about our latest offerings and promotions.
(A) instead of
(B) following
(C) so that
(D) according to

22 ------- limited marketing, the musical attracted a sizable audience on its opening night.
(A) By
(B) Even though
(C) During
(D) In spite of

23 The presentation will be more effective ------- it includes more charts.
(A) if
(B) unlike
(C) else
(D) just

24 ------- uses the stapler last is requested to return it to the mail room.
(A) Whoever
(B) Whatever
(C) Everyone
(D) Whose

빈출 어휘 | 부사 2

✓ PART 5 어휘 문제에 자주 출제되는 어휘를 예문과 함께 확실히 익혀두세요.

01 especially 특별히, 특히
be **especially** designed for beginners
초보자들을 위해 특별히 설계되다
파 special 특별한

02 rapidly 빠르게
rapidly increase production using automation
자동화를 사용하여 생산을 빠르게 늘리다
파 rapid 빠른

03 enthusiastically 열정적으로
participate in discussions **enthusiastically**
토론에 열정적으로 참여하다
파 enthusiastic 열정적인

04 accordingly 그에 알맞게, 적절히
get paid **accordingly** for the role
역할에 알맞게 보수를 받다

05 politely 정중하게
respond **politely** to customer complaints
고객 불만에 정중하게 답변하다
파 polite 정중한 반 rudely 무례하게

06 correctly 정확하게, 올바르게
identify the cause of the problem **correctly**
문제의 원인을 정확하게 파악하다
파 correct 정확한, 올바른 반 incorrectly 부정확하게

07 unusually 보통과는 달리, 대단히
receive an **unusually** large order
보통과는 달리 많은 주문을 받다
파 unusual 특이한

08 extremely 극히, 극도로
show **extremely** impressive results
극히 인상적인 결과를 보여주다
파 extreme 극도의

09 successfully 성공적으로
close the deal with the client **successfully**
고객과 거래를 성공적으로 마무리하다
파 successful 성공적인

10 seamlessly 매끄럽게
seamlessly integrate with existing systems
기존 시스템과 매끄럽게 통합되다
파 seamless 매끄러운

11 equally 동등하게
distribute resources **equally** among all departments
모든 부서에 자원을 동등하게 배분하다
파 equal 동등한

12 strictly 엄격히
strictly enforce the new regulations
새로운 규정들을 엄격히 시행하다
파 strict 엄격한 동 rigidly 엄격하게

13 heavily 많이, 심하게
invest **heavily** in healthcare infrastructure
의료 기반 시설에 많이 투자하다
파 heavy 무거운

14 eventually 결국, 마침내
eventually succeed in achieving their goal
결국 그들의 목표를 달성하는 데 성공하다

15 punctually 정시에
arrive **punctually** for the scheduled meeting
예정된 회의에 정시에 도착하다
파 punctual 시간을 잘 지키는

16 continuously 지속적으로
continuously monitor the progress
진행 상황을 지속적으로 관찰하다
파 continuous 지속적인

17 increasingly 점점 더, 갈수록 더

become **increasingly** popular with consumers
소비자들에게 점점 더 인기 있게 되다

파 **increase** 증가하다 반 **decreasingly** 점점 감소하여

18 initially 처음에

initially target the local market
처음에 지역 시장을 목표로 삼다

파 **initial** 처음의

19 consequently 결과적으로, 그 결과로

consequently affect the performance
결과적으로 성과에 영향을 미치다

파 **consequence** 결과

20 consistently 일관되게

consistently apply guidelines across all branches
모든 지점에 걸쳐 지침을 일관되게 적용하다

파 **consistent** 일관된 반 **inconsistently** 일관성 없이

토익 실전문제

01 Both countries are ------- attractive as potential locations for the new factory.
(A) exactly (B) steadily
(C) punctually (D) equally

02 The consultant ------- identified the company's problem as one of low staff motivation.
(A) occasionally (B) correctly
(C) sharply (D) highly

03 Participation in the weekly brainstorming sessions is ------- voluntary for the sales staff.
(A) entirely (B) immediately
(C) successfully (D) openly

04 With the event a month away, organizers are growing ------- concerned by the lack of interest.
(A) abruptly (B) initially
(C) increasingly (D) precisely

05 Concert attendees are ------- prohibited from filming the musicians during their performances.
(A) voluntarily (B) strictly
(C) nearly (D) freely

06 Mr. Banerjee ------- declined the invitation to appear on the television talk show.
(A) extremely (B) politely
(C) diligently (D) greatly

07 According to the plan, the first three floors of the building will ------- be occupied by retail stores.
(A) seamlessly (B) previously
(C) eventually (D) closely

08 The chain restaurant will need lots of capital to expand ------- across the country.
(A) rapidly (B) generally
(C) positively (D) distinctly

정답·해석·해설 p.165

DAY 12 비교 구문

매회 0~1문제 출제

거북이는 달팽이만큼 빠르다.
　　　　원급 구문

토끼는 거북이보다 빠르다.
　　　　비교급 구문

셋 중 토끼가 가장 빠르다.
　　　　최상급 구문

비교 구문에는 '거북이'와 '달팽이'처럼 비교하는 두 대상이 동등할 때 쓰는 원급 구문, '토끼'와 '거북이'처럼 두 개의 비교 대상 중 하나가 더 우월할 때 쓰는 비교급 구문, 그리고 '토끼'처럼 셋 이상의 비교 대상 중 하나가 가장 뛰어날 때 쓰는 최상급 구문이 있습니다.

기출포인트 01 원급·비교급·최상급의 형태

● 형용사나 부사가 1음절 단어이거나, -er, -y, -ow, -some으로 끝나는 2음절 단어일 때는 다음과 같은 형태를 가집니다.

원급(형용사나 부사의 일반 형태)	비교급(원급 + -er)	최상급(원급 + -est)
fast(빠른)	faster	fastest
narrow(좁은)	narrower	narrowest

● 형용사나 부사가 -able, -ful, -ous, -ive 등으로 끝나거나, 3음절 이상의 단어일 때는 다음과 같은 형태를 가집니다.

원급(형용사나 부사의 일반 형태)	비교급(more + 원급)	최상급(most + 원급)
professional(전문적인)	more professional	most professional
reasonable(합리적인)	more reasonable	most reasonable

● 어떤 형용사와 부사는 -er/-est를 쓰지 않고 고유의 비교급/최상급 형태를 가집니다.

원급	비교급	최상급
good/well(좋은/잘)	better	best
bad(나쁜)	worse	worst
many/much(많은)	more	most
little(적은)	less	least

실전 Check-up

01 The ValuePlus supermarket is ------- to our office than ShopSmart Plaza.

(A) closer　　　　(B) close

02 GrandLux Tower is the ------- of the buildings in the downtown business district.

(A) tall　　　　(B) tallest

정답·해석·해설 p.166

기출포인트 02 원급 구문

- '~만큼 -한'이라는 의미로 두 대상의 동등함을 나타내는 원급 구문은 'as + 형용사/부사 + as'를 씁니다.

  The running shoes are **as expensive as** the designer sunglasses. 그 운동화는 그 유명 브랜드 선글라스만큼 비싸다.

  This inexpensive camera captures images **as clearly as** professional equipment.
  이 비싸지 않은 카메라는 전문 장비만큼 선명하게 이미지를 담아낸다.

- '~만큼 많은/적은 명사'라는 의미를 나타내는 원급 구문은 'as + many/much/few/little + 명사 + as'를 씁니다.

  The store will provide customers with **as many samples as** they request.
  　　　　　　　　　　　　　　　　　　　　　　　　　명사
  그 상점은 고객이 요청하는 만큼 많은 견본품을 제공할 것이다.

기출포인트 03 비교급 구문

- '~보다 -한'이라는 의미로 두 대상 중 한쪽이 우월함을 나타내는 비교급 구문은 '형용사/부사의 비교급 + than'을 씁니다. 따라서 문장에 than이 나오면 앞에는 형용사/부사의 비교급이 와야 합니다.

  Fresh fruit tastes **sweeter than** canned fruit. 신선한 과일은 통조림 과일보다 더 달다.

  The train runs **more frequently than** the bus on weekends. 기차는 주말에 버스보다 더 자주 운행된다.

- 형용사나 부사의 비교급을 강조하는 표현으로는 much, even, still, far(훨씬) 등이 있습니다.

  Our products are **much cheaper** than similar items at other stores.
  　　　　　　　　　　　　비교급
  우리 제품들은 다른 상점들의 유사한 물건들보다 훨씬 더 저렴하다.

실전 Check-up

01 The team completed the project as ------- as expected.

(A) quicker　　　　(B) quickly

02 With recent price reductions, international flights have become ------- than they were last year.

(A) more affordable　　　　(B) affordable

정답·해석·해설 p.166

기출포인트 04 최상급 구문

- '~ 중에 가장 -한'이라는 의미로 셋 이상의 대상들 중 하나가 우월함을 나타내는 최상급 구문은 'the + 형용사/부사의 최상급 + of ~/in ~/that절'을 씁니다.

My sister lives **the most happily of all my family members**. 내 여동생은 우리 가족 구성원들 중에 가장 행복하게 살고 있다.

The car's ride is **the smoothest that I've ever experienced**. 그 차의 주행감은 내가 지금까지 경험해 본 것 중에 가장 부드럽다.

기출포인트 05 토익에 잘 나오는 비교급·최상급 표현

- 비교급이 포함된 표현은 다음과 같습니다.

more than + 명사 ~보다 많은	no longer 더 이상 ~ 않다
less than + 명사 ~보다 적은	other than ~ 이외에
no later than 늦어도 ~까지	rather than ~보다는
no sooner ~ than - ~하자마자 -하다	the + 비교급 ~, the + 비교급 - ~하면 할수록 더 -하다

I prefer tea **rather than** coffee in the morning. 나는 아침에 커피보다는 차를 선호한다.

The higher you climb, **the colder** it gets. 높이 올라갈수록 더 추워진다.

- 최상급이 포함된 표현은 다음과 같습니다.

one of the + 최상급 + 복수 명사 가장 ~한 사람/것 중 하나	the + 서수 + 최상급 몇 번째로 가장 ~한

She is **one of the most respected scientists** in her field. 그녀는 그녀의 분야에서 가장 존경받는 과학자 중 한 명이다.

This company is **the second oldest** manufacturer in the industry. 이 회사는 그 산업에서 두 번째로 오래된 제조업체이다.

실전 Check-up

01. When launching a startup, securing funding is the ------- prerequisite for first-year survival.
    (A) essentially   (B) most essential

02. The recent survey showed that ------- than 30 percent of people prefer digital books to print ones.
    (A) longer   (B) more

정답·해석·해설 p.166

3초컷 정답 공식

자주 출제되는 정답 공식을 적용하여 빈칸에 가장 알맞은 보기를 고르세요.

정답공식 01 no와 than 사이에 빈칸이 있으면 later가 정답일 확률이 높다!

01 Guests must check out no ------- than 11 A.M. to avoid additional charges.
(A) later (B) late
(C) lateness (D) latest

02 Vendors are required to confirm their booth reservations no ------- than two weeks prior to the event.
(A) latest (B) later
(C) lately (D) late

정답공식 02 빈칸 뒤에 than이 있으면 비교급이 정답이다!

03 The demand for electric vehicles is ------- now than ever.
(A) height (B) high
(C) highly (D) higher

04 Consumer interest in organic and locally sourced food is ------- than it was a decade ago.
(A) strong (B) strongly
(C) strength (D) stronger

정답공식 03 문장에 '(out) of all ~'이 있으면 최상급을 정답으로 고른다!

05 Of all the candidates interviewed, Ms. Johnson has the ------- qualifications for the position.
(A) better (B) best
(C) good (D) well

06 The company acquired the ------- market share out of all competitors.
(A) significance (B) more significant
(C) most significant (D) significant

정답공식 04 빈칸이 the와 variety/selection 사이에 있으면 widest가 정답이다!

07 The Polyglot Haven Bookstore carries the ------- variety of foreign language publications in the city.
(A) widely (B) widen
(C) widest (D) wider

08 The ------- selection of travel packages makes this agency a top choice for vacationers.
(A) widen (B) widely
(C) width (D) widest

HACKERS TEST

빈칸에 가장 알맞은 보기를 고르세요.

01 The new printer works as ------- as the previous model while using less energy.
(A) effective
(B) effectively
(C) more effective
(D) effectiveness

02 All contractors should complete the renovation work no ------- than the first week of July.
(A) later
(B) late
(C) lateness
(D) latest

03 The GreenLeaf Restaurant features the ------- variety of vegetarian options in the city.
(A) width
(B) wider
(C) widely
(D) widest

04 As of next week, the office building will no ------- be accessible on weekends without special permission.
(A) longer
(B) long
(C) longing
(D) longest

05 Of all the products in our catalog, the KitchenMaster Pro 3000 has been the ------- one this season.
(A) popularity
(B) more popular
(C) most popular
(D) popular

06 This year's conference had more attendees ------- last year's event.
(A) than
(B) that
(C) from
(D) of

07 The orientation has been pushed back by 30 minutes ------- the meeting room is still being used by the finance department.
(A) whereas
(B) though
(C) unless
(D) because

08 Our Web site should be as ------- as the competitor's platform to entice more customers.
(A) more attractive
(B) attractively
(C) attractive
(D) most attractive

09 The network's decision to move the late show to an earlier time slot allowed it to reach a ------- audience than before.
(A) broaden
(B) broadly
(C) broadest
(D) broader

10 Compared to other marketing strategies, social media advertising has performed the ------- this year.
(A) successfully
(B) most successfully
(C) more successfully
(D) successful

11 The error causing processing delays for applications should be ------- immediately.
(A) address
(B) addressed
(C) addressing
(D) addresses

12 The Braxton Copper Mine was once one of the ------- worksites, but safety improvements have greatly reduced workplace accidents.
(A) dangers
(B) most dangerous
(C) dangerously
(D) more dangerously

13 The Parkview Residence apartment is as ------- as a typical suburban house despite being in the city center.
(A) spacious
(B) spaciously
(C) more spacious
(D) spaciousness

14 ABC Inc.'s quarterly profits will be ------- than originally estimated, according to the CEO's recent announcement.
(A) low
(B) lower
(C) lowest
(D) lowering

15 The architect designed the building with the ------- windows to maximize natural light in the workspace.
(A) largest
(B) largely
(C) larger
(D) largeness

16 The videos of lectures posted on the Web site have been edited, so they will be slightly ------- than the live lectures.
(A) short
(B) shorter
(C) shortly
(D) shortest

17 Investors are the ------- cautious about stock prices when evaluating a company.
(A) either
(B) some
(C) most
(D) much

18 The warranty does not cover malfunctions ------- those caused by technical defects.
(A) prior to
(B) other than
(C) along with
(D) according to

19 Bronson Heavy Machinery has implemented the ------- safety protocols in the entire industry.
(A) strictest
(B) stricter
(C) strict
(D) strictly

20 Sunlight Hotel has received the highest customer satisfaction rating ------- all the accommodation facilities listed on Trivv.
(A) about
(B) along
(C) of
(D) under

21 The group enjoyed the cruise organized by Stellar Travel, calling it the ------- holiday ever.
(A) most memorable
(B) memorize
(C) memorable
(D) memorably

22 ------- purchasing a car for his daily commute, Mr. Sufi has decided to take advantage of public transportation.
(A) Compared to
(B) Rather than
(C) Even though
(D) As long as

23 Myson Publishing paid ------- than 500 dollars to rent a booth at the book fair.
(A) less
(B) further
(C) rather
(D) under

24 The Silverleaf National Park trails will be accessible ------- the wildfire recovery efforts are completed.
(A) in spite of
(B) as soon as
(C) owing to
(D) in order to

빈출 어휘 | 어구

✅ PART 5 어휘 문제에 자주 출제되는 어휘를 예문과 함께 확실히 익혀두세요.

01 comply with ~을 준수하다, 따르다
The product **complies with** all environmental regulations.
그 제품은 모든 환경 규정을 준수한다.

02 replace A with B A를 B로 교체하다
The technician will **replace** the laptop's battery **with** a new one.
기술자는 노트북 배터리를 새것으로 교체할 것이다.

03 follow the instructions 지시를 따르다
Please **follow the instructions** to complete the setup process.
설치 절차를 완료하기 위해 지시를 따르세요.

04 host an event 행사를 주최하다
Our team was selected to **host an event** during the festival.
우리 팀이 축제 동안 행사를 주최하도록 선정되었다.

05 familiarize oneself with ~에 익숙해지다
The interns **familiarized themselves with** the company's policies.
인턴들은 회사의 정책에 익숙해졌다.

06 conduct a survey 설문조사를 실시하다
Ms. Hayes **conducted a survey** to assess employee satisfaction.
Ms. Hayes는 직원 만족도를 평가하기 위해 설문조사를 실시했다.

07 a series of 일련의
The doctor performed **a series of** medical tests to determine the patient's condition.
의사는 환자의 상태를 판단하기 위해 일련의 의료 검사들을 실시했다.

08 a range of 다양한
The tablet has **a range of** advanced features.
그 태블릿은 다양한 고급 기능을 갖추고 있다.

09 a variety of 다양한, 여러 종류의
The community center offered **a variety of** programs for senior citizens.
지역사회 센터는 노인들을 위한 다양한 프로그램을 제공했다.

10 sales figures 판매 수치
The managers discussed the monthly **sales figures** in the meeting.
관리자들은 회의에서 월별 판매 수치에 대해 논의했다.

11 safety protocol 안전 규약
Factory workers are required to observe the **safety protocol**.
공장 근로자들은 안전 규약을 준수하도록 요구된다.

12 until further notice 추후 공지가 있을 때까지
Wait **until further notice** to board the aircraft.
비행기에 탑승하기 위해 추후 공지가 있을 때까지 기다려주세요.

13 in response to ~에 대응하여
An updated model was released **in response to** market demand.
시장 수요에 대응하여 업데이트된 모델이 출시되었다.

14 be eligible for ~을 받을 자격이 있다
The customer **is eligible for** a full refund within 30 days.
그 고객은 30일 이내에 전액 환불을 받을 자격이 있다.

15 be pleased to ~하게 되어 기쁘다
Crofton Department Store **is pleased to** announce its summer sale.
Crofton 백화점은 여름 할인 판매를 발표하게 되어 기쁘다.

16 be attributed to ~의 덕분이다, ~에 기인하다
The success of the project **is attributed to** the team's efforts.
프로젝트의 성공은 팀의 노력 덕분이다.

17 be willing to ~할 의향이 있다

We **are willing to** work overtime next week.
우리는 다음 주에 초과 근무를 할 의향이 있다.

18 be famous for ~으로 유명하다

The owner of the bakery **is famous for** her cheesecake.
그 빵집의 주인은 그녀의 치즈케이크로 유명하다.

19 be responsible for ~을 담당하다, ~에 책임이 있다

The receptionist **is responsible for** keeping track of all appointments.
접수원은 모든 예약을 관리하는 것을 담당한다.

20 be urged to ~하도록 촉구받다

Mr. Yang **was urged to** reconsider his decision to retire.
Mr. Yang은 은퇴하기로 한 결정을 재고하도록 촉구받았다.

토익 실전문제

01 All staff, without exception, will participate in a ------- of development seminars.

(A) kind
(B) range
(C) member
(D) lack

02 The island is ------- for its beautiful beaches, clear blue waters, and relaxing atmosphere.

(A) interested
(B) famous
(C) responsible
(D) capable

03 The city of Lindberg will ------- an event to promote the annual chess tournament.

(A) host
(B) compare
(C) assume
(D) follow

04 The financial report highlighted sales ------- that reflected the company's overseas growth.

(A) designs
(B) supplies
(C) workers
(D) figures

05 The government will hold a ------- of public forums to gather additional input on its policy proposal.

(A) note
(B) series
(C) lecture
(D) possibility

06 Only members of Hoyts Retail's loyalty program are ------- for the discount.

(A) optional
(B) essential
(C) difficult
(D) eligible

07 The facility manager would like to remind everyone to ------- themselves with the building's emergency exits.

(A) distribute
(B) conduct
(C) collaborate
(D) familiarize

08 Applicants who do not ------- with the listed requirements will not be considered for the job.

(A) connect
(B) provide
(C) comply
(D) associate

정답·해석·해설 p.169

한 권으로 끝내는 해커스 토익 600+ LC+RC+VOCA

PART 6

DAY 13 문맥 파악 문제: 문법
DAY 14 문맥 파악 문제: 어휘
DAY 15 문맥 파악 문제: 문장

PART 6 알아보기

PART 6는 131번부터 146번까지 총 16문제로, 각 지문 내 4개의 빈칸에 알맞은 문법 사항이나 어휘, 또는 문장을 4개의 보기 중에서 골라 채우는 파트입니다. 16문제 중 문법 문제가 평균 7~8문제, 어휘 문제가 평균 4~5문제, 문장 고르기 문제가 4문제 출제됩니다.

PART 6 미리 보기

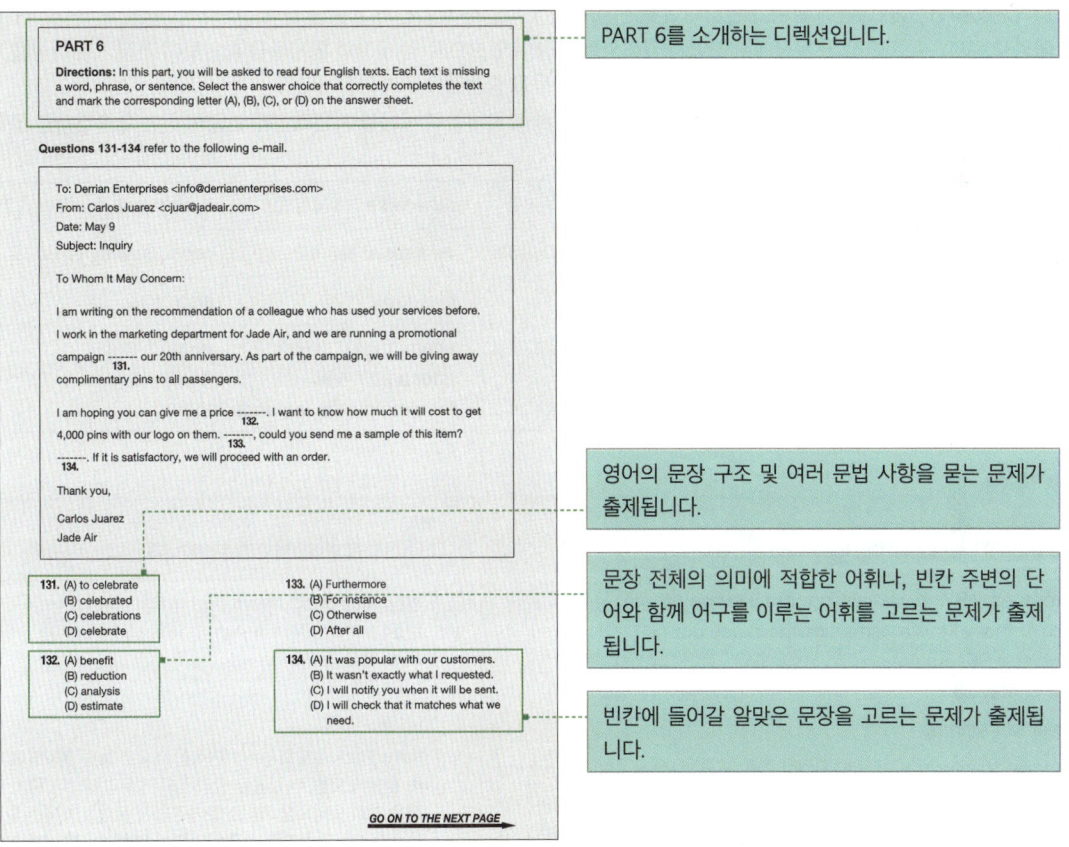

PART 6 학습 전략

- **PART 6에 자주 나오는 문제 유형별 최신 경향 및 전략 익히기**
  PART 6에서는 시제, 대명사, 접속부사, 명사 어휘 문제가 문맥 파악 문제로 자주 출제됩니다. 따라서 빈출 유형의 최신 경향 및 전략을 중점적으로 학습하면 목표 점수를 더욱 쉽고 빠르게 달성할 수 있습니다.

- **PART 6에 자주 출제되는 기출 어휘 익히기**
  어휘 문제는 문장을 해석한 뒤 문맥상 가장 알맞은 의미의 보기를 정답으로 골라야 하므로, PART 6에 자주 출제되는 기출 어휘를 꼭 익혀두어야 합니다.

문맥 파악 문제: 문법

문맥을 파악해서 풀어야 하는 문법 문제는 주변 또는 전체 문맥에 맞는 적절한 문법 사항을 고르는 문제입니다. PART 6 전체 16문제 중 매회 7~8문제가 문법 문제로 출제되는데 약 3~4문제가 문맥 파악 문제입니다.

최신 경향 및 전략

문맥 파악이 필요한 문법 문제로는 주로 시제, 대명사, 접속부사가 출제됩니다.

- **시제 문제**: 빈칸 주변에 쓰인 동사의 시제를 확인하여 빈칸에 들어갈 동사의 시제를 예상합니다. 만약 주변 문장에 날짜가 언급되어 있다면 지문 상단에 날짜가 언급되어 있는지도 함께 확인하여 시간의 흐름을 파악합니다.
- **대명사 문제**: 주로 빈칸 앞 문장에 빈칸에서 가리키는 대상이 있으므로 앞 문장의 명사들을 확인하여 가리키는 대상을 찾습니다. 이때, 빈칸에서 가리키는 대상의 수(단수/복수), 인칭 등을 중점적으로 확인합니다.
- **접속부사 문제**: 빈칸이 있는 문장과 그 앞 문장의 의미 관계를 파악하여 내용을 자연스럽게 연결해 주는 접속부사를 고릅니다. PART 6에 자주 출제되는 접속부사는 다음과 같습니다.

역접	however 그러나	even so 그렇기는 하지만	otherwise 그렇지 않으면	in contrast 그와 대조적으로
인과	therefore/thus 그러므로	for that reason 그 이유로	as a result 결과적으로	consequently 결과적으로
추가	in addition 게다가	furthermore 더욱이	moreover 게다가, 더욱이	also 게다가
기타	in particular 특히 in the meantime 그동안 unfortunately 불행히도	above all 무엇보다도, 특히 then 그러고 나서 likewise 마찬가지로	alternatively 그 대신에 after all 결국에는 for example/for instance 예를 들어	instead 대신에 finally 마침내

Example

Question 01 refers to the following e-mail.

From: Amy Blend <amyb@righttrackrailways.com>
To: Anthony Martin <amartin@mailplace.com>
Subject: RE: Inquiry
Date: May 23

Dear Mr. Martin,

I regret to inform you that Right Track Railways cannot refund tickets for trains missed due to personal reasons. Our company policy allows refunds only when we fail to provide the service promised. ------, we would like to offer you a 10 percent discount on your next trip. Thank you for your understanding.

01 (A) However
　 (B) Likewise
　 (C) In particular
　 (D) For instance

해석
01번은 다음 이메일에 관한 문제입니다.

발신: Amy Blend <amyb@righttrackrailways.com>
수신: Anthony Martin <amartin@mailplace.com>
제목: 회신: 문의
날짜: 5월 23일

Mr. Martin께,

Right Track 철도회사는 개인적인 이유로 놓친 열차표에 대해 환불해 드릴 수 없음을 알리게 되어 유감입니다. 당사 규정은 저희가 약속한 서비스를 제공하지 못했을 때에만 환불을 허용합니다. 01그러나, 귀하의 다음 여행에 10퍼센트 할인을 제공하고자 합니다. 양해해 주셔서 감사합니다.

01 (A) 그러나
　 (B) 마찬가지로
　 (C) 특히
　 (D) 예를 들어

해설 접속부사 채우기 주변 문맥 파악　　　　　　　　　　　　　　　　　　　　　　　　　　　　　　　　　　　정답 (A)
빈칸이 콤마와 함께 문장의 맨 앞에 온 접속부사 자리이므로, 앞 문장과 빈칸이 있는 문장의 의미 관계를 파악하여 정답을 선택한다. 앞부분에서 개인적인 이유로 놓친 열차표에 대해 환불해 줄 수 없다고 한 반면, 빈칸을 포함한 문장에서는 다음 여행에 10퍼센트 할인을 제공하고자 한다고 했으므로, 상반되는 내용을 나타낼 때 사용되는 (A) However(그러나)가 정답이다.

어휘
regret v. 유감스럽게 생각하다　personal adj. 개인적인　understanding n. 양해, 이해

HACKERS PRACTICE

빈칸에 가장 알맞은 보기를 고르세요.

Question 01 refers to the following memo.

TO: All store managers
FROM: Marissa Hamlett, vice president of operations
DATE: June 1
SUBJECT: New point-of-sale system

Bucky's Superstore ------ a new point-of-sale system at all branches on July 28. Store managers and staff members, particularly those assigned to the checkout registers, will need to be trained on how to use it. The new system will allow us to track sales and inventory. This will reduce the risk of stores running out of stock.

---

01 (A) installing
(B) will install
(C) is installed
(D) has installed

Question 02 refers to the following advertisement.

Are you looking for a quick, reliable, and affordable way to transform your office or home? True Colors specializes in painting the interiors of both commercial and residential properties, including offices, stores, and apartments. ------, our competitive pricing ensures that you can achieve a fresh look without exceeding your budget. So for fast and dependable service, call True Colors today at 555-2902. There is no job we can't handle.

---

02 (A) Moreover
(B) Unfortunately
(C) Otherwise
(D) Thus

Question 03 refers to the following e-mail.

TO: Norma Jennings <n_jennings@unitedmail.com>
FROM: Larry Keith <l.keith@str.com>
DATE: January 5
SUBJECT: Truck Rental

Dear Ms. Jennings,

Thank you for choosing Simons Truck Rental. The moving truck you requested for ------ upcoming relocation to Los Angeles may be picked up for use. Please visit our branch on Wilshire Road before 10 A.M. on January 17 to pick up the vehicle. Note that you will be required to show a valid driver's license for anyone who will be operating the vehicle. When you return the truck, one of our employees will inspect it. If there is any damage, the cost of repairs will be charged to the credit card you provided when making the reservation. Thank you.

---

03 (A) my
(B) our
(C) your
(D) their

정답·해석·해설 p.171

HACKERS TEST

빈칸에 가장 알맞은 보기를 고르세요.

Questions 01-04 refer to the following notice.

Notice to all Diego Corporation employees

The staff lunchroom will be inaccessible ------- (01) June 4 and June 7 to allow for some renovations. The primary improvement will be the addition of a window to one of the walls to let in more sunlight. Moreover, the old appliances will be replaced with modern ones. ------- (02), a much larger stainless-steel refrigerator will be installed.

In the meantime, ------- (03) Conference Rooms 1 and 2 during your lunch break. ------- (04). We appreciate your patience.

01
(A) since
(B) with
(C) into
(D) between

02
(A) Even so
(B) Otherwise
(C) For example
(D) However

03
(A) utilizes
(B) utilizing
(C) utilization
(D) utilize

04
(A) Those schedules have been posted on the doors.
(B) Both spaces are reserved for that specific purpose.
(C) Some staff members have asked for more time.
(D) The breaks were supposed to last less than an hour.

Questions 05-08 refer to the following letter.

Kendra Sampson
338 West Elm Drive
Burlington, Vermont 05402

Dear Ms. Sampson,

We are writing to notify you that your subscription to *Literature Now* ------- on June 1. If you do not renew before this date, your credit card will no longer be ------- for future issues. However, if you wish to continue your subscription, please contact us at 555-3922.

-------. For starters, you will be able to enjoy more articles by some of today's leading writers. You can also save 24 dollars over the course of the year with our May renewal discount. We hope you continue to subscribe to our -------.

Sincerely,

Literature Now Team

05 (A) expired
(B) expiring
(C) will expire
(D) is expired

06 (A) charging
(B) charged
(C) charges
(D) charge

07 (A) Trial subscriptions typically run for a six-month period.
(B) You can expect to receive the latest issue within just a few weeks.
(C) Our records indicate that you have been a reader for two years.
(D) There are plenty of reasons to renew your subscription.

08 (A) publication
(B) message
(C) installment
(D) episode

Questions 09-12 refer to the following article.

ALICE SPRINGS (August 26)—Owler Inc. was chosen for an upcoming energy project by Alice Springs City Council. It will install solar panels at all local public schools. -------. The project begins on October 1 at Gillen High School, which will be ------- with 225 panels. -------, Owler Inc. is scheduled to move on to East Side Elementary School and Braitling Middle School. When installed, the panels will result in thousands of dollars in annual savings for each school. "We chose Owler Inc. because of its low fees and ------- experience," said Alice Springs mayor Tanya McCrindle.

09 (A) Several environmental groups indicated their support for the project.
(B) Each company was assigned to work on a different school building.
(C) They apologized to parents for the additional delay.
(D) The winner of the contract will remain anonymous.

10 (A) equipping
(B) equip
(C) equipped
(D) equips

11 (A) Instead
(B) Then
(C) Yet
(D) Alternatively

12 (A) extensive
(B) routine
(C) predictable
(D) objective

Questions 13-16 refer to the following e-mail.

TO: Andrea Stinton <stinton.a@kuvarik.com>
FROM: Leroy Wauters <wauters.l@kuvarik.com>
SUBJECT: Recent inspection
DATE: November 17

Dear Ms. Stinton,

Yesterday, I ------- a mandatory inspection of the Kuvarik production plant in Donetsk. Though most items on the checklist were satisfactory, I discovered two potential ------- issues. First of all, we need to add three more fire extinguishers due to a change in regulations last year. -------. Secondly, I saw that some handrails are missing along one stairway. ------- would be essential in the event of an emergency. Please contact me so we can discuss ordering replacements.

Regards,

Leroy Wauters
Facility Manager

13. (A) scheduled
    (B) postponed
    (C) canceled
    (D) conducted

14. (A) service
    (B) safety
    (C) productivity
    (D) personnel

15. (A) If this isn't done promptly, we will be issued a fine.
    (B) The regulations require that we update our employee handbook.
    (C) New employees were trained to use the fire extinguishers.
    (D) As expected, we met our production quota last year.

16. (A) It
    (B) That
    (C) Theirs
    (D) They

문맥 파악 문제: 어휘

문맥을 파악해서 풀어야 하는 어휘 문제는 주변 또는 전체 문맥에 맞는 적절한 어휘를 고르는 문제입니다. PART 6 전체 16문제 중 매회 4~5문제가 어휘 문제로 출제되는데 약 3~4문제가 문맥 파악 문제입니다.

최신 경향 및 전략

1. 문맥 파악이 필요한 어휘 문제로는 명사, 동사, 형용사, 부사가 출제되며, 명사 어휘가 가장 많이 출제됩니다.
2. 주로 빈칸의 주변 문장에 단서가 되는 어휘나 표현이 포함되어 있으므로 빈칸 주변 문장을 확인합니다.
3. 명사 어휘 문제에서 빈칸 앞에 정관사(the), 소유격(your, his/her, their 등), 지시대명사/지시형용사(this, these, those 등)가 있으면 가리키는 대상이 앞 문장에 언급되어 있으므로 빈칸 앞 문장을 먼저 확인합니다.
4. 자주 나오는 어휘들을 익혀두면 도움이 됩니다.
   * PART 6에 자주 출제되는 어휘는 VOCA(시험장에도 들고 가는 토익 기출 VOCA) DAY 11~17에서 학습할 수 있습니다.

Example

Question 01 refers to the following letter.

February 2
Ingrid Helgarson
43 Thompson Avenue
Lansing, MI 48920

Dear Ms. Helgarson,

Our records indicate that you have been a regular customer at Aberdeen Grocers for the past four years. We appreciate your ------- .
01
To help us enhance our products and services, we would like to request that you complete a questionnaire on our Web site at www.aberdeengrocers.com.

We assure you that any personal information will be kept confidential and used solely for evaluating our performance. Thank you for your participation.

Yours truly,
Aberdeen Grocers Customer Service Team

01 (A) concern
(B) business
(C) donation
(D) understanding

해석
01번은 다음 편지에 관한 문제입니다.

2월 2일
Ingrid Helgarson
43번지 Thompson가
랜싱, 미시간 주 48920

Ms. Helgarson께,

저희의 기록은 귀하께서 지난 4년 동안 Aberdeen 식료 잡화점의 단골 고객이었음을 보여줍니다. **01귀하의 이용에 감사드립니다.**

저희의 제품과 서비스를 향상시키는 데 도움을 주실 수 있도록, 귀하께 저희의 웹사이트 www.aberdeengrocers.com에서 설문지를 작성해 주실 것을 요청하고 싶습니다.

개인 정보는 비밀로 유지될 것이고 오직 저희의 성과를 평가하는 데에만 사용될 것이라는 점을 귀하께 보장드립니다. 귀하의 참여에 감사드립니다.

Aberdeen 식료 잡화점 고객 서비스팀

01 (A) 우려
(B) 이용
(C) 기부
(D) 이해

해설 명사 어휘 고르기 주변 문맥 파악 　　　　　　　　　　　　　　　　　　　　　　　　　　　　정답 (B)
'귀하의 _____ 에 감사드립니다'라는 문맥이므로 모든 보기가 정답의 후보이다. 빈칸이 있는 문장만으로 정답을 고를 수 없으므로 주변 문맥이나 전체 문맥을 파악한다. 앞 문장에서 귀하, 즉 Ms. Helgarson이 지난 4년 동안 단골 고객이었다고 했으므로, Ms. Helgarson에게 그동안의 이용에 감사를 표한다는 것을 알 수 있다. 따라서 명사 (B) business((고객의) 이용)가 정답이다. (A) concern은 '우려', (C) donation은 '기부', (D) understanding은 '이해'라는 의미이다.

어휘
indicate v. 보여주다　appreciate v. 감사하다, 감상하다　questionnaire n. 설문지　assure v. 보장하다, 확언하다　confidential adj. 비밀의, 기밀의　participation n. 참여

HACKERS PRACTICE

빈칸에 가장 알맞은 보기를 고르세요.

Question 01 refers to the following announcement.

Maincore Diving Center

Congratulations on completing the three-day scuba diving course at Maincore Diving Center. It is our hope that you found it to be a ------- experience. We don't want you to forget your time with us. As a final requirement for certification, you will perform your first deepwater dive tomorrow. Please be sure to follow the procedures you have been taught to avoid injuries and accidents. The staff at the center will assist you in selecting your equipment.

---

01 (A) memorable
(B) sensitive
(C) mandatory
(D) reasonable

Question 02 refers to the following e-mail.

To: Winston Wheeler <w.wheeler@ata.com>
From: Matt Nicholson < m.nicholson@northshire.com>
Subject: Re: Projectors
Date: December 9

Dear Mr. Wheeler,

Thank you for providing me with the information about the projectors I requested. I appreciate your taking the time to ------- some of the brands available in your shop. Unfortunately, the ones suggested are too expensive. Nevertheless, I would like to know more about the speaker system you suggested. Could you send me the technical details for the speaker system? Thank you.

Matt Nicholson
IT Department Head, Northshire University

---

02 (A) replace
(B) improve
(C) recommend
(D) test

Question 03 refers to the following information.

Replacing printer ink cartridges is expensive. Moreover, disposing of them is harmful to the environment. Fortunately, most ink cartridges can be refilled and reused. Doing this is better than throwing them away because it saves money. It also reduces waste in landfills. Our office supply store has ink-refilling stations at all branches. We will confirm that your cartridge is ------- in good condition. If so, we will refill it at half the price of a new one.

---

03 (A) rarely
(B) frequently
(C) barely
(D) still

HACKERS TEST

빈칸에 가장 알맞은 보기를 고르세요.

Questions 01-04 refer to the following advertisement.

Kelli Corporation is proud to introduce its newly ------- Hava-Go hair dryer. The company's most portable model, the Hava-Go is cordless and weighs only 500 grams. These ------- make it very easy to use. -------. When fully charged, its battery lasts for up to 100 minutes. So you can dry your hair wherever you are.

------- a Hava-Go now. It's sold at electronics stores such as Ciao Mall and by online retailers, including GoodsSupply.com. Don't miss out on this amazing device!

01 (A) releases
 (B) releasing
 (C) released
 (D) release

02 (A) containers
 (B) machines
 (C) accessories
 (D) features

03 (A) The device is also ideal for traveling.
 (B) The design will be updated later this month.
 (C) A model name hasn't yet been chosen.
 (D) They're only being supplied to major hotel chains.

04 (A) Lend
 (B) Connect
 (C) Estimate
 (D) Purchase

Questions 05-08 refer to the following press release.

NEW YORK (January 28)—An advertisement for TymTech's newest laptop was named Best TV Ad at this year's Worldwide Marketing Awards. The ------- (05) advertisement was made by Telerana Associates.

------- (06) the world-famous athlete Wanda Vilanova, the 30-second advertisement was broadcast on stations across North America. English, Spanish, and French versions were created. "We ------- (07) considered cultural differences. Thus, we ensured that all three versions were effective," said Harold Martel, the director of Telerana Associates.

According to TymTech, the advertisement has resulted in record sales for the company. -------. (08)

05 (A) controversial
(B) sample
(C) winning
(D) canceled

06 (A) Starred
(B) Star
(C) Starring
(D) Stars

07 (A) carefully
(B) barely
(C) roughly
(D) randomly

08 (A) Vouchers were sent to all winners of the competition.
(B) The Worldwide Marketing Awards will make a decision soon.
(C) It plans to hire Telerana Associates again for future campaigns.
(D) This record was later broken by one of its main competitors.

Questions 09-12 refer to the following article.

September 9, Mexico City—Compensa Solutions has announced the ------- of Valeria Gomez. -------. Speaking to reporters, spokesperson Thomas Walden described Ms. Gomez as a terrific addition to the senior management of the firm. "We are ------- to welcome Ms. Gomez as our new chief marketing officer and hope that she can help us enter new markets with her extensive knowledge and years of experience," he said. ------- Ms. Gomez has not held an executive position before, she stated that she is prepared for the challenge.

09 (A) retirement
(B) appointment
(C) investment
(D) accomplishment

10 (A) They offer superior products and services.
(B) The company's sales have climbed steadily for over a year.
(C) A list of open positions at the firm is available through the Web site.
(D) The statement was made at a press conference yesterday.

11 (A) please
(B) pleased
(C) pleases
(D) pleasing

12 (A) While
(B) In spite of
(C) During
(D) Because

Questions 13-16 refer to the following announcement.

Sortix Digital Security Consultancy

URGENT ANNOUNCEMENT

Alephnet, makers of the Zeno operating system, will stop providing support for older versions of its platform. -------13-------, the company will not provide software updates for Zeno-10 anymore. So please upgrade to Zeno-11. -------14------- you fail to do this, your computer will be vulnerable to security threats. In general, Zeno-11 provides better security compared to the -------15------- platform. To ensure the stability of your system, we strongly urge you to update immediately. -------16-------. In case you have any additional questions, please contact us at cs@sortix.com.

13
(A) As a result
(B) Instead
(C) Once
(D) However

14
(A) By
(B) If
(C) Until
(D) Whether

15
(A) previous
(B) faulty
(C) proposed
(D) expensive

16
(A) Act now before this special promotion expires.
(B) We will send you a reminder as soon as one is available.
(C) The company has recalled several of its products.
(D) For installation instructions and support, refer to our Web site.

DAY 15 문맥 파악 문제: 문장

문맥을 파악해서 풀어야 하는 문장 문제는 주변 또는 전체 문맥에 맞는 적절한 문장을 고르는 문제입니다. PART 6 전체 16문제 중 매회 4문제 출제됩니다.

최신 경향 및 전략

1. 빈칸이 지문 처음에 제시되면 주로 지문의 주제나 목적을 나타내는 문장이 출제되며, 빈칸이 지문 중간이나 뒷부분에 제시되면 주로 빈칸 앞뒤 내용에 대한 요약, 강조, 첨가, 부연 설명, 이유, 결과와 관련된 문장이 출제됩니다.
2. 보기 내에 대명사(it, that, these 등)나 지시형용사(this, those 등)가 있다면 보기의 주변 문맥에 언급된 명사와 일치하는지 확인하고, 보기 내에 연결어(however, yet, also 등)가 있다면 빈칸의 앞뒤 문맥에 맞는 연결어인지 확인합니다.
3. 지문의 주제에서 벗어나거나, 앞뒤 문장과의 논리적 흐름이 어색하거나, 문장에서 지칭하는 대상이 앞뒤 문장의 대상과 불일치하는 오답에 유의합니다.

Example

Question 01 refers to the following article.

July 14—The St. Louis Restaurant Association will begin offering a monthly subscription plan on August 1. The goal is to promote the city's lesser-known restaurants.

When people sign up, they will be asked to indicate their preferred types of foods. Subscribers will receive a voucher for two entrées at a different restaurant each month and will be billed a monthly fee of only 20 dollars. -------. The St. Louis Restaurant Association is optimistic that the subscription model will lead to an overall increase in customers for its members.

01 (A) Association members can choose from vouchers with a range of values.
(B) Each restaurant specializes in a different type of international cuisine.
(C) Late payments will result in additional charges.
(D) This price is much lower than that of a regular two-person meal.

해석
01번은 다음 기사에 관한 문제입니다.

7월 14일—St. Louis 식당 협회는 8월 1일에 월간 구독 플랜을 제공하기 시작할 것이다. 목적은 이 도시의 덜 알려진 식당들을 홍보하는 것이다.

사람들이 가입할 때, 그들은 그들이 선호하는 음식의 종류를 표시하도록 요구받을 것이다. 가입자들은 매월 다른 식당에서의 두 개의 메인 요리 쿠폰을 받을 것이며 월 요금 20달러만이 청구될 것이다. ⁰¹이 가격은 일반적인 2인분 식사의 가격보다 훨씬 더 적다. St. Louis 식당 협회는 이 구독 모델이 회원들을 위한 전반적인 고객 증가로 이어질 것이라고 낙관한다.

01 (A) 협회 회원들은 다양한 값의 쿠폰 중에서 선택할 수 있다.
(B) 각각의 식당은 다양한 종류의 국제 요리를 전문으로 한다.
(C) 늦은 지불은 추가 요금을 야기할 것이다.
(D) 이 가격은 일반적인 2인분 식사의 가격보다 훨씬 더 적다.

해설 알맞은 문장 고르기 **정답 (D)**
앞 문장 "Subscribers will receive a voucher for two entrées ~ and will be billed a monthly fee of only 20 dollars."에서 가입자들은 두 개의 메인 요리 쿠폰을 받을 것이며 월 요금 20달러만이 청구될 것이라고 했으므로, 빈칸에는 요리 쿠폰의 가격과 관련된 내용이 들어가야 함을 알 수 있다. 따라서 (D)가 정답이다.

어휘
association n. 협회 value n. 값 specialize in ~을 전문으로 하다 late payment 늦은 지불 additional adj. 추가의 regular adj. 일반적인, 보통의 meal n. 식사

HACKERS PRACTICE

빈칸에 가장 알맞은 보기를 고르세요.

Question 01 refers to the following letter.

Dear Ms. Sunders,

At Edildburgh Technologies, our remarkable growth and innovative strategies have positioned us as a leader in the technology sector. Without the support of our shareholders, we would not have become one of the top electronics companies in Western Europe. -----01-----.
Enclosed is an invitation to the event.

Jasper Diaz
President, Edildburgh Technologies

---

01 (A) In addition, our company is now considering forming a partnership with its rival.
(B) Therefore, we want to show our appreciation for your support with a party.
(C) Our stock value has increased significantly over the past year.
(D) Thanks for expressing an interest in joining our team.

Question 02 refers to the following announcement.

COME TO THE FIRST-EVER ALGERIAN TRADE SHOW!

More than 200 Algerian manufacturers are scheduled to showcase their products at the Maktub Convention Center in November. Minister of Trade and Industry Samir Klouchi will open the exhibition on November 1. The month-long event aims to support local businesses. -----02-----.

---

02 (A) The event will last for one week.
(B) Submit your feedback forms by the end of today.
(C) It concludes on November 30 with a 15-minute fireworks show.
(D) Booths must be cleaned up by 8:00 P.M. each day.

Question 03 refers to the following e-mail.

To: Muscle Mass Gym <customerservice@mmg.com>
From: Oscar Perry <o.perry@tmail.com>
Date: September 4
Subject: Request

To Whom It May Concern:

-----03-----. I need to request the cancellation as I will be moving overseas. My membership is fully paid until the end of the year. However, since I will be unable to use it after October 1, I would like to get a refund for the unused portion. I look forward to your quick reply.

Regards,

Oscar Perry

---

03 (A) I wish to make a complaint about your fitness class instructor.
(B) My records show that I was charged an additional fee for September.
(C) I would like to cancel my membership with your establishment effective October 1.
(D) I appreciate that you processed my membership application so quickly.

HACKERS TEST

빈칸에 가장 알맞은 보기를 고르세요.

Questions 01-04 refer to the following announcement.

An Announcement for Cliffdale Ridge Manor Residents

This is to inform you that the new ------- permits will be available on August 26. These must be placed on all vehicles left in our underground garage.

They will include a bar code that can be ------- scanned. To receive one, turn in your old pass at Cliffdale Ridge Manor's maintenance office. ------- you get your new permit, stick it to the interior of your vehicle's front windshield. -------.

---

01 (A) parking
(B) construction
(C) trash
(D) access

02 (A) easy
(B) easily
(C) ease
(D) easiest

03 (A) Even if
(B) By the time
(C) Before
(D) As soon as

04 (A) The maintenance crew will complete the work next week.
(B) The safety inspection will be similar to last year's.
(C) Vehicles should be kept in good repair.
(D) Be sure to check that it is clearly visible.

Questions 05-08 refer to the following advertisement.

If you are looking to upgrade your wardrobe this fall, why not get a Winchester casual jacket by Edward Dormer? This jacket revives the brand's iconic look, -------(05) was popular in the 1940s. We take great pride in producing this premium clothing item. Each jacket is handcrafted using durable -------(06). These include high-quality leather, wool, and cotton. A special coating -------(07) to make each jacket wind-resistant and waterproof. -------(08). You can find this jacket online or at any of our store branches around the country.

05
(A) that
(B) who
(C) which
(D) when

06
(A) cases
(B) devices
(C) tools
(D) materials

07
(A) applying
(B) is applied
(C) is applying
(D) to apply

08
(A) Therefore, it will keep your body warm and dry.
(B) However, the jacket comes with several accessories.
(C) The first leather jackets appeared in the early 20th century.
(D) Mr. Dormer has owned the same jacket for years.

Questions 09-12 refer to the following e-mail.

To: Blair McKay <b.mckay@rdedental.com>
From: Nancy Tang <n.tang@goldhotel.com>
Subject: Business luncheon
Date: December 12

Dear Mr. McKay,

I just received your e-mail. -------(09)-------. The room you are considering renting can fit up to 50 people. Adding 10 more will not be a problem. Because you chose our buffet-style menu, we can easily adjust the -------(10)------- of food. I also agree with your idea to select flowers that match your company logo. I -------(11)------- with our florist that this is possible, and he plans to use blue and orange flowers. I am ready to prepare the final draft of the agreement, and -------(12)------- will be faxed to your office today.

Sincerely,

Nancy Tang
Gold Hotel

09 (A) We sincerely appreciate your assistance.
(B) There have been changes to the room you rented.
(C) We can certainly accommodate your request.
(D) Our manager will contact you regarding your concerns.

10 (A) amount
(B) type
(C) price
(D) quality

11 (A) will confirm
(B) am confirming
(C) have confirmed
(D) had confirmed

12 (A) it
(B) them
(C) those
(D) its

Questions 13-16 refer to the following information.

Sign up for the Middletown Art Exhibition!

Middletown's 8th Annual Art Exhibition will be held from August 1 to 14. Local painters, sculptors, and photographers are ------- to participate. The event will include artwork from numerous artists. Emerson Gallery and city hall have been selected as the sites to ------- the art. Residents will be able to view the exhibits at these locations free of charge for two weeks. -------.
                                                                                                    13   **14**   **15**

In order to join the event, visit www.middletown.gov/artexhibit_apply. Note that the deadline for applications is January 15. We will review ------- by February 20. All selected artists will be notified the following day.
                                                                                            16

13 (A) invite
(B) inviting
(C) invited
(D) invites

14 (A) store
(B) display
(C) judge
(D) package

15 (A) All works will be returned to the artists after this period.
(B) The cost of admission will be announced next month.
(C) A number of exhibition sites are currently being considered.
(D) The organizers were praised for the success of the event.

16 (A) that
(B) these
(C) it
(D) both

한 권으로 끝내는 해커스 토익 600+ LC+RC+VOCA

PART 7

- **DAY 16** 이메일/편지 및 메시지 대화문
- **DAY 17** 양식 및 광고
- **DAY 18** 기사 및 안내문
- **DAY 19** 공고 및 회람
- **DAY 20** 다중 지문

PART 7 알아보기

PART 7은 147번부터 200번까지 총 54문제로, 제시된 지문과 관련된 질문들에 대해 4개의 보기 중에서 가장 적절한 답을 선택하는 파트입니다. 단일 지문 10개에서 29문제, 이중 지문 2세트에서 10문제, 삼중 지문 3세트에서 15문제가 출제됩니다.

PART 7 미리 보기

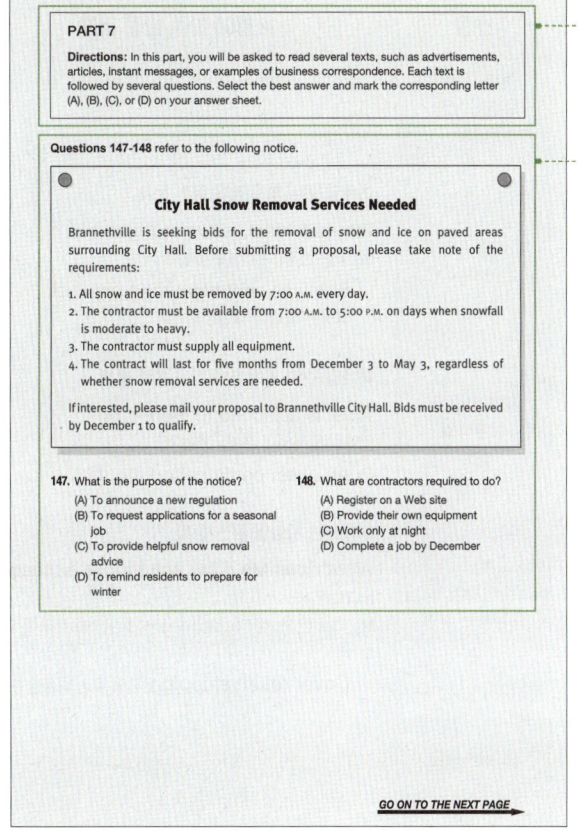

PART 7을 소개하는 디렉션입니다.

지문과 함께, 지문을 읽고 풀어야 하는 2~5개의 문제가 출제됩니다.

PART 7 학습 전략

- **지문 유형별로 자주 나오는 지문 흐름과 빈출 문제 익히기**
  PART 7은 지문 유형에 따른 전형적인 흐름이 있으며, 자주 출제되는 문제 또한 정해진 편입니다. 실제 시험에서 더욱 쉽게 지문의 내용을 파악하여 정확하게 문제를 풀 수 있도록, 지문별 흐름과 빈출 문제를 꼭 학습해야 합니다.

- **지문 유형별 자주 나오는 표현 익히기**
  PART 7의 지문 내용을 빠르게 파악하기 위해서는 지문의 흐름을 알려주는 표현을 익혀두어야 합니다.

DAY 16 이메일/편지 및 메시지 대화문

1. 이메일/편지

이메일/편지는 비즈니스나 개인 생활과 관련된 제품 구매, 서비스 이용, 고객 항의, 회사 생활 등에 관한 정보를 주고받는 편지글 형식의 지문입니다. PART 7에서 매회 7~8개 정도 출제됩니다.

지문 흐름과 빈출 문제

이메일	흐름	흐름에 따른 빈출 문제
TO: Mobile Accessories <service@maccessories.com> FROM: Naomi Clay <naomic@deftmail.com> DATE: January 17 SUBJECT: Order 34928 To Whom It May Concern: **I'm writing to** inform you that I received the wrong product in my order this morning.	받는 사람, 보내는 사람, 날짜	
	이메일/편지를 쓴 이유	**이메일/편지의 목적을 묻는 문제** Why did Ms. Clay write the e-mail? Ms. Clay는 왜 이메일을 썼는가? → She was sent the wrong product. 잘못된 물품을 배송받았다.
Unfortunately, it includes a case for the Athena 8 phone rather than the one for the Athena 7 that I ordered. **I have attached** an image of the order confirmation for your reference.	세부 사항 및 첨부파일 설명	**이메일/편지에 첨부된 것을 묻는 문제** What is attached to the e-mail? 이메일에 무엇이 첨부되었는가? → An order confirmation 주문 확인서
I will send back the one I mistakenly received. However, as this was your error, **I think you should cover the cost of return shipping. Please let me know** if this is possible. I look forward to your prompt response. Regards, Naomi Clay	수신자에게 요청하는 사항	**요청하는 사항을 묻는 문제** What does Ms. Clay ask Mobile Accessories to do? Ms. Clay는 Mobile Accessories사에 무엇을 하도록 요청하는가? → Cover return shipping 반품 배송 비용을 부담한다.
	보내는 사람	

해석 p.180

이메일/편지에서 지문의 흐름을 알려주는 표현들을 알아두면 도움이 됩니다.

- **이메일/편지의 목적**: I'm pleased to ~ ~하게 되어 기쁩니다
  I'm writing to ~ ~하기 위해 이메일/편지를 씁니다
- **동봉된 것**: I have attached/enclosed ~ 저는 ~을 첨부/동봉했습니다
- **요청 사항**: Could you ~? ~해 주실 수 있으신가요?
  Please let me know ~ ~을 알려 주시기 바랍니다
  I would appreciate ~ ~해 주시면 감사하겠습니다

자주 나오는 표현

제품 구매 및 서비스 이용	bill n. 요금 고지서, 청구서; v. 청구하다	reminder n. 상기시키는 것
	renewal n. 갱신	subscription n. 구독
	discount n. 할인	satisfy v. 충족시키다
	make a change 변경하다	reward n. 보상
	account n. 계정	available adj. 구입할 수 있는, 이용할 수 있는
고객 항의	query n. 문의	occur v. 발생하다
	inattentive adj. 부주의한	cancellation n. 취소
	breakage n. 파손	faulty adj. 흠이 있는
	delay v. 지연시키다; n. 지연	inconvenience n. 불편
	refund v. 환불하다; n. 환불	shipment n. 수송, 발송
회사 생활	attach v. 첨부하다	initiative n. (새로운) 계획
	branch n. 지사, 분점	substitute v. 대신하다, 교체되다
	budget n. 예산	approval n. 승인
	supplier n. 공급업체	extension n. 연장
	adjustment n. 조정	oversee v. 감독하다
	production n. 생산	contract n. 계약서
	efficiency n. 효율(성), 능률	supervisor n. 감독관, 관리자
	forward v. 전달하다	corporate adj. 법인의
	issue n. 문제, 사안; v. 발행하다	plant n. 공장
	prioritize v. 우선적으로 처리하다	notify v. 알리다, 통지하다

HACKERS PRACTICE

지문을 읽고 주어진 질문에 가장 알맞은 보기를 고르세요.

Question 01 refers to the following letter.

Brian Lanzotti
343 Ewing Drive
San Diego, CA 91911

Dear Mr. Lanzotti,

Thank you for signing up with Obsatron Security. To activate your home alarm, enter your master code on the keypad. As a reminder, this code should be changed every three months. If the alarm goes off, we will be notified and attempt to reach you. Therefore, please keep your contact information up-to-date. You can do this by logging in to your Obsatron account on our Web site. Thank you.

Sincerely,

David Wendt
Obsatron Customer Assistance Manager

01 What is Mr. Lanzotti asked to do?

(A) Update his contact information as needed
(B) Call an emergency number immediately
(C) Replace the keypad of a security system
(D) Learn some important safety procedures

Question 02 refers to the following e-mail.

To: Reggie Bartlett <regbart@somepost.com>
From: Customer Service <custservice@forteelectric.com>
Subject: May
Attachment: Bill
Date: June 1

Dear Mr. Bartlett,

I have attached your electricity bill for May. Please check the amounts to ensure accuracy and make your payment by June 10. You can do so by bank transfer or credit card at www.forteelectric.com/payments. If you have any questions regarding your bill or our services, contact one of our customer service agents at 555-0022. Thank you for your continued business.

Sincerely,

Forte Electric
Customer Service

02 What is attached to the e-mail?

(A) A monthly statement
(B) A legal agreement
(C) A payment receipt
(D) A cancellation notice

2. 메시지 대화문

메시지 대화문은 두 명 이상의 화자가 회사 생활이나 일상 생활과 관련된 주제에 관한 메시지를 주고받는 대화 형식의 지문입니다. PART 7에서 매회 2개 출제됩니다.

지문 흐름과 빈출 문제

메시지 대화문	흐름	흐름에 따른 빈출 문제
Leo Henderson [10:48 A.M.] My flight from San Diego has been delayed for five hours. I won't arrive in Chicago until 6:30 P.M. So I'll miss the regional managers' meeting scheduled for four o'clock this afternoon. **Shelly Summers [10:50 A.M.]** I'm sorry to hear that. Is there anything I can do to help? **Leo Henderson [10:52 A.M.]** <mark>Could you</mark> please inform the director?	연락한 목적	**대화자가 연락한 목적을 묻는 문제** Why did Mr. Henderson contact Ms. Summers? Mr. Henderson은 왜 Ms. Summers에게 연락했는가? → To notify her of a schedule change 일정 변동을 알리기 위해
Shelly Summers [10:53 A.M.] I'll call the director right now. He may want to reschedule. Let me check.	요청하는 사항	**요청 사항을 묻는 문제** What has Ms. Summers been asked to do? Ms. Summers는 무엇을 하도록 요청되었는가? → Contact the director 이사에게 연락한다.
Shelly Summers [10:59 A.M.] Yes, **he wants to reschedule for tomorrow morning at 8:30 A.M.** He would like all regional managers in attendance. **Will that work for you?** **Leo Henderson [11:02 A.M.]** <mark>That works.</mark> **Shelly Summers [11:04 A.M.]** Sounds great! Have a good flight!	요청 사항에 대한 답변	**특정 어구의 의도를 묻는 문제** At 11:02 A.M., what does Mr. Henderson mean when he writes, "That works"? 오전 11시 2분에, Mr. Henderson이 "That works"라고 썼을 때, 그가 의도한 것은? → The new schedule is acceptable. 새로운 일정이 받아들여질 수 있다.

해석 p.180

메시지 대화문에서 지문의 흐름을 알려주는 표현들을 알아두면 도움이 됩니다.

- **요청 사항**: Could you ~? ~해 주실 수 있으신가요?
  Do you mind ~? ~해 주실 수 있으신가요?
  Can you help me with ~? ~을 도와주실 수 있나요?
- **제안 사항**: Would you like me to ~? ~해 드릴까요?
  What about ~? ~은 어때요?
  I would like 사람 to ~ 저는 [사람]이 ~하는 것이 좋을 것 같아요
  Why don't we ~? ~하는 게 어때요?

자주 나오는 표현

회사 생활	out of stock 재고가 떨어진	run out of ~을 다 써버리다
	place an order 주문하다	office supply 사무용품
	supply closet 비품 창고	promotion n. 승진, 홍보
	status n. 상황	on one's way to ~로 오는 중에
	pick up ~을 사가다/사오다	trade fair 무역 박람회
	confirm v. 확인하다	stop by ~에 들르다
	rush adj. 급한; v. 서두르다	figure out ~을 알아내다
일상생활	service v. 정비하다, 점검하다; n. 서비스	reschedule v. 일정을 변경하다
	commute v. 통근하다; n. 통근	proceed v. 진행하다
	landlord n. 집주인	form n. 양식
	upcoming adj. 다가오는	charge n. 요금; v. 청구하다
	post v. 게시하다	forum n. (온라인 커뮤니티의) 토론방
	invite v. 초대하다	registration n. 등록
	reach out to ~에 연락을 취하다	shift n. (교대) 근무 시간

작성자의 의도를 물을 때 나오는 표현

긍정/동의	Got it. / Noted. 알겠습니다.	Will do. 그렇게 할게요.
	Definitely. / Absolutely. 물론이죠.	Same here. 저도 마찬가지입니다.
	(That) Makes sense. / Sounds good. / That sounds reasonable. / That works. 말이 되네요.	
부정/거절	I don't know. 모르겠네요.	Not at all. 전혀 그렇지 않아요.
	Not really. 그렇진 않아요.	I don't think so. 그렇게 생각하지 않아요.
	Not yet. 아직이요.	No need. 필요 없어요.

HACKERS PRACTICE

지문을 읽고 주어진 질문에 가장 알맞은 보기를 고르세요.

Question 01 refers to the following text-message chain.

Jerry Mills [10:48 A.M.]
Ms. Daniels, do you mind if I leave work early tomorrow afternoon? I need to pick up my parents at the airport.

Pearl Daniels [10:50 A.M.]
That's fine. Have you finished the financial report?

Jerry Mills [10:53 A.M.]
Not yet. I'm planning to work on it this afternoon.

Pearl Daniels [10:54 A.M.]
Could you get it done by the end of your shift today? I'll be using it in my upcoming presentation to the board.

Jerry Mills [10:55 A.M.]
No problem.

---

01 At 10:53 A.M., what does Mr. Mills mean when he writes, "Not yet"?

(A) He has not submitted a leave request.
(B) He intends to reschedule a presentation.
(C) He has not completed an assignment.
(D) He plans to work extra hours tomorrow.

Question 02 refers to the following online chat discussion.

Bastian Guthrie [4:35 P.M.]
I don't think it's in our best interest to keep working with JEPN Manufacturing. The rush order we received last week had to be returned because many of the components were faulty.

Marie Holcomb [4:44 P.M.]
What about finding a replacement supplier?

Bastian Guthrie [4:48 P.M.]
I have a list of manufacturers on my computer. They will probably charge more than JEPN, but switching will save us money in the long run.

Marie Holcomb [4:49 P.M.]
Makes sense.

---

02 At 4:49 P.M., what does Ms. Holcomb mean when she writes, "Makes sense"?

(A) She thinks that a supplier is reliable.
(B) She hopes JEPN will offer better service.
(C) She intends to provide an updated list.
(D) She feels that costs will be reduced.

HACKERS TEST

지문을 읽고 주어진 질문에 가장 알맞은 보기를 고르세요.

Questions 01-03 refer to the following e-mail.

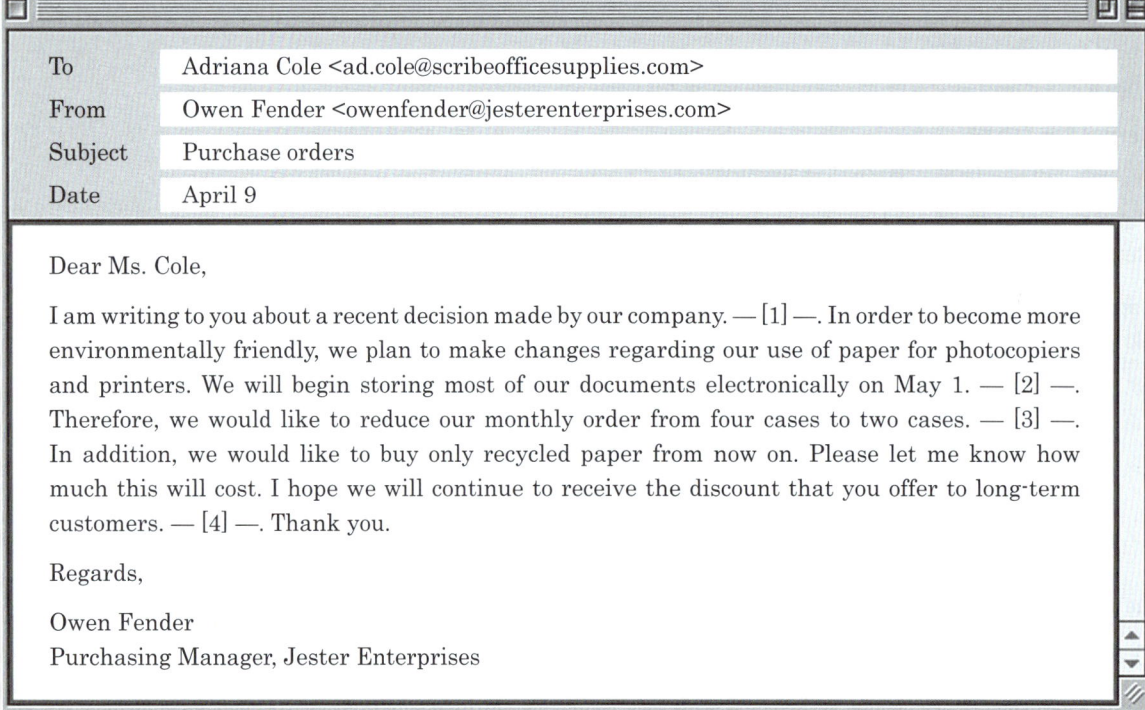

To: Adriana Cole <ad.cole@scribeofficesupplies.com>
From: Owen Fender <owenfender@jesterenterprises.com>
Subject: Purchase orders
Date: April 9

Dear Ms. Cole,

I am writing to you about a recent decision made by our company. — [1] —. In order to become more environmentally friendly, we plan to make changes regarding our use of paper for photocopiers and printers. We will begin storing most of our documents electronically on May 1. — [2] —. Therefore, we would like to reduce our monthly order from four cases to two cases. — [3] —. In addition, we would like to buy only recycled paper from now on. Please let me know how much this will cost. I hope we will continue to receive the discount that you offer to long-term customers. — [4] —. Thank you.

Regards,

Owen Fender
Purchasing Manager, Jester Enterprises

01 Why was the e-mail written?

(A) To make an adjustment to a regular order
(B) To inquire about new products
(C) To submit a complaint about a policy
(D) To request a higher discount

02 What is mentioned about Jester Enterprises?

(A) Its manager has decided to reduce operating expenses.
(B) It will not keep its current photocopiers and printers.
(C) Its environmental efforts have received positive publicity.
(D) It has not been paying the full price for paper.

03 In which of the positions marked [1], [2], [3], and [4] does the following sentence best belong?

"However, we will still require a supply of paper for various purposes."

(A) [1]
(B) [2]
(C) [3]
(D) [4]

Questions 04-05 refer to the following text-message chain.

Daniel Miller [3:40 P.M.]
Hey, are you going to Ms. Downing's promotion party? Apparently, the whole office is invited to meet up at Finlay's Grill tonight after work.

Elaine Larue [3:43 P.M.]
I don't know. I'm feeling pretty tired today. Plus, you are the only person I've gotten to know since I started here. I'd feel uncomfortable going to the party alone.

Daniel Miller [3:44 P.M.]
Why don't we go together? It'll be a good opportunity for you to meet people. I've got a few things to finish up, but I should be ready to go by 7:00 P.M.

Elaine Larue [3:45 P.M.]
That sounds good. Let's meet in the lobby at 7:10 P.M.

04 At 3:43 P.M., what does Ms. Larue mean when she writes, "I don't know"?

(A) She was not sent an invitation.
(B) She does not plan to go to a party.
(C) She will leave a staff gathering early.
(D) She needs the address of a venue.

05 What does Mr. Miller suggest?

(A) Attending an event together
(B) Finishing a task ahead of schedule
(C) Meeting at a nearby restaurant
(D) Inviting another staff member

Questions 06-09 refer to the following letter.

March 12
Nelly Garrison
493 22nd Street
Portland, OR 97246

Dear Ms. Garrison,

Thank you for coming in last Friday to interview for the associate curator position here at the Weston Archeological Institute. We were impressed with your background and would like to offer you the position.

I have enclosed the employment contract. It specifies the salary discussed during the interview and the benefits package I mentioned. If our offer is acceptable to you, please sign the contract and forward it to our personnel department.

Your starting day will be April 15. You will go through an orientation with another curator, Arnold Hazelton. The training period will last one week, and Mr. Hazelton will direct you through various tasks during that time. You will begin your regular duties the week after. Mr. Hazelton will give you more details on your first day.

We would appreciate receiving a response by March 20. You may call me at 555-3029.

Sincerely yours,

Marsha Kent
WAI Head of Personnel

06 What did Ms. Garrison do last week?
(A) Took a tour of an educational facility
(B) Called a number to inquire about a job
(C) Participated in an orientation session
(D) Attended a job interview at an institute

07 What is attached to the letter?
(A) A legal agreement
(B) A training manual
(C) A work schedule
(D) An application form

08 What will Mr. Hazelton do on April 15?
(A) Interview several job applicants
(B) Begin training an employee
(C) Resign from his duties at the institute
(D) Join a workshop organized by the personnel department

09 The word "direct" in paragraph 3, line 2, is closest in meaning to
(A) apply
(B) guide
(C) operate
(D) demonstrate

Questions 10-13 refer to the following online chat discussion.

Mimi Pearson [3:40 P.M.]	Is anyone else having trouble with the new word processing software?
Donald Platt [3:42 P.M.]	I am. I've been waiting for someone from IT.
Grace Helmsley [3:43 P.M.]	I confirmed with an IT employee that they are working on the problem. They just finished here on the second floor. Louis and some others were having problems, too.
Louis Jones [3:46 P.M.]	My software is working fine now. You just have to update your operating system for the installation to work.
Mimi Pearson [3:47 P.M.]	That's not the problem. I was able to install it just fine. I'm having trouble figuring out how to use the software.
Donald Platt [3:48 P.M.]	Mimi, there's a user manual on the company Intranet.
Grace Helmsley [3:49 P.M.]	You can also click on the Help button in the toolbar.
Mimi Pearson [3:50 P.M.]	I didn't know there were instructions. I'll look at them later. I'll try Grace's suggestion first as I need to print a file right away.
Louis Jones [3:52 P.M.]	The company should really provide training. But first I'll ask around to see who feels they need it.

10 What is mentioned about Ms. Helmsley?

(A) She spoke to a member of the IT department.
(B) She works on the third floor of a building.
(C) She required an operating system update.
(D) She finds the software complicated.

11 At 3:47 P.M., what does Ms. Pearson mean when she writes, "That's not the problem"?

(A) She did not understand an explanation.
(B) She installed the new software.
(C) She thought an issue was resolved.
(D) She could not contact an employee from IT.

12 Why does Ms. Pearson decide not to look at the software instructions right away?

(A) She can't turn her computer on.
(B) She can't find them.
(C) She works far from Mr. Platt.
(D) She is in a hurry.

13 What most likely will Mr. Jones do next?

(A) Print a document for a coworker
(B) Inquire about some second-floor employees
(C) Confirm the schedule of a training session
(D) Speak with some other staff members

DAY 17 양식 및 광고

1. 양식

양식은 초대장, 일정표, 광고지, 청구서/영수증 등 생활 속에서 자주 사용되는 다양한 서식 형태의 지문입니다. PART 7에서 매회 5~6개 정도 출제됩니다.

지문 흐름과 빈출 문제

초대장

Blue Bay Release Party

You are invited to attend the release party for *Blue Bay*, a jazz album by saxophonist Jay Delong.

The event will take place on June 9 from 6 P.M. to 10 P.M. at the Starry Hills Event Center, 994 Santa Monica Boulevard, Los Angeles.

The event will feature live performances by guest musicians Joelle Baker, Paul Massa, and The Pinstripes. Food and beverages will be served to attendees throughout the evening. As space is limited, only one additional guest may accompany each invitee. **Please inform us before May 30 if you plan on attending** by contacting Cole Anderson at cander@marinproductions.com.

해석 p.184

흐름
- 행사 제목
- 행사 종류 언급
- 행사의 날짜, 시간, 장소 안내
- 행사에 대한 세부 내용

흐름에 따른 빈출 문제

양식의 목적을 묻는 문제
What type of event is the invitation most likely for?
초대장은 어떤 행사를 위한 것 같은가?
→ A promotional event for a music album
음악 앨범을 위한 홍보 행사

양식에 언급된 세부 내용에 대해 (불)일치하는 것을 묻는 문제
What is true about Mr. Delong?
Mr. Delong에 대해 사실인 것은?
→ He will be joined by other musicians.
다른 음악가들과 함께 공연할 것이다.

수신자가 요청받은 사항을 묻는 문제
What are invitees instructed to do?
초대된 사람들은 무엇을 하라고 지시받는가?
→ Confirm attendance in advance
미리 참석을 확정한다.

양식에서 지문의 흐름을 알려주는 표현들을 알아두면 도움이 됩니다.

- **양식의 목적**: You are invited to ~ 귀하를 ~에 초대합니다
  Join us for ~ ~에 저희와 함께해 주시기 바랍니다
- **요청 사항**: You should ~ ~하셔야 합니다
  Be sure to ~ 반드시 ~ 해 주세요
  Please confirm your attendance. 귀하의 참석 여부를 확인해 주시기 바랍니다.
  Please inform us if you plan on attending. 참석하실 계획이라면 저희에게 알려주십시오.

자주 나오는 표현

초대장	register for ~에 등록하다	festival n. 축제
	limited adj. 한정된, 제한된	admission n. 입장료
	attendee n. 참석자	anniversary n. 기념일
	session n. (특정한 활동을 위한) 시간	ceremony n. 기념식
일정표	feature v. 특별히 포함하다, 출연시키다; n. 특징	presenter n. 발표자
	be postponed to ~으로 연기되다	feel free to 마음대로 ~하다
	appearance n. 출연	time slot 시간대
	required adj. 필수의	cover v. 다루다
청구서/영수증	quote n. 견적(서)	tax n. 세금
	quantity n. 수량	estimate v. 견적을 내다, 추산하다; n. 견적(서)
	receipt n. 영수증	deposit n. 보증금
	subtotal n. 소계	payment n. 결제
후기	worthwhile adj. 가치 있는	rate v. 평가하다, 등급을 매기다
	uncomfortable adj. 불쾌한	unpleasant adj. 불쾌한
	resolve v. 해결하다	disappointed adj. 실망한
	outstanding adj. 뛰어난	regret n. 후회, 유감
웹페이지	based adj. 본사를 둔, 기반을 둔	passionate adj. 열정적인
	individualized adj. 개별화된	leading adj. 최고의, 선두의
	prestigious adj. 명망 높은	advanced adj. 고급의
	make arrangements 준비하다	consultation n. 상담

HACKERS PRACTICE

지문을 읽고 주어진 질문에 가장 알맞은 보기를 고르세요.

Question 01 refers to the following receipt.

Ronson Home Supplies
167 Caldwell Boulevard, Twin Lakes, NM 86515
555-8863
Date: 08/08   Time: 5:26 P.M.

A refund or exchange will only be issued upon presentation of this receipt.

93432-B	Electric Fan	$ 34.99
88822-F	HDMI Cable	$ 18.50
	Subtotal	$ 53.49
	5% Sales Tax	$ 2.67
	Total	$ 56.16
	Cash	$ 60.00
	Change	$ 3.84

Thank you for visiting Ronson Home Supplies.
Please tell us what you thought of your shopping experience today by completing our online survey at www.ronsonhome.com or by calling our customer center at 555-9933.

---

01 What are customers asked to do?

(A) Sign up as members on a Web site
(B) Provide feedback about a store
(C) Call a service center for coupons
(D) Buy raffle tickets for a free device

Question 02 refers to the following schedule.

Dianne Brennan
Schedule – July 8

9:30 A.M. – 10:30 A.M.
Meet with the design team to discuss changes to the company logo.

11:00 A.M. – 12:30 P.M.
Review applications for the marketing assistant position, and create a list of candidates to be interviewed.

1:30 P.M. – 2:30 P.M.
Reserve a booth for the National Appliance Trade Show at the Stanford Center (from Friday to Sunday).

3:00 P.M. – 4:00 P.M.
Finalize the features to be emphasized by the presenter during the new dishwasher model launch.

---

02 What is true about the event at the Stanford Center?

(A) It has been held annually for several years.
(B) It is expected to attract over a thousand visitors.
(C) It will include activities for job seekers.
(D) It will take place over a three-day period.

2. 광고

광고는 상품, 서비스, 상점 등을 홍보하는 일반 광고나 일할 사람을 찾는 구인 광고 형식의 지문입니다. PART 7에서 매회 2~3개 정도 출제됩니다.

지문 흐름과 빈출 문제

광고	흐름	흐름에 따른 빈출 문제
SheerYou—Dewdrop Skincare's Newest Product **Are you looking for** a gentle and effective way to keep your skin hydrated? We are proud to unveil SheerYou, our latest moisturizer.	광고되는 것 소개	**광고되는 것을 묻는 문제** What is being advertised? 무엇이 광고되고 있는가? → A skincare product 스킨 케어 제품
It has been scientifically proven to restore the natural moisture of the skin, making it look brighter and healthier. **Created by dermatologists using only natural ingredients**, SheerYou is our gentlest yet most powerful moisturizer.	제품의 특징	**광고되는 제품이나 서비스에 대해 묻는 문제** What is mentioned about SheerYou? SheerYou에 대해 언급된 것은? → It does not include artificial substances. 인공적인 물질들을 포함하지 않는다.
To celebrate its release, we are offering a special deal for the month of June. Anyone who purchases SheerYou will receive a complimentary three-ounce bottle of Floria. This is the signature **perfume** of Jenna Harvel, star of the popular TV drama *Broken Hearts*.	구매 시 받는 혜택	**구매 혜택을 묻는 문제** What is provided for free? 무엇이 무료로 제공되는가? → A bottle of perfume 향수 한 병
For a list of stores that sell Dewdrop's merchandise, please visit www.dewdropskin.com/vendors. 해석 p.185	추가 정보 안내	

광고에서 지문의 흐름을 알려주는 표현들을 알아두면 도움이 됩니다.

- **광고되는 것 소개**: [일반 광고] Are you looking for ~? ~을 찾고 계신가요?
  - [일반 광고] Take advantage of ~ ~을 이용해 보세요
  - [일반 광고] We offer ~ 저희는 ~을 제공합니다
  - [일반 광고] Visit us to ~ ~하기 위해 저희를 방문하세요
  - [구인 광고] 회사/기관 is looking for ~ [회사/기관]이 ~를 찾고 있습니다
  - [구인 광고] 회사/기관 is hiring ~ [회사/기관]이 ~를 채용하고 있습니다

자주 나오는 표현

일반 광고	advantage n. 이점	recognized adj. 인정받는
	guarantee n. 보증(서), 보장; v. 보장하다	professional n. 전문가; adj. 전문적인
	at no cost 무료로	expert n. 전문가
	bulk order 대량 주문	specialize v. 전문적으로 다루다
	purchase v. 구입하다; n. 구입	suitable adj. 적합한
	sign up ~에 가입하다, 등록하다	for free 무료로
	benefit n. 이점, 혜택	convenient adj. 편리한
	directly adv. 곧바로	exclusively adv. 오직, 독점적으로
	customized adj. 맞춤형의	effective adj. 효과적인
	membership n. 회원권	innovative adj. 혁신적인
	real estate 부동산	on one's behalf ~을 대신하여
	reside v. 거주하다	agent n. 중개인, 대리인
	negotiate v. 협상하다	community n. 지역 사회
	property n. 건물, 소유지	commercial adj. 상업의
구인 광고	job seeker 구직자	responsibility n. 책무, 책임
	candidate n. 후보자, 지원자	qualification n. 자격
	internship n. 인턴직	applicant n. 지원자
	opening n. 일자리	experienced adj. 숙련된
	reference letter 추천서	interview n. 면접; v. 면접하다
	role n. 임무, 역할	compensation n. 보상, 보수

HACKERS PRACTICE

지문을 읽고 주어진 질문에 가장 알맞은 보기를 고르세요.

Question 01 refers to the following advertisement.

Get in shape today at Phoenix Fitness!

Visit us on Ballard Street in Elmwood, between Pita Wraps and Gilbert's Cycles, to see our enlarged exercise facilities and newly renovated locker rooms and lobby! To celebrate the completion of our renovations, present this flyer to get a 50 percent discount on a one-year membership! In addition, all new members get a trial session with one of our professional trainers.

This promotion is valid until February 15 at the Elmwood branch exclusively.

Phoenix Fitness
18 Ballard Street, Elmwood
Tel. 555-3243

---

01 What is being offered by Phoenix Fitness?

(A) A membership discount
(B) A facility tour
(C) A free consultation
(D) A complimentary item

Question 02 refers to the following job advertisement.

Job Opening for Veterinarians

Haven for Animals is a veterinary clinic dedicated to providing quality healthcare to pets. Since opening our establishment in San Diego 15 years ago, we have expanded into Los Angeles and San Francisco. We are looking for five experienced veterinarians to join our team. We offer a high starting salary and a comprehensive benefits package.

Qualifications:
- A veterinary medicine degree
- A license to practice veterinary medicine

Applications should be sent to www.haven.com/hr by December 16.

---

02 What is indicated about Haven for Animals?

(A) It first opened in Los Angeles.
(B) It was founded over a decade ago.
(C) It is looking to hire veterinary assistants.
(D) It plans to renovate a facility.

HACKERS TEST

지문을 읽고 주어진 질문에 가장 알맞은 보기를 고르세요.

Questions 01-02 refer to the following advertisement.

The 35th Annual Western Canada Vintage Auto Show
Friday and Saturday, July 7-8, 10 A.M.-9 P.M.

Visit downtown Vernon for this year's vintage auto show, with over 400 vehicles on display!

You can gain admission at no cost, and souvenirs will be available for purchase from numerous vendors. Take advantage of the many food booths to get hot dogs, burgers, fries, soft drinks, and much more!

And don't forget to enter our raffle to win a vintage sports car! Purchase tickets for the draw at the fair's help desk on both days. For further information, visit www.wcvintageautoshow.com.

01 What is NOT indicated about the auto show?

(A) It will take place over a two-day period.
(B) It is held every year.
(C) It is hosted at a venue in the suburbs.
(D) It does not charge a fee for attendance.

02 According to the advertisement, what can visitors do at the help desk?

(A) Register for a vehicle test drive
(B) Request a copy of a publication
(C) Request vendor information
(D) Participate in a prize draw

Questions 03-05 refer to the following form.

Thank you, Nadia Abdulhak, for choosing Frontward Car Rental. We want to know whether you were satisfied with your experience of renting a Gallapot Mini from May 7 to 13. After completing this form, please click SUBMIT.

1) The variety of available rental options was suitable.	● Agree	○ Disagree
2) The reservation system was convenient.	○ Agree	● Disagree
3) The quality of service when picking up the vehicle was satisfactory.	● Agree	○ Disagree
4) The vehicle performed reliably.	○ Agree	● Disagree
5) The quality of service when returning the vehicle was satisfactory.	○ Agree	● Disagree

Additional Comments

When I picked up the car from your Fairfield location, the staff member was very helpful. However, when the vehicle broke down on Highway 99 two days later, your company took about three hours to resolve the situation. I was also disappointed that no refund was offered at your Danbury location when I returned the automobile.

SUBMIT

03 What is the purpose of the form?

(A) To determine interest in a product
(B) To grant a refund for a payment
(C) To request feedback on a service
(D) To confirm a reservation for an event

04 What aspect of the business was Ms. Abdulhak pleased with?

(A) The simplicity of the booking process
(B) The customer service skills of an employee
(C) The fuel efficiency of the Gallapot Mini
(D) The conditions of a contract

05 What is indicated about Frontward Car Rental?

(A) It allows clients to pick up and return vehicles at different branches.
(B) It has established a team of automobile mechanics in Danbury.
(C) It made the decision to close down its location in Fairfield.
(D) It requires customers to submit a report in the event of an accident.

Questions 06-09 refer to the following job advertisement.

MediTek Incorporated
Are you looking for an exciting career opportunity?

For over 30 years, MediTek Incorporated has been supplying the most advanced medical equipment to hospitals and clinics across the country. We are currently looking for someone to help with the development of promotional materials, including print, television, and online advertisements.

The successful candidate will have the choice of working out of our Oakland, Chicago, or Detroit branch. We plan to conduct all interviews in the first week of August. Those who make it to this stage of the application process will be sent an e-mail with the date and time, as well as instructions on how to set up the necessary video-chat software.

Visit www.meditek.com/applications for more information about the position. To apply, complete and submit the online application form. Please note that at least two letters of recommendation from former employers must be provided. All applicants must submit their documents by July 25.

---

06 For whom is the advertisement most likely intended?

(A) Technicians
(B) Marketing assistants
(C) Real estate agents
(D) Accountants

07 What is true about MediTek Incorporated?

(A) It operates both hospitals and clinics.
(B) It has expanded into another country.
(C) It distributes products through retailers.
(D) It has opened branches in multiple cities.

08 What is suggested about the interviews?

(A) They will be scheduled over the phone.
(B) They will not be conducted in person.
(C) They will not be required for some positions.
(D) They will begin at the end of August.

09 According to the advertisement, what must be included with an application?

(A) A work sample
(B) Training certificates
(C) Professional references
(D) A résumé

Questions 10-13 refer to the following Web page.

---

www.refurnish.com

| Home | **About** | Feedback | Contact Us |

At ReFurnish, we collect, clean, and repair pre-owned furniture to make it suitable for a new home. Unlike other secondhand furniture stores, we are highly selective, only offering prestigious brands with a reputation for quality.

If you have furniture you want to sell, send an e-mail to purchases@refurnish.com that includes a brief description and a photograph of the piece. One of our representatives will then visit your home to negotiate the amount we will pay. After payment is made, we will make arrangements to have the piece delivered to our store.

Anyone looking to buy furniture should stop by our showroom at 3746 Walker Street in downtown San Francisco. We have a wide variety of items in stock, with new pieces arriving every day. You should click here to check out the feedback from our previous clients. We're sure you will be impressed by what they have to say!

---

10 The word "collect" in paragraph 1, line 1, is closest in meaning to

(A) deposit
(B) gather
(C) connect
(D) present

11 What is true about ReFurnish?

(A) It manufactures custom furniture for clients.
(B) Its inventory is limited to specific brands.
(C) It offers both new and used items for sale.
(D) Its merchandise has gained national attention.

12 According to the Web page, what do ReFurnish employees do during a home visit?

(A) They discuss a price with a seller.
(B) They take some pictures of an item.
(C) They confirm the arrival of a delivery.
(D) They show a piece to potential buyers.

13 What are customers advised to do online?

(A) Post questions about a service
(B) Find the location of a store
(C) Check the status of an order
(D) Read reviews of a business

DAY 18 기사 및 안내문

1. 기사

기사는 사회, 환경, 비즈니스와 관련된 다양한 분야의 새로운 소식을 전달하는 신문이나 잡지 형태의 지문입니다. PART 7에서 매회 2~3개 정도 출제됩니다.

지문 흐름과 빈출 문제

기사	흐름	흐름에 따른 빈출 문제
Former Factory Finds New Life By Gregory McKenna (April 3)—**Yesterday, chairperson of the Grand Prairie Arts Council Belinda Blair announced that** following extensive renovations, the abandoned factory formerly operated by XLT Industries has been converted into a 3,000-square-meter cultural complex.	기사의 주제	**기사의 주제를 묻는 문제** What is the article mainly about? 기사는 주로 무엇에 대한 것인가? → The opening of a cultural facility 문화 시설의 개장

The new Grand Prairie Cultural Center features a performing arts facility with seating for 1,500 people.
 	
"**This project would not have been possible without the support of Mayor Wilma Brown and local businesses like Keystone Bank**," said Belinda Blair.
 	
The center opens to the public on August 5.
 	
해석 p.188
	기사의 세부 내용	**기사에 언급된 특정 사항에 대해 추론할 수 있는 것을 묻는 문제**
		What is suggested about Ms. Blair's project?
		Ms. Blair의 프로젝트에 대해 암시되는 것은?
		→ It received funding from private companies.
		  사기업으로부터 자금을 받았다.
		
		기사에 언급된 사람을 묻는 문제
		Who is Ms. Brown?
		Ms. Brown은 누구인가?
		→ A city official
		  시 공무원

기사에서 지문의 흐름을 알려주는 표현들을 알아두면 도움이 됩니다.

- **기사의 주제**: 사람/기관 announced that ~ [사람/기관]이 ~이라고 발표했다
  - 사람/기관 will hold ~ [사람/기관]이 ~을 열 것이다
  - 사람/기관 recently launched ~ [사람/기관]이 최근에 ~을 시작했다/출시했다
  - 사람/기관 recently published ~ [사람/기관]이 최근에 ~을 발표했다/출간했다
- **인용**: "~," said 사람 [사람]이 "~"이라고 말했다
  - 사람 explains, "~" [사람]이 "~"이라고 설명한다
  - 사람 pointed out, "~" [사람]이 "~"이라고 지적했다

자주 나오는 표현

사회	celebrate v. 기념하다, 축하하다	society n. 협회, 단체
	occasion n. 행사	support n. 지원, 지지; v. 지지하다
	generation n. 세대	present v. 수여하다, 주다
	sector n. 분야, 부문	concern n. 관심사, 우려
	mark v. 기념하다	growth n. 증가
환경	effort n. 노력	reduce v. 줄이다
	eco-friendly adj. 친환경적인	sustainability n. 지속 가능성
	vital adj. 필수적인	solar adj. 태양광을 이용한
	long-term adj. 장기적인	emission n. 배기가스
비즈니스	major adj. 주요한	shareholder n. 주주
	expand v. 확대하다	revenue n. 수익, 소득
	accomplish v. 완수하다	anticipate v. 예상하다
	vice president 부사장	appreciate v. 높이 평가하다, 고마워하다
	cite v. 인용하다, 언급하다	strategy n. 전략
	opportunity n. 기회	remark v. 언급하다
	phase n. 단계	manufacturer n. 제조업체
	compete v. 경쟁하다	acquire v. 인수하다
	headquarters n. 본사	investor n. 투자자
	relocation n. 이전	retail outlet 소매판매점
	bankruptcy n. 파산	press release 보도 자료

HACKERS PRACTICE

지문을 읽고 주어진 질문에 가장 알맞은 보기를 고르세요.

Question 01 refers to the following article.

Business Buzz Weekly
Sustainability and Your Business
By Jonathan Demarco
November 14

Increasingly aware of the importance of environmental sustainability, businesses are taking steps to adopt green methods of production. Nonetheless, Evelyn Harris, a senior researcher at the Center for Sustainable Economics, pointed out, "Cost is a major factor to consider." Replacing factory equipment with eco-friendly devices, for example, can be a very expensive task. Subsequently, a company may try to recover this cost by increasing the price of goods. And ultimately, consumers are more likely to buy a product based on its price, not on how it was produced.

01 What most likely is Ms. Harris's job?

(A) Environmental consultant
(B) Economics researcher
(C) Factory manager
(D) Marketing expert

Question 02 refers to the following press release.

Market Reports

Sept. 8—Beale Apparel has announced that it will be launching a new line of sportswear. The move is an apparent attempt to capture a share of the growing market for athletic wear. The new line will be sold at the company's retail outlets beginning in June of next year.

Marketing director Rita Murphy says the timing of the launch is deliberate. It will coincide with the 43rd World Summer Sports Games to be held in Athens, Greece that month. Millions of international viewers will see the company's products worn by the US athletes.

02 What is the purpose of the press release?

(A) To reveal the location of an upcoming event
(B) To introduce a new sportswear product line
(C) To promote a special sale
(D) To announce a sponsorship for a sports event

2. 안내문

안내문은 제품, 업체/시설, 행사 등 실생활에서 접할 수 있는 다양한 소재에 관한 정보를 제공하는 지문입니다. PART 7에서 매회 1~2개 정도 출제됩니다.

지문 흐름과 빈출 문제

안내문	흐름	흐름에 따른 빈출 문제

Important: Please Read Before Assembly
 	
Thank you for purchasing our Outdoor Adventure Tent.
 	
Before setting it up for the first time, carefully unpack all components and check that none are missing. For optimal assembly, spread out the parts on a soft surface like grass. Begin by positioning the main frame on its side, as specified in the illustration below. Take care not to force any connections or excessively tighten the poles, as doing so could compromise the tent's structural integrity.
 	
To access detailed maintenance tips, please visit our official **Web site** at www.wildgeartrek.com.
 	
해석 p.188
	안내문에서 설명하는 것 소개
	
	세부 안내 사항
		안내문의 주제를 묻는 문제
		What kind of item is most likely being discussed?
		논의되고 있는 제품의 종류는 무엇일 것 같은가?
		→ A tent
		  텐트
		
		안내문이 있을 만한 곳을 묻는 문제
		Where is the information most likely found?
		안내문은 어디에서 찾을 수 있을 것 같은가?
		→ In a product's instruction manual
		  제품의 설명서에
		
		얻을 수 있는 정보를 묻는 문제
		What can be found on a Web site?
		웹사이트에서 무엇을 확인할 수 있는가?
		→ Tips for maintenance
		  유지 관리를 위한 팁

안내문에서 지문의 흐름을 알려주는 표현들을 알아두면 도움이 됩니다.

- **안내문의 주제**: Thank you for purchasing ~ ~을 구입해 주셔서 감사합니다
- 주의 사항: Do not ~ ~하지 마십시오
  - Avoid ~ ~하지 마십시오
  - 상품 must be ~ 상품은 반드시 ~되어야 합니다
- **얻을 수 있는 정보**: To ~, please visit our Web site ~을 하기 위해서, 웹사이트를 방문해 주세요
  - To ~, speak to ~ ~을 하기 위해서, ~에게 이야기해 주세요

자주 나오는 표현

제품 안내	unpack v. 포장을 풀다	maintenance n. 유지 (관리)
	component n. 부품	coverage n. 보장
	damage n. 손상; v. 손상을 주다	remove v. 제거하다, 없애다
	warranty n. 품질 보증(서)	user-friendly adj. 사용하기 쉬운
	appliance n. 기구, 장치	improvement n. 개선, 향상
	portable adj. 휴대용의, 휴대가 쉬운	launch v. 출시하다; n. 출시
	come with ~이 딸려 있다	newsletter n. 소식지
	verify v. 확인하다	container n. 용기, 그릇
	loss n. 분실	step n. 단계
	assemble v. 조립하다	up-to-date adj. 최신의, 첨단의
업체/시설 안내	remodel v. 개조하다, 고치다	complex n. 복합 건물, 단지
	allow v. 허용하다	guideline n. 지침, 가이드라인
	enable v. 가능하게 하다	office space 사무실 공간
	premium adj. 고급의, 우수한	follow v. 따르다
	on-site adj. 현장의, 현지의	chain n. (상점·호텔 등의) 체인
행사 안내	accommodate v. 수용하다	winner n. 우승자, 승리자
	participant n. 참가자	award n. 상; v. 수여하다
	attendant n. 안내원, 종업원	mandatory adj. 의무적인
	complimentary adj. 무료의	recreational adj. 오락의
	host v. 주최하다	workshop n. 워크숍

HACKERS PRACTICE

지문을 읽고 주어진 질문에 가장 알맞은 보기를 고르세요.

Question 01 refers to the following information.

> Judith Weber, the author of the best-selling book *Working Together*, will conduct a workshop at the Bridgeport Business Institute on July 17 from 1 to 5 P.M. The focus will be on improving communication skills, and she will provide tips on how to effectively interact with coworkers. Ms. Weber will also conduct exercises to give participants the chance to put what they have learned into action.
>
> Please note that this is the first in a series of workshops that will be led by Ms. Weber. To find out the dates and times of future sessions, please visit our Web site at www.bridgeportbusiness.com.

01 What can be found on a Web site?

(A) A feedback form
(B) A venue map
(C) A speaker biography
(D) A session schedule

Question 02 refers to the following instruction.

> Product Assembly
>
> Before you begin assembling your computer desk from Wellington Furniture, take note of the following. It is important to match up the provided metal screws with the right holes. The product comes with different-sized screws. Each type of screw is designed for a different component of the desk. Do not attempt to put a screw in the wrong hole, as you will risk cracking the wood and damaging it. To avoid this, please refer to the illustration on Page 8 of this assembly guide. It explicitly indicates which screws should be used in the different holes.

02 According to the instructions, what must be avoided when assembling the desk?

(A) Applying too much pressure to the wood
(B) Using a screw in the incorrect location
(C) Attaching a component from another product
(D) Assembling the parts in the wrong order

HACKERS TEST

지문을 읽고 주어진 질문에 가장 알맞은 보기를 고르세요.

Questions 01-02 refer to the following instructions.

Maxwell's Frozen Breakfast Sandwich
[Contains bread, sausage, egg, cheese | Serving size: 250 grams]

Keep the item frozen until you are ready to heat it.

Microwave Heating Instructions
1. Remove from plastic wrapper, and place in a microwave-safe container.
2. Heat on LOW for two minutes.
3. Turn product over, and heat on HIGH for three minutes.

Oven Heating Instructions
1. Remove from plastic wrapper, and wrap in foil.
2. Place on a baking sheet, and bake at 350 degrees for 20 minutes.

CAUTION: Do not refreeze any uneaten portions of the sandwich. Doing so may pose a health risk.

01 What is stated about the product?
(A) It includes five ingredients.
(B) It is suitable for a vegetarian diet.
(C) It can be heated using only one method.
(D) It can be cooked while it is still frozen.

02 What do the instructions advise customers to do?
(A) Avoid putting leftovers in the freezer
(B) Take note of the expiration date
(C) Wait 20 minutes before eating
(D) Limit consumption to one serving

Questions 03-05 refer to the following article.

Casa Bella Announces Plans to Launch in India
By Reena Singh

Casa Bella, the major Italian furniture retailer, has announced plans to open its first branch in India. The company intends to construct the store in Mumbai, with the opening scheduled for March. — [1] —. The store will offer the same products and services as its other global branches.

In addition to the Mumbai outlet, stores in other Indian cities are planned. According to company representative Daniella Fieri, the growth of the Indian economy has made the country an attractive target. — [2] —. Ms. Fieri also said that because the company already operates a production plant in India, the shipping costs for stores will be low. Furniture industry experts have high expectations, and the company's stock value has increased by nearly 10 percent. — [3] —.

If the retail outlets in India are successful, Casa Bella will likely expand into Southeast Asia. The retailer is already a market leader in Europe and North America. — [4] —.

03 What is the article mainly about?

(A) An opportunity for investment in a business
(B) An expansion plan of a retail company
(C) A merger between two companies in India
(D) A decision to discontinue product lines

04 What is NOT indicated about Casa Bella?

(A) It has a strong market position in two continents.
(B) It manufactures some goods in India.
(C) It offers free shipping to customers.
(D) It reported an increase in its stock value.

05 In which of the positions marked [1], [2], [3], and [4] does the following sentence best belong?

"This is because Indian consumers now spend more on items for the home."

(A) [1]
(B) [2]
(C) [3]
(D) [4]

Questions 06-09 refer to the following information.

The Sonnenville Public Swimming Pool

We hope you enjoy yourself here at the Sonnenville Public Swimming Pool. To ensure that everyone has a pleasant and safe time, please take note of the following:

1. Food and beverages are not permitted in the facility except at the snack bar.
2. Children under 10 years of age must be accompanied by an adult.
3. Diving and jumping into the pool are not allowed.

Two lifeguards will be on duty at their stations when the pool is open. Anyone not following the guidelines may be asked to leave the facility.

The Sonnenville Public Swimming Pool is open from 7 A.M. to 9 P.M. from Monday through Friday, from 6 A.M. to 9 P.M. on Saturday, and from 8 A.M. to 9 P.M. on Sunday. The facility also offers a wide variety of swimming classes for people of all ages and levels. To get information on times, fees, and instructors or to enroll in a course, speak to one of our staff members at the front desk.

06 What is the purpose of the information?
(A) To update members on policy changes
(B) To notify visitors of guidelines
(C) To announce new operation hours
(D) To promote a swimming competition

07 What is NOT indicated about the Sonnenville Public Swimming Pool?
(A) It sells snack items to visitors.
(B) It requires parents to accompany all children.
(C) It does not allow visitors to dive.
(D) It employs a couple of lifeguards.

08 On which day does the pool open the earliest?
(A) Monday
(B) Friday
(C) Saturday
(D) Sunday

09 How can visitors register for a class?
(A) By contacting an instructor
(B) By filling out an application
(C) By going to a service desk
(D) By sending an e-mail

Questions 10-13 refer to the following article.

LiteraLegends Offers New Authors the Opportunity for Publication

There is hope for authors trying to get their works published! Founded just five years ago, LiteraLegends is a Web site that offers writers an opportunity to publish their novels, short stories, poetry, and nonfiction works. Authors simply upload their works to the site, and members can download them for their reading pleasure.

LiteraLegends CEO Sam Ashoka explained, "First-time writers usually offer their work for free. If members like what they read, they leave a positive review." If a work becomes popular, the author then has the option of charging members for downloads. The price can be as low as $2.99 or as high as $35.99. LiteraLegends charges a 20 percent commission fee and also helps promote authors to traditional publishing companies.

Well-known author of *The Believers*, Meridiana Chase, was contracted by a publishing house after developing a significant readership for her works on LiteraLegends. "Some works have been downloaded over a million times," Ashoka also remarked. "LiteraLegends hopes to bring a high level of success to new authors."

10 In paragraph 1, line 1, the word "Founded" is closest in meaning to

(A) Discovered
(B) Established
(C) Searched
(D) Revealed

11 What is mentioned about LiteraLegends?

(A) It offers services on other Web sites.
(B) It requires customers to pay in advance.
(C) It forms partnerships with other companies.
(D) It allows users to provide feedback.

12 How does LiteraLegends generate revenue?

(A) By charging for memberships
(B) By taking sales commissions
(C) By collecting subscription fees
(D) By running advertisements

13 Who is Meridiana Chase?

(A) A company spokesperson
(B) A literary critic
(C) A book author
(D) A marketing expert

DAY 19 공고 및 회람

1. 공고

공고는 행사 소개 및 시설 이용 안내 등과 관련된 일반 공고나 회사의 새로운 방침, 사내 행사 등을 알리는 사내 공고 형식의 지문입니다. PART 7에서 매회 1~2개 정도 출제됩니다.

지문 흐름과 빈출 문제

공고	흐름	흐름에 따른 빈출 문제
We're Moving! After 25 years at the same location, **Nickel Books has decided to** move to 3408 Polson Street.	공고를 쓴 이유	**공고의 목적을 묻는 문제** What is the purpose of the notice? 공고의 목적은 무엇인가? → To announce a store relocation 가게 이전을 알리기 위해
The reason is that the storeroom of our current building does not have enough space for our growing inventory. The new location will open on April 30. To celebrate, we'll be offering a 15 percent discount on all books and magazines from May 1 to 15. In addition, anyone making a purchase of 25 dollars and over will receive a free tote bag with our logo. *From Exit 5 of Panhurst Station, walk straight for about two blocks. **We will be located above a restaurant called Color Kitchen and will occupy the second and third floors of the building.**	세부 공고 내용	**공고에 언급된 특정 사항에 대해 (불)일치하는 것을 묻는 문제** What is indicated about Nickel Books? Nickel Books에 대해 언급된 것은? → It will share a building with another business. 다른 사업체와 건물을 공유할 것이다.
Please make sure to check our Web site at www.nickelbooks.com for a map. 해석 p.191	요청하는 사항 및 연락처 안내	**요청 사항을 묻는 문제** What are the customers asked to do? 고객들은 무엇을 하도록 요청받는가? → Check a Web site for a map 지도를 위해 웹사이트를 확인한다.

공고에서 지문의 흐름을 알려주는 표현들을 알아두면 도움이 됩니다.

- **공고의 목적**: 사람/기관/지역 has decided to ~ [사람/기관/지역]이 ~하기로 결정했습니다
  사람/기관/지역 will be holding ~ [사람/기관/지역]이 ~을 개최할 것입니다
  행사 will be held ~ [행사]가 열릴 것입니다
  We would like to ~ 저희는 ~하고 싶습니다

- **요청 사항**: Please make sure ~ 반드시 ~해 주십시오
  Please note ~ ~을 유념하세요
  You must ~ 여러분은 꼭 ~해야 합니다
  사람 needs to ~ [사람]은 ~할 필요가 있습니다

자주 나오는 표현

일반 공고		
	gather v. 모이다, 집합하다	security n. 보안, 안전
	donate v. 기부하다	organization n. 단체
	exit n. 출구; v. 나가다	venue n. 행사장, 장소
	switch v. 전환하다, 바꾸다	cooperation n. 협조
	charitable adj. 자선의	automatically adv. 자동으로
	transition n. 전환	local n. 현지인, 주민; adj. 현지의
	participating adj. 참여하는	disruption n. 방해
	great deals 할인, 구매 혜택	outage n. 정전
	minimize v. 최소화하다	postpone v. 연기하다, 미루다
	installation n. 설치, 설비	investigate v. 살피다, 조사하다
	city council 시의회	official adj. 공식적인; n. 관계자, 공무원
	exhibit n. 전시(품); v. 전시하다	inform v. 알리다, 통지하다

사내 공고		
	laboratory n. 실험실	manual n. 설명서, 지침서
	accident n. 사고	direction n. 지시
	operate v. 작동하다	properly adv. 제대로
	overview n. 개요, 개관	safety equipment 안전 장비
	distribute v. 분배하다, 나누어 주다	adhere to ~을 준수하다
	duty n. 의무, 직무	manager n. 관리자
	inaccessible adj. 접근할 수 없는	board meeting 이사회 회의
	undertake v. (일·책임을) 맡다, 착수하다	instruction n. 지시, 설명

HACKERS PRACTICE

지문을 읽고 주어진 질문에 가장 알맞은 보기를 고르세요.

Question 01 refers to the following notice.

Customer Advisory

We would like to advise our customers that the following electronic banking services will be suspended on Sunday, July 8, from 12 A.M. to 8 A.M.

- Automated teller machines (ATMs)
- Online fund transfers and bill payments
- Online usage of credit and debit cards

During this time, clients may continue to check their account balances online. We regret any inconvenience this disruption may cause, but it is necessary for the installation of a software update that will ensure the security of our electronic banking system.

---

01 What is the purpose of the notice?

(A) To explain a recent policy change
(B) To provide details about weekend hours
(C) To request updates of personal information
(D) To announce a temporary service interruption

Question 02 refers to the following announcement.

Annual Awards Ceremony

On January 18, the company will be holding its annual awards ceremony to acknowledge employees who have excelled in their duties. Certificates and gift cards will be distributed to the top-performing staff.

Project managers are encouraged to recommend any team member they feel deserves recognition. A copy of the nomination form and detailed instructions on how to fill it out will be sent to you by e-mail early next week. Please make sure to drop off the completed form at the human resources office by December 30. Any nominations received after this date will not be considered.

---

02 What must managers do to nominate a team member for an award?

(A) Send an e-mail to a manager
(B) Review detailed evaluations
(C) Submit a form by a deadline
(D) Gather employee opinions

2. 회람

회람은 회사 방침 및 경영, 시설 이용, 사내 행사 등과 관련된 공지 사항 및 새로운 소식을 회사 내에서 전달하는 지문입니다. PART 7에서 가끔 1개 정도 출제됩니다.

지문 흐름과 빈출 문제

회람

MEMO

To: All Employees
From: Spencer Buffone, Building Services Manager
Date: March 6
Subject: Notice

I'd like to inform you of the annual exterior window cleaning at our office building.

On March 12, we will be cleaning the windows from the 11th to 20th floors between 10 A.M. and 5 P.M.

We ask our employees to close all windows fully on that day. If you have any questions, please contact the building services team at extension 2966.

해석 p.192

흐름

받는 사람,
보내는 사람,
날짜

회람을 쓴 이유

회람의
세부 내용

흐름에 따른 빈출 문제

글을 쓴 이유를 묻는 문제
Why did Mr. Buffone send the memo?
Mr. Buffone은 왜 회람을 보냈는가?
→ To announce a project
작업을 공지하기 위해

추후 일정 계획을 묻는 문제
What will happen on March 12?
3월 12일에 무슨 일이 있을 것인가?
→ Cleaning will begin on the upper floors.
청소가 상층부에서 시작될 것이다.

의무 및 권장 사항을 묻는 문제
What are the employees told to do?
직원들은 무엇을 하라고 당부받는가?
→ Close all windows
모든 창문을 닫는다.

회람에서 지문의 흐름을 알려주는 표현들을 알아두면 도움이 됩니다.

- **회람의 주제 및 목적**: I'd like to inform ~ ~을 알리고자 합니다
  To announce/inform ~ ~을 알리기 위해
- **추후 일정 계획**: On 날짜/시간, we will ~ [날짜/시간]에, 우리는 ~할 것입니다
  ~ is expected to resume on 날짜/시간 [날짜/시간]에 ~이 재개될 것으로 예상됩니다
- **의무 및 권장 사항**: We ask/encourage our employees to ~ 우리는 직원들이 ~하기를 요청/권장합니다
  You should ~ 여러분은 ~해야 합니다

자주 나오는 표현

회사 방침 및 경영	expense n. 경비	payroll n. 급료 지불 총액
	go into effect 시행되다	accounting n. 회계
	process n. 절차; v. 처리하다	policy n. 정책
	committee n. 위원회	note v. 유의하다
	fund n. 자금, 기금	encourage v. 권장하다
	partner n. 협력사; v. 제휴를 맺다	division n. 부, 부서
	address v. 다루다, 연설하다; n. 연설, 강연	administrative adj. 행정의, 관리의
	personnel n. 직원, 인원	merger n. 합병, 합동
	procedure n. 절차, 과정	employ v. 고용하다, 사용하다
	transfer v. 옮기다, 이동하다; n. 전근, 이동	acceptable adj. 받아들일 수 있는, 허용 가능한
시설 이용	lobby n. 로비	measure n. 조치
	detour v. 우회하다, 돌아가다; n. 우회로, 우회	renovation n. 개조, 보수
	entrance n. 입구, 입장	temporary adj. 임시의
	locate v. (어떤 장소를) 찾아내다, 위치를 정하다	spacious adj. 넓은, 광대한
	facility n. 시설	workspace n. 작업 공간
	repair n. 수리, 보수; v. 수리하다	inspection n. 점검
	flooring n. 바닥재	no later than 늦어도 ~까지
사내 행사	retreat n. (회사) 야유회	cater v. 음식을 조달하다
	suggestion n. 제안, 제의	fundraising n. 모금 활동; adj. 모금의
	annual adj. 연례의	training n. 교육, 훈련

HACKERS PRACTICE

지문을 읽고 주어진 질문에 가장 알맞은 보기를 고르세요.

Question 01 refers to the following memo.

MEMO

To: All Staff Members
From: Human Resources Department
Date: September 16
Subject: Dress code

While it is true that Farnham-Price Company allows its personnel to dress casually for daily work in the office, you should wear acceptable clothing for a business setting when attending meetings with clients. The clothing you wear directly affects the impressions potential and current clients have of the company. Please feel free to direct any questions about this policy to me.

---

01 What are staff members instructed to do?

(A) Dress professionally for interactions with clients
(B) Complete a questionnaire about dress code
(C) Arrive punctually for meetings with customers
(D) Review recent changes to a corporate policy

Question 02 refers to the following memo.

To: All Staff Members
From: Michael Lewis
Date: December 10
Subject: Year-End Party

As you know, our law firm's annual year-end party is taking place on December 17. I'd like to inform you that it will be held at the Harborview Hotel rather than the Pullman Conference Center as originally planned. We were forced to make this adjustment because there was a fire at the conference center, and the damage will take several weeks to repair.

If you have any questions, please contact me. Thank you.

---

02 What is the purpose of the memo?

(A) To correct an error in a schedule
(B) To extend an invitation to an event
(C) To explain the reason for a social gathering
(D) To announce a change of venue

HACKERS TEST

지문을 읽고 주어진 질문에 가장 알맞은 보기를 고르세요.

Questions 01-02 refer to the following memo.

MEMO

To: All Staff
From: Michael Reni, Office Manager
Date: May 15
Subject: Reminders

There have been several recent instances in which staff members working overtime failed to set the alarm when they left the building. This creates a significant security risk for our company. Therefore, the last person to leave the office must ensure that the security alarm is activated.

In addition, please note that you should turn off all lights, air-conditioning units, and office equipment before you go. Leaving these on overnight increases the monthly electricity bill, and our company is trying to cut back on unnecessary expenses.

We encourage our employees to make an effort to follow these policies. Thank you for your cooperation.

---

01 What is indicated about the employees?
(A) Some worked longer than scheduled.
(B) Several were recently hired.
(C) All were given security badges.
(D) Many moved to a new office.

02 What is true about the company?
(A) It has replaced a senior manager.
(B) It is trying to reduce expenses.
(C) It plans to install a security alarm.
(D) It purchased equipment recently.

Questions 03-05 refer to the following notice.

Before entering the Iceland Heritage Gallery, please review our guidelines. These apply to all ticketholders. Following these will ensure that all visitors have an enjoyable experience.

- Please note that taking photographs of the pieces on display is not permitted.
- Large bags may not be brought beyond the lobby. You may store baggage and other belongings in one of our lockers near the gift shop.
- People who visit our garden are asked to use the designated waste bins to dispose of any garbage.
- We ask that you begin proceeding to the gallery's exit 15 minutes before closing. An announcement will be made at this time.

Visit www.icelandheritage.com for more information about our facility and upcoming exhibits.

03 What is true about the gallery?
(A) It allows visitors to take pictures of artwork on display.
(B) It includes a storage area for personal belongings.
(C) It partners with artists in several countries.
(D) It intends to increase the size of its outdoor garden.

04 The phrase "Please note" in paragraph 2, line 1, is closest in meaning to
(A) try again
(B) account for
(C) take over
(D) be aware

05 According to the notice, why will an announcement be made?
(A) To offer details about an interactive experience
(B) To notify visitors that a facility is about to close
(C) To remind ticketholders about a special offer
(D) To provide information about upcoming events

Questions 06-09 refer to the following memo.

MEMO

To: All Staff
From: Nina Summers, Manager
Date: October 3
Subject: Lobby

As discussed during last month's staff meeting, the lobby renovation project will begin as scheduled on October 10. — [1] —. During this time, employees and visitors will need to enter the building through the back entrance.

Throughout the week of October 17 to 24, only the elevator on the west side of the building will be in operation. Since elevator access will be limited during this time, we recommend that only those with mobility issues use it. — [2] —. If you are able to take the stairs, please do so.

Full elevator access is expected to resume on October 25, but the remodeling work in the lobby will continue until November 4. — [3] —. Please remind all clients and visitors that the lobby is being renovated and will be blocked off. — [4] —. A security guard will be in the area while the project is ongoing.

Thank you for your patience as we work on our lobby!

---

06 Why did Ms. Summers send the memo?

(A) To offer a solution to a problem
(B) To announce the opening of a facility
(C) To confirm the extension of a deadline
(D) To give information about a plan

07 What is recommended for some employees?

(A) Checking a building floor plan
(B) Waiting in the lobby
(C) Assisting visitors
(D) Taking the stairs

08 What will happen on October 25?

(A) Some machinery will be activated.
(B) A company event will be held.
(C) Some furniture will be relocated.
(D) A building inspection will be conducted.

09 In which of the positions marked [1], [2], [3], and [4] does the following sentence best belong?

"This will ensure that no one accesses this area without permission."

(A) [1]
(B) [2]
(C) [3]
(D) [4]

Questions 10-13 refer to the following announcement.

The company will be holding a webinar on August 17 from 2:30 P.M. to 3:30 P.M. The manager of each branch must make arrangements for all full-time employees to participate. If any of your workers are unable to take part due to leave or other reasons, please notify the human resources department at our company headquarters.

The webinar has been organized to provide details about the upcoming modifications to our firm's health insurance policy. There are several improvements that are sure to make our staff happy, including full coverage of prescription costs. The webinar will be led by Kyle Polanski, who has been in charge of the health insurance project since May. This was his first assignment when he started working here, and he has achieved impressive results.

You must ensure that all employees have properly installed the latest version of Team Chat on their workstations by August 15. This is the program we will be using for the webinar. Thank you.

10 Who is the announcement most likely intended for?

(A) Branch managers
(B) Business owners
(C) Part-time workers
(D) Corporate trainers

11 What will be discussed in the webinar?

(A) Upgrades to office equipment
(B) Improvements to a company facility
(C) Changes to an employee benefit
(D) Ways to increase worker efficiency

12 What is implied about Mr. Polanski?

(A) He manages the human resources team.
(B) He is a former insurance firm employee.
(C) He has overseen multiple major projects.
(D) He was hired several months ago.

13 What must employees do by August 15?

(A) Install a software application
(B) Register for an online session
(C) Sign up for a health checkup
(D) Review a training manual

DAY 20 다중 지문

다중 지문은 2개 또는 3개의 관련 있는 지문이 한 세트로 구성된 형태입니다. PART 7 다중 지문 전체 5세트 중 이중 지문은 매회 2세트, 삼중 지문은 매회 3세트 출제됩니다.

최신 경향 및 전략

1. 다중 지문은 다음과 같은 지문 조합이 자주 출제됩니다.

후기 & 이메일	시설 이용 후 불만을 제기한 고객의 후기 & 시설 관리자가 고객에게 보상을 제안하는 이메일
웹페이지 & 이메일	직원 모집 관련 웹페이지 & 지원자에게 채용 세부 사항을 안내하는 이메일
일정표 & 이메일 & 안내문	세미나 일정표 & 참가자가 참석 취소 및 변경을 요청하는 이메일 & 세미나 참석 관련 규정을 설명하는 안내문
이메일 & 요청서 & 이메일	고객에게 예약을 확정하는 이메일 & 고객의 예약 변경 요청서 & 업체가 변경 요청을 승인하는 이메일

2. 5개의 문제 중 1~2문제는 두 개 이상의 지문에서 각각 단서를 찾아 조합해야 정답을 찾을 수 있는 연계 문제로 출제되며, 연계 문제는 주로 5문제 중 3~5번째 문제로 출제됩니다.
3. 정답의 단서를 두 개 이상의 지문에서 찾아야 하는 연계 문제는 다음과 같이 출제됩니다.

이중 지문

지문 1	Brookdale 호텔에 투숙한 Celeste Morgan이 호텔에 새로 생긴 시설이 기대에 못 미쳤다고 쓴 후기
지문 2	Brookdale 호텔이 Celeste Morgan에게 스파 시설 이용에 불편을 끼쳐 죄송하다고 사과하며, 무료 숙박권을 보상으로 제공한다는 이메일
연계 문제와 정답	질문 Brookdale 호텔에 새로 생긴 시설은 무엇인가? 정답 스파 시설

삼중 지문

지문 1	Otis 대학교에서 열리는 직무 교육 세미나 일정표
지문 2	9월 8일 세미나 참석 예정이었던 Lester Wells가 일정 충돌로 인해 8월 22일에 참석 취소 의사를 밝히는 이메일
지문 3	참석자가 행사 5일 전까지 취소 신청하면 환불 가능하며, 환불은 행사일 이후 15일 이내에 처리된다는 안내문
연계 문제와 정답	질문 Mr. Wells에 대해 사실인 것은? 정답 9월 중에 환불을 받을 수 있다.

Example

Question 01 refers to the following Web page and e-mail.

| HOME | Job Listings | Sign in | Contact Us | Help |

Talle Centrum Contact Center

We have been the leading provider of contact center services for global companies for over 20 years. We are seeking individuals interested in joining our team of customer service agents.

RESPONSIBILITIES
- Handling customer service calls for corporate clients

QUALIFICATIONS
- A minimum of two years of college is required
- Must be willing to work flexible hours

COMPENSATION
- $12.50 per hour plus performance bonuses
- Health insurance

The application deadline is July 10.

From: Dennis Carlsen <d.carlsen@tallecentrum.com>
To: Angela Lakmal <lakmal@pointmail.com>
Date: August 16
Subject: Your Employment Confirmation at Talle Centrum

Dear Ms. Lakmal,

Thank you for stopping by on August 10 to discuss your employment. **As agreed, you will be taking on the role of a full-time customer service agent here at our center in Colombo.** Compensation will be as advertised. Your start date will be on September 18. If you have any concerns, please call me at 555-2795.

Sincerely,

Dennis Carlsen, Human Resources Manager

01 What is indicated about Ms. Lakmal?

(A) She will earn a bonus for every sale.
(B) She will receive extra pay for good work.
(C) She will have to earn a professional certificate.
(D) She will be working mostly at night.

HACKERS PRACTICE

지문을 읽고 주어진 질문에 가장 알맞은 보기를 고르세요.

Question 01 refers to the following article and letter.

Greenfield City to Introduce New Community Center Hours

August 10—In a press release issued on August 4, Greenfield City Council announced plans to extend the operating hours of the community centers run by the municipal government. This decision is based on responses in questionnaires distributed in May to solicit feedback from residents on city services. The press release specified that the Oakwood and Selma community centers will remain open until 8:30 P.M., while the Belleville and Blanchard centers will close at 8:00 P.M. and 9:00 P.M., respectively. The new schedules will take effect on August 15.

August 12
Wilma Gomez
Department of Public Services
387 Paterson Street
Greenfield, MA 02125

Dear Ms. Gomez,

I am contacting you regarding the recently announced changes to the hours of operation of our city's community centers. In general, I am in favor of the plan because I have signed up for a number of programs since I retired last year. However, I was disappointed to learn that the community center nearest to my apartment building would only be staying open for an additional 30 minutes—until 8:00 P.M. I would like to ask that your department reconsider this decision and ensure that all of the community centers have their operating hours extended by the same amount of time. Thank you.

Sincerely,

Adam Ferris

---

01 Which community center is closest to Mr. Ferris's residence?

(A) Oakwood Community Center
(B) Selma Community Center
(C) Belleville Community Center
(D) Blanchard Community Center

Question 02 refers to the following information, form, and e-mail.

How does Buzzchain work?

Buzzchain is a network of consumers who review products and provide assistance with online marketing. To join, sign up and let us know what kinds of products you are interested in. We will notify you when a product is available for review. You will be sent either a free sample or a voucher that can be exchanged at a store near you.

As a member, you will earn points for every review you complete. Redeem your points for products and services on our partner Web site, www.linkchange.com.

Buzzchain Reviewer: Sean Morgan
Product name: Limba Air
Attachment: Product_Photo.jpg

Buzzchain Reviewer ID: M90746
Category: Household products

Is this your first time using the product?
Yes.

What is your overall opinion of the product?
I received a package of two scents, Berry Fresh and Crisp Sheets. I didn't like the first one, but I might buy the second.

To: Buzzchain Customer Service <service@buzzchain.com>
From: Sean Morgan <s.morgan@mynetmail.com>
Subject: Inquiry
Date: May 14

To Whom It May Concern,

I recently completed my first review. However, when I visited the Linkchange Web site, I realized that I did not have enough points for the beach sandals I wanted. Could you send me some more products to review as soon as possible?

Thank you.

Sean Morgan

---

02 What is true about Mr. Morgan?

(A) He is a frequent user of air fresheners.
(B) He expressed an interest in household items.
(C) He is unqualified to perform a review.
(D) He designs product packaging.

HACKERS TEST

지문을 읽고 주어진 질문에 가장 알맞은 보기를 고르세요.

Questions 01-05 refer to the following advertisement and form.

Glisten Plan Pricing

Stream hours of high-quality background music at multiple retail locations, with each song licensed for public use. Choose easy monthly payments or a one-time annual fee for greater savings.

Glisten Beat	Glisten Rhythm	Glisten Harmony
$9.99 a month or $100 a year per location Includes a 5-day free trial	$15.99 a month or $150 a year per location Includes a 15-day free trial	$24.99 a month or $250 a year per location Includes a 30-day free trial
• Choose from several custom radio stations or create your own playlists • Control the listening experience from your mobile device	• All features of the Glisten Beat package • The ability to create audio advertisements to support your marketing activities • Customize music per region or store	• All features of the Glisten Rhythm package • Access to music experts who create playlists in support of your brand • Allow your guests to request music using our smartphone application

The plans above are only available to businesses with fewer than five locations. If you operate five or more, please contact us at 555-3092 to develop a package that is suitable for you.

GLISTEN
www.glisten.com

Company: Coax Clothing
Address: 1228 Willow Wood Drive
Hubbard, OH 44425
Contact: Andy Lewis
E-mail: a.lewis@mailbot.com

Web site (optional): www.coaxclothing.com
Title: Marketing Director
Phone: 555-9946

Preferred Plan:
☒ Glisten Beat   ☐ Glisten Rhythm   ☐ Glisten Harmony

Your trial period begins upon completion of the application process.

Payment Scheme:
☐ One-time charge   ☒ Monthly

Clicking on SUBMIT will take you to the payment page.

| Please check your e-mail for a confirmation message. To view our refund policy or other terms and conditions, click here. | RESET | SUBMIT |

01 For whom is the advertisement intended?

(A) Professional musicians
(B) Software programmers
(C) Recording technicians
(D) Store owners

02 What is NOT included with every payment plan?

(A) A free trial
(B) Radio stations
(C) Custom playlists
(D) Guest access

03 What can users on the most expensive plan do?

(A) Broadcast video advertisements
(B) Send messages through social media
(C) Get expert help with music selections
(D) Take advantage of additional discounts

04 What is indicated about Coax Clothing?

(A) It will pay 100 dollars a year.
(B) It has fewer than five locations.
(C) Its trial period lasts for one month.
(D) Its initial payment is due in 15 days.

05 Why should Mr. Lewis check his e-mail?

(A) To read the terms and conditions
(B) To verify his registration
(C) To receive his monthly invoice
(D) To receive a temporary password

Questions 06-10 refer to the following letter and schedule.

Dawn Taylor
42 Coote Road
Bluff Hill, Napier 4110
New Zealand

Dear Ms. Taylor,

I am honored by your request that I speak at the event in February marking the 100th year of the New Zealand Sailing Society (NZSS). As a former NZSS president, I am familiar with the club's history. And it has been a pleasure to watch it evolve in the years since I stepped down from my leadership position.

Regrettably, I am unable to participate because I will be taking part in a sailing race on the same day. In my place, I would like to recommend Brenda Wilson, a yachting enthusiast and an accomplished public speaker. Another good choice would be Ling Zhang, who has broken some world records for solo sailing. Alison Scott also comes to mind. Her grandfather was an original member of the NZSS, so she has some interesting stories about the society's early days. Let me know if one of these people seems suitable to speak at the event, and I will provide you with that person's e-mail address.

Kind regards,
Patrick Patel

Schedule of Events for 100 Years of Smooth Sailing:
An Anniversary Celebration of the New Zealand Sailing Society

<u>Location</u>: Walter Donahue Clubhouse
<u>Date</u>: February 28

Time	Event	Speaker
5:00-5:20 P.M.	Opening speech: Welcome Fellow Sailors	Dominika Gladstone
5:20-5:50 P.M.	Main address: Why Sailing Matters	Ling Zhang
6:00-7:30 P.M.	Dinner banquet in the Ketch Room	
7:30-8:00 P.M.	Slideshow: The NZSS Over the Years	Winny Baxter
8:00-8:30 P.M.	NZSS quiz with prizes for the winners	David Young
8:40-9:00 P.M.	Fireworks display over Breakwater Harbor	

06 What is the main purpose of the letter?

(A) To suggest holding an event
(B) To turn down an invitation
(C) To review some qualifications
(D) To ask for a change in date

07 In the letter, the word "original" in paragraph 2, line 5, is closest in meaning to

(A) unique
(B) new
(C) first
(D) authentic

08 What did Mr. Patel probably do?

(A) Sent Ms. Zhang's contact details to an event organizer
(B) Provided Ms. Taylor with a suitable topic for a lecture
(C) Gave a speech about Ms. Scott's background
(D) Taught Ms. Wilson how to sail

09 According to the schedule, when will attendees begin playing a game?

(A) At 5:00 P.M.
(B) At 6:00 P.M.
(C) At 8:00 P.M.
(D) At 8:40 P.M.

10 What will NOT take place at 100 Years of Smooth Sailing?

(A) An outdoor show
(B) A product demonstration
(C) A visual presentation
(D) An opening talk

Questions 11-15 refer to the following e-mail, invoice, and letter.

From	Claude Symonds <cs100@edgeattire.com>
To	Sheila Bryant <bryant@edgeattire.com>
Date	August 6
Subject	Fredericton Style Expo

Hi Sheila,

As we discussed, the Fredericton Style Expo is the perfect opportunity to promote our clothing to potential buyers. To get us ready for the expo, I'd like you to do the following. First, please rent us a booth for the entire duration of the event. Be sure to ask about the availability of storage space to hold our clothing and accessories. Also, I think we should have one or two models at the booth wearing our outfits. Please contact the modeling agency we worked with previously to find suitable candidates. Thanks.

Best,
Claude

Fredericton Style Expo

Renter: Edge Attire
Contact: Sheila Bryant, 555-4096

Booth size: 4x4 (square meters)
Rental charge: $320 ($80 daily rental fee x 4 days)
Deposit: $45

Terms: Booth rentals include four event tickets, one table, two chairs, one electrical outlet, one set of lights, and one standard sign. The following are available for an extra fee:

Additional outlets, tables, and chairs: $20 per day
Custom sign: $50 installation fee
Storage rental: $15 per day

September 27
Fredericton Style Expo
5 Bulkley Street
Shelburne, NS B0T 1W0

Dear Fredericton Style Expo,

Our company participated in your recent event as an exhibitor. We requested a standard booth and a storage locker for the items used in our display. However, when I checked our final bill, I noticed that we were also charged for a custom sign. Please refund me the amount we were mistakenly charged as soon as possible. I would also like to be notified when this has been done. You can reach me at 555-3938. Thank you.

Yours truly,

Claude Symonds
Edge Attire

11 What is the purpose of the e-mail?

(A) To assign some tasks
(B) To adjust a schedule
(C) To address some complaints
(D) To confirm a price

12 What can be concluded about the Fredericton Style Expo?

(A) It lasted for a period of four days.
(B) It charged a fee to exhibitors who opened late.
(C) It partnered with a modeling agency.
(D) It promoted exhibitors' products on its Web site.

13 What is indicated about Edge Attire in the invoice?

(A) It can send several people to take part in the expo.
(B) It must give up the deposit that was paid in advance.
(C) It must pay an extra fee to choose a booth location.
(D) It can upgrade to a larger option free of charge.

14 How much was Mr. Symonds overcharged?

(A) $15
(B) $45
(C) $50
(D) $320

15 Why does Mr. Symonds ask that a Fredericton Style Expo representative contact him?

(A) To explain why a bill was inaccurate
(B) To inform him that a refund has been completed
(C) To clarify how to request a discount
(D) To tell him where a payment can be submitted

Questions 16-20 refer to the following Web page, e-mail, and review.

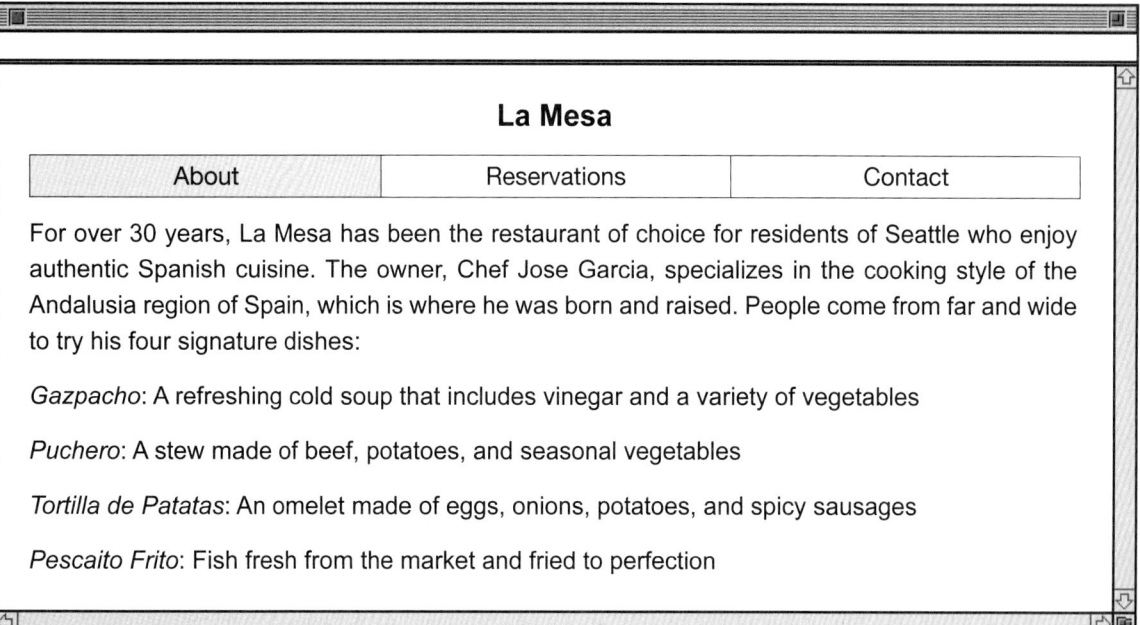

La Mesa

| About | Reservations | Contact |

For over 30 years, La Mesa has been the restaurant of choice for residents of Seattle who enjoy authentic Spanish cuisine. The owner, Chef Jose Garcia, specializes in the cooking style of the Andalusia region of Spain, which is where he was born and raised. People come from far and wide to try his four signature dishes:

Gazpacho: A refreshing cold soup that includes vinegar and a variety of vegetables

Puchero: A stew made of beef, potatoes, and seasonal vegetables

Tortilla de Patatas: An omelet made of eggs, onions, potatoes, and spicy sausages

Pescaito Frito: Fish fresh from the market and fried to perfection

---

From	Sally Mendez <s.mendez@lamesa.com>
To	Kyle Graves <k.graves@aceair.com>
Subject	Service Request
Date	August 2

Dear Mr. Graves,

One of the air-conditioning units in our restaurant is not working properly. The air conditioner in the kitchen that your employee fixed last month is fine, but now the one in the private dining room has stopped working completely. Would you be able to send another technician to the restaurant to deal with this problem? We open at 11:30 A.M. each day, so it would be great if your technician could come early in the morning.

I'd like this to be done as soon as possible. The private dining room is the only option we have to accommodate groups of 15 or more, as none of the tables in the main dining room are large enough. Thanks.

Sincerely,

Sally Mendez
General Manager, La Mesa

Restaurant: La Mesa
Reviewer: David Porter
Date: August 5
Score: 4/5

I arranged for La Mesa to host the retirement party for my company's CEO on August 4. Overall, the service was excellent—especially considering that there were 18 people in our party sitting together. The server assigned to us was friendly and efficient. With regard to the food, most of us were very happy with the dishes we ordered. I especially liked that the chef obviously tried to use authentic Spanish cooking methods and seasonings. However, I had the seafood dish, one of the chef's signature dishes, and it was a little overcooked.

16 What is mentioned about Mr. Garcia?

(A) He operates several restaurants.
(B) He was born in Spain.
(C) He recently relocated to Seattle.
(D) He has attended culinary school.

17 According to the e-mail, what happened last month?

(A) A kitchen was remodeled.
(B) An employee was promoted.
(C) An appliance was repaired.
(D) A menu was updated.

18 What does Ms. Mendez ask Mr. Graves to do?

(A) Order some equipment
(B) Send a worker
(C) Repair some furniture
(D) Confirm a reservation

19 What is suggested about Mr. Porter?

(A) He is organizing another event with his coworkers.
(B) He has decided not to eat a meal at La Mesa again.
(C) He will be retiring from his company in the near future.
(D) He was not seated in the main area of the restaurant.

20 Which dish did Mr. Porter most likely order?

(A) Gazpacho
(B) Puchero
(C) Tortilla de Patatas
(D) Pescaito Frito

MEMO

한 권으로 끝내는
해커스 토익 600+plus
LC + RC + VOCA

정답·해석·해설
해설집

해커스 어학연구소

저작권자 © 2025, 해커스 어학연구소 이 책 및 음성파일의 모든 내용, 이미지, 디자인, 편집 형태에 대한 저작권은 저자에게 있습니다.
서면에 의한 저자와 출판사의 허락 없이 내용의 일부 혹은 전부를 인용, 발췌하거나 복제, 배포할 수 없습니다.

PART 1

DAY 01 사람 중심 사진

1. 1인 사진

HACKERS PRACTICE			p.31
01 (D)	02 (C)	03 (D)	04 (A)

01 1인 사진 　　　　　　　　　🎧 미국 / 호주

(A) He is opening a door.
(B) He is wiping a window.
(C) He is watering a plant.
(D) He is using a copy machine.

open v. 열다   wipe v. 닦다   water v. 물을 주다   copy machine 복사기

해석 (A) 그는 문을 열고 있다.
(B) 그는 창문을 닦고 있다.
(C) 그는 식물에 물을 주고 있다.
(D) 그는 복사기를 사용하고 있다.

해설 (A) [×] opening(열고 있다)은 남자의 동작과 무관하므로 오답이다. 사진에 있는 문(door)을 사용하여 혼동을 주었다.
(B) [×] wiping(닦고 있다)은 남자의 동작과 무관하므로 오답이다. 사진에 있는 창문(window)을 사용하여 혼동을 주었다.
(C) [×] watering(물을 주고 있다)은 남자의 동작과 무관하므로 오답이다. 사진에 있는 화분(plant)을 사용하여 혼동을 주었다.
(D) [○] 남자가 복사기를 사용하고 있는 모습을 가장 잘 묘사한 정답이다.

02 1인 사진 　　　　　　　　　🎧 영국 / 캐나다

(A) Some furniture is being displayed.
(B) A woman is paying for a purchase.
(C) A woman is inspecting an item.
(D) Some clothing is being folded.

display v. 진열하다, 전시하다   pay for ~의 값을 지불하다
purchase n. 구매(품)   inspect v. 살펴보다, 검사하다
clothing n. 옷, 의류   fold v. 접다

해석 (A) 가구가 진열되고 있다.
(B) 한 여자가 구매품의 값을 지불하고 있다.
(C) 한 여자가 물품을 살펴보고 있다.
(D) 옷이 접히고 있다.

해설 (A) [×] 사진에 진열되고 있는(being displayed) 가구가 없으므로 오답이다.
(B) [×] paying(값을 지불하고 있다)은 여자의 동작과 무관하므로 오답이다. 사진의 장소인 옷 가게와 관련된 purchase(구매품)를 사용하여 혼동을 주었다.
(C) [○] 여자가 물품을 살펴보고 있는 모습을 가장 잘 묘사한 정답이다.
(D) [×] 사진에서 옷(clothing)은 보이지만 접히고 있는(being folded) 모습은 아니므로 오답이다.

03 1인 사진 　　　　　　　　　🎧 캐나다 / 영국

(A) The man is stirring a beverage.
(B) The man is checking a receipt.
(C) The man is lifting a chair.
(D) The man is looking down at a phone.

stir v. 저어 섞다, 휘젓다   beverage n. 음료   check v. 확인하다
receipt n. 영수증   lift v. 들어 올리다   look down at ~을 내려다보다

해석 (A) 남자가 음료를 저어 섞고 있다.
(B) 남자가 영수증을 확인하고 있다.
(C) 남자가 의자를 들어 올리고 있다.
(D) 남자가 휴대전화를 내려다보고 있다.

해설 (A) [×] stirring(저어 섞고 있다)은 남자의 동작과 무관하므로 오답이다. 사진에 있는 음료(beverage)를 사용하여 혼동을 주었다.
(B) [×] 사진에서 영수증(receipt)을 확인할 수 없으므로 오답이다.
(C) [×] lifting a chair(의자를 들어 올리고 있다)는 남자의 동작과 무관하므로 오답이다.
(D) [○] 남자가 휴대전화를 내려다보고 있는 모습을 가장 잘 묘사한 정답이다.

04 1인 사진 　　　　　　　　　🎧 호주 / 미국

(A) The woman is kneeling to work with a wire.
(B) The woman is plugging in a tool.
(C) The woman is packing supplies into boxes.
(D) The woman is mopping the floor.

kneel v. 무릎을 꿇다   wire n. 전선, 철사   plug in ~의 전원을 연결하다
tool n. 도구   pack v. 포장하다, 싸다   supplies n. 물품
mop v. 대걸레로 닦다

해석 (A) 여자가 전선으로 작업하기 위해 무릎을 꿇고 있다.
(B) 여자가 도구의 전원을 연결하고 있다.
(C) 여자가 물품을 상자 안에 넣어 포장하고 있다.
(D) 여자가 바닥을 대걸레로 닦고 있다.

해설 (A) [○] 여자가 전선으로 작업하기 위해 무릎을 꿇고 있는 모습을 가장 잘 묘사한 정답이다.
(B) [×] plugging in a tool(도구의 전원을 연결하고 있다)은 여자의 동작과 무관하므로 오답이다.
(C) [×] 사진에 상자(boxes)가 없으므로 오답이다.
(D) [×] mopping(대걸레로 닦고 있다)은 여자의 동작과 무관하므로 오답이다.

2. 2인 이상 사진

HACKERS PRACTICE			p.33
01 (D)	02 (B)	03 (B)	04 (C)

01 2인 이상 사진   영국 / 캐나다

(A) They are exiting a building.
(B) A man is closing a window.
(C) A woman is reaching for a handrail.
(D) They are going up some stairs.

exit v. 나가다   reach for ~을 향해 손을 뻗다   handrail n. 난간
go up 올라가다   stair n. 계단

해석 (A) 그들은 건물을 나가고 있다.
(B) 한 남자가 창문을 닫고 있다.
(C) 한 여자가 난간을 향해 손을 뻗고 있다.
(D) 그들은 계단을 올라가고 있다.

해설 (A) [×] exiting a building(건물을 나가고 있다)은 사람들의 동작과 무관하므로 오답이다.
(B) [×] 사진에 창문을 닫고 있는(closing a window) 남자가 없으므로 오답이다.
(C) [×] 사진에 난간을 향해 손을 뻗고 있는(reaching for a handrail) 여자가 없으므로 오답이다.
(D) [○] 사람들이 계단을 올라가고 있는 모습을 가장 잘 묘사한 정답이다.

02 2인 이상 사진   호주 / 미국

(A) One of the men is typing on a computer.
(B) Some people are attending a presentation.
(C) One of the men is pointing at a whiteboard.
(D) Some people are looking at a monitor.

attend v. 참석하다   presentation n. 발표   point at ~을 가리키다

해석 (A) 남자들 중 한 명이 컴퓨터로 타자를 치고 있다.
(B) 몇몇 사람들이 발표에 참석하고 있다.
(C) 남자들 중 한 명이 화이트보드를 가리키고 있다.
(D) 몇몇 사람들이 모니터를 보고 있다.

해설 (A) [×] 사진에 컴퓨터로 타자를 치고 있는(typing on a computer) 남자가 없으므로 오답이다.
(B) [○] 몇몇 사람들이 발표에 참석하고 있는 모습을 가장 잘 묘사한 정답이다.
(C) [×] 사진에 화이트보드를 가리키고 있는(pointing at a whiteboard) 남자가 없으므로 오답이다.
(D) [×] 사람들이 모니터(monitor)를 보고 있는 것이 아니라, 발표자를 보고 있으므로 오답이다.

03 2인 이상 사진   미국 / 호주

(A) A cashier is putting fruit in a bag.
(B) A customer is handing an item to a cashier.
(C) A customer is taking out a credit card.
(D) A cashier is arranging some beverages.

take out 꺼내다   arrange v. 정리하다, 배열하다   beverage n. 음료

해석 (A) 계산원이 과일을 가방에 넣고 있다.
(B) 손님이 계산원에게 물품을 건네고 있다.
(C) 손님이 신용카드를 꺼내고 있다.
(D) 계산원이 음료를 정리하고 있다.

해설 (A) [×] putting fruit in a bag(과일을 가방에 넣고 있다)은 계산원의 동작과 무관하므로 오답이다.
(B) [○] 손님이 계산원에게 물품을 건네고 있는 모습을 가장 잘 묘사한 정답이다.
(C) [×] 사진에서 신용카드(credit card)를 확인할 수 없으므로 오답이다.
(D) [×] arranging some beverages(음료를 정리하고 있다)는 계산원의 행동과 무관하므로 오답이다.

04 2인 이상 사진   캐나다 / 영국

(A) A cabinet is being stocked with containers.
(B) The woman is placing a cup on a shelf.
(C) The man is leaning over a table.
(D) Some dishes have been left in a sink.

cabinet n. 수납장   stock v. 채우다   container n. 그릇, 용기   shelf n. 선반
lean over ~ 위로 몸을 구부리다

해석 (A) 수납장이 그릇들로 채워지고 있다.
(B) 여자가 컵을 선반 위에 놓고 있다.
(C) 남자가 탁자 위로 몸을 구부리고 있다.
(D) 몇몇 접시들이 싱크대 안에 남겨져 있다.

해설 (A) [×] 사진에서 수납장(cabinet)은 보이지만 채워지고 있는(being stocked) 모습은 아니므로 오답이다.
(B) [×] placing a cup on a shelf(컵을 선반 위에 놓고 있다)는 여자의 동작과 무관하므로 오답이다.
(C) [○] 남자가 탁자 위로 몸을 구부리고 있는 모습을 가장 잘 묘사한 정답이다.
(D) [×] 사진에서 싱크대(sink)를 확인할 수 없으므로 오답이다. 사진의 장소인 주방과 관련된 dishes(접시들)를 사용하여 혼동을 주었다.

HACKERS TEST   p.34

01 (A)	02 (D)	03 (B)	04 (A)	05 (B)
06 (D)	07 (C)	08 (D)	09 (C)	10 (D)
11 (A)	12 (D)			

01 1인 사진   미국

(A) A man is using a laptop.
(B) A man is boarding an airplane.
(C) A man is reading a magazine.
(D) A man is taking off his jacket.

board v. 탑승하다   take off (옷을) 벗다

해석 (A) 남자가 노트북 컴퓨터를 사용하고 있다.
(B) 남자가 비행기에 탑승하고 있다.
(C) 남자가 잡지를 읽고 있다.
(D) 남자가 재킷을 벗고 있다.

해설 (A) [○] 남자가 노트북 컴퓨터를 사용하고 있는 모습을 가장 잘 묘사한 정답이다.
(B) [×] boarding(탑승하고 있다)은 남자의 동작과 무관하므로 오답이다. 사진의 장소인 공항과 관련된 airplane(비행기)을 사용하여 혼동을 주었다.
(C) [×] 사진에 잡지(magazine)가 없으므로 오답이다.
(D) [×] 남자가 재킷을 입고 있지 않은 상태인데, 재킷을 벗고 있다(taking off)고 잘못 묘사한 오답이다.

02 2인 이상 사진   호주

(A) A man is looking in a toolbox.
(B) They are repairing a window.
(C) They are lifting up a board.
(D) A man is holding a piece of paper.

toolbox n. 공구통   repair v. 수리하다   lift v. 들어 올리다   board n. 판자
hold v. 쥐다, 잡다

해석 (A) 한 남자가 공구통을 들여다보고 있다.
    (B) 그들은 창문을 수리하고 있다.
    (C) 그들은 판자를 들어 올리고 있다.
    (D) 한 남자가 종이 한 장을 쥐고 있다.

해설 (A) [x] 사진에 공구통(toolbox)이 없으므로 오답이다.
    (B) [x] repairing(수리하고 있다)은 사람들의 동작과 무관하므로 오답이다. 사진에 있는 창문(window)을 사용하여 혼동을 주었다.
    (C) [x] 사진에 판자(board)가 없으므로 오답이다.
    (D) [o] 한 남자가 종이 한 장을 쥐고 있는 모습을 가장 잘 묘사한 정답이다.

03 1인 사진   영국

(A) She is cutting a vegetable.
(B) She is drinking from a glass.
(C) She is washing some dishes.
(D) She is opening a refrigerator.

vegetable n. 채소   glass n. 유리잔   refrigerator n. 냉장고

해석 (A) 그녀는 채소를 자르고 있다.
    (B) 그녀는 유리잔에 든 것을 마시고 있다.
    (C) 그녀는 몇몇 접시들을 씻고 있다.
    (D) 그녀는 냉장고를 열고 있다.

해설 (A) [x] cutting(자르고 있다)은 여자의 동작과 무관하므로 오답이다. 사진에 있는 채소(vegetable)를 사용하여 혼동을 주었다.
    (B) [o] 여자가 유리잔에 든 것을 마시고 있는 모습을 가장 잘 묘사한 정답이다.
    (C) [x] washing(씻고 있다)은 여자의 동작과 무관하므로 오답이다. 사진에 있는 접시들(dishes)을 사용하여 혼동을 주었다.
    (D) [x] opening(열고 있다)은 여자의 동작과 무관하므로 오답이다.

04 2인 이상 사진   캐나다

(A) They are shaking hands.
(B) A railing is being installed.
(C) A staircase is being cleaned.
(D) They are entering a store.

shake hands 악수하다   railing n. 난간   install v. 설치하다
staircase n. 계단

해석 (A) 그들은 악수하고 있다.
    (B) 난간이 설치되고 있다.
    (C) 계단이 청소되고 있다.
    (D) 그들은 가게에 들어가고 있다.

해설 (A) [o] 사람들이 악수하고 있는 모습을 가장 잘 묘사한 정답이다.
    (B) [x] 사진에서 난간(railing)은 보이지만 설치되고 있는(being installed) 모습은 아니므로 오답이다.
    (C) [x] 사진에서 계단(staircase)은 보이지만 청소되고 있는(being cleaned) 모습은 아니므로 오답이다.
    (D) [x] entering a store(가게에 들어가고 있다)는 사람들의 동작과 무관하므로 오답이다.

05 2인 이상 사진   영국

(A) Some people are standing next to each other.
(B) One of the women is giving a presentation.
(C) Some people are watching a movie.
(D) One of the men is moving a desk.

next to each other 나란히   presentation n. 발표   move v. 옮기다

해석 (A) 몇몇 사람들이 나란히 서 있다.
    (B) 여자들 중 한 명이 발표를 하고 있다.
    (C) 몇몇 사람들이 영화를 보고 있다.
    (D) 남자들 중 한 명이 책상을 옮기고 있다.

해설 (A) [x] 사진에 나란히 서 있는(standing next to each other) 사람들이 없으므로 오답이다.
    (B) [o] 여자들 중 한 명이 발표를 하고 있는 모습을 가장 잘 묘사한 정답이다.
    (C) [x] 사람들이 영화(movie)를 보고 있는 것이 아니라, 발표를 보고 있으므로 오답이다.
    (D) [x] 사진에 책상을 옮기고 있는(moving a desk) 남자가 없으므로 오답이다.

06 1인 사진   미국

(A) A woman is pressing a button.
(B) A woman is making a phone call.
(C) A woman is purchasing from a vendor.
(D) A woman is facing a machine.

press v. 누르다   make a phone call 전화를 걸다   vendor n. 노점상
face v. 마주 보다   machine n. 기계

해석 (A) 한 여자가 버튼을 누르고 있다.
    (B) 한 여자가 전화를 걸고 있다.
    (C) 한 여자가 노점상에게서 구매하고 있다.
    (D) 한 여자가 기계를 마주 보고 있다.

해설 (A) [x] pressing a button(버튼을 누르고 있다)은 여자의 동작과 무관하므로 오답이다.
    (B) [x] making a phone call(전화를 걸고 있다)은 여자의 동작과 무관하므로 오답이다.
    (C) [x] 사진에 노점상(vendor)이 없으므로 오답이다.
    (D) [o] 여자가 기계를 마주 보고 있는 모습을 가장 잘 묘사한 정답이다.

07 1인 사진   캐나다

(A) He is picking up a device.
(B) He is sipping from a bottle.
(C) Some footwear has been placed on a table.
(D) Some cushions have been laid on the floor.

pick up 들어 올리다, 집다   device n. 장치   sip v. 조금씩 마시다
bottle n. 병   footwear n. 신발   lay v. 놓다

해석 (A) 그는 장치를 들어 올리고 있다.
    (B) 그는 병에 든 것을 조금씩 마시고 있다.
    (C) 몇몇 신발들이 탁자 위에 놓여 있다.
    (D) 몇몇 쿠션들이 바닥에 놓여 있다.

해설 (A) [x] 남자가 장치(device)를 들어 올리고 있는 것이 아니라, 의류를 들고 있으므로 오답이다.
    (B) [x] sipping(조금씩 마시고 있다)은 남자의 동작과 무관하므로 오답

이다. 사진에 있는 병(bottle)을 사용하여 혼동을 주었다.
(C) [o] 몇몇 신발들이 탁자 위에 놓여 있는 모습을 가장 잘 묘사한 정답이다.
(D) [x] 사진에서 바닥에 놓여 있는(have been laid on the floor) 쿠션들을 확인할 수 없으므로 오답이다.

08 2인 이상 사진 〔영국〕

(A) An item of luggage has been left in a van.
(B) Water has spilled from a vase.
(C) One of the women is sweeping a room.
(D) A man is waiting at a counter.

luggage n. 여행용 짐, 수하물 van n. 승합차 spill v. 쏟아지다
sweep v. 쓸다

해석 (A) 여행용 짐 하나가 승합차 안에 놓여 있다.
(B) 물이 꽃병에서 쏟아져 있다.
(C) 여자들 중 한 명이 방을 쓸고 있다.
(D) 한 남자가 카운터에서 기다리고 있다.

해설 (A) [x] 사진에 승합차(van)가 없으므로 오답이다.
(B) [x] 물(Water)이 꽃병에서 쏟아져 있는 것이 아니라, 꽃병에 담겨 있으므로 오답이다.
(C) [x] 사진에 방을 쓸고 있는(sweeping a room) 여자가 없으므로 오답이다.
(D) [o] 남자가 카운터에서 기다리고 있는 모습을 가장 잘 묘사한 정답이다.

09 1인 사진 〔호주〕

(A) The woman is loading garbage onto a truck.
(B) The woman is closing the door of a car.
(C) The woman is walking on a pedestrian crosswalk.
(D) The woman is leaving a parking lot.

load v. 싣다 garbage n. 쓰레기 pedestrian crosswalk 보행자 횡단보도
leave v. 떠나다 parking lot 주차장

해석 (A) 여자가 쓰레기를 트럭에 싣고 있다.
(B) 여자가 자동차의 문을 닫고 있다.
(C) 여자가 보행자 횡단보도에서 걷고 있다.
(D) 여자가 주차장을 떠나고 있다.

해설 (A) [x] loading(싣고 있다)은 여자의 동작과 무관하므로 오답이다. 사진에 있는 트럭(truck)을 사용하여 혼동을 주었다.
(B) [x] closing(닫고 있다)은 여자의 동작과 무관하므로 오답이다. 사진에 있는 자동차(car)를 사용하여 혼동을 주었다.
(C) [o] 여자가 보행자 횡단보도에서 걷고 있는 모습을 가장 잘 묘사한 정답이다.
(D) [x] 사진에서 주차장(parking lot)을 확인할 수 없으므로 오답이다.

10 2인 이상 사진 〔미국〕

(A) Some chairs have been propped against a wall.
(B) The man is writing on a notepad.
(C) The woman is touching a screen.
(D) Some documents are scattered on a tabletop.

prop v. 받치다 notepad n. 메모장 touch v. 만지다 screen n. 화면
scatter v. 흩어지게 하다 tabletop n. 테이블 윗면

해석 (A) 몇몇 의자들이 벽에 기대어 받쳐져 있다.
(B) 남자가 메모장에 글자를 쓰고 있다.
(C) 여자가 화면을 만지고 있다.
(D) 몇몇 서류들이 테이블 윗면에 흩어져 있다.

해설 (A) [x] 사진에서 의자들(chairs)은 보이지만 벽에 기대어 받쳐져 있는(have been propped against a wall) 모습은 아니므로 오답이다.
(B) [x] writing(쓰고 있다)은 남자의 동작과 무관하므로 오답이다. 사진에 있는 메모장(notepad)을 사용하여 혼동을 주었다.
(C) [x] touching(만지다)은 여자의 동작과 무관하므로 오답이다. 사진에 있는 화면(screen)을 사용하여 혼동을 주었다.
(D) [o] 서류들이 테이블 윗면에 흩어져 있는 모습을 가장 잘 묘사한 정답이다.

11 1인 사진 〔캐나다〕

(A) He is clearing snow from a roof.
(B) He is installing a fence around a house.
(C) A shovel is lying in the corner of a garden.
(D) Trees are growing on both sides of the walkway.

clear v. 치우다, 청소하다 roof n. 지붕 fence n. 울타리 shovel n. 삽
lie v. 놓여 있다 corner n. 구석, 모퉁이 on both sides of ~의 양쪽에서
walkway n. 보도, 산책길

해석 (A) 그는 지붕에서 눈을 치우고 있다.
(B) 그는 집 주위에 울타리를 설치하고 있다.
(C) 삽이 정원의 구석에 놓여 있다.
(D) 나무들이 보도의 양쪽에서 자라고 있다.

해설 (A) [o] 남자가 지붕에서 눈을 치우고 있는 모습을 가장 잘 묘사한 정답이다.
(B) [x] installing(설치하고 있다)은 남자의 동작과 무관하므로 오답이다.
(C) [x] 사진에서 정원(garden)을 확인할 수 없으므로 오답이다.
(D) [x] 사진에서 보도(walkway)를 확인할 수 없으므로 오답이다.

12 2인 이상 사진 〔호주〕

(A) One of the women is wiping a cup with a cloth.
(B) Some jackets have been folded on a chair.
(C) One of the women is holding some flowers.
(D) Some books are arranged close to the window.

wipe v. 닦다 cloth n. 천 fold v. 접다 arrange v. 정리하다
close to ~ 가까이에

해석 (A) 여자들 중 한 명이 천으로 컵을 닦고 있다.
(B) 몇몇 재킷들이 의자 위에 접혀 있다.
(C) 여자들 중 한 명이 꽃들을 들고 있다.
(D) 몇몇 책들이 창문 가까이에 정리되어 있다.

해설 (A) [x] 사진에 컵을 닦고 있는(wiping a cup) 여자가 없으므로 오답이다. 사진에 있는 컵(cup)을 사용하여 혼동을 주었다.
(B) [x] 사진에서 접혀 있는(have been folded) 재킷을 확인할 수 없으므로 오답이다.
(C) [x] 사진에 꽃들을 들고 있는(holding some flowers) 여자가 없으므로 오답이다. 사진에 있는 꽃들(flowers)을 사용하여 혼동을 주었다.
(D) [o] 몇몇 책들이 창문 가까이에 정리되어 있는 모습을 가장 잘 묘사한 정답이다.

DAY 02 사물/풍경 중심 사진

1. 실내 사진

HACKERS PRACTICE p.37
01 (B)   02 (A)   03 (C)   04 (D)

01 실내 사진  캐나다 / 영국

(A) The floor is being swept.
(B) Sofas have been arranged for display.
(C) There is a lamp next to a table.
(D) There are some pillows on a bed.

sweep v. 쓸다   arrange v. 배열하다, 정돈하다   for display 전시용으로
pillow n. 베개

해석 (A) 바닥이 쓸리고 있다.
(B) 소파들이 전시용으로 배열되어 있다.
(C) 등이 탁자 옆에 있다.
(D) 몇몇 베개들이 침대 위에 있다.

해설 (A) [×] 사진에서 바닥(floor)은 보이지만 쓸리고 있는(being swept) 모습은 아니므로 오답이다.
(B) [○] 소파들이 전시용으로 배열되어 있는 모습을 가장 잘 묘사한 정답이다.
(C) [×] 등(lamp)이 탁자 옆에 있는 것이 아니라, 천장에 매달려 있으므로 오답이다.
(D) [×] 베개들(pillows)이 침대 위가 아니라, 소파 위에 있으므로 오답이다.

02 실내 사진  영국 / 캐나다

(A) Some light fixtures are hanging from the ceiling.
(B) Some chairs are pushed against a wall.
(C) There are eating utensils on a table.
(D) There is a potted plant in front of a window.

light fixture 조명 기구   ceiling n. 천장   push v. 밀다
eating utensil 식사용 도구   potted plant 화분에 심은 식물

해석 (A) 몇몇 조명 기구들이 천장에 매달려 있다.
(B) 몇몇 의자들이 벽에 기대어 밀려 있다.
(C) 식사용 도구들이 탁자 위에 있다.
(D) 화분에 심은 식물이 창문 앞에 있다.

해설 (A) [○] 몇몇 조명 기구들이 천장에 매달려 있는 모습을 가장 잘 묘사한 정답이다.
(B) [×] 사진에서 의자들(chairs)은 보이지만 벽에 기대어 밀려 있는(are pushed against a wall) 모습은 아니므로 오답이다.
(C) [×] 사진에 식사용 도구들(eating utensils)이 없으므로 오답이다. 사진에 있는 탁자(table)를 사용하여 혼동을 주었다.
(D) [×] 화분에 심은 식물(potted plant)이 창문 앞이 아니라, 조리대 위에 있으므로 오답이다. 사진에 있는 창문(window)을 사용하여 혼동을 주었다.

03 실내 사진 호주 / 미국

(A) A decoration is positioned on a windowsill.
(B) Magazines have been piled on the floor.
(C) Books have been organized on shelves.
(D) A worker is standing next to a bookcase.

decoration n. 장식품   windowsill n. 창턱   pile v. 쌓다   bookcase n. 책장

해석 (A) 장식품이 창턱 위에 놓여 있다.
(B) 잡지들이 바닥에 쌓여 있다.
(C) 책들이 선반에 정리되어 있다.
(D) 직원이 책장 옆에 서 있다.

해설 (A) [×] 사진에 장식품(decoration)이 없으므로 오답이다.
(B) [×] 사진에서 바닥에 쌓여 있는(have been piled on the floor) 잡지들이 없으므로 오답이다.
(C) [○] 책들이 선반에 정리되어 있는 모습을 가장 잘 묘사한 정답이다.
(D) [×] 사진에 직원(worker)이 없으므로 오답이다. 사진에 있는 책장(bookcase)을 사용하여 혼동을 주었다.

04 실내 사진  미국 / 호주

(A) Plants are being moved onto a balcony.
(B) Some rolling chairs are occupied.
(C) A room is being prepared for a meeting.
(D) A screen has been mounted on a wall.

rolling chair 바퀴 달린 의자   occupy v. (자리를) 차지하다
prepare v. 준비하다   mount v. 설치하다, 장착하다

해석 (A) 식물들이 발코니 위로 옮겨지고 있다.
(B) 몇몇 바퀴 달린 의자들이 자리가 차 있다.
(C) 방이 회의를 위해 준비되고 있다.
(D) 스크린이 벽에 설치되어 있다.

해설 (A) [×] 사진에서 식물들(Plants)은 보이지만 옮겨지고 있는(being moved) 모습은 아니므로 오답이다.
(B) [×] 사진에서 바퀴 달린 의자들(rolling chairs)은 보이지만 자리가 차 있는(are occupied) 모습은 아니므로 오답이다.
(C) [×] 사진에서 회의를 위해 준비되고 있는(being prepared for a meeting) 방을 확인할 수 없으므로 오답이다. 사진의 장소인 회의실과 관련된 meeting(회의)을 사용하여 혼동을 주었다.
(D) [○] 스크린이 벽에 설치되어 있는 모습을 가장 잘 묘사한 정답이다.

2. 야외 사진

HACKERS PRACTICE p.39
01 (D)   02 (C)   03 (A)   04 (B)

01 야외 사진  미국 / 호주

(A) A bicycle is being sprayed with water.
(B) Signs have been posted on a wall.
(C) A car is being towed.
(D) Bikes have been placed on a rack.

spray v. 뿌리다   post v. 게시하다   tow v. 견인하다   rack n. 거치대, 선반

해석 (A) 자전거에 물이 뿌려지고 있다.
(B) 표지판들이 벽에 게시되어 있다.

(C) 자동차가 견인되고 있다.
(D) 자전거들이 거치대에 놓여 있다.

해설 (A) [x] 사진에서 자전거(bicycle)는 보이지만 물이 뿌려지고 있는 (being sprayed with water) 모습은 아니므로 오답이다.
(B) [x] 사진에 표지판들(Signs)이 없으므로 오답이다.
(C) [x] 사진에서 자동차(car)는 보이지만 견인되고 있는(being towed) 모습은 아니므로 오답이다.
(D) [o] 자전거들이 거치대에 놓여 있는 모습을 가장 잘 묘사한 정답이다.

02 야외 사진   호주 / 미국

(A) A truck is stopped in a tunnel.
(B) A pedestrian is crossing a street.
(C) Traffic cones are set up on a road.
(D) Vehicles are lined up in a row.

traffic cone 원뿔형의 도로 표지   vehicle n. 차량   in a row 일렬로

해설 (A) 트럭이 터널 안에 멈춰 있다.
(B) 보행자가 거리를 건너고 있다.
(C) 원뿔형의 도로 표지들이 도로에 세워져 있다.
(D) 차량들이 일렬로 세워져 있다.

해설 (A) [x] 사진에서 트럭(truck)은 보이지만 터널 안에 멈춰 있는(is stopped in a tunnel) 모습은 아니므로 오답이다.
(B) [x] 사진에 보행자(pedestrian)가 없으므로 오답이다.
(C) [o] 원뿔형의 도로 표지들이 도로에 세워져 있는 모습을 가장 잘 묘사한 정답이다.
(D) [x] 사진에 일렬로 세워져 있는(are lined up in a row) 차량들이 없으므로 오답이다.

03 야외 사진   캐나다 / 영국

(A) There are picnic tables covered by roofs.
(B) Diners are having a meal.
(C) There are leaves scattered in a field.
(D) Trees provide shade on a patio.

cover v. 덮다   roof n. 지붕   diner n. 식사 손님   scatter v. 흩어지게 하다
field n. 들판   provide v. 제공하다   shade n. 그늘   patio n. 테라스

해설 (A) 지붕으로 덮여 있는 피크닉 탁자들이 있다.
(B) 식사 손님들이 식사를 하고 있다.
(C) 들판에 흩어져 있는 나뭇잎들이 있다.
(D) 나무들이 테라스 위에 그늘을 제공한다.

해설 (A) [o] 피크닉 탁자들이 지붕으로 덮여 있는 모습을 가장 잘 묘사한 정답이다.
(B) [x] 사진에 식사 손님들(Diners)이 없으므로 오답이다.
(C) [x] 사진에서 흩어져 있는(scattered) 나뭇잎들을 확인할 수 없으므로 오답이다.
(D) [x] 사진의 장소가 테라스(patio)가 아니므로 오답이다. Trees provide shade(나무들이 그늘을 제공한다)까지만 듣고 정답으로 선택하지 않도록 주의한다.

04 야외 사진   영국 / 캐나다

(A) A ship is passing under a bridge.
(B) Buildings are overlooking the coastline.
(C) A motorcycle is parked near the waterfront.
(D) People are walking along the shore.

pass v. 지나가다   overlook v. 내려다보다   coastline n. 해안선
waterfront n. 물가   shore n. 해안, 기슭

해설 (A) 배가 다리 밑을 지나가고 있다.
(B) 건물들이 해안선을 내려다보고 있다.
(C) 오토바이가 물가 근처에 주차되어 있다.
(D) 사람들이 해안을 따라 걷고 있다.

해설 (A) [x] 사진에서 다리 밑을 지나가고 있는(passing under a bridge) 배를 확인할 수 없으므로 오답이다.
(B) [o] 건물들이 해안선을 내려다보고 있는 모습을 가장 잘 묘사한 정답이다.
(C) [x] 사진에서 물가 근처에 주차된(is parked near the waterfront) 오토바이를 확인할 수 없으므로 오답이다.
(D) [x] 사진에서 해안을 따라 걷고 있는(walking along the shore) 사람들을 확인할 수 없으므로 오답이다.

HACKERS TEST   p.40

01 (C)	02 (D)	03 (C)	04 (A)	05 (C)
06 (D)	07 (B)	08 (A)	09 (C)	10 (D)
11 (C)	12 (B)			

01 야외 사진   캐나다

(A) Equipment is being repaired at an airport.
(B) Ramps are connected to a building.
(C) Clouds are scattered across the sky.
(D) Luggage is being unloaded from a plane.

equipment n. 장비   ramp n. 경사로   connect v. 연결되다
scatter v. 흩어지게 하다   luggage n. 수하물   unload v. 짐을 내리다

해설 (A) 장비가 공항에서 수리되고 있다.
(B) 경사로들이 건물에 연결되어 있다.
(C) 구름들이 하늘 곳곳에 흩어져 있다.
(D) 수하물이 비행기에서 내려지고 있다.

해설 (A) [x] 사진에서 장비(Equipment)가 보이지만 수리되고 있는(being repaired) 모습은 아니므로 오답이다.
(B) [x] 사진에서 건물에 연결된(are connected to a building) 경사로들을 확인할 수 없으므로 오답이다.
(C) [o] 구름들이 하늘 곳곳에 흩어져 있는 모습을 가장 잘 묘사한 정답이다.
(D) [x] 사진에서 수하물(Luggage)을 확인할 수 없으므로 오답이다. 사진에 있는 비행기(plane)를 사용하여 혼동을 주었다.

02 실내 사진   미국

(A) A clock has been propped up on a desk.
(B) Sunlight is being blocked by some blinds.
(C) A television is set up on a cabinet.
(D) There are some windows by a seating area.

prop up 기대어 세우다   sunlight n. 햇빛   block v. 가리다, 막다
set up 세우다, 설치하다   cabinet n. 장식장, 진열장   seating area 좌석 공간

해설 (A) 시계가 책상 위에 기대어 세워져 있다.
(B) 햇빛이 몇몇 블라인드들에 의해 가려지고 있다.
(C) 텔레비전이 장식장 위에 세워져 있다.

(D) 몇몇 창문들이 좌석 공간 옆에 있다.

해설 (A) [x] 사진에서 책상 위에 기대어 세워져 있는(has been propped up on a desk) 시계를 확인할 수 없으므로 오답이다.
(B) [x] 햇빛이 몇몇 블라인드에 의해 가려지고 있지(being blocked by some blinds) 않으므로 오답이다.
(C) [x] 텔레비전(television)이 장식장 위에 세워져 있는 것이 아니라, 벽에 걸려 있으므로 오답이다.
(D) [o] 몇몇 창문들이 좌석 공간 옆에 있는 모습을 가장 잘 묘사한 정답이다.

03 실내 사진 호주

(A) Books have fallen onto the floor.
(B) There is a picture between two light fixtures.
(C) Flowers have been placed in a vase.
(D) Mugs are stacked on a coffee table.

fall v. 떨어지다   light fixture 조명 기구   mug n. 머그잔   stack v. 쌓다

해설 (A) 책들이 바닥 위로 떨어져 있다.
(B) 그림이 두 개의 조명 기구 사이에 있다.
(C) 꽃들이 꽃병에 놓여 있다.
(D) 머그잔들이 커피 탁자 위에 쌓여 있다.

해설 (A) [x] 사진에서 책들(Books)은 보이지만 바닥 위로 떨어져 있는(have fallen onto the floor) 모습은 아니므로 오답이다.
(B) [x] 사진에 조명 기구(light fixtures)가 없으므로 오답이다.
(C) [o] 꽃들이 꽃병에 놓여 있는 상태를 가장 잘 묘사한 정답이다.
(D) [x] 사진에서 쌓여 있는(are stacked) 머그잔을 확인할 수 없으므로 오답이다.

04 실내 사진 영국

(A) Some plants have been hung from the ceiling.
(B) Some pots are being arranged in a greenhouse.
(C) A tree has been cut down near the entrance.
(D) Some vegetables are growing in a field.

hang v. 걸다, 매달다   ceiling n. 천장   pot n. 화분   greenhouse n. 온실
cut down 베어내다, 잘라내다   entrance n. 입구   grow v. 자라다

해설 (A) 몇몇 식물들이 천장에 걸려 있다.
(B) 몇몇 화분들이 온실에 배열되고 있다.
(C) 나무가 입구 근처에 베어져 있다.
(D) 몇몇 채소들이 들판에서 자라고 있다.

해설 (A) [o] 몇몇 식물들이 천장에 걸려 있는 모습을 가장 잘 묘사한 정답이다.
(B) [x] 사진에서 화분들(pots)은 보이지만 배열되고 있는(being arranged) 모습은 아니므로 오답이다.
(C) [x] 사진에 나무(tree)가 없으므로 오답이다.
(D) [x] 사진에서 채소들(vegetables)을 확인할 수 없고, 사진의 장소가 들판(field)이 아니므로 오답이다.

05 실내 사진 호주

(A) Some curtains have been rolled up.
(B) A carpet covers part of the floor.
(C) Some boxes have been left open.
(D) A chair is positioned under an overhead light.

roll up 말아 올리다   part of ~의 일부   leave v. (~한 채로) 두다
position v. 놓다, 두다   overhead light 천장 조명

해설 (A) 몇몇 커튼들이 말아 올려져 있다.
(B) 카펫이 바닥의 일부를 덮고 있다.
(C) 몇몇 상자들이 열린 채로 있다.
(D) 의자가 천장 조명 아래에 배치되어 있다.

해설 (A) [x] 사진에서 커튼들(curtains)은 보이지만 말아 올려져 있는(have been rolled up) 모습은 아니므로 오답이다.
(B) [x] 사진에 카펫(carpet)이 없으므로 오답이다.
(C) [o] 몇몇 상자들이 열린 채로 있는 모습을 가장 잘 묘사한 정답이다.
(D) [x] 사진에서 천장 조명(overhead light)을 확인할 수 없으므로 오답이다. 사진에 있는 의자(chair)를 사용하여 혼동을 주었다.

06 야외 사진 미국

(A) There is heavy traffic on a road.
(B) A wire is being attached to a pole.
(C) There is a structure behind some trees.
(D) Some trucks are parked side by side.

heavy traffic 많은 교통량   wire n. 전선   attach v. 부착하다   pole n. 기둥
structure n. 구조물   side by side 나란히

해설 (A) 도로에 교통량이 많다.
(B) 전선이 기둥에 부착되고 있다.
(C) 구조물이 몇몇 나무들 뒤에 있다.
(D) 몇몇 트럭들이 나란히 주차되어 있다.

해설 (A) [x] 사진에서 많은 교통량(heavy traffic)을 확인할 수 없으므로 오답이다. 사진에 있는 도로(road)를 사용하여 혼동을 주었다.
(B) [x] 사진에 전선(wire)은 보이지만 기둥에 부착되고 있는(being attached to a pole) 모습은 아니므로 오답이다.
(C) [x] 구조물(structure)이 나무 뒤에 있는 것이 아니라, 앞에 있으므로 오답이다.
(D) [o] 몇몇 트럭들이 나란히 주차되어 있는 모습을 가장 잘 묘사한 정답이다.

07 실내 사진 영국

(A) A blanket has been folded in a basket.
(B) A hat has been laid on a bed.
(C) A suitcase has been unzipped.
(D) A phone is mounted beside a lamp.

blanket n. 담요   fold v. 접다   suitcase n. 여행 가방
unzip v. ~의 지퍼를 열다   mount v. 설치하다, 장착하다

해설 (A) 담요가 바구니 안에 접혀 있다.
(B) 모자가 침대 위에 놓여 있다.
(C) 여행 가방의 지퍼가 열려 있다.
(D) 전화기가 등 옆에 설치되어 있다.

해설 (A) [x] 사진에 바구니(basket)가 없으므로 오답이다.
(B) [o] 모자가 침대 위에 놓여 있는 모습을 가장 잘 묘사한 정답이다.
(C) [x] 여행 가방(suitcase)의 지퍼가 열려 있는 것이 아니라, 닫혀 있으므로 오답이다.
(D) [x] 전화기(phone)가 등 옆에 설치된 것이 아니라, 탁자 위에 있으므로 오답이다.

08 야외 사진

(A) Some boats are tied up to a dock.
(B) Some people are fishing from a pier.
(C) Some ropes are lying on a deck.
(D) Some ships are sailing in the same direction.

tie up (배를) 묶어 두다 dock n. 부두, 선창 pier n. 부두, 방파제
rope n. 밧줄 deck n. 갑판 sail v. 항해하다 direction n. 방향

해석 (A) 몇몇 배들이 부두에 묶여 있다.
(B) 몇몇 사람들이 부두에서 낚시하고 있다.
(C) 몇몇 밧줄들이 갑판 위에 놓여 있다.
(D) 몇몇 배들이 같은 방향으로 항해하고 있다.

해설 (A) [ㅇ] 몇몇 배들이 부두에 묶여 있는 모습을 가장 잘 묘사한 정답이다.
(B) [×] 사진에 낚시하고 있는(fishing) 사람들이 없으므로 오답이다.
(C) [×] 사진에서 갑판 위에 놓여 있는(lying on a deck) 밧줄들을 확인할 수 없으므로 오답이다.
(D) [×] 사진에서 배들(ships)은 보이지만 같은 방향으로 항해하는 (sailing in the same direction) 모습은 아니므로 오답이다.

09 야외 사진

(A) Building materials are stored in a warehouse.
(B) A path is paved with bricks.
(C) Tires are leaning against a building.
(D) A fence borders a parking area.

material n. 자재, 재료 store v. 보관하다 warehouse n. 창고
path n. 길, 통로 pave v. 포장하다 brick n. 벽돌 fence n. 울타리
border v. 둘러싸다, ~의 경계를 이루다 parking area 주차장

해석 (A) 건축 자재가 창고 안에 보관되어 있다.
(B) 길이 벽돌로 포장되어 있다.
(C) 타이어들이 건물에 기대어 있다.
(D) 울타리가 주차장을 둘러싸고 있다.

해설 (A) [×] 사진에 건축 자재(Building materials)가 없고, 사진의 장소가 창고(warehouse) 내부가 아니므로 오답이다.
(B) [×] 사진에 벽돌로 포장된(is paved with bricks) 길이 없으므로 오답이다.
(C) [ㅇ] 타이어들이 건물에 기대어 있는 모습을 가장 잘 묘사한 정답이다.
(D) [×] 사진에 울타리(fence)가 없으므로 오답이다.

10 실내 사진

(A) A wooden crate has been filled with food.
(B) A store is full of shoppers.
(C) Fruits and vegetables are being washed.
(D) Products are being displayed on shelves.

wooden adj. 나무로 된 crate n. (운반용) 상자 fill v. 채우다
shopper n. 쇼핑객

해석 (A) 나무로 된 상자가 음식으로 채워져 있다.
(B) 가게가 쇼핑객들로 가득 차 있다.
(C) 과일과 채소들이 씻기고 있다.
(D) 상품들이 선반에 진열되어 있다.

해설 (A) [×] 사진에 나무로 된 상자(wooden crate)가 없으므로 오답이다.
(B) [×] 사진에 쇼핑객들(shoppers)이 없으므로 오답이다.
(C) [×] 사진에서 과일과 채소(Fruits and vegetables)는 보이지만 씻기고 있는(being washed) 모습은 아니므로 오답이다.
(D) [ㅇ] 상품들이 선반에 진열되어 있는 모습을 가장 잘 묘사한 정답이다.

11 야외 사진

(A) Some trees are surrounding a shed.
(B) Some tools are being reorganized outdoors.
(C) A plastic bucket is set on a workbench.
(D) A lid is being removed from a container.

surround v. 둘러싸다 shed n. 헛간 reorganize v. 재정리하다
outdoors adv. 야외에서 bucket n. 양동이, 들통 workbench n. 작업대
lid n. 뚜껑 remove v. 제거하다, 치우다 container n. 용기, 그릇

해석 (A) 몇몇 나무들이 헛간을 둘러싸고 있다.
(B) 몇몇 도구들이 야외에서 재정리되고 있다.
(C) 플라스틱 양동이가 작업대 위에 놓여 있다.
(D) 뚜껑이 용기에서 제거되고 있다.

해설 (A) [×] 사진에서 헛간(shed)을 확인할 수 없으므로 오답이다. 사진에 보이는 나무들(trees)을 사용하여 혼동을 주었다.
(B) [×] 사진에서 도구들(tools)은 보이지만 재정리되고 있는(being reorganized) 모습은 아니므로 오답이다.
(C) [ㅇ] 플라스틱 양동이가 작업대 위에 놓여 있는 모습을 가장 잘 묘사한 정답이다.
(D) [×] 사진에서 뚜껑(lid)과 용기(container)는 보이지만 뚜껑이 제거되고 있는(being removed) 모습은 아니므로 오답이다.

12 야외 사진

(A) A box has been put in front of the door.
(B) A table has been left near the vehicle.
(C) Some trash is being swept into a dustpan.
(D) A truck is being towed into a garage.

trash n. 쓰레기 dustpan n. 쓰레받기 tow v. 견인하다 garage n. 차고

해석 (A) 상자가 문 앞에 놓여 있다.
(B) 탁자가 차량 근처에 놓여 있다.
(C) 쓰레기가 쓰레받기 안으로 쓸리고 있다.
(D) 트럭이 차고 안으로 견인되고 있다.

해설 (A) [×] 사진에 상자(box)가 없으므로 오답이다.
(B) [ㅇ] 탁자가 차량 근처에 놓여 있는 모습을 가장 잘 묘사한 정답이다.
(C) [×] 사진에서 쓰레기(trash)를 확인할 수 없으므로 오답이다.
(D) [×] 사진에서 트럭(truck)은 보이지만 견인되고 있는(being towed) 모습은 아니므로 오답이다.

PART 2

DAY 03 의문사 의문문: Who, What/Which

1. Who 의문문

HACKERS PRACTICE				p.45
01 (C)	02 (A)	03 (B)	04 (B)	05 (B)
06 (A)				

01 Who 의문문   미국 → 호주 / 영국 → 캐나다

Who's working on the proposal?
(A) A couple of hours more.
(B) Because the first one was rejected.
(C) Someone from the sales department.

proposal n. 제안서   sales department 영업부

해석 누가 제안서를 작업하고 있나요?
(A) 몇 시간 더요.
(B) 첫 번째 것이 거절되었기 때문이에요.
(C) 영업부의 누군가요.

해설 (A) [x] 누가 제안서를 작업하고 있는지 물었는데, 시간으로 응답했으므로 오답이다.
(B) [x] 누가 제안서를 작업하고 있는지 물었는데, 이유로 응답했으므로 오답이다. 질문의 the proposal(제안서)을 가리킬 수 있는 one(것)을 사용하여 혼동을 주었다.
(C) [o] 영업부의 누군가라는 말로, 누가 제안서를 작업하고 있는지를 언급했으므로 정답이다.

02 Who 의문문   호주 → 미국 / 캐나다 → 영국

Who's going to drive us to the movie?
(A) Paul will give us a ride.
(B) It's a popular film.
(C) She failed her driving test.

give a ride 태워주다   popular adj. 인기 있는

해석 누가 우리를 영화관에 태워다 줄 건가요?
(A) Paul이 우리를 태워줄 거예요.
(B) 인기 있는 영화예요.
(C) 그녀는 운전면허 시험을 통과하지 못했어요.

해설 (A) [o] Paul이 우리를 태워줄 것이라는 말로, 우리를 영화관에 태워다 줄 사람을 언급했으므로 정답이다.
(B) [x] 질문의 movie(영화관)와 관련 있는 film(영화)을 사용하여 혼동을 준 오답이다.
(C) [x] drive - driving의 유사 발음 어휘를 사용하여 혼동을 준 오답이다.

03 Who 의문문   미국 → 영국 / 영국 → 미국

Who should I talk to about the deadline?
(A) After you turn it in.
(B) One of our supervisors.
(C) He should too.

deadline n. 마감 기한   turn in 제출하다   supervisor n. 관리자

해석 마감 기한에 대해 누구에게 이야기해야 할까요?
(A) 그것을 제출한 후에요.
(B) 우리 관리자들 중 한 명이요.
(C) 그도 해야 해요.

해설 (A) [x] 마감 기한에 대해 누구에게 이야기해야 하는지를 물었는데, 시점으로 응답했으므로 오답이다.
(B) [o] 관리자들 중 한 명이라며, 마감 기한에 대해 이야기해야 할 사람을 언급했으므로 정답이다.
(C) [x] 질문의 should를 반복 사용하여 혼동을 준 오답이다.

04 Who 의문문   호주 → 영국 / 캐나다 → 미국

Who edited the press release?
(A) I'm less stressed than before.
(B) Susan worked on it.
(C) The second edition.

edit v. 편집하다   press release 보도 자료   edition n. 판

해석 보도 자료를 누가 편집했나요?
(A) 저는 전보다 스트레스를 덜 받아요.
(B) Susan이 그것을 작업했어요.
(C) 두 번째 판이요.

해설 (A) [x] press - stressed의 유사 발음 어휘를 사용하여 혼동을 준 오답이다.
(B) [o] Susan이 그것을 작업했다며, 보도 자료를 편집한 사람을 언급했으므로 정답이다.
(C) [x] edited - edition의 유사 발음 어휘를 사용하여 혼동을 준 오답이다.

05 Who 의문문   영국 → 캐나다 / 미국 → 호주

Who took this photo for the article?
(A) I'll take some pictures for you.
(B) My assistant did.
(C) The Daily Business News is free.

article n. 기사, 글   assistant n. 조수   free adj. 무료의

해석 누가 기사의 이 사진을 찍었나요?
(A) 당신을 위해 사진을 몇 장 찍어 드릴게요.
(B) 제 조수가 했어요.
(C) The Daily Business News지는 무료예요.

해설 (A) [x] 질문의 photo(사진)와 같은 의미인 pictures(사진)를 사용하여 혼동을 준 오답이다.
(B) [o] 내 조수가 했다는 말로, 기사의 사진을 찍은 사람을 언급했으므로 정답이다.
(C) [x] 질문의 article(기사)에서 연상할 수 있는 신문 이름과 관련된 The Daily Business News지를 사용하여 혼동을 준 오답이다.

06 Who 의문문   캐나다 → 미국 / 호주 → 영국

Who is Juan flying to Spain with?
(A) We're going together.
(B) The flight just landed.

(C) No, an economy seat.

fly v. 비행기로 가다   flight n. 비행기, 항공편   land v. 착륙하다
economy seat 일반석

해석 Juan은 누구와 함께 비행기로 스페인에 갈 건가요?
(A) 우리는 함께 갈 거예요.
(B) 그 항공기는 방금 착륙했어요.
(C) 아니요, 일반석이요.

해설 (A) [o] 우리는 함께 갈 것이라는 말로, Juan이 누구와 함께 비행기로 스페인에 갈 것인지를 언급했으므로 정답이다.
(B) [x] 질문의 flying(비행기로 가다)과 관련된 flight(항공기)을 사용하여 혼동을 준 오답이다.
(C) [x] 의문사 의문문에 No로 응답했으므로 오답이다. 질문의 flying(비행기로 가다)에서 연상할 수 있는 economy seat(일반석)을 사용하여 혼동을 주었다.

2. What/Which 의문문

HACKERS PRACTICE p.47

01 (B)   02 (B)   03 (A)   04 (C)   05 (C)
06 (C)

01 What 의문문 호주 → 미국 / 캐나다 → 영국

What's the price of that kitchen knife?
(A) The kitchen was remodeled.
(B) It's 20 dollars.
(C) With a credit card.

remodel v. 개조하다, 리모델링하다   credit card 신용카드

해석 부엌칼의 가격은 얼마인가요?
(A) 주방이 개조되었어요.
(B) 20달러예요.
(C) 신용 카드로요.

해설 (A) [x] 질문의 kitchen을 반복 사용하여 혼동을 준 오답이다.
(B) [o] 20달러라는 말로, 부엌칼의 가격을 언급했으므로 정답이다.
(C) [x] 질문의 price(가격)에서 연상할 수 있는 credit card(신용카드)를 사용하여 혼동을 준 오답이다.

02 What 의문문 미국 → 호주 / 영국 → 캐나다

What time do you generally take your break?
(A) I'll have some coffee, thanks.
(B) At about 3 o'clock.
(C) For a coworker.

generally adv. 보통, 일반적으로   break n. 휴식 (시간)   coworker n. 동료

해석 당신은 보통 몇 시에 휴식 시간을 갖나요?
(A) 저는 커피를 마실게요, 고마워요.
(B) 3시쯤에요.
(C) 동료를 위해서요.

해설 (A) [x] 질문의 break(휴식 시간)에서 연상할 수 있는 coffee(커피)를 사용하여 혼동을 준 오답이다.
(B) [o] 3시쯤이라며, 자신이 보통 휴식 시간을 갖는 시각을 언급했으므로 정답이다.
(C) [x] 보통 몇 시에 휴식 시간을 갖는지를 물었는데, 이와 관련 없는 동료를 위해서라는 말로 응답했으므로 오답이다.

03 Which 의문문 캐나다 → 영국 / 호주 → 미국

Which floor is the engineering team on?
(A) They're on the seventh.
(B) The accounting department.
(C) Yes, the update is complete.

floor n. 층, 바닥   engineering n. 기술   accounting n. 회계
complete adj. 완료된

해석 어느 층에 기술팀이 있나요?
(A) 그들은 7층에 있어요.
(B) 회계 부서요.
(C) 네, 업데이트는 완료되었어요.

해설 (A) [o] 그들은 7층에 있다는 말로, 기술팀이 있는 층을 언급했으므로 정답이다.
(B) [x] 질문의 team(팀)과 관련 있는 department(부서)를 사용하여 혼동을 준 오답이다.
(C) [x] 의문사 의문문에 Yes로 응답했으므로 오답이다. 질문의 engineering team(기술팀)에서 연상할 수 있는 update(업데이트)를 사용하여 혼동을 주었다.

04 What 의문문 캐나다 → 미국 / 호주 → 영국

What should I do to improve my overall health?
(A) It's quite an improvement.
(B) During my annual checkup.
(C) You could start with regular exercise.

overall adj. 전반적인   annual adj. 연례의, 매년의   checkup n. 건강 진단
regular adj. 규칙적인   exercise n. 운동

해석 전반적인 건강을 개선하려면 무엇을 해야 하나요?
(A) 그건 상당한 개선이에요.
(B) 연례 건강 진단 중이에요.
(C) 규칙적인 운동부터 시작할 수 있어요.

해설 (A) [x] improve - improvement의 유사 발음 어휘를 사용하여 혼동을 준 오답이다.
(B) [x] 질문의 health(건강)와 관련 있는 checkup(건강 진단)을 사용하여 혼동을 준 오답이다.
(C) [o] 규칙적인 운동부터 시작할 수 있다는 말로, 전반적인 건강을 개선하려면 무엇을 해야 하는지 방법을 언급했으므로 정답이다.

05 What 의문문 영국 → 캐나다 / 미국 → 호주

What type of food should we order for dinner?
(A) The order took three weeks to arrive.
(B) Thanks for making dinner.
(C) I enjoy Mexican.

order v. 주문하다; n. 주문품

해석 저녁 식사로 어떤 종류의 음식을 주문해야 할까요?
(A) 주문품이 도착하는 데 3주가 걸렸어요.
(B) 저녁 식사를 만들어줘서 고마워요.
(C) 저는 멕시코 음식을 좋아해요.

해설 (A) [x] 질문의 order(주문하다)를 '주문품'이라는 의미의 명사로 반복 사용하여 혼동을 준 오답이다.
(B) [x] 질문의 dinner를 반복 사용하여 혼동을 준 오답이다.
(C) [o] 멕시코 음식을 좋아한다는 말로, 저녁 식사로 멕시코 음식을 주문하자는 것을 간접적으로 전달했으므로 정답이다.

06 What 의문문

영국 → 호주 / 미국 → 캐나다

What do you think of the upcoming conference?
(A) At the convention center.
(B) Next Friday, I believe.
(C) It'll be beneficial.

conference n. 회의, 회담   beneficial adj. 유익한, 이로운

해석 다가오는 회의에 대해 어떻게 생각하나요?
(A) 컨벤션 센터에서요.
(B) 다음 주 금요일인 것 같아요.
(C) 그것은 유익할 거예요.

해설 (A) [×] 다가오는 회의에 대해 어떻게 생각하는지 물었는데, 장소로 응답했으므로 오답이다.
(B) [×] 다가오는 회의에 대해 어떻게 생각하는지 물었는데, 요일로 응답했으므로 오답이다.
(C) [○] 그것은 유익할 것이라는 말로, 다가오는 회의에 대해 어떻게 생각하는지를 언급했으므로 정답이다.

HACKERS TEST   p.48

01 (A)	02 (B)	03 (A)	04 (A)	05 (C)
06 (C)	07 (A)	08 (A)	09 (C)	10 (C)
11 (C)	12 (C)	13 (C)	14 (B)	15 (A)
16 (A)	17 (B)	18 (C)	19 (B)	20 (B)
21 (C)	22 (C)	23 (C)	24 (B)	25 (B)

01 Who 의문문

캐나다 → 미국

Who created that logo?
(A) Mr. Davis, I guess.
(B) Four years ago.
(C) No, that was your project.

create v. 만들다, 창작하다

해석 누가 그 로고를 만들었나요?
(A) Mr. Davis인 것 같아요.
(B) 4년 전에요.
(C) 아니요, 그것은 당신의 프로젝트였습니다.

해설 (A) [○] Mr. Davis라는 말로, 로고를 만든 사람을 언급했으므로 정답이다.
(B) [×] 누가 로고를 만들었는지를 물었는데, 시점으로 응답했으므로 오답이다.
(C) [×] 의문사 의문문에 No로 응답했으므로 오답이다.

02 Which 의문문

영국 → 호주

Which hotel are you staying at for your vacation?
(A) Stay as long as you like.
(B) The one you recommended.
(C) An executive suite.

recommend v. 추천하다   executive suite (호텔의) 고급 특실

해석 휴가 때 어떤 호텔에 묵을 예정인가요?
(A) 원하는 만큼 묵으세요.
(B) 당신이 추천한 곳이요.
(C) 고급 특실이요.

해설 (A) [×] 질문의 staying을 Stay로 반복 사용하여 혼동을 준 오답이다.
(B) [○] 당신이 추천한 곳이라는 말로, 휴가 때 묵을 예정인 호텔을 언급했으므로 정답이다.
(C) [×] 질문의 hotel(호텔)과 관련 있는 executive suite(고급 특실)를 사용하여 혼동을 준 오답이다.

03 What 의문문

호주 → 미국

What do you need to buy at the mall?
(A) Some winter clothes.
(B) No, we don't have any.
(C) We missed the sale.

miss v. 놓치다   sale n. 할인 판매

해석 쇼핑몰에서 무엇을 사야 하나요?
(A) 겨울옷 몇 벌이요.
(B) 아니요, 우리는 아무것도 갖고 있지 않아요.
(C) 우리는 할인 판매를 놓쳤어요.

해설 (A) [○] 겨울옷 몇 벌이라며, 쇼핑몰에서 사야 하는 것을 언급했으므로 정답이다.
(B) [×] 의문사 의문문에 No로 응답했으므로 오답이다.
(C) [×] 질문의 mall(쇼핑몰)과 관련 있는 sale(할인 판매)을 사용하여 혼동을 준 오답이다.

04 Which 의문문

미국 → 캐나다

Which chef can handle the banquet tomorrow?
(A) Chef Morales is available.
(B) Sorry, you're not on the list.
(C) I booked a table for four.

handle v. 담당하다, 처리하다   banquet n. 연회   book v. 예약하다

해석 어느 주방장이 내일 연회를 담당할 수 있나요?
(A) Morales 주방장이 가능해요.
(B) 죄송해요, 당신은 명단에 없어요.
(C) 저는 네 명을 위한 테이블을 예약했어요.

해설 (A) [○] Morales 주방장이 가능하다는 말로, Morales 주방장이 내일 연회를 담당할 수 있음을 간접적으로 전달했으므로 정답이다.
(B) [×] banquet(연회)과 관련된 list(명단)를 사용하여 혼동을 준 오답이다.
(C) [×] 질문의 chef(주방장)에서 연상할 수 있는 식당과 관련된 booked(예약했다)를 사용하여 혼동을 준 오답이다.

05 Who 의문문

호주 → 영국

Who qualifies for the annual membership discount?
(A) It's the original price.
(B) She filled out an application form.
(C) Current university students.

qualify for ~할 자격이 있다   original adj. 원래의   fill out 작성하다   current adj. 현재의

해석 누가 연간 회원권 할인을 받을 자격이 있나요?
(A) 이것은 원래 가격이에요.
(B) 그녀는 신청서를 작성했어요.
(C) 현재 대학생들이요.

해설 (A) [×] 질문의 discount(할인)와 관련 있는 price(가격)를 사용하여 혼동을 준 오답이다.
(B) [×] 누가 연간 회원권 할인을 받을 자격이 있는지를 물었는데, 이와 관련이 없는 그녀는 신청서를 작성했다고 응답했으므로 오답이다.
(C) [○] 현재 대학생들이라는 말로, 연간 회원권 할인을 받을 자격이 있는 사람을 언급했으므로 정답이다.

06 What 의문문
미국 → 호주

What is the best way to get to the airport?
(A) About 20 kilometers from here.
(B) To reserve a later flight.
(C) A taxi would be the easiest.

reserve v. 예약하다   flight n. 항공편

해석 공항에 가는 가장 좋은 방법은 무엇인가요?
(A) 여기에서 약 20킬로미터 떨어져 있어요.
(B) 더 늦은 항공편을 예약하기 위해서요.
(C) 택시가 가장 쉬울 거예요.

해설 (A) [x] 질문의 get to the airport(공항에 가다)에서 연상할 수 있는 이동 거리와 관련된 20 kilometers(20킬로미터)를 사용하여 혼동을 준 오답이다.
(B) [x] airport(공항)와 관련 있는 flight(항공편)을 사용하여 혼동을 준 오답이다.
(C) [o] 택시가 가장 쉬울 것이라는 말로, 공항에 가는 가장 좋은 방법을 언급했으므로 정답이다.

07 Who 의문문
캐나다 → 영국

Who wants a map to the auditorium?
(A) I've been there before.
(B) The lights are too bright.
(C) Check the audio system.

auditorium n. 강당   check v. 점검하다, 확인하다

해석 누가 강당으로 가는 지도를 원하나요?
(A) 저는 전에 그곳에 가봤어요.
(B) 조명이 너무 밝아요.
(C) 오디오 시스템을 점검하세요.

해설 (A) [o] 전에 그곳에 가봤다는 말로, 자신은 강당으로 가는 지도를 원하지 않는다는 것을 간접적으로 전달했으므로 정답이다.
(B) [x] auditorium(강당)에서 연상할 수 있는 lights(조명)를 사용하여 혼동을 준 오답이다.
(C) [x] auditorium - audio의 유사 발음 어휘를 사용하여 혼동을 준 오답이다.

08 What 의문문
영국 → 호주

What do you think about the new user manual?
(A) It's very well written.
(B) No, I don't think so.
(C) On a personal vacation.

manual n. 설명서

해석 새로운 사용자 설명서에 대해 어떻게 생각하나요?
(A) 그것은 매우 잘 쓰여 있어요.
(B) 아니요, 그렇게 생각하지 않아요.
(C) 개인 휴가 중이에요.

해설 (A) [o] 그것은 매우 잘 쓰여 있다는 말로, 사용자 설명서에 대해 어떻게 생각하는지를 언급했으므로 정답이다.
(B) [x] 의문사 의문문에 No로 응답했으므로 오답이다. 질문의 think를 반복 사용하여 혼동을 주었다.
(C) [x] 사용자 설명서에 대해 어떻게 생각하는지를 물었는데, 이와 관련이 없는 개인 휴가 중이라는 말로 응답했으므로 오답이다.

09 Who 의문문
호주 → 캐나다

Who's preparing the training program for the new employees?
(A) It's supposed to rain tomorrow.
(B) A new computer program.
(C) Grace was assigned that task.

prepare v. 준비하다   be supposed to ~할 예정이다, ~하기로 되어 있다
assign v. 배정하다   task n. 업무

해석 누가 새로운 직원들을 위한 교육 프로그램을 준비하고 있나요?
(A) 내일 비가 올 예정이에요.
(B) 새로운 컴퓨터 프로그램이요.
(C) Grace가 그 업무에 배정되었어요.

해설 (A) [x] training - to rain의 유사 발음 어휘를 사용하여 혼동을 준 오답이다.
(B) [x] 질문의 program을 반복 사용하여 혼동을 준 오답이다.
(C) [o] Grace가 그 업무에 배정되었다는 말로, 새로운 직원들을 위한 교육 프로그램을 준비할 사람을 언급했으므로 정답이다.

10 Which 의문문
영국 → 캐나다

Which art class are you taking at the community center?
(A) Twenty students in total.
(B) The center opens at 10 A.M.
(C) The pottery one.

pottery n. 도예, 도자기

해석 지역 문화 회관에서 어느 미술 수업을 듣고 있나요?
(A) 총 20명의 학생들이요.
(B) 회관은 오전 10시에 문을 열어요.
(C) 도예 수업이요.

해설 (A) [x] 질문의 class(수업)와 관련 있는 students(학생들)를 사용하여 혼동을 준 오답이다.
(B) [x] 질문의 center를 반복 사용하여 혼동을 준 오답이다.
(C) [o] 도예 수업이라는 말로, 지역 문화 회관에서 듣고 있는 미술 수업을 언급했으므로 정답이다.

11 Who 의문문
캐나다 → 미국

Who can give the presentation at the trade fair?
(A) Within 90 days.
(B) A successful presentation.
(C) I think Jane is free that day.

presentation n. 발표

해석 누가 무역 박람회에서 발표를 할 수 있나요?
(A) 90일 이내예요.
(B) 성공적인 발표요.
(C) Jane이 그날 시간이 있는 것 같아요.

해설 (A) [x] 누가 무역 박람회에서 발표를 할 수 있는지를 물었는데, 이와 관련이 없는 90일 이내라는 말로 응답했으므로 오답이다.
(B) [x] 질문의 presentation을 반복 사용하여 혼동을 준 오답이다.
(C) [o] Jane이 그날 시간이 있는 것 같다는 말로, Jane이 무역 박람회에서 발표를 할 수 있음을 간접적으로 전달했으므로 정답이다.

12 What 의문문
영국 → 호주

What time does the next train depart?
(A) You can wait at Gate 22.
(B) Part of the time.
(C) It leaves at 4 P.M.

depart v. 출발하다   gate n. 승강장, 출입문   part n. 일부

해석 다음 기차가 몇 시에 출발하나요?
　　(A) 22번 승강장에서 기다리시면 돼요.
　　(B) 그 시간 중 일부요.
　　(C) 그것은 오후 4시에 떠나요.

해설 (A) [×] 질문의 train(기차)과 관련된 Gate(승강장)를 사용하여 혼동을 준 오답이다.
　　(B) [×] 질문의 time을 반복 사용하여 혼동을 준 오답이다.
　　(C) [○] 그것이 오후 4시에 떠난다는 말로, 다음 기차가 출발하는 시간을 언급했으므로 정답이다.

13 Which 의문문   캐나다 → 영국

Which local restaurant serves the best Italian food?
(A) I need to get some rest tonight.
(B) The servings are pretty large.
(C) My favorite is just down the street.

serve v. 제공하다   serving n. (음식의) 1인분

해석 어느 현지 음식점이 최고의 이탈리아 음식을 제공하나요?
　　(A) 전 오늘 밤 휴식을 좀 취해야 해요.
　　(B) 1인분이 꽤 많아요.
　　(C) 제가 가장 좋아하는 곳은 길 바로 아래에 있어요.

해설 (A) [×] restaurant - rest의 유사 발음 어휘를 사용하여 혼동을 준 오답이다.
　　(B) [×] serves - servings의 유사 발음 어휘를 사용하여 혼동을 준 오답이다.
　　(C) [○] 가장 좋아하는 곳은 길 바로 아래에 있다는 말로, 최고의 이탈리아 음식을 제공하는 현지 음식점을 언급했으므로 정답이다.

14 Who 의문문   미국 → 호주

Who has the schedule for next year's seminars?
(A) I think it starts in February.
(B) The office assistant.
(C) About communication skills.

schedule n. 일정표   office assistant 사무 보조원   communication n. 소통

해석 내년 세미나들의 일정표를 누가 가지고 있죠?
　　(A) 제 생각에 그건 2월에 시작해요.
　　(B) 사무 보조원이요.
　　(C) 소통 기술들에 대해서요.

해설 (A) [×] 질문의 schedule(일정표)에서 연상할 수 있는 February(2월)를 사용하여 혼동을 준 오답이다.
　　(B) [○] 사무 보조원이라며, 내년 세미나들의 일정표를 가지고 있는 사람을 언급했으므로 정답이다.
　　(C) [×] 질문의 seminars(세미나들)에서 연상할 수 있는 communication skills(소통 기술들)를 사용하여 혼동을 준 오답이다.

15 Which 의문문   캐나다 → 미국

Which article did you end up revising?
(A) The one on global warming.
(B) No, I need to revise it.
(C) Probably next week.

revise v. 수정하다

해석 어느 기사를 결국 수정하게 되었나요?
　　(A) 지구 온난화에 대한 것이요.
　　(B) 아니요, 저는 그것을 수정해야 해요.
　　(C) 아마 다음 주예요.

해설 (A) [○] 지구 온난화에 대한 것이라는 말로, 수정하게 된 기사를 언급했으므로 정답이다.
　　(B) [×] 의문사 의문문에 No로 응답했으므로 오답이다. 질문의 revising을 revise로 반복 사용하여 혼동을 준 오답이다.
　　(C) [×] 어느 기사를 결국 수정하게 되었는지를 물었는데, 시점으로 응답했으므로 오답이다.

16 What 의문문   영국 → 캐나다

What was your impression of the house that we toured?
(A) The backyard was impressive.
(B) Tours start near the entrance.
(C) I'll be home all day.

impression n. 느낌, 인상   tour v. 둘러보다, 유람하다   backyard n. 뒤뜰

해석 우리가 둘러본 집에 대한 당신의 느낌은 어땠나요?
　　(A) 뒤뜰이 인상적이었어요.
　　(B) 관광은 입구 근처에서 시작해요.
　　(C) 전 종일 집에 있을 거예요.

해설 (A) [○] 뒤뜰이 인상적이었다는 말로, 둘러본 집에 대한 느낌을 언급했으므로 정답이다.
　　(B) [×] toured - Tours의 유사 발음 어휘를 사용하여 혼동을 준 오답이다.
　　(C) [×] 질문의 house(집)와 관련 있는 home(집에)을 사용하여 혼동을 준 오답이다.

17 Who 의문문   미국 → 영국

Who's in charge of assembling the new machine?
(A) To change the password.
(B) I'll put it together.
(C) Some heavy equipment.

in charge of ~을 담당하는   put together 조립하다
heavy equipment 중장비

해석 새 기계를 조립하는 것을 누가 담당하나요?
　　(A) 비밀번호를 변경하기 위해서요.
　　(B) 제가 조립할 거예요.
　　(C) 몇몇 중장비요.

해설 (A) [×] 새 기계를 조립하는 것을 누가 담당하는지를 물었는데, 이와 관련 없는 비밀번호를 변경하기 위해서라는 말로 응답했으므로 오답이다.
　　(B) [○] 자신이 조립할 것이라는 말로, 새 기계를 조립하는 것을 누가 담당하는지를 언급했으므로 정답이다.
　　(C) [×] 질문의 machine(기계)과 관련 있는 equipment(장비)를 사용하여 혼동을 준 오답이다.

18 What 의문문   영국 → 호주

What still needs to be done for the workshop?
(A) The shop across the street.
(B) It was very informative.
(C) Just print the handouts.

handout n. 유인물

해석 워크숍을 위해 아직도 무엇이 완료되어야 하나요?
　　(A) 길 건너편에 있는 상점이요.
　　(B) 매우 유익했어요.
　　(C) 유인물을 인쇄만 하세요.

해설 (A) [×] workshop - shop의 유사 발음 어휘를 사용하여 혼동을 준 오답이다.

(B) [×] 질문의 workshop(워크숍)에서 연상할 수 있는 informative (유익한)를 사용하여 혼동을 준 오답이다.
(C) [○] 유인물을 인쇄만 하라는 말로, 워크숍을 위해 완료되어야 하는 것을 언급했으므로 정답이다.

19 What 의문문 　　　　　　　　　　　호주 → 미국

What will be the program coordinator's role in the project?
(A) Yes, I started the project.
(B) I haven't decided yet.
(C) They have to reprogram it.

coordinator n. 진행자, 조정자　role n. 역할
reprogram v. (컴퓨터 등의) 프로그램을 다시 짜다

해석　그 프로젝트에서 프로그램 진행자의 역할은 무엇이 될 것인가요?
　　(A) 네, 제가 그 프로젝트를 시작했어요.
　　(B) 아직 결정하지 않았어요.
　　(C) 그들은 그것의 프로그램을 다시 짜야 해요.
해설　(A) [×] 질문의 project를 반복 사용하여 혼동을 준 오답이다.
　　(B) [○] 아직 결정하지 않았다는 말로, 프로젝트에서 프로그램 진행자의 역할이 무엇이 될지 아직 모른다는 것을 간접적으로 전달했으므로 정답이다.
　　(C) [×] program - reprogram의 유사 발음 어휘를 사용하여 혼동을 준 오답이다.

20 Who 의문문 　　　　　　　　　　　영국 → 캐나다

Who can repair the air conditioner in my room?
(A) The repairs were expensive.
(B) I can do that today.
(C) It's a popular model.

air conditioner 에어컨　repairs n. 수리비　popular adj. 인기 있는
model n. (상품의) 모델, 모형

해석　누가 제 방에 있는 에어컨을 수리할 수 있나요?
　　(A) 수리비가 비쌌어요.
　　(B) 제가 오늘 할 수 있어요.
　　(C) 인기 있는 모델이에요.
해설　(A) [×] repair - repairs의 유사 발음 어휘를 사용하여 혼동을 준 오답이다.
　　(B) [○] 자신이 오늘 할 수 있다는 말로, 자신이 에어컨을 수리할 수 있다는 것을 전달했으므로 정답이다.
　　(C) [×] 질문의 air conditioner(에어컨)에서 연상할 수 있는 model(모델)을 사용하여 혼동을 준 오답이다.

21 What 의문문 　　　　　　　　　　　호주 → 미국

What did the team leader suggest during the meeting?
(A) No, it has been addressed.
(B) We meet several times a week.
(C) He said we must reduce costs.

address v. 해결하다　reduce v. 줄이다　cost n. 비용

해석　팀장이 회의 중에 무엇을 제안했나요?
　　(A) 아니요, 그것은 해결되었어요.
　　(B) 우리는 일주일에 여러 번 만나요.
　　(C) 그는 우리가 비용을 줄여야 한다고 말했어요.
해설　(A) [×] 의문사 의문문에 No로 응답했으므로 오답이다. 질문의 meeting(회의)에서 연상할 수 있는 addressed(해결되었다)를 사용하여 혼동을 주었다.

(B) [×] 팀장이 회의 중에 무엇을 제안했는지를 물었는데, 이와 관련 없는 우리는 일주일에 여러 번 만난다는 말로 응답했으므로 오답이다.
(C) [○] 그는 우리가 비용을 줄여야 한다고 말했다는 말로, 팀장이 회의 중에 제안한 것을 언급했으므로 정답이다.

22 What 의문문 　　　　　　　　　　　영국 → 미국

What are you giving Derek for his birthday?
(A) 27 years old.
(B) At nine in the evening.
(C) I'm getting him a new wallet.

give v. (선물로) 주다　get v. 사주다

해석　Derek의 생일에 무엇을 줄 건가요?
　　(A) 27살이요.
　　(B) 저녁 9시에요.
　　(C) 저는 그에게 새 지갑을 사줄 거예요.
해설　(A) [×] 질문의 birthday(생일)에서 연상할 수 있는 27 years old(27살)를 사용하여 혼동을 준 오답이다.
　　(B) [×] Derek의 생일에 무엇을 선물할 것인지를 물었는데, 시간으로 응답했으므로 오답이다.
　　(C) [○] 그에게 새 지갑을 사줄 것이라는 말로, Derek의 생일에 줄 것을 언급했으므로 정답이다.

23 Which 의문문 　　　　　　　　　　　캐나다 → 영국

Which brand of oven are you planning to buy?
(A) Various vehicle brands.
(B) I plan to bake some bread this afternoon.
(C) Doesn't HomeTek make great appliances?

appliance n. 가전제품

해석　어느 브랜드의 오븐을 구매할 계획인가요?
　　(A) 다양한 차량 브랜드요.
　　(B) 오늘 오후에 빵을 좀 구울 계획이에요.
　　(C) HomeTek사가 훌륭한 가전제품을 만들지 않나요?
해설　(A) [×] 질문의 brand를 brands로 반복 사용하여 혼동을 준 오답이다.
　　(B) [×] 질문의 oven(오븐)과 관련 있는 bake(굽다)를 사용하여 혼동을 준 오답이다.
　　(C) [○] HomeTek사가 훌륭한 가전제품을 만들지 않냐고 되물어, HomeTek사의 오븐을 구매할 계획이라는 것을 간접적으로 전달했으므로 정답이다.

24 Who 의문문 　　　　　　　　　　　미국 → 호주

Who will conduct the customer survey?
(A) The survey responses were surprising.
(B) The marketing team.
(C) Several customer complaints.

conduct v. 실시하다　survey n. 설문조사

해석　누가 고객 설문조사를 실시할 건가요?
　　(A) 설문조사 응답이 놀라웠어요.
　　(B) 마케팅팀이요.
　　(C) 몇몇 고객 불만이요.
해설　(A) [×] 질문의 survey를 반복 사용하여 혼동을 준 오답이다.
　　(B) [○] 마케팅팀이라는 말로, 누가 고객 설문조사를 실시할 것인지를 언급했으므로 정답이다.
　　(C) [×] 질문의 customer를 반복 사용하여 혼동을 준 오답이다.

25 Which 의문문   캐나다 → 미국

> Which part of the city should I look for an apartment in?
> (A) The one with two bedrooms.
> **(B) Everyone seems to like the downtown area.**
> (C) The building has just been renovated.
>
> apartment n. 아파트   bedroom n. 침실   downtown adj. 도심의, 중심가의
> renovate v. 개조하다, 보수하다

해석 도시의 어느 지역에서 아파트를 찾아봐야 하나요?
    (A) 침실이 두 개인 것이요.
    (B) 모든 사람들이 도심 지역을 좋아하는 것 같아요.
    (C) 그 건물은 막 개조되었어요.

해설 (A) [×] 질문의 apartment(아파트)와 관련 있는 bedrooms(침실)를 사용하여 혼동을 준 오답이다.
    (B) [○] 모든 사람들이 도심 지역을 좋아하는 것 같다는 말로, 아파트를 찾아봐야 하는 지역이 도시의 어느 지역인지 언급했으므로 정답이다.
    (C) [×] 질문의 apartment(아파트)와 관련 있는 building(건물)을 사용하여 혼동을 준 오답이다.

DAY 04 의문사 의문문: Where, When

1. Where 의문문

HACKERS PRACTICE   p.51

| 01 (C) | 02 (B) | 03 (A) | 04 (B) | 05 (C) |
| 06 (C) |

01 Where 의문문   캐나다 → 영국 / 호주 → 미국

> Where can I get a resident parking permit?
> (A) To pay a parking fine.
> (B) About 50 dollars per month.
> **(C) From the building manager.**
>
> resident n. 거주민   permit n. 허가증   fine n. 벌금

해석 거주민 주차 허가증을 어디에서 받을 수 있나요?
    (A) 주차 벌금을 내기 위해서요.
    (B) 한 달에 약 50달러요.
    (C) 건물 관리인으로부터요.

해설 (A) [×] 질문의 parking을 반복 사용하여 혼동을 준 오답이다.
    (B) [×] 거주민 주차 허가증을 어디에서 받을 수 있는지를 물었는데, 비용으로 응답했으므로 오답이다.
    (C) [○] 건물 관리인으로부터라는 말로, 거주민 주차 허가증을 어디에서 받을 수 있는지를 언급했으므로 정답이다.

02 Where 의문문   영국 → 캐나다 / 미국 → 호주

> Where will the conference be held?
> (A) We are attending together.
> **(B) In Berlin, I believe.**
> (C) About a week ago.
>
> conference n. 회의   attend v. 참석하다

해석 회의는 어디에서 열릴 건가요?
    (A) 우리는 함께 참석할 거예요.
    (B) 베를린에서인 것 같아요.
    (C) 약 일주일 전에요.

해설 (A) [×] 질문의 conference(회의)와 관련 있는 attending(참석하다)을 사용하여 혼동을 준 오답이다.
    (B) [○] 베를린에서인 것 같다는 말로, 회의가 열릴 장소를 언급했으므로 정답이다.
    (C) [×] 회의가 어디에서 열릴지를 물었는데, 시점으로 응답했으므로 오답이다.

03 Where 의문문   호주 → 미국 / 캐나다 → 영국

> Where did you get the quarterly report?
> **(A) Jane had an extra one.**
> (B) To the company headquarters.
> (C) Report the problem immediately.
>
> quarterly adj. 분기의   extra adj. 여분의   headquarters n. 본사
> immediately adv. 즉시

해석 당신은 분기 보고서를 어디에서 얻었나요?
    (A) Jane이 여분의 것을 가지고 있었어요.
    (B) 회사 본사로요.
    (C) 문제를 즉시 보고하세요.

해설 (A) [○] Jane이 여분의 것을 가지고 있었다는 말로, 분기 보고서를 얻은 출처를 언급했으므로 정답이다.
    (B) [×] 분기 보고서를 어디에서 얻었는지를 물었는데, 장소로 응답했으므로 오답이다.
    (C) [×] 질문의 report(보고서)를 '보고하다'라는 의미의 동사로 반복 사용하여 혼동을 준 오답이다.

04 Where 의문문   영국 → 캐나다 / 미국 → 호주

> Where is the revised copy of the partnership agreement?
> (A) Please make another copy.
> **(B) Our lawyer is reviewing it.**
> (C) It is valid for one year.
>
> revised adj. 수정된   copy n. 사본, 복사   partnership n. 제휴, 동업
> agreement n. 계약(서)   valid adj. 유효한

해석 제휴 계약서의 수정본은 어디에 있나요?
    (A) 다른 사본을 만들어주세요.
    (B) 우리 변호사가 검토 중이에요.
    (C) 그건 1년 동안 유효해요.

해설 (A) [×] 질문의 copy를 반복 사용하여 혼동을 준 오답이다.
    (B) [○] 우리 변호사가 검토 중이라는 말로, 제휴 계약서의 수정본이 어디에 있는지 언급했으므로 정답이다.
    (C) [×] 질문의 agreement(계약서)에서 연상할 수 있는 valid(유효한)를 사용하여 혼동을 준 오답이다.

05 Where 의문문   호주 → 미국 / 캐나다 → 영국

> Where is the information center located?
> (A) A lot of different shops.
> (B) The parking lot was empty today.
> **(C) To the left of the south entrance.**
>
> information center 안내소   parking lot 주차장

해석 안내소는 어디에 위치해 있나요?
    (A) 여러 다른 가게들이요.
    (B) 오늘 주차장이 비었어요.
    (C) 남쪽 입구의 왼쪽이에요.

해설 (A) [×] 안내소는 어디에 위치해 있는지를 물었는데, 이와 관련 없는 여

러 다른 가게들이라는 말로 응답했으므로 오답이다.
(B) [x] 안내소는 어디에 위치해 있는지를 물었는데, 이와 관련 없는 오늘 주차장이 비었다는 말로 응답했으므로 오답이다.
(C) [o] 남쪽 입구의 왼쪽이라며, 안내소의 위치를 언급했으므로 정답이다.

06 Where 의문문
호주 → 미국 / 캐나다 → 영국

Where can I purchase a colorful scarf like yours?
(A) I prefer the yellow one.
(B) Make sure to dress warmly.
(C) It was a birthday present.

purchase v. 구매하다   colorful adj. 형형색색의

해석 당신 것과 같은 형형색색의 스카프는 어디에서 구매할 수 있나요?
(A) 저는 노란 것이 더 좋아요.
(B) 따뜻하게 입는 것을 잊지 마세요.
(C) 그건 생일 선물이었어요.

해설 (A) [x] scarf(스카프)를 가리킬 수 있는 one(것)을 사용하여 혼동을 준 오답이다.
(B) [x] 질문의 scarf(스카프)에서 연상할 수 있는 dress warmly(따뜻하게 입다)를 사용하여 혼동을 준 오답이다.
(C) [o] 생일 선물이었다는 말로, 스카프를 어디에서 구매할 수 있는지 모른다는 것을 간접적으로 전달했으므로 정답이다.

2. When 의문문

HACKERS PRACTICE   p.53

| 01 (C) | 02 (A) | 03 (A) | 04 (B) | 05 (B) |
| 06 (A) |

01 When 의문문
영국 → 호주 / 미국 → 캐나다

When is the performance evaluation due?
(A) About the team's evaluation.
(B) To the department head.
(C) By next Monday.

performance evaluation 업무 평가   due adj. ~하기로 되어 있는, 예정된

해석 업무 평가는 언제까지 하기로 되어 있나요?
(A) 팀의 평가에 관해서요.
(B) 부서장에게요.
(C) 다음 주 월요일까지요.

해설 (A) [x] 질문의 evaluation을 반복 사용하여 혼동을 준 오답이다.
(B) [x] 질문의 performance evaluation(업무 평가)에서 연상할 수 있는 department head(부서장)를 사용하여 혼동을 준 오답이다.
(C) [o] 다음 주 월요일까지라는 말로, 업무 평가를 언제까지 하기로 되어 있는지를 언급했으므로 정답이다.

02 When 의문문
호주 → 캐나다 / 캐나다 → 호주

When is a good time to meet for dinner?
(A) In about an hour.
(B) At the restaurant, maybe.
(C) The food was great.

해석 언제 저녁 식사를 하러 만나는 게 좋을까요?
(A) 약 한 시간 후에요.
(B) 아마도 식당에서요.
(C) 음식이 훌륭했어요.

해설 (A) [o] 약 한 시간 후라는 말로, 저녁 식사를 하러 만나기 좋은 시간을 언급했으므로 정답이다.
(B) [x] 질문의 dinner(저녁 식사)에서 연상할 수 있는 장소와 관련된 restaurant(식당)를 사용하여 혼동을 준 오답이다.
(C) [x] 질문의 dinner(저녁 식사)와 관련 있는 food(음식)를 사용하여 혼동을 준 오답이다.

03 When 의문문
미국 → 호주 / 영국 → 캐나다

When will the orientation for new staff be conducted?
(A) Tomorrow after lunch.
(B) To explain the policy.
(C) Several new hires.

orientation n. 예비 교육   policy n. 방침   hire n. 신입 사원

해석 신입 사원을 위한 예비 교육은 언제 진행될 예정인가요?
(A) 내일 점심 식사 후에요.
(B) 방침을 설명하기 위해서요.
(C) 여러 신입 사원들이요.

해설 (A) [o] 내일 점심 식사 후라는 말로, 예비 교육이 진행되는 시점을 언급했으므로 정답이다.
(B) [x] 질문의 orientation(예비 교육)에서 연상할 수 있는 explain the policy(방침을 설명하다)를 사용하여 혼동을 준 오답이다.
(C) [x] 질문의 new를 반복 사용하여 혼동을 준 오답이다.

04 When 의문문
캐나다 → 호주 / 호주 → 캐나다

When did you do the store's inventory?
(A) No. We're out of stock.
(B) On September 13.
(C) The shop across the street.

inventory n. 재고 조사   out of stock 재고가 없는

해석 가게 재고 조사를 언제 했나요?
(A) 아니요. 저희는 재고가 없어요.
(B) 9월 13일에요.
(C) 길 건너편에 있는 가게요.

해설 (A) [x] 의문사 의문문에 No로 응답했으므로 오답이다. 질문의 the store's inventory(가게 재고 조사)에서 연상할 수 있는 out of stock(재고가 없는)을 사용하여 혼동을 주었다.
(B) [o] 9월 13일이라는 말로, 재고 조사를 한 날짜를 언급했으므로 정답이다.
(C) [x] 질문의 store(가게)와 같은 의미인 shop(가게)을 사용하여 혼동을 준 오답이다. When을 Where로 혼동하여 이를 정답으로 선택하지 않도록 주의한다.

05 When 의문문
미국 → 캐나다 / 영국 → 호주

When do you plan to pick up the dry cleaning?
(A) Please pick me up from the airport.
(B) I finish work at 4 P.M. today.
(C) We should clean the house soon.

pick up 찾아오다, ~를 (차에) 태우다

해석 드라이클리닝 한 세탁물을 언제 찾아올 계획인가요?
(A) 공항에서 저를 태워 가 주세요.
(B) 오늘 오후 4시에 일을 마쳐요.
(C) 우리는 곧 집을 청소해야 해요.

해설 (A) [x] 질문의 pick up을 반복 사용하여 혼동을 준 오답이다.

(B) [○] 오늘 오후 4시에 일을 마친다는 말로, 오늘 오후 4시 이후에 드라이클리닝 한 세탁물을 찾아올 수 있음을 간접적으로 전달했으므로 정답이다.
(C) [×] cleaning - clean의 유사 발음 어휘를 사용하여 혼동을 준 오답이다.

06 When 의문문
캐나다 → 영국 / 호주 → 미국

When can we use the office?
(A) Once the renovations are complete.
(B) That's a relief.
(C) Come in and sit wherever you like.

renovation n. 보수공사 complete adj. 완료된, 완전한

해석 사무실을 언제 사용할 수 있나요?
(A) 보수공사가 완료되는 대로요.
(B) 그건 다행이네요.
(C) 들어와서 원하는 곳에 앉으세요.

해설 (A) [○] 보수공사가 완료되는 대로라는 말로, 사무실을 사용할 수 있는 시점을 언급했으므로 정답이다.
(B) [×] 사무실을 언제 사용할 수 있는지를 물었는데, 이와 관련이 없는 그건 다행이라는 말로 응답했으므로 오답이다.
(C) [×] 사무실을 언제 사용할 수 있는지를 물었는데, 이와 관련이 없는 들어와서 원하는 곳에 앉으라고 응답했으므로 오답이다.

HACKERS TEST
p.54

01 (C)	02 (A)	03 (B)	04 (C)	05 (A)
06 (C)	07 (B)	08 (C)	09 (A)	10 (B)
11 (B)	12 (B)	13 (A)	14 (C)	15 (B)
16 (A)	17 (B)	18 (A)	19 (B)	20 (A)
21 (B)	22 (A)	23 (A)	24 (A)	25 (C)

01 When 의문문
캐나다 → 미국

When is the product launch going to be held?
(A) Consumers seem to like the device.
(B) Here's the lunch menu.
(C) At the end of the month.

product n. 제품 launch n. 출시 (행사)

해석 제품 출시 행사는 언제 열릴 건가요?
(A) 소비자들은 그 장치를 좋아하는 것 같아요.
(B) 여기 점심 메뉴가 있어요.
(C) 이번 달 말에요.

해설 (A) [×] 질문의 product launch(제품 출시 행사)와 관련 있는 device(장치)를 사용하여 혼동을 준 오답이다.
(B) [×] launch - lunch의 유사 발음 어휘를 사용하여 혼동을 준 오답이다.
(C) [○] 이번 달 말에라는 말로, 제품 출시 행사가 열리는 시점을 언급했으므로 정답이다.

02 Where 의문문
영국 → 호주

Where's the nearest pharmacy?
(A) Across from the bookstore.
(B) My family doctor.
(C) From 9 A.M. to 7 P.M.

pharmacy n. 약국 family doctor 주치의

해석 가장 가까운 약국은 어디에 있나요?
(A) 서점 건너편이에요.
(B) 저의 주치의요.
(C) 오전 9시부터 오후 7시까지요.

해설 (A) [○] 서점 건너편이라는 말로, 가장 가까운 약국이 있는 위치를 언급했으므로 정답이다.
(B) [×] 가장 가까운 약국이 어디에 있는지를 물었는데, 사람으로 응답했으므로 오답이다.
(C) [×] 가장 가까운 약국이 어디에 있는지를 물었는데, 시간으로 응답했으므로 오답이다.

03 When 의문문
호주 → 미국

When can you show us the survey results?
(A) A marketing plan.
(B) As soon as I've reviewed them.
(C) More than 50 people responded.

result n. 결과 review v. 검토하다 respond v. 응답하다

해석 설문 조사 결과를 언제 보여줄 수 있나요?
(A) 마케팅 계획이요.
(B) 제가 검토하는 대로요.
(C) 50명이 넘는 사람들이 응답했어요.

해설 (A) [×] 설문 조사 결과를 언제 보여줄 수 있는지를 물었는데, 이와 관련이 없는 마케팅 계획이라는 말로 응답했으므로 오답이다.
(B) [○] 자신이 검토하는 대로라는 말로, 설문 조사 결과를 보여줄 수 있는 시점을 언급했으므로 정답이다.
(C) [×] 질문의 survey results(설문 조사 결과)에서 연상할 수 있는 responded(응답했다)를 사용하여 혼동을 준 오답이다.

04 Where 의문문
영국 → 캐나다

Where's the emergency medical kit?
(A) He's a trained medical worker.
(B) The second Tuesday of the month.
(C) It's in one of the storeroom closets.

emergency medical kit 응급 의료용 키트 storeroom n. 창고

해석 응급 의료용 키트는 어디에 있나요?
(A) 그는 훈련된 의료 종사자예요.
(B) 매월 두 번째 화요일이요.
(C) 창고 수납장 중 하나에 있어요.

해설 (A) [×] 질문의 medical을 반복 사용하여 혼동을 준 오답이다.
(B) [×] 응급 의료용 키트가 어디에 있는지를 물었는데, 요일로 응답했으므로 오답이다. 질문의 Where를 When으로 혼동하여 이를 정답으로 선택하지 않도록 주의한다.
(C) [○] 창고 수납장 중 하나에 있다는 말로, 응급 의료용 키트가 있는 위치를 언급했으므로 정답이다.

05 When 의문문
캐나다 → 영국

When are you planning to leave for Bali?
(A) On Tuesday.
(B) I'll pack your luggage.
(C) They leave at noon.

pack v. 싸다, 포장하다 luggage n. 짐, 수하물

해석 발리로 언제 떠날 계획인가요?
(A) 화요일에요.
(B) 제가 당신의 짐을 쌀게요.
(C) 그들은 정오에 떠나요.

해설 (A) [o] 화요일이라는 말로, 발리로 떠나는 요일을 언급했으므로 정답이다.
(B) [x] 질문의 leave(떠나다)에서 연상할 수 있는 여행과 관련된 luggage(짐)를 사용하여 혼동을 준 오답이다.
(C) [x] 질문의 leave를 반복 사용하여 혼동을 준 오답이다.

06 Where 의문문 호주 → 영국

Where are we going to open another branch?
(A) At the beginning of August.
(B) Our Seoul office is closed.
(C) The CEO still hasn't decided.

branch n. 지점   beginning n. 초(반), 처음   decide v. 결정하다

해석 우리는 어디에 또 다른 지점을 열 예정인가요?
(A) 8월 초예요.
(B) 우리의 서울 사무실은 문을 닫았어요.
(C) 최고 경영자가 아직 결정하지 못했어요.

해설 (A) [x] 어디에 또 다른 지점을 열 예정인지를 물었는데, 시점으로 응답했으므로 오답이다. 질문의 Where를 When으로 혼동하여 이를 정답으로 선택하지 않도록 주의한다.
(B) [x] 질문의 branch(지점)와 관련 있는 Seoul office(서울 사무실)를 사용하여 혼동을 준 오답이다.
(C) [o] 최고 경영자가 아직 결정하지 못했다는 말로, 어디에 또 다른 지점을 열 예정인지 모른다는 것을 간접적으로 전달했으므로 정답이다.

07 When 의문문 미국 → 영국

When is the deadline for the blueprint revisions?
(A) The building on Aspen Road.
(B) At 10 A.M. tomorrow.
(C) No. I don't need any help.

deadline n. 마감 기한   blueprint n. 설계도

해석 설계도 수정의 마감 기한이 언제인가요?
(A) Aspen 도로에 있는 건물이요.
(B) 내일 오전 10시에요.
(C) 아니요. 저는 도움이 필요하지 않아요.

해설 (A) [x] 설계도 수정의 마감일이 언제인지 시점을 물었는데, 장소로 응답했으므로 오답이다. 질문의 When을 Where로 혼동하여 이를 정답으로 선택하지 않도록 주의한다.
(B) [o] 내일 오전 10시이라는 말로, 설계도 수정의 마감 기한이 언제인지 언급했으므로 정답이다.
(C) [x] 의문사 의문문에 No로 응답했으므로 오답이다.

08 Where 의문문 캐나다 → 미국

Where did this amazing painting come from?
(A) To hang in the dining room.
(B) The artist is world-famous.
(C) The Sanderson Gallery.

painting n. 그림   hang v. 걸다   artist n. 화가
world-famous adj. 세계적으로 유명한

해석 이 멋진 그림은 어디에서 왔나요?
(A) 식당에 걸기 위해서요.
(B) 그 화가는 세계적으로 유명해요.
(C) Sanderson 미술관이요.

해설 (A) [x] 질문의 painting(그림)에서 연상할 수 있는 hang(걸다)을 사용하여 혼동을 준 오답이다.
(B) [x] 질문의 painting(그림)과 관련 있는 artist(화가)를 사용하여 혼동을 준 오답이다.
(C) [o] Sanderson 미술관이라는 말로, 그림이 온 출처를 언급했으므로 정답이다.

09 When 의문문 미국 → 캐나다

When did we hire the accountant?
(A) He started here last month.
(B) It was a long hiring process.
(C) In the company's account.

accountant n. 회계사   account n. 계좌

해석 우리는 그 회계사를 언제 채용했나요?
(A) 그는 여기에서 지난달에 시작했어요.
(B) 긴 채용 과정이었어요.
(C) 회사의 계좌에서요.

해설 (A) [o] 그가 여기에서 지난달에 시작했다는 말로, 회계사를 채용한 시점을 언급했으므로 정답이다.
(B) [x] hire – hiring의 유사 발음 어휘를 사용하여 혼동을 준 오답이다.
(C) [x] 질문의 accountant(회계사)에서 연상할 수 있는 company's account(회사의 계좌)를 사용하여 혼동을 준 오답이다.

10 Where 의문문 호주 → 미국

Where's this shipment of chairs and tables going?
(A) It will take only three hours.
(B) To the distribution center in Seattle.
(C) About a hundred people will be there.

shipment n. 수송품, 적하물   distribution center 물류 센터

해석 이 의자와 탁자 수송품은 어디로 가나요?
(A) 3시간만 걸릴 거예요.
(B) 시애틀에 있는 물류 센터로요.
(C) 약 100명의 사람들이 그곳에 있을 거예요.

해설 (A) [x] 의자와 탁자 수송품이 어디로 가는지 장소를 물었는데, 시간으로 응답했으므로 오답이다. 질문의 Where를 When으로 혼동하여 이를 정답으로 선택하지 않도록 주의한다.
(B) [o] 시애틀에 있는 물류 센터라는 말로, 의자와 탁자 수송품이 가는 장소를 언급했으므로 정답이다.
(C) [x] 의자와 탁자 수송품이 어디로 가는지 장소를 물었는데, 이와 관련이 없는 약 100명의 사람들이 그곳에 있을 거라는 말로 응답했으므로 오답이다.

11 When 의문문 미국 → 캐나다

When is ShoreTech's new phone coming out?
(A) He's back from a recent holiday.
(B) On Friday.
(C) With a long battery life.

come out (상품이 시장에) 나오다   recent adj. 최근, 최신

해설 ShoreTech사의 새로운 휴대전화는 언제 나오나요?
(A) 그는 최근 휴가에서 돌아왔어요.
(B) 금요일이에요.
(C) 긴 배터리 수명을 가지고요.

해설 (A) [x] 질문의 new(새로운)와 관련 있는 recent(최근)를 사용하여 혼동을 준 오답이다.
(B) [o] 금요일이라며, ShoreTech사의 새로운 휴대전화가 나올 요일을 언급했으므로 정답이다.
(C) [x] 질문의 phone(휴대전화)에서 연상할 수 있는 battery life(배터리 수명)를 사용하여 혼동을 준 오답이다.

12 Where 의문문　　　🎧 호주 → 캐나다

Where are we supposed to meet for the workshop?
(A) Were there enough people?
(B) In Room 304.
(C) Once the workshop ends.

be supposed to ~하기로 되어 있다　workshop n. 연수, 워크숍

해석　우리는 연수를 위해 어디에서 모이기로 되어 있나요?
　　　(A) 그곳에 사람들이 충분히 있었나요?
　　　(B) 304호실에서요.
　　　(C) 연수가 끝나자마자요.

해설　(A) [×] 연수를 위해 어디에서 모이기로 되어 있는지를 물었는데, 이와 관련이 없는 그곳에 사람들이 충분히 있었는지를 되물었으므로 오답이다.
　　　(B) [○] 304호실에서라는 말로, 연수를 위해 모이기로 한 장소를 언급했으므로 정답이다.
　　　(C) [×] 연수를 위해 어디에서 모이기로 되어 있는지를 물었는데, 시점으로 응답했으므로 오답이다. 질문의 workshop을 반복 사용하여 혼동을 주었다.

13 When 의문문　　　🎧 영국 → 캐나다

When will the technician finish his repair work?
(A) He completed it this morning.
(B) At the electronics store.
(C) On a factory machine.

technician n. 기술자　complete v. 완료하다
electronics store 전자제품 매장

해석　기술자는 언제 수리 작업을 끝낼 건가요?
　　　(A) 그는 그것을 오늘 아침에 완료했어요.
　　　(B) 전자제품 매장에서요.
　　　(C) 공장 기계 위에요.

해설　(A) [○] 오늘 아침에 완료했다는 말로, 기술자가 이미 수리 작업을 끝냈음을 전달했으므로 정답이다. 미래 시점을 묻는 When 의문문에 과거 시점을 사용하여 이미 완료되었음을 나타내는 응답도 정답이 될 수 있음을 알아둔다.
　　　(B) [×] 기술자가 언제 수리 작업을 끝낼지를 물었는데, 장소로 응답했으므로 오답이다. 질문의 When을 Where로 혼동하여 이를 정답으로 선택하지 않도록 주의한다.
　　　(C) [×] 기술자가 언제 수리 작업을 끝낼지를 물었는데, 위치로 응답했으므로 오답이다. 질문의 When을 Where로 혼동하여 이를 정답으로 선택하지 않도록 주의한다.

14 Where 의문문　　　🎧 호주 → 미국

Where should I set up the intern's workstation?
(A) A three-month internship.
(B) Meet me at the train station.
(C) This floor is already too crowded.

set up 마련하다, 설치하다　workstation n. 작업 장소
crowded adj. (사람·물건 등으로) 꽉 찬, 붐비는

해석　인턴의 작업 장소를 어디에 마련해야 하나요?
　　　(A) 3개월 인턴직이요.
　　　(B) 저와 기차역에서 만나요.
　　　(C) 이 층은 이미 너무 꽉 찼어요.

해설　(A) [×] intern - internship의 유사 발음 어휘를 사용하여 혼동을 준 오답이다.
　　　(B) [×] workstation - station의 유사 발음 어휘를 사용하여 혼동을 준 오답이다.
　　　(C) [○] 이 층은 이미 너무 꽉 찼다는 말로, 이 층에 인턴의 작업 장소를 마련할 수 없음을 간접적으로 전달했으므로 정답이다.

15 When 의문문　　　🎧 영국 → 호주

When was that documentary about the whales aired?
(A) It was an episode about whales.
(B) Last Wednesday night.
(C) Yes, that's the one.

air v. 방송하다　episode n. (1회) 방송분, 에피소드

해석　고래에 관한 그 다큐멘터리는 언제 방송되었나요?
　　　(A) 그건 고래에 관한 방송분이었어요.
　　　(B) 지난 수요일 밤이요.
　　　(C) 네, 바로 그거예요.

해설　(A) [×] 질문의 whales를 반복 사용하여 혼동을 준 오답이다.
　　　(B) [○] 지난 수요일 밤이라는 말로, 고래에 관한 그 다큐멘터리가 방송된 시점을 언급했으므로 정답이다.
　　　(C) [×] 의문사 의문문에 Yes로 응답했으므로 오답이다.

16 When 의문문　　　🎧 캐나다 → 영국

When do you want to discuss the design changes?
(A) Now would be perfect.
(B) Several modifications.
(C) Yes, she is the designer.

discuss v. 논의하다, 토론하다　modification n. 수정 사항, 변경

해석　디자인 수정에 대해 언제 논의하고 싶은가요?
　　　(A) 지금이 딱 좋을 것 같아요.
　　　(B) 몇 가지 수정 사항이요.
　　　(C) 네, 그녀가 디자이너예요.

해설　(A) [○] 지금이 딱 좋을 것 같다는 말로, 디자인 수정을 논의하고 싶은 시점을 언급했으므로 정답이다.
　　　(B) [×] changes(수정)와 관련 있는 modifications(수정 사항)를 사용하여 혼동을 준 오답이다.
　　　(C) [×] 의문사 의문문에 Yes로 응답했으므로 오답이다.

17 Where 의문문　　　🎧 미국 → 호주

Where does the company conduct its board meetings?
(A) Only if you get bored.
(B) Mr. Lewis would probably know.
(C) I'll inform her about that.

conduct v. 실시하다　board meeting 이사회　bored adj. 지루한
inform v. 알리다

해석　회사는 어디에서 이사회를 실시하나요?
　　　(A) 만약 당신이 지루해할 경우에만요.
　　　(B) Mr. Lewis가 아마 아실 거예요.
　　　(C) 제가 그녀에게 그것에 대해 알려줄게요.

해설　(A) [×] board - bored의 유사 발음 어휘를 사용하여 혼동을 준 오답이다.
　　　(B) [○] Mr. Lewis가 아마 알 거라는 말로, 회사가 어디에서 이사회를 실시하는지 모른다는 것을 간접적으로 전달했으므로 정답이다.
　　　(C) [×] 회사가 이사회를 실시하는 장소를 물었는데, 이와 관련이 없는 자신이 그녀에게 그것에 대해 알려주겠다는 말로 응답했으므로 오답이다.

18 When 의문문   호주 → 영국

When is your dental appointment scheduled for?
(A) **Early next week.**
(B) Yes, for a checkup.
(C) Sure. Ask the dentist.

appointment n. 예약 scheduled adj. 예정된 checkup n. 검진

해석 당신의 치과 예약은 언제로 예정되어 있나요?
(A) 다음 주 초예요.
(B) 네, 검진을 위해서요.
(C) 물론이죠. 치과 의사에게 물어보세요.

해설 (A) [o] 다음 주 초라는 말로, 치과 예약이 예정된 시점을 언급했으므로 정답이다.
(B) [x] 의문사 의문문에 Yes로 응답했으므로 오답이다. 질문의 dental appointment(치과 예약)에서 연상할 수 있는 checkup(검진)을 사용하여 혼동을 주었다.
(C) [x] 질문의 dental - dentist의 유사 발음 어휘를 사용하여 혼동을 준 오답이다.

19 Where 의문문   영국 → 캐나다

Where is the farmers' market being held?
(A) The booths open at 8 A.M. each morning.
(B) **It always takes place in the same venue.**
(C) Only local residents will be participating.

farmers' market 농산물 직판장 take place (행사 등이) 열리다, 일어나다
venue n. 장소 local adj. 지역의 resident n. 주민

해석 농산물 직판장은 어디에서 열리나요?
(A) 부스는 매일 아침 8시에 열어요.
(B) 그건 항상 같은 장소에서 열려요.
(C) 지역 주민들만 참여할 거예요.

해설 (A) [x] 농산물 직판장이 열리는 장소를 물었는데, 시간으로 응답했으므로 오답이다.
(B) [o] 그건 항상 같은 장소에서 열린다는 말로, 농산물 직판장이 어디에서 열리는지에 대한 정보를 간접적으로 제공했으므로 정답이다.
(C) [x] 농산물 직판장이 열리는 장소를 물었는데, 이와 관련이 없는 지역 주민들만 참여할 것이라는 말로 응답했으므로 오답이다.

20 When 의문문   캐나다 → 호주

When should I post the job advertisement?
(A) **Check with our team leader.**
(B) Of course. I'll take care of it.
(C) On our firm's Web site.

post v. 게시하다 job advertisement 구인 광고 team leader 팀장
take care of ~을 처리하다 firm n. 회사

해석 구인 광고를 언제 게시해야 하나요?
(A) 우리 팀장님에게 확인해 보세요.
(B) 물론이죠. 제가 처리할게요.
(C) 우리 회사 웹사이트에서요.

해설 (A) [o] 우리 팀장님에게 확인해 보라는 말로, 구인 광고를 언제 게시해야 하는지 모른다는 것을 간접적으로 전달했으므로 정답이다.
(B) [x] 구인 광고를 언제 게시해야 하는지를 물었는데, 이와 관련이 없는 자신이 처리하겠다는 말로 응답했으므로 오답이다.
(C) [x] 질문의 job advertisement(구인 광고)에서 연상할 수 있는 firm's Web site(회사 웹사이트)를 사용하여 혼동을 준 오답이다.

21 Where 의문문   미국 → 호주

Where's the store manager?
(A) I'll accompany him.
(B) **She's away on vacation.**
(C) A store catalog.

accompany v. 동행하다, 동반하다 on vacation 휴가 중인
catalog n. 카탈로그, 목록

해석 매장 관리자는 어디에 있나요?
(A) 제가 그와 동행할게요.
(B) 그녀는 휴가 중이라 자리에 없어요.
(C) 매장 카탈로그요.

해설 (A) [x] 매장 관리자가 어디에 있는지를 물었는데, 이와 관련이 없는 자신이 그와 동행하겠다는 말로 응답했으므로 오답이다.
(B) [o] 그녀는 휴가 중이라 자리에 없다는 말로, 매장 관리자가 어디에 있는지를 언급했으므로 정답이다.
(C) [x] 질문의 store를 반복 사용하여 혼동을 준 오답이다.

22 When 의문문   캐나다 → 미국

When do you think someone can stop by to pick up my box?
(A) **Is it ready to ship?**
(B) It has a few of my personal belongings.
(C) Yes, it's already on the way.

stop by 들르다 pick up 가져가다, 찾아오다
ship v. (배·트럭 등으로) 보내다, 수송하다 personal belongings 개인 소지품

해석 누군가가 제 상자를 가지러 언제 들를 수 있다고 생각하시나요?
(A) 보낼 준비가 되어 있나요?
(B) 그것은 제 개인 소지품 몇 개를 담고 있어요.
(C) 네, 그것은 이미 오는 중이에요.

해설 (A) [o] 보낼 준비가 되어 있는지 되물어, 가져갈 상자에 대한 추가 정보를 요구한 정답이다.
(B) [x] box(상자)를 가리킬 수 있는 It(그것)을 사용하여 혼동을 준 오답이다.
(C) [x] 의문사 의문문에 Yes로 응답했으므로 오답이다.

23 Where 의문문   영국 → 미국

Where is the application form for the seminar?
(A) **On our department's Web page.**
(B) I've worked there for a while.
(C) As soon as the talk begins.

application form 신청서 talk n. 강연

해석 세미나의 신청서는 어디에 있나요?
(A) 우리 부서의 웹페이지예요.
(B) 저는 한동안 그곳에서 일해왔어요.
(C) 강연이 시작되자마자요.

해설 (A) [o] 우리 부서의 웹페이지에라며, 세미나 신청서가 어디에 있는지를 언급했으므로 정답이다.
(B) [x] 질문의 seminar(세미나)를 나타낼 수 있는 there(그곳에서)를 사용하여 혼동을 준 오답이다.
(C) [x] 세미나 신청서가 어디에 있는지를 물었는데, 시점으로 응답했으므로 오답이다.

24 When 의문문 호주 → 미국

When did you find out that the clients want to renew the contract?
(A) During a business lunch.
(B) Some clients asked for a discount.
(C) My contact information.

renew v. 연장하다, 갱신하다   client n. 고객   contact information 연락처

해석 고객들이 계약을 연장하기를 원한다는 것을 언제 알게 되었나요?
(A) 사업상의 점심 식사 동안이에요.
(B) 몇몇 고객들이 할인을 요청했어요.
(C) 제 연락처요.

해설 (A) [o] 사업상의 점심 식사 동안이라는 말로, 고객들이 계약을 연장하기를 원한다는 것을 알게 된 시점을 언급했으므로 정답이다.
(B) [x] 질문의 clients를 반복 사용하여 혼동을 준 오답이다.
(C) [x] contract – contact의 유사 발음 어휘를 사용하여 혼동을 준 오답이다.

25 Where 의문문 영국 → 캐나다

Where do we go after watching the product demonstration?
(A) The other members of our division.
(B) That movie was very interesting.
(C) To the main lobby.

demonstration n. 시연   division n. 부서

해석 제품 시연을 본 이후에 우리는 어디에 가나요?
(A) 우리 부서의 다른 사원들이요.
(B) 그 영화는 매우 흥미로웠어요.
(C) 중앙 로비요.

해설 (A) [x] 제품 시연을 본 이후에 갈 장소를 물었는데, 사람으로 응답했으므로 오답이다.
(B) [x] 질문의 watching(보다)에서 연상할 수 있는 영상과 관련된 movie(영화)를 사용하여 혼동을 준 오답이다.
(C) [o] 중앙 로비라는 말로, 제품 시연을 본 이후에 갈 장소를 언급했으므로 정답이다.

DAY 05 의문사 의문문: Why, How

1. Why 의문문

HACKERS PRACTICE p.57

01 (C)   02 (A)   03 (C)   04 (C)   05 (B)
06 (B)

01 Why 의문문 미국 → 호주 / 영국 → 캐나다

Why did the server take your meal back?
(A) I'll treat you to dinner tonight.
(B) Can I see the menu?
(C) He gave me the wrong dish.

server n. 종업원   meal n. 식사   treat v. 대접하다

해석 왜 종업원이 당신의 식사를 다시 가져갔나요?
(A) 제가 오늘 저녁 식사를 당신에게 대접할게요.
(B) 메뉴를 볼 수 있을까요?
(C) 그가 제게 요리를 잘못 가져다주었어요.

해설 (A) [x] 질문의 meal(식사)과 관련 있는 dinner(저녁 식사)를 사용하여 혼동을 준 오답이다.
(B) [x] 질문의 meal(식사)과 관련 있는 menu(메뉴)를 사용하여 혼동을 준 오답이다.
(C) [o] 그가 요리를 잘못 가져다주었다는 말로, 종업원이 식사를 다시 가져간 이유를 언급했으므로 정답이다.

02 Why 의문문 캐나다 → 영국 / 호주 → 미국

Why is the furnace not turning on?
(A) I'll call a repairperson.
(B) Sure, I'll turn up the heat.
(C) Yes. In the basement.

furnace n. 보일러   repairperson n. 수리공   basement n. 지하실

해석 왜 보일러가 켜지지 않고 있나요?
(A) 수리공을 부를게요.
(B) 물론이죠, 온도를 높이겠습니다.
(C) 네, 지하실에서요.

해설 (A) [o] 수리공을 부르겠다는 말로, 보일러가 켜지지 않고 있는 이유를 모른다는 것을 간접적으로 전달했으므로 정답이다.
(B) [x] 이유를 묻는 질문에 Sure로 응답했으므로 오답이다. 질문의 furnace(보일러)에서 연상할 수 있는 heat(온도)을 사용하여 혼동을 주었다.
(C) [x] 의문사 의문문에 Yes로 응답했으므로 오답이다.

03 Why 의문문 미국 → 캐나다 / 영국 → 호주

Why hasn't the hallway carpet been replaced yet?
(A) It's a lovely design.
(B) I need to replace my laptop.
(C) Because the new one hasn't arrived yet.

hallway n. 복도   replace v. 교체하다   laptop n. 노트북

해석 복도 카펫은 왜 아직 교체되지 않았나요?
(A) 그건 멋진 디자인이에요.
(B) 저는 노트북을 교체해야 해요.
(C) 새것이 아직 도착하지 않았기 때문이에요.

해설 (A) [x] 복도 카펫이 아직 교체되지 않은 이유를 물었는데, 이와 관련 없는 멋진 디자인이라는 말로 응답했으므로 오답이다.
(B) [x] replaced – replace의 유사 발음 어휘를 사용하여 혼동을 준 오답이다.
(C) [o] 새것이 아직 도착하지 않았기 때문이라는 말로, 복도 카펫이 아직 교체되지 않은 이유를 언급했으므로 정답이다.

04 Why 의문문 호주 → 영국 / 캐나다 → 미국

Why did Ms. Peters travel to Chicago this week?
(A) She'll return next week.
(B) I found the trip very stressful.
(C) There is a problem at our factory.

trip n. 출장   stressful adj. 스트레스를 일으키는

해석 Ms. Peters는 왜 이번 주에 시카고에 갔나요?
(A) 그녀는 다음 주에 돌아올 거예요.
(B) 그 출장은 정말 스트레스를 일으켰어요.
(C) 우리 공장에 문제가 있어요.

해설 (A) [x] 질문의 travel(가다)에서 연상할 수 있는 return(돌아오다)을 사용하여 혼동을 준 오답이다.

(B) [x] 질문의 travel(가다)과 관련 있는 trip(출장)을 사용하여 혼동을 준 오답이다.
(C) [o] 우리 공장에 문제가 있다는 말로, Ms. Peters가 이번 주에 시카고에 간 이유를 언급했으므로 정답이다.

05 Why 의문문
미국 → 영국 / 영국 → 미국

Why is the product being recalled?
(A) I can't recall the name.
(B) Because of safety concerns.
(C) It's one of the leading brands.

recall v. 회수하다, 리콜하다, 기억해 내다   concern n. 우려
leading adj. 선도적인

해석 제품이 왜 회수되고 있나요?
(A) 저는 이름이 기억나지 않아요.
(B) 안전상의 우려 때문이에요.
(C) 그것은 선도적인 브랜드 중 하나예요.

해설 (A) [x] recalled - recall의 유사 발음 어휘를 사용하여 혼동을 준 오답이다.
(B) [o] 안전상의 우려 때문이라는 말로, 제품이 회수되고 있는 이유를 언급했으므로 정답이다.
(C) [x] 질문의 product(제품)와 관련 있는 brand(브랜드)를 사용하여 혼동을 준 오답이다.

06 Why 의문문
호주 → 영국 / 캐나다 → 미국

Why hasn't the customer database been updated?
(A) You should not share your password.
(B) I had a problem with my computer.
(C) It took 20 minutes.

customer n. 고객

해석 고객 데이터베이스는 왜 업데이트되지 않았나요?
(A) 비밀번호를 공유하면 안 됩니다.
(B) 제 컴퓨터에 문제가 있었어요.
(C) 20분이 걸렸어요.

해설 (A) [x] 고객 데이터베이스가 업데이트되지 않은 이유를 물었는데, 이와 관련이 없는 비밀번호를 공유하면 안 된다고 응답했으므로 오답이다.
(B) [o] 컴퓨터에 문제가 있었다는 말로, 고객 데이터베이스가 업데이트되지 않은 이유를 언급했으므로 정답이다.
(C) [x] 고객 데이터베이스가 업데이트되지 않은 이유를 물었는데, 시간으로 응답했으므로 오답이다.

2. How 의문문

HACKERS PRACTICE   p.59

01 (A)   02 (C)   03 (C)   04 (B)   05 (C)
06 (C)

01 How 의문문
호주 → 미국 / 캐나다 → 영국

How should I send you the photographs?
(A) By text message.
(B) Four copies, please.
(C) Yes. I took some yesterday.

photograph n. 사진   text message 문자 메시지   copy n. 사본

해석 사진을 어떻게 보내드려야 하나요?

(A) 문자 메시지로요.
(B) 사본 네 장을 부탁합니다.
(C) 네. 제가 어제 몇 장 찍었어요.

해설 (A) [o] 문자 메시지로라는 말로, 사진을 보내는 수단을 언급했으므로 정답이다.
(B) [x] 질문의 photographs(사진)에서 연상할 수 있는 copies(사본)를 사용하여 혼동을 준 오답이다.
(C) [x] 의문사 의문문에 Yes로 응답했으므로 오답이다. 질문의 photographs(사진)를 나타낼 수 있는 some(몇 장)을 사용하여 혼동을 주었다.

02 How 의문문
영국 → 캐나다 / 미국 → 호주

How many hats are on display?
(A) Yes, I helped set up the display.
(B) It looks good on you.
(C) There are six on the front table.

display n. 진열, 전시   set up 준비하다

해석 몇 개의 모자가 진열되어 있나요?
(A) 네, 제가 진열 준비를 도왔어요.
(B) 그건 당신에게 잘 어울려요.
(C) 앞 테이블에는 여섯 개가 있어요.

해설 (A) [x] 질문의 display를 반복 사용하여 혼동을 준 오답이다.
(B) [x] 질문의 hats(모자)에서 연상할 수 있는 looks good on(~와 잘 어울리다)을 사용하여 혼동을 준 오답이다.
(C) [o] 앞 테이블에 여섯 개가 있다는 말로, 진열되어 있는 모자의 수를 언급했으므로 정답이다.

03 How 의문문
캐나다 → 미국 / 호주 → 영국

How can we reserve a booth at the trade show?
(A) The reservation was canceled.
(B) Over 300 participants.
(C) By e-mailing the venue.

reserve v. 예약하다   reservation n. 예약   participant n. 참가자

해석 무역 박람회에서 부스를 어떻게 예약할 수 있나요?
(A) 그 예약은 취소되었어요.
(B) 300명이 넘는 참가자들이요.
(C) 행사장에 이메일을 보내세요.

해설 (A) [x] reserve - reservation의 유사 발음 어휘를 사용하여 혼동을 준 오답이다.
(B) [x] 질문의 trade show(무역 박람회)에서 연상할 수 있는 participants(참가자들)를 사용하여 혼동을 준 오답이다.
(C) [o] 행사장에 이메일을 보내라는 말로, 무역 박람회에서 부스를 예약할 수 있는 방법을 언급했으므로 정답이다.

04 How 의문문
영국 → 호주 / 미국 → 캐나다

How is the Westwood branch of our store doing?
(A) The store has a large parking lot.
(B) Sales have declined lately.
(C) A new branch recently opened.

decline v. 감소하다   branch n. 지점

해석 우리 가게의 Westwood 지점은 어떻게 되고 있나요?
(A) 그 가게에는 넓은 주차장이 있어요.
(B) 최근 매출이 감소했어요.
(C) 최근에 새로운 지점이 개장했어요.

해설 (A) [x] 질문의 store를 반복 사용하여 혼동을 준 오답이다.
(B) [o] 최근 매출이 감소했다는 말로, 우리 가게의 Westwood 지점이 어떻게 되고 있는지를 언급했으므로 정답이다.
(C) [x] 질문의 branch를 반복 사용하여 혼동을 준 오답이다.

05 How 의문문 캐나다 → 호주 / 호주 → 캐나다

How long does it take to get to Bryce Park?
(A) It's 30 meters long.
(B) To watch a soccer game.
(C) About an hour by car.

get to ~에 가다, 도착하다   about prep. 약

해석 Bryce 공원까지 가는 데 얼마나 걸리나요?
(A) 길이가 30미터예요.
(B) 축구 경기를 보기 위해서요.
(C) 자동차로 약 1시간이요.

해설 (A) [x] 질문의 long을 반복 사용하여 혼동을 준 오답이다.
(B) [x] Bryce 공원까지 가는 데 얼마나 걸리는지를 물었는데, 이와 관련이 없는 축구 경기를 보기 위해서라고 응답했으므로 오답이다.
(C) [o] 자동차로 약 1시간이라는 말로, Bryce 공원까지 가는 데 걸리는 시간을 언급했으므로 정답이다.

06 How 의문문 미국 → 캐나다 / 영국 → 호주

How much will the folding tables cost?
(A) We'll go for a picnic.
(B) Fold the sweater neatly.
(C) At least 60 dollars each.

neatly adv. 단정하게

해석 접이식 탁자의 가격은 얼마인가요?
(A) 소풍을 갈 거예요.
(B) 스웨터를 깔끔하게 접으세요.
(C) 각각 최소 60달러예요.

해설 (A) [x] 질문의 folding tables(접이식 탁자)에서 연상할 수 있는 picnic(소풍)을 사용하여 혼동을 준 오답이다.
(B) [x] 질문의 folding을 fold로 반복 사용하여 혼동을 준 오답이다.
(C) [o] 각각 최소 60달러라는 말로, 접이식 탁자의 가격을 언급했으므로 정답이다.

HACKERS TEST p.60

01 (C)	02 (A)	03 (B)	04 (C)	05 (A)
06 (B)	07 (A)	08 (C)	09 (A)	10 (A)
11 (C)	12 (C)	13 (B)	14 (A)	15 (C)
16 (B)	17 (A)	18 (C)	19 (A)	20 (B)
21 (A)	22 (C)	23 (C)	24 (A)	25 (B)

01 Why 의문문 호주 → 영국

Why was the workshop postponed?
(A) About marketing strategies.
(B) No, yesterday afternoon.
(C) Not enough people registered.

postpone v. 연기하다, 미루다   strategy n. 전략, 계획

해석 워크숍은 왜 연기되었나요?
(A) 마케팅 전략들에 대해서요.
(B) 아니요, 어제 오후에요.
(C) 충분한 사람들이 등록하지 않았어요.

해설 (A) [x] 질문의 workshop(워크숍)에서 연상할 수 있는 marketing strategies(마케팅 전략들)를 사용하여 혼동을 준 오답이다.
(B) [x] 의문사 의문문에 No로 응답했으므로 오답이다.
(C) [o] 충분한 사람들이 등록하지 않았다는 말로, 워크숍이 연기된 이유를 언급했으므로 정답이다.

02 How 의문문 영국 → 캐나다

How often are the reports published?
(A) Once every month.
(B) A financial consultant is working on it.
(C) Yes, they should be created.

publish v. 발행하다   financial adj. 재무의
consultant n. 컨설턴트, 자문 위원   create v. 제작하다

해석 보고서는 얼마나 자주 발행되나요?
(A) 매달 한 번씩이요.
(B) 재무 컨설턴트가 그것을 작업하고 있어요.
(C) 네, 그것들은 제작되어야 해요.

해설 (A) [o] 매달 한 번씩이라는 말로, 보고서가 발행되는 빈도를 언급했으므로 정답이다.
(B) [x] 보고서가 얼마나 자주 발행되는지를 물었는데, 이와 관련이 없는 재무 컨설턴트가 그것을 작업하고 있다는 말로 응답했으므로 오답이다.
(C) [x] 의문사 의문문에 Yes로 응답했으므로 오답이다. 질문의 reports(보고서)를 나타낼 수 있는 they(그것들)를 사용하여 혼동을 주었다.

03 How 의문문 호주 → 미국

How did you get the idea to start a delivery service?
(A) Terry will get a job.
(B) My friend suggested it.
(C) I appreciate the offer.

suggest v. 제안하다

해석 배달 서비스를 시작할 아이디어를 어떻게 얻으셨나요?
(A) Terry가 직장을 구할 거예요.
(B) 제 친구가 이것을 제안했어요.
(C) 제안해 주셔서 감사해요.

해설 (A) [x] 배달 서비스를 시작할 아이디어를 어떻게 얻었는지를 물었는데, 이와 관련이 없는 Terry가 직장을 구할 거라는 말로 응답했으므로 오답이다.
(B) [o] 자신의 친구가 제안했다는 말로, 배달 서비스를 시작할 아이디어를 얻은 방법을 언급했으므로 정답이다.
(C) [x] 배달 서비스를 시작할 아이디어를 어떻게 얻었는지를 물었는데, 이와 관련이 없는 제안해 주셔서 감사하다는 말로 응답했으므로 오답이다.

04 Why 의문문 미국 → 캐나다

Why isn't the printer working?
(A) Print your name at the top.
(B) In my home office.
(C) It's out of paper.

print v. 작성하다, 인쇄하다   out of 떨어져서, 동나서

해석 프린터가 왜 작동하지 않나요?
(A) 상단에 이름을 작성해 주세요.

(B) 제 재택 사무실이에요.
(C) 종이가 떨어졌어요.

해설 (A) [×] printer – Print의 유사 발음 어휘를 사용하여 혼동을 준 오답이다.
(B) [×] 질문의 printer(프린터)에서 연상할 수 있는 office(사무실)를 사용하여 혼동을 준 오답이다.
(C) [o] 종이가 떨어졌다는 말로, 프린터가 작동하지 않는 이유를 언급했으므로 정답이다.

05 Why 의문문   호주 → 영국

Why did you buy a backpack instead of a suitcase?
(A) **It's more convenient.**
(B) Let's pack them with clothes.
(C) At a local luggage shop.

suitcase n. 여행 가방   convenient adj. 편리한   luggage n. 가방

해설 여행 가방 대신 왜 배낭을 구매하셨나요?
(A) 더 편리해요.
(B) 그것들에 옷을 챙겨 넣읍시다.
(C) 지역 가방 가게에서요.

해설 (A) [o] 더 편리하다는 말로, 여행 가방 대신 배낭을 구매한 이유를 언급했으므로 정답이다.
(B) [×] backpack – pack의 유사 발음 어휘를 사용하여 혼동을 준 오답이다.
(C) [×] 질문의 buy a backpack(배낭을 구매하다)에서 연상할 수 있는 luggage shop(가방 가게)을 사용하여 혼동을 준 오답이다.

06 How 의문문   미국 → 영국

How often does the subway train come?
(A) How many tickets do you need?
(B) **Every 10 minutes.**
(C) Right down the road.

subway train 지하철

해설 지하철은 얼마나 자주 오나요?
(A) 표가 몇 장 필요하신가요?
(B) 10분마다요.
(C) 길 바로 아래요.

해설 (A) [×] 질문의 subway train(지하철)에서 연상할 수 있는 tickets(표)를 사용하여 혼동을 준 오답이다.
(B) [o] 10분마다라는 말로, 지하철이 오는 빈도를 언급했으므로 정답이다.
(C) [×] 지하철이 얼마나 자주 오는지를 물었는데, 위치로 응답했으므로 오답이다.

07 Why 의문문   캐나다 → 영국

Why are you waiting for Ms. Anderson?
(A) **We need to talk about production rates.**
(B) You can wait by the door.
(C) Yes, tell her for me.

production n. 생산   rate n. 비율   wait v. 기다리다

해설 당신은 왜 Ms. Anderson을 기다리고 있나요?
(A) 우리는 생산율에 대해 논의해야 해요.
(B) 문 옆에서 기다리시면 돼요.
(C) 네, 저 대신 그녀에게 말해 주세요.

해설 (A) [o] 생산율에 대해 논의해야 한다는 말로, Ms. Anderson을 기다리고 있는 이유를 언급했으므로 정답이다.
(B) [×] waiting – wait의 유사 발음 어휘를 사용하여 혼동을 준 오답이다.
(C) [×] 의문사 의문문에 Yes로 응답했으므로 오답이다. 질문의 Ms. Anderson을 나타낼 수 있는 her(그녀)를 사용하여 혼동을 주었다.

08 How 의문문   미국 → 호주

How many chairs do we need for the dinner party?
(A) By invitation only.
(B) Just put them in that room.
(C) **Nine in total.**

invitation n. 초대장   in total 모두 합해서

해설 만찬 모임을 위해 몇 개의 의자가 필요한가요?
(A) 초대장으로만요.
(B) 그것들을 저 방에 두세요.
(C) 모두 합해서 9개요.

해설 (A) [×] 질문의 dinner party(만찬 모임)에서 연상할 수 있는 invitation(초대장)을 사용하여 혼동을 준 오답이다.
(B) [×] 만찬 모임을 위해 얼마나 많은 의자가 필요한지 물었는데, 이와 관련이 없는 그것들을 저 방에 두라는 말로 응답했으므로 오답이다. 질문의 chairs(의자)를 나타낼 수 있는 them(그것들)을 사용하여 혼동을 주었다.
(C) [o] 모두 합해서 9개라는 말로, 필요한 의자의 수를 전달했으므로 정답이다.

09 Why 의문문   캐나다 → 영국

Why was the sales meeting rescheduled?
(A) **Well, the manager didn't give a reason.**
(B) Update the price list.
(C) Be sure to review the agenda.

reschedule v. ~의 일정을 변경하다   give a reason 이유를 대다
price list 가격표   agenda n. 안건, 의제

해설 영업 회의의 일정은 왜 변경되었나요?
(A) 음, 관리자가 이유를 대지 않았어요.
(B) 가격표를 갱신하세요.
(C) 반드시 안건을 검토하세요.

해설 (A) [o] 관리자가 이유를 대지 않았다는 말로, 영업 회의의 일정이 변경된 이유를 모른다는 것을 간접적으로 전달했으므로 정답이다.
(B) [×] 질문의 sales(영업의)에서 연상할 수 있는 판매와 관련된 price list(가격표)를 사용하여 혼동을 준 오답이다.
(C) [×] 질문의 meeting(회의)과 관련 있는 agenda(안건)를 사용하여 혼동을 준 오답이다.

10 How 의문문   미국 → 호주

How did you learn about our research?
(A) **Through a Web site.**
(B) About health products.
(C) A challenging course.

challenging adj. 힘든, 해내기 어려운   course n. 강의, 강좌

해설 당신은 우리의 연구에 대해 어떻게 알게 되었나요?
(A) 웹사이트를 통해서요.
(B) 건강 제품들에 대해서요.
(C) 힘든 강의요.

해설 (A) [o] 웹사이트를 통해서라는 말로, 연구에 대해 알게 된 방법을 언급했으므로 정답이다.

(B) [x] 연구에 대해 어떻게 알게 되었는지를 물었는데, 이와 관련이 없는 건강 제품들에 대해서라는 말로 응답했으므로 오답이다.
(C) [x] 연구에 대해 어떻게 알게 되었는지를 물었는데, 이와 관련이 없는 힘든 강의라는 말로 응답했으므로 오답이다.

11 Why 의문문 　　　　　　　　　　호주 → 영국

Why aren't we beginning the discussion now?
(A) I don't know when it is.
(B) I found it very informative.
(C) We're waiting for Helen.

discussion n. 논의, 토론　informative adj. 유익한

해석 우리는 왜 지금 논의를 시작하지 않고 있나요?
(A) 저는 그게 언제인지 모르겠어요.
(B) 그것이 매우 유익하다고 생각했어요.
(C) 우리는 Helen을 기다리는 중이에요.

해설 (A) [x] 질문의 now(지금)와 관련 있는 when(언제)을 사용하고, discussion(논의)을 나타낼 수 있는 it(그것)을 사용하여 혼동을 준 오답이다.
(B) [x] 질문의 discussion(논의)에서 연상할 수 있는 informative(유익한)를 사용하여 혼동을 준 오답이다.
(C) [o] Helen을 기다리는 중이라는 말로, 논의를 시작하지 않고 있는 이유를 언급했으므로 정답이다.

12 How 의문문 　　　　　　　　　　미국 → 캐나다

How far away is the supermarket from here?
(A) We'll get groceries in an hour.
(B) I'm here until March.
(C) Only five or six blocks.

get v. 사다　grocery n. 식료품

해석 슈퍼마켓은 여기에서 얼마나 멀리 있나요?
(A) 우리는 한 시간 후에 식료품을 살 거예요.
(B) 저는 3월까지 여기에 있어요.
(C) 대여섯 블록밖에 안 돼요.

해설 (A) [x] 질문의 supermarket(슈퍼마켓)과 관련 있는 groceries(식료품)를 사용하여 혼동을 준 오답이다.
(B) [x] 질문의 here를 반복 사용하여 혼동을 준 오답이다.
(C) [o] 대여섯 블록밖에 안 된다는 말로, 슈퍼마켓이 얼마나 멀리 있는지 거리를 언급했으므로 정답이다.

13 Why 의문문 　　　　　　　　　　캐나다 → 호주

Why is the store on North Avenue closed today?
(A) The nearest one is on Broad Street.
(B) Because it's being renovated.
(C) Yes, a notification will be posted.

renovate v. 보수공사하다　notification n. 공지　post v. 게시하다

해석 North가에 있는 매장은 왜 오늘 문을 닫았나요?
(A) 가장 가까운 건 Broad가에 있어요.
(B) 보수공사 중이기 때문이에요.
(C) 네, 공지가 게시될 거예요.

해설 (A) [x] North가에 있는 매장이 왜 오늘 문을 닫았는지를 물었는데, 이와 관련이 없는 가장 가까운 건 Broad가에 있다는 말로 응답했으므로 오답이다. 질문의 store(매장)를 나타낼 수 있는 one(것)을 사용하여 혼동을 주었다.
(B) [o] 보수공사 중이기 때문이라는 말로, North가에 있는 매장이 문을 닫은 이유를 언급했으므로 정답이다.

(C) [x] 의문사 의문문에 Yes로 응답했으므로 오답이다.

14 How 의문문 　　　　　　　　　　미국 → 캐나다

How long will you be visiting your cousin in Hartford?
(A) Only for a few days.
(B) Thanks for visiting me.
(C) Every chance I get.

visit v. 방문하다　chance n. 기회

해석 Hartford에 있는 사촌을 얼마나 오랫동안 방문할 예정인가요?
(A) 며칠 만이요.
(B) 방문해 주셔서 감사합니다.
(C) 기회가 있을 때마다요.

해설 (A) [o] 며칠 만이라는 말로, 사촌을 방문하는 기간을 언급했으므로 정답이다.
(B) [x] 질문의 visiting을 반복 사용하여 혼동을 준 오답이다.
(C) [x] 사촌을 얼마나 오랫동안 방문할 예정인지를 물었는데, 빈도로 응답했으므로 오답이다.

15 Why 의문문 　　　　　　　　　　호주 → 영국

Why hasn't the air conditioner been replaced?
(A) A new order was placed this morning.
(B) The antique is in good condition.
(C) Have you seen the cost estimate?

air conditioner 에어컨　replace v. 교체하다　estimate n. 견적서

해석 에어컨이 왜 교체되지 않았나요?
(A) 오늘 아침에 새 주문이 이루어졌어요.
(B) 골동품이 상태가 좋아요.
(C) 비용 견적서를 보셨나요?

해설 (A) [x] 질문의 replaced(교체되다)에서 연상할 수 있는 제품과 관련된 order(주문)를 사용하여 혼동을 준 오답이다.
(B) [x] conditioner - condition의 유사 발음 어휘를 사용하여 혼동을 준 오답이다.
(C) [o] 비용 견적서를 보았는지 되물어 비용이 비싸서 교체되지 않았음을 간접적으로 전달했으므로 정답이다.

16 How 의문문 　　　　　　　　　　영국 → 캐나다

How's the building design coming along?
(A) From the architectural designer.
(B) The initial draft is nearly complete.
(C) Come early to get a seat, please.

come along 되어 가다　initial adj. 초기의　draft n. 도면, 원고

해석 건물 디자인은 어떻게 되어 가고 있나요?
(A) 건축 디자이너로부터요.
(B) 초기 도면이 거의 다 끝났어요.
(C) 자리를 잡으려면 일찍 오세요.

해설 (A) [x] design - designer의 유사 발음 어휘를 사용하여 혼동을 준 오답이다.
(B) [o] 초안이 거의 다 끝났다는 말로, 건물 디자인이 어떻게 되어 가고 있는지 전달했으므로 정답이다.
(C) [x] coming - Come의 유사 발음 어휘를 사용하여 혼동을 준 오답이다.

17 Why 의문문 　　　　　　　　　　호주 → 미국

Why are the orchestra members meeting tomorrow morning?

(A) Because they need to discuss the season's schedule.
(B) I met with her recently as well.
(C) They loved the performance.

orchestra n. 오케스트라   meet v. 모이다, 만나다   discuss v. 논의하다
schedule n. 일정   recently adv. 최근에   as well 또한
performance n. 공연

해석 오케스트라 회원들은 왜 내일 아침에 모이나요?
(A) 그들은 시즌 일정에 대해 논의할 필요가 있기 때문이에요.
(B) 저 또한 최근에 그녀와 만났어요.
(C) 그들은 그 공연을 좋아했어요.

해설 (A) [o] 시즌 일정에 대해 논의할 필요가 있기 때문이라는 말로, 오케스트라 회원들이 내일 아침에 모이는 이유를 언급했으므로 정답이다.
(B) [x] meeting - met의 유사 발음 어휘를 사용하여 혼동을 준 오답이다.
(C) [x] 질문의 orchestra(오케스트라)와 관련 있는 performance(공연)를 사용하여 혼동을 준 오답이다.

18 How 의문문   🔊 영국 → 미국

How can I watch movies with this streaming app?
(A) I thought the ending was good.
(B) To make space on my phone.
(C) By signing up for a membership.

membership n. 회원권

해석 이 스트리밍 앱으로 어떻게 영화를 볼 수 있나요?
(A) 저는 결말이 좋다고 생각했어요.
(B) 제 휴대전화에 공간을 만들기 위해서요.
(C) 회원 가입을 해서요.

해설 (A) [x] 질문의 movies(영화)와 관련 있는 ending(결말)을 사용하여 혼동을 준 오답이다.
(B) [x] 질문의 app(앱)과 관련 있는 phone(휴대전화)을 사용하여 혼동을 준 오답이다.
(C) [o] 회원 가입을 해서라는 말로, 스트리밍 앱으로 영화를 볼 수 있는 방법을 언급했으므로 정답이다.

19 Why 의문문   🔊 캐나다 → 영국

Why was the publication deadline extended?
(A) Because we found some errors.
(B) They're extending the office hours.
(C) You missed the deadline.

deadline n. 마감일, 기한   extend v. 연장하다

해석 출판 마감일은 왜 연장되었나요?
(A) 우리가 몇몇 오류를 발견했기 때문이에요.
(B) 그들은 근무 시간을 연장하고 있어요.
(C) 당신은 마감일을 놓쳤어요.

해설 (A) [o] 자신들이 몇몇 오류를 발견했기 때문이라는 말로, 마감일이 연장된 이유를 언급했으므로 정답이다.
(B) [x] extended - extending의 유사 발음 어휘를 사용하여 혼동을 준 오답이다.
(C) [x] 질문의 deadline을 반복 사용하여 혼동을 준 오답이다.

20 How 의문문   🔊 미국 → 캐나다

How many volunteers do you need for the expo?
(A) I can be there when it opens.
(B) Three or four would be great.
(C) On Sunday night.

volunteer n. 자원봉사자

해석 박람회를 위해 몇 명의 자원봉사자들이 필요한가요?
(A) 개장할 때 저는 그곳에 있을 수 있어요.
(B) 3명이나 4명이면 좋을 것 같아요.
(C) 일요일 밤에요.

해설 (A) [x] 박람회를 위해 몇 명의 자원봉사자들이 필요한지를 물었는데, 이와 관련이 없는 개장할 때 그곳에 있을 수 있다는 내용으로 응답했으므로 오답이다. 질문의 expo(박람회)를 나타낼 수 있는 it(그것)을 사용하여 혼동을 주었다.
(B) [o] 3명이나 4명이면 좋을 것 같다는 말로, 박람회를 위해 필요한 자원봉사자들의 수를 언급했으므로 정답이다.
(C) [x] 박람회를 위해 몇 명의 자원봉사자들이 필요한지를 물었는데, 시점으로 응답했으므로 오답이다.

21 Why 의문문   🔊 호주 → 미국

Why does your team require additional members?
(A) Because we will have a lot of work.
(B) The personnel manager has the form.
(C) It doesn't charge any extra fees.

additional adj. 추가적인, 추가의   personnel n. 인사과   charge v. 부과하다

해석 당신의 팀은 왜 추가적인 팀원을 필요로 하나요?
(A) 왜냐하면 저희에게 많은 업무가 있을 것이어서요.
(B) 인사 관리자가 양식을 가지고 있어요.
(C) 그것은 추가 요금을 부과하지 않아요.

해설 (A) [o] 자신들에게 많은 업무가 있을 것이라는 말로 추가적인 팀원을 필요로 하는 이유를 언급했으므로 정답이다.
(B) [x] 질문의 members(팀원)와 관련 있는 personnel manager(인사 관리자)를 사용하여 혼동을 준 오답이다.
(C) [x] 질문의 additional(추가적인)과 같은 의미인 extra(추가의)를 사용하여 혼동을 준 오답이다.

22 How 의문문   🔊 영국 → 호주

How much will it cost to repaint the reception area?
(A) I've requested an estimate.
(B) From a new receptionist.
(C) Should we hang the painting here?

repaint v. 다시 칠하다   reception area 접수 구역, 로비   estimate n. 견적

해석 접수 구역을 다시 칠하는 데 비용이 얼마나 들까요?
(A) 제가 견적을 요청했어요.
(B) 새 접수원으로부터요.
(C) 여기에 그림을 걸어야 할까요?

해설 (A) [o] 자신이 견적을 요청했다는 말로, 접수 구역을 다시 칠하는 데 드는 비용이 얼마인지 모른다는 것을 간접적으로 전달했으므로 정답이다.
(B) [x] reception - receptionist의 유사 발음 어휘를 사용하여 혼동을 준 오답이다.
(C) [x] 질문의 repaint(다시 칠하다)에서 연상할 수 있는 painting(그림)을 사용하여 혼동을 준 오답이다.

23 Why 의문문   🔊 호주 → 캐나다

Why was the baseball game canceled?
(A) I'll meet you at the stadium.
(B) My favorite team won the championship.
(C) Because it was raining too heavily.

cancel v. 취소하다   championship n. 선수권 대회

해석 야구 경기가 왜 취소되었나요?
(A) 경기장에서 만나겠습니다.
(B) 제가 좋아하는 팀이 선수권 대회에서 이겼어요.
(C) 비가 너무 많이 내리고 있어서요.

해설 (A) [×] 질문의 baseball game(야구 경기)과 관련 있는 stadium(경기장)을 사용하여 혼동을 준 오답이다.
(B) [×] 질문의 baseball game(야구 경기)에서 연상할 수 있는 championship(선수권 대회)을 사용하여 혼동을 준 오답이다.
(C) [○] 비가 너무 많이 내리고 있어서라는 말로, 야구 경기가 취소된 이유를 언급했으므로 정답이다.

24 How 의문문   미국 → 캐나다

How do our employees feel about the new leave policy?
(A) No one has complained yet.
(B) For about two weeks in June.
(C) My leave was approved.

employee n. 직원   complain v. 불평하다

해석 우리 직원들은 새로운 휴가 정책에 대해 어떻게 생각하나요?
(A) 아직 아무도 불평하지 않았어요.
(B) 6월에 약 2주 동안이요.
(C) 제 휴가가 승인되었어요.

해설 (A) [○] 아직 아무도 불평하지 않았다는 말로, 직원들은 새로운 휴가 정책에 대해 만족하고 있다는 것을 간접적으로 전달했으므로 정답이다.
(B) [×] 직원들은 새로운 휴가 정책에 대해 어떻게 생각하는지를 물었는데, 기간으로 응답했으므로 오답이다.
(C) [×] 질문의 leave를 반복 사용하여 혼동을 준 오답이다.

25 Why 의문문   호주 → 영국

Why did the staff find it difficult to follow the instructions?
(A) Most of the collections.
(B) There were no examples included.
(C) The director of the company.

staff n. 직원   instruction n. 지시, 설명   collection n. 수집품, 소장품
include v. 포함하다   director n. 관리자, 책임자

해석 직원들은 왜 지시 사항들을 따르는 것이 어렵다고 느꼈나요?
(A) 수집품들의 대부분이요.
(B) 아무런 예시들이 포함되어 있지 않았어요.
(C) 그 회사의 관리자요.

해설 (A) [×] 직원들이 지시 사항들을 따르는 것을 어렵다고 느낀 이유를 물었는데, 이와 관련이 없는 수집품들의 대부분이라는 말로 응답했으므로 오답이다.
(B) [○] 아무런 예시들이 포함되어 있지 않았다는 말로, 직원들이 지시 사항들을 따르는 것을 어렵다고 느낀 이유를 언급했으므로 정답이다.
(C) [×] 질문의 staff(직원들)와 관련 있는 director(관리자)를 사용하여 혼동을 준 오답이다.

DAY 06 일반 의문문 및 선택 의문문

1. 일반 의문문

HACKERS PRACTICE   p.63

| 01 (B) | 02 (A) | 03 (B) | 04 (B) | 05 (C) |
| 06 (A) |

01 일반 의문문   호주 → 미국 / 캐나다 → 영국

Did you know that our branch in Portland closed?
(A) The closing ceremony.
(B) No. I wasn't aware of that.
(C) I've only visited the city once.

aware adj. 알고 있는

해석 포틀랜드에 있는 우리 지점이 폐업했다는 것을 알고 있었나요?
(A) 폐막식이요.
(B) 아니요. 저는 그것을 알지 못했어요.
(C) 저는 그 도시를 한 번만 방문했어요.

해설 (A) [×] closed - closing의 유사 발음 어휘를 사용하여 혼동을 준 오답이다.
(B) [○] No로 포틀랜드에 있는 우리 지점이 폐업했다는 것을 알고 있지 못했음을 전달했으므로 정답이다.
(C) [×] 포틀랜드에 있는 지점이 폐업했다는 것을 알고 있었는지를 물었는데, 이와 관련이 없는 자신이 그 도시를 한 번만 방문했다는 말로 응답했으므로 오답이다.

02 일반 의문문   영국 → 호주 / 미국 → 캐나다

Can you attend the company workshop?
(A) Yes. I plan to.
(B) Sometimes I do.
(C) On advertising strategies.

attend v. 참석하다   advertising n. 광고, 광고업

해석 당신은 회사 워크숍에 참석할 수 있나요?
(A) 네, 그럴 계획이에요.
(B) 저는 종종 그래요.
(C) 광고 전략들에 대해서요.

해설 (A) [○] Yes로 회사 워크숍에 참석할 수 있음을 전달했으므로 정답이다.
(B) [×] 질문의 주체인 you를 나타낼 수 있는 I를 사용하고, attend(참석하다)를 나타낼 수 있는 do(하다)를 사용하여 혼동을 준 오답이다.
(C) [×] 질문의 company workshop(회사 워크숍)에서 연상할 수 있는 advertising strategies(광고 전략들)를 사용하여 혼동을 준 오답이다.

03 일반 의문문   캐나다 → 영국 / 호주 → 미국

Is Sarah looking for a part-time job?
(A) I work at a convenience store.
(B) No. She doesn't have time right now.
(C) Fill out this application form.

part-time adj. 시간제의   convenience store 편의점

해석 Sarah는 시간제 일자리를 찾고 있나요?
(A) 저는 편의점에서 일해요.
(B) 아니요. 그녀는 지금 시간이 없어요.
(C) 이 지원서를 작성하세요.

해설 (A) [x] 질문의 part-time job(시간제 일자리)에서 연상할 수 있는 convenience store(편의점)를 사용하여 혼동을 준 오답이다.
(B) [o] No로 Sarah는 시간제 일자리를 찾고 있지 않음을 전달한 후, 그녀는 지금 시간이 없다는 부연 설명을 했으므로 정답이다.
(C) [x] 질문의 part-time job(시간제 일자리)과 관련 있는 application form(지원서)을 사용하여 혼동을 준 오답이다.

04 일반 의문문 　　미국 → 캐나다 / 영국 → 호주

Have you chosen a color for the carpet?
(A) My car is parked over there.
(B) I was hoping you could help me.
(C) Oh, that color really suits you.

suit v. 어울리다

해석 카펫 색상을 선택하셨나요?
(A) 제 차는 저기에 주차되어 있어요.
(B) 당신이 저를 도와줄 수 있기를 바라고 있었어요.
(C) 아, 그 색상이 당신에게 정말 잘 어울려요.

해설 (A) [x] carpet - car의 유사 발음 어휘를 사용하여 혼동을 준 오답이다.
(B) [o] 당신이 도와줄 수 있기를 바라고 있었다는 말로, 카펫 색상을 선택하지 못했다는 것을 간접적으로 전달했으므로 정답이다.
(C) [x] 질문의 color를 반복 사용하여 혼동을 준 오답이다.

05 일반 의문문 　　호주 → 영국 / 캐나다 → 미국

Are you thinking of taking a course abroad?
(A) It's somewhere in Sydney.
(B) A return ticket, please.
(C) I can't really afford to.

abroad adv. 해외에서, 해외로　　return ticket 왕복표
afford to ~할 여유가 있다, ~할 형편이 된다

해석 당신은 해외에서 수업을 들을 생각이 있나요?
(A) 그것은 시드니 어딘가에 있어요.
(B) 왕복표를 주세요.
(C) 저는 그럴 여유가 없어요.

해설 (A) [x] 질문의 abroad(해외에서)와 관련 있는 Sydney(시드니)를 사용하여 혼동을 준 오답이다.
(B) [x] 질문의 abroad(해외에서)와 관련 있는 return ticket(왕복표)을 사용하여 혼동을 준 오답이다.
(C) [o] 그럴 여유가 없다는 말로 해외에서 수업을 들을 생각이 없음을 간접적으로 전달했으므로 정답이다.

06 일반 의문문 　　미국 → 캐나다 / 영국 → 호주

Do you want to review the agreement before we sign it?
(A) Let me see it.
(B) Oh, the view is lovely.
(C) It is the first contract he's written.

agreement n. 계약서

해석 당신은 우리가 계약서에 서명을 하기 전에 검토하기를 원하세요?
(A) 그것을 보여 주세요.
(B) 아, 전망이 아름답네요.
(C) 그것은 그가 작성한 첫 번째 계약서예요.

해설 (A) [o] 그것을 보여 달라는 말로, 계약서에 서명을 하기 전에 검토하기를 원한다는 것을 전달했으므로 정답이다.
(B) [x] review - view의 유사 발음 어휘를 사용하여 혼동을 준 오답이다.
(C) [x] 질문의 agreement(계약서)와 같은 의미인 contract(계약서)를 사용하여 혼동을 준 오답이다.

2. 선택 의문문

HACKERS PRACTICE p.65

01 (A)　　02 (A)　　03 (A)　　04 (B)　　05 (A)
06 (C)

01 선택 의문문 　　영국 → 호주 / 미국 → 캐나다

Would you like to sit inside the café or on the patio?
(A) I'm fine with either.
(B) How about ordering some coffee?
(C) The line was really long.

patio n. 파티오(보통 집 뒤쪽에 만드는 테라스)　　order v. 주문하다

해석 카페 내부에 앉고 싶으세요, 아니면 파티오에 앉고 싶으세요?
(A) 어느 쪽이든 괜찮아요.
(B) 커피를 주문하는 게 어때요?
(C) 줄이 정말 길었어요.

해설 (A) [o] 어느 쪽이든 괜찮다는 말로, 둘 다 선택했으므로 정답이다.
(B) [x] 질문의 café(카페)와 관련 있는 coffee(커피)를 사용하여 혼동을 준 오답이다.
(C) [x] 카페 내부에 앉고 싶은지 파티오에 앉고 싶은지를 물었는데, 이와 관련이 없는 줄이 정말 길었다는 말로 응답했으므로 오답이다.

02 선택 의문문 　　호주 → 미국 / 캐나다 → 영국

Will you call a taxi, or should I?
(A) Let's take the bus.
(B) A fare of 15 dollars.
(C) Ask the driver about that.

fare n. 요금

해석 당신이 택시를 부를 건가요, 아니면 제가 불러야 할까요?
(A) 버스를 탑시다.
(B) 15달러의 요금이에요.
(C) 그것에 대해 운전사에게 물어보세요.

해설 (A) [o] 버스를 타자는 말로, 자신이 택시를 부르는 것과 상대방이 택시를 부르는 것 둘 다 선택하지 않은 정답이다.
(B) [x] 질문의 taxi(택시)와 관련 있는 fare(요금)를 사용하여 혼동을 준 오답이다.
(C) [x] 질문의 taxi(택시)와 관련 있는 driver(운전사)를 사용하여 혼동을 준 오답이다.

03 선택 의문문 　　영국 → 미국 / 미국 → 영국

Should we close the deal on Thursday or Friday?
(A) We need to confirm with the client.
(B) Yes, that sounds perfect.
(C) Do you need my payment details?

close the deal 거래·협상을 마무리하다　　confirm v. 확인하다

해석 거래를 목요일에 마무리할까요, 아니면 금요일에 마무리할까요?
(A) 고객에게 확인해야 해요.
(B) 네, 그거 좋네요.
(C) 제 지급 세부 정보가 필요하신가요?

해설 (A) [o] 고객에게 확인해야 한다는 말로, 목요일과 금요일 둘 다 선택하지 않은 정답이다.
(B) [x] 선택 의문문에 Yes로 응답했으므로 오답이다.
(C) [x] 거래를 목요일에 마무리할지 금요일에 마무리할지를 물었는데,

DAY 06 일반 의문문 및 선택 의문문　29

이와 관련이 없는 자신의 지급 세부 정보가 필요하냐고 물었으므로 오답이다.

04 선택 의문문 캐나다 → 영국 / 호주 → 미국

Is the air conditioner being fixed today or tomorrow?
(A) Pass me the remote control.
(B) It'll be done after lunch today.
(C) It's really hot this summer.

fix v. 수리하다, 고치다 remote control 리모컨

해석 에어컨이 오늘 수리되나요, 아니면 내일 수리되나요?
(A) 리모컨을 건네주세요.
(B) 오늘 점심 이후에 완료될 거예요.
(C) 올여름은 정말 덥네요.

해설 (A) [x] 질문의 air conditioner(에어컨)와 관련 있는 remote control (리모컨)을 사용하여 혼동을 준 오답이다.
(B) [o] 오늘 점심 이후에 완료될 것이라는 말로, 에어컨이 오늘 수리될 것임을 선택했으므로 정답이다.
(C) [x] 질문의 air conditioner(에어컨)에서 연상할 수 있는 hot(더운)을 사용하여 혼동을 준 오답이다.

05 선택 의문문 미국 → 캐나다 / 영국 → 호주

Do you want to go cycling or hiking this weekend?
(A) I'd like to relax at home.
(B) Lock your bike up over there.
(C) The trail is two kilometers long.

lock up 자물쇠로 잠그다 trail n. 등산로, 오솔길

해석 이번 주말에 자전거를 타러 가고 싶으세요, 아니면 하이킹을 하러 가고 싶으세요?
(A) 집에서 쉬고 싶어요.
(B) 자전거를 저기에 자물쇠로 잠그세요.
(C) 등산로는 2킬로미터예요.

해설 (A) [o] 집에서 쉬고 싶다는 말로, 자전거를 타러 가는 것과 하이킹을 하러 가는 것 둘 다 선택하지 않은 정답이다.
(B) [x] 질문의 cycling(자전거를 타다)과 관련 있는 bike(자전거)를 사용하여 혼동을 준 오답이다.
(C) [x] 질문의 hiking(하이킹을 하다)과 관련 있는 trail(등산로)을 사용하여 혼동을 준 오답이다.

06 선택 의문문 캐나다 → 호주 / 호주 → 캐나다

Should I buy this tablet or a different one?
(A) I downloaded several books.
(B) I already have this model.
(C) It depends on the features you want.

model n. 모델, 모형 feature n. 기능, 특징

해석 이 태블릿을 사야 할까요, 아니면 다른 모델을 사야 할까요?
(A) 저는 여러 책을 다운로드했어요.
(B) 저는 이미 이 모델을 가지고 있어요.
(C) 그것은 당신이 원하는 기능에 달려 있어요.

해설 (A) [x] 질문의 tablet(태블릿)에서 연상할 수 있는 downloaded(다운로드했다)를 사용하여 혼동을 준 오답이다.
(B) [x] 질문의 tablet(태블릿)과 관련 있는 model(모델)을 사용하여 혼동을 준 오답이다.
(C) [o] 그것은 당신이 원하는 기능에 달려 있다는 말로, 이 태블릿과 다른 모델 둘 다 선택하지 않은 정답이다.

HACKERS TEST p.66

01 (B)	02 (B)	03 (A)	04 (B)	05 (B)
06 (C)	07 (B)	08 (C)	09 (B)	10 (A)
11 (C)	12 (A)	13 (B)	14 (B)	15 (B)
16 (B)	17 (A)	18 (A)	19 (A)	20 (A)
21 (C)	22 (C)	23 (A)	24 (B)	25 (A)

01 일반 의문문 미국 → 호주

Can we get a discount at the amusement park?
(A) On that ride.
(B) Yes. I have a coupon.
(C) To the nearby park.

discount n. 할인 ride n. 놀이 기구

해석 우리가 놀이공원에서 할인을 받을 수 있나요?
(A) 저 놀이 기구 위에요.
(B) 네. 저는 쿠폰이 있어요.
(C) 가까운 공원으로요.

해설 (A) [x] 질문의 amusement park(놀이공원)와 관련 있는 ride(놀이 기구)를 사용하여 혼동을 준 오답이다.
(B) [o] Yes로 놀이공원에서 할인을 받을 수 있음을 전달한 후, 쿠폰이 있다는 부연 설명을 했으므로 정답이다.
(C) [x] 질문의 park를 반복 사용하여 혼동을 준 오답이다.

02 선택 의문문 캐나다 → 영국

Should I call the CEO or meet with her?
(A) No, it's quite cool outside.
(B) You'd better see her in person.
(C) It was a pleasure to meet you.

quite adv. 꽤, 상당히 had better (~하는 것이) 좋을 것이다 in person 직접
pleasure n. 영광, 기쁨

해석 제가 최고경영자에게 전화를 해야 하나요, 아니면 만나야 하나요?
(A) 아니요, 밖은 꽤 시원합니다.
(B) 당신은 그녀를 직접 보는 게 좋을 거예요.
(C) 당신을 만나 뵙게 되어 영광이었어요.

해설 (A) [x] 선택 의문문에 No로 응답했으므로 오답이다. call - cool의 유사 발음 어휘를 사용하여 혼동을 주었다.
(B) [o] 직접 보는 게 좋을 것이라는 말로, 만나는 것을 선택했으므로 정답이다.
(C) [x] 질문의 meet을 반복 사용하여 혼동을 준 오답이다.

03 일반 의문문 영국 → 호주

Does the shop stay open all night?
(A) No. It closes at midnight.
(B) Yes, here's the booking form.
(C) It takes five minutes to get to the station.

midnight n. 자정 booking n. 예약 station n. 역

해석 그 상점은 밤새 열려 있나요?
(A) 아니요. 자정에 문을 닫아요.
(B) 네, 여기 예약 양식이 있어요.
(C) 역까지 가는 데 5분이 걸려요.

해설 (A) [o] No로 상점이 밤새 열려 있지 않음을 전달한 후, 자정에 문을 닫는다는 부연 설명을 했으므로 정답이다.

(B) [x] 상점이 밤새 열려 있는지를 물었는데, 이와 관련이 없는 예약 양식이 있다고 응답했으므로 오답이다. Yes만 듣고 정답으로 고르지 않도록 주의한다.
(C) [x] 상점이 밤새 열려 있는지를 물었는데, 이와 관련이 없는 역까지 가는 데 5분이 걸린다고 응답했으므로 오답이다.

04 선택 의문문 〔캐나다 → 미국〕

Would you like to have the meeting on Thursday or Friday?
(A) A detailed assessment.
(B) Friday's fine.
(C) I submitted that yesterday.

detailed adj. 상세한   assessment n. 평가   submit v. 제출하다

해석 회의를 목요일에 하는 것이 좋으신가요, 아니면 금요일에 하는 것이 좋으신가요?
(A) 상세한 평가요.
(B) 금요일이 좋아요.
(C) 저는 그것을 어제 제출했어요.

해설 (A) [x] 질문의 meeting(회의)에서 연상할 수 있는 assessment(평가)를 사용하여 혼동을 준 오답이다.
(B) [o] 금요일이 좋다는 말로, 금요일을 선택했으므로 정답이다.
(C) [x] 질문의 Thursday or Friday(목요일 아니면 금요일)와 관련 있는 yesterday(어제)를 사용하여 혼동을 준 오답이다.

05 일반 의문문 〔영국 → 캐나다〕

Are you willing to work on weekends if necessary?
(A) I usually leave by six.
(B) Sorry, I can't.
(C) I really enjoyed it.

on weekends 주말에, 주말마다   enjoy v. 즐기다

해석 만약 필요하다면 주말에 일할 의향이 있나요?
(A) 저는 보통 6시에는 퇴근해요.
(B) 죄송해요, 저는 그럴 수 없어요.
(C) 저는 그것을 정말 즐겼어요.

해설 (A) [x] 만약 필요하다면 주말에 일할 의향이 있는지를 물었는데, 이와 관련이 없는 보통 6시에는 퇴근한다고 응답했으므로 오답이다. 질문의 work(일하다)에서 연상할 수 있는 직장과 관련된 leave(퇴근하다)를 사용하여 혼동을 주었다.
(B) [o] Sorry로 주말에 일할 의향이 없음을 전달한 후, 그럴 수 없다는 부연 설명을 했으므로 정답이다.
(C) [x] 만약 필요하다면 주말에 일할 의향이 있는지를 물었는데, 이와 관련이 없는 그것을 정말 즐겼다고 응답했으므로 오답이다.

06 선택 의문문 〔미국 → 호주〕

Are you looking for the same brand of vehicle or a different one?
(A) Many great features.
(B) I paid with credit card.
(C) The same brand.

vehicle n. 차량   feature n. 기능, 특징

해석 같은 브랜드의 차량을 찾고 계신가요, 아니면 다른 브랜드를 찾고 계신가요?
(A) 여러 훌륭한 기능들이요.
(B) 신용카드로 결제했어요.
(C) 같은 브랜드요.

해설 (A) [x] 질문의 vehicle(차량)에서 연상할 수 있는 features(기능들)를 사용하여 혼동을 준 오답이다.
(B) [x] 같은 브랜드의 차량을 찾고 있는지 다른 브랜드를 찾고 있는지를 물었는데, 이와 관련이 없는 신용카드로 결제했다고 응답했으므로 오답이다.
(C) [o] 같은 브랜드라는 말로, 같은 브랜드의 차량을 선택했으므로 정답이다.

07 일반 의문문 〔영국 → 미국〕

Is your assistant giving a presentation this afternoon?
(A) Join the weekly meeting.
(B) No. Not today.
(C) By the marketing team.

assistant n. 조수, 보조

해석 당신의 조수가 오늘 오후에 발표를 하나요?
(A) 주간 회의에 참여하세요.
(B) 아니요. 오늘은 아니에요.
(C) 마케팅팀에 의해서요.

해설 (A) [x] 질문의 presentation(발표)에서 연상할 수 있는 meeting(회의)을 사용하여 혼동을 준 오답이다.
(B) [o] No로 조수가 오늘 오후에 발표를 하지 않음을 전달했으므로 정답이다.
(C) [x] 조수가 오늘 오후에 발표를 하는지를 물었는데, 이와 관련이 없는 마케팅팀에 의해서라고 응답했으므로 오답이다.

08 선택 의문문 〔호주 → 영국〕

Do you want to take a break, or are you able to keep working?
(A) I'll take two, please.
(B) No, we worked on it before.
(C) I'm a little tired, actually.

break n. 휴식, 중단

해석 당신은 휴식을 취하고 싶나요, 아니면 계속 일할 수 있나요?
(A) 두 개 주세요.
(B) 아니요, 우리는 전에 그것을 작업했어요.
(C) 사실은, 좀 피곤해요.

해설 (A) [x] 질문의 take를 반복 사용하여 혼동을 준 오답이다.
(B) [x] working – worked의 유사 발음 어휘를 사용하여 혼동을 준 오답이다.
(C) [o] 좀 피곤하다는 말로, 휴식을 취하는 것을 간접적으로 선택했으므로 정답이다.

09 일반 의문문 〔미국 → 호주〕

Does the hotel have a swimming pool?
(A) No. But it's close to the beach.
(B) A free room upgrade.
(C) Make the booking online.

beach n. 해변

해석 호텔에 수영장이 있나요?
(A) 아니요. 하지만 해변에 가까워요.
(B) 무료 객실 업그레이드요.
(C) 온라인으로 예약하세요.

해설 (A) [o] No로 호텔에 수영장이 없음을 전달한 후, 하지만 호텔이 해변에 가깝다는 부연 설명을 했으므로 정답이다.
(B) [x] 질문의 hotel(호텔)과 관련 있는 room upgrade(객실 업그레이

드)를 사용하여 혼동을 준 오답이다.
(C) [×] 질문의 hotel(호텔)과 관련 있는 booking(예약)을 사용하여 혼동을 준 오답이다.

10 선택 의문문 호주 → 미국

Do you take credit card or only cash?
(A) Both are acceptable.
(B) The total is 19 dollars.
(C) Here's your receipt.

credit card 신용카드 acceptable adj. 받아들일 수 있는 total n. 총액
receipt n. 영수증

해석 신용카드를 받으시나요, 아니면 현금만 받으시나요?
  (A) 둘 다 받을 수 있어요.
  (B) 총액은 19달러예요.
  (C) 여기 당신의 영수증이요.
해설 (A) [○] 둘 다 받을 수 있다는 말로, 신용카드와 현금 둘 다 선택했으므로 정답이다.
  (B) [×] 질문의 cash(현금)와 관련 있는 total(총액)을 사용하여 혼동을 준 오답이다.
  (C) [×] 질문의 credit card(신용카드)와 관련 있는 receipt(영수증)를 사용하여 혼동을 준 오답이다.

11 일반 의문문 미국 → 캐나다

Did you see our new billboard?
(A) To advertise our products.
(B) Oh, I'm still on the board.
(C) Yes. On the Seaward Building.

billboard n. 광고판, 게시판

해석 우리의 새 광고판을 보았나요?
  (A) 제품을 광고하기 위해서요.
  (B) 아, 저는 아직 이사회에 있어요.
  (C) 네, Seaward 건물에서요.
해설 (A) [×] 질문의 billboard(광고판)와 관련 있는 advertise(광고하다)를 사용하여 혼동을 준 오답이다.
  (B) [×] billboard - board의 유사 발음 어휘를 사용하여 혼동을 준 오답이다.
  (C) [○] Yes로 새 광고판을 보았음을 전달한 후, Seaward 건물에서라는 부연 설명을 했으므로 정답이다.

12 선택 의문문 호주 → 미국

Will Robert attend the seminar, or will he be out of town?
(A) He should be able to go.
(B) It was held downtown.
(C) A list of invited speakers.

out of town 도시를 떠난 speaker n. 연사, 발표자

해석 Robert는 세미나에 참석할 건가요, 아니면 도시를 떠나 있을 건가요?
  (A) 그는 갈 수 있을 거예요.
  (B) 그것은 시내에서 열렸어요.
  (C) 초청 연사 명단이요.
해설 (A) [○] 그가 갈 수 있을 거라는 말로, 세미나에 참석하는 것을 선택했으므로 정답이다.
  (B) [×] town - downtown의 유사 발음 어휘를 사용하여 혼동을 준 오답이다.
  (C) [×] 질문의 seminar(세미나)와 관련 있는 speakers(연사)를 사용하여 혼동을 준 오답이다.

13 일반 의문문 영국 → 캐나다

Are there still tickets available for the concert on Friday?
(A) At the music hall.
(B) They are sold out.
(C) An hour-long show.

sold out 매진된

해석 금요일 콘서트 표가 아직 구매 가능한가요?
  (A) 음악회장에서요.
  (B) 그것들은 매진되었어요.
  (C) 한 시간짜리 공연이에요.
해설 (A) [×] 질문의 concert(콘서트)와 관련 있는 music hall(음악회장)을 사용하여 혼동을 준 오답이다.
  (B) [○] 그것들은 매진되었다는 말로, 금요일 콘서트 표가 남아있지 않음을 전달했으므로 정답이다.
  (C) [×] 질문의 concert(콘서트)와 관련 있는 show(공연)를 사용하여 혼동을 준 오답이다.

14 선택 의문문 캐나다 → 미국

Are you going to prepare the food yourself or have it catered?
(A) With delicious food.
(B) My friend will make it.
(C) They need specific dates.

cater v. (가게 등이) 음식을 제공하다 specific adj. 특정한

해석 당신이 음식을 직접 준비할 건가요, 아니면 그것을 제공받을 건가요?
  (A) 맛있는 음식과 함께요.
  (B) 제 친구가 만들거예요.
  (C) 그들은 특정 날짜를 필요로 해요.
해설 (A) [×] 질문의 food를 반복 사용하여 혼동을 준 오답이다.
  (B) [○] 친구가 만들 것이라는 말로, 음식을 직접 준비하는 것과 제공받는 것 둘 다 선택하지 않은 정답이다.
  (C) [×] 질문의 prepare(준비하다)에서 연상할 수 있는 need(필요로 하다)를 사용하여 혼동을 준 오답이다.

15 일반 의문문 미국 → 영국

Do you plan on advertising the new product?
(A) The busiest month of the year.
(B) Yes. We will run TV commercials.
(C) Well, about the recruitment plans.

plan v. 계획하다; n. 계획 advertise v. 광고하다
commercial n. 광고; adj. 상업의

해석 당신의 신제품을 광고할 계획이세요?
  (A) 일 년 중 가장 바쁜 달이요.
  (B) 네, 우리는 TV 광고를 내보낼 거예요.
  (C) 음, 채용 계획에 대해서요.
해설 (A) [×] 신제품을 광고할 계획인지 물었는데, 이와 관련이 없는 일 년 중 가장 바쁜 달이라는 말로 응답했으므로 오답이다.
  (B) [○] Yes로 신제품을 광고할 계획임을 전달한 후, TV 광고를 내보낼 것이라는 부연 설명을 했으므로 정답이다.
  (C) [×] 질문의 plan을 plans로 반복 사용하여 혼동을 준 오답이다.

16 선택 의문문 캐나다 → 영국

Do we need to pay the bill today, or can we do it later?
(A) Including tax.

(B) Either is fine.
(C) Try not to arrive late.

pay v. 지불하다, 보수를 지급하다   bill n. 청구서   include v. 포함하다
tax n. 세금

해석 우리가 청구서를 지불해야 할까요, 아니면 나중에 해도 되나요?
(A) 세금을 포함해서요.
(B) 둘 중 어느 쪽이든 괜찮아요.
(C) 늦게 도착하지 않도록 해보세요.

해설 (A) [x] 질문의 bill(청구서)과 관련 있는 tax(세금)를 사용하여 혼동을 준 오답이다.
(B) [o] 둘 중 어느 쪽이든 괜찮다는 말로, 둘 다 선택했으므로 정답이다.
(C) [x] later – late의 유사 발음 어휘를 사용하여 혼동을 준 오답이다.

17 일반 의문문   영국 → 호주

Have you read the notice from the president yet?
(A) What is it about?
(B) He just went to his office.
(C) Just press that button.

notice n. 공지; v. 주목하다   president n. 회장, 대통령
press v. 누르다

해석 회장님의 공지를 이미 읽어봤나요?
(A) 무엇에 관한 것이죠?
(B) 그는 방금 그의 사무실로 갔어요.
(C) 그냥 그 버튼을 누르세요.

해설 (A) [o] 공지가 무엇에 관한 것인지를 되물어 아직 공지를 읽지 않았음을 간접적으로 전달했으므로 정답이다.
(B) [x] 질문의 president(회장)와 관련 있는 office(사무실)를 사용하여 혼동을 준 오답이다.
(C) [x] president – press that의 유사 발음 어휘를 사용하여 혼동을 준 오답이다.

18 선택 의문문   호주 → 캐나다

Is Carol leading today's yoga class, or is Dan?
(A) It has been canceled, actually.
(B) A certified fitness coach.
(C) I was just reading about that.

lead v. 진행하다, 이끌다   certified adj. 공인된, 인증받은

해석 Carol이 오늘 요가 수업을 진행하나요, 아니면 Dan인가요?
(A) 사실, 그건 취소되었어요.
(B) 공인된 운동 코치요.
(C) 저는 방금 그것에 대해 읽고 있었어요.

해설 (A) [o] 사실 그건 취소되었다는 말로, 둘 중 누구도 요가 수업을 진행하지 않을 것임을 간접적으로 전달했으므로 정답이다.
(B) [x] 질문의 yoga class(요가 수업)와 관련 있는 fitness coach(운동 코치)를 사용하여 혼동을 준 오답이다.
(C) [x] leading – reading의 유사 발음 어휘를 사용하여 혼동을 준 오답이다.

19 일반 의문문   미국 → 호주

Has Donald found a position at another company?
(A) No. He's still looking for one.
(B) To attend an upcoming job fair.
(C) That's the correct position.

position n. 직장, 위치   upcoming adj. 다가오는   correct adj. 맞는

해석 Donald가 다른 회사에 직장을 구했나요?
(A) 아니요. 그는 아직도 찾고 있어요.
(B) 다가오는 직업 박람회에 참석하기 위해서요.
(C) 거기가 맞는 위치예요.

해설 (A) [o] No로 Donald가 다른 회사에 직장을 구하지 못했음을 전달한 후, 아직도 찾고 있다는 부연 설명을 했으므로 정답이다.
(B) [x] 질문의 position(직장)과 관련 있는 job fair(직업 박람회)를 사용하여 혼동을 준 오답이다.
(C) [x] 질문의 position(직장)을 '위치'라는 의미의 명사로 반복 사용하여 혼동을 준 오답이다.

20 선택 의문문   캐나다 → 미국

Would you like to meet for lunch or dinner on Thursday?
(A) How about breakfast instead?
(B) A very healthy dish.
(C) That's a great choice.

healthy adj. 건강에 좋은, 건강한   dish n. 요리   choice n. 선택

해석 목요일에 점심 식사를 위해 만나고 싶은가요, 아니면 저녁 식사를 위해 만나고 싶은가요?
(A) 대신에 아침 식사는 어때요?
(B) 매우 건강에 좋은 요리요.
(C) 그건 좋은 선택이에요.

해설 (A) [o] 대신에 아침 식사는 어떠냐는 말로, 점심 식사와 저녁 식사 둘 다 선택하지 않은 정답이다.
(B) [x] 질문의 lunch or dinner(점심 식사 또는 저녁 식사)와 관련 있는 dish(요리)를 사용하여 혼동을 준 오답이다.
(C) [x] 목요일에 점심 식사를 위해 만나고 싶은지 저녁 식사를 위해 만나고 싶은지를 물었는데, 이와 관련이 없는 그건 좋은 선택이라는 말로 응답했으므로 오답이다.

21 일반 의문문   영국 → 호주

Are you looking to buy car insurance?
(A) The car needs some new parts.
(B) Look in the trunk first.
(C) Thanks, but I don't need any.

look to ~을 생각해 보다   buy insurance 보험에 가입하다   part n. 부품

해석 자동차 보험에 가입하는 것을 생각해 보고 있나요?
(A) 그 차는 새로운 부품들이 필요해요.
(B) 트렁크를 먼저 들여다보세요.
(C) 감사합니다만, 전 필요하지 않아요.

해설 (A) [x] 질문의 car를 반복 사용하고, car(자동차)와 관련 있는 parts(부품들)를 사용하여 혼동을 준 오답이다.
(B) [x] looking – Look in의 유사 발음 어휘를 사용하고, car(자동차)와 관련 있는 trunk(트렁크)를 사용하여 혼동을 준 오답이다.
(C) [o] 고맙지만 필요하지 않다는 말로 자동차 보험에 가입하는 것을 생각해 보고 있지 않다는 것을 간접적으로 전달했으므로 정답이다.

22 선택 의문문   캐나다 → 영국

Should I give you a tour of the property, or do you want to look around yourself?
(A) To purchase a home.
(B) We enjoyed the tour.
(C) Whatever you prefer.

give a tour of ~을 구경시켜 주다   property n. 건물   look around 둘러보다

해석 제가 건물을 구경시켜 드릴까요, 아니면 당신 혼자서 둘러보시겠어요?

(A) 집을 구매하기 위해서요.
(B) 우리는 관광을 즐겼어요.
(C) 당신이 선호하는 대로요.

해설 (A) [x] 질문의 property(건물)에서 연상할 수 있는 home(집)을 사용하여 혼동을 준 오답이다.
(B) [x] 질문의 tour를 반복 사용하여 혼동을 준 오답이다.
(C) [o] 당신이 선호하는 대로라는 말로, 둘 다 선택했으므로 정답이다.

23 일반 의문문 　　　　　　　　　　　　　🔊 영국 → 캐나다

Is Ms. Chen transferring to our overseas branch office?
(A) That's what I heard.
(B) No, the bank transferred the funds.
(C) She used to live in my neighborhood.

transfer v. 전근 가다, 이체하다　overseas adj. 해외의

해석 Ms. Chen이 해외 지사로 전근을 가나요?
(A) 저는 그렇게 들었어요.
(B) 아니요, 은행이 자금을 이체했어요.
(C) 그녀는 제 근처에 살았어요.

해설 (A) [o] 그렇게 들었다는 말로, Ms. Chen이 해외 지사로 전근을 갈 것임을 전달했으므로 정답이다.
(B) [x] 질문의 transferring(전근 가다)을 '이체하다'라는 의미의 동사로 반복 사용하여 혼동을 준 오답이다.
(C) [x] Ms. Chen이 해외 지사로 전근을 가는지를 물었는데, 이와 관련이 없는 그녀가 자신의 근처에 살았다고 응답했으므로 오답이다. 질문의 Ms. Chen을 나타낼 수 있는 She(그녀)를 사용하여 혼동을 주었다.

24 선택 의문문 　　　　　　　　　　　　　🔊 캐나다 → 호주

Does the client want the device installed or just left at reception?
(A) Several clients complained.
(B) I'm waiting to hear back.
(C) We will hire a receptionist.

install v. 설치하다　reception n. 접수처　complain v. 불평하다
receptionist n. 접수원

해석 고객이 장치가 설치되기를 원하나요, 아니면 그냥 접수처에 놔두길 원하나요?
(A) 여러 고객들이 불평했어요.
(B) 회신을 기다리고 있어요.
(C) 우리는 접수원을 고용할 거예요.

해설 (A) [x] 질문의 client를 clients로 반복 사용하여 혼동을 준 오답이다.
(B) [o] 회신을 기다리고 있다는 말로, 고객이 장치가 설치되기를 원하는지 그냥 접수처에 놔두길 원하는지 모른다는 것을 간접적으로 전달했으므로 정답이다.
(C) [x] reception - receptionist의 유사 발음 어휘를 사용하여 혼동을 준 오답이다.

25 선택 의문문 　　　　　　　　　　　　　🔊 미국 → 호주

Do you have a copy of the report, or should I print one?
(A) There's an extra one on my desk.
(B) Report to my supervisor.
(C) The printer was delivered.

deliver v. 배달하다

해석 당신은 보고서의 사본을 가지고 있나요, 아니면 제가 한 부를 출력해야 하나요?
(A) 제 책상 위에 여분의 것이 있어요.
(B) 제 상사에게 보고해 주세요.
(C) 프린터가 배달되었어요.

해설 (A) [o] 책상 위에 여분의 것이 있다는 말로, 사본을 가지고 있는 것을 선택했으므로 정답이다.
(B) [x] 질문의 report(보고서)를 '보고하다'라는 의미의 동사로 사용하여 혼동을 준 오답이다.
(C) [x] print - printer의 유사 발음 어휘를 사용하여 혼동을 준 오답이다.

DAY 07 부정 의문문 및 부가 의문문

1. 부정 의문문

HACKERS PRACTICE 　　　　　　　　　　　　p.69

01 (B)　02 (C)　03 (C)　04 (A)　05 (C)
06 (A)

01 부정 의문문 　　　　　　　　　🔊 영국 → 호주 / 미국 → 캐나다

Doesn't the company have a policy on overtime?
(A) At the human resources department.
(B) Yes, up to 10 hours per week.
(C) To discuss the new project schedule.

policy n. 정책　overtime n. 초과 근무

해석 회사에 초과 근무에 관한 정책이 있지 않나요?
(A) 인사부에서요.
(B) 네, 일주일에 최대 10시간이요.
(C) 새 프로젝트 일정을 논의하기 위해서요.

해설 (A) [x] 질문의 company(회사)와 관련 있는 human resources department(인사부)를 사용하여 혼동을 준 오답이다.
(B) [o] Yes로 회사에 초과 근무에 관한 정책이 있음을 전달한 후, 일주일에 최대 10시간이라는 부연 설명을 했으므로 정답이다.
(C) [x] 질문의 company(회사)와 관련 있는 project schedule(프로젝트 일정)을 사용하여 혼동을 준 오답이다.

02 부정 의문문 　　　　　　　　　🔊 캐나다 → 영국 / 호주 → 미국

Didn't the manager approve the purchase?
(A) Thanks, I left it on my desk.
(B) The store is on Elm Street.
(C) Yes. I'll place the order now.

approve v. 승인하다　purchase n. 구매

해석 관리자가 구매를 승인하지 않았나요?
(A) 감사합니다, 제 책상 위에 두었어요.
(B) 그 가게는 Elm가에 있어요.
(C) 네. 제가 지금 주문할게요.

해설 (A) [x] 관리자가 구매를 승인하지 않았는지를 물었는데, 이와 관련이 없는 책상 위에 두고 왔다고 응답했으므로 오답이다.
(B) [x] 질문의 purchase(구매)에서 연상할 수 있는 store(가게)를 사용하여 혼동을 준 오답이다.
(C) [o] Yes로 관리자가 구매를 승인했다고 전달한 후, 자신이 지금 주문할 것이라고 부연 설명을 했으므로 정답이다.

03 부정 의문문
미국 → 캐나다 / 영국 → 호주

Wasn't our photocopier repaired today?
(A) I'm glad you could fix it.
(B) Take a look at this picture.
(C) Are you having a problem using it?

photocopier n. 복사기 repair v. 수리하다, 고치다 fix v. 수리하다, 고치다

해석 우리 복사기가 오늘 수리되지 않았나요?
(A) 당신이 그것을 수리할 수 있어서 기쁘네요.
(B) 이 사진을 한번 보세요.
(C) 그것을 사용하는 데 문제가 있나요?

해설 (A) [x] 질문의 repaired(수리하다)와 같은 의미인 fix(수리하다)를 사용하여 혼동을 준 오답이다.
(B) [x] 질문의 photocopier(복사기)에서 연상할 수 있는 picture(사진)를 사용하여 혼동을 준 오답이다.
(C) [o] 그것을 사용하는 데 문제가 있는지 되물어, 복사기가 수리되었는 것을 간접적으로 전달했으므로 정답이다.

04 부정 의문문
호주 → 미국 / 캐나다 → 영국

Haven't we hired too many workers?
(A) No. We need even more.
(B) The workspace over there.
(C) I already interviewed him.

hire v. 고용하다 workspace n. 작업 공간

해석 우리가 너무 많은 근로자들을 고용하지 않았나요?
(A) 아니요. 우리는 훨씬 더 많이 필요해요.
(B) 저쪽에 있는 작업 공간이요.
(C) 저는 이미 그를 면접했어요.

해설 (A) [o] No로 너무 많은 근로자들을 고용하지 않았음을 전달한 후, 근로자들이 훨씬 더 많이 필요하다는 부연 설명을 했으므로 정답이다.
(B) [x] 질문의 workers(근로자들)에서 연상할 수 있는 workspace(작업 공간)를 사용하여 혼동을 준 오답이다.
(C) [x] 질문의 hired(고용했다)에서 연상할 수 있는 interviewed(면접했다)를 사용하여 혼동을 준 오답이다.

05 부정 의문문
영국 → 미국 / 미국 → 영국

Shouldn't employees park behind the store?
(A) The most experienced employee.
(B) No. We don't provide any refunds.
(C) Yes. It's a new policy.

employee n. 직원 experienced adj. 경험이 많은 provide v. 제공하다

해석 직원들이 가게 뒤에 주차해야 하지 않나요?
(A) 가장 경험이 많은 직원이요.
(B) 아니요. 저희는 어떤 환불도 제공하지 않습니다.
(C) 네. 그것은 새로운 정책이에요.

해설 (A) [x] 질문의 employees를 employee로 반복 사용하여 혼동을 준 오답이다.
(B) [x] 질문의 store(가게)에서 연상할 수 있는 refunds(환불)를 사용하여 혼동을 준 오답이다.
(C) [o] Yes로 직원들이 가게 뒤에 주차해야 함을 전달한 후, 그것은 새로운 정책이라는 부연 설명을 했으므로 정답이다.

06 부정 의문문
미국 → 영국 / 영국 → 미국

Aren't there more staples in the storage closet?
(A) I haven't ordered them yet.
(B) Store them in the warehouse.
(C) To buy some office supplies.

storage closet 수납장 order v. 주문하다 warehouse n. 창고
office supplies 사무용품

해석 수납장에 스테이플러 심이 더 없나요?
(A) 아직 그것들을 주문하지 않았어요.
(B) 그것들을 창고에 보관하세요.
(C) 몇몇 사무용품을 사기 위해서요.

해설 (A) [o] 아직 그것들을 주문하지 않았다는 말로, 수납장에 스테이플러 심이 더 없음을 간접적으로 전달했으므로 정답이다.
(B) [x] storage - Store의 유사 발음 어휘를 사용하여 혼동을 준 오답이다.
(C) [x] 질문의 staples(스테이플러 심)와 관련 있는 office supplies(사무용품)를 사용하여 혼동을 준 오답이다.

2. 부가 의문문

HACKERS PRACTICE
p.71

01 (A) 02 (A) 03 (A) 04 (C) 05 (B)
06 (A)

01 부가 의문문
호주 → 미국 / 캐나다 → 영국

The food we ordered hasn't been served, has it?
(A) No. Not yet.
(B) Yes. Let's do that.
(C) I enjoy cooking.

serve v. 서빙하다, 제공하다

해석 우리가 주문한 음식이 서빙되지 않았죠, 그렇죠?
(A) 아니요. 아직요.
(B) 네. 그렇게 합시다.
(C) 저는 요리하는 것을 즐겨요.

해설 (A) [o] No로 주문한 음식이 서빙되지 않았다고 전달했으므로 정답이다.
(B) [x] 주문한 음식이 서빙되지 않았는지를 물었는데, 이와 관련이 없는 그렇게 하자는 말로 응답했으므로 오답이다.
(C) [x] 질문의 food(음식)와 관련 있는 cooking(요리하다)을 사용하여 혼동을 준 오답이다.

02 부가 의문문
미국 → 캐나다 / 영국 → 호주

There's a vacant office on this floor, right?
(A) Yes. It's across the hall.
(B) The floor was just waxed.
(C) No, I left it in my office.

vacant adj. 비어 있는 wax v. 왁스를 바르다

해석 이 층에 비어 있는 사무실이 있죠, 그렇죠?
(A) 네. 복도 건너편에 있어요.
(B) 바닥에 왁스를 방금 발랐어요.
(C) 아니요, 제 사무실에 두고 왔어요.

해설 (A) [o] Yes로 이 층에 비어 있는 사무실이 있음을 전달한 후, 복도 건너편에 있다는 부연 설명을 했으므로 정답이다.
(B) [x] 질문의 floor를 반복 사용하여 혼동을 준 오답이다.
(C) [x] 질문의 office를 반복 사용하여 혼동을 준 오답이다.

03 부가 의문문
📢 호주 → 캐나다 / 캐나다 → 호주

Ms. Lee will be on leave next Thursday, won't she?
(A) Let me check the schedule.
(B) Submit a leave request.
(C) I'd prefer to do it today.

on leave 휴가 중인 submit v. 제출하다

해석 Ms. Lee가 다음 주 목요일에 휴가 중일 거죠, 그렇지 않나요?
(A) 일정표를 확인해 볼게요.
(B) 휴가 신청서를 제출하세요.
(C) 저는 오늘 하는 것을 선호해요.

해설 (A) [○] 일정표를 확인해 보겠다는 말로, Ms. Lee가 다음 주 목요일에 휴가 중일지 모른다는 것을 간접적으로 전달했으므로 정답이다.
(B) [×] 질문의 leave를 반복 사용하여 혼동을 준 오답이다.
(C) [×] Ms. Lee가 다음 주 목요일에 휴가 중일지를 물었는데, 이와 관련이 없는 자신은 오늘 하는 것을 선호한다는 말로 응답했으므로 오답이다.

04 부가 의문문
📢 영국 → 호주 / 미국 → 캐나다

The play starts at six, doesn't it?
(A) I enjoyed the performance.
(B) Because he's my favorite actor.
(C) No. The tickets say seven.

play n. 연극 performance n. 공연

해석 연극이 6시에 시작하죠, 그렇지 않나요?
(A) 저는 공연을 즐겼어요.
(B) 그는 제가 가장 좋아하는 배우이기 때문이에요.
(C) 아니요. 표에 7시라고 적혀 있어요.

해설 (A) [×] 질문의 play(연극)와 관련 있는 performance(공연)를 사용하여 혼동을 준 오답이다.
(B) [×] 연극이 6시에 시작하는지를 물었는데 이유로 답했으므로 오답이다. 질문의 play(연극)와 관련 있는 actor(배우)를 사용하여 혼동을 주었다.
(C) [○] No로 연극이 6시에 시작하지 않음을 전달한 후, 표에 7시라고 적혀 있다는 부연 설명을 했으므로 정답이다.

05 부가 의문문
📢 캐나다 → 영국 / 호주 → 미국

There's a café in this hotel, isn't there?
(A) The room overlooks the ocean.
(B) Near the main entrance.
(C) You must check out by noon.

overlook v. 내려다보다 entrance n. 입구

해석 이 호텔에 카페가 있죠, 그렇지 않나요?
(A) 객실에서 바다가 내려다보여요.
(B) 정문 입구 근처예요.
(C) 당신은 정오까지 체크아웃해야 해요.

해설 (A) [×] 질문의 hotel(호텔)과 관련 있는 room(객실)을 사용하여 혼동을 준 오답이다.
(B) [○] 정문 입구 근처에라는 말로, 호텔에 카페가 있다는 것을 전달했으므로 정답이다.
(C) [×] 질문의 hotel(호텔)과 관련 있는 check out(체크아웃하다)을 사용하여 혼동을 준 오답이다.

06 부가 의문문
📢 미국 → 캐나다 / 영국 → 호주

Our client accepted our proposal, didn't he?
(A) He still has a few concerns.
(B) By improving customer service.
(C) I'll read your proposal soon.

accept v. 수락하다 proposal n. 제안 concern n. 걱정
improve v. 개선하다

해석 우리 고객이 우리의 제안을 수락했죠, 그렇지 않나요?
(A) 그는 아직 몇 가지 걱정이 있어요.
(B) 고객 서비스를 개선함으로써요.
(C) 저는 곧 당신의 제안서를 읽을 거예요.

해설 (A) [○] 그는 아직 몇 가지 걱정이 있다는 말로, 고객이 제안을 수락하지 않았음을 간접적으로 전달했으므로 정답이다.
(B) [×] 질문의 client(고객)와 관련 있는 customer service(고객 서비스)를 사용하여 혼동을 준 오답이다.
(C) [×] 질문의 proposal을 반복 사용하여 혼동을 준 오답이다.

HACKERS TEST
p.72

01 (A)	02 (B)	03 (B)	04 (A)	05 (B)
06 (B)	07 (C)	08 (A)	09 (A)	10 (B)
11 (C)	12 (B)	13 (A)	14 (A)	15 (C)
16 (C)	17 (C)	18 (A)	19 (C)	20 (B)
21 (C)	22 (A)	23 (C)	24 (C)	25 (C)

01 부정 의문문
📢 호주 → 영국

Didn't you submit the report the other day?
(A) No. I'm still working on it.
(B) At the port, actually.
(C) Every other day.

submit v. 제출하다 port n. 항구

해석 당신은 며칠 전에 보고서를 제출하지 않았나요?
(A) 아니요. 아직 작업 중이에요.
(B) 실은, 항구에서요.
(C) 이틀에 한 번이요.

해설 (A) [○] No로 며칠 전에 보고서를 제출하지 않았음을 전달한 후, 아직 작업 중이라는 부연 설명을 했으므로 정답이다.
(B) [×] report – port의 유사 발음 어휘를 사용하여 혼동을 준 오답이다.
(C) [×] 질문의 other day를 반복 사용하여 혼동을 준 오답이다.

02 부가 의문문
📢 미국 → 캐나다

You are going to reserve a hotel room today, aren't you?
(A) A reservation policy.
(B) Yes. I'll do it as soon as I get home.
(C) The lobby was really crowded.

reserve v. 예약하다 policy n. 정책 crowded adj. 붐비는, 혼잡한

해석 당신은 오늘 호텔 객실을 예약할 거죠, 그렇지 않나요?
(A) 예약 정책이요.
(B) 네. 집에 도착하는 대로 그것을 할 거예요.
(C) 로비는 정말 붐볐어요.

해설 (A) [×] reserve – reservation의 유사 발음 어휘를 사용하여 혼동을 준 오답이다.
(B) [○] Yes로 오늘 호텔 객실을 예약할 것임을 전달한 후, 집에 도착하는 대로 그것을 할 것이라는 부연 설명을 했으므로 정답이다.

(C) [×] 질문의 hotel(호텔)과 관련 있는 lobby(로비)를 사용하여 혼동을 준 오답이다.

03 부정 의문문
🔊 캐나다 → 영국

Isn't the vending machine out of order?
(A) The order arrived yesterday.
(B) No. It has been repaired.
(C) Try the cheapest one.

vending machine 자판기   out of order 고장 난   repair v. 수리하다
try v. 써 보다, 입어보다   cheap adj. 값이 싼

해석 자판기가 고장 난 것 아닌가요?
(A) 주문품은 어제 도착했어요.
(B) 아니요. 그건 수리되었어요.
(C) 가장 값이 싼 것을 써 보세요.

해설 (A) [×] 질문의 order를 반복 사용하여 혼동을 준 오답이다.
(B) [○] No로 자판기가 고장 나지 않았음을 전달한 후, 그건 수리되었다는 부연 설명을 했으므로 정답이다.
(C) [×] 자판기가 고장 난 것 아닌지를 물었는데, 이와 관련이 없는 가장 값이 싼 것을 써 보라는 말로 응답했으므로 오답이다.

04 부가 의문문
🔊 미국 → 영국

That was an interesting seminar, wasn't it?
(A) Yes. It was better than I expected.
(B) I'm not interested, thanks.
(C) In the auditorium.

expect v. 기대하다, 예상하다   auditorium n. 강당

해석 그것은 흥미로운 세미나였어요, 그렇지 않나요?
(A) 네. 제가 기대했던 것보다 더 좋았어요.
(B) 고맙지만, 저는 관심이 없어요.
(C) 강당에서요.

해설 (A) [○] Yes로 흥미로운 세미나였다고 전달한 후, 기대했던 것보다 더 좋았다는 부연 설명을 했으므로 정답이다.
(B) [×] interesting - interested의 유사 발음 어휘를 사용하여 혼동을 준 오답이다.
(C) [×] 질문의 seminar(세미나)에서 연상할 수 있는 auditorium(강당)을 사용하여 혼동을 준 오답이다.

05 부정 의문문
🔊 호주 → 미국

Hasn't Aisle 5 been restocked?
(A) A shipment of merchandise.
(B) It's not done yet.
(C) They placed a large order.

restock v. 재고를 다시 채우다   shipment n. 발송(물), 선적
merchandise n. 제품, 상품

해석 5번 통로에 재고가 다시 채워지지 않았나요?
(A) 제품의 발송물이요.
(B) 그건 아직 완료되지 않았어요.
(C) 그들은 대량 주문을 넣었어요.

해설 (A) [×] 질문의 restocked(재고가 다시 채워졌다)와 관련 있는 merchandise(제품)를 사용하여 혼동을 준 오답이다.
(B) [○] 그건 아직 완료되지 않았다는 말로, 5번 통로에 재고가 다시 채워지지 않았음을 전달했으므로 정답이다.
(C) [×] 질문의 restocked(재고가 다시 채워졌다)에서 연상할 수 있는 order(주문)를 사용하여 혼동을 준 오답이다.

06 부정 의문문
🔊 영국 → 호주

Can't the property owner meet us at the construction site?
(A) We manage several properties.
(B) Yes. She'll be there in an hour.
(C) The owner of the building.

property n. 부동산, 자산   owner n. 소유주   construction n. 건설, 공사
site n. 현장   manage v. 관리하다

해석 부동산 소유주는 건설 현장에서 우리를 만날 수 없나요?
(A) 우리는 여러 부동산을 관리해요.
(B) 네. 그녀는 한 시간 후에 그곳에 있을 거예요.
(C) 그 건물의 소유주요.

해설 (A) [×] 질문의 property를 properties로 반복 사용하여 혼동을 준 오답이다.
(B) [○] Yes로 부동산 소유자가 건설 현장에서 우리를 만날 수 있음을 전달한 후, 그녀가 한 시간 후에 그곳에 있을 거라는 부연 설명을 했으므로 정답이다.
(C) [×] 질문의 owner를 반복 사용하여 혼동을 준 오답이다.

07 부가 의문문
🔊 캐나다 → 호주

Jim signed up for a fitness class last week, didn't he?
(A) A qualified fitness instructor.
(B) There are 10 participants.
(C) That's what I heard.

qualified adj. 자격을 갖춘   instructor n. 강사

해석 Jim이 지난주에 피트니스 수업에 등록했죠, 그렇지 않나요?
(A) 자격을 갖춘 피트니스 강사요.
(B) 참가자가 10명 있어요.
(C) 저도 그렇게 들었어요.

해설 (A) [×] 질문의 fitness를 반복 사용하여 혼동을 준 오답이다.
(B) [×] 질문의 fitness class(피트니스 수업)와 관련 있는 participants(참가자)를 사용하여 혼동을 준 오답이다.
(C) [○] 그렇게 들었다는 말로, Jim이 지난주에 피트니스 수업에 등록했음을 간접적으로 전달했으므로 정답이다.

08 부정 의문문
🔊 미국 → 캐나다

Didn't you receive the latest sales figures?
(A) Yes. From my manager.
(B) I already finished the report.
(C) To figure out the problem.

sales figures 판매 수치   figure out ~을 알아내다

해석 최신 판매 수치를 받지 않았나요?
(A) 네. 제 관리자로부터요.
(B) 저는 이미 보고서를 끝냈어요.
(C) 문제를 알아내기 위해서요.

해설 (A) [○] Yes로 최신 판매 수치를 받았음을 전달한 후, 자신의 관리자로부터라는 부연 설명을 했으므로 정답이다.
(B) [×] 질문의 sales figures(판매 수치)에서 연상할 수 있는 report(보고서)를 사용하여 혼동을 준 오답이다.
(C) [×] 질문의 figures(수치)를 '알아내다'라는 의미의 동사로 반복 사용하여 혼동을 준 오답이다.

09 부가 의문문
🔊 캐나다 → 영국

You'll be joining us on the cruise, won't you?

(A) That's the plan.
(B) No, I won't be working.
(C) You'll have a great time.

cruise n. 유람선 여행   plan n. 계획

해석 당신은 우리와 함께 유람선 여행을 갈 거죠, 그렇지 않나요?
(A) 그게 계획이에요.
(B) 아니요, 저는 일하고 있지 않을 거예요.
(C) 당신은 좋은 시간을 보낼 거예요.

해설 (A) [○] 그게 계획이라는 말로, 함께 유람선 여행을 갈 것임을 전달했으므로 정답이다.
(B) [×] 질문의 won't를 반복 사용하여 혼동을 준 오답이다.
(C) [×] 질문의 cruise(유람선 여행)에서 연상할 수 있는 great time(좋은 시간)을 사용하여 혼동을 준 오답이다.

10 부정 의문문   미국 → 호주

Isn't Mr. Hadley giving the presentation on Monday?
(A) New company products.
(B) Yes, I think so.
(C) I changed my topic.

presentation n. 발표   product n. 상품

해석 Mr. Hadley는 월요일에 발표를 할 것이지 않나요?
(A) 새로운 회사 제품들이요.
(B) 네, 그런 것 같아요.
(C) 저는 주제를 바꿨어요.

해설 (A) [×] 질문의 presentation(발표)에서 연상할 수 있는 company products(회사 제품들)를 사용하여 혼동을 준 오답이다.
(B) [○] Yes로 Mr. Hadley가 월요일에 발표를 할 것임을 전달했으므로 정답이다.
(C) [×] 질문의 presentation(발표)과 관련 있는 topic(주제)을 사용하여 혼동을 준 오답이다.

11 부가 의문문   캐나다 → 미국

The old computers aren't being replaced, are they?
(A) There are many commuters.
(B) It's about five years old.
(C) New ones arrive this week.

replace v. 교체하다, 대신하다   commuter n. 통근자

해석 오래된 컴퓨터들이 교체되고 있지 않죠, 그렇죠?
(A) 통근자들이 많이 있어요.
(B) 그것은 5년 정도 됐어요.
(C) 이번 주에 새 것들이 도착해요.

해설 (A) [×] computers - commuters의 유사 발음 어휘를 사용하여 혼동을 준 오답이다.
(B) [×] 질문의 old를 반복 사용하여 혼동을 준 오답이다.
(C) [○] 이번 주에 새 것들이 도착한다는 말로, 오래된 컴퓨터들이 교체될 것임을 간접적으로 전달했으므로 정답이다.

12 부정 의문문   영국 → 미국

Didn't you pay the electricity bill already?
(A) Make sure to unplug the fan.
(B) No. I'll take care of it today.
(C) All major credit cards.

electricity bill 전기 요금   unplug v. 플러그를 뽑다

해석 전기 요금을 이미 지불하지 않았나요?
(A) 반드시 선풍기 플러그를 뽑으세요.
(B) 아니요. 제가 오늘 처리할게요.
(C) 모든 주요 신용카드들이요.

해설 (A) [×] 질문의 electricity bill(전기 요금)에서 연상할 수 있는 전기 제품과 관련된 fan(선풍기)을 사용하여 혼동을 준 오답이다.
(B) [○] No로 전기 요금을 아직 지불하지 않았음을 전달한 후, 자신이 오늘 처리하겠다는 부연 설명을 했으므로 정답이다.
(C) [×] 질문의 pay(지불하다)에서 연상할 수 있는 credit cards(신용카드)를 사용하여 혼동을 준 오답이다.

13 부가 의문문   호주 → 영국

We're driving together to Montreal, right?
(A) Yes. I'm looking forward to it.
(B) You still have to get one.
(C) Another rental car company.

rental car 렌터카

해석 우리는 몬트리올로 함께 운전해 갈 거죠, 그렇죠?
(A) 네. 저는 그것을 기대하고 있어요.
(B) 당신은 여전히 하나를 받아야 해요.
(C) 다른 렌터카 회사요.

해설 (A) [○] Yes로 몬트리올로 함께 운전해서 간다는 것을 전달한 후, 그것을 기대하고 있다는 부연 설명을 했으므로 정답이다.
(B) [×] 몬트리올로 함께 운전해 갈 것인지를 물었는데, 이와 관련이 없는 여전히 하나를 받아야 한다는 말로 응답했으므로 오답이다.
(C) [×] 질문의 driving(운전해 가다)과 관련된 rental car(렌터카)를 사용하여 혼동을 준 오답이다.

14 부정 의문문   미국 → 캐나다

Haven't you chosen a destination for your holiday yet?
(A) Do you have any suggestions?
(B) An hour-long tour.
(C) My holiday was too short.

destination n. 여행지, 목적지   suggestion n. 추천, 제안

해석 당신은 아직 휴가를 위한 여행지를 선택하지 않았나요?
(A) 추천할 곳이 있으신가요?
(B) 한 시간짜리 관광이요.
(C) 제 휴가는 너무 짧았어요.

해설 (A) [○] 추천할 곳이 있는지 되물어, 휴가를 위한 여행지에 대한 추가 정보를 요구한 정답이다.
(B) [×] 질문의 destination(여행지)에서 연상할 수 있는 tour(관광)를 사용하여 혼동을 준 오답이다.
(C) [×] 질문의 holiday를 반복 사용하여 혼동을 준 오답이다.

15 부가 의문문   호주 → 영국

This mall is pretty crowded, isn't it?
(A) Not as delicious as I expected.
(B) It's such a cloudy day.
(C) Yes. There are a lot of shoppers.

mall n. 쇼핑몰   pretty adv. 꽤   crowded adj. 붐비는   shopper n. 쇼핑객

해석 이 쇼핑몰은 꽤 붐비네요, 그렇지 않나요?
(A) 제가 기대했던 만큼 맛있지 않아요.
(B) 정말 흐린 날이에요.
(C) 네. 쇼핑객들이 많네요.

해설 (A) [×] 이 쇼핑몰이 꽤 붐빈다고 했는데, 이와 관련이 없는 기대했던 것만큼 맛있지 않다고 응답했으므로 오답이다.
(B) [×] crowded – cloudy의 유사 발음 어휘를 사용하여 혼동을 준 오답이다.
(C) [o] Yes로 이 쇼핑몰이 꽤 붐빈다는 것을 전달한 후, 쇼핑객들이 많다는 부연 설명을 했으므로 정답이다.

16 부정 의문문
영국 → 캐나다

Haven't any letters arrived today?
(A) Her arrival has been delayed.
(B) Let me listen to it.
(C) Two were delivered.

arrival n. 도착 delay v. 지연시키다 deliver v. 배달하다

해석 오늘 편지가 하나도 도착하지 않았나요?
(A) 그녀의 도착이 지연되었어요.
(B) 제가 그걸 들어볼게요.
(C) 두 통이 배달되었어요.

해설 (A) [×] arrived – arrival의 유사 발음 어휘를 사용하여 혼동을 준 오답이다.
(B) [×] 편지가 도착하지 않았는지를 물었는데, 이와 관련이 없는 자신이 그걸 들어보겠다는 말로 응답했으므로 오답이다.
(C) [o] 두 통이 배달되었다는 말로, 편지가 도착했음을 전달했으므로 정답이다.

17 부가 의문문
호주 → 캐나다

Our software application will be released soon, won't it?
(A) A mobile application.
(B) With another software developer.
(C) Yes. On August 14.

release v. 출시하다 developer n. 개발자

해석 우리 소프트웨어 애플리케이션이 곧 출시될 예정이에요, 그렇지 않나요?
(A) 휴대전화 애플리케이션이요.
(B) 다른 소프트웨어 개발자와 함께요.
(C) 네. 8월 14일이에요.

해설 (A) [×] 질문의 application을 반복 사용하여 혼동을 준 오답이다.
(B) [×] 질문의 software를 반복 사용하여 혼동을 준 오답이다.
(C) [o] Yes로 소프트웨어 애플리케이션이 곧 출시될 예정임을 전달한 후, 8월 14일에라는 부연 설명을 했으므로 정답이다.

18 부정 의문문
영국 → 호주

Aren't the flowers in this shop a bit disappointing?
(A) I can't find anything good either.
(B) By trimming off the leaves.
(C) A recently appointed board member.

trim off 다듬다 appoint v. 임명하다

해석 이 가게의 꽃들이 조금 실망스럽지 않은가요?
(A) 저도 좋은 것을 찾을 수가 없어요.
(B) 나뭇잎들을 다듬어서요.
(C) 최근에 임명된 이사회 구성원이요.

해설 (A) [o] 자신도 좋은 것을 찾을 수가 없다는 말로, 가게의 꽃들이 조금 실망스럽다는 말에 간접적으로 동의했으므로 정답이다.
(B) [×] 질문의 flowers(꽃들)와 관련 있는 leaves(나뭇잎들)를 사용하여 혼동을 준 오답이다.
(C) [×] disappointing – appointed의 유사 발음 어휘를 사용하여 혼동을 준 오답이다.

19 부가 의문문
캐나다 → 미국

I should make a reservation for next week's luncheon, shouldn't I?
(A) The menu was updated.
(B) It was very successful.
(C) No. I already did that.

make a reservation 예약을 하다 luncheon n. 오찬

해석 다음 주의 오찬을 위해 제가 예약을 해야 하죠, 그렇지 않나요?
(A) 그 메뉴는 업데이트되었어요.
(B) 그것은 매우 성공적이었어요.
(C) 아니요. 제가 이미 그것을 했어요.

해설 (A) [×] 질문의 luncheon(오찬)과 관련 있는 menu(메뉴)를 사용하여 혼동을 준 오답이다.
(B) [×] 다음 주의 오찬을 위해 자신이 예약을 해야 하는지를 물었는데, 이와 관련이 없는 그것이 매우 성공적이었다는 말로 응답했으므로 오답이다. 질문의 luncheon(오찬)을 나타낼 수 있는 It(그것)을 사용하여 혼동을 주었다.
(C) [o] No로 오찬을 위해 예약을 할 필요가 없음을 전달한 후, 자신이 이미 예약했다는 부연 설명을 했으므로 정답이다.

20 부정 의문문
미국 → 호주

Isn't the company picnic being held next weekend?
(A) The venue holds concerts.
(B) Yes. At Meyer Park.
(C) The company president.

company picnic 회사 야유회 hold v. 열다, 개최하다 venue n. 장소 president n. 사장

해석 회사 야유회가 다음 주말에 열리지 않나요?
(A) 그 장소에서 콘서트가 열려요.
(B) 네. Meyer 공원에서요.
(C) 회사 사장이요.

해설 (A) [×] held – hold의 유사 발음 어휘를 사용하여 혼동을 준 오답이다.
(B) [o] Yes로 회사 야유회가 다음 주말에 열린다는 것을 전달한 후, Meyer 공원에서라는 부연 설명을 했으므로 정답이다.
(C) [×] 질문의 company(회사)를 반복 사용하여 혼동을 준 오답이다.

21 부가 의문문
캐나다 → 영국

Ms. Woodward is being promoted to team leader, isn't she?
(A) Yes, we need to promote our products.
(B) I would appreciate it if you did.
(C) Nothing has been confirmed yet.

promote v. 승진시키다, 홍보하다 appreciate v. 고마워하다, 진가를 알아보다 confirm v. 확정하다

해석 Ms. Woodward는 팀장으로 승진될 거예요, 그렇지 않나요?
(A) 네, 우리의 제품들을 홍보해야 해요.
(B) 그렇게 해 주시면 고맙겠습니다.
(C) 아직 아무것도 확정되지 않았어요.

해설 (A) [×] promoted – promote의 유사 발음 어휘를 사용하여 혼동을 준 오답이다.
(B) [×] Ms. Woodward가 팀장으로 승진될 것인지를 물었는데, 이와 관련이 없는 그렇게 해 주면 고맙겠다는 말로 응답했으므로 오답이다.
(C) [o] 아직 아무것도 확정되지 않았다는 말로, Ms. Woodward가 팀장으로 승진될지 모른다는 것을 간접적으로 전달했으므로 정답이다.

22 부정 의문문
🔊 미국 → 영국

Shouldn't you e-mail the proposal to our client?
(A) No. Myra will do that.
(B) An important client.
(C) By regular mail.

client n. 고객 regular mail 일반 우편

해석 당신이 고객에게 제안서를 이메일로 보내야 하지 않나요?
(A) 아니요. Myra가 그것을 할 거예요.
(B) 중요한 고객이요.
(C) 일반 우편으로요.

해설 (A) [o] No로 자신이 고객에게 제안서를 이메일로 보낼 필요가 없음을 전달한 후, Myra가 그것을 할 것이라는 부연 설명을 했으므로 정답이다.
(B) [x] 질문의 client를 반복 사용하여 혼동을 준 오답이다.
(C) [x] e-mail – mail의 유사 발음 어휘를 사용하여 혼동을 준 오답이다.

23 부가 의문문
🔊 호주 → 미국

Most of our company's profits come from the Spanish market, right?
(A) An increase in profits.
(B) Just the travel receipts, thanks.
(C) That's correct.

profit n. 수익, 이익

해석 우리 회사의 수익 대부분은 스페인 시장에서 나오죠, 그렇죠?
(A) 수익의 증가요.
(B) 출장 영수증만요, 고마워요.
(C) 맞아요.

해설 (A) [x] 질문의 profits를 반복 사용하여 혼동을 준 오답이다.
(B) [x] 질문의 Spanish market(스페인 시장)에서 연상할 수 있는 travel(출장)을 사용하여 혼동을 준 오답이다.
(C) [o] 맞다는 말로, 회사 수익의 대부분이 스페인 시장에서 나온다고 전달했으므로 정답이다.

24 부가 의문문
🔊 영국 → 캐나다

Our clients have already been to the factory, haven't they?
(A) No, I don't believe so.
(B) Production started last week.
(C) In just a few minutes.

factory n. 공장 production n. 생산, 생산량

해석 우리 고객들은 이미 공장에 가 보았죠, 그렇지 않나요?
(A) 아니요, 아닌 것 같아요.
(B) 생산은 지난주에 시작했어요.
(C) 몇 분 후에요.

해설 (A) [o] No로 고객들이 공장에 가 보지 않았음을 전달했으므로 정답이다.
(B) [x] 질문의 factory(공장)와 관련 있는 production(생산)을 사용하여 혼동을 준 오답이다.
(C) [x] 고객들이 이미 공장에 가 보았는지를 물었는데, 이와 관련이 없는 몇 분 후에라고 응답했으므로 오답이다.

25 부가 의문문
🔊 호주 → 미국

Mr. Dixon will approve the marketing budget, won't he? 🔊

(A) No, he won't be able to join us.
(B) The budget was exceeded.
(C) He said he'll check it this afternoon.

approve v. 승인하다 budget n. 예산안, 예산 exceed v. 초과하다, 넘다

해석 Mr. Dixon은 마케팅 예산안을 승인할 거예요, 그렇지 않나요?
(A) 아니요, 그는 우리와 함께하지 못할 거예요.
(B) 예산이 초과되었어요.
(C) 그는 오늘 오후에 그것을 확인하겠다고 말했어요.

해설 (A) [x] Mr. Dixon이 마케팅 예산안을 승인할 것인지를 물었는데, 이와 관련이 없는 그는 우리와 함께하지 못할 것이라는 말로 응답했으므로 오답이다.
(B) [x] 질문의 budget을 반복 사용하여 혼동을 준 오답이다.
(C) [o] 그가 오늘 오후에 그것을 확인하겠다고 말했다는 말로, Mr. Dixon이 마케팅 예산안을 승인할지 모른다는 것을 간접적으로 전달했으므로 정답이다.

DAY 08 제안/제공/요청 의문문 및 평서문

1. 제안/제공/요청 의문문

HACKERS PRACTICE p.75

01 (B)   02 (C)   03 (B)   04 (C)   05 (B)
06 (A)

01 제안 의문문
🔊 캐나다 → 영국 / 호주 → 미국

Why don't we hire a new graphic designer?
(A) I really like that design.
(B) Yes. We're busy these days.
(C) Who did you hire?

hire v. 고용하다, 채용하다

해석 새로운 그래픽 디자이너를 고용하는 게 어때요?
(A) 저 디자인이 정말 마음에 들어요.
(B) 네. 우리는 요즘 바쁘죠.
(C) 누구를 고용했나요?

해설 (A) [x] designer – design의 유사 발음 어휘를 사용하여 혼동을 준 오답이다.
(B) [o] Yes로 제안을 수락한 후, 우리는 요즘 바쁘다는 말로 제안을 수락한 이유를 제시했으므로 정답이다.
(C) [x] 질문의 hire를 반복 사용하여 혼동을 준 오답이다.

02 요청 의문문
🔊 미국 → 캐나다 / 영국 → 호주

Could you help me choose a camera?
(A) I bought it years ago.
(B) Sure, you can borrow mine.
(C) What will it be used for?

borrow v. 빌리다

해석 제가 카메라를 고르는 것을 도와주시겠어요?
(A) 저는 그것을 몇 년 전에 샀어요.
(B) 당연하죠, 당신은 제 것을 빌려도 돼요.
(C) 어떤 용도로 사용될 건가요?

해설 (A) [x] 질문의 choose(고르다)에서 연상할 수 있는 선택과 관련된

bought(샀다)를 사용하여 혼동을 준 오답이다.
(B) [x] 카메라를 고르는 것을 도와줄 수 있는지를 물었는데, 이와 관련이 없는 자신의 것을 빌려도 된다는 말로 응답했으므로 오답이다. Sure까지만 듣고 정답으로 고르지 않도록 주의한다.
(C) [o] 어떤 용도로 사용될 것인지를 되물어, 요청을 간접적으로 수락했으므로 정답이다.

03 제안 의문문
호주 → 영국 / 캐나다 → 미국

How about trying these muffins I made?
(A) We have some blueberry ones.
(B) No, thanks. I have a stomachache.
(C) You should try them soon.

stomachache n. 복통

해석 제가 만든 이 머핀을 드셔보시는 것이 어때요?
(A) 우리는 블루베리 머핀이 있어요.
(B) 아니요, 괜찮아요. 저는 복통이 있어요.
(C) 당신이 빨리 그것들을 먹어봐야 해요.

해설 (A) [x] 머핀을 먹어보는 것이 어떤지를 물었는데, 이와 관련이 없는 블루베리 머핀이 있다는 말로 응답했으므로 오답이다. 질문의 muffins(머핀)를 나타낼 수 있는 ones(것들)를 사용하여 혼동을 주었다.
(B) [o] No, thanks로 제안을 거절한 후, 복통이 있다는 말로 제안을 거절한 이유를 제시했으므로 정답이다.
(C) [x] 질문의 trying을 try로 반복 사용하여 혼동을 준 오답이다.

04 제공 의문문
미국 → 호주 / 영국 → 캐나다

Do you want me to contact a plumber?
(A) A part of the contract.
(B) Inside one of the pipes.
(C) If you don't mind.

plumber n. 배관공   contract n. 계약서

해석 제가 배관공에게 연락하기를 원하시나요?
(A) 계약서의 일부요.
(B) 파이프들 중 하나의 안쪽에요.
(C) 당신이 괜찮다면요.

해설 (A) [x] contact - contract의 유사 발음 어휘를 사용하여 혼동을 준 오답이다.
(B) [x] 질문의 plumber(배관공)와 관련 있는 pipes(파이프들)를 사용하여 혼동을 준 오답이다.
(C) [o] 당신이 괜찮다면이라는 말로, 배관공에게 연락해 주겠다는 제공을 수락했으므로 정답이다.

05 요청 의문문
캐나다 → 호주 / 호주 → 캐나다

Can you take some time to review the building plans?
(A) It's just a preview.
(B) Show them to me after lunch.
(C) Yes, it has a lovely view.

review v. 검토하다; n. 검토   building plan 건축 설계도
preview n. 예고, 미리 보기   view n. 전망

해석 건축 설계도를 검토할 시간을 내주실 수 있나요?
(A) 그것은 단지 예고일 뿐이에요.
(B) 점심시간 후에 제게 그것들을 보여주세요.
(C) 네, 그것은 아름다운 전망을 가지고 있어요.

해설 (A) [x] review - preview의 유사 발음 어휘를 사용하여 혼동을 준 오답이다.
(B) [o] 점심시간 후에 보여 달라는 말로, 건축 설계도를 검토할 시간을

내달라는 요청을 간접적으로 수락한 정답이다.
(C) [x] 질문의 building(건축)에서 연상할 수 있는 view(전망)를 사용하여 혼동을 준 오답이다.

06 제안 의문문
미국 → 캐나다 / 영국 → 호주

Would you like some coffee before the presentation?
(A) I already had some this morning.
(B) Well, the presentation was quite helpful.
(C) Yes, please turn on the projector.

presentation n. 발표   turn on ~을 켜다

해석 발표 전에 커피를 좀 드시겠어요?
(A) 저는 오늘 아침에 이미 마셨어요.
(B) 음, 발표가 꽤 도움이 되었어요.
(C) 네, 프로젝터를 켜주세요.

해설 (A) [o] 오늘 아침에 이미 마셨다는 말로, 발표 전에 커피를 주겠다는 제안을 간접적으로 거절했으므로 정답이다.
(B) [x] 질문의 presentation을 반복 사용하여 혼동을 준 오답이다.
(C) [x] 질문의 presentation(발표)에서 연상할 수 있는 projector(프로젝터)를 사용하여 혼동을 준 오답이다.

2. 평서문

HACKERS PRACTICE   p.77

01 (B)   02 (B)   03 (A)   04 (A)   05 (B)
06 (A)

01 평서문
영국 → 호주 / 미국 → 캐나다

The marketing budget should be increased.
(A) It costs over 3,000 dollars.
(B) We don't have the funds.
(C) It's a good advertisement.

budget n. 예산   increase v. 증가시키다; n. 증가   fund n. 자금, 기금

해석 마케팅 예산이 증가되어야 합니다.
(A) 그것은 3,000달러 넘게 들어요.
(B) 우리는 자금이 없어요.
(C) 그것은 좋은 광고예요.

해설 (A) [x] 질문의 budget(예산)과 관련 있는 cost((값·비용이) 들다)를 사용하여 혼동을 준 오답이다.
(B) [o] 우리는 자금이 없다는 말로, 마케팅 예산이 증가되어야 한다는 의견에 반대했으므로 정답이다.
(C) [x] 질문의 marketing(마케팅)과 관련 있는 advertisement(광고)를 사용하여 혼동을 준 오답이다.

02 평서문
캐나다 → 미국 / 호주 → 영국

We've been asked to revise the installation manual.
(A) It's an annual report.
(B) Really? When is it due?
(C) It's easy to install.

revise v. 수정하다, 변경하다   installation n. 설치   manual n. 안내서
annual adj. 연례의, 연간의

해석 우리는 설치 안내서를 수정해달라는 요청을 받았어요.
(A) 그것은 연례 보고서예요.
(B) 정말요? 언제까지 해야 하나요?

(C) 그것은 설치하기 쉬워요.

해설 (A) [x] manual – annual의 유사 발음 어휘를 사용하여 혼동을 준 오답이다.
(B) [o] 언제까지 해야 하는지를 되물어, 설치 안내서 수정에 대한 추가 정보를 요구한 정답이다.
(C) [x] installation – install의 유사 발음 어휘를 사용하여 혼동을 준 오답이다.

03 평서문   미국 → 영국 / 영국 → 미국

It's quite cold outside today.
(A) Right. I'll wear a heavy coat.
(B) The hourly weather forecast.
(C) Who called for me?

quite adv. 꽤, 상당히   coat n. 외투, 코트

해설 오늘 바깥이 꽤 춥네요.
(A) 맞아요. 저는 두꺼운 외투를 입을 거예요.
(B) 시간별 일기 예보요.
(C) 누가 저를 찾았나요?

해설 (A) [o] Right으로 오늘 바깥이 꽤 추운 것이 맞다고 한 후, 두꺼운 외투를 입을 것이라고 했으므로 정답이다.
(B) [x] 질문의 cold(추운)에서 연상할 수 있는 날씨와 관련된 weather forecast(일기 예보)를 사용하여 혼동을 준 오답이다.
(C) [x] cold – called의 유사 발음 어휘를 사용하여 혼동을 준 오답이다.

04 평서문   호주 → 미국 / 캐나다 → 영국

Please turn down the volume of the television.
(A) Sure. Let me find the remote.
(B) Change the channel.
(C) It's a new TV show.

turn down 줄이다   volume n. 음량, 볼륨

해설 텔레비전 음량을 줄여주세요.
(A) 물론이죠. 리모컨을 찾아 볼게요.
(B) 채널을 바꾸세요.
(C) 새로운 텔레비전 쇼예요.

해설 (A) [o] Sure로 요청을 수락한 후, 리모컨을 찾아 보겠다는 부연 설명을 했으므로 정답이다.
(B) [x] 질문의 television(텔레비전)과 관련 있는 channel(채널)을 사용하여 혼동을 준 오답이다.
(C) [x] 질문의 television(텔레비전)과 관련 있는 TV show(텔레비전 쇼)를 사용하여 혼동을 준 오답이다.

05 평서문   영국 → 캐나다 / 미국 → 호주

I left my umbrella in my apartment.
(A) On the seventh floor.
(B) You can share mine.
(C) Don't forget to call me.

leave v. 두고 오다, 떠나다   share v. 함께 쓰다, 공유하다

해설 저는 우산을 아파트에 두고 왔어요.
(A) 7층에요.
(B) 제 것을 함께 쓰셔도 돼요.
(C) 제게 전화하는 것을 잊지 마세요.

해설 (A) [x] 질문의 apartment(아파트)에서 연상할 수 있는 seventh floor(7층)를 사용하여 혼동을 준 오답이다.
(B) [o] 자신의 것을 함께 써도 된다는 말로, 우산을 두고 왔다는 문제점에 대한 해결책을 제시했으므로 정답이다.
(C) [x] 우산을 아파트에 두고 왔다고 했는데, 이와 관련이 없는 자신에게 전화하는 것을 잊지 말라고 응답했으므로 오답이다.

06 평서문   호주 → 캐나다 / 캐나다 → 호주

The company's sales increased sharply this year.
(A) Our employees have worked hard.
(B) Well, within the next year.
(C) Ms. Henry will accompany you.

sharply adv. 급격히   accompany v. 함께 가다, 동반하다

해설 올해 회사의 매출이 급격히 증가했어요.
(A) 우리 직원들이 열심히 일했어요.
(B) 음, 내년 안으로요.
(C) Ms. Henry가 당신과 함께 갈 거예요.

해설 (A) [o] 직원들이 열심히 일했다는 말로, 올해 회사의 매출이 급격히 증가한 이유를 언급했으므로 정답이다.
(B) [x] 질문의 year를 반복 사용하여 혼동을 준 오답이다.
(C) [x] company – accompany의 유사 발음 어휘를 사용하여 혼동을 준 오답이다.

HACKERS TEST   p.78

01 (C)	02 (B)	03 (A)	04 (A)	05 (C)
06 (B)	07 (C)	08 (C)	09 (B)	10 (C)
11 (B)	12 (B)	13 (B)	14 (C)	15 (C)
16 (B)	17 (A)	18 (B)	19 (B)	20 (A)
21 (C)	22 (B)	23 (B)	24 (B)	25 (C)

01 요청 의문문   미국 → 호주

Can you set up more chairs in the lobby?
(A) What an interesting hobby!
(B) Set it against the wall.
(C) I'll get some from the storage room.

interesting adj. 흥미로운   set against ~에 기대어 놓다   storage room 창고

해설 로비에 더 많은 의자들을 놓아 주시겠어요?
(A) 정말 흥미로운 취미네요!
(B) 그것을 벽에 기대어 놓아 주세요.
(C) 창고에서 몇 개 가져올게요.

해설 (A) [x] lobby – hobby의 유사 발음 어휘를 사용하여 혼동을 준 오답이다.
(B) [x] 질문의 set를 반복 사용하여 혼동을 준 오답이다.
(C) [o] 창고에서 몇 개 가져오겠다는 말로, 로비에 더 많은 의자들을 놓아 달라는 요청을 간접적으로 수락한 정답이다.

02 평서문   호주 → 영국

X-Tech will install the security alarm for free.
(A) The fire alarm was activated.
(B) We'll save a lot of money, then.
(C) No, there is no charge.

activate v. 작동시키다, 활성화시키다

해설 X-Tech사가 무료로 보안 경보기를 설치해 줄 거예요.
(A) 화재경보기가 작동됐어요.

(B) 그럼 우리는 많은 돈을 절약하겠네요.
(C) 아니요, 요금은 없어요.

해설 (A) [×] 질문의 alarm을 반복 사용하여 혼동을 준 오답이다.
(B) [○] 그럼 많은 돈을 절약하겠다는 말로, X-Tech사가 무료로 보안 경보기를 설치해 줄 것이라는 말에 추가 의견을 전달했으므로 정답이다.
(C) [×] 질문의 for free(무료로)에서 연상할 수 있는 charge(요금)를 사용하여 혼동을 준 오답이다.

03 평서문   미국 → 캐나다

Let's buy some fresh bread from that bakery.
(A) OK. Good idea.
(B) Some fresh strawberries.
(C) By taking baking lessons.

fresh adj. 갓 만든, 신선한   bakery n. 빵집

해설 그 빵집에서 갓 만든 빵을 좀 삽시다.
(A) 알겠어요. 좋은 생각이에요.
(B) 신선한 딸기들이요.
(C) 제빵 수업을 들음으로써요.

해설 (A) [○] OK로 제안을 수락한 후, 좋은 생각이라는 말로 추가 의견을 전달했으므로 정답이다.
(B) [×] 질문의 fresh를 '신선한'이라는 의미의 형용사로 반복 사용하여 혼동을 준 오답이다.
(C) [×] 질문의 bread(빵)와 관련 있는 baking(제빵)을 사용하여 혼동을 준 오답이다.

04 제안 의문문   캐나다 → 영국

Why don't you read the instruction manual?
(A) Yes, I think I will.
(B) She's the instructor.
(C) Read my e-mail.

instruction manual 사용 설명서   instructor n. 강사

해설 사용 설명서를 읽는 게 어때요?
(A) 네, 그래야겠어요.
(B) 그녀는 강사예요.
(C) 제 이메일을 읽어보세요.

해설 (A) [○] Yes로 제안을 수락한 후, 그래야겠다는 부연 설명을 했으므로 정답이다.
(B) [×] instruction - instructor의 유사 발음 어휘를 사용하여 혼동을 준 오답이다.
(C) [×] 질문의 read를 반복 사용하여 혼동을 준 오답이다.

05 제공 의문문   미국 → 호주

Do you want me to buy you a ticket for the music festival?
(A) It cost me 30 dollars.
(B) On the main stage.
(C) No. I have to work that day.

festival n. 축제   stage n. 무대

해설 제가 당신에게 음악 축제 표를 사주기를 원하시나요?
(A) 저에게 30달러가 들었어요.
(B) 메인 무대에서요.
(C) 아니요. 저는 그날 일해야 해요.

해설 (A) [×] 질문의 buy(사다)와 관련 있는 cost((값·비용이) 들다)를 사용하여 혼동을 준 오답이다.
(B) [×] 질문의 music festival(음악 축제)과 관련 있는 stage(무대)를 사용하여 혼동을 준 오답이다.
(C) [○] No로 제공을 거절한 후, 그날 일해야 한다는 말로 제공을 거절한 이유를 제시했으므로 정답이다.

06 평서문   캐나다 → 미국

The movie *Tiger Park* has gotten good reviews.
(A) Our film class is canceled.
(B) That's why tickets have sold out.
(C) In the modern art exhibit.

cancel v. 취소하다

해설 영화 *Tiger Park*는 좋은 평가를 받았어요.
(A) 우리 영화 수업이 취소되었어요.
(B) 그래서 표가 매진되었군요.
(C) 현대 미술 전시회에서요.

해설 (A) [×] 질문의 movie(영화)와 같은 의미인 film(영화)을 사용하여 혼동을 준 오답이다.
(B) [○] 그래서 표가 매진되었다는 말로, 영화 *Tiger Park*가 좋은 평가를 받은 것에 대한 추가 정보를 제공했으므로 정답이다.
(C) [×] 영화 *Tiger Park*가 좋은 평가를 받았다고 말했는데, 이와 관련이 없는 현대 미술 전시회에서라고 응답했으므로 오답이다.

07 제안 의문문   영국 → 호주

Would it be OK to hold the meeting here?
(A) This is the sales report.
(B) Under the table.
(C) The conference room would be better.

hold v. (회의를) 열다, 개최하다

해설 이곳에서 회의를 열어도 괜찮을까요?
(A) 이것이 영업 보고서예요.
(B) 탁자 아래에요.
(C) 회의실이 더 좋을 것 같아요.

해설 (A) [×] 질문의 meeting(회의)에서 연상할 수 있는 회의 자료와 관련된 sales report(매출 보고서)를 사용하여 혼동을 준 오답이다.
(B) [×] 이곳에서 회의를 열어도 괜찮은지 물었는데, 이와 관련이 없는 탁자 아래에라고 응답했으므로 오답이다.
(C) [○] 회의실이 더 좋을 것 같다는 말로, 이곳에서 회의를 열자는 제안을 간접적으로 거절했으므로 정답이다.

08 평서문   캐나다 → 호주

Polson Industries is closing this fall.
(A) Only some of the time.
(B) You can go if you want to.
(C) Yes. I saw a news report about that.

news report 뉴스 보도

해설 Polson사가 이번 가을에 폐업할 예정이에요.
(A) 가끔씩만이요.
(B) 원하신다면 가져도 돼요.
(C) 네. 그것에 관한 뉴스 보도를 봤어요.

해설 (A) [×] Polson사가 이번 가을에 폐업할 예정이라고 했는데, 이와 관련이 없는 가끔씩만이라는 말로 응답했으므로 오답이다.
(B) [×] Polson사가 이번 가을에 폐업할 예정이라고 했는데, 이와 관련이 없는 원한다면 가도 된다는 말로 응답했으므로 오답이다.
(C) [○] Yes로 Polson사가 폐업할 예정임을 전달한 후, 그것에 관한 뉴스 보도를 봤다는 부연 설명을 했으므로 정답이다.

09 평서문
영국 → 호주

I won't be able to complete my project today.
(A) The other assignment.
(B) Try to finish it tomorrow.
(C) For the video presentation.

complete v. 완료하다; adj. 완벽한   presentation n. 발표, 제시

해석 저는 오늘 프로젝트를 완료하지 못할 거예요.
(A) 다른 과제요.
(B) 내일 끝내도록 해 보세요.
(C) 영상 발표를 위해서요.

해설 (A) [×] 질문의 project(프로젝트)와 관련 있는 assignment(과제)를 사용하여 혼동을 준 오답이다.
(B) [○] 내일 끝내도록 해 보라는 말로, 문제점에 대한 해결책을 제시했으므로 정답이다.
(C) [×] 질문의 project(프로젝트)에서 연상할 수 있는 presentation(발표)을 사용하여 혼동을 준 오답이다.

10 제안 의문문
캐나다 → 미국

Would you like to have dinner on Friday?
(A) Oh, the pasta was great.
(B) Several new restaurants.
(C) How about Thursday instead?

instead adv. 대신에

해석 금요일에 저녁 식사를 하실래요?
(A) 아, 파스타가 훌륭했어요.
(B) 몇몇 새로운 식당들이요.
(C) 대신에 목요일은 어떤가요?

해설 (A) [×] 질문의 dinner(저녁 식사)에서 연상할 수 있는 pasta(파스타)를 사용하여 혼동을 준 오답이다.
(B) [×] 질문의 dinner(저녁 식사)와 관련 있는 restaurants(식당들)를 사용하여 혼동을 준 오답이다.
(C) [○] 대신에 목요일은 어떤지를 되물어, 금요일에 저녁 식사를 하자는 제안을 간접적으로 거절한 정답이다.

11 평서문
영국 → 캐나다

The company plans to hire more engineers.
(A) Well, it's higher than expected.
(B) It's about time.
(C) Applicants at the front desk.

hire v. 고용하다   applicant n. 지원자

해석 회사는 더 많은 기술자들을 고용할 계획이에요.
(A) 음, 예상했던 것보다 더 높아요.
(B) 그럴 때가 됐네요.
(C) 안내 데스크에 있는 지원자들이요.

해설 (A) [×] hire – higher의 유사 발음 어휘를 사용하여 혼동을 준 오답이다.
(B) [○] 그럴 때가 됐다는 말로, 회사가 더 많은 기술자들을 고용할 계획이라는 말에 대한 의견을 제시했으므로 정답이다.
(C) [×] 질문의 hire(고용하다)와 관련 있는 Applicants(지원자들)를 사용하여 혼동을 준 오답이다.

12 제공 의문문
호주 → 영국

Do you want me to make some coffee?
(A) Where do you keep the coffee?
(B) No. Not right now.
(C) At the café down the street.

keep v. 보관하다

해석 제가 커피를 좀 만들어 드릴까요?
(A) 커피를 어디에 보관하시나요?
(B) 아니요. 지금은 괜찮아요.
(C) 길 아래 카페에서요.

해설 (A) [×] 질문의 coffee를 반복 사용하여 혼동을 준 오답이다.
(B) [○] No로 제공을 거절한 후, 지금은 괜찮다는 부연 설명을 했으므로 정답이다.
(C) [×] 질문의 coffee(커피)에서 연상할 수 있는 café(카페)를 사용하여 혼동을 준 오답이다.

13 요청 의문문
영국 → 미국

Could you give me an update on the marketing campaign?
(A) Most of the new advertisements.
(B) The entire team will get an e-mail.
(C) I updated the software.

update n. 최신 정보, 업데이트; v. 업데이트하다

해석 마케팅 캠페인에 대한 최신 정보를 주시겠어요?
(A) 대부분의 새로운 광고들이요.
(B) 팀 전체가 이메일을 받을 거예요.
(C) 제가 소프트웨어를 업데이트했어요.

해설 (A) [×] 질문의 marketing campaign(마케팅 캠페인)과 관련 있는 advertisements(광고들)를 사용하여 혼동을 준 오답이다.
(B) [○] 팀 전체가 이메일을 받을 거라는 말로, 최신 정보를 달라는 요청을 간접적으로 수락한 정답이다.
(C) [×] 질문의 update를 '업데이트하다'라는 의미의 동사 updated로 반복 사용하여 혼동을 준 오답이다.

14 평서문
캐나다 → 미국

I recently moved into a larger office on the top floor.
(A) Our office receptionist.
(B) The relocation was canceled.
(C) That's a nice upgrade.

move into ~로 이사하다   receptionist n. 접수 담당자
relocation n. 이전, 이주

해석 저는 최근에 최상층의 더 넓은 사무실로 이사했어요.
(A) 우리 사무실의 접수 담당자요.
(B) 이전이 취소됐어요.
(C) 괜찮은 개선이네요.

해설 (A) [×] 질문의 office를 반복 사용하여 혼동을 준 오답이다.
(B) [×] 질문의 moved into(~로 이사했다)와 관련 있는 relocation(이전)을 사용하여 혼동을 준 오답이다.
(C) [○] 괜찮은 개선이라는 말로, 최근에 최상층의 더 넓은 사무실로 이사했다는 말에 대한 의견을 제시했으므로 정답이다.

15 요청 의문문
영국 → 캐나다

Would you mind giving Antonio our newsletter?
(A) An interesting article.
(B) It's published monthly.
(C) Of course not. I'll do it in a minute.

newsletter n. 소식지, 회보   publish v. 발행하다, 출판하다
in a minute 잠시 후, 곧, 즉시

해석 Antonio에게 우리의 소식지를 줄 수 있나요?
  (A) 흥미로운 기사요.
  (B) 그것은 매달 발행돼요.
  (C) 물론이죠. 잠시 후에 할게요.

해설 (A) [x] 질문의 newsletter(소식지)와 관련 있는 article(기사)을 사용하여 혼동을 준 오답이다.
  (B) [x] 질문의 newsletter(소식지)와 관련 있는 published(발행된다)를 사용하여 혼동을 준 오답이다.
  (C) [o] Of course not으로 요청을 수락한 후, 잠시 후에 하겠다고 부연 설명을 했으므로 정답이다.

16 제안 의문문 호주 → 미국

Why don't we visit a museum this afternoon?
(A) The tour group enjoyed the exhibit.
(B) That sounds like a lot of fun.
(C) Please greet the visitors.

visit v. 방문하다 exhibit n. 전시회, 전시품; v. 전시하다
greet v. 맞이하다, 인사하다

해석 우리 오늘 오후에 박물관을 방문하는 게 어때요?
  (A) 그 여행 단체는 전시회를 즐겼어요.
  (B) 그것은 정말 재미있을 것 같아요.
  (C) 방문객들을 맞이해 주세요.

해설 (A) [x] 질문의 museum(박물관)과 관련 있는 exhibit(전시회)을 사용하여 혼동을 준 오답이다.
  (B) [o] 그것은 정말 재미있을 것 같다는 말로, 박물관을 방문하자는 제안을 수락한 정답이다.
  (C) [x] visit - visitors의 유사 발음 어휘를 사용하여 혼동을 준 오답이다.

17 제공 의문문 미국 → 호주

Would you like me to close the window?
(A) Yes, thanks.
(B) It closes at 10.
(C) The door is locked, I think.

lock v. 잠그다

해석 창문을 닫아 드릴까요?
  (A) 네, 감사합니다.
  (B) 그곳은 10시에 마감해요.
  (C) 제 생각엔 문이 잠겨 있는 것 같아요.

해설 (A) [o] Yes로 제공을 수락한 후, 감사하다고 부연 설명을 했으므로 정답이다.
  (B) [x] close - closes의 유사 발음 어휘를 사용하여 혼동을 준 오답이다.
  (C) [x] 질문의 close(닫다)에서 연상할 수 있는 locked(잠기다)를 사용하여 혼동을 준 오답이다.

18 평서문 호주 → 캐나다

We just hired several new accountants.
(A) By logging in to the account.
(B) When is their first day?
(C) A recruitment plan.

accountant n. 회계사 account n. 계정 recruitment n. 채용

해석 우리는 몇몇 새로운 회계사들을 막 고용했어요.
  (A) 계정에 로그인함으로써요.
  (B) 그들의 첫 출근일은 언제인가요?
  (C) 채용 계획이요.

해설 (A) [x] accountants - account의 유사 발음 어휘를 사용하여 혼동을 준 오답이다.
  (B) [o] 그들의 첫 출근일이 언제인지를 되물어, 새로운 회계사들을 고용했다는 것에 대한 추가 정보를 요구한 정답이다.
  (C) [x] 질문의 hired(고용했다)와 관련 있는 recruitment(채용)를 사용하여 혼동을 준 오답이다.

19 요청 의문문 영국 → 호주

Could you cancel my subscription over the phone?
(A) The latest phone model.
(B) Certainly. But it will take a few minutes.
(C) Here's a magazine to read.

subscription n. 구독 over the phone 전화상으로

해석 제 구독을 전화상으로 취소해 주시겠어요?
  (A) 최신 휴대전화 모델이요.
  (B) 그럼요. 하지만 그것은 몇 분 걸릴 거예요.
  (C) 여기 읽을 잡지가 있어요.

해설 (A) [x] 질문의 phone을 반복 사용하여 혼동을 준 오답이다.
  (B) [o] Certainly로 요청을 수락한 후, 몇 분 걸릴 것이라고 부연 설명을 했으므로 정답이다.
  (C) [x] 질문의 subscription(구독)과 관련 있는 magazine(잡지)을 사용하여 혼동을 준 오답이다.

20 평서문 캐나다 → 미국

Our Web site isn't functioning right now.
(A) Yes. I notified the IT department.
(B) Just download the file.
(C) For an online payment.

function v. 작동하다; n. 기능 notify v. 알리다 payment n. 결제

해석 우리 웹사이트가 지금 작동하지 않고 있어요.
  (A) 네. 제가 IT 부서에 알렸어요.
  (B) 파일을 다운로드만 하세요.
  (C) 온라인 결제를 위해서요.

해설 (A) [o] Yes로 웹사이트가 작동하지 않고 있다는 것을 전달한 후, 자신이 IT 부서에 알렸다는 추가 정보를 제공했으므로 정답이다.
  (B) [x] 질문의 Web site(웹사이트)와 관련 있는 download the file(파일을 다운로드하다)을 사용하여 혼동을 준 오답이다.
  (C) [x] 질문의 Web site(웹사이트)와 관련 있는 online(온라인)을 사용하여 혼동을 준 오답이다.

21 평서문 영국 → 캐나다

I don't think the new copy machine has been delivered.
(A) I got enough copies of that.
(B) A two-dollar delivery fee.
(C) It's set up on the second floor.

deliver v. 배달하다 delivery fee 배달료

해석 새 복사기가 배달되지 않은 것 같아요.
  (A) 그것의 복사본을 충분히 가지고 있어요.
  (B) 2달러의 배달료요.
  (C) 그것은 2층에 설치되어 있어요.

해설 (A) [x] 질문의 copy machine(복사기)과 관련 있는 copies(복사본)를 사용하여 혼동을 준 오답이다.
  (B) [x] 질문의 delivered(배달되었다)와 관련 있는 delivery fee(배달료)

를 사용하여 혼동을 준 오답이다.
(C) [o] 그것은 2층에 설치되어 있다는 말로, 새 복사기가 배달되었다고 전달했으므로 정답이다.

22 제안 의문문
호주 → 영국

Would you like to borrow this book when I finish reading it?
(A) You can borrow it.
(B) If you don't mind.
(C) From the local library.

local adj. 지역의

해석 제가 이 책을 다 읽고 나면 빌리시겠어요?
(A) 당신이 그것을 빌리셔도 돼요.
(B) 당신이 괜찮으시다면요.
(C) 지역 도서관에서요.

해설 (A) [x] 질문의 borrow를 반복 사용하여 혼동을 준 오답이다.
(B) [o] 당신이 괜찮다면이라는 말로, 책을 빌리겠냐는 제안을 수락했으므로 정답이다.
(C) [x] 질문의 book(책)에서 연상할 수 있는 library(도서관)를 사용하여 혼동을 준 오답이다.

23 요청 의문문
미국 → 영국

Could you pick up the brochures from the print shop?
(A) Pick me up at eight.
(B) I have a dentist appointment.
(C) The printer seems fine, thanks.

pick up ~을 찾아오다, ~를 (차에) 태우러 가다　appointment n. 약속

해석 인쇄소에서 소책자를 찾아와 주시겠어요?
(A) 8시에 저를 태우러 오세요.
(B) 저는 치과 예약이 있어요.
(C) 프린터는 괜찮아 보여요, 고마워요.

해설 (A) [x] 질문의 pick up을 반복 사용하여 혼동을 준 오답이다.
(B) [o] 치과 예약이 있다는 말로, 인쇄소에서 소책자를 찾아와 달라는 요청을 간접적으로 거절한 정답이다.
(C) [x] print - printer의 유사 발음 어휘를 사용하여 혼동을 준 오답이다.

24 평서문
캐나다 → 영국

You should work with a real estate agent to find a good apartment.
(A) Just across the hall.
(B) I appreciate your suggestion.
(C) You made the right decision.

real estate agent 부동산 중개인　appreciate v. 감사하다
suggestion n. 제안

해석 좋은 아파트를 찾으려면 부동산 중개인과 함께 일하는 게 좋아요.
(A) 복도 바로 맞은편이에요.
(B) 당신의 제안에 감사드려요.
(C) 당신은 옳은 선택을 했어요.

해설 (A) [x] 부동산 중개인과 함께 일하는 게 좋다고 말했는데, 이와 관련이 없는 복도 바로 맞은편이라고 응답했으므로 오답이다.
(B) [o] 제안에 감사드린다는 말로, 부동산 중개인과 함께 일하는 게 좋다는 제안을 수락한 정답이다.
(C) [x] 부동산 중개인과 함께 일하는 게 좋다고 말했는데, 이와 관련이 없는 당신은 옳은 선택을 했다고 응답했으므로 오답이다.

25 평서문
미국 → 캐나다

Our company has decided to let employees work from home.
(A) I'll be home by five at the latest.
(B) Several employee benefits.
(C) I'd like to do that if possible.

employee n. 직원　work from home 재택 근무하다　benefit n. 혜택

해석 우리 회사는 직원들이 재택근무를 할 수 있게 하기로 결정했어요.
(A) 늦어도 5시까지는 집에 도착할 거예요.
(B) 여러 가지 직원 혜택이요.
(C) 저는 가능하다면 그것을 하고 싶어요.

해설 (A) [x] 질문의 home을 반복 사용하여 혼동을 준 오답이다.
(B) [x] 질문의 employees를 employee로 반복 사용하여 혼동을 준 오답이다.
(C) [o] 가능하다면 그것을 하고 싶다는 말로, 회사가 직원들이 재택근무를 할 수 있게 하기로 결정했다는 말에 대한 의견을 제시했으므로 정답이다.

PART 3

DAY 09 전체 대화 관련 문제

1. 주제/목적 문제

HACKERS PRACTICE p.83

01 (A)   02 (A)   03 (A)

---

[01] 미국 → 캐나다 / 영국 → 호주
Question 01 refers to the following conversation.

W: This is Theresa from Appliance Mart. **01 I'm calling to remind you about the appointment to repair your air conditioner** this Saturday.
M: Oh, no. I got the dates confused, and I have another appointment downtown in the morning. Is it possible for the repair crew to come over after 2 P.M.?
W: Certainly. Our crew will arrive at around 5 P.M. The entire process will only last about 45 minutes.

remind v. 상기시키다, 생각나게 하다 appointment n. 예약, 약속
crew n. 작업반 entire adj. 전체의 process n. 과정, 절차

해석
01번은 다음 대화에 관한 문제입니다.

여: 저는 Appliance Mart에서 근무하는 Theresa입니다. 01이번 주 토요일에 고객님의 에어컨을 수리하기로 한 예약이 있음을 상기시켜 드리기 위해 전화드렸습니다.
남: 아, 안 돼요. 날짜를 혼동해서, 제가 아침에 시내에서 다른 예약이 있어요. 수리 작업반이 오후 2시 이후에 오는 게 가능한가요?
여: 물론입니다. 저희 작업반이 저녁 5시쯤 도착할 것입니다. 전체 과정은 45분 정도밖에 안 걸릴 거예요.

01 목적 문제
해석 여자는 왜 전화를 하고 있는가?
  (A) 상기시켜 주기 위해
  (B) 업그레이드를 제공하기 위해
  (C) 환불을 요청하기 위해
  (D) 고장을 설명하기 위해

해설 전화의 목적을 묻는 문제이므로, 대화의 초반을 반드시 듣는다. 여자가 "I'm calling to remind you about the appointment to repair your air conditioner this Saturday."라며 이번 주 토요일에 남자의 집에 에어컨을 수리하기로 한 예약이 있음을 상기시켜 주고 싶다고 하였다. 따라서 (A)가 정답이다.

어휘 reminder n. 상기시키는 것 refund n. 환불, 상환액
malfunction n. 고장, 기능 불량

---

[02] 영국 → 호주 / 미국 → 캐나다
Question 02 refers to the following conversation.

W: Hi, Michael. **02 I need to complete our expense summary** for last month. Can you give me the receipts from your trip to St. Paul?
M: Unfortunately, the receipts are in my luggage at home. When's the summary due?
W: Mr. Brown is expecting it tomorrow afternoon.
M: I will bring them tomorrow and give them to you first thing in the morning.

expense n. 지출, 비용, 경비 receipt n. 영수증
unfortunately adv. 안타깝게도, 불행하게도
expect v. 기대하다, 예상하다, 기다리다 first thing 무엇보다도 먼저

해석
02번은 다음 대화에 관한 문제입니다.

여: 안녕하세요, Michael. 02저는 지난달의 지출 보고서를 마무리해야 해요. 당신의 St. Paul 출장에서의 영수증들을 주실 수 있나요?
남: 안타깝게도, 영수증들은 집에 있는 여행 가방 안에 있어요. 보고서 마감일이 언제인가요?
여: Mr. Brown은 내일 오후에 그걸 기대하고 있어요.
남: 내일 그것들을 가져와서 아침에 무엇보다도 먼저 드릴게요.

02 주제 문제
해석 화자들은 주로 무엇에 대해 이야기하고 있는가?
  (A) 보고서를 끝내는 것
  (B) 영수증을 출력하는 것
  (C) 주문을 확인하는 것
  (D) 여행 가방을 찾아가는 것

해설 대화의 주제를 묻는 문제이므로 대화의 초반을 반드시 듣는다. 여자가 "I need to complete our expense summary"라며 지출 보고서를 마무리해야 한다고 한 뒤, 지출 보고서를 끝내기 위해 필요한 남자의 영수증에 관한 내용으로 대화가 이어지고 있다. 따라서 (A)가 정답이다.

어휘 confirm v. 확인하다, 사실임을 보여주다, 확정하다

---

[03] 캐나다 → 영국 / 호주 → 미국
Question 03 refers to the following conversation.

M: Hello, Ms. Florence. **03 I was wondering if any buyers contacted you** about the retail space I put on the market.
W: I've shown it to a few people so far, but no one has been interested in purchasing it. I think it's because of the high price.
M: I see. I'm going to check the prices of other properties in the area and then call you back.

contact v. 연락하다 retail n. 소매 space n. 공간, 자리
purchase v. 구매하다 property n. 부동산, 건물

해석
03번은 다음 대화에 관한 문제입니다.

남: 안녕하세요, Ms. Florence. 03제가 시장에 내놓은 소매 공간에 대해 연락한 구매자가 있는지 궁금합니다.
여: 지금까지 몇 명에게 보여드렸지만, 아무도 그것을 구매하는 데 관심을 보이지 않았어요. 높은 가격 때문인 것 같아요.
남: 알겠습니다. 이 지역의 다른 부동산들의 가격을 확인한 후 다시 전화드릴게요.

03 목적 문제
해석 전화의 목적은 무엇인가?
  (A) 구매자들의 관심에 대해 문의하기 위해

(B) 가격을 협상하기 위해
(C) 날짜를 확인하기 위해
(D) 설명을 제공하기 위해

해설 전화의 목적을 묻는 문제이므로, 대화의 초반을 반드시 듣는다. 남자가 "I was wondering if any buyers contacted you about the retail space I put on the market."이라며 자신이 시장에 내놓은 소매 공간에 대해 연락한 구매자가 있는지 궁금하다고 한 것을 통해, 남자가 구매자들의 관심에 대해 문의하기 위해 전화하고 있음을 알 수 있다. 따라서 (A)가 정답이다.

어휘 inquire v. 문의하다 negotiate v. 협상하다 instruction n. 설명

2. 화자/장소 문제

HACKERS PRACTICE p.85
01 (A)   02 (B)   03 (C)

[01] 캐나다 → 미국 / 호주 → 영국
Question 01 refers to the following conversation.

M: Hi, Beth. ⁰¹Have you had a chance to organize the books in the reference section?
W: ⁰¹Not yet. I was putting up some signs with information about our summer reading program for local children.
M: I see. You seem really busy these days. I'll help you get those books in order.

organize v. 정리하다, 조직하다   reference n. 참고 문헌
section n. 부문, 구획   put up 게시하다, 내붙이다   sign n. 표지판

해석
01번은 다음 대화에 관한 문제입니다.
남: 안녕하세요, Beth. ⁰¹혹시 참고 문헌 부문에 있는 책들을 정리하셨나요?
여: ⁰¹아직 안 했어요. 지역 어린이들을 위한 여름 독서 프로그램에 관한 정보가 있는 표지판을 게시하고 있었어요.
남: 그렇군요. 요즘 정말 바빠 보이네요. 제가 그 책들을 정리하는 것을 도와드릴게요.

01 장소 문제
해석 대화는 어디에서 일어나는가?
(A) 도서관에서
(B) 미술관에서
(C) 극장에서
(D) 공원에서

해설 대화에서 장소와 관련된 표현을 놓치지 않고 듣는다. 남자가 "Have you had a chance to organize the books in the reference section?"이라며 참고 문헌 부문에 있는 책들을 정리했는지 묻자, 여자가 "Not yet. I was putting up some signs with information about our summer reading program for local children."이라며 아직 안 했다고 한 후, 지역 어린이들을 위한 여름 독서 프로그램에 관한 정보가 있는 표지판을 게시하고 있었다고 한 것을 통해 도서관에서 대화가 일어나고 있음을 알 수 있다. 따라서 (A)가 정답이다.

[02] 호주 → 영국 / 캐나다 → 미국
Question 02 refers to the following conversation.

M: Good morning. My name is Kevin Gould. I have an appointment with Ms. Brent, the regional director. ⁰²I'm here to be interviewed for the market researcher job.
W: Oh, Ms. Brent is currently in a conference call, and it's taking longer than expected. Do you mind waiting until she's finished?
M: No. I can wait here until she is available.

appointment n. 약속   currently adv. 현재   conference call 전화 회의

해석
02번은 다음 대화에 관한 문제입니다.
남: 안녕하세요. 제 이름은 Kevin Gould입니다. 저는 지사장님이신 Ms. Brent와 약속이 있습니다. ⁰²저는 여기에 시장 조사원 직무에 대한 면접을 보기 위해 왔어요.
여: 오, Ms. Brent는 현재 전화 회의 중이시고, 예상보다 시간이 오래 걸리고 있습니다. 그녀가 끝날 때까지 기다리셔도 괜찮으신가요?
남: 네. 그녀가 가능할 때까지 여기서 기다릴 수 있어요.

02 화자 문제
해석 남자는 누구인 것 같은가?
(A) 비서
(B) 지원자
(C) 임원
(D) 발표자

해설 대화에서 신분 및 직업과 관련된 표현을 놓치지 않고 듣는다. 남자가 "I'm here to be interviewed for the market researcher job."이라며 시장 조사원 직무에 대한 면접을 보기 위해 왔다고 한 것을 통해 남자가 면접을 보러 온 지원자임을 알 수 있다. 따라서 (B)가 정답이다.

어휘 secretary n. 비서   applicant n. 지원자   executive n. 임원

[03] 미국 → 호주 / 영국 → 캐나다
Question 03 refers to the following conversation.

W: Did the ink cartridges arrive yet?
M: Unfortunately, no. They were supposed to come this morning, but I was notified that they won't get here until tomorrow.
W: That's a problem. ⁰³I have a meeting at 10 to go over some legal documents for an upcoming court case.
M: Just put the files on a USB drive. I'll take it to the print shop across the street.

notify v. 통지하다   legal document 법률 문서   court case 법정 사건

해석
03번은 다음 대화에 관한 문제입니다.
여: 잉크 카트리지가 이미 도착했나요?
남: 안타깝게도, 아니요. 그것들이 오늘 아침에 오기로 되어 있었는데, 내일까지 여기에 도착하지 않을 거라고 통지받았어요.
여: 그건 문제네요. ⁰³저는 다가오는 법정 사건을 위한 몇몇 법률 문서를 검토하는 회의가 10시에 있어요.
남: 파일을 USB 저장 장치에 담아두세요. 제가 그것을 길 건너편의 인쇄소에 가져갈게요.

03 화자 문제
해석 화자들은 어디에서 일하는 것 같은가?
(A) 배송 회사에서
(B) 출판 회사에서
(C) 법률 사무소에서
(D) 부동산 중개소에서

해설 대화에서 신분 및 직업과 관련된 표현을 놓치지 않고 듣는다. 여자가 "I have a meeting at 10 to go over some legal documents for an upcoming court case."라며 다가오는 법정 사건을 위한 몇몇 법률 문

서를 검토하는 회의가 10시에 있다고 한 말을 통해 화자들이 법률 사무소에서 일한다는 것을 알 수 있다. 따라서 (C)가 정답이다.

어휘 shipping n. 배송   real estate agency 부동산 중개소

HACKERS TEST   p.86

01 (D)	02 (D)	03 (B)	04 (A)	05 (A)
06 (C)	07 (D)	08 (B)	09 (C)	10 (B)
11 (A)	12 (C)	13 (C)	14 (B)	15 (D)
16 (C)	17 (A)	18 (B)	19 (D)	20 (A)
21 (D)	22 (D)	23 (A)	24 (B)	

[01-03] 캐나다 → 영국

Questions 01-03 refer to the following conversation.

M: Sorry I'm so late. ⁰¹There have been a lot of tech support requests at our bank today.
W: I understand. I called you because I dropped my laptop, and now it won't turn on. But ⁰¹/⁰²I need to access a file on it to get ready for an important client meeting about a loan.
M: I'll try to retrieve the file from the hard drive now. But repairing your laptop may take a few days.
W: Got it. ⁰³Could I get another one to use in the meantime?

support n. 지원   request n. 요청   laptop n. 노트북   access v. 접근하다
loan n. 대출   retrieve v. 복구하다   repair v. 수리하다

해석
01-03번은 다음 대화에 관한 문제입니다.

남: 이렇게 늦어서 죄송합니다. ⁰¹오늘 우리 은행에 기술 지원 요청이 많았어요.
여: 이해해요. 제가 노트북을 떨어뜨렸고, 이제 그것이 켜지지 않아서 전화했어요. 하지만 ⁰¹/⁰²대출 관련 중요한 고객 미팅을 준비하기 위해 거기에 있는 파일에 접근해야 해요.
남: 지금 하드디스크 드라이브에서 그 파일을 복구해 볼게요. 하지만 노트북을 수리하는 데는 며칠 걸릴 수 있어요.
여: 알겠어요. ⁰³그동안 사용할 다른 노트북을 받을 수 있을까요?

01 장소 문제
해석 대화는 어디에서 일어나는 것 같은가?
(A) 광고 대행사에서
(B) 전자제품 회사에서
(C) 건축 회사에서
(D) 금융 기관에서
해설 대화에서 장소와 관련된 표현을 놓치지 않고 듣는다. 남자가 "There have been a lot of tech support requests at our bank today."라며 오늘 우리 은행에 기술 지원 요청이 많았다고 하자, 여자가 "I need to access a file on it to get ready for an important client meeting about a loan"이라며 대출 관련 중요한 고객 미팅을 준비하기 위해 노트북에 있는 파일에 접근해야 한다고 하였다. 따라서 (D)가 정답이다.

어휘 agency n. 대행사   electronics n. 전자제품
architectural adj. 건축의, 건축학의   financial adj. 금융의
institution n. 기관

02 이유 문제
해석 여자는 왜 파일에 접근해야 하는가?
(A) 평가를 수행하기 위해

(B) 제안을 검토하기 위해
(C) 직위에 지원하기 위해
(D) 미팅을 준비하기 위해
해설 질문의 핵심 어구(access a file)가 언급된 내용을 주의 깊게 듣는다. 여자가 "I need to access a file on it to get ready for an important client meeting about a loan"이라며 대출 관련 중요한 고객 미팅을 준비하기 위해 노트북에 있는 파일에 접근해야 한다고 하였다. 따라서 (D)가 정답이다.

어휘 perform v. 수행하다   evaluation n. 평가   proposal n. 제안
apply v. 지원하다

[Paraphrasing]
get ready for ~을 준비하다 → prepare for ~을 준비하다

03 요청 문제
해석 여자는 무엇을 요청하는가?
(A) 사용 설명서
(B) 대체 기기
(C) 소프트웨어 업그레이드
(D) 계정 비밀번호
해설 여자의 말에서 요청과 관련된 표현이 포함된 문장을 주의 깊게 듣는다. 여자가 "Could I get another one to use in the meantime?"이라며 그동안 사용할 다른 노트북을 받을 수 있을지를 물었다. 따라서 (B)가 정답이다.

어휘 instruction manual 사용 설명서   replacement n. 대체, 교체
device n. 기기   account n. 계정

[04-06] 미국 → 캐나다

Questions 04-06 refer to the following conversation.

W: Excuse me. I need to see your identification before letting you inside.
M: Oh, ⁰⁴I'm from the *International Sun* newspaper. Here's my badge. ⁰⁵I'm supposed to write about the championship tennis match taking place this afternoon between Maria Isner and Sue Williams.
W: Yes, everything looks fine. You can go ahead. But ⁰⁶it would be best if you wore your badge for the rest of the day. You shouldn't keep it in your bag.

identification n. 신분증   badge n. 배지, 신분증   championship n. 선수권
match n. 경기   rest n. 나머지

해석
04-06번은 다음 대화에 관한 문제입니다.

여: 실례합니다. 제가 당신을 들여보내드리기 전에 신분증을 봐야 해요.
남: 아, ⁰⁴저는 *International Sun* 신문사에서 왔어요. 여기 제 배지가 있어요. ⁰⁵저는 오늘 오후에 있을 Maria Isner와 Sue Williams의 테니스 선수권 경기에 대해 글을 쓰기로 되어 있어요.
여: 네, 모든 것이 괜찮아 보이네요. 들어가셔도 됩니다. 하지만 ⁰⁶오늘 남은 시간 동안 배지를 착용하는 것이 좋겠어요. 가방에 넣어두지 마세요.

04 화자 문제
해석 남자는 어느 산업에서 일하는 것 같은가?
(A) 언론
(B) 소프트웨어
(C) 패션
(D) 금융
해설 대화에서 신분 및 직업과 관련된 표현을 놓치지 않고 듣는다. 남자가 "I'm from the *International Sun* newspaper"라며 *International Sun* 신문사에서 왔다고 한 것을 통해 남자가 언론 산업에서 일한다는 것을 알 수 있다. 따라서 (A)가 정답이다.

어휘 journalism n. 언론   finance n. 금융

05 다음에 할 일 문제
해석 오후에 무슨 일이 일어날 것 같은가?
(A) 스포츠 게임
(B) 모금 행사
(C) 기자 회견
(D) 사진 촬영

해설 질문의 핵심 어구(in the afternoon)와 관련된 내용을 주의 깊게 듣는다. 여자가 "I'm supposed to write about the championship tennis match taking place this afternoon"이라며 오늘 오후에 있을 테니스 선수권 경기에 대해 글을 쓰기로 되어 있다고 한 것을 통해 오후에 스포츠 게임이 일어날 것임을 알 수 있다. 따라서 (A)가 정답이다.

어휘 fundraiser n. 모금 행사   press conference 기자 회견
photo shoot (광고용) 사진 촬영

[Paraphrasing]
championship tennis match 테니스 선수권 경기 → sports game 스포츠 게임

06 제안 문제
해석 여자는 남자에게 무엇을 해야 한다고 제안하는가?
(A) 구역을 떠난다.
(B) 입장권을 산다.
(C) 배지를 착용한다.
(D) 가방을 확인한다.

해설 남자의 말에서 제안과 관련된 표현이 언급된 다음을 주의 깊게 듣는다. 여자가 "it would be best if you wore your badge for the rest of the day"라며 오늘 남은 시간 동안 배지를 착용하는 것이 좋겠다고 하였다. 따라서 (C)가 정답이다.

[07-09] 🎧 호주 → 미국
Questions 07-09 refer to the following conversation.

M: ⁰⁷**What would you like to do during your personal training sessions at our gym?**
W: My friend suggested working out with weights. Um, ⁰⁸**I plan to come in for three hours every Saturday**.
M: Hmm . . . ⁰⁸**Exercising one day a week for that long increases the risk of injury. Maybe you should consider coming more often.**
W: Then, how about Tuesday, Thursday, and Saturday evenings for an hour? I could start at 7 P.M.
M: Perfect. ⁰⁹**Please give me your e-mail address** so I can send you a customized workout plan before our first session.

session n. 시간, 기간   gym n. 체육관   work out 운동하다   risk n. 위험
injury n. 부상   customized adj. 맞춤형의

해석
07-09번은 다음 대화에 관한 문제입니다.
남: ⁰⁷저희 체육관에서 개인 트레이닝 수업 시간 동안 무엇을 하고 싶으세요?
여: 제 친구가 중량을 이용해서 운동하는 것을 추천했어요. 음, ⁰⁸저는 매주 토요일마다 3시간씩 오려고 계획하고 있어요.
남: 흠... ⁰⁸일주일에 하루 그렇게 오래 운동하는 것은 부상 위험을 증가시킵니다. 더 자주 오시는 것을 고려해 보셔야 할 거예요.
여: 그렇다면, 화요일, 목요일, 그리고 토요일 저녁에 한 시간씩 어떨까요? 저는 오후 7시에 시작할 수 있어요.
남: 완벽해요. 첫 수업 전에 맞춤형 운동 계획을 보내드릴 수 있도록 ⁰⁹이메일 주소를 주세요.

07 장소 문제
해석 화자들은 어디에 있는 것 같은가?
(A) 가구점에
(B) 병원에
(C) 맞춤 양복점에
(D) 헬스장에

해설 화자들이 있는 장소를 묻는 문제이므로, 장소와 관련된 표현을 놓치지 않고 듣는다. 남자가 "What would you like to do during your personal training sessions at our gym?"이라며 우리 체육관에서 개인 트레이닝 수업 시간 동안 무엇을 하고 싶은지 물어본 것을 통해 화자들이 헬스장에 있음을 알 수 있다. 따라서 (D)가 정답이다.

어휘 furniture n. 가구   medical clinic 병원   tailor's shop 맞춤 양복점

08 이유 문제
해석 남자는 왜 일정이 변경되어야 한다고 생각하는가?
(A) 초과하여 예약을 받는 것을 방지하기 위해
(B) 안전 위험을 줄이기 위해
(C) 할인의 자격을 얻기 위해
(D) 무료 수업을 받기 위해

해설 질문의 핵심 어구(schedule)와 관련된 내용을 주의 깊게 듣는다. 여자가 "I plan to come in for three hours every Saturday"라며 매주 토요일마다 3시간씩 오려고 계획하고 있다고 하자, 남자가 "Exercising one day a week for that long increases the risk of injury. Maybe you should consider coming more often."이라며 일주일에 하루 그렇게 오래 운동하는 것은 부상 위험을 증가시킨다고 한 후, 더 자주 오는 것을 고려해 보라고 하였다. 따라서 (B)가 정답이다.

어휘 overbook v. 초과하여 예약을 받다   reduce v. 줄이다   safety n. 안전
qualify for ~의 자격을 얻다   discount n. 할인

09 요청 문제
해석 남자는 무엇을 요청하는가?
(A) 선불
(B) 계좌번호
(C) 연락처 정보
(D) 사업 청구서

해설 남자의 말에서 요청과 관련된 표현이 언급된 다음을 주의 깊게 듣는다. 남자가 여자에게 "Please give me your e-mail address"라며 이메일 주소를 달라고 하였다. 따라서 (C)가 정답이다.

어휘 advance payment 선불   account n. 계좌   invoice n. 청구서

[10-12] 🎧 영국 → 캐나다
Questions 10-12 refer to the following conversation.

W: ¹⁰**The door to your right leads to our largest event hall.** It can comfortably seat up to 200 people and also has an excellent multimedia system.
M: It's wonderful, but our banquet is not going to be very large. We only have 50 guests, so ¹⁰**could I see a smaller hall?**
W: Well, we do have three smaller halls. ¹¹**However, they've already been rented for the day you requested.** If your date is flexible, we may be able to accommodate you. For instance, one of the smaller halls is available on June 5.
M: ¹²**We should be able to delay the banquet by a week.**

comfortably adv. 수월하게, 편안하게
flexible adj. (마음대로) 바꿀 수 있는, 탄력적인
accommodate v. 공간을 제공하다, 수용하다

해석
10-12번은 다음 대화에 관한 문제입니다.
여: ¹⁰오른쪽 문은 저희의 가장 큰 행사장으로 이어집니다. 200명까지 수월하게 수용할 수 있고, 훌륭한 멀티미디어 시스템도 있습니다.
남: 멋지네요, 하지만 저희 연회는 아주 크지는 않을 거예요. 저희는 손님이 50명 정도밖에 없어서, ¹⁰더 작은 행사장을 볼 수 있을까요?
여: 그게, 더 작은 행사장들이 세 개 있긴 합니다. ¹¹하지만, 고객님께서 요청하신 날짜에는 이미 대여되었어요. 만약 날짜를 바꿀 수 있으시다면, 고객님께 공간을 제공할 수 있을 거예요. 예를 들어, 작은 행사장 중 하나가 6월 5일에 이용할 수 있어요.
남: ¹²연회를 일주일까지는 연기할 수 있을 거예요.

10 주제 문제
해석 대화는 주로 무엇에 관한 것인가?
(A) 손님 목록 정하기
(B) 행사 장소 예약하기
(C) 장비 대여하기
(D) 가구 설치하기

해설 대화의 주제를 묻는 문제이므로, 대화의 초반을 반드시 듣는다. 여자가 "The door to your right leads to our largest event hall."이라며 오른쪽 문이 가장 큰 행사장으로 이어진다고 하자, 남자가 "could I see a smaller hall?"이라며 더 작은 행사장을 볼 수 있을지 물은 후, 장소 예약에 대한 내용으로 대화가 이어지고 있다. 따라서 (B)가 정답이다.

어휘 venue n. 장소 equipment n. 장비

11 문제점 문제
해석 여자는 무슨 문제를 언급하는가?
(A) 공간이 이용할 수 없다.
(B) 요금이 지불되지 않았다.
(C) 가격이 인상되었다.
(D) 준비가 되지 않았다.

해설 여자의 말에서 부정적인 표현이 언급된 주변을 주의 깊게 듣는다. 여자가 "However, they[smaller halls]'ve already been rented for the day you requested."라며 남자가 요청한 날짜에는 더 작은 행사장들이 이미 대여되었다고 하였다. 따라서 (A)가 정답이다.

어휘 space n. 공간 unavailable adj. 이용할 수 없는, 구할 수 없는 increase v. 인상하다 preparation n. 준비

12 언급 문제
해석 남자는 연회에 관해 무엇을 말하는가?
(A) 음식이 제공될 것이다.
(B) 확장될 수 있다.
(C) 연기될 수 있다.
(D) 비용이 많이 들지 않을 것이다.

해설 질문의 핵심 어구(banquet)가 언급된 주변을 주의 깊게 듣는다. 남자가 "We should be able to delay the banquet by a week."이라며 연회를 일주일까지는 연기할 수 있을 것이라고 하였다. 따라서 (C)가 정답이다.

어휘 cater v. 음식·서비스 등을 제공하다 expand v. 확장하다 postpone v. 연기하다, 미루다 inexpensive adj. 비용이 많이 들지 않는

Paraphrasing
delay the banquet 연회를 연기하다 → be postponed 연기되다

[13-15] 캐나다 → 영국
Questions 13-15 refer to the following conversation.

M: Hi. ¹³I'm calling to ask if you dry-clean silk items. I'd like to drop off a silk shirt today.
W: Sure. We can clean delicate fabrics for an extra charge of 5 dollars per item.
M: I see. ¹⁴Can I pick the shirt up tomorrow at around 3 P.M.? I want to wear it to my firm's year-end party tomorrow evening.
W: We can perform a rush service for 8 dollars extra. So your total will be 18 dollars.
M: That's fine. ¹⁵I'll stop by in 20 minutes.

drop off 맡기다, 갖다 주다   delicate adj. 섬세한, 민감한   fabric n. 직물
perform v. 시행하다   rush adj. 빠른, 급한

해석
13-15번은 다음 대화에 관한 문제입니다.
남: 안녕하세요. ¹³실크 제품을 드라이클리닝 하시는지 문의하기 위해 전화드려요. 저는 오늘 실크 셔츠를 맡기고 싶어요.
여: 그럼요. 저희는 품목당 5달러의 추가 요금으로 섬세한 직물들을 세탁해 드릴 수 있습니다.
남: 그렇군요. ¹⁴제가 셔츠를 내일 오후 3시 정도에 받을 수 있을까요? 저는 내일 저녁 우리 회사의 연말 파티에 그것을 입고 가고 싶어요.
여: 8달러 추가로 빠른 서비스를 시행해 드릴 수 있어요. 그러면 총액은 18달러가 될 겁니다.
남: 좋아요. ¹⁵20분 후에 들를게요.

13 화자 문제
해석 여자는 어디에서 일하는가?
(A) 사진관에서
(B) 백화점에서
(C) 세탁 시설에서
(D) 택배회사에서

해설 대화에서 신분 및 직업과 관련된 표현을 놓치지 않고 듣는다. 남자가 여자에게 "I'm calling to ask if you dry-clean silk items. I'd like to drop off a silk shirt today."라며 실크 제품을 드라이클리닝 하는지 문의하기 위해 전화한다고 한 후, 오늘 실크 셔츠를 맡기고 싶다고 한 말을 통해, 여자가 세탁 시설에서 일한다는 것을 알 수 있다. 따라서 (C)가 정답이다.

어휘 delivery service 택배회사

14 언급 문제
해석 남자는 물품에 대해 무엇을 말하는가?
(A) 이전에 사용된 적이 없다.
(B) 회사 행사를 위해 필요하다.
(C) 온라인으로 구입되었다.
(D) 현재 구할 수 없다.

해설 질문의 핵심 어구(item)와 관련된 내용을 주의 깊게 듣는다. 남자가 "Can I pick the shirt up tomorrow at around 3 P.M.? I want to wear it to my firm's year-end party tomorrow evening."이라며 셔츠를 내일 오후 3시 정도에 받을 수 있을지 물은 후, 내일 저녁 회사의 연말 파티에 그것을 입고 가고 싶다고 하였다. 따라서 (B)가 정답이다.

Paraphrasing
firm's year-end party 회사의 연말 파티 → company event 회사 행사

15 다음에 할 일 문제
해석 남자는 20분 후에 무엇을 할 것인가?
(A) 파티에 참석한다.
(B) 계정을 생성한다.
(C) 전화를 한다.
(D) 가게를 방문한다.

해설 질문의 핵심 어구(in 20 minutes)가 언급된 주변을 주의 깊게 듣는다. 남자가 "I'll stop by in 20 minutes."라며 20분 후에 들르겠다고 하였다. 따라서 (D)가 정답이다.

어휘 place v. (~을) 하다, 놓다

Paraphrasing
stop by 들르다 → Visit 방문하다

[16-18] 호주 → 미국 → 영국
Questions 16-18 refer to the following conversation with three speakers.

M: Amanda, ¹⁶**the launch of our company's latest smart TV is next week, right?**
W1: I think it's on September 7. But we'd better make sure. ¹⁷**We've still got a lot of promotional materials to prepare for the event.** Oh, ¹⁸**here comes Tanya. Let's check with her.**
M: Tanya, when will we be revealing our new TV?
W2: The event is scheduled for September 9. ¹⁸**I just spoke with our department head and confirmed the date.**
M: Got it. That should give us enough time to get ready.

launch n. 출시   promotional material 홍보 자료   reveal v. 공개하다
schedule v. 예정하다   confirm v. 확인하다

해석
16-18번은 다음 세 명의 대화에 관한 문제입니다.
남: Amanda, ¹⁶우리 회사의 최신 스마트 TV 출시가 다음 주죠, 그렇죠?
여1: 9월 7일인 것 같아요. 하지만 확실히 해두는 게 좋겠어요. ¹⁷행사를 위한 홍보 자료를 아직 많이 준비해야 해요. 오, ¹⁸Tanya가 오네요. 그녀와 확인해 봅시다.
남: Tanya, 우리는 언제 새 TV를 공개하나요?
여2: 행사는 9월 9일로 예정되어 있어요. ¹⁸방금 우리 부서장님과 대화하고 날짜를 확인했어요.
남: 알겠어요. 준비할 시간이 충분하겠네요.

16 주제 문제
해석 대화는 주로 무엇에 관한 것인가?
(A) 화상 회의
(B) 취업 면접
(C) 제품 출시
(D) 교육 기간
해설 대화의 주제를 묻는 문제이므로, 대화의 초반을 반드시 듣는다. 남자가 "the launch of our company's latest smart TV is next week, right?"라며 회사의 최신 스마트 TV 출시가 다음 주인지 물은 후, 제품 출시에 대한 내용으로 대화가 이어지고 있다. 따라서 (C)가 정답이다.
어휘 conference n. 회의   session n. 기간, (수업) 과정

17 화자 문제
해석 화자들은 어느 부서에서 일하는 것 같은가?
(A) 마케팅
(B) 연구
(C) 인사
(D) 회계
해설 대화에서 신분 및 직업과 관련된 표현을 놓치지 않고 듣는다. 여자1이 "We've still got a lot of promotional materials to prepare for the event."라며 행사를 위한 홍보 자료를 아직 많이 준비해야 한다고 한 것을 통해, 화자들이 마케팅 부서에서 일하고 있음을 알 수 있다. 따라서 (A)가 정답이다.
어휘 research n. 연구   personnel n. 인사(과)   accounting n. 회계

18 특정 세부 사항 문제
해석 Tanya는 최근에 무엇을 했는가?
(A) 고객을 만났다.
(B) 관리자와 대화했다.
(C) 기기를 구매했다.
(D) 예약을 했다.
해설 대화에서 Tanya의 말을 주의 깊게 듣는다. 여자1이 "here comes Tanya. Let's check with her."라며 Tanya가 오니까 그녀와 확인해 보자고 한 것을 통해 여자2가 Tanya라는 것을 알 수 있고, 여자2가 "I just spoke with our department head and confirmed the date."라며 방금 부서장과 대화하고 날짜를 확인했다고 하였다. 따라서, (B)가 정답이다.
어휘 booking n. 예약

[19-21] 미국 → 호주
Questions 19-21 refer to the following conversation.

W: Hello. My name is Hannah Long, and I work at the Sapphire Medical Center. ¹⁹**I'm calling to remind you about your upcoming appointment with us.**
M: Thanks for contacting me. I'm supposed to come in on Thursday at 10 A.M., right?
W: That's correct. ²⁰**I sent you an e-mail with some instructions about the medical test.** It includes guidelines about what you can and cannot eat the night before.
M: OK. Is there anything else?
W: Yes. Since this is your first visit to our facility, ²¹**please bring your health insurance card.**
M: I'll be sure to do that.

medical center 병원   instructions n. 지침, 설명
health insurance 건강 보험

해석
19-21번은 다음 대화에 관한 문제입니다.
여: 안녕하세요. 제 이름은 Hannah Long이고, Sapphire 병원에서 일합니다. ¹⁹귀하에게 다가오는 저희와의 예약에 대해 상기시켜 드리기 위해 전화 드렸어요.
남: 연락해 주셔서 감사해요. 제가 목요일 오전 10시에 가기로 되어 있죠, 맞나요?
여: 맞습니다. ²⁰제가 의료 검사에 관한 몇 가지 지침이 담긴 이메일을 보내드렸어요. 그것은 귀하께서 전날 밤에 드실 수 있는 것과 드실 수 없는 것에 대한 지침을 포함합니다.
남: 알겠어요. 다른 것이 더 있나요?
여: 네. 이번이 저희 시설에 첫 방문이시기 때문에, ²¹건강 보험 카드를 가져와 주세요.
남: 반드시 그렇게 할게요.

19 목적 문제
해석 여자는 왜 전화하고 있는가?
(A) 일정을 변경하기 위해
(B) 오류를 사과하기 위해
(C) 행사를 광고하기 위해
(D) 상기시켜 주기 위해
해설 전화의 목적을 묻는 문제이므로, 대화의 초반을 반드시 듣는다. 여자가 "I'm calling to remind you about your upcoming appointment with us."라며 다가오는 예약에 대해 상기시키기 위해 전화했다고 하였다. 따라서 (D)가 정답이다.
어휘 reminder n. 상기시켜 주는 것

20 특정 세부 사항 문제
해석 여자는 남자에게 무엇을 이메일로 보냈는가?
(A) 검사에 대한 지침
(B) 진료 기록

(C) 검사 결과
(D) 병원으로 가는 길 안내

해설 질문의 핵심 어구(e-mail)가 언급된 주변을 주의 깊게 듣는다. 여자가 "I sent you an e-mail with some instructions about the medical test."라며 의료 검사에 관한 몇 가지 지침이 담긴 이메일을 보냈다고 하였다. 따라서 (A)가 정답이다.

어휘 medical record 진료 기록 examination n. 검사 directions n. 길 안내

21 요청 문제

해설 여자는 남자에게 무엇을 하라고 요청하는가?
(A) 애플리케이션을 다운로드한다.
(B) 의사에게 전화한다.
(C) 문서를 발송한다.
(D) 카드를 가져온다.

해설 여자의 말에서 요청과 관련된 표현이 언급된 다음을 주의 깊게 듣는다. 여자가 남자에게 "please bring your health insurance card"라며 건강 보험 카드를 가져와 달라고 하였다. 따라서 (D)가 정답이다.

[22-24] 🎧 호주 → 영국

Questions 22-24 refer to the following conversation.

M: Thank you for tuning in to YBC Radio. On today's episode of *Technology News*, I have a very special guest. ²²**Dianne Webb is a biologist who is trying to find a treatment for cancer.** Welcome, Ms. Webb.

W: Thank you for having me. The project I'm working on shows a lot of promise. As a result, ²³**we received a significant grant from the government. We plan to use it to expand our laboratory.**

M: That's exciting. Are you making much progress?

W: Yes. And ²⁴**we'll be publishing a status report on May 10** with a summary of my team's findings.

tune in 청취하다, 채널을 맞추다   biologist n. 생물학자
significant adj. 상당한, 중요한   grant n. 보조금
status report 진행 상황 보고서   finding n. 연구 결과

해석
22-24번은 다음 대화에 관한 문제입니다.
남: YBC 라디오를 청취해 주셔서 감사합니다. 오늘의 *Technology News* 에피소드에는 매우 특별한 게스트가 있습니다. ²²Dianne Webb은 암 치료법을 찾고자 노력하고 있는 생물학자입니다. Ms. Webb, 환영합니다.
여: 초대해 주셔서 감사합니다. 제가 진행 중인 프로젝트는 많은 가능성을 보여주고 있습니다. 그 결과, ²³저희는 정부로부터 상당한 보조금을 받았습니다. 저희는 그것을 실험실을 확장하는 데 사용할 계획입니다.
남: 그거 흥미롭군요. 많은 진전을 이루고 계신가요?
여: 네. ²⁴그리고 5월 10일에 제 팀의 연구 결과 요약과 함께 진행 상황 보고서를 발표할 예정입니다.

22 화자 문제

해설 여자는 누구인 것 같은가?
(A) 강사
(B) 공무원
(C) 프로그래머
(D) 연구원

해설 대화에서 신분 및 직업과 관련된 표현을 놓치지 않고 듣는다. 남자가 "Dianne Webb is a biologist who is trying to find a treatment for cancer."라며 Dianne Webb이 암 치료법을 찾고자 노력하고 있는 생물학자라고 한 것을 통해 여자가 연구원이라는 것을 알 수 있다. 따라서 (D)가 정답이다.

어휘 instructor n. 강사   official n. 공무원   researcher n. 연구원

23 특정 세부 사항 문제

해설 여자에 따르면, 보조금은 무엇을 위해 사용될 것인가?
(A) 시설을 확장하는 것
(B) 장치를 수리하는 것
(C) 직원을 채용하는 것
(D) 캠페인에 착수하는 것

해설 여자의 말에서 질문의 핵심 어구(grant)가 언급된 주변을 주의 깊게 듣는다. 여자가 "we received a significant grant from the government. We plan to use it to expand our laboratory."라며 정부로부터 상당한 보조금을 받았고, 그것을 실험실을 확장하는 데 사용할 계획이라고 하였다. 따라서 (A)가 정답이다.

어휘 expand v. 확장하다   facility n. 시설   employee n. 직원
launch v. 착수하다, 시작하다

24 다음에 할 일 문제

해설 5월 10일에 무슨 일이 일어날 것인가?
(A) 프로젝트가 완료될 것이다.
(B) 문서가 발표될 것이다.
(C) 팀이 새로 발령될 것이다.
(D) 검사가 수행될 것이다.

해설 질문의 핵심 어구(May 10)가 언급된 주변을 주의 깊게 듣는다. 여자가 "we'll be publishing a status report on May 10"이라며 5월 10일에 진행 상황 보고서를 발표할 예정이라고 한 것을 통해 문서가 발표될 것임을 알 수 있다. 따라서 (B)가 정답이다.

어휘 publish v. 발표하다, 공개하다   reassign v. 새로 발령내다
inspection n. 검사, 점검

DAY 10 세부 사항 관련 문제

1. 세부 사항 문제

HACKERS PRACTICE   p.89

01 (B)   **02** (D)   **03** (A)

[01] 🎧 캐나다 → 미국 / 호주 → 영국

Question 01 refers to the following conversation.

M: Hello. I need to purchase a TV stand for my house. Can you make some recommendations?

W: I'm happy to help you. What is your budget?

M: I don't have a specific budget. But I want something that will match the décor of my living room.

W: I see. ⁰¹**Could you tell me about the furniture in that room?**

recommendation n. 추천, 권고   specific adj. 구체적인, 특정한
budget n. 예산, 비용; v. 예산을 세우다
match v. (색깔·무늬·스타일이 서로) 맞다   décor n. 인테리어, 실내장식

해석
01번은 다음 대화에 관한 문제입니다.
남: 안녕하세요. 제가 집에 놓을 텔레비전 받침대를 구입해야 하는데요. 추천을 해주실 수 있을까요?
여: 도와드릴 수 있어서 기쁩니다. 예산이 어떻게 되시나요?
남: 구체적인 예산은 없어요. 하지만 제 거실 인테리어와 어울리는 것이 필요해요.
여: 알겠습니다. ⁰¹그 방의 가구에 대해 말씀해 주시겠어요?

01 다음에 할 일 문제

해석 남자는 다음에 무엇을 할 것 같은가?
(A) 제품을 살펴본다.
(B) 비치 가구를 설명한다.
(C) 비용을 계산한다.
(D) 약속을 잡는다.

해설 대화의 마지막 부분을 주의 깊게 듣는다. 여자가 "Could you tell me about the furniture in that room[living room]?"이라며 거실의 가구에 대해 말해달라고 하였다. 따라서 (B)가 정답이다.

어휘 describe v. 설명하다, 묘사하다   furnishing n. 비치 가구, 세간
calculate v. 계산하다

> **Paraphrasing**
> tell ~ about ~ furniture 가구에 대해 말하다 → Describe ~ furnishings 비치 가구를 설명하다

[02] 호주 → 영국 / 캐나다 → 미국

Question 02 refers to the following conversation.

M: Are you busy, Leena? I'm wondering if you could make arrangements for my upcoming trip. ⁰²**I have to meet some important clients from August 8 to 12 in Chicago.**
W: Of course, Mr. Sanders. Is there a specific hotel that you'd like to stay at in Chicago?
M: Anywhere downtown is fine. Please e-mail me the details later this afternoon. Thanks in advance!

make arrangements ~를 준비하다   upcoming adj. 다가오는, 곧 나올
specific adj. 특정한

해석
02번은 다음 대화에 관한 문제입니다.

남: 바쁜가요, Leena? 당신이 다가오는 출장 준비를 해줄 수 있는지 궁금해요. ⁰²저는 8월 8일부터 12일까지 시카고에서 중요한 고객들을 만나야 해요.
여: 물론이죠, Mr. Sanders. 시카고에 계시는 동안 묵고 싶으신 특정 호텔이 있으신가요?
남: 시내라면 어디든지 괜찮아요. 세부 사항들을 오늘 오후 제게 이메일로 보내주세요. 미리 고마워요!

02 이유 문제

해석 남자는 왜 시카고에 가는가?
(A) 그는 친척들을 방문하길 원한다.
(B) 그는 모임에서 연설해야 한다.
(C) 그는 조사를 수행해야 한다.
(D) 그는 고객들과 만나야 한다.

해설 남자의 말에서 질문의 핵심 어구(Chicago)가 언급된 주변을 주의 깊게 듣는다. 남자가 "I have to meet some important clients from August 8 to 12 in Chicago."라며 8월 8일부터 12일까지 시카고에서 중요한 고객들을 만나야 한다고 하였다. 따라서 (D)가 정답이다.

어휘 relative n. 친척   gathering n. 모임   conduct v. 수행하다
research n. 조사, 연구

[03] 미국 → 캐나다 / 영국 → 호주

Question 03 refers to the following conversation.

W: Hey, Mike. I heard that our sales seminar has been postponed until next month. The speaker was suddenly called away on an urgent business trip.
M: Really? ⁰³**I'm just worried because I was hoping to learn some new techniques to sell products before the trade show** in Denver.
W: Well, maybe you can check the materials he left behind.
M: I suppose I could. Besides, there are a number of Web sites on the topic, too.

postpone v. 연기하다, 미루다   business trip 출장   technique n. 기술

해석
03번은 다음 대화에 관한 문제입니다.

여: 저기, Mike. 우리 영업 세미나가 다음 달로 연기되었다고 들었어요. 발표자가 갑자기 긴급한 출장에 불려 갔대요.
남: 정말이요? 덴버에서 열리는 ⁰³그 무역 박람회 전에 제품을 판매하는 새로운 기술을 좀 배우고 싶었는데 걱정이네요.
여: 흠, 아마도 그가 남기고 간 자료들을 확인할 수 있을 거예요.
남: 그럴 수도 있을 것 같네요. 게다가, 그 주제에 대한 웹사이트들도 많이 있으니까요.

03 문제점 문제

해석 남자는 무엇에 관해 걱정하는가?
(A) 그는 판매 기술을 배우지 못할 것이다.
(B) 그는 덴버로 통근할 수 없다.
(C) 그는 자료를 가져올 것을 잊었다.
(D) 그는 행사를 위한 연설자를 찾지 못하고 있다.

해설 남자의 말에서 부정적인 표현이 언급된 다음을 주의 깊게 듣는다. 남자가 "I'm just worried because I was hoping to learn some new techniques to sell products before the trade show"라며 무역 박람회 전에 제품을 판매하는 새로운 기술을 배우고 싶었기 때문에 걱정이라고 하였다. 따라서 (A)가 정답이다.

어휘 be unable to ~할 수 없다   forget v. 잊다

2. 의도 파악 문제

HACKERS PRACTICE p.91

01 (C)   02 (D)   03 (C)

[01] 캐나다 → 영국 / 호주 → 미국

Question 01 refers to the following conversation.

M: Hello. I'm here to take the written exam to renew my driver's license.
W: OK. Just note that many people are ahead of you.
M: Oh . . . When do you think I'll be able to take the test? ⁰¹**I need to leave at 4 P.M.**
W: I doubt you'll be finished by then. ⁰¹**We are open on Saturday, though.** That might be best for you.

renew v. 갱신하다   license n. 면허증, 면허

해석
01번은 다음 대화에 관한 문제입니다.

남: 안녕하세요. 저는 운전면허증을 갱신하기 위해 필기시험을 치르려고 이곳에 왔어요.
여: 알겠습니다. 당신 앞에 많은 사람들이 있다는 점만 유념해 주세요.
남: 아... 제가 언제 시험을 칠 수 있을 것 같나요? ⁰¹저는 오후 4시에는 떠나야 해요.
여: 당신이 그때까지 끝낼 수 있을지 의문이에요. ⁰¹하지만 저희는 토요일에도 열려 있어요. 그것이 아마 당신에게 가장 좋을 거예요.

01 의도 파악 문제

해석 여자는 왜 "그것이 아마 당신에게 가장 좋을 거예요"라고 말하는가?

(A) 남자에게 줄에 들어가 서라고 조언하기 위해
(B) 신청서가 지금 작성될 수 있다고 알려주기 위해
(C) 남자가 나중에 다시 와야 한다고 제안하기 위해
(D) 남자의 제안에 동의하기 위해

해설 질문의 인용어구(That might be best for you)가 언급된 주변을 주의 깊게 듣는다. 남자가 "I need to leave at 4 P.M."이라며 오후 4시에는 떠나야 한다고 하자, 여자가 "We are open on Saturday, though."라며 토요일에도 열려 있다고 한 것을 통해 남자가 나중에 다시 와야 한다고 제안하기 위함임을 알 수 있다. 따라서 (C)가 정답이다.

어휘 get in line 줄에 들어가 서다   indicate v. 알리다
application n. 신청서, 지원서   agree with ~에 동의하다
suggestion n. 제안

[02] 영국 → 호주 / 미국 → 캐나다
Question 02 refers to the following conversation.

W: Kyle, it's Lisa Griggs from accounting. I just want to remind you that we're supposed to give a presentation next Friday. ⁰²**We should probably start preparing for it soon.**
M: ⁰²**I agree.** After all, our company president will be attending. Why don't we start sometime today? When are you free?
W: Now is a good time. I won't be available later in the afternoon because I have a meeting.

accounting n. 회계   remind v. 상기시키다   attend v. 참석하다

해석
02번은 다음 대화에 관한 문제입니다.
여: Kyle, 회계팀의 Lisa Griggs입니다. 우리가 다음 주 금요일에 발표를 하기로 되어 있다는 것을 상기시켜 드리려고 해요. ⁰²우리는 아마 곧 그것을 준비하기 시작해야 할 거예요.
남: ⁰²동의해요. 어쨌든, 우리 회사의 대표 이사가 참석할 거예요. 오늘 언젠가 시작하는 게 어때요? 언제가 가능하신가요?
여: 지금이 좋은 시간이에요. 저는 오후에는 회의가 있어서 시간이 안 될 거예요.

02 의도 파악 문제
해설 남자는 "우리 회사의 대표 이사가 참석할 거예요"라고 말할 때 무엇을 의도하는가?
(A) 임원이 연락되어야 한다.
(B) 지원을 받을 것이다.
(C) 발표가 연기되었다.
(D) 업무가 중요하다.

해설 질문의 인용어구(our company president will be attending)가 언급된 주변을 주의 깊게 듣는다. 여자가 "We should probably start preparing for it[presentation] soon."이라며 아마 곧 발표를 준비하기 시작해야 할 것이라고 하자, 남자가 "I agree."라며 동의한다고 한 후, 회사의 대표 이사가 참석할 것이라고 한 것을 통해 업무가 중요함을 알 수 있다. 따라서 (D)가 정답이다.

어휘 executive n. 임원   assistance n. 지원, 도움   assignment n. 업무, 과제

[03] 캐나다 → 미국 / 호주 → 영국
Question 03 refers to the following conversation.

M: How's your team doing with developing the advertising campaign, Denise? Our CEO wants us to start promoting our products on social media soon.
W: We're going to need more time. ⁰³**Our main competitor just launched some online videos that are very similar to ours. So I decided that my team should start again.**
M: We don't want to look like we are copying them. ⁰³**Don't worry. I'll explain the situation to our CEO.**

advertising n. 광고   promote v. 홍보하다   competitor n. 경쟁사
launch v. 개시하다   similar adj. 비슷한, 유사한   copy v. 베끼다

해석
03번은 다음 대화에 관한 문제입니다.
남: 당신 팀의 광고 캠페인 개발은 어떻게 진행되고 있나요, Denise? 우리 최고 경영자는 우리가 곧 소셜 미디어에서 제품 홍보를 시작하기를 원해요.
여: 시간이 더 필요할 거예요. ⁰³우리의 주요 경쟁사가 우리의 것과 매우 비슷한 온라인 동영상을 방금 개시했어요. 그래서 우리 팀이 다시 시작해야 한다고 결정을 내렸어요.
남: 우리가 그것들을 베끼는 것처럼 보이고 싶지는 않죠. ⁰³걱정하지 마세요. 우리 최고 경영자에게 상황을 설명할게요.

03 의도 파악 문제
해설 남자는 왜 "우리가 그것들을 베끼는 것처럼 보이고 싶지는 않죠"라고 말하는가?
(A) 초대를 거절하기 위해
(B) 계획을 변경하기 위해
(C) 결정에 대한 지지를 보여주기 위해
(D) 온라인 캠페인을 칭찬하기 위해

해설 질문의 인용어구(We don't want to look like we are copying them)가 언급된 주변을 주의 깊게 듣는다. 여자가 "Our main competitor just launched some online videos that are very similar to ours. So I decided that my team should start again."이라며 주요 경쟁사가 자사의 것과 매우 비슷한 온라인 동영상을 방금 개시했다고 한 후, 자신의 팀이 다시 시작해야 한다고 결정을 내렸다고 하자, 남자가 "Don't worry. I'll explain the situation to our CEO."라며 걱정하지 말라고 한 후, 최고 경영자에게 상황을 설명하겠다고 하였다. 따라서 (C)가 정답이다.

어휘 decline v. 거절하다   invitation n. 초대   support n. 지지
decision n. 결정   praise v. 칭찬하다

3. 시각 자료 문제

HACKERS PRACTICE   p.93

01 (C)   02 (C)   03 (B)

[01] 미국 → 호주 / 영국 → 캐나다
Question 01 refers to the following conversation and pie chart.

W: Isaac, can you explain the details of our hair salon's plan to attract customers in March?
M: ⁰¹**We're going to discount our services by up to 50 percent** for the month.
W: Which services are going to be featured?
M: All of them, but ⁰¹**we've chosen to give the biggest discount to the service preferred by over 20 percent of our customers.** It has the highest profit margin.

feature v. 포함하다   profit margin 이윤

해석
01번은 다음 대화와 원그래프에 관한 문제입니다.
여: Isaac, 3월에 고객들을 끌어모으기 위한 우리 미용실의 계획에 대한 세부

사항들을 설명해줄 수 있나요?

남: 그달에는 ⁰¹우리 서비스들을 50퍼센트까지 할인할 거예요.

여: 어떤 서비스들이 포함될 건가요?

남: 모두 다 이긴 한데, ⁰¹우리 고객들 중 20퍼센트 이상에 의해 선호되는 서비스에 가장 큰 할인을 주기로 결정했어요. 그것이 가장 이윤이 높거든요.

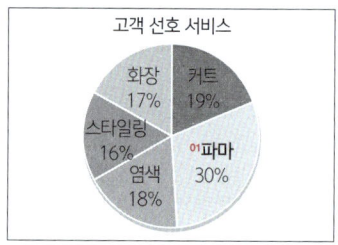

01 시각 자료 문제

해석 시각 자료를 보아라. 어떤 서비스가 50퍼센트 할인될 것인가?
(A) 화장
(B) 커트
(C) 파마
(D) 스타일링

해설 제시된 원그래프의 정보를 확인한 후 질문의 핵심어구(50 percent off)와 관련된 내용을 주의 깊게 듣는다. 남자가 "We're going to discount our services by up to 50 percent"라며 서비스들을 50퍼센트까지 할인할 것이라고 한 뒤, "we've chosen to give the biggest discount to the service preferred by over 20 percent of our customers"라며 고객들 중 20퍼센트 이상에 의해 선호되는 서비스에 가장 큰 할인을 주기로 결정했다고 했으므로, 50퍼센트 할인되는 서비스는 파마 서비스임을 원그래프에서 알 수 있다. 따라서 (C)가 정답이다.

[02] 🎧 호주 → 영국 / 캐나다 → 미국

Question 02 refers to the following conversation and price list.

M: Could you go over this list of furniture for our new lounge? Here you go.
W: These are good choices. However, I'm not sure we can afford all of them.
M: In that case, ⁰²I suggest not buying the 250-dollar piece since we already have one.
W: OK, good. I'm comfortable with that.

go over ~을 검토하다　lounge n. 휴게실　afford v. ~을 살 여유가 되다
comfortable adj. 납득할 수 있는, 편안한

해석
02번은 다음 대화와 가격표에 관한 문제입니다.

남: 새 휴게실을 위한 가구 목록을 검토해 주시겠어요? 여기 있어요.

여: 좋은 선택들이에요. 하지만, 저는 우리가 그것들을 모두 살 여유가 되는지 모르겠어요.

남: 그렇다면, ⁰²이미 250달러짜리가 있으니 그건 사지 않는 것을 제안해요.

여: 네, 좋아요. 그것에 납득할 수 있네요.

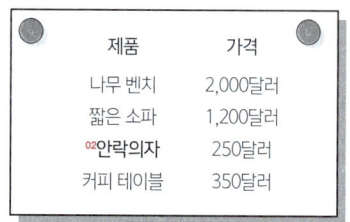

02 시각 자료 문제

해석 시각 자료를 보아라. 어떤 제품이 구매되지 않을 것인가?
(A) 나무 벤치
(B) 짧은 소파
(C) 안락의자
(D) 커피 테이블

해설 제시된 가격표의 정보를 확인한 후 질문의 핵심 어구(will not be purchased)와 관련된 내용을 주의 깊게 듣는다. 남자가 "I suggest not buying the 250-dollar piece since we already have one."이라며 이미 250달러짜리가 있으니 그것을 사지 않는 것을 제안한다고 했으므로, 구매되지 않을 제품이 안락의자임을 가격표에서 알 수 있다. 따라서 (C)가 정답이다.

[03] 🎧 캐나다 → 미국 / 호주 → 영국

Question 03 refers to the following conversation and directory.

M: My sales presentations for the clients in Berlin didn't go well. Most of them already use electronic locks that are similar to the ones we sell.
W: That's unfortunate. It seems our competitor, SecureForce, has many customers in Europe. We need to rethink our sales strategy.
M: Absolutely. I'm going to bring this up at our meeting this Wednesday.
W: Good idea. Also, ⁰³I'll call our market researcher to request a report on our European competition.

electronic adj. 전자의　rethink v. 재고하다　strategy n. 전략
bring up 말을 꺼내다

해석
03번은 다음 대화와 전화번호부에 관한 문제입니다.

남: 베를린에 있는 고객들을 위한 영업 발표가 별로 좋지는 않았어요. 그들 대부분은 우리가 판매하는 것과 유사한 전자 자물쇠를 이미 사용하고 있어요.

여: 안타깝네요. 우리의 경쟁사인 SecureForce가 유럽에 많은 고객을 보유하고 있는 것 같네요. 우리는 우리의 판매 전략을 재고해야 돼요.

남: 물론이에요. 이번 주 수요일 회의에서 제가 이것에 대해 말을 꺼낼게요.

여: 좋은 생각이에요. 또한, ⁰³우리 시장 조사 담당자에게 전화해서 유럽의 경쟁에 대한 보고서를 요청할게요.

부서	내선 번호
영업	310
시장 조사	⁰³455
보안	562
제품 디자인	640

03 시각 자료 문제

해석 시각 자료를 보아라. 여자는 어느 내선 번호로 전화할 것인가?
(A) 310
(B) 455
(C) 562
(D) 640

해설 제시된 전화번호부의 정보를 확인한 후 질문의 핵심 어구(dial)와 관련된 내용을 주의 깊게 듣는다. 여자가 "I'll call our market researcher"라며 시장 조사 담당자에게 전화하겠다고 했으므로, 여자가 전화할 내선 번호가 455임을 전화번호부에서 알 수 있다. 따라서 (B)가 정답이다.

HACKERS TEST

p.94

01 (A)	02 (A)	03 (C)	04 (D)	05 (C)
06 (B)	07 (A)	08 (B)	09 (A)	10 (D)
11 (B)	12 (C)	13 (D)	14 (B)	15 (C)
16 (D)	17 (C)	18 (B)	19 (D)	20 (A)
21 (A)				

[01-03] 호주 → 미국

Questions 01-03 refer to the following conversation.

M: Hi. ⁰¹Can you please tell me where the baking dishes are located?

W: ⁰¹Those are in Aisle 1, next to the fruit and vegetable section. And just to let you know, we now carry the popular Presto line of cookware.

M: Oh, ⁰²I already went to your Web site to print a coupon for another brand.

W: That's good. Also, ⁰³if you brought your own shopping bag, you can get an additional 5 percent discount.

M: Thanks for letting me know.

baking dish 제빵 접시   aisle n. 열, 통로   cookware n. 조리기구
additional adj. 추가(의)

해석
01-03번은 다음 대화에 관한 문제입니다.

남: 안녕하세요. ⁰¹여기 제빵 접시가 어디에 있는지 알려주실 수 있나요?
여: ⁰¹그것들은 1번 통로에 있어요, 과일과 채소 구역 옆에요. 그리고 그저 알려드리는 건데, 저희는 이제 인기 있는 Presto 조리기구 라인을 취급합니다.
남: 아, ⁰²저는 이미 다른 브랜드의 쿠폰을 인쇄하기 위해 귀사의 웹사이트를 방문했어요.
여: 잘됐네요. 그리고 ⁰³만약 고객님 자신의 장바구니를 가져오셨다면, 5퍼센트 추가 할인을 받으실 수 있어요.
남: 알려주셔서 감사해요.

01 장소 문제

해석 화자들은 어디에 있는 것 같은가?
(A) 슈퍼마켓에
(B) 빵집에
(C) 식당에
(D) 카페에

해설 대화에서 장소와 관련된 표현을 놓치지 않고 듣는다. 남자가 "Can you please tell me where the baking dishes are located?"라며 제빵 접시가 어디에 있는지 묻자, 여자가 "Those[baking dishes] are in Aisle 1, next to the fruit and vegetable section."이라며 제빵 접시가 과일과 채소 구역 옆 1번 통로에 있다고 하였다. 이를 통해, 화자들이 슈퍼마켓에 있음을 알 수 있다. 따라서 (A)가 정답이다.

02 이유 문제

해석 남자는 왜 웹사이트에 방문했는가?
(A) 쿠폰을 받기 위해
(B) 주문을 하기 위해
(C) 가격을 확인하기 위해
(D) 비밀번호를 바꾸기 위해

해설 질문의 핵심 어구(Web site)가 언급된 주변을 주의 깊게 듣는다. 남자가 "I already went to your Web site to print a coupon for another brand."라며 다른 브랜드의 쿠폰을 인쇄하기 위해 웹사이트를 방문했다고 하였다. 따라서 (A)가 정답이다.

03 특정 세부 사항 문제

해석 추가 할인을 받기 위해 무엇이 필요한가?
(A) 작성이 완료된 설문조사
(B) 회원 카드
(C) 장바구니
(D) 판매 영수증

해설 질문의 핵심 어구(additional discount)와 관련된 내용을 주의 깊게 듣는다. 여자가 "if you brought your own shopping bag, you can get an additional 5 percent discount"라며 만약 남자가 자신의 장바구니를 가져왔다면, 5퍼센트 추가 할인을 받을 수 있다고 하였다. 따라서 (C)가 정답이다.

어휘 survey n. 설문조사   sales receipt 판매 영수증

[04-06] 영국 → 캐나다

Questions 04-06 refer to the following conversation.

W: Hi. ⁰⁴I just looked at some products in your online store, and I'm interested in the crystal chandelier. If I order it, will your store take care of the installation?

M: Yes. ⁰⁵We are providing free installation for all orders made this month.

W: That's good to know. But before deciding, ⁰⁶I'd like to check the price at another store nearby, just to compare. I want to make sure I'm getting the best deal.

installation n. 설치   deal n. 거래

해석
04-06번은 다음 대화에 관한 문제입니다.

여: 안녕하세요. ⁰⁴저는 방금 당신의 온라인 상점에서 몇몇 제품들을 보았는데, 크리스털 샹들리에에 관심이 생겼어요. 제가 그것을 주문하면, 당신의 가게에서 설치를 처리해 주시나요?
남: 네. ⁰⁵저희는 이번 달에 이루어진 모든 주문 건에 대해 무료 설치를 제공하고 있어요.
여: 알게 되어 좋네요. 하지만 결정하기 전에, ⁰⁶단지 비교를 하기 위해서 근처에 있는 다른 상점의 가격을 확인해 보고 싶어요. 제가 가장 좋은 거래를 하고 있는지 확실히 하기를 원해요.

04 특정 세부 사항 문제

해석 여자는 이미 무엇을 했는가?
(A) 조명을 구입했다.
(B) 이메일을 보냈다.
(C) 배달을 받았다.
(D) 온라인 상점을 둘러보았다.

해설 질문의 핵심 어구(woman already do)와 관련된 내용을 주의 깊게 듣는다. 여자가 "I just looked at some products in your online store"라며 방금 온라인 상점에서 몇몇 제품들을 보았다고 하였다. 따라서 (D)가 정답이다.

어휘 browse v. 둘러보다

[Paraphrasing]
looked at ~ products in ~ online store 온라인 상점에서 제품들을 보았다
→ browsed an online store 온라인 상점을 둘러보았다

05 특정 세부 사항 문제

해석 상점은 이번 달에 무엇을 제공하는가?
(A) 연장된 보증
(B) 더 빠른 배송
(C) 무료 설치
(D) 상품권

해설 남자의 말에서 질문의 핵심 어구(provide this month)와 관련된 내용을

주의 깊게 듣는다. 남자가 "We are providing free installation for all orders made this month."라며 이번 달에 이루어진 모든 주문 건에 대해 무료 설치를 제공하고 있다고 하였다. 따라서 (C)가 정답이다.

어휘 extended adj. 연장된 warranty n. 보증 expedite v. 더 신속히 처리하다
installation n. 설치 gift certificate 상품권

06 이유 문제

해석 여자는 왜 다른 가게를 방문할 계획인가?
(A) 환불을 요청하기 위해
(B) 가격을 비교하기 위해
(C) 샘플을 얻기 위해
(D) 불만을 제기하기 위해

해설 질문의 핵심 어구(plan to visit another store)와 관련된 내용을 주의 깊게 듣는다. 여자가 "I'd like to check the price at another store nearby, just to compare"라며 비교를 하기 위해서 근처에 있는 다른 상점의 가격을 확인해 보고 싶다고 하였다. 따라서 (B)가 정답이다.

어휘 refund n. 환불 compare v. 비교하다 complaint n. 불만

[07-09] 캐나다 → 영국 → 미국

Questions 07-09 refer to the following conversation with three speakers.

M: Oh, hello. I didn't know you two were in here.
W1: Hi, Ted. We're just finalizing the blueprint for the Franklin property. ⁰⁷**The deadline to send it to the client was yesterday, but we missed it.** Do you need to use the conference room?
M: Yes, actually. ⁰⁸**I'm going to conduct a workshop for some new staff members at 4 P.M.**
W1: That's half an hour from now.
M: I have to set up the projector and rearrange the tables. When do you think you'll be finished, Ann?
W2: We'll be done in a few minutes. After that, ⁰⁹**I'll give you a hand with moving the tables**.

finalize v. 마무리하다 blueprint n. 설계도, 청사진
property n. 건물, 부동산 miss v. 놓치다 conduct v. 진행하다, 수행하다
rearrange v. 재배치하다 give a hand 도와주다

해석
07-09번은 다음 세 명의 대화에 관한 문제입니다.

남: 아, 안녕하세요. 두 분이 여기 계시는지 몰랐어요.
여1: 안녕하세요, Ted. 저희는 지금 막 Franklin 건물에 대한 설계도를 마무리하고 있어요. ⁰⁷고객에게 그것을 보내는 마감 기한이 어제였는데, 우리가 그것을 놓쳤어요. 회의실을 사용하셔야 하나요?
남: 사실, 그래요. ⁰⁸저는 오후 4시에 몇몇 새로운 직원들을 위한 워크숍을 진행할 거예요.
여1: 그건 지금으로부터 30분 후인데요.
남: 프로젝터를 설치하고 책상들을 재배치해야 해요. 언제 끝날 것 같나요, Ann?
여2: 우리는 몇 분 안에 끝날 거예요. 그 후에, ⁰⁹제가 책상을 옮기는 것을 도와드릴게요.

07 문제점 문제

해석 무슨 문제가 언급되는가?
(A) 마감 기한을 놓쳤다.
(B) 건물이 손상되었다.
(C) 기기가 제대로 작동하지 않고 있다.
(D) 결정이 승인되지 않았다.

해설 대화에서 부정적인 표현이 언급된 주변을 주의 깊게 듣는다. 여자1이 "The deadline to send it[blueprint] to the client was yesterday, but we missed it."이라며 고객에게 설계도를 보내는 기한이 어제였는데, 놓쳤다고 하였다. 따라서 (A)가 정답이다.

어휘 damage v. 손상시키다 properly adv. 제대로, 적절하게

08 다음에 할 일 문제

해석 남자는 오후 4시에 무엇을 할 것인가?
(A) 건물을 보여준다.
(B) 워크숍을 이끈다.
(C) 문서를 읽는다.
(D) 설계도를 인쇄한다.

해설 남자의 말에서 질문의 핵심 어구(4 P.M.)가 언급된 주변을 주의 깊게 듣는다. 남자가 "I'm going to conduct a workshop for some new staff members at 4 P.M."이라며 오후 4시에 몇몇 새로운 직원들을 위한 워크숍을 진행할 것이라고 하였다. 따라서 (B)가 정답이다.

어휘 document n. 문서

Paraphrasing
conduct 진행하다 → lead 이끌다

09 제안 문제

해석 Ann은 남자를 위해 무엇을 해주겠다고 제안하는가?
(A) 가구를 옮긴다.
(B) 장비를 교체한다.
(C) 회의실을 예약한다.
(D) 직원에게 연락한다.

해설 여자2[Ann]의 말에서 남자를 위해 해주겠다고 언급한 내용을 주의 깊게 듣는다. 여자2[Ann]가 남자에게 "I'll give you a hand with moving the tables"라며 책상을 옮기는 것을 도와주겠다고 하였다. 따라서 (A)가 정답이다.

어휘 replace v. 교체하다 reserve v. 예약하다 contact v. 연락하다

Paraphrasing
tables 책상 → furniture 가구

[10-12] 영국 → 호주

Questions 10-12 refer to the following conversation.

W: Hello. ¹⁰**I need some landscaping work done at my home.** ¹⁰/¹¹**One of my coworkers suggested that I try your company.** Are you taking on new clients?
M: Yes, ¹²**but we wouldn't be able to work on your property for another four weeks**. This is our busiest time of year, so we have a lot of other jobs booked right now.
W: That's not a problem, as I'm willing to wait until then. In fact, I'm still trying to decide precisely what I want done, so some extra time would be helpful.

landscaping n. 조경 take on 맡다 book v. 예약하다
willing adj. 기꺼이 ~하려는 precisely adv. 정확히

해석
10-12번은 다음 대화에 관한 문제입니다.

여: 안녕하세요. ¹⁰제 집에 조경 작업이 필요해요. ¹⁰/¹¹동료들 중 한 명이 당신의 회사를 이용해 보라고 제안했어요. 새 고객을 받고 계신가요?
남: 네, ¹²하지만 앞으로 4주 동안 당신의 건물 작업을 할 수 없을 것 같아요. 일 년 중 가장 바쁜 시기라서, 지금 예약된 다른 일들이 많거든요.
여: 저는 그때까지 기꺼이 기다릴 수 있으니까, 그건 문제가 되지 않아요. 사실, 저는 정확히 어떤 작업이 되기를 원하는지 결정하려 하고 있어서, 약간의 추가 시간이 도움이 될 것 같아요.

10 화자 문제
해석 남자는 어디에서 일하는 것 같은가?
(A) 원예용품 상점에서
(B) 건축 회사에서
(C) 부동산 중개소에서
(D) 조경 회사에서

해설 대화에서 신분 및 직업과 관련된 표현을 놓치지 않고 듣는다. 여자가 "I need some landscaping work done at my home. One of my coworkers suggested that I try your company."라며 집에 조경 작업이 필요하다고 한 후, 남자의 회사를 이용해 보라는 제안을 받았다고 하였다. 이를 통해 남자가 조경 회사에서 일한다는 것을 알 수 있다. 따라서 (D)가 정답이다.

어휘 architectural adj. 건설의 real estate 부동산

11 방법 문제
해석 여자는 업체에 대해 어떻게 알게 되었는가?
(A) 인터넷을 검색함으로써
(B) 동료와 대화함으로써
(C) 라디오를 들음으로써
(D) 이웃에게 물어봄으로써

해설 질문의 핵심 어구(business)와 관련된 내용을 주의 깊게 듣는다. 여자가 "One of my coworkers suggested that I try your company."라며 동료들 중 한 명이 남자의 회사를 이용해 보라고 제안했다고 하였다. 따라서 (B)가 정답이다.

어휘 search v. 검색하다 colleague n. 동료

> **Paraphrasing**
> one of my coworkers 나의 동료들 중 한 명 → a colleague 동료

12 문제점 문제
해석 남자는 무슨 문제를 언급하는가?
(A) 약속 일정을 다시 잡아야 한다.
(B) 서비스가 최근 중단되었다.
(C) 프로젝트가 한 달 동안 시작될 수 없다.
(D) 결정이 나지 않았다.

해설 남자의 말에서 부정적인 표현이 언급된 다음을 주의 깊게 듣는다. 남자가 "but we wouldn't be able to work on your property for another four weeks"라며 앞으로 4주 동안 여자의 건물 작업을 할 수 없을 것 같다고 하였다. 따라서 (C)가 정답이다.

어휘 discontinue v. 중단하다

> **Paraphrasing**
> wouldn't be able to work ~ for another four weeks 앞으로 4주 동안 작업을 할 수 없다 → A project cannot begin for a month 프로젝트가 한 달 동안 시작될 수 없다

[13-15] 🎧 호주 → 미국
Questions 13-15 refer to the following conversation.

M: Good afternoon, Ms. Pao. This is Harold Pearce, the curator of the Elm Museum. As we discussed, ¹³**I'd like to feature your three most recent sculptures in an art exhibit starting on May 15**.
W: Of course. I have them stored at my studio right now. When do you need them by?
M: ¹⁴**Why don't I send someone to pick them up on Saturday, May 2?**
W: Oh . . . I'm teaching classes on the weekends.
M: In that case, ¹⁵**our staff will transport them to the museum on Thursday**, April 30.

feature v. (특징으로) 포함하다 sculpture n. 조각 exhibit n. 전시

store v. 보관하다 transport v. 운송하다

해석
13-15번은 다음 대화에 관한 문제입니다.

남: 안녕하세요, Ms. Pao. 저는 Elm 박물관의 큐레이터인 Harold Pearce예요. 논의했던 대로, ¹³5월 15일부터 시작하는 미술 전시회에 귀하의 가장 최근 조각품 세 점을 포함하고 싶습니다.
여: 물론이죠. 지금 제 작업실에 보관하고 있어요. 언제까지 필요하신가요?
남: ¹⁴5월 2일 토요일에 제가 누군가를 보내서 그것들을 가져가도록 하는 건 어떨까요?
여: 아... 저는 주말에 수업을 가르치고 있어요.
남: 그렇다면, ¹⁵저희 직원이 4월 30일 목요일에 그것들을 박물관으로 운송하겠습니다.

13 특정 세부 사항 문제
해석 남자는 무엇을 하고 싶어 하는가?
(A) 박물관 입장권을 보낸다.
(B) 온라인 서비스를 사용한다.
(C) 견학을 신청한다.
(D) 조각품을 전시한다.

해설 대화에서 남자의 말을 주의 깊게 듣는다. 남자가 "I'd like to feature your three most recent sculptures in an art exhibit starting on May 15"라며 5월 15일부터 시작하는 미술 전시회에 여자의 가장 최근 조각품 세 점을 포함하고 싶다고 하였다. 따라서 (D)가 정답이다.

어휘 pass n. 입장권 register v. 신청하다 display v. 전시하다

14 의도 파악 문제
해석 여자는 왜 "저는 주말에 수업을 가르치고 있어요"라고 말하는가?
(A) 일정을 확인하기 위해
(B) 문제점을 지적하기 위해
(C) 지연을 설명하기 위해
(D) 요구를 하기 위해

해설 질문의 인용어구(I'm teaching classes on the weekends)가 언급된 주변을 주의 깊게 듣는다. 남자가 "Why don't I send someone to pick them[sculptures] up on Saturday, May 2?"라며 5월 2일 토요일에 누군가를 보내서 조각품을 가져가도록 하는 건 어떠냐는 물음에 여자가 주말에 수업을 가르치고 있다고 한 것을 통해 주말에 가능하지 않다는 문제점을 지적하려고 한다는 것을 알 수 있다. 따라서 (B)가 정답이다.

어휘 confirm v. 확인하다 indicate v. 지적하다 delay n. 지연, 지체 make a demand 요구하다

15 다음에 할 일 문제
해석 목요일에 무슨 일이 일어날 것인가?
(A) 그림이 판매될 것이다.
(B) 상이 수여될 것이다.
(C) 물품들이 이동될 것이다.
(D) 공지가 이루어질 것이다.

해설 질문의 핵심 어구(Thursday)가 언급된 주변을 주의 깊게 듣는다. 남자가 "our staff will transport them to the museum on Thursday"라며 직원이 목요일에 조각품을 박물관으로 운송하겠다고 한 것을 통해 목요일에 물품들이 이동될 것임을 알 수 있다. 따라서 (C)가 정답이다.

어휘 painting n. 그림 announcement n. 공지

[16-18] 🎧 미국 → 호주
Questions 16-18 refer to the following conversation.

W: Excuse me, ¹⁶**I'm supposed to attend a seminar on developing mobile applications. I'm one of the speakers**, actually. Where is the Walberg Auditorium?
M: Just take the elevator up to the third floor and turn

right when you exit. By the way, ¹⁷**there's a map of the conference center in the pamphlet that all participants are given.**
W: Thanks for letting me know. One more thing . . . I heard that speakers at this event won't be charged for parking. Is that correct?
M: Yes. ¹⁸**Just talk to the receptionist on the main floor before you leave.**

develop v. 개발하다　speaker n. 연사, 발표자　exit v. 나가다
participant n. 참가자　receptionist n. 접수원

해석
16-18번은 다음 대화에 관한 문제입니다.
여: 실례합니다. ¹⁶저는 모바일 애플리케이션 개발에 관한 세미나에 참석하기로 되어 있어요. 사실 저는 연사 중 한 명이에요. Walberg 강당이 어디에 있나요?
남: 엘리베이터를 타고 3층으로 올라가서, 나오시면서 오른쪽으로 가시면 됩니다. 그건 그렇고, ¹⁷모든 참가자에게 제공되는 팸플릿에 회의장의 지도가 있어요.
여: 알려주셔서 감사합니다. 한 가지 더요... 이 행사의 연사들은 주차비가 부과되지 않는다고 들었는데요. 맞나요?
남: 네. ¹⁸떠나기 전에 메인 층에 있는 접수원과 이야기하세요.

16 화자 문제
해석 여자는 어떤 산업에서 일하는 것 같은가?
(A) 보험
(B) 마케팅
(C) 운송
(D) 소프트웨어

해설 대화에서 신분 및 직업과 관련된 표현을 놓치지 않고 듣는다. 여자가 "I'm supposed to attend a seminar on developing mobile applications. I'm one of the speakers"라며 자신이 모바일 애플리케이션 개발에 관한 세미나에 참석하기로 되어 있다고 한 후, 자신이 연사 중 한 명이라고 하였다. 이를 통해 여자가 소프트웨어 업계에서 일하고 있음을 알 수 있다. 따라서 (D)가 정답이다.

어휘 insurance n. 보험　transportation n. 운송

17 특정 세부 사항 문제
해석 남자에 따르면, 모든 회의 참가자는 무엇을 받는가?
(A) 양식
(B) 이름표
(C) 책자
(D) 기기

해설 남자의 말에서 질문의 핵심 어구(conference participants receive)와 관련된 내용을 주의 깊게 듣는다. 남자가 "there's a map of the conference center in the pamphlet that all participants are given"이라며 모든 참가자에게 제공되는 팸플릿에 회의장의 지도가 있다고 하였다. 따라서 (C)가 정답이다.

어휘 brochure n. 책자　device n. 기기

[Paraphrasing]
pamphlet 팸플릿 → brochure 책자

18 특정 세부 사항 문제
해석 남자는 여자에게 무엇을 하라고 말하는가?
(A) 정책을 확인한다.
(B) 접수원과 이야기한다.
(C) 애플리케이션을 설치한다.
(D) 시간표를 인쇄한다.

해설 남자의 말에서 질문의 핵심 어구(woman ~ do)와 관련된 내용을 주의 깊게 듣는다. 남자가 "Just talk to the receptionist on the main floor before you leave."라며 떠나기 전에 메인 층에 있는 접수원과 이야기하라고 하였다. 따라서 (B)가 정답이다.

어휘 install v. 설치하다　timetable n. 시간표

[19-21] 캐나다 → 영국
Questions 19-21 refer to the following conversation and room layout.

M: Hello. My name is David Wilkes, and ¹⁹**I was told to check in for the new hire orientation. Where should I go now?**
W: Hold on . . . OK, ¹⁹/²⁰**you have been assigned to one of the tables closest to the hall entrance.** ²⁰**It's right next to the window.**
M: Thanks. Do you know what activity is scheduled first?
W: ²¹**In a few minutes, the CEO will give a welcome speech on the stage.** After that, each group will do some customer service role-playing exercises.
M: ²¹**I'll head over now.** Thanks for your help.

check in for ~에 출석하다　new hire 신입사원
orientation n. 예비 교육, 오리엔테이션　assign v. 배정하다
entrance n. 입구　schedule v. 예정하다　speech n. 연설

해석
19-21번은 다음 대화와 방 배치도에 관한 문제입니다.
남: 안녕하세요. 제 이름은 David Wilkes이고, ¹⁹신입사원 예비 교육에 출석하라고 들었어요. 지금 어디로 가야 하나요?
여: 잠시만요... 네, ¹⁹/²⁰당신은 홀 입구에서 가장 가까운 탁자 중 하나에 배정되었어요. ²⁰창문 바로 옆이에요.
남: 감사합니다. 첫 번째로 예정된 활동이 무엇인지 아시나요?
여: ²¹몇 분 후에, 최고 경영자가 무대에서 환영 연설을 할 거예요. 그 후에, 각 그룹은 고객 서비스 역할극 연습을 할 거예요.
남: ²¹지금 바로 가볼게요. 도와주셔서 감사합니다.

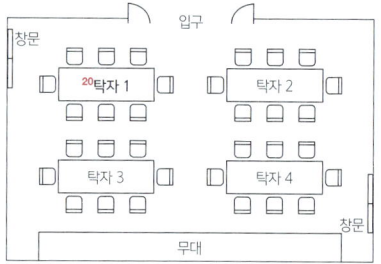

19 화자 문제
해석 남자는 누구인가?
(A) 교육 진행자
(B) 세미나 발표자
(C) 학생 인턴
(D) 새로 온 직원

해설 대화에서 신분 및 직업과 관련된 표현을 놓치지 않고 듣는다. 남자가 "I was told to check in for the new hire orientation. Where should I go now?"라며 자신이 신입사원 예비 교육에 참석 등록을 하라고 들었다고 하면서 지금 어디로 가야 하는지 묻자, 여자가 "you have been assigned to one of the tables closest to the hall entrance"라며 홀 입구에서 가장 가까운 탁자 중 하나에 배정되었다고 한 것을 통해 남자는 새로 온 직원이라는 것을 알 수 있다. 따라서 (D)가 정답이다.

어휘 coordinator n. 진행자, 조정자

20 시각 자료 문제

해석 시각 자료를 보아라. 남자는 어느 탁자에 배정되었는가?
   (A) 탁자 1
   (B) 탁자 2
   (C) 탁자 3
   (D) 탁자 4

해설 제시된 방 배치도의 정보를 확인한 후 질문의 핵심 어구(table)가 언급된 주변을 주의 깊게 듣는다. 여자가 "you have been assigned to one of the tables closest to the hall entrance. It's right next to the window."라며 남자가 홀 입구에서 가장 가까운 탁자 중 하나에 배정되었다고 했으므로, 남자가 배정된 탁자가 탁자 1임을 방 배치도에서 알 수 있다. 따라서 (A)가 정답이다.

21 다음에 할 일 문제

해석 남자는 다음에 무엇을 할 것 같은가?
   (A) 연설을 듣는다.
   (B) 시연을 본다.
   (C) 줄을 선다.
   (D) 유인물을 읽는다.

해설 대화의 마지막 부분을 주의 깊게 듣는다. 여자가 "In a few minutes, the CEO will give a welcome speech on the stage."라며 몇 분 후에 최고 경영자가 무대에서 환영 연설을 할 것이라고 하자, 남자가 "I'll head over now."라며 지금 바로 가겠다고 하였다. 따라서 (A)가 정답이다.

어휘 demonstration n. 시연

DAY 11 회사 업무 및 사무기기 관련 대화

HACKERS PRACTICE   p.97

| 01 (B) | 02 (A) | 03 (D) | 04 (C) |

[01-02] 🎧 미국 → 캐나다 / 영국 → 호주

Questions 01-02 refer to the following conversation.

W: Sanjiv, ⁰¹**I need you to help Johanna look over a contract** for one of our clients.
M: Sure, I can do that. I've worked with her on some other cases in the past, and we seem to make a good team.
W: I know. Johanna asked to work with you specifically. As you have experience with international contracts, she thought you'd be helpful.
M: No problem. ⁰²**I'll give her a call right now.**

contract n. 계약(서); v. 계약하다, 수축하다   case n. 사건, 경우
specifically adv. 특별히, 분명히

해석
01-02번은 다음 대화에 관한 문제입니다.

여: Sanjiv, ⁰¹Johanna가 우리 고객들 중 한 분의 **계약서를 검토하는 걸 도와주세요.**
남: 물론이죠, 할 수 있어요. 전에 몇몇 다른 사건에서 그녀와 함께 일했는데, 우리는 호흡이 잘 맞는 것 같아요.
여: 알아요. Johanna가 특별히 당신과 일할 것을 요청했어요. 당신이 국제 계약에 대한 경험이 있으니, 그녀가 당신이 도움이 될 거라고 생각했대요.
남: 알겠어요. ⁰²그녀에게 지금 바로 전화할게요.

01 요청 문제

해설 여자는 남자에게 무엇을 해달라고 요청하는가?
   (A) 고객 기록을 갱신한다.
   (B) 법률 계약을 검토한다.
   (C) 지원자를 면접한다.
   (D) 다른 나라로 여행 간다.

해설 여자의 말에서 요청과 관련된 표현이 언급된 다음을 주의 깊게 듣는다. 여자가 남자에게 "I need you to help Johanna look over a contract"라며 Johanna가 계약서를 검토하는 것을 도와주라고 요청하였다. 따라서 (B)가 정답이다.

어휘 agreement n. 계약

02 다음에 할 일 문제

해석 남자는 다음에 무엇을 할 것 같은가?
   (A) 동료에게 전화한다.
   (B) 서류를 복사한다.
   (C) 보고서를 작성한다.
   (D) 사례를 조사한다.

해설 대화의 마지막 부분을 주의 깊게 듣는다. 남자가 "I'll give her[Johanna] a call right now."라며 지금 바로 Johanna에게 전화하겠다고 한 것을 통해 남자가 동료에게 전화할 것임을 알 수 있다. 따라서 (A)가 정답이다.

어휘 research v. 조사하다, 연구하다

[03-04] 🎧 호주 → 영국 / 캐나다 → 미국

Questions 03-04 refer to the following conversation.

M: Hi, Edna. It's Aaron. I'm at the furniture store looking for a new desk for Mr. Richards, ⁰³**but I misplaced the note with his office measurements**. I've been trying to contact him, but there's **no response**. Do you know where he is?
W: ⁰⁴**Mr. Richards is showing some clients around the manufacturing plant.**
M: Will that take long?
W: Oh, if you wait just a few minutes, I will go into his office and measure it for you.

misplace v. 잃어버리다, 두고 오다   contact v. 연락하다
measurement n. 치수, 측정   manufacturing adj. 제조(업)의
plant n. 공장

해석
03-04번은 다음 대화에 관한 문제입니다.

남: 안녕하세요, Edna. Aaron이에요. Mr. Richards의 새 책상을 보러 가구점에 와 있는데, ⁰³그의 사무실 치수가 적힌 메모를 잃어버렸어요. 그에게 연락해 보고 있는데, 응답이 없네요. 그가 어디에 있는지 아시나요?
여: ⁰⁴Mr. Richards는 몇몇 고객들에게 제조 공장을 구경시켜 주고 있어요.
남: 오래 걸릴 것 같나요?
여: 아, 몇 분만 기다리시면, 제가 그의 사무실로 가서 치수를 재드릴게요.

03 문제점 문제

해설 남자는 어떤 문제를 언급하는가?
   (A) 그는 회의에 늦었다.
   (B) 그는 장비를 손상시켰다.
   (C) 그는 정책을 알지 못한다.
   (D) 그는 정보를 잃어버렸다.

해설 남자의 말에서 부정적인 표현이 언급된 다음을 주의 깊게 듣는다. 남자가 "but I misplaced the note with his office measurements"라며 사무실 치수가 적힌 메모를 잃어버렸다고 하였다. 따라서 (D)가 정답이다.

어휘 damage v. 손상시키다, 손해를 입히다   be unaware of ~을 알지 못하다
lose v. 잃어버리다, 분실하다

04 언급 문제

해설 여자는 Mr. Richards에 대해 무엇을 말하는가?

(A) 그는 몇몇 사무실 가구들을 구입했다.
(B) 그는 도움을 요청하기 위해 전화했다.
(C) 그는 제조 시설에 있다.
(D) 그는 몇몇 고객들을 기다리고 있다.

해설 여자의 말에서 질문의 핵심 어구(Mr. Richards)가 언급된 주변을 주의 깊게 듣는다. 여자가 "Mr. Richards is showing some clients around the manufacturing plant."라며 Mr. Richards가 몇몇 고객들에게 제조 공장을 구경시켜 주고 있다고 하였다. 따라서 (C)가 정답이다.

[Paraphrasing]
manufacturing plant 제조 공장 → manufacturing facility 제조 시설

HACKERS TEST   p.98

01 (C)	02 (B)	03 (D)	04 (A)	05 (B)
06 (D)	07 (C)	08 (B)	09 (A)	10 (D)
11 (B)	12 (A)	13 (B)	14 (A)	15 (D)
16 (C)	17 (D)	18 (A)	19 (C)	20 (A)
21 (D)				

[01-03] 영국 → 호주
Questions 01-03 refer to the following conversation.

W: ⁰¹**What is this blueprint still doing on my desk, Henry? I thought I told you to send it to Agrippa Incorporated.**
M: Actually, ⁰²**Mr. Carter called me while you were out yesterday afternoon. He requested some revisions to the blueprint** in order to make room for additional equipment.
W: I see. How big are the changes?
M: ⁰³**I measured the space this morning**, and we will only need to revise one-third of the floor plan. It won't take long.

blueprint n. 청사진   additional adj. 추가의   equipment n. 장비
measure v. 측정하다   floor plan 평면도

해석
01-03번은 다음 대화에 관한 문제입니다.
여: ⁰¹이 청사진이 왜 아직 제 책상 위에 있는 건가요, Henry? 제가 당신에게 그것을 Agrippa사로 보내라고 말했다고 생각하는데요.
남: 사실, ⁰²어제 오후에 당신이 나가 있는 동안 Mr. Carter가 저에게 전화하셨어요. 그가 추가 장비를 위한 공간을 만들기 위해 청사진에 몇몇 수정을 요청했어요.
여: 그렇군요. 변경 사항이 얼마나 큰가요?
남: ⁰³오늘 아침에 제가 그 공간을 측정해 보았는데, 평면도의 3분의 1만 수정하면 될 거예요. 오래 걸리지 않을 거예요.

01 특정 세부 사항 문제
해석 여자는 남자에게 무엇을 하라고 말했는가?
(A) 청사진 마무리하기
(B) 고객에게 연락하기
(C) 서류를 보내기
(D) 기록을 업데이트하기
해설 대화에서 질문의 핵심 어구(tell the man to do)와 관련된 내용을 주의 깊게 듣는다. 여자가 "What is this blueprint still doing on my desk, Henry? I thought I told you to send it to Agrippa Incorporated."라며 청사진이 왜 아직 자신의 책상 위에 있는지 물은 후, 남자에게 그것을 Agrippa사로 보내라고 말했다고 생각했다고 한 것을 통해 여자가 남

자에게 서류를 보내라고 말했음을 알 수 있다. 따라서 (C)가 정답이다.

02 이유 문제
해석 Mr. Carter는 왜 남자에게 연락했는가?
(A) 프로젝트를 위한 장비를 주문하기 위해
(B) 도면에 대한 변경을 요청하기 위해
(C) 물품 비용을 확인하기 위해
(D) 일정에 관한 문제를 설명하기 위해
해설 질문의 핵심 어구(Mr. Carter contact)와 관련된 내용을 주의 깊게 듣는다. 남자가 "Mr. Carter called me while you were out yesterday afternoon. He requested some revisions to the blueprint"라며 어제 오후에 여자가 나가 있는 동안 Mr. Carter가 전화했고, 그가 청사진에 몇몇 수정을 요청했다고 하였다. 따라서 (B)가 정답이다.

어휘 supplies n. 물품   issue n. 문제

03 특정 세부 사항 문제
해석 남자는 오늘 아침에 무엇을 했다고 말하는가?
(A) 파일을 다운로드했다.
(B) 자금을 이체했다.
(C) 수정을 했다.
(D) 측정을 했다.
해설 남자의 말에서 질문의 핵심 어구(this morning)가 언급된 주변을 주의 깊게 듣는다. 남자가 "I measured the space this morning"이라며 오늘 아침에 그 공간을 측정해 보았다고 하였다. 따라서 (D)가 정답이다.

어휘 transfer v. 이체하다   fund n. 자금   measurement n. 측정

[04-06] 미국 → 캐나다 → 호주
Questions 04-06 refer to the following conversation with three speakers.

W: How do you two feel about our studio's reception area? ⁰⁴**I'm worried that it looks too outdated.** Maybe we should consider changing the wall colors or decorations.
M1: Personally, I like how the reception area is now. That being said, ⁰⁵**I think the furniture is in need of replacement.** It's looking pretty worn out.
M2: ⁰⁵**I agree with Dale. Replacing the sofa and chairs is a good idea.**
W: Yeah, I see what you mean. ⁰⁶**Should I start searching online for some options?**
M2: Yes. If you don't mind.

reception n. 접수처, 응접   outdated adj. 시대에 뒤처진, 구식인
decoration n. 장식   furniture n. 가구   in need of ~을 필요로 하는
replacement n. 교체

해석
04-06번은 다음 세 명의 대화에 관한 문제입니다.
여: 두 분은 우리 스튜디오의 접수처 구역에 대해 어떻게 생각하세요? ⁰⁴저는 그곳이 너무 시대에 뒤처진 것처럼 보여서 걱정이에요. 아마 벽지 색상이나 장식을 바꾸는 것을 고려해봐야 할 것 같아요.
남1: 개인적으로, 저는 접수처 구역이 현재 모습 그대로 마음에 들어요. 그렇지만, ⁰⁵가구는 교체를 필요로 한다고 생각해요. 그건 꽤 낡아 보여요.
남2: ⁰⁵저도 Dale에 동의해요. 소파와 의자를 교체하는 것은 좋은 생각이에요.
여: 네, 여러분이 무슨 뜻으로 말하는지 알겠어요. ⁰⁶제가 몇몇 선택지를 온라인에서 찾아보기 시작할까요?
남2: 네. 괜찮으시다면요.

04 문제점 문제
해석 여자는 무엇에 대해 걱정하는가?

(A) 공간의 외관
(B) 건물의 크기
(C) 진열대의 위치
(D) 로고의 색상

해설 여자의 말에서 부정적인 표현이 언급된 다음을 주의 깊게 듣는다. 여자가 "I'm worried that it[reception area] looks too outdated."라며 접수 구역이 너무 시대에 뒤떨어진 것처럼 보여서 걱정이라고 하였다. 따라서 (A)가 정답이다.

어휘 appearance n. 외관, 겉모습

05 특정 세부 사항 문제
해석 남자들은 무엇을 바꾸고 싶어 하는가?
(A) 장식
(B) 가구
(C) 장비
(D) 식물

해설 질문의 핵심 어구(change)와 관련된 내용을 주의 깊게 듣는다. 남자 1이 "I think the furniture is in need of replacement"라며 가구는 교체를 필요로 한다고 생각한다고 하자, 남자 2가 "I agree with Dale. Replacing the sofa and chairs is a good idea."라며 자신도 Dale에 동의한다며 소파와 의자를 교체하는 것은 좋은 생각이라고 하였다. 따라서 (B)가 정답이다.

06 제안 문제
해석 여자는 무엇을 해주겠다고 제안하는가?
(A) 고객들과 예산을 논의한다.
(B) 추가 근무를 한다.
(C) 도구들을 수거한다.
(D) 몇몇 물품을 찾아본다.

해설 여자의 말에서 제안과 관련된 표현이 언급된 다음을 주의 깊게 듣는다. 여자가 "Should I start searching online for some options?"라며 자신이 몇몇 선택지를 온라인에서 찾아보기 시작할지 묻고 있다. 따라서 (D)가 정답이다.

어휘 discuss v. 논의하다   shift n. (교대) 근무   collect v. 수거하다
search for ~을 찾다

[07-09] 캐나다 → 영국
Questions 07-09 refer to the following conversation.

M: ⁰⁷I was trying to print some copies of our new survey forms, but it seems the printer is out of ink. Do you know where we keep the cartridges?
W: They're usually in the storage cupboard, but I think we're out. ⁰⁸I'm going to the office supply store after lunch, so I can get some while I'm there.
M: Perfect. ⁰⁹Could you also pick up some additional things from the store? I'm running low on pens, folders, and a couple of other items.
W: Of course. ⁰⁹Just e-mail me a list of what you need within the next 30 minutes, and I'll be sure to get everything for you.

survey form 설문지   cupboard n. 벽장, 찬장
office supply store 사무용품점   run low 떨어져 가다

해석
07-09번은 다음 대화에 관한 문제입니다.
남: ⁰⁷우리의 새 설문지들을 몇 부 인쇄하려고 했는데, 프린터에 잉크가 다 떨어진 것 같아요. 우리가 카트리지를 어디에 보관하는지 알고 있나요?
여: 그것들은 보통 보관 벽장에 있는데, 제 생각엔 다 떨어진 것 같아요. ⁰⁸제가 점심 식사 후에 사무용품점에 갈 거라서, 그곳에 있는 동안 몇 개 사

올 수 있어요.
남: 잘됐네요. ⁰⁹몇몇 추가적인 용품들도 가게에서 사다 주실 수 있나요? 저는 펜, 서류철, 그리고 몇 가지 다른 물품들이 떨어져 가고 있거든요.
여: 물론이죠. 앞으로 30분 안에 ⁰⁹당신이 필요한 것의 목록을 이메일로 보내 주시면, 제가 당신을 위해 꼭 모든 걸 사 오도록 할게요.

07 문제점 문제
해석 남자의 문제는 무엇인가?
(A) 그는 설문지를 찾을 수 없다.
(B) 그는 주문하는 것을 잊었다.
(C) 그는 문서들을 인쇄할 수 없다.
(D) 그는 배송 송장을 잃어버렸다.

해설 남자의 말에서 부정적인 표현이 언급된 주변을 주의 깊게 듣는다. 남자가 "I was trying to print some copies of our new survey forms, but it seems the printer is out of ink."라며 새 설문지들을 몇 부 인쇄하려고 했는데, 프린터에 잉크가 다 떨어진 것 같다고 하였다. 따라서 (C)가 정답이다.

어휘 place an order 주문하다   invoice n. 송장

08 특정 세부 사항 문제
해석 여자는 오늘 오후에 어디에 가는가?
(A) 복사 센터에
(B) 용품점에
(C) 음식점에
(D) 보관 시설에

해설 여자의 말에서 질문의 핵심 어구(going this afternoon)와 관련된 내용을 주의 깊게 듣는다. 여자가 "I'm going to the office supply store after lunch"라며 점심 식사 후에 사무용품점에 갈 것이라고 하였다. 따라서 (B)가 정답이다.

어휘 dining establishment 음식점

09 특정 세부 사항 문제
해석 남자는 여자에게 무엇을 보낼 것 같은가?
(A) 웹사이트의 링크
(B) 대금 청구서
(C) 상품 번호
(D) 물품 목록

해설 질문의 핵심 어구(send)와 관련된 내용을 주의 깊게 듣는다. 남자가 "Could you also pick up some additional things from the store?"라며 몇몇 추가적인 용품들도 가게에서 사다 줄 수 있냐고 묻자, 여자가 "Just e-mail me a list of what you need"라며 필요한 것의 목록을 이메일로 보내달라고 하였다. 따라서 (D)가 정답이다.

어휘 billing statement 대금 청구서

Paraphrasing
a list of what ~ need 필요한 것의 목록 → A list of items 물품 목록

[10-12] 미국 → 캐나다
Questions 10-12 refer to the following conversation.

W: ¹⁰I finished the revisions to the manual for the Rafal Blender . . . uh, the product we designed together. ¹¹Can you check if any other parts need to be revised?
M: I've got a meeting with a client. ¹¹It's likely going to take a couple of hours. If you need it done right away, ¹²why don't you ask Patrick to do it?
W: ¹²Good idea. I'll go and talk to him about this.

manual n. 설명서   blender n. 믹서기, 분쇄기
design v. 설계하다, 디자인하다   revise v. 수정하다, 변경하다

해석
10-12번은 다음 대화에 관한 문제입니다.
여: ¹⁰저는 Rafal 믹서기... 아, 우리가 함께 설계한 제품에 대한 설명서의 수정을 마쳤어요. ¹¹다른 부분들도 수정이 필요한지 확인해 주실 수 있나요?
남: 저는 고객과의 회의가 있어요. ¹¹아마 몇 시간 정도 걸릴 거예요. 지금 당장 그것이 필요하다면, ¹²Patrick에게 그것을 하도록 요청해 보시는 게 어때요?
여: ¹²좋은 생각이에요. 가서 이 일에 대해 그와 이야기해 볼게요.

10 화자 문제
해석 화자들은 어떤 산업에서 일하는 것 같은가?
(A) 건축
(B) 출판
(C) 교육
(D) 전자제품

해설 대화에서 신분 및 직업과 관련된 표현을 놓치지 않고 듣는다. 여자가 남자에게 "I finished the revisions to the manual for the Rafal Blender ~ we designed together."라며 우리가 함께 설계한 믹서기 제품에 대한 설명서의 수정을 마쳤다고 한 것을 통해 화자들이 전자제품 산업에서 일한다는 것을 알 수 있다. 따라서 (D)가 정답이다.

어휘 architecture n. 건축 publishing n. 출판 electronics n. 전자제품

11 의도 파악 문제
해석 남자가 "저는 고객과의 회의가 있어요"라고 말할 때 무엇을 의도하는가?
(A) 준비할 시간이 필요하다.
(B) 도울 수 없다.
(C) 약속을 변경했다.
(D) 기다릴 생각이 없다.

해설 질문의 인용어구(I've got a meeting with a client)가 언급된 주변을 주의 깊게 듣는다. 여자가 "Can you check if any other parts need to be revised?"라며 다른 부분들도 수정이 필요한지 확인해 줄 수 있냐고 하자, 남자가 "I've got a meeting with a client. It's likely going to take a couple of hours."라며 자신은 고객과의 회의가 있고, 아마 몇 시간 정도 걸릴 것이라고 한 것을 통해 여자를 도울 수 없음을 알 수 있다. 따라서 (B)가 정답이다.

어휘 appointment n. 약속

12 다음에 할 일 문제
해석 여자는 다음에 무엇을 할 것 같은가?
(A) 동료와 이야기한다.
(B) 영수증을 준비한다.
(C) 몇몇 계획을 평가한다.
(D) 계약서에 서명한다.

해설 대화의 마지막 부분을 주의 깊게 듣는다. 남자가 "why don't you ask Patrick to do it?"이라며 Patrick에게 그것을 하도록 요청해 보는 게 어떠냐고 하자, 여자가 "Good idea. I'll go and talk to him about this."라며 좋은 생각이라고 한 후, 가서 이 일에 대해 그와 이야기해 보겠다고 하였다. 따라서 (A)가 정답이다.

어휘 coworker n. 동료

[13-15] 호주 → 영국
Questions 13-15 refer to the following conversation.

M: Unfortunately, ¹³**I can't give you a passing score on your inspection today**, Ms. Berry.
W: Really? I was sure I double-checked everything. What in particular is the issue?
M: The chandelier in the lobby isn't working properly. It needs to be dealt with.
W: Hmm . . . we must have missed that. Fortunately, ¹⁴**I bought the light fixture at a nearby store**. I'll replace it.
M: Great. ¹⁵**I'll come back next Monday to make sure it has been fixed.** If it looks good, then your business will be ready to open.

unfortunately adv. 유감스럽게도 inspection n. 검사 deal with 해결하다
light fixture 조명 기구 nearby adj. 근처의 replace v. 교체하다, 대신하다
business n. 상점, 사업체

해석
13-15번은 다음 대화에 관한 문제입니다.
남: 유감스럽게도, ¹³오늘 귀하의 검사에서 합격점을 드릴 수 없어요, Ms. Berry.
여: 정말인가요? 저는 모든 것을 재확인했다고 확신했는데요. 무엇이 특별히 문제인가요?
남: 로비의 샹들리에가 제대로 작동하지 않아요. 이것이 해결되어야 합니다.
여: 흠... 저희가 그것을 놓쳤나 봐요. 다행히도, ¹⁴제가 근처의 상점에서 그 조명 기구를 구입했어요. 그것을 교체할게요.
남: 좋아요. ¹⁵다음 주 월요일에 그것이 수리되었는지 확인하기 위해 다시 올게요. 만약 그것이 괜찮아 보인다면, 귀하의 상점을 열 준비가 된 거예요.

13 화자 문제
해석 남자는 누구인 것 같은가?
(A) 부동산 중개인
(B) 감독관
(C) 설계자
(D) 투자자

해설 대화에서 신분 및 직업과 관련된 표현을 놓치지 않고 듣는다. 남자가 "I can't give you a passing score on your inspection today"라며 오늘 검사에서 합격점을 줄 수 없다고 한 것을 통해 남자가 감독관임을 알 수 있다. 따라서 (B)가 정답이다.

어휘 realtor n. 부동산 중개인 inspector n. 감독관 investor n. 투자자

14 언급 문제
해석 조명 기구에 대해 무엇이 언급되는가?
(A) 근처에서 구입되었다.
(B) 여러 가지 크기로 나온다.
(C) 2층에 위치해 있다.
(D) 제조자에 의해서 회수되었다.

해설 질문의 핵심 어구(light fixture)가 언급된 주변을 주의 깊게 듣는다. 여자가 "I bought the light fixture at a nearby store"라며 근처의 상점에서 그 조명 기구를 구입했다고 하였다. 따라서 (A)가 정답이다.

어휘 multiple adj. 여러 가지 recall v. 회수하다 manufacturer n. 제조자

15 이유 문제
해석 남자는 왜 다음 주에 돌아올 것인가?
(A) 더 많은 용품을 배달하기 위해
(B) 오래된 배선을 제거하기 위해
(C) 시 공무원과 만나기 위해
(D) 문제를 점검하기 위해

해설 남자의 말에서 질문의 핵심 어구(return next week)와 관련된 내용을 주의 깊게 듣는다. 남자가 "I'll come back next Monday to make sure it[light fixture] has been fixed."라며 다음 주 월요일에 조명 기구가 수리되었는지 확인하기 위해 다시 오겠다고 하였다. 따라서 (D)가 정답이다.

어휘 remove v. 제거하다 wiring n. 배선 official n. 공무원

[16-18] 미국 → 캐나다

Questions 16-18 refer to the following conversation.

W: Hey, Walter. [16]**About the materials you put up during your presentation yesterday** . . .
M: You mean the charts showing our Toronto stores' performance over the past three years?
W: Right. [17]**I'm going to be taking part in a meeting this afternoon about our Bendale office, which we are considering closing.** I think your information would be helpful.
M: Of course. Do you need me to go over them with you before your meeting?
W: That would be great. [18]**I'll reserve us one of the conference rooms now so that we can discuss them.**
M: Sounds good.

material n. 자료, 재료   put up 제시하다, 내놓다   chart n. 도표
take part in 참여하다   helpful adj. 도움이 되는   go over 검토하다
reserve v. 예약하다, 남겨 두다

해석
16-18번은 다음 대화에 관한 문제입니다.
여: 안녕하세요, Walter. [16]당신이 어제 발표 중에 제시하신 자료들에 관해서요...
남: 지난 3년간 토론토 매장들의 실적을 보여주는 도표를 말씀하시는 건가요?
여: 맞아요. [17]저는 오늘 오후에 Bendale 영업소에 관한 회의에 참여할 예정인데, 그곳은 우리가 폐쇄를 고려하고 있어요. 당신의 정보가 도움이 될 것 같아요.
남: 물론이죠. 회의 전에 제가 그것들을 함께 검토해 드릴까요?
여: 그거 좋겠네요. [18]우리가 그것들에 대해 논의할 수 있도록 지금 회의실 중 하나를 예약할게요.
남: 좋아요.

16 주제 문제
해석 화자들은 주로 무엇에 대해 이야기하고 있는가?
(A) 출장
(B) 투자 전략
(C) 발표 자료
(D) 고객 의견

해설 대화의 주제를 묻는 문제이므로, 대화의 초반을 반드시 듣는다. 여자가 "About the materials you put up during your presentation yesterday"라며 남자가 어제 발표 중에 제시한 자료들에 관한 것이라고 한 후, 발표 자료에 대한 내용으로 대화가 이어지고 있다. 따라서 (C)가 정답이다.

어휘 business trip 출장   feedback n. 의견

17 언급 문제
해석 Bendale 영업소에 관해 무엇이 언급되는가?
(A) 행사를 주최할 것이다.
(B) 직원이 부족하다.
(C) 확장될 수도 있다.
(D) 문을 닫을 수도 있다.

해설 질문의 핵심 어구(Bendale office)가 언급된 주변을 주의 깊게 듣는다. 여자가 "I'm going to be taking part in a meeting this afternoon about our Bendale office, which we are considering closing."이라며 오늘 오후에 Bendale 영업소에 관한 회의에 참여할 예정인데, 그곳은 폐쇄를 고려하고 있다고 하였다. 따라서 (D)가 정답이다.

어휘 understaffed adj. 직원이 부족한

18 다음에 할 일 문제
해석 여자는 다음에 무엇을 할 것 같은가?
(A) 회의실을 예약한다.
(B) 약속 시간을 변경한다.
(C) 매장 관리자에게 연락한다.
(D) 일정표를 조정한다.

해설 대화의 마지막 부분을 주의 깊게 듣는다. 여자가 "I'll reserve us one of the conference rooms now so that we can discuss them[charts]."이라며 그 도표들에 대해 논의할 수 있도록 지금 회의실 중 하나를 예약하겠다고 하였다. 따라서 (A)가 정답이다.

어휘 book v. 예약하다   contact v. 연락하다   adjust v. 조정하다, 조절하다

[19-21] 호주 → 영국

Questions 19-21 refer to the following conversation and floor plan.

M: Deborah, I just want to let you know that [19]**workers will be setting up a new fire sprinkler system on the third floor next week**.
W: Really? When will they be working in my office?
M: On Monday. Would you mind using the conference room as a temporary workspace that day?
W: Hmm . . . [20]**I have a meeting with a new client on Monday. Why don't I use the empty office right next to the storage area?**
M: Sure. [21]**No one has been using it since Mr. Hobbs moved to our Seattle office last month.**
W: Great. I'll put some of my things in there on Friday afternoon.

fire sprinkler 화재 스프링클러   temporary adj. 임시의
workspace n. 작업 공간   empty adj. 빈

해석
19-21번은 다음 대화와 평면도에 관한 문제입니다.
남: Deborah, [19]작업자들이 다음 주에 3층에 새로운 화재 스프링클러 시스템을 설치할 것이라는 점을 당신에게 알려드리고 싶어요.
여: 정말요? 그들이 제 사무실에서는 언제 작업할 예정인가요?
남: 월요일이에요. 그날 회의실을 임시 작업 공간으로 사용해도 괜찮으시겠어요?
여: 흠... [20]저는 월요일에 새로운 고객과 회의가 있어요. 제가 창고 구역 바로 옆의 빈 사무실을 사용하는 게 어떨까요?
남: 물론이죠. [21]지난달에 Mr. Hobbs가 우리 시애틀 사무실로 이전한 후로 아무도 그곳을 사용하고 있지 않아요.
여: 좋아요. 금요일 오후에 그곳에 제 물건 몇 개를 놓아둘게요.

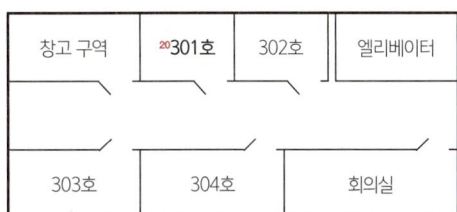

19 다음에 할 일 문제
해석 다음 주에 무슨 일이 일어날 것 같은가?
(A) 작업 공간이 다시 페인트칠 될 것이다.
(B) 창고 구역이 청소될 것이다.
(C) 몇몇 장비가 설치될 것이다.
(D) 몇몇 컴퓨터가 업데이트될 것이다.

해설 질문의 핵심 어구(next week)가 언급된 주변을 주의 깊게 듣는다. 남자가 "workers will be setting up a new fire sprinkler system on the third floor next week"이라며 작업자들이 다음 주에 3층에 새로운 화재 스프링클러 시스템을 설치할 것이라고 하였다. 따라서 (C)가 정답이다.

어휘 equipment n. 장비 install v. 설치하다

[Paraphrasing]
fire sprinkler system 화재 스프링클러 시스템 → Some equipment 몇몇 장비

20 시각 자료 문제

해석 시각 자료를 보아라. 여자는 월요일에 어떤 방을 사용할 것인가?
(A) 301호
(B) 302호
(C) 303호
(D) 304호

해설 제시된 평면도의 정보를 확인한 후 질문의 핵심 어구(Monday)가 언급된 주변을 주의 깊게 듣는다. 여자가 "I have a meeting with a new client on Monday. Why don't I use the empty office right next to the storage area?"라며 월요일에 새로운 고객과 회의가 있다고 한 후, 자신이 창고 구역 바로 옆의 빈 사무실을 사용하는 게 어떠냐고 했으므로, 여자가 월요일에 사용할 방은 301호임을 평면도에서 알 수 있다. 따라서 (A)가 정답이다.

21 언급 문제

해석 Mr. Hobbs에 대해 무엇이 언급되는가?
(A) 다른 회사에 입사했다.
(B) 휴가를 가기로 결정했다.
(C) 고객 회의를 준비했다.
(D) 다른 지점으로 옮겼다.

해설 질문의 핵심 어구(Mr. Hobbs)가 언급된 주변을 주의 깊게 듣는다. 남자가 "No one has been using it since Mr. Hobbs moved to our Seattle office last month."라며 지난달에 Mr. Hobbs가 시애틀 사무실로 이전한 후로 아무도 그곳을 사용하고 있지 않다고 하였다. 따라서 (D)가 정답이다.

어휘 firm n. 회사, 기업

[Paraphrasing]
moved 이전했다 → transferred 옮겼다

DAY 12 인사 및 사내 행사 관련 대화

HACKERS PRACTICE   p.101

01 (D)   02 (C)   03 (B)   04 (C)

[01-02] 🎧 호주 → 미국 / 캐나다 → 영국

Questions 01-02 refer to the following conversation.

M: Ms. Whittier, I noticed that I have to lead a lot of training sessions next month. ⁰¹Since you're the head of the human resources department, I'd like to discuss this with you.
W: Well, ⁰²Janice Light will be flying to France to offer training to overseas staff. That means someone else needs to lead her sessions.
M: Right, but both of her workshops are assigned to me. Can I ask another staff member to cover one?
W: OK. I'm fine with that.

lead v. 이끌다, 인솔하다   training n. 교육
human resources department 인사부   overseas adj. 해외의

assign v. 배정하다, 맡기다   cover v. 대신하다

해석 01-02번은 다음 대화에 관한 문제입니다.

남: Ms. Whittier, 제가 다음 달에, 많은 교육을 이끌어야 한다는 것을 확인했어요. ⁰¹당신이 인사부 책임자이니, 당신과 이에 대해 논의하고 싶어요.
여: 음, ⁰²Janice Light가 해외 직원들에게 교육을 제공하기 위해 프랑스로 갈 거예요. 그것은 다른 누군가가 그녀의 수업을 이끌 필요가 있다는 것을 의미해요.
남: 맞아요, 하지만 그녀의 워크숍 두 개가 모두 제게 배정되었어요. 다른 직원에게 한 개를 대신해 달라고 부탁해도 될까요?
여: 알겠어요. 저는 괜찮아요.

01 화자 문제

해석 여자는 누구인가?
(A) 개인 비서
(B) 여행사 직원
(C) 기업 자문 위원
(D) 부서 책임자

해설 대화에서 신분 및 직업과 관련된 표현을 놓치지 않고 듣는다. 남자가 여자에게 "Since you're the head of the human resources department, I'd like to discuss this with you."라며 여자가 인사부 책임자이니 이에 대해 논의하고 싶다고 한 것을 통해 여자가 부서 책임자임을 알 수 있다. 따라서 (D)가 정답이다.

어휘 assistant n. 비서   corporate adj. 기업의   consultant n. 자문 위원

02 이유 문제

해석 Janice Light는 왜 프랑스로 이동할 것인가?
(A) 조직을 이끌기 위해
(B) 연구를 수행하기 위해
(C) 교육을 제공하기 위해
(D) 일자리를 위한 면접을 보기 위해

해설 질문의 핵심 어구(Janice Light)가 언급된 주변을 주의 깊게 듣는다. 여자가 "Janice Light will be flying to France to offer training to overseas staff"라며 Janice Light가 해외 직원들에게 교육을 제공하기 위해 프랑스로 갈 것이라고 하였다. 따라서 (C)가 정답이다.

어휘 conduct v. 수행하다   research n. 연구   interview v. 면접을 보다

[03-04] 🎧 영국 → 캐나다 / 미국 → 호주

Questions 03-04 refer to the following conversation.

W: Good afternoon. ⁰³One of our senior managers is retiring, and I am arranging a party for him. Does your hotel have a reception hall big enough for 120 people?
M: Definitely. Just last weekend, we hosted an event with 150 people.
W: Let's go ahead and make the reservation, then. Oh, before I forget . . . Could you set up a microphone and speaker for us?
M: No problem. And ⁰⁴there will be no additional charge for the audio system.

arrange v. 준비하다, 마련하다   host v. 주최하다, 접대하다
additional charge 추가 요금

해석

03-04번은 다음 대화에 관한 문제입니다.

여: 안녕하세요. ⁰³저희 고위 관리자들 중 한 분이 은퇴하시는데, 제가 그 분을 위해 파티를 준비하고 있어요. 당신의 호텔에 120명의 사람들을 위한

충분히 큰 연회장이 있나요?
남: 물론입니다. 저희는 바로 지난주에 150명이 참석한 행사를 주최했어요.
여: 그럼, 지금 예약을 진행할게요. 아, 제가 잊기 전에... 저희를 위해 마이크와 스피커를 설치해 주실 수 있나요?
남: 문제없습니다. 그리고 ⁰⁴음향 시스템에 대한 추가 요금은 없을 것입니다.

03 특정 세부 사항 문제

해석 어떤 종류의 행사가 계획되고 있는가?
(A) 시상식
(B) 은퇴 기념 파티
(C) 음악 공연
(D) 기업 회의

해설 질문의 핵심 어구(event)와 관련된 내용을 주의 깊게 듣는다. 여자가 "One of our senior managers is retiring, and I am arranging a party for him."이라며 고위 관리자들 중 한 명이 은퇴하는데 그를 위해 파티를 준비하고 있다고 하였다. 따라서 (B)가 정답이다.

어휘 retirement n. 은퇴

04 특정 세부 사항 문제

해석 무엇이 추가 요금 없이 이용 가능할 것인가?
(A) 주문 제작 메뉴
(B) 주차 대행 서비스
(C) 음향 시스템
(D) 전문 사진가

해설 질문의 핵심 어구(no additional charge)가 언급된 주변을 주의 깊게 듣는다. 남자가 "there will be no additional charge for the audio system"이라며 음향 시스템에 대한 추가 비용은 없을 것이라고 하였다. 따라서 (C)가 정답이다.

어휘 customized adj. 주문 제작한, 맞춤형의

HACKERS TEST   p.102

01 (D)	02 (C)	03 (B)	04 (A)	05 (D)
06 (D)	07 (D)	08 (D)	09 (D)	10 (D)
11 (C)	12 (C)	13 (D)	14 (D)	15 (D)
16 (B)	17 (C)	18 (D)	19 (B)	20 (C)
21 (A)				

[01-03] 🎧 미국 → 호주

Questions 01-03 refer to the following conversation.

W: ⁰¹**Thank you for coming to our hotel for an interview today**, Mr. Anders. Your résumé shows that you have over three years of relevant experience.
M: That's right. ⁰²**I handled all of the bookkeeping at my former company. I also assisted with filing tax returns.**
W: That's good to hear. I should mention that ⁰³**whoever we hire for this position will have to visit our company's headquarters in Chicago several times a year**. Will that be an issue for you?
M: Not at all.

어휘 résumé n. 이력서   relevant adj. 관련된   experience n. 경험
handle v. 처리하다, 다루다   assist with ~을 돕다   file v. 제출하다
tax return 소득 신고서   headquarters n. 본사

해석
01-03번은 다음 대화에 관한 문제입니다.

여: ⁰¹오늘 우리 호텔에 면접을 보러 와주셔서 감사합니다, Mr. Anders. 귀하의 이력서를 보니 3년 이상의 관련 경험이 있으시네요.
남: 맞습니다. ⁰²저는 이전 회사에서 모든 장부 기재를 처리했습니다. 또한 소득 신고서 제출을 도왔습니다.
여: 좋네요. 말씀드려야 할 것이 있는데, ⁰³이 직책에 채용되는 사람은 누구든 일 년에 몇 번 시카고에 있는 우리 회사 본사를 방문해야 합니다. 그것이 당신에게 문제가 될까요?
남: 전혀요.

01 장소 문제

해석 대화는 어디에서 일어나고 있는가?
(A) 출판사에서
(B) 금융 기관에서
(C) 관공서에서
(D) 숙박 시설에서

해설 대화에서 장소와 관련된 표현을 놓치지 않고 듣는다. 여자가 남자에게 "Thank you for coming to our hotel for an interview today"라며 오늘 호텔에 면접을 보러 와줘서 감사하다고 하였다. 이를 통해 호텔에서 대화가 이루어지고 있음을 알 수 있다. 따라서 (D)가 정답이다.

어휘 financial institution 금융 기관   government office 관공서
accommodation facility 숙박 시설

02 특정 세부 사항 문제

해석 남자는 어떤 직책에 지원하고 있는가?
(A) 컨설턴트
(B) 판매원
(C) 회계사
(D) 기술자

해설 질문의 핵심 어구(position)와 관련된 내용을 주의 깊게 듣는다. 남자가 "I handled all of the bookkeeping at my former company. I also assisted with filing tax returns."라며 자신이 이전 회사에서 모든 장부 기재를 처리했고, 소득 신고서 제출을 도왔다고 하였다. 따라서 (C)가 정답이다.

어휘 salesperson n. 판매원   accountant n. 회계사   technician n. 기술자

03 특정 세부 사항 문제

해석 여자는 그 직책에 대해 무엇을 강조하는가?
(A) 최근에 만들어졌다.
(B) 가끔 출장을 요구한다.
(C) 관리직이다.
(D) 재택근무를 포함할 것이다.

해설 질문의 핵심 어구(position)가 언급된 주변을 주의 깊게 듣는다. 여자가 "whoever we hire for this position will have to visit our company's headquarters in Chicago several times a year"라며 이 직책에 채용되는 사람은 누구든 일 년에 몇 번 시카고에 있는 회사 본사를 방문해야 한다고 하였다. 따라서 (B)가 정답이다.

어휘 recently adv. 최근에   occasional adj. 가끔의
management n. 관리, 경영   work from home 재택근무를 하다

[04-06] 🎧 캐나다 → 미국

Questions 04-06 refer to the following conversation.

M: ⁰⁴**When does the guest speaker for tomorrow's investment seminar arrive?**
W: Mr. Nelson should be at the convention center by 10 A.M. at the latest. ⁰⁵**His flight arrives at Seattle Airport at 7 A.M.**, and he's planning to take a taxi from there.
M: Perfect. That'll give him about an hour for any last-minute preparations.

W: Right. And if he needs to, he can stop by his hotel before his presentation. That reminds me . . . ⁰⁶I should call there now to make sure there are no issues with his booking.

investment n. 투자(액)   last-minute adj. 막바지의   preparation n. 준비
stop by 들르다

해석
04-06번은 다음 대화에 관한 문제입니다.
남: ⁰⁴내일 투자 세미나를 위한 초청 연사는 언제 도착하나요?
여: Mr. Nelson은 늦어도 오전 10시까지 컨벤션 센터에 도착할 거예요. ⁰⁵그의 비행기는 오전 7시에 시애틀 공항에 도착하고, 그는 그곳에서 택시를 탈 계획이에요.
남: 완벽해요. 그러면 그에게 막바지 준비를 위한 약 한 시간이 생기겠네요.
여: 맞아요. 그리고 필요하다면, 그는 발표 전에 호텔에 들를 수도 있어요. 그러고 보니... ⁰⁶지금 그곳에 전화해서 그의 예약에 문제가 없는지 확인해야겠어요.

04 특정 세부 사항 문제
해석 세미나의 주제는 무엇인가?
(A) 금융
(B) 관광
(C) 교통
(D) 보건
해설 질문의 핵심 어구(topic of the seminar)와 관련된 내용을 주의 깊게 듣는다. 남자가 "When does the guest speaker for tomorrow's investment seminar arrive?"라며 내일 투자 세미나를 위한 초청 연사가 언제 도착하는지 물었다. 따라서 (A)가 정답이다.
어휘 finance n. 금융   tourism n. 관광   transportation n. 교통   health care 보건

05 방법 문제
해석 Mr. Nelson은 어떻게 시애틀로 이동하는가?
(A) 기차로
(B) 자동차로
(C) 버스로
(D) 비행기로
해설 질문의 핵심 어구(Seattle)가 언급된 주변을 주의 깊게 듣는다. 여자가 "His[Mr. Nelson's] flight arrives at Seattle Airport at 7 A.M."이라며 Mr. Nelson의 비행기는 오전 7시에 시애틀 공항에 도착한다고 하였다. 따라서 (D)가 정답이다.

06 다음에 할 일 문제
해석 여자는 다음에 무엇을 할 것 같은가?
(A) 운전기사에게 전화한다.
(B) 호텔에 방문한다.
(C) 세미나에 참석한다.
(D) 예약을 확인한다.
해설 대화의 마지막 부분을 주의 깊게 듣는다. 여자가 "I should call there[hotel] now to make sure there are no issues with his booking."이라며 지금 호텔에 전화해서 예약에 문제가 없는지 확인해야겠다고 하였다. 따라서 (D)가 정답이다.

[07-09] 영국 → 호주
Questions 07-09 refer to the following conversation.

W: ⁰⁷We need to decide which applicant to hire for the software engineer position. What's your opinion of the three people we interviewed?
M: For me, Mike Dunlop is the best option. ⁰⁸I'm particularly impressed by the fact that he designed a successful language-learning app on his own. It shows that he's highly motivated.
W: I agree. We need someone who is willing to take the initiative.
M: In that case, ⁰⁹I'll call Beth in the legal department this afternoon and have her prepare a contract for him to review.

applicant n. 지원자   impressed adj. 감명을 받은   design v. 설계하다
successful adj. 성공적인   take the initiative 앞장을 서다
legal department 법무 부서   contract n. 계약서

해석
07-09번은 다음 대화에 관한 문제입니다.
여: ⁰⁷우리는 소프트웨어 기술자 직책에 어떤 지원자를 채용할지 결정해야 해요. 우리가 면접을 본 세 사람에 대한 당신의 의견은 어떤가요?
남: 제게는 Mike Dunlop이 가장 좋은 선택이에요. ⁰⁸저는 그가 혼자서 성공적인 언어 학습 앱을 설계했다는 사실에 특히 감명받았어요. 그것은 그가 매우 의욕적이라는 것을 보여줍니다.
여: 동의해요. 우리는 앞장설 의향이 있는 사람이 필요해요.
남: 그렇다면, ⁰⁹오늘 오후에 법무 부서의 Beth에게 전화해서 그가 검토할 계약서를 준비하도록 할게요.

07 주제 문제
해설 대화는 주로 무엇에 관한 것인가?
(A) 설문조사 실시하기
(B) 소프트웨어 프로그램 개선하기
(C) 직원 진급시키기
(D) 지원자 선정하기
해설 대화의 주제를 묻는 문제이므로, 대화의 초반을 반드시 듣는다. 여자가 "We need to decide which applicant to hire for the software engineer position. What's your opinion of the three people we interviewed?"라며 소프트웨어 기술자 직책에 어떤 지원자를 채용할지 결정해야 하는데 면접을 본 세 사람에 대한 의견이 어떤지 물은 후, 지원자 선정에 대한 내용으로 대화가 이어지고 있다. 따라서 (D)가 정답이다.
어휘 promote v. 진급시키다, 승진시키다   candidate n. 지원자

08 언급 문제
해설 Mike Dunlop에 대해 무엇이 언급되는가?
(A) 그는 몇 가지 지시를 받았다.
(B) 그는 면접 일정을 미뤘다.
(C) 그는 언어학을 전공했다.
(D) 그는 애플리케이션을 개발했다.
해설 질문의 핵심 어구(Mike Dunlop)와 관련된 내용을 주의 깊게 듣는다. 남자가 "I'm particularly impressed by the fact that he[Mike Dunlop] designed a successful language-learning app on his own."이라며 Mike Dunlop이 혼자서 성공적인 언어 학습 앱을 설계했다는 사실에 특히 감명받았다고 하였다. 따라서 (D)가 정답이다.
어휘 receive v. 받다   instructions n. 지시
push back (회의 등의 시간·날짜를 뒤로) 미루다   major in ~을 전공하다

09 다음에 할 일 문제
해설 남자는 오후에 무엇을 할 것인가?
(A) 고객과 대화한다.
(B) 프로그램을 설치한다.
(C) 계약서를 수정한다.
(D) 동료와 이야기한다.
해설 질문의 핵심 어구(afternoon)가 언급된 주변을 주의 깊게 듣는다. 남자가 "I'll call Beth in the legal department this afternoon and have her

prepare a contract"라며 오늘 오후에 법무 부서의 Beth에게 전화해서 계약서를 준비하도록 하겠다고 하였다. 따라서 (D)가 정답이다.

[10-12] 캐나다 → 미국 → 영국

Questions 10-12 refer to the following conversation with three speakers.

> M: Is everything ready for Mr. Henderson's party on Friday? ¹⁰**He is being recognized for his accomplishments as a writer at the *Boston Times***, so I want everything to go smoothly for him.
> W1: Actually, ¹¹**we ran into an unforeseen problem**.
> W2: Yeah. ¹¹**The owner of Oakridge Restaurant just called to cancel our reservation.**
> M: Really? Why?
> W1: The private room we reserved for Friday was double-booked. However, the owner said he would take 25 percent off our total bill if we hold the event on a different night.
> M: ¹²**Why don't you check if there is a room available on Saturday?**
> W2: Sure thing.
>
> recognize v. 인정하다, 인식하다 accomplishment n. 업적, 성취
> smoothly adv. 순조롭게, 매끄럽게 run into (곤경 등을) 만나다
> unforeseen adj. 예상하지 못한

해석
10-12번은 다음 세 명의 대화에 관한 문제입니다.

남: 금요일에 있을 Mr. Henderson의 파티를 위한 모든 것이 준비되었나요? ¹⁰그가 *Boston Times*지의 기자로서 그의 업적을 인정받고 있는 만큼, 그를 위해 모든 것이 순조롭게 진행되었으면 해요.
여1: 사실, ¹¹예상하지 못한 문제를 만났어요.
여2: 네. ¹¹Oakridge 식당 주인이 우리의 예약을 취소하기 위해 방금 전화했어요.
남: 정말요? 왜요?
여1: 금요일에 우리가 예약했던 개인실이 이중 예약이 되었어요. 하지만, 주인이 만약 우리가 행사를 다른 날 밤에 연다면 우리의 총 청구 금액에서 25퍼센트를 할인해 주겠다고 말했어요.
남: ¹²토요일에 이용할 수 있는 방이 있는지 확인해 보는 것이 어떨까요?
여2: 알겠습니다.

10 특정 세부 사항 문제

해석 Mr. Henderson은 누구인가?
(A) 회사 회장
(B) 식당 주인
(C) 개인 비서
(D) 신문 기자

해설 질문 대상(Mr. Henderson)의 신분 및 직업과 관련된 표현을 놓치지 않고 듣는다. 남자가 "He[Mr. Henderson] is being recognized for his accomplishments as a writer at the *Boston Times*"라며 Mr. Henderson이 *Boston Times*지의 기자로서 그의 업적을 인정받고 있다고 한 것을 통해 Mr. Henderson이 신문 기자임을 알 수 있다. 따라서 (D)가 정답이다.

어휘 secretary n. 비서

11 문제점 문제

해석 여자들은 무엇에 대해 걱정하는가?
(A) 후기
(B) 메뉴
(C) 예약

(D) 지불금

해설 여자들의 말에서 부정적인 표현이 언급된 주변을 주의 깊게 듣는다. 여자1이 "we ran into an unforeseen problem"이라며 예상하지 못한 문제를 만났다고 하자, 여자2가 "The owner of Oakridge Restaurant just called to cancel our reservation."이라며 Oakridge 식당 주인이 예약을 취소하기 위해 방금 전화했다고 한 것을 통해 여자들이 예약에 대해 걱정하고 있음을 알 수 있다. 따라서 (C)가 정답이다.

어휘 payment n. 지불(금)

12 제안 문제

해석 남자는 무엇을 제안하는가?
(A) 다른 장소를 선택하기
(B) 파티 초대장을 업데이트하기
(C) 기념행사를 연기하기
(D) 할인에 관해 물어보기

해설 남자의 말에서 제안과 관련된 표현이 언급된 다음을 주의 깊게 듣는다. 남자가 "Why don't you check if there is a room available on Saturday?"라며 토요일에 이용할 수 있는 방이 있는지 확인해보는 것이 어떠냐고 한 것을 통해 남자가 행사를 연기하는 것을 제안함을 알 수 있다. 따라서 (C)가 정답이다.

어휘 venue n. 장소 invitation n. 초대장, 초청 celebration n. 기념행사, 축하연

[13-15] 미국 → 캐나다

Questions 13-15 refer to the following conversation.

> W: Derek, you were on leave last week, right? That means ¹³**you missed the big announcement. Brenda Johnson received a promotion!**
> M: I heard the news this morning. She's taking over the marketing team, right?
> W: Exactly. And apparently one of her goals is closer cooperation with us and the other sales representatives.
> M: What makes you say that?
> W: Well, ¹⁴/¹⁵**she asked me to present our sales team's suggestions for future advertising campaigns to her senior staff.** ¹⁵**But I don't know if I'll have time.** I'm really busy these days.
> M: The two teams need to work together. ¹⁵**Please make this a priority.** It's very important.
>
> leave n. 휴가 announcement n. 발표 promotion n. 승진
> department n. 부서 apparently adv. 보아하니, 듣자 하니
> cooperation n. 협력 sales representative 영업 담당자
> priority n. 우선 (사항)

해석
13-15번은 다음 대화에 관한 문제입니다.

여: Derek, 지난주에 휴가 중이셨죠, 그렇죠? 그러면 ¹³큰 발표를 놓쳤다는 뜻이네요. Brenda Johnson이 승진했어요!
남: 오늘 아침에 그 소식을 들었어요. 그녀는 마케팅팀을 맡게 되는 거죠, 그렇죠?
여: 맞아요. 그리고 보아하니 그녀의 목표 중 하나는 우리와 다른 영업 담당자들과의 더 긴밀한 협력이에요.
남: 왜 그렇게 말씀하시나요?
여: 음, ¹⁴/¹⁵그녀는 제게 우리 영업팀의 향후 광고 캠페인에 대한 제안을 그녀의 선임 직원들에게 발표해달라고 요청했어요. ¹⁵하지만 제가 시간이 있을지 모르겠네요. 요즘 정말 바쁘거든요.
남: 두 팀이 함께 일해야 해요. ¹⁵이것을 우선시해 주세요. 그건 매우 중요해요.

13 특정 세부 사항 문제

해석 여자에 따르면, 발표는 무엇에 관한 것이었는가?

DAY 12 인사 및 사내 행사 관련 대화 69

(A) 실적 평가
(B) 프로젝트 마감일
(C) 회사의 확장
(D) 동료의 승진

해설 여자의 말에서 질문의 핵심 어구(announcement)가 언급된 주변을 주의 깊게 듣는다. 여자가 "you missed the big announcement. Brenda Johnson received a promotion!"이라며 남자가 큰 발표를 놓쳤는데 Brenda Johnson이 승진했다고 하였다. 따라서 (D)가 정답이다.

어휘 performance n. 실적, 성과 evaluation n. 평가 expansion n. 확장

14 화자 문제

해설 화자들은 어느 부서에서 일하는가?
(A) 마케팅
(B) 영업
(C) 법무
(D) 인사

해설 대화에서 신분 및 직업과 관련된 표현을 놓치지 않고 듣는다. 여자가 "she[Brenda Johnson] asked me to present our sales team's suggestions for future advertising campaigns to her senior staff"라며 Brenda Johnson이 우리 영업팀의 향후 광고 캠페인에 대한 제안을 선임 직원들에게 발표해달라고 한 것을 통해 화자들이 영업 부서에서 일한다는 것을 알 수 있다. 따라서 (B)가 정답이다.

어휘 personnel n. 인사

15 의도 파악 문제

해설 남자가 "두 팀이 함께 일해야 해요"라고 말할 때 무엇을 의도하는가?
(A) 여자는 회의 일정을 잡아야 한다.
(B) 여자는 캠페인 계획을 수정해야 한다.
(C) 회사는 선임 직원을 승진시켜야 한다.
(D) 여자는 발표를 해야 한다.

해설 질문의 인용어구(The two teams need to work together)가 언급된 주변을 주의 깊게 듣는다. 여자가 "she[Brenda Johnson] asked me to present our sales team's suggestions for future advertising campaigns to her senior staff. But I don't know if I'll have time."이라며 Brenda Johnson이 영업팀의 향후 광고 캠페인에 대한 제안을 선임 직원들에게 발표해달라고 했지만 자신에게 시간이 있을지 모르겠다고 하자, 남자가 "Please make this[to present our sales team's suggestions] a priority."라며 발표를 우선시해 달라고 하였다. 이는 두 팀이 함께 일해야 하니 발표가 중요하다는 것이므로, 여자가 발표를 해야 한다는 것임을 알 수 있다. 따라서 (D)가 정답이다.

[16-18] 호주 → 영국
Questions 16-18 refer to the following conversation.

M: ¹⁶**What do you think about holding our firm's annual team-building seminar at the Walden Lake Resort instead of at the Langley Convention Center?** That way, our team leaders can spend more time together.
W: It sounds great, ¹⁷**but booking hotel rooms for over 20 people will be quite costly. We'd probably end up going over our budget for this event.**
M: It might be worth it, though. That resort specializes in corporate retreats, so ¹⁸**it offers a number of exercises and training sessions. You can find descriptions of them on its Web site.**

costly adj. 많은 비용이 드는 budget n. 예산
specialize in ~을 전문으로 하다 corporate adj. 회사의 retreat n. 야유회

해석
16-18번은 다음 대화에 관한 문제입니다.

남: ¹⁶우리 회사의 연례 팀 빌딩 세미나를 Langley 컨벤션 센터 대신 Walden Lake 리조트에서 개최하는 것에 대해 어떻게 생각하세요? 그러면 우리 팀 리더들이 더 많은 시간을 함께 보낼 수 있을 거예요.
여: 좋은 것 같지만, ¹⁷20명이 넘는 사람들을 위해 호텔 객실을 예약하는 것은 꽤 비용이 많이 들 것입니다. 우리는 아마도 이 행사를 위한 예산을 초과하게 될 거예요.
남: 그래도 가치가 있을 거예요. ¹⁸그 리조트는 회사 야유회를 전문으로 해서 여러 가지 활동과 교육 과정을 제공해요. 웹사이트에서 그것들에 대한 설명을 찾을 수 있어요.

16 제안 문제

해설 남자는 무엇을 할 것을 제안하는가?
(A) 교육 과정을 연기하기
(B) 회사 행사를 이전하기
(C) 팀 리더를 새로 발령하기
(D) 프로젝트 예산을 확인하기

해설 남자의 말에서 제안과 관련된 표현이 언급된 다음을 주의 깊게 듣는다. 남자가 "What do you think about holding our firm's annual team-building seminar at the Walden Lake Resort instead of at the Langley Convention Center?"라며 회사의 연례 팀 빌딩 세미나를 Langley 컨벤션 센터 대신 Walden Lake 리조트에서 개최하는 것에 대해 어떻게 생각하는지 묻고 있다. 따라서 (B)가 정답이다.

어휘 delay v. 연기하다, 미루다 relocate v. 이전하다, 이동하다
reassign v. 새로 발령내다, 다시 맡기다

17 문제점 문제

해설 여자는 무슨 문제를 언급하는가?
(A) 과정이 어려울 것이다.
(B) 목적지가 멀다.
(C) 비용이 높을 것이다.
(D) 정책이 불공평하다.

해설 여자의 말에서 부정적인 표현이 언급된 주변을 주의 깊게 듣는다. 여자가 "but booking hotel rooms for over 20 people will be quite costly. We'd probably end up going over our budget for this event."라며 20명이 넘는 사람들을 위해 호텔 객실을 예약하는 것은 꽤 비용이 많이 들 것이라고 한 후, 행사를 위한 예산을 초과하게 될 것이라고 하였다. 따라서 (C)가 정답이다.

어휘 process n. 과정, 절차 destination n. 목적지 cost n. 비용, 값

18 특정 세부 사항 문제

해설 남자에 따르면, 웹사이트에서 무엇을 찾을 수 있는가?
(A) 숙박 시설 가격
(B) 서비스 후기
(C) 장소까지의 길 안내
(D) 활동에 대한 세부 사항

해설 남자의 말에서 질문의 핵심 어구(Web site)가 언급된 주변을 주의 깊게 듣는다. 남자가 "it[resort] offers a number of exercises and training sessions. You can find descriptions of them on its Web site."라며 그 리조트는 여러 가지 활동과 교육 과정을 제공한다고 한 후, 웹사이트에서 그것들에 대한 설명을 찾을 수 있다고 한 것을 통해 웹사이트에서 활동에 대한 세부 사항을 찾을 수 있음을 알 수 있다. 따라서 (D)가 정답이다.

[19-21] 영국 → 호주
Questions 19-21 refer to the following conversation and schedule.

W: Did you make the final seating chart for Friday's shareholder meeting?
M: Yeah. However, something's come up. ¹⁹**Our CEO informed me that she cannot attend the meeting.**

Now, we need to figure out how to fill our 11:30 slot.
W: That certainly changes things. Do you have any ideas on what to add to the schedule?
M: Hmm . . . Oh! [20]**Why don't we play the promotional movie our PR team put together recently?** It's about 45 minutes long and highlights our major upcoming product lines.
W: Perfect. And [21]**let's print out nametags for attendees to wear** before we forget.

shareholder n. 주주   figure out 생각해 내다, 이해하다   slot n. 자리
promotional adj. 홍보용의   put together (이것저것을 모아) 준비하다, 만들다
highlight v. 강조하다   nametag n. 이름표

해석
19-21번은 다음 대화와 일정표에 관한 문제입니다.
여: 금요일 주주 총회를 위한 최종 좌석 배치도를 만들었나요?
남: 네, 하지만, 일이 생겼어요. [19]우리 최고 경영자가 회의에 참석할 수 없다고 저에게 알렸어요. 이제, 11시 30분 자리를 어떻게 채울지 생각해 내야 해요.
여: 그것이 확실히 상황을 바꾸네요. 일정에 무엇을 추가할지에 대한 아이디어가 있나요?
남: 음... 아! [20]홍보팀이 최근에 준비한 홍보용 영화를 재생하는 것은 어때요? 그것은 약 45분 분량이고, 우리의 향후 주요 제품 라인을 강조해요.
여: 완벽해요. 그리고 잊기 전에 [21]참석자가 착용할 이름표를 인쇄하기로 해요.

시간	연설	연사
오전 10시 30분	인력 혁신	Margot Hatch
오전 11시 30분	[19]세계적 확장	Cynthia Bloom
오후 12시 15분	점심시간	
오후 1시 30분	재정 예측	Gerald Fines
오후 2시 45분	국내 시장	Pete Strass

19 시각 자료 문제
해석 시각 자료를 보아라. 어떤 연설이 대체될 것인가?
(A) 인력 혁신
(B) 세계적 확장
(C) 재정 예측
(D) 국내 시장

해설 제시된 일정표의 정보를 확인한 후 질문의 핵심 어구(talk ~ replaced)와 관련된 내용을 주의 깊게 듣는다. 남자가 "Our CEO informed me that she cannot attend the meeting. Now, we need to figure out how to fill our 11:30 slot."이라며 최고 경영자가 회의에 참석할 수 없다고 알렸다고 한 후, 11시 30분 자리를 어떻게 채울지 생각해 내야 한다고 하였으므로 대체될 연설은 세계적 확장임을 일정표에서 알 수 있다. 따라서 (B)가 정답이다.

20 제안 문제
해석 남자는 무엇을 권장하는가?
(A) 시간대를 조정하기
(B) 다른 연사를 초대하기
(C) 영상을 보여주기
(D) 참석자들에게 알리기

해설 남자의 말에서 제안과 관련된 표현이 언급된 다음을 주의 깊게 듣는다. 남자가 "Why don't we play the promotional movie our PR team put together recently?"라며 홍보팀이 최근에 준비한 홍보용 영화를 재생하는 것은 어떠냐고 하였다. 따라서 (C)가 정답이다.

어휘 adjust v. 조정하다   time slot 시간대   invite v. 초대하다   notify v. 알리다

Paraphrasing
play the promotional movie 홍보용 영화를 재생하다 → Showing a video 영상을 보여주기

21 특정 세부 사항 문제
해석 여자는 무엇을 인쇄할 것인가?
(A) 손님 이름표
(B) 기업 안내서
(C) 좌석 배치도
(D) 회의 진행표

해설 질문의 핵심 어구(print)가 언급된 주변을 주의 깊게 듣는다. 여자가 "let's print out nametags for attendees to wear"라며 참석자가 착용할 이름표를 인쇄하자고 하였다. 따라서 (A)가 정답이다.

어휘 brochure n. 안내서

DAY 13 마케팅/판매/재무 관련 대화

HACKERS PRACTICE   p.105

01 (D)   **02** (D)   **03** (D)   **04** (B)

[01-02] 캐나다 → 영국 / 호주 → 미국
Questions 01-02 refer to the following conversation.

M: [01]**Thanks for meeting with us, Ms. Davidson. We appreciate the chance to show you** how our company's newest face-toning device works.
W: No problem. This is exactly the kind of beauty product that customers at my stores are interested in. Oh, it's much smaller than I expected.
M: That's actually one of its selling points. And [02]**I want to point out that we offer a five-year comprehensive warranty**. This shows our confidence in the product.

appreciate v. 고맙게 생각하다, 진가를 알다   chance n. 기회, 가능성
selling point (판매 시) 상품의 강조점   point out 언급하다, 지적하다
comprehensive adj. 종합적인, 포괄적인   warranty n. 품질 보증
confidence n. 자신감, 신뢰

해석
01-02번은 다음 대화에 관한 문제입니다.
남: [01]저희와 만나주셔서 감사합니다, Ms. Davidson. 저희 회사의 최신 얼굴 토닝 기기가 어떻게 작동하는지 보여드릴 기회를 주셔서 감사하게 생각합니다.
여: 천만에요. 이것은 제 가게의 고객들이 관심을 두는 바로 그런 종류의 미용 제품이에요. 아, 생각했던 것보다 훨씬 작네요.
남: 사실 그게 상품의 강조점 중 하나입니다. 그리고 [02]저희가 5년짜리 종합 품질 보증을 제공한다는 점을 언급하고 싶습니다. 이것은 제품에 대한 저희의 자신감을 보여줍니다.

01 이유 문제
해석 남자는 왜 여자를 방문하고 있는가?
(A) 제휴를 논의하기 위해
(B) 면접을 진행하기 위해
(C) 계약을 협상하기 위해
(D) 제품을 소개하기 위해

해설 질문의 핵심 어구(visiting the woman)와 관련된 내용을 주의 깊게 듣는다. 남자가 "Thanks for meeting with us, Ms. Davidson. We appreciate the chance to show you how our company's newest face-toning device works."라며 만나주어서 감사하다고 한 후, 자사의 최신 얼굴 토닝 기기가 어떻게 작동하는지 보여줄 기회를 주어서 감사하게 생각한다고 하였다. 따라서 (D)가 정답이다.

어휘 partnership n. 제휴, 협력   negotiate v. 협상하다

02 특정 세부 사항 문제
해석 남자는 그의 회사가 무엇을 제공한다고 말하는가?
(A) 연간 회원 자격
(B) 무료 액세서리
(C) 소프트웨어 업그레이드
(D) 연장된 품질 보증

해설 질문의 핵심 어구(company provides)와 관련된 내용을 주의 깊게 듣는다. 남자가 "I want to point out that we[our company] offer a five-year comprehensive warranty"라며 자사가 5년짜리 종합 품질 보증을 제공한다는 점을 언급하고 싶다고 하였다. 따라서 (D)가 정답이다.

어휘 annual adj. 연간의   complimentary adj. 무료의   extended adj. 연장한

[03-04] 미국 → 호주 / 영국 → 캐나다
Questions 03-04 refer to the following conversation.

W: Jake, would you mind helping me put up the new price tags? 03**Our clothing boutique's annual summer sale starts tomorrow.** We need to get everything ready for the customers.
M: Sure. And once we are done, 04**maybe we should put a sign in the front window**. That way, everyone who walks by will know that we are having a sale.
W: I was thinking the same thing.

put up 붙이다, 세우다   price tag 가격표   boutique n. 부티크, 양품점
sign n. 표지판

해석
03-04번은 다음 대화에 관한 문제입니다.
여: Jake, 새 가격표를 붙이는 것을 도와줄 수 있나요? 03우리 의류 부티크의 연례 여름 할인 판매가 내일 시작돼요. 고객들을 위해 모든 것을 준비해야 해요.
남: 물론이죠. 그리고 일을 마치면, 04우리는 아마도 앞쪽 창문에 표지판을 붙여야 할 거예요. 그렇게 하면, 지나가는 모든 사람들이 우리가 할인을 하고 있다는 것을 알게 될 거예요.
여: 저도 같은 생각을 하고 있었어요.

03 다음에 할 일 문제
해석 여자에 따르면, 내일 무슨 일이 일어날 것인가?
(A) 거리가 폐쇄될 것이다.
(B) 제품이 출시될 것이다.
(C) 상점이 이전할 것이다.
(D) 판촉 활동이 시작될 것이다.

해설 여자의 말에서 질문의 핵심 어구(tomorrow)가 언급된 주변을 주의 깊게 듣는다. 여자가 "Our clothing boutique's annual summer sale starts tomorrow."라며 우리 의류 부티크의 연례 여름 할인 판매가 내일 시작된다고 한 것을 통해 내일 판촉 활동이 시작될 것임을 알 수 있다. 따라서 (D)가 정답이다.

어휘 launch v. 출시하다   relocate v. 이전하다   promotion n. 판촉 활동

04 제안 문제
해석 남자는 무엇을 권장하는가?
(A) 제품 배열하기
(B) 안내문 게시하기
(C) 창문 청소하기
(D) 상점 방문하기

해설 남자의 말에서 제안과 관련된 표현이 언급된 다음을 주의 깊게 듣는다. 남자가 "maybe we should put a sign in the front window"라며 아마도 앞쪽 창문에 표지판을 붙여야 할 것이라고 하였다. 따라서 (B)가 정답이다.

어휘 arrange v. 배열하다, 정돈하다   post v. 게시하다

Paraphrasing
put a sign 표지판을 붙이다 → Posting a notice 안내문 게시하기

HACKERS TEST   p.106

01 (B)	02 (A)	03 (C)	04 (A)	05 (A)
06 (D)	07 (C)	08 (B)	09 (A)	10 (A)
11 (A)	12 (A)	13 (C)	14 (D)	15 (D)
16 (B)	17 (B)	18 (C)	19 (A)	20 (C)
21 (D)				

[01-03] 캐나다 → 미국
Questions 01-03 refer to the following conversation.

M: Over the last month, 01**our boutique has only sold a few dresses from the Joyce Cho Collection**. We may want to consider replacing that line with items from other designers.
W: Yes, I know that it hasn't been doing well, but I think that's because it hasn't been properly promoted. 02**Maybe we should consider making a post to draw attention to it on our social media page.**
M: That's a great idea. I'll take care of that now. 03**Could you create the inventory list for the merchandise we received this morning while I do that?**

line n. 제품군   properly adv. 제대로, 적절히   attention n. 관심, 주목
inventory n. 재고, 재고 조사   merchandise n. 상품

해석
01-03번은 다음 대화에 관한 문제입니다.
남: 지난 한 달 동안, 01우리 부티크는 Joyce Cho 컬렉션의 드레스를 몇 벌밖에 팔지 못했어요. 우리는 그 제품군을 다른 디자이너들의 물건들로 교체하는 것을 고려해야 할 수도 있겠어요.
여: 네, 저는 그것이 잘 안 팔리고 있다는 것을 알지만, 그건 제대로 홍보되지 않았기 때문이라고 생각해요. 02아마도 우리 소셜 미디어 페이지에 그것에 대한 관심을 끌기 위한 게시물을 올리는 것을 고려해야 할 것 같아요.
남: 좋은 생각이네요. 제가 지금 그것을 처리할게요. 03제가 그것을 하는 동안 당신은 오늘 아침에 받은 상품의 재고 목록을 작성해 주시겠어요?

01 문제점 문제
해석 무엇이 문제인가?
(A) 부티크가 현재 문을 열지 않았다.
(B) 의류 제품군이 잘 팔리지 않고 있다.
(C) 드레스가 교환될 수 없다.
(D) 구매품이 환불될 수 없다.

해설 대화에서 부정적인 표현이 언급된 주변을 주의 깊게 듣는다. 남자가 "our boutique has only sold a few dresses from the Joyce Cho Collection"이라며 우리 부티크가 Joyce Cho 컬렉션의 드레스를 몇 벌밖에 팔지 못했다고 하였다. 따라서 (B)가 정답이다.

02 제안 문제
해석 여자는 무엇을 하는 것을 제안하는가?

(A) 온라인으로 광고하기
(B) 할인을 제공하기
(C) 직원을 고용하기
(D) 공간을 확장하기

해설 여자의 말에서 제안과 관련된 표현이 언급된 다음을 주의 깊게 듣는다. 여자가 "Maybe we should consider making a post to draw attention to it[Joyce Cho Collection] on our social media page."라며 소셜 미디어 페이지에 Joyce Cho 컬렉션에 대한 관심을 끌기 위한 게시물을 올리는 것을 고려해야 할 것 같다고 하였다. 따라서 (A)가 정답이다.

03 요청 문제

해석 남자는 여자에게 무엇을 하라고 요청하는가?
(A) 고객을 돕는다.
(B) 디자인을 만든다.
(C) 목록을 작성한다.
(D) 거래를 처리한다.

해설 남자의 말에서 요청과 관련된 표현이 언급된 다음을 주의 깊게 듣는다. 남자가 여자에게 "Could you create the inventory list for the merchandise ~?"라며 상품의 재고 목록을 작성해달라고 요청하였다. 따라서 (C)가 정답이다.

어휘 transaction n. 거래, 매매

[04-06] 영국 → 캐나다
Questions 04-06 refer to the following conversation.

W: Hi. ⁰⁴I'm building a wall around my client's property, and he wants me to use bricks made from recycled materials. Do you sell those here?
M: We do. They're right over here.
W: I'm a little worried that they might get damaged easily.
M: Many people think that, but ⁰⁵surprisingly, these bricks are much stronger than traditional ones.
W: That's good to hear. I'll need about 3,000 of them. How much will shipping cost? The property is within the city limits.
M: ⁰⁶With that large of an order, I won't charge you for delivery. I just need the address and a contact number.

property n. 부지, 부동산   recycle v. 재활용하다   material n. 재료
traditional adj. 기존의, 전통적인   limit n. 경계
charge v. (요금·값을) 청구하다

해석
04-06번은 다음 대화에 관한 문제입니다.

여: 안녕하세요. ⁰⁴제 의뢰인의 부지 둘레에 벽을 짓고 있는데, 그는 제가 재활용된 재료로 만들어진 벽돌을 사용하기를 원하세요. 여기서 그런 것을 판매하나요?
남: 네, 판매합니다. 바로 여기 있어요.
여: 그것들이 쉽게 손상될까 봐 조금 걱정돼요.
남: 많은 사람들이 그렇게 생각하지만, ⁰⁵놀랍게도 이 벽돌들은 기존 벽돌들보다 훨씬 더 튼튼합니다.
여: 좋네요. 3,000개 정도 필요할 거예요. 배송 비용은 얼마인가요? 그 부지는 시 경계 내에 있어요.
남: ⁰⁶그렇게 큰 주문이라면, 배송료를 청구하지 않을게요. 주소와 연락처만 필요합니다.

04 화자 문제
해설 여자는 어떤 종류의 업체에서 일하는가?
(A) 건설 회사
(B) 조경 서비스 업체

(C) 인테리어 디자인 회사
(D) 부동산 중개소

해설 대화에서 신분 및 직업과 관련된 표현을 놓치지 않고 듣는다. 여자가 "I'm building a wall around my client's property"라며 의뢰인의 부지 둘레에 벽을 짓고 있다고 한 것을 통해 여자가 건설 회사에서 일한다는 것을 알 수 있다. 따라서 (A)가 정답이다.

어휘 landscaping n. 조경

05 특정 세부 사항 문제
해석 남자는 제품에 관해 무엇이 놀랍다고 말하는가?
(A) 내구성
(B) 외관
(C) 무게
(D) 가격

해설 남자의 말에서 질문의 핵심 어구(surprising about a product)와 관련된 내용을 주의 깊게 듣는다. 남자가 "surprisingly, these bricks[bricks made from recycled materials] are much stronger than traditional ones"라며 놀랍게도 재활용 재료로 만들어진 벽돌들이 기존 벽돌들보다 훨씬 더 튼튼하다고 하였다. 따라서 (A)가 정답이다.

어휘 durability n. 내구성   appearance n. 외관, 외형   weight n. 무게

06 특정 세부 사항 문제
해석 여자는 대량 주문을 하면 무엇을 받을 것인가?
(A) 특별 선물
(B) 상품권
(C) 회원 등급 상향
(D) 무료 서비스

해설 질문의 핵심 어구(receive for placing a large order)와 관련된 내용을 주의 깊게 듣는다. 남자가 "With that large of an order, I won't charge you for delivery."라며 그렇게 큰 주문이라면, 배송료를 청구하지 않겠다고 한 것을 통해 여자가 대량 주문을 하면 무료 서비스를 받을 것임을 알 수 있다. 따라서 (D)가 정답이다.

어휘 gift certificate 상품권

[07-09] 호주 → 영국
Questions 07-09 refer to the following conversation.

M: Sally, ⁰⁷tenants are complaining about the lack of security cameras in our apartment building. I think it's time for us to install some.
W: Sure, but how expensive would it be? ⁰⁸Since I'm managing our budget, I have to approve any expenses.
M: I researched several local companies online that can set everything up for under 10,000 dollars.
W: Oh, that sounds reasonable, but how long would it take for the equipment to be installed?
M: They could do it within two days, I believe. ⁰⁹I'll call those companies this afternoon and confirm that, though.

tenant n. 세입자   complain v. 불평하다   lack n. 부족
approve v. 승인하다   reasonable adj. 합리적인   equipment n. 장비

해석
07-09번은 다음 대화에 관한 문제입니다.

남: Sally, ⁰⁷세입자들이 우리 아파트 건물에 보안 카메라가 부족한 것에 대해 불평하고 있어요. 몇 개를 설치해야 할 때라고 생각해요.
여: 그럼요, 그런데 얼마나 비쌀까요? ⁰⁸제가 예산을 관리하고 있어서, 모든 경비를 승인해야 해요.

남: 제가 1만 달러 미만으로 모든 것을 설치할 수 있는 지역 회사 몇 군데를 온라인으로 조사했어요.
여: 아, 그건 합리적인 것 같은데, 장비를 설치하는 데는 얼마나 걸릴까요?
남: 제 생각엔, 그들이 이틀 안에 그것을 할 수 있을 것 같아요. 그래도, [09]제가 오늘 오후에 그 회사들에 전화해서 확인해 볼게요.

07 주제 문제

해석 화자들은 주로 무엇에 대해 이야기하고 있는가?
(A) 임대료 인상
(B) 세입자 공지사항
(C) 보안 장비
(D) 온라인 데이터

해설 대화의 주제를 묻는 문제이므로, 대화의 초반을 반드시 듣는다. 남자가 "tenants are complaining about the lack of security cameras in our apartment building"이라며 세입자들이 아파트 건물에 보안 카메라가 부족한 것에 대해 불평하고 있다고 한 후, 보안 장비에 대한 내용으로 대화가 이어지고 있다. 따라서 (C)가 정답이다.

어휘 rent n. 임대료   increase n. 인상

Paraphrasing
security cameras 보안 카메라 → Security equipment 보안 장비

08 특정 세부 사항 문제

해석 여자는 무엇을 하는 것을 담당하는가?
(A) 거주민들과 소통하기
(B) 예산을 감독하기
(C) 직원들에게 업무를 배정하기
(D) 기계를 설치하기

해설 질문의 핵심 어구(in charge of doing)와 관련된 내용을 주의 깊게 듣는다. 여자가 "Since I'm managing our budget, I have to approve any expenses."라며 자신이 예산을 관리하고 있어서 모든 경비를 승인해야 한다고 한 말을 통해 여자가 예산 감독을 담당함을 알 수 있다. 따라서 (B)가 정답이다.

어휘 communicate v. 소통하다   oversee v. 감독하다   machinery n. 기계

Paraphrasing
managing ~ budget 예산을 관리하다 → Overseeing a budget 예산을 감독하기

09 다음에 할 일 문제

해석 남자는 오늘 오후에 무엇을 할 것이라고 말하는가?
(A) 업체들에 연락한다.
(B) 사용자 설명서를 읽는다.
(C) 소프트웨어 프로그램을 설치한다.
(D) 서비스를 홍보한다.

해설 남자의 말에서 질문의 핵심 어구(this afternoon)가 언급된 주변을 주의 깊게 듣는다. 남자가 "I'll call those companies this afternoon and confirm that"이라며 오늘 오후에 그 회사들에 전화해서 확인해 보겠다고 하였다. 따라서 (A)가 정답이다.

어휘 manual n. 설명서

Paraphrasing
call ~ companies 회사들에 전화하다 → Contact businesses 업체들에 연락하다

[10-12] 미국 → 캐나다

Questions 10-12 refer to the following conversation.

W: [10]I think we need to find a way to attract more customers to our hair shop.
M: [11]What about making some flyers? We could distribute them around the neighborhood to attract new customers.
W: I've been considering that for a while. [11]It's a cost-effective and easy way to advertise our business.
M: In that case, [12]I will start working on the design of the flyer now. I'll show you what I've come up with in a couple of hours.

attract v. 끌어모으다   flyer n. 전단   distribute v. 나누어 주다
neighborhood n. 인근, 근처   cost-effective adj. 비용 효율이 높은
come up with ~을 생각해 내다

해석
10-12번은 다음 대화에 관한 문제입니다.
여: [10]우리 미용실에 더 많은 고객을 끌어모을 방법을 찾아야 할 것 같아요.
남: [11]전단을 만드는 것은 어떨까요? 우리는 새로운 고객을 끌어모으기 위해 인근 곳곳에 그것들을 나누어줄 수 있어요.
여: 저도 얼마 동안 그것을 고려하고 있었어요. [11]그것은 우리 업체를 홍보하는 데 비용 효율이 높고 쉬운 방법이에요.
남: 그렇다면, [12]지금 전단 디자인 작업을 시작할게요. 두어 시간 후에 제가 생각해 낸 것을 보여드릴게요.

10 장소 문제

해석 화자들이 어디에 있는 것 같은가?
(A) 미용실에
(B) 식료품점에
(C) 인쇄소에
(D) 건강 휴양 시설에

해설 대화에서 장소와 관련된 표현을 놓치지 않고 듣는다. 여자가 "I think we need to find a way to attract more customers to our hair shop."이라며 우리 미용실에 더 많은 고객을 끌어모을 방법을 찾아야 할 것 같다고 한 것을 통해 화자들이 미용실에 있음을 알 수 있다. 따라서 (A)가 정답이다.

어휘 hair salon 미용실   grocery store 식료품점   print shop 인쇄소
health spa 건강 휴양 시설

11 의도 파악 문제

해석 여자는 왜 "저도 얼마 동안 그것을 고려하고 있었어요"라고 말하는가?
(A) 제안에 동의를 표현하기 위해
(B) 선택에 대한 불확실성을 나타내기 위해
(C) 문제에 대한 해결책을 소개하기 위해
(D) 과제에 대한 도움을 요청하기 위해

해설 질문의 인용어구(I've been considering that for a while)가 언급된 주변을 주의 깊게 듣는다. 남자가 "What about making some flyers?"라며 전단을 만드는 것은 어떨지 묻자, 여자가 "It's a cost-effective and easy way to advertise our business."라며 그것이 업체를 홍보하는 데 비용 효율이 높고 쉬운 방법이라고 한 것을 통해, 전단을 만들자는 제안에 동의를 표현하기 위함임을 알 수 있다. 따라서 (A)가 정답이다.

어휘 express v. 표현하다   agreement n. 동의   proposal n. 제안
uncertainty n. 불확실성

12 제안 문제

해석 남자는 무엇을 해주겠다고 제안하는가?
(A) 디자인을 만든다.
(B) 재료를 구매한다.
(C) 전단을 배포한다.
(D) 고객을 만난다.

해설 남자의 말에서 제안과 관련된 표현이 언급된 다음을 주의 깊게 듣는다. 남자가 "I will start working on the design of the flyer now"라며 지금 전단 디자인 작업을 시작하겠다고 하였다. 따라서 (A)가 정답이다.

어휘 hand out 배포하다, 나눠주다

[13-15] 호주 → 영국 → 미국

Questions 13-15 refer to the following conversation with three speakers.

M: This is Greg Wilkins from Hartford Bank. [13]**I'm calling regarding your inquiry about a loan to open a second branch of your café.**
W1: Thanks for calling back. My partner and I are both on the line.
W2: Right. [14]**We're interested in the low-interest loan for small businesses that is advertised on your home page.**
M: OK. You need to first apply for the loan.
W1: Got it. [15]**Should we apply in person at your bank?**
M: Actually, [15]**I can e-mail you the document you need to fill out.**

regarding prep. ~에 관하여 inquiry n. 문의 loan n. 대출
branch n. 지점 be on the line 통화 중이다 low-interest adj. 저금리의
in person 직접 document n. 서류 fill out 작성하다

해석
13-15번은 다음 세 명의 대화에 관한 문제입니다.
남: 저는 Hartford 은행에서 근무하는 Greg Wilkins입니다. [13]카페의 두 번째 지점을 열기 위한 대출 관련 귀하의 문의에 관하여 전화드렸습니다.
여1: 다시 전화해 주셔서 감사합니다. 제 동업자와 저 둘 다 통화 중이에요.
여2: 맞아요. [14]저희는 귀사의 홈페이지에 광고된 소규모 사업체를 위한 저금리 대출에 관심이 있어요.
남: 네. 먼저 대출을 신청하셔야 합니다.
여: 알겠습니다. [15]은행에서 직접 신청해야 하나요?
남: 사실, [15]작성하셔야 하는 서류를 제가 이메일로 보내드릴 수 있습니다.

13 이유 문제
해석 여자들은 왜 돈을 빌리고 싶어 하는가?
(A) 시설을 개선하기 위해
(B) 차량을 구매하기 위해
(C) 사업을 확장하기 위해
(D) 제품을 개발하기 위해

해설 질문의 핵심 어구(borrow money)와 관련된 내용을 주의 깊게 듣는다. 남자가 "I'm calling regarding your inquiry about a loan to open a second branch of your café."라며 카페의 두 번째 지점을 열기 위한 대출 관련 여자들의 문의에 관하여 전화했다고 하였다. 따라서 (C)가 정답이다.

어휘 facility n. 시설 purchase v. 구매하다 vehicle n. 차량
expand v. 확장하다

14 방법 문제
해석 여자들은 어떻게 서비스에 대해 알게 되었는가?
(A) 소책자를 읽음으로써
(B) 동료와 이야기함으로써
(C) 지점에 전화함으로써
(D) 웹사이트에 접속함으로써

해설 질문의 핵심 어구(learn about a service)와 관련된 내용을 주의 깊게 듣는다. 여자2가 "We're interested in the low-interest loan for small businesses that is advertised on your home page."라며 자신들이 홈페이지에 광고된 소규모 사업체를 위한 저금리 대출에 관심이 있다고 하였다. 따라서 (D)가 정답이다.

어휘 pamphlet n. 소책자, 팸플릿 branch n. 지점 access v. 접속하다

15 특정 세부 사항 문제
해석 남자는 이메일로 무엇을 보낼 것인가?
(A) 납입 일정
(B) 영업 허가증
(C) 재정 기록
(D) 신청서

해설 질문의 핵심 어구(send in an e-mail)와 관련된 내용을 주의 깊게 듣는다. 여자1이 "Should we apply in person at your bank?"라며 은행에서 직접 신청해야 하는지 묻자, 남자가 "I can e-mail you the document you need to fill out"이라며 작성해야 하는 서류를 이메일로 보내줄 수 있다고 하였다. 따라서 (D)가 정답이다.

어휘 operating license 영업 허가증 financial adj. 재정의
application form 신청서

[16-18] 영국 → 호주

Questions 16-18 refer to the following conversation.

W: Hi, [16]**this is Andrea Proctor, purchaser for FML. I'd like to make an order for five more desktop computers** with the 22-inch LCD screens, please.
M: OK, five desktops with LCD monitors will cost a total of 4,540 dollars including tax and shipping. That's at the regular retail price.
W: Actually, [17]**I believe my company received the wholesale rate for our previous purchases. I know this isn't as large as our usual orders, but I think we still qualify.**
M: Oh, yes. I just looked at our records, and FML is eligible for our wholesale discount. I apologize for the misunderstanding. Your total will be 4,039 dollars. [18]**I will charge that amount to your company's account.**

purchaser n. 구매 담당자 retail adj. 소매의 wholesale adj. 도매의
rate n. 가격 previous adj. 이전의, 바로 앞의 qualify v. 자격이 있다
eligible adj. 자격이 있는 charge v. 청구하다; n. 요금 account n. 계좌

해석
16-18번은 다음 대화에 관한 문제입니다.
여: 안녕하세요, [16]FML사의 구매 담당자인 Andrea Proctor입니다. 22인치 LCD 화면을 갖춘 탁상용 컴퓨터를 다섯 대 더 주문하고 싶습니다.
남: 네, LCD 모니터를 갖춘 탁상용 컴퓨터 다섯 대는 세금과 운송비를 포함해 총 4,540달러일 것입니다. 이것은 정상 소매가입니다.
여: 사실, [17]저희 회사는 이전 구매에서 도매가를 받았던 것 같아요. 이번이 평소 주문만큼 많지 않은 건 알지만, 여전히 자격이 있다고 생각해요.
남: 아, 네. 제가 방금 기록을 살펴보았고, FML사는 저희의 도매 할인을 받으실 자격이 있습니다. 오해가 있었던 점 사과드립니다. 총금액은 4,039달러가 될 것입니다. [18]귀사의 계좌에 해당 금액을 청구하겠습니다.

16 특정 세부 사항 문제
해석 여자는 무엇을 하고 싶어 하는가?
(A) 몇몇 화면들을 수리한다.
(B) 사무용 장비를 구매한다.
(C) 계좌를 개설한다.
(D) 비용 견적을 받는다.

해설 질문의 핵심 어구(want to do)와 관련된 내용을 주의 깊게 듣는다. 여자가 "this is Andrea Proctor, purchaser for FML. I'd like to make an order for five more desktop computers"라며 자신이 FML사의 구매 담당자이며, 탁상용 컴퓨터를 다섯 대 더 주문하고 싶다고 하였다. 따라서 (B)가 정답이다.

어휘 estimate n. 견적

17 언급 문제
해석 여자는 그녀의 회사에 관해 무엇을 말하는가?
(A) 손상된 물품을 받았다.
(B) 더 낮은 가격을 받을 자격이 있다.
(C) 매주 주문을 한다.
(D) 잘못된 모델을 주문했다.

해설 여자의 말에서 질문의 핵심 어구(company)가 언급된 주변을 주의 깊게 듣는다. 여자가 "I believe my company received the wholesale rate for our previous purchases. I know this isn't as large as our usual orders, but I think we still qualify."라며 자신의 회사는 이전 구매에서 도매가를 받았던 것 같다고 한 후, 이번이 평소 주문만큼 많지 않은 건 알지만, 여전히 자격이 있다고 생각한다고 하였다. 따라서 (B)가 정답이다.

18 다음에 할 일 문제
해석 남자는 무엇을 할 것이라고 말하는가?
(A) 창고에 연락한다.
(B) 주문을 더 신속히 처리한다.
(C) 계좌에 청구한다.
(D) 컴퓨터를 설치한다.

해설 대화의 마지막 부분을 주의 깊게 듣는다. 남자가 "I will charge that amount to your company's account."라며 여자 회사의 계좌에 해당 금액을 청구하겠다고 하였다. 따라서 (C)가 정답이다.

어휘 expedite v. 더 신속히 처리하다

[19-21] 🎧 캐나다 → 미국
Questions 19-21 refer to the following conversation and pie chart.

> M: ¹⁹**Sales have greatly improved since you took over the Collingwood branch of our hardware store chain**, Rebecca.
> W: I appreciate that, Mr. Samson.
> M: ²⁰**The product category that makes up 20 percent of your total sales in the quarterly report surprised me.** That's much higher than in our other locations.
> W: It's because of an in-store promotion we held in April.
> M: Interesting. I'd like to do something similar at all our stores.
> W: ²¹**Why don't I prepare a summary about the promotion? I'll give it to you by Thursday.**

hardware store 철물점 chain n. 체인점 quarterly report 분기별 보고서
in-store adj. 매장 내의 promotion n. 판촉 활동, 홍보 similar adj. 비슷한

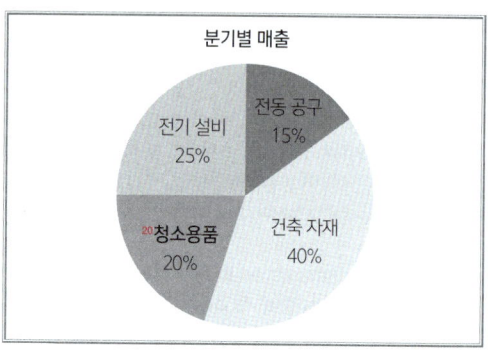

해석
19-21번은 다음 대화와 원그래프에 관한 문제입니다.
남: ¹⁹당신이 우리 철물점 체인점 중 Collingwood 지점을 맡은 이후로 매출이 크게 향상되었네요, Rebecca.
여: 감사합니다, Mr. Samson.
남: ²⁰분기별 보고서에서 총매출의 20퍼센트를 차지하는 제품군이 저를 놀라게 했어요. 그건 우리의 다른 지점들보다 훨씬 높은 수치예요.
여: 그건 4월에 저희가 개최한 매장 내 판촉 활동 때문이에요.
남: 흥미롭네요. 저는 우리의 모든 매장에서 비슷한 일을 하고 싶군요.
여: ²¹제가 판촉 활동에 대한 요약본을 준비해 드릴까요? 목요일까지 드릴게요.

19 화자 문제
해석 여자는 누구인 것 같은가?
(A) 지점 관리자
(B) 상점 점원
(C) 경영 컨설턴트
(D) 영업 담당자

해설 대화에서 신분 및 직업과 관련된 표현을 놓치지 않고 듣는다. 남자가 "Sales have greatly improved since you took over the Collingwood branch of our hardware store chain"이라며 여자가 철물점 체인점 중 Collingwood 지점을 맡은 이후로 매출이 크게 향상되었다고 한 것을 통해 여자가 지점 관리자임을 알 수 있다. 따라서 (A)가 정답이다.

어휘 supervisor n. 관리자 clerk n. 점원, 직원

20 시각 자료 문제
해석 시각 자료를 보아라. 어느 제품군이 남자를 놀라게 했는가?
(A) 전동 공구
(B) 건축 자재
(C) 청소용품
(D) 전기 설비

해설 제시된 원그래프의 정보를 확인한 후 질문의 핵심 어구(product category surprised the man)와 관련된 내용을 주의 깊게 듣는다. 남자가 "The product category that makes up 20 percent of your total sales in the quarterly report surprised me."라며 분기별 보고서에서 총매출의 20퍼센트를 차지하는 제품군이 자신을 놀라게 했다고 하였다. 원그래프에서 총매출의 20퍼센트를 차지하는 제품군은 청소용품임을 알 수 있다. 따라서 (C)가 정답이다.

21 제안 문제
해석 여자는 남자에게 무엇을 주겠다고 제안하는가?
(A) 이력서
(B) 청구서
(C) 사진
(D) 요약본

해설 여자의 말에서 제안과 관련된 표현이 언급된 내용을 주의 깊게 듣는다. 여자가 "Why don't I prepare a summary about the promotion? I'll give it to you by Thursday."라며 자신이 판촉 활동에 대한 요약본을 준비하겠다며 남자에게 그것을 목요일까지 주겠다고 하였다. 따라서 (D)가 정답이다.

어휘 invoice n. 청구서 photograph n. 사진

DAY 14 일상생활 관련 대화

HACKERS PRACTICE   p.109

01 (A)   02 (C)   03 (B)   04 (C)

[01-02] 🎧 미국 → 호주 / 영국 → 캐나다
Questions 01-02 refer to the following conversation.

W: Do you know what you would like to order today?
M: Actually, ⁰¹do you have any recommendations? I can't decide what to get.
W: You should try the cheese pizza. It has a delicious crust, a savory sauce, and three different types of cheese. It is one of our most popular options.
M: That sounds perfect. But ⁰²please give me a few more minutes to look at the menu. I need to select a beverage.

order v. 주문하다 recommendation n. 추천 decide v. 결정하다
savory adj. 풍미 있는 popular adj. 인기 있는 select v. 선택하다

해석
01-02번은 다음 대화에 관한 문제입니다.
여: 오늘 무엇을 주문하시겠습니까?
남: 실은, ⁰¹추천하실 게 있나요? 무엇을 주문할지 결정하지 못하겠어요.
여: 치즈피자를 드셔 보세요. 맛있는 크러스트, 풍미 있는 소스, 그리고 세 가지 다른 종류의 치즈가 들어갑니다. 저희 가게에서 가장 인기 있는 메뉴 중 하나입니다.
남: 딱 좋네요. 하지만 ⁰²메뉴를 볼 시간을 몇 분만 더 주세요. 음료를 골라야 해요.

01 이유 문제
해석 남자는 왜 도움이 필요한가?
(A) 무엇을 주문해야 할지 확신이 없다.
(B) 몇몇 재료를 확인하고 싶다.
(C) 잘못된 주문품을 받았다.
(D) 식사를 받지 못했다.
해설 남자의 말에서 질문의 핵심 어구(need assistance)와 관련된 내용을 주의 깊게 듣는다. 남자가 "do you have any recommendations? I can't decide what to get."이라며 추천할 것이 있는지 물으며, 무엇을 주문할지 결정하지 못하겠다고 하였다. 따라서 (A)가 정답이다.
어휘 assistance n. 도움, 원조, 지원 uncertain adj. 확신이 없는, 잘 모르는
receive v. 받다, 받아들이다

02 다음에 할 일 문제
해석 남자는 다음에 무엇을 할 것 같은가?
(A) 오늘의 특선 요리에 대해 묻는다.
(B) 저녁 식사 주문을 요청한다.
(C) 메뉴를 다시 살펴본다.
(D) 그의 음식이 도착하기를 기다린다.
해설 대화의 마지막 부분을 주의 깊게 듣는다. 남자가 "please give me a few more minutes to look at the menu"라며 메뉴를 볼 시간을 몇 분만 더 달라고 하였다. 따라서 (C)가 정답이다.
어휘 today's special 오늘의 특선 요리 review v. 살펴보다, 논평하다

[Paraphrasing]
look at 보다 → Review 살펴보다

[03-04] 🎧 캐나다 → 영국 / 호주 → 미국
Questions 03-04 refer to the following conversation.

M: Hello, Ms. Glenn. ⁰³Now that I have arrived at your house, what seems to be wrong with your dishwasher?
W: Water leaks from it while it's running. I'm worried that the water will ruin my wood floor.
M: I see. This DryMore 3XC model has a weak bottom seal. Fortunately, ⁰⁴that's fairly easy to fix. It shouldn't take me more than an hour.
W: Oh, great.

dishwasher n. 식기 세척기 leak v. 새다 run v. 작동하다 ruin v. 망치다
weak adj. 약한 seal n. 밀폐 부분

해석
03-04번은 다음 대화에 관한 문제입니다.
남: 안녕하세요, Ms. Glenn. ⁰³이제 제가 당신의 집에 도착했으니 말인데, 당신의 식기 세척기에 어떤 문제가 있는 것 같나요?
여: 그것이 작동하는 동안 물이 새어 나와요. 물이 제 나무 바닥을 망칠까 봐 걱정돼요.
남: 알겠습니다. 이 DryMore 3XC 모델은 바닥 밀폐 부분이 약해요. 다행스럽게도, ⁰⁴저것은 꽤 고치기 쉬워요. 한 시간 이상 걸리지는 않을 거예요.
여: 아, 좋아요.

03 장소 문제
해석 화자들은 어디에 있는 것 같은가?
(A) 상점에
(B) 거주지에
(C) 사무실에
(D) 공장에
해설 대화에서 장소와 관련된 표현을 놓치지 않고 듣는다. 남자가 "Now that I have arrived at your[Ms. Glenn's] house"라며 이제 Ms. Glenn의 집에 도착했다고 한 것을 통해, 화자들은 거주지에 있음을 알 수 있다. 따라서 (B)가 정답이다.
어휘 residence n. 거주지 factory n. 공장

04 다음에 할 일 문제
해석 남자는 다음에 무엇을 할 것 같은가?
(A) 제품을 주문한다.
(B) 가전제품을 옮긴다.
(C) 수리를 한다.
(D) 기술자에게 전화한다.
해설 대화의 마지막 부분을 주의 깊게 듣는다. 남자가 "that[DryMore 3XC model]'s fairly easy to fix. It shouldn't take me more than an hour."라며 DryMore 3XC model이 꽤 고치기 쉬우며 1시간 이상 걸리지는 않을 것이라고 하였다. 따라서 (C)가 정답이다.
어휘 appliance n. 가전제품 repair n. 수리

HACKERS TEST   p.110

01 (A)	02 (B)	03 (D)	04 (C)	05 (B)
06 (C)	07 (B)	08 (A)	09 (A)	10 (A)
11 (B)	12 (D)	13 (A)	14 (A)	15 (D)
16 (C)	17 (A)	18 (A)	19 (B)	20 (A)
21 (D)				

[01-03] 영국 → 호주

Questions 01-03 refer to the following conversation.

W: ⁰¹**I saw your school's advertisement in the newspaper for the painting class starting next week. How do I register for it?**
M: Oh, ⁰²**the person who handles registration is Ms. Wells, and she's out for lunch right now**. She will be back in about 15 minutes. Do you mind waiting?
W: So her break ends at 1? ⁰³**I need to leave here by 1:30 at the latest because I have a meeting with an important client.** Will I have enough time to sign up?
M: Don't worry. The process won't take more than 20 minutes.

advertisement n. 광고 register v. 등록하다, 신고하다
registration n. 등록 process n. 과정, 절차

해석
01-03번은 다음 대화에 관한 문제입니다.
여: ⁰¹다음 주에 시작하는 미술 수업에 대한 그쪽 학교의 광고를 신문에서 보았습니다. 어떻게 등록하나요?
남: 아, ⁰²등록을 담당하는 사람은 Ms. Wells이고, 지금은 점심을 먹으러 나갔습니다. 그녀는 약 15분 뒤에 돌아올 것입니다. 기다려 주시겠습니까?
여: 그럼 그녀의 휴식 시간은 1시에 끝나는 건가요? ⁰³저는 중요한 고객과 미팅이 있어서 늦어도 1시 30분까지는 여기를 떠나야 해요. 등록할 시간이 충분할까요?
남: 걱정하지 마세요. 그 과정은 20분 이상 걸리지 않을 거예요.

01 화자 문제
해석 남자는 어디에서 일하는 것 같은가?
(A) 학교 사무실에서
(B) 광고 대행사에서
(C) 컨벤션 센터에서
(D) 미술관에서

해설 대화에서 신분 및 직업과 관련된 표현을 놓치지 않고 듣는다. 여자가 "I saw your school's advertisement ~ for the painting class starting next week. How do I register for it?"이라며 다음 주에 시작하는 미술 수업에 대한 남자 학교의 광고를 봤다고 한 후, 어떻게 등록하는지 묻는 것을 통해, 남자가 학교 사무실에서 일한다는 것을 알 수 있다. 따라서 (A)가 정답이다.

02 언급 문제
해석 남자는 Ms. Wells에 대해 무엇을 말하는가?
(A) 그녀는 수업에 등록했다.
(B) 그녀는 현재 자리에 없다.
(C) 그녀는 유명한 화가이다.
(D) 그녀는 일자리 면접을 보았다.

해설 남자의 말에서 질문의 핵심 어구(Ms. Wells)가 언급된 주변을 주의 깊게 듣는다. 남자가 "the person who handles registration is Ms. Wells, and she's out for lunch right now"라며 등록을 담당하는 사람은 Ms. Wells이며 그녀는 지금 점심을 먹으러 나갔다고 하였다. 따라서 (B)가 정답이다.

어휘 well-known adj. 유명한, 친숙한

03 이유 문제
해석 여자는 왜 1시 30분까지 떠나야 하는가?
(A) 워크숍을 준비하기 위해
(B) 과제를 제출하기 위해
(C) 발표를 하기 위해
(D) 고객을 만나기 위해

해설 여자의 말에서 질문의 핵심 어구(1:30)가 언급된 주변을 주의 깊게 듣는다. 여자가 "I need to leave here by 1:30 at the latest because I have a meeting with an important client."라며 중요한 고객과 미팅이 있어서 늦어도 1시 30분까지는 여기를 떠나야 한다고 하였다. 따라서 (D)가 정답이다.

어휘 submit v. 제출하다 assignment n. 과제 presentation n. 발표 customer n. 고객

Paraphrasing
client 고객 → customer 고객

[04-06] 미국 → 캐나다

Questions 04-06 refer to the following conversation.

W: I'd like one adult ski pass for the day, please.
M: OK. And in case you didn't know, ⁰⁴**all passes are half off. This is because it was 50 years ago today that our resort first opened.** So they're only 12 dollars.
W: That's good to hear. Oh . . . I forgot to tell you that I need a pair of rental boots as well. ⁰⁵**I brought skis**, but my boots recently broke.
M: No problem. That'll be 40 dollars. ⁰⁶**You'll just have to complete this rental form.**

rental n. 대여, 임대 complete v. 작성하다

해석
04-06번은 다음 대화에 관한 문제입니다.
여: 일일 성인 스키 입장권 하나 주세요.
남: 네. 그리고 고객님께서 모르실 경우에 대비해서, ⁰⁴모든 입장권이 반값이에요. 우리 리조트가 50년 전 오늘 처음 개장했기 때문이에요. 그래서 단지 12달러입니다.
여: 좋은 소식이네요. 아... 대여 부츠 한 켤레도 필요하다고 말씀드리는 것을 잊었어요. ⁰⁵스키는 가져왔지만, 제 부츠가 최근에 망가졌어요.
남: 문제없어요. 40달러 되겠습니다. ⁰⁶이 대여 양식을 작성해 주시기만 하면 돼요.

04 이유 문제
해석 왜 할인이 제공되고 있는가?
(A) 공휴일을 기리기 위해
(B) 행사를 홍보하기 위해
(C) 기념일을 축하하기 위해
(D) 제품 출시를 기념하기 위해

해설 질문의 핵심 어구(discount ~ offered)와 관련된 내용을 주의 깊게 듣는다. 남자가 "all passes are half off. This is because it was 50 years ago today that our resort first opened."라며 모든 입장권이 반값이며, 리조트가 50년 전 오늘 처음 개장했기 때문이라고 하였다. 따라서 (C)가 정답이다.

어휘 recognize v. 인정하다, 승인하다 commemorate v. 기념하다 launch n. 출시

05 특정 세부 사항 문제
해석 여자는 무엇을 가져왔다고 말하는가?
(A) 신용카드
(B) 장비
(C) 음식
(D) 정기권

해설 여자의 말에서 질문의 핵심 어구(brought)가 언급된 주변을 주의 깊게 듣는다. 여자가 "I brought skis"라며 스키는 가져왔다고 하였다. 따라서 (B)가 정답이다.

Paraphrasing
skis 스키 → equipment 장비

06 다음에 할 일 문제
해석 여자는 다음에 무엇을 할 것 같은가?
(A) 앱을 다운로드한다.
(B) 강사를 만난다.
(C) 서류를 작성한다.
(D) 지도를 확인한다.

해설 대화의 마지막 부분을 주의 깊게 듣는다. 남자가 여자에게 "You'll just have to complete this rental form."이라며 대여 양식을 작성하기만 하면 된다고 하였다. 따라서 (C)가 정답이다.

어휘 instructor n. 강사

Paraphrasing
complete ~ rental form 대여 양식을 작성하다 → Fill out ~ paperwork 서류를 작성한다

[07-09] 🎧 캐나다 → 미국
Questions 07-09 refer to the following conversation.

M: ⁰⁷**I'm finished fixing the leaky pipe in the bathroom**, Ms. Rowe. You shouldn't have any more trouble with it.
W: Great. Um, one more thing. I recently noticed that my kitchen faucet isn't working properly. ⁰⁸**Could you take a look at it?**
M: I don't have any appointments this afternoon. ⁰⁸**Why don't you show me where the kitchen is?**
W: Of course. Oh, and once you've figured out the problem, ⁰⁹**let me know the expected cost before you begin any repairs.**

leaky adj. 새는 faucet n. 수도꼭지 take a look at ~을 (고치기 위해) 보다
appointment n. 예약, 약속 figure out ~을 알아내다
expected adj. 예상되는

해석
07-09번은 다음 대화에 관한 문제입니다.

남: Ms. Rowe, ⁰⁷저는 화장실에 새는 파이프를 수리하는 것을 끝냈습니다. 그것에 더 이상의 문제는 없을 거예요.
여: 좋아요. 음, 하나 더요. 저는 주방 수도꼭지가 제대로 작동하고 있지 않다는 것을 최근에 알았어요. ⁰⁸그것을 봐주시겠어요?
남: 저는 오늘 오후에 예약이 없어요. ⁰⁸부엌이 어디 있는지 보여주시겠어요?
여: 물론이죠. 아, 그리고 문제가 무엇인지 알아내시면, ⁰⁹수리를 시작하시기 전에 저에게 예상 비용을 알려 주세요.

07 화자 문제
해석 남자는 누구인 것 같은가?
(A) 목수
(B) 배관공
(C) 청소부
(D) 전기 기사

해설 대화에서 신분 및 직업과 관련된 표현을 놓치지 않고 듣는다. 남자가 "I'm finished fixing the leaky pipe in the bathroom"이라며 화장실에 새는 파이프를 수리하는 것을 끝냈다고 한 것을 통해 남자가 배관공임을 알 수 있다. 따라서 (B)가 정답이다.

어휘 carpenter n. 목수 plumber n. 배관공 electrician n. 전기 기사

08 의도 파악 문제
해석 남자가 "저는 오늘 오후에 예약이 없어요"라고 말할 때 무엇을 의도하는가?
(A) 작업을 수행할 것이다.
(B) 고객에게 확인할 것이다.
(C) 나중에 돌아올 것이다.
(D) 동료를 기다릴 것이다.

해설 질문의 인용어구(I don't have any appointments this afternoon)가 언급된 주변을 주의 깊게 듣는다. 여자가 "Could you take a look at it[faucet]?"이라며 수도꼭지를 봐줄 수 있는지 묻자, 남자가 "Why don't you show me where the kitchen is?"라며 부엌이 어디 있는지 보여달라고 한 것을 통해 남자가 수도꼭지 점검 작업을 수행할 것임을 알 수 있다. 따라서 (A)가 정답이다.

09 요청 문제
해석 여자는 무엇을 요청하는가?
(A) 가격 견적
(B) 부품 목록
(C) 사업 계약
(D) 프로젝트 일정

해설 여자의 말에서 요청과 관련된 표현이 언급된 다음을 주의 깊게 듣는다. 여자가 "let me know the expected cost before you begin any repairs"라며 수리를 시작하기 전에 예상 비용을 알려 달라고 하였다. 따라서 (A)가 정답이다.

어휘 estimate n. 견적 component n. 부품 contract n. 계약

[10-12] 🎧 영국 → 호주
Questions 10-12 refer to the following conversation.

W: Hello. My name is Julia Mendez, and ¹⁰**I brought some clothes here yesterday to be altered**. I'm wondering if they're finished yet.
M: Let me check . . . Sorry, Ms. Mendez, they aren't ready. Our records show that you aren't scheduled to pick up your garments until tomorrow. ¹¹**Did you contact us in advance to request that they be done early?**
W: No, I didn't. I just thought I'd check on my way home from work.
M: I see. Well, ¹²**you'll have to come back at the scheduled time.** Your items will be ready for you then.

alter v. (옷을 몸에 맞게) 고치다 wonder v. 궁금하다, ~일지 모르겠다
pick up 수거하다 garment n. 옷, 의복 in advance 사전에, 미리

해석
10-12번은 다음 대화에 관한 문제입니다.

여: 안녕하세요. 제 이름은 Julia Mendez이고, ¹⁰어제 이곳에 옷 몇 벌을 고치려고 가지고 왔습니다. 아직 다 안 끝났는지 궁금해서요.
남: 확인해 볼게요... 죄송합니다, Ms. Mendez, 그것들은 아직 준비되지 않았어요. 저희 기록에는 고객님께서 내일은 되어야 옷들을 수거하실 예정이라고 나옵니다. ¹¹그것들이 일찍 완료되도록 요청하기 위해 사전에 연락하셨나요?
여: 아니요, 그러지 않았어요. 그냥 회사에서 집으로 가는 길에 확인하려고 했던 거예요.
남: 알겠습니다. 그럼, ¹²예정된 시간에 다시 오셔야 할 거예요. 그때는 고객님의 물품들이 준비되어 있을 겁니다.

10 특정 세부 사항 문제
해석 여자는 어제 무엇을 했는가?
(A) 물품을 맡겼다.
(B) 옷을 구매했다.
(C) 사업체에 전화했다.
(D) 재택근무를 했다.

해설 여자의 말에서 질문의 핵심 어구(yesterday)가 언급된 주변을 주의 깊게 듣는다. 여자가 "I brought some clothes here yesterday to be altered"라며 어제 이곳에 옷 몇 벌을 고치려고 가지고 왔다고 하였다. 따라서 (A)가 정답이다.

어휘 work from home 재택근무를 하다

11 특정 세부 사항 문제
해석 남자는 여자에게 무엇에 관해 묻는가?
(A) 그녀가 받은 서비스가 무엇인지
(B) 그녀가 요청을 했는지
(C) 그녀가 현재 어디에 사는지
(D) 그녀가 언제 지불했는지

해설 질문의 핵심 어구(ask the woman about)와 관련된 내용을 주의 깊게 듣는다. 남자가 "Did you contact us in advance to request that they[garments] be done early?"라며 옷들이 일찍 완료되도록 요청하기 위해 사전에 연락했는지 물었다. 따라서 (B)가 정답이다.

어휘 request n. 요청

12 특정 세부 사항 문제
해석 남자는 여자에게 무엇을 하라고 말하는가?
(A) 추가 요금을 지불한다.
(B) 의류를 검사한다.
(C) 온라인으로 확인한다.
(D) 나중에 돌아온다.

해설 질문의 핵심 어구(tell the woman to do)와 관련된 내용을 주의 깊게 듣는다. 남자가 "you'll have to come back at the scheduled time"이라며 예정된 시간에 다시 와야 할 것이라고 하였다. 따라서 (D)가 정답이다.

어휘 fee n. 요금

Paraphrasing
come back 다시 오다 → Returning 돌아오기

[13-15] 캐나다 → 미국 → 영국
Questions 13-15 refer to the following conversation with three speakers.

M: ¹³**What a great movie. I'm glad we decided to see it.** The special effects were amazing.
W1: I know. Now, let's grab something to eat.
M: ¹⁴**I heard that a Chinese restaurant called The Beijing House just opened near here. We should go there.**
W2: Oh, that place has gotten good reviews.
M: Yeah. Plus, it's not too far. I know how to get there by subway.
W2: ¹⁵**Let's head to the subway station.** There's an entrance at the end of this block.

special effects 특수 효과

해석
13-15번은 다음 세 명의 대화에 관한 문제입니다.
남: ¹³정말 좋은 영화예요. 우리가 그것을 보기로 결정했던 것이 기쁘네요. 특수 효과가 훌륭했어요.
여1: 맞아요. 이제, 무언가를 먹으러 가요.
남: ¹⁴The Beijing House라는 이름의 중국 식당이 이 근처에 막 문을 열었다고 들었어요. 우리는 거기에 가야 해요.
여2: 아, 그곳은 좋은 후기를 받았네요.
남: 네. 게다가, 너무 멀지 않아요. 지하철로 그곳에 가는 방법을 알고 있어요.
여2: ¹⁵지하철역으로 갑시다. 이 블록 끝에 입구가 있어요.

13 특정 세부 사항 문제
해석 화자들은 무엇을 했는가?
(A) 영화를 보았다.
(B) 콘서트에 참석했다.
(C) 전시를 보았다.
(D) 박물관에 갔다.

해설 질문의 핵심 어구(speakers do)와 관련된 내용을 주의 깊게 듣는다. 남자가 여자에게 "What a great movie. I'm glad we decided to see it."이라며 정말 좋은 영화라며 그것을 보기로 결정했던 것이 기쁘다고 하였다. 따라서 (A)가 정답이다.

어휘 attend v. 참석하다 view v. 보다

14 제안 문제
해석 남자는 무엇을 제안하는가?
(A) 시설에 방문하기
(B) 버스를 기다리기
(C) 길을 물어보기
(D) 후기를 읽기

해설 남자의 말에서 제안과 관련된 표현이 언급된 다음을 주의 깊게 듣는다. 남자가 "I heard that a Chinese restaurant ~ just opened near here. We should go there."라며 중국 식당이 이 근처에 막 문을 열었다고 들었다고 한 후, 거기에 가야 한다고 하였다. 따라서 (A)가 정답이다.

어휘 establishment n. 시설, 기관 direction n. 길, 방향

15 다음에 할 일 문제
해석 화자들은 다음에 무엇을 할 것 같은가?
(A) 주문을 한다.
(B) 택시를 탄다.
(C) 표를 구매한다.
(D) 역으로 걸어간다.

해설 대화의 마지막 부분을 주의 깊게 듣는다. 여자2가 "Let's head to the subway station."이라며 지하철역으로 가자고 하였다. 따라서 (D)가 정답이다.

어휘 order n. 주문

Paraphrasing
head to ~로 가다 → Walk to ~로 걸어가다

[16-18] 호주 → 미국
Questions 16-18 refer to the following conversation.

M: ¹⁶**You've reached customer assistance for Grenada Capital.** How may I assist you?
W: Hi. My name's Claudia Bruno. I recently tried checking my account statements online. But I can't view them since I forgot my password.
M: In that case, I'll need you to answer a security question, Ms. Bruno. ¹⁷**Could you tell me the name of your first school?**
W: That would be Baker Elementary School.
M: Great. So . . . ¹⁸**I've sent you an e-mail that will allow you to change your password. You should click on the link in the e-mail and then enter a new password on the Web page that opens.**
W: Thank you.

assistance n. 지원, 도움 assist v. 돕다 account n. 계좌, 계정 statement n. 명세서 enter v. 입력하다

해석
16-18번은 다음 대화에 관한 문제입니다.

남: ¹⁶Grenada Capital사의 고객 지원부에 연락하셨습니다. 어떻게 도와드릴까요?
여: 안녕하세요. 제 이름은 Claudia Bruno입니다. 최근에 온라인으로 계좌 명세서를 확인하는 것을 시도했어요. 하지만 제가 비밀번호를 잊어서 볼 수가 없어요.
남: 그런 경우에는 보안 질문에 답하셔야 합니다, Ms. Bruno. ¹⁷고객님의 첫 학교 이름을 제게 말해주시겠어요?
여: Baker 초등학교일 거예요.
남: 좋습니다. 그럼... ¹⁸고객님께서 비밀번호를 바꾸실 수 있도록 해드릴 이메일을 보내드렸습니다. 이메일에 있는 링크를 클릭하시고 나서 열리는 웹 페이지에 새로운 비밀번호를 입력하셔야 합니다.
여: 감사합니다.

16 화자 문제
해석 남자는 어느 부서에서 일하는 것 같은가?
(A) 회계
(B) 마케팅
(C) 고객 서비스
(D) 인사
해설 대화에서 신분 및 직업과 관련된 표현을 놓치지 않고 듣는다. 남자가 "You've reached customer assistance for Grenada Capital."이라며 Grenada Capital사의 고객 지원부에 연락했다고 한 것을 통해 남자가 고객 서비스 부서에서 일한다는 것을 알 수 있다. 따라서 (C)가 정답이다.

17 요청 문제
해석 남자는 어떤 정보를 요청하는가?
(A) 학교 이름
(B) 출생일
(C) 거래 금액
(D) 계좌 번호
해설 남자의 말에서 요청과 관련된 표현이 언급된 다음을 주의 깊게 듣는다. 남자가 "Could you[Ms. Bruno] tell me the name of your first school?"이라며 Ms. Bruno의 첫 학교 이름을 말해달라고 하였다. 따라서 (A)가 정답이다.
어휘 transaction n. 거래

18 특정 세부 사항 문제
해석 남자는 여자에게 무엇을 하도록 안내하는가?
(A) 비밀번호를 변경한다.
(B) 이메일에 답장한다.
(C) 파일을 다운로드한다.
(D) 지점에 간다.
해설 질문의 핵심 어구(instruct the woman to do)와 관련된 내용을 주의 깊게 듣는다. 남자가 "I've sent you an e-mail that will allow you to change your password. You should ~ enter a new password on the Web page that opens."라며 비밀번호를 바꿀 수 있도록 해줄 이메일을 보냈다고 한 후, 열리는 웹페이지에서 새로운 비밀번호를 입력해야 한다고 하였다. 따라서 (A)가 정답이다.
어휘 branch n. 지점

[19-21] 영국 → 호주
Questions 19-21 refer to the following conversation and logo designs.

W: ¹⁹**Thanks for buying me lunch today, Greg. I'm really enjoying the food at this restaurant.**
M: No problem. And ²⁰**I'm sorry I had to cancel our plans last weekend**. I've been really busy since I joined my local community center's basketball league. My team has been practicing a lot.
W: I understand. Are you having fun playing basketball?
M: Yeah. And I'm helping to design a new logo for the team. Here . . . Look at this picture on my phone. ²¹**Which logo do you prefer?**
W: ²¹**The one with the ball on top of the net seems best.**

cancel v. 취소하다   community center 주민 센터

해석
19-21번은 다음 대화와 로고 디자인에 관한 문제입니다.
여: ¹⁹오늘 점심을 사줘서 고마워요, Greg. 저는 이 식당의 음식을 정말 즐기고 있어요.
남: 별말씀을요. 그리고 ²⁰지난 주말에 우리의 계획을 취소해서 미안해요. 지역 주민 센터의 농구 리그에 가입한 이후로 정말 바빴어요. 팀이 연습을 많이 하고 있거든요.
여: 이해해요. 농구를 하는 게 재미있나요?
남: 네. 그리고 저는 팀을 위한 새로운 로고를 디자인하는 것을 돕고 있어요. 여기요... 제 휴대전화에 있는 이 사진을 보세요. ²¹어느 로고를 선호하시나요?
여: ²¹공이 네트 위에 있는 로고가 가장 좋아 보여요.

19 장소 문제
해석 화자들은 어디에 있는 것 같은가?
(A) 식료품점에
(B) 식당에
(C) 경기장에
(D) 주민 센터에
해설 대화에서 장소와 관련된 표현을 놓치지 않고 듣는다. 여자가 "Thanks for buying me lunch today, Greg. I'm really enjoying the food at this restaurant."라며 오늘 점심을 사줘서 고맙다고 한 후, 이 식당의 음식을 정말 즐기고 있다고 한 것을 통해 화자들은 식당에 있음을 알 수 있다. 따라서 (B)가 정답이다.
어휘 grocery store 식료품점   stadium n. 경기장

20 특정 세부 사항 문제
해석 남자는 무엇에 대해 사과하는가?
(A) 약속을 취소한 것
(B) 행사를 잊어버린 것
(C) 물건을 잃어버린 것
(D) 연습을 놓친 것
해설 질문의 핵심 어구(apologize for)와 관련된 내용을 주의 깊게 듣는다. 남자가 "I'm sorry I had to cancel our plans last weekend"라며 지난 주말에 계획을 취소해서 미안하다고 하였다. 따라서 (A)가 정답이다.
어휘 appointment n. 약속   misplace v. 잃어버리다

21 시각 자료 문제

해석 시각 자료를 보아라. 여자가 선호하는 옵션은 무엇인가?
(A) 옵션 1
(B) 옵션 2
(C) 옵션 3
(D) 옵션 4

해설 제시된 로고 디자인의 정보를 확인한 후 질문의 핵심 어구(woman prefer)와 관련된 내용을 주의 깊게 듣는다. 남자가 "Which logo do you prefer?"라며 여자가 어느 로고를 선호하는지 묻자, 여자가 "The one[logo] with the ball on top of the net seems best."라며 공이 네트 위에 있는 로고가 가장 좋아 보인다고 하였다. 로고 디자인에서 공이 네트 위에 있는 옵션은 옵션 4임을 알 수 있다. 따라서 (D)가 정답이다.

DAY 15 여행 및 여가 관련 대화

HACKERS PRACTICE　　　p.113

| 01 (B) | 02 (C) | 03 (D) | 04 (A) |

[01-02]　영국 → 캐나다 / 미국 → 호주

Questions 01-02 refer to the following conversation.

W: Hi, I'd like to buy a train ticket to Bellingham. ⁰¹I think I can get a discount if I pay with this credit card. Could you check for me?
M: Unfortunately, that promotion ended last month. But ⁰²if you purchase a ticket for a standard seat, I can offer you an upgrade at no additional charge.
W: That would be great. ⁰²Please give me a ticket for the 10 A.M. train.

discount n. 할인　standard adj. 일반적인, 보통의　seat n. 좌석
upgrade n. 상승, 향상; v. (좌석·객실 등의) 등급을 높여주다
additional adj. 추가적인　charge n. 요금

해석
01-02번은 다음 대화에 관한 문제입니다.
여: 안녕하세요, Bellingham행 기차표를 사고 싶어요. ⁰¹이 신용카드로 결제하면 할인을 받을 수 있을 것 같은데요. 확인해 주시겠어요?
남: 유감스럽게도, 그 프로모션은 지난달에 끝났어요. 하지만 ⁰²일반석 표를 구매하시면, 추가 요금 없이 좌석 등급을 높여드릴 수 있어요.
여: 그거 좋네요. ⁰²오전 10시 기차표로 주세요.

01 요청 문제

해설 여자는 무엇을 요청하는가?
(A) 배달
(B) 할인
(C) 영수증
(D) 환불

해설 여자의 말에서 요청과 관련된 표현이 언급된 주변을 주의 깊게 듣는다. 여자가 "I think I can get a discount if I pay with this credit card. Could you check for me?"라며 이 신용카드로 결제하면 할인을 받을 수 있을 것 같다고 한 후, 확인해 줄 수 있는지 물었다. 따라서 (B)가 정답이다.

어휘 delivery n. 배달　receipt n. 영수증

02 다음에 할 일 문제

해설 남자가 다음에 무엇을 할 것 같은가?
(A) 카드를 발급한다.
(B) 요금을 지불한다.
(C) 좌석의 등급을 높여준다.
(D) 일정을 확인한다.

해설 대화의 마지막 부분을 주의 깊게 듣는다. 남자가 "if you purchase a ticket for a standard seat, I can offer you an upgrade at no additional charge"라며 일반석 표를 구매하면, 추가 요금 없이 좌석 등급을 높여줄 수 있다고 하자, 여자가 "Please give me a ticket for the 10 A.M. train."이라며 오전 10시 기차표로 달라고 하였다. 따라서 (C)가 정답이다.

어휘 issue v. 발급하다　fare n. 요금

[03-04]　호주 → 미국 / 캐나다 → 영국

Questions 03-04 refer to the following conversation.

M: ⁰³How are you enjoying the dessert festival so far?
W: It's great. There are so many different types of desserts, and everything looks delicious.
M: Look over there. ⁰⁴That booth is run by the famous pastry chef Kenta Yamada. Why don't we go try his tarts? I heard they're amazing.
W: That sounds like a great idea. I've always wanted to taste his pastries. Let's go!

booth n. 부스, 작은 공간　pastry chef 파티시에　run v. 운영하다

해석
03-04번은 다음 대화에 관한 문제입니다.
남: ⁰³지금까지 디저트 축제를 어떻게 즐기고 있나요?
여: 좋아요. 매우 다양한 종류의 디저트가 있고, 모든 것이 맛있어 보여요.
남: 저기를 보세요. ⁰⁴저 부스는 유명한 파티시에 Kenta Yamada가 운영하는 곳이에요. 그의 타르트를 먹어보러 가는 게 어때요? 그것들이 놀랍다고 들었어요.
여: 좋은 생각이네요. 저는 항상 그의 페이스트리를 맛보고 싶었어요. 가요!

03 장소 문제

해설 화자들은 어디에 있는 것 같은가?
(A) 워크숍에
(B) 파티에
(C) 결혼식에
(D) 축제에

해설 대화에서 장소와 관련된 표현을 놓치지 않고 듣는다. 남자가 "How are you enjoying the dessert festival so far?"라며 지금까지 디저트 축제를 어떻게 즐기고 있는지 물은 것을 통해 화자들이 축제에 있음을 알 수 있다. 따라서 (D)가 정답이다.

어휘 contest n. 대회, 시합

04 언급 문제

해설 Kenta Yamada에 대해 무엇이 언급되는가?
(A) 유명하다.
(B) 늦게 도착했다.
(C) 바쁜 일정이 있다.
(D) 행사를 개최했다.

해설 질문의 핵심 어구(Kenta Yamada)와 관련된 내용을 주의 깊게 듣는다. 남자가 "That booth is run by the famous pastry chef Kenta Yamada."라며 저 부스는 유명한 파티시에 Kenta Yamada가 운영하는 곳이라고 하였다. 따라서 (A)가 정답이다.

어휘 well-known adj. 유명한　organize v. 개최하다

HACKERS TEST   p.114

01 (C)	02 (C)	03 (A)	04 (A)	05 (D)
06 (C)	07 (A)	08 (B)	09 (A)	10 (B)
11 (D)	12 (A)	13 (D)	14 (A)	15 (D)
16 (A)	17 (A)	18 (B)	19 (A)	20 (B)
21 (C)				

[01-03] 호주 → 미국
Questions 01-03 refer to the following conversation.

M: 01Do you plan on visiting Tahoe again for your vacation this summer? You said that you had a lot of fun there last year.
W: No. 01I'm taking my husband and kids to San Diego to attend a science expo.
M: Oh, that's wonderful. 02The weather there is pleasant nearly all year round. 03Have you booked a hotel yet?
W: 03I did, but then a friend of ours offered to let us stay at her home, so I canceled the reservation.

expo n. 박람회, 전시회   pleasant adj. 쾌적한, 즐거운

해석
01-03번은 다음 대화에 관한 문제입니다.
남: 01올해 여름휴가 때 다시 타호를 방문할 계획인가요? 당신이 작년에 그곳에서 아주 즐거운 시간을 보냈다고 말했었어요.
여: 아니요. 01과학 박람회에 참석하기 위해 남편과 아이들을 데리고 샌디에이고에 갈 거예요.
남: 아, 그거 멋지네요. 02거기 날씨는 거의 일년 내내 쾌적하잖아요. 03호텔은 이미 예약했나요?
여: 03예약을 했는데, 우리 친구 중 한 명이 그녀의 집에 머무를 수 있도록 해 줘서 취소했어요.

01 특정 세부 사항 문제
해석 여자는 휴가 동안 무엇을 할 계획인가?
(A) 콘서트에 간다.
(B) 박물관을 견학한다.
(C) 박람회에 참석한다.
(D) 미술관에 방문한다.

해설 여자의 말에서 질문의 핵심 어구(planning to do during her vacation)와 관련된 내용을 주의 깊게 듣는다. 남자가 "Do you plan on visiting Tahoe again for your vacation this summer?"라며 올해 여름휴가 때 다시 타호를 방문할 계획인지 묻자, 여자가 "I'm taking my husband and kids to San Diego to attend a science expo."라며 과학 박람회에 참석하기 위해 샌디에이고에 갈 것이라고 하였다. 따라서 (C)가 정답이다.

어휘 tour v. 견학하다, 여행하다

02 언급 문제
해석 남자는 샌디에이고에 대해 무엇을 말하는가?
(A) 가족 행사를 많이 개최한다.
(B) 많은 명소들을 포함한다.
(C) 기후가 좋다.
(D) 가격이 알맞은 호텔들이 있다.

해설 남자의 말에서 질문의 핵심 어구(San Diego)와 관련된 내용을 주의 깊게 듣는다. 남자가 "The weather there[San Diego] is pleasant"라며 샌디에이고는 날씨가 쾌적하다고 하였다. 따라서 (C)가 정답이다.

어휘 host v. 개최하다   attraction n. 명소, 명물, 끌림   climate n. 기후

affordable adj. 가격이 알맞은
[Paraphrasing]
weather ~ is pleasant 날씨가 쾌적하다 → has a good climate 기후가 좋다

03 특정 세부 사항 문제
해석 여자는 여행 계획에 대해 무엇을 바꾸었는가?
(A) 숙박 형태
(B) 교통 수단
(C) 체류 기간
(D) 출발 날짜

해설 대화에서 질문의 핵심 어구(change about her travel plan)와 관련된 내용을 주의 깊게 듣는다. 남자가 "Have you booked a hotel yet?"이라며 호텔을 이미 예약했는지 묻자, 여자가 "I did, but then a friend of ours offered to let us stay at her home, so I canceled the reservation."이라며 호텔을 예약했지만 친구가 자신의 집에 머물게 해 주겠다고 제안하여 예약을 취소했다고 말했다. 따라서 (A)가 정답이다.

어휘 accommodation n. 숙박   transportation n. 교통   departure n. 출발

[04-06] 영국 → 캐나다
Questions 04-06 refer to the following conversation.

W: 04I'm getting our tickets for the football game next weekend. There are still some seats available on the upper level and in the back row of the main level.
M: Are there any closer to the field?
W: No. It's a popular game. 05Eva Torres, a famous singer, is doing a special halftime show, so everyone's trying to go.
M: Got it. I'd prefer the main level. But 06since our friend Anita is going with us, maybe you should call and get her opinion too.
W: 06I'll do that now.

upper adj. 상부의, 높은 쪽의   field n. 경기장   popular adj. 인기 있는
halftime n. 하프 타임(운동 경기 전반전이 끝난 뒤의 중간 휴식 시간)
opinion n. 의견

해석
04-06번은 다음 대화에 관한 문제입니다.
여: 04저는 다음 주말 축구 경기 표를 사고 있어요. 아직 상층과 본관층의 뒷줄에 일부 좌석이 있어요.
남: 경기장에 더 가까운 좌석은 없나요?
여: 없어요. 그건 인기 있는 경기예요. 05유명 가수인 Eva Torres가 특별 하프 타임 쇼를 할 예정이어서 모두가 가려고 해요.
남: 알겠어요. 저는 본관층을 선호해요. 하지만 06우리의 친구 Anita가 함께 가니까, 아마도 전화해서 그녀의 의견도 들어봐야 할 것 같아요.
여: 06지금 그렇게 할게요.

04 특정 세부 사항 문제
해석 여자는 무엇을 하고 있는가?
(A) 표 구매하기
(B) 좌석 등급 높이기
(C) 앱 다운로드하기
(D) 일정 확인하기

해설 여자의 말에서 질문의 핵심 어구(woman doing)와 관련된 내용을 주의 깊게 듣는다. 여자가 "I'm getting our tickets for the football game next weekend."라며 다음 주말 축구 경기 표를 사고 있다고 하였다. 따라서 (A)가 정답이다.

어휘 purchase v. 구매하다

Paraphrasing
getting ~ tickets 표를 사다 → Purchasing tickets 표 구매하기

05 이유 문제
해석 행사가 왜 많은 관심을 끌었는가?
(A) 지역 주민들에게는 무료이다.
(B) 웹사이트에서 홍보되었다.
(C) 유명 운동선수를 특별히 포함할 것이다.
(D) 음악 공연을 포함한다.

해설 질문의 핵심 어구(event attracted much interest)와 관련된 내용을 주의 깊게 듣는다. 여자가 "Eva Torres, a famous singer, is doing a special halftime show, so everyone's trying to go."라며 유명 가수인 Eva Torres가 특별 하프 타임 쇼를 할 예정이어서 모두가 가려고 한다고 하였다. 따라서 (D)가 정답이다.

어휘 resident n. 주민 promote v. 홍보하다 athlete n. 운동선수
musical adj. 음악의 performance n. 공연

06 다음에 할 일 문제
해석 여자는 다음에 무엇을 할 것인가?
(A) 경기를 관람한다.
(B) 예약을 취소한다.
(C) 친구에게 연락한다.
(D) 비밀번호를 입력한다.

해설 대화의 마지막 부분을 주의 깊게 듣는다. 남자가 "since our friend Anita is going with us, maybe you should call and get her opinion too"라며 친구 Anita가 함께 가니까, 아마도 전화해서 그녀의 의견도 들어봐야 할 것 같다고 하자, 여자가 "I'll do that now."라며 지금 그렇게 하겠다고 하였다. 따라서 (C)가 정답이다.

어휘 cancel v. 취소하다 booking n. 예약 contact v. 연락하다
enter v. 입력하다

[07-09] 미국 → 호주
Questions 07-09 refer to the following conversation.

W: Wow, it's so cold today. ⁰⁷I planned to go jogging, but I think it would be smarter to stay indoors.
M: How about coming to the Museum of Ancient History with me? They have an indoor parking garage, so we wouldn't have to step outside at all.
W: Hmm. ⁰⁸I saw a report on TV that said the museum recently opened some new exhibits. I wouldn't mind seeing them.
M: Right. ⁰⁹My coworker saw those displays the other day and said they were really excellent.

indoors adv. 실내에서 ancient adj. 고대의 exhibit n. 전시회; v. 전시하다
coworker n. 회사 동료, 협력자

해석
07-09번은 다음 대화에 관한 문제입니다.
여: 와, 오늘은 정말 춥네요. ⁰⁷조깅하러 가려고 계획했었는데, 실내에 있는 것이 더 현명할 것 같네요.
남: 저와 함께 고대사 박물관에 가는 건 어때요? 거기에는 실내 주차장이 있어서, 야외로 전혀 나가지 않아도 될 거예요.
여: 흠. ⁰⁸최근에 박물관에서 몇몇 새로운 전시회를 열었다는 보도를 텔레비전에서 보긴 했어요. 그것들을 보는 것도 괜찮을 것 같네요.
남: 맞아요. ⁰⁹며칠 전에 제 회사 동료가 그 전시회를 봤는데 정말 훌륭했다고 말했어요.

07 특정 세부 사항 문제
해석 여자는 원래 오늘 무슨 활동을 하려고 계획했는가?
(A) 운동하기
(B) 공부하기
(C) 관광하기
(D) 청소하기

해설 여자의 말에서 질문의 핵심 어구(originally plan to do today)와 관련된 내용을 주의 깊게 듣는다. 여자가 "I planned to go jogging, but I think it would be smarter to stay indoors."라며 조깅하러 가려고 계획했었는데, 실내에 있는 것이 더 현명할 것 같다고 하였다. 따라서 (A)가 정답이다.

어휘 sightsee v. 관광하다

08 언급 문제
해석 여자는 박물관에 대해 무엇을 말하는가?
(A) 주차 시설들을 갖추고 있지 않다.
(B) 텔레비전 프로그램에 방영되었다.
(C) 최근에 확장을 했다.
(D) 오늘은 방문객들에게 개방되지 않는다.

해설 여자의 말에서 질문의 핵심 어구(museum)가 언급된 주변을 주의 깊게 듣는다. 여자가 "I saw a report on TV that said the museum recently opened some new exhibits."라며 박물관에서 몇몇 새로운 전시회들을 열었다는 보도를 텔레비전에서 보았다고 하였다. 따라서 (B)가 정답이다.

어휘 facility n. 시설 feature v. 방영하다, 출연하다 expansion n. 확장

09 방법 문제
해석 남자는 전시회에 관해 어떻게 알게 됐는가?
(A) 동료로부터
(B) 라디오 프로그램에서
(C) 신문 기사에서
(D) 박물관 회보를 통해

해설 질문의 핵심 어구(displays)가 언급된 주변을 주의 깊게 듣는다. 남자가 "My coworker saw those displays ~ and said they were really excellent."라며 회사 동료가 전시회를 봤는데 정말 훌륭했다고 말했다고 하였다. 따라서 (A)가 정답이다.

어휘 colleague n. 동료 article n. 기사, 조항

Paraphrasing
coworker 회사 동료 → colleague 동료

[10-12] 호주 → 영국 → 미국
Questions 10-12 refer to the following conversation with three speakers.

M: Hi. This is Brett Roberts calling. ¹⁰I'm supposed to return the car I rented by 11 A.M. today. Could I do this in the early afternoon instead?
W1: Let me transfer you to the Speedy Auto customer service department.
W2: Hello. My name is Danielle. Would you be able to return the car by 1 P.M.?
M: That's fine. ¹¹The meeting with my client will end before noon.
W2: OK. ¹²Just as a reminder, the vehicle has to be brought back to the branch you rented it from. Um, the one on Fifth Street.
M: Got it. Thanks, Danielle.

transfer v. 연결하다, 전환하다
customer service department 고객 서비스 부서 client n. 고객
vehicle n. 차량 branch n. 지점

해석
10-12번은 다음 세 명의 대화에 관한 문제입니다.

남: 안녕하세요. Brett Roberts입니다. ¹⁰제가 빌린 차를 오늘 오전 11시까지 반납해야 하는데요. 대신 이른 오후에 반납할 수 있을까요?
여1: Speedy Auto사의 고객 서비스 부서로 연결해 드리겠습니다.
여2: 안녕하세요. 제 이름은 Danielle입니다. 오후 1시까지 차를 반납하실 수 있으신가요?
남: 괜찮습니다. ¹¹고객과의 회의는 정오 전에 끝날 거예요.
여2: 네. ¹²상기시켜 드리자면, 차량은 빌리셨던 지점으로 반납하셔야 합니다. 음, 5번가에 있는 곳이요.
남: 알겠습니다. 고마워요, Danielle.

10 목적 문제
해석 남자는 왜 전화하고 있는가?
(A) 예약을 하기 위해
(B) 임대 기간을 연장하기 위해
(C) 할인을 요청하기 위해
(D) 결제 방식을 변경하기 위해

해설 전화의 목적을 묻는 문제이므로, 대화의 초반을 반드시 듣는다. 남자가 "I'm supposed to return the car I rented by 11 A.M. today. Could I do this in the early afternoon instead?"라며 빌린 차를 오늘 오전 11시까지 반납해야 한다고 한 후, 대신 이른 오후에 반납할 수 있는지 물었다. 따라서 (B)가 정답이다.

어휘 reservation n. 예약 extend v. 연장하다 rental period 임대 기간 payment n. 결제, 지급 method n. 방식

11 다음에 할 일 문제
해석 남자는 오전에 무엇을 할 것인가?
(A) 계정에 로그인한다.
(B) 계약서에 서명한다.
(C) 차량을 선택한다.
(D) 고객과 만난다.

해설 질문의 핵심 어구(morning)와 관련된 내용을 주의 깊게 듣는다. 남자가 "The meeting with my client will end before noon."이라며 고객과의 회의가 정오 전에 끝날 것이라고 한 것을 통해 남자가 오전에 고객과 만날 것임을 알 수 있다. 따라서 (D)가 정답이다.

어휘 account n. 계정 contract n. 계약서

12 특정 세부 사항 문제
해석 Danielle은 남자에게 무엇에 대해 상기시키는가?
(A) 반납 위치
(B) 약속 시간
(C) 현장 점검
(D) 지점 폐쇄

해설 Danielle의 말에서 질문의 핵심 어구(remind)와 관련된 내용을 주의 깊게 듣는다. 여자2[Danielle]가 "Just as a reminder, the vehicle has to be brought back to the branch you rented it from."이라며 상기시켜 준다며 차량을 빌렸던 지점으로 반납해야 한다고 하였다. 따라서 (A)가 정답이다.

어휘 location n. 위치 appointment n. 약속 on-site adj. 현장의 inspection n. 점검 closure n. 폐쇄

[13-15] 🎧 영국 → 호주
Questions 13-15 refer to the following conversation.

W: ¹³**It was a surprise to see you at the Wildlife Foundation's charity dinner last night, Chris.**
M: Yeah. I had no idea you were going. Did you enjoy yourself? ↷

W: I did. But ¹⁴**I was annoyed by how small the parking lot at the venue was**. It was full by the time I arrived, so I had to pay to use the garage across the street.
M: Check your e-mail. ¹⁵**The event organizers are asking for the parking receipts of everyone in your situation. They will reimburse you.**

charity n. 자선 foundation n. 재단 annoyed adj. 짜증이 난 garage n. 주차장 reimburse v. 환급하다, 상환하다

해석
13-15번은 다음 대화에 관한 문제입니다.

여: ¹³어젯밤 Wildlife 재단의 자선 만찬에서 당신을 보게 되어 놀랐어요, Chris.
남: 네. 당신이 갈 줄은 몰랐어요. 즐거우셨나요?
여: 그랬어요. 하지만 ¹⁴행사장의 주차장이 얼마나 작았는지에 짜증이 났어요. 제가 도착했을 때는 이미 가득 차서 길 건너편에 있는 주차장을 이용하느라 돈을 지불해야 했어요.
남: 이메일을 확인해 보세요. ¹⁵행사 주최 측에서 당신과 같은 상황에 놓인 모든 사람들의 주차 영수증을 요청하고 있어요. 그들이 환급해 줄 거예요.

13 주제 문제
해석 대화는 주로 무엇에 관한 것인가?
(A) 공연
(B) 워크숍
(C) 세미나
(D) 모금 행사

해설 대화의 주제를 묻는 문제이므로, 대화의 초반을 반드시 듣는다. 여자가 "It was a surprise to see you at the Wildlife Foundation's charity dinner last night, Chris."라며 어젯밤 Wildlife 재단의 자선 만찬에서 Chris를 보게 되어 놀랐다고 말한 후, 모금 행사에 대한 내용으로 대화가 이어지고 있다. 따라서 (D)가 정답이다.

어휘 fundraiser n. 모금 행사

Paraphrasing
charity dinner 자선 만찬 → fundraiser 모금 행사

14 특정 세부 사항 문제
해석 무엇이 여자를 신경 쓰이게 했는가?
(A) 행사장의 위치
(B) 행사의 길이
(C) 물건의 비용
(D) 시설의 크기

해설 질문의 핵심 어구(bothered)와 관련된 내용을 주의 깊게 듣는다. 여자가 "I was annoyed by how small the parking lot at the venue was"라며 행사장의 주차장이 얼마나 작았는지에 짜증이 났다고 하였다. 따라서 (D)가 정답이다.

어휘 facility n. 시설

15 의도 파악 문제
해석 남자는 왜 "이메일을 확인해 보세요"라고 말하는가?
(A) 피드백이 요청되었음을 암시하기 위해
(B) 정보가 부정확함을 시사하기 위해
(C) 허가가 필요함을 강조하기 위해
(D) 환급이 가능함을 나타내기 위해

해설 질문의 인용어구(Check your e-mail)가 언급된 주변을 주의 깊게 듣는다. 남자가 "The event organizers are asking for the parking receipts ~. They will reimburse you."라며 행사 주최 측에서 주차 영수증을 요청하고 있다고 한 후, 그들이 환급해 줄 것이라고 하였다. 따라서 (D)가 정답이다.

어휘 imply v. 암시하다　inaccurate adj. 부정확한　stress v. 강조하다
permission n. 허가　indicate v. 나타내다　reimbursement n. 환급, 상환

[16-18] 🎧 캐나다 → 영국

Questions 16-18 refer to the following conversation.

M: Good morning. ¹⁶**I need to get to Harrisburg today. Could you tell me when the next bus departs from here?**
W: Hold on while I check our system . . . Um, it leaves at 10 A.M. and arrives there at 1 P.M.
M: ¹⁷**The wedding I'm attending doesn't start until 4.** I don't want to get there too early and have to wait around. Is there one at noon?
W: ¹⁸**I'm very sorry, but there are no seats left.** There are still several on the one departing at 11 o'clock, though. Would that work for you?
M: That should be OK. Please give me one ticket.

depart v. 출발하다　hold on 기다리다　arrive v. 도착하다

해석
16-18번은 다음 대화에 관한 문제입니다.
남: 좋은 아침입니다. ¹⁶저는 오늘 Harrisburg에 가야 하는데요. 여기서 다음 버스가 언제 출발하는지 말씀해 주시겠어요?
여: 제가 시스템을 확인하는 동안 기다려 주세요... 음, 오전 10시에 출발해서 오후 1시에 그곳에 도착합니다.
남: ¹⁷제가 참석하는 결혼식은 4시가 되어서야 시작해요. 너무 일찍 도착해서 기다리고 싶지는 않아요. 정오에 출발하는 것이 있나요?
여: ¹⁸정말 죄송합니다만, 남은 좌석이 없습니다. 하지만 11시에 출발하는 버스에는 아직 여러 자리가 남아 있습니다. 괜찮으신가요?
남: 괜찮을 것 같습니다. 표 한 장 주세요.

16 장소 문제
해석 화자들은 어디에 있는 것 같은가?
(A) 버스 터미널에
(B) 지하철역에
(C) 공항에
(D) 택시 승차장에
해설 대화에서 장소와 관련된 표현을 놓치지 않고 듣는다. 남자가 "I need to get to Harrisburg today. Could you tell me when the next bus departs from here?"라며 Harrisburg에 가야 하는데 여기서 다음 버스가 언제 출발하는지 묻는 것을 통해 화자들은 버스 터미널에 있다는 것을 알 수 있다. 따라서 (A)가 정답이다.
어휘 taxi stand 택시 승차장

17 이유 문제
해석 남자는 왜 Harrisburg에 가는가?
(A) 콘서트에 참여하기 위해
(B) 면접에 참여하기 위해
(C) 결혼식에 참석하기 위해
(D) 회의에 참석하기 위해
해설 남자의 말에서 질문의 핵심 어구(traveling to Harrisburg)와 관련된 내용을 주의 깊게 듣는다. 남자가 "The wedding I'm attending doesn't start until 4."라며 자신이 참석하는 결혼식은 4시가 되어서야 시작한다고 하였다. 따라서 (C)가 정답이다.
어휘 participate in ~에 참여하다　conference n. 회의

18 문제점 문제
해석 여자는 무슨 문제를 언급하는가?
(A) 가방이 분실되었다.
(B) 표가 매진되었다.
(C) 차량이 제대로 작동하지 않았다.
(D) 승객들이 늦게 도착했다.
해설 여자의 말에서 부정적인 표현이 언급된 주변을 주의 깊게 듣는다. 여자가 "I'm very sorry, but there are no seats left."라며 미안하지만 남은 좌석이 없다고 하였다. 따라서 (B)가 정답이다.
어휘 misplaced adj. 분실된　sold out 매진된
malfunction v. 제대로 작동하지 않다

[19-21] 🎧 미국 → 캐나다

Questions 19-21 refer to the following conversation and seating chart.

W: Welcome to the Riverfront Arts Center. How can I help you?
M: Hello. ¹⁹**I'd like to buy a ticket for the Friday evening play**, All Along the Dock.
W: We still have seats available in all of our sections.
M: Wonderful. ²⁰**I'd like to sit in the middle section, as close to the stage as possible, please.**
W: OK. I'll put you in seat 14F. Your ticket will cost 25 dollars.
M: Here's my credit card. Could I get a receipt as well?
W: Of course. And ²¹**I would suggest arriving here at least 30 minutes early**. Sometimes the line at the entrance can be quite long.

play n. 연극　section n. 구역　stage n. 무대　receipt n. 영수증
entrance n. 입구

해석
19-21번은 다음 대화와 좌석 배치도에 관한 문제입니다.
여: Riverfront 예술 회관에 오신 것을 환영합니다. 어떻게 도와드릴까요?
남: 안녕하세요. ¹⁹금요일 저녁 연극인 All Along the Dock의 표를 구매하고 싶습니다.
여: 여전히 모든 구역에 이용할 수 있는 좌석이 있어요.
남: 좋습니다. ²⁰중앙 구역에 앉고 싶고, 가능한 한 무대에 가까운 자리로 부탁립니다.
여: 알겠습니다. 14F 자리로 해드리겠습니다. 표는 25달러입니다.
남: 여기 제 신용 카드가 있습니다. 영수증도 받을 수 있을까요?
여: 물론입니다. 그리고 ²¹적어도 30분 일찍 도착하시는 것을 제안해 드려요. 때때로 입구의 줄이 꽤 길 수 있습니다.

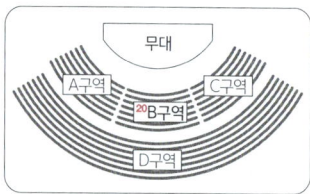

19 특정 세부 사항 문제
해석 남자는 어떤 종류의 행사를 위한 표를 원하는가?
(A) 연극
(B) 음악 축제
(C) 시상식
(D) 영화 상영
해설 질문의 핵심 어구(ticket)가 언급된 주변을 주의 깊게 듣는다. 남자가 "I'd like to buy a ticket for the Friday evening play"라며 금요일 저녁 연극의 표를 구매하고 싶다고 하였다. 따라서 (A)가 정답이다.
어휘 awards ceremony 시상식　screening n. (영화) 상영

20 시각 자료 문제

해석 시각 자료를 보아라. 남자는 어느 구역에 앉기를 원하는가?
(A) A구역
(B) B구역
(C) C구역
(D) D구역

해설 제시된 좌석 배치도의 정보를 확인한 후 질문의 핵심 어구(section ~ sit in)와 관련된 내용을 주의 깊게 듣는다. 남자가 "I'd like to sit in the middle section, as close to the stage as possible, please."라며 중앙 구역에 앉고 싶고, 가능한 한 무대에 가까운 자리로 부탁한다고 하였다. 좌석 배치도에서 중앙 구역이면서 무대에 가까운 구역은 B구역임을 알 수 있다. 따라서 (B)가 정답이다.

21 제안 문제

해석 여자는 무엇을 제안하는가?
(A) 결제 영수증 보관하기
(B) 등급 상향에 대한 비용을 지불하기
(C) 장소에 일찍 도착하기
(D) 온라인 후기를 읽기

해설 여자의 말에서 제안과 관련된 표현이 언급된 내용을 주의 깊게 듣는다. 여자가 "I would suggest arriving here at least 30 minutes early"라며 적어도 30분 일찍 도착하는 것을 제안한다고 하였다. 따라서 (C)가 정답이다.

어휘 save v. 보관하다, 저장하다   venue n. 장소

PART 4

DAY 16 음성 메시지 및 회의 발췌

1. 음성 메시지

담화 흐름과 빈출 문제 🎧 캐나다 p.118

해석 안녕하세요, Mr. Kim. 저는 GlobalTrip에서 근무하는 Renaldo Rolenti입니다. 귀하의 패키지여행 할인에 대한 문의에 답변하고 싶습니다. 저희 웹사이트에서 그것을 예약하신 것으로 확인되는데, 이 판촉 행사는 저희 스마트폰 애플리케이션을 통해 예약하신 경우에만 이용 가능합니다. 그저 애플리케이션을 설치하시고 일반 요금의 15퍼센트를 절약하기 위한 할인 코드를 입력하시면 됩니다. 귀하는 그 후에 확인 이메일을 받으실 것입니다. 귀하의 이전 예약을 취소하시는 것을 잊지 마세요. 그렇게 하면, 이중으로 요금이 부과되지 않을 것입니다. 궁금한 점이 있으시면 알려주세요.

어휘 inquiry n. 문의 discount n. 할인 promotion n. 판촉 행사
save v. 절약하다 regular adj. 일반적인

HACKERS PRACTICE p.119

01 (C) 02 (D) 03 (C) 04 (B)

[01-02] 🎧 영국 / 미국

Questions 01-02 refer to the following telephone message.

⁰¹**I'm calling from Pearson's to let you know that the item you ordered will arrive** at our store tomorrow morning. You can pick up your new guitar from our shop at any time during our regular business hours. Make sure to bring your receipt when you do this. ⁰²**Just show it to the staff at our customer service desk**, and they will get your item for you. Thank you.

business hours 영업시간 receipt n. 영수증

해석
01-02번은 다음 전화 메시지에 관한 문제입니다.
⁰¹귀하께서 주문하신 상품이 내일 오전에 저희 매장에 도착할 예정임을 알려드리기 위해 Pearson's에서 전화드립니다. 정규 영업시간 중에 언제든지 저희 매장에서 새 기타를 찾아가실 수 있습니다. 찾아가실 때 영수증을 꼭 가져오시길 바랍니다. ⁰²그것을 고객 서비스 데스크의 직원에게 보여주시기만 하면, 그들이 귀하의 상품을 가져다 드릴 것입니다. 감사합니다.

01 목적 문제

해석 화자는 왜 전화하고 있는가?
(A) 환불 과정을 설명하기 위해
(B) 배송 주소를 확인하기 위해
(C) 주문에 대한 최신 정보를 제공하기 위해
(D) 특별 할인 내용을 설명하기 위해

해설 전화 메시지의 목적을 묻는 문제이므로, 지문의 초반을 반드시 듣는다. "I'm calling from Pearson's to let you know that the item you ordered will arrive at our store tomorrow morning."이라며 청자가 주문한 상품이 내일 오전에 매장에 도착할 예정임을 알려주기 위해 Pearson's에서 전화했다고 하였다. 따라서 (C)가 정답이다.

어휘 refund n. 환불 confirm v. 확인하다 describe v. 설명하다

02 특정 세부 사항 문제

해석 청자는 고객 서비스 데스크에서 무엇을 해야 하는가?
(A) 양식을 작성한다.
(B) 상품을 살펴본다.
(C) 결제를 한다.
(D) 영수증을 보여준다.

해설 질문의 핵심 어구(customer service desk)가 언급된 주변을 주의 깊게 듣는다. "Just show it[receipt] to the staff at our customer service desk"라며 영수증을 고객 서비스 데스크의 직원에게 보여주기만 하면 된다고 하였다. 따라서 (D)가 정답이다.

어휘 fill out 작성하다 examine v. 살펴보다, 조사하다 payment n. 결제
present v. 보여주다, 제시하다

[Paraphrasing]
show 보여주다 → Present 보여주다

[03-04] 🎧 호주 / 캐나다

Questions 03-04 refer to the following recorded message.

Good morning. ⁰³**This is Daniel at the reception desk. A large package has just been delivered for you. You may pick it up before 6 P.M., or have a member of the staff bring it up to your apartment.** After 6 P.M., it will be transferred to our storage room. We usually only keep large items for up to 15 days. ⁰⁴**Please inform us in advance if you'd like us to keep it for longer.** Thank you.

reception desk 접수처, 프런트 transfer v. 옮기다, 이동하다
storage room 창고 inform v. 알리다 in advance 미리, 사전에

해석
03-04번은 다음 녹음 메시지에 관한 문제입니다.
안녕하세요. ⁰³저는 접수처의 Daniel입니다. 큰 소포가 방금 귀하 앞으로 배송되었습니다. 오후 6시 이전에 가져가시거나 직원이 귀하의 아파트로 가져다드리도록 요청하실 수 있습니다. 오후 6시 이후, 그것은 저희의 창고로 옮겨질 것입니다. 저희는 보통 대형 물품을 15일 동안만 보관합니다. ⁰⁴저희가 그것을 더 오래 보관하기를 원하시면 미리 저희에게 알려주시길 바랍니다. 감사합니다.

03 화자 문제

해석 화자는 어디에서 일하는가?
(A) 여행사에서
(B) 사무용 건물에서
(C) 주거용 건물에서
(D) 배송 회사에서

해설 지문에서 신분 및 직업과 관련된 표현을 놓치지 않고 듣는다. "This is Daniel at the reception desk. A large package has just been delivered for you. You may pick it up before 6 P.M., or have a member of the staff bring it up to your apartment."라며 자신은 접수처의 Daniel인데, 큰 소포가 방금 당신 앞으로 배송되었으며, 오후 6시 이전에 그것을 가져가거나 직원이 당신의 아파트로 가져다주도록 요청할 수 있다고 하였다. 이를 통해 화자는 주거용 건물에서 일한다는 것을 알 수 있다. 따라서 (C)가 정답이다.

어휘 travel agency 여행사 residential adj. 주거(용)의

[Paraphrasing]
apartment 아파트 → residential building 주거용 건물

04 요청 문제

해석 화자는 청자에게 무엇을 하라고 요청하는가?
(A) 요금을 지불한다.
(B) 알림을 제공한다.
(C) 참석을 확인한다.
(D) 매뉴얼을 재검토한다.

해설 지문에서 요청과 관련된 표현이 언급된 주변을 주의 깊게 듣는다. "Please inform us in advance if you'd like us to keep it[package] for longer."라며 소포를 더 오래 보관하기를 원한다면 미리 알려주길 바란다고 하였다. 따라서 (B)가 정답이다.

어휘 settle v. (돈을) 지불하다, 해결하다   notification n. 알림, 통지
attendance n. 참석, 출석   review v. 재검토하다

Paraphrasing
inform 알리다 → Provide notification 알림을 제공하다

2. 회의 발췌

담화 흐름과 빈출 문제   [호주]   p.120

해설 안녕하세요. 저는 오늘 기술부에서 온 공무원 그룹이 우리의 연구 시설을 둘러볼 예정이기 때문에 이 회의를 소집했습니다. 그들이 여러분의 연구실 구역을 방문할 때, 시간을 내서 여러분이 무슨 일을 하고 있는지 설명해 주시기 바랍니다. 그들이 우리가 여기서 하고 있는 연구와 그것이 왜 중요한지에 대해 이해하는 것은 매우 중요합니다. 우리가 방문객들에게 좋은 인상을 주어야 한다는 것을 명심하세요. 아시다시피, 우리 기금의 대부분은 정부로부터 나옵니다.

어휘 official n. (고위) 공무원   laboratory n. 연구실   significant adj. 중요한
impression n. 인상   funding n. 기금

HACKERS PRACTICE   p.121

01 (C)   **02** (A)   **03** (C)   **04** (B)

[01-02]   [미국 / 영국]

Questions 01-02 refer to the following excerpt from a meeting.

⁰¹**I called this meeting to start our work on the advertisement for our company's newest camera model.** Before we get started, though, I'd like you to learn more about our main rival's latest camera. We need to clearly differentiate between the two products in our advertisement. I'll give each of you a brochure about that device. ⁰²**Please go through it carefully**, and we will discuss it next week.

call a meeting 회의를 소집하다   advertisement n. 광고
differentiate v. 차별화하다, 구별하다   brochure n. 브로슈어, 안내 책자
go through ~을 검토하다

해설 01-02번은 다음 회의 발췌에 관한 문제입니다.

⁰¹저는 우리 회사의 최신 카메라 모델을 위한 광고 작업을 시작하기 위해 이 회의를 소집했습니다. 하지만 시작하기 전에, 저는 여러분이 우리의 주요 경쟁 업체의 최신 카메라에 대해 더 알아보셨으면 합니다. 우리는 광고에서 두 제품을 명확하게 차별화해야 합니다. 해당 기기에 대한 브로슈어를 여러분 각자에게 드리겠습니다. ⁰²그것을 꼼꼼히 검토해 주시고, 우리는 다음 주에 그것을 논의하겠습니다.

01 주제 문제

해설 화자는 주로 무엇에 대해 이야기하고 있는가?
(A) 제품 개선
(B) 직원 성과 검토
(C) 광고 제작
(D) 설문조사 실시

해설 회의의 주제를 묻는 문제이므로, 지문의 초반을 반드시 듣는다. "I called this meeting to start our work on the advertisement for our company's newest camera model."이라며 회사의 최신 카메라 모델에 대한 광고 작업을 시작하기 위해 이 회의를 소집했다고 하였다. 따라서 (C)가 정답이다.

어휘 improve v. 개선하다, 향상시키다   performance n. 성과, 공연
conduct v. 실시하다

Paraphrasing
work on the advertisement 광고 작업 → Creating an advertisement 광고 제작

02 요청 문제

해설 청자들은 무엇을 하도록 요청받는가?
(A) 자료를 읽는다.
(B) 샘플을 개발한다.
(C) 회의에 참석한다.
(D) 몇몇 오류를 수정한다.

해설 지문에서 요청과 관련된 표현이 언급된 주변을 주의 깊게 듣는다. "Please go through it[brochure] carefully"라며 브로슈어를 꼼꼼히 검토해 달라고 하였다. 따라서 (A)가 정답이다.

어휘 material n. 자료, 재료

Paraphrasing
go through 검토하다 → Read 읽다

[03-04]   [캐나다 / 호주]

Questions 03-04 refer to the following excerpt from a meeting.

⁰³**Summer will be here soon, and that means we're about to get very busy at our resort.** Before this happens, we need to hire several front desk clerks. ⁰⁴**The goal is to have them start work on May 20.** I have one concern, though. ⁰⁴**That does not give us much time to find suitable candidates.** So if you know of someone with relevant experience who is looking for a job, please notify me immediately.

clerk n. 직원   suitable adj. 적합한   candidate n. 후보자
relevant adj. 관련된   experience n. 경력, 경험   notify v. 알리다
immediately adv. 즉시

해설 03-04번은 다음 회의 발췌에 관한 문제입니다.

⁰³여름이 곧 다가올 것이고, 그것은 우리 리조트가 매우 바빠질 것을 의미합니다. 이렇게 되기 전에, 안내 데스크 직원을 몇 명 고용해야 합니다. ⁰⁴목표는 그들이 5월 20일부터 일을 시작하게 하는 것입니다. 하지만, 한 가지 걱정이 있습니다. ⁰⁴우리가 적합한 후보자를 찾을 시간이 많지 않다는 것입니다. 따라서 관련된 경력이 있는 구직자를 알고 계신다면, 즉시 저에게 알려주시길 바랍니다.

03 화자 문제

해설 화자는 어떤 업계에서 일하는 것 같은가?
(A) 투자
(B) 교통
(C) 숙박 시설
(D) 엔터테인먼트

해설 지문에서 신분 및 직업과 관련된 표현을 놓치지 않고 듣는다. "Summer will be here soon, and that means we're about to get very busy at our resort."라며 여름이 곧 다가올 것이고, 그것은 우리 리조트가 매우 바빠질 것을 의미한다고 하였다. 이를 통해 화자가 숙박 시설인 리조트에서 일한다는 것을 알 수 있다. 따라서 (C)가 정답이다.

어휘 investment n. 투자   transportation n. 교통
accommodation n. 숙박 시설

Paraphrasing
resort 리조트 → Accommodation 숙박 시설

04 의도 파악 문제

해석 남자는 "한 가지 걱정이 있습니다"라고 말할 때 무엇을 의도하는가?
(A) 일이 너무 고되다.
(B) 일정이 빠듯하다.
(C) 지원자가 적합하지 않다.
(D) 시설에 인원이 부족하다.

해설 질문의 인용어구(I have one concern)가 언급된 주변을 주의 깊게 듣는다. "The goal is to have them[front desk clerks] start work on May 20."라며 목표는 안내 데스크 직원들이 5월 20일부터 일을 시작하게 하는 것이라고 한 후, "That does not give us much time to find suitable candidates."라며 적합한 후보자를 찾을 시간이 많지 않다고 하였다. 따라서 (B)가 정답이다.

어휘 demanding adj. 고된, 힘든   tight adj. 빠듯한   applicant n. 지원자
unsuitable adj. 적합하지 않은   understaffed adj. 인원이 부족한

Paraphrasing
not give us much time to find suitable candidates 우리가 적합한 후보자를 찾을 시간이 많지 않다 → A schedule is tight 일정이 빠듯하다

HACKERS TEST   p.122

01 (C)	02 (C)	03 (C)	04 (D)	05 (A)
06 (D)	07 (B)	08 (B)	09 (D)	10 (B)
11 (B)	12 (C)	13 (C)	14 (B)	15 (D)
16 (B)	17 (A)	18 (D)	19 (A)	20 (C)
21 (A)				

[01-03] 호주

Questions 01-03 refer to the following excerpt from a meeting.

> ⁰¹**We've decided to introduce a dress code for workers in our store.** All of you will be required to wear a blue shirt with our logo on it. ⁰²**This will be provided to you on Thursday.** The goal of the policy change is to make staff more visible to shoppers. I'd also like to remind you that we'll be collecting customer feedback next month. ⁰³**I will now go over the questionnaire we want them to fill out.**

dress code 복장 규정   policy n. 규정   visible adj. (눈에) 보이는
questionnaire n. 설문지   fill out 작성하다

해석
01-03번은 다음 회의 발췌에 관한 문제입니다.

⁰¹우리는 매장에서 일하는 직원들을 위한 복장 규정을 도입하기로 결정했습니다. 여러분 모두는 우리 로고가 있는 파란색 셔츠를 착용해야 할 것입니다. ⁰²이것은 목요일에 여러분에게 제공될 것입니다. 이 규정 변화의 목표는 직원들이 쇼핑객들에게 더 잘 보이도록 하기 위함입니다. 또한 다음 달에 고객 피드백을 수집할 것이라는 점을 상기시켜 드리고 싶습니다. ⁰³이제 그들이 작성하기를 바라는 설문지를 살펴보겠습니다.

01 청자 문제

해석 청자들은 누구인 것 같은가?
(A) 청소 직원들
(B) 배달 기사들
(C) 매장 점원들
(D) 보안 요원들

해설 지문에서 신분 및 직업과 관련된 표현을 놓치지 않고 듣는다. "We've decided to introduce a dress code for workers in our store."라며 우리는 매장에서 일하는 직원들을 위한 복장 규정을 도입하기로 결정했다고 했으므로 청자들이 매장 점원들임을 알 수 있다. 따라서 (C)가 정답이다.

어휘 delivery n. 배달   clerk n. 점원   security n. 보안

02 특정 세부 사항 문제

해석 청자들에게 무엇이 제공될 것인가?
(A) 명찰
(B) 직원 수칙
(C) 의류 제품
(D) 상품권

해설 질문의 핵심 어구(be provided to the listeners)와 관련된 내용을 주의 깊게 듣는다. "This[a blue shirt] will be provided to you on Thursday."라며 파란색 셔츠가 목요일에 청자들에게 제공될 것이라고 하였다. 따라서 (C)가 정답이다.

어휘 employee manual 직원 수칙

03 특정 세부 사항 문제

해석 다음에 무엇이 논의될 것 같은가?
(A) 면접 과정
(B) 계절 프로모션
(C) 고객 설문조사
(D) 팀빌딩 활동

해설 질문의 핵심 어구(be discussed next)와 관련된 내용을 주의 깊게 듣는다. 지문 마지막에서 "I will now go over the questionnaire we want them[shoppers] to fill out."이라며 이제 쇼핑객들이 작성하기를 바라는 설문지를 살펴보겠다고 하였다. 따라서 (C)가 정답이다.

어휘 process n. 과정   survey n. 설문조사

Paraphrasing
questionnaire 설문지 → survey 설문조사

[04-06] 영국

Questions 04-06 refer to the following telephone message.

> Good afternoon. ⁰⁴**This is Teresa from Rushbar Hospital.** When you came to our facility two days ago, I forgot to tell you to create an online account. ⁰⁵**You will need one to arrange appointments moving forward.** Could you visit our Web site and take care of this? ⁰⁶**If you need help setting it up, please call me back at 555-1879.** Thank you.

account n. 계정   appointment n. 예약

해석
04-06번은 다음 전화 메시지에 관한 문제입니다.

안녕하세요. ⁰⁴저는 Rushbar 병원에서 근무하는 Teresa입니다. 이틀 전에 저희 시설에 오셨을 때, 온라인 계정을 만드시라고 말씀드리는 것을 잊었습니다. ⁰⁵앞으로 예약을 잡으시려면 그것이 필요하실 겁니다. 저희 웹사이트를 방문하셔서 이것을 처리해 주시겠어요? ⁰⁶설정하는 데 도움이 필요하시면, 555-1879로 저에게 다시 전화해 주세요. 감사합니다.

04 화자 문제

해석 화자는 어디에서 일하는가?
(A) 보험 회사에서

(B) 은행에서
(C) 약국에서
(D) 병원에서

해설 지문에서 신분 및 직업과 관련된 표현을 놓치지 않고 듣는다. "This is Teresa from Rushbar Hospital."이라며 자신은 Rushbar 병원에서 근무하는 Teresa라고 한 것을 통해, 화자가 병원에서 일한다는 것을 알 수 있다. 따라서 (D)가 정답이다.

어휘 pharmacy n. 약국   medical center 병원

Paraphrasing
Hospital 병원 → medical center 병원

05 언급 문제
해석 화자는 온라인 계정에 대해 무엇을 언급하는가?
(A) 일정 관리 기능을 포함한다.
(B) 검사 결과를 제공한다.
(C) 청구서 지급이 가능하다.
(D) 채팅 프로그램을 특별히 포함한다.

해설 질문의 핵심 어구(online account)와 관련된 내용을 주의 깊게 듣는다. "You will need one[an online account] to arrange appointments moving forward."라며 앞으로 예약을 잡으려면 온라인 계정이 필요할 것이라고 하였다. 따라서 (A)가 정답이다.

어휘 scheduling n. 일정 관리   function n. 기능   bill n. 청구서
payment n. 지급

06 이유 문제
해석 청자는 왜 전화를 다시 걸 것 같은가?
(A) 예약을 하기 위해
(B) 정보를 수정하기 위해
(C) 비밀번호를 물어보기 위해
(D) 도움을 요청하기 위해

해설 질문의 핵심 어구(return a call)와 관련된 내용을 주의 깊게 듣는다. "If you need help setting it[an online account] up, please call me back at 555-1879."라며 온라인 계정을 설정하는 데 도움이 필요하면, 다시 전화해 달라고 하였다. 따라서 (D)가 정답이다.

어휘 correct v. 수정하다   assistance n. 도움

Paraphrasing
help 도움 → assistance 도움

[07-09] 🎧 미국
Questions 07-09 refer to the following excerpt from a meeting.

> Before we end our meeting, I have a quick announcement. ⁰⁷Since our current accounting software is running slowly and freezing often, I want to make a change and have a new application installed on your computers. ⁰⁸There will be workshops all next week on how to use it. I have asked Ms. Lauren from the IT department to lead these. ⁰⁹She will send out an e-mail tomorrow with the days and times that everyone will meet.
>
> current adj. 현재의, 현행의   application n. 응용 프로그램, 신청서

해석
07-09번은 다음 회의 발췌에 관한 문제입니다.
회의를 마치기 전에, 한 가지 간단한 발표가 있습니다. ⁰⁷우리가 현재 사용하는 회계 소프트웨어가 느리게 실행되고 자주 멈추기 때문에, 저는 변경을 해서 새로운 응용 프로그램이 여러분의 컴퓨터에 설치되기를 원합니다. ⁰⁸다음 주 내내 이것을 사용하는 방법에 대한 워크숍이 있을 예정입니다. 저는 IT 부서의 Ms. Lauren에게 이것들을 이끌어 달라고 요청했습니다. ⁰⁹내일 그녀는 모두가 만날 날짜와 시간이 적힌 이메일을 보낼 것입니다.

07 이유 문제
해석 화자는 왜 변경을 하고 싶어 하는가?
(A) 직원들에게 너무 많은 업무가 있다.
(B) 소프트웨어 프로그램이 문제를 일으키고 있다.
(C) 부서장이 사임하는 것을 고려하고 있다.
(D) 기술자들이 업그레이드를 권장한다.

해설 질문의 핵심 어구(make a change)가 언급된 주변을 주의 깊게 듣는다. "Since our current accounting software is running slowly and freezing often, I want to make a change"라며 현재 사용하는 회계 소프트웨어가 느리게 실행되고 자주 멈추기 때문에 변경을 하고 싶다고 하였다. 따라서 (B)가 정답이다.

어휘 assignment n. 업무   cause v. 일으키다   resign v. 사임하다, 사직하다
recommend v. 권장하다, 추천하다

Paraphrasing
running slowly and freezing often 느리게 실행되고 자주 멈추고 있다 → causing problems 문제를 일으키고 있다

08 다음에 할 일 문제
해석 다음 주에 무슨 일이 일어날 것인가?
(A) 전자 기기들이 교체될 것이다.
(B) 교육 세션들이 열릴 것이다.
(C) 추가 직원들이 고용될 것이다.
(D) 직원 평가가 실시될 것이다.

해설 질문의 핵심 어구(next week)가 언급된 주변을 주의 깊게 듣는다. "There will be workshops all next week on how to use it[a new application]."이라며 다음 주 내내 새로운 응용 프로그램을 사용하는 방법에 대한 워크숍이 있을 것이라고 하였다. 따라서 (B)가 정답이다.

어휘 electronic adj. 전자의   replace v. 교체하다

09 방법 문제
해석 Ms. Lauren은 어떻게 일정을 공유할 것인가?
(A) 공지를 게시함으로써
(B) 전화를 함으로써
(C) 회의를 개최함으로써
(D) 이메일을 보냄으로써

해설 질문의 핵심 어구(share a schedule)와 관련된 내용을 주의 깊게 듣는다. "She[Ms. Lauren] will send out an e-mail tomorrow with the days and times that everyone will meet."이라며 내일 Ms. Lauren이 모두가 만날 날짜와 시간이 적힌 이메일을 보낼 것이라고 하였다. 따라서 (D)가 정답이다.

어휘 post v. 게시하다, 공고하다

[10-12] 🎧 캐나다
Questions 10-12 refer to the following excerpt from a meeting.

> Today, ¹⁰I want to discuss our company's upcoming service fee changes. Starting next week, we will increase the cost of our deluxe cable TV package from 35 dollars a month to 45 dollars a month. It's still a great deal because of the premium channels we've added. In the long term, customer satisfaction will increase. But, well... challenges are expected. ¹¹So, we may need to overcome some objections. ¹²If you receive any calls about this matter, transfer them to one of our customer service specialists. They are trained to handle these situations.
>
> upcoming adj. 다가오는   fee n. 요금   deluxe adj. 고급의
> satisfaction n. 만족도   challenge n. 어려움   overcome v. 극복하다
> objection n. 이의, 반대   transfer v. 돌리다, 전달하다   specialist n. 전문가
> handle v. 처리하다

해석

10-12번은 다음 회의 발췌에 관한 문제입니다.

오늘, ¹⁰저는 우리 회사의 다가오는 서비스 요금 변경에 대해 논의하고자 합니다. 다음 주부터, 우리는 고급 케이블 TV 패키지의 비용을 월 35달러에서 월 45달러로 인상할 것입니다. 우리가 추가한 프리미엄 채널들 때문에 이것은 여전히 좋은 거래입니다. 장기적으로, 고객 만족도가 증가할 것입니다. 그러나, 음... 어려움이 예상됩니다. ¹¹그래서 우리는 몇 가지 이의를 극복해야 할 수도 있습니다. ¹²만약 여러분이 이 문제에 관한 전화를 받으면, 우리의 고객 서비스 전문가들 중 한 명에게 돌려주십시오. 그들은 이러한 상황들을 처리하도록 교육받았습니다.

10 특정 세부 사항 문제
해석 화자에 따르면, 무엇이 바뀔 것인가?
  (A) 반품 정책
  (B) 서비스 요금
  (C) 생산 계약
  (D) 전화번호

해설 질문의 핵심 어구(will be changed)와 관련된 내용을 주의 깊게 듣는다. "I want to discuss our company's upcoming service fee changes."라며 다가오는 서비스 요금 변경에 대해 논의하고자 한다고 하였다. 따라서 (B)가 정답이다.

어휘 policy n. 정책 production n. 생산

11 의도 파악 문제
해석 화자는 "어려움이 예상됩니다"라고 말할 때 무엇을 의도하는가?
  (A) 더 많은 직원이 필요하다.
  (B) 고객들이 불평할 수 있다.
  (C) 추가 시간이 필요하다.
  (D) 비용이 증가할 수 있다.

해설 질문의 인용어구(challenges are expected)가 언급된 주변을 주의 깊게 듣는다. "So, we may need to overcome some objections."라며 우리는 고객들의 몇 가지 이의를 극복해야 할 수도 있다고 한 것을 통해 고객이 불평할 수 있음을 알 수 있다. 따라서 (B)가 정답이다.

어휘 extra adj. 추가의 expense n. 비용, 지출

12 요청 문제
해석 청자들은 무엇을 하도록 요청받는가?
  (A) 서류를 검토한다.
  (B) 책임자에게 연락한다.
  (C) 전화를 돌린다.
  (D) 구독을 홍보한다.

해설 지문의 중후반에서 요청과 관련된 표현이 포함된 문장을 주의 깊게 듣는다. "If you receive any calls about this matter[objections], transfer them to one of our customer service specialists."라며 만약 고객들의 이의에 관한 전화를 받으면, 우리의 고객 서비스 전문가들 중 한 명에게 돌려 달라고 하였다. 따라서 (C)가 정답이다.

어휘 director n. 책임자 promote v. 홍보하다 subscription n. 구독

[13-15] 영국
Questions 13-15 refer to the following recorded message.

¹³**Thank you for calling the Apollo Mall.** Our facility is open from 9 A.M. to 9 P.M. every day of the week. ¹³**We have over 100 different stores**, ranging from small gift shops to designer clothing boutiques. Beginning in March, ¹⁴**we will be renovating our cinema**. During this period, all of our stores will remain open, but the mall's south entrance will be blocked off. Accordingly, ¹⁵**we encourage visitors to avoid using the south parking lot**, as they will have to walk to the west entrance to access the mall.

range v. ~범위에 이르다 boutique n. 부티크 renovate v. 수리하다
block off 막다, 차단하다 lot n. 구역 access v. 들어가다, 접근하다

해석

13-15번은 다음 녹음 메시지에 관한 문제입니다.

¹³Apollo 쇼핑몰에 전화 주셔서 감사합니다. 저희 시설은 오전 9시부터 오후 9시까지 일주일 내내 영업합니다. ¹³저희는 작은 선물 가게부터 디자이너 의상 부티크에 이르는 100개 이상의 다양한 상점들이 있습니다. 3월부터, ¹⁴저희는 영화관을 수리할 예정입니다. 이 기간 동안 모든 상점들은 계속 문을 열겠지만, 쇼핑몰의 남쪽 출입구는 막힐 것입니다. 이에 따라, 고객님들이 쇼핑몰에 들어오기 위해 서쪽 출입구까지 걸어오셔야 할 것이기 때문에, ¹⁵저희는 방문객들이 남쪽 주차구역 이용을 피해 주시기를 권장하는 바입니다.

13 화자 문제
해석 화자는 어떤 종류의 업체에서 일하는가?
  (A) 디자인 회사
  (B) 놀이동산
  (C) 쇼핑 단지
  (D) 영화 제작사

해설 지문에서 신분 및 직업과 관련된 표현을 놓치지 않고 듣는다. "Thank you for calling the Apollo Mall."이라며 Apollo 쇼핑몰에 전화 주셔서 감사하다고 한 후, "We have over 100 different stores"라며 쇼핑몰에 100개 이상의 다양한 상점들이 있다고 한 것을 통해 화자는 쇼핑 단지에서 일하고 있음을 알 수 있다. 따라서 (C)가 정답이다.

어휘 amusement park 놀이동산 complex n. 단지 production n. 제작

Paraphrasing
Mall 쇼핑몰 → shopping complex 쇼핑 단지

14 특정 세부 사항 문제
해석 화자에 따르면, 무엇이 수리될 것인가?
  (A) 주차장
  (B) 영화관
  (C) 선물 가게
  (D) 의상 부티크

해설 질문의 핵심 어구(renovated)가 언급된 주변을 주의 깊게 듣는다. "we will be renovating our cinema"라며 영화관을 수리할 예정이라 하였다. 따라서 (B)가 정답이다.

Paraphrasing
cinema 영화관 → movie theater 영화관

15 제안 문제
해석 화자는 무엇을 제안하는가?
  (A) 티켓을 미리 구매하기
  (B) 특정한 날에 방문하기
  (C) 로열티 클럽에 가입하기
  (D) 특정 구역을 피하기

해설 지문의 중후반에서 제안과 관련된 표현이 포함된 문장을 주의 깊게 듣는다. "we encourage visitors to avoid using the south parking lot"이라며 방문객들에게 남쪽 주차구역 이용을 피해 주기를 권장한다고 하였다. 따라서 (D)가 정답이다.

어휘 sign up 가입하다

Paraphrasing
avoid using the south parking lot 남쪽 주차구역 이용을 피하다 → Avoiding a specific lot 특정 구역을 피하기

[16-18] 캐나다
Questions 16-18 refer to the following telephone message.

This is Eric Seymour from the city building commission.

[16]I'm replying to your inquiry about how to apply for a permit to build a second branch of your bakery. The application form can be downloaded from our Web site. [17]You must then submit the completed form along with the building blueprints at our office. [18]Your request will be reviewed, and you'll be notified of our decision within one month of the submission date. If you have any further questions, please feel free to contact me.

inquiry n. 문의, 질문　permit n. 허가, 증명서; v. 허락하다
application form 신청서　blueprint n. 청사진　notify v. 통지하다
submission n. 제출, 항복　further adj. 추가의; adv. 더 나아가

해석
16-18번은 다음 전화 메시지에 관한 문제입니다.
저는 도시 건축 위원회의 Eric Seymour입니다. [16]제과점의 두 번째 지점을 세우기 위한 허가를 신청하는 방법에 대한 귀하의 문의에 답변드립니다. 신청서는 저희 웹사이트에서 다운로드할 수 있습니다. [17]그런 다음 작성된 양식과 함께 건물 청사진을 저희 사무실에 제출하셔야 합니다. [18]귀하의 요청은 검토될 것이며, 제출 날짜부터 한 달 이내에 저희의 결정을 통지받으실 것입니다. 추가적인 질문이 있으시면, 언제든지 저에게 연락해 주십시오.

16 청자 문제
해석 청자는 누구일 것 같은가?
(A) 안전 검사관
(B) 사업주
(C) 웹 디자이너
(D) 금융 상담가

해설 지문에서 신분 및 직업과 관련된 표현을 놓치지 않고 듣는다. "I'm replying to your inquiry about how to apply for a permit to build a second branch of your bakery."라며 제과점의 두 번째 지점을 세우기 위한 허가를 신청하는 방법에 대한 귀하의 문의에 답변한다고 한 것을 통해 청자가 사업주임을 알 수 있다. 따라서 (B)가 정답이다.

어휘 safety inspector 안전 검사관　financial adj. 금융의
consultant n. 상담가, 컨설턴트

17 특정 세부 사항 문제
해석 청자는 무엇을 하도록 요구되는가?
(A) 사무실을 방문한다.
(B) 결정을 확인한다.
(C) 통지를 보낸다.
(D) 예약을 한다.

해설 질문의 핵심 어구(required to do)와 관련된 내용을 주의 깊게 듣는다. "You must then submit the completed form along with the building blueprints at our office."라며 작성된 양식과 함께 건물 청사진을 화자의 사무실에 제출해야 한다고 하였다. 따라서 (A)가 정답이다.

어휘 notification n. 통지

18 특정 세부 사항 문제
해석 화자에 따르면, 무엇이 완료되는 데 한 달이 걸릴 것인가?
(A) 안전 검사
(B) 비용 견적
(C) 건설 프로젝트
(D) 신청서 검토

해설 질문의 핵심 어구(one month)가 언급된 주변을 주의 깊게 듣는다. "Your request will be reviewed, and you'll be notified of our decision within one month of the submission date."라며 요청이 검토될 것이며, 제출 날짜부터 한 달 이내에 결정을 통지받을 것이라고 하였다. 따라서 (D)가 정답이다.

어휘 estimate n. 견적

[19-21] 미국
Questions 19-21 refer to the following excerpt from a meeting and product list.

[19]I'd like to begin with the recent focus group. We got a lot of useful input on our new line of makeup tables. Most participants felt that the model with one round mirror had a stylish design. [20]They also liked the one with three mirrors, but some said it was too expensive. We should reduce that model's price by 10 percent. [21]However, I'm concerned about one issue. Many participants pointed out that our packaging materials are not environmentally friendly. We'll need a plan to address this issue.

focus group 포커스 그룹(상품 개발 등에 대해 토의하는 소비자 그룹)
input n. 의견　concerned adj. 걱정하는　point out 지적하다
material n. 재료　address v. 해결하다, 다루다

해석
19-21번은 다음 회의 발췌와 제품 목록에 관한 문제입니다.
[19]저는 최근 포커스 그룹으로 이야기를 시작하고 싶습니다. 우리는 새로운 화장대 라인에 대한 여러 유용한 의견을 얻었습니다. 대부분의 참가자들은 하나의 둥근 거울이 있는 모델이 세련된 디자인을 가졌다고 느꼈습니다. [20]그들은 또한 세 개의 거울이 있는 것도 좋아했지만, 일부는 그것이 너무 비싸다고 말했습니다. 우리는 그 모델의 가격을 10퍼센트 인하해야 합니다. [21]하지만, 저는 한 가지 문제가 걱정됩니다. 많은 참가자들이 우리의 포장 재료가 환경 친화적이지 않다고 지적했습니다. 우리는 이 문제를 해결하기 위한 계획이 필요할 것입니다.

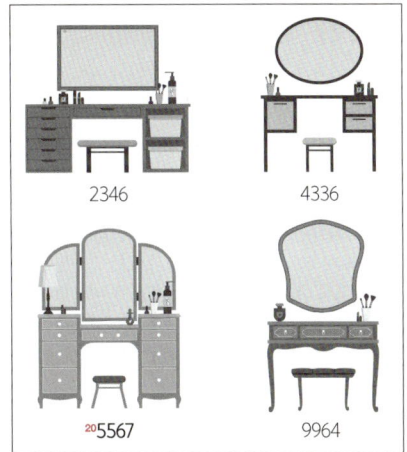

2346　4336
[20]5567　9964

19 주제 문제
해석 화자는 주로 무엇에 대해 이야기하는가?
(A) 포커스 그룹의 의견
(B) 고객으로부터의 문의
(C) 제품 라인의 판매
(D) 디자인 개선

해설 회의의 주제를 묻는 문제이므로, 지문의 초반을 반드시 듣는다. "I'd like to begin with the recent focus group. We got a lot of useful input on our new line of makeup tables."라며 최근 포커스 그룹으로 이야기를 시작하고 싶다고 한 후, 우리는 새로운 화장대 라인에 대한 여러 유용한 의견을 얻었다고 하였다. 따라서 (A)가 정답이다.

어휘 inquiry n. 문의　sale n. 판매　improvement n. 개선

20 시각 자료 문제
해석 시각 자료를 보아라. 어떤 모델의 가격이 인하될 것 같은가?

(A) 2346
(B) 4336
(C) 5567
(D) 9964

해설 제시된 제품 목록의 정보를 확인한 후 질문의 핵심 어구(be reduced in price)와 관련된 내용을 주의 깊게 듣는다. "They[participants] also liked the one with three mirrors, but some said it was too expensive. We should reduce that model's price by 10 percent."라며 참가자들이 세 개의 거울이 있는 것도 좋아했지만, 일부는 그것이 너무 비싸다고 말했다고 한 후, 그 모델의 가격을 10퍼센트 인하해야 한다고 하였으므로, 가격이 인하될 모델이 5567 모델임을 제품 목록에서 알 수 있다. 따라서 (C)가 정답이다.

21 문제점 문제

해설 화자는 무엇에 대해 걱정하는가?
(A) 포장 재료
(B) 배송 일정
(C) 생산 비용
(D) 마케팅 방법

해설 화자의 말에서 부정적인 표현이 언급된 다음을 주의 깊게 듣는다. "However, I'm concerned about one issue. Many participants pointed out that our packaging materials are not environmentally friendly."라며 한 가지 문제가 걱정된다고 한 후, 많은 참가자들이 우리의 포장 재료가 환경 친화적이지 않다고 지적했다고 하였다. 따라서 (A)가 정답이다.

어휘 method n. 방법

DAY 17 공지 및 관광 안내

1. 공지

담화 흐름과 빈출 문제 🎧 캐나다   p.124

해설 쇼핑객 여러분, 주목해 주십시오. Fresh 슈퍼마켓에 와 주셔서 감사합니다. 매장이 수리로 인해 5월 13일부터 16일까지 문을 닫을 것이라는 점을 알려드립니다. 저희는 농산물 구역 근처에 조제 식품 판매점을 설치할 것입니다. 불편에 사과드리며 매장의 변화가 모든 고객분들께 개선된 쇼핑 경험으로 이어지길 바랍니다. 5월 17일에 조제 식품 판매점의 개점을 축하하기 위해, 저희는 무료 샘플과 다음 방문 시 사용할 수 있는 쿠폰을 드릴 예정입니다. 고객 서비스 창구에 있는 저희 직원 중 한 명에게 쿠폰을 요청하시기 바랍니다.

어휘 renovation n. 수리, 개조   deli n. 조제 식품 판매점, 조제 식품
produce n. 농산물; v. 생산하다   section n. 구역   improve v. 개선하다
celebrate v. 축하하다, 기념하다   pick up ~을 받다, 구매하다

HACKERS PRACTICE   p.125

01 (B)   **02** (D)   **03** (C)   **04** (C)

[01-02] 🎧 미국 / 영국
Questions 01-02 refer to the following announcement.

⁰¹**Attention passengers on Flight 813 to Toronto. Due to a technical problem, your departure gate has been changed.** You will now be boarding at Gate 26 instead of Gate 18. If you have any questions, airport employees are available to assist you. ⁰²**Please proceed to the new gate immediately, as boarding will begin in just a few minutes.** Thank you for your cooperation.

passenger n. 승객   technical adj. 기술적인   departure n. 출발
gate n. 탑승구, 출입구   board v. 탑승하다, 타다   assist v. 돕다, 지원하다
proceed v. 이동하다, 진행하다   cooperation n. 협조

해설 01-02번은 다음 공지에 관한 문제입니다.

⁰¹토론토행 813편 승객 여러분께 안내드립니다. 기술적 문제로 인해, 출발 탑승구가 변경되었습니다. 이제 여러분은 18번 탑승구 대신 26번 탑승구에서 탑승하실 것입니다. 궁금한 점이 있으시면, 공항 직원이 여러분을 도와드릴 수 있습니다. ⁰²몇 분 후에 탑승이 시작될 예정이므로, 즉시 새로운 탑승구로 이동해 주시기 바랍니다. 협조해 주셔서 감사합니다.

01 장소 문제
해설 공지는 어디에서 이루어지고 있는가?
(A) 기차역에서
(B) 공항에서
(C) 호텔에서
(D) 쇼핑센터에서

해설 지문에서 장소와 관련된 표현을 놓치지 않고 듣는다. "Attention passengers on Flight 813 to Toronto. Due to a technical problem, your departure gate has been changed."라며 기술적 문제로 인해 토론토행 813편의 출발 탑승구가 변경되었다고 승객들에게 안내한 것을 통해 공지가 공항에서 이루어지고 있음을 알 수 있다. 따라서 (B)가 정답이다.

02 다음에 할 일 문제
해설 청자들은 다음에 무엇을 할 것 같은가?
(A) 무료 물품을 가지러 간다.
(B) 결제를 한다.
(C) 직원과 이야기한다.
(D) 다른 위치로 이동한다.

해설 지문의 마지막 부분을 주의 깊게 듣는다. "Please proceed to the new gate immediately, as boarding will begin in just a few minutes."라며 몇 분 후에 탑승이 시작될 예정이므로 즉시 새로운 탑승구로 이동해달라고 하였다. 따라서 (D)가 정답이다.

어휘 collect v. 가지러 가다, 모으다   complimentary adj. 무료의
payment n. 결제   location n. 위치, 장소

[Paraphrasing]
proceed to the new gate 새로운 탑승구로 이동하다 → Go to a different location 다른 위치로 이동한다

[03-04] 🎧 호주 / 캐나다
Questions 03-04 refer to the following announcement.

⁰³**I'd like to announce that a new bonus system will be implemented at our auto dealership.** Each time one of you sells a vehicle, you will receive a 1,000-dollar payment from the company. ⁰⁴**I know some of you are concerned about the very low number of customers these days.** But the company is planning to run several new TV commercials soon. These will likely lead to an increase in sales at our branch.

implement v. 시행하다   auto n. 자동차   dealership n. 대리점
payment n. 지급, 지불   concerned adj. 걱정하는   commercial n. 광고
branch n. 지점

해설 03-04번은 다음 공지에 관한 문제입니다.

⁰³우리 자동차 대리점에서 새로운 보너스 제도가 시행될 예정임을 알려드리고자 합니다. 여러분 중 한 분께서 자동차 한 대를 판매할 때마다, 회사로부터

1,000달러의 지급금을 받을 것입니다. ⁰⁴요즘 매우 적은 고객 수에 대해 몇몇 분들이 걱정하고 계신다는 것을 알고 있습니다. 하지만 회사에서 곧 여러 개의 새로운 TV 광고를 방영할 계획입니다. 이는 우리 지점의 매출 증가로 이어질 가능성이 높습니다.

03 목적 문제
해석 공지의 목적은 무엇인가?
(A) 채용 계획을 제시하기 위해
(B) 고객 서비스 제도를 설명하기 위해
(C) 인센티브 프로그램을 소개하기 위해
(D) 회사의 확장을 발표하기 위해

해설 공지의 목적을 묻는 문제이므로 지문의 초반을 반드시 듣는다. "I'd like to announce that a new bonus system will be implemented at our auto dealership."이라며 자동차 대리점에서 새로운 보너스 제도가 시행될 예정이라고 하였다. 따라서 (C)가 정답이다.

어휘 recruitment n. 채용   describe v. 설명하다, 묘사하다
customer service 고객 서비스   incentive n. 인센티브, 장려책
announce v. 발표하다   expansion n. 확장

> **Paraphrasing**
> bonus system 보너스 제도 → incentive program 인센티브 프로그램

04 문제점 문제
해석 화자는 어떤 걱정을 언급하는가?
(A) 판매 전략이 효과가 없다.
(B) 광고가 부정적인 의견을 받았다.
(C) 업체가 고객을 거의 끌어모으지 못했다.
(D) 보너스 지급이 지연될 것이다.

해설 남자의 말에서 부정적인 표현이 언급된 주변을 주의 깊게 듣는다. "I know some of you are concerned about the very low number of customers these days."라며 매우 적은 고객 수에 대해 요즘 몇몇 사람들이 걱정하고 있다는 것을 알고 있다고 하였다. 따라서 (C)가 정답이다.

어휘 strategy n. 전략   ineffective adj. 효과가 없는   negative adj. 부정적인
attract v. 끌어모으다   delay v. 지연시키다, 연기하다

> **Paraphrasing**
> the very low number of customers 매우 적은 고객 수 → has attracted few customers 고객을 거의 끌어모으지 못했다

2. 관광 안내

담화 흐름과 빈출 문제 🔊 미국   p.126

해석 안녕하세요, 여러분. 제가 오늘 오후 동안 여러분의 가이드가 될 것입니다. Glendale에서 사람들이 가장 많이 방문하는 곳 중 하나인, Arvada 밀랍 인형 박물관에 오신 것을 환영합니다. Arvada는 전 세계 유명인들의 동상 100여 개를 보유하고 있습니다. 그 동상들은 움직일 수 있고 말을 할 수 있게 하는 컴퓨터 기반의 기술이 장착되어 있습니다. 조각상들이 입고 있는 옷은 동상들이 나타내는 실제 인물들에게 제공받은 것이기 때문에 특별합니다. 관람을 시작하기 전에, 음식과 음료는 박물관 내에서 허용되지 않음을 다시 한 번 알려드립니다. 또한, 그 어떤 전시된 물품도 만지지 말아 주십시오. 좋습니다, 저를 따라오시면, A 전시장에서부터 출발하겠습니다.

어휘 wax n. 밀랍, 왁스   statue n. 동상, 조각상
computerized adj. 컴퓨터 기반의, 컴퓨터화된   technology n. 기술
actual adj. 실제의   represent v. 나타내다, 대표하다   beverage n. 음료

HACKERS PRACTICE   p.127
| 01 (B) | 02 (D) | 03 (D) | 04 (C) |

[01-02] 🔊 호주 / 캐나다
Questions 01-02 refer to the following talk.

> Welcome to the Gemstone Center. ⁰¹**Today, I will be showing you the exhibits** of mineral specimens at this facility. You will see gemstones such as rubies and sapphires from all over the world. And ⁰²**we have set up the displays so that you can get very close to the stones.** This makes it easier to see all of their unique features.
>
> gemstone n. 보석(의 원석)   exhibit n. 전시품, 전시   mineral n. 광물
> specimen n. 표본, 견본   feature n. 특징   set up 준비하다, 설치하다
> display n. 전시, 진열; v. 전시하다   unique adj. 고유한, 독특한
> feature n. 특징

해석
01-02번은 다음 담화에 관한 문제입니다.
Gemstone 센터에 오신 것을 환영합니다. ⁰¹오늘, 저는 여러분께 이 시설의 광물 표본 전시품들을 보여드릴 것입니다. 여러분은 전 세계에서 온 루비와 사파이어 같은 보석들을 보실 것입니다. 그리고 ⁰²저희는 여러분께서 보석에 매우 가까이 다가가실 수 있도록 전시를 준비했습니다. 이는 그것들의 모든 고유한 특징을 더 쉽게 볼 수 있게 합니다.

01 화자 문제
해석 화자는 누구일 것 같은가?
(A) 광산 기술자
(B) 관광 가이드
(C) 가게 점원
(D) 보석 분석가

해설 지문에서 신분 및 직업과 관련된 표현을 놓치지 않고 듣는다. "Today, I will be showing you the exhibits of mineral specimens at this facility."라며 오늘 이 시설의 광물 표본 전시품들을 보여줄 것이라고 한 것을 통해 화자가 관광 가이드임을 알 수 있다. 따라서 (B)가 정답이다.

어휘 mining adj. 광산의; n. 광업   engineer n. 기술자, 엔지니어
clerk n. 점원, 직원   analyst n. 분석가

02 특정 세부 사항 문제
해석 화자는 방문객들이 무엇을 할 수 있다고 말하는가?
(A) 제한된 구역에 들어간다.
(B) 짧은 설명을 듣는다.
(C) 보석이 깎이는 것을 관찰한다.
(D) 물건들을 가까이에서 살펴본다.

해설 질문의 핵심 어구(visitors can do)와 관련된 내용을 주의 깊게 듣는다. "we have set up the displays so that you can get very close to the stones"라며 보석에 매우 가까이 다가갈 수 있도록 전시를 준비했다고 하였다. 따라서 (D)가 정답이다.

어휘 access v. 들어가다, 접근하다   restricted adj. 제한된
presentation n. 설명, 발표

> **Paraphrasing**
> get very close to the stones 보석에 매우 가까이 다가가다 → Examine items closely 물건들을 가까이에서 살펴본다

[03-04] 🔊 영국 / 미국
Questions 03-04 refer to the following tour information.

> I hope all of you have enjoyed the tour so far. ⁰³**We've now arrived at our final destination, Porec Studio.** Paintings and sculptures by some of the country's most celebrated artists are on display here. Please note that ⁰⁴**the facility is currently undergoing renovations, so some rooms are inaccessible to the public.** For

your safety, please do not walk into these. Remember to stay with the group at all times as well.

so far 지금까지   destination n. 목적지   sculpture n. 조각품
celebrated adj. 유명한   on display 전시되어 있는   undergo v. 받다, 겪다
renovation n. 수리   inaccessible adj. 들어갈 수 없는, 접근할 수 없는

해석
03-04번은 다음 관광 안내에 관한 문제입니다.
지금까지 여러분 모두에게 즐거운 관광이 되셨기를 바랍니다. 03저희는 이제 최종 목적지인 Porec 스튜디오에 도착했습니다. 이곳에는 국내에서 가장 유명한 예술가들 중 몇 명의 그림과 조각품이 전시되어 있습니다. 04시설이 현재 수리 중이므로, 일부 전시실은 일반인이 들어갈 수 없다는 점을 유의해 주시길 바랍니다. 04여러분의 안전을 위해, 이곳에는 들어가지 마시길 바랍니다. 항상 그룹과 함께 계셔야 한다는 점 또한 기억해 주시길 바랍니다.

03 장소 문제
해석 청자들은 어디에 있는가?
(A) 공원에
(B) 극장에
(C) 도서관에
(D) 미술관에

해설 지문에서 장소와 관련된 표현을 놓치지 않고 듣는다. "We've now arrived at our final destination, Porec Studio. Paintings and sculptures by some of the country's most celebrated artists are on display here."라며 최종 목적지인 Porec 스튜디오에는 국내에서 가장 유명한 예술가들 중 몇 명의 그림과 조각품이 전시되어 있다고 한 것을 통해 청자들이 미술관에 있음을 알 수 있다. 따라서 (D)가 정답이다.

어휘 art gallery 미술관

04 특정 세부 사항 문제
해석 화자는 청자들에게 무엇을 하지 말라고 말하는가?
(A) 너무 크게 이야기한다.
(B) 사진을 찍는다.
(C) 특정 구역에 들어간다.
(D) 입구를 막는다.

해설 질문의 핵심 어구(not to do)와 관련된 내용을 주의 깊게 듣는다. "the facility is currently undergoing renovations, so some rooms are inaccessible to the public. For your safety, please do not walk into these."라며 시설이 현재 수리 중이므로 일부 전시실은 일반인이 들어갈 수 없다고 한 후, 안전을 위해 이곳에 들어가지 말라고 하였다. 따라서 (C)가 정답이다.

어휘 certain adj. 특정한   block v. 막다, 차단하다

HACKERS TEST p.128

01 (D)	02 (C)	03 (B)	04 (D)	05 (B)
06 (B)	07 (B)	08 (D)	09 (B)	10 (A)
11 (C)	12 (A)	13 (D)	14 (D)	15 (C)
16 (A)	17 (D)	18 (B)	19 (D)	20 (B)
21 (A)

[01-03] 영국
Questions 01-03 refer to the following announcement.

I have an important announcement. 01This month, five workers were injured by our factory's machines. To ensure we don't have any more accidents, 02the human resources team has just created a safety video. It is an hour long and covers a variety of topics. 03We will all watch it together during the safety workshop scheduled for Friday afternoon. Afterward, any questions you might have will be answered.

injure v. 부상을 입다   factory n. 공장   accident n. 사고
human resources team 인사팀   cover v. 다루다   a variety of 다양한
scheduled adj. 예정된

해석
01-03번은 다음 공지에 관한 문제입니다.
중요한 공지가 있습니다. 01이번 달에, 5명의 작업자가 우리 공장의 기계로 인해 부상을 입었습니다. 더 이상 어떠한 사고도 발생하지 않도록 하기 위해, 02인사팀이 이제 막 안전 영상을 제작하였습니다. 그것은 1시간짜리이며 다양한 주제를 다룹니다. 03우리는 모두 금요일 오후로 예정된 안전 워크숍 동안 그것을 함께 시청할 것입니다. 그 후에, 여러분들이 가질 수 있는 어떤 질문이든 답변해 드리겠습니다.

01 특정 세부 사항 문제
해석 화자에 따르면, 이번 달에 무슨 일이 일어났는가?
(A) 안전 검사
(B) 장비 고장
(C) 직원 회의
(D) 작업 사고

해설 질문의 핵심 어구(this month)가 언급된 주변을 주의 깊게 듣는다. "This month, five workers were injured by our factory's machines."라며 이번 달에 5명의 작업자가 공장의 기계로 인해 부상을 입었다고 하였다. 따라서 (D)가 정답이다.

어휘 inspection n. 검사   malfunction n. 고장; v. 제대로 작동하지 않다

02 특정 세부 사항 문제
해석 인사팀은 최근에 무엇을 했는가?
(A) 안내서를 수정했다.
(B) 정책을 변경했다.
(C) 영상을 제작했다.
(D) 일정을 업데이트했다.

해설 질문의 핵심 어구(human resources team)가 언급된 주변을 주의 깊게 듣는다. "the human resources team has just created a safety video"라며 인사팀이 이제 막 안전 영상을 제작했다고 하였다. 따라서 (C)가 정답이다.

어휘 produce v. (영화·연극 등을) 제작하다

Paraphrasing
created a ~ video 영상을 제작했다 → Produced a video 영상을 제작했다

03 다음에 할 일 문제
해석 금요일 오후에 무슨 일이 일어날 것인가?
(A) 이사회 회의
(B) 교육 시간
(C) 시설 보수
(D) 공장 견학

해설 질문의 핵심 어구(Friday afternoon)가 언급된 주변을 주의 깊게 듣는다. "We will all watch it[safety video] together during the safety workshop scheduled for Friday afternoon."이며 금요일 오후로 예정된 안전 워크숍 동안 안전 영상을 함께 시청할 것이라고 하였다. 따라서 (B)가 정답이다.

어휘 board n. 이사회

[04-06] 미국
Questions 04-06 refer to the following announcement.

> **04Good evening, Montcalm Resort guests.** A pair of snow goggles has been found in the lobby. If you believe you are the owner of this item, **05please proceed to the lost-and-found desk, which is located on the second floor next to the ski rental shop.** **06In order to prove that you are the owner, you must give a brief description of the item.** For example, you should be able to state the color of the item and the brand name.

snow goggles 스키용 고글   owner n. 주인   prove v. 증명하다, 입증하다
lost-and-found 분실물 보관소   description n. 묘사, 설명   state v. 말하다

해석
04-06번은 다음 공지에 관한 문제입니다.
04안녕하세요, Montcalm 리조트의 손님 여러분. 스키용 고글 한 개가 로비에서 발견되었습니다. 만약 이 제품의 주인이라고 생각되신다면, 052층 스키 대여점 옆에 위치한 분실물 보관소 데스크로 가시기 바랍니다. 06당신이 주인이라는 것을 증명하기 위해서, 이 물건에 대한 간단한 묘사를 해 주셔야 합니다. 예를 들어, 물건의 색상과 상표명을 말씀해 주실 수 있어야 합니다.

04 청자 문제
해석 청자들은 누구인 것 같은가?
(A) 식당 고객들
(B) 행사 참석자들
(C) 비행기 승객들
(D) 리조트 손님들

해설 지문에서 신분 및 직업과 관련된 표현을 놓치지 않고 듣는다. "Good evening, Montcalm Resort guests."라며 Montcalm 리조트의 손님들에게 인사한 것을 통해 청자들은 리조트 손님들임을 알 수 있다. 따라서 (D)가 정답이다.

어휘 attendee n. 참석자

05 특정 세부 사항 문제
해석 2층에 무엇이 위치해 있는가?
(A) 식당
(B) 대여점
(C) 매표소
(D) 휴게실

해설 질문의 핵심 어구(on the second floor)가 언급된 주변을 주의 깊게 듣는다. "please proceed to the lost-and-found desk, which is located on the second floor next to the ski rental shop"이라며 2층 스키 대여점 옆에 위치한 분실물 보관소 데스크로 가라고 하였다. 따라서 (B)가 정답이다.

06 요청 문제
해석 분실물의 주인은 무엇을 하도록 요청받는가?
(A) 연락처를 제공한다.
(B) 묘사를 한다.
(C) 영수증을 제출한다.
(D) 사진이 부착된 신분증을 보여준다.

해설 지문에서 요청과 관련된 표현이 포함된 문장을 주의 깊게 듣는다. "In order to prove that you are the owner, you must give a brief description of the item."이라며 주인이라는 것을 증명하기 위해서, 물건에 대한 간단한 묘사를 해야 한다고 하였다. 따라서 (B)가 정답이다.

어휘 contact information 연락처   photo identification 사진이 부착된 신분증

[07-09] 캐나다
Questions 07-09 refer to the following talk.

> My name is Richard White, and I'll be your guide throughout your tour of the Huffington Science Museum. This month, the museum has a very special exhibit entitled Life of Dinosaurs. **07The exhibition is unique because it showcases a rare collection of fossils.** Today's tour has attracted a lot of interest. **08I don't want to cause any inconvenience for the other visitors, so as I show you around, please try to avoid blocking the walkways.** Now, let's make our way to the exhibit's first display, and **09please remember that taking pictures isn't allowed inside the facility.**

entitle v. ~라는 제목을 붙이다   rare adj. 희귀한, 드문   collection n. 수집품
fossil n. 화석   walkway n. 통로

해석
07-09번은 다음 담화에 관한 문제입니다.
제 이름은 Richard White이고, 저는 Huffington 과학 박물관을 투어하는 내내 여러분의 가이드가 되어 드릴 것입니다. 이번 달에, 박물관에서 '공룡들의 삶'이라는 제목의 굉장히 특별한 전시회를 엽니다. 07이 전시회는 희귀한 화석 수집품을 전시하기 때문에 특별합니다. 오늘 투어는 많은 관심을 끌었습니다. 08저는 다른 방문객들에게 어떤 불편도 끼치고 싶지 않기 때문에, 제가 여러분을 안내할 때, 통로를 막지 않도록 해 주세요. 이제, 전시회의 첫 번째 전시품을 보기 위해 출발하겠습니다. 그리고 09시설 내부에서는 사진 촬영이 허용되지 않는다는 것을 기억해 주시기 바랍니다.

07 언급 문제
해석 화자는 전시회에 관해 무엇을 말하는가?
(A) 본관 층에 위치해 있다.
(B) 희귀한 화석들을 포함하고 있다.
(C) 곧 준비가 완료될 것이다.
(D) 새로운 기술에 관한 것이다.

해설 질문의 핵심 어구(exhibit)와 관련된 내용을 주의 깊게 듣는다. "The exhibition is unique because it showcases a rare collection of fossils."라며 이 전시회는 희귀한 화석 수집품을 전시하기 때문에 특별하다고 하였다. 따라서 (B)가 정답이다.

어휘 be located on ~에 위치하다   include v. 포함하다
complete v. 준비를 완료하다, 끝마치다   technology n. 기술

08 의도 파악 문제
해석 화자가 "오늘 투어는 많은 관심을 끌었습니다"라고 말할 때 무엇을 의도하는가?
(A) 활동이 지연될 것이다.
(B) 특별 행사가 계획되어 있다.
(C) 투어가 한 번 더 실시될 것이다.
(D) 공간이 붐빌 것이다.

해설 질문의 인용어구(Today's tour has attracted a lot of interest)가 언급된 주변을 주의 깊게 듣는다. 화자가 "I don't want to cause any inconvenience for the other visitors, so as I show you around, please try to avoid blocking the walkways."라며 다른 방문객들에게 어떤 불편도 끼치고 싶지 않기 때문에 자신이 안내할 때 통로를 막지 않도록 해 달라고 한 것을 통해 공간이 붐빌 것임을 알 수 있다. 따라서 (D)가 정답이다.

어휘 crowded adj. 붐비는

09 특정 세부 사항 문제
해석 화자에 따르면, 무엇이 허용되지 않는가?
(A) 전시품 만지기

(B) 사진 찍기
(C) 전시품 근처에서 먹기
(D) 배낭 가져오기

해설 질문의 핵심 어구(not allowed)가 언급된 주변을 주의 깊게 듣는다. "please remember that taking pictures isn't allowed inside the facility"라며 시설 내부에서는 사진 촬영이 허용되지 않는다는 것을 기억해 달라고 하였다. 따라서 (B)가 정답이다.

어휘 backpack n. 배낭

Paraphrasing
taking pictures 사진 촬영 → Taking photographs 사진 찍기

[10-12] 영국
Questions 10-12 refer to the following announcement.

> Thank you for using the Gilmore City Subway system. Did you know you can save 20 percent on transit fees by signing up for a monthly pass? ¹⁰**You can also claim the cost of your pass on your annual tax return, which may reduce the amount of taxes you owe.** And ¹¹**anyone who purchases a transit pass this month will get 30 percent off.** ¹²**To purchase one, simply download and install the Gilmore Transit mobile app and then follow the instructions.**
>
> transit fee 교통비 sign up 신청하다 monthly pass 한 달 정기권
> claim v. 청구하다, 신청하다 tax return 소득세 신고
> owe v. 지불할 의무가 있다

해석
10-12번은 다음 공지에 관한 문제입니다.
Gilmore시 지하철 시스템을 이용해 주셔서 감사합니다. 한 달 정기권을 신청하면 교통비를 20퍼센트 절약할 수 있다는 것을 알고 계셨나요? ¹⁰여러분은 또한 연간 소득세 신고 시 정기권 비용을 청구할 수 있는데, 이는 당신이 납부해야 하는 세금을 줄여줄 수 있습니다. 그리고 ¹¹이번 달에 대중교통 정기권을 구입하시는 분들은 30퍼센트의 할인을 받을 것입니다. ¹²대중교통 정기권을 구매하려면, 그저 Gilmore 교통 모바일 앱을 다운로드하고 설치한 다음 지시 사항을 따르세요.

10 언급 문제
해설 화자는 정기권에 대해 무엇을 말하는가?
(A) 세금 혜택을 제공한다.
(B) 자동으로 갱신된다.
(C) 모든 교통 시스템에서 쓰일 수 있다.
(D) 역 직원에게 보여야 한다.

해설 질문의 핵심 어구(pass)가 언급된 주변을 주의 깊게 듣는다. "You can ~ claim the cost of your pass on your annual tax return, which may reduce the amount of taxes you owe."라며 연간 소득세 신고 시 정기권 비용을 청구할 수 있는데, 이는 납부해야 하는 세금을 줄여줄 수 있다고 하였다. 따라서 (A)가 정답이다.

어휘 renew v. 갱신되다, 재개하다 automatically adv. 자동으로
benefit n. 혜택

11 특정 세부 사항 문제
해설 청자들은 이번 달에 구매를 하면 무엇을 받을 수 있는가?
(A) 일일권
(B) 교통 지도
(C) 추가 할인
(D) 시설 회원권

해설 질문의 핵심 어구(make a purchase this month)와 관련된 내용을 주의 깊게 듣는다. "anyone who purchases ~ this month will get 30 percent off"라며 이번 달에 구입한 사람들은 30퍼센트의 할인을 받을

것이라고 하였다. 따라서 (C)가 정답이다.

어휘 receive v. 받다, 받아들이다 facility n. 시설, 설비

12 방법 문제
해설 청자들은 어떻게 정기권을 구매할 수 있는가?
(A) 애플리케이션을 설치함으로써
(B) 매표소를 방문함으로써
(C) 상담 전화를 함으로써
(D) 양식을 다운로드함으로써

해설 질문의 핵심 어구(buy a pass)와 관련된 내용을 주의 깊게 듣는다. "To purchase one[transit pass], simply download and install the Gilmore Transit mobile app and then follow the instructions."라며 대중교통 이용권을 구입하려면 Gilmore 교통 모바일 앱을 다운로드하고 설치한 다음 지시 사항을 따르라고 하였다. 따라서 (A)가 정답이다.

어휘 ticket counter 매표소 hotline n. 상담 전화 form n. 양식

[13-15] 캐나다
Questions 13-15 refer to the following talk.

> ¹³**We'd like to inform everyone that Eurasia Travel will be introducing nine new destinations** around Europe next year. In addition, ¹⁴**we will be upgrading our ships. The goal is to include better amenities for our passengers. You will be able to explore the night sky using telescopes.** We will also add poolside movie screens and new restaurants. ¹⁵**Visit our Web site for more information on the cost of tickets.** Thanks for your attention, and enjoy your cruise.
>
> destination n. 여행지 explore v. 탐험하다, 답사하다

해석
13-15번은 다음 담화에 관한 문제입니다.
¹³Eurasia 여행사는 내년에 유럽 전역에 9개의 새로운 여행지를 도입할 예정임을 모든 분들께 알려드립니다. 더불어, ¹⁴저희는 선박을 업그레이드할 것입니다. 목표는 승객들을 위한 더 나은 편의 시설을 갖추는 것입니다. 여러분께서는 망원경을 이용하여 밤하늘을 탐험하실 수 있게 될 것입니다. 저희는 또한 수영장 옆에 영화 스크린과 새로운 식당을 추가할 것입니다. ¹⁵표의 가격에 관한 더 많은 정보를 위해서는 저희 웹사이트를 방문해주시기 바랍니다. 관심 가져 주셔서 감사드리며, 즐거운 유람선 여행이 되길 바랍니다.

13 목적 문제
해설 담화의 주된 목적은 무엇인가?
(A) 지연에 관한 세부 사항을 알리기 위해
(B) 특별 행사를 홍보하기 위해
(C) 경로 정보를 제공하기 위해
(D) 향후 서비스를 알리기 위해

해설 담화의 목적을 묻는 문제이므로, 지문의 초반을 반드시 듣는다. "We'd like to inform everyone that Eurasia Travel will be introducing nine new destinations"라며 Eurasia 여행사가 9개의 새로운 여행지를 도입할 예정임을 모든 분들께 알린다고 한 후, 선박이 어떻게 업그레이드될 것인지에 대한 내용으로 지문이 이어지고 있다. 따라서 (D)가 정답이다.

어휘 detail n. 세부 사항 promote v. 홍보하다 route n. 경로

14 특정 세부 사항 문제
해설 화자에 따르면, 무엇이 업그레이드된 선박에 추가될 것인가?
(A) 콘서트홀
(B) 스포츠 활동을 위한 장비
(C) 어린이 놀이터
(D) 하늘을 관찰하기 위한 장치

해설 질문의 핵심 어구(added to the upgraded ships)와 관련된 내용을 주의 깊게 듣는다. "we will be upgrading our ships. ~ You will be able to explore the night sky using telescopes."라며 선박을 업그레이드 할 것이며, 망원경을 이용하여 밤하늘을 탐험할 수 있게 될 것이라고 하였다. 따라서 (D)가 정답이다.

어휘 observe v. 관찰하다

15 특정 세부 사항 문제

해설 온라인에서 어떤 정보를 찾을 수 있는가?
(A) 출발 날짜
(B) 식당 메뉴
(C) 표 가격
(D) 구인 목록

해설 질문의 핵심 어구(information ~ online)와 관련된 내용을 주의 깊게 듣는다. "Visit our Web site for more information on the cost of tickets."라며 표의 가격에 관한 더 많은 정보를 위해서는 웹사이트를 방문해 달라고 하였다. 따라서 (C)가 정답이다.

어휘 departure n. 출발, 떠남 listing n. 목록, 기재

> Paraphrasing
> cost of tickets 표의 가격 → Ticket prices 표 가격

[16-18] 미국

Questions 16-18 refer to the following announcement.

> Excuse me, everybody, ¹⁶I've got some news about our next company retreat. On Friday, we will be going to Grover County Park. Buses will take everyone to the park at 9:30 A.M., and ¹⁷we will begin with an hour-long nature walk. So be sure to wear comfortable clothing. Then, ¹⁸we'll enjoy lunch prepared by Deli Delights and listen to speeches by the department heads. After that, you'll be divided into teams for some group games. The goal is to give everyone a chance to learn more about their colleagues.

retreat n. 야유회 hour-long adj. 한 시간 동안의
nature walk 자연 관찰 산책 divide into ~으로 나누다 colleague n. 동료

해설
16-18번은 다음 공지에 관한 문제입니다.

실례합니다, 여러분, ¹⁶저는 우리의 다음번 회사 야유회에 관한 몇 가지 소식이 있습니다. 금요일에, 우리는 Grover County 공원으로 갈 것입니다. 버스가 오전 9시 30분에 모두를 공원으로 데려다 줄 것이고, ¹⁷우리는 한 시간 동안의 자연 관찰 산책으로 시작할 것입니다. 그러므로 반드시 편안한 옷을 입어 주십시오. 그리고 나서, ¹⁸우리는 Deli Delights사에서 준비한 점심을 먹고 부서장들의 연설을 들을 것입니다. 그 후에, 여러분은 몇 가지 단체 게임을 위해 팀으로 나뉠 것입니다. 목표는 모두에게 동료들에 대해 더 알 수 있는 기회를 주는 것입니다.

16 주제 문제

해설 공지는 주로 무엇에 대한 것인가?
(A) 회사 야유회
(B) 지역 축제
(C) 개장식
(D) 자선 모금 행사

해설 공지의 주제를 묻는 문제이므로, 지문의 초반을 반드시 듣는다. "I've got some news about our next company retreat."라며 다음번 회사 야유회에 관한 몇 가지 소식이 있다고 한 후, 회사 야유회에 대한 구체적인 내용으로 지문이 이어지고 있다. 따라서 (A)가 정답이다.

어휘 opening n. 개장식 charity n. 자선 fundraiser n. 모금 행사

17 이유 문제

해설 화자는 왜 청자들에게 편안하게 옷을 입으라고 말하는가?
(A) 경주에 참가할 것이다.
(B) 건축 현장을 방문할 것이다.
(C) 공원을 청소할 것이다.
(D) 산책을 갈 것이다.

해설 질문의 핵심 어구(dress comfortably)와 관련된 내용을 주의 깊게 듣는다. "we will begin with an hour-long nature walk. So be sure to wear comfortable clothing."이라며 한 시간 동안의 자연 관찰 산책으로 시작할 것이므로 반드시 편안한 옷을 입어 달라고 하였다. 따라서 (D)가 정답이다.

어휘 go for a walk 산책을 가다

18 특정 세부 사항 문제

해설 청자들은 연설 후에 무엇을 할 것인가?
(A) 점심시간을 가진다.
(B) 그룹으로 나누어진다.
(C) 직장으로 돌아간다.
(D) 주최자를 만난다.

해설 질문의 핵심 어구(after ~ speeches)와 관련된 내용을 주의 깊게 듣는다. "we'll ~ listen to speeches ~. After that, you'll be divided into teams for some group games."라며 연설을 들을 것이며, 그 후에 단체 게임을 위해 팀으로 나뉠 것이라고 하였다. 따라서 (B)가 정답이다.

어휘 break up into ~으로 나누어지다, 분리되다 organizer n. 주최자

> Paraphrasing
> be divided into teams 팀으로 나뉘다 → Break up into groups 그룹으로 나누어진다

[19-21] 호주

Questions 19-21 refer to the following tour information and schedule.

> ¹⁹Before we begin, please put on one of these protective helmets. They reduce the risk of injury. Our tour starts at the assembly line. This is where you will see how the drones our company produces are put together. ²⁰And you will get to meet Mr. Walton, who is in charge of this entire facility. He will be waiting for us in the testing area. ²¹When the tour is over, I will give each of you a 25-dollar gift certificate, and you can use it to purchase any Bezel product. Thank you very much for taking an interest in our company.

protective adj. 보호용 risk n. 위험 injury n. 부상 assembly n. 조립
put together ~을 조립하다 in charge of ~을 담당하는 facility n. 시설
gift certificate 상품권

해설
19-21번은 다음 관광 안내와 일정표에 관한 문제입니다.

¹⁹시작하기 전에, 이 보호 헬멧 중 하나를 착용해 주세요. 그것들은 부상의 위험을 줄입니다. 우리 견학은 조립 라인에서 시작할 것입니다. 이곳은 여러분이 우리 회사가 생산하는 드론이 어떻게 조립되는지 볼 수 있는 곳입니다. ²⁰그리고 이 시설 전체를 담당하는 Mr. Walton을 만나게 될 것입니다. 그는 시험 구역에서 우리를 기다리고 있을 것입니다. ²¹견학이 끝나면, 저는 여러분 각자에게 25달러 상품권을 드릴 것이며, 여러분은 그것을 Bezel 제품을 구매하는 데 사용하실 수 있습니다. 우리 회사에 관심을 가져 주셔서 대단히 감사합니다.

Bezel 드론 공장 견학 일정표	
조립 구역	오후 1시 30분
시험 구역	²⁰오후 2시
포장 구역	오후 2시 30분
배송 구역	오후 3시

19 요청 문제

해석 화자는 청자들에게 무엇을 하라고 요청하는가?
  (A) 부상을 보고한다.
  (B) 양식을 작성한다.
  (C) 신분증을 착용한다.
  (D) 안전 장비를 착용한다.

해설 지문에서 요청과 관련된 표현이 언급된 다음을 주의 깊게 듣는다. "Before we begin, please put on one of these protective helmets."라며 시작하기 전에 보호 헬멧 중 하나를 착용해 달라고 하였다. 따라서 (D)가 정답이다.

어휘 report v. 보고하다 ID badge 신분증 gear n. 장비

20 시각 자료 문제

해석 시각 자료를 보아라. 청자들은 언제 Mr. Walton을 만날 것인가?
  (A) 오후 1시 30분에
  (B) 오후 2시에
  (C) 오후 2시 30분에
  (D) 오후 3시에

해설 제시된 일정표의 정보를 확인한 후 질문의 핵심 어구(meet Mr. Walton)가 언급된 주변을 주의 깊게 듣는다. "And you will get to meet Mr. Walton, who is in charge of this entire facility. He will be waiting for us in the testing area."라며 시설 전체를 담당하는 Mr. Walton을 만나게 될 것이라고 한 후, 그가 시험 구역에서 우리를 기다리고 있을 것이라고 했으므로, 청자들이 오후 2시에 Mr. Walton을 만날 것임을 일정표에서 알 수 있다. 따라서 (B)가 정답이다

21 특정 세부 사항 문제

해석 화자는 청자들에게 무엇을 줄 것인가?
  (A) 상품권
  (B) 견본품
  (C) 카탈로그
  (D) 지도

해설 질문의 핵심 어구(give)가 언급된 주변을 주의 깊게 듣는다. "When the tour is over, I will give each of you a 25-dollar gift certificate"라며 견학이 끝나면 각자에게 25달러 상품권을 줄 것이라고 하였다. 따라서 (A)가 정답이다.

어휘 voucher n. 상품권

Paraphrasing
gift certificate 상품권 → voucher 상품권

DAY 18 연설 및 강연

1. 연설

담화 흐름과 빈출 문제 🎧 미국   p.130

해설 여러분, 환영합니다. 오늘 여러분의 신입 교육의 일환으로, 각기 다른 생산 단계들을 보여드리기 위해 우리 아이스크림 공장을 견학시켜 드리겠습니다. 그러나 먼저, 저는 아이스크림을 제조할 때 반드시 지켜야 할 몇 가지 중요한 원칙들에 대해 이야기하고자 합니다. 우리는 우리 완제품의 안전과 품질을 보장하기 위해 식품안전청의 공정 지침을 따릅니다. 이에 따라, 보관용 용기와 냉장고를 포함하여 사용되는 장비는 소독되어야 합니다. 이제, 공장을 안내해 드리겠습니다.

어휘 principle n. 원칙, 원리 sanitize v. 소독하다

HACKERS PRACTICE   p.131

01 (C) **02** (A) **03** (D) **04** (A)

[01-02] 🎧 호주 / 캐나다
Questions 01-02 refer to the following speech.

⁰¹Thank you for gathering for this party tonight. It has been another successful year for Grandforth Hotels. Occupancy rates are up 20 percent from last year. Not to mention, our Havana branch, which just opened this spring, has received over 1,000 positive reviews. I especially want to acknowledge the contributions of our head of marketing, Clara Snow. ⁰²She will now give a short speech.

gather v. (사람들이) 모이다 successful adj. 성공적인
occupancy n. (호텔·비행기 등의) 점유(이용)율 acknowledge v. 인정하다
contribution n. 공헌

해석
01-02번은 다음 연설에 관한 문제입니다.
⁰¹오늘 밤 이 파티에 모여주셔서 감사합니다. 올해는 Grandforth 호텔에게 또 한 번의 성공적인 한 해였습니다. 점유율은 작년보다 20퍼센트 증가했습니다. 말할 것도 없이, 이번 봄에 이제 막 개장한 우리의 Havana 지점은 1,000건이 넘는 긍정적인 후기를 받았습니다. 저는 특히 마케팅 책임자 Clara Snow의 공헌을 인정하고 싶습니다. ⁰²이제 그녀가 짧은 연설을 할 것입니다.

01 목적 문제

해석 행사의 목적은 무엇인가?
  (A) 신입 직원을 교육하기 위해
  (B) 새로운 호텔 지점을 개설하기 위해
  (C) 회사의 성공을 축하하기 위해
  (D) 직원의 승진을 발표하기 위해

해설 행사의 목적을 묻는 문제이므로, 지문의 초반을 주의 깊게 듣는다. "Thank you for gathering for this party tonight. It has been another successful year for Grandforth Hotels."라며 파티에 모여줘서 감사하다고 한 후, Grandforth 호텔이 성공적인 한 해를 보냈다고 하였다. 따라서 (C)가 정답이다.

어휘 celebrate v. 축하하다 promotion n. 승진

Paraphrasing
another successful year for ~ Hotels 호텔에게 또 한 번의 성공적인 한 해 → the company's success 회사의 성공

02 다음에 할 일 문제

해석 Clara Snow는 다음에 무엇을 할 것 같은가?
  (A) 연설을 한다.
  (B) 시범을 보여준다.
  (C) 수상자를 발표한다.
  (D) 장치를 설치한다.

해설 질문의 핵심 어구(do next)와 관련된 내용을 주의 깊게 듣는다. "She[Clara Snow] will now give a short speech."라며 이제 Clara Snow가 짧은 연설을 할 것이라고 하였다. 따라서 (A)가 정답이다.

어휘 demonstration n. 시범, 시연 device n. 장치

Paraphrasing
give a ~ speech 연설을 하다 → Make a speech 연설을 한다

[03-04] 영국 / 미국
Questions 03-04 refer to the following talk.

> ⁰³I'd like to welcome you to Rosewood Corporation's monthly board meeting. This morning, we are going to hear updates on current building projects from our department heads. Also, next month will be our staff awards dinner, and I'd like to find out which of you will be attending. ⁰⁴I am going to pass out a form for you to confirm attendance. OK, let's start with a report on the Berlin Towers project from Sue Ling.

어휘 corporation n. 회사, 기업 monthly adj. 월례의; adv. 한 달에 한 번
board meeting 이사회 회의 current adj. 현재의 department n. 부서
form n. 양식 confirm v. 확인하다 attendance n. 참석, 출석
report n. 보고

해석
03-04번은 다음 담화에 관한 문제입니다.

⁰³Rosewood사의 월례 이사회 회의에 오신 것을 환영합니다. 오늘 아침에는, 부서 책임자들로부터 현재 건설 프로젝트에 대한 최신 정보를 들을 것입니다. 또한, 다음 달에는 직원 시상식 만찬이 예정되어 있는데, 여러분 중 어떤 분이 참석하실 것인지 알고 싶습니다. ⁰⁴참석 여부를 확인하기 위한 양식을 나눠드리겠습니다. 그럼, Berlin Towers 프로젝트에 관한 Sue Ling의 보고로 시작하겠습니다.

03 장소 문제
해석 청자들은 어디에 있는 것 같은가?
(A) 시상식에
(B) 은퇴 기념 파티에
(C) 직원 오리엔테이션에
(D) 이사회 회의에

해설 지문에서 장소와 관련된 표현을 놓치지 않고 듣는다. "I'd like to welcome you to Rosewood Corporation's monthly board meeting."이라며 Rosewood사의 월례 이사회에 온 것을 환영한다고 한 것을 통해 청자들이 있는 장소는 이사회 회의임을 알 수 있다. 따라서 (D)가 정답이다.

어휘 awards ceremony 시상식 retirement n. 은퇴, 퇴직
orientation n. 오리엔테이션, 예비 교육

04 이유 문제
해석 화자는 왜 양식을 나눠 줄 것인가?
(A) 참석 여부를 확인하기 위해
(B) 의견을 모으기 위해
(C) 회원권을 만들기 위해
(D) 약속 일정을 잡기 위해

해설 질문의 핵심 어구(pass out a form)가 언급된 주변을 주의 깊게 듣는다. "I am going to pass out a form for you to confirm attendance."라며 참석 여부를 확인할 수 있게 양식을 나눠줄 거라고 하였다. 따라서 (A)가 정답이다.

어휘 appointment n. 약속, 예약

2. 강연

담화 흐름과 빈출 문제 호주   p.132

해석 안녕하세요. 저희 투자 회사에서 휴가를 신청하는 절차를 방금 변경해서, 저는 여러분이 무엇을 하셔야 하는지에 대해 설명하고자 합니다. 더 이상 상사에게 휴가를 요청하는 이메일을 보내지 마십시오. 대신, 회사의 인트라넷 시스템을 사용하여 온라인 요청 양식을 작성하십시오. 이는 승인 또는 거절되기 전에 인사부 책임자인 David Reynolds에 의해 검토될 것입니다. 결정은 2영업일 이내에 이루어질 것입니다. 요청서 제출에 문제가 있으시다면, 안내를 위해 직원 안내서를 참고하시기 바랍니다.

어휘 request v. 신청하다; n. 신청서 leave n. 휴가 investment n. 투자
supervisor n. 상사, 상관 approve v. 승인하다 reject v. 거절하다
business day 영업일 guidance n. 안내

HACKERS PRACTICE   p.133

01 (B)   **02** (C)   **03** (A)   **04** (D)

[01-02] 영국 / 미국
Questions 01-02 refer to the following talk.

> ⁰¹Today, I'll show you how to take better photos of food. It's best to take them near a window where there's plenty of natural light. Avoid using a flash, as it can change the food's color. ⁰²If you send me your photos afterward, I'll give you detailed feedback on how to take better ones next time. You can do this through the photography app we used last week. I look forward to seeing your work.

plenty of 많은 natural light 자연광 avoid v. ~하지 않도록 하다, 피하다
afterward adv. 나중에 detailed adj. 자세한, 상세한

해석
01-02번은 다음 담화에 관한 문제입니다.

⁰¹오늘, 여러분들에게 더 좋은 음식 사진을 찍는 방법을 보여드리겠습니다. 자연광이 많은 창가 근처에서 찍는 것이 가장 좋습니다. 플래시는 음식의 색을 바꿀 수 있으므로 사용하지 않도록 해주세요. ⁰²나중에 여러분의 사진을 저에게 보내주시면, 다음에 더 좋은 사진을 찍는 방법에 대해 자세한 의견을 드리겠습니다. 지난주에 사용한 사진 앱을 통해 이것을 하실 수 있습니다. 여러분의 작품을 기대하고 있습니다.

01 주제 문제
해석 화자는 어떤 종류의 사진에 대해 이야기하고 있는가?
(A) 인물 사진
(B) 음식
(C) 풍경
(D) 여행

해설 담화의 주제를 묻는 문제이므로, 지문의 초반을 반드시 듣는다. "Today, I'll show you how to take better photos of food."라며 오늘은 더 좋은 음식 사진을 찍는 방법을 보여준다고 한 후, 음식 사진을 잘 찍는 방법에 대한 내용으로 이어지고 있다. 따라서 (B)가 정답이다.

어휘 portrait n. 인물 사진, 초상화 landscape n. 풍경

02 특정 세부 사항 문제
해석 청자들이 의견을 원한다면 무엇을 해야 하는가?
(A) 그들의 사진을 인화한다.
(B) 수업에 참여한다.
(C) 모바일 앱을 사용한다.
(D) 화자에게 전화한다.

해설 질문의 핵심 어구(feedback)가 언급된 주변을 주의 깊게 듣는다. "If you send me your photos afterward, I'll give you detailed feedback on how to take better ones next time. You can do this through the photography app"이라며 자신에게 사진을 보내주면 다음에 더 좋은 사진을 찍는 방법에 대한 자세한 의견을 줄 것인데, 이것은 사진 앱을 통해서 할 수 있다고 하였다. 따라서 (C)가 정답이다.

어휘 print a photo 사진을 인화하다

[Paraphrasing]
photography app 사진 앱 → mobile app 모바일 앱

[03-04] 캐나다 / 호주
Questions 03-04 refer to the following instructions.

⁰³In order to identify areas for improvement, we need to document every step of our manufacturing process. The goal is to improve efficiency and increase productivity. We will need to gather and analyze lots of data, both manually and through the use of cameras. ⁰⁴I've broken the project down into different tasks that are assigned to individual members of the team. You'll see this information now if you look up at the screen.

identify v. 확인하다, 알아보다 improvement n. 개선
document v. 기록하다, 서류로 입증하다 manufacturing n. 제조(업)
process n. 공정, 과정 efficiency n. 효율성 productivity n. 생산성
gather v. 수집하다, 모으다 analyze v. 분석하다 manually adv. 수동으로
break ~ down ~을 분류하다, 나누다 task n. 작업, 과제
assign v. 할당하다, 배정하다 individual adj. 개별의, 개인의

해석
03-04번은 다음 설명에 관한 문제입니다.

⁰³개선이 필요한 영역을 확인하기 위해, 우리는 제조 공정의 모든 단계를 기록해야 합니다. 목표는 효율성을 개선하고 생산성을 높이는 것입니다. 우리는 수동으로 그리고 카메라 사용을 통해, 많은 데이터를 수집하고 분석해야 할 것입니다. ⁰⁴이 프로젝트를 팀의 개별 구성원들에게 할당된 여러 가지 작업으로 분류했습니다. 지금 화면을 보시면 이 정보를 확인하실 수 있습니다.

03 주제 문제
해석 무엇이 주로 논의되고 있는가?
(A) 공정 기록
(B) 직원 교육
(C) 생산 일정 관리
(D) 공장 이전

해설 설명의 주제를 묻고 있으므로 지문의 초반을 반드시 듣는다. "In order to identify areas for improvement, we need to document every step of our manufacturing process."라며 개선이 필요한 영역을 확인하기 위해 제조 공정의 모든 단계를 기록해야 한다고 한 후, 공정의 기록에 대한 내용으로 지문이 이어지고 있다. 따라서 (A)가 정답이다.

어휘 relocate v. 이전하다 factory n. 공장

04 특정 세부 사항 문제
해석 청자는 화면을 봄으로써 무엇을 알 수 있는가?
(A) 회사의 목표
(B) 절차의 단계
(C) 그룹 프로젝트의 일정표
(D) 팀 구성원들의 할당된 임무

해설 질문의 핵심 어구(looking at a screen)와 관련된 내용을 주의 깊게 듣는다. "I've broken the project down into different tasks that are assigned to individual members of the team. You'll see this information now if you look up at the screen."이라며 프로젝트를 팀의 개별 구성원들에게 할당된 여러 가지 작업으로 분류했으며, 화면으로 이 정보를 확인할 수 있다고 하였다. 따라서 (D)가 정답이다.

어휘 procedure n. 절차, 수순 assignment n. (할당된) 임무, 과제

> **Paraphrasing**
> tasks that are assigned to ~ members of the team 팀의 구성원들에게 할당된 작업 → The assignments of team members 팀 구성원들의 할당된 임무

HACKERS TEST   p.134

01 (C)	02 (A)	03 (A)	04 (A)	05 (B)
06 (C)	07 (B)	08 (C)	09 (D)	10 (B)
11 (C)	12 (A)	13 (C)	14 (B)	15 (C)
16 (D)	17 (B)	18 (A)	19 (C)	20 (C)
21 (D)				

[01-03] 영국
Questions 01-03 refer to the following talk.

Good afternoon, everyone. ⁰¹I'd like to congratulate you all on being promoted to sales team managers. You now qualify for a number of additional benefits. ⁰²These include annual bonuses based on the performance of your team as well as stock options. ⁰³Please go through the relevant section of the management handbook by Monday. Hazel Collins from human resources will meet with you on that day to discuss everything in detail.

promote v. 승진시키다 qualify v. 자격이 있다 benefit n. 혜택
performance n. 성과, 실적 go through ~을 살펴보다 relevant adj. 관련된

해석
01-03번은 다음 담화에 관한 문제입니다.

안녕하세요, 여러분. ⁰¹여러분 모두가 영업팀 관리자로 승진하신 것을 축하하고 싶습니다. 이제 여러분은 여러 추가 혜택을 받을 자격이 있습니다. ⁰²이것들은 스톡옵션뿐만 아니라 팀의 성과에 따른 연례 보너스도 포함합니다. ⁰³월요일까지 관리 안내서의 관련 부분을 살펴봐 주세요. 인사과의 Hazel Collins가 그날 여러분을 만나 모든 것을 자세히 논의할 것입니다.

01 청자 문제
해석 청자들은 어느 부서에서 일하는 것 같은가?
(A) 법무
(B) 재무
(C) 영업
(D) 인사

해설 지문에서 신분 및 직업과 관련된 표현을 놓치지 않고 듣는다. "I'd like to congratulate you all on being promoted to sales team managers."라며 여러분 모두가 영업팀 관리자로 승진한 것을 축하하고 싶다고 한 것을 통해 청자들이 영업 부서에서 일한다는 것을 알 수 있다. 따라서 (C)가 정답이다.

02 언급 문제
해석 화자는 보너스에 대해 무엇을 언급하는가?
(A) 일 년에 한 번 지급된다.
(B) 근속 연수를 기준으로 한다.
(C) 모든 직원이 받을 수 있다.
(D) 새로운 유형의 혜택이다.

해설 질문의 핵심 어구(bonuses)가 언급된 주변을 주의 깊게 듣는다. "These[additional benefits] include annual bonuses based on the performance of your team"이라며 추가 혜택이 팀의 성과에 따른 연례 보너스도 포함한다고 하였다. 따라서 (A)가 정답이다.

어휘 seniority n. 근속 연수

> **Paraphrasing**
> annual 연례의 → once a year 일 년에 한 번

03 요청 문제
해석 화자는 청자들에게 월요일까지 무엇을 하라고 요청하는가?
(A) 설명서를 검토한다.

(B) 선택지를 고른다.
(C) 팀을 구성한다.
(D) 관리자에게 연락한다.

해설 지문에서 요청과 관련된 표현이 언급된 주변을 주의 깊게 듣는다. "Please go through the relevant section of the management handbook by Monday."라며 월요일까지 관리 안내서의 관련 부분을 살펴봐 달라고 하였다. 따라서 (A)가 정답이다.

Paraphrasing
go through ~ handbook 안내서를 살펴보다 → Review a manual 설명서를 검토하다

[04-06] 호주
Questions 04-06 refer to the following talk.

⁰⁴Welcome to our annual marketing conference. Our goal is to explore how companies can advertise their products online. ⁰⁵Unlike in previous years, many of the speakers at today's event are researchers from other countries. So you will be able to develop a global perspective. Before we begin, however, I have to announce a change. ⁰⁶The projector in the main hall is not working. Therefore, the closing ceremony will take place in Room 401 instead.

explore v. 탐구하다, 탐험하다   advertise v. 광고하다   previous adj. 이전의
perspective n. 관점   closing ceremony 폐회식

해설
04-06번은 다음 담화에 관한 문제입니다.
⁰⁴저희 연례 마케팅 컨퍼런스에 오신 것을 환영합니다. 우리의 목표는 회사들이 온라인에서 그들의 제품들을 광고하는 법을 탐구하는 것입니다. ⁰⁵이전 연도들과 달리, 오늘 행사의 많은 연사들은 다른 국가들에서 온 연구원들입니다. 그러므로 여러분은 국제적인 관점을 발달시키실 수 있을 것입니다. 하지만, 저희가 시작하기 전에, 저는 한 가지 변경 사항을 알려드려야 합니다. ⁰⁶중앙 홀의 프로젝터가 작동하지 않습니다. 따라서, 폐회식은 대신 401호에서 열릴 것입니다.

04 특정 세부 사항 문제
해석 컨퍼런스의 중점이 무엇인가?
(A) 온라인 광고
(B) 작업장 안전
(C) 웹사이트 디자인
(D) 인사 관리

해설 질문의 핵심 어구(conference)가 언급된 주변을 주의 깊게 듣는다. "Welcome to our annual marketing conference. Our goal is to explore how companies can advertise their products online."이라며 연례 마케팅 컨퍼런스에 오신 것을 환영한다고 한 후, 컨퍼런스의 목표는 회사들이 온라인에서 그들의 제품들을 광고하는 법을 탐구하는 것이라고 하였다. 따라서 (A)가 정답이다.

어휘 safety n. 안전

Paraphrasing
advertise ~ products online 온라인에서 제품들을 광고하다 → Online advertising 온라인 광고

05 특정 세부 사항 문제
해석 올해의 컨퍼런스는 이전 것들과 어떻게 다른가?
(A) 더 많은 연사들이 참여한다.
(B) 국제적인 연구자들을 특별히 포함한다.
(C) 더 긴 강연들을 포함할 것이다.
(D) 다른 장소에서 열리고 있다.

해설 질문의 핵심 어구(different from previous ones)와 관련된 내용을 주의 깊게 듣는다. "Unlike in previous years, many of the speakers at today's event are researchers from other countries."라며 이전 연도들과 달리, 오늘 행사의 많은 연사들은 다른 국가들에서 온 연구원들이라고 하였다. 따라서 (B)가 정답이다.

어휘 lecture n. 강연

Paraphrasing
from other countries 다른 국가들에서 온 → international 국제적인

06 이유 문제
해석 왜 폐회식이 이전되었는가?
(A) 공간이 청소되지 않았다.
(B) 활동이 변경되었다.
(C) 기계가 제대로 작동하지 않았다.
(D) 시설이 개방되지 않았다.

해설 질문의 핵심 어구(closing ceremony)가 언급된 주변을 주의 깊게 듣는다. "The projector in the main hall is not working. Therefore, the closing ceremony will take place in Room 401 instead."라며 중앙 홀의 프로젝터가 작동하지 않아서 폐회식은 대신 401호에서 열릴 것이라고 하였다. 따라서 (C)가 정답이다.

어휘 malfunction v. 제대로 작동하지 않다

[07-09] 미국
Questions 07-09 refer to the following talk.

This year, ⁰⁷our company will hold a bake sale to raise funds for establishing the Playroom of Hope at the Hurles Children's Hospital. ⁰⁸Employees from all departments are asked to volunteer by baking items, such as cupcakes and cookies, at home for the sale. We will rent a booth at the Hillside Farmers' Market. Staff will sell these items there, and the money raised will be given to the hospital. ⁰⁹I plan to send you all an e-mail describing the hospital's objectives regarding this project.

raise v. (자금·사람 등을) 모으다   fund n. 기금   establish v. 설립하다
objective n. 목적, 목표

해설
07-09번은 다음 담화에 관한 문제입니다.
올해, ⁰⁷우리 회사는 Hurles 어린이 병원에 희망의 놀이방을 설립하기 위한 기금을 모으기 위해 빵 판매 행사를 개최할 것입니다. ⁰⁸모든 부서의 직원분들께 판매를 위해 컵케이크와 쿠키와 같은 품목들을 집에서 구워서 자원봉사해 줄 것을 요청합니다. 우리는 Hillside 농산물 시장에서 부스를 빌릴 것입니다. 직원들이 그곳에서 이 물품들을 판매할 것이고, 모금된 돈은 병원에 기부될 것입니다. ⁰⁹저는 여러분 모두에게 이 프로젝트에 관한 병원의 목적을 설명하는 이메일을 보내드릴 계획입니다.

07 특정 세부 사항 문제
해석 회사는 무엇을 할 것인가?
(A) 도시에서 회의를 개최한다.
(B) 모금 행사를 주최한다.
(C) 병원 관계자들과 만난다.
(D) 새로운 상품을 출시한다.

해설 질문의 핵심 어구(company ~ do)와 관련된 내용을 주의 깊게 듣는다. "our company will hold a bake sale to raise funds"라며 회사가 기금을 모으기 위해 빵 판매 행사를 개최할 것이라고 하였다. 이를 통해 회사가 모금 행사를 준비할 것임을 알 수 있다. 따라서 (B)가 정답이다.

어휘 fundraising n. 모금

08 요청 문제
해석 청자들은 무엇을 하도록 요청받는가?

(A) 제품에 대한 아이디어를 제시한다.
(B) 중고 책과 장난감을 기부한다.
(C) 집에서 만든 음식을 준비한다.
(D) 놀이 구역에서 자원봉사 한다.

해설 지문에서 요청과 관련된 표현이 언급된 주변을 주의 깊게 듣는다. "Employees from all departments are asked to volunteer by baking items, such as cupcakes and cookies, at home for the sale."이라며 모든 부서의 직원분들에게 판매를 위해 컵케이크와 쿠키와 같은 품목들을 집에서 구워서 자원봉사해 줄 것을 요청한다고 하였다. 따라서 (C)가 정답이다.

어휘 come up with ~을 제시하다, 내놓다 donate v. 기부하다

09 특정 세부 사항 문제
해설 화자는 이메일에 무엇을 포함시킬 것인가?
(A) 자원봉사자들을 위한 일정표
(B) 보수 공사 시간표
(C) 장비에 대한 신청서
(D) 프로젝트 목표의 목록

해설 질문의 핵심 어구(e-mail)가 언급된 주변을 주의 깊게 듣는다. "I plan to send you all an e-mail describing the hospital's objectives regarding this project."라며 이 프로젝트에 관한 병원의 목적을 설명하는 이메일을 보낼 계획이라고 하였다. 따라서 (D)가 정답이다.

어휘 timetable n. 시간표

Paraphrasing
objectives regarding this project 이 프로젝트에 관한 목적 → project goals 프로젝트 목표

[10-12] 캐나다
Questions 10-12 refer to the following speech.

[10]I'm Jamie Dunn, the lead designer of the Robo Sweeper—a device that cleans floors all by itself. It has been a huge success, and today Duva Tech is introducing a follow-up version, the Robo Sweeper Plus. As head of one of the teams involved in this product, [11]I can say that it is faster, quieter, and more energy efficient than the original. I'm already using one at home. In just a moment, [12]my assistant will show you how the Robo Sweeper Plus works.

by itself 스스로 head n. 책임자 involve v. 관여하다
energy efficient 에너지 효율적인

해설 10-12번은 다음 연설에 관한 문제입니다.
[10]저는 바닥을 스스로 청소하는 기기인 Robo Sweeper의 수석 디자이너 Jamie Dunn입니다. 이것은 큰 성공을 거두고, 오늘 Duva Tech사는 후속 버전인 Robo Sweeper Plus를 소개합니다. 이 제품에 관여한 팀들 중 하나의 책임자로서, [11]저는 이것이 기존의 것보다 더 빠르고, 조용하며, 에너지 효율적이라고 말씀드릴 수 있습니다. 저는 이미 집에서 이것을 사용하고 있습니다. 잠시 후, [12]저의 조수가 여러분께 Robo Sweeper Plus가 어떻게 작동하는지 보여드릴 것입니다.

10 화자 문제
해설 화자는 누구인가?
(A) 마케팅 전문가
(B) 제품 디자이너
(C) 뉴스 기자
(D) 유지보수 책임자

해설 지문에서 신분 및 직업과 관련된 표현을 놓치지 않고 듣는다. "I'm Jamie Dunn, the lead designer of the Robo Sweeper"라며 자신이 Robo Sweeper의 수석 디자이너 Jamie Dunn이라고 한 것을 통해 화자는 제품 디자이너임을 알 수 있다. 따라서 (B)가 정답이다.

어휘 reporter n. 기자 maintenance n. 유지보수

11 의도 파악 문제
해설 화자는 왜 "저는 이미 집에서 이것을 사용하고 있습니다"라고 말하는가?
(A) 제품이 감당할 수 있는 비용임을 나타내기 위해
(B) 서비스의 편리함을 보여주기 위해
(C) 모델의 장점을 강조하기 위해
(D) 기기의 기능을 설명하기 위해

해설 질문의 인용어구(I'm already using one at home)가 언급된 주변을 주의 깊게 듣는다. "I can say that it[Robo Sweeper Plus] is faster, quieter, and more energy efficient than the original."이라며 Robo Sweeper Plus가 기존의 것보다 더 빠르고, 조용하며, 에너지 효율적이라고 말할 수 있다고 한 것을 통해 모델의 장점을 강조하기 위함임을 알 수 있다. 따라서 (C)가 정답이다.

어휘 indicate v. 나타내다 affordability n. 감당할 수 있는 비용
convenience n. 편리함 stress v. 강조하다 advantage n. 장점, 이점
function n. 기능

12 다음에 할 일 문제
해설 조수는 다음에 무엇을 할 것인가?
(A) 기기를 보여준다.
(B) 방문객들을 실험실로 안내한다.
(C) 무료 샘플들을 나눠준다.
(D) 새로 나올 제품들을 설명한다.

해설 지문의 마지막 부분을 주의 깊게 듣는다. "my assistant will show you how the Robo Sweeper Plus works"라며 자신의 조수가 Robo Sweeper Plus가 어떻게 작동하는지 보여줄 것이라고 하였다. 따라서 (A)가 정답이다.

어휘 demonstrate v. 보여주다, 설명하다

Paraphrasing
show 보여주다 → Demonstrate 보여주다

[13-15] 미국
Questions 13-15 refer to the following talk.

[13]Today, I'll be talking about how to conduct interviews. Since [14]it's your job to hire new workers, you must be able to determine which applicants are best suited to particular positions. When interviewing people, pay close attention to how they present themselves. If you do not feel like a candidate is talking enough, try asking general questions about their past work experience. This is an effective way to get individuals to talk at length about something they are familiar with. Now, [15]I'd like you all to find a partner for a role-playing exercise. Ask each other questions as if you were interviewing a real applicant.

determine v. 결정하다 pay attention to ~에 주목하다
candidate n. 지원자, 후보자

해설 13-15번은 다음 담화에 관한 문제입니다.
[13]오늘, 저는 어떻게 면접을 진행하는지에 대해 이야기할 것입니다. 새로운 [14]직원을 고용하는 것이 여러분의 업무이기 때문에, 여러분은 어느 지원자가 특정 직책에 가장 적합한지 결정하실 수 있어야 합니다. 사람들을 면접할 때, 그들이 자신을 어떻게 표현하는지에 주목하십시오. 만약 지원자가 충분히 이야기를 하고 있지 않다고 느껴진다면, 그들에게 과거 업무 경험에 관한 일반적인 질문을 해보십시오. 이것은 사람들이 그들이 익숙한 것에 대해 상세히 이야기하게 하는 효과적인 방법입니다. 이제, [15]저는 여러분 모두가 역할극 연습

을 위해 파트너를 찾으시길 바랍니다. 마치 실제 지원자를 면접하는 것처럼 서로에게 질문을 하십시오.

13 주제 문제
해석 담화의 주제는 무엇인가?
(A) 예산 삭감
(B) 업무 평가
(C) 면접 방법
(D) 초과근무 시간

해설 담화의 주제를 묻는 문제이므로, 지문의 초반을 반드시 듣는다. "Today, I'll be talking about how to conduct interviews."라며 오늘 면접을 어떻게 진행하는지에 대해 이야기할 것이라고 한 후, 면접 방법에 대한 내용으로 지문이 이어지고 있다. 따라서 (C)가 정답이다.

어휘 reduction n. 삭감, 감소 method n. 방법

Paraphrasing
how to conduct interviews 어떻게 면접을 진행하는지 → Interviewing methods 면접 방법

14 청자 문제
해석 청자들은 누구인 것 같은가?
(A) 고객 서비스 담당자들
(B) 인사 담당 직원들
(C) 교육 전문가들
(D) 경영 자문 위원들

해설 지문에서 신분 및 직업과 관련된 표현을 놓치지 않고 듣는다. "Since it's your job to hire new workers"라며 새로운 직원을 고용하는 것이 여러분의 업무라고 한 것을 통해 청자들이 인사 담당 직원들임을 알 수 있다. 따라서 (B)가 정답이다.

어휘 specialist n. 전문가 consultant n. 자문 위원, 고문

15 이유 문제
해석 화자는 왜 청자들이 파트너를 찾기를 원하는가?
(A) 설문지를 완성하기 위해
(B) 지원자에 관해 논의하기 위해
(C) 연습에 참여하기 위해
(D) 발표를 준비하기 위해

해설 질문의 핵심 어구(find a partner)가 언급된 주변을 주의 깊게 듣는다. "I'd like you all to find a partner for a role-playing exercise"라며 여러분 모두가 역할극 연습을 위해 파트너를 찾길 바란다고 하였다. 따라서 (C)가 정답이다.

어휘 questionnaire n. 설문지 exercise n. 연습

[16-18] 🎧 호주
Questions 16-18 refer to the following talk.

I'm glad all of you are here for this ceremony hosted by the International Eco-Business Association. The prize for this year's Most Eco-Friendly Company goes to BioPro Incorporated. I am very pleased to give this prize to ¹⁶**the company's president, Mr. Adrian Miller.** ¹⁷**BioPro is a major manufacturer of all-natural cosmetics.** And the high demand for its products has encouraged other companies to follow its example. ¹⁸**We hope BioPro will successfully achieve its objective of expanding into Europe and Asia** and inspire more companies to develop eco-friendly products.

manufacturer n. 제조사 cosmetic n. 화장품 demand n. 수요
expand v. 확장하다 inspire v. 영감을 주다

해석 16-18번은 다음 담화에 관한 문제입니다.
여러분 모두가 국제 친환경 기업 협회가 주최한 이 기념식에 참석해 주셔서 기쁩니다. 올해의 최우수 친환경 기업상은 BioPro사에 돌아갑니다. 저는 ¹⁶이 회사의 회장인 Mr. Adrian Miller께 이 상을 수여하게 되어 매우 기쁩니다. ¹⁷BioPro사는 천연 재료로만 만든 화장품의 주요 제조사입니다. 그리고 그 회사의 제품에 대한 높은 수요는 다른 회사들이 본받도록 독려했습니다. ¹⁸저희는 BioPro가 유럽과 아시아로 확장하겠다는 목표를 성공적으로 달성하고 더 많은 기업들이 친환경 제품을 개발하도록 영감을 주기를 희망합니다.

16 특정 세부 사항 문제
해석 Adrian Miller는 누구인 것 같은가?
(A) 행사 진행자
(B) 유명한 연구원
(C) 학교 설립자
(D) 기업 지도자

해설 질문 대상(Adrian Miller)의 신분 및 직업과 관련된 표현을 놓치지 않고 듣는다. "the company's president, Mr. Adrian Miller"라며 Mr. Adrian Miller가 회사의 회장이라고 하였다. 따라서 (D)가 정답이다.

어휘 founder n. 설립자

17 언급 문제
해석 화자는 BioPro사에 대해 무엇을 말하는가?
(A) 최소한의 포장재를 사용한다.
(B) 천연 제품들을 만든다.
(C) 훌륭한 서비스를 제공한다.
(D) 환경 단체들을 후원한다.

해설 질문의 핵심 어구(BioPro)가 언급된 주변을 주의 깊게 듣는다. "BioPro is a major manufacturer of all-natural cosmetics."라며 BioPro사는 천연 재료로만 만든 화장품의 주요 제조사라고 하였다. 따라서 (B)가 정답이다.

어휘 sponsor v. 후원하다, 협찬하다

18 특정 세부 사항 문제
해석 화자에 따르면, BioPro사의 목표는 무엇인가?
(A) 해외 확장
(B) 비용 절감
(C) 효율성 향상
(D) 직원 채용

해설 질문의 핵심 어구(BioPro's goal)와 관련된 내용을 주의 깊게 듣는다. "We hope BioPro will successfully achieve its objective of expanding into Europe and Asia"라며 BioPro사가 유럽과 아시아로 확장하겠다는 목표를 성공적으로 달성하기를 희망한다고 하였다. 따라서 (A)가 정답이다.

어휘 improve v. 향상시키다 efficiency n. 효율성

[19-21] 🎧 영국
Questions 19-21 refer to the following talk and flowchart.

In this workshop, ¹⁹**we are going to continue with our discussion of why creating and following a budget is important for small business owners.** In fact, this can be the difference between whether an enterprise succeeds or fails. ²⁰**During the last session, we talked about the need to determine your priorities, so today we will turn to the next step in the process.** But before we get started, I would like you to read through this summary of the key points we will cover this afternoon. ²¹**I'll hand out a copy to each of you now.**

DAY 18 연설 및 강연 105

enterprise n. 기업, 회사 succeed v. 성공하다 process n. 과정
cover v. 다루다, 덮다 summary n. 개요, 요약

Paraphrasing
hand out a copy 사본을 나눠 주다 → distribute a document 문서를 배부하다

해석
19-21번은 다음 담화와 업무 흐름도에 관한 문제입니다.

이번 워크숍에서, ¹⁹우리는 소규모 사업체 소유주들에게 예산을 세우고 따르는 것이 왜 중요한지에 대한 논의를 계속할 것입니다. 사실, 이것은 기업이 성공할지 실패할지에 대한 차이점이 될 수 있습니다. ²⁰지난 시간에는, 우선순위를 결정하는 것의 필요성에 대해 이야기했으므로, 오늘 우리는 이 과정의 다음 단계로 넘어갈 것입니다. 하지만 시작하기 전에, 저는 여러분들이 오늘 오후에 우리가 다루게 될 핵심 요점들의 개요를 읽어보시길 바랍니다. ²¹지금 여러분 각자에게 사본을 나눠드리겠습니다.

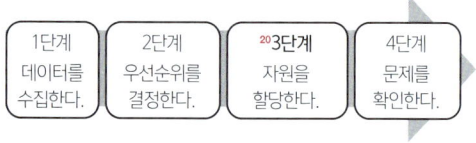

19 주제 문제
해석 화자는 주로 무엇에 대해 이야기하고 있는가?
(A) 채용
(B) 생산
(C) 회계
(D) 마케팅

해설 담화의 주제를 묻는 문제이므로, 지문의 초반을 반드시 듣는다. "we are going to continue with our discussion of why creating and following a budget is important for small business owners"라며 소규모 사업체 소유주들에게 예산을 세우고 따르는 것이 왜 중요한지에 대한 논의를 계속하겠다고 한 후, 회계에 대한 내용으로 지문이 이어지고 있다. 따라서 (C)가 정답이다.

어휘 recruitment n. 채용, 모집 accounting n. 회계

20 시각 자료 문제
해석 시각 자료를 보아라. 오늘 어떤 단계가 논의될 것인가?
(A) 1단계
(B) 2단계
(C) 3단계
(D) 4단계

해설 제시된 흐름도의 정보를 확인한 후 질문의 핵심 어구(step will be discussed today)와 관련된 내용을 주의 깊게 듣는다. "During the last session, we talked about the need to determine your priorities, so today we will turn to the next step in the process."라며 지난 시간에는 우선순위를 결정하는 것의 필요성에 대해 이야기했으므로, 오늘은 이 과정의 다음 단계로 넘어갈 것이라고 하였다. 우선순위를 결정하는 것의 다음 단계는 3단계임을 흐름도에서 알 수 있다. 따라서 (C)가 정답이다.

21 다음에 할 일 문제
해석 다음에 무슨 일이 일어날 것 같은가?
(A) 시연이 진행될 것이다.
(B) 질문이 대답 될 것이다.
(C) 조수가 소개될 것이다.
(D) 문서가 배부될 것이다.

해설 지문의 마지막 부분을 주의 깊게 듣는다. "I'll hand out a copy to each of you now."라며 지금 여러분 각자에게 사본을 나눠 주겠다고 하였다. 따라서 (D)가 정답이다.

어휘 demonstration n. 시연 distribute v. 배부하다

DAY 19 방송 및 보도

1. 방송

담화 흐름과 빈출 문제 캐나다 p.136

해석 여러분은 시카고 최고의 라디오 방송 중 하나인 COOL 105.1의 Ricky Doyle을 듣고 계십니다. 이 지역의 기상 상황에 대한 업데이트를 할 시간입니다. 심한 눈보라가 도시를 향해 오고 있으며 오후 8시경에 엄습할 것으로 예상됩니다. 최고 10인치의 눈이 밤사이에 쌓일 수 있습니다. 도로가 미끄러울 테니, 내일 운전을 하신다면 반드시 조심하시기 바랍니다. 이번 주말이면 다시 맑은 하늘을 보게 될 것입니다. 다음에 이어질 인기 영화 In His way에 대한 비평을 위해 채널을 고정하세요.

어휘 blizzard n. 눈보라 hit v. (폭풍 등이) 엄습하다; n. 인기 작품
accumulate v. 쌓이다, 모으다 careful adj. 조심하는, 주의 깊은
slippery adj. 미끄러운

HACKERS PRACTICE p.137
01 (B) **02** (A) **03** (A) **04** (B)

[01-02] 호주 / 캐나다
Questions 01-02 refer to the following broadcast.

You're listening to Westville's own WGGT 97.3 radio. I'm your host, Harold LaRoche. Today, ⁰¹I'll be interviewing our city's newly hired parks and recreation department supervisor, Jane Kearney. Ms. Kearney will discuss plans for several upcoming events, including the summer arts festival and the regional tennis competition. And after that, our listeners are encouraged to call our station and ask questions directly to Ms. Kearney. Now, ⁰²let's hear some commercials.

host n. 진행자 hire v. 채용하다 recreation n. 레크리에이션, 오락
supervisor n. 관리자, 감독관 upcoming adj. 다가오는
regional adj. 지역의 competition n. 대회, 경쟁
station n. 방송국, 스튜디오 commercial n. 광고

해석
01-02번은 다음 방송에 관한 문제입니다.

여러분은 Westville의 자체 WGGT 라디오 97.3을 듣고 계십니다. 저는 진행자인 Harold LaRoche입니다. 오늘, ⁰¹저는 새로 채용된 우리 시의 공원 및 레크리에이션 부서 관리자인 Jane Kearney를 인터뷰할 예정입니다. Ms. Kearney는 여름 예술 축제와 지역 테니스 대회를 포함한 여러 다가오는 행사에 대한 계획을 논의할 예정입니다. 그리고 그 후, 청취자분들께서는 저희 방송국에 전화하셔서 Ms. Kearney에게 직접 질문을 하도록 권장됩니다. 이제, ⁰²광고를 들어보겠습니다.

01 특정 세부 사항 문제
해석 Jane Kearney는 누구일 것 같은가?
(A) 영화감독
(B) 시 공무원
(C) 인사 담당자
(D) 부동산 중개인

해설 질문 대상(Jane Kearney)의 신분 및 직업과 관련된 표현을 놓치지 않

고 듣는다. "I'll be interviewing our city's newly hired parks and recreation department supervisor, Jane Kearney"라며 Jane Kearney가 새로 채용된 우리 시의 공원 및 레크리에이션 부서 관리자라고 하였다. 따라서 (B)가 정답이다.

어휘 director n. 감독, 관리자   official n. 공무원, 관계자
personnel manager 인사 담당자   real estate agent 부동산 중개인

[Paraphrasing]
city's ~ department supervisor 시의 ~ 부서 관리자 → A city official 시 공무원

02 다음에 할 일 문제

해석 청자들은 다음에 무엇을 들을 것 같은가?
(A) 광고
(B) 음악 공연
(C) 날씨 업데이트
(D) 교통 정보

해설 질문의 핵심 어구(hear next)와 관련된 내용을 주의 깊게 듣는다. "let's hear some commercials"라며 광고를 들을 것이라고 하였다. 따라서 (A)가 정답이다.

어휘 advertisement n. 광고   performance n. 공연   traffic n. 교통

[Paraphrasing]
some commercials 광고 → An advertisement 광고

[03-04] 영국 / 미국
Questions 03-04 refer to the following broadcast and chart.

> ⁰³**In entertainment news, the popular band Northern Arc has released its second album.** Titled *Out of the Wind*, it features 15 new songs. It is available in stores across the country and can also be ordered from the band's Web site. To promote the album, Northern Arc will launch a four-city tour in August. And ⁰⁴**the show in Olympia will feature famed guitarist Janice Polson as a special guest.** Tickets for these concerts will go on sale next week.

entertainment n. 연예(계), 오락   popular adj. 유명한
release v. 발매하다, 출시하다   available adj. 구할 수 있는, 이용할 수 있는
promote v. 홍보하다, 촉진하다   launch v. 시작하다, 착수하다
famed adj. 유명한   guitarist n. 기타 연주자

해석
03-04번은 다음 방송과 표에 관한 문제입니다.
⁰³연예계 소식으로는, 인기 밴드 Northern Arc가 두 번째 앨범을 발매했습니다. *Out of the Wind*라는 제목으로, 그것은 15곡의 신곡을 수록하고 있습니다. 그것은 전국 매장에서 구할 수 있고 또한 밴드의 웹사이트에서도 주문할 수 있습니다. 앨범을 홍보하기 위해, Northern Arc는 8월에 네 개 도시 투어를 시작할 것입니다. 그리고 ⁰⁴올림피아에서의 공연에는 유명 기타 연주자 Janice Polson이 특별 게스트로 특별히 포함될 것입니다. 이 콘서트들의 티켓은 다음 주부터 판매될 예정입니다.

Northern Arc – 콘서트 날짜	
시애틀	8월 10일
올림피아	⁰⁴8월 13일
포틀랜드	8월 15일
밴쿠버	8월 18일

03 목적 문제

해석 방송의 목적은 무엇인가?
(A) 앨범 발매를 알리기 위해
(B) 최근 콘서트를 리뷰하기 위해
(C) 밴드의 기념일을 축하하기 위해
(D) 음악가의 경력을 설명하기 위해

해설 방송의 목적을 묻는 문제이므로, 지문의 초반을 주의 깊게 듣는다. "In entertainment news, the popular band Northern Arc has released its second album."이라며 연예계 소식으로는 인기 밴드 Northern Arc가 두 번째 앨범을 발매했다고 하였다. 따라서 (A)가 정답이다.

어휘 announce v. 알리다, 발표하다   celebrate v. 축하하다
anniversary n. 기념일   describe v. 설명하다   career n. 경력, 직업

[Paraphrasing]
released ~ album 앨범을 발매했다 → the release of an album 앨범 발매

04 시각 자료 문제

해석 시각 자료를 보아라. Janice Polson은 언제 Northern Arc와 함께 공연할 것인가?
(A) 8월 10일
(B) 8월 13일
(C) 8월 15일
(D) 8월 18일

해설 제시된 일정표의 정보를 확인한 후 질문의 핵심 어구(Janice Polson perform with Northern Arc)와 관련된 내용을 주의 깊게 듣는다. "the show in Olympia will feature famed guitarist Janice Polson as a special guest"라며 올림피아에서의 공연에는 유명 기타 연주자 Janice Polson이 특별 게스트로 특별히 포함될 것이라고 했고, 올림피아에서의 공연은 8월 13일임을 일정표에서 알 수 있다. 따라서 (B)가 정답이다.

2. 보도

담화 흐름과 빈출 문제   영국   p.138

해석 Lanton Electronics사가 이번 분기에 큰 매출 성장을 발표했습니다. 첨단 소음 차단 기술을 특징으로 하는 그 회사의 최신 무선 헤드폰이 고객들 사이에서 특히 인기를 끌고 있습니다. 인터뷰에서, CEO인 Alan Park는 연구 개발팀의 구성원들의 노고에 감사를 표하고 싶다고 말했습니다. 그는 혁신에 대한 그들의 헌신이 회사의 성공에 핵심적인 역할을 했다고 말했습니다. 그는 또한 회사가 내년에 제품군을 확장할 계획이라고 밝혔습니다. 전문가들은 Lanton Electronics사가 앞으로 몇 달 동안 꾸준한 성장을 계속해서 보일 것이라고 예측합니다.

어휘 quarter n. 분기   wireless adj. 무선의   dedication n. 헌신
play a key role 핵심적인 역할을 하다   expand v. 확장하다
steady adj. 꾸준한

HACKERS PRACTICE   p.139

01 (C)   **02** (B)   **03** (D)   **04** (A)

[01-02] 캐나다 / 호주
Questions 01-02 refer to the following business report.

> Now, here's the business news. ⁰¹**Carwin Electronics has reported receiving many complaints about its newest electric fan.** Users have noted that the product occasionally makes an unusually loud noise, especially when used for long periods. ⁰²**Sarah Mitchell from the company's public relations team** stated that the sound does not indicate a safety issue or a problem with the fan's performance. She added that the product remains popular because it's both reliable and affordable.

complaint n. 불만   electric adj. 전기의   fan n. 선풍기, 팬
occasionally adv. 종종, 때때로   unusually adv. 비정상적으로
noise n. 소음   period n. 시간, 기간   public relations 홍보

indicate v. 나타내다, 보여주다 performance n. 성능, 성과
reliable adj. 신뢰할 수 있는, 믿을 수 있는
affordable adj. 저렴한, 가격이 알맞은

seafood n. 해산물 explain v. 설명하다 current adj. 현재의
delay n. 지연 equipment n. 장비 load v. (짐을) 싣다
unload v. (짐을) 내리다 cargo n. 화물

해석
01-02번은 다음 비즈니스 보도에 관한 문제입니다.

이제, 비즈니스 뉴스를 전해드리겠습니다. **01**Carwin Electronics사는 자사의 최신 전기 선풍기에 대한 많은 불만이 접수되고 있다고 보고했습니다. 사용자들은 이 제품이 특히 장시간 사용할 때 종종 비정상적으로 큰 소음을 낸다고 지적했습니다. **02**회사 홍보팀의 Sarah Mitchell은 이 소음이 안전 문제나 선풍기 성능의 문제를 나타내는 것은 아니라고 말했습니다. 그녀는 이 제품이 신뢰할 수 있고 저렴하기 때문에 여전히 인기가 있다고 덧붙였습니다.

01 주제 문제
해석 보도는 주로 무엇에 관한 것인가?
(A) 제품 출시
(B) 공장 확장
(C) 고객 불만
(D) 가격 책정 전략

해설 보도의 주제를 묻는 문제이므로 지문의 초반을 주의 깊게 듣는다. "Carwin Electronics has reported receiving many complaints about its newest electric fan."이라며 Carwin Electronics사가 자사의 최신 전기 선풍기에 대해 많은 불만이 접수되고 있다고 보고했다고 하였다. 따라서 (C)가 정답이다.

어휘 launch n. 출시, 개시 expansion n. 확장, 확대 pricing n. 가격 책정
strategy n. 전략

Paraphrasing
complaints about its newest electric fan 자사의 최신 전기 선풍기에 대한 불만 → Customer complaints 고객 불만

02 특정 세부 사항 문제
해석 Sarah Mitchell은 누구인가?
(A) 영업 사원
(B) 홍보 담당자
(C) 유지보수 관리자
(D) 고객 서비스 직원

해설 질문 대상(Sarah Mitchell)의 신분 및 직업과 관련된 표현을 놓치지 않고 듣는다. "Sarah Mitchell from the company's public relations team"이라며 회사 홍보팀의 Sarah Mitchell이라고 하였다. 따라서 (B)가 정답이다.

어휘 sales associate 영업 사원 representative n. 담당자, 대리인
maintenance n. 유지보수 agent n. 직원, 대리인

Paraphrasing
the company's public relations team 회사 홍보팀 → A public relations representative 홍보 담당자

[03-04] 미국 / 영국
Questions 03-04 refer to the following news report.

Here's today's local news update. **03**The city of Harrisburg is building a new port to speed up the delivery of goods. The project is expected to help businesses operate more efficiently when it opens next year. **04**In an interview, Martin Blake, the owner of a seafood import company, explained that the current port is too small, and this often causes delays. The new port will have more space for containers and better equipment for loading and unloading cargo.

local adj. 지역의 port n. 항구 delivery n. 배송, 배달 goods n. 상품, 제품
operate v. 운영하다 efficiently adv. 효율적으로 owner n. 소유주

해석
03-04번은 다음 뉴스 보도에 관한 문제입니다.

오늘의 최신 지역 뉴스입니다. **03**Harrisburg시는 상품 배송 속도를 높이기 위해 새 항구를 건설하고 있습니다. 이 프로젝트는 내년에 개장하면 기업들이 더 효율적으로 운영할 수 있도록 도울 것으로 기대됩니다. **04**인터뷰에서, 한 해산물 수입 업체의 소유주인 Martin Blake는 현재 항구가 너무 작고, 이는 종종 지연을 초래한다고 설명했습니다. 새 항구는 컨테이너를 위한 더 많은 공간과 화물을 싣고 내리기 위한 더 나은 장비를 갖추게 될 것입니다.

03 목적 문제
해석 보도의 목적은 무엇인가?
(A) 시 정책의 변경을 논의하기 위해
(B) 상품 수입의 지연을 설명하기 위해
(C) 사업주를 소개하기 위해
(D) 항구의 건설을 발표하기 위해

해설 보도의 목적을 묻는 문제이므로, 지문의 초반을 주의 깊게 듣는다. "The city of Harrisburg is building a new port to speed up the delivery of goods."라며 Harrisburg시는 상품 배송 속도를 높이기 위해 새 항구를 건설하고 있다고 하였다. 따라서 (D)가 정답이다.

어휘 policy n. 정책 construction n. 건설

Paraphrasing
building a new port 새 항구를 건설하고 있다 → the construction of a port 항구의 건설

04 특정 세부 사항 문제
해석 Martin Blake가 인터뷰에서 언급한 문제는 무엇인가?
(A) 시설이 충분히 크지 않다.
(B) 작업자를 구할 수 없다.
(C) 위치가 접근하기 어렵다.
(D) 수입은 비용이 너무 많이 든다.

해설 질문의 핵심 어구(Martin Blake mention in the interview)와 관련된 내용을 주의 깊게 듣는다. "In an interview, Martin Blake ~ explained that the current port is too small"이라며 Martin Blake가 인터뷰에서 현재 항구가 너무 작다고 설명했다고 하였다. 따라서 (A)가 정답이다.

어휘 facility n. 시설 inaccessible adj. 접근하기 어려운
costly adj. 비용이 많이 드는

Paraphrasing
the current port is too small 현재 항구가 너무 작다 → A facility is not large enough 시설이 충분히 크지 않다

HACKERS TEST

01 (C)	02 (C)	03 (A)	04 (D)	05 (C)
06 (A)	07 (B)	08 (A)	09 (B)	10 (A)
11 (A)	12 (B)	13 (C)	14 (B)	15 (A)
16 (C)	17 (D)	18 (B)	19 (C)	20 (B)
21 (D)				

[01-03] 호주
Questions 01-03 refer to the following report.

In business news, **01**the dry cleaner chain Fresh Fabric will be opening 14 new locations next month in cities across Texas, including Dallas and Houston.

The company had originally intended to open over 30 branches. ⁰²**However, it had to change its plans due to a lack of affordable commercial spaces. Rents have been increasing throughout the region.** But ⁰³**Leanne Wilson, who established Fresh Fabric 10 years ago**, expressed confidence that the issue is temporary.

chain n. 체인점   originally adv. 원래, 본래   intend v. 의도하다, 작정하다
affordable adj. (가격 등이) 알맞은, 감당할 수 있는   establish v. 설립하다
express v. 나타내다, 표현하다   temporary adj. 일시적인

해석 01-03번은 다음 보도에 관한 문제입니다.

비즈니스 뉴스에서는, ⁰¹드라이클리닝 체인점 Fresh Fabric이 다음 달 댈러스와 휴스턴을 포함한 텍사스 전역의 도시들에 14개의 새로운 지점을 열 예정입니다. 그 회사는 원래 30개 이상의 지점을 열려고 의도했습니다. ⁰²하지만, 가격이 알맞은 상업 공간의 부족으로 인해 계획을 변경해야 했습니다. 임대료는 그 지역 전체에 걸쳐 상승해 왔습니다. 그러나 ⁰³10년 전 Fresh Fabric을 설립한 Leanne Wilson은 이 문제가 일시적이라는 확신을 나타냈습니다.

01 주제 문제
해석 보도는 주로 무엇에 관한 것인가?
(A) 프로그램 출시
(B) 본사 이전
(C) 회사 확장
(D) 산업 동향
해설 보도의 주제를 묻는 문제이므로 지문의 초반을 주의 깊게 듣는다. "the dry cleaner chain Fresh Fabric will be opening 14 new locations next month in cities across Texas"라며 드라이클리닝 체인점 Fresh Fabric이 다음 달 텍사스 전역의 도시들에 14개의 새로운 지점을 열 예정이라고 하였다. 따라서 (C)가 정답이다.
어휘 launch n. 출시   relocation n. 이전   expansion n. 확장

02 문제점 문제
해석 Fresh Fabric은 어떤 문제에 직면했는가?
(A) 불충분한 직원 교육
(B) 증가된 경쟁
(C) 높은 임대료
(D) 감소된 수익
해설 화자의 말에서 부정적인 표현이 언급된 다음을 주의 깊게 듣는다. "However, it[Fresh Fabric] had to change its plans due to a lack of affordable commercial spaces. Rents have been increasing throughout the region."이라며 가격이 알맞은 상업 공간의 부족으로 인해 계획을 변경해야 했다고 한 후, 임대료가 그 지역 전체에 걸쳐 상승해 왔다고 하였다. 따라서 (C)가 정답이다.
어휘 insufficient adj. 불충분한   rental fee 임대료   profit n. 수익, 이익

03 특정 세부 사항 문제
해석 Leanne Wilson은 누구일 것 같은가?
(A) 회사 창립자
(B) 부동산 소유자
(C) 금융 상담가
(D) 기자
해설 질문 대상(Leanne Wilson)의 신분 및 직업과 관련된 표현을 놓치지 않고 듣는다. "Leanne Wilson, who established Fresh Fabric 10 years ago"라며 Leanne Wilson이 10년 전 Fresh Fabric을 설립했다고 하였다. 따라서 (A)가 정답이다.
어휘 founder n. 창립자, 설립자   property n. 부동산   journalist n. 기자

[04-06] 미국
Questions 04-06 refer to the following report.

⁰⁴**At a press conference this morning, Norton Pharmaceuticals revealed its newest product, NanoFlu.** Spokesperson Michael Sanderson said that this medication has fewer side effects than similar products on the market. ⁰⁵**This was confirmed during testing by researchers at the Clearwater Medical Center.** Mr. Sanderson also stated that the retail price of NanoFlu has not been determined yet. ⁰⁶**It will be discussed during a press conference on June 20**, the day before the product becomes available in stores.

press conference 기자 회견   pharmaceuticals n. 제약 회사
reveal v. 공개하다   spokesperson n. 대변인   medication n. 약물, 약
side effect 부작용   similar adj. 비슷한

해석 04-06번은 다음 보도에 관한 문제입니다.

⁰⁴오늘 아침 기자 회견에서, Norton 제약 회사는 자사의 최신 제품인 NanoFlu를 공개했습니다. 대변인 Michael Sanderson은 이 약물이 시장에 있는 유사한 제품들보다 부작용이 더 적다고 말했습니다. ⁰⁵이는 실험 중에 Clearwater 의료 센터의 연구원들에 의해 확인되었습니다. Mr. Sanderson은 또한 NanoFlu의 소매가격이 아직 결정되지 않았다고 말했습니다. ⁰⁶이것은 제품이 매장에서 이용 가능해지기 하루 전인 6월 20일에 있을 기자 회견에서 논의될 것입니다.

04 이유 문제
해석 Norton 제약회사는 왜 기자 회견을 열었는가?
(A) 불만을 해결하기 위해
(B) 대변인을 소개하기 위해
(C) 동업을 설명하기 위해
(D) 제품을 발표하기 위해
해설 질문의 핵심 어구(press conference)가 언급된 주변을 주의 깊게 듣는다. "At a press conference this morning, Norton Pharmaceuticals revealed its newest product, NanoFlu."라며 오늘 아침 기자 회견에서 Norton 제약 회사가 자사의 최신 제품인 NanoFlu를 공개했다고 하였다. 따라서 (D)가 정답이다.
어휘 address v. 해결하다   complaint n. 불만, 항의   partnership n. 동업, 제휴

05 언급 문제
해석 Clearwater 의료 센터에 대해 무엇이 언급되었는가?
(A) 연구실을 확장했다.
(B) 연구원들을 고용했다.
(C) 실험을 수행했다.
(D) 치료법을 개발했다.
해설 질문의 핵심 어구(Clearwater Medical Center)가 언급된 주변을 주의 깊게 듣는다. "This was confirmed during testing by researchers at the Clearwater Medical Center."라며 NanoFlu가 유사한 제품들보다 부작용이 더 적다는 것이 실험 중에 Clearwater 의료 센터의 연구원들에 의해 확인되었다고 하였다. 따라서 (C)가 정답이다.
어휘 laboratory n. 연구실   treatment n. 치료법

06 특정 세부 사항 문제
해석 6월 20일 기자 회견에서 무엇이 논의될 것인가?
(A) 가격 책정
(B) 마케팅
(C) 판매
(D) 유통
해설 질문의 핵심 어구(June 20)가 언급된 주변을 주의 깊게 듣는다.

"It[the retail price of NanoFlu] will be discussed during a press conference on June 20"이라며 NanoFlu의 소매가격이 6월 20일에 있을 기자 회견에서 논의될 것이라고 하였다. 따라서 (A)가 정답이다.

어휘 pricing n. 가격 책정 distribution n. 유통

[07-09] 캐나다
Questions 07-09 refer to the following podcast.

> Hello, I'm your host, Steve Clayborn, and this is *Job Talk*, the weekly podcast for job seekers. ⁰⁷**Today, I'm focusing on the skills you need for a job interview.** ⁰⁸**Recruiter Lionel Wesley has agreed to take time out of his hectic schedule to provide some tips. He usually declines these requests.** Also, ⁰⁹**next month I'll be holding a live broadcast of my show**, and you'll be able to practice your interview skills with me.
>
> host n. 진행자; v. 열다, 주최하다   job seeker 구직자
> recruiter n. 채용 담당자   hectic adj. 정신없이 바쁜   live broadcast 생방송

해석
07-09번은 다음 팟캐스트에 관한 문제입니다.

안녕하세요, 저는 여러분의 진행자 Steve Clayborn이고, 이것은 구직자들을 위한 주간 팟캐스트인 *Job Talk*입니다. ⁰⁷오늘, 저는 취업 면접에 필요한 기술에 초점을 둘 것입니다. ⁰⁸채용 담당자인 Lionel Wesley께서 그의 정신없이 바쁜 일정 중에 시간을 내어 몇 가지 조언을 주시기로 동의했습니다. 그는 보통 이런 요청을 거절합니다. 또한, ⁰⁹다음 달에 저는 제 쇼의 생방송을 할 것이므로, 여러분은 저와 함께 면접 기술을 연습하실 수 있을 겁니다.

07 주제 문제
해석 이번 주 팟캐스트의 주제는 무엇인가?
(A) 은퇴 계획
(B) 취업 면접 기술
(C) 채용 절차
(D) 직원 교육 방법

해설 팟캐스트의 주제를 묻는 문제이므로, 지문의 초반을 반드시 듣는다. "Today, I'm focusing on the skills you need for a job interview."라며 오늘, 취업 면접에 필요한 기술에 초점을 둘 것이라고 한 후, 취업 면접 기술에 대한 방송의 내용으로 지문이 이어지고 있다. 따라서 (B)가 정답이다.

어휘 procedure n. 절차

08 의도 파악 문제
해석 화자는 왜 "그는 보통 이런 요청을 거절합니다"라고 말하는가?
(A) 게스트가 매우 바쁘다는 것을 암시하기 위해
(B) 인터뷰가 취소되었음을 명시하기 위해
(C) 실수가 발생했음을 나타내기 위해
(D) 지원자가 자격이 있음을 보여주기 위해

해설 질문의 인용어구(He usually declines these requests)가 언급된 주변을 주의 깊게 듣는다. "Recruiter Lionel Wesley has agreed to take time out of his hectic schedule to provide some tips."라며 인사 담당자인 Lionel Wesley가 그의 정신없이 바쁜 일정 중에 시간을 내어 몇 가지 조언을 주기로 동의했다고 하였다. 그 후, 그는 보통 이런 요청을 거절한다고 했으므로, 그가 매우 바쁘다는 것을 암시하기 위함임을 알 수 있다. 따라서 (A)가 정답이다.

어휘 suggest v. 암시하다   specify v. 명시하다   qualified adj. 자격이 있는

09 다음에 할 일 문제
해석 화자는 다음 달에 무엇을 할 것인가?
(A) 청취자들의 전화에 응답한다.
(B) 생방송을 한다.
(C) 상을 받는다.
(D) 이전 회차를 올린다.

해설 질문의 핵심 어구(next month)가 언급된 주변을 주의 깊게 듣는다. "next month I'll be holding a live broadcast of my show"라며 다음 달에는 자신의 쇼의 생방송을 할 것이라고 하였다. 따라서 (B)가 정답이다.

[10-12] 영국
Questions 10-12 refer to the following broadcast.

> This is *Arts Expression* with Michelle Frommer. ¹⁰**The Classical Art Museum will be exhibiting works by the famous sculptor Yang Xu. The exhibition will run from January 20 to 23.** ¹¹**Mr. Xu's pieces will be displayed in Maxwell Hall, which is the biggest exhibition room in the museum.** Tickets for this event are now available through the museum's mobile application and Web site. Additionally, ¹²**we're giving away free tickets to five lucky listeners who send a text message to our radio station** before the end of the show.
>
> classical art 고전 미술   exhibit v. 전시하다   sculptor n. 조각가
> run v. 진행하다, 운영하다   display v. 전시하다
> additionally adv. 추가적으로   give away 증정하다, 나눠주다

해석
10-12번은 다음 방송에 관한 문제입니다.

Michelle Frommer와 함께하는 *Arts Expression*입니다. ¹⁰고전 미술 미술관이 유명한 조각가 Yang Xu의 작품들을 전시할 예정입니다. 이 전시는 1월 20일부터 23일까지 진행될 거예요. ¹¹Mr. Xu의 작품들은 Maxwell홀에 전시될 것인데, 그곳은 그 미술관에서 가장 큰 전시실이죠. 이 행사의 입장권은 현재 미술관의 모바일 애플리케이션과 웹사이트를 통해 구매 가능합니다. 추가적으로, ¹²저희는 방송이 끝나기 전에 저희 라디오 방송국으로 문자를 보내 주시는 다섯 명의 행운의 청취자들에게 무료입장권을 증정할 것입니다.

10 특정 세부 사항 문제
해석 화자는 주로 어떤 종류의 행사에 대해 이야기하는가?
(A) 전시회
(B) 연극
(C) 수업
(D) 축제

해설 질문의 핵심 어구(type of event)와 관련된 내용을 주의 깊게 듣는다. "The Classical Art Museum will be exhibiting works by the famous sculptor Yang Xu. The exhibition will run from January 20 to 23."라며 고전 미술 미술관이 유명한 조각가 Yang Xu의 작품들을 전시할 예정이라고 한 후, 이 전시는 1월 20일부터 23일까지 진행될 것이라고 하였다. 따라서 (A)가 정답이다.

11 언급 문제
해석 화자는 Maxwell홀에 대해 무엇을 말하는가?
(A) 매우 넓다.
(B) 입구 근처에 있다.
(C) 보수될 것이다.
(D) 매각될 것이다.

해설 질문의 핵심 어구(Maxwell Hall)가 언급된 주변을 주의 깊게 듣는다. "Mr. Xu's pieces will be displayed in Maxwell Hall, which is the biggest exhibition room in the museum."이라며 Mr. Xu의 작품들은 Maxwell홀에 전시될 것인데, 그곳은 그 미술관에서 가장 큰 전시실이라고 하였다. 따라서 (A)가 정답이다.

어휘 spacious adj. 넓은, 널찍한

Paraphrasing
biggest exhibition room 가장 큰 전시실 → very spacious 매우 넓다

12 방법 문제
해석 일부 청취자들은 어떻게 행사의 무료입장권을 받을 수 있는가?
(A) 웹사이트를 방문함으로써
(B) 문자 메시지를 보냄으로써
(C) 이메일에 답장함으로써
(D) 전화를 걺으로써

해설 질문의 핵심 어구(free tickets)가 언급된 주변을 주의 깊게 듣는다. "we're giving away free tickets to five lucky listeners who send a text message to our radio station"이라며 라디오 방송국으로 문자를 보내 주는 다섯 명의 행운의 청취자들에게 무료입장권을 증정할 것이라고 하였다. 따라서 (B)가 정답이다.

[13-15] 캐나다
Questions 13-15 refer to the following podcast.

> As you know, ¹³**I always try to give you tips on cutting everyday expenses in my podcast**. One of my listeners asked me for advice on how to create a household budget, so that's what I want to discuss today. ¹⁴**The most important step is the first one. You should write down each expense in the order of largest to smallest.** I'll now explain what to do next. But before I do, I have a quick reminder. ¹⁵**You can download a copy of my free e-book on my Web site.** It includes lots of money-saving suggestions.

cut v. 줄이다, 삭감하다 expense n. 지출, 돈 order n. 순서

해석
13-15번은 다음 팟캐스트에 관한 문제입니다.
아시다시피, ¹³저는 항상 제 팟캐스트에서 일상적인 지출을 줄이는 것에 대한 조언을 드리려고 노력합니다. 저의 청취자 중 한 명이 가계 예산을 세우는 방법에 대한 조언을 요청했기 때문에, 오늘은 그것에 대해 논의하고 싶습니다. ¹⁴가장 중요한 단계는 첫 번째 단계입니다. 여러분은 각 지출을 가장 큰 것부터 가장 작은 것의 순서대로 적어야 합니다. 이제 다음에 무엇을 해야 할지에 대해 설명해 드리겠습니다. 하지만 그 전에, 간단히 상기시켜 드릴 것이 있습니다. ¹⁵제 웹사이트에서 무료 전자책 사본을 다운로드하실 수 있습니다. 그것은 여러 돈을 아낄 수 있는 제안을 포함하고 있습니다.

13 주제 문제
해석 화자의 팟캐스트의 중점은 무엇인가?
(A) 자료를 공유하는 방법
(B) 집을 정리하는 방법
(C) 지출을 줄이는 방법
(D) 책을 출판하는 방법

해설 팟캐스트의 주제를 묻고 있으므로 지문의 초반을 반드시 듣는다. "I always try to give you tips on cutting everyday expenses in my podcast"라며 자신이 항상 팟캐스트에서 일상적인 지출을 줄이는 것에 대한 조언을 주려고 노력한다고 한 후, 가계 예산을 세우는 방법에 대한 내용으로 이어지고 있다. 따라서 (C)가 정답이다.

어휘 tidy v. 정리하다, 정돈하다

14 특정 세부 사항 문제
해석 화자는 무엇을 강조하는가?
(A) 서비스 비용 지불하기
(B) 목록 작성하기
(C) 쿠폰 사용하기
(D) 동영상 시청하기

해설 질문의 핵심 어구(emphasize)와 관련된 내용을 주의 깊게 듣는다. "The most important step is the first one. You should write down each expense in the order of largest to smallest."라며 가장 중요한 단계는 첫 번째 단계라고 한 후, 각 지출을 가장 큰 것에서 가장 작은 것의 순서대로 적어야 한다고 하였다. 따라서 (B)가 정답이다.

Paraphrasing
write down ~ in the order 순서대로 적다 → Making a list 목록 작성하기

15 방법 문제
해석 청취자들은 어떻게 무료 전자책을 받을 수 있는가?
(A) 웹사이트를 방문함으로써
(B) 애플리케이션을 다운로드함으로써
(C) 이메일을 보냄으로써
(D) 설문조사를 완료함으로써

해설 질문의 핵심 어구(receive a free e-book)와 관련된 내용을 주의 깊게 듣는다. "You can download a copy of my free e-book on my Web site."라며 자신의 웹사이트에서 무료 전자책 사본을 다운로드할 수 있다고 하였다. 따라서 (A)가 정답이다.

[16-18] 영국
Questions 16-18 refer to the following business report.

> ¹⁶**Earlier this afternoon, the city council approved Rosemount Incorporated's bid to build a soccer arena downtown.** This will be the company's largest construction project ever. However, Rosemount's CEO, Amy Smith, stated that the company is ready for the challenge. ¹⁷**The project is estimated to cost 90 million dollars and will provide work to nearly 1,000 skilled laborers from the local community.** Construction of the facility will begin on May 13 and will take 12 months to finish. As of now, ¹⁸**the city's soccer team expects to play its opening match in the completed stadium next year.**

council n. 의회 bid n. 입찰 arena n. 경기장 estimate v. 추정하다
as of now 현재로서는

해석
16-18번은 다음 비즈니스 보도에 관한 문제입니다.
¹⁶오늘 오후 일찍, 시 의회는 시내에 축구 경기장을 짓는 Rosemount사의 입찰을 승인했습니다. 이것은 그 회사의 역대 가장 큰 건설 프로젝트가 될 것입니다. 하지만, Rosemount사의 최고 경영자인 Amy Smith는 회사가 그 도전을 위한 준비가 되었다고 밝혔습니다. ¹⁷이 프로젝트는 9천만 달러의 비용이 들 것으로 추정되었으며 지역 사회의 거의 1,000명의 숙련된 노동자들에게 일자리를 제공할 것입니다. 이 시설의 공사는 5월 13일에 시작할 것이며 완공까지 12개월이 걸릴 것입니다. 현재로서는, ¹⁸시립 축구팀이 내년에 완공된 경기장에서 개막전을 치를 것으로 기대하고 있습니다.

16 특정 세부 사항 문제
해석 오늘 오후에 무엇이 발표되었는가?
(A) 계약 연장
(B) 기업 합병
(C) 시설 건설
(D) 모금 결과

해설 질문의 핵심 어구(this afternoon)가 언급된 주변을 주의 깊게 듣는다. "Earlier this afternoon, the city council approved Rosemount Incorporated's bid to build a soccer arena downtown."이라며 오늘 오후 일찍, 시 의회가 시내에 축구 경기장을 짓는 Rosemount사의 입찰을 승인했다고 하였다. 따라서 (C)가 정답이다.

어휘 extension n. 연장 merger n. 합병 fundraising n. 모금

17 특정 세부 사항 문제
해석 화자에 따르면, 그 프로젝트는 지역 사회에 어떻게 영향을 끼칠 것인가?
(A) 더 많은 관광객을 유치할 것이다.
(B) 세금을 낮출 것이다.
(C) 교통 체증을 초래할 것이다.
(D) 더 많은 일자리를 만들 것이다.

해설 질문의 핵심 어구(community)가 언급된 주변을 주의 깊게 듣는다. "The project is estimated to ~ provide work to nearly 1,000 skilled laborers from the local community."라며 이 프로젝트는 지역 사회의 거의 1,000명의 숙련된 노동자들에게 일자리를 제공할 것이라고 하였다. 따라서 (D)가 정답이다.

어휘 lower v. 낮추다, 내리다

18 다음에 할 일 문제
해석 내년에 무슨 일이 일어날 것 같은가?
(A) 주민들이 투표를 할 것이다.
(B) 스포츠팀이 새 경기장을 사용할 것이다.
(C) 회사가 지역 지점을 열 것이다.
(D) 건축가들이 도면을 완성할 것이다.

해설 질문의 핵심 어구(next year)가 언급된 주변을 주의 깊게 듣는다. "the city's soccer team expects to play its opening match in the completed stadium next year"라며 시립 축구팀이 내년에 완공된 경기장에서 개막전을 치를 것으로 기대하고 있다고 하였다. 따라서 (B)가 정답이다.

어휘 take a vote 투표를 하다 branch n. 지점 architect n. 건축가

[19-21] 호주
Questions 19-21 refer to the following broadcast and weather forecast.

Now for the local news update. ¹⁹**The Cranbrook Food Festival will take place on June 11 as scheduled, even though rain is expected.** But it will now be held in the Westport Community Center's main hall rather than in Tanner Park. The event will feature dishes prepared by over 25 local restaurants. ²⁰**The names of the establishments involved are included in the promotional poster that has been put up around town.** ²¹**The organizers are looking for people to set up the booths for the event.** Please call 555-0939 if you're interested in volunteering.

schedule v. 예정하다 establishment n. 업체, 점포
promotional adj. 홍보의 organizer n. 주최 측

해석
19-21번은 다음 방송과 일기 예보에 관한 문제입니다.

이제 최신 지역 뉴스입니다. ¹⁹비가 예상됨에도 불구하고, Cranbrook 음식 축제는 예정대로 6월 11일에 개최될 것입니다. 그러나 그것은 이제 Tanner 공원이 아닌 Westport 커뮤니티 센터의 메인 홀에서 열릴 예정입니다. 이 행사는 25개가 넘는 지역 식당에서 준비한 요리들을 선보일 것입니다. ²⁰참여하는 업체들의 이름은 마을 곳곳에 게시된 홍보 포스터에 포함되어 있습니다. ²¹주최 측은 행사를 위한 부스를 설치할 사람들을 찾고 있습니다. 자원하는 데에 관심이 있으시면 555-0939로 전화해 주세요.

화요일	☀
수요일	☁
¹⁹목요일	☂
금요일	☀

19 시각 자료 문제
해석 시각 자료를 보아라. 어떤 날에 행사가 개최될 것인가?
(A) 화요일
(B) 수요일
(C) 목요일
(D) 금요일

해설 제시된 일기 예보의 정보를 확인한 후 질문의 핵심 어구(the event be held)와 관련된 내용을 주의 깊게 듣는다. "The Cranbrook Food Festival will take place on June 11 as scheduled, even though rain is expected."라며 비가 예상됨에도 불구하고, Cranbrook 음식 축제는 예정대로 6월 11일에 개최될 것이라고 하였으므로 행사가 개최되는 날이 목요일임을 일기 예보에서 알 수 있다. 따라서 (C)가 정답이다.

20 특정 세부 사항 문제
해석 화자에 따르면, 포스터에는 무엇이 포함되어 있는가?
(A) 행사장의 지도
(B) 참가자 목록
(C) 식당의 메뉴
(D) 행사 일정

해설 질문의 핵심 어구(included on a poster)와 관련된 내용을 주의 깊게 듣는다. "The names of the establishments involved are included in the promotional poster that has been put up around town."이라며 참여하는 업체들의 이름은 마을 곳곳에 게시된 홍보 포스터에 포함되어 있다고 하였다. 따라서 (B)가 정답이다.

어휘 venue n. 행사장, 장소

21 이유 문제
해석 주최 측은 왜 자원봉사자들을 필요로 하는가?
(A) 교통정리를 하기 위해
(B) 표를 걷기 위해
(C) 음식을 준비하기 위해
(D) 부스를 마련하기 위해

해설 질문의 핵심 어구(need volunteers)와 관련된 내용을 주의 깊게 듣는다. "The organizers are looking for people to set up the booths for the event."라며 주최 측은 행사를 위한 부스를 설치할 사람들을 찾고 있다고 하였다. 따라서 (D)가 정답이다.

어휘 direct traffic 교통정리를 하다 arrange v. 마련하다

[Paraphrasing]
set up 설치하다 → arrange 마련하다

DAY 20 광고 및 소개

1. 광고

담화 흐름과 빈출 문제 호주 p.142

해석 Baroness 호텔에서는, 오늘날의 출장 여행객들이 필요로 하는 것들을 이해합니다. 전 세계 40개 이상의 도시들에서 호텔을 운영하는 Baroness 호텔 체인점은 우수한 서비스와 작은 부분까지 신경 쓰는 것으로 유명합니다. 그리고 이제, 저희는 전 세계 모든 지점에 비즈니스 센터를 추가했습니다. 이곳들은 무료 인터넷, 회의 및 모임실, 그리고 복사기의 이용을 제공합니다. 게다가, 단골 고객들께서는 객실 업그레이드와 자동차 대여

를 위한 포인트를 획득하실 수 있는 저희의 회원 프로그램을 이용하실 수 있습니다. Baroness 호텔에 관해 더 알고 싶거나 예약하고 싶으시면, 저희 웹사이트 www.baronesshotels.com을 방문해 주십시오.

어휘 operate v. 운영하다, 작동하다   access n. 이용, 접근
frequent guest 단골 고객   take advantage of ~을 이용하다, 활용하다

HACKERS PRACTICE   p.143

| 01 (D) | 02 (D) | 03 (B) | 04 (A) |

[01-02]   미국 / 영국
Questions 01-02 refer to the following advertisement.

Do you wish doing accounting work were easier? If so, you need the FinancePro software from Crevice Industries. This program makes it easy to fill out tax forms. Also, ⁰¹it includes many innovative features, such as enabling users to communicate with each other through an instant messaging system. ⁰²Buy this software before February 15 to take advantage of the 55-dollar introductory price offered by Crevice Industries. Otherwise, you will have to pay 65 dollars.

accounting n. 회계   fill out 작성하다   innovative adj. 혁신적인
feature n. 기능, 특징   enable v. ~할 수 있게 하다
communicate v. 소통하다   instant messaging 인스턴트 메시지 보내기
take advantage of ~을 이용하다
introductory price 출시 특별가, 시험 구독료

해석
01-02번은 다음 광고에 관한 문제입니다.

회계 업무가 더 쉬워지기를 원하시나요? 만약 그렇다면, Crevice Industries 사의 FinancePro 소프트웨어가 필요합니다. 이 프로그램은 세금 신고서를 작성하기 쉽게 만들어 줍니다. 또한, ⁰¹그것은 인스턴트 메시지 보내기 시스템을 통해 사용자들이 서로 소통할 수 있게 하는 것과 같은 많은 혁신적인 기능을 포함합니다. ⁰²2월 15일 이전에 이 소프트웨어를 구매하여 Crevice Industries사에서 제공하는 55달러의 출시 특별가를 이용하세요. 그렇지 않으면, 65달러를 지불하셔야 합니다.

01 특정 세부 사항 문제
해석 프로그램의 기능은 무엇인가?
    (A) 온라인 데이터베이스에 연결된다.
    (B) 모바일 기기에서 작동한다.
    (C) 월간 최신 정보를 받는다.
    (D) 채팅 프로그램을 포함한다.

해설 질문의 핵심 어구(feature of the program)와 관련된 내용을 주의 깊게 듣는다. "it[the program] includes many innovative features, such as enabling users to communicate with each other through an instant messaging system"이라며 프로그램이 인스턴트 메시지 보내기 시스템과 같은 사용자들이 서로 소통할 수 있는 혁신적인 기능을 포함한다고 하였다. 따라서 (D)가 정답이다.

어휘 connect v. 연결하다   function v. 작동하다, 기능하다

Paraphrasing
includes ~ an instant messaging system 인스턴트 메시지 보내기 시스템을 포함하는 ~ → includes a chat program 채팅 프로그램을 포함하다

02 특정 세부 사항 문제
해석 Crevice Industries는 2월 15일에 무엇을 할 것인가?
    (A) 서비스를 개선한다.
    (B) 시험을 완료한다.
    (C) 제품을 출시한다.
    (D) 가격을 인상한다.

해설 질문의 핵심 어구(February 15)와 관련된 내용을 주의 깊게 듣는다. "Buy this software before February 15 to take advantage of the 55-dollar introductory price offered by Crevice Industries. Otherwise, you will have to pay 65 dollars."라며 2월 15일 이전에 소프트웨어를 구매하면 55달러의 출시 특별가로 이용할 수 있지만, 그 이후에는 65달러를 지불해야 한다고 하였다. 따라서 (D)가 정답이다.

어휘 improve v. 개선하다   complete v. 완료하다   trial n. 시험, 실험
release v. 출시하다

[03-04]   캐나다 / 호주
Questions 03-04 refer to the following advertisement.

⁰³Looking for a way to protect your home or office? LokTek Industries can help! Our innovative A800 package is perfect for securing your business or residence. It uses advanced sensors to monitor cameras and alarms, and it automatically notifies the police if an unauthorized person enters the building. ⁰⁴To get a free site inspection and estimate, call 555-2020 now. You can also visit our showroom in Bentley Plaza if you want to learn more about our new system.

protect v. 보호하다   innovative adj. 혁신적인
perfect for ~에 안성맞춤인, ~에 제격인   secure v. 보호하다
residence n. 거주지   advanced adj. 첨단의, 고급의
monitor v. 모니터링하다, 추적 관찰하다   alarm n. 경보기, 경보
automatically adv. 자동으로   notify v. 신고하다, 알리다
unauthorized adj. 허가받지 않은   site n. 현장, 위치   inspection n. 점검
estimate n. 견적; v. 추정하다   showroom n. 전시실, 진열실

해석
03-04번은 다음 광고에 관한 문제입니다.

⁰³집이나 사무실을 보호할 방법을 찾고 계신가요? LokTek Industries사가 도와드릴 수 있습니다! 저희의 혁신적인 A800 패키지는 귀하의 사업체나 거주지를 보호하는 데 안성맞춤입니다. 그것은 카메라와 경보기를 모니터링하기 위해 첨단 센서를 사용하여, 허가받지 않은 사람이 건물에 들어오면 자동으로 경찰에 신고합니다. ⁰⁴무료 현장 점검과 견적을 받으시려면, 지금 555-2020으로 전화하세요. 저희의 새로운 시스템에 대해 더 알고 싶으시면 Bentley Plaza에 있는 저희 전시실을 방문하실 수도 있습니다.

03 주제 문제
해석 무엇이 광고되고 있는가?
    (A) 재활용 서비스
    (B) 보안 시스템
    (C) 소프트웨어 프로그램
    (D) 컨설팅 사업

해설 광고의 주제를 묻는 문제이므로, 지문의 초반을 반드시 듣는다. "Looking for a way to protect your home or office? LokTek Industries can help! Our innovative A800 package is perfect for securing your business or residence."라며 LokTek Industries사가 사업체와 거주지를 보호하는 서비스를 제공한다고 하였다. 따라서 (B)가 정답이다.

어휘 recycling n. 재활용   security n. 보안   consulting n. 컨설팅, 자문

Paraphrasing
a way to protect your home or office 집이나 사무실을 보호할 방법, securing your business or residence 사업체나 거주지를 보호하는 것 → A security system 보안 시스템

04 이유 문제
해석 청자들은 왜 회사에 즉시 전화해야 하는가?
    (A) 무료 서비스를 받기 위해
    (B) 특별 할인을 받기 위해

(C) 제품을 구매하기 위해
(D) 위치를 찾기 위해

해설 질문의 핵심 어구(call a company right away)가 언급된 주변을 주의 깊게 듣는다. "To get a free site inspection and estimate, call 555-2020 now."라며 무료 현장 점검과 견적을 받으려면 지금 555-2020으로 전화하라고 하였다. 따라서 (A)가 정답이다.

어휘 discount n. 할인   purchase v. 구매하다   location n. 위치, 장소

Paraphrasing
get a free site inspection and estimate 무료 현장 점검과 견적을 받다
→ receive a free service 무료 서비스를 받다

2. 소개

담화 흐름과 빈출 문제 [미국]   p.144

해석 오늘 모두 와주셔서 감사합니다. 이번 달부터, 우리는 팀 발전에 관한 일련의 워크숍을 개최할 것입니다. 오늘 오전의 진행자는 Shamara Wymer입니다. 그녀는 조직 심리학에 대한 상담가로서 15년 이상 일해왔습니다. Ms. Wymer는 이 분야에 있어서 전문가이고, 저는 여러분들이 그녀로부터 많이 배울 것이라고 확신합니다. 오늘의 워크숍에서, 그녀는 팀의 의무와 개인의 책임에 관해 논의할 것입니다. 여러분들은 팀 구성원 간 의사소통의 중요성에 대해 배울 것입니다. 세션이 끝날 때, 각자 최근에 출간된 그녀의 출판물, Building Effective Teams를 받으실 것입니다. 오늘 와주셔서 정말 감사드립니다, Ms. Wymer.

어휘 facilitator n. 진행자   organizational psychology 조직 심리학
commitment n. 의무, 헌신   accountability n. 책임, 의무

HACKERS PRACTICE   p.145

01 (D)   02 (B)   03 (C)   04 (A)

[01-02] [캐나다 / 호주]
Questions 01-02 refer to the following introduction.

> ⁰¹Greenhill Library is once again hosting a series of special seminars for local residents this year. Because of the strong interest, we had to move this session to a larger room. ⁰²Today's event is the first workshop in the series, and the topic is nutrition. We invited a registered dietitian to share practical tips on healthy eating and smart grocery shopping. We're excited to begin the program and hope you learn a lot.

host v. 개최하다; n. 진행자   local adj. 지역의   resident n. 주민
topic n. 주제   nutrition n. 영양   registered adj. 공인된, 등록된
dietitian n. 영양사   practical adj. 실용적인   grocery shopping 장보기

해석
01-02번은 다음 소개에 관한 문제입니다.

⁰¹Greenhill 도서관은 올해 다시 한번 지역 주민들을 위한 특별 세미나 시리즈를 개최하고 있습니다. 많은 관심 덕분에, 이번 세션을 더 큰 공간으로 옮겨야 했습니다. ⁰²오늘 행사는 시리즈의 첫 번째 워크숍이며, 주제는 영양입니다. 건강한 식습관과 현명한 장보기에 대한 실용적인 팁을 공유하기 위해 공인된 영양사분을 초대했습니다. 프로그램을 시작하게 되어 기쁘고 여러분에게서 많은 것을 배우시길 바랍니다.

01 장소 문제
해설 담화는 어디에서 일어나고 있는가?
(A) 피트니스 센터에서
(B) 병원에서
(C) 대학교에서
(D) 도서관에서

해설 담화가 이루어지는 장소를 묻는 문제이므로, 장소와 관련된 표현을 놓치지 않고 듣는다. "Greenhill Library is once again hosting a series of special seminars for local residents this year."라며 Greenhill 도서관이 올해 다시 한번 지역 주민들을 위한 특별 세미나 시리즈를 개최한다고 한 것을 통해 담화가 도서관에서 일어나고 있음을 알 수 있다. 따라서 (D)가 정답이다.

02 특정 세부 사항 문제
해설 화자에 따르면, 행사의 주제는 무엇인가?
(A) 안전
(B) 영양
(C) 요리
(D) 운동

해설 질문의 핵심 어구(topic of the event)와 관련된 내용을 주의 깊게 듣는다. "Today's event is the first workshop in the series, and the topic is nutrition."이라며 (특별 세미나) 시리즈의 첫 번째 워크숍인 오늘 행사의 주제는 영양이라고 하였다. 따라서 (B)가 정답이다.

[03-04] [영국 / 미국]
Questions 03-04 refer to the following introduction.

> Our next speaker for today's seminar needs no introduction. ⁰³Devon Baker has worked at Floppy Basics as a shoe designer for over a decade. The company is known for its casual footwear with customizable and stylish designs. Today, she will talk to you about fostering creativity in the workplace. Before we begin, ⁰⁴please take a few minutes to take a look at some of her shoe designs, which are on display at the back of the room.

introduction n. 소개   decade n. 10년   casual adj. 캐주얼의, 평상복의
footwear n. 신발   customizable adj. 주문 제작이 가능한
stylish adj. 유행을 따르는, 멋진   foster v. 육성하다, 키우다
creativity n. 창의성   workplace n. 직장   on display 전시된

해석
03-04번은 다음 소개에 관한 문제입니다.

오늘 세미나의 다음 연사는 소개가 필요 없습니다. ⁰³Devon Baker는 Floppy Basics사에서 10년 넘게 신발 디자이너로 일해 왔습니다. 이 회사는 주문 제작이 가능하며 유행을 따르는 디자인을 갖춘 캐주얼 신발로 알려져 있습니다. 오늘, 그녀는 여러분께 직장에서 창의성을 육성하는 것에 대해 이야기할 것입니다. 시작하기 전에, ⁰⁴잠시 시간을 내어 방 뒤쪽에 전시된 그녀의 신발 디자인을 봐주시길 바랍니다.

03 특정 세부 사항 문제
해설 Devon Baker는 누구인가?
(A) 상담가
(B) 교수
(C) 신발 디자이너
(D) 패션 기자

해설 질문 대상(Devon Baker)의 신분 및 직업과 관련된 표현을 놓치지 않고 듣는다. "Devon Baker has worked at Floppy Basics as a shoe designer for over a decade."라며 Devon Baker가 Floppy Basics사에서 10년 넘게 신발 디자이너로 일해 왔다고 하였다. 따라서 (C)가 정답이다.

어휘 consultant n. 상담가, 자문 위원   professor n. 교수   journalist n. 기자

Paraphrasing
a shoe designer 신발 디자이너 → A footwear designer 신발 디자이너

04 다음에 할 일 문제

해석 청자들은 다음에 무엇을 할 것 같은가?
(A) 디자인을 본다.
(B) 회사 비디오를 본다.
(C) 발표를 듣는다.
(D) 설문지를 작성한다.

해설 질문의 핵심 어구(do next)와 관련된 내용을 주의 깊게 듣는다. "please take a few minutes to take a look at some of her shoe designs, which are on display at the back of the room"이라며 잠시 시간을 내어 방 뒤쪽에 전시된 그녀의 신발 디자인을 봐달라고 하였다. 따라서 (A)가 정답이다.

어휘 presentation n. 발표 fill out 작성하다, 기입하다 questionnaire n. 설문지

[Paraphrasing]
take a look at some of her shoe designs 그녀의 신발 디자인을 보다
→ Look at some designs 디자인을 본다

HACKERS TEST p.146

01 (C)	02 (B)	03 (D)	04 (C)	05 (D)
06 (D)	07 (D)	08 (B)	09 (A)	10 (C)
11 (B)	12 (B)	13 (D)	14 (B)	15 (B)
16 (C)	17 (D)	18 (B)	19 (A)	20 (D)
21 (B)				

[01-03] 영국
Questions 01-03 refer to the following introduction.

⁰¹**I'm excited to welcome Maria Lopez, the new head chef here at our restaurant.** She has over 15 years of experience working at respected dining establishments around the world. ⁰²**Her last position was manager of London's most popular dining facility.** She will spend the next two weeks modifying our menu to have a Spanish theme. ⁰³**Once she has created a new selection of entrées and desserts, everyone will be trained on how to cook them. This will take place sometime next week.**

respected adj. 훌륭한, 높이 평가되는 dining establishment 식당
modify v. 수정하다 entrée n. 주요리

해석
01-03번은 다음 소개에 관한 문제입니다.

⁰¹저는 이곳 우리 식당의 새로운 수석 요리사, Maria Lopez를 환영하게 되어 기쁩니다. 그녀는 전 세계의 훌륭한 식당들에서 15년 넘게 일한 경력이 있습니다. ⁰²그녀의 마지막 직책은 런던의 가장 유명한 식당의 관리자였습니다. 그녀는 스페인 테마를 갖추기 위해 우리 메뉴를 수정하는 데 앞으로 2주를 보낼 것입니다. ⁰³그녀가 새로운 주요리와 디저트 종류들을 만들고 나면, 여러분 모두 그것들을 요리하는 방법에 대해 교육받게 될 것입니다. 이것은 다음 주 중에 진행될 예정입니다.

01 장소 문제

해석 청자들은 어디에 있는 것 같은가?
(A) 빵집에
(B) 식료품점에
(C) 식당에
(D) 출장 연회업체에

해설 지문에서 장소와 관련된 표현을 놓치지 않고 듣는다. "I'm excited to welcome Maria Lopez, the new head chef here at our restaurant."라며 이곳 우리 식당에서 새로운 수석 요리사 Maria Lopez를 환영하게 되어 기쁘다고 하였다. 따라서 (C)가 정답이다.

어휘 grocery n. 식료품 catering n. 출장 연회(업)

[Paraphrasing]
restaurant 식당 → dining establishment 식당

02 특정 세부 사항 문제

해석 Maria Lopez는 런던에서 무엇을 했는가?
(A) 시설을 견학했다.
(B) 사업체를 관리했다.
(C) 회사를 설립했다.
(D) 학위를 취득했다.

해설 질문의 핵심 어구(Maria Lopez ~ London)와 관련된 내용을 주의 깊게 듣는다. "Her[Maria Lopez's] last position was manager of London's most popular dining facility."라며 Maria Lopez의 마지막 직책은 런던의 가장 유명한 식당의 관리자였다고 하였다. 따라서 (B)가 정답이다.

어휘 facility n. 시설 manage v. 관리하다

03 다음에 할 일 문제

해석 청자들은 다음 주에 무엇을 할 것인가?
(A) 시설에 방문한다.
(B) 오찬에 참여한다.
(C) 계약서를 검토한다.
(D) 교육을 받는다.

해설 지문의 마지막 부분을 주의 깊게 듣는다. "Once she[Maria Lopez] has created a new selection of entrées and desserts, everyone will be trained on how to cook them. This will take place sometime next week."이라며 Maria Lopez가 새로운 주요리와 디저트 종류들을 만들고 나면, 청자들 모두 그것들을 요리하는 방법에 대해 교육받게 될 것이라고 한 후, 이것은 다음 주 중에 진행될 예정이라고 하였다. 따라서 (D)가 정답이다.

어휘 establishment n. 시설, 기관 luncheon n. 오찬

[04-06] 캐나다
Questions 04-06 refer to the following advertisement.

Everyone knows it can be difficult to manage both your professional and home life. And that's where Alito Incorporated comes in! ⁰⁴**Let us take care of your household cleaning tasks.** ⁰⁵**If you are a first-time customer, one of our specialists will visit your home to discuss your needs and recommend a package. There is no charge for this.** So don't delay. ⁰⁶**Consider downloading our mobile application today to set up a time that works for you.** We know you will be completely satisfied with our services.

home life 가정생활 household n. 가정 specialist n. 전문가
completely adv. 완전히 satisfied adj. 만족하는

해석
04-06번은 다음 광고에 관한 문제입니다.

직장 생활과 가정생활을 모두 관리하기가 어려울 수 있다는 것은 누구나 알고 있습니다. 그리고 바로 그곳이 Alito사가 등장하는 지점입니다! ⁰⁴당신의 가정 청소 작업을 저희가 책임지겠습니다. ⁰⁵귀하가 새로운 고객이시라면, 저희 전문가 중 한 명이 귀하의 집을 방문하여 필요한 사항에 대해 논의하고 패키지를 추천해 드릴 것입니다. 이에 대한 요금은 없습니다. 그러니 지체하지 마세요. ⁰⁶오늘 저희 모바일 애플리케이션을 다운로드하여 귀하에게 맞는 시간을 설정하는 것을 고려해 보세요. 저희는 귀하가 저희 서비스에 완전히 만족하실 것이라고 확신합니다.

04 주제 문제

해석 어떤 종류의 업체가 광고되고 있는가?
(A) 부동산 관리 회사
(B) 조경 회사
(C) 청소 서비스
(D) 실내 장식 회사

해설 광고의 주제를 묻는 문제이므로, 지문의 초반을 반드시 듣는다. "Let us take care of your household cleaning tasks."라며 당신의 가정 청소 작업을 저희가 책임지겠다고 한 후, 청소 서비스에 대한 내용으로 이어지고 있다. 따라서 (C)가 정답이다.

어휘 property management 부동산 관리 landscaping n. 조경 firm n. 회사

05 특정 세부 사항 문제

해석 새로운 고객들은 무엇을 받게 될 것인가?
(A) 체험권
(B) 상품권
(C) 정보 안내 책자
(D) 무료 상담

해설 질문의 핵심 어구(first-time customers receive)와 관련된 내용을 주의 깊게 듣는다. "If you are a first-time customer, one of our specialists will visit your home to discuss your needs and recommend a package. There is no charge for this."라며 새로운 고객이라면, 전문가 중 한 명이 집을 방문하여 필요한 사항에 대해 논의하고 패키지를 추천해 줄 것이라고 한 후, 이에 대한 요금은 없다고 하였다. 따라서 (D)가 정답이다.

어휘 trial membership 체험권 consultation n. 상담

06 제안 문제

해석 화자는 무엇을 제안하는가?
(A) 리뷰를 읽기
(B) 패키지를 업그레이드하기
(C) 사무실에 방문하기
(D) 앱을 설치하기

해설 지문의 중후반에서 제안과 관련된 표현이 언급된 다음을 주의 깊게 듣는다. "Consider downloading our mobile application today to set up a time that works for you."라며 오늘 모바일 애플리케이션을 다운로드하여 맞는 시간을 설정하는 것을 고려하라고 하였다. 따라서 (D)가 정답이다.

[Paraphrasing]
downloading ~ application 애플리케이션을 다운로드하는 것 → Installing an app 앱을 설치하기

[07-09] 🎧 미국

Questions 07-09 refer to the following introduction.

> ⁰⁷As the organizer of the National Linguistics Conference, I'm pleased to introduce our keynote speaker, Wilma Parker. A professor at Bakersfield University, she is also a leading researcher in the field of ancient North African languages. In fact, ⁰⁸it was just announced that she will receive funding from the government for her new research on the development of early Egyptian writing systems. Before Ms. Parker comes up on stage, ⁰⁹I want to remind everyone that the order of the presentations this afternoon has been changed. The updated schedule was posted yesterday. Now, please welcome Ms. Parker.

linguistics n. 언어학 keynote speaker 기조연설자 leading adj. 선두적인
researcher n. 연구원 field n. 분야 ancient adj. 고대의

해석 07-09번은 다음 소개에 관한 문제입니다.

⁰⁷전국 언어학 학회의 주최자로서, 저는 저희의 기조연설자인 Wilma Parker를 소개하게 되어 기쁩니다. Bakersfield 대학의 교수인 그녀는 또한 고대 북아프리카 언어 분야의 선두적인 연구원이기도 합니다. 사실, ⁰⁸그녀가 초기 이집트 문자 체계의 발전에 관한 그녀의 새로운 연구에 대해 정부로부터 재정 지원을 받게 될 것이라고 방금 발표되었습니다. Ms. Parker가 무대에 오르기 전에, ⁰⁹저는 모든 분들께 오늘 오후 발표 순서가 변경되었다는 것을 상기시켜 드리고 싶습니다. 업데이트된 일정은 어제 게시되었습니다. 이제, Ms. Parker를 환영해 주시기 바랍니다.

07 화자 문제

해석 화자는 누구인 것 같은가?
(A) 사업주
(B) 대학생
(C) 수상자
(D) 행사 주최자

해설 지문에서 신분 및 직업과 관련된 표현을 놓치지 않고 듣는다. "As the organizer of the National Linguistics Conference, I'm pleased to introduce our keynote speaker"라며 전국 언어학 학회의 주최자로서 기조연설자를 소개하게 되어 기쁘다고 했으므로 화자는 행사 주최자임을 알 수 있다. 따라서 (D)가 정답이다.

어휘 award recipient 수상자

08 특정 세부 사항 문제

해석 화자에 따르면, 무엇이 방금 발표되었는가?
(A) 연구 제안
(B) 정부 재정 지원
(C) 취업 제안
(D) 산업 규제

해설 질문의 핵심 어구(just announced)가 언급된 주변을 주의 깊게 듣는다. "it was just announced that she[Ms. Parker] will receive funding from the government for her new research on the development of early Egyptian writing systems"라며 Ms. Parker가 초기 이집트 문자 체계의 발전에 관한 그녀의 새로운 연구에 대해 정부로부터 재정 지원을 받게 될 것이라고 방금 발표되었다고 하였다. 따라서 (B)가 정답이다.

어휘 proposal n. 제안 employment n. 취업 offer n. 제안
regulation n. 규제

[Paraphrasing]
receive funding from the government 정부로부터 재정 지원을 받다
→ Government funding 정부 재정 지원

09 특정 세부 사항 문제

해석 화자는 청자들에게 무엇에 대해 상기시키는가?
(A) 일정이 변경되었다.
(B) 발표가 취소되었다.
(C) 웹사이트가 업데이트될 것이다.
(D) 회의가 연장될 것이다.

해설 질문의 핵심 어구(remind)가 언급된 주변을 주의 깊게 듣는다. "I want to remind everyone that the order of the presentations this afternoon has been changed. The updated schedule was posted yesterday."라며 모든 분들에게 오늘 오후 발표 순서가 변경되었다는 것을 상기시키고 싶다고 한 후, 업데이트된 일정은 어제 게시되었다고 하였다. 따라서 (A)가 정답이다.

[10-12] 🎧 캐나다
Questions 10-12 refer to the following introduction.

> It's a pleasure to welcome you all to the Stein Institute Convention. ¹⁰**The topic for today is renewable energy**, which can replace gas, coal, and oil. We have a number of great speakers lined up, including Morgan O'Malley, a renowned solar panel designer. ¹¹**He will give a talk on a new type of solar panel that he recently developed.** Oh, one more thing. ¹²**You may want to ask questions during a talk.** But, well . . . Each speaker has only 30 minutes. ¹²**So we'd like to avoid any interruptions.** Thank you for your understanding.
>
> renewable energy 재생 가능 에너지   coal n. 석탄   line up 준비하다
> solar panel 태양 전지판   give a talk 강연하다

해석
10-12번은 다음 소개에 관한 문제입니다.
Stein 연구소 학회에 여러분 모두를 환영하게 되어 기쁩니다. ¹⁰오늘의 주제는 가스, 석탄, 그리고 석유를 대체할 수 있는 **재생 가능 에너지입니다**. 저명한 태양 전지판 설계자인 Morgan O'Malley를 포함하여, 여러 훌륭한 연사들이 준비되어 있습니다. ¹¹그는 그가 최근에 개발한 새로운 유형의 태양 전지판에 대해 강연할 것입니다. 아, 한 가지 더 말씀드리겠습니다. ¹²여러분은 강연 중에 질문을 하고 싶으실 수도 있습니다. 하지만, 음... 각 연사에게 30분만 주어집니다. ¹²그래서 저희는 어떠한 방해도 방지하고 싶습니다. 이해해 주셔서 감사합니다.

10 주제 문제
해석 학회의 주제는 무엇인가?
(A) 재무 관리
(B) 기업 브랜딩
(C) 재생 가능 에너지
(D) 건축 설계

해설 학회의 주제가 무엇인지 묻는 문제이므로, 지문의 초반을 반드시 듣는다. "The topic for today is renewable energy"라며 오늘의 주제는 재생 가능 에너지라고 하였다. 따라서 (C)가 정답이다.

어휘 financial adj. 재무의   architectural adj. 건축의

11 언급 문제
해석 Morgan O'Malley에 대해 무엇이 언급되는가?
(A) 그는 건설 프로젝트에 참여했다.
(B) 그는 새로운 장치를 개발했다.
(C) 그는 정부 프로그램을 이끌었다.
(D) 그는 산업 행사를 조직했다.

해설 질문의 핵심 어구(Morgan O'Malley)에 관련된 내용을 주의 깊게 듣는다. "He[Morgan O'Malley] will give a talk on a new type of solar panel that he recently developed."라며 Morgan O'Malley가 최근에 그가 개발한 새로운 유형의 태양 전지판에 대해 강연할 것이라고 하였다. 따라서 (B)가 정답이다.

어휘 construction n. 건설   organize v. 조직하다

12 의도 파악 문제
해석 화자는 "각 연사에게 30분만 주어집니다"라고 말할 때 무엇을 의도하는가?
(A) 일정이 수정되어야 한다.
(B) 질문은 자제되어야 한다.
(C) 주제가 변경될 것이다.
(D) 업무가 완료될 수 없다.

해설 질문의 인용어구(Each speaker has only 30 minutes)가 언급된 주변을 주의 깊게 듣는다. "You may want to ask questions during a talk."라며 여러분은 강연 중에 질문을 하고 싶으실 수도 있다고 한 후, "So we'd like to avoid any interruptions."라며 어떠한 방해도 방지하고 싶다고 한 것을 통해 강연 중에 질문이 자제되어야 한다는 의도임을 알 수 있다. 따라서 (B)가 정답이다.

[13-15] 🎧 미국
Questions 13-15 refer to the following advertisement.

> ¹³**Do you wish you could enjoy high-quality fashion items at affordable prices? Visit Megan's Apparel during our clearance sale**, from April 10 to 20! ¹⁴**Megan's Apparel is moving into a new location next month**, so we need to clear out as much inventory as possible. If savings of 30 to 50 percent are not enough to bring you in, ¹⁵**we are also giving away free T-shirts. You just need to spend over 100 dollars to receive one.** Don't miss out!
>
> high-quality adj. 고급의, 우수한   affordable adj. 저렴한, 알맞은
> clearance sale 재고 정리 세일   inventory n. 재고
> give away 나누어 주다, 거저 주다

해석
13-15번은 다음 광고에 관한 문제입니다.
¹³저렴한 가격에 고급 의류 상품을 즐길 수 있기를 원하십니까? 4월 10일부터 20일까지 진행되는 저희의 재고 정리 세일 동안 Megan's Apparel을 방문하세요! ¹⁴Megan's Apparel은 다음 달에 새로운 장소로 옮기기 때문에, 가능한 한 많은 재고를 정리해야 합니다. 만약 30퍼센트에서 50퍼센트의 절약이 여러분을 이곳으로 오게 하기에 충분하지 않다면, ¹⁵저희는 무료 티셔츠 또한 나누어 드리고 있습니다. 여러분은 티셔츠를 받으시기 위해 단지 100달러 넘게 소비하시면 됩니다. 놓치지 마세요!

13 주제 문제
해석 어떤 종류의 업체가 광고되고 있는가?
(A) 원예 상점
(B) 스포츠용품점
(C) 슈퍼마켓
(D) 의류 소매점

해설 광고의 주제를 묻는 문제이므로, 지문의 초반을 반드시 듣는다. "Do you wish you could enjoy high-quality fashion items at affordable prices? Visit Megan's Apparel during our clearance sale"이라며 저렴한 가격에 고급 의류 상품을 즐길 수 있기를 원한다면 재고 정리 세일 동안 Megan's Apparel을 방문하라고 하였다. 따라서 (D)가 정답이다.

어휘 gardening n. 원예   retailer n. 소매점

14 언급 문제
해석 사업체에 관해 무엇이 언급되는가?
(A) 여러 지점이 있다.
(B) 이전할 계획이다.
(C) 새로운 재고가 있다.
(D) 임시 직원을 고용한다.

해설 질문의 핵심 어구(the business)와 관련된 내용을 주의 깊게 듣는다. "Megan's Apparel is moving into a new location next month"라며 Megan's Apparel이 다음 달에 새로운 장소로 옮긴다고 하였다. 따라서 (B)가 정답이다.

어휘 relocate v. 이전하다   temporary adj. 임시의, 일시적인

> Paraphrasing
> is moving into a new location 새로운 장소로 옮길 것이다 → relocate 이전하다

15 방법 문제
해석 고객들은 어떻게 무료 물품을 받을 수 있는가?

(A) 추첨에 참여함으로써
(B) 최소한의 구매를 함으로써
(C) 피드백 양식을 작성함으로써
(D) 가게에 일찍 도착함으로써

해설 질문의 핵심 어구(receive a free item)와 관련된 내용을 주의 깊게 듣는다. "we are also giving away free T-shirts. You just need to spend over 100 dollars to receive one."이라며 자신들이 무료 티셔츠 또한 나누어 주고 있는데, 티셔츠를 받기 위해 단지 100달러 넘게 소비하면 된다고 하였다. 따라서 (B)가 정답이다.

어휘 enter v. 참여하다, 출전하다   drawing n. 추첨   minimum adj. 최소한의

[16-18] 호주

Questions 16-18 refer to the following introduction.

¹⁶Paula Pine has been invited to our factory today to explain how to operate our new industrial printers. Ms. Pine works for the manufacturer that builds this equipment and is an expert in both its design and operation. This morning, she will go over the various functions of each machine. After that, Ms. Pine will also explain how to properly maintain them over time. ¹⁷Be sure to listen carefully to all of the information, as it will be fairly technical. But ¹⁸first, Ms. Pine will provide some basic safety tips for handling the machinery.

operate v. 작동시키다   industrial adj. 산업용의   expert n. 전문가
function n. 기능

해석
16-18번은 다음 소개에 관한 문제입니다.

¹⁶새로운 산업용 인쇄기를 작동시키는 방법을 설명해 주기 위해 오늘 우리 공장으로 Paula Pine이 초청되었습니다. Ms. Pine은 이 장비를 만든 제조업체에서 근무하고 있고, 그것의 설계 및 작동 모두에 관한 전문가입니다. 오늘 아침에, 그녀는 각 기계의 다양한 기능에 대해 다룰 것입니다. 그 후에, Ms. Pine은 또한 시간이 지남에 따라 그것들을 어떻게 적절히 유지 보수해야 하는지도 설명해 줄 것입니다. ¹⁷모든 정보가 상당히 기술적이기 때문에, 주의 깊게 듣기를 바랍니다. 하지만 ¹⁸먼저, Ms. Pine은 그 기계를 다루기 위한 몇몇 기본적인 안전상 조언을 줄 것입니다.

16 이유 문제

해설 Paula Pine은 왜 공장에 초청되었는가?
(A) 설명서를 수정하기 위해
(B) 제품들을 배달하기 위해
(C) 장비에 대해 이야기하기 위해
(D) 점검을 하기 위해

해설 질문의 핵심 어구(Paula Pine ~ invited)가 언급된 주변을 주의 깊게 듣는다. "Paula Pine has been invited to our factory today to explain how to operate our new industrial printers."라며 새로운 산업용 인쇄기를 작동시키는 방법을 설명해 주기 위해 Paula Pine이 공장으로 초청되었다고 하였다. 따라서 (C)가 정답이다.

어휘 edit v. 수정하다   equipment n. 장비   inspection n. 점검

Paraphrasing
explain how to operate ~ industrial printers 산업용 인쇄기를 작동시키는 방법을 설명하다 → discuss some equipment 장비에 대해 이야기하다

17 요청 문제

해설 화자는 청자들에게 무엇을 하라고 요청하는가?
(A) 기계를 조립한다.
(B) 발표를 연습한다.
(C) 세미나에 등록한다.
(D) 세심한 주의를 기울인다.

해설 지문의 중후반에서 요청과 관련된 표현이 포함된 문장을 주의 깊게 듣는다. "Be sure to listen carefully to all of the information, as it will be fairly technical."이라며 모든 정보가 기술적이기 때문에 주의 깊게 듣기를 바란다고 하였다. 따라서 (D)가 정답이다.

어휘 assemble v. 조립하다   practice v. 연습하다   sign up 등록하다

Paraphrasing
listen carefully 주의 깊게 듣다 → Pay close attention 세심한 주의를 기울이다

18 특정 세부 사항 문제

해설 화자에 따르면, 무엇이 처음으로 다루어질 것인가?
(A) 장치 디자인
(B) 안전 조치
(C) 프로젝트 세부 사항
(D) 마감 날짜

해설 질문의 핵심 어구(covered first)와 관련된 내용을 주의 깊게 듣는다. "first, Ms. Pine will provide some basic safety tips for handling the machinery"라며 먼저 Ms. Pine이 그 기계를 다루기 위한 몇몇 기본적인 안전상 조언을 줄 것이라고 하였다. 따라서 (B)가 정답이다.

[19-21] 영국

Questions 19-21 refer to the following advertisement and product list.

If you are suffering from back pain, Swift Corporation has the solution! ¹⁹Based on feedback gathered from our customers last year, we've designed our best massage chair. ²⁰Like many of our other models, the SwiftLux includes a heating function and a custom massage pattern option. But it is our first to respond to voice commands. Best of all, we're offering it at a 25 percent discount. Just sign up for the newly launched Swift Loyalty Club. ²¹Once your account is created, you will receive a digital coupon to use for your purchase.

gather v. 수집하다   custom adj. 맞춤형의   command n. 명령

해석
19-21번은 다음 광고와 제품 목록에 관한 문제입니다.

만약 당신이 허리 통증으로 고통받고 계신다면, Swift사가 해결책을 가지고 있습니다! ¹⁹작년에 저희 고객들로부터 수집한 의견을 기반으로, 저희는 최고의 마사지 의자를 설계했습니다. ²⁰저희의 다른 여러 모델들과 마찬가지로, SwiftLux는 온열 기능과 맞춤형 마사지 패턴 옵션을 포함하고 있습니다. 하지만 이것은 음성 명령에 반응하는 저희의 첫 번째 제품입니다. 무엇보다도, 저희는 그것을 25퍼센트 할인된 가격에 제공하고 있습니다. 새롭게 출시된 Swift Loyalty Club에 가입하기만 하면 됩니다. ²¹계정이 생성되면, 귀하는 구매에 사용하실 수 있는 디지털 쿠폰을 받게 되실 것입니다.

Swift사 제품 목록			
모델 #	기능		
	온열 기능	맞춤형 패턴	음성 명령
XR485	✓		
SC837		✓	
VP938	✓	✓	
²⁰WS127	✓	✓	✓

19 특정 세부 사항 문제

해설 Swift사는 작년에 무엇을 했는가?
(A) 의견을 수집했다.
(B) 디자이너를 고용했다.
(C) 앱을 출시했다.

(D) 생산을 증가시켰다.

해설 질문의 핵심 어구(last year)가 언급된 주변을 주의 깊게 듣는다. "Based on feedback gathered from our customers last year, we've designed our best massage chair."라며 작년에 고객들로부터 수집한 의견을 기반으로 최고의 마사지 의자를 설계했다고 하였다. 따라서 (A)가 정답이다.

어휘 launch v. 출시하다

[Paraphrasing]
feedback gathered 수집한 의견 → collected feedback 의견을 수집했다

20 시각 자료 문제

해석 시각 자료를 보아라. 어느 제품이 홍보되고 있는가?
(A) XR485
(B) SC837
(C) VP938
(D) WS127

해설 제시된 제품 목록의 정보를 확인한 후 질문의 핵심 어구(being promoted)와 관련된 내용을 주의 깊게 듣는다. "Like many of our other models, the SwiftLux includes a heating function and a custom massage pattern option. But it is our first to respond to voice commands."라며 다른 여러 모델들과 마찬가지로, SwiftLux는 온열 기능과 맞춤형 마사지 패턴 옵션을 포함하고 있으며, 음성 명령에 반응하는 첫 번째 제품이라고 하였다. 이 세 가지 기능을 모두 포함하는 제품은 WS127임을 제품 목록에서 알 수 있다. 따라서 (D)가 정답이다.

21 방법 문제

해석 청자들은 어떻게 할인 자격을 받을 수 있는가?
(A) 계정을 업그레이드함으로써
(B) 멤버십을 생성함으로써
(C) 설문을 완성함으로써
(D) 제품을 리뷰함으로써

해설 질문의 핵심 어구(qualify for a discount)와 관련된 내용을 주의 깊게 듣는다. "Once your account is created, you will receive a digital coupon to use for your purchase."라며 계정이 생성되면 구매에 사용할 수 있는 디지털 쿠폰을 받게 될 것이라고 하였다. 따라서 (B)가 정답이다.

[Paraphrasing]
account is created 계정이 생성되다 → creating a membership 멤버십 생성하기

PART 5

DAY 01 명사

기출 포인트 01~02

실전 Check-up p.156

01 (B) **02** (A)

01 명사 자리 채우기
해석 사람들은 이 목록에 그들의 이름을 추가함으로써 행사 참여의 의사를 나타낼 수 있다.
해설 소유격 인칭대명사(their)의 꾸밈을 받으면서 동사(may indicate)의 목적어 자리에 올 수 있는 것은 명사이므로 명사 (B) intention(의사)이 정답이다. 동사 (A)는 명사 자리에 올 수 없다.
어휘 indicate v. 나타내다 participate in ~에 참여하다

02 명사 자리 채우기
해석 연체료를 피하기 위해서는 매달 15일 이전에 지불이 이루어져야 한다.
해설 부정관사(A)와 동사(should be made) 사이에 올 수 있는 것은 명사이므로 명사 (A) payment(지불)가 정답이다. 동사 또는 과거분사 (B)는 명사 자리에 올 수 없다.
어휘 avoid v. 피하다 late fee 연체료

기출 포인트 03~04

실전 Check-up p. 157

01 (B) **02** (B)

01 가산 명사와 불가산 명사 구별하여 채우기
해석 Riverside 극단은 다음 주말에 곧 있을 여름 상연 작품을 위한 오디션을 개최할 것이다.
해설 빈칸은 동사(is holding)의 목적어 자리이므로 모든 보기가 정답의 후보이다. audition(오디션)은 가산 명사이고 빈칸 앞에 부정관사(a(n))가 없으므로 복수형 (B) auditions가 정답이다.
어휘 hold v. 개최하다 upcoming adj. 곧 있을, 다가오는
production n. 상연 작품, 연출

02 가산 명사와 불가산 명사 구별하여 채우기
해석 그 회사는 일 년에 두 번 각 직원의 평가를 실시할 것이다.
해설 빈칸은 전치사(of)의 목적어 자리이므로 모든 보기가 정답의 후보이다. 수량 표현 each 뒤에는 단수 가산 명사가 오므로 (B) worker가 정답이다.
어휘 evaluation n. 평가

기출 포인트 05

실전 Check-up p. 158

01 (B) **02** (B)

01 사람명사와 사물/추상명사 구별하여 채우기
해석 이 웹사이트에 대한 주된 불평은 스마트폰에서의 형편없는 디스플레이이다.
해설 빈칸은 형용사(main)의 수식을 받는 명사 자리이므로 모든 보기가 정답의 후보이다. '이 웹사이트에 대한 주된 불평'이라는 의미가 되어야 하므로 추상명사 (B) complaint(불평)가 정답이다. 사람명사 (A) complainer (투덜대는 사람)를 쓸 경우 '이 웹사이트에 대한 주된 투덜대는 사람'이라는 어색한 의미가 된다.
어휘 main adj. 주된 display n. 디스플레이(컴퓨터 화면에 나타나는 정보)

02 사람명사와 사물/추상명사 구별하여 채우기
해석 그녀는 마케팅 관리자의 조수로 3년 동안 일해 왔다.
해설 부정관사(an)와 전치사(to) 사이에 올 수 있는 것은 명사이므로 모든 보기가 정답의 후보이다. '그녀는 마케팅 관리자의 조수로 일해 왔다'라는 의미가 되어야 하므로 사람명사 (B) assistant(조수)가 정답이다. 추상명사 (A) assistance(원조, 보조)를 쓸 경우 '그녀는 마케팅 관리자의 원조로 일해 왔다'라는 어색한 의미가 된다.
어휘 director n. 관리자

3초컷 정답 공식 p.159

01 (B) **02** (C) **03** (D) **04** (D) **05** (D)
06 (D) **07** (A) **08** (B)

01 명사 자리 채우기
해석 그 강좌의 강사는 정보 기술 분야에서 10년이 넘는 경력을 가지고 있다.
해설 정관사(The)와 전치사(of) 사이에 올 수 있는 것은 명사이므로 명사 (B) instructor(강사)가 정답이다. 동사 (A)와 (D), 형용사 (C)는 명사 자리에 올 수 없다.
어휘 technology n. 기술 instruct v. 가르치다, 지시하다
instructive adj. 유익한, 교육적인

02 명사 자리 채우기
해석 특별 행사를 위한 회의실 사용은 건물 관리인의 승인을 필요로 한다.
해설 정관사(the)와 전치사(of) 사이에 오면서 동사(requires)의 목적어 자리에 올 수 있는 것은 명사이므로 명사 (C) permission(승인, 허가)이 정답이다. 형용사 (A)와 (D), 동사 또는 과거분사 (B)는 명사 자리에 올 수 없다.
어휘 require v. 필요로 하다 administrator n. 관리인
permissive adj. 관대한, 자유방임적인 permit v. 허용하다
permissible adj. 허용되는

03 명사 자리 채우기
해석 Dana Peters에 의해 쓰인 잡지 기사는 인공지능 분야의 발전에 대한 정보를 포함하고 있다.
해설 빈칸은 전치사(about)의 목적어 자리이므로 명사 (D) developments(발전)가 정답이다. 동사 (A)와 (C), 동사 또는 형용사 (B)는 명사 자리에 올 수 없다.
어휘 article n. 기사 field n. 분야 artificial intelligence 인공 지능

04 명사 자리 채우기
해석 대부분의 환자들은 Hawthorne 병원에서 그들이 받는 치료의 질에 대해 높은 수준의 만족감을 표현한다.
해설 빈칸은 전치사(of)의 목적어 자리이므로 명사 (D) satisfaction(만족감)이 정답이다. 동사 (A)와 (B), 동사 또는 형용사 (C)는 명사 자리에 올 수 없다.

어휘 quality n. 질, 우수함

05 가산 명사와 불가산 명사 구별하여 채우기
해석 Huntington 호텔은 수상 스포츠와 관광여행을 포함하여 투숙객들을 위해 다양한 여가 활동들을 준비한다.
해설 빈칸은 전치사(of)의 목적어 자리이므로 명사 (A)와 (D)가 정답의 후보이다. a variety of(다양한) 뒤에는 복수 가산 명사가 와야 하므로 activity(활동)의 복수형 (D) activities가 정답이다. 형용사 (B)와 부사 (C)는 명사 자리에 올 수 없다.
어휘 sightseeing n. 관광, 구경 active adj. 활동적인

06 가산 명사와 불가산 명사 구별하여 채우기
해석 설문조사에 따르면, 많은 직원들이 사무실에 출근하는 것보다 원격으로 근무하는 것을 선호한다.
해설 빈칸은 전치사(of)의 목적어 자리이므로 명사 (A), (B), (D)가 정답의 후보이다. a number of(많은) 뒤에는 복수 가산 명사가 와야 하므로 employee(직원)의 복수형 (D) employees가 정답이다. 동사 (C)는 명사 자리에 올 수 없다.
어휘 prefer v. 선호하다 remotely adv. 원격으로

07 사람명사와 사물/추상명사 구별하여 채우기
해석 생산성을 평가하기 위해, 검토가 실시될 것이다.
해설 부정관사(a)와 동사(will be conducted) 사이에 올 수 있는 것은 명사이므로 명사 (A)와 (B)가 정답의 후보이다. '생산성을 평가하기 위해 검토가 실시되다'라는 의미가 되어야 하므로 추상명사 (A) review(검토)가 정답이다. 사람명사 (B) reviewer(검토자, 비평가)를 쓸 경우 '생산성을 평가하기 위해 검토자가 실시되다'라는 어색한 의미가 된다. to 부정사 (C), 동사 또는 과거분사 (D)는 명사 자리에 올 수 없다.
어휘 assess v. 평가하다, 산정하다 productivity n. 생산성
conduct v. 실시하다

08 사람명사와 사물/추상명사 구별하여 채우기
해석 회사의 전략 기획 세션 동안 모든 직원에게 적극적인 참여가 권장된다.
해설 형용사(Active)와 동사(is recommended) 사이에 올 수 있는 것은 명사이므로 명사 (A)와 (B)가 정답의 후보이다. '직원에게 적극적인 참여가 권장되다'라는 의미가 되어야 하므로 추상명사 (B) participation(참여, 참가)이 정답이다. 사람명사 (A) participant(참가자)를 쓸 경우 '직원에게 적극적인 참가자가 권장되다'라는 어색한 의미가 된다. 동사 (C), 동사 또는 과거분사 (D)는 명사 자리에 올 수 없다.
어휘 recommend v. 권장하다 strategic adj. 전략적인

HACKERS TEST   p.160

01 (C)	02 (C)	03 (C)	04 (D)	05 (D)
06 (A)	07 (D)	08 (D)	09 (C)	10 (C)
11 (B)	12 (A)	13 (D)	14 (A)	15 (C)
16 (C)	17 (A)	18 (D)	19 (D)	20 (B)
21 (D)	22 (B)	23 (B)	24 (B)	

01 명사 자리 채우기 정답 공식 02
해석 젊은 사람들은 즐거움과 기회로 인해 대도시들에 끌린다.
해설 전치사(by)의 목적어 자리에 올 수 있는 것은 명사이므로 명사 (C) excitement(즐거움)가 정답이다. 동사 (A), 동사 또는 형용사 (B), 형용사 (D)는 명사 자리에 올 수 없다.
어휘 draw v. 끌다, 유인하다 opportunity n. 기회

02 사람명사와 사물/추상명사 구별하여 채우기
해석 그 강당은 최대 300명의 수용 능력을 가진다.
해설 동사(has)의 목적어 자리에 올 수 있으면서 형용사(maximum)의 꾸밈을 받을 수 있는 것은 명사이므로 명사 (C)와 (D)가 정답의 후보이다. '강당은 최대 300명의 수용 능력을 가진다'라는 의미가 되어야 하므로 추상명사 (C) occupancy(수용 능력, 점유)가 정답이다. 사람명사 (D) occupant(입주자)를 쓸 경우 '강당은 최대 300명의 입주자를 가진다'라는 어색한 의미가 된다. 동사 또는 과거분사 (A)와 동사 (B)는 명사 자리에 올 수 없다. maximum을 명사로 보고, (A) occupied가 과거분사로 쓰여 maximum을 수식하는 구조로 본다 해도, '그 강당은 300명의 점유된 최대를 가진다'라는 어색한 문맥이 된다.
어휘 auditorium n. 강당 maximum adj. 최대의; n. 최대

03 가산 명사와 불가산 명사 구별하여 채우기
해석 Mr. Louis는 마케팅에 큰 관심이 있는 유능한 직원이다.
해설 전치사(with)의 목적어 역할을 하면서 형용사(strong)의 꾸밈을 받을 수 있는 것은 명사이므로 명사 (B)와 (C)가 정답의 후보이다. 빈칸 앞에 부정관사(a)가 있으므로 단수 명사 (C) interest(관심)가 정답이다. 동사 또는 과거분사 (A)와 동사 (D)는 명사 자리에 올 수 없다.
어휘 competent adj. 유능한

04 명사 자리 채우기 정답 공식 01
해석 Thurmond 철도사는 그것의 서비스 확장을 위한 충분한 자금을 모을 수 있었다.
해설 정관사(the) 다음에 오면서 빈칸 앞 전치사(for)의 목적어 자리에 올 수 있는 것은 명사이므로 명사 (D) expansion(확장)이 정답이다. 동사 (A), 동사 또는 과거분사 (B), 형용사 (C)는 명사 자리에 올 수 없다.
어휘 capital n. 자금 expand v. 확장하다 expandable adj. 확장할 수 있는

05 사람명사와 사물/추상명사 구별하여 채우기 정답 공식 04
해석 모든 이메일 문의들은 고객 서비스 담당자들에 의해 검토되고 적합한 부서로 발송된다.
해설 동사(are reviewed)의 주어 역할을 하면서 전치사구(by ~ agents)의 꾸밈을 받을 수 있는 것은 명사이므로 명사 (B)와 (D)가 정답의 후보이다. 빈칸 앞의 e-mail과 함께 '이메일 문의'라는 의미를 만드는 추상명사 (D) inquiries(문의)가 정답이다. 사람명사 (B) inquirers(문의자)를 쓸 경우 '이메일 문의자들이 검토되다'라는 어색한 의미가 된다. 동사 또는 과거분사 (A), to 부정사 (C)는 명사 자리에 올 수 없다. 동사 또는 과거분사 (A)는 명사 자리에 올 수 없다. to 부정사 (C)가 e-mail을 수식하는 구조로 본다 해도, 단수 명사 e-mail과 복수 동사 are reviewed가 수일치되지 않으므로 답이 될 수 없다.
어휘 appropriate adj. 적합한 department n. 부서

06 사람명사와 사물/추상명사 구별하여 채우기
해석 Milkins사는 BG Holdings사의 전 부사장과 2년 계약을 협상할 것이다.
해설 동사(negotiate)의 목적어 역할을 하면서, '관사 + 형용사'(a two-year)의 꾸밈을 받을 수 있는 것은 명사이므로 명사 (A)와 (D)가 정답의 후보이다. 'Milkins사는 계약을 협상할 것이다'라는 의미가 되어야 하므로 추상명사 (A) contract(계약(서))가 정답이다. 사람명사 (D) contractor(계약자)를 쓸 경우 'Milkins사는 계약자를 협상할 것이다'라는 어색한 의미가 된다. 형용사 (B), 동사 또는 과거분사 (C)는 명사 자리에 올 수 없다.
어휘 negotiate v. 협상하다 former adj. (이)전의 vice president 부사장

07 명사 자리 채우기 정답 공식 02
해석 창이 국제공항에 도착하면, 승객들은 세관과 입국 심사를 지나 이동할 것이다.
해설 전치사(upon)의 목적어 자리에 올 수 있는 명사 (D) arrival(도착)이 정답이다. 동사 (A)와 (C), 동사 또는 과거분사 (B)는 전치사의 목적어 자리에 올 수 없다.
어휘 passenger n. 승객 proceed v. (특정 방향으로) 이동하다, 나아가다
customs n. 세관, 관세 immigration n. 입국 심사, 출입국 관리소

08 명사 자리 채우기
해석 최고 경영자가 산티아고에 회의를 가 있는 동안, 그의 비서인 Mr. Hale이 그를 대신해서 모든 공식적인 연락을 처리할 것이다.

해설 빈칸 앞의 형용사(official)의 꾸밈을 받을 수 있는 것은 명사이므로 명사 (D) communications(연락)가 정답이다. 동사 (A)와 (B), 형용사 (C)는 명사 자리에 올 수 없다.

어휘 handle v. 처리하다, 다루다 official adj. 공식적인, 공인된
on one's behalf ~를 대신해서 communicate v. 의사소통을 하다
communicative adj. 의사 전달의

09 가산 명사와 불가산 명사 구별하여 채우기
해석 이사는 초기 제안을 좋아했지만 그것을 개선하기 위해 몇 가지 제안을 했다.

해설 빈칸 앞의 수량 형용사(a few)의 꾸밈을 받을 수 있는 것은 명사이므로 명사 (B)와 (C)가 정답의 후보이다. 수량 표현 a few 뒤에는 복수 가산 명사가 오므로 (C) suggestions(제안)가 정답이다. 동사 (A), 동사 또는 과거분사 (D)는 명사 자리에 올 수 없다.

어휘 initial adj. 초기의, 최초의 proposal n. 제안, 계획안
improve v. 개선하다, 향상시키다

10 사람명사와 사물/추상명사 구별하여 채우기
해석 50명이 넘는 젊은 예술가들이 현대미술관에 의해 후원되는 미술 대회에 참가할 것이다.

해설 전치사(in)의 목적어 역할을 하면서 부정관사(a) 다음에 올 수 있는 것은 명사이므로 명사 (A)와 (C)가 정답의 후보이다. 빈칸 앞의 painting과 함께 '미술 대회'라는 의미를 만드는 추상명사 (C) contest(대회)가 정답이다. 사람명사 (A) contestant(경쟁자)를 쓸 경우 '예술가들이 미술 경쟁자에 참가하다'라는 어색한 의미가 된다. 형용사 (B), 동사 또는 과거분사 (D)는 명사 자리에 올 수 없다.

어휘 sponsor v. 후원하다

11 명사 자리 채우기
해석 작문 워크숍이 끝날 무렵에, 참가자들은 문법에 대한 완전한 이해를 얻게 될 것이다.

해설 동사(have gained)의 목적어 자리에 오면서 형용사(thorough)의 꾸밈을 받을 수 있는 것은 명사이므로 명사 (B) comprehension(이해)이 정답이다. 동사 (A)와 (D), 부사 (C)는 명사 자리에 올 수 없다.

어휘 thorough adj. 완전한, 철저한

12 명사 자리 채우기
해석 Vector 역사 재단은 다른 유사 기관들과 친밀한 동반자 관계를 수립하는 것에 중점을 둔다.

해설 동사(puts)의 목적어 자리에 올 수 있는 것은 명사이므로 명사 (A) emphasis(중점, 강조)가 정답이다. 동사 (B), 동사 또는 과거분사 (C), 부사 (D)는 명사 자리에 올 수 없다. 참고로, put emphasis on(~에 중점을 두다)을 관용구로 외워둔다.

어휘 partnership n. 동반자 관계, 협력, 제휴

13 사람명사와 사물/추상명사 구별하여 채우기
해석 베개와 담요는 승무원에 의해 그것들을 요청하는 여행자들에게 제공될 수 있다.

해설 빈칸은 전치사(to)의 목적어 자리이므로 명사 (C)와 (D)가 정답의 후보이다. 그것들(them), 즉 베개와 담요(Pillows and blankets)를 요청할(requesting) 수 있는 주체는 사람이므로 사람명사 (D) travelers(여행자)가 정답이다. 동사 (A), 동사 또는 과거분사 (B)는 명사 자리에 올 수 없다.

어휘 request v. 요청하다

14 가산 명사와 불가산 명사 구별하여 채우기
해석 Julia Sacks의 많은 작품들은 오늘날 최고의 소설 작가들에게 영감을 주었다.

해설 수량 형용사(Many)의 꾸밈을 받으면서 동사(inspired)의 주어 자리에 올 수 있는 것은 명사이므로 명사 (A)와 (C)가 정답의 후보이다. many(많은) 뒤에는 복수 명사가 오므로 work(작품)의 복수형 (A) works가 정답이다. 동사 또는 과거분사 (B), to 부정사 (D)는 형용사의 꾸밈을 받을 수 없다.

어휘 inspire v. 영감을 주다 top adj. 최고의 fiction n. 소설

15 명사 자리 채우기
해석 고객들이 우리의 제품 특징에 대해 추가 정보가 필요하다면, 그들은 무료 상담 전화로 연락할 수 있다.

해설 형용사(additional)의 꾸밈을 받을 수 있는 것은 명사이므로 명사 (C) information(정보)이 정답이다. 동사 (A)와 (B), 동사 또는 과거분사 (D)는 명사 자리에 올 수 없다.

어휘 additional adj. 추가적인 feature n. 특징 toll-free adj. 무료의
hotline n. 상담 전화

16 명사 자리 채우기 [정답 공식 01]
해석 Alpine Footwear사의 등산화에 대한 후기는 다른 회사의 것들과 비교하여 이 제품들의 내구성을 강조한다.

해설 정관사(the)와 전치사(of) 사이에 오면서 동사(stress)의 목적어 자리에 올 수 있는 것은 명사이므로 명사 (C) durability(내구성)가 정답이다. 형용사 (A), 부사 (B), 형용사의 비교급 (D)는 명사 자리에 올 수 없다.

어휘 stress v. 강조하다 compared to ~과 비교하여

17 사람명사와 사물/추상명사 구별하여 채우기
해석 공무원들은 지역 사업 공동체 내에서 협력을 증진시키기를 희망한다.

해설 동사(increase)의 목적어 자리에 올 수 있는 명사 (A)와 (C)가 정답의 후보이다. '지역 사업 공동체 내에서 협력을 증진시키다'라는 의미이므로 추상명사 (A) collaboration(협력)이 정답이다. 사람명사 (C) collaborator(협력자)를 쓸 경우 '지역 사업 공동체 내에서 협력자를 증진시키다'라는 어색한 의미가 된다. 형용사 (B)와 동사 (D)는 명사 자리에 올 수 없다.

어휘 official n. 공무원, 관리 collaborative adj. 협력하는, 공동의

18 가산 명사와 불가산 명사 구별하여 채우기
해석 Mr. Johnson의 책무는 마케팅 부서를 감독하고 새로운 비즈니스 전략을 개발하는 것을 포함한다.

해설 동사(include)의 주어 자리이고 전치사구(of Mr. Johnson)의 꾸밈을 받고 있으므로 명사 (A)와 (B)가 정답의 후보이다. 동사(include)가 복수이므로 복수형 (B) responsibilities가 정답이다. 부사 (C)와 형용사 (D)는 명사 자리에 올 수 없다.

어휘 responsibly adv. 책임감 있게 responsible adj. 책임지고 있는

19 사람명사와 사물/추상명사 구별하여 채우기
해석 기술자에 따르면, 사무실 통신망 설치는 완료하는 데 3일까지 걸릴 수 있다.

해설 정관사(the)와 전치사(of) 사이에 올 수 있는 것은 명사이므로 명사 (C)와 (D)가 정답의 후보이다. '사무실 통신망 설치는 완료하는 데 3일까지 걸릴 수 있다'라는 의미이므로 추상명사 (D) installation(설치)이 정답이다. 사람명사 (C) installer(설치하는 사람)를 쓸 경우 '사무실 통신망 설치하는 사람을 완료하는 데 3일까지 걸릴 수 있다'라는 어색한 의미가 된다. 동사 (A), 동사 또는 과거분사 (B)는 명사 자리에 올 수 없다.

어휘 technician n. 기술자, 기사 office network 사무실 통신망
up to (특정한 수·정도)까지
complete v. 완료하다, 끝마치다; adj. 전부의, 완전한

20 가산 명사와 불가산 명사 구별하여 채우기
해석 이사회가 현재 경제 상태에 가장 수익성이 높은 것들을 결정하기 위해 투자 옵션들을 평가할 것이다.

해설 빈칸은 동사(will evaluate)의 목적어 자리이므로, 빈칸 앞 명사

investment와 함께 '투자 옵션'이라는 의미의 복합 명사 investment option을 만드는 명사 (A)와 (B)가 정답의 후보이다. option(선택권)은 반드시 앞에 한정사가 오거나 복수형으로 쓰이는 가산 명사이므로 복수형 (B) options가 정답이다. 부사 (C)와 형용사 (D)는 명사 자리에 올 수 없다.

어휘 board of directors 이사회 evaluate v. 평가하다 investment n. 투자 profitable adj. 수익성이 좋은 economy n. 경제 상태

21 사람명사와 사물/추상명사 구별하여 채우기
해석 판매 사원들은 고객들에게 우리의 최신 잡지의 구독을 권하는 데 다음 주에 메일을 보낼 것이다.

해설 빈칸은 4형식 동사 offer(offering)의 직접 목적어 자리이므로 목적어 자리에 올 수 있는 명사 (C)와 (D)가 정답의 후보이다. 참고로, offer는 'offer A B'의 형태로 쓰여 'A에게 B를 권하다'라는 의미를 나타낸다. '고객들에게 최신 잡지의 구독을 권하다'라는 의미가 되어야 하므로 추상명사 (D) subscriptions(구독, 가입)가 정답이다. 사람명사 (C) subscribers(구독자)를 쓸 경우 '고객들에게 최신 잡지의 구독자들을 권하다'라는 어색한 의미가 된다. 동사 (A), 동사 또는 과거분사 (B)는 명사 자리에 올 수 없다.

어휘 spend v. (시간·돈 등을) 보내다, 쓰다

22 가산 명사와 불가산 명사 구별하여 채우기 [정답 공식 03]
해석 많은 방문자들이 입구에서의 긴 대기 시간에 대해 불평했다.

해설 빈칸은 전치사(of)의 목적어 자리이므로 명사 (A)와 (B), 동명사 (C)가 정답의 후보이다. a number of(많은) 뒤에는 복수 가산 명사가 와야 하므로 visitor(방문자)의 복수형 (B) visitors가 정답이다. 동사 (D)는 명사 자리에 올 수 없다.

어휘 complain v. 불평하다 entrance n. 입구

23 명사 자리 채우기
해석 Velmora 협회의 가입은 사업주들에게만 가능하다.

해설 빈칸은 동사(is)의 주어 자리이고 전치사구(into ~ Association)의 꾸밈을 받고 있으므로 명사 (B) Acceptance(가입)가 정답이다. 동사 (A), 동사 또는 과거분사 (C), 부사 (D)는 명사 자리에 올 수 없다.

어휘 association n. 협회 business owner 사업주 accept v. 받아들이다 acceptably adv. 받아들일 수 있게, 마음에 들게

24 가산 명사와 불가산 명사 구별하여 채우기
해석 그 소매 체인점은 남미 및 서아프리카의 몇몇 장난감 제조사와 계약을 맺고 있다.

해설 빈칸 앞의 수량 형용사(several)와 빈칸 뒤의 전치사구(in ~ Africa)의 꾸밈을 받을 수 있는 것은 명사이므로 명사 (A), (B), (D)가 정답의 후보이다. several(몇몇의) 뒤에는 복수 가산 명사가 와야 하므로 manufacturer(제조사)의 복수형 (B) manufacturers가 정답이다. (D) manufacture(제조)는 불가산 명사이므로 답이 될 수 없다. 참고로, (D)가 '제품'이라는 의미의 가산 명사일 때는 복수형으로 쓰인다. 동사 또는 과거분사 (C)는 명사 자리에 올 수 없다.

어휘 manufacture v. 제조하다

빈출 어휘 명사 1

토익 실전문제   p.163

| 01 (C) | 02 (A) | 03 (D) | 04 (A) | 05 (D) |
| 06 (B) | 07 (C) | 08 (A) | | |

01 명사 어휘 고르기
해석 Westfield 은행은 다음 달에 하트포드 시내에 새로운 지점을 개설할 것이다.

해설 '은행이 새로운 지점을 개설하다'라는 문맥이므로 (C) branch(지점, 지사)가 정답이다. (A) decline은 '감소, 하락', (B) aspect는 '측면, 양상', (D) regulation은 '규정, 규칙'이라는 의미이다.

어휘 downtown n. 시내

02 명사 어휘 고르기
해석 웹사이트에 있는 제품 설명이 우리가 받은 실제 상품과 일치하지 않는다.

해설 '웹사이트에 있는 제품 설명이 실제 상품과 일치하지 않다'라는 문맥이므로 (A) description(설명, 묘사)이 정답이다. (B) committee는 '위원회', (C) ticket은 '표', (D) volume은 '양'이라는 의미이다.

어휘 match v. 일치하다 actual adj. 실제의 merchandise n. 상품

03 명사 어휘 고르기
해석 Parkwell 산업은 마케팅 부서에 즉시 채워져야 할 비어 있는 일자리가 있다.

해설 '마케팅 부서에 비어 있는 일자리가 있다'라는 문맥이므로 (D) position(일자리, 직책)이 정답이다. (A) registration은 '등록, 신청', (B) assignment는 '과제', (C) nomination은 '지명'이라는 의미이다.

어휘 vacant adj. 비어 있는 immediately adv. 즉시

04 명사 어휘 고르기
해석 비록 11월 3일이 팀의 연구 과제 마감 기한이지만, 추가 시간이 필요할 수도 있다.

해설 '비록 11월 3일이 팀의 연구 과제 마감 기한이지만, 추가 시간이 필요할 수도 있다'라는 문맥이므로 (C) deadline(마감 기한)이 정답이다. (A) report는 '보고서', (B) decision은 '결정', (D) outline은 '개요'라는 의미이다.

어휘 additional adj. 추가의 require v. 필요로 하다

05 명사 어휘 고르기
해석 그 소유주들은 그들의 요가 스튜디오를 위한 적합한 위치를 찾기 위해 부동산 중개인을 고용했다.

해설 '적합한 위치를 찾기 위해 부동산 중개인을 고용했다'라는 문맥이므로 (D) location(위치, 장소)이 정답이다. (A) contract는 '계약', (B) transaction은 '거래', (C) itinerary는 '여행 일정'이라는 의미이다.

어휘 hire v. 고용하다 real estate agent 부동산 중개인 suitable adj. 적합한

06 명사 어휘 고르기
해석 그 소프트웨어 제품은 개발의 마지막 단계에 있다.

해설 '소프트웨어 제품은 개발의 마지막 단계에 있다'라는 문맥이므로 (B) phase(단계, 국면)가 정답이다. (A) scene은 '장면', (C) result는 '결과', (D) issue는 '문제, 쟁점'이라는 의미이다.

어휘 development n. 개발

07 명사 어휘 고르기
해석 Deerwood 연구소는 연금 계획에 제안된 변경 사항에 대한 직원들의 의견을 모을 것이다.

해설 '변경 사항에 대한 직원들의 의견을 모으다'라는 문맥이므로 (C) feedback(의견, 피드백)이 정답이다. (A) practice는 '관행, 연습', (B) effort는 '노력', (D) admission은 '입학, 입장'이라는 의미이다.

어휘 gather v. 모으다 proposed adj. 제안된 pension plan 연금 계획

08 명사 어휘 고르기
해석 이사회는 Ms. Jensen의 아시아 시장으로의 사업 확장을 위한 제안을 다음 주에 검토할 것이다.

해설 '이사회는 사업 확장을 위한 제안을 검토할 것이다'라는 문맥이므로 (A) proposal(제안(서), 제의)이 정답이다. (B) episode는 '사건, 에피소드', (C) technique는 '기술, 기법', (D) presence는 '참석, 존재'라는 의미이다.

어휘 expand v. 확장하다 operation n. 사업

DAY 02 대명사

기출 포인트 01

실전 Check-up
p.164

01 (A) **02** (A)

01 격에 맞는 인칭대명사 채우기
해석 Ms. Breen은 그녀가 오늘 오후에 현장에서 돌아오면 프로젝트에 대한 최신 정보를 제공할 것이다.
해설 빈칸은 when이 이끄는 부사절의 주어 자리이므로, 주어 역할을 할 수 있는 주격 인칭대명사 (A) she가 정답이다. (B) her가 소유격 인칭대명사로 쓰일 경우, 뒤에 명사가 와야 하므로 답이 될 수 없고, 목적격 인칭대명사로 쓰일 경우, 주어 자리에 올 수 없다.
어휘 job site 현장

02 격에 맞는 인칭대명사 채우기
해석 Ms. Patel은 Mr. Cho를 면접했고 그를 공석에 채용하기로 결정했다.
해설 빈칸은 to 부정사(to hire)의 목적어 자리이므로 목적어 자리에 올 수 있는 목적격 인칭대명사 (A) him이 정답이다. 소유격 인칭대명사 (B) his는 목적어 자리에 올 수 없다. (B)를 '그의 것'이라는 의미의 소유대명사로 본다 해도, '그의 것을 공석에 채용하기로 결정했다'라는 어색한 문맥을 만든다.
어휘 hire v. 채용하다 open position 공석

기출 포인트 02~03

실전 Check-up
p.165

01 (B) **02** (A)

01 재귀대명사 채우기
해석 창고 관리자 자신이 배송 지연에 대해 사과하기 위해 전화했다.
해설 이 문장은 주어(The manager of the warehouse)와 동사(called)를 갖춘 완전한 절이므로 빈칸은 수식어 거품으로 보아야 한다. '창고 관리자 자신이 배송 지연에 대해 사과하기 위해 전화했다'라는 의미가 되어야 하므로 강조 용법의 재귀대명사 (B) himself가 정답이다. 참고로, 강조 용법의 재귀대명사는 부사 역할을 하여 강조하고자 하는 말 바로 뒤나 문장 맨 뒤에 올 수 있다. 주격 인칭대명사 (A)는 수식어 거품 자리에 올 수 없다.
어휘 warehouse n. 창고 apologize v. 사과하다 delay n. 지연

02 지시대명사 those 채우기
해석 이 선반에 있는 제품들은 다른 선반들에 있는 것들보다 저렴하다.
해설 빈칸은 전치사(than)의 목적어이면서 전치사구(on the other shelves)의 꾸밈을 받는 명사 자리이므로 모든 보기가 정답의 후보이다. '이 선반에 있는 제품들은 다른 선반들에 있는 것들보다 저렴하다'라는 의미가 되어야 하므로 앞에 나온 복수 명사(The products)를 대신하는 지시대명사 (A) those가 정답이다. 지시대명사 (B)는 앞에 나온 단수 명사를 대신해서 사용한다.

기출 포인트 04

실전 Check-up
p.166

01 (A) **02** (B)

01 부정대명사 채우기
해석 대부분의 고객들은 서비스에 만족했지만, 몇몇은 배송 시간에 대해 불평했다.
해설 빈칸은 but이 이끄는 절의 주어 자리로 명사가 와야 하므로 모든 보기가 정답의 후보이다. '대부분의 고객들은 서비스에 만족했지만, 몇몇은 배송 시간에 대해 불평했다'라는 의미가 되어야 하므로 주로 긍정문에 쓰이는 부정대명사 (A) some(몇몇, 약간)이 정답이다. (B) any는 주로 부정문, 의문문, 조건문에 쓰인다.
어휘 satisfied adj. 만족하는 complain v. 불평하다

02 부정대명사 채우기
해석 그들은 두 종류의 천을 주문했는데, 하나는 의자용이고 나머지 하나는 커튼용이었다.
해설 '그들이 두 종류의 천을 주문했는데, 하나는 의자용이고 나머지 하나는 커튼용이었다'라는 의미가 되어야 하므로, 빈칸 앞의 the와 함께 '나머지 하나'라는 의미의 부정대명사 the other를 만드는 (B) other가 정답이다. (A) each는 '각각'이라는 의미이므로 문맥상 어색하다.
어휘 fabric n. 천, 직물

3초컷 정답 공식
p.167

01 (A) **02** (B) **03** (B) **04** (C) **05** (D)
06 (A) **07** (B) **08** (D)

01 격에 맞는 인칭대명사 채우기
해석 저희는 다음 달 회의에 귀하의 참석을 확인하고자 합니다.
해설 명사(attendance) 앞에서 형용사처럼 쓰일 수 있는 인칭대명사는 소유격이므로 (A) your가 정답이다. 주격 또는 목적격 인칭대명사 (B), 소유대명사 (C), 재귀대명사 (D)는 명사를 꾸밀 수 없다.
어휘 confirm v. 확인하다 attendance n. 참석

02 격에 맞는 인칭대명사 채우기
해석 Ms. Lee의 재정상의 조언은 투자자로서의 그녀의 경험에 기반을 둔다.
해설 명사(experience) 앞에서 형용사처럼 쓰일 수 있는 인칭대명사는 소유격이므로 (B) her가 정답이다. 주격 인칭대명사 (A), 재귀대명사 (C), 소유대명사 (D)는 명사를 꾸밀 수 없다.
어휘 financial adj. 재정상의, 금융의 investor n. 투자자

03 격에 맞는 인칭대명사 채우기
해석 나의 동료가 최근에 국제 지사의 관리자로 승진했다.
해설 전치사(of)의 목적어 자리에 올 수 있는 소유대명사 (B), 목적격 인칭대명사 (C), 재귀대명사 (D)가 정답의 후보이다. 명사(colleague)가 관사(A)와 함께 쓰여 '나의 동료'라는 소유의 의미를 나타낼 때는 '관사 + 명사 + of + 소유대명사'의 형태로 쓰이므로 소유대명사 (B) mine이 정답이다. 목적격 인칭대명사 (C)와 재귀대명사 (D)는 소유대명사 자리에 올 수 없다. 소유격 인칭대명사 (A)는 뒤에 명사가 필요하므로 단독으로 쓰일 수 없다.
어휘 colleague n. 동료 promote v. 승진시키다 international adj. 국제적인

04 격에 맞는 인칭대명사 채우기
해석 저희 대표자가 다음 주에 배송 세부 사항에 대해 당신에게 연락할 것입니다.
해설 전치사(of)의 목적어 자리에 올 수 있는 목적격 인칭대명사 (B), 소유대명사 (C), 재귀대명사 (D)가 정답의 후보이다. 명사(representative)가 관사(A)와 함께 쓰여 '우리 대표자'라는 소유의 의미를 나타낼 때는 '관사 + 명사 + of + 소유대명사'의 형태로 쓰이므로 소유대명사 (C) ours가 정답이다. 목적격 인칭대명사 (B)와 재귀대명사 (D)는 소유대명사 자리에 올 수 없다. 소유격 인칭대명사 (A)는 뒤에 명사가 필요하므로 단독으로

쓰일 수 없다.

어휘 representative n. 대표자 detail n. 세부 사항

05 재귀대명사 채우기
해석 보건 전문가들은 그 분야의 최신 지침에 자신들을 익숙하게 해야 한다.

해설 동사(familiarize)의 목적어 자리에 올 수 있는 목적격 인칭대명사 (A), 소유대명사 (C), 재귀대명사 (D)가 정답의 후보이다. '전문가들이 지침에 자신들을 익숙하게 하다'라는 의미가 되어야 하므로 동사 familiarize와 함께 쓰여 '~에 익숙하게 하다'라는 의미의 어구 familiarize oneself with를 만드는 재귀대명사 (D) themselves가 정답이다.

어휘 health-care n. 보건, 의료 서비스 professional n. 전문가
guideline n. 지침

06 재귀대명사 채우기
해석 우리는 업무차 해외로 출장을 떠나기 전에 현지 관습과 전통에 자신들을 익숙하게 해야 한다.

해설 동사(familiarize)의 목적어 자리에 올 수 있는 재귀대명사 (A)와 목적격 인칭대명사 (B)가 정답의 후보이다. '우리가 현지 관습과 전통에 자신들을 익숙하게 하다'라는 의미가 되어야 하므로 동사 familiarize와 함께 쓰여 '~에 익숙하게 하다'라는 의미의 어구 familiarize oneself with를 만드는 재귀대명사 (A) ourselves가 정답이다.

어휘 custom n. 관습

07 지시대명사 those 채우기
해석 Colville 마을은 이 지역 사회의 풍부한 역사에 대해 더 알고 싶은 사람들을 위해 가이드 투어를 제공한다.

해설 빈칸은 전치사(for)의 목적어이면서 관계절(who ~ history)의 꾸밈을 받는 명사 자리이므로 모든 보기가 정답의 후보이다. 관계절의 동사(want)가 복수 동사이므로 복수 명사를 대신하는 지시대명사 (B) those가 정답이다. 관계절의 동사(want)가 복수 동사이므로 단수 취급되는 지시대명사 (A), 부정대명사 (C)와 (D)는 답이 될 수 없다.

어휘 community n. 지역 사회

08 지시대명사 those 채우기
해석 유효한 티켓을 소지한 사람들만 입장이 허용될 것이다.

해설 빈칸은 형용사(Only)와 관계절(who ~ entry)의 꾸밈을 받는 명사 자리이고, 관계절의 동사(have)가 복수 동사이므로 복수 명사를 대신하는 지시대명사 (C)와 (D)가 정답의 후보이다. '티켓을 소지한 사람들'이라는 의미가 되어야 하므로 '~한 사람들'이라는 의미로 쓰이는 지시대명사 (D) those가 정답이다. 지시대명사 (C) these는 '~한 사람들'이라는 의미로 쓰일 수 없다.

어휘 valid adj. 유효한 entry n. 입장(할 수 있는 권리·기회)

HACKERS TEST   p.168

01 (D)	02 (D)	03 (C)	04 (C)	05 (B)
06 (A)	07 (A)	08 (B)	09 (C)	10 (A)
11 (B)	12 (C)	13 (D)	14 (B)	15 (D)
16 (A)	17 (C)	18 (D)	19 (D)	20 (D)
21 (C)	22 (B)	23 (B)	24 (B)	

01 격에 맞는 인칭대명사 채우기
해석 행사장은 우리의 전문적인 행사 기획자들에 의해 장식될 것이다.

해설 명사구(expert ~ planners) 앞에서 형용사처럼 명사를 꾸밀 수 있는 인칭대명사는 소유격이므로 소유격 인칭대명사 (D) our가 정답이다. 목적격 인칭대명사 (A), 주격 인칭대명사 (B), 재귀대명사 (C)는 명사를 꾸밀 수 없다.

어휘 decorate v. 장식하다, 꾸미다 expert adj. 전문적인; n. 전문가

02 재귀대명사 채우기
해석 Mr. Adams는 한국에서 온 Calterna 기술사의 직원들을 돕는 것에 직접 자원했다.

해설 이 문장은 주어(Mr. Adams)와 동사(volunteered)를 갖춘 완전한 절이므로 빈칸은 수식어 거품으로 보아야 한다. 'Mr. Adams는 직원들을 돕는 것에 직접 자원했다'라는 의미가 되어야 하므로 강조 용법의 재귀대명사 (D) himself가 정답이다. 참고로, 강조 용법의 재귀대명사는 부사 역할을 하여 강조하고자 하는 말 바로 뒤나 문장 맨 뒤에 올 수 있다. 주격 인칭대명사 (A), 목적격 인칭대명사 (B), 소유격 인칭대명사 또는 소유대명사 (C)는 수식어 거품 자리에 올 수 없다.

어휘 volunteer v. 자원하다 assist v. 돕다 representative n. 직원, 대표

03 격에 맞는 인칭대명사 채우기 [정답공식 01]
해석 기조연설자인 Melanie Allen은 그녀의 연설문 초안을 목요일에 행사 위원회에 보낼 것이다.

해설 명사(speech) 앞에서 형용사처럼 쓸 수 있는 인칭대명사는 소유격이므로 (C) her가 정답이다. 주격 인칭대명사 (A), 목적격 인칭대명사 (B), 재귀대명사 (D)는 명사를 꾸밀 수 없다.

어휘 keynote speaker 기조연설자 draft n. 초안 committee n. 위원회

04 지시대명사 those 채우기 [정답공식 04]
해석 컨퍼런스에 일찍 등록하는 사람들은 숙박에 15퍼센트의 할인을 받을 것이다.

해설 빈칸은 관계절(who ~ conference)의 꾸밈을 받는 명사 자리이고 관계절의 동사(register)가 복수 동사이므로 복수 명사를 대신하는 (A)와 (C)가 정답의 후보이다. '컨퍼런스에 일찍 등록하는 사람들'이라는 의미가 되어야 하므로 '~한 사람들'이라는 의미로 쓰이는 지시대명사 (C) Those가 정답이다. 목적격 인칭대명사 (A)와 소유격 인칭대명사 (B)는 '~한 사람들'이라는 의미로 쓰일 수 없다. 지시대명사 (D)는 단수 명사를 대신해서 사용한다.

어휘 accommodation n. 숙박

05 격에 맞는 인칭대명사 채우기
해석 만약 여러분이 여행에 참여하는 데 관심이 있으시다면, 안내 데스크에서 등록하세요.

해설 If절에 동사(are)만 있고, 주어가 없으므로 주어 역할을 할 수 있는 주격 인칭대명사 (B)와 소유대명사 (C)가 정답의 후보이다. '만약 여러분이 여행에 참여하는 데 관심이 있다면'이라는 의미가 되어야 하므로 주격 인칭대명사 (B) you가 정답이다. 소유대명사 (C)를 쓸 경우 '만약 여러분의 것이 여행에 참여하는 데 관심이 있다면'이라는 어색한 문맥을 만든다. 소유격 인칭대명사 (A)는 주어 역할을 할 수 없다. 재귀대명사 (D)는 목적어가 주어와 같은 사람이나 사물을 지칭할 때나, 주어나 목적어를 강조할 때 쓰인다.

어휘 join v. 참여하다, 가입하다 tour n. 여행

06 지시대명사 those 채우기
해석 Mr. Tolentino에 의해 제시된 의견은 회계 부서의 다른 직원의 것들과 달랐다.

해설 'Mr. Tolentino에 의해 제시된 의견은 다른 직원의 것들과 달랐다'라는 문맥이므로, 앞에 나온 복수 명사(opinions)를 대신해서 사용할 수 있는 지시대명사 (A) those가 정답이다. 참고로, 지시대명사 that/those가 앞에 나온 명사를 대신해서 사용될 때에는 that/those 뒤에 반드시 수식어(전치사구, 관계절, 분사)가 온다는 것을 알아둔다. (B) they는 주격 인칭대명사로 주어 자리에 쓰이고, (C) this는 단수 명사 앞에서 지시형용사로 쓰여 '이 –'라는 의미를 갖거나 단수 명사를 대신하는 지시대명사로 쓰인다. (D) their는 소유격 인칭대명사로 명사 앞에 와야 한다.

어휘 opinion n. 의견 differ from ~과 다르다

07 격에 맞는 인칭대명사 채우기 [정답 공식 02]

해석 그 관리자는 재고 조사를 돕기 위해 그녀의 조수를 불렀다.

해설 빈칸은 전치사(of)의 목적어이면서 전치사구(to help ~ count)의 꾸밈을 받는 명사 자리이므로 소유대명사 (A), 목적격 인칭대명사 (B), 재귀대명사 (D)가 정답의 후보이다. 명사(assistant)가 관사(an)와 함께 쓰여 '그녀의 조수'라는 소유의 의미를 나타낼 때는 '관사 + 명사 + of + 소유대명사'의 형태로 쓰이므로 소유대명사 (A) hers가 정답이다. 목적격 인칭대명사 (B)와 재귀대명사 (D)는 소유대명사 자리에 올 수 없다. 주격 인칭대명사 (C)는 목적어 자리에 올 수 없다.

어휘 supervisor n. 관리자, 감독관 inventory count 재고 조사

08 부정대명사 채우기

해석 Greenville시의 여러 버스들이 나쁜 상태였기 때문에, 시장은 Trek 교통으로부터 몇몇을 구입하기로 결정했다.

해설 빈칸 앞 to 부정사(to purchase)의 목적어 자리에 오면서 빈칸 뒤 전치사(from) 앞에 올 수 있는 것은 명사이므로 부정대명사 (B) some(몇몇, 약간)이 정답이다. (A) other와 (C) every는 형용사로만 쓰이므로 명사 자리에 올 수 없고, (D) couple은 가산 명사로, 빈칸 앞에 한정사가 오지 않았으므로 답이 될 수 없다.

어휘 mayor n. 시장

09 재귀대명사 채우기

해석 Marina는 반 친구들과 함께하기보다는 혼자 힘으로 몇 가지 발레 스텝을 연습했다.

해설 전치사(by)의 목적어 자리에 올 수 있는 목적격 인칭대명사 (B), 재귀대명사 (C), 소유대명사 (D)가 정답의 후보이다. '혼자 힘으로 발레 스텝을 연습하다'라는 의미가 되어야 하므로, 전치사 by와 함께 쓰여 '혼자 힘으로, 스스로'라는 의미의 어구 by oneself를 만드는 재귀대명사 (C) herself가 정답이다. (B)와 (D)를 쓰면 각각 '그녀/그녀의 것에 의해 연습하다'라는 어색한 문맥이 된다. 주격 인칭대명사 (A)는 전치사 다음에 올 수 없다.

어휘 practice v. 연습하다 step n. (댄스의) 스텝 rather than ~보다는

10 격에 맞는 인칭대명사 채우기 [정답 공식 01]

해석 Mr. Tang은 홍콩으로 여행을 가기 전에 공항 장기 주차 시설에 그의 차량을 놔두었다.

해설 명사(vehicle) 앞에서 형용사처럼 쓰일 수 있는 인칭대명사는 소유격이므로 (A) his가 정답이다. 재귀대명사 (B), 주격 인칭대명사 (C), 목적격 인칭대명사 (D)는 명사를 꾸밀 수 없다.

어휘 vehicle n. 차량, 탈것 long-term adj. 장기적인 parking n. 주차 facility n. 시설, 기관

11 부정형용사 채우기

해석 우리는 공급업체로부터 이번 주에 몇몇 제품들의 배송을 기다리고 있다.

해설 빈칸 뒤의 명사(deliveries)를 꾸밀 수 있는 부정형용사 (A)와 (B), 지시형용사 (C)가 정답의 후보이다. '몇몇 제품들의 배송을 기다리고 있다'라는 의미가 되어야 하므로 부정형용사 (B) several(몇몇의, 약간의)이 정답이다. (A)는 주로 부정문, 의문문, 조건문에 쓰인다. (C)는 뒤에 단수 명사가 오므로 답이 될 수 없다. 부정대명사 (D)는 형용사 자리에 올 수 없고, '하나의'라는 의미의 수량 형용사로 본다 해도, 뒤에 단수 명사가 오므로 답이 될 수 없다.

어휘 expect v. 기다리다 delivery n. 배송, 배달 supplier n. 공급업체

12 재귀대명사 채우기

해석 Jackson시는 오락 시설에 돈을 더 투자함으로써 그것 자체를 활기찬 도시로 변화시켰다.

해설 동사(has transformed)의 목적어 자리에 올 수 있는 목적격 인칭대명사 (A), 재귀대명사 (B)와 (C)가 정답의 후보이다. 'Jackson시가 그것 자체를 활기찬 도시로 변화시켰다'라는 의미가 되어야 하므로 주어(Jackson City)와 목적어가 동일한 대상을 가리킬 때 목적어 자리에 올 수 있는 재귀대명사 중 단수 주어인 Jackson City와 함께 쓰일 수 있는 (C) itself가 정답이다. 재귀대명사 (B)는 주어가 복수일 때 쓰인다. 목적격 인칭대명사 (A)는 'Jackson시가 그것(Jackson시가 아닌 다른 시)을 활기찬 도시로 변화시켰다'라는 어색한 문맥을 만든다. (A)를 주격 인칭대명사로 본다 해도, 주격 인칭대명사는 목적어 자리에 올 수 없으므로 답이 될 수 없다. 소유격 인칭대명사 (D)는 목적어 자리에 올 수 없다.

어휘 transform v. 변화시키다 vibrant adj. 활기찬 recreational adj. 오락의

13 격에 맞는 인칭대명사 채우기

해석 플로리다로 떠나기 전에, Anderson 코치는 선수들에게 그들이 평상시의 연습을 계속해야만 한다고 말했다.

해설 that으로 시작하는 명사절(that ~ practice)에 주어가 없으므로 주어로 쓰일 수 있는 소유대명사 (C)와 주격 인칭대명사 (D)가 정답의 후보이다. '그들이 연습을 계속해야만 한다'라는 의미가 되어야 하므로 주격 인칭대명사 (D) they가 정답이다. (C)를 쓰면 '그들의 것이 연습을 계속해야만 한다'라는 어색한 의미가 된다. 목적격 인칭대명사 (A)는 타동사 또는 전치사의 목적어 자리에 쓰이고, 소유격 인칭대명사 (B)는 형용사처럼 명사 앞에 쓰여 '~의'라고 해석된다.

어휘 coach n. (스포츠 팀의) 코치 usual adj. 평상시의 practice n. 연습

14 지시대명사 that 채우기

해석 새 소프트웨어의 품질은 이전 버전의 것보다 훨씬 좋다.

해설 빈칸은 전치사(than)의 목적어이면서 전치사구(of ~ version)의 꾸밈을 받는 명사 자리이므로 지시대명사 (A), (B), (C)가 정답의 후보이다. '새 소프트웨어의 품질은 이전 버전의 것보다 훨씬 좋다'라는 의미가 되어야 하므로 앞에 나온 단수 명사(quality)를 대신하는 지시대명사 (B) that이 정답이다. 지시대명사 (A)와 (C)는 앞에 나온 복수 명사를 대신해서 사용한다. 주격 인칭대명사 (D)는 목적어 자리에 올 수 없다.

15 재귀대명사 채우기

해석 투자자들을 유치하지 못한 채, Mr. Meyers는 스스로 새 사업에 자금을 대기로 선택했다.

해설 전치사(by)의 목적어 자리에 올 수 있는 목적격 인칭대명사 (B), 소유대명사 (C), 재귀대명사 (D)가 정답의 후보이다. '스스로 새 사업에 자금을 대다'라는 의미가 되어야 하므로, 전치사 by와 함께 쓰여 '스스로, 혼자 힘으로'라는 의미의 어구 by oneself를 만드는 재귀대명사 (D) himself가 정답이다. (B)와 (C)를 쓰면 각각 '그/그의 것에 의해 자금을 대다'라는 어색한 문맥이 된다. 주격 인칭대명사 (A)는 전치사 다음에 올 수 없다.

어휘 attract v. 유치하다, 끌어들이다 finance v. 자금을 대다; n. 자금

16 사람명사와 사물/추상명사 구별하여 채우기

해석 두 연구기관 간의 성공적인 협력이 의학 분야에서 큰 발전으로 이어졌다.

해설 빈칸은 형용사(successful)의 꾸밈을 받는 명사 자리이므로 명사 (A)와 (B)가 정답의 후보이다. '두 연구기관 간의 성공적인 협력'이라는 의미가 되어야 하므로 추상명사 (A) partnership(협력, 제휴)이 정답이다. 사람명사 (B) partner(동업자)를 쓸 경우 '두 연구기관 간의 성공적인 동업자'라는 어색한 의미가 된다. 동사 또는 과거분사 (C)는 명사 자리에 올 수 없고, to 부정사 (D)는 형용사의 꾸밈을 받을 수 없다.

어휘 breakthrough n. 큰 발전; adj. 획기적인, 중요한

17 부정대명사 채우기

해석 다섯 명의 후보자들 중 한 명만이 그 자리에 선발될 것이다.

해설 빈칸은 형용사(Only)와 전치사구(of ~ candidates)의 꾸밈을 받는 명사 자리이므로 부정대명사 (A), (C), (D)가 정답의 후보이다. '다섯 명의 후보자들 중 한 명만이 그 자리에 선발될 것이다'라는 의미가 되어야 하므로, 정해지지 않은 단수 가산 명사를 대신하는 부정대명사 (C) one(어떤 하나)이 정답이다. (A)는 '각각', (D)는 '또 다른 하나'라는 의미이므로 문맥상 어색하다. (B)는 형용사로만 쓰이므로 동사(will be selected)의 주어 자리에 올 수 없다.

어휘 candidate n. 후보자 position n. 자리, 직위

18 지시형용사 these 채우기

해석 우리는 내일 있을 고객 회의를 위해 이 문서들을 검토해야 한다.

해설 빈칸은 뒤의 명사(documents)를 수식하는 형용사 자리이므로 지시형용사 (A), (B), (D)가 정답의 후보이다. 빈칸은 복수 명사 앞에 있으므로 (D) these가 정답이다. (A)와 (B)는 단수 명사 앞에 오므로 답이 될 수 없고, 주격 또는 목적격 인칭대명사 (C)는 형용사 자리에 올 수 없다.

19 격에 맞는 인칭대명사 채우기

해석 그녀가 프로젝트를 일정보다 앞서 완수했기 때문에 Ms. Lewis는 이번 분기에 실적 보너스를 받았다.

해설 빈칸은 because가 이끄는 부사절의 주어 자리이므로, 주어 역할을 할 수 있는 소유대명사 (B)와 주격 인칭대명사 (D)가 정답의 후보이다. '그녀가 프로젝트를 일정보다 앞서 완수했기 때문에'라는 의미이므로 주격 인칭대명사 (D) she가 정답이다. 소유대명사 (B)를 쓸 경우 '그녀의 것이 프로젝트를 일정보다 앞서 완수했기 때문에'라는 어색한 의미를 만들기 때문에 답이 될 수 없다. 목적격 인칭대명사 (A)는 주어 자리에 올 수 없고, 재귀대명사 (C)는 주어와 목적어가 같은 대상일 때 목적어 자리에 오므로 답이 될 수 없다.

어휘 performance n. 실적, 성과 quarter n. 분기 complete v. 완수하다, 완료하다

20 명사 자리 채우기

해석 경영진은 올 4월에 Hollman 부동산의 사업 10주년 기념 행사를 계획하고 있다.

해설 부정관사(a)와 전치사(of) 사이에 오면서 동사(is planning)의 목적어 자리에 올 수 있는 것은 명사이므로 명사 (D) celebration(기념 행사)이 정답이다. 동사 (A)와 (B), 동사 또는 과거분사 (C)는 명사 자리에 올 수 없다.

어휘 management n. 경영진 realty n. 부동산

21 지시대명사 those 채우기 [정답 공식 04]

해석 행사 주최자는 휠체어 접근이 필요한 사람들에게 특별한 지원을 제공할 것이다.

해설 빈칸은 전치사(to)의 목적어이면서 관계절(who ~ access)의 꾸밈을 받는 명사 자리이므로 모든 보기가 정답의 후보이다. '휠체어 접근이 필요한 사람들'이라는 의미가 되어야 하므로 '~한 사람들'이라는 의미로 쓰이는 지시대명사 (C) those가 정답이다. 부정대명사 (A), 목적격 인칭대명사 (B), 주격 또는 목적격 인칭대명사 (D)는 '~한 사람들'이라는 의미로 쓰일 수 없다.

어휘 assistance n. 지원 require v. 필요로 하다 access n. 접근

22 부정대명사 채우기

해석 그 가게는 두 모델의 장치를 판매하는데, 그중 하나는 가벼운 반면 나머지 하나는 더 내구성이 있다.

해설 빈칸은 while이 이끄는 부사절의 주어 자리이고, 부사절의 동사(is)가 단수 동사이므로 단수 주어가 될 수 있는 부정대명사 (A)와 (D)가 정답의 후보이다. '하나는 가벼운 반면 나머지 하나는 더 내구성이 있다'라는 의미가 되어야 하므로 (D) the other(나머지 하나)가 정답이다. (B)는 복수 취급하는 대명사로만 쓰이므로 단수 동사 앞에 올 수 없다. (C)는 형용사로만 쓰이므로 주어 자리에 올 수 없다.

어휘 lightweight adj. 가벼운 durable adj. 내구성 있는

23 재귀대명사 채우기 [정답 공식 03]

해석 마케팅 팀원들은 출시 행사 전에 새 제품 기능에 자신들을 익숙하게 해야 한다.

해설 동사(familiarize)의 목적어 자리에 올 수 있는 소유대명사 (A)와 재귀대명사 (B)가 정답의 후보이다. '마케팅 팀원들이 새 제품 기능에 자신들을 익숙하게 하다'라는 의미가 되어야 하므로 동사 familiarize와 함께 쓰여 '~에 익숙하게 하다'라는 의미의 어구 familiarize oneself with를 만드는 재귀대명사 (B) themselves가 정답이다.

어휘 feature n. 기능 launch n. 출시

24 부정대명사 채우기

해석 몇몇 손님들은 창가 좌석을 선호하는 반면, 다른 몇 명은 통로 근처에 앉는 것을 선택한다.

해설 빈칸은 while이 이끄는 부사절의 주어 자리이고, 부사절의 동사(choose)가 복수 동사이므로 복수 주어가 될 수 있는 부정대명사 (B) others가 정답이다. (A)는 형용사로만 쓰이므로 주어 자리에 올 수 없다. 부정대명사 (C)와 (D)는 단수 취급하는 대명사로만 쓰이므로 복수 동사 앞에 올 수 없다.

어휘 prefer v. 선호하다 aisle n. 통로

빈출 어휘 명사 2

토익 실전문제

| 01 (A) | 02 (B) | 03 (D) | 04 (A) | 05 (C) |
| 06 (A) | 07 (C) | 08 (B) | | |

01 명사 어휘 고르기

해석 고객들은 제품의 내구성에 대해 염려한다면 서면 보증을 요청해야 한다.

해설 '제품의 내구성에 대해 염려한다면 서면 보증을 요청해야 한다'라는 문맥이므로 (A) guarantee(보증, 보장)가 정답이다. (B) margin은 '여유, 차익', (C) decline은 '감소, 하락', (D) certainty는 '확실성, 확신'이라는 의미이다.

어휘 concerned adj. 염려하는, 관련된 durability n. 내구성, 지속성

02 명사 어휘 고르기

해석 정책은 이사회 구성원들의 과반수가 동의하지 않으면 시행될 수 없다.

해설 '정책은 이사회 구성원들의 과반수가 동의하지 않으면 시행될 수 없다'라는 문맥이므로 (B) majority(과반수, 대다수)가 정답이다. (A) regulation은 '규정, 통제', (C) statement는 '성명, 명세서', (D) procedure는 '절차, 과정'이라는 의미이다.

어휘 policy n. 정책, 방침 implement v. 시행하다, 실행하다

03 명사 어휘 고르기

해석 그 최고 경영자는 도전적인 프로젝트를 예정보다 앞서 완료하기 위한 팀의 헌신을 칭찬했다.

해설 '최고 경영자가 팀의 헌신을 칭찬하다'라는 문맥이므로 (D) dedication(헌신, 전념)이 정답이다. (A) profitability는 '수익성', (B) investment는 '투자', (C) basis는 '단위, 기초'라는 의미이다.

어휘 praise v. 칭찬하다 challenging adj. 도전적인

04 명사 어휘 고르기

해석 성공적인 제품 개발은 디자인팀과 기술팀 간의 긴밀한 협업을 필요로 한다.

해설 '제품 개발은 디자인팀과 기술팀 간의 긴밀한 협업을 필요로 한다'라는 문맥이므로 (A) collaboration(협업, 협력)이 정답이다. (B) strategy는 '전략', (C) organization은 '단체, 조직', (D) enrollment는 '등록, 가입'이라는 의미이다.

어휘 successful adj. 성공적인 require v. 필요로 하다 close adj. 긴밀한

05 명사 어휘 고르기

해석 발표 중에, Mr. Park는 연구 결과에 대한 간략한 개요를 제공할 것이다.

해설 '발표 중에 연구 결과에 대한 간략한 개요를 제공하다'라는 문맥이므로 (C) overview(개요, 개관)가 정답이다. (A) performance는 '성과, 수행', (B) recommendation은 '추천, 권고', (D) promotion은 '홍보, 승진'이라는 의미이다.

어휘 brief adj. 간략한 finding n. 결과, 발견

06 명사 어휘 고르기

해석 Dr. Carter의 재생 에너지 기술에 대한 전문 지식은 그를 인기 있는 산업 자문가로 만들었다.

해설 'Dr. Carter의 전문 지식이 그를 인기 있는 자문가로 만들었다'라는 문맥이므로 (A) expertise(전문 지식, 전문 기술)가 정답이다. (B) response는 '응답, 반응', (C) delivery는 '배달, 전달', (D) allocation은 '할당, 배분'이라는 의미이다.

어휘 renewable adj. 재생 가능한 sought-after adj. 인기 있는, 수요가 많은

07 명사 어휘 고르기

해석 저희가 당신의 환급을 신속히 처리할 수 있도록 각 비용을 정확하게 분류해 주세요.

해설 '환급을 신속히 처리할 수 있도록 각 비용을 정확하게 분류하다'라는 문맥이므로 (C) expense(비용, 경비)가 정답이다. (A) event는 '행사', (B) inventory는 '재고, 목록', (D) description은 '설명, 묘사'라는 의미이다.

어휘 categorize v. 분류하다, 범주화하다 accurately adv. 정확하게
process v. 처리하다 reimbursement n. 환급, 상환

08 명사 어휘 고르기

해석 비록 컴퓨터는 배송되었지만, 소프트웨어의 설치는 이틀 더 걸릴 것으로 예상된다.

해설 '컴퓨터는 배송되었지만, 소프트웨어의 설치는 이틀 더 걸릴 것이다'라는 문맥이므로 (B) installation(설치, 시설)이 정답이다. (A) association은 '협회', (C) phase는 '단계, 국면', (D) foundation은 '기초'라는 의미이다.

어휘 deliver v. 배송하다, 전달하다 expect v. 예상하다

DAY 03 형용사와 부사

기출 포인트 01~03

실전 Check-up   p.172

01 (A)   02 (B)

01 형용사 자리 채우기

해석 제품들은 구매일로부터 30일의 기간 후에는 환불이 불가능하다.

해설 빈칸이 be동사(are) 다음에 왔으므로 be동사의 보어 자리에 올 수 있는 모든 보기가 정답의 후보이다. '제품들은 구매일로부터 30일의 기간 후에는 환불이 불가능하다'라는 의미가 되어야 하므로 형용사 (A) refundable(환불 가능한)이 정답이다. 명사 (B)를 쓸 경우 '제품들은 구매일로부터 30일의 기간 후에는 환불이 아니다'라는 어색한 문맥이 된다.

02 형용사 자리 채우기

해석 사업 개발 관리자는 새로운 사업 기회를 발견하는 것에 책임이 있다.

해설 '관리자는 기회를 발견하는 것에 책임이 있다'라는 의미가 되어야 하므로 빈칸 앞의 be동사(is)와 뒤의 전치사 for와 함께 '~에 책임이 있다'라는 의미의 어구 'be responsible for'를 만드는 형용사 (B) responsible이 정답이다. 명사 (A)를 is의 보어로 본다 해도, '관리자는 기회를 발견하는 것에 책임이다'라는 어색한 문맥을 만든다.

어휘 identify v. 발견하다, 찾다 opportunity n. 기회 responsibility n. 책임

기출 포인트 04~06

실전 Check-up   p.173

01 (B)   02 (A)

01 부사 자리 채우기

해석 Mr. Chase는 워크숍을 이끌어 달라는 초청을 정중히 거절했고 대안을 제안했다.

해설 동사(declined)를 꾸밀 수 있는 것은 부사이므로 부사 (B) kindly(정중히)가 정답이다. 명사 또는 형용사 (A)는 동사를 꾸밀 수 없다.

어휘 decline v. 거절하다 invitation n. 초청, 초대 suggest v. 제안하다
alternative n. 대안, 양자택일 kind n. 종류; adj. 친절한

02 시간 부사 자리 채우기

해석 마케팅팀은 이번 분기 예산 보고서를 이미 완료했다.

해설 빈칸은 동사(has completed)를 꾸미는 부사 자리이고, '마케팅팀은 이번 분기 예산 보고서를 이미 완료했다'라는 의미가 되어야 하므로 시간 부사 (A) already(이미)가 정답이다. (B) soon(곧)을 쓸 경우 '마케팅팀은 이번 분기 예산 보고서를 곧 완료했다'라는 어색한 문맥이 된다.

어휘 budget n. 예산 quarter n. 분기

기출 포인트 07

실전 Check-up   p.174

01 (A)   02 (B)

01 문맥에 어울리는 형용사 채우기

해석 여러 차례의 시도 후에, 연구원들은 마침내 성공적인 실험을 수행했다.

해설 빈칸 뒤의 명사(experiment)를 꾸밀 수 있는 것은 형용사이므로 모든 보기가 정답의 후보이다. '여러 차례의 시도 후에, 연구원들은 마침내 성공적인 실험을 수행했다'라는 의미가 되어야 하므로 형용사 (A) successful(성공적인)이 정답이다. 형용사 (B) successive(연속적인)를 쓸 경우 '여러 차례의 시도 후에, 연구원들은 마침내 연속적인 실험을 수행했다'라는 어색한 의미가 된다.

어휘 attempt n. 시도 experiment n. 실험

02 문맥에 어울리는 부사 채우기

해석 위원회는 결정을 내리기 전에 제안서를 면밀히 검토했다.

해설 동사(reviewed)를 꾸밀 수 있는 것은 부사이므로 모든 보기가 정답의 후보이다. '결정을 내리기 전에 제안서를 면밀히 검토하다'라는 의미가 되어야 하므로 부사 (B) closely(면밀히, 자세히)가 정답이다. 부사 (A) close(가까이에)를 쓸 경우 물리적인 거리의 가까움을 의미하기 때문에 어색한 문맥이 된다.

어휘 committee n. 위원회 review v. 검토하다 proposal n. 제안서

3초컷 정답 공식   p.175

01 (D)   02 (A)   03 (C)   04 (A)   05 (D)
06 (A)   07 (B)   08 (C)

01 형용사 자리 채우기

해석 Ms. Davis는 전 세계 생태계에 끼치는 지구 온난화의 영향에 대한 유익한 강의를 했다.

해설 빈칸 뒤의 명사(lecture)를 꾸밀 수 있는 것은 형용사이므로 형용사 (D) instructive(유익한)가 정답이다. 동사 (A)와 (C), 부사 (B)는 형용사 자리에 올 수 없다.

어휘 lecture n. 강의, 강연 impact n. 영향, 효과 global warming 지구 온난화
ecosystem n. 생태계 instruct v. 지시하다, 가르치다

02 형용사 자리 채우기

해석 업무 현장 안전을 향상시키기 위해 엄격한 규정이 다음 달에 시행될 것이다.

해설 빈칸 뒤의 명사(regulations)를 꾸밀 수 있는 것은 형용사이므로 형용사 (A) strict(엄격한)가 정답이다. 부사 (B), 명사 (C)와 (D)는 형용사 자리에 올 수 없다.

어휘 regulation n. 규정 implement v. 시행하다 workplace n. 업무 현장 stricture n. 비난

03 형용사 자리 채우기

해석 그 정책은 직원들의 일정을 훨씬 더 유연하게 만들어, 그들이 직장 생활과 개인 생활을 더 효과적으로 균형 잡을 수 있게 했다.

해설 동사 make는 목적어와 목적격 보어를 가지는 동사이며, 동사(made) 뒤에 목적어(employees' schedules)가 있으므로 빈칸은 목적격 보어 자리이다. 따라서 동사 make의 목적격 보어 자리에 올 수 있는 명사 (A)와 (D), 형용사 (C)가 정답의 후보이다. '그 정책은 직원들의 일정을 훨씬 더 유연하게 만들었다'라는 의미가 되어야 하므로 형용사 (C) flexible(유연한)이 정답이다. 참고로, 부사(more)는 형용사나 부사를 수식할 수 있다. 부사 (B)는 보어 자리에 올 수 없다.

어휘 balance v. 균형 잡다 effectively adv. 효과적으로 flexibility n. 융통성 flex n. 굴곡성; v. (준비 운동으로서) 굽히다

04 형용사 자리 채우기

해석 고객 정보를 무단 접근으로부터 안전하게 유지하는 것은 회사의 책임이다.

해설 동사 keep은 목적어와 목적격 보어를 가지는 동사이며, 동사(keep) 뒤에 목적어(customer information)가 있으므로 빈칸은 목적격 보어 자리이다. 따라서 동사 keep의 목적격 보어 자리에 올 수 있는 형용사 (A)와 현재분사 (D)가 정답의 후보이다. '고객 정보를 안전하게 유지하다'라는 의미가 되어야 하므로 형용사 (A) secure(안전한)가 정답이다. 현재분사 (D) securing(확보하는)을 쓸 경우 '확보하는 고객 정보를 유지하다'라는 어색한 의미가 된다. 명사 (B) security(안전)를 쓸 경우 목적어를 2개 갖는 4형식 동사 keep(~을 위해 -을 남겨 두다)이 되어 '고객 정보를 위해 안전을 남겨 두다'라는 어색한 문맥이 된다. 부사 (C)는 보어 자리에 올 수 없다.

어휘 responsibility n. 책임 unauthorized access 무단 접근 secure adj. 안전한

05 부사 자리 채우기

해석 웹사이트는 시스템 정비를 위해 오전 2시부터 오전 4시까지 잠시 폐쇄될 것이다.

해설 동사(will be closed)를 꾸밀 수 있는 것은 부사이므로 부사 (D) briefly(잠시)가 정답이다. 명사 (A), 동명사 또는 현재분사 (B), 형용사 (C)는 동사를 꾸밀 수 없다.

어휘 maintenance n. 정비

06 부사 자리 채우기

해석 그 회사는 편리하게 상업 지구에 지점을 열었다.

해설 동사(has opened)를 꾸밀 수 있는 것은 부사이므로 부사 (A) conveniently(편리하게)가 정답이다. 형용사 (B), 명사 (C)와 (D)는 동사를 꾸밀 수 없다.

어휘 district n. 지구, 지역

07 시간 부사 자리 채우기

해석 디지털 결제 방법의 발전에도 불구하고, 일부 소비자들은 여전히 현금 사용을 선호한다.

해설 빈칸은 동사(prefer)를 꾸미는 부사 자리이고, '디지털 결제 방법의 발전에도 불구하고, 일부 소비자들은 여전히 현금 사용을 선호한다'라는 의미가 되어야 하므로 시간 부사 (A) still(여전히, 아직)이 정답이다. (B)와 (C)를 쓸 경우 각각 '디지털 결제 방법의 발전에도 불구하고, 일부 소비자들은 한때/곧 현금 사용을 선호한다'라는 어색한 문맥이 된다. (D) ago(~ 전에)는 시간 표현 바로 다음에 와서 현재를 기준으로 그 시간 이전에 일어난 일을 나타낸다.

어휘 advancement n. 발전 payment n. 결제 consumer n. 소비자

08 시간 부사 자리 채우기

해석 비록 그 식당은 작년에 개조되었지만, 새로운 규정을 충족시키기 위해 추가적인 개선이 여전히 필요하다.

해설 빈칸은 동사(needs)를 꾸미는 부사 자리이고, '비록 식당이 개조되었지만, 추가적인 개선이 여전히 필요하다'라는 의미가 되어야 하므로 시간 부사 (C) still(여전히, 아직)이 정답이다. (A) nearly(거의)를 쓸 경우 '비록 식당이 개조되었지만, 추가적인 개선이 거의 필요하다'라는 어색한 문맥이 된다. 강조 부사 (B)는 동사를 꾸밀 수 없고, (D)는 주로 부정문이나 의문문에 쓰인다.

어휘 renovate v. 개조하다, 보수하다 further adj. 추가적인 meet v. 충족시키다

HACKERS TEST p.176

01 (C)	02 (C)	03 (A)	04 (D)	05 (A)
06 (C)	07 (A)	08 (B)	09 (C)	10 (D)
11 (C)	12 (B)	13 (D)	14 (C)	15 (D)
16 (B)	17 (A)	18 (B)	19 (D)	20 (A)
21 (B)	22 (C)	23 (C)	24 (A)	

01 형용사 자리 채우기 [정답 공식 01]

해석 기획 위원회의 대표자들은 행사를 월말까지 연기하자는 공동의 결정을 내렸다.

해설 빈칸 뒤의 명사(decision)를 꾸밀 수 있는 것은 형용사이므로 형용사 (C) collective(공동의)가 정답이다. 동사 (A), 명사 (B), 부사 (D)는 명사를 꾸밀 수 없다.

어휘 committee n. 위원회 representative n. 대표자, 대리인 postpone v. 연기하다, 미루다 collect v. 모으다, 수집하다 collection n. 수집품, 수집, 모금 collectively adv. 집합적으로, 총괄하여

02 부사 자리 채우기

해석 이 스마트 워치는 오직 운동선수들을 위해서만 제조되었으며 많은 특화된 기능이 있다.

해설 동사(is manufactured)를 꾸밀 수 있는 것은 부사이므로 부사 (C) exclusively(오직 ~만, 전적으로)가 정답이다. 동명사, 현재분사, 전치사 (A), 형용사 (B), 명사 (D)는 동사를 꾸밀 수 없다.

어휘 manufacture v. 제조하다, 생산하다 function n. 기능 excluding prep. ~을 제외하고 exclusion n. 제외, 배제

03 형용사 자리 채우기 [정답 공식 02]

해석 정부로부터의 추가 재정 지원은 그 연구 프로젝트를 가능하게 만들 것이다.

해설 동사 make는 목적어와 목적격 보어를 가지는 동사이며, 동사(make) 뒤에 목적어(the research project)가 있으므로 빈칸은 목적격 보어 자리이다. 따라서 동사 make의 목적격 보어 자리에 올 수 있는 형용사 (A), 명사 (C)와 (D)가 정답의 후보이다. '추가 재정 지원이 그 연구 프로젝트를 가능하게 만들다'라는 의미가 되어야 하므로 형용사 (A) possible(가능한)이 정답이다. 명사 (C)와 (D)를 쓸 경우 각각 '추가 재정 지원이 그 연구 프로젝트를 가능성/가능성들로 만들다'라는 어색한 문맥이 된다. 부사 (B)는 보어 자리에 올 수 없다.

어휘 funding n. 재정 지원

04 문맥에 어울리는 형용사 채우기

해석 정부는 시골 지역의 교육 접근성을 확대하는 데 있어 상당한 진전을 이루었다.

해설 빈칸 뒤의 명사(progress)를 꾸밀 수 있는 것은 형용사이므로 형용사 (C)와 (D)가 정답의 후보이다. '정부가 교육 접근성을 확대하는 데 있어 상당

한 진전을 이루다'라는 의미가 되어야 하므로 형용사 (D) considerable (상당한)이 정답이다. 형용사 (C)를 쓸 경우 '정부가 교육 접근성을 확대하는 데 있어 사려 깊은 진전을 이루다'라는 어색한 의미가 된다. 동사 (A)는 형용사 자리에 올 수 없고, to 부정사 (B)는 형용사 역할을 할 때 명사를 뒤에서 꾸민다.

어휘 progress n. 진전, 발전 expand v. 확대하다 access n. 접근성

05 빈도 부사 자리 채우기
해석 저희 고객 서비스 부서는 항상 귀하의 구매에 관한 모든 질문을 도와드릴 준비가 되어 있습니다.
해설 '항상 질문을 도와줄 준비가 되어 있다'라는 의미가 되어야 하므로 빈도 부사 (A) always(항상)가 정답이다. 부사 (B) formerly(이전에), (C) shortly(곧), (D) early(일찍)를 쓸 경우 어색한 문맥이 된다.

06 형용사 자리 채우기
해석 그들의 보통 일과의 일부로, 기술자들은 공장 설비의 보수 점검을 실시한다.
해설 빈칸 뒤의 명사(routine)를 꾸밀 수 있는 것은 형용사이므로 형용사 (C) normal(보통의)이 정답이다. 명사 (A), 부사 (B), 동사 (D)는 명사를 꾸밀 수 없다.
어휘 routine n. 일과, 일상적인 일 conduct v. 실시하다
 maintenance n. 보수, 유지 inspection n. 점검, 조사
 equipment n. 설비, 장비

07 부사 자리 채우기 [정답공식 03]
해석 텍사스에 있는 Bloomfield 과학 도서관은 다음 달 학술 회의를 개최할 준비가 완전히 되어 있다.
해설 동사(is prepared)를 꾸밀 수 있는 것은 부사이므로 부사 (A) completely(완전히, 완벽하게)가 정답이다. 동사 또는 형용사 (B), 동사 또는 과거분사 (C), 명사 (D)는 동사를 꾸밀 수 없다.
어휘 academic adj. 학술적인, 학구적인

08 형용사 자리 채우기 [정답공식 02]
해석 일정을 따르는 것은 그룹 프로젝트에 참여하는 직원들을 생산적이게 유지할 수 있다.
해설 동사 keep은 목적어와 목적격 보어를 가지는 동사이며, 동사(can keep) 뒤에 목적어(employees)가 있으므로 빈칸은 목적격 보어 자리이다. 따라서 동사 keep의 목적격 보어 자리에 올 수 있는 형용사 (A) productive(생산적인)가 정답이다. 명사 (B), 명사 또는 동사 (C)와 (D)는 동사 keep의 목적격 보어 자리에 올 수 없다. 참고로, involved in group projects는 앞에 나온 명사 employees를 수식하는 수식어 거품이다.
어휘 productivity n. 생산성 produce n. 농산물; v. 생산하다

09 문맥에 어울리는 부사 채우기
해석 이 직책을 위해, 우리는 최소 5년의 관련 업계 경험을 가진 매우 자질이 있는 전문가가 필요하다.
해설 형용사(qualified)를 꾸밀 수 있는 것은 부사이므로 모든 보기가 정답의 후보이다. '매우 자질이 있는 전문가가 필요하다'라는 의미가 되어야 하므로 부사 (C) highly(매우, 대단히)가 정답이다. (A) higher(더 높게), (B) high(높게), (D) highest(가장 높게)를 쓸 경우 물리적인 높이가 높다는 것을 의미하기 때문에 어색한 문맥이 된다.
어휘 position n. 직책 qualified adj. 자질이 있는 relevant adj. 관련된

10 형용사 자리 채우기
해석 그 영화 평론가는 그의 주간 칼럼에서 인기 있는 할리우드 제작물에 비판적인 것으로 알려져 있다.
해설 '그 영화 평론가는 할리우드 제작물에 비판적인 것으로 알려져 있다'라는 의미가 되어야 하므로 빈칸 앞의 be동사(being)와 뒤의 전치사 of와 함께 '~에 대해 비판적이다'라는 의미의 어구 'be critical of'를 만드는 형용사 (D) critical이 정답이다. 명사 (B)를 be동사(being)의 보어로 본다 해도, '그 영화 평론가는 할리우드 제작물에 비판으로 알려져 있다'라는 어색한 의미를 만든다. 동사 (A)와 부사 (C)는 be동사와 함께 해당 표현을 만들 수 없다.
어휘 reviewer n. 평론가 production n. 제작물, 작품 criticize v. 비판하다
 critically adv. 비판적으로

11 시간 부사 자리 채우기
해석 Millions of Viewers가 곧 흥미로운 에피소드가 있는 새로운 시즌으로 돌아올 것이다.
해설 빈칸은 동사(will return)를 꾸미는 부사 자리이고, 'Millions of Viewers가 곧 새로운 시즌으로 돌아올 것이다'라는 의미가 되어야 하므로 시간 부사 (C) soon(곧)이 정답이다. (A) usually(보통), (B) so(너무), (D) almost(거의)를 쓸 경우 각각 'Millions of Viewers가 보통/너무/거의 새로운 시즌으로 돌아올 것이다'라는 어색한 문맥이 된다.

12 문맥에 어울리는 형용사 채우기
해석 직원들은 연말 전에 회사 데이터베이스에 있는 그들의 개인적인 정보를 업데이트하도록 요구된다.
해설 빈칸 뒤의 명사(information)를 꾸밀 수 있는 것은 형용사이므로 형용사 (B)와 (C)가 정답의 후보이다. '그들의 개인적인 정보'라는 의미가 되어야 하므로 형용사 (B) personal(개인적인)이 정답이다. 형용사 (C)를 쓸 경우 '그들의 매력적인 정보'라는 어색한 의미가 된다. 명사 (A)와 (D)는 형용사 자리에 올 수 없다.
어휘 be required to ~하도록 요구되다

13 재귀대명사 채우기
해석 Linford 시장은 직접 도심 지역의 교통 혼잡을 줄이기 위한 계획을 개발했다.
해설 이 문장은 주어(Mayor Linford), 동사(developed), 목적어(the plan)를 갖춘 완전한 절이므로 빈칸은 수식어 거품으로 보아야 한다. 'Linford 시장은 직접 도심 지역의 교통 혼잡을 줄이기 위한 계획을 개발했다'라는 의미가 되어야 하므로 강조 용법의 재귀대명사 (D) himself가 정답이다. 참고로, 강조 용법의 재귀대명사는 부사 역할을 하여 강조하고자 하는 말 바로 뒤나 문장 맨 뒤에 올 수 있다. 주격 인칭대명사 (A), 소유격 인칭대명사 또는 소유대명사 (B), 목적격 인칭대명사 (C)는 수식어 거품 자리에 올 수 없다.
어휘 develop v. 개발하다 traffic congestion 교통 혼잡

14 문맥에 어울리는 형용사 채우기
해석 시장 동향을 분석한 후, 그 회사는 새로운 지역으로 확장하는 것이 유리할 것임을 발견했다.
해설 빈칸이 be동사(be) 다음에 왔으므로 be동사의 보어 자리에 올 수 있는 형용사 (A)와 (C), 명사 (B)가 정답의 후보이다. '회사가 새로운 지역으로 확장하는 것이 유리하다'라는 의미가 되어야 하므로 형용사 (C) profitable(유리한, 이익이 있는)이 정답이다. 형용사 (A)를 쓸 경우 '회사가 새로운 지역으로 확장하는 것이 능숙하다'라는 어색한 문맥이 된다. 명사 (B)를 쓸 경우 '회사가 새로운 지역으로 확장하는 것이 이익들이다'라는 어색한 문맥이 된다. 부사 (D)는 보어 자리에 올 수 없다.
어휘 analyze v. 분석하다 expand v. 확장하다

15 부사 자리 채우기
해석 소비자 지출 감소 때문에 작년 4분기 동안 고급 자동차의 판매량이 상당히 감소했다.
해설 동사(fell)를 꾸밀 수 있는 것은 부사이므로 부사 (D) significantly(상당히)가 정답이다. 현재분사 또는 동명사 (A), 동사 (B), 형용사 (C)는 동사를 꾸밀 수 없다. 추가로, fall(떨어지다), rise(상승하다)와 자주 함께 쓰이는 부사 dramatically(극적으로)와 gradually(점진적으로)도 함께 알아둔다.
어휘 vehicle n. 자동차 quarter n. 분기 reduction n. 감소

16 형용사 자리 채우기

해석 환자들이 그들의 건강을 유지하고 싶다면 의사의 권고를 따르는 것은 필수적이다.

해설 빈칸이 be동사(is) 다음에 왔으므로 보어 자리에 올 수 있는 명사 (A)와 (C), 형용사 (B)가 정답의 후보이다. '환자들이 의사의 권고를 따르는 것은 필수적이다'라는 의미가 되어야 하므로 형용사 (B) essential(필수적인)이 정답이다. 명사 (A)와 (C)를 쓸 경우 각각 '환자들이 의사의 권고를 따르는 것은 본질/요점이다'라는 어색한 문맥이 된다. 부사 (D)는 보어 자리에 올 수 없다.

어휘 recommendation n. 권고, 추천 essence n. 본질
essential adj. 필수적인; n. 요점 essentially adv. 근본적으로

17 시간 부사 자리 채우기 〔정답공식 04〕

해석 최근의 경제 침체에도 불구하고, TechNova사는 국제 시장에서 강한 입지를 여전히 유지하고 있다.

해설 빈칸은 동사(maintains)를 꾸미는 부사 자리이므로 부사 (A), (C), (D)가 정답의 후보이다. '경제 침체에도 불구하고, TechNova사는 강한 입지를 여전히 유지하다'라는 의미가 되어야 하므로 시간 부사 (A) still(여전히, 아직)이 정답이다. (C) seldom(거의 ~않다)을 쓸 경우 '경제 침체에도 불구하고, TechNova사는 강한 입지를 거의 유지하지 않다'라는 어색한 문맥이 된다. (D) too(너무)를 쓸 경우 '경제 침체에도 불구하고, TechNova사는 강한 입지를 너무 유지하다'라는 어색한 문맥이 되며, too는 주로 형용사나 부사를 꾸민다. 전치사 (B) due to(~때문에)는 부사 자리에 올 수 없다.

어휘 economic downturn 경제 침체 international adj. 국제의

18 형용사 자리 채우기

해석 그 배송 관리자는 Destinations사 소프트웨어 애플리케이션이 고객들의 소포를 추적하는 데 유용할 것이라고 믿는다.

해설 빈칸이 be동사(be) 다음에 왔으므로 보어 자리에 올 수 있는 형용사 (B)와 명사 (D), 진행형을 만드는 현재분사 (C)가 정답의 후보이다. '애플리케이션이 고객들의 소포를 추적하는 데 유용하다'라는 의미가 되어야 하므로 형용사 (B) useful(유용한)이 정답이다. 현재분사 (C)를 쓸 경우 '애플리케이션이 사용하고 있을 것이다'라는 어색한 문맥이 된다. 명사 (D) user는 가산 명사이고 빈칸 앞에 부정관사 a(n)이 없으므로 답이 될 수 없다. 동사 (A)는 보어 자리에 올 수 없다.

어휘 track v. 추적하다 package n. 소포

19 시간 부사 자리 채우기

해석 Elmsborough 도시 의회는 한때 산업 지역이었던 부지에 공원을 건설하는 계획을 발표했다.

해설 빈칸은 동사(was)를 꾸미는 부사 자리이고, '한때 산업 지역이었던 부지에 공원을 건설하다'라는 의미가 되어야 하므로 시간 부사 (D) once(한때, 이전에)가 정답이다. 시간 부사 (A) ago(~ 전에)는 시간 표현 바로 다음에 와서 현재를 기준으로 그 시간 이전에 일어난 일을 나타낸다. (B) here(지금, 이 시점에)와 (C) approximately(대략)을 쓸 경우 각각 '지금/대략 산업 지역이었던 부지에 공원을 건설하다'라는 어색한 문맥이 된다.

어휘 council n. 의회 announce v. 발표하다 site n. 부지, 장소

20 가산 명사와 불가산 명사 구별하여 채우기

해석 상세한 설명서 덕분에 가구의 조립이 쉬웠다.

해설 빈칸은 동사(was)의 주어 자리이므로 명사 (A), (B), (D)가 정답의 후보이다. assembly(조립)는 앞에 부정관사가 올 수 없고 복수형으로 쓰일 수 없는 불가산 명사이므로 (A) assembly가 정답이다. 명사 (D)는 '상세한 설명서 덕분에 가구의 조립공이 쉬웠다'라는 어색한 문맥을 만들기 때문에 답이 될 수 없다. 동사 (C)는 명사 자리에 올 수 없다.

어휘 instruction n. 설명서, 지시 assemble v. 조립하다, 모으다
assembler n. 조립공, 조립 기술자

21 문맥에 어울리는 부사 채우기

해석 새 사무실 건물의 건설은 내부 마감 작업만 남아 있어, 거의 완료되었다.

해설 '사무실 건물의 건설이 거의 완료되었다'라는 의미가 되어야 하므로 부사 (B) nearly(거의)가 정답이다. (A) near(가까이), (C) nearer(더 가까이), (D) nearest(가장 가깝게)는 공간이나 시간적 거리를 나타내는 표현이지만 진행 정도를 나타낼 수 없으므로 답이 될 수 없다.

어휘 construction n. 건설 finishing work 마감 작업

22 형용사 자리 채우기

해석 최종 합의는 계약서에 서명을 진행하기 전에 당사자 모두에게 수용 가능해야 한다.

해설 '최종 합의는 당사자 모두에게 수용 가능해야 한다'라는 의미가 되어야 하므로 빈칸 앞의 be동사(be)와 뒤의 전치사 to와 함께 '~에게 수용 가능하다'라는 의미의 어구 'be acceptable to'를 만드는 형용사 (C) acceptable이 정답이다. 명사 (D)를 be의 보어로 본다 해도, '최종 합의는 당사자 모두에게 수락이어야 한다'라는 어색한 의미를 만든다. 동사 (A)와 (B)는 be동사와 함께 해당 표현을 만들 수 없다.

어휘 agreement n. 합의 party n. 당사자 proceed v. 진행하다
contract n. 계약

23 부사 자리 채우기

해석 많은 정비공은 자동차 엔진이 더욱 부드럽게 작동하는 데 도움이 되도록 다른 어떤 브랜드보다 Haskell사의 엔진 오일 사용을 추천한다.

해설 빈칸 앞의 부사(more)와 함께 쓰여 동사 run(작동하다)을 꾸밀 수 있는 부사 (C) smoothly(부드럽게)가 정답이다. 동사 (A), 형용사 smooth(부드러운)의 비교급 (B), 최상급 (D)는 동사를 꾸밀 수 없다.

어휘 mechanic n. 정비공, 기계공 run v. 작동하다, 기능하다
smooth v. 매끈하게 하다, 반듯하게 펴다; adj. 부드러운

24 숫자 표현과 함께 쓰이는 부사 자리 채우기

해석 엘리베이터 수리 작업은 거의 90퍼센트 완료되어 다음 주까지 끝날 것이다.

해설 형용사 역할을 하는 수 표현(90)을 꾸밀 수 있는 부사 (A) almost(거의)가 정답이다. (B) seldom은 '거의 ~ 않다', (C) frequently는 '종종'이라는 의미이다. 시간 부사 (D) ago(~ 전에)는 시간 표현 바로 다음에 와서 현재를 기준으로 그 시간 이전에 일어난 일을 나타낸다.

어휘 repair n. 수리 complete adj. 완료된

빈출 어휘   명사 3

토익 실전문제 p.179

01 (B)	02 (A)	03 (C)	04 (D)	05 (C)
06 (D)	07 (C)	08 (A)		

01 명사 어휘 고르기

해석 Ms. Takahashi는 방문하는 임원들을 위해 Arden Heights 호텔을 마지막 순간에 예약했다.

해설 '임원들을 위해 호텔을 예약했다'라는 문맥이므로 '예약하다'라는 의미의 'make a reservation'을 완성하는 (B) reservation(예약, 보류)이 정답이다. (A) requirement는 '요구 사항', (C) treatment는 '대우, 치료', (D) accommodation은 '숙박 시설'이라는 의미이다.

어휘 last-minute adj. 마지막 순간의, 막바지의 executive n. 임원, 경영진

02 명사 어휘 고르기

해석 그 소프트웨어는 대량의 고객 데이터를 빠르게 분석할 수 있는 우리의 역량을 향상시킨다.

해설 '소프트웨어가 데이터를 분석할 수 있는 역량을 향상시키다'라는 문맥이

므로 (A) capability(역량, 능력)가 정답이다. (B) longevity는 '수명, 장수', (C) resolution은 '결단력', (D) deadline은 '마감 기한'이라는 의미이다.

어휘 enhance v. 향상시키다   analyze v. 분석하다   volume n. 양, 부피

03 명사 어휘 고르기

해석 기술적인 문제 때문에, 그 기계의 작동은 수리팀이 도착할 때까지 중단되어야 했다.

해설 '기계의 작동이 수리팀이 도착할 때까지 중단되어야 했다'라는 문맥이므로 (C) operation(작동, 운영)이 정답이다. (A) location은 '위치, 장소', (B) status는 '상태, 지위', (D) break는 '휴식, 중단'이라는 의미이다.

어휘 technical adj. 기술적인   issue n. 문제, 쟁점   pause v. 중단하다, 멈추다

04 명사 어휘 고르기

해석 회사는 휴가철 동안 스마트폰의 판매를 촉진하기 위해 특별 홍보를 진행할 것이다.

해설 '회사가 스마트폰의 판매를 촉진하기 위해 특별 홍보를 진행할 것이다'라는 문맥이므로 (D) promotion(홍보, 승진)이 정답이다. (A) statement는 '성명, 명세서', (B) creation은 '창작(물)', (C) conservation은 '보존, 보호'라는 의미이다.

어휘 boost v. 촉진하다, 증진시키다   sale n. 판매

05 명사 어휘 고르기

해석 구직자들은 면접 전에 그들의 교육 증명서를 제출해야 한다.

해설 '구직자들이 교육 증명서를 제출해야 한다'라는 문맥이므로 명사 credential(자격 증명, 신임장)의 복수형 (C) credentials가 정답이다. (A)의 instruction은 '설명, 지시', (B)의 reaction은 '반응', (D)의 registration은 '등록, 신청'이라는 의미이다.

어휘 job applicant 구직자

06 명사 어휘 고르기

해석 새로 고용된 직원들은 그들의 직업상의 책무를 효과적으로 처리하도록 훈련받아야 한다.

해설 '직원들이 직업상의 책무를 효과적으로 처리하다'라는 문맥이므로 명사 responsibility(책무, 책임)의 복수형 (D) responsibilities가 정답이다. (A)의 talk는 '대화, 연설', (B)의 component는 '구성 요소', (C)의 reminder는 '알림, 상기시키는 것'이라는 의미이다.

어휘 handle v. 처리하다   professional adj. 직업상의, 직업적인   effectively adv. 효과적으로

07 명사 어휘 고르기

해석 가구 소매상은 고객들이 제품 조립을 하는 데 도움이 되도록 상세한 설명서를 제공한다.

해설 '고객들이 제품 조립을 하는 데 도움이 되도록 설명서를 제공하다'라는 문맥이므로 (C) assembly(조립, 집회)가 정답이다. (A) direction은 '지시, 방향', (B) contact는 '연락', (D) coverage는 '보도'라는 의미이다.

어휘 retailer n. 소매상   detailed adj. 상세한   manual n. 설명서

08 명사 어휘 고르기

해석 임대 계약서의 몇 가지 조항들은 좋은 상태로 건물을 유지하는 것에 대한 세입자의 의무를 명시한다.

해설 '임대 계약서의 몇 가지 조항들이 좋은 상태로 건물을 유지하는 것에 대한 의무를 명시하다'라는 문맥이므로 명사 provision(조항, 규정)의 복수형 (A) provisions가 정답이다. (B)의 characteristic은 '특성', (C)의 priority는 '우선순위', (D)의 recommendation은 '추천, 권고'라는 의미이다.

어휘 rental adj. 임대의   contract n. 계약서   specify v. 명시하다   tenant n. 세입자   duty n. 의무   property n. 건물

DAY 04 전치사

기출 포인트 01

실전 Check-up   p.180

01 (A)   02 (B)

01 전치사 채우기

해석 그 영업팀은 다음 주에 중요한 회의를 위해 서울로 이동할 것이다.

해설 빈칸은 명사(Seoul)를 목적어로 가지는 전치사 자리이다. '서울로 이동하다'라는 의미가 되어야 하므로 전치사 (A) to(~로)가 정답이다. 동사 또는 형용사 (B) last는 전치사 자리에 올 수 없다.

어휘 travel v. 이동하다, 가다   important adj. 중요한

02 전치사 채우기

해석 그 의사는 오늘 오후 4시까지 환자들과 예약이 있다.

해설 빈칸은 명사(4 P.M.)를 목적어로 가지는 전치사 자리이다. '오후 4시까지 환자들과 예약이 있다'라는 의미가 되어야 하므로 전치사 (B) until이 정답이다. 형용사 또는 부사 (A) still은 전치사 자리에 올 수 없다.

어휘 appointment n. 예약   patient n. 환자

기출 포인트 02

실전 Check-up   p.181

01 (A)   02 (A)

01 in/on/at 구별하여 채우기

해석 에어컨 시스템은 밤에 절전 모드로 설정될 수 있다.

해설 시점(night) 앞에는 전치사 at을 쓰므로 전치사 (A) at이 정답이다. (B) on은 날짜·요일·특정한 날 앞에 온다.

어휘 sleep mode 절전 모드

02 전치사 채우기

해석 Coster 보안회사는 근무 시간 동안 개인적인 사유로 인한 휴대폰의 사용을 허용하지 않는다.

해설 빈칸은 명사구(working hours)를 목적어로 취하는 전치사 자리이다. '근무 시간 동안 개인적인 사유로 인한 휴대폰의 사용을 허용하지 않는다'라는 의미가 되어야 하므로 기간을 나타내는 전치사 (A) during(~ 동안)이 정답이다. (B) without은 '~ 없이'라는 의미이다.

어휘 working hours 근무 시간

기출 포인트 03~04

실전 Check-up   p.182

01 (B)   02 (A)

01 전치사 채우기

해석 그 고객은 회의를 위해 마닐라에서 도쿄에 있는 회사 본사로 비행기를 타고 가고 있다.

해설 장소를 나타내는 명사(Manila)를 목적어로 취하면서, '회사 본사로'(to the company's main office)라는 도착지를 나타내는 문맥과 자연스럽게 연결되는 전치사 (B) from(~에서, ~으로부터)이 정답이다. (A) by는 '~ 함으로써, ~에 의해'라는 의미이다.

어휘 client n. 고객, 의뢰인   main office 본사

02 전치사 채우기

해석 시간 관리에 관한 워크숍이 3번 강의실에서 열릴 것이다.

해설 빈칸은 명사구(time management)를 목적어로 취하면서, '시간 관리에 관한 워크숍'이라는 의미가 되어야 하므로 전치사 (A) about(~에 관한, ~에 대한)이 정답이다. (B) following은 '~에 이어'라는 의미이다.

어휘 management n. 관리

3초컷 정답 공식 p.183

| 01 (C) | 02 (B) | 03 (A) | 04 (D) | 05 (A) |
| 06 (C) | 07 (A) | 08 (B) | | |

01 전치사 채우기

해석 세계 시장에서 스마트폰 브랜드들 사이에 경쟁이 증가하고 있다.

해설 빈칸은 명사구(smartphone brands)를 목적어로 가지는 전치사 자리이므로 모든 보기가 정답의 후보이다. '스마트폰 브랜드들 사이에 경쟁이 증가하다'라는 의미가 되어야 하므로 (C) among(사이에)이 정답이다. (A) within은 '~내에', (B) from은 '~에서, ~으로부터', (D) over는 '~ 동안, ~하는 내내'라는 의미이다.

어휘 competition n. 경쟁 global adj. 세계적인, 전 세계의

02 전치사 채우기

해석 그 자선단체는 홍수로 피해를 입은 가족들 사이에 보급품을 분배했다.

해설 빈칸은 명사구(the families)를 목적어로 가지는 전치사 자리이므로 모든 보기가 정답의 후보이다. '홍수로 피해를 입은 가족들 사이에 보급품을 분배하다'라는 의미가 되어야 하므로 (B) among(사이에)이 정답이다. (A) between은 '사이에'라는 뜻이지만, 두 개의 대상 사이를 나타낼 때 쓰인다. (C) toward는 '~ 쪽으로, ~을 향하여', (D) despite는 '~에도 불구하고'라는 의미이다.

어휘 charity n. 자선단체 distribute v. 분배하다 supply n. 보급품, 물자

03 전치사 채우기

해석 그 IT 부서는 최신 소프트웨어 업데이트 이래로 어떠한 시스템 오류도 보고 받지 않았다.

해설 빈칸은 명사구(the latest software update)를 목적어로 가지는 전치사 자리이므로 모든 보기가 정답의 후보이다. '최신 소프트웨어 업데이트 이래로 어떠한 시스템 오류도 보고 받지 않았다'라는 의미가 되어야 하므로 시점을 나타내는 전치사 (A) since(~ 이래로)가 정답이다. (B) outside는 '~ 밖에', (C) to는 '~으로, ~ 쪽으로', (D) throughout은 '~ 동안, ~하는 내내'라는 의미이다.

04 전치사 채우기

해석 Ms. Park는 2020년 설립 이래로 Greenest Organics사에서 마케팅 부장으로 일해 왔다.

해설 빈칸은 명사구(its founding in 2020)를 목적어로 가지는 전치사 자리이므로 모든 보기가 정답의 후보이다. '설립 이래로 마케팅 부장으로 일해 왔다'라는 의미가 되어야 하므로 시점을 나타내는 전치사 (D) since(~ 이래로)가 정답이다. (A) along은 '~을 따라', (B) until은 '~까지', (C) before는 '~ 전에'라는 의미이다.

어휘 founding n. 설립

05 전치사 채우기

해석 Ferndale 간이 식당의 인기 있는 점심 특선 메뉴는 평일 오후 12시에서 1시까지만 이용 가능하다.

해설 이 문장은 주어(The Ferndale ~ special), 동사(is), 보어(available)를 갖춘 완전한 절이므로, ___ ~ weekdays는 수식어 거품으로 보아야 한다. 이 수식어 거품은 동사가 없는 거품구이므로 거품구를 이끌 수 있는 모든 보기가 정답의 후보이다. '오후 12시에서 1시까지'라는 의미가 되어야 하므로 빈칸 뒤의 to와 함께 from A to B(A에서 B까지)를 만드는 (A) from(~에서, ~으로부터)이 정답이다. 전치사 (C) between(사이에)도 해석상 그럴듯해 보이지만, (C)는 두 개의 대상 사이의 관계나 위치, 또는 시간을 나타내며 보통 between A and B(A와 B 사이에)의 형태로 쓰이기 때문에 답이 될 수 없다. (B) with는 '~을 가지고, ~과 함께', (D) for는 '~ 동안, ~을 위해'라는 의미이다.

어휘 diner n. 간이 식당, 작은 식당 available adj. 이용 가능한 weekday n. 평일

06 전치사 채우기

해석 교육 세션은 한 시간의 점심 휴식 시간과 함께, 오전 9시와 오후 4시 사이에 열릴 것이다.

해설 이 문장은 주어(The training session)와 동사(will be held)를 갖춘 완전한 절이므로, ___ ~ break는 수식어 거품으로 보아야 한다. 이 수식어 거품은 동사가 없는 거품구이므로 거품구를 이끌 수 있는 모든 보기가 정답의 후보이다. '오전 9시와 오후 4시 사이에'라는 의미가 되어야 하므로 빈칸 뒤의 and와 함께 between A and B(A와 B 사이에)를 만드는 (C) between(사이에)이 정답이다. (A) to는 '~으로, ~ 쪽으로', (B) over는 '~ 동안, ~하는 내내', (D) like는 '~처럼'이라는 의미이다.

07 전치사 채우기

해석 어떤 문제에 대해서든 돕기 위해 영업시간 동안 지원팀이 이용 가능하다.

해설 이 문장은 주어(The support team), 동사(is), 보어(available)를 모두 갖춘 완전한 절이므로, ___ ~ hours는 수식어 거품으로 보아야 한다. 이 수식어 거품은 동사가 없는 거품구이므로 거품구를 이끌 수 있는 모든 보기가 정답의 후보이다. '영업시간 동안 지원팀이 이용 가능하다'라는 의미가 되어야 하고, business hours라는 명사구가 와서 '언제 일어나는지'를 나타내고 있으므로 전치사 (A) during(~ 동안)이 정답이다. (B) toward는 '~ 쪽으로, ~을 향하여', (C) against는 '~에 반대하여, ~에 기대어', (D) by는 '~까지'라는 의미이다.

어휘 business hours 영업시간 assist v. 돕다, 지원하다

08 전치사 채우기

해석 환불은 5영업일 이내에 처리되어 귀하의 계좌로 보내질 것입니다.

해설 이 문장은 주어(The refund)와 동사(will be ~ sent)를 모두 갖춘 완전한 절이므로, ___ ~ days는 수식어 거품으로 보아야 한다. 이 수식어 거품은 동사가 없는 거품구이므로 거품구를 이끌 수 있는 모든 보기가 정답의 후보이다. '5영업일 이내에'라는 의미가 되어야 하므로 전치사 (B) within(~ 이내에)이 정답이다. (A) into는 '~ 안으로', (C) across는 '~을 가로질러', (D) between은 '사이에'라는 의미이다.

어휘 process v. 처리하다 account n. 계좌 business day 영업일

HACKERS TEST p.184

01 (A)	02 (D)	03 (A)	04 (C)	05 (D)
06 (A)	07 (D)	08 (A)	09 (B)	10 (A)
11 (A)	12 (B)	13 (A)	14 (D)	15 (B)
16 (C)	17 (B)	18 (A)	19 (D)	20 (A)
21 (D)	22 (A)	23 (A)	24 (C)	

01 in/on/at 구별하여 채우기

해석 도서관 카드를 신청하려면, 2층에 있는 서비스 창구로 향하세요.

해설 '2층에 있는 서비스 창구'라는 의미가 되기 위해 the second floor 앞에 올 수 있는 전치사는 표면 위 일직선상의 지점을 나타내야 하므로 (A) on(~ 위에)이 정답이다. (B) as는 '~로서'라는 의미로 신분이나 자격을 나타내고, (C) at은 '~에'라는 의미이지만 층 앞에 쓰일 수 없다. (D) against는 '~에 반대하여, ~에 기대어'라는 의미로 의견 등에 대한 반대나 물건이 기대어 놓인 상태를 나타낸다.

어휘 apply for ~을 신청하다 proceed to ~으로 향하다, 나아가다

02 전치사 채우기
해석 Richard Lucas의 신간 Lens Explorer의 무료 사본이 El Patio 박물관에서 열리는 그의 사진 전시회 동안 관람객들에게 배포될 것이다.
해설 '무료 사본이 사진 전시회 동안 배포될 것이다'라는 의미가 되어야 하므로 기간을 나타내는 전치사 (D) during(~ 동안)이 정답이다. (A) toward는 '~ 쪽으로, ~을 향하여'라는 의미로 방향을 나타낸다. (B) between은 '사이에'라는 의미로 기간을 나타낼 수 있지만 두 가지의 사이의 기간을 나타낸다. (C) since는 '~ 이래로'라는 의미로 시점을 나타내며 주로 현재완료 시제와 함께 쓰인다.
어휘 exhibit n. 전시회

03 전치사 채우기
해석 Bobby Ortega는 그의 뛰어난 리더십과 조직 기술 때문에 공장 관리자로 선택되었다.
해설 이 문장은 필수성분(Bobby Ortega ~ plant supervisor)을 갖춘 완전한 절이므로 ___ his ~ skills는 수식어 거품으로 보아야 한다. 이 수식어 거품은 동사가 없는 거품구이므로 거품구를 이끌 수 있는 모든 보기가 정답의 후보이다. '뛰어난 리더십과 조직 기술 때문에 공장 관리자로 선택되었다'라는 의미가 되어야 하므로 전치사 (A) due to(~ 때문에, ~으로 인해)가 정답이다. (B) despite는 '~에도 불구하고', (C) except는 '~을 제외하고는', (D) against는 '~에 반대하여, ~에 기대어'라는 의미이다.
어휘 plant n. 공장, 식물 supervisor n. 관리자 organizational skill 조직 기술

04 전치사 채우기
해석 모든 이동 수단과 숙박 시설에 더하여, 그 패키지 여행은 매일 두 끼의 식사를 포함한다.
해설 패키지 여행(the tour package)은 이동 수단과 숙박 시설(transportation and accommodations), 그리고 식사를 포함한다(includes ~ meals)는 내용이므로 부가를 나타내는 (C) In addition to(~에 더하여)가 정답이다. (A) Prior to는 '~ 전에', (B) In spite of는 '~에도 불구하고', (D) According to는 '~에 따라'라는 의미이다.
어휘 transportation n. 이동 수단 accommodation n. 숙박 시설 include v. 포함하다

05 전치사 채우기 정답공식 04
해석 정비팀은 오늘 영업시간 동안 모든 수리를 완료하기로 예정되어 있다.
해설 이 문장은 주어(The maintenance team), 동사(is scheduled to complete), 목적어(all repairs)를 모두 갖춘 완전한 절이므로 ___ ~ today는 수식어 거품으로 보아야 한다. 이 수식어 거품은 동사가 없는 거품구이므로 거품구를 이끌 수 있는 모든 보기가 정답의 후보이다. '오늘 영업시간 동안'이라는 의미가 되어야 하므로 전치사 (D) during(~ 동안)이 정답이다. 전치사 (A) through는 '~을 통과하여, ~을 통해', (B) until은 '~까지', (C) along은 '~을 따라'라는 의미이다.
어휘 maintenance n. 정비, 유지, 관리 schedule v. 예정하다, 계획하다 complete v. 완료하다 repair n. 수리

06 전치사 채우기
해석 불법 주차에 대한 벌금을 인상하려는 시 정부의 결정에 대해 아는 사람은 거의 없다.
해설 빈칸은 명사구(the city government's decision)를 목적어로 가지는 전치사 자리이고, '불법 주차에 대한 벌금을 인상하려는 시 정부의 결정'이라는 의미가 되어야 하므로 전치사 (A) about(~에 관한, ~에 대한)이 정답이다. (B) at은 '~에', (C) with는 '~을 가지고, ~과 함께', (D) toward는 '~ 쪽으로, ~을 향하여'라는 의미이다.
어휘 fine n. 벌금 illegal adj. 불법적인

07 전치사 채우기 정답공식 03
해석 오후 1시에서 4시까지 매일 운영하는 Urban Travel사의 Greenwich 마을의 가이드 투어는 방문객들에게 인기가 있다.
해설 빈칸은 명사구(1 P.M.)를 목적어로 가지는 전치사 자리이므로 모든 보기가 정답의 후보이다. '오후 1시에서 4시까지'라는 의미가 되어야 하므로 빈칸 뒤의 to와 함께 from A to B(A에서 B까지)를 만드는 (D) from(~에서, ~으로부터)이 정답이다. (A) until은 '~까지', (B) before는 '~ 전에', (C) by는 '~까지'라는 의미이다.

08 전치사 채우기
해석 공항은 도심 가까이에 있어서, 여행객들이 비행기를 빨리 타러 가기에 용이하게 한다.
해설 빈칸은 명사구(the city center)를 목적어로 가지는 전치사 자리이므로 모든 보기가 정답의 후보이다. '공항이 도심 가까이에 있다'라는 의미가 되어야 하므로 전치사 (A) near(~ 가까이, ~ 근처에)가 정답이다. (B) for는 '~을 위해', (C) following은 '~에 이어', (D) outside는 '~ 밖에'라는 의미이다.
어휘 city center 도심

09 전치사 채우기
해석 Riverpoint 물류 회사의 주가는 긍정적인 분기 결과에 대한 발표 후에 크게 상승했다.
해설 빈칸은 명사구(the announcement ~ results)를 목적어로 가지는 전치사 자리이므로 모든 보기가 정답의 후보이다. '주가가 긍정적인 분기 결과에 대한 발표 후에 크게 상승했다'라는 의미가 되어야 하므로 전치사 (B) after(~ 후에)가 정답이다. (A) from은 '~에서, ~으로부터', (C) about은 '~에 관한, ~에 대한', (D) despite는 '~에도 불구하고'라는 의미이다.
어휘 stock price 주가 significantly adv. 크게, 상당히 announcement n. 발표 quarterly adj. 분기의

10 전치사 채우기
해석 재료는 포장 뒷면의 영양 정보 위에 기재되어 있다.
해설 빈칸은 명사구(the nutritional ~ package)를 목적어로 가지는 전치사 자리이므로 모든 보기가 정답의 후보이다. '재료가 영양 정보 위에 기재되어 있다'라는 의미가 되어야 하므로 전치사 (A) above(~ 위에)가 정답이다. (B) into는 '~ 안으로', (C) out은 '밖으로', (D) until은 '~까지'라는 의미이다.
어휘 ingredient n. 재료 list v. 기재하다, 기입하다 nutritional information 영양 정보 package n. 포장

11 형용사 자리 채우기
해석 금융 전문가들은 국제 경제가 경기 침체에서 빠져나왔다는 확실한 징후를 보지 못했다.
해설 빈칸 뒤의 명사(indications)를 꾸밀 수 있는 것은 형용사이므로 형용사 (A) firm(확실한, 확고한)이 정답이다. 부사 (B), 명사 또는 동사 (C), 명사 (D)는 명사를 꾸밀 수 없다. 부사 (B)가 동사(have not seen)를 꾸미는 것으로 본다 해도, '징후를 단호하게 보지 못했다'라는 어색한 문맥이 되며, 부사가 동사를 꾸밀 때는 동사와 목적어 사이에 올 수 없고 '동사 + 목적어'의 앞이나 뒤에 와야 한다.
어휘 financial adj. 금융의 expert n. 전문가 indication n. 징후, 표시 recession n. 경기 침체, 불황

12 전치사 채우기 정답공식 02
해석 Pullman Design사는 지난여름 새로운 사무실로의 이전 이래로 20명이 넘는 새로운 직원을 고용했다.
해설 빈칸은 명사구(the move ~ office)를 목적어로 가지는 전치사 자리이므로 모든 보기가 정답의 후보이다. '이전 이래로 20명이 넘는 새로운 직원을 고용했다'라는 의미가 되어야 하므로 전치사 (B) since(~ 이래로)가 정답이다. (A) by는 '~까지', (C) with는 '~을 가지고, ~과 함께', (D) outside는 '~ 밖에'라는 의미이다.
어휘 hire v. 고용하다 employee n. 직원

13 전치사 채우기
해석 노점상들은 길 양쪽을 따라 좌판을 설치하도록 허락되지만, 보행자들을 위해 중앙은 비워두어야 한다.
해설 빈칸은 명사구(either side of the lane)를 목적어로 가지는 전치사 자리이므로 모든 보기가 정답의 후보이다. '노점상들은 길 양쪽을 따라 좌판을 설치하도록 허락된다'라는 의미가 되어야 하므로 전치사 (A) along(~을 따라)이 정답이다. (B) below(~ 아래에)와 (D) over(~ 위에)는 위치를, (C) toward(~ 쪽으로, ~을 향해)는 방향을 나타낸다.
어휘 vendor n. 노점상, 행상인 permit v. 허락하다, 허용하다 set up 설치하다
stall n. 좌판, 마구간 lane n. 길, 도로, 차선 pedestrian n. 보행자

14 전치사 채우기
해석 Coleman 미술관 방문객들은 메인 주차장이 재포장되는 동안 건물 뒤에 주차하도록 지시받았다.
해설 빈칸은 명사(the building)를 목적어로 가지는 전치사 자리이므로 모든 보기가 정답의 후보이다. '주차장이 재포장되는 동안 건물 뒤에 주차하다'라는 의미가 되어야 하므로 전치사 (D) behind(~ 뒤에)가 정답이다. (A) between은 '사이에'라는 뜻이지만, 두 개의 대상 사이를 나타낼 때 쓰인다. (B) through는 '~을 통과하여, ~을 통해'라는 의미이다. (C) among은 '사이에'라는 의미이지만, 세 개 이상의 대상 사이를 나타낼 때 쓰인다.
어휘 instruct v. 지시하다 repave v. 재포장하다

15 전치사 채우기
해석 이 동네의 주택 가격은 지난 5년 동안 30퍼센트 상승했다.
해설 빈칸은 명사구(the last five years)를 목적어로 가지는 전치사 자리이므로 모든 보기가 정답의 후보이다. '주택 가격이 지난 5년 동안 상승했다'라는 의미가 되어야 하므로 전치사 (B) over(~ 동안, ~하는 내내)가 정답이다. (A) about은 '~에 관한, ~에 대한', (C) into는 '~ 안으로', (D) until은 '~까지'라는 의미이다.
어휘 housing price 주택 가격 neighborhood n. 동네, 이웃

16 전치사 채우기
해석 노트북 안에 유일하게 교체 가능한 부품은 배터리와 하드 드라이브이다.
해설 빈칸은 명사(the laptop)를 목적어로 가지는 전치사 자리이므로 모든 보기가 정답의 후보이다. '노트북 안에 유일하게 교체 가능한 부품'이라는 의미가 되어야 하므로 전치사 (C) inside(~ 안에)가 정답이다. (A) between은 '사이에', (B) above는 '~ 위에', (D) after는 '~ 후에'라는 의미이다.
어휘 replaceable adj. 교체 가능한 component n. 부품, 구성품

17 전치사 채우기
해석 모든 대여 장비는 사용하신 날 오후 5시까지 반드시 반납해 주십시오.
해설 빈칸은 명사구(5 P.M. on the day of use)를 목적어로 가지는 전치사 자리이므로 모든 보기가 정답의 후보이다. '모든 대여 장비는 오후 5시까지 반납해 주십시오'라는 의미가 되어야 하므로 전치사 (B) by(~까지)가 정답이다. (A) in은 '~에'라는 의미이지만 시각 앞에 쓰일 수 없고, (C) to는 '~으로, ~ 쪽으로'라는 의미이다. (D) within은 '~ 이내에'라는 의미로, 뒤에 기간 표현이 온다.

18 전치사 채우기
해석 Ms. Safi는 치과 예약 때문에 오늘 오후에 고객들을 만날 수 없을 것이다.
해설 빈칸은 명사구(her dental appointment)를 목적어로 가지는 전치사 자리이므로 모든 보기가 정답의 후보이다. '치과 예약 때문에 고객들을 만날 수 없다'라는 의미가 되어야 하므로 전치사 (A) because of(~ 때문에)가 정답이다. (B) according to는 '~에 따라', (C) such as는 '~과 같은', (D) in spite of는 '~에도 불구하고'라는 의미이다.
어휘 appointment n. 예약

19 부사 자리 채우기
해석 Mr. Dreyfuss는 은퇴했음에도 불구하고 그는 관광 산업 행사들에서 여전히 두드러지게 활동 중이다.
해설 2형식 동사 remains의 보어 자리에 온 형용사(active)를 꾸밀 수 있는 것은 부사이므로 부사 (D) noticeably(두드러지게)가 정답이다. 명사 또는 동사 (A), 동사 또는 과거분사 (B), 형용사 (C)는 형용사를 꾸밀 수 없다.
어휘 remain v. 여전히 ~이다 active adj. 활동 중의, 활발한
tourism industry 관광 산업 retire v. 은퇴하다
noticeable adj. 두드러지는, 뚜렷한

20 전치사 채우기
해석 바쁜 일정에도 불구하고, Ms. Harris는 다음 달 생명공학 학회의 기조연설자가 되는 것에 동의했다.
해설 이 문장은 주어(Ms. Harris), 동사(has agreed to be), 보어(the keynote ~ conference)를 갖춘 완전한 절이므로, ___ ~ schedule은 수식어 거품으로 보아야 한다. 이 수식어 거품은 동사가 없는 거품구이므로 거품구를 이끌 수 있는 모든 보기가 정답의 후보이다. '바쁜 일정에도 불구하고, 학회의 기조연설자가 되는 것에 동의했다'라는 의미가 되어야 하므로 전치사 (A) Despite(~에도 불구하고)가 정답이다. (B) Across는 '~을 가로질러', (C) Above는 '~ 위에', (D) Between은 '사이에'라는 의미이다.
어휘 keynote speaker 기조연설자 bioengineering n. 생명공학
conference n. 학회, 회의

21 전치사 채우기
해석 집주인은 바닥용 타일 선택을 제외하고는 수리 계획의 모든 측면을 승인했다.
해설 빈칸은 명사구(the choice ~ tiles)를 목적어로 가지는 전치사 자리이므로 모든 보기가 정답의 후보이다. '집주인은 바닥용 타일 선택을 제외하고는 수리 계획의 모든 측면을 승인했다'라는 의미가 되어야 하므로 전치사 (D) except for(~을 제외하고는)가 정답이다. (A) according to는 '~에 따라', (B) near는 '~ 가까이, ~ 근처에', (C) against는 '~에 반대하여, ~에 기대어'라는 의미이다.
어휘 approve of ~을 승인하다 renovation n. 수리

22 전치사 채우기 정답 공식 01
해석 Charlie Curran은 이번 금요일의 패널 토론에 참여하도록 선정된 기업 리더들 사이에 한 명이다.
해설 빈칸은 명사구(the business ~ talk)를 목적어로 가지는 전치사 자리이므로 모든 보기가 정답의 후보이다. 'Charlie Curran은 선정된 기업 리더들 사이에 한 명이다'라는 의미가 되어야 하므로 (C) among(사이에)이 정답이다. (A) onto는 '~ 위로, ~ 쪽으로', (B) through는 '~을 통과하여, ~을 통해', (D) for는 '~ 동안, ~을 위해'라는 의미이다.
어휘 select v. 선정하다, 고르다 participate v. 참여하다

23 전치사 채우기 정답 공식 04
해석 지원서를 받은 후 3영업일 이내에, 저희 팀이 면접 일정을 잡기 위해 연락드릴 것입니다.
해설 이 문장은 주어(our team), 동사(will contact), 목적어(you)를 모두 갖춘 완전한 절이므로, ___ ~ application은 수식어 거품으로 보아야 한다. 이 수식어 거품은 동사가 없는 거품구이므로 거품구를 이끌 수 있는 모든 보기가 정답의 후보이다. '3영업일 이내에'라는 의미가 되어야 하므로 전치사 (A) Within(~ 이내에)이 정답이다. 전치사 (B) Besides는 '~ 외에도', (C) Over는 '~ 동안, ~하는 내내', (D) Behind는 '~ 뒤에'라는 의미이다.
어휘 application n. 지원서 contact v. 연락하다 schedule v. 일정을 잡다

24 전치사 채우기
해석 시장이 Quantanet사에게는 너무 도전적이어서, 그 사업은 이익을 늘리려는 소유주의 노력에도 불구하고 실패했다.

해설 빈칸 앞의 사업이 실패했다(the business failed)는 내용은 이익을 늘리려는 소유주의 노력(the owner's efforts to increase profits)과 상반되는 내용이므로 양보를 나타내는 전치사 (C) in spite of(~에도 불구하고)가 정답이다. (A) due to는 '~ 때문에, ~으로 인해', (B) except for는 '~을 제외하고는', (D) in addition to는 '~에 더하여'라는 의미이다.

어휘 challenging adj. 도전적인, 어려운 owner n. 소유주

빈출 어휘 — 명사 4

토익 실전문제
p.187

| 01 (C) | 02 (A) | 03 (A) | 04 (B) | 05 (D) |
| 06 (C) | 07 (B) | 08 (D) | | |

01 명사 어휘 고르기

해석 새로운 공항 보안 정책은 기내 반입용 수하물에 대한 추가 규제를 포함한다.

해설 '공항 보안 정책이 수하물에 대한 추가 규제를 포함하다'라는 문맥이므로 명사 restriction(규제, 제한)의 복수형 (C) restrictions가 정답이다. (A)의 option은 '선택권, 옵션', (B)의 reentry는 '재입장, 복귀', (D)의 preparation은 '준비'라는 의미이다.

어휘 security n. 보안 measure n. 정책 carry-on adj. 기내 반입용의 luggage n. 수하물

02 명사 어휘 고르기

해석 Dr. Patel은 예방 의학을 전문으로 하는 존경받는 의료 전문가이다.

해설 '예방 의학을 전문으로 하는 존경받는 의료 전문가이다'라는 문맥이므로 (A) practitioner(전문가, 개업의)가 정답이다. (B) proficiency는 '능숙함, 숙달', (C) association은 '제휴, 협회', (D) position은 '직책, 일자리'라는 의미이다.

어휘 respected adj. 존경받는 healthcare adj. 의료의 preventive adj. 예방의 medicine n. 의학

03 명사 어휘 고르기

해석 그 발전소는 에너지 수요가 절정기인 동안 최대 생산 능력으로 가동된다.

해설 '발전소가 최대 생산 능력으로 가동되다'라는 문맥이므로 (A) capacity(생산 능력, 수용력)가 정답이다. (B) warranty는 '보증(서)', (C) adjustment는 '조정, 적응', (D) resistance는 '저항(력)'이라는 의미이다.

어휘 power plant 발전소 operate v. 가동되다 full adj. 최대의 peak adj. 절정기의 demand n. 수요

04 명사 어휘 고르기

해석 Oakwood 골프 클럽은 이 지역의 사업체들을 위한 기업 회원권 패키지를 제공한다.

해설 '지역의 사업체들을 위한 기업 회원권 패키지를 제공하다'라는 문맥이므로 (B) membership(회원(권), 회원 자격)이 정답이다. (A) authorization은 '승인, 허가', (C) formula는 '제조법, 공식', (D) disclosure는 '공개, 폭로'라는 의미이다.

어휘 corporate adj. 기업의 business n. 사업체

05 명사 어휘 고르기

해석 분기별 재정 보고서는 작년과 비교하여 수입이 15퍼센트 증가했다는 것을 보여준다.

해설 '수입이 15퍼센트 증가했다'라는 문맥이므로 (D) revenue(수입, 매출)가 정답이다. (A) specification은 '명세서, 사양', (B) circumstance는 '상황, 환경', (C) feedback은 '의견, 피드백'이라는 의미이다.

어휘 quarterly adj. 분기별의 financial adj. 재정의 compared to ~과 비교하여

06 명사 어휘 고르기

해석 우리 회사의 사명은 자동차 산업을 위한 지속 가능한 제품을 개발하는 것이다.

해설 '회사의 사명이 지속 가능한 제품을 개발하는 것이다'라는 문맥이므로 (C) mission(사명, 임무)이 정답이다. (A) application은 '신청', (B) evaluation은 '평가', (D) approval은 '승인'이라는 의미이다.

어휘 sustainable adj. 지속 가능한 automotive adj. 자동차의

07 명사 어휘 고르기

해석 그 최고 경영자는 회사의 전 세계적인 영향력을 확장하는 데 있어 Ms. Garcia의 중요한 성과를 인정했다.

해설 '회사의 전 세계적인 영향력을 확장하는 데 있어 중요한 성과를 인정하다'라는 문맥이므로 (B) accomplishment(성과, 업적)가 정답이다. (A) guide는 '안내', (C) payment는 '지급', (D) criticism은 '비판'이라는 의미이다.

어휘 recognize v. 인정하다 significant adj. 중요한, 상당한 expand v. 확장하다 reach n. 영향력

08 명사 어휘 고르기

해석 지역 주민들의 강한 반대에도 불구하고, 시의회는 건설 프로젝트를 승인했다.

해설 '지역 주민들의 강한 반대에도 불구하고, 시의회가 프로젝트를 승인했다'라는 문맥이므로 (D) opposition(반대, 대립)이 정답이다. (A) opportunity는 '기회', (B) usage는 '사용', (C) enrollment는 '등록'이라는 의미이다.

어휘 resident n. 주민, 거주자 city council 시의회 construction n. 건설

DAY 05 동사의 형태와 수일치

기출 포인트 01

실전 Check-up
p.188

01 (A) 02 (B)

01 조동사 다음에 동사원형 채우기

해석 방문객들은 매월 첫 번째 일요일에 무료로 미술관에 입장할 수 있다.

해설 조동사(can) 다음에 올 수 있는 것은 동사원형이므로 동사원형 (A) enter(입장하다)가 정답이다. 동사의 3인칭 단수형 (B)는 조동사 다음의 동사원형 자리에 올 수 없다.

어휘 gallery n. 미술관 for free 무료로

02 'have동사 + p.p.' 채우기

해석 마케팅 이사는 회사의 분기 보고서를 발표했다.

해설 빈칸이 have동사인 has 뒤에 있으므로, the company's quarterly report를 목적어로 취하면서 has와 함께 완료형 동사를 만드는 과거분사 (B) presented(발표하다)가 정답이다. 동사원형 (A)는 has와 함께 쓰일 수 없다.

기출 포인트 02~04

실전 Check-up
p.189

01 (A) 02 (A)

01 주어와 수일치하는 동사 채우기

해석 각 제안서는 부서 관리자와 경영 위원회 모두의 승인이 필요하다.

해설 문장에 주어(Each proposal)만 있고 동사가 없으므로 모든 보기가 정답의 후보이다. 'each + 단수 명사'는 단수 취급하므로 단수 동사 (A) needs(필요하다)가 정답이다. 복수 동사 (B)는 복수 주어와 함께 써야 한다.

어휘 proposal n. 제안서 approval n. 승인, 인가 department n. 부서 executive adj. 경영의, 행정의 committee n. 위원회

02 주어와 수일치하는 동사 채우기

해석 최신 카탈로그들은 우리 회사의 웹사이트에서 온라인 열람이 가능하다.

해설 문장에 주어(The current catalogs)만 있고 동사가 없으므로 모든 보기가 정답의 후보이다. 주어(The current catalogs)가 복수이므로 복수 동사 (A) are가 정답이다. 단수 동사 (B)는 단수 주어와 함께 써야 한다.

기출 포인트 05

실전 Check-up   p.190

01 (B)   02 (A)

01 주어와 수일치하는 동사 채우기

해석 많은 음악가들이 주말 저녁에 도심의 재즈 클럽에서 정기적으로 공연한다.

해설 문장에 주어(A number of musicians)만 있고 동사가 없으므로 모든 보기가 정답의 후보이다. 빈칸 앞에 복수 주어로 취급하는 'a number of + 복수 명사(musicians)'가 있으므로 복수 동사 (B) perform(공연하다)이 정답이다. 단수 동사 (A)는 단수 주어와 함께 써야 한다.

02 주어와 수일치하는 동사 채우기

해석 일부 식당들은 새로운 모바일 앱을 통해 배달 서비스를 제공한다.

해설 문장에 주어(Some of the restaurants)만 있고 동사가 없으므로 모든 보기가 정답의 후보이다. some of 뒤의 명사에 동사를 수일치하는 표현으로, 뒤에 복수 명사(the restaurants)가 있으므로 복수 동사 (A) offer(제공하다)가 정답이다. 단수 동사 (B)는 단수 주어와 함께 써야 한다.

어휘 delivery n. 배달

3초컷 정답 공식   p.191

| 01 (D) | 02 (C) | 03 (A) | 04 (B) | 05 (A) |
| 06 (C) | 07 (A) | 08 (B) | | |

01 조동사 다음에 동사원형 채우기

해석 새로운 정책은 다음 달부터 모든 직원에게 영향을 끼칠 것이다.

해설 조동사(will) 다음에 올 수 있는 것은 동사원형이므로 동사원형 (D) affect(영향을 끼치다)가 정답이다. 동명사 또는 현재분사 (A), 동사의 3인칭 단수형 (B), 동사의 과거형 또는 과거분사 (C)는 조동사 다음의 동사원형 자리에 올 수 없다.

어휘 policy n. 정책

02 조동사 다음에 동사원형 채우기

해석 직원들은 사무실에 있는 동안 항상 그들의 신분증을 착용해야 한다.

해설 조동사(should) 다음에 올 수 있는 것은 동사원형이므로 동사원형 (C) wear(착용하다)가 정답이다. 동사의 3인칭 단수형 (A), 동명사 또는 현재분사 (B), 과거분사 (D)는 조동사 다음의 동사원형 자리에 올 수 없다.

어휘 ID card 신분증 at all times 항상, 언제나

03 동사 자리 채우기

해석 제품을 제대로 조립하기 위해, 설명서를 주의 깊게 읽으십시오.

해설 이 문장은 주어가 없는 명령문이므로, 명령문의 동사 자리에 올 수 있는 동사원형 (A) read(읽다)가 정답이다. 동명사 또는 현재분사 (B), 동사의 3인칭 단수형 (C), to 부정사 (D)는 명령문의 동사 자리에 올 수 없다.

어휘 assemble v. 조립하다 properly adv. 제대로, 적절히 instruction n. 설명서, 지시

04 동사 자리 채우기

해석 예약을 할 때 식이 제한 사항을 명시해 주십시오.

해설 이 문장은 주어가 없는 명령문이므로, 명령문의 동사 자리에 올 수 있는 동사원형 (B) specify(명시하다)가 정답이다. 동사의 3인칭 단수형 (A), 동명사 또는 현재분사 (C), 명사 (D)는 명령문의 동사 자리에 올 수 없다.

어휘 dietary adj. 식이 요법의, 음식의 restriction n. 제한 (사항) reservation n. 예약

05 주어와 수일치하는 동사 채우기

해석 건축가 Jennifer Wu는 전 세계 도시 개발 프로젝트를 위한 지속 가능한 건물 디자인을 만든다.

해설 문장에 동사가 없으므로 동사 (A), (B), (C)가 정답의 후보이다. 주어(Architect Jennifer Wu)가 단수이므로 단수 동사 (A) creates(만들다)가 정답이다. 복수 동사 (B)와 (C)는 복수 주어와 함께 써야 한다. 명사 (D)는 동사 자리에 올 수 없다.

어휘 architect n. 건축가 sustainable adj. 지속 가능한 urban adj. 도시의

06 주어와 수일치하는 동사 채우기

해석 Melodify Tech사는 스트리밍 음악 서비스에 대해 3개월 무료 체험 기간을 준다.

해설 문장에 동사가 없으므로 동사 (B), (C), (D)가 정답의 후보이다. 주어(Melodify Tech)가 단수이므로 단수 동사 (C) grants(주다)가 정답이다. 복수 동사 (B)와 (D)는 복수 주어와 함께 써야 한다. 동명사 또는 현재분사 (A)는 동사 자리에 올 수 없다.

어휘 trial period 체험 기간

07 주어와 수일치하는 동사 채우기

해석 투어에 참여하기를 원하는 박물관 관람객들은 안내 데스크에서 등록해야 한다.

해설 빈칸은 명사(Museum patrons)를 꾸미는 주격 관계절(who ~ tour)의 동사 자리이므로 동사 (A), (B), (D)가 정답의 후보이다. 주격 관계절의 동사는 선행사(Museum patrons)와 수일치하므로 복수 동사 (A) wish(원하다)가 정답이다. 단수 동사 (B)와 (D)는 단수 선행사와 함께 써야 한다. to 부정사 (C)는 동사 자리에 올 수 없다.

어휘 patron n. 이용자, 고객

08 주어와 수일치하는 동사 채우기

해석 정품 소프트웨어를 소유한 사람들은 무료로 최신판 업그레이드를 받을 자격이 자동으로 주어진다.

해설 빈칸은 명사(Those)를 꾸미는 주격 관계절(who ~ software)의 동사 자리이므로 동사 (A), (B), (D)가 정답의 후보이다. 주격 관계절의 동사는 선행사(Those)와 수일치하므로 복수 동사 (B) own(소유하다)이 정답이다. 단수 동사 (A)와 (D)는 단수 선행사와 함께 써야 한다. 동명사 또는 현재분사 (C)는 동사 자리에 올 수 없다.

어휘 automatically adv. 자동으로 qualify v. 자격이 있다 latest adj. 최신의

HACKERS TEST   p.192

01 (C)	02 (D)	03 (A)	04 (A)	05 (B)
06 (A)	07 (B)	08 (C)	09 (A)	10 (D)
11 (C)	12 (A)	13 (B)	14 (A)	15 (A)
16 (D)	17 (D)	18 (D)	19 (C)	20 (D)
21 (D)	22 (A)	23 (D)	24 (A)	

01 조동사 다음에 동사원형 채우기 [정답 공식 01]
해석 Grand Azure 호텔은 3박 넘게 묵는 손님들에게 무료 셔틀 서비스를 제공할 것이다.

해설 조동사(will) 다음에 올 수 있는 것은 동사원형이므로 동사원형 (C) provide(제공하다)가 정답이다. 동사의 3인칭 단수형 (A), 동명사 또는 현재분사 (B), 동사의 과거형 또는 과거분사 (D)는 조동사 다음의 동사원형 자리에 올 수 없다.

02 'be동사 + -ing' 채우기
해석 최고경영자는 내년에 아시아 시장에서 사업을 확장하는 것을 고려하고 있다.

해설 be동사(is) 뒤에 올 수 있는 명사 (C)와 현재분사 (D)가 정답의 후보이다. '최고경영자는 아시아 시장에서 사업을 확장하는 것을 고려하고 있다'라는 의미가 되어야 하므로 현재진행 시제를 만드는 (D) considering이 정답이다. (C) consideration을 쓸 경우 '최고경영자는 고려 사항이다'라는 어색한 의미를 만들기 때문에 답이 될 수 없다. 동사원형 (A)와 동사의 3인칭 단수형 (B)는 be동사 뒤에 올 수 없다.

어휘 expand v. 확장하다 operation n. 사업, 운영

03 주어와 수일치하는 동사 채우기 [정답 공식 03]
해석 Greenleaf Organic Food사는 건강을 의식하는 전국의 소비자들에게 현지에서 공급받은 제품을 유통한다.

해설 문장에 동사가 없으므로 동사 (A), (B), (D)가 정답의 후보이다. 주어(Greenleaf Organic Food)가 단수이므로 단수 동사 (A) distributes(유통하다)가 정답이다. 복수 동사 (B)와 (D)는 복수 주어와 함께 써야 한다. 동명사 또는 현재분사 (C)는 동사 자리에 올 수 없다.

어휘 health-conscious adj. 건강을 의식하는 nationwide adv. 전국적으로

04 동사 자리 채우기 [정답 공식 02]
해석 다가오는 웨비나에 등록하고 자리를 확보하려면 웹사이트를 방문하세요.

해설 이 문장은 주어가 없는 명령문이므로, 명령문의 동사 자리에 올 수 있는 동사원형 (A) visit(방문하다)가 정답이다. 동사의 3인칭 단수형 (B), 동명사 또는 현재분사 (C), 동사의 과거형 또는 과거분사 (D)는 명령문의 동사 자리에 올 수 없다.

어휘 sign up 등록하다 upcoming adj. 다가오는 secure v. 확보하다

05 주어와 수일치하는 동사 채우기
해석 여러 사용자들이 새로운 온라인 결제 시스템에 대해 끊임없이 불평한다.

해설 문장에 주어(Several users)만 있고 동사가 없으므로 동사 (A), (B), (C)가 정답의 후보이다. 주어(Several users)가 복수이므로 복수 동사 (B) complain(불평하다)이 정답이다. 단수 동사 (A)와 (C)는 단수 주어와 함께 써야 한다. 동명사 또는 현재분사 (D)는 동사 자리에 올 수 없다.

어휘 constantly adv. 끊임없이, 거듭 payment n. 결제

06 사람명사와 사물/추상명사 구별하여 채우기
해석 Ms. Lindstrom의 블로그는 식물 돌보기에 경험이 적은 정원사들을 위한 유용한 안내서로의 역할을 한다.

해설 빈칸은 동사(serves)의 보어이면서 형용사(useful)의 꾸밈을 받는 명사 자리이므로 명사 (A)와 (B)가 정답의 후보이다. '블로그가 유용한 안내서로의 역할을 하다'라는 의미가 되어야 하므로 사물명사 (A) guide(안내서)가 정답이다. 사람명사 (B) guider(지도자)를 쓸 경우 '블로그가 유용한 지도자로의 역할을 하다'라는 어색한 의미가 된다. 동사 또는 과거분사 (C)는 명사 자리에 올 수 없다. to 부정사 (D)는 형용사의 꾸밈을 받을 수 없다.

어휘 useful adj. 유용한 gardener n. 정원사

07 동사 자리 채우기
해석 고객 만족도 설문조사는 개선된 서비스 응답 시간이 필요하다는 것을 보여주는 것 같이 보인다.

해설 문장에 동사가 없으므로 동사 (B) appears(~인 것 같이 보이다)가 정답이다. to 부정사 (A), 동명사 또는 현재분사 (C), 명사 (D)는 동사 자리에 올 수 없다.

어휘 satisfaction n. 만족도 survey n. 설문조사 response n. 응답

08 주어와 수일치하는 동사 채우기
해석 우리는 혼잡 시간 동안 방문객들이 지정된 주차 구역을 이용할 것을 권장한다.

해설 문장에 동사가 없으므로 동사 (A)와 (B)가 정답의 후보이다. 주어(We)가 복수이므로 복수 동사 (A) recommend(권장하다)가 정답이다. 단수 동사 (B)는 단수 주어와 함께 써야 한다. 동명사 또는 현재분사 (C)와 명사 (D)는 동사 자리에 올 수 없다.

어휘 designated adj. 지정된

09 주어와 수일치하는 동사 채우기 [정답 공식 04]
해석 추가 수하물을 부치는 것을 선택하는 승객들은 추가 요금이 부과될 것이다.

해설 빈칸은 명사(Passengers)를 꾸미는 주격 관계절(who ~ luggage)의 동사 자리이므로 동사 (A), (B), (D)가 정답의 후보이다. 주격 관계절의 동사는 선행사(Passengers)와 수일치하므로 복수 동사 (A) choose(선택하다)가 정답이다. 단수 동사 (B)와 (D)는 단수 선행사와 함께 써야 한다. 동명사 또는 현재분사 (C)는 동사 자리에 올 수 없다.

어휘 passenger n. 승객 check v. (비행기 등을 탈 때 수하물을) 부치다 luggage n. 수하물 charge v. 부과하다 extra fee 추가 요금

10 주어와 수일치하는 동사 채우기
해석 그 지원자들은 인상적인 학력과 관련 경험을 가지고 있다.

해설 문장에 동사가 없으므로 동사 (A), (B), (D)가 정답의 후보이다. 주어(The candidates)가 복수이므로 복수 동사 (D) have(가지다)가 정답이다. 단수 동사 (A)와 (B)는 단수 주어와 함께 써야 한다. 동명사 또는 현재분사 (C)는 동사 자리에 올 수 없다.

어휘 candidate n. 지원자 impressive adj. 인상적인 educational background 학력 relevant adj. 관련된

11 주어와 수일치하는 동사 채우기
해석 그 문화 축제는 20개의 다양한 나라들로부터의 전통 공연을 특징으로 한다.

해설 문장에 동사가 없으므로 동사 (B)와 (C)가 정답의 후보이다. 주어(The cultural festival)가 단수이므로 단수 동사 (C) features(~을 특징으로 하다)가 정답이다. 복수 동사 (B)는 복수 주어와 함께 써야 한다. 동명사 또는 현재분사 (A)는 동사 자리에 올 수 없다. 빈칸 앞에 be동사가 없으므로 현재진행 시제를 만드는 (D)는 답이 될 수 없다.

어휘 traditional adj. 전통적인 performance n. 공연

12 주어와 수일치하는 동사 채우기
해석 업데이트된 안전 절차에 관한 공지가 모든 작업장 구역에 게시되었다.

해설 문장에 주어(The notice)만 있고 동사가 없으므로 동사 (A), (B), (D)가 정답의 후보이다. 주어(The notice)가 단수이므로 단수 동사 (A) has been posted(게시되었다)가 정답이다. 복수 동사 (B)와 (D)는 복수 주어와 함께 써야 한다. 동명사 또는 현재분사 (C)는 동사 자리에 올 수 없다. 참고로, 주어와 동사 사이에 있는 수식어 거품(regarding ~ procedures)은 동사의 수 결정에 아무런 영향을 주지 않는다.

어휘 notice n. 공지 procedure n. 절차 workshop n. 작업장

13 전치사 채우기
해석 박물관의 관람객들은 관장으로부터의 특별 허가 없이는 사진을 찍는 것이 허용되지 않는다.

해설 빈칸은 명사구(special ~ the curator)를 목적어로 가지는 전치사 자리이므로 모든 보기가 정답의 후보이다. '허가 없이는 사진을 찍는 것이 허

용되지 않는다'라는 의미가 되어야 하므로 전치사 (B) without(~ 없이)이 정답이다. (A) across는 '~을 가로질러', (C) over는 '~ 위에', (D) within은 '~ 이내에'라는 의미이다.

어휘 permit v. 허용하다, 허락하다 photograph n. 사진
permission n. 허가, 승인 curator n. (도서관·박물관 등의) 관장

14 주어와 수일치하는 동사 채우기
해석 그 차량의 이후 모델들은 이전 모델들보다 더 나은 연비를 가지는 경향이 있다.
해설 문장에 주어(Later models)만 있고 동사가 없으므로 동사 (A), (B), (C)가 정답의 후보이다. 주어(Later models)가 복수이므로 복수 동사 (A) tend가 정답이다. 참고로, tend to는 '~하는 경향이 있다'라는 의미이다. 단수 동사 (B)와 (C)는 단수 주어와 함께 써야 한다. to 부정사 (D)는 동사 자리에 올 수 없다. 참고로, 주어와 동사 사이에 있는 수식어 거품(of the vehicle)은 동사의 수 결정에 아무런 영향을 주지 않는다.
어휘 vehicle n. 차량 fuel efficiency 연비

15 주어와 수일치하는 동사 채우기
해석 Business Monthly의 6월호는 NexTech Solutions사의 최고경영자인 James Wilson과의 인터뷰를 포함한다.
해설 문장에 주어(The June issue)만 있고 동사가 없으므로 동사 (A)와 (B)가 정답의 후보이다. 주어(The June issue)가 단수이므로 단수 동사 (A) includes(포함하다)가 정답이다. 복수 동사 (B)는 복수 주어와 함께 써야 한다. 동명사 또는 현재분사 (C)와 to 부정사 (D)는 동사 자리에 올 수 없다.
어휘 issue n. 호, 발행물

16 주어와 수일치하는 동사 채우기
해석 온도 기록은 올해 3월이 비정상적으로 따뜻했다는 것을 나타낸다.
해설 문장에 주어(Temperature records)만 있고 동사가 없으므로 동사 (B)와 (D)가 정답의 후보이다. 주어(Temperature records)가 복수이므로 복수 동사 (D) indicate(나타내다)가 정답이다. 단수 동사 (B)는 단수 주어와 함께 써야 한다. 명사 (A)와 동명사 또는 현재분사 (C)는 동사 자리에 올 수 없다.
어휘 temperature n. 온도 unusually adv. 비정상적으로

17 주어와 수일치하는 동사 채우기 [정답 공식 03]
해석 David Clark는 대학원생들에게 매 학기 국제 경제학을 가르친다.
해설 문장에 주어(David Clark)만 있고 동사가 없으므로 동사 (B)와 (D)가 정답의 후보이다. 주어(David Clark)가 단수이므로 단수 동사 (D) teaches(가르치다)가 정답이다. 복수 동사 (B)는 복수 주어와 함께 써야 한다. to 부정사 (A)와 동명사 또는 현재분사 (C)는 동사 자리에 올 수 없다.
어휘 economics n. 경제학 graduate student 대학원생 semester n. 학기

18 주어와 수일치하는 동사 채우기
해석 모든 공연자들은 연극 개막일 전에 추가 리허설을 요구한다.
해설 문장에 주어(All of the performers)만 있고 동사가 없으므로 동사 (A), (B), (D)가 정답의 후보이다. all은 of 뒤의 명사에 동사를 수일치하는 표현으로, 뒤에 복수 명사(performers)가 있으므로 복수 동사 (B) demand(요구하다)가 정답이다. 단수 동사 (A)와 (D)는 단수 주어와 함께 써야 한다. 동명사 또는 현재분사 (C)는 동사 자리에 올 수 없다.
어휘 rehearsal n. 리허설 opening night (연극·영화 등의 개막·개봉) 첫날 밤

19 주어와 수일치하는 동사 채우기
해석 모든 부서는 이번 주말까지 월간 보고서를 제출하도록 요구된다.
해설 문장에 주어(Every department)만 있고 동사가 없으므로 동사 (A), (C), (D)가 정답의 후보이다. 'every + 단수 명사'는 단수 취급하므로 단수 동사 (C) is required(요구되다)가 정답이다. 복수 동사 (A)와 (D)는 복수 주어와 함께 써야 한다. 동명사 또는 현재분사 (B)는 동사 자리에 올 수 없다.
어휘 department n. 부서 submit v. 제출하다

20 'have동사 + p.p.' 채우기
해석 Spart-Gym은 더 많은 고객들을 끌어들이기 위해 다가오는 행사를 홍보했다.
해설 빈칸이 has와 명사구(its upcoming event) 사이에 있으므로, its upcoming event를 목적어로 취하면서 has와 함께 완료형 동사를 만드는 과거분사 (D) publicized가 정답이다. 명사 (A) publicity를 쓸 경우 'Spart-Gym은 홍보를 가지고 있다'라는 어색한 문맥이 된다. 동명사 또는 현재분사 (B), 형용사 (C)는 has 다음에 올 수 없다. (C)를 '대중'이라는 의미의 명사로 본다 해도, 'Spart-Gym은 대중을 가지고 있다'라는 어색한 의미를 만들기 때문에 답이 될 수 없다.
어휘 upcoming adj. 다가오는 attract v. 끌어들이다 publicity n. 홍보, 광고
publicize v. 홍보하다, 알리다 public adj. 공공의; n. 대중

21 주어와 수일치하는 동사 채우기
해석 몇몇 기술자들이 시스템 안정성을 유지하기 위해 영업시간 외의 시간 동안 원격으로 일한다.
해설 문장에 주어(A few technicians)만 있고 동사가 없으므로 모든 보기가 정답의 후보이다. 'a few + 복수 명사'는 복수 취급하므로 복수 동사 (D) work(일하다)가 정답이다. 단수 동사 (A), (B), (C)는 단수 주어와 함께 써야 한다.
어휘 remotely adv. 원격으로, 멀리서 maintain v. 유지하다, 관리하다
stability n. 안정성 off-hours n. 영업시간 외의 시간

22 주어와 수일치하는 동사 채우기 [정답 공식 04]
해석 경비 보고서를 늦게 제출하는 사람들은 그다음 달이 되어서야 상환받을 것이다.
해설 빈칸은 명사(Those)를 꾸미는 주격 관계절(who ~ late)의 동사 자리이므로 동사 (A), (B), (D)가 정답의 후보이다. 주격 관계절의 동사는 선행사(Those)와 수일치하므로 복수 동사 (A) submit(제출하다)가 정답이다. 단수 동사 (B)와 (D)는 단수 선행사와 함께 써야 한다. 동명사 또는 현재분사 (C)는 동사 자리에 올 수 없다.
어휘 expense n. 경비 reimburse v. 상환하다

23 주어와 수일치하는 동사 채우기
해석 Help-A-Neighbor 단체의 회원들은 다양한 지역 자선단체들을 후원한다.
해설 문장에 동사가 없으므로 동사 (B)와 (D)가 정답의 후보이다. 주어(The members)가 복수이므로 복수 동사 (D) support(후원하다, 지원하다)가 정답이다. 단수 동사 (B)는 단수 주어와 함께 써야 한다. 형용사 (A)와 동명사 또는 현재분사 (C)는 동사 자리에 올 수 없다. 참고로, 주어와 동사 사이에 있는 수식어 거품(of ~ Organization)은 동사의 수 결정에 아무런 영향을 주지 않는다.
어휘 organization n. 단체, 기관 charitable adj. 자선의, 너그러운
supportive adj. 지지하는, 보완적인

24 주어와 수일치하는 동사 채우기
해석 증가하는 국제 관광객들의 수는 그 나라의 세계적인 평판을 반영한다.
해설 문장에 주어(The increasing ~ tourists)만 있고 동사가 없으므로 동사 (A), (B), (D)가 정답의 후보이다. 빈칸 앞에 단수 주어로 취급하는 'the number of + 복수 명사(tourists)'가 있으므로 단수 동사 (A) reflects(반영하다)가 정답이다. 복수 동사 (B)와 (D)는 복수 주어와 함께 써야 한다. 동명사 또는 현재분사 (C)는 동사 자리에 올 수 없다.
어휘 international adj. 국제적인 tourist n. 관광객 reputation n. 평판

빈출 어휘   동사 1

토익 실전문제   p.195

| 01 (D) | 02 (B) | 03 (B) | 04 (A) | 05 (B) |
| 06 (A) | 07 (B) | 08 (C) | | |

01 동사 어휘 고르기
해석 실내 장식가와의 약속은 수요일 아침으로 일정이 변경되어야 했다.

해설 '약속이 수요일 아침으로 일정이 변경되다'라는 문맥이므로 동사 reschedule(일정을 변경하다)의 p.p.형 (D) rescheduled가 정답이다. (A)의 expand는 '확장하다', (B)의 cancel은 '취소하다', (C)의 admit는 '인정하다'라는 의미이다.

어휘 appointment n. 약속   interior decorator 실내 장식가

02 동사 어휘 고르기
해석 Novoris사는 칠레의 새 채굴 프로젝트를 위해 현재 기술자들을 모집하고 있다.

해설 'Novoris사는 채굴 프로젝트를 위해 기술자들을 모집하고 있다'라는 문맥이므로 be동사(is)와 함께 현재 진행형을 완성하는 recruit(모집하다)의 현재분사 (B) recruiting이 정답이다. (A)의 insist는 '주장하다', (C)의 submit는 '제출하다', (D)의 compose는 '작곡하다'라는 의미이다.

어휘 presently adv. 현재, 지금   mining n. 채굴

03 동사 어휘 고르기
해석 극장 전체에 사용된 벽 패널은 과도한 소음을 흡수하도록 설계되었다.

해설 '벽 패널이 과도한 소음을 흡수하도록 설계되다'라는 문맥이므로 (B) absorb(흡수하다)가 정답이다. (A) press는 '누르다', (C) wrap은 '감싸다', (D) protect는 '보호하다'라는 의미이다.

어휘 panel n. 패널(넓은 직사각형의 목 판 또는 합판)   design v. 설계하다   excessive adj. 과도한

04 동사 어휘 고르기
해석 Nolan 학원의 강사들은 학생들이 안전하게 차량을 운전하는 법을 배우는 것을 보장하기 위한 조치를 취한다.

해설 '안전하게 차량을 운전하는 법을 배우는 것을 보장하기 위한 조치를 취하다'라는 문맥이므로 (A) ensure(보장하다)가 정답이다. (B) achieve는 '달성하다', (C) predict는 '예측하다', (D) assign은 '배정하다'라는 의미이다.

어휘 instructor n. 강사   step n. 조치   operate v. 운전하다

05 동사 어휘 고르기
해석 그 미술관 전시는 전국의 여러 유망한 젊은 예술가들의 작품들을 특별히 포함할 것이다.

해설 '미술관 전시가 유망한 젊은 예술가들의 작품들을 특별히 포함하다'라는 문맥이므로 (B) feature(특별히 포함하다, 특징으로 삼다)가 정답이다. (A) occupy는 '차지하다', (C) transfer는 '옮기다', (D) organize는 '조직하다'라는 의미이다.

어휘 exhibit n. 전시   promising adj. 유망한, 전도유망한

06 동사 어휘 고르기
해석 Ms. Porter는 오염된 강을 깨끗이 하기 위한 자금을 요청하기 위해 5월 11일에 시의회에게 연설할 것이다.

해설 '자금을 요청하기 위해 시의회에게 연설하다'라는 문맥이므로 (A) address(연설하다, 다루다)가 정답이다. (B) present는 '제시하다', (C) outline은 '개요를 말하다', (D) declare는 '선언하다'라는 의미이다.

어휘 council n. 의회   request v. 요청하다   fund n. 자금   polluted adj. 오염된

07 동사 어휘 고르기
해석 과도하게 스트레스 받는 것을 피하기 위해, Ms. Gomez는 개인 생활과 직업 생활의 균형을 맞추기 위해 지속적인 노력을 한다.

해설 '개인 생활과 직업 생활의 균형을 맞추기 위해 지속적인 노력을 하다'라는 문맥이므로 (B) balance(균형을 맞추다)가 정답이다. (A) determine은 '결정하다', (C) involve는 '관련시키다', (D) collect는 '수집하다'라는 의미이다.

어휘 avoid v. 피하다   constant adj. 지속적인   personal adj. 개인의   professional adj. 직업적인

08 동사 어휘 고르기
해석 30개가 넘는 팀이 3일간의 버뮤다 요트 경주에 참가할 것인데, 이것은 5월 25일에 시작할 것이다.

해설 '30개가 넘는 팀이 버뮤다 요트 경주에 참가할 것인데, 이것은 5월 25일에 시작할 것이다'라는 문맥이므로 (C) commence(시작하다)가 정답이다. (A) monitor는 '감시하다', (B) announce는 '발표하다', (D) disclose는 '공개하다'라는 의미이다.

어휘 compete v. 참가하다, 겨루다   sailboat n. 요트

DAY 06   동사의 종류와 태

기출 포인트 01

실전 Check-up   p.196

| 01 (B) | 02 (B) |

01 자동사와 타동사 구별하여 채우기
해석 품질 관리팀은 각 제품이 고객들에게 배송되기 전에 그것을 승인해야 한다.

해설 '품질 관리팀이 각 제품을 승인해야 한다'라는 문맥이므로 (B) approve(승인하다)가 정답이다. (A) agree(동의하다)도 해석상 그럴듯해 보이지만 자동사이므로 목적어(each product)와 함께 쓰이기 위해서는 전치사가 필요하다.

어휘 quality-control team 품질 관리팀   ship v. 배송하다

02 자동사와 타동사 구별하여 채우기
해석 많은 지역 주민이 주거 지역 근처에 새 고속도로를 건설하는 것에 반대한다.

해설 '주민들이 고속도로를 건설하는 것에 반대하다'라는 문맥이므로 (B) object(반대하다)가 정답이다. (A) oppose(반대하다)도 해석상 그럴듯해 보이지만 타동사이므로 빈칸 뒤의 전치사(to)와 함께 쓰일 수 없다.

어휘 resident n. 주민, 거주자   construction n. 건설, 공사   highway n. 고속도로   residential area 주거 지역

기출 포인트 02

실전 Check-up   p.197

| 01 (A) | 02 (B) |

01 태에 맞는 동사 채우기
해석 그 기술자는 장비가 제대로 작동하고 있는지 확실히 하기 위해 그것을 주의 깊게 점검했다.

해설 문장에 주어(The technician)만 있고 동사가 없으므로 모든 보기가 정답의 후보이다. '장비를 점검하다'라는 능동의 의미가 되어야 하므로 능동태 동사 (A) inspected가 정답이다.

어휘 technician n. 기술자 equipment n. 장비
ensure v. 확실히 하다, 보장하다 function v. 작동하다, 기능하다
properly adv. 제대로, 적절하게

02 태에 맞는 동사 채우기
해석 승객들은 그들이 남겨두었을지도 모르는 물품들이 있는지 그들의 주변을 확인하도록 상기된다.

해설 문장에 주어(Passengers)만 있고 동사가 없으므로 모든 보기가 정답의 후보이다. '주변을 확인하도록 상기되다'라는 수동의 의미가 되어야 하므로 수동태 (B) are reminded가 정답이다.

어휘 passenger n. 승객 surrounding n. 주변 remind v. 상기시키다

기출 포인트 03~04

실전 Check-up   p.198

01 (A)   02 (A)

01 태에 맞는 동사 채우기
해석 정부 조사관은 운영 책임자에 의해 연구 시설을 안내받을 것이다.

해설 문장에 주어(The government inspector)만 있고 동사가 없으므로 be동사(be)와 함께 동사를 만드는 모든 보기가 정답의 후보이다. 목적어가 없고 '정부 조사관은 운영 책임자에 의해 연구 시설을 안내받을 것이다'라는 수동의 의미가 되어야 하므로 수동태를 만드는 과거분사 (A) escorted가 정답이다.

어휘 inspector n. 조사관 escort v. 안내하다

02 수동태 관용 표현 채우기
해석 관리자는 대부분의 훈련생들의 성과에 만족했다.

해설 '훈련생들의 성과에 만족했다'라는 의미가 되어야 하므로 '~에 만족하다'라는 표현을 만드는 (A) satisfied가 정답이다.

어휘 supervisor n. 관리자, 감독관 performance n. 성과, 실적
trainee n. 훈련생, 실습생

3초컷 정답 공식   p.199

01 (B)   02 (A)   03 (C)   04 (A)   05 (A)
06 (D)   07 (C)   08 (D)

01 태에 맞는 동사 채우기
해석 해안 지역을 강타한 허리케인에 의해 여러 역사적 건물들이 훼손되었다.

해설 문장에 주어(Several historical buildings)만 있고 동사가 없으므로 be동사(were)와 함께 동사를 만드는 현재분사 (A)와 과거분사 (B)가 정답의 후보이다. 목적어가 없고 '허리케인에 의해 건물들이 훼손되었다'라는 수동의 의미가 되어야 하므로 수동태를 만드는 과거분사 (B) damaged가 정답이다. 동사원형 (C)와 3인칭 단수형 (D)는 be동사와 함께 동사를 만들 수 없다. (C)와 (D)를 명사로 본다 해도 '허리케인에 의해 건물들이 훼손/훼손들이다'라는 어색한 의미를 만들기 때문에 답이 될 수 없다.

어휘 historical adj. 역사적인 coastal adj. 해안의, 연안의 damage v. 훼손하다

02 태에 맞는 동사 채우기
해석 고대 문서가 지하실에서 고고학자들에 의해 발견되었다.

해설 문장에 주어(The ancient manuscript)만 있고 동사가 없으므로 be동사(was)와 함께 동사를 만드는 과거분사 (A)와 현재분사 (B)가 정답의 후보이다. 목적어가 없고 '고대 문서가 고고학자들에 의해 발견되었다'라는 수동의 의미가 되어야 하므로 수동태를 만드는 과거분사 (A) discovered가 정답이다. 동사원형 (C)와 to 부정사 (D)는 be동사와 함께 동사를 만들 수 없다.

어휘 manuscript n. 문서, 원고 archaeologist n. 고고학자
underground adj. 지하의 chamber n. ~실, 방

03 태에 맞는 동사 채우기
해석 참가자들은 오리엔테이션 세션을 위해 최소 15분 일찍 도착하도록 권장된다.

해설 문장에 주어(Participants)만 있고 동사가 없으므로 동사 (B), (C), (D)가 정답의 후보이다. '참가자들이 일찍 도착하도록 권장된다'라는 수동의 의미가 되어야 하므로 수동태 (C) are encouraged가 정답이다. 동명사 또는 현재분사 (A)는 동사 자리에 올 수 없다.

어휘 participant n. 참가자

04 태에 맞는 동사 채우기
해석 이 인사 고과는 기밀로 여겨지며 승인되지 않은 직원과 공유되어서는 안 된다.

해설 문장에 주어(This performance review)만 있고 동사가 없으므로 be동사(is)와 함께 동사를 만드는 과거분사 (A)와 현재분사 (C)가 정답의 후보이다. 목적어가 없고 '인사 고과가 기밀로 여겨지다'라는 수동의 의미가 되어야 하므로 수동태를 만드는 과거분사 (A) considered가 정답이다. 명사 (B)와 형용사 (D)는 be동사와 함께 동사를 만들 수 없다.

어휘 performance review 인사 고과 confidential adj. 기밀의, 비밀의
unauthorized adj. 승인되지 않은 personnel n. 직원, 인원

05 태에 맞는 동사 채우기
해석 Ms. Tanaka는 해외 확장 팀의 팀장으로 임명되었다.

해설 문장에 주어(Ms. Tanaka)만 있고 동사가 없으므로 동사 (A), (B), (D)가 정답의 후보이다. 'Ms. Tanaka가 팀장으로 임명되었다'라는 수동의 의미가 되어야 하므로 수동태 (A) was appointed가 정답이다. 동명사 또는 현재분사 (C)는 동사 자리에 올 수 없다.

어휘 international expansion 해외 확장

06 태에 맞는 동사 채우기
해석 중세 성곽은 독특한 건축적 특징과 역사적 중요성 때문에 보물로 여겨진다.

해설 문장에 주어(The medieval castle)만 있고 동사가 없으므로 동사 (C)와 (D)가 정답의 후보이다. '성곽이 보물로 여겨지다'라는 수동의 의미가 되어야 하므로 수동태 (D) is regarded가 정답이다. to 부정사 (A)와 동명사 또는 현재분사 (B)는 동사 자리에 올 수 없다.

어휘 medieval adj. 중세의 castle n. 성곽, 성 treasure n. 보물
unique adj. 독특한 architectural adj. 건축의 feature n. 특징
significance n. 중요성

07 태에 맞는 동사 채우기
해석 고급 리조트는 장관을 이루는 바다 전망이 있는 개인 섬에 위치해 있다.

해설 문장에 주어(The luxury resort)만 있고 동사가 없으므로 동사 (A), (B), (C)가 정답의 후보이다. '고급 리조트가 개인 섬에 위치해 있다'라는 수동의 의미가 되어야 하므로 수동태 (C) is situated가 정답이다. to 부정사 (D)는 동사 자리에 올 수 없다.

어휘 private adj. 개인의, 사적인 spectacular adj. 장관을 이루는
view n. 전망, 경치

08 태에 맞는 동사 채우기
해석 회사의 본사는 도쿄 시내에 위치해 있으며, 여러 교통 시설 근처에 있다.

해설 문장에 주어(The main office ~ company)만 있고 동사가 없으므로 동사 (A), (B), (D)가 정답의 후보이다. '본사는 시내에 위치해 있다'라는 수동의 의미가 되어야 하므로 수동태 (D) is located가 정답이다. to 부정사 (C)는 동사 자리에 올 수 없다.

어휘 main office 본사, 본점

HACKERS TEST

p.200

01 (B)	02 (D)	03 (B)	04 (D)	05 (C)
06 (A)	07 (B)	08 (C)	09 (D)	10 (B)
11 (C)	12 (D)	13 (C)	14 (A)	15 (B)
16 (A)	17 (B)	18 (C)	19 (B)	20 (D)
21 (A)	22 (D)	23 (A)	24 (D)	

01 태에 맞는 동사 채우기

해석 인사부는 채용 과정을 시작하기 전에 경영진으로부터 승인을 얻는다.

해설 문장에 주어(The human resources department)만 있고 동사가 없으므로 동사 (B)와 (C)가 정답의 후보이다. 빈칸 뒤에 목적어(approval)가 있고 '인사부가 경영진으로부터 승인을 얻다'라는 능동의 의미가 되어야 하므로 능동태 동사 (B) obtains가 정답이다. to 부정사 (A)와 동명사 또는 현재분사 (D)는 동사 자리에 올 수 없다.

어휘 approval n. 승인, 허가 hiring process 채용 과정

02 태에 맞는 동사 채우기 [정답 공식 01]

해석 연구 시설에 접근하려고 하는 모든 방문객은 도착 시 보안 요원에 의해 확인되어야 한다.

해설 문장에 주어(All visitors seeking ~ facility)만 있고 동사가 없으므로 be 동사(be)와 함께 동사를 만드는 현재분사 (C)와 과거분사 (D)가 정답의 후보이다. 목적어가 없고 '보안 요원에 의해 확인되다'라는 수동의 의미가 되어야 하므로 수동태를 만드는 과거분사 (D) checked가 정답이다. 동사원형 (A)와 3인칭 단수형 (B)는 be동사와 함께 동사를 만들 수 없다.

어휘 seek v. (~하려고) 하다 access n. 접근, 입장 facility n. 시설
security n. 보안 personnel n. 요원 arrival n. 도착

03 태에 맞는 동사 채우기 [정답 공식 03]

해석 Summit View 식당 주인은 지역 사업 협회의 회장으로 선출되었다.

해설 문장에 주어(The Summit ~ owner)만 있고 동사가 없으므로 동사 (B), (C), (D)가 정답의 후보이다. '식당 주인이 협회의 회장으로 선출되었다'라는 수동의 의미가 되어야 하므로 수동태 (B) was elected가 정답이다. 동명사 또는 현재분사 (A)는 동사 자리에 올 수 없다.

어휘 head n. 회장, 책임자 community n. 지역 사회 association n. 협회

04 태에 맞는 동사 채우기

해석 놀이공원의 입장료는 14시간 동안 놀이 기구의 무제한 이용을 포함한다.

해설 문장에 주어(The admission ~ park)만 있고 동사가 없으므로 동사 (C)와 (D)가 정답의 후보이다. 빈칸 뒤에 목적어(unlimited access)가 있고 '놀이공원의 입장료가 무제한 이용을 포함하다'라는 능동의 의미이므로 능동태 (D) includes(포함하다)가 정답이다. 형용사 (A)와 동명사 또는 현재분사 (B)는 동사 자리에 올 수 없다.

어휘 amusement park 놀이공원 unlimited adj. 무제한의, 무한정의
access n. 이용, 접근 ride n. 놀이 기구, 탈것

05 태에 맞는 동사 채우기

해석 Midlands 공예 축제에 참가하는 판매자들은 모든 품목의 가격을 명확히 보여주도록 지시받았다.

해설 문장에 주어(Vendors ~ Festival)만 있고 동사가 없으므로 be동사(been)와 함께 동사를 만드는 과거분사 (C)와 be동사의 보어 자리에 올 수 있는 형용사 (D)가 정답의 후보이다. 목적어가 없고 '판매자들이 가격을 보여주도록 지시받다'라는 수동의 의미가 되어야 하므로 수동태를 만드는 과거분사 (C) instructed가 정답이다. 형용사 (D)를 쓸 경우 '판매자들이 가격을 보여주도록 유익했다'라는 어색한 문맥이 된다. 동사원형 (A)와 3인칭 단수형 (B)는 be동사와 함께 동사를 만들 수 없다.

어휘 vendor n. 판매자, 노점상 display v. 보여주다

06 수동태 관용 표현 채우기

해석 임상 시험에 참여하는 자원봉사자들은 의학 검사 전 12시간 동안 음식을 먹지 않도록 요구받는다.

해설 문장에 주어(Volunteers ~ trial)만 있고 동사가 없으므로 모든 보기가 정답의 후보이다. '자원봉사자들이 음식을 먹지 않도록 요구받다'라는 의미가 되어야 하므로 '~하도록 요구받다'라는 표현을 만드는 (A) are required가 정답이다.

어휘 clinical trial 임상 시험

07 태에 맞는 동사 채우기

해석 내일 취업 박람회를 위한 물품들이 이미 행사 장소로 운송되었다.

해설 문장에 주어(The materials ~ fair)만 있고 동사가 없으므로 동사 (B), (C), (D)가 정답의 후보이다. '물품들이 행사 장소로 운송되다'라는 수동의 의미가 되어야 하므로 수동태 (B) were transported가 정답이다. 동명사 또는 현재분사 (A)는 동사 자리에 올 수 없다.

어휘 material n. 물품, 자료, 재료 venue n. (행사 등의) 장소

08 태에 맞는 동사 채우기 [정답 공식 04]

해석 안내 데스크는 용이한 접근을 위해 쇼핑몰 중앙에 위치해 있다.

해설 문장에 주어(The information desk)만 있고 동사가 없으므로 모든 보기가 정답의 후보이다. '안내 데스크가 쇼핑몰 중앙에 위치해 있다'라는 수동의 의미가 되어야 하므로 수동태 (C) is located가 정답이다.

어휘 access n. 접근, 이용

09 태에 맞는 동사 채우기

해석 위원회는 9월에 개최될 국제 무역 포럼을 조직하고 있다.

해설 문장에 주어(The committee)만 있고 동사가 없으므로 be동사(is)와 함께 동사를 만드는 과거분사 (C)와 현재분사 (D)가 정답의 후보이다. 빈칸 뒤에 목적어(an international trade forum)가 있고 '위원회가 포럼을 조직하다'라는 능동의 의미가 되어야 하므로 능동태를 만드는 현재분사 (D) organizing이 정답이다. 동사 (A)와 (B)는 be동사와 함께 동사를 만들 수 없다.

어휘 committee n. 위원회 international adj. 국제적인

10 형용사 자리 채우기

해석 주기적인 정비를 위해 웹 서버를 정지시키는 것은 시스템 오류를 방지할 수 있기 때문에 필수적이다.

해설 빈칸 뒤의 명사(maintenance)를 꾸밀 수 있는 것은 형용사이므로 형용사 (B) periodic(주기적인)이 정답이다. 명사 (A)와 (D), 부사 (C)는 형용사 자리에 올 수 없다.

어휘 shut down 정지시키다, 폐쇄하다 maintenance n. 정비, 유지
vital adj. 필수적인 period n. 기간 periodically adv. 주기적으로

11 태에 맞는 동사 채우기

해석 물가 인상으로 인해, 생활비가 올해 내내 꾸준히 오르고 있다.

해설 문장에 주어(the cost of living)만 있고 동사가 없으므로 be동사(been)와 함께 동사를 만드는 현재분사 (C)와 과거분사 (D)가 정답의 후보이다. '생활비가 오르고 있다'라는 능동의 의미가 되어야 하므로 능동태를 만드는 현재분사 (C) rising이 정답이다. 참고로, rise(오르다, 상승하다)는 목적어를 갖지 않는 자동사이므로 수동태로 쓰일 수 없다. 동사원형 (A)와 과거 시제 동사 (B)는 be동사와 함께 동사를 만들 수 없다.

어휘 inflation n. 물가 인상

12 태에 맞는 동사 채우기 [정답 공식 02]

해석 필요한 모든 영수증이 첨부된 경우에만 당신의 환급 요청이 유효하다고 여겨질 것입니다.

해설 문장에 주어(Your reimbursement request)만 있고 동사가 없으므로 모든 보기가 정답의 후보이다. 목적어가 없고 '환급 요청이 유효하다고 여겨지다'라는 수동의 의미가 되어야 하므로 수동태 (D) will be considered가 정답이다.

어휘 reimbursement n. 환급, 상환 request n. 요청 valid adj. 유효한
receipt n. 영수증 attach v. 첨부하다

13 수동태 관용 표현 채우기
해석 만약 당신이 저희 제품에 불만족한다면, 전액 환불을 위해 30일 이내에 그것들을 반품할 수 있습니다.
해설 If절(If ~ products)에 주어(you)만 있고 동사가 없으므로 동사 (B)와 (C)가 정답의 후보이다. '만약 제품에 불만족한다면'이라는 의미가 되어야 하므로 '~에 불만족하다'라는 표현을 만드는 (C) are dissatisfied가 정답이다. 동명사 또는 현재분사 (A)와 명사 (D)는 동사 자리에 올 수 없다.
어휘 return v. 반품하다 full refund 전액 환불

14 태에 맞는 동사 채우기
해석 우리의 채용팀은 현재 여러 IT 부서 공석을 위한 잠재적 후보자들을 면접하고 있다.
해설 문장에 주어(Our recruitment team)만 있고 동사가 없으므로 be동사(is)와 함께 동사를 만드는 현재분사 (A)와 과거분사 (C)가 정답의 후보이다. 빈칸 뒤에 목적어(potential candidates)가 있고 '잠재적 후보자들을 면접하다'라는 능동의 의미가 되어야 하므로 능동태를 만드는 현재분사 (A) interviewing이 정답이다. 동사의 3인칭 단수형 또는 명사 (B), 동사원형 또는 명사 (D)는 be동사와 함께 동사를 만들 수 없다.
어휘 recruitment n. 채용 currently adv. 현재, 지금 potential adj. 잠재적인
candidate n. 후보자 opening n. 공석, 결원

15 태에 맞는 동사 채우기 [정답 공식 04]
해석 회사의 주요 생산 시설들은 주요 대도시 지역 외곽의 산업 지구에 위치해 있다.
해설 문장에 주어(The company's ~ facilities)만 있고 동사가 없으므로 모든 보기가 정답의 후보이다. '생산 시설들이 산업 지구에 위치해 있다'라는 수동의 의미가 되어야 하므로 수동태 (B) are situated가 정답이다.
어휘 production n. 생산 facility n. 시설 metropolitan adj. 대도시의

16 수동태 관용 표현 채우기
해석 Horizon BioTech 실험실은 자세한 표본 분석을 위해 고급 현미경을 갖추고 있다.
해설 '고급 현미경을 갖추고 있다'라는 의미가 되어야 하므로 '~을 갖추고 있다'라는 표현을 만드는 (A) equipped가 정답이다. 동사의 3인칭 단수형 (B)와 동사원형 (D)는 be동사 뒤에 올 수 없다.
어휘 advanced adj. 고급의, 첨단의 microscope n. 현미경
detailed adj. 자세한 specimen n. 표본 analysis n. 분석

17 주어와 수일치하는 동사 채우기
해석 이 제비뽑기의 당첨자는 Serenity 스파로부터 1년 회원권 패키지를 받는다.
해설 문장에 주어(The winner ~ raffle)만 있고 동사가 없으므로 동사 (A)와 (B)가 정답의 후보이다. 주어(The winner ~ raffle)가 단수이므로 단수 동사 (B) receives가 정답이다. 복수 동사 (A)는 복수 주어와 함께 써야 한다. 동명사 또는 현재분사 (C)와 to 부정사 (D)는 동사 자리에 올 수 없다.
어휘 raffle n. 제비뽑기 membership n. 회원권

18 수동태 관용 표현 채우기
해석 여행객들은 이 산악 지역에서 갑작스러운 기상 상태 변화에 놀랄 수도 있다.
해설 '여행객들이 기상 상태 변화에 놀랄 수도 있다'라는 의미가 되어야 하므로 '~에 놀라다'라는 표현을 만드는 (C) frightened가 정답이다. 동사원형 (A)와 동사의 3인칭 단수형 (B)는 be동사 뒤에 올 수 없다.
어휘 weather condition 기상 상태 mountainous region 산악 지역, 산간 지대

19 수동태 관용 표현 채우기
해석 다양한 산업 분야의 저명한 연사들이 회의에서 그들의 전문 지식을 공유할 것을 요청받았다.
해설 문장에 주어(Distinguished speakers ~ industries)만 있고 동사가 없으므로 동사 (A), (B), (D)가 정답의 후보이다. '전문 지식을 공유할 것을 요청받다'라는 의미가 되어야 하므로 '~할 것을 요청받다'라는 표현을 만드는 (B) were invited가 정답이다. 동명사 또는 현재분사 (C)는 동사 자리에 올 수 없다.
어휘 distinguished adj. 저명한, 뛰어난 various adj. 다양한 share v. 공유하다
expertise n. 전문 지식

20 태에 맞는 동사 채우기
해석 Mr. Powell은 오늘 사무실에 없지만, 그는 어떤 비상사태에도 그의 휴대전화로 연락될 수 있다.
해설 절(he ~ emergencies)에 주어(he)만 있고 동사가 없으므로 모든 보기가 정답의 후보이다. '그가 휴대전화로 연락될 수 있다'라는 수동의 의미가 되어야 하므로 수동태 (D) can be reached가 정답이다.
어휘 emergency n. 비상사태

21 태에 맞는 동사 채우기 [정답 공식 02]
해석 고객들은 우리의 서비스를 개선하는 데 도움이 되도록 그들의 쇼핑 경험에 대한 의견을 제공하도록 권장된다.
해설 문장에 주어(Customers)만 있고 동사가 없으므로 be동사(are)와 함께 동사를 만드는 과거분사 (A)와 현재분사 (C)가 정답의 후보이다. '의견을 제공하도록 권장되다'라는 수동의 의미가 되어야 하므로 수동태를 만드는 과거분사 (A) encouraged(권장하다)가 정답이다. 동사원형 (B)와 명사 (D)는 be동사와 함께 동사를 만들 수 없다.
어휘 feedback n. 의견 improve v. 개선하다

22 태에 맞는 동사 채우기
해석 주민들은 주말에만 대형 가구를 시의 폐기물 처리 센터에 가져갈 수 있다.
해설 문장에 주어(Residents)만 있고 동사가 없으므로 동사 (B), (C), (D)가 정답의 후보이다. 빈칸 뒤에 목적어(large pieces of furniture)가 있고 '대형 가구를 가져갈 수 있다'라는 능동의 의미가 되어야 하므로 능동태 동사 (D) can bring이 정답이다. 동명사 또는 현재분사 (A)는 동사 자리에 올 수 없다.
어휘 waste disposal 폐기물 처리

23 수동태 관용 표현 채우기
해석 Innovative Solutions사는 지역 사업을 지원하기 위한 다양한 지역사회 봉사활동에 관련되어 있다.
해설 문장에 주어(Innovative Solutions Inc.)만 있고 동사가 없으므로 동사 (A)와 (C)가 정답의 후보이다. 'Innovative Solutions사가 봉사활동에 관련되어 있다'라는 수동의 의미가 되어야 하므로 '~에 관련되다'라는 표현을 만드는 (A) is involved가 정답이다. to 부정사 (B)와 명사 (D)는 동사 자리에 올 수 없다.
어휘 outreach program 봉사활동 support v. 지원하다

24 태에 맞는 동사 채우기
해석 구조물의 수리가 완료되었으므로 Georgetown 다리에 차량이 접근하는 것을 막는 장벽들이 제거되었다.
해설 문장에 주어(The barriers ~ Bridge)만 있고 동사가 없으므로 동사 (B), (C), (D)가 정답의 후보이다. '장벽들이 제거되다'라는 수동의 의미가 되어야 하므로 수동태 (D) were removed가 정답이다. 동명사 또는 현재분사 (A)는 동사 자리에 올 수 없다.
어휘 barrier n. 장벽, 장애물 access v. 접근하다 structure n. 구조물, 건축물

빈출 어휘 동사 2

토익 실전문제
p.203

| 01 (C) | 02 (B) | 03 (B) | 04 (C) | 05 (C) |
| 06 (B) | 07 (A) | 08 (D) | | |

01 동사 어휘 고르기
해석 마케팅 계획에 대한 모든 변경 사항은 본사의 Mr. Osborne에 의해 승인되어야 한다.
해설 '변경 사항이 Mr. Osborne에 의해 승인되어야 한다'라는 문맥이므로 동사 approve(승인하다)의 p.p.형 (C) approved가 정답이다. (A)의 donate는 '기부하다', (B)의 respond는 '응답하다, 대답하다', (D)의 elect는 '선출하다'라는 의미이다.
어휘 head office 본사

02 동사 어휘 고르기
해석 새로운 메시징 앱은 사용자들의 개인 메시지를 보호할 것을 약속한다.
해설 '메시징 앱이 개인 메시지를 보호할 것을 약속하다'라는 문맥이므로 (B) protect(보호하다)가 정답이다. (A) showcase는 '선보이다', (C) lease는 '임대하다', (D) return은 '반환하다'라는 의미이다.
어휘 personal adj. 개인의 communication n. 메시지, 통신

03 동사 어휘 고르기
해석 그 음식 공급사가 우리 손님들을 위한 채식주의 옵션을 제공할 것인지 확인해 주세요.
해설 '채식주의 옵션을 제공할 것인지 확인하다'라는 문맥이므로 (B) confirm(확인하다)이 정답이다. (A) regard는 '여기다', (C) demonstrate는 '보여주다', (D) transfer는 '이동하다'라는 의미이다.
어휘 caterer n. 음식 공급사 vegetarian adj. 채식주의의

04 동사 어휘 고르기
해석 Bradford 마을은 주민들에게 도서관과 대형 레크리에이션 센터를 포함한 여러 편의시설을 제공한다.
해설 '마을이 주민들에게 여러 편의시설을 제공하다'라는 문맥이므로 offer(제공하다)의 3인칭 단수형 (C) offers가 정답이다. (A)의 advise는 '조언하다, 충고하다', (B)의 continue는 '계속하다', (D)의 transform은 '변형시키다, 변화시키다'라는 의미이다.
어휘 amenity n. 편의시설 resident n. 주민

05 동사 어휘 고르기
해석 연구원들이 실험 결과를 분석하는 데 몇 주가 걸렸다.
해설 '실험 결과를 분석하는 데 몇 주가 걸리다'라는 문맥이므로 (C) analyze(분석하다)가 정답이다. (A) postpone은 '연기하다', (B) relieve는 '완화하다', (D) admire는 '감탄하다'라는 의미이다.
어휘 researcher n. 연구원 experiment n. 실험

06 동사 어휘 고르기
해석 그 운동 프로그램은 사람들의 체중 관련 질병이 생기는 위험을 줄이는 것을 목표로 한다.
해설 '운동 프로그램이 질병이 생기는 위험을 줄이는 것을 목표로 하다'라는 문맥이므로 (B) reduce(줄이다)가 정답이다. (A) omit은 '생략하다', (C) compensate는 '보상하다', (D) ignore는 '무시하다'라는 의미이다.
어휘 workout n. 운동 aim v. 목표로 하다 risk n. 위험
develop v. (병·문제가) 생기다 disease n. 질병

07 동사 어휘 고르기
해석 종업원들은 팁을 받고 각 근무 시간 후에 그것들을 자기끼리 나눈다.
해설 '종업원들이 팁을 받고 그것들을 자기끼리 나누다'라는 문맥이므로 (A) divide(나누다)가 정답이다. (B) access는 '접근하다', (C) concentrate는 '집중하다', (D) convince는 '설득하다'라는 의미이다.
어휘 shift n. 근무 시간

08 동사 어휘 고르기
해석 개방형 설계를 사용하는 것은 사무실에서 우리가 가진 제한된 공간을 최대화할 수 있게 한다.
해설 '사무실에서 제한된 공간을 최대화할 수 있게 하다'라는 문맥이므로 (D) maximize(최대화하다)가 정답이다. (A) undergo는 '받다, 겪다', (B) devise는 '고안하다', (C) conduct는 '수행하다'라는 의미이다.
어휘 open floor plan 개방형 설계(칸막이나 벽 없이 트인 공간)
limited adj. 제한된, 한정된

DAY 07 동사의 시제

기출 포인트 01

실전 Check-up
p.204

| 01 (B) | 02 (A) |

01 올바른 시제의 동사 채우기
해석 그녀는 날씨가 좋을 때 종종 자전거를 타고 출근한다.
해설 문장에 동사가 없으므로 모든 보기가 정답의 후보이다. 그녀가 날씨가 좋을 때 종종 자전거를 타고 출근한다는 일상적으로 반복되는 동작을 나타내는 문맥이므로 현재 시제 (B) rides가 정답이다.
어휘 bicycle n. 자전거

02 올바른 시제의 동사 채우기
해석 행사 주최자들은 이번 달 말까지 모든 초대장을 보낼 것이다.
해설 문장에 동사가 없으므로 모든 보기가 정답의 후보이다. 미래를 나타내는 시간 표현(by the end of this month)이 있으므로 미래 시제 (A) will send가 정답이다. 과거 시제 (B)는 미래를 나타내는 표현과 함께 쓰일 수 없다.
어휘 event n. 행사, 사건 organizer n. 주최자, 기획자 invitation n. 초대장

기출 포인트 02

실전 Check-up
p.205

| 01 (B) | 02 (A) |

01 올바른 시제의 동사 채우기
해석 바로 지금, 부서 관리자는 프로젝트 책임자들과 워크숍을 하고 있다.
해설 문장에 동사가 없으므로 모든 보기가 정답의 후보이다. 현재진행을 나타내는 표현(Right now)이 있으므로 현재진행 시제 (B) is conducting이 정답이다. 과거 시제 (A)는 현재진행을 나타내는 표현과 함께 쓰일 수 없다.
어휘 department n. 부서, 과

02 올바른 시제의 동사 채우기
해석 그 프로젝터가 작동을 멈췄을 때 그녀는 이사회에 발표를 하고 있었다.
해설 주절(She ~ board)에 주어(She)만 있고 동사가 없으므로 모든 보기가 정답의 후보이다. 주절은 when이 이끄는 종속절(when ~ working)과 같은 시점에 일어났고, 종속절에 과거 시제 동사(stopped)가 쓰였으므로 과거진행 시제 (A) was giving이 정답이다.
어휘 presentation n. 발표 board n. 이사회, 위원회

기출 포인트 03

실전 Check-up p.206

01 (B)　　**02** (B)

01 올바른 시제의 동사 채우기
해석 지난 달에 온라인 서비스를 시작한 이래로 많은 고객이 그것에 등록했다.
해설 문장에 주어(Many customers)만 있고 동사가 없으므로 모든 보기가 정답의 후보이다. 현재완료를 나타내는 표현인 'since + 과거 시간 표현'(~한 이래로)이 있으므로 현재완료 시제 (B) have registered가 정답이다. 과거진행 시제 (A)는 현재완료를 나타내는 표현과 함께 쓰일 수 없다.

02 올바른 시제의 동사 채우기
해석 Ms. Aydin이 회의장에 도착했을 즈음에, 기조연설자는 이미 그의 발표를 끝냈었다.
해설 주절(the keynote speaker ~ already)에 주어(the keynote speaker)만 있고 동사가 없으므로 모든 보기가 정답의 후보이다. 주절에서 나타내는 사건, 즉 기조연설자가 발표를 끝마친 시점은 by the time이 이끄는 절(Ms. Aydin ~ venue)에서 나타내는 사건, 즉 Ms. Aydin이 회의장에 도착한 것보다 먼저 일어난 일이다. by the time이 이끄는 절에 과거 시제 동사(arrived)가 쓰였으므로 과거의 특정 시점 이전에 발생한 일을 나타내는 과거완료 시제 (B) had finished가 정답이다. 과거 시제 (A)는 과거의 특정 시점 이전에 발생한 일을 표현할 수 없다.
어휘 venue n. 장소　keynote speaker 기조연설자

3초컷 정답 공식 p.207

| 01 (B) | 02 (A) | 03 (C) | 04 (A) | 05 (C) |
| 06 (B) | 07 (A) | 08 (D) | | |

01 올바른 시제의 동사 채우기
해석 여행 일정표에 따르면, 그 단체는 다음 주 일요일에 이스탄불에 있는 몇몇 유적지를 관광할 것이다.
해설 문장에 동사가 없으므로 동사 (A), (B), (C)가 정답의 후보이다. 미래를 나타내는 표현인 next Sunday(다음 주 일요일)가 있으므로 미래 시제 (B) will tour가 정답이다. 현재완료 시제 (A)와 과거 시제 (C)는 미래를 나타내는 표현과 함께 쓰일 수 없다. 동명사 또는 현재분사 (D)는 동사 자리에 올 수 없다.
어휘 according to ~에 따르면　itinerary n. 여행 일정표　historic site 유적지

02 올바른 시제의 동사 채우기
해석 Fifth Street 체육관은 다음 달에 많은 기구를 교체할 것이다.
해설 문장에 주어(The Fifth Street Fitness Center)만 있고 동사가 없으므로 모든 보기가 정답의 후보이다. 미래를 나타내는 표현인 next month(다음 달)가 있으므로 미래 시제를 나타낼 수 있는 현재진행 시제 (A) is replacing이 정답이다. 참고로, 현재진행 시제는 예정된 일이나 곧 일어나려고 하는 일을 표현하여 미래를 나타낼 수 있다는 점을 알아 둔다.
어휘 equipment n. 기구, 장비

03 올바른 시제의 동사 채우기
해석 연구원들에 의해 화학 실험이 실시되고 있는 동안에는 실험실 구역에 들어가지 마십시오.
해설 while이 이끄는 종속절(while ~ staff)에 주어(chemical tests)만 있고 동사가 없으므로 모든 보기가 정답의 후보이다. 종속절은 주절(Please ~ area)과 같은 시점에 일어났고, 주절에 현재 시제 동사(do not enter)가 쓰였으므로 현재진행 시제 (C) are being이 정답이다.
어휘 laboratory n. 실험실　chemical adj. 화학의

conduct v. 실시하다, 수행하다　research n. 연구

04 올바른 시제의 동사 채우기
해석 기술자들이 새 장비를 설치하고 있던 동안 전원이 갑자기 나갔다.
해설 while이 이끄는 종속절(while ~ equipment)에 주어(the technicians)만 있고 동사가 없으므로 모든 보기가 정답의 후보이다. 종속절은 주절(The power suddenly failed)과 같은 시점에 일어났고, 주절에 과거 시제 동사(failed)가 쓰였으므로 과거진행 시제 (A) were installing이 정답이다.
어휘 fail v. 작동이 안 되다, 고장 나다　technician n. 기술자

05 올바른 시제의 동사 채우기
해석 그 지원팀은 올해 초 이래로 5,000건이 넘는 문의를 처리해 왔다.
해설 주절(The support team ~ inquiries)에 주어(The support team)만 있고 동사가 없으므로 모든 보기가 정답의 후보이다. 현재완료를 나타내는 표현인 'since + 과거 시간 표현'(~ 이래로)이 있으므로 현재완료 시제 (C) has handled가 정답이다.
어휘 support n. 지원　inquiry n. 문의, 질문

06 올바른 시제의 동사 채우기
해석 3개월 전에 처음 문을 연 이래로, Nelson 서점은 고객층의 규모를 늘려왔다.
해설 주절(Nelson Bookstore ~ customer base)에 주어(Nelson Bookstore)만 있고 동사가 없으므로 동사 (B), (C), (D)가 정답의 후보이다. 현재완료와 함께 쓰이는 표현인 'since + 주어 + 과거 시제'(~한 이래로)이 있으므로 현재완료 시제 (B) has increased가 정답이다. to 부정사 (A)는 동사 자리에 올 수 없다.

07 올바른 시제의 동사 채우기
해석 그 공급 회사가 여러 마감 기한을 놓친 후에 계약이 해지되었다.
해설 종속절(after ~ deadlines)에 주어(the supplier)만 있고 동사가 없으므로 모든 보기가 정답의 후보이다. 주절(The agreement was terminated)의 동사(was terminated)의 시제가 과거이므로 종속절에는 과거 시제 또는 과거완료 시제가 와야 하는데, 보기에 과거완료 시제가 없으므로 과거 시제 (A) missed가 정답이다.
어휘 agreement n. 계약, 협정　terminate v. 해지하다　supplier n. 공급 회사

08 올바른 시제의 동사 채우기
해석 직원들이 새로운 안전 절차를 배운 후에, 작업장 사고가 감소했다.
해설 종속절(After ~ procedures)에 주어(the employees)만 있고 동사가 없으므로 모든 보기가 정답의 후보이다. 주절(workplace accidents decreased)의 동사(decreased)의 시제가 과거이므로 종속절에는 과거 시제 또는 과거완료 시제가 와야 하는데, 보기에 과거 시제가 없으므로 과거완료 시제 (D) had learned가 정답이다.
어휘 procedure n. 절차　workplace n. 작업장　accident n. 사고

HACKERS TEST p.208

01 (A)	02 (D)	03 (A)	04 (C)	05 (A)
06 (B)	07 (D)	08 (A)	09 (A)	10 (C)
11 (C)	12 (D)	13 (A)	14 (C)	15 (D)
16 (A)	17 (B)	18 (C)	19 (B)	20 (C)
21 (A)	22 (C)	23 (D)	24 (A)	

01 올바른 시제의 동사 채우기
해석 매일, La Mirina의 요리사들은 몇 대에 걸쳐서 전해진 전통적인 요리법을 따른다.
해설 문장에 주어(Chefs at La Mirina)만 있고 동사가 없으므로 동사 (A)와

(D)가 정답의 후보이다. 현재를 나타내는 표현인 Every day(매일)가 있으므로, 현재 시제 (A) follow가 정답이다. 명사 (B)와 to 부정사 (C)는 동사 자리에 올 수 없다.

어휘 traditional adj. 전통적인 recipe n. 요리법 pass down 전해주다, 물려주다 for generations 몇 대에 걸쳐서

02 올바른 시제의 동사 채우기 [정답공식 01]
해석 Marvin Gray는 전국 투어를 시작하기 전 다음 주 금요일에 그의 새 소설을 출간할 것이다.
해설 문장에 주어(Marvin Gray)만 있고 동사가 없으므로 동사 (B), (C), (D)가 정답의 후보이다. 미래를 나타내는 표현인 next Friday(다음 주 금요일)가 있으므로 미래 시제를 나타낼 수 있는 현재진행 시제 (D) is releasing이 정답이다. 참고로, 현재진행 시제는 예정된 일이나 곧 일어나려고 하는 일을 표현하여 미래를 나타낼 수 있다는 점을 알아 둔다. 동명사 또는 현재분사 (A)는 동사 자리에 올 수 없다.

어휘 novel n. 소설 nationwide adj. 전국적인 release v. 출간하다, 발매하다

03 올바른 시제의 동사 채우기
해석 경비원이 창고 근처에서 의심스러운 움직임을 발견했을 때 부지를 순찰하고 있었다.
해설 주절(The security guard ~ premises)에 주어(The security guard)만 있고 동사가 없으므로 동사 (A), (C), (D)가 정답의 후보이다. 주절은 when이 이끄는 종속절(when ~ warehouse)과 같은 시점에 일어났고, 종속절에 과거 시제 동사(noticed)가 쓰였으므로 과거진행 시제 (A) was patrolling이 정답이다. to 부정사 (B)는 동사 자리에 올 수 없다.

어휘 premises n. 부지 suspicious adj. 의심스러운 patrol v. 순찰하다

04 올바른 시제의 동사 채우기 [정답공식 01]
해석 다음 주까지, 참여하는 판매자들을 위한 주차 요금이 적용되지 않을 것이다.
해설 주절(parking ~ vendors)에 주어(parking fees)만 있고 동사가 없으므로 모든 보기가 정답의 후보이다. 미래를 나타내는 표현인 'until + 미래 시간 표현'(~까지)이 있으므로 미래 시제 (C) will be waived가 정답이다.

어휘 vendor n. 판매자, 노점상 waive v. (규칙 따위를) 적용하지 않다

05 올바른 시제의 동사 채우기 [정답공식 02]
해석 동쪽 부속 건물에서 공사가 진행되는 동안, 모든 직원은 서쪽 입구를 이용하도록 요청받는다.
해설 while이 이끄는 종속절(While ~ wing)에 주어(the construction)만 있고 동사가 없으므로 모든 보기가 정답의 후보이다. 종속절은 주절(all ~ entrance)과 같은 시점에 일어났고, 주절에 현재 시제 동사(are asked)가 쓰였으므로 현재진행 시제 (A) is taking이 정답이다.

어휘 construction n. 공사, 건설 wing n. 부속 건물 entrance n. 입구

06 올바른 시제의 동사 채우기
해석 Mr. Yilmaz는 Global Financial Partners사의 재무 이사로 6년 동안 일해 왔다.
해설 문장에 주어(Mr. Yilmaz)만 있고 동사가 없으므로 (A), (B), (D)가 정답의 후보이다. 현재완료를 나타내는 표현인 'for + 기간'(~ 동안)이 있으므로 현재완료 시제 (B) has worked가 정답이다. 동명사 또는 현재분사 (C)는 동사 자리에 올 수 없다.

어휘 financial adj. 재무의, 재정상의

07 올바른 시제의 동사 채우기 [정답공식 04]
해석 승객들이 수많은 불만을 제기한 후, SkyWave 항공사는 탑승수속을 변경했다.
해설 종속절(after ~ complaints)에 주어(passengers)만 있고 동사가 없으므로 모든 보기가 정답의 후보이다. 주절(SkyWave Airlines ~ procedures)의 동사(changed)의 시제가 과거이므로 종속절에는 과거 시제 또는 과거완료 시제가 와야 하는데, 보기에 과거완료 시제가 없으므로 과거 시제 (D) filed가 정답이다.

어휘 boarding procedure 탑승수속 numerous adj. 수많은, 다수의 complaint n. 불만, 항의

08 올바른 시제의 동사 채우기
해석 현재, Veltrix Solutions사는 마케팅 직무에 대한 지원서를 받고 있다.
해설 문장에 주어(Veltrix Solutions)만 있고 동사가 없으므로 모든 보기가 정답의 후보이다. 현재진행을 나타내는 표현인 Currently(현재, 지금)가 있으므로 현재진행 시제 (A) is accepting이 정답이다.

어휘 application n. 지원서, 신청서 position n. 직무, 직위

09 올바른 시제의 동사 채우기
해석 시장 조사원들이 부정적인 소비자 의견을 보고했기 때문에 제품 출시가 지연되었다.
해설 종속절(because ~ feedback)에 주어(market researchers)만 있고 동사가 없으므로 모든 보기가 정답의 후보이다. 주절(The product ~ delayed)의 동사(was delayed)의 시제가 과거이므로 종속절에는 과거 시제 또는 과거완료 시제가 와야 하는데, 보기에 과거완료 시제가 없으므로 과거 시제 (A) reported가 정답이다.

어휘 product launch 제품 출시 delay v. 지연시키다 market researcher 시장 조사원

10 올바른 시제의 동사 채우기 [정답공식 03]
해석 최고 경영자가 합병을 발표한 이래로 그 회사의 주가는 30퍼센트 상승했다.
해설 주절(The ~ 30 percent)에 주어(The firm's stock price)만 있고 동사가 없으므로 동사 (B), (C), (D)가 정답의 후보이다. 현재완료를 나타내는 표현인 'since + 주어 + 과거 시제'(~한 이래로)가 있으므로 현재완료 시제 (C) has increased가 정답이다. to 부정사 (A)는 동사 자리에 올 수 없다.

어휘 firm n. 회사 stock price 주가 merger n. 합병

11 올바른 시제의 동사 채우기
해석 내년 즈음에, Veridian Innovations사는 유럽 전역에 20개의 소매점을 개점하게 될 것이다.
해설 문장에 주어(Veridian Innovations)만 있고 동사가 없으므로 모든 보기가 정답의 후보이다. 미래완료 시제와 함께 쓰이는 표현 'by + 미래 시간 표현'(~ 즈음에)이 왔으므로 미래완료 시제 (C) will have opened가 정답이다.

어휘 retail store 소매점

12 올바른 시제의 동사 채우기
해석 지난 몇 달 동안, Ms. Saer는 그녀의 깊은 컴퓨터 공학 지식으로 동료들에게 깊은 인상을 줘 왔다.
해설 문장에 주어(Ms. Saer)만 있고 동사가 없으므로 동사 (A)와 (D)가 정답의 후보이다. 현재완료를 나타내는 표현인 'over the past + 기간'(지난 ~ 동안)이 있으므로 현재완료 시제 (D) has impressed가 정답이다. 동명사 또는 현재분사 (B)와 형용사 (C)는 동사 자리에 올 수 없다.

어휘 colleague n. 동료 knowledge n. 지식

13 올바른 시제의 동사 채우기
해석 과학자들이 새로운 화합물을 실험하고 있었을 때 화재 경보가 울렸다.
해설 종속절(as ~ chemical compound)에 주어(the scientists)만 있고 동사가 없으므로 모든 보기가 정답의 후보이다. as가 이끄는 종속절은 주절(The fire alarm went off)과 같은 시점에 일어났고, 주절에 과거 시제 동사(went off)가 쓰였으므로 과거진행 시제 (A) were testing이 정답이다.

어휘 fire alarm 화재 경보 go off (경보기 등이) 울리다 chemical compound 화합물

14 올바른 시제의 동사 채우기

해석 Mr. Moore는 직원들과 상의해 오면서 다음 회의에서 다뤄질 필요가 있는 많은 안건들을 찾아냈다.

해설 빈칸 앞에 등위접속사(and)가 왔으므로 빈칸에는 동사가 와서 and 앞의 동사구(has been talking)와 대등하게 연결되어야 한다. 따라서 동사 (A), (B), (C)가 정답의 후보이다. 빈칸 뒤에 목적어(a number of issues)가 있고, Mr. Moore가 직원들과 상의해 왔다(Mr. Moore has been talking with the staff)고 했으므로, 방금 완료된 일을 뜻하는 현재완료 (C) has identified가 정답이다. 현재 시제 (A)는 일반적인 사실이나 일상적으로 반복되는 동작을 나타낼 때 사용되고, 수동태 동사 (B)는 빈칸 뒤에 목적어가 있으므로 답이 될 수 없다. 동명사 또는 현재분사 (D)는 동사 자리에 올 수 없다. (D) being identified를 has been과 함께 현재완료 진행 시제를 만드는 –ing형으로 보더라도 수동형이기 때문에 뒤에 목적어가 올 수 없다.

어휘 a number of 많은, 다수의   issue n. 안건, 주제
address v. 다루다, 고심하다

15 올바른 시제의 동사 채우기

해석 한 달 후에, Jensen Sportswear사는 여름 시즌을 위한 반바지와 수영복 라인을 출시할 것이다.

해설 문장에 주어(Jensen Sportswear)만 있고 동사가 없으므로 동사 (C)와 (D)가 정답의 후보이다. 미래를 나타내는 표현인 In one month(한 달 후에)가 있으므로 미래 시제 (D) will launch가 정답이다. 형용사 (A)와 명사 또는 현재분사 (B)는 동사 자리에 올 수 없다.

16 올바른 시제의 동사 채우기

해석 현재, 우리의 싱가포르 지점은 대규모의 보수를 진행하고 있다.

해설 문장에 주어(our branch ~ Singapore)만 있고 동사가 없으므로 모든 보기가 정답의 후보이다. 현재진행을 나타내는 표현인 at present(현재)가 있으므로 현재진행 시제 (A) is undergoing이 정답이다.

어휘 renovation n. 보수   undergo v. 진행하다, 겪다

17 올바른 시제의 동사 채우기

해석 시청자들이 참신한 콘텐츠의 부족에 대해 불평하자마자, Spotlight Network사는 그해 가을에 새로운 프로그램들을 도입했다.

해설 Once로 시작하는 종속절(Once ~ content)에 동사가 없으므로 동사 (A)와 (B)가 정답의 후보이다. 주절(the Spotlight Network ~ that fall)의 동사(introduced)가 과거 시제이고 '시청자들이 참신한 콘텐츠의 부족에 대해 불평하자마자, 새로운 프로그램들을 도입했다'라는 의미가 되어야 하므로 시청자들이 불평을 한 것도 이미 과거에 일어난 일이다. 따라서 이미 끝난 과거의 동작이나 상태를 나타내는 과거 시제 (B) complained가 정답이다. 동명사 또는 현재분사 (C)와 (D)는 동사 자리에 올 수 없다.

어휘 viewer n. 시청자   lack n. 부족   original adj. 참신한
content n. 콘텐츠, 내용   introduce v. 도입하다

18 올바른 시제의 동사 채우기

해석 오늘 밤 10시에, 공장 근로자들은 야간 근무 생산을 시작하고 있을 것이다.

해설 문장에 주어(the factory workers)만 있고 동사가 없으므로 동사 (B), (C), (D)가 정답의 후보이다. 미래를 나타내는 표현인 At 10 P.M. tonight(오늘 밤 10시에)이 있으므로 미래진행 시제 (C) will be starting이 정답이다. to 부정사 (A)는 동사 자리에 올 수 없다.

어휘 night shift 야간 근무   production n. 생산

19 올바른 시제의 동사 채우기

해석 Mr. Davis는 YHW Rails사가 특별 반값 할인을 발표하기 전에 그의 티켓에 대해 전액을 지불했다.

해설 주절(Mr. Davis ~ tickets)에 주어(Mr. Davis)만 있고 동사가 없으므로 모든 보기가 정답의 후보이다. 주절에서 나타내는 사건, 즉 Mr. Davis가 티켓에 대해 전액을 지불한 시점은 before가 이끄는 절(before ~ offer)에서 나타내는 사건, 즉 YHW Rails사가 특별 반값 할인을 발표한 것보다 먼저 일어난 일이다. before가 이끄는 절에 과거 시제 동사(announced)가 쓰였으므로 과거의 특정 시점 이전에 발생한 일을 표현할 수 있는 과거완료 시제 (B) had paid가 정답이다.

어휘 announce v. 발표하다, 알리다   half-price adj. 반값의   offer n. 할인, 제안

20 격에 맞는 인칭대명사 채우기

해석 Ms. Lewis는 어제 그녀가 5월 말에 본사로 전근될 것이라고 밝혔다.

해설 that절에 동사(will be transferring)만 있고, 주어가 없으므로 주어 역할을 할 수 있는 소유대명사 (B)와 주격 인칭대명사 (D)가 정답의 후보이다. '그녀가 5월 말에 본사로 전근될 것이다'라는 의미가 되어야 하므로 주격 인칭대명사 (D) she가 정답이다. 소유대명사 (B)를 쓸 경우 '그녀의 것이 5월 말에 본사로 전근될 것이다'라는 어색한 문맥을 만든다. 목적격 또는 소유격 인칭대명사 (A)는 주어 역할을 할 수 없다. 재귀대명사 (C)는 목적어가 주어와 같은 사람이나 사물을 지칭할 때나, 주어나 목적어를 강조할 때 쓰인다.

어휘 reveal v. 밝히다, 드러내다   transfer v. 전근 가다, 이동하다
head office 본사

21 태, 시제에 맞는 동사 채우기

해석 웹 개발자는 사람들이 온라인으로 친구들과 연락하는 것을 돕기 위해 소셜 네트워크 사이트를 10년 전에 만들었다.

해설 과거 시간 표현(10 years ago)이 있으므로 과거 동사 (A)와 (C)가 정답의 후보이다. '웹 개발자가 소셜 네트워크 사이트를 만들었다'라는 능동의 의미이므로 능동태 동사 (A) created가 정답이다. to 부정사 (D)는 동사 자리에 올 수 없다.

어휘 stay in touch 연락하다

22 올바른 시제의 동사 채우기 정답공식 04

해석 그 건축가가 건물 계획을 완성한 후, 건설이 즉시 시작되었다.

해설 종속절(After ~ plans)에 주어(the architect)만 있고 동사가 없으므로 모든 보기가 정답의 후보이다. 주절(construction began immediately)의 동사(began)의 시제가 과거이므로 종속절에는 과거 시제 또는 과거완료 시제가 와야 하는데, 보기에 과거 시제가 없으므로 과거완료 시제 (C) had finalized가 정답이다.

어휘 architect n. 건축가   construction n. 건설   immediately adv. 즉시, 바로

23 올바른 시제의 동사 채우기

해석 다가오는 6월부터 8월까지, IT 부서는 회사 전체의 네트워크 인프라를 업그레이드하고 있을 것이다.

해설 문장에 주어(the IT department)만 있고 동사가 없으므로 동사 (A), (C), (D)가 정답의 후보이다. 미래를 나타내는 표현인 From this coming June to August(다가오는 6월부터 8월까지)가 있으므로 미래진행 시제 (D) will be upgrading이 정답이다. 동명사 또는 현재분사 (B)는 동사 자리에 올 수 없다.

어휘 entire adj. 전체의, 모든   infrastructure n. 인프라, 기반 시설

24 올바른 시제의 동사 채우기 정답공식 02

해석 그 회사가 대규모의 구조 조정을 겪고 있는 동안 투자자들은 그들의 지원을 철회했다.

해설 while이 이끄는 종속절(while ~ restructuring)에 주어(the company)만 있고 동사가 없으므로 모든 보기가 정답의 후보이다. 종속절은 주절(The investors ~ support)과 같은 시점에 일어났고, 주절에 과거 시제 동사(withdrew)가 쓰였으므로 과거진행 시제 (A) was going이 정답이다.

어휘 investor n. 투자자   withdraw v. 철회하다, 빼다   support n. 지원
restructuring n. 구조 조정

빈출 어휘 동사 3

토익 실전문제   p.211

01 (C) 02 (A) 03 (B) 04 (C) 05 (D)
06 (C) 07 (B) 08 (A)

01 동사 어휘 고르기
해석 그 학부장은 새로운 강사들이 그들의 수업을 어떻게 관리하는지 관찰할 것이다.
해설 '강사들이 수업을 어떻게 관리하는지 관찰하다'라는 문맥이므로 (C) observe(관찰하다, 지켜보다)가 정답이다. (A) stimulate는 '활발하게 하다, 자극하다', (B) obey는 '복종하다', (D) claim은 '주장하다'라는 의미이다.
어휘 faculty n. 학부   manage v. 관리하다

02 동사 어휘 고르기
해석 교통부는 밤에 보행자와 운전자들을 도로 사고로부터 보호하기 위해 새로운 규정을 시행했다.
해설 '교통부가 새로운 규정을 시행했다'라는 문맥이므로 동사 implement(시행하다)의 과거형 (A) implemented가 정답이다. (B)의 supply는 '공급하다', (C)의 gather는 '모으다', (D)의 neglect는 '소홀히 하다, 무시하다'라는 의미이다.
어휘 regulation n. 규정, 규제   pedestrian n. 보행자
motorist n. (자동차) 운전자   accident n. 사고, 재난

03 동사 어휘 고르기
해석 Ms. Tanner는 아직 무역 박람회를 위한 보스턴 출장에 대한 여행 계획을 마무리하지 않았다.
해설 '출장에 대한 여행 계획을 마무리하지 않았다'라는 문맥이므로 동사 finalize(마무리하다)의 p.p.형 (B) finalized가 정답이다. (A)의 rank는 '순위를 매기다', (C)의 maximize는 '최대화하다', (D)의 regulate는 '규제하다'라는 의미이다.
어휘 trip n. 출장   trade n. 무역

04 동사 어휘 고르기
해석 정부는 대규모 투자를 하는 외국 기업에 대한 일부 세금을 면제할 계획이다.
해설 '기업에 대한 세금을 면제할 계획이다'라는 문맥이므로 (C) waive(면제하다)가 정답이다. (A) acquire는 '취득하다, 얻다', (B) possess는 '갖추다, 소유하다', (D) wield는 '행사하다'라는 의미이다.
어휘 tax n. 세금   foreign adj. 외국의   firm n. 기업   investment n. 투자

05 동사 어휘 고르기
해석 부모님과 손님은 그 뒤에 있는 채로, 첫 스무 줄은 졸업반에 의해 채워질 것이다.
해설 '첫 스무 줄이 졸업반에 의해 채워지다'라는 문맥이므로 동사 occupy(채우다, 차지하다)의 p.p.형 (D) occupied가 정답이다. (A)의 represent는 '대표하다', (B)의 evaluate는 '평가하다', (C)의 screen은 '심사하다, 가리다'라는 의미이다.
어휘 row n. 줄

06 동사 어휘 고르기
해석 Brightland 제과점은 이번 주말 자선 행사를 위해 도넛 100상자를 기부하기로 약속했다.
해설 '제과점이 도넛 100상자를 기부하기로 약속하다'라는 문맥이므로 동사 pledge(약속하다)의 p.p.형 (C) pledged가 정답이다. (A)의 relocate는 '이전하다', (B)의 support는 '지원하다', (D)의 encourage는 '격려하다'라는 의미이다.

어휘 donate v. 기부하다   charity n. 자선

07 동사 어휘 고르기
해석 Hyman 제약 회사의 아시아 시장에서의 매출이 작년에 급증했고, 이는 상당한 이익 증가로 이어졌다.
해설 '제약 회사의 매출이 급증하여 이익 증가로 이어졌다'라는 문맥이므로 soar((가치·물가 등이) 급증하다, 치솟다)의 과거형 (B) soared가 정답이다. (A)의 estimate는 '추정하다', (C)의 surface는 '나타나다', (D)의 reschedule은 '일정을 변경하다'라는 의미이다.
어휘 sales n. 매출(액)   result in ~으로 이어지다   significant adj. 상당한
boost n. 증가   profit n. 이익

08 동사 어휘 고르기
해석 시장은 도시 전역의 역사적 가치가 있는 건물을 보존하는 데 전념하는 대책 위원회를 만들었다.
해설 '건물을 보존하는 데 전념하는 대책 위원회를 만들었다'라는 문맥이므로 동사 preserve(보존하다)의 동명사형 (A) preserving이 정답이다. (B)의 attract는 '끌어들이다', (C)의 revise는 '수정하다', (D)의 postpone은 '연기하다'라는 의미이다.
어휘 task force 대책 위원회   dedicate to ~에 전념하다   historical adj. 역사적인
value n. 가치

DAY 08 to 부정사와 동명사

기출 포인트 01~02

실전 Check-up   p.212

01 (B) 02 (A)

01 to 부정사 채우기
해석 Ms. Turner는 연례 야유회에 도착한 첫 번째 사람이다.
해설 이 문장은 주어(Ms. Turner), 동사(is), 보어(the first person)를 갖춘 완전한 절이므로, ___ ~ retreat는 수식어 거품으로 보아야 한다. 이 수식어 거품은 동사가 없는 거품구이므로, 거품구를 이끌며 명사 the first person 뒤에서 명사를 꾸미는 형용사 역할을 하는 to 부정사 (B) to arrive가 정답이다. 동사 (A)는 형용사 자리에 올 수 없다.
어휘 annual adj. 연례의, 매년의   retreat n. 야유회

02 to 부정사 채우기
해석 지역 단체를 위한 기금을 모으기 위해, Doyle 은행의 Mayville 지점은 종종 특별 행사를 주최한다.
해설 이 문장은 주어(the Mayville ~ Bank), 동사(hosts), 목적어(special events)를 갖춘 완전한 절이므로, ___ ~ groups는 수식어 거품으로 보아야 한다. 이 수식어 거품은 동사가 없는 거품구이므로, 거품구를 이끌며 '지역 단체를 위한 기금을 모으기 위해'라는 의미의 목적을 나타내는 to 부정사 (A) To raise가 정답이다. 동사 (B)는 수식어 거품을 이끌 수 없다.
어휘 branch n. 지점, 지사   host v. 주최하다, 개최하다

기출 포인트 03~05

실전 Check-up   p.213

01 (A) 02 (A)

01 동명사 채우기
해석 균형 잡힌 식단을 따르는 것은 최상의 건강을 유지하는 것에 필수적이다.

해설 동사(is)의 주어 자리에 올 수 있고 명사구(a balanced diet)를 목적어로 가질 수 있는 동명사 (A) Following이 정답이다. 동사 (B)는 주어 자리에 올 수 없다.

어휘 balanced adj. 균형 잡힌   diet n. 식단, 식이요법   essential adj. 필수적인
optimal adj. 최상의

02 동명사와 명사 구별하여 채우기

해설 그 강사는 장비를 사용하는 올바른 방법을 시연하는 것을 고집했다.

해설 전치사(on)의 목적어 자리에 올 수 있는 모든 보기가 정답의 후보이다. 빈칸 뒤에 목적어(the correct way)가 있으므로 목적어를 가질 수 있는 동명사 (A) demonstrating이 정답이다. 명사 (B) demonstration은 목적어를 가질 수 없으므로 답이 될 수 없다.

어휘 instructor n. 강사, 지도자   insist v. 고집하다, 주장하다
equipment n. 장비, 기구   demonstrate v. 시연하다, 설명하다
demonstration n. 설명, 시위

기출 포인트 06~07

실전 Check-up   p.214

01 (B)   02 (A)

01 to 부정사와 동명사 구별하여 채우기

해설 Sunrise 타워는 전자 청구서를 도입하여, 거주자들이 온라인으로 공과금을 납부할 수 있게 허가하고 있다.

해설 동사 allow(allowing)의 목적격 보어 자리에 올 수 있는 to 부정사 (B) to pay가 정답이다. 동명사 또는 현재분사 (A)는 allow의 목적격 보어 자리에 올 수 없다.

어휘 adopt v. 도입하다, 채택하다   electronic adj. 전자의
invoice n. 청구서를 보내다   resident n. 거주자, 주민   utility bill 공과금

02 to 부정사와 동명사 구별하여 채우기

해설 그 여행사 직원은 돈을 절약하기 위해 비수기 동안 여행할 것을 제안했다.

해설 동사 suggest(suggested)의 목적어 자리에 올 수 있는 동명사 (A) traveling이 정답이다. to 부정사 (B)는 suggest의 목적어 자리에 올 수 없다.

어휘 off-season n. 비수기, 한가한 시기   save v. 절약하다, 저축하다

3초컷 정답 공식   p.215

01 (C)   02 (B)   03 (A)   04 (D)   05 (A)
06 (C)   07 (D)   08 (D)

01 to 부정사와 동명사 구별하여 채우기

해설 Pinnacle Technologies사는 내년에 시카고에 새 연수원을 열 것을 계획한다.

해설 동사 plan(plans)의 목적어 자리에 올 수 있는 to 부정사 (C) to open이 정답이다. 동사 (A)와 (B)는 목적어 자리에 올 수 없고, 동명사 또는 현재분사 (D)는 plan의 목적어 자리에 올 수 없다.

02 to 부정사와 동명사 구별하여 채우기

해설 우리는 고객들에게 최고 품질의 서비스를 제공하길 원한다.

해설 동사 want의 목적어 자리에 올 수 있는 to 부정사 (B) to provide가 정답이다. (D) provision(공급)을 쓸 경우, 명사(provision)와 명사구(our customers)가 특별한 연결어 없이 나란히 오게 되므로 답이 될 수 없다. 동명사 또는 현재분사 (A)는 want의 목적어 자리에 올 수 없고, 동사 또는 과거분사 (C)는 목적어 자리에 올 수 없다.

어휘 provide v. 제공하다   provision n. 공급, 제공

03 to 부정사 채우기

해설 그 역사적 문서들은 너무 훼손되어서 특수 장비 없이는 읽을 수 없었다.

해설 빈칸 앞의 too와 함께 '너무 ~해서 ~할 수 없다'라는 의미를 완성하는 to 부정사 (A) to read가 정답이다. 동사 (B), (C), (D)는 부사 too와 함께 해당 표현을 만들 수 없다.

어휘 historical adj. 역사적인   document n. 문서
deteriorated adj. 훼손된, 악화된

04 to 부정사와 동명사 구별하여 채우기

해설 그 등산로는 우기 동안 너무 위험해서 하이킹을 할 수 없다.

해설 빈칸 앞의 too와 함께 '너무 ~해서 ~할 수 없다'라는 의미를 완성하는 to 부정사 (D) to hike가 정답이다. 명사 (A), 동사 또는 과거분사 (B), 동사 (C)는 부사 too와 함께 해당 표현을 만들 수 없다.

어휘 mountain trail 등산로   rainy season 우기

05 to 부정사와 동명사 구별하여 채우기

해설 그녀는 계산에서 심각한 실수를 한 것에 대해 사과했다.

해설 전치사(for)의 목적어 자리에 올 수 있고 명사구(a serious mistake in her calculations)를 목적어로 가질 수 있는 동명사 (A) making이 정답이다. 동사 (B)와 (C), to 부정사 (D)는 전치사의 목적어 자리에 올 수 없다.

어휘 apologize v. 사과하다   serious adj. 심각한   mistake n. 실수
calculation n. 계산

06 to 부정사와 동명사 구별하여 채우기

해설 직원들은 다가오는 합병에 관한 세부사항을 외부인들과 논의하는 것에 대해 경고를 받았다.

해설 전치사(against)의 목적어 자리에 올 수 있고 명사구(the details ~ merger)를 목적어로 가질 수 있는 동명사 (C) discussing이 정답이다. to 부정사 (A), 동사 (B)와 (D)는 전치사의 목적어 자리에 올 수 없다.

어휘 warn v. 경고하다, 주의를 주다   merger n. 합병   outsider n. 외부인

07 동명사 채우기

해설 요리사 Martinez는 전통적인 요리법과 현대적인 요리법을 결합함으로써 독특한 요리를 만들어낸다.

해설 전치사(by)의 목적어 자리에 올 수 있고 명사구(techniques from ~ cuisine)를 목적어로 가질 수 있는 동명사 (D) combining이 정답이다. 동사 (A)와 (C), 동사 또는 과거분사 (B)는 전치사의 목적어 자리에 올 수 없다.

어휘 unique adj. 독특한   cuisine n. 요리법   combine v. 결합하다

08 to 부정사와 동명사 구별하여 채우기

해설 기술자들은 외부로부터의 소리를 차단하는 소재를 사용함으로써 소음을 줄였다.

해설 전치사(by)의 목적어 자리에 올 수 있고 명사구(materials ~ outside)를 목적어로 가질 수 있는 동명사 (D) using이 정답이다. to 부정사 (A), 동사 (B), 동사 또는 과거분사 (C)는 전치사의 목적어 자리에 올 수 없다.

어휘 material n. 소재, 재료   block v. 차단하다, 막다

HACKERS TEST   p.216

01 (C)	02 (C)	03 (C)	04 (D)	05 (D)
06 (D)	07 (A)	08 (C)	09 (B)	10 (D)
11 (C)	12 (B)	13 (C)	14 (B)	15 (B)
16 (A)	17 (D)	18 (D)	19 (D)	20 (B)
21 (B)	22 (A)	23 (D)	24 (A)	

01 to 부정사 채우기
해석 Vellonix 컴퓨터는 대용량 비디오 파일의 빠른 처리를 가능하게 하기 위해 강력한 칩을 갖추고 있다.

해설 이 문장은 주어(The Vellonix computer)와 동사(is equipped)를 갖춘 완전한 절이므로, ___ ~ files는 수식어 거품으로 보아야 한다. 이 수식어 거품은 동사가 없는 거품구이므로, 거품구를 이끌며 '대용량 비디오 파일의 빠른 처리를 가능하게 하기 위해'라는 의미의 목적을 나타내는 to 부정사 (C) to enable이 정답이다. 동사 (A)와 (B), 동사 또는 과거분사 (D)는 수식어 거품을 이끌 수 없다. (D)를 명사(chips)를 꾸미는 과거분사로 본다 해도, 뒤에 목적어(the rapid ~ files)가 있으므로 답이 될 수 없다.

어휘 be equipped with ~을 갖추고 있다 rapid adj. 빠른 processing n. 처리

02 동명사와 명사 구별하여 채우기 [정답 공식 03]
해석 이러한 질환들의 의학적 원인을 알아내는 우리의 목표를 달성하기 위해서는 추가 자금이 필요하다.

해설 전치사(of)의 목적어 자리에 올 수 있는 것은 명사이므로 명사 (A)와 명사 역할을 하는 동명사 (C)가 정답의 후보이다. 빈칸 다음에 온 목적어(the medical causes)를 가질 수 있는 것은 동명사이므로 (C) determining이 정답이다. 명사 (A)는 목적어를 가질 수 없다. 동사 또는 과거분사 (B)와 동사 (D)는 전치사의 목적어 자리에 올 수 없다.

어휘 medical adj. 의학적인 condition n. 질환, 문제
determine v. 알아내다, 밝히다

03 to 부정사와 동명사 구별하여 채우기 [정답 공식 02]
해석 그 고급 물리학 교과서는 너무 기술적이고 복잡해서 사전 지식 없이는 이해할 수 없다.

해설 빈칸 앞의 too와 함께 '너무 ~해서 ~할 수 없다'라는 의미를 완성하는 to 부정사 (C) to understand가 정답이다. 동명사 또는 현재분사 (A), 동사 또는 과거분사 (B), 동사 (D)는 부사 too와 함께 해당 표현을 만들 수 없다.

어휘 advanced adj. 고급의 physics n. 물리학 technical adj. 기술적인
complex adj. 복잡한 prior knowledge 사전 지식

04 to 부정사 채우기
해석 시 의회는 대중교통을 개선하려는 5개년 계획을 발표했다.

해설 이 문장은 주어(The city council), 동사(announced), 목적어(a five-year plan)를 갖춘 완전한 절이므로, ___ ~ transportation은 수식어 거품으로 보아야 한다. 이 수식어 거품은 동사가 없는 거품구이므로, 거품구를 이끌며 명사 plan 뒤에서 명사를 꾸미는 형용사 역할을 하는 to 부정사 (D) to improve가 정답이다. 동사 (A), (B), (C)는 형용사 자리에 올 수 없다. (C)를 명사(plan)를 꾸미는 과거분사로 본다 해도, 뒤에 목적어(public transportation)가 있으므로 답이 될 수 없다.

어휘 council n. 의회 announce v. 발표하다 transportation n. 교통, 운송

05 동명사 채우기 [정답 공식 04]
해석 그 발표자는 세션 내내 질문함으로써 청중의 주의를 끌었다.

해설 전치사(by)의 목적어 자리에 올 수 있고 명사(questions)를 목적어로 가질 수 있는 동명사 (D) asking이 정답이다. 동사 (A)와 (B), 동사 또는 과거분사 (C)는 전치사의 목적어 자리에 올 수 없다.

어휘 presenter n. 발표자 engage v. (주의·관심을) 끌다, 사로잡다
audience n. 청중, 관객 session n. (특정한 활동을 위한) 세션, 시간

06 to 부정사의 동사원형 채우기
해석 회사는 직원들의 발표 기술 향상을 돕기 위해 Nina Chou에 의해 주최되는 세미나에 참여하라고 요청했다.

해설 동사 invite(invited)의 목적격 보어 자리에는 to 부정사가 와야 하므로, to 다음의 빈칸에 올 수 있는 동사원형 (D) participate가 정답이다.

어휘 organize v. 주최하다, 조직하다 improve v. 향상시키다

07 동명사 채우기
해석 몇 번의 시도가 있었지만, Mr. Phelps는 추가 직원 고용의 필요성을 경영진에게 납득시키는 데 성공했다.

해설 전치사(in)의 목적어 자리에 올 수 있고 명사(management)를 목적어로 가질 수 있는 동명사 (A) convincing이 정답이다. 동사 (B), 동사 또는 과거분사 (C), to 부정사 (D)는 전치사의 목적어 자리에 올 수 없다.

어휘 attempt n. 시도 succeed in ~에 성공하다 management n. 경영진
additional adj. 추가의

08 to 부정사 채우기
해석 주의 산만을 최소화하기 위해, Janzyll사는 업무 중에 전화와 인터넷의 사적인 사용을 막는다.

해설 이 문장은 주어(Janzyll Incorporated), 동사(discourages), 목적어(the personal use ~ Internet)를 갖춘 완전한 절이므로, ___ distractions는 수식어 거품으로 보아야 한다. 이 수식어 거품은 동사가 없는 거품구이므로, 거품구를 이끌며 '주의 산만을 최소화하기 위해'라는 의미의 목적을 나타내는 to 부정사 (C) To minimize가 정답이다. 동사 (A), (B), (D)는 수식어 거품을 이끌 수 없다.

어휘 distraction n. 주의 산만, 집중 방해 discourage v. 막다, 좌절시키다

09 동명사 채우기
해석 마케팅 부서는 우리의 소식지를 구독한 고객들에게 홍보 이메일을 보내는 것을 계속할 것이다.

해설 동사 keep의 목적어 자리에 올 수 있는 동명사 (B) sending이 정답이다. 동사 (A)와 (D), 동사 또는 과거분사 (C)는 목적어 자리에 올 수 없다.

어휘 promotional adj. 홍보의, 판촉의 subscribe v. 구독하다
newsletter n. 소식지

10 to 부정사와 동명사 구별하여 채우기
해석 그 직원은 회사 내부 데이터베이스의 기밀 자료를 외부 판매 회사들에게 공유한 것을 부인했다.

해설 동사 deny(denied)의 목적어 자리에 올 수 있는 동명사 (D) sharing이 정답이다. to 부정사 (A)는 deny의 목적어 자리에 올 수 없고, 동사 또는 과거분사 (B)와 동사 (C)는 목적어 자리에 올 수 없다. (C)를 '몫'이라는 의미의 명사로 본다 해도, 명사는 목적어(any confidential data)를 가질 수 없으므로 답이 될 수 없다.

어휘 confidential adj. 기밀의 vendor n. (특정 제품의) 판매 회사
share v. 공유하다

11 부사 자리 채우기
해석 전동 공구들은 심각한 부상의 위험을 최소화하기 위해 조심스럽게 다루어져야 한다.

해설 빈칸 앞의 동사(should be handled)를 꾸밀 수 있는 것은 부사이므로 부사 (C) cautiously(조심스럽게)가 정답이다. 형용사 (A), 명사 또는 동사 (B), 형용사의 비교급 (D)는 동사를 꾸밀 수 없다.

어휘 power tool 전동 공구 minimize v. 최소화하다 risk n. 위험
serious adj. 심각한 injury n. 부상 cautious adj. 조심스러운, 신중한
caution n. 주의, 경고; v. 주의를 주다

12 to 부정사와 동명사 구별하여 채우기 [정답 공식 01]
해석 Novexia사는 토론토 시내에 새로운 주력 상점을 짓기로 결정했다.

해설 동사 decide(decided)의 목적어 자리에 올 수 있는 to 부정사 (B) to build가 정답이다. 동명사 또는 현재분사 (A)와 동명사의 완료형 (D)는 decide의 목적어 자리에 올 수 없고, 동사 (C)는 목적어 자리에 올 수 없다.

어휘 flagship store 주력 상점 downtown n. 시내

13 to 부정사와 동명사 구별하여 채우기
해석 많은 졸업생은 국제적인 경험을 쌓고 직업 전망을 향상시키기 위해 해외로 이주하는 것을 고려한다.

해설 동사 consider의 목적어 자리에 올 수 있는 동명사 (C) moving이 정답이다. 동사 (A)와 (B)는 목적어 자리에 올 수 없고, to 부정사 (D)는 consider의 목적어 자리에 올 수 없다.

어휘 graduate n. 졸업생 abroad adv. 해외로, 외국으로
career prospect 직업 전망

14 to 부정사와 동명사 구별하여 채우기
해석 소비자들은 약초 보조 식품을 먹기 전에 전문의와 상담하도록 권고된다.

해설 빈칸은 수동태로 쓰인 5형식 동사(encourage)의 목적격 보어 자리이다. encourage는 to 부정사를 목적격 보어로 취하는 동사이므로 (B) to consult가 정답이다. 명사 (A), 동명사 또는 현재분사 (C), 동사 또는 명사 (D)는 encourage의 목적어 자리에 올 수 없다.

어휘 medical professional 전문의 prior to ~ 전에
herbal supplement 약초 보조 식품

15 to 부정사와 동명사 구별하여 채우기
해석 운전자들은 혼잡 시간대에 Brookdale가에 진입하는 것을 피하도록 권고된다.

해설 동사 avoid의 목적어 자리에 올 수 있는 동명사 (B) entering이 정답이다. 동사 (A)와 (D)는 목적어 자리에 올 수 없고, to 부정사 (C)는 avoid의 목적어 자리에 올 수 없다.

어휘 rush hour 혼잡 시간대

16 to 부정사와 동명사 구별하여 채우기 정답 공식 01
해석 자연 재해 이후, 마을 주민들은 정부 지원으로 그들의 집을 재건하길 희망한다.

해설 동사 hope의 목적어 자리에 올 수 있는 to 부정사 (A) to rebuild가 정답이다. 동명사 또는 현재분사 (B)는 hope의 목적어 자리에 올 수 없고, 동사 (C)와 (D)는 목적어 자리에 올 수 없다.

어휘 disaster n. 재해, 재난 assistance n. 지원, 도움

17 to 부정사의 in order to 채우기
해석 고객들은 배송 지연을 방지하기 위해 그들이 제공하는 주소를 확인하도록 상기된다.

해설 이 문장은 필수성분(Customers ~ address)을 갖춘 완전한 절이므로, ___ ~ shipment는 수식어 거품으로 보아야 한다. 따라서 수식어 거품을 이끌 수 있는 모든 보기가 정답의 후보이다. 이 수식어 거품은 동사 (prevent)만 있고 주어가 없으며 '배송 지연을 방지하기 위해'라는 의미가 되어야 하므로, 목적을 나타내는 to 부정사를 만들기 위해 동사원형 (prevent) 앞에 to가 와야 한다. 따라서 목적을 나타내는 to 부정사 대신 쓰일 수 있는 (D) in order to가 정답이다. 전치사 (A), (B), (C)는 뒤에 명사가 와야 한다. 참고로, to 부정사가 목적을 나타낼 때는 to 대신 in order to를 쓸 수 있음을 알아 둔다.

어휘 remind v. 상기시키다 prevent v. 방지하다 delay n. 지연
shipment n. 배송

18 동명사와 명사 구별하여 채우기
해석 환경 과학자들은 플라스틱 폐기물을 부적절하게 버리는 것이 해양 생태계에 영향을 끼친다고 경고한다.

해설 that절(that ~ ecosystems) 안에 주어가 없으므로 주어 자리에 올 수 있는 동명사 (A)와 명사 (D)가 정답의 후보이다. 빈칸 뒤에 목적어(plastic waste)가 있으므로 목적어를 가질 수 있는 동명사 (A) discarding이 정답이다. 명사 (D) discarder는 목적어를 가질 수 없으므로 답이 될 수 없다. 형용사 (B)와 동사 또는 과거분사 (C)는 주어 자리에 올 수 없다.

어휘 waste n. 폐기물 improperly adv. 부적절하게 marine adj. 해양의
ecosystem n. 생태계 discard v. 버리다 discarder n. 버리는 사람

19 동명사 채우기
해설 위원회는 더 안전한 작업 환경을 보장하기 위해 안전 매뉴얼을 수정하는 것의 중요성을 강조했다.

해설 전치사(of)의 목적어 자리에 올 수 있고 명사구(the safety manual)를 목적어로 가질 수 있는 동명사 (D) revising이 정답이다. 동사 (A)와 (B), 동사 또는 과거분사 (C)는 전치사의 목적어 자리에 올 수 없다.

어휘 committee n. 위원회 emphasize v. 강조하다 ensure v. 보장하다
revise v. 수정하다

20 동명사 채우기
해설 지원서를 작성하는 것을 끝내면, 인사과에 제출해 주십시오.

해설 동사 finish의 목적어 자리에 올 수 있는 동명사 (B) filling이 정답이다. 동사 (A)와 (D), 동사 또는 과거분사 (C)는 목적어 자리에 올 수 없다.

어휘 application form 지원서 submit v. 제출하다 HR department 인사과

21 올바른 시제의 동사 채우기
해설 Lara Karowski가 심하게 무릎 부상을 입었을 때 지난해의 배드민턴 결승전에서 우승할 가능성이 낮아졌다.

해설 주절에 주어(Lara Karowski's chances ~ finals)만 있고 동사가 없으므로 동사 (A), (B), (D)가 정답의 후보이다. 과거를 나타내는 표현인 last year(지난해)가 있으므로 과거 시제 (B) diminished가 정답이다. 부사 (C)는 동사 자리에 올 수 없다.

어휘 finals n. 결승전 injure v. 부상을 입다

22 to 부정사 채우기
해설 오케스트라 단원들은 다가오는 시즌을 위해 그들과 합류할 재능 있는 음악가들을 찾고 있다고 언급했다.

해설 that절(that ~ season)은 주어(they), 동사(were searching for), 목적어(talented musicians)를 갖춘 완전한 절이므로, ___ ~ season은 수식어 거품으로 보아야 한다. 이 수식어 거품은 동사가 없는 거품구이므로, 거품구를 이끌며 명사구 talented musicians 뒤에서 명사를 꾸미는 형용사 역할을 하는 to 부정사 (A) to join이 정답이다. 동사 (B), (C), (D)는 형용사 자리에 올 수 없다.

어휘 search for ~을 찾다 talented adj. 재능 있는

23 동명사와 명사 구별하여 채우기
해설 학생들은 스포츠가 일상적인 학업 스트레스로부터 해방감을 제공하기 때문에 그것들에 참여하도록 권장된다.

해설 동사(offer)의 목적어 자리에 올 수 있는 동명사 (C)와 명사 (D)가 정답의 후보이다. 부정관사(a) 다음에 올 수 있는 것은 명사이므로 명사 (D) release가 정답이다. 동명사 (C)는 부정관사 다음에 올 수 없다. 형용사 (A), 동사 또는 과거분사 (B)는 명사 자리에 올 수 없다.

어휘 releasable adj. 해방할 수 있는 release n. 해방(감); v. 해방하다, 공개하다

24 to 부정사와 동명사 구별하여 채우기 정답 공식 01
해설 예상치 못한 폭풍으로 인해, 행사 주최자들은 야외 콘서트의 일정을 변경하기로 결정했다.

해설 동사 decide(decided)의 목적어 자리에 올 수 있는 to 부정사 (A) to reschedule이 정답이다. 동명사 또는 현재분사 (B)는 decide의 목적어 자리에 올 수 없고, 동사 (C)와 (D)는 목적어 자리에 올 수 없다.

어휘 outdoor adj. 야외의 reschedule v. 일정을 변경하다

빈출 어휘 | 형용사 1

토익 실전문제 p.219

01 (B)	02 (A)	03 (C)	04 (C)	05 (B)
06 (D)	07 (C)	08 (A)		

01 형용사 어휘 고르기
해석 디자인 팀은 여러 유용한 아이디어를 생산한 매우 가치 있는 토론을 했다.
해설 '유용한 아이디어를 생산한 매우 가치 있는 토론을 하다'라는 문맥이므로

(B) valuable(가치 있는, 귀중한)이 정답이다. (A) vague는 '모호한', (C) redundant는 '불필요한, 중복되는', (D) available은 '이용 가능한, 구할 수 있는'이라는 의미이다.

어휘 discussion n. 토론, 논의

02 형용사 어휘 고르기
해석 Madison사는 그것이 개발한 시장을 변화시키는 서비스로 인해 매우 혁신적이라고 여겨진다.
해설 'Madison사가 시장을 변화시키는 서비스로 인해 매우 혁신적이라고 여겨지다'라는 문맥이므로 (A) innovative(혁신적인)가 정답이다. (B) conditional은 '조건부의', (C) permanent는 '상설의, 영구적인', (D) restricted는 '제한된, 한정된'이라는 의미이다.

어휘 extremely adv. 매우 develop v. 개발하다

03 형용사 어휘 고르기
해석 직원은 많은 업무량 때문에 교육 과정에 참여하는 것에 대한 제한된 기회를 가졌다.
해설 '많은 업무량 때문에 교육 과정에 참여하는 것에 대한 제한된 기회를 가지다'라는 문맥이므로 (C) limited(제한된)가 정답이다. (A) advanced는 '선진의, 고급의', (B) exact는 '정확한, 정밀한', (D) tense는 '긴장된'이라는 의미이다.

04 형용사 어휘 고르기
해석 Mr. Achebe는 그의 인기 있는 주간 소식지에서 수집된 자료를 사용하여 베스트셀러 책을 출판했다.
해설 '인기 있는 주간 소식지에서 수집된 자료를 사용하여 베스트셀러 책을 출판하다'라는 문맥이므로 (C) popular(인기 있는, 대중적인)가 정답이다. (A) certain은 '확실한', (B) delicate는 '섬세한', (D) mandatory는 '의무적인, 필수적인'이라는 의미이다.

어휘 publish v. 출판하다 material n. 자료 gather v. 수집하다, 모으다

05 형용사 어휘 고르기
해석 성공적인 시행 후에, 그 회사는 원격 근무를 허용하기 위해 공식적인 정책을 변경했다.
해설 '시행 후에, 회사가 원격 근무를 허용하기 위해 공식적인 정책을 변경하다'라는 문맥이므로 (B) official(공식적인)이 정답이다. (A) distant는 '멀리 떨어진', (C) exclusive는 '전용의, 독점적인', (D) noble은 '고귀한, 고결한'이라는 의미이다.

어휘 trial run 시행 allow v. 허용하다 remote work 원격 근무

06 형용사 어휘 고르기
해석 Vertex Solutions사는 공사의 환경적인 영향을 평가하기 위해 폭넓은 연구를 수행했다.
해설 'Vertex Solutions사가 환경적인 영향을 평가하기 위해 폭넓은 연구를 수행하다'라는 문맥이므로 (D) extensive(폭넓은, 광범위한)가 정답이다. (A) fragile은 '손상되기 쉬운', (B) knowledgeable은 '지식이 풍부한', (C) potential은 '잠재적인'이라는 의미이다.

어휘 conduct v. 수행하다, 실시하다 evaluate v. 평가하다
environmental adj. 환경적인 impact n. 영향 construction n. 공사

07 형용사 어휘 고르기
해석 창고 관리자는 새로운 주문을 하기 전에 재고 기록이 정확한지 확인했다.
해설 '창고 관리자가 재고 기록이 정확한지 확인하다'라는 문맥이므로 (C) accurate(정확한)가 정답이다. (A) vacant는 '비어 있는, 사람이 없는', (B) deliberate는 '의도적인', (D) leading은 '선도적인'이라는 의미이다.

어휘 warehouse n. 창고 verify v. 확인하다, 입증하다
inventory n. 재고, 물품 목록

08 형용사 어휘 고르기
해석 프로젝트 관리자는 직원을 다섯 개의 별개 팀으로 나누었고, 각 팀이 한 단계를 처리했다.
해설 '관리자가 직원을 다섯 개의 별개 팀으로 나누었고, 각 팀이 한 단계를 처리했다'라는 문맥이므로 (A) distinct(별개의, 독특한)가 정답이다. (B) rigorous는 '엄격한, 철저한', (C) frequent는 '잦은, 빈번한', (D) terminal은 '끝의, 종말의'라는 의미이다.

어휘 separate v. 나누다, 분리하다 handle v. 처리하다, 다루다
phase n. 단계, 국면

DAY 09 분사

기출 포인트 01~02

실전 Check-up   p.220
01 (A)   02 (B)

01 분사 채우기
해석 채용 담당자들은 일자리에 필요한 자격을 보여준 지원자들에게 연락할 것이다.
해설 빈칸 앞의 명사(applicants)를 꾸밀 수 있는 것은 형용사이므로 현재분사 (A) demonstrating이 정답이다. 동사 (B)는 형용사 자리에 올 수 없다.

어휘 recruiter n. 채용 담당자 applicant n. 지원자 qualification n. 자격
position n. 일자리 demonstrate v. 보여주다

02 분사 채우기
해석 Wiltshire 아파트 단지의 거주자들은 그들에게 배정된 자리에만 주차하도록 요청받는다.
해설 빈칸 뒤의 명사(spots)를 꾸밀 수 있는 것은 형용사이므로 과거분사 (B) assigned가 정답이다. 동사 (A)는 형용사 자리에 올 수 없다.

어휘 resident n. 거주자 spot n. 자리, 장소 assign v. 배정하다, 할당하다

기출 포인트 03~04

실전 Check-up   p.221
01 (B)   02 (A)

01 현재분사와 과거분사 구별하여 채우기
해석 그 골동품 가게는 빅토리아 시대의 여러 마음을 빼앗는 물건들을 전시한다.
해설 빈칸 뒤의 명사(items)를 꾸밀 수 있는 것은 형용사이므로 모든 보기가 정답의 후보이다. 꾸밈을 받는 명사(items)와 분사가 '마음을 빼앗는 물건들'이라는 의미의 능동 관계이므로 현재분사 (B) charming이 정답이다. 과거분사 (A) charmed를 쓸 경우 '마음을 빼앗긴 물건들'이라는 어색한 문맥이 된다.

어휘 antique n. 골동품 era n. 시대 charm v. ~의 마음을 빼앗다

02 현재분사와 과거분사 구별하여 채우기
해석 그 영업사원은 회의에 명함을 가져오지 않았다는 것을 깨달았을 때 당황했다.
해설 빈칸이 동사(felt) 뒤에 왔으므로 주격 보어 자리에 올 수 있는 모든 보기가 정답의 후보이다. '명함을 가져오지 않았다는 것을 깨달았을 때 당황했다'라는 의미가 되어야 하므로 과거분사 (A) embarrassed(당황해하는)가 정답이다. 참고로, The salesperson(그 영업사원)이 감정을 느끼는 주체이므로 과거분사가 왔다. 타동사(embarrass)의 현재분사는 뒤에 목적어를 가져야 하는데, 빈칸 뒤에 목적어가 없으므로 현재분사 (B)는 답이 될 수 없다.

어휘 realize v. 깨닫다 business card 명함

기출 포인트 05~06

실전 Check-up p.222

01 (B) 02 (A)

01 현재분사와 과거분사 구별하여 채우기
해석 그 고객은 지난주에 받은 손상된 물품에 대한 환불을 요청했다.
해설 빈칸 뒤의 명사(item)를 꾸밀 수 있는 것은 형용사이므로 모든 보기가 정답의 후보이다. '손상된 물품'이라는 의미가 되어야 하므로 과거분사 (B) damaged가 정답이다.
어휘 request v. 요청하다

02 분사구문 채우기
해석 고객의 의견에 영감을 받아, 팀은 제품에 여러 개선을 했다.
해설 이 문장은 주어(the team), 동사(made), 목적어(several improvements)를 갖춘 완전한 절이므로, ____ ~ feedback은 수식어 거품으로 보아야 한다. 따라서 수식어 거품이 될 수 있는 분사구문을 만드는 모든 보기가 정답의 후보이다. '고객의 의견에 영감을 받다'라는 수동의 의미가 되어야 하므로 과거분사 (A) Inspired가 정답이다.
어휘 improvement n. 개선, 향상 inspire v. 영감을 주다

3초컷 정답 공식 p.223

01 (D) 02 (C) 03 (A) 04 (C) 05 (A)
06 (D) 07 (A) 08 (C)

01 현재분사와 과거분사 구별하여 채우기
해석 우리는 새로운 프로젝트팀에 합류할 숙련된 기술자들을 찾고 있다.
해설 빈칸 뒤의 명사(engineers)를 꾸밀 수 있는 것은 형용사이므로 현재분사 (B)와 과거분사 (D)가 정답의 후보이다. 꾸밈을 받는 명사(engineers)와 분사가 '숙련된 기술자들'이라는 의미의 수동 관계이므로 과거분사 (D) experienced가 정답이다. 현재분사 (B) experiencing을 쓸 경우 '경험하는 기술자들'이라는 어색한 문맥이 된다. 동사 또는 명사 (A)와 (C)는 형용사 자리에 올 수 없다.

02 현재분사와 과거분사 구별하여 채우기
해석 그녀는 인공 지능 분야에서 선도적인 전문가이다.
해설 빈칸 뒤의 명사(expert)를 꾸밀 수 있는 것은 형용사이므로 과거분사 (B)와 현재분사 (C)가 정답의 후보이다. 꾸밈을 받는 명사(expert)와 분사가 '선도적인 전문가'라는 의미의 능동 관계이므로 현재분사 (C) leading이 정답이다. 과거분사 (B)를 쓸 경우 '선도된 전문가'라는 어색한 문맥이 된다. 동사 또는 명사 (A)와 명사 (D)는 형용사 자리에 올 수 없다.
어휘 field n. 분야 artificial intelligence 인공 지능 lead v. 이끌다; n. 선두

03 현재분사와 과거분사 구별하여 채우기
해석 진행 중인 수리로 인해, 도서관은 이번 달에 제한된 시간으로 운영될 것이다.
해설 빈칸 뒤의 명사(hours)를 꾸밀 수 있는 것은 형용사이므로 과거분사 (A)와 현재분사 (B)가 정답의 후보이다. 꾸밈을 받는 명사(hours)와 분사가 '제한된 시간'이라는 의미의 수동 관계이므로 과거분사 (A) limited가 정답이다. 현재분사 (B) limiting을 쓸 경우 '제한하는 시간'이라는 어색한 문맥이 된다. 동사 또는 명사 (C)와 (D)는 형용사 자리에 올 수 없다.
어휘 ongoing adj. 진행 중인 renovation n. 수리 limit v. 제한하다; n. 한계

04 현재분사와 과거분사 구별하여 채우기
해석 TechVista Solutions사는 신규 구독자들에게 제한된 시간 동안 무료 체험을 제공하고 있다.
해설 빈칸 뒤의 명사(time)를 꾸밀 수 있는 것은 형용사이므로 현재분사 (A)와 과거분사 (C)가 정답의 후보이다. 꾸밈을 받는 명사(time)와 분사가 '제한된 시간'이라는 의미의 수동 관계이므로 과거분사 (C) limited가 정답이다. 동사 또는 명사 (B)는 형용사 자리에 올 수 없고, to 부정사 (D)는 명사를 뒤에서 꾸며주므로 답이 될 수 없다.
어휘 subscriber n. 구독자

05 현재분사와 과거분사 구별하여 채우기
해석 안건 목록에 남아 있는 항목들은 다음 회의에서 논의될 것이다.
해설 빈칸 뒤의 명사(items)를 꾸밀 수 있는 것은 형용사이므로 현재분사 (A)와 과거분사 (C)가 정답의 후보이다. 꾸밈을 받는 명사(items)와 분사가 '남아 있는 항목들'이라는 의미의 능동 관계이므로 현재분사 (A) remaining이 정답이다. 과거분사 (C) remained를 쓸 경우 해석상 그럴듯해 보이지만, 동사 remain(남다)은 자동사이므로 수동형인 과거분사로 쓰일 수 없다. 동사 (B)와 (D)는 형용사 자리에 올 수 없다.
어휘 agenda n. 안건 목록

06 현재분사와 과거분사 구별하여 채우기
해석 일정에 남아 있는 변경 사항들은 이메일로 모든 직원에게 전달될 것이다.
해설 빈칸 뒤의 명사(changes)를 꾸밀 수 있는 것은 형용사이므로 과거분사 (C)와 현재분사 (D)가 정답의 후보이다. 꾸밈을 받는 명사(changes)와 분사가 '남아 있는 변경 사항들'이라는 의미의 능동 관계이므로 현재분사 (D) remaining이 정답이다. 과거분사 (C) remained를 쓸 경우 해석상 그럴듯해 보이지만, 동사 remain(남다)은 자동사이므로 수동형인 과거분사로 쓰일 수 없다. 동사 (A)와 명사 (B)는 형용사 자리에 올 수 없다.
어휘 communicate v. 전달하다, 의사소통을 하다

07 현재분사와 과거분사 구별하여 채우기
해석 국제 전문가들에 의해 진행된 강의들은 세 가지 언어로 번역될 것이다.
해설 빈칸 앞의 명사(Lectures)를 꾸밀 수 있는 것은 형용사이므로 과거분사 (A)와 현재분사 (D)가 정답의 후보이다. 꾸밈을 받는 명사(Lectures)와 분사가 '진행된 강의들'이라는 의미의 수동 관계이므로 과거분사 (A) conducted가 정답이다. 현재분사 (D) conducting을 쓸 경우 '진행하는 강의들'이라는 어색한 문맥이 된다. 동사 또는 명사 (B)와 (C)는 형용사 자리에 올 수 없다.
어휘 lecture n. 강의, 강연 international adj. 국제적인 translate v. 번역하다, 통역하다 conduct v. (특정한 활동을) 하다; n. 행동

08 현재분사와 과거분사 구별하여 채우기
해석 회계부에 의해 수집된 자료에 따르면, 회사 수익이 이번 분기에 15퍼센트 증가했다.
해설 빈칸 앞의 명사(data)를 꾸밀 수 있는 것은 형용사이므로 현재분사 (B), 과거분사 (C), 형용사 (D)가 정답의 후보이다. 꾸밈을 받는 명사(data)와 분사가 '수집된 자료'라는 의미의 수동 관계이므로 과거분사 (C) collected가 정답이다. 현재분사 (B)와 형용사 (D)를 쓸 경우 각각 '회계부에 의해 수집하는/집합적인 자료'라는 어색한 문맥이 된다.
어휘 revenue n. 수익, 수입 quarter n. 분기 finance department 회계부

HACKERS TEST p.224

01 (C)	02 (B)	03 (A)	04 (A)	05 (D)
06 (C)	07 (B)	08 (A)	09 (B)	10 (C)
11 (B)	12 (B)	13 (B)	14 (C)	15 (B)
16 (C)	17 (B)	18 (D)	19 (A)	20 (D)
21 (B)	22 (B)	23 (B)	24 (D)	

01 현재분사와 과거분사 구별하여 채우기 [정답공식 01]

해석 그 회사는 회의에서 그들의 지식을 공유하기 위해 선도적인 전문가들을 초대했다.

해설 빈칸 뒤의 명사(professionals)를 꾸밀 수 있는 것은 형용사이므로 현재분사 (C)와 과거분사 (D)가 정답의 후보이다. 꾸밈을 받는 명사(professionals)와 분사가 '선도적인 전문가들'이라는 의미의 능동 관계이므로 현재분사 (C) leading이 정답이다. 과거분사 (D)를 쓸 경우 '선도된 전문가'라는 어색한 문맥이 된다. 명사 (A)와 동사 (B)는 형용사 자리에 올 수 없다.

어휘 professional n. 전문가 share v. 공유하다 conference n. 회의

02 분사 채우기

해석 학교 이사회는 다음 학기부터 시작하는 연장된 학교 운영 시간에 대한 제안을 승인했다.

해설 빈칸 뒤의 명사(school day)를 꾸밀 수 있는 것은 형용사이므로 과거분사 (B) extended가 정답이다. 동사 (A), 명사 (C)와 (D)는 형용사 자리에 올 수 없다.

어휘 approve v. 승인하다 proposal n. 제안 semester n. 학기
extend v. 연장하다 extender n. 늘이는 것 extension n. 확대

03 현재분사와 과거분사 구별하여 채우기

해석 새로운 고객들을 유인하는 것은 기존 고객들을 유지하는 것보다 비용이 더 많이 든다.

해설 빈칸 뒤의 명사(ones)를 꾸밀 수 있는 것은 형용사이므로 현재분사 (A)와 과거분사 (B)가 정답의 후보이다. 꾸밈을 받는 명사(ones)와 분사가 '기존 고객들'이라는 의미의 능동 관계이므로 현재분사 (A) existing이 정답이다. 과거분사 (B) existed를 쓸 경우 해석상 그럴듯해 보이지만, 동사 exist(현존하다, 있다)는 자동사이므로 수동형인 과거분사로 쓰일 수 없다. 동사 (C)와 명사 (D)는 형용사 자리에 올 수 없다.

어휘 attract v. 유인하다, 끌어모으다 retain v. 유지하다 existence n. 존재

04 현재분사와 과거분사 구별하여 채우기 [정답공식 02]

해석 Lakeside 식당의 계절 메뉴는 여름 동안 제한된 시간 동안 이용 가능할 것이다.

해설 빈칸 뒤의 명사(time)를 꾸밀 수 있는 것은 형용사이므로 과거분사 (A)와 현재분사 (C)가 정답의 후보이다. 꾸밈을 받는 명사(time)와 분사가 '제한된 시간'이라는 의미의 수동 관계이므로 과거분사 (A) limited가 정답이다. 현재분사 (C) limiting을 쓸 경우 '제한하는 시간'이라는 어색한 문맥이 된다. 동사 또는 명사 (B)와 명사 (D)는 형용사 자리에 올 수 없다.

어휘 seasonal adj. 계절의 available adj. 이용 가능한

05 분사구문 채우기

해석 경찰대에서의 수년간의 노고에 경의를 표하며 Dane Evans에게 특별 상이 수여되었다.

해설 이 문장은 주어(A special award)와 동사(was presented)를 모두 갖춘 완전한 절이므로, ____ him ~ force는 수식어 거품으로 보아야 한다. 따라서 수식어 거품이 될 수 있는 과거분사 (B)와 현재분사 (D)가 정답의 후보이다. 빈칸 뒤에 목적어(him)가 있고, 주절의 주어(A special award)와 분사가 '특별 상이 경의를 표하다'라는 의미의 능동 관계이므로 동사 honor(경의를 표하다)의 현재분사 (D) honoring이 정답이다. 과거분사 (B) honored는 수동의 의미를 나타내므로 답이 될 수 없다. 형용사 (A), 동사 또는 명사 (C)는 수식어 거품을 이끌 수 없다.

어휘 present v. 수여하다, 주다 service n. 노고, 봉사

06 현재분사와 과거분사 구별하여 채우기

해석 Westbrook Industries사의 1분기 결과는 이전 예측과 비교하면 꽤 실망스럽게 했다.

해설 빈칸이 동사(were) 뒤에 왔으므로 주격 보어 자리에 올 수 있는 과거분사 (B)와 현재분사 (C), 명사 (D)가 정답의 후보이다. '결과가 실망스럽게 했다'라는 의미가 되어야 하므로 현재분사 (C) disappointing이 정답이다. 과거분사 (B)를 쓸 경우 '결과가 실망스러워했다'라는 어색한 문맥이 된다. 명사 (D)는 '실망스러운 것'이라는 의미로 쓰일 때, 가산 명사이므로 부정관사와 함께 써야 한다. 동사 (A)는 주격 보어 자리에 올 수 없다.

어휘 projection n. 예측, 추정

07 전치사 채우기

해석 전기 차량 충전소는 건물 주차장의 중앙출입구 옆에 위치해 있다.

해설 빈칸은 명사구(the main ~ lot)를 목적어로 가지는 전치사 자리이므로 모든 보기가 정답의 후보이다. '충전소는 중앙출입구 옆에 위치해 있다'라는 의미가 되어야 하므로 전치사 (B) beside(~ 옆에)가 정답이다. (A) from은 '~에서, ~로부터', (C) throughout은 '~ 도처에, ~ 동안', (D) down은 '아래로'라는 의미이다.

어휘 electric adj. 전기의 charging station 충전소 main entrance 중앙출입구

08 분사구문 채우기

해석 수학에서 뛰어난 재능을 보여주었기 때문에, Lisa는 일류 대학교의 장학금을 제공받았다.

해설 이 문장은 주어(Lisa), 동사(was offered), 목적어(a scholarship)를 갖춘 완전한 절이므로, ____ ~ mathematics는 수식어 거품으로 보아야 한다. 따라서 보기 중 수식어 거품이 될 수 있는 분사구문을 만드는 현재분사 (A) Displaying이 정답이다. 동사 또는 명사 (B)와 (C), 명사 (D)는 수식어 거품을 이끌 수 없다.

어휘 exceptional adj. 뛰어난 talent n. 재능 scholarship n. 장학금
prestigious adj. 일류의, 명망 있는 display v. 보여주다; n. 전시, 진열
displayer n. 전시하는 사람

09 현재분사와 과거분사 구별하여 채우기

해석 그 연구 시설은 가장 가까운 마을에서 배로 여섯 시간 떨어진, 섬의 고립된 지역에 위치해 있다.

해설 빈칸 뒤의 명사(area)를 꾸밀 수 있는 것은 형용사이므로 과거분사 (B)와 현재분사 (C)가 정답의 후보이다. 꾸밈을 받는 명사(area)와 분사가 '고립된 지역'이라는 의미의 수동 관계이므로 과거분사 (B) secluded가 정답이다. 현재분사 (C) secluding을 쓸 경우 '고립하는 지역'이라는 어색한 문맥이 된다. 동사 (A)는 형용사 자리에 올 수 없고, to 부정사 (D)는 명사를 뒤에서 꾸며주므로 답이 될 수 없다.

어휘 facility n. 시설 located adj. 위치한 seclude v. 고립시키다

10 분사구문 채우기

해석 수제 가구를 전문으로 해서, 그 지역 장인 공방은 상품들의 뛰어난 품질로 인정을 받았다.

해설 이 문장은 주어(the local artisan studio), 동사(has gained), 목적어(recognition)를 갖춘 완전한 절이므로, ____ in handcrafted furniture는 수식어 거품으로 보아야 한다. 따라서 보기 중 수식어 거품이 될 수 있는 분사구문을 만드는 현재분사 (C) Specializing이 정답이다. 동사 (A)와 (B), 명사 (D)는 수식어 거품을 이끌 수 없다.

어휘 handcrafted adj. 수제의 artisan n. 장인 recognition n. 인정
exceptional adj. 뛰어난

11 현재분사와 과거분사 구별하여 채우기

해석 치과 협회의 회원 자격은 최소 3년의 전문적인 진료 경험이 있는 면허가 있는 치과의사들로 엄격히 제한된다.

해설 빈칸 뒤의 명사(dentists)를 꾸밀 수 있는 것은 형용사이므로 과거분사 (B)와 현재분사 (C)가 정답의 후보이다. 꾸밈을 받는 명사(dentists)와 분사가 '면허가 있는 치과의사들'이라는 의미의 수동 관계이므로 과거분사 (B) licensed가 정답이다. 현재분사 (C) licensing을 쓸 경우 '면허를 주는 치과의사들'이라는 어색한 문맥이 된다. 동사 또는 명사 (A)와 (D)는 형용사 자리에 올 수 없다.

어휘 membership n. 회원 자격 dental adj. 치과의 association n. 협회
strictly adv. 엄격히 professional adj. 전문적인

practice n. (의사·변호사 등의) 영업, 업무
license v. 면허를 주다, 허가하다; n. 면허

12 분사구문 채우기
해석 그 나라의 침체된 경제는 사람들이 직장을 구하기 어렵게 만들었는데, 이는 더 많은 시민들이 해외에서 직장을 찾는 결과를 낳았다.

해설 이 문장은 주어(The stagnant economy), 동사(has made), 목적어(it), 목적격 보어(hard)를 갖춘 완전한 절이므로, ____ ~ overseas는 수식어 거품으로 보아야 한다. 따라서 보기 중 수식어 거품을 이끌 수 있는 현재분사 (B)와 과거분사 (C)가 정답의 후보이다. 주절의 주어와 분사구문이 '더 많은 시민들이 해외에서 직장을 찾는 결과를 낳다'라는 능동 관계이므로 빈칸 뒤의 in과 결합해 '~이라는 결과를 낳다'라는 능동의 의미를 만드는 현재분사 (B) resulting이 정답이다. 동사 또는 명사 (A)와 (D)는 수식어 거품이 될 수 없다.

어휘 stagnant adj. 침체된, 고여 있는   citizen n. 시민
overseas adv. 해외에서, 해외로

13 분사 채우기
해석 큰 액수의 돈과 관련된 결정들은 정식 회의에서 모든 동업자와 논의되어야 한다.

해설 이 문장은 주어(Decisions)와 동사(must be discussed)를 갖춘 완전한 절이므로, ____ large sums of money는 수식어 거품으로 보아야 한다. 보기 중 수식어 거품을 이끌 수 있는 현재분사 (B) involving이 정답이다. 동사 (A), (C), (D)는 수식어 거품이 될 수 없다.

어휘 sum n. 액수   discuss v. 논의하다, 토론하다   formal adj. 정식의, 정중한
partner n. 동업자

14 현재분사와 과거분사 구별하여 채우기 [정답 공식 01]
해석 우리의 프로젝트는 환경 지속 가능성 분야의 숙련된 전문가 팀에 의해 이끌어질 것이다.

해설 빈칸 뒤의 명사(specialists)를 꾸밀 수 있는 것은 형용사이므로 현재분사 (A)와 과거분사 (C)가 정답의 후보이다. 꾸밈을 받는 명사(specialists)와 분사가 '숙련된 전문가'라는 의미의 수동 관계이므로 과거분사 (C) experienced가 정답이다. 현재분사 (A) experiencing을 쓸 경우 '경험하는 전문가'라는 어색한 문맥이 된다. 동사 또는 명사 (B)와 (D)는 형용사 자리에 올 수 없다.

어휘 specialist n. 전문가   environmental adj. 환경의
sustainability n. 지속 가능성

15 현재분사와 과거분사 구별하여 채우기
해석 투자자들은 업계 침체에도 불구하고 분기별 수익이 15퍼센트 증가했다는 것에 놀랐다.

해설 빈칸이 동사(were) 뒤에 왔으므로 주격 보어 자리에 올 수 있는 과거분사 (B)와 현재분사 (C)가 정답의 후보이다. '투자자들이 놀랐다'라는 의미가 되어야 하므로 과거분사 (B) surprised가 정답이다. 참고로, The investors(투자자들)가 감정을 느끼는 주체이므로 과거분사가 왔다. 동사 (A)와 부사 (D)는 주격 보어 자리에 올 수 없다.

어휘 investor n. 투자자   quarterly adj. 분기별의   profit n. 수익
downturn n. 침체

16 현재분사와 과거분사 구별하여 채우기 [정답 공식 04]
해석 유명한 건축가인 Jonathan Green에 의해 설계된 타워는 도시의 랜드마크가 되었다.

해설 빈칸 앞의 명사(The tower)를 꾸밀 수 있는 것은 형용사이므로 현재분사 (B), 과거분사 (C), 형용사 (D)가 정답의 후보이다. 꾸밈을 받는 명사(The tower)와 분사가 '유명한 건축가에 의해 설계된 타워'라는 의미의 수동 관계이므로 과거분사 (C) designed가 정답이다. 현재분사 (B)와 형용사 (D)를 쓸 경우 각각 '유명한 건축가에 의해 설계하는/설계할 수 있는 타워'라는 어색한 문맥이 된다. 동사 또는 명사 (A)는 형용사 자리에 올 수 없다.

어휘 architect n. 건축가   landmark n. 랜드마크, 주요 지형지물

17 to 부정사 채우기
해석 Ms. Goodman은 그녀가 믹서기를 구매했던 가게를 방문하기 위해 차를 몰고 패서디나로 갔다.

해설 빈칸 다음에 동사원형(visit)이 왔고 '가게를 방문하기 위해 차를 몰고 갔다'라는 의미가 되어야 하므로 목적을 나타내는 to 부정사를 만들 수 있는 (B) to가 정답이다. 전치사 (A), (C), (D)는 뒤에 명사가 와야 한다. 빈칸 뒤의 visit을 '방문'이라는 의미의 명사로 보더라도, 뒤에 오는 명사(the store)와 특별한 연결어 없이 나란히 오게 되므로 전치사 (A), (C), (D)는 답이 될 수 없다.

어휘 blender n. 믹서기, 분쇄기

18 분사 채우기
해석 모금 만찬에 참석하는 손님들은 등록과 착석을 위해 최소 30분 일찍 도착해야 한다.

해설 빈칸 앞의 명사(Guests)를 꾸밀 수 있는 것은 형용사이므로 현재분사 (D) attending이 정답이다. 동사 (A)와 (B), 명사 (C)는 형용사 자리에 올 수 없다.

어휘 fundraising n. 모금   registration n. 등록   attendance n. 출석, 참석

19 현재분사와 과거분사 구별하여 채우기 [정답 공식 02]
해석 우리 고객 서비스 부서는 국경일로 인해 제한된 시간 동안 운영된다.

해설 빈칸 뒤의 명사(hours)를 꾸밀 수 있는 것은 형용사이므로 과거분사 (A)와 현재분사 (C)가 정답의 후보이다. 꾸밈을 받는 명사(hours)와 분사가 '제한된 시간'이라는 의미의 수동 관계이므로 과거분사 (A) limited가 정답이다. 현재분사 (C) limiting을 쓸 경우 '제한하는 시간'이라는 어색한 문맥이 된다. 동사 또는 명사 (B)와 명사 (D)는 형용사 자리에 올 수 없다.

어휘 department n. 부서   national holiday 국경일

20 현재분사와 과거분사 구별하여 채우기 [정답 공식 03]
해석 식료품 저장실에 주말 내내 지속될 만큼 충분한 음식이 남아있다.

해설 이 문장은 가주어(There), 동사(is), 진주어(enough food)를 모두 갖춘 완전한 절이므로, ____ ~ weekend는 수식어 거품으로 보아야 한다. 따라서 수식어 거품이 될 수 있는 과거분사 (C)와 현재분사 (D)가 정답의 후보이다. 주절의 주어(enough food)와 분사가 '충분한 음식이 남아있다'라는 의미의 능동 관계이므로 동사 remain(남다)의 현재분사 (D) remaining이 정답이다. 과거분사 (C) remained를 쓸 경우 해석상 그럴듯해 보이지만, 동사 remain(남다)은 자동사이므로 수동형인 과거분사로 쓰일 수 없다. 동사 (A)와 명사 (B)는 수식어 거품을 이끌 수 없다.

어휘 pantry n. 식료품 저장실   last v. 지속되다   remainder n. 나머지

21 현재분사와 과거분사 구별하여 채우기
해석 그 팀은 최종 디자인이 그들의 모든 요구사항을 충족했다는 것에 만족스러워했다.

해설 빈칸이 동사(was) 뒤에 왔으므로 주격 보어 자리에 올 수 있는 현재분사 (A)와 과거분사 (B)가 정답의 후보이다. '그 팀이 만족스러워했다'라는 의미가 되어야 하므로 과거분사 (B) satisfied가 정답이다. 참고로, The team(그 팀)이 감정을 느끼는 주체이므로 과거분사가 왔다. 동사 (C)와 (D)는 주격 보어 자리에 올 수 없다.

어휘 meet v. 충족시키다   requirement n. 요구사항

22 분사 채우기
해석 운전 중 휴대전화 사용을 금지하는 법은 주의가 산만해진 운전자들과 관련된 사고를 줄이려는 의도가 있다.

해설 빈칸 뒤의 명사(drivers)를 꾸밀 수 있는 것은 형용사이므로 과거분사 (B) distracted가 정답이다. 동사 (A)와 (D), 명사 (C)는 형용사 자리에 올 수 없다.

어휘 ban v. 금지하다   be intended to ~할 의도가 있다   accident n. 사고
distract v. 산만하게 하다, 주의를 딴 데로 돌리다

23 분사 채우기

해석 흥미로워하는 분석가들은 회사의 5년 재무 계획에 대해 상세한 질문을 했다.

해설 빈칸 뒤의 명사(analysts)를 꾸밀 수 있는 것은 형용사이므로 과거분사 (B) interested가 정답이다. 참고로, analysts(분석가들)이 감정을 느끼는 주체이므로 과거분사가 왔다. 부사 (A), 동사 또는 명사 (C)와 (D)는 형용사 자리에 올 수 없다.

어휘 analyst n. 분석가 projection n. 계획, 예측
interest v. ~의 관심을 끌다; n. 관심

24 현재분사와 과거분사 구별하여 채우기

해석 소프트웨어 설치 방법에 관한 지침은 첨부된 파일에 포함되어 있다.

해설 빈칸 뒤의 명사(file)를 꾸밀 수 있는 것은 형용사이므로 현재분사 (B)와 과거분사 (D)가 정답의 후보이다. '첨부된 파일'이라는 의미가 되어야 하므로 과거분사 (D) attached가 정답이다. 참고로, attached file은 '첨부된 파일'이라는 의미의 표현으로 자주 쓰이는 점을 알아 둔다. 동사 (A)와 (C)는 형용사 자리에 올 수 없다.

어휘 install v. 설치하다

빈출 어휘 | 형용사 2

토익 실전문제
p.227

| 01 (A) | 02 (D) | 03 (D) | 04 (A) | 05 (C) |
| 06 (B) | 07 (C) | 08 (B) | | |

01 형용사 어휘 고르기

해석 그 건축가는 타워의 설계 문제가 해결하기 아주 복잡한 문제가 아니라고 말했다.

해설 '문제가 해결하기 아주 복잡한 문제가 아니다'라는 문맥이므로 (A) complicated(복잡한)가 정답이다. (B) adequate는 '충분한, 적절한'이라는 의미로, 주로 해결책이나 설명, 자원, 사람의 능력 등이 충분하거나 적절하다고 할 때 쓴다. (C) distributed는 '분배된', (D) popular는 '인기 있는, 대중적인'이라는 의미이다.

어휘 architect n. 건축가 issue n. 문제 design n. 설계 solve v. 해결하다

02 형용사 어휘 고르기

해석 비즈니스 클래스에서 제공되는 추가로 다리를 뻗을 수 있는 공간은 긴 비행을 더 편안하게 만들었다.

해설 '다리를 뻗을 수 있는 공간이 긴 비행을 더 편안하게 만들다'라는 문맥이므로 (D) comfortable(편안한)이 정답이다. (A) humble은 '겸손한', (B) clever는 '영리한', (C) adaptable은 '적응성 있는, 적응할 수 있는'이라는 의미이다.

어휘 offer v. 제공하다, 제안하다 flight n. 비행

03 형용사 어휘 고르기

해석 두 그룹은 타협 없이는 해결될 수 없는 상충하는 요구를 가지고 있다.

해설 '타협 없이는 해결될 수 없는 상충하는 요구를 가지고 있다'라는 문맥이므로 (D) conflicting(상충하는)이 정답이다. (A) crowded는 '붐비는', (B) anonymous는 '익명의', (C) absorbed는 '~에 몰두한'이라는 의미이다.

어휘 demand n. 요구 resolve v. 해결하다 compromise n. 타협

04 형용사 어휘 고르기

해석 Kiva 통신 회사의 올해 25퍼센트의 시장 점유율을 얻겠다는 목표는 대부분의 투자자들에게 야심 찬 것으로 보인다.

해설 'Kiva 통신 회사의 목표가 투자자들에게 야심 찬 것으로 보이다'라는 문맥이므로 (A) ambitious(야심 찬)가 정답이다. (B) extensive는 '폭넓은, 광범위한', (C) absolute는 '완전한, 절대적인', (D) mutual은 '상호간의, 서로의'라는 의미이다.

어휘 obtain v. 얻다, 획득하다 market share 시장 점유율 investor n. 투자자

05 형용사 어휘 고르기

해석 제조 공장의 건설은 많은 일자리를 창출하고 지역 경제에 유리한 영향을 미칠 것이다.

해설 '제조 공장의 건설이 지역 경제에 유리한 영향을 미칠 것이다'라는 문맥이므로 (C) favorable(유리한, 호의적인)이 정답이다. (A) respectful은 '존경하는', (B) mandatory는 '의무적인, 필수적인', (D) voluntary는 '자발적인'이라는 의미이다.

어휘 construction n. 건설, 건축 manufacturing n. 제조
create v. 창출하다, 만들다

06 형용사 어휘 고르기

해석 우리 영업팀의 시연은 여러 무역 박람회 참석자들이 회사의 제품을 주문하도록 설득할 만큼 충분히 설득력 있었다.

해설 '영업팀의 시연이 박람회 참석자들이 회사의 제품을 주문하도록 설득할 만큼 충분히 설득력 있다'라는 문맥이므로 (B) persuasive(설득력 있는)가 정답이다. (A) certified는 '공인된', (C) durable은 '내구성이 있는, 오래가는', (D) predictable은 '예측할 수 있는'이라는 의미이다.

어휘 demonstration n. 시연 convince v. 설득하다 attendee n. 참석자

07 형용사 어휘 고르기

해석 Glasgow Antiques는 오래되고 손상된 물품들을 원래 상태로 복원할 수 있는 것으로 알려져 있다.

해설 '오래되고 손상된 물품들을 원래 상태로 복원할 수 있다'라는 문맥이므로 (C) original(원래의, 독창적인)이 정답이다. (A) extra는 '추가의', (B) impartial은 '공정한', (D) bright는 '밝은'이라는 의미이다.

어휘 restore v. 복원하다 damaged adj. 손상을 입은

08 형용사 어휘 고르기

해석 가게 관리자는 배송품을 내리는 데 걸리는 과도한 시간에 불만을 느낀다.

해설 '배송품을 내리는 데 걸리는 과도한 시간에 불만을 느끼다'라는 문맥이므로 (B) excessive(과도한)가 정답이다. (A) confidential은 '기밀의', (C) dynamic은 '역동적인', (D) advanced는 '선진의, 고급의'라는 의미이다.

어휘 unload v. (짐을) 내리다

DAY 10 등위/상관접속사와 관계절

기출 포인트 01

실전 Check-up
p.228

01 (A) 02 (A)

01 등위접속사 채우기

해석 Mr. Anders와 그의 동료들은 5월 15일에 베를린에서 열리는 Continental 책 박람회에 참석할 것이다.

해설 명사구(Mr. Anders)와 명사구(his associates)를 대등하게 연결해 주는 등위접속사가 필요하고 'Mr. Anders와 그의 동료들'이라는 의미가 되어야 하므로 등위접속사 (A) and(그리고)가 정답이다. (B) but은 '그러나, 하지만'이라는 의미이다.

어휘 associate n. 동료 attend v. 참석하다

02 상관접속사 채우기

해석 등록된 사용자들은 연구 논문을 인쇄물과 오디오 형태 둘 다로 다운로드

할 수 있다.

해설 등위접속사 and와 맞는 짝인 (A) both(둘 다)가 정답이다. (B)는 or와 함께 상관접속사 either A or B(A 또는 B 중 하나)의 형태로 쓰인다.

어휘 registered adj. 등록된 user n. 사용자 research article 연구 논문

기출 포인트 02~03

실전 Check-up   p.229

01 (A)   02 (B)

01 관계대명사 채우기

해석 어제 도착한 가구는 사용 전에 조립되어야 한다.

해설 이 문장은 주어(The furniture), 동사(needs), 목적어(to be assembled)를 갖춘 완전한 절이므로, ___ arrived yesterday는 수식어 거품으로 보아야 한다. 이 수식어 거품은 빈칸 앞의 명사(The furniture)를 선행사로 갖는 관계절이므로 모든 보기가 정답의 후보이다. 선행사가 사물이고 빈칸 뒤에 주어가 없는 불완전한 절이 왔으므로 주격 관계대명사 (A) which가 정답이다. (B) who는 사물을 선행사로 가질 수 없다.

어휘 furniture n. 가구 assemble v. 조립하다

02 관계대명사 채우기

해석 미술관이 전시회에서 소개한 여러 예술가들은 국제적인 인정을 받았다.

해설 이 문장은 주어(Several artists), 동사(have gained), 목적어(international recognition)를 갖춘 완전한 절이므로, ___ ~ exhibition은 수식어 거품으로 보아야 한다. 이 수식어 거품은 빈칸 앞의 명사구(Several artists)를 선행사로 갖는 관계절이므로 모든 보기가 정답의 후보이다. 선행사가 사람이고 빈칸 뒤에 목적어가 없는 불완전한 절이 왔으므로 목적격 관계대명사 (B) whom이 정답이다. (A) which는 사람을 선행사로 가질 수 없다.

어휘 exhibition n. 전시회 gain v. 얻다, 획득하다 recognition n. 인정, 인식

기출 포인트 04

실전 Check-up   p.230

01 (A)   02 (B)

01 관계대명사 채우기

해석 공원이 내려다보이는 아파트들은 다른 것들보다 더 비싸다.

해설 이 문장은 주어(The apartments), 동사(are), 보어(more expensive)를 갖춘 완전한 절이므로, ___ ~ park는 수식어 거품으로 보아야 한다. 이 수식어 거품은 빈칸 앞의 명사(The apartments)를 선행사로 갖는 관계절이므로 모든 보기가 정답의 후보이다. 관계절 내에 동사(overlook)가 있고 주어가 없으므로 주격 관계대명사 (A) that이 정답이다. 목적격 관계대명사 (B) whom은 사물을 선행사로 가질 수 없고, 목적어가 생략된 불완전한 절을 이끌기 때문에 답이 될 수 없다.

어휘 overlook v. 내려다보다 expensive adj. 비싼

02 관계대명사 채우기

해석 본사가 파리에 있는, 그 도시에 기반을 둔 한 회사가 뉴욕에 지점을 열 것이다.

해설 이 문장은 주어(A Paris-based company), 동사(is opening), 목적어(a branch)를 갖춘 완전한 절이므로, ___ ~ city는 수식어 거품으로 보아야 한다. 빈칸 뒤에 선행사(A Paris-based company)가 소유하는 명사(headquarters)가 있으므로 소유격 관계대명사 (B) whose가 정답이다. 관계대명사 (A)는 뒤에 불완전한 절이 와야 한다.

어휘 headquarters n. 본사, 본부 branch n. 지점, 지사

3초컷 정답 공식   p.231

| 01 (B) | 02 (C) | 03 (A) | 04 (B) | 05 (A) |
| 06 (B) | 07 (B) | 08 (A) |

01 등위접속사 채우기

해석 그 기계는 대용량을 처리할 만큼 충분히 강력하지 않지만, 더 작은 작업에는 잘 작동한다.

해설 절(The machine ~ volumes)과 절(it ~ tasks)을 대등하게 연결해 주는 등위접속사가 필요하고 '그 기계는 대용량을 처리할 만큼 충분히 강력하지 않지만, 더 작은 작업에는 잘 작동한다'라는 의미가 되어야 하므로 등위접속사 (B) but(하지만, 그러나)이 정답이다. (D) or는 '또는'이라는 의미이다. 전치사 (A) to와 (C) between은 절과 절을 연결할 수 없다.

어휘 powerful adj. 강력한 handle v. 처리하다, 다루다 volume n. 양, 분량

02 등위접속사 채우기

해석 메인가는 지금 붐비지 않지만, 오늘 늦게는 붐빌 것이다.

해설 절(Main Avenue ~ moment)과 절(it ~ today)을 대등하게 연결해 주는 등위접속사가 필요하고 '메인가는 지금 붐비지 않지만, 오늘 늦게는 붐빌 것이다'라는 의미가 되어야 하므로 등위접속사 (C) but(하지만, 그러나)이 정답이다. (A) nor는 neither와 함께 neither A nor B(A도 B도 아닌)의 상관접속사 형태로 쓰인다. 전치사 (B) with와 (D) by는 절과 절을 연결할 수 없다.

어휘 crowded adj. 붐비는, 혼잡한 at the moment 지금, 현재

03 관계대명사 채우기

해석 교육 프로그램에 참여하는 모든 직원은 수료증을 받을 것이다.

해설 이 문장은 주어(All employees), 동사(will receive), 목적어(a certificate of completion)를 갖춘 완전한 절이므로, ___ ~ program은 수식어 거품으로 보아야 한다. 이 수식어 거품은 빈칸 앞의 명사구(All employees)를 선행사로 갖는 관계절이므로 모든 보기가 정답의 후보이다. 선행사가 사람이고 빈칸 뒤에 주어가 없는 불완전한 절이 왔으므로 주격 관계대명사 (A) who가 정답이다. 목적격 관계대명사 (B) whom은 목적어가 생략된 불완전한 절을 이끌기 때문에 답이 될 수 없다. (C) whose는 뒤에 선행사가 소유하는 명사가 와야 한다. (D) which는 사람을 선행사로 가질 수 없다.

어휘 participate v. 참여하다 certificate of completion 수료증

04 관계대명사 채우기

해석 디자인 변경을 요청한 고객은 추가 비용을 부담하기로 동의했다.

해설 이 문장은 주어(The client), 동사(has agreed), 목적어(to cover ~ costs)를 갖춘 완전한 절이므로, ___ ~ change는 수식어 거품으로 보아야 한다. 이 수식어 거품은 빈칸 앞의 명사(The client)를 선행사로 갖는 관계절이므로 관계대명사 (B) that이 정답이다. 목적격 관계대명사 (A) whom은 목적어가 생략된 불완전한 절을 이끌기 때문에 답이 될 수 없다. (C) which는 사람을 선행사로 가질 수 없고, (D) whose는 뒤에 선행사가 소유하는 명사가 와야 한다.

어휘 request v. 요청하다 cover v. 부담하다, 메우다 additional adj. 추가적인

05 관계대명사 채우기

해석 Nova 대학교는 연구 프로젝트가 지속 가능성에 초점을 맞추는 학과들에 보조금을 제공할 것이다.

해설 이 문장은 주어(Nova University), 동사(will provide), 목적어(grants)를 갖춘 완전한 절이므로, ___ ~ sustainability는 수식어 거품으로 보아야 한다. 빈칸 뒤에 선행사(departments)가 소유하는 명사구(research projects)가 있으므로 소유격 관계대명사 (A) whose가 정답이다. 지시대명사 (B)는 관계절을 이끌 수 없다. 관계대명사 (C)와 (D)는 뒤에 불완전한 절이 와야 한다.

어휘 grant n. 보조금 focus on ~에 초점을 맞추다 sustainability n. 지속 가능성

06 관계대명사 채우기

해석 우리의 보증은 일련번호가 온라인에 등록된 제품들을 보장한다.

해설 이 문장은 주어(Our warranty), 동사(covers), 목적어(products)를 갖춘 완전한 절이므로, ____ ~ online은 수식어 거품으로 보아야 한다. 빈칸 뒤에 선행사(products)가 소유하는 명사구(serial numbers)가 있으므로 소유격 관계대명사 (B) whose가 정답이다. 형용사 또는 부사 (A)는 관계절을 이끌 수 없다. 관계대명사 (C)와 (D)는 뒤에 불완전한 절이 와야 한다.

어휘 warranty n. 보증, 보증서 cover v. 보장하다 serial number 일련번호

07 관계대명사 채우기

해석 그 최고 경영자는 회의에서 회사의 새로운 제품 라인을 발표했는데, 그곳에는 500명이 넘는 업계 전문가들이 참석했다.

해설 이 문장은 주어(The CEO), 동사(unveiled), 목적어(the company's new product line)를 갖춘 완전한 절이므로, ____ ~ professionals은 수식어 거품으로 보아야 한다. 이 수식어 거품은 동사(was attended)가 있으나 주어가 없는 불완전한 절이고, 빈칸 앞에 콤마가 있는 것으로 보아 빈칸 이하가 앞에 나온 사물 명사(the conference)에 대해 부가 설명을 해주는 계속적 용법으로 쓰였다는 것을 알 수 있다. 따라서 주격 관계대명사 (B) which가 정답이다. (A) that은 사물 선행사를 가질 수 있지만, 콤마 바로 뒤에 올 수 없다. (C) whose는 뒤에 선행사가 소유하는 명사가 와야 한다. 재귀대명사 (D)는 수식어 거품을 이끌 수 없다.

어휘 unveil v. 발표하다 conference n. 회의 attend v. 참석하다, 참여하다 professional n. 전문가

08 관계대명사 채우기

해석 20년 넘게 경제학을 가르쳐온 Kim 교수는 지난달에 새 교재를 출판했다.

해설 이 문장은 주어(Professor Kim), 동사(published), 목적어(a new textbook)를 갖춘 완전한 절이므로, ____ ~ 20 years는 수식어 거품으로 보아야 한다. 이 수식어 거품은 동사(has been teaching)가 있으나 주어가 없는 불완전한 절이고, 빈칸 앞에 콤마가 있는 것으로 보아 빈칸 이하가 앞에 나온 사람 명사구(Professor Kim)에 대해 부가 설명을 해주는 계속적 용법으로 쓰였다는 것을 알 수 있다. 따라서 주격 관계대명사 (A) who가 정답이다. (B) which는 사람을 선행사로 가질 수 없다. (C) that은 사람 선행사를 가질 수 있지만, 콤마 바로 뒤에 올 수 없다. (D) whose는 뒤에 선행사가 소유하는 명사가 와야 한다.

어휘 economics n. 경제학 publish v. 출판하다, 발행하다 textbook n. 교재, 교과서

HACKERS TEST   p.232

01 (A)	02 (B)	03 (C)	04 (A)	05 (B)
06 (B)	07 (A)	08 (B)	09 (A)	10 (A)
11 (C)	12 (B)	13 (C)	14 (D)	15 (B)
16 (A)	17 (A)	18 (D)	19 (B)	20 (C)
21 (B)	22 (D)	23 (C)	24 (D)	

01 등위접속사 채우기

해석 Lakeford 지점은 월요일에 휴업할 것이므로, 고객들은 가까운 지점을 방문하도록 요청된다.

해설 절(The Lakeford branch ~ Monday)과 절(customers ~ locations)을 연결할 수 있는 접속사가 필요하므로 등위접속사 (A)와 (C)가 정답의 후보이다. 'Lakeford 지점이 월요일에 휴업할 것이므로, 고객들은 가까운 지점을 방문하도록 요청된다'라는 의미가 되어야 하므로 인과 관계를 나타내는 등위접속사 (A) so(그러므로, 그래서)가 정답이다. (C) or는 '또는'이라는 의미이다. 전치사 (B) about(~에 대해), 형용사 또는 부사 (D) even(평평한; ~조차, 훨씬)은 절과 절을 연결할 수 없다. 참고로, 등위접속사 so는 오직 절과 절을 연결할 수 있으며, 단어나 구는 연결하지 못한다.

어휘 close v. 휴업하다, 끝내다 nearby adj. 가까운; adv. 가까이에

02 상관접속사 채우기

해석 승객들은 셀프 서비스 키오스크에서 체크인하거나 항공사의 모바일 앱을 사용할 수 있다.

해설 등위접속사 or와 맞는 짝인 (B) either(둘 중 하나의)가 정답이다. (A)와 (C)는 함께 상관접속사 neither A nor B(A도 B도 아닌)의 형태로 쓰인다. (D)는 and와 함께 상관접속사 both A and B(A와 B 둘 다)의 형태로 쓰인다.

어휘 passenger n. 승객 airline n. 항공사

03 관계대명사 채우기

해석 마을의 외곽에 농장을 소유한 가족이 있는 Ms. Ku에 의해 여러 상자의 과일이 기부되었다.

해설 이 문장은 주어(Several crates of fruit)와 동사(were donated)를 갖춘 완전한 절이므로, ____ ~ town은 수식어 거품으로 보아야 한다. 빈칸 뒤에 선행사(Ms. Ku)가 소유하는 명사(family)가 있으므로 소유격 관계대명사 (C) whose가 정답이다. 대명사 (A)와 (D), 지시대명사 또는 지시형용사 (B)는 수식어 거품을 이끌 수 없다.

어휘 crate n. 상자, 나무 상자 donate v. 기부하다, 기증하다

04 등위접속사 채우기

해석 모든 Kentworth 공장 방문객은 경비실에서 서명을 하고 손님용 출입증을 받아 가는 것이 요구된다.

해설 to 부정사구(to sign in at the security office)와 to 부정사구(to pick up a guest pass)를 대등하게 연결해 주는 등위접속사가 필요하므로 등위접속사 (A)와 (B)가 정답의 후보이다. '경비실에서 서명을 하고 손님용 출입증을 받아 가는 것이 요구된다'라는 의미가 되어야 하므로 (A) and(그리고)가 정답이다. 참고로, 해당 문장은 빈칸과 pick 사이에 to 부정사가 생략된 구조임을 알아둔다. (B) yet은 '그러나'라는 의미이다. 전치사 (C)는 접속사 자리에 올 수 없다. (D) which는 '어떤'이라는 의미의 의문사, 또는 사물을 선행사로 하는 관계대명사이다.

어휘 sign in 서명하다 security office 경비실 pick up ~을 받다, 얻다 pass n. 출입증

05 관계대명사 채우기 [정답 공식 04]

해석 고객들은 그들이 하는 각 구매마다 포인트를 받을 것이고, 그것은 그들이 상점에서 판매되는 다른 제품들을 사는 데 쓸 수 있다.

해설 이 문장은 주어(Customers), 동사(will receive), 목적어(points)를 갖춘 완전한 절이므로, ____ ~ store는 수식어 거품으로 보아야 한다. 이 수식어 거품은 동사(can use)가 있으나 목적어가 없는 불완전한 절이고, 빈칸 앞에 콤마가 있는 것으로 보아 빈칸 이하가 앞에 나온 사물 명사(points)에 대해 부가 설명을 해주는 계속적 용법으로 쓰였다는 것을 알 수 있다. 따라서 목적격 관계대명사 (B) which가 정답이다. 의문사 (A), 지시대명사 또는 지시형용사 (C)는 수식어 거품을 이끌 수 없다. (D) that은 사물 선행사를 가질 수 있지만, 콤마 바로 뒤에 올 수 없다.

어휘 purchase n. 구매

06 상관접속사 채우기

해석 Tim Kelly는 그의 소셜 미디어 피드와 잡지 기사 둘 다에서 소비자 가전 제품을 평가한다.

해설 상관접속사 both와 맞는 짝인 (B) and가 정답이다. 등위접속사 (A) so는 오직 절과 절을 연결할 수 있으며, 단어나 구는 연결하지 못한다. 부사 (C) not(~이 아니다)은 접속사 자리에 올 수 없다. 전치사 또는 접속사 (D) than(~보다)은 어색한 의미를 만들기 때문에 답이 될 수 없다.

어휘 evaluate v. 평가하다 appliance n. 가전제품

07 관계대명사 채우기
해석 7월 18일까지 Oriang Health 스파의 설문조사를 완료한 사람들에게 상품권이 주어질 것이다.
해설 이 문장은 주어(Gift certificates)와 동사(will be given)를 갖춘 완전한 절이므로, ___ complete ~ July 18은 수식어 거품으로 보아야 한다. 이 수식어 거품은 지시대명사 those를 뒤에서 꾸미는 관계절이므로 관계대명사 (A) who가 정답이다. 주격 인칭대명사 (B), 의문사 (C), 소유대명사(D)는 관계대명사 자리에 올 수 없다. 참고로, those who는 '~하는 사람들'이라는 의미로 자주 쓰이는 표현임을 알아둔다.
어휘 gift certificate 상품권 complete v. 완료하다 survey n. (설문)조사

08 등위접속사 채우기 [정답공식 01]
해석 영업팀은 제품을 홍보하는 것을 훌륭히 잘 해냈지만, 그 기기는 기술적 문제로 인해 인기가 없었다.
해설 절(The sales team ~ the product)과 절(the device ~ technical issues)을 대등하게 연결해 주는 등위접속사가 필요하고 '영업팀은 제품을 홍보하는 것을 훌륭히 잘 해냈지만, 그 기기는 인기가 없었다'라는 의미가 되어야 하므로 등위접속사 (B) but(하지만, 그러나)이 정답이다. (A) and는 '그리고', (C) so는 '그래서, 그러므로'라는 의미이다. 전치사 (D)는 접속사 자리에 올 수 없다.
어휘 promote v. 홍보하다 device n. 기기, 장치 technical adj. 기술적인 issue n. 문제

09 관계대명사 채우기 [정답공식 02]
해석 프로젝트를 도왔던 그 인턴은 정규직 일자리를 제안받았다.
해설 이 문장은 주어(The intern), 동사(was offered), 목적어(a full-time job)를 갖춘 완전한 절이므로, ___ ~ project는 수식어 거품으로 보아야 한다. 이 수식어 거품은 빈칸 앞의 명사(The intern)를 선행사로 갖는 관계절이므로 관계대명사 (A), (B), (C)가 정답의 후보이다. 선행사가 사람이고 빈칸 뒤에 주어가 없는 불완전한 절이 왔으므로 주격 관계대명사 (A) who가 정답이다. 참고로, 이 문장은 목적어를 2개 가지는 4형식 동사 offer가 수동태로 쓰이면서 목적어 1개가 뒤에 그대로 남아 있는 구조이다. (B) which는 사람을 선행사로 가질 수 없다. (C) whose는 뒤에 선행사가 소유하는 명사가 와야 한다. 지시대명사 또는 지시형용사 (D) this는 수식어 거품을 이끌 수 없다.
어휘 assist v. 돕다, 조력하다 full-time adj. 정규직의

10 상관접속사 채우기
해석 현재 투자자들과 잠재적인 투자자들 둘 다 3월 15일에 주주 총회에 참석하도록 요청받는다.
해설 등위접속사 and와 맞는 짝인 (A) Both(둘 다)가 정답이다. 한정사 또는 대명사 (B) Each는 접속사 자리에 올 수 없다. (C) Either는 or과 함께 상관접속사 either A or B(A 또는 B 중 하나)의 형태로 쓰인다. 지시대명사 또는 지시형용사 (D) This는 접속사 자리에 올 수 없다.
어휘 current adj. 현재의, 지금의 prospective adj. 잠재적인, 장래의 investor n. 투자자 shareholders n. 주주

11 관계대명사 채우기
해석 모든 기술자는 지난주에 보고된 문제들을 바로잡기 위해 일하고 있다.
해설 이 문장은 주어(All technicians)와 동사(are working)를 갖춘 완전한 절이므로, ___ ~ week는 수식어 거품으로 보아야 한다. 이 수식어 거품은 빈칸 앞의 명사(the problems)를 선행사로 갖는 관계절이므로 관계대명사 (A), (B), (C)가 정답의 후보이다. 관계절 내에 동사(were reported)가 있고 주어가 없으므로 주격 관계대명사 (C) that이 정답이다. (A) who는 선행사가 사람일 때 쓸 수 있고, (B) whose는 뒤에 선행사가 소유하는 명사가 와야 한다. 부사 (D) ahead(앞에)는 수식어 거품을 이끌 수 없다.
어휘 technician n. 기술자 fix v. 바로잡다, 고치다 report v. 보고하다

12 관계대명사 채우기
해석 우리가 무역 박람회에서 만난 그 회사 대표들은 가치 있는 동업 기회를 제안했다.
해설 이 문장은 주어(The company representatives), 동사(offered), 목적어(valuable partnership opportunities)를 갖춘 완전한 절이므로, ___ ~ show는 수식어 거품으로 보아야 한다. 이 수식어 거품은 빈칸 앞의 명사구(The company representatives)를 선행사로 갖는 관계절이므로 관계대명사 (B), (C), (D)가 정답의 후보이다. 선행사가 사람이고 빈칸 뒤에 목적어가 없는 불완전한 절이 왔으므로 목적격 관계대명사 (B) whom이 정답이다. (C) which는 사람을 선행사로 가질 수 없다. 관계대명사 (D) whose는 뒤에 선행사가 소유하는 명사가 와야 한다. 목적격 인칭대명사 (A)는 수식어 거품을 이끌 수 없다.
어휘 representative n. 대표, 담당자 trade show 무역 박람회 valuable adj. 가치 있는, 귀중한 partnership n. 동업 opportunity n. 기회

13 관계대명사 채우기 [정답공식 03]
해석 사진이 올해 잡지 표지로 선정된 사진작가는 10,000달러의 상금을 받을 것이다.
해설 이 문장은 주어(The photographer), 동사(will be given), 목적어(a cash prize of 10,000 dollars)를 갖춘 완전한 절이므로, ___ ~ cover는 수식어 거품으로 보아야 한다. 빈칸 뒤에 선행사(The photographer)가 소유하는 명사(image)가 있으므로 소유격 관계대명사 (C) whose가 정답이다. 관계대명사 (A)는 뒤에 불완전한 절이 와야 한다. 전치사 (B) as (~ 같이), 형용사 또는 부사 (D) even(평평한; ~조차, 훨씬)은 수식어 거품을 이끌 수 없다. (B)를 '~하기 때문에'라는 의미의 부사절 접속사로 본다 해도, 부사절 접속사는 주절의 주어와 동사 사이에 올 수 없으므로 답이 될 수 없다.
어휘 cash prize 상금

14 상관접속사 채우기
해석 식당 관리자도 소유주도 내일 예정된 화재 안전 점검에 대해 통보받지 못했다.
해설 상관접속사 Neither와 맞는 짝인 (D) nor가 정답이다. (A) of는 '~의'라는 의미로 소유관계를 나타내는 전치사이다. (B) both와 (C) and는 상관접속사 both A and B(A와 B 둘 다)의 형태로 쓰인다.
어휘 owner n. 소유주 notify v. 통보하다, 알리다 inspection n. 점검, 검사

15 관계대명사 채우기 [정답공식 04]
해석 그 기관은 새로운 복리후생 제도를 발표했는데, 그것은 직원들에게 잘 받아들여졌다.
해설 이 문장은 주어(The organization), 동사(announced), 목적어(a new benefits package)를 갖춘 완전한 절이므로, ___ ~ employees는 수식어 거품으로 보아야 한다. 이 수식어 거품은 동사(was received)가 있으나 주어가 없는 불완전한 절이고, 빈칸 앞에 콤마가 있는 것으로 보아 빈칸 이하가 앞에 나온 사물 명사구(a new benefits package)에 대해 부가 설명을 해주는 계속적 용법으로 쓰였다는 것을 알 수 있다. 따라서 주격 관계대명사 (B) which가 정답이다. (A) that은 사물 선행사를 가질 수 있지만, 콤마 바로 뒤에 올 수 없다. 의문사 (C)와 부정대명사 (D)는 수식어 거품을 이끌 수 없다.
어휘 organization n. 기관 announce v. 발표하다, 공지하다 benefits package 복리후생 제도

16 관계대명사 채우기 [정답공식 02]
해석 광고된 것과 다른 직무에 지원하고자 하는 입사 지원자들은 별도의 지원서를 제출해야 한다.
해설 이 문장은 주어(Job candidates), 동사(must submit), 목적어(separate applications)를 갖춘 완전한 절이므로, ___ ~ advertised는 수식어 거품으로 보아야 한다. 이 수식어 거품은 빈칸 앞의 명사구(Job candidates)를 선행사로 갖는 관계절이므로 모든 보기가 정답의 후보이다. 선행사가 사람이고 빈칸 뒤에 주어가 없는 불완전한 절이 왔으므로 주격 관계대명사 (A) who가 정답이다. (B) which는 사람을 선행사

로 가질 수 없다. 목적격 관계대명사 (C) whom은 목적어가 생략된 불완전한 절을 이끌기 때문에 답이 될 수 없다. (D) whose는 뒤에 선행사가 소유하는 명사가 와야 한다.

어휘 candidate n. 지원자, 후보자 advertise v. 광고하다 submit v. 제출하다
application n. 지원서

17 등위접속사 채우기
해석 5년 근무 기념일로, 직원들은 손목시계, 만년필, 또는 고급 가죽 지갑을 선물로 선택할 수 있다.
해설 동사(may select)의 목적어인 명사(wristwatch), 명사구(fountain pen), 명사구(premium leather wallet)를 대등하게 연결해 주는 등위접속사가 필요하고 '손목시계, 만년필, 또는 고급 가죽 지갑을 선택할 수 있다'라는 의미가 되어야 하므로 등위접속사 (A) or(또는)가 정답이다. 등위접속사 (B)는 '그러나, 하지만'이라는 의미이고, (C)는 오직 절과 절을 연결할 수 있으며, 단어나 구는 연결할 수 없다. (D)는 neither와 함께 상관접속사 neither A nor B(A도 B도 아닌)의 형태로 쓰인다.
어휘 service n. 근무 anniversary n. 기념일 wristwatch n. 손목시계
fountain pen 만년필 premium adj. 고급의, 프리미엄의 leather n. 가죽

18 격에 맞는 인칭대명사 채우기
해석 SkyNet 텔레비전은 그것의 유명한 여름 영화제가 다음 달 로스앤젤레스에서 생방송으로 중계될 것이라고 발표했다.
해설 명사구(summer film festival) 앞에서 형용사처럼 명사를 꾸밀 수 있는 인칭대명사는 소유격이므로 소유격 인칭대명사 (D) its가 정답이다. 주격 또는 목적격 인칭대명사 (A), 소유격 관계대명사 (B), 주격 인칭대명사 (C)는 명사를 꾸밀 수 없다. (B)를 의문형용사로 본다 해도 '누구의 유명한 여름 영화제'라는 어색한 의미를 만들기 때문에 답이 될 수 없다.
어휘 prestigious adj. 유명한, 일류의 film festival 영화제
broadcast v. 중계하다, 방송하다 live adv. 생방송으로

19 상관접속사 채우기
해석 사회 활동뿐만 아니라 스포츠에 참여하는 성인들은 스트레스를 덜 받는 것으로 널리 인식된다.
해설 전치사 in 다음의 명사구(sports, social activities)를 연결하는 자리이므로 'B뿐만 아니라 A도'라는 뜻의 (B) as well as가 정답이다. (A) within은 '~ 이내에'라는 의미로 기간을 나타내는 전치사이고, (C) accordingly는 '따라서', (D) ever는 '어느 때고, 언제든'이라는 의미를 나타내는 부사이다.
어휘 recognize v. 인식하다 engage in ~에 참여하다

20 관계대명사 채우기
해석 Ms. Dawson은 올해 연례 사무실 파티를 준비하고 있는 그룹의 일원이다.
해설 이 문장은 주어(Ms. Dawson), 동사(is), 보어(part of the group)를 갖춘 완전한 절이므로, ___ ~ this year는 수식어 거품으로 보아야 한다. 이 수식어 거품은 빈칸 앞의 명사(the group)를 선행사로 갖는 관계절이므로 관계대명사 (C) that이 정답이다. 부사 (A)와 주격 인칭대명사 (D)는 수식어 거품을 이끌 수 없다. (B) whose는 뒤에 선행사가 소유하는 명사가 와야 한다.
어휘 organize v. 준비하다, 조직하다 annual adj. 연례의

21 주어와 수일치하는 동사 채우기
해석 원격 근무를 선택한 사람들은 최근 연구에서 더 높은 직무 만족도를 보고한다.
해설 빈칸은 명사(Those)를 꾸미는 주격 관계절(who ~ work)의 동사 자리이므로 동사 (A)와 (B)가 정답의 후보이다. 주격 관계절의 동사는 선행사(Those)와 수일치하므로 복수 동사 (B) opt(선택하다)가 정답이다. 단수 동사 (A)는 단수 선행사와 함께 써야 한다. 동명사 또는 현재분사 (C)와 to 부정사 (D)는 동사 자리에 올 수 없다.
어휘 remote adj. 원격의, 먼 satisfaction n. 만족(도) study n. 연구, 조사

22 부사 자리 채우기
해석 제조업체들은 운영비를 많이 낮출 방법들을 찾고 있다.
해설 to 부정사(to lower)를 꾸밀 수 있는 것은 부사이므로 부사 (D) considerably(많이, 상당히)가 정답이다. 동명사 또는 현재분사 (A), 형용사 (B)와 (C)는 to 부정사를 꾸밀 수 없다.
어휘 manufacturer n. 제조업체 lower v. 낮추다; adj. 더 낮은
operating cost 운영비, 경영비 considerate adj. 사려 깊은
considerable adj. 상당한

23 관계대명사 채우기
해석 지난달에 주문했던 그 장비가 마침내 창고에 도착했다.
해설 이 문장은 주어(The equipment)와 동사(has ~ arrived)를 갖춘 완전한 절이므로, ___ ~ month는 수식어 거품으로 보아야 한다. 이 수식어 거품은 빈칸 앞의 명사(The equipment)를 선행사로 갖는 관계절이므로 관계대명사 (A), (B), (C)가 정답의 후보이다. 선행사가 사물이고 빈칸 뒤에 주어가 없는 불완전한 절이 왔으므로 주격 관계대명사 (C) which가 정답이다. (A) who와 (B) whom은 사물을 선행사로 가질 수 없다. 의문사 (D)는 수식어 거품을 이끌 수 없다.
어휘 equipment n. 장비 order v. 주문하다 warehouse n. 창고

24 상관접속사 채우기
해석 계약 조건은 서명일 이후에는 협상의 여지가 있지도 조정 가능하지도 않다.
해설 등위접속사 nor와 맞는 짝인 (D) neither(둘 중 어느 것도 아닌)가 정답이다. (A)는 and와 함께 상관접속사 both A and B(A와 B 둘 다)의 형태로 쓰이며, (B)는 or와 함께 상관접속사 either A or B(A 또는 B 중 하나)의 형태로 쓰인다. 빈도 부사 (C) often(종종, 자주)은 두 단어를 연결할 수 없다.
어휘 contract term 계약 조건 negotiable adj. 협상의 여지가 있는
adjustable adj. 조정 가능한

빈출 어휘 부사 1

토익 실전문제

| 01 (D) | 02 (B) | 03 (C) | 04 (C) | 05 (D) |
| 06 (A) | 07 (A) | 08 (B) | | |

01 부사 어휘 고르기
해석 개발업자는 이전에 쇼핑센터가 차지했던 부지에 연립 주택을 지었다.
해설 '이전에 쇼핑센터가 차지했던 부지에 연립 주택을 짓다'라는 문맥이므로 (D) previously(이전에)가 정답이다. (A) seriously는 '진지하게, 진심으로', (B) gradually는 '차츰, 서서히', (C) particularly는 '특히'라는 의미이다.
어휘 developer n. 개발업자 townhouse n. 연립 주택 lot n. 부지
occupy v. 차지하다, 점유하다

02 부사 어휘 고르기
해석 Arqua사는 잠재적인 공격을 방지하기 위해 보안 업데이트를 신속히 설치하라고 사용자들에게 조언했다.
해설 '보안 업데이트를 신속히 설치하라고 조언하다'라는 문맥이므로 (B) promptly(신속히)가 정답이다. (A) justly는 '공정하게', (C) evenly는 '고르게, 균등하게', (D) abundantly는 '풍부하게'라는 의미이다.
어휘 install v. 설치하다 security n. 보안 potential adj. 잠재적인
attack n. 공격

03 부사 어휘 고르기
해석 하루짜리 워크숍은 정확히 오전 10시에 시작할 것이므로, 참가자들은 늦지 않도록 권장된다.

해설 '워크숍이 정확히 오전 10시에 시작하다'라는 문맥이므로 (C) precisely(정확히)가 정답이다. (A) closely는 '면밀히, 긴밀히', (B) smoothly는 '매끄럽게', (D) confidentially는 '기밀로, 비밀리에'라는 의미이다.

어휘 participant n. 참가자

04 부사 어휘 고르기

해석 챔피언십 농구 경기는 많은 대중의 관심을 끌었기 때문에, 표가 완전히 매진되었다.

해설 '경기가 많은 대중의 관심을 끌어서 표가 완전히 매진되다'라는 문맥이므로 (C) completely(완전히)가 정답이다. (A) regularly는 '정기적으로', (B) directly는 '직접, 곧장', (D) generally는 '일반적으로'라는 의미이다.

어휘 a great deal of 많은 public adj. 대중의 attention n. 관심

05 부사 어휘 고르기

해석 계획에 대한 모든 변경은 적용되기 전에 고객과 철저히 논의되어야 한다.

해설 '계획에 대한 모든 변경이 고객과 철저히 논의되다'라는 문맥이므로 (D) thoroughly(철저히)가 정답이다. (A) seemingly는 '겉보기에', (B) independently는 '독립적으로', (C) easily는 '쉽게'라는 의미이다.

어휘 discuss v. 논의하다 client n. 고객 apply v. 적용하다

06 부사 어휘 고르기

해석 Ms. Roberts는 마케팅 보고서를 마감일까지 완료하기 위해 부지런히 일했다.

해설 '보고서를 마감일까지 완료하기 위해 부지런히 일하다'라는 문맥이므로 (A) diligently(부지런히)가 정답이다. (B) obviously는 '분명히, 명백하게', (C) clearly는 '명확하게, 분명히', (D) distinctly는 '뚜렷하게'라는 의미이다.

어휘 complete v. 완료하다 deadline n. 마감일

07 부사 어휘 고르기

해석 패스트패션 회사들은 소비자들의 관심을 유지하기 위해 새로운 의류 상품을 자주 소개한다.

해설 '패스트패션 회사들이 새로운 의류 상품을 자주 소개하다'라는 문맥이므로 (A) frequently(자주, 빈번히)가 정답이다. (B) accidentally는 '우연히', (C) unexpectedly는 '뜻밖에, 예상치 않게', (D) nearly는 '거의'라는 의미이다.

어휘 introduce v. 소개하다 consumer n. 소비자

08 부사 어휘 고르기

해석 자유 무역 협정이 시행되었으므로 많은 식료품의 비용이 상당히 더 낮다.

해설 '자유 무역 협정이 시행되었으므로 식료품의 비용이 상당히 더 낮다'라는 문맥이므로 (B) considerably(상당히)가 정답이다. (A) extensively는 '광범위하게', (C) attentively는 '주의 깊게', (D) elsewhere는 '다른 곳에'라는 의미이다.

어휘 trade n. 무역 agreement n. 협정 implement v. 시행하다

DAY 11 부사절과 명사절

기출 포인트 01

실전 Check-up p.236

01 (B)   02 (A)

01 부사절 접속사 채우기

해석 눈보라가 사무실로의 이동을 어렵게 만들 것이기 때문에, 관리자는 내일 모두가 원격으로 근무하도록 결정했다.

해설 빈칸은 동사(will make)가 있는 거품절(___ the snowstorm ~ difficult)을 이끄는 부사절 접속사 자리이므로 이유를 나타내는 부사절 접속사 (B) Since가 정답이다. 전치사 (A)는 거품절을 이끌 수 없다.

어휘 snowstorm n. 눈보라 remotely adv. 원격으로

02 부사절 접속사 채우기

해석 군중은 국가대표 축구팀 선수들이 경기장에 입장하는 동안 큰 소리로 환호했다.

해설 빈칸은 동사(were entering)가 있는 거품절(___ the members ~ stadium)을 이끄는 부사절 접속사 자리이므로 시간을 나타내는 부사절 접속사 (A) while이 정답이다. 전치사 (B)는 거품절을 이끌 수 없다.

어휘 crowd n. 군중 stadium n. 경기장

기출 포인트 02

실전 Check-up p.237

01 (A)   02 (A)

01 부사절 접속사 채우기

해석 3층 보수공사가 완료되는 대로 Griswold 공공 도서관의 어린이 열람실이 열릴 것이다.

해설 빈칸은 동사(are finished)가 있는 거품절(___ the third-floor ~ finished)을 이끄는 부사절 접속사 자리이므로 모든 보기가 정답의 후보이다. '3층 보수공사가 완료되는 대로 Griswold 공공 도서관의 어린이 열람실이 열릴 것이다'라는 의미가 되어야 하므로 시간을 나타내는 부사절 접속사 (A) once(~하는 대로)가 정답이다. (B) so that은 '~할 수 있도록'이라는 의미이다.

어휘 reading room 열람실

02 부사절 접속사 채우기

해석 비록 NX 스마트폰의 최신 버전이 많은 기능을 포함하고 있지만, 이전 모델보다 인기가 덜하다.

해설 빈칸은 동사(includes)가 있는 거품절(___ the latest version ~ features)을 이끄는 부사절 접속사 자리이고, '비록 NX 스마트폰의 최신 버전이 많은 기능을 포함하고 있지만, 이전 모델보다 인기가 덜하다'라는 의미가 되어야 하므로 양보를 나타내는 부사절 접속사 (A) Although(비록 ~이지만, ~일지라도)가 정답이다. (B) Until은 '~할 때까지'라는 의미이다.

어휘 feature n. 기능 predecessor n. 이전 모델, 전임자

기출 포인트 03~04

실전 Check-up p.238

01 (A)   02 (B)

01 명사절 접속사 채우기

해석 고객들이 온라인 쇼핑을 선호하는지 매장 내 경험을 선호하는지는 소매업체들에게 중요한 정보이다.

해설 빈칸은 동사(is)의 주어 역할을 하는 명사절(___ customers ~ experiences)을 이끄는 명사절 접속사 자리이므로 명사절 접속사 (A) Whether(~인지 아닌지)가 정답이다. 부사절 접속사 (B)는 명사절을 이끌 수 없다.

어휘 prefer v. 선호하다 in-store adj. 매장 내의 crucial adj. 중요한 retailer n. 소매업체

02 명사절 접속사 채우기

해석 최근 시장 조사는 소비자 선호가 더 친환경적인 제품으로 바뀌고 있다는

것을 시사한다.
해설 빈칸은 동사(suggests)의 목적어 역할을 하는 명사절(___ consumer ~ products)을 이끄는 명사절 접속사 자리이므로 명사절 접속사 (B) that(~라는 것)이 정답이다. 부사절 접속사 (A)는 명사절을 이끌 수 없다.
어휘 consumer preference 소비자 선호   shift v. 바뀌다
eco-friendly adj. 친환경적인

기출 포인트 05

실전 Check-up   p.239
01 (A)   **02** (B)

01 명사절 접속사 채우기
해설 시의회는 새 커뮤니티 센터에 자금을 제공할지 아닐지 결정할 것이다.
해설 빈칸은 동사(will determine)의 목적어 역할을 하는 명사절(___ ~ center)을 이끄는 명사절 접속사 자리이므로 명사절 접속사 (A) whether(~인지 아닌지)가 정답이다. 부사절 접속사 (B)는 명사절 접속사를 이끌 수 없다.
어휘 determine v. 결정하다

02 명사절 접속사 채우기
해설 그녀의 유일한 관심사는 그 계약이 1년 더 갱신될지 아닐지였다.
해설 빈칸은 동사(was)의 보어 역할을 하는 명사절(___ the contract ~ year)을 이끄는 명사절 접속사 자리이므로 명사절 접속사 (B) if(~인지 아닌지)가 정답이다. 부사절 접속사 (A)는 명사절을 이끌 수 없다.
어휘 concern n. 관심사, 우려   contract n. 계약   renew v. 갱신하다

기출 포인트 06

실전 Check-up   p.240
01 (A)   **02** (B)

01 의문사 채우기
해설 그 설문조사는 소비자들에게 텔레비전을 구매할 때 그들이 어느 기능들을 가장 중요하게 생각하는지에 대해 물었다.
해설 빈칸은 전치사(about)의 목적어 역할을 하는 명사절(___ features ~ television)을 이끌면서 뒤에 나온 명사(features)를 꾸밀 수 있는 의문형용사 자리이므로 의문형용사 (A) which가 정답이다. 명사절 접속사 (B)는 뒤에 완전한 절이 와야 하므로 답이 될 수 없다.
어휘 survey n. 설문조사   consumer n. 소비자   feature n. 기능, 특징

02 복합관계대명사 채우기
해설 작가에 의해 제출되는 무엇이든 간에 출판 전에 잡지 편집자에게 검토를 받아야 한다.
해설 동사(must be reviewed)의 주어 역할을 하는 절(___ ~ writer)의 맨 앞에 올 수 있는 것은 명사절 접속사이므로 복합관계대명사 (B) Whatever가 정답이다. 부정대명사 또는 부정형용사 (A)는 절을 이끌 수 없다.
어휘 editor n. 편집자   publication n. 출판

3초컷 정답 공식   p.241
01 (C)   **02** (D)   **03** (B)   **04** (D)   **05** (D)
06 (A)   **07** (C)   **08** (D)

01 부사절 접속사 채우기
해설 우리가 유럽에 지사를 연 이래로 우리의 국제 고객층이 빠르게 확장했다.
해설 빈칸은 동사(opened)가 있는 거품절(___ we opened ~ Europe)을 이끄는 부사절 접속사 자리이고, '유럽에 지사를 연 이래로 국제 고객층이 빠르게 확장했다'라는 의미가 되어야 하므로 시간을 나타내는 부사절 접속사 (C) since(~한 이래로)가 정답이다. 전치사 (A), (B), (D)는 거품절을 이끌 수 없다.
어휘 client base 고객층   expand v. 확장하다   rapidly adv. 빠르게

02 부사절 접속사 채우기
해설 회사의 구조조정 정책이 시행된 이래로 6개월이 되었다.
해설 빈칸은 동사(were implemented)가 있는 거품절(___ the company's restructuring ~ implemented)을 이끄는 부사절 접속사 자리이고, '회사의 구조조정 정책이 시행된 이래로 6개월이 되었다'라는 의미가 되어야 하므로 시간을 나타내는 부사절 접속사 (D) since(~한 이래로)가 정답이다. (A) before는 '~하기 전에', (B) until은 '~할 때까지', (C) while은 '~하는 동안'이라는 의미이다.
어휘 restructuring n. 구조조정   policy n. 정책
implement v. 시행하다, 이행하다

03 부사절 접속사 채우기
해설 시설 관리과가 새로운 투숙객들이 도착하기 전에 방을 청소할 수 있도록 모든 투숙객은 오후 12시까지 체크아웃해야 한다.
해설 빈칸은 동사(can clean up)가 있는 거품절(___ housekeeping ~ arrive)을 이끄는 부사절 접속사 자리이고, '시설 관리과가 방을 청소할 수 있도록 모든 투숙객은 오후 12시까지 체크아웃해야 한다'라는 의미가 되어야 하므로 목적을 나타내는 부사절 접속사 (B) so that(~할 수 있도록)이 정답이다. 형용사 또는 부사 (A)와 접속부사 (D)는 거품절을 이끌 수 없다. (C) as if는 '마치 ~처럼'이라는 의미이다.
어휘 housekeeping n. 시설 관리과

04 부사절 접속사 채우기
해설 그 행사는 더 많은 사람들을 수용할 수 있도록 더 큰 컨벤션 센터로 옮겨졌다.
해설 빈칸은 동사(could accommodate)가 있는 거품절(___ it ~ people)을 이끄는 부사절 접속사 자리이고, '그 행사가 더 많은 사람들을 수용할 수 있도록 더 큰 컨벤션 센터로 옮겨졌다'라는 의미가 되어야 하므로 목적을 나타내는 부사절 접속사 (D) so that(~할 수 있도록)이 정답이다. (A) if는 '만약 ~이라면', (B) when은 '~할 때'라는 의미이다. 전치사 (C)는 거품절을 이끌 수 없다.
어휘 accommodate v. 수용하다

05 부사절 접속사 채우기
해설 주방 수리가 이루어지는 동안 식당은 금요일 저녁에 문을 닫을 것이다.
해설 빈칸은 동사(is taking place)가 있는 거품절(___ the kitchen ~ place)을 이끄는 부사절 접속사 자리이고, '주방 수리가 이루어지는 동안'이라는 의미가 되어야 하므로 시간을 나타내는 부사절 접속사 (D) while(~하는 동안)이 정답이다. (A) until은 '~할 때까지', (C) though는 '비록 ~이지만, ~일지라도'라는 의미이다. 부사 (B)는 거품절을 이끌 수 없다.
어휘 renovation n. 수리   take place 이루어지다

06 부사절 접속사 채우기
해설 승객들은 비행기가 난기류를 겪는 동안 침착함을 유지했다.
해설 빈칸은 동사(was experiencing)가 있는 거품절(___ the airplane ~ turbulence)을 이끄는 부사절 접속사 자리이고, '승객들은 비행기가 난기류를 겪는 동안 침착함을 유지했다'라는 의미가 되어야 하므로 시간을 나타내는 부사절 접속사 (A) while(~하는 동안)이 정답이다. 등위접속사 (B) so는 '그래서, 그러므로'라는 의미이다. 부사절 접속사 (C) until은 '~할 때까지'라는 의미이다. 형용사 또는 부사 (D)는 거품절을 이끌 수

없다.

어휘 passenger n. 승객 calm adj. 침착한 turbulence n. 난기류

07 명사절 접속사 채우기
해석 그 계약은 송장을 받은 후 30일 이내에 대금이 지급되어야 한다는 것을 분명히 명시한다.

해설 빈칸은 동사(states)의 목적어 역할을 하는 명사절(___ payment ~ invoice)을 이끄는 명사절 접속사 자리이므로 명사절 접속사 (C) that (~라는 것)이 정답이다. 의문사 (A) what 뒤에는 불완전한 절이 와야 하므로 답이 될 수 없다. 등위접속사(B)와 (D)는 명사절을 이끌 수 없다.

어휘 contract n. 계약 explicitly adv. 명시적으로 state v. 명시하다, 기술하다 payment n. 대금, 지불 invoice n. 송장, 청구서

08 명사절 접속사 채우기
해석 우리가 등산로로 떠나기 전에, 여행 가이드는 우리가 하이킹 여행을 위해 물을 가져올 것을 제안했다.

해설 빈칸은 동사(suggested)의 목적어 역할을 하는 명사절(___ we ~ trip)을 이끄는 명사절 접속사 자리이므로 명사절 접속사 (D) that(~라는 것)이 정답이다. 전치사 (A)와 (C)는 명사절을 이끌 수 없다. 의문사 (B) 뒤에는 불완전한 절이 와야 하므로 답이 될 수 없다.

어휘 depart v. 떠나다 mountain trail 등산로

HACKERS TEST
p.242

01 (D)	02 (A)	03 (B)	04 (A)	05 (A)
06 (A)	07 (B)	08 (B)	09 (C)	10 (C)
11 (C)	12 (A)	13 (D)	14 (D)	15 (C)
16 (B)	17 (C)	18 (B)	19 (B)	20 (A)
21 (C)	22 (D)	23 (A)	24 (A)	

01 부사절 접속사 채우기
해석 만약 사람들이 많은 질문을 가지고 있는 게 아니라면 발표는 일정보다 일찍 끝날 것이다.

해설 이 문장은 주어(The presentation)와 동사(will finish)를 갖춘 완전한 절이므로, ___ ~ questions는 수식어 거품으로 보아야 한다. 이 수식어 거품은 동사(have)가 있는 거품절이므로, 거품절을 이끌 수 있는 부사절 접속사 (C)와 (D)가 정답의 후보이다. '만약 사람들이 많은 질문을 가지고 있는 게 아니라면 발표가 일찍 끝날 것이다'라는 의미가 되어야 하므로 조건을 나타내는 부사절 접속사 (D) unless(만약 ~아니라면)가 정답이다. 부사절 접속사 (C) once는 '~하는 대로'라는 의미이다. 전치사 (A)와 (B)는 거품절이 아닌 거품구를 이끌며, (A)가 접속부사일 경우 수식어 거품을 이끌 수 없다.

어휘 presentation n. 발표 ahead of ~보다 일찍 besides prep. ~ 외에; adv. ~뿐만 아니라

02 의문사 채우기
해석 보고서는 회사가 다음 분기에 마케팅 노력을 어디에 집중해야 하는지 보여준다.

해설 빈칸은 동사(indicates)의 목적어 역할을 하는 명사절(___ the company ~ quarter)을 이끄는 명사절 접속사 자리이므로 모든 보기가 정답의 후보이다. 빈칸 뒤에 완전한 절이 왔으므로 의문부사 (A) where가 정답이다. 의문대명사 (B), (C), (D) 뒤에는 불완전한 절이 와야 하므로 답이 될 수 없다.

03 부사절 접속사 채우기 [정답 공식 01]
해석 지난봄에 우리가 새 소셜 미디어 관리자를 고용한 이래로 우리 회사의 온라인상에서의 존재감이 극적으로 향상되었다.

해설 빈칸은 동사(hired)가 있는 거품절(___ we hired ~ spring)을 이끄는 부사절 접속사 자리이고, '새 소셜 미디어 관리자를 고용한 이래로 회사의 존재감이 향상되었다'라는 의미가 되어야 하므로 시간을 나타내는 부사절 접속사 (B) since(~한 이래로)가 정답이다. 부사절 접속사 (C) until은 '~할 때까지'라는 의미이다. 전치사 (A)와 (D)는 거품절을 이끌 수 없다.

어휘 presence n. 존재감 dramatically adv. 극적으로

04 부사절 접속사 채우기
해석 다음 주까지 제품이 배송될 수 없음에도 불구하고 미용실의 공급업체는 헤어 제품 대금의 전액 지급을 요청했다.

해설 빈칸은 동사(cannot be shipped)가 있는 거품절(___ they ~ week)을 이끄는 부사절 접속사 자리이고, '다음 주까지 제품이 배송될 수 없음에도 불구하고 제품 대금의 전액 지급을 요청했다'라는 의미가 되어야 하므로 양보를 나타내는 부사절 접속사 (A) even though(비록 ~이지만, ~일지라도)가 정답이다. (C) as soon as는 '~하자마자'라는 의미이다. 전치사 (B)와 (D)는 거품절을 이끌 수 없다.

어휘 salon n. 미용실, 상점 supplier n. 공급업체 in full 전액으로, 완전히

05 부사절 접속사 채우기 [정답 공식 03]
해석 Wesleyville행 열차는 그곳의 역이 보수되고 있는 동안 Jaspers에 정차하지 않을 것이다.

해설 빈칸은 동사(is being renovated)가 있는 거품절(___ the station ~ renovated)을 이끄는 부사절 접속사 자리이고, '열차는 그곳의 역이 보수되고 있는 동안 정차하지 않을 것이다'라는 의미가 되어야 하므로 시간을 나타내는 부사절 접속사 (A) while(~하는 동안)이 정답이다. (D) until은 '~할 때까지'라는 의미이다. 부사 또는 전치사 (B)와 부사 (C)는 거품절을 이끌 수 없다.

어휘 bound for ~행의, ~을 향한 station n. 역

06 의문사 채우기
해석 그 관리자는 누가 주말 동안 기꺼이 일할 것인지 알고 싶어한다.

해설 빈칸은 to 부정사(to know)의 목적어 역할을 하는 명사절(___ might ~ the weekend)을 이끄는 명사절 접속사 자리이므로 명사절 접속사 (A), (B), (C)가 정답의 후보이다. '누가 주말 동안 기꺼이 일할 것인지 알고 싶어한다'라는 의미가 되어야 하고 빈칸 뒤에 불완전한 절이 왔으므로 의문대명사 (A) who가 정답이다. 의문부사 (B)와 (C)는 뒤에 완전한 절이 와야 하므로 답이 될 수 없다. 지시대명사 또는 지시형용사 (D)는 명사절을 이끌 수 없다.

어휘 be willing to 기꺼이 ~하다

07 부사절 접속사 채우기
해석 상품권은 상품권 보유자가 그것을 온라인에서 활성화한 후에 사용될 수 있다.

해설 빈칸은 동사(activates)가 있는 거품절(___ the cardholder ~ online)을 이끄는 부사절 접속사 자리이고, '상품권은 그것을 온라인에서 활성화한 후에 사용될 수 있다'라는 의미가 되어야 하므로 시간을 나타내는 부사절 접속사 (B) after(~한 후에)가 정답이다. (C) while은 '~하는 동안'이라는 의미이다. 형용사 또는 부사 (A)와 부사 (D)는 거품절을 이끌 수 없다.

어휘 gift card 상품권 cardholder n. 카드 소지자 activate v. 활성화시키다, 작동시키다

08 의문사 채우기
해석 그 요리사는 요리 수업 참가자들에게 정통 이탈리아 요리를 어떻게 준비할지 보여줄 것이다.

해설 빈칸은 동사(will show)의 목적어 역할을 하는 '의문사 + to 부정사'의 의문사 자리이므로 모든 보기가 정답의 후보이다. '정통 이탈리아 요리를 어떻게 준비할지 보여줄 것이다'라는 의미가 되어야 하므로 의문부사 (B) how가 정답이다. 의문사 (A), (C), (D)를 쓸 경우 각각 '정통 이탈리아 요리를 무엇을/어떤 것을/누구를 준비할지 보여줄 것이다'라는 어색한 문맥이 된다.

어휘 authentic adj. 정통의 dish n. 요리

09 명사절 접속사 채우기 정답공식 04
해석 건물의 화재 경보 테스트가 토요일 오전 8시에 있을 것이라고 거주자들에게 알려주세요.
해설 빈칸은 동사(inform)의 목적어 역할을 하는 명사절(___ a test ~ 8 A.M.)을 이끄는 명사절 접속사 자리이므로 명사절 접속사 (C) that(~라는 것)이 정답이다. 대명사 또는 형용사 (A)와 부사 (B)는 명사절을 이끌 수 없다. 의문사 (D) which 뒤에는 불완전한 절이 와야 하므로 답이 될 수 없다.
어휘 inform v. 알리다, 통지하다 resident n. 거주자, 주민 fire alarm 화재 경보

10 현재분사와 과거분사 구별하여 채우기
해석 전국 테니스 대회에 참가하는 모든 선수는 늦어도 6월 3일까지 대회에 등록하도록 요구된다.
해설 빈칸 앞의 명사(All players)를 꾸밀 수 있는 것은 형용사이므로 현재분사 (A)와 과거분사 (C)가 정답의 후보이다. 꾸밈을 받는 명사(All players)와 분사가 '참가하는 모든 선수'라는 의미의 능동 관계이므로 현재분사 (A) competing이 정답이다. 과거분사 (C) competed를 쓸 경우 '참가되는 모든 선수'라는 어색한 문맥이 된다. 동사 (B)와 (D)는 형용사 자리에 올 수 없다.
어휘 tournament n. 대회 compete v. 참가하다

11 명사절 접속사 채우기
해석 Paskow 식품이 직원 규모를 줄여야 할지 아닐지가 고려되고 있다.
해설 빈칸은 동사(is being considered)의 주어 역할을 하는 명사절(___ Paskow Foods ~ workforce)을 이끄는 명사절 접속사 자리이므로 명사절 접속사 (C) Whether(~인지 아닌지)가 정답이다. (D) If도 명사절 접속사로 쓰일 수 있지만, 주어 자리에는 올 수 없다. 전치사 (A)와 빈도 부사 (B)는 명사절을 이끌 수 없다.
어휘 performance n. 성과 workforce n. 직원, 노동자

12 전치사 채우기
해석 소유주 Sylvia Aspen은 증가하는 고객의 수 때문에 카페에 종업원을 더 고용하기로 결정했다.
해설 이 문장은 필수성분(Owner Sylvia Aspen ~ servers)을 갖춘 완전한 절이므로, ___ the increasing ~ customers는 수식어 거품으로 보아야 한다. 이 수식어 거품은 동사가 없는 거품구이므로, 보기 중 거품구를 이끌 수 있는 전치사 (C) due to(~ 때문에)가 정답이다. 부사절 접속사 (A) whereas(~한 반면에), (B) so that(~할 수 있도록), (D) because(~ 하기 때문에)는 뒤에 절을 이끈다.
어휘 hire v. 고용하다 server n. 종업원, 웨이터

13 부사절 접속사 채우기
해석 Fast Mail사는 받기로 예정된 사람들에게 물품을 배달하지 못할 때 소포와 문서를 보낸 사람들에게 돌려보낸다.
해설 빈칸 앞에 주어(Fast Mail)와 동사(returns)가 있는 절이 있고 빈칸 뒤에도 주어(it)와 동사(fails)가 있는 절이 있으므로 두 개의 절을 연결해주는 등위접속사 (C)와 부사절 접속사 (D)가 정답의 후보이다. '받기로 예정된 사람들에게 물품을 배달하지 못할 때 소포와 문서를 보낸 사람들에게 돌려보낸다'라는 의미가 되어야 하므로 시간을 나타내는 부사절 접속사 (D) when(~할 때)이 정답이다. (C) or(또는)를 쓰면 어색한 문맥이 된다. (A) still은 '아직도, 여전히'라는 의미로 시간을 나타내는 부사이다. (B) where는 명사절을 이끄는 의문부사이다.
어휘 intended adj. 예정된, 의도된 recipient n. 받는 사람, 수취인

14 의문사 채우기
해석 소셜 네트워크 사이트들의 출현과 함께, 대부분의 회사들은 그들이 광고하는 방법에 변화를 주었다.
해설 빈칸은 전치사(in)의 목적어 역할을 하는 명사절(___they advertise)을 이끄는 명사절 접속사 자리이므로 의문부사 (D) how가 정답이다. 전치사 (A), 등위접속사 또는 부사 (B), 접속부사 (C)는 명사절을 이끌 수 없다.
어휘 advent n. 출현 make a change ~에 변화를 주다, 변경하다
advertise v. 광고하다

15 부사절 접속사 채우기
해석 다른 국가들이 손실을 입은 반면, 그 나라의 주식 시장은 이익을 달성했다.
해설 빈칸은 동사(suffered)가 있는 거품절(___ ~ losses)을 이끄는 부사절 접속사 자리이므로 양보를 나타내는 부사절 접속사 (C) whereas(~한 반면에)가 정답이다. 접속부사 (A)는 수식어 거품을 이끌 수 없다. (B)는 접속부사일 경우 수식어 거품을 이끌 수 없고, 전치사일 경우 거품절이 아닌 거품구를 이끈다. 전치사 (D)도 마찬가지로 거품절이 아닌 거품구를 이끈다.
어휘 stock n. 주식, 재고 achieve v. 달성하다, 성취하다 gain n. 이익, 수익
nation n. 국가 suffer losses 손실을 입다 concerning prep. ~에 관한

16 명사절 접속사 채우기 정답공식 04
해석 국영 언론사는 실업률이 5년 만에 가장 낮은 수준으로 떨어졌다는 것을 보도했다.
해설 빈칸은 동사(reported)의 목적어 역할을 하는 명사절(___ unemployment rates ~ years)을 이끄는 명사절 접속사 자리이므로 명사절 접속사 (B) that(~라는 것)이 정답이다. 의문사 (A) which와 (C) what 뒤에는 불완전한 절이 와야 하므로 답이 될 수 없다. 부사 또는 전치사 (D)는 명사절을 이끌 수 없다.
어휘 national adj. 국영의, 국립의 news agency 언론사
unemployment rate 실업률

17 부사절 접속사 채우기
해석 보상금 청구 신청이 부서에 의해 검토될 때까지는 그 어떠한 대금도 보험 가입자에게 지급될 수 없다.
해설 빈칸은 동사(has been examined)가 있는 거품절(___ the claim ~ department)을 이끄는 부사절 접속사 자리이므로 시간을 나타내는 부사절 접속사 (C) until(~할 때까지)이 정답이다. 접속부사 (A), 전치사 또는 접속부사 (B), 전치사 (D)는 거품절을 이끌 수 없다.
어휘 insurance subscriber 보험가입자 claim n. (보상금에 대한) 청구 신청
examine v. 검토하다

18 명사절 접속사 채우기
해석 재고 관리자는 소비자 수요에 기반하여 어떤 품목들이 먼저 재입고되어야 하는지를 결정해야 한다.
해설 빈칸은 to 부정사(to determine)의 목적어 역할을 하는 명사절(___ items ~ demand)을 이끌면서 뒤에 나온 명사(items)를 꾸밀 수 있는 의문형용사 자리이므로 의문형용사 (B) which가 정답이다. 복합관계대명사 (A)와 의문대명사 (C)는 뒤에 명사가 올 수 없으므로 답이 될 수 없다. 지시대명사 또는 지시형용사 (D)는 명사절을 이끌 수 없다.
어휘 inventory n. 재고 restock v. 재입고하다 demand n. 수요

19 부사절 접속사 채우기
해석 직원 수칙의 사본은 사람들이 그것을 자세히 살피기를 원하는 경우에 대비하여 온라인에 게시되었다.
해설 빈칸은 동사(want)가 있는 거품절(___ people ~ it)을 이끄는 부사절 접속사 자리이므로 부사절 접속사 (A)와 (B)가 정답의 후보이다. '직원 수칙의 사본은 사람들이 그것을 자세히 살피기를 원하는 경우에 대비하여 온라인에 게시되었다'라는 의미가 되어야 하므로 조건을 나타내는 부사절 접속사 (B) in case(~에 대비하여, ~의 경우)가 정답이다. (A) even if는 '비록 ~이지만, ~일지라도'라는 의미이다. 전치사 (C)와 (D)는 거품절이 아닌 거품구를 이끈다.
어휘 copy n. 사본 manual n. 수칙, 설명서 post v. 게시하다
on behalf of ~을 대표하여 aside from ~ 이외에

20 부사절 접속사 채우기

해석 그날 비가 오지 않는 한 Beaton 낙농회사의 연례 회사 소풍이 토요일에 Maple 공원에서 열릴 것이다.

해설 빈칸은 동사(does)가 있는 거품절(___ it ~ day)을 이끄는 부사절 접속사 자리이므로 부사절 접속사 (A)와 (B)가 정답의 후보이다. '그날 비가 오지 않는 한 회사 소풍이 토요일에 열릴 것이다'라는 의미가 되어야 하므로 조건을 나타내는 부사절 접속사 (A) as long as(~하는 한)가 정답이다. (B) whereas는 '~한 반면에'라는 의미이다. 부사 (C)와 상관접속사 (D)는 거품절을 이끌 수 없다.

어휘 annual adj. 연례의   take place 열리다, 발생하다

21 부사절 접속사 채우기   정답공식 02

해석 당사의 최신 제품들과 홍보 활동들을 알려드릴 수 있도록 동봉된 고객 정보지를 작성해 주십시오.

해설 빈칸은 동사(can let)가 있는 거품절(___ we ~ promotions)을 이끄는 부사절 접속사 자리이고, '당사의 최신 제품들과 홍보 활동들을 알려드릴 수 있도록 동봉된 고객 정보지를 작성해 주십시오'라는 의미가 되어야 하므로 목적을 나타내는 부사절 접속사 (C) so that(~할 수 있도록)이 정답이다. 전치사 (A), (B), (D)는 거품절이 아닌 거품구를 이끈다.

어휘 enclosed adj. 동봉된   latest adj. 최신의   offering n. (팔 물건의) 제공   promotion n. 홍보, 판촉

22 전치사 채우기

해석 제한된 마케팅에도 불구하고, 그 뮤지컬은 상연 첫날밤에 상당한 관객을 끌어모았다.

해설 빈칸은 명사구(limited marketing)를 목적어로 가지는 전치사 자리이므로 전치사 (A), (C), (D)가 정답의 후보이다. '제한된 마케팅에도 불구하고, 그 뮤지컬은 상당한 관객을 끌어모았다'라는 의미가 되어야 하므로 전치사 (D) In spite of(~에도 불구하고)가 정답이다. (A) By는 '~까지', (C) During은 '~동안'이라는 의미이다. 부사절 접속사 (B)는 명사구를 목적어로 가질 수 없다.

어휘 attract v. 끌어모으다, 유치하다   sizable adj. 상당한, 큰   audience n. 관객, 청중   opening night 상연 첫날밤

23 부사절 접속사 채우기

해석 만약 그 발표가 더 많은 도표들을 포함한다면 그것은 더 효과적일 것이다.

해설 빈칸은 동사(includes)가 있는 거품절(___ ~ charts)을 이끄는 부사절 접속사 자리이므로 조건을 나타내는 부사절 접속사 (A) if(만약 ~이라면)가 정답이다. 전치사 또는 형용사 (B), 부사 (C), 형용사 또는 부사 (D)는 거품절을 이끌 수 없다.

어휘 effective adj. 효과적인   chart n. 도표, 차트   unlike prep. ~과 달리; adj. 서로 다른   else adv. 또 다른   just adj. 공정한; adv. 단지

24 명사절 접속사 채우기

해석 스테이플러를 마지막으로 사용하는 사람이 누구든 간에 그것을 우편실로 반납하도록 요구된다.

해설 동사(is requested)의 주어 자리에 온 절(___ ~ last)의 맨 앞에 올 수 있는 것은 명사절 접속사이므로 복합관계대명사 (A)와 (B)가 정답의 후보이다. '스테이플러를 마지막으로 사용하는 사람이 누구든 간에 그것을 우편실로 반납하도록 요구된다'라는 의미가 되어야 하므로 (A) Whoever(누구든 간에)가 정답이다. 복합관계대명사 (B) Whatever(무엇이든 간에)는 사물을 지칭할 때 쓰이므로 답이 될 수 없다. 대명사 (C)는 절을 이끌 수 없다. 의문형용사 (D)는 '누구의'라는 의미로 뒤에 명사가 와야 한다.

어휘 stapler n. 스테이플러   mail room 우편실

빈출 어휘 | 부사 2

토익 실전문제   p.245

01 (D)	02 (B)	03 (A)	04 (C)	05 (B)
06 (B)	07 (C)	08 (A)		

01 부사 어휘 고르기

해석 두 나라 모두 새로운 공장의 잠재적 위치로서 동등하게 매력적이다.

해설 '두 나라 모두 공장의 위치로서 동등하게 매력적이다'라는 문맥이므로 (D) equally(동등하게)가 정답이다. (A) exactly는 '정확히', (B) steadily는 '착실하게, 꾸준히', (C) punctually는 '정시에'라는 의미이다.

어휘 attractive adj. 매력적인   potential adj. 잠재적인   location n. 위치

02 부사 어휘 고르기

해석 상담가는 그 회사의 문제를 직원들의 낮은 동기 부여라고 정확하게 파악했다.

해설 '회사의 문제를 직원들의 낮은 동기 부여라고 정확하게 파악하다'라는 문맥이므로 (B) correctly(정확하게, 올바르게)가 정답이다. (A) occasionally는 '가끔', (C) sharply는 '날카롭게', (D) highly는 '매우'라는 의미이다.

어휘 identify v. 파악하다, 식별하다   motivation n. 동기 부여

03 부사 어휘 고르기

해석 주간 브레인스토밍 세션의 참여는 영업 직원들에게 전적으로 자발적이다.

해설 '세션의 참여는 직원들에게 전적으로 자발적이다'라는 문맥이므로 (A) entirely(전적으로, 완전히)가 정답이다. (B) immediately는 '즉시', (C) successfully는 '성공적으로', (D) openly는 '공개적으로'라는 의미이다.

어휘 participation n. 참여   voluntary adj. 자발적인

04 부사 어휘 고르기

해석 행사가 한 달 앞으로 다가오면서, 주최자들은 관심 부족으로 인해 점점 더 걱정하고 있다.

해설 '행사가 다가오면서, 주최자들은 관심 부족으로 인해 점점 더 걱정하고 있다'라는 문맥이므로 (C) increasingly(점점 더, 갈수록 더)가 정답이다. (A) abruptly는 '갑자기', (B) initially는 '처음에', (D) precisely는 '정확히'라는 의미이다.

어휘 organizer n. 주최자   grow v. ~하게 되다   concerned adj. 걱정하는   lack n. 부족

05 부사 어휘 고르기

해석 콘서트 참석자들은 공연 중 연주자들을 촬영하는 것이 엄격히 금지된다.

해설 '콘서트 참석자들은 연주자들을 촬영하는 것이 엄격히 금지된다'라는 문맥이므로 (B) strictly(엄격히)가 정답이다. (A) voluntarily는 '자발적으로', (C) nearly는 '거의', (D) freely는 '자유롭게'라는 의미이다.

어휘 attendee n. 참석자   prohibit v. 금지하다   film v. 촬영하다   performance n. 공연

06 부사 어휘 고르기

해석 Mr. Banerjee는 텔레비전 토크쇼에 출연하라는 초대를 정중하게 거절했다.

해설 '토크쇼에 출연하라는 초대를 정중하게 거절하다'라는 문맥이므로 (B) politely(정중하게)가 정답이다. (A) extremely는 '극히, 극도로', (C) diligently는 '부지런히', (D) greatly는 '매우'라는 의미이다.

어휘 decline v. 거절하다   invitation n. 초대   appear v. 출연하다

07 부사 어휘 고르기

해석 계획에 따르면, 건물의 첫 세 층은 결국 소매점들이 차지하게 될 것이다.

해설 '계획에 따르면, 건물의 첫 세 층은 결국 소매점들이 차지하게 될 것이다'라는 문맥이므로 (C) eventually(결국, 마침내)가 정답이다. (A) seamlessly는 '매끄럽게', (B) previously는 '이전에', (D) closely는 '면밀히'라는 의미이다.

어휘 occupy v. 차지하다 retail adj. 소매의

08 부사 어휘 고르기

해석 그 식당 체인점은 전국적으로 빠르게 확장하기 위해 많은 자본이 필요할 것이다.

해설 '체인점이 빠르게 확장하기 위해 많은 자본이 필요하다'라는 문맥이므로 (A) rapidly(빠르게)가 정답이다. (B) generally는 '일반적으로', (C) positively는 '긍정적으로', (D) distinctly는 '뚜렷하게'라는 의미이다.

어휘 capital n. 자본 expand v. 확장하다

DAY 12 비교 구문

기출 포인트 01

실전 Check-up   p.246

01 (A)   02 (B)

01 비교급 표현 채우기

해석 ValuePlus 슈퍼마켓은 ShopSmart 쇼핑센터보다 우리 사무실에서 더 가깝다.

해설 빈칸은 be동사(is)의 주격 보어 자리이고 빈칸 뒤에 than(~보다)이 왔으므로 형용사 close(가까운)의 비교급 (A) closer가 정답이다.

02 최상급 표현 채우기

해석 GrandLux 타워는 도심 상업 지구의 건물 중에서 가장 높은 건물이다.

해설 'GrandLux 타워는 도심 상업 지구의 건물 중에서 가장 높은 건물이다'라는 의미가 되어야 하고, 빈칸 앞에 최상급과 함께 쓰이는 the가 있으므로 형용사 tall(높은)의 최상급 (B) tallest가 정답이다.

어휘 downtown adj. 도심(지)의, 중심가의 district n. 지구, 지역

기출 포인트 02~03

실전 Check-up   p.247

01 (B)   02 (A)

01 원급 표현 채우기

해석 그 팀은 기대했던 것만큼 빠르게 프로젝트를 완료했다.

해설 동사(completed)를 꾸밀 수 있고 빈칸 뒤의 as(~만큼)와 함께 원급 표현을 만드는 부사의 원급 (B) quickly(빠르게)가 정답이다. 형용사의 비교급 (A)는 원급 표현과 함께 쓰일 수 없다.

어휘 complete v. 완료하다

02 비교급 표현 채우기

해석 최근의 가격 인하로, 국제선 항공편은 작년에 그랬던 것보다 더 저렴해졌다.

해설 동사(have become)의 보어 자리에 올 수 있고 빈칸 뒤의 than(~보다)과 함께 비교급 표현을 만드는 형용사 affordable(저렴한)의 비교급 (A) more affordable이 정답이다. 형용사의 원급 (B)는 비교급 표현과 함께 쓰일 수 없다.

어휘 reduction n. 인하, 감소

기출 포인트 04~05

실전 Check-up   p.248

01 (B)   02 (B)

01 최상급 표현 채우기

해석 창업을 시작할 때, 자금을 확보하는 것은 1년 차 생존을 위한 가장 필수적인 전제 조건이다.

해설 빈칸 뒤의 명사(prerequisite)를 꾸밀 수 있는 것은 형용사이므로 형용사 essential(필수적인)의 최상급 (B) most essential이 정답이다. 부사 (A)는 명사를 꾸밀 수 없다.

어휘 launch v. 시작하다 startup n. 창업 secure v. 확보하다
prerequisite n. 전제 조건, 필수 요건

02 비교급 표현 채우기

해석 최근 설문조사는 30퍼센트보다 많은 사람들이 인쇄 도서보다 디지털 도서를 선호한다는 것을 보여준다.

해설 빈칸 뒤의 than(~보다)과 함께 비교급 표현을 만드는 모든 보기가 정답의 후보이다. '30퍼센트보다 많은 사람들이 디지털 도서를 선호한다'라는 의미가 되어야 하므로 (B) more가 정답이다.

어휘 survey n. 설문 조사

3초컷 정답 공식   p.249

01 (A)   02 (B)   03 (D)   04 (D)   05 (B)
06 (C)   07 (C)   08 (D)

01 비교급 표현 채우기

해석 투숙객들은 추가 요금을 피하기 위해 늦어도 오전 11시까지 체크아웃해야 한다.

해설 빈칸 앞의 no와 빈칸 뒤의 than과 함께 '늦어도 ~까지'라는 의미를 만드는 (A) later가 정답이다. 형용사 또는 부사의 원급 (B), 명사 (C), 형용사 또는 부사의 최상급 (D)는 no, than과 함께 표현을 만들 수 없다.

어휘 check out 체크아웃하다 additional adj. 추가의 charge n. 요금

02 비교급 표현 채우기

해석 판매자들은 늦어도 행사 2주 전까지 그들의 부스 예약을 확정해야 한다.

해설 빈칸 앞의 no와 빈칸 뒤의 than과 함께 '늦어도 ~까지'라는 의미를 만드는 (B) later가 정답이다. 형용사 또는 부사의 최상급 (A), 부사 (C), 형용사 또는 부사의 원급 (D)는 no, than과 함께 표현을 만들 수 없다.

어휘 vendor n. 판매자 confirm v. 확정하다, 확인하다 reservation n. 예약
prior to ~ 전에, ~에 앞서

03 비교급 표현 채우기

해석 전기 자동차에 대한 수요는 지금 그 어느 때보다도 더 높다.

해설 be동사(is)의 보어 자리에 올 수 있고 빈칸 뒤의 than(~보다)과 함께 비교급 표현을 만드는 형용사 high(높은)의 비교급 (D) higher가 정답이다. 명사 (A)와 형용사 또는 부사의 원급 (B)는 비교급 표현과 함께 쓰일 수 없다. 부사 (C)는 be동사의 보어 자리에 올 수 없다.

어휘 demand n. 수요 electric vehicle 전기 자동차

04 비교급 표현 채우기

해석 유기농 식품과 현지 생산된 식품에 대한 소비자 관심은 10년 전에 그랬던 것보다 더 강하다.

해설 be동사(is)의 보어 자리에 올 수 있고 빈칸 뒤의 than(~보다)과 함께 비교

급 표현을 만드는 형용사 strong(강한)의 비교급 (D) stronger가 정답이다. 형용사의 원급 (A)와 명사 (C)는 비교급 표현과 함께 쓰일 수 없다. 부사 (B)는 be동사의 보어 자리에 올 수 없다.

어휘 organic adj. 유기농의 locally sourced 현지 생산된

05 최상급 표현 채우기
해석 면접을 본 모든 후보자들 중에서, Ms. Johnson은 그 직책에 가장 좋은 자격을 가지고 있다.
해설 빈칸 뒤의 명사(qualifications)를 꾸밀 수 있는 것은 형용사이므로 모든 보기가 정답의 후보이다. '모든 후보자들 중에서 Ms. Johnson이 그 직책에 가장 좋은 자격을 가지고 있다'라는 의미가 되어야 하고, 빈칸 앞에 최상급과 함께 쓰이는 the가 있으므로 최상급을 만드는 (B) best가 정답이다.
어휘 candidate n. 후보자 qualification n. 자격, 자질

06 최상급 표현 채우기
해석 그 회사는 모든 경쟁업체들 중에서 가장 중요한 시장 점유율을 얻었다.
해설 빈칸 뒤의 명사구(market share)를 꾸밀 수 있는 것은 형용사이므로 비교급 (B), 최상급 (C), 원급 (D)가 정답의 후보이다. '그 회사가 모든 경쟁업체들 중에서 가장 중요한 시장 점유율을 얻었다'라는 의미가 되어야 하고, 빈칸 앞에 최상급과 함께 쓰이는 the가 있으므로 형용사 significant(중요한)의 최상급 (C) most significant가 정답이다. 명사 (A)는 형용사 자리에 올 수 없다.
어휘 acquire v. 얻다, 획득하다 market share 시장 점유율
competitor n. 경쟁업체

07 최상급 표현 채우기
해석 Polyglot Haven 서점은 이 도시에서 가장 다양한 종류의 외국어 출판물을 취급한다.
해설 빈칸 뒤의 명사(variety)를 꾸밀 수 있는 것은 형용사이므로 형용사의 최상급 (C)와 비교급 (D)가 정답의 후보이다. '가장 다양한 종류의 외국어 출판물을 취급하다'라는 의미가 되어야 하고, 빈칸 앞에 최상급과 함께 쓰이는 the가 있으므로 형용사 wide(다양한, 광범위한)의 최상급 (C) widest가 정답이다. 부사 (A)와 동사 (B)는 형용사 자리에 올 수 없다.
어휘 carry v. 취급하다, 판매하다 publication n. 출판물

08 최상급 표현 채우기
해석 여행 패키지의 가장 다양한 선택지가 이 여행사를 휴가객들에게 최고의 선택으로 만든다.
해설 빈칸 뒤의 명사(selection)를 꾸밀 수 있는 것은 형용사이므로 형용사 wide(다양한, 광범위한)의 최상급 (D) widest가 정답이다. 동사 (A), 부사 (B), 명사 (C)는 형용사 자리에 올 수 없다.
어휘 vacationer n. 휴가객

HACKERS TEST p.250

01 (B)	02 (A)	03 (D)	04 (A)	05 (C)
06 (A)	07 (D)	08 (C)	09 (D)	10 (B)
11 (B)	12 (B)	13 (A)	14 (B)	15 (A)
16 (B)	17 (C)	18 (B)	19 (A)	20 (C)
21 (B)	22 (B)	23 (A)	24 (B)	

01 원급 표현 채우기
해석 새로운 프린터는 더 적은 에너지를 사용하면서도 이전 모델만큼 효과적으로 작동한다.
해설 동사(works)를 꾸밀 수 있고 빈칸 뒤의 as(~만큼)와 함께 원급 표현을 만드는 부사의 원급 (B) effectively(효과적으로)가 정답이다. 형용사의 원급 (A), 형용사의 비교급 (C), 명사 (D)는 동사를 꾸밀 수 없다.

어휘 previous adj. 이전의

02 비교급 표현 채우기 정답공식 01
해석 모든 도급업자들은 늦어도 7월 첫 주까지 수리 작업을 완료해야 한다.
해설 빈칸 앞의 no와 빈칸 뒤의 than과 함께 '늦어도 ~까지'라는 의미를 만드는 (A) later가 정답이다. 형용사 또는 부사의 원급 (B), 명사 (C), 형용사 또는 부사의 최상급 (D)는 no, than과 함께 표현을 만들 수 없다.
어휘 contractor n. 도급업자, 계약자 renovation n. 수리

03 최상급 표현 채우기 정답공식 04
해석 GreenLeaf 식당은 이 도시에서 가장 다양한 종류의 채식주의 선택지를 특징으로 한다.
해설 빈칸 뒤의 명사(variety)를 꾸밀 수 있는 것은 형용사이므로 형용사의 비교급 (B)와 최상급 (D)가 정답의 후보이다. '가장 다양한 종류의 채식주의 선택지를 특징으로 한다'라는 의미가 되어야 하고, 빈칸 앞에 최상급과 함께 쓰이는 the가 있으므로 형용사 wide(다양한, 광범위한)의 최상급 (D) widest가 정답이다. 명사 (A)와 부사 (C)는 형용사 자리에 올 수 없다.
어휘 vegetarian adj. 채식주의의

04 비교급 표현 채우기
해석 다음 주부터, 사무실 건물은 특별 허가 없이는 주말에 더 이상 이용 가능하지 않을 것이다.
해설 빈칸 앞의 no와 함께 '더 이상 ~ 않다'라는 의미를 만드는 (A) longer가 정답이다. 형용사의 원급 (B), 명사 또는 형용사 (C), 형용사의 최상급 (D)는 no와 함께 표현을 만들 수 없다.
어휘 accessible adj. 이용 가능한 permission n. 허가
longing n. 갈망; adj. 갈망하는

05 최상급 표현 채우기 정답공식 03
해석 우리 카탈로그의 모든 제품 중에서, KitchenMaster Pro 3000이 이번 시즌에 가장 인기 있는 것이었다.
해설 빈칸 뒤의 명사(one)를 꾸밀 수 있는 것은 형용사이므로 형용사의 비교급 (B), 최상급 (C), 원급 (D)가 정답의 후보이다. '모든 제품 중에서 KitchenMaster Pro 3000이 이번 시즌에 가장 인기 있는 것이었다'라는 의미가 되어야 하고, 빈칸 앞에 최상급과 함께 쓰이는 the가 있으므로 최상급 (C) most popular가 정답이다.
어휘 catalog n. 카탈로그, (물품·책 등의) 목록

06 비교급 표현 채우기
해석 올해의 학회에는 작년의 행사보다 더 많은 참석자가 있었다.
해설 빈칸 앞에 비교급(more)이 있으므로 비교급 표현을 만드는 (A) than(~보다)이 정답이다. 지시대명사 또는 지시형용사 (B), 전치사 (C)와 (D)는 비교급과 함께 표현을 만들 수 없다.
어휘 conference n. 학회, 회의 attendee n. 참석자

07 부사절 접속사 채우기
해석 회의실이 아직 회계부에 의해 사용되고 있기 때문에 오리엔테이션이 30분 연기되었다.
해설 빈칸은 동사(is being used)가 있는 거품절(___ the meeting room ~ department)을 이끄는 부사절 접속사 자리이고, '회의실이 아직 회계부에 의해 사용되고 있기 때문에 오리엔테이션이 30분 연기되었다'라는 의미가 되어야 하므로 이유를 나타내는 부사절 접속사 (D) because(~하기 때문에)가 정답이다. (A) whereas는 '~한 반면에', (B) though는 '비록 ~이지만, ~일지라도', (C) unless는 '만약 ~이 아니라면'이라는 의미이다.
어휘 push back 연기하다 finance department 회계부

08 원급 표현 채우기
해석 우리 웹사이트는 더 많은 고객을 유인하기 위해 경쟁사의 플랫폼만큼 매력적이어야 한다.

해설 be동사(be)의 보어 자리에 올 수 있고 빈칸 뒤의 as(~만큼)와 함께 원급 표현을 만드는 형용사의 원급 (C) attractive(매력적인)가 정답이다. 형용사의 비교급 (A)와 최상급 (D)는 원급 표현과 함께 쓰일 수 없다. 부사 (B)는 be동사의 보어 자리에 올 수 없다.

어휘 entice v. 유인하다   attractively adv. 보기 좋게

09 비교급 표현 채우기 [정답공식 02]

해석 늦은 시간의 프로그램을 더 이른 시간대로 옮기기로 한 그 방송사의 결정은 그것을 이전보다 더 폭넓은 시청자에게 다가가는 것을 가능하게 했다.

해설 명사(audience)를 앞에서 꾸밀 수 있는 형용사의 최상급 (C)와 비교급 (D)가 정답의 후보이다. 빈칸 뒤의 than과 함께 비교급 표현을 만드는 형용사 broad(폭넓은)의 비교급 (D) broader가 정답이다. 최상급 (C)는 than과 함께 쓸 수 없고 앞에 정관사(the)가 와야 한다. 동사 (A)와 부사 (B)는 명사를 꾸밀 수 없다.

어휘 network n. 방송사, 방송망   time slot 시간대   allow v. ~을 가능하게 하다
reach v. (~에) 다가가다, 이르다   audience n. 시청자, 관중, 청중

10 최상급 표현 채우기

해석 다른 마케팅 전략들과 비교하여, 소셜 미디어 광고가 올해 가장 성공적으로 행해졌다.

해설 빈칸 앞의 동사(has performed)를 꾸밀 수 있는 것은 부사이므로 부사의 원급 (A), 최상급 (B), 비교급 (C)가 정답의 후보이다. '다른 마케팅 전략들과 비교하여, 소셜 미디어 광고가 올해 가장 성공적으로 행해졌다'라는 의미가 되어야 하고, 빈칸 앞에 최상급과 함께 쓰이는 the가 있으므로 부사 successfully(성공적으로)의 최상급 (B) most successfully가 정답이다. 형용사 (D)는 부사 자리에 올 수 없다.

어휘 compared to ~과 비교하여   strategy n. 전략

11 태에 맞는 동사 채우기

해석 지원서들의 처리 지연을 일으키는 오류는 즉시 해결되어야 한다.

해설 be동사(be) 다음에 올 수 있는 모든 보기가 정답의 후보이다. '오류가 해결되어야 한다'라는 수동의 의미가 되어야 하므로 빈칸 앞의 be동사(be)와 함께 수동태를 만드는 동사 address(해결하다, 다루다)의 과거분사 (B) addressed가 정답이다. 명사 (A)와 (D)는 be동사 다음에 올 수는 있지만, 보어로서 주어와 동격 관계가 되어 '오류는 주소/주소들이 되어야 한다'라는 어색한 문맥을 만든다.

어휘 delay n. 지연   immediately adv. 즉시

12 최상급 표현 채우기

해석 Braxton 구리 광산은 한때 가장 위험한 작업장들 중 하나였지만, 안전 개선으로 작업장 사고가 크게 줄었다.

해설 빈칸 뒤의 명사(worksites)를 꾸밀 수 있는 것은 형용사이므로 형용사 dangerous(위험한)의 최상급 (B) most dangerous가 정답이다. 참고로, 최상급 관련 표현 'one of the + 최상급 + 복수 명사(가장 ~한 사람/것 중 하나)'를 알아둔다. 명사 (A), 부사 (C), 부사의 비교급 (D)는 형용사 자리에 올 수 없다.

어휘 mine n. 광산   worksite n. 작업장   improvement n. 개선, 향상
workplace n. 작업장, 일터

13 원급 표현 채우기

해석 Parkview Residence 아파트는 도심에 위치해 있음에도 불구하고 전형적인 교외 주택만큼 넓다.

해설 be동사(is)의 보어 자리에 올 수 있고 빈칸 뒤의 as(~만큼)와 함께 원급 표현을 만드는 형용사의 원급 (A) spacious(넓은)가 정답이다. 부사 (B)는 be동사의 보어 자리에 올 수 없다. 형용사의 비교급 (C)는 원급 표현과 함께 쓰일 수 없다. 명사 (D)는 원급 표현과 쓰이기 위해서는 'as + many/much/few/little + 명사 + as'의 형태로 쓰여야 한다.

어휘 typical adj. 전형적인, 대표적인   suburban adj. 교외의
spaciousness n. 넓음

14 비교급 표현 채우기 [정답공식 02]

해석 최고 경영자의 최근 발표에 따르면, ABC사의 분기별 수익은 원래 추정된 것보다 더 낮을 것이다.

해설 be동사(be)의 보어 자리에 올 수 있고 빈칸 뒤의 than(~보다)과 함께 비교급 표현을 만드는 형용사 low(낮은)의 비교급 (B) lower가 정답이다. 형용사의 원급 (A)와 (D), 최상급 (C)는 비교급 표현과 함께 쓰일 수 없다.

어휘 quarterly adj. 분기별의   profit n. 수익, 이익
estimate v. 추정하다, 추산하다   announcement n. 발표
lowering adj. (날씨가) 험악한

15 최상급 표현 채우기

해석 그 건축가는 작업 공간의 자연광을 극대화하기 위해 가장 큰 창문들이 있는 건물을 설계했다.

해설 빈칸 뒤의 명사(windows)를 꾸밀 수 있는 것은 형용사이므로 형용사의 최상급 (A)와 비교급 (C)가 정답의 후보이다. '가장 큰 창문들이 있는 건물'이라는 의미가 되어야 하고, 빈칸 앞에 최상급과 함께 쓰이는 the가 있으므로 형용사 large(큰)의 최상급 (A) largest가 정답이다. 부사 (B)와 명사 (D)는 형용사 자리에 올 수 없다.

어휘 architect n. 건축가   maximize v. 극대화하다   natural light 자연광
workspace n. 작업 공간

16 비교급 표현 채우기 [정답공식 02]

해석 웹사이트에 게시된 강의 영상들은 편집되었으므로, 실제 강의보다 약간 더 짧을 것이다.

해설 be동사(be)의 보어 자리에 올 수 있고 빈칸 뒤의 than(~보다)과 함께 비교급 표현을 만드는 형용사 short(짧은)의 비교급 (B) shorter가 정답이다. 형용사의 원급 (A)와 최상급 (D)는 비교급 표현과 함께 쓰일 수 없다. 부사 (C)는 be동사의 보어 자리에 올 수 없다.

어휘 lecture n. 강의   edit v. 편집하다   slightly adv. 약간

17 최상급 표현 채우기

해석 투자자들은 회사를 평가할 때 주가에 대해 가장 신중하다.

해설 '투자자들이 회사를 평가할 때 주가에 대해 가장 신중하다'라는 의미가 되어야 하고, 빈칸 앞에 최상급과 함께 쓰이는 the가 있으므로 최상급을 만드는 (C) most가 정답이다. 부사 (A) either는 부정문에서 '~도'라는 의미이고, 한정사 (B) some은 '약간'이라는 의미이다. 부사 (D) much는 '훨씬'이라는 의미로, 비교급을 강조하는 강조 부사로 쓰인다.

어휘 investor n. 투자자   evaluate v. 평가하다

18 비교급 표현 채우기

해석 그 보증서는 기술적 결함으로 인한 것 이외에 고장은 보장하지 않는다.

해설 '그 보증서는 기술적 결함으로 인한 것 이외에 고장은 보장하지 않는다'라는 의미가 되어야 하므로 비교급 표현 (B) other than(~ 이외에)이 정답이다. 전치사 (A) prior to(~ 전에), (C) along with(~에 덧붙여), (D) according to(~에 따르면)는 어색한 문맥을 만든다.

어휘 warranty n. 보증서   cover v. 보장하다   malfunction n. 고장, 오작동
defect n. 결함

19 최상급 표현 채우기

해석 Bronson 중장비사는 전체 산업에서 가장 엄격한 안전 규약을 시행해 왔다.

해설 빈칸 뒤의 명사구(safety protocols)를 꾸밀 수 있는 것은 형용사이므로 형용사의 최상급 (A), 비교급 (B), 원급 (C)가 정답의 후보이다. '전체 산업에서 가장 엄격한 안전 규약을 시행하다'라는 의미가 되어야 하고, 빈칸 앞에 최상급과 함께 쓰이는 the가 있으므로 형용사 strict(엄격한)의 최상급 (A) strictest가 정답이다. 부사 (D)는 형용사 자리에 올 수 없다.

어휘 implement v. 시행하다   protocol n. 규약   industry n. 산업

20 최상급 표현 채우기

해석 Sunlight 호텔은 Trivv에 등록된 모든 숙박 시설들 중에서 가장 높은 고

객 만족도 평가를 받았다.

해설 빈칸은 명사구(all the ~ Trivv)를 목적어로 가지는 전치사 자리이므로 모든 보기가 정답의 후보이다. '모든 숙박 시설들 중에서 가장 높은 고객 만족도 평가를 받다'라는 의미가 되어야 하므로 전치사 (C) of(~중에서)가 정답이다. (A) about은 '~에 관한', (B) along은 '~을 따라' (D) under는 '~ 아래에'라는 의미이다.

어휘 satisfaction n. 만족(도) rating n. 평가, 등급
accommodation facility 숙박 시설

21 최상급 표현 채우기

해석 그 그룹은 Stellar 여행사에 의해 준비된 유람선 여행을 즐겼으며, 그것을 여태껏 가장 기억에 남는 휴가라고 일컬었다.

해설 빈칸 뒤의 명사(holiday)를 꾸밀 수 있는 것은 형용사이므로 memorable (기억에 남는)의 최상급 (A) most memorable이 정답이다. 형용사의 원급 (C)는 최상급 표현과 함께 쓰일 수 없다. 동사 (B)와 부사 (D)는 명사를 꾸밀 수 없다.

어휘 cruise n. 유람선 여행 memorize v. 암기하다
memorably adv. 기억할 만하게

22 비교급 표현 채우기

해석 일상적인 출퇴근을 위해 자동차를 구매하기보다는, Mr. Sufi는 대중교통을 이용하기로 결정했다.

해설 동명사구(purchasing a car) 앞에 올 수 있고, '출퇴근을 위해 자동차를 구매하기보다는, 대중교통을 이용하기로 결정했다'라는 의미가 되어야 하므로 비교급 표현 (B) Rather than(~보다는)이 정답이다. 전치사 (A)는 '~과 비교하여'라는 의미이다. 부사절 접속사 (C)와 (D)는 뒤에 동명사구가 아닌 절이 와야 한다.

어휘 commute n. 출퇴근 take advantage of ~을 이용하다

23 비교급 표현 채우기

해석 Myson Publishing사는 도서전에서 부스를 빌리는 데 500달러보다 적게 지불했다.

해설 빈칸 뒤에 비교급 표현을 만드는 than이 있으므로 '~보다 적은'이라는 표현을 만드는 (A) less가 정답이다. (B) further는 '더 멀리에'라는 의미이다. (C) rather는 '오히려, 차라리'라는 의미로, than과 함께 '~보다는'이라는 의미의 비교급 표현으로 자주 쓰이는 점을 알아 둔다. 전치사 (D)는 비교급 표현과 함께 쓰일 수 없다.

어휘 book fair 도서전

24 부사절 접속사 채우기

해석 산불 복구 작업이 완료되자마자 Silverleaf 국립공원 등산로가 접근 가능해질 것이다.

해설 빈칸은 동사(are completed)가 있는 거품절(___ the wildfire ~ completed)을 이끄는 부사절 접속사 자리이고, '산불 복구 작업이 완료되자마자 등산로가 접근 가능해질 것이다'라는 의미가 되어야 하므로 시간을 나타내는 부사절 접속사 (B) as soon as(~하자마자)가 정답이다. 전치사 (A)와 (C)는 거품절을 이끌 수 없고, (D)는 뒤에 동사원형이 와야 한다.

어휘 trail n. 등산로, 둘레길 wildfire n. 산불 recovery n. 복구

빈출 어휘 | 어구

토익 실전문제 p.253

| 01 (B) | 02 (B) | 03 (A) | 04 (D) | 05 (B) |
| 06 (D) | 07 (B) | 08 (C) | | |

01 명사 관련 어구 완성하기

해석 모든 직원은 예외 없이 다양한 개발 세미나에 참여할 것이다.

해설 '모든 직원이 다양한 세미나에 참여하다'라는 문맥에서 빈칸 앞의 부정관사(a)와 뒤의 전치사(of)와 함께 쓰여 '다양한'이라는 어구를 이루는 (B) range가 정답이다. (a range of: 다양한) (A) kind는 '종류'라는 의미로, 'a kind of + 단수 명사 (일종의)', 'kinds of 복수 명사(~의 여러 종류)'의 형태로 써야 한다. (C) member는 '구성원', (D) lack은 '부족'이라는 의미이다.

어휘 participate v. 참여하다 development n. 개발

02 형용사 관련 어구 완성하기

해석 그 섬은 아름다운 해변, 맑고 푸른 바다, 그리고 휴식을 취할 수 있는 분위기로 유명하다.

해설 '그 섬이 아름다운 해변으로 유명하다'라는 문맥이므로 빈칸 앞의 be동사(is)와 뒤의 전치사(for)와 함께 '~으로 유명하다'라는 의미의 어구 be famous for를 만드는 형용사 (B) famous(유명한)가 정답이다. (C) responsible도 전치사 for와 함께 쓰일 수 있지만, '~을 담당하는, ~에 책임이 있는'이라는 의미로 어색한 문맥이 되므로 답이 될 수 없다. (A) interested는 '~에 관심 있는'이라는 의미로 전치사 in과 함께 쓰이며, (D) capable은 '~을 할 수 있는'이라는 의미로 전치사 of와 함께 쓰인다.

어휘 atmosphere n. 분위기

03 동사 관련 어구 완성하기

해석 Lindberg시는 연례 체스 대회를 홍보하기 위한 행사를 주최할 것이다.

해설 'Lindberg시가 행사를 주최할 것이다'라는 문맥이므로 빈칸 뒤의 an event와 함께 '행사를 주최하다'라는 의미의 어구 host an event를 만드는 동사 (A) host(주최하다)가 정답이다. (B) compare는 '비교하다', (C) assume은 '추정하다, 가정하다', (D) follow는 '따르다'라는 의미이다.

어휘 promote v. 홍보하다 annual adj. 연례의 tournament n. 대회

04 명사 관련 어구 완성하기

해석 그 재무 보고서는 회사의 해외 성장을 반영하는 판매 수치를 강조했다.

해설 '회사의 해외 성장을 반영하는 판매 수치를 강조하다'라는 문맥이므로 빈칸 앞의 명사(sales)와 함께 '판매 수치'라는 의미의 어구 sales figures를 만드는 명사 figure(수치)의 복수형 (D) figures가 정답이다. (A)의 design은 '디자인', (B)의 supply는 '공급량', (C)의 worker는 '근로자'라는 의미이다.

어휘 financial adj. 재무의 highlight v. 강조하다 reflect v. 반영하다
overseas adj. 해외의

05 명사 관련 어구 완성하기

해석 정부는 정책 제안에 대한 추가 의견을 수집하기 위해 일련의 공개 포럼을 개최할 것이다.

해설 '정부가 의견을 수집하기 위해 일련의 포럼을 개최하다'라는 문맥에서 빈칸 앞의 부정관사(a)와 뒤의 전치사(of)와 함께 쓰여 '일련의'라는 어구를 이루는 (B) series가 정답이다. (a series of: 일련의) (A) note는 '메모', (C) lecture는 '강의', (D) possibility는 '가능성'이라는 의미이다.

어휘 public adj. 공개의 gather v. 수집하다 input n. 의견, 입력

06 형용사 관련 어구 완성하기

해석 Hoyts 소매점의 고객 보상 프로그램 회원들만 그 할인을 받을 자격이 있다.

해설 '프로그램 회원들만 그 할인을 받을 자격이 있다'라는 문맥이므로 빈칸 앞의 be동사(are)와 뒤의 전치사(for)와 함께 '~을 받을 자격이 있다'라는 의미의 어구 be eligible for를 만드는 형용사 (D) eligible(자격이 있는)이 정답이다. (B) essential과 (C) difficult도 전치사 for와 함께 쓰일 수 있지만, 각각 '~에 필수적인', '~에게 어려운'이라는 의미로 어색한 문맥이 되므로 답이 될 수 없다. (A) optional(선택적인)은 '~을 받을 자격이 있다'라는 의미의 어구를 만들 수 없다.

어휘 loyalty program 고객 보상 프로그램

07 동사 관련 어구 완성하기

해석 시설 관리자는 모든 사람들에게 건물의 비상구에 익숙해질 것을 상기시키고 싶어 한다.

해설 '관리자가 사람들에게 건물의 비상구에 익숙해질 것을 상기시키다'라는 문맥이므로 빈칸 뒤의 재귀대명사(themselves)와 전치사(with)와 함께 '~에 익숙해지다'라는 의미의 어구를 이루는 (D) familiarize(익숙하게 하다)가 정답이다. (familiarize oneself with: ~에 익숙해지다) (A) distribute는 '분배하다', (B) conduct는 '실시하다', (C) collaborate는 '협력하다'라는 의미이다.

어휘 facility n. 시설   emergency n. 비상   exit n. 출구

08 동사 관련 어구 완성하기

해석 명시된 요구 사항을 준수하지 않는 지원자들은 그 일자리에 고려되지 않을 것이다.

해설 '요구 사항을 준수하지 않는 지원자들은 그 일자리에 고려되지 않을 것이다'라는 문맥이므로 빈칸 뒤의 전치사(with)와 함께 '~을 준수하다, 따르다'라는 의미의 어구를 이루는 (C) comply(준수하다)가 정답이다. (A) connect는 '연결하다', (B) provide는 '제공하다', (D) associate는 '연관시키다'라는 의미이다. connect와 associate도 전치사 with와 함께 쓰일 수 있지만, 각각 '~과 연결하다', '~과 어울리다'라는 의미로 어색한 문맥이 되므로 답이 될 수 없다.

어휘 applicant n. 지원자   requirement n. 요구 사항

PART 6

DAY 13 문맥 파악 문제: 문법

HACKERS PRACTICE   p.257

01 (B)   02 (A)   03 (C)

01번은 다음 회람에 관한 문제입니다.

> 수신: 모든 매장 관리자들
> 발신: Marissa Hamlett, 운영 부사장
> 날짜: 6월 1일
> 제목: 새로운 판매 시스템
>
> 01Bucky's 대형 슈퍼는 7월 28일에 모든 지점에 새로운 판매 시스템을 설치할 것입니다. 매장 관리자들과 직원들, 특히 계산대에 배치된 사람들은 그것을 사용하는 방법에 대해 교육받아야 할 것입니다. 새로운 시스템은 우리가 매출과 재고를 추적할 수 있게 할 것입니다. 이것은 매장에서 재고가 품절되는 위험을 줄일 것입니다.

point-of-sale adj. 판매의, 매장의 branch n. 지점
assign v. (사람 등을) 배치하다 checkout register 계산대 train v. 교육하다
track v. 추적하다, 확인하다 inventory n. 재고 out of stock 품절된

01 올바른 시제의 동사 채우기 전체 문맥 파악

해설 문장에 주어(Bucky's Superstore)만 있고 동사가 없으므로 동사 (B), (C), (D)가 정답의 후보이다. 빈칸이 있는 문장만으로 정답을 고를 수 없으므로 주변 문맥이나 전체 문맥을 파악한다. '7월 28일에 모든 지점에 새로운 판매 시스템을 설치하다'라는 문장이고, 앞부분에서 회람이 6월 1일에 쓰였음을 확인할 수 있으므로 새로운 시스템이 도입되는 시점이 미래임을 알 수 있다. 따라서 미래 시제 (B) will install이 정답이다.

02번은 다음 광고에 관한 문제입니다.

> 당신의 사무실이나 집을 바꾸어 놓을 빠르고, 믿을 만하고, 저렴한 방법을 찾고 있나요? True Colors사는 사무실, 상점, 아파트를 포함한 상업용 및 주거용 부동산의 내부 도색을 전문으로 합니다. 02게다가, 저희의 경쟁력 있는 가격 책정은 당신이 예산을 초과하지 않으면서 새로운 모습을 연출할 수 있도록 보장합니다. 그러니 빠르고 믿을 만한 서비스를 위해, 오늘 555-2902로 True Colors사에 전화하세요. 저희가 처리하지 못하는 일은 없습니다.

look for ~을 찾다 reliable adj. 믿을 만한, 신뢰할 수 있는
affordable adj. 저렴한, 가격이 알맞은 transform v. 바꾸어 놓다
specialize in ~을 전문으로 하다 interior n. 내부
commercial adj. 상업용의, 영리적인 residential adj. 주거용의, 거주하기 좋은
competitive adj. 경쟁력 있는 exceed v. 초과하다
dependable adj. 믿을 만한, 신뢰할 수 있는 handle v. 처리하다, 다루다

02 접속부사 채우기 주변 문맥 파악

해설 빈칸이 콤마와 함께 문장의 맨 앞에 온 접속부사 자리이므로, 앞 문장과 빈칸이 있는 문장의 의미 관계를 파악하여 정답을 선택한다. 앞 문장에서 True Colors사는 상업용 및 주거용 부동산의 내부 도색을 전문으로 한다고 했고, 빈칸이 있는 문장에서는 회사의 경쟁력 있는 가격 책정은 예산을 초과하지 않으면서 새로운 모습을 연출할 수 있도록 보장한다고 했으므로 앞에서 언급된 내용에 추가 정보를 덧붙일 때 사용되는 접속부사 (A) Moreover(게다가, 더욱이)가 정답이다.

어휘 unfortunately adv. 불행히도 otherwise adv. 그렇지 않으면, 달리

thus adv. 그러므로

03번은 다음 이메일에 관한 문제입니다.

> 수신: Norma Jennings <n_jennings@unitedmail.com>
> 발신: Larry Keith <l.keith@str.com>
> 날짜: 1월 5일
> 제목: 트럭 대여
>
> Ms. Jennings께,
> Simons 트럭 대여사를 선택해 주셔서 감사합니다. 03곧 있을 로스앤젤레스로의 귀하의 이사를 위해 요청하신 이사 트럭을 가져가서 사용하실 수 있습니다. 1월 17일 오전 10시 이전에 Wilshire로에 있는 저희 지점을 방문하여 차량을 가져가시기 바랍니다. 차량을 운전하는 모든 분의 유효한 운전 면허증을 제시해 주셔야 합니다. 트럭을 반납하실 때, 저희 직원 중 한 명이 그것을 점검할 것입니다. 그것에 손상이 있는 경우, 예약 시 귀하가 제공하신 신용카드로 수리 비용이 청구될 것입니다. 감사합니다.

request v. 요청하다 upcoming adj. 곧 있을, 다가오는
relocation n. 이사, 이전 operate v. 운전하다 inspect v. 점검하다
damage n. 손상

03 인칭대명사 채우기 전체 문맥 파악

해설 '곧 있을 ___의 이사'라는 문맥에서 빈칸이 명사구(upcoming relocation)를 꾸미는 형용사 자리이므로, 형용사처럼 명사를 앞에서 꾸밀 수 있는 소유격 대명사인 모든 보기가 정답의 후보이다. 빈칸이 있는 문장만으로 정답을 고를 수 없으므로 주변 문맥이나 전체 문맥을 파악한다. 편지의 수신자가 Ms. Jennings이고, 앞 문장에서 Simons 트럭 대여사를 선택해 줘서 고맙다고 한 뒤, 뒷부분에서 트럭에 손상이 있는 경우, 예약 시 제공한 신용카드로 수리 비용이 청구될 것이라고 했으므로 이사를 가는 사람은 Ms. Jennings, 즉 편지의 수신자임을 알 수 있다. 따라서 편지의 수신자를 가리키는 2인칭 대명사 (C) your가 정답이다.

HACKERS TEST   p.258

01 (D)	02 (C)	03 (D)	04 (B)	05 (C)
06 (B)	07 (D)	08 (A)	09 (A)	10 (C)
11 (D)	12 (A)	13 (D)	14 (B)	15 (A)
16 (D)				

01-04번은 다음 공고에 관한 문제입니다.

> 모든 Diego사 직원들에게 알림
>
> 01직원 구내식당은 몇 가지 보수 공사를 가능하게 하기 위해 6월 4일과 6월 7일 사이에 이용할 수 없을 것입니다. 주요 개선점은 더 많은 햇빛이 들어오게 하기 위해 벽 중 하나에 창문을 추가하는 것이 될 것입니다. 더욱이, 오래된 가전제품들은 최신의 것들로 교체될 것입니다. 02예를 들어, 훨씬 더 큰 스테인리스제의 냉장고가 설치될 것입니다.
> 03그동안에, 여러분의 점심시간 동안에 회의실 1과 2를 이용하십시오. 04두 공간 모두 이 특정 목적을 위해 남겨두었습니다. 여러분의 인내심에 감사드립니다.

inaccessible adj. 이용할 수 없는 allow for ~을 가능하게 하다, 감안하다
renovation n. 보수 공사, 수리 primary adj. 주요한, 주된
improvement n. 개선(점) appliance n. 가전제품, 기기
replace v. 교체하다 in the meantime 그동안

01 전치사 채우기
해설 빈칸은 명사구(June 4 and June 7)를 목적어로 취하는 전치사 자리이다. '구내식당은 6월 4일에서 6월 7일 사이에 이용할 수 없을 것이다'라는 의미가 되어야 하므로 등위접속사 and와 함께 쓰여 between A and B(A와 B 사이에) 구문을 만드는 전치사 (D) between(~ 사이에)이 정답이다. (A) since는 '~ 이후로', (B) with는 '~과 함께', (C) into는 '~ 안으로'라는 의미이다.

02 접속부사 채우기 주변 문맥 파악
해설 빈칸이 콤마와 함께 문장의 맨 앞에 온 접속부사 자리이므로, 앞 문장과 빈칸이 있는 문장의 의미 관계를 파악하여 정답을 선택한다. 앞 문장에서 오래된 가전제품들은 최신의 것들로 교체될 것이라고 했고, 빈칸이 있는 문장에서는 훨씬 더 큰 스테인리스제의 냉장고가 설치될 것이라고 했으므로, 앞에서 말한 내용에 대한 예시를 언급하는 문장에서 사용되는 (C) For example(예를 들어)이 정답이다.

어휘 even so 그렇기는 하지만   otherwise adv. 그렇지 않으면
however adv. 그러나

03 동사 자리 채우기
해설 전치사구(In the meantime) 뒤에 나온 절이 주어가 없는 명령문이므로, 명령문의 동사 자리에 올 수 있는 동사원형 (D) utilize(이용하다)가 정답이다. 3인칭 단수 동사 (A), 동명사 또는 현재분사 (B), 명사 (C)는 명령문의 동사 자리에 올 수 없다.

04 알맞은 문장 고르기
해석 (A) 그 일정들은 문에 게시되었습니다.
(B) 두 공간 모두 이 특정 목적을 위해 남겨두었습니다.
(C) 몇몇 직원들은 더 많은 시간을 요청했습니다.
(D) 휴식은 한 시간보다 적게 지속되기로 되어 있었습니다.

해설 앞 문장 '(utilize) Conference Rooms 1 and 2 during your lunch break'에서 점심시간 동안에 회의실 1과 2를 이용하라고 했으므로, 빈칸에는 두 개의 회의실 모두 점심시간 동안 사용될 목적을 위해 남겨두었다는 내용이 들어가야 함을 알 수 있다. 따라서 (B)가 정답이다.

어휘 post v. 게시하다   reserve v. 남겨두다, 예약하다   specific adj. 특정한
be supposed to ~하기로 되어 있다   last v. 지속되다, 계속되다

05-08번은 다음 편지에 관한 문제입니다.

Kendra Sampson
338번지 West Elm로
벌링턴시, 버몬트주 05402

Ms. Sampson께,

05저희는 귀하께 *Literature Now*지의 구독이 6월 1일에 만료될 것임을 알리기 위해 편지를 씁니다. 06이날 전에 연장하지 않으신다면, 향후 발행물에 대해 귀하의 신용카드에 더 이상 요금이 청구되지 않을 것입니다. 하지만, 만약 귀하께서 구독을 연장하고 싶으시다면, 555-3922로 저희에게 연락해 주세요.

07귀하의 구독을 연장해야 할 많은 이유가 있습니다. 우선, 오늘날의 몇몇 최고 작가들의 글을 더 많이 즐길 수 있게 될 것입니다. 귀하께서는 또한 5월 갱신 할인으로 일 년 동안 24달러를 절약하실 수 있습니다. 08저희는 귀하께서 저희의 출판물을 계속해서 구독해 주시기를 바랍니다.

*Literature Now*지 팀 드림

notify v. 알리다, 통지하다   subscription n. 구독, 가입
renew v. 연장하다, 갱신하다   for starters 우선, 먼저   article n. 글, 기사
leading adj. 최고의, 선두적인   renewal n. 갱신

05 올바른 시제의 동사 채우기 주변 문맥 파악
해설 that절(that ~ June 1)에 주어(your subscription to *Literature Now*)만 있고 동사가 없으므로 동사 (A), (C), (D)가 정답의 후보이다. 빈칸이 있는 문장만으로 정답을 고를 수 없으므로 주변 문맥이나 전체 문맥을 파악한다. 뒤 문장에서 미래 시제(will ~ be)를 사용해서 이날 전에 연장하지 않는다면, 신용카드에 더 이상 요금이 청구되지 않을 것이라고 했으므로, 구독이 만료되는 시점이 미래임을 알 수 있다. 따라서 미래 시제 (C) will expire가 정답이다.

06 'be동사 + p.p.' 채우기
해설 빈칸이 be동사(be) 다음에 왔으므로 진행형을 만드는 현재분사 (A)와 수동태를 만드는 과거분사 (B)가 정답의 후보이다. '신용카드에 더 이상 요금이 청구되지 않을 것이다'라는 수동의 의미가 되어야 하므로 빈칸 앞의 be동사와 함께 수동태를 만드는 과거분사 (B) charged가 정답이다. 현재분사 (A)는 미래 진행형을 만들어서 '신용카드에 더 이상 요금이 청구되지 않고 있는 중일 것이다'라는 어색한 문맥을 만든다. 3인칭 단수 동사 (C)와 동사원형 (D)는 be동사 다음에 올 수 없다. (C)와 (D)를 '요금'이라는 의미의 명사로 본다 해도, '신용카드에 더 이상 요금이 아닐 것이다'라는 어색한 의미를 만들기 때문에 답이 될 수 없다.

07 알맞은 문장 고르기
해석 (A) 시험 구독은 보통 6개월의 기간 동안 계속됩니다.
(B) 귀하께서는 단 몇 주 내에 최신 호를 받을 것으로 기대할 수 있습니다.
(C) 저희의 기록은 귀하가 2년 동안 구독자였다고 나타납니다.
(D) 귀하의 구독을 연장해야 할 많은 이유가 있습니다.

해설 뒤 문장 'For starters, you will be able to enjoy more articles by some of today's leading writers.'에서 우선, 오늘날의 몇몇 최고 작가들의 글을 더 많이 즐길 수 있게 될 것이라고 한 후, 뒷부분에서 할인을 받아 금액도 절약할 수 있다고 했으므로 빈칸에는 구독을 연장해야 할 많은 이유가 있다고 안내하는 내용이 들어가야 함을 알 수 있다. 따라서 (D)가 정답이다.

어휘 trial adj. 시험의, 시험적인   typically adv. 보통, 일반적으로
latest adj. 최신의, 최근의   indicate v. 나타내다   plenty of 많은

08 명사 어휘 고르기
해설 '저희의 출판물을 계속해서 구독해 주기를 바란다'라는 문맥이므로 (A) publication(출판물)이 정답이다. (B) message는 '메시지', (C) installment는 '할부금', (D) episode는 '사건, 에피소드'라는 의미이다.

09-12번은 다음 기사에 관한 문제입니다.

ALICE SPRINGS (8월 26일)—다가오는 에너지 프로젝트를 위해 Owler사가 Alice Springs 시의회에 의해 선정되었다. 그것은 모든 지역 공립 학교에 태양 전지판을 설치할 것이다. 09몇몇 환경 단체들이 이 프로젝트에 대해 지지를 나타냈다. 10이 프로젝트는 10월 1일에 Gillen 고등학교에서 시작되는데, 이곳에는 225개의 전지판들이 갖춰질 것이다. 11그러고 나서, Owler사는 East Side 초등학교와 Braitling 중학교로 넘어갈 것이다. 설치되면, 그 전지판들은 각 학교에 수천만 달러의 연간 비용 절감을 가져올 것이다. 12"저희는 Owler사의 낮은 비용과 폭넓은 경험 때문에 그곳을 선택했습니다."라고 Alice Springs 시장 Tanya McCrindle이 말했다.

city council 시의회   install v. 설치하다   solar panel 태양 전지판
annual adj. 연간의, 연례의

09 알맞은 문장 고르기
해석 (A) 몇몇 환경 단체들이 이 프로젝트에 대해 지지를 나타냈다.
(B) 각 회사는 다른 학교 건물에서 일하도록 배정되었다.
(C) 그들은 추가적인 지연에 대해 부모들에게 사과했다.
(D) 계약을 따낸 사람은 익명으로 남을 것이다.

해설 앞 문장 'It will install solar panels at all local public schools.'에서 그것, 즉 Owler사가 모든 지역 공립 학교에 태양 전지판을 설치할 것이라고 했으므로 빈칸에는 이러한 환경 프로젝트에 대한 반응과 관련된 내용이 와야 함을 알 수 있다. 따라서 (A)가 정답이다.

어휘 indicate v. 나타내다   support n. 지지, 지원   assign v. 배정하다
apologize v. 사과하다   delay n. 지연, 지체; v. 연기하다
anonymous adj. 익명인

10 수동태 관용 표현 채우기
해설 관계절(which ~ panels)에 동사가 없으므로 be동사(be)와 함께 동사를 만드는 현재분사 (A)와 과거분사 (C)가 정답의 후보이다. '이곳에는 225개의 전지판들이 갖춰질 것이다'라는 의미가 되어야 하므로 '~을 갖추고 있다'라는 표현을 만드는 (C) equipped가 정답이다. 동사원형 (B)와 동사의 3인칭 단수형 (D)는 be동사 뒤에 올 수 없다.

11 접속부사 채우기 주변 문맥 파악
해설 빈칸이 콤마와 함께 문장의 맨 앞에 온 접속부사 자리이므로, 앞 문장과 빈칸이 있는 문장의 의미 관계를 파악하여 정답을 선택한다. 앞 문장에서 이 프로젝트는 10월 1일에 Gillen 고등학교에서 시작된다고 했고, 빈칸이 있는 문장에서는 Owler사가 East Side 초등학교와 Braitling 중학교로 넘어갈 것이라고 했으므로, 앞 문장의 내용에 이어질 다음 과정을 설명할 때 사용되는 (B) Then(그러고 나서)이 정답이다.
어휘 instead adv. 대신에 yet adv. 아직 alternatively adv. 그 대신에

12 형용사 어휘 고르기
해설 'Owler사의 낮은 비용과 폭넓은 경험'이라는 문맥이므로 (A) extensive(폭넓은)가 정답이다. (B) routine은 '일상적인, 보통의', (C) predictable은 '예측할 수 있는', (D) objective는 '객관적인'이라는 의미이다.

13-16번은 다음 이메일에 관한 문제입니다.

수신: Andrea Stinton <stinton.a@kuvarik.com>
발신: Leroy Wauters <wauters.l@kuvarik.com>
제목: 최근 점검
날짜: 11월 17일

Ms. Stinton께,

¹³어제, 저는 도네츠크에 있는 Kuvarik사 생산 공장에 대한 의무 점검을 실시했습니다. ¹⁴체크리스트에 있는 많은 항목들이 만족스러웠지만, 저는 두 가지의 잠재적 안전 문제들을 발견했습니다. 우선, 우리는 작년의 규제 변경으로 인해 소화기 세 대를 더 추가해야 합니다. ¹⁵이것이 즉시 행해지지 않으면, 우리는 벌금을 부과받을 것입니다. 두 번째로, 한 계단에 난간의 일부가 없는 것을 발견했습니다. ¹⁶그것들은 긴급 상황이 발생할 경우에 필수적일 것입니다. 대체품 주문에 대해 논의할 수 있도록 저에게 연락해 주시기 바랍니다.

Leroy Wauters 드림
시설 관리자

mandatory adj. 의무적인, 필수의 inspection n. 점검, 검사
satisfactory adj. 만족스러운 discover v. 발견하다, 깨닫다
potential adj. 잠재적인, 가능성이 있는 fire extinguisher 소화기
regulation n. 규제, 규정 handrail n. 난간 stairway n. 계단
essential adj. 필수적인; n. 필수적인 것 emergency n. 긴급 상황
order v. 주문하다 replacement n. 대체품

13 동사 어휘 고르기 주변 문맥 파악
해설 '어제, 생산 공장에 대한 의무 점검을 ___했다'라는 문맥이므로 모든 보기가 정답의 후보이다. 빈칸이 있는 문장만으로 정답을 고를 수 없으므로 주변 문맥이나 전체 문맥을 파악한다. 뒤 문장에서 체크리스트에 있는 많은 항목들이 만족스러웠지만, 잠재적 문제들을 발견했다고 했으므로 이 메일의 작성자인 Mr. Wauters가 어제 점검을 실시했다는 것을 알 수 있다. 따라서 동사 conduct(실시하다)의 과거 시제 (D) conducted가 정답이다.
어휘 schedule v. 일정을 잡다 postpone v. 연기하다 cancel v. 취소하다

14 명사 관련 어구 완성하기 전체 문맥 파악
해설 빈칸은 빈칸 뒤의 명사(issues)와 복합 명사를 이루어 동사(discovered)의 목적어 역할을 하는 명사 자리이다. '두 가지의 잠재적 ___ 문제들을 발견했다'라는 문맥이므로 모든 보기가 정답의 후보이다. 빈칸이 있는 문장만으로 정답을 고를 수 없으므로 주변 문맥이나 전체 문맥을 파악한다.

뒤 문장에서 작년의 규제 변경으로 인해 소화기 세 대를 더 추가해야 한다고 했고, 뒷부분에서 한 계단에 난간의 일부가 없는 것을 발견했다고 했으므로 두 가지의 잠재적 안전 문제들을 발견했음을 알 수 있다. 따라서 (B) safety(안전)가 정답이다.
어휘 service n. 업무, 서비스 productivity n. 생산성 personnel n. 인사

15 알맞은 문장 고르기
해설 (A) 이것이 즉시 행해지지 않으면, 우리는 벌금을 부과받을 것입니다.
(B) 규정은 우리가 직원 안내서를 업데이트하기를 요구합니다.
(C) 신입 직원들은 소화기를 사용할 수 있도록 교육받았습니다.
(D) 예상했던 대로, 우리는 지난해 생산 할당량을 달성했습니다.
해설 앞 문장 'we need to add three more fire extinguishers due to a change in regulations last year.'에서 작년의 규제 변경으로 인해 소화기 세 대를 더 추가해야 한다고 했으므로 빈칸에는 이것이 즉시 행해지지 않으면 어떻게 되는지에 관한 내용이 들어가야 함을 알 수 있다. 따라서 (A)가 정답이다.
어휘 promptly adv. 즉시 issue v. (벌금을) 부과하다 fine n. 벌금
handbook n. 안내서, 입문서 meet v. 달성하다, 만나다 quota n. 할당량

16 인칭대명사 채우기 주변 문맥 파악
해설 빈칸은 동사(would be)의 주어 자리이므로 주어 자리에 올 수 있는 인칭대명사인 모든 보기가 정답의 후보이다. 빈칸이 있는 문장만으로 정답을 고를 수 없으므로 주변 문맥이나 전체 문맥을 파악한다. '___은 긴급 상황이 발생할 경우에 필수적일 것이다'라는 문맥이고, 앞 문장에서 '한 계단에 난간의 일부가 없는 것을 발견했다(I saw that some handrails are missing along one stairway)'라고 했으므로, 복수 사물 명사(some handrails)를 가리키는 주격 인칭대명사 (D) They(그것들)가 정답이다. 인칭대명사 (A) It과 지시대명사 (B) That은 단수 명사를 가리킨다. 소유대명사 (C) Theirs는 '그들의 것'이라는 의미로 어색한 문맥을 만든다.

DAY 14 문맥 파악 문제: 어휘

HACKERS PRACTICE p.263

01 (A)   02 (C)   03 (D)

01번은 다음 공고에 관한 문제입니다.

Maincore 다이빙 센터
Maincore 다이빙 센터에서 3일간의 스쿠버 다이빙 강습을 끝내신 것을 축하합니다. ⁰¹여러분께 기억할 만한 경험이 되셨기를 바랍니다. 저희와의 시간을 잊지 않으시면 좋겠습니다. 자격증을 위한 마지막 요건으로, 내일 여러분은 처음으로 심해 다이빙을 할 것입니다. 부상과 사고를 방지하기 위해 배운 절차를 반드시 준수해 주시기 바랍니다. 센터 직원들은 여러분의 장비 선택을 도와줄 것입니다.

requirement n. 요건, 필요 certification n. 자격증
deepwater adj. 심해의, 깊은 물의 procedure n. 절차 equipment n. 장비

01 형용사 어휘 고르기 주변 문맥 파악
해설 '___한 경험이 되었기를 바란다'라는 문맥이므로 모든 보기가 정답의 후보이다. 빈칸이 있는 문장만으로 정답을 고를 수 없으므로 주변 문맥이나 전체 문맥을 파악한다. 뒤 문장에서 저희, 즉 Maincore 다이빙 센터와의 시간을 잊지 않으면 좋겠다고 했으므로, 스쿠버 다이빙 강습이 기억할 만한 경험이 되었기를 바란다는 것임을 알 수 있다. 따라서 (A) memorable(기억할 만한)이 정답이다. (B) sensitive는 '세심한', (C) mandatory는 '의무적인', (D) reasonable은 '합리적인'이라는 의미이다.

02번은 다음 이메일에 관한 문제입니다.

수신: Winston Wheeler <w.wheeler@ata.com>
발신: Matt Nicholson < m.nicholson@northshire.com>
제목: 회신: 프로젝터
날짜: 12월 9일

Mr. Wheeler께,

제가 요청했던 프로젝터에 관한 정보를 제공해 주셔서 감사합니다. 02시간을 내어 귀하의 가게에서 구매 가능한 몇몇 브랜드를 추천해 주셔서 감사드립니다. 유감스럽게도, 제안된 것들은 너무 비쌉니다. 그럼에도 불구하고, 저는 귀하께서 추천하셨던 스피커에 대해 더 알고 싶습니다. 스피커 시스템에 대한 기술적인 세부 사항을 보내주실 수 있나요? 감사합니다.

Matt Nicholson 드림
정보통신기술 학과장, Northshire 대학교

projector n. 프로젝터, 영사기   unfortunately adv. 유감스럽게도
technical adj. 기술적인   detail n. 세부 사항

02 동사 어휘 고르기 주변 문맥 파악

해설 '시간을 내어 가게에서 구매 가능한 몇몇 브랜드를 ___해 주어 감사하다'라는 문맥이므로 모든 보기가 정답의 후보이다. 빈칸이 있는 문장만으로 정답을 고를 수 없으므로 주변 문맥이나 전체 문맥을 파악한다. 뒤 문장에서 유감스럽게도 제안된 것들이 너무 비싸다고 했으므로, Mr. Wheeler가 가게에서 구매 가능한 몇몇 브랜드를 추천해 주었음을 알 수 있다. 따라서 (C) recommend(추천하다)가 정답이다. (A) replace는 '교체하다', (B) improve는 '개선하다, 향상시키다', (D) test는 '시험하다'라는 의미이다.

03번은 다음 안내문에 관한 문제입니다.

프린터 잉크 카트리지를 교체하는 것은 비쌉니다. 게다가, 그것들을 버리는 것은 환경에 해롭습니다. 다행히도, 대부분의 잉크 카트리지는 다시 채워지고 재사용될 수 있습니다. 이렇게 하는 것은 돈을 절약하기 때문에 버리는 것보다 낫습니다. 그것은 또한 쓰레기 매립지의 폐기물을 줄입니다. 저희 사무용품 매장은 모든 지점에 잉크 재충전소가 있습니다. 03저희는 여러분의 카트리지가 여전히 양호한 상태인지 확인할 것입니다. 만약 그렇다면, 새 것의 절반 가격으로 재충전해 드릴 것입니다.

dispose v. 버리다, 없애다   refill v. 다시 채우다   reuse v. 재사용하다
waste n. 폐기물, 쓰레기   landfill n. 쓰레기 매립지   condition n. 상태

03 부사 어휘 고르기 주변 문맥 파악

해설 '카트리지가 ____ 양호한 상태인지 확인할 것이다'라는 문맥이므로 (B), (C), (D)가 정답의 후보이다. 빈칸이 있는 문장만으로 정답을 고를 수 없으므로 주변 문맥이나 전체 문맥을 파악한다. 뒤 문장에서 만약 그렇다면 새 것의 절반 가격으로 재충전해 주겠다고 했으므로 카트리지가 여전히 양호한 상태인지 확인할 것임을 알 수 있다. 따라서 (D) still(여전히)이 정답이다. (A) rarely는 '드물게, 좀처럼 ~하지 않는', (B) frequently는 '자주, 흔히', (C) barely는 '간신히, 겨우'라는 의미이다.

HACKERS TEST   p.264

01 (C)	02 (D)	03 (A)	04 (D)	05 (C)
06 (C)	07 (A)	08 (C)	09 (B)	10 (D)
11 (B)	12 (A)	13 (A)	14 (B)	15 (A)
16 (D)				

01-04번은 다음 광고에 관한 문제입니다.

01Kelli사는 새롭게 출시된 Hava-Go 헤어 드라이어를 소개하게 되어 자랑스럽습니다. 당사에서 가장 휴대가 쉬운 모델인 Hava-Go는 무선이며 무게가 단 500그램입니다. 02이러한 특징들은 그것을 매우 사용하기 쉽게 만들어 줍니다. 03그 기기는 또한 여행에도 이상적입니다. 완전히 충전되면, 그것의 배터리는 100분까지 지속됩니다. 그래서 여러분이 어디에 있든 머리를 말릴 수 있습니다.

04지금 Hava-Go를 구입하세요. 그것은 Ciao 쇼핑몰과 같은 전자제품 매장들이나 GoodsSupply.com을 포함한 온라인 상점들에서 판매됩니다. 이 놀라운 기기를 놓치지 마세요!

introduce v. 소개하다   portable adj. 휴대가 쉬운   cordless adj. 무선인
weigh v. 무게가 ~이다   charged adj. 충전된   last v. 지속되다

01 현재분사와 과거분사 구별하여 채우기

해설 빈칸 뒤의 명사(Hava-Go hair dryer)를 꾸미면서 빈칸 앞의 부사(newly)의 꾸밈을 받을 수 있는 것은 형용사이므로 현재분사 (B)와 과거분사 (C)가 정답의 후보이다. 꾸밈을 받는 명사(Hava-Go hair dryer)와 분사가 '출시된 Hava-Go 헤어 드라이어'라는 의미의 수동 관계이므로 과거분사 (C) released가 정답이다. 현재분사 (B) releasing을 쓸 경우 '출시하는 Hava-Go 헤어 드라이어'라는 어색한 문맥이 된다. 동사 또는 명사 (A)와 (D)는 형용사 자리에 올 수 없다.

어휘 release v. 출시하다, 공개하다; n. 출시, 공개

02 명사 어휘 고르기 주변 문맥 파악

해설 '이러한 ____은 그것을 매우 사용하기 쉽게 만들어 준다'라는 문맥이므로 모든 보기가 정답의 후보이다. 빈칸이 있는 문장만으로 정답을 고를 수 없으므로 주변 문맥이나 전체 문맥을 파악한다. 앞 문장에서 Hava-Go 헤어 드라이어가 무선이며 무게가 단 500그램이라고 했으므로 Hava-Go 헤어 드라이어의 이러한 특징들이 그것을 매우 사용하기 쉽게 만들어 준다는 것을 알 수 있다. 따라서 (D) features(특징들)가 정답이다. (A) containers는 '용기', (B) machines는 '기계', (C) accessories는 '액세서리, 부품'이라는 의미이다.

03 알맞은 문장 고르기

해석 (A) 그 기기는 또한 여행에도 이상적입니다.
    (B) 그 디자인은 이번 달 후반에 업데이트될 것입니다.
    (C) 모델명은 아직 정해지지 않았습니다.
    (D) 그것들은 대형 호텔 체인들에만 공급되고 있습니다.

해설 앞부분에서 Hava-Go 헤어 드라이어가 휴대 및 사용이 쉬운 기기라고 한 후, 뒤 문장 'When fully charged, its battery lasts for up to 100 minutes.'에서 완전히 충전되면 배터리가 100분까지 지속된다고 했으므로, 빈칸에는 이 기기가 휴대가 쉬우며 장시간 사용할 수 있다는 장점과 관련된 내용이 들어가야 함을 알 수 있다. 따라서 (A)가 정답이다.

어휘 ideal adj. 이상적인   supply v. 공급하다

04 동사 어휘 고르기 주변 문맥 파악

해설 '지금 Hava-Go를 ____하라'라는 문맥이므로 (A), (B), (D)가 정답의 후보이다. 빈칸이 있는 문장만으로 정답을 고를 수 없으므로 주변 문맥이나 전체 문맥을 파악한다. 뒤 문장에서 그것, 즉 Hava-Go 헤어 드라이기가 전자제품 매장이나 온라인 상점들에서 판매된다고 했으므로, 지금 Hava-Go를 구입하라는 것임을 알 수 있다. 따라서 (D) Purchase(구입하다)가 정답이다. (A) Lend는 '빌려주다', (B) Connect는 '연결하다', (C) Estimate는 '추정하다'라는 의미이다.

05-08번은 다음 보도 자료에 관한 문제입니다.

뉴욕 (1월 28일)—TymTech사의 최신 노트북에 대한 광고가 올해 전 세계 마케팅 시상식에서 최고의 TV 광고로 선정되었다. 05이 우승한 광고는 Telerana Associates사에 의해 제작되었다.

⁰⁶세계적으로 유명한 운동선수 Wanda Vilanova에게 주연을 맡긴 그 30초짜리 광고는 북미 전역의 방송국들에서 방송되었다. 영어, 스페인어, 그리고 프랑스어 버전들이 만들어졌다. ⁰⁷"저희는 문화적 차이들을 세심하게 고려했습니다. 따라서, 저희는 세 가지 버전이 모두 확실히 효과적이게 했습니다."라고 Telerana Associates사의 임원인 Harold Martel이 말했다.

TymTech사에 따르면, 그 광고는 회사에 최고 기록의 매출을 냈다. ⁰⁸그것은 향후 캠페인들을 위해 Telerana Associates사를 다시 고용할 계획이다.

world-famous adj. 세계적으로 유명한 broadcast v. 방송하다
station n. 방송국 ensure v. 확실히 ~하게 하다 effective adj. 효과적인
result in (어떠한 결과를) 내다, 낳다 record adj. 최고 기록의, 기록적인

05 형용사 어휘 고르기 주변 문맥 파악

해설 '이 ___ 광고는 Telerana Associates사에 의해 제작되었다'라는 문맥이므로 모든 보기가 정답의 후보이다. 빈칸이 있는 문장만으로 정답을 고를 수 없으므로 주변 문맥이나 전체 문맥을 파악한다. 앞 문장에서 TymTech사의 최신 노트북에 대한 광고가 올해 전 세계 마케팅 시상식에서 최고의 TV 광고로 선정되었다고 했으므로 이 우승한 광고가 Telerana Associates사에 의해 제작된 것을 알 수 있다. 따라서 (C) winning(우승한)이 정답이다. (A) controversial은 '논란이 많은', (B) sample은 '견본의', (D) canceled는 '취소된'이라는 의미이다.

06 현재분사와 과거분사 구별하여 채우기

해설 이 문장은 주어(the 30-second advertisement)와 동사(was broadcast)를 갖춘 완전한 절이므로, ___ ~ Wanda Vilanova는 수식어 거품으로 보아야 한다. 보기 중 수식어 거품이 될 수 있는 과거분사 (A)와 현재분사 (C)가 정답의 후보이다. 빈칸 다음에 목적어(the world-famous ~ Wanda Vilanova)가 있고, 주절의 주어(the 30-second advertisement)와 분사구문이 'Wanda Vilanova에게 주연을 맡긴 30초짜리 광고'라는 의미의 능동 관계이므로 현재분사 (C) Starring이 정답이다. 동사 또는 명사 (B)와 (D)는 수식어 거품을 이끌 수 없다.

어휘 star v. 주연을 맡기다; n. 인기인, 스타

07 부사 어휘 고르기 주변 문맥 파악

해설 '우리는 문화적 차이들을 ___ 고려했다'라는 문맥이므로 모든 보기가 정답의 후보이다. 빈칸이 있는 문장만으로 정답을 고를 수 없으므로 주변 문맥이나 전체 문맥을 파악한다. 앞 문장에서 광고의 영어, 스페인어, 그리고 프랑스어 버전들이 만들어졌다고 했고, 뒤 문장에서 세 가지 버전이 모두 확실히 효과적이도록 했다고 했으므로 문화적 차이들을 세심하게 고려했다는 것을 알 수 있다. 따라서 (A) carefully(세심하게)가 정답이다. (B) barely는 '거의 ~아니게', (C) roughly는 '대충, 거칠게', (D) randomly는 '무작위로'라는 의미이다.

08 알맞은 문장 고르기

해석 (A) 대회의 모든 우승자들에게 상품권이 발송되었다.
(B) 전 세계 마케팅 시상식은 곧 결정을 내릴 것이다.
(C) 그것은 향후 캠페인들을 위해 Telerana Associates사를 다시 고용할 계획이다.
(D) 이 기록은 나중에 그것의 주요 경쟁사들 중 하나에 의해 깨졌다.

해설 앞 문장 'According to TymTech, the advertisement has resulted in record sales for the company.'에서 TymTech사에 따르면, 그 광고, 즉 Telerana Associates사에 의해 제작된 광고가 회사에 최고 기록의 매출을 냈다고 했으므로, 빈칸에는 추후 캠페인을 위해 TymTech사가 다시 Telerana Associates사를 고용할 것이라는 내용이 들어가야 함을 알 수 있다. 따라서 (C)가 정답이다.

어휘 voucher n. 상품권 competition n. 대회, 경쟁 competitor n. 경쟁사

09-12번은 다음 기사에 관한 문제입니다.

⁰⁹9월 9일, 멕시코시티―Compensa Solutions사는 Valeria Gomez의 임명을 발표했다. ¹⁰그 발표는 어제 기자회견에서 이루어졌다. 기자들과 이야기하면서, 대변인 Thomas Walden은 Ms. Gomez를 회사의 고위 관리직에 훌륭한 추가 인력이라고 설명했다. ¹¹"저희는 Ms. Gomez를 새로운 최고 마케팅 책임자로 맞이하게 되어 기쁘며 그녀가 폭넓은 지식과 수년간의 경험을 통해 저희가 새로운 시장에 진출하도록 도울 수 있기를 희망합니다."라고 그는 말했다. ¹²Ms. Gomez는 이전에 이사직을 맡았던 적이 없지만, 그녀는 도전에 대해 그녀가 준비되어 있다고 말했다.

announce v. 발표하다 describe v. 설명하다, 묘사하다 terrific adj. 훌륭한
addition n. 추가 (인력) senior management 고위 관리직
chief adj. 최고의 extensive adj. 폭넓은 state v. 말하다, 서술하다
challenge n. 도전

09 명사 어휘 고르기 전체 문맥 파악

해설 'Compensa Solutions사는 Valeria Gomez의 ___을 발표했다'라는 문맥이므로 모든 보기가 정답의 후보이다. 빈칸이 있는 문장만으로 정답을 고를 수 없으므로 주변 문맥이나 전체 문맥을 파악한다. 뒷부분에서 대변인 Thomas Walden이 Ms. Gomez를 새로운 최고 마케팅 책임자로 맞이하게 되었다고 했으므로 Compensa Solutions사가 Ms. Gomez의 임명을 발표했음을 알 수 있다. 따라서 (B) appointment(임명)가 정답이다. (A) retirement는 '은퇴, 퇴직', (C) investment는 '투자', (D) accomplishment는 '업적'이라는 의미이다.

10 알맞은 문장 고르기

해석 (A) 그들은 우수한 상품과 서비스를 제공한다.
(B) 회사의 매출은 1년 넘게 꾸준히 올랐다.
(C) 회사의 공석 목록은 웹사이트에서 확인 가능하다.
(D) 그 발표는 어제 기자회견에서 이루어졌다.

해설 앞 문장 'September 9, Mexico City―Compensa Solutions has announced the (appointment) of Valeria Gomez.'에서 Compensa Solutions사가 Valeria Gomez의 임명을 발표했다고 했고, 뒤 문장 'Speaking to reporters, spokesperson Thomas Walden described Ms. Gomez as a terrific addition to the senior management of the firm.'에서 기자들과 이야기하면서, 대변인 Thomas Walden은 Ms. Gomez를 회사의 고위 관리직에 훌륭한 추가 인력이라고 설명했다고 했으므로 빈칸에는 발표가 기자들이 있는 자리에서 이루어졌다는 내용이 들어가야 함을 알 수 있다. 따라서 (D)가 정답이다.

어휘 superior adj. 우수한 climb v. 오르다 steadily adv. 꾸준히
open position 공석 statement n. 발표, 성명
press conference 기자회견

11 현재분사와 과거분사 구별하여 채우기

해설 be동사(are)의 보어 자리에 올 수 있는 과거분사 (B)와 현재분사 (D)가 정답의 후보이다. 'Ms. Gomez를 맞이하게 되어 기쁘다'라는 의미가 되어야 하므로 과거분사 (B) pleased가 정답이다. 현재분사 (D)를 쓸 경우 'Ms. Gomez를 맞이하게 되어 기쁘게 하다'라는 어색한 의미가 된다. 동사 (A)와 (C)는 보어 자리에 올 수 없다. 참고로, We(우리)가 감정을 느끼는 주체이므로 과거분사가 왔다.

12 부사절 접속사 채우기

해설 이 문장은 주어(she), 동사(stated), 목적어(that she is ~ challenge)를 갖춘 완전한 절이므로 ___ ~ before는 수식어 거품으로 보아야 한다. 이 수식어 거품은 동사(has not held)가 있는 거품절이므로, 부사절 접속사 (A)와 (D)가 정답의 후보이다. 'Ms. Gomez는 이전에 이사직을 맡았던 적이 없지만, 그녀는 도전에 대해 그녀가 준비되어 있다고 말했다'라는 의미가 되어야 하므로 (A) While(~하지만, ~한 반면)이 정답이다. (D) Because는 '~때문에'라는 의미이다. 전치사 (B) In spite of(~에도 불구하고)와 (C) During(~동안)은 거품절을 이끌 수 없다.

13-16번은 다음 공고에 관한 문제입니다.

> **Sortix 디지털 보안 자문 회사**
> **긴급 공지**
>
> Zeno 운영체제의 제조업체인 Alephnet사가 그것의 플랫폼의 이전 버전들에 대한 지원을 제공하는 것을 중단할 것입니다. ¹³결과적으로, 그 회사는 Zeno-10의 소프트웨어 업데이트를 더 이상 제공하지 않을 것입니다. 그러므로 Zeno-11로 업그레이드하십시오. ¹⁴만약 이것을 하지 않는다면, 여러분의 컴퓨터들이 보안 위협에 취약해질 것입니다. ¹⁵전반적으로, Zeno-11은 이전의 플랫폼에 비해 더 나은 보안을 제공합니다. 여러분의 시스템 안정성을 보장하기 위해, 저희는 여러분께 즉시 업데이트하는 것을 강력히 권고합니다. ¹⁶설치 지침 및 지원을 위해서, 저희의 웹사이트를 참고하십시오. 추가 질문이 있는 경우에는, cs@sortix.com으로 저희에게 연락 주십시오.

support n. 지원 vulnerable adj. 취약한 threat n. 위협
stability n. 안정성 urge v. 권고하다, 촉구하다 immediately adv. 즉시

13 접속부사 채우기 주변 문맥 파악
해설 빈칸이 콤마와 함께 문장의 맨 앞에 온 접속부사 자리이므로, 앞 문장과 빈칸이 있는 문장의 의미 관계를 파악하여 정답을 선택한다. 앞 문장에서 Zeno 운영체제의 제조업체가 그것의 플랫폼의 이전 버전들에 대한 지원을 제공하는 것을 중단할 것이라고 했고, 빈칸이 있는 문장에서는 그 회사가 Zeno-10의 소프트웨어 업데이트를 더 이상 제공하지 않을 것이라고 했으므로, 앞에서 말한 내용에 따른 결과를 언급하는 내용의 문장에서 사용되는 (A) As a result(결과적으로)가 정답이다.

어휘 instead adv. 대신에 once adv. 한 번, 언젠가; conj. ~하자마자
however adv. 그러나

14 부사절 접속사 채우기
해설 이 문장은 필수성분(your computer will be vulnerable)을 갖춘 완전한 절이므로, ___ you fail to do this는 수식어 거품으로 보아야 한다. 이 수식어 거품은 동사(fail)가 있는 거품절이므로, 거품절을 이끌 수 있는 부사절 접속사 (B), (C), (D)가 정답의 후보이다. '만약 이것을 하지 않는다면, 컴퓨터들이 보안 위협에 취약해질 것이다'라는 의미가 되어야 하므로 조건을 나타내는 부사절 접속사 (B) If(만약 ~라면)가 정답이다. (C) Until과 (D) Whether는 각각 '이것을 하지 않을 때까지/이것을 안 하든 말든, 컴퓨터들이 보안 위협에 취약해질 것이다'라는 어색한 문맥을 만든다. 전치사 (A) By(~함으로써, ~에 의해)는 거품절을 이끌 수 없다.

15 형용사 어휘 고르기 전체 문맥 파악
해설 'Zeno-11은 ___ 플랫폼에 비해 더 나은 보안을 제공한다'라는 문맥이므로 모든 보기가 정답의 후보이다. 빈칸이 있는 문장만으로 정답을 고를 수 없으므로 주변 문맥이나 전체 문맥을 파악한다. 앞부분에서 Zeno-10의 소프트웨어 업데이트를 더 이상 제공하지 않을 것이므로 Zeno-11로 업그레이드하라고 했으므로 Zeno-10은 Zeno-11의 이전의 플랫폼이라는 것을 알 수 있다. 따라서 (A) previous(이전의)가 정답이다. (B) faulty는 '흠이 있는, 불완전한', (C) proposed는 '제안된', (D) expensive는 '비싼, 돈이 많이 드는'이라는 의미이다.

16 알맞은 문장 고르기
해석 (A) 이 특별 판촉이 끝나기 전에 지금 행동하십시오.
(B) 저희는 이용 가능해지는 즉시 여러분께 알림을 보내겠습니다.
(C) 그 회사는 여러 제품을 회수했습니다.
(D) 설치 지침 및 지원을 위해서, 저희의 웹사이트를 참고하십시오.

해설 앞 문장 'To ensure the stability of your system, we strongly urge you to update immediately.'에서 시스템의 안정성을 보장하기 위해 즉시 업데이트하는 것을 강력히 권고한다고 했고, 뒤 문장 'In case you have any additional questions, please contact us at cs@sortix.com.'에서 추가 질문이 있는 경우에는 이메일로 연락하라고 했으므로 빈칸에는 업데이트에 대한 정보를 얻을 수 있는 방법과 관련된 내용이 들어가야 함을 알 수 있다. 따라서 (D)가 정답이다.

어휘 expire v. 끝나다 reminder n. (상기시켜 주는) 알림, 메모
recall v. 회수하다, 리콜하다 instruction n. 지침 refer to ~을 참고하다

DAY 15 문맥 파악 문제: 문장

HACKERS PRACTICE p.269

01 (B) **02** (C) **03** (C)

01번은 다음 편지에 관한 문제입니다.

> Ms. Sunders께,
>
> Edildburgh Technologies사에서는, 저희의 놀라운 성장과 혁신적인 전략이 우리를 기술 분야의 선두 주자로 자리를 잡게 했습니다. 저희 주주들의 지지가 없었다면, 저희는 서유럽 최고의 전자 회사 중 하나가 되지 못했을 것입니다. ⁰¹따라서, 파티를 열어 여러분의 지원에 감사를 표하고자 합니다.
>
> 동봉되어 있는 것은 행사 초청장입니다.
>
> Jasper Diaz 드림
> 사장, Edildburgh Technologies사

remarkable adj. 놀라운, 주목할 만한 growth n. 성장
innovative adj. 혁신적인 strategy n. 전략 position v. 자리를 잡다
shareholder n. 주주 enclose v. 동봉하다

01 알맞은 문장 고르기
해석 (A) 또한, 당사는 현재 경쟁사와 파트너십을 맺는 것을 고려하고 있습니다.
(B) 따라서, 파티를 열어 여러분의 지원에 감사를 표하고자 합니다.
(C) 지난 1년 동안 주가가 크게 상승했습니다.
(D) 저희 팀에 합류하는 것에 관심을 표해 주셔서 감사합니다.

해설 뒤 문장 'Enclosed is an invitation to the event.'에서 동봉되어 있는 것은 행사 초청장이라고 했으므로, 빈칸에는 행사를 열 것이라는 내용이 들어가야 함을 알 수 있다. 따라서 (B)가 정답이다.

어휘 appreciation n. 감사, 감상 stock value 주가
significantly adv. 크게, 상당히 express v. 표하다, 나타내다

02번은 다음 공고에 관한 문제입니다.

> **사상 첫 알제리 무역 박람회로 오세요!**
>
> 11월에 Maktub 컨벤션 센터에서 200개가 넘는 알제리 제조업체가 그들의 제품을 전시할 예정입니다. Samir Klouchi 무역산업부 장관이 11월 1일에 전시회를 개막할 것입니다. 한 달 동안 계속되는 행사는 지역 사업을 지원하는 것을 목표로 합니다. ⁰²이것은 11월 30일에 15분간의 불꽃놀이와 함께 막을 내립니다.

manufacturer n. 제조업체 exhibition n. 전시(회)
aim to ~하는 것을 목표로 하다

02 알맞은 문장 고르기
해석 (A) 행사는 일주일 동안 진행될 것입니다.
(B) 오늘 중으로 피드백 의견을 제출하세요.
(C) 이것은 11월 30일에 15분간의 불꽃놀이와 함께 막을 내립니다.
(D) 부스는 매일 오후 8시까지 청소되어야 합니다.

해설 앞부분에서 무역산업부 장관이 11월 1일에 전시회를 개막할 것이라고 한 후, 앞 문장 'The month-long event aims to support local businesses.'에서 한 달 동안 계속되는 행사는 지역 사업을 지원하는 것을 목표로 한다고 했으므로, 빈칸에는 이 행사의 진행 정보와 관련된 내용이 들어가야 함을 알 수 있다. 따라서 (C)가 정답이다. (A)가 The event

(행사)를 언급해서 언뜻 보기에 정답인 것으로 착각할 수 있지만, 행사가 한 달 동안 계속된다는 것과 행사가 일주일 동안 진행된다는 것은 전체 문맥상 어울리지 않으므로 답이 될 수 없다.

어휘 firework n. 불꽃놀이

03번은 다음 이메일에 관한 문제입니다.

수신: Muscle Mass 체육관 <customerservice@mmg.com>
발신: Oscar Perry <o.perry@tmail.com>
날짜: 9월 4일
제목: 요청

관계자분께:

03저는 10월 1일부로 귀 시설의 회원권을 해지하고 싶습니다. 제가 해외로 이주할 것이기 때문에 해지를 요청해야 합니다. 제 회원권은 올해 말까지 완전히 납부되어 있습니다. 그러나, 10월 1일 이후에는 사용할 수 없기 때문에, 사용되지 않는 부분에 대해 환불을 받고 싶습니다. 빠른 회신을 기다리겠습니다.

Oscar Perry 드림

---

cancellation n. 해지, 취소 overseas adv. 해외로
unused adj. 사용되지 않은, 쓴 적이 없는 portion n. 부분, 일부

03 알맞은 문장 고르기

해석 (A) 운동 수업 강사에 대해 불만을 제기하고 싶습니다.
(B) 제 기록은 9월에 추가 요금이 청구되었다는 것을 보여줍니다.
(C) 저는 10월 1일부로 귀 시설의 회원권을 해지하고 싶습니다.
(D) 제 회원권 신청을 신속하게 처리해 주셔서 감사합니다.

해설 뒤 문장 'I need to request the cancellation as I will be moving overseas.'에서 자신이 해외로 이주할 것이기 때문에 해지를 요청해야 한다고 했으므로, 빈칸에는 회원권 해지에 관한 내용이 들어가야 함을 알 수 있다. 따라서 (C)가 정답이다.

어휘 complaint n. 불만, 불평, 항의 fitness n. 운동, 건강 charge v. 청구하다
establishment n. 시설, 기관 effective adj. ~부로 (유효한), 효과적인
process v. 처리하다 application n. 신청

HACKERS TEST p.270

01 (A)	02 (B)	03 (D)	04 (D)	05 (C)
06 (D)	07 (B)	08 (A)	09 (C)	10 (A)
11 (C)	12 (A)	13 (C)	14 (B)	15 (A)
16 (B)				

01-04번은 다음 공고에 관한 문제입니다.

Cliffdale Ridge Manor 주민들에 대한 공고

01이것은 여러분에게 새로운 주차 허가증이 8월 26일에 이용 가능할 것임을 알려드리기 위함입니다. 그것들은 지하 차고에 있는 모든 차량에 붙여져야 합니다.

02그것들은 쉽게 스캔될 수 있는 바코드를 포함할 것입니다. 그것을 받기 위해서는, Cliffdale Ridge Manor의 관리 사무실에서 여러분의 이전 출입증을 반납하십시오. 03여러분의 새로운 허가증을 받자마자, 차량의 앞쪽 전면 유리창 내부에 그것을 부착하십시오. 04그것이 명확히 보이는지 반드시 확인하십시오.

---

permit n. 허가증; v. 허용하다 available adj. 이용 가능한
place v. ~을 붙이다, 두다 underground adj. 지하의
turn in ~을 반납하다, 제출하다 maintenance n. 관리
interior n. 내부; adj. 내부의 vehicle n. 차량 windshield n. 전면 유리창

01 명사 관련 어구 완성하기 주변 문맥 파악

해설 '새로운 ____ 허가증이 이용 가능할 것이다'라는 문맥이므로 모든 보기가 정답의 후보이다. 빈칸이 있는 문장만으로 정답을 고를 수 없으므로 주변 문맥이나 전체 문맥을 파악한다. 뒤 문장에서 그것들은 지하 차고에 있는 모든 차량에 붙여져야 한다고 했으므로 새로운 주차 허가증이 이용 가능할 것이라는 것을 알 수 있다. 따라서 빈칸 뒤의 명사 permits와 함께 '주차 허가증'이라는 의미의 어구인 parking permits를 만드는 (A) parking(주차)이 정답이다. (B) construction(건설, 공사), (C) trash(쓰레기), (D) access(입장, 접근)는 '주차 허가증'이라는 의미의 어구를 만들 수 없다.

02 부사 자리 채우기

해설 동사(can be scanned)를 꾸밀 수 있는 것은 부사이므로 부사 (B) easily(쉽게)가 정답이다. 형용사 (A), 명사 또는 동사 (C), 형용사의 최상급 (D)는 동사를 꾸밀 수 없다.

어휘 easy adj. 쉬운 ease n. 쉬움; v. 수월하게 하다, 편하게 해주다

03 부사절 접속사 채우기

해설 이 문장은 주절(stick it ~ windshield)이 주어가 없는 명령문으로 동사(stick)와 목적어(it)를 갖추고 있으므로, ____ ~ permit은 수식어 거품으로 보아야 한다. 빈칸은 동사(get)가 있는 거품절을 이끄는 부사절 접속사 자리이므로 모든 보기가 정답의 후보이다. '새로운 허가증을 받자마자 차량의 앞쪽 전면 유리창 내부에 그것을 부착하라'라는 의미가 되어야 하므로 시간을 나타내는 부사절 접속사 (D) As soon as(~하자마자)가 정답이다. (A) Even if는 '비록 ~일지라도', (B) By the time은 '~할 때까지', (C) Before는 '~하기 전에'라는 의미이다.

04 알맞은 문장 고르기

해석 (A) 관리조가 다음 주에 작업을 완료할 것입니다.
(B) 안전 점검은 지난해의 것과 유사할 것입니다.
(C) 차량들은 수리가 잘 되어 있어야 합니다.
(D) 그것이 명확히 보이는지 반드시 확인하십시오.

해설 앞 문장 '(As soon as) you receive your new permit, stick it to the interior of your vehicle's front windshield.'에서 새로운 허가증을 받자마자, 차량의 앞쪽 전면 유리창 내부에 그것을 부착하라고 했으므로, 빈칸에는 허가증 부착 후 해야 할 일과 관련된 내용이 들어가야 함을 알 수 있다. 따라서 (D)가 정답이다.

어휘 crew n. (공동 작업에 종사하는) 조, 반 inspection n. 점검
in good repair 수리가 잘 되어 있는, 상태가 좋은 visible adj. 보이는

05-08번은 다음 광고에 관한 문제입니다.

이번 가을에 옷장을 업그레이드하려면, Edward Dormer사의 Winchester 캐주얼 재킷은 어떠신가요? 05이 재킷은 브랜드의 상징적인 모습을 환기시키는데, 이는 1940년대에 인기가 있었습니다. 저희는 이 프리미엄 의류 제품을 생산하는 것에 큰 자부심을 가지고 있습니다. 06각 재킷은 내구성 있는 재료들로 수작업으로 만들어졌습니다. 그것들은 고급 가죽, 양모, 면을 포함합니다. 07각 재킷이 방풍 및 방수가 되도록 하기 위해 특수한 코팅이 칠해져 있습니다. 08따라서, 그것은 당신의 몸을 계속 따뜻하고, 물기 없게 유지해 줄 것입니다. 이 재킷은 온라인이나 전국에 있는 저희 매장 지점 어디에서나 찾으실 수 있습니다.

---

wardrobe n. 옷장 revive v. 환기시키다, 되살아나게 하다
iconic adj. 상징적인 handcraft v. 손으로 만들다 durable adj. 내구성 있는
high-quality adj. 고급의 leather n. 가죽 wool n. 양모, 모직
cotton n. 면 wind-resistant adj. 바람을 막아주는
waterproof adj. 방수의

05 관계대명사 채우기

해설 이 문장은 주어(This jacket), 동사(revives), 목적어(the brand's ~ look)를 갖춘 완전한 절이므로, ____ ~ 1940s는 수식어 거품으로 보아야 한다. 이 수식어 거품은 빈칸 앞의 명사(the brand's ~ look)를 선행

사로 갖는 관계절이므로 관계대명사 (A), (B), (C)가 정답의 후보이다. 빈칸 뒤에 동사가 있으므로 주격 관계대명사 (C) which가 정답이다. 관계대명사 (A) that은 콤마(,) 바로 뒤에 올 수 없다. (B) who는 사물을 선행사로 가질 수 없다. 관계부사 (D) 뒤에는 완전한 절이 와야 한다.

06 명사 어휘 고르기 _주변 문맥 파악_
해설 '각 재킷은 내구성 있는 ___으로 수작업으로 만들어졌다'라는 문맥이므로 모든 보기가 정답의 후보이다. 빈칸이 있는 문장만으로 정답을 고를 수 없으므로 주변 문맥이나 전체 문맥을 파악한다. 뒤 문장에서 그것들은 고급 가죽, 양모, 면을 포함한다고 했으므로 각 재킷이 내구성 있는 재료로 수작업으로 만들어졌음을 알 수 있다. 따라서 (D) materials(재료들, 소재들)가 정답이다. (A) cases는 '덮개, 용기', (B) devices는 '장치', (C) tools는 '도구, 공구'라는 의미이다.

07 태에 맞는 동사 채우기
해설 문장에 주어(A ~ coating)만 있고 동사가 없으므로 동사 (B)와 (C)가 정답의 후보이다. 주어(A special coating)와 동사(apply)가 '특수한 코팅이 칠해져 있다'라는 수동의 의미가 되어야 하므로 수동태 동사 (B) is applied가 정답이다.
어휘 apply v. 칠하다, 적용하다

08 알맞은 문장 고르기
해석 (A) 따라서, 그것은 당신의 몸을 계속 따뜻하고, 물기 없게 유지해 줄 것입니다.
(B) 하지만, 그 재킷은 몇몇 액세서리와 함께 제공됩니다.
(C) 최초의 가죽 재킷들은 20세기 초에 등장했습니다.
(D) Mr. Dormer는 수년 동안 같은 재킷을 소유해 왔습니다.
해설 앞 문장 'A special coating (is applied) to make each jacket wind-resistant and waterproof.'에서 각 재킷이 방풍 및 방수가 되도록 하기 위해 특수한 코팅이 칠해져 있다고 했으므로 빈칸에는 따라서 그것, 즉 재킷이 몸을 계속 따뜻하고, 물기 없게 유지해 줄 것이라는 내용이 들어가야 함을 알 수 있다. 따라서 (A)가 정답이다.
어휘 appear v. 등장하다 own v. 소유하다

09-12번은 다음 이메일에 관한 문제입니다.

수신: Blair McKay <b.mckay@rdedental.com>
발신: Nancy Tang <n.tang@goldhotel.com>
제목: 비즈니스 오찬
날짜: 12월 12일

Mr. McKay께,

저는 방금 귀하의 이메일을 받았습니다. ⁰⁹저희는 귀하의 요청 사항을 확실히 수용할 수 있습니다. 귀하가 빌리시려고 고려하시는 방은 50명까지 수용할 수 있습니다. 10명을 더 추가하는 것은 문제가 되지 않을 것입니다. ¹⁰귀하가 저희의 뷔페 형식 메뉴를 선택하셨기 때문에, 저희는 음식의 양을 쉽게 조정할 수 있습니다. 귀사의 로고와 어울리는 꽃을 선택하자는 귀하의 아이디어에도 동의합니다. ¹¹저는 저희의 플로리스트와 이것이 가능하다는 것을 확인했고, 그는 파란색과 주황색 꽃을 사용할 계획입니다. ¹²저는 계약서의 최종안을 마련할 준비가 되어 있고, 이것은 오늘 귀하의 사무실에 팩스로 보내질 것입니다.

Nancy Tang 드림
Gold 호텔

rent v. 빌리다 adjust v. 조정하다, 조절하다 match v. 어울리다
florist n. 플로리스트, 꽃집 주인 final draft 최종안
agreement n. 계약서, 합의 fax v. 팩스로 보내다

09 알맞은 문장 고르기
해석 (A) 저희는 진심으로 귀하의 도움에 감사드립니다.
(B) 귀하께서 빌리신 방에 변경 사항들이 생겼습니다.
(C) 저희는 귀하의 요청 사항을 확실히 수용할 수 있습니다.
(D) 저희 관리자가 귀하의 우려와 관련하여 귀하께 연락할 것입니다.
해설 뒷부분에서 10명을 더 추가하는 것은 문제가 되지 않을 것이라고 했으므로, 빈칸에는 명단에 10명을 추가해달라는 요청 사항을 수용할 수 있다는 것과 관련된 내용이 들어가야 함을 알 수 있다. 따라서 (C)가 정답이다.
어휘 accommodate v. 수용하다

10 명사 어휘 고르기 _주변 문맥 파악_
해설 '음식의 ___을 쉽게 조정할 수 있다'라는 문맥이므로 모든 보기가 정답의 후보이다. 빈칸이 있는 문장만으로 정답을 고를 수 없으므로 주변 문맥이나 전체 문맥을 파악한다. 앞 문장에서 10명을 더 추가하는 것은 문제가 되지 않을 것이라고 했으므로 음식의 양 또한 쉽게 조정할 수 있다는 것을 알 수 있다. 따라서 (A) amount(양)가 정답이다. (B) type은 '종류', (C) price는 '가격', (D) quality는 '질'이라는 의미이다.

11 올바른 시제의 동사 채우기
해설 문장에 주어(I)만 있고 동사가 없으므로 모든 보기가 정답의 후보이다. and로 시작하는 종속절(and he plans ~ flowers)에서 그, 즉 플로리스트가 파란색과 주황색 꽃을 사용할 계획이라고 했으므로 플로리스트와 이것, 즉 회사의 로고와 어울리는 꽃을 선택하는 것이 가능하다는 것을 이미 확인했음을 알 수 있다. 따라서 과거에 발생한 일이 현재까지 영향을 미치거나 방금 완료된 것을 표현할 때 사용되는 현재완료 시제 (C) have confirmed가 정답이다.
어휘 confirm v. 확인하다

12 격에 맞는 인칭대명사 채우기
해설 and로 시작하는 절(___ will ~ today)에 동사(will be faxed)만 있고, 주어가 없으므로 주어 역할을 할 수 있는 주격 인칭대명사 (A)와 지시대명사 (C)가 정답의 후보이다. 명사(final draft)를 가리키는 인칭대명사가 필요하므로 주격 인칭대명사 (A) it이 정답이다. 지시대명사 (C)는 앞에 나온 복수 명사를 대신해서 사용한다. 목적격 인칭대명사 (B)와 소유격 인칭대명사 (D)는 주어 자리에 올 수 없다.

13-16번은 다음 안내문에 관한 문제입니다.

Middletown 미술 전시회에 신청하세요!
Middletown의 제8회 연례 미술 전시회가 8월 1일부터 14일까지 열릴 것입니다. ¹³지역 화가들, 조각가들, 그리고 사진작가들이 참가하도록 요청됩니다. 이 행사는 수많은 예술가들의 예술품을 포함할 것입니다. ¹⁴Emerson 미술관과 시청이 예술 작품을 전시할 장소로 선정되었습니다. 주민들은 이 장소들에서 전시회를 2주 동안 무료로 볼 수 있을 것입니다. ¹⁵모든 작품은 이 기간 이후에 예술가들에게 돌려보내질 것입니다.

행사에 참여하기 위해서는, www.middletown.gov/artexhibit_apply를 방문하십시오. 신청서들의 마감일은 1월 15일임을 유념하십시오. ¹⁶저희는 2월 20일까지 이것들을 검토할 것입니다. 선정된 모든 예술가는 다음 날 통보받을 것입니다.

sign up for ~에 신청하다 exhibition n. 전시회 sculptor n. 조각가
participate v. 참가하다 site n. 장소 view v. 보다 exhibit n. 전시회
location n. 장소 free of charge 무료로 application n. 신청서
notify v. 통보하다, 알리다

13 'be동사 + p.p.' 채우기
해설 빈칸이 be동사(are) 다음에 왔으므로 진행형을 만드는 현재분사 (B)와 수동태를 만드는 과거분사 (C)가 정답의 후보이다. '지역 화가들, 조각가들, 그리고 사진작가들이 참가하도록 요청된다'라는 수동의 의미가 되어야 하므로 동사 invite(요청하다)의 과거분사 (C) invited가 정답이다. 현재분사 (B)를 쓸 경우 '지역 화가들, 조각가들, 그리고 사진작가들이 참석하기 위해서 초대하고 있다'라는 어색한 문맥이 된다. (B)를 '유혹적인'이라는 의미의 형용사나 '초대하는 것'이라는 의미의 동명사로 본다 해도 어색한 문맥이 되어 답이 될 수 없다. 동사 (A)와 (D)는 be동사 뒤에 올 수 없다.

14 동사 어휘 고르기 주변 문맥 파악

해설 'Emerson 미술관과 시청이 예술 작품을 ___할 장소로 선정되었다'라는 문맥이므로 모든 보기가 정답의 후보이다. 빈칸이 있는 문장만으로 정답을 고를 수 없으므로 주변 문맥이나 전체 문맥을 파악한다. 뒤 문장에서 주민들이 이 장소들에서 전시회를 2주 동안 무료로 볼 수 있다고 했으므로 Emerson 미술관과 시청이 예술 작품을 전시할 장소로 선정되었다는 것을 알 수 있다. 따라서 (B) display(전시하다)가 정답이다. (A) store는 '보관하다, 저장하다', (C) judge는 '평가하다, 판단하다', (D) package는 '포장하다'라는 의미이다.

15 알맞은 문장 고르기

해석 (A) 모든 작품은 이 기간 이후에 예술가들에게 돌려보내질 것입니다.
(B) 입장료는 다음 달에 발표될 것입니다.
(C) 현재 여러 전시 장소들이 고려되고 있습니다.
(D) 주최 측들은 행사의 성공에 대해 찬사를 받았습니다.

해설 앞 문장 'Residents will be able to view the exhibits at these locations free of charge for two weeks.'에서 주민들이 이 장소들, 즉 Emerson 미술관과 시청에서 전시회를 2주 동안 무료로 볼 수 있다고 했으므로, 빈칸에는 이 기간, 즉 2주가 지난 이후에 일어날 일에 관한 내용이 들어가야 함을 알 수 있다. 따라서 (A)가 정답이다.

어휘 work n. 작품 period n. 기간 admission n. 입장 organizer n. 주최 측

16 지시대명사 these 채우기 주변 문맥 파악

해설 동사(will review)의 목적어 자리에 올 수 있는 것은 명사이므로 모든 보기가 정답의 후보이다. 빈칸이 있는 문장만으로 정답을 고를 수 없으므로 주변 문맥이나 전체 문맥을 파악한다. 앞 문장에서 신청서들의 마감일이 1월 15일임을 유념하라고 했고, '2월 20일까지 신청서들을 검토할 것이다'라는 의미가 되어야 하므로 앞에 나온 복수 명사(applications)를 대신하는 지시대명사 (B) these가 정답이다. 지시대명사 (A)와 인칭대명사 (C)는 앞에 나온 단수 명사를 대신해서 사용한다. 대명사 (D) both는 '둘 다'라는 의미로 어색한 문맥을 만든다.

PART 7

DAY 16 이메일/편지 및 메시지 대화문

1. 이메일/편지

지문 흐름과 빈출 문제   p.276

수신: Mobile Accessories사 <service@maccessories.com>
발신: Naomi Clay <naomic@deftmail.com>
날짜: 1월 17일
제목: 주문 34928

관계자분께,

저는 오늘 아침에 제 주문에서 잘못된 제품을 받았음을 알려드리기 위해 이메일을 씁니다.

유감스럽게도, 그것은 제가 주문한 Athena 7의 휴대폰 케이스가 아니라 Athena 8의 휴대폰 케이스를 포함합니다.

저는 참고를 위해 주문 확인서의 이미지를 첨부했습니다.

저는 제가 잘못 받은 것을 돌려보내겠습니다. 하지만, 이것은 귀사의 실수였으므로, **저는 귀사가 반품 배송 비용을 부담해야 한다고 생각합니다.** 이것이 가능한지 제게 알려주시기 바랍니다. 빠른 답변을 기다리겠습니다.

Naomi Clay 드림

inform v. 알리다, 통지하다   **attach** v. 첨부하다, 붙이다
confirmation n. 확인서   **reference** n. 참고, 참조
mistakenly adv. 잘못하여, 실수로   **cover** v. 부담하다, 보장하다
shipping n. 배송, 운송

HACKERS PRACTICE   p.278

01 (A)   **02** (A)

01번은 다음 편지에 관한 문제입니다.

Brian Lanzotti
343 Ewing가
샌디에이고, 캘리포니아주 91911

Mr. Lanzotti께,

Obsatron Security에 가입해 주셔서 감사합니다. 가정용 경보 장치를 활성화하려면, 키패드에 마스터 코드를 입력하십시오. 상기시켜 드리자면, 이 코드는 3개월마다 변경되어야 합니다. 알람이 울리면, 저희는 알림을 받고 귀하에게 연락을 시도할 것입니다. 따라서, ⁰¹연락처 정보를 최신으로 유지해 주시기 바랍니다. 저희 웹사이트에서 귀하의 Obsatron 계정에 로그인함으로써 이것을 하실 수 있습니다. 감사합니다.

David Wendt 드림
Obsatron사 고객 지원 관리자

sign up ~에 가입하다   **activate** v. 활성화시키다, 작동시키다
enter v. 입력하다, 기입하다   **go off** (경보기 등이) 울리다
notify v. 알리다, 통지하다   **attempt** v. 시도하다   **reach** v. 연락하다
up-to-date adj. 최신의, 최근의   **account** n. 계정

01 육하원칙 문제
해석 Mr. Lanzotti는 무엇을 하도록 요청받는가?
(A) 필요한 경우 그의 연락처 정보를 업데이트한다.
(B) 긴급 전화번호로 즉시 전화한다.
(C) 보안 시스템의 키패드를 교체한다.
(D) 몇몇 중요한 보안 절차를 익힌다.

해설 지문의 'please keep your contact information up-to-date'에서 연락처 정보를 최신으로 유지해 주기 바란다고 했으므로 (A)가 정답이다.

어휘 **immediately** adv. 즉시, 즉각적으로   **procedure** n. 절차

Paraphrasing
keep ~ contact information up-to-date 연락처 정보를 최신으로 유지하다
→ Update ~ contact information 연락처 정보를 업데이트하다

02번은 다음 이메일에 관한 문제입니다.

수신: Reggie Bartlett <regbart@somepost.com>
발신: 고객 서비스 <custservice@forteelectric.com>
제목: 5월
첨부: 청구서
날짜: 6월 1일

Mr. Bartlett께,

⁰²귀하의 5월 전기 요금 고지서를 첨부했습니다. 정확성을 보장하기 위해 금액을 확인하시고 6월 10일까지 납부해 주십시오. 귀하는 www.forteelectric.com/payments에서 은행 송금 혹은 신용카드로 그것을 하실 수 있습니다. 만약 귀하께서 귀하의 고지서나 저희 서비스에 관해 문의 사항이 있으시다면, 555-0022로 저희 고객 서비스 담당자 중 한 명에게 연락하십시오. 귀하의 지속적인 이용에 감사드립니다.

Forte Electric사
고객 서비스 드림

electricity bill 전기 요금 고지서   **ensure** v. 보장하다   **accuracy** n. 정확성
payment n. 납부, 결제   **transfer** n. 송금   **regarding** prep. ~에 관해
agent n. 담당자, 대리인   **continued** adj. 지속적인   **business** n. 이용, 거래

02 육하원칙 문제
해석 이메일에 무엇이 첨부되었는가?
(A) 월간 명세서
(B) 법적 계약서
(C) 결제 영수증
(D) 취소 통지서

해설 'I have attached your electricity bill for May.'에서 5월 전기 요금 고지서를 첨부했다고 했으므로 (A)가 정답이다.

어휘 **statement** n. 명세서, 설명서   **legal** adj. 법적인   **receipt** n. 영수증

2. 메시지 대화문

지문 흐름과 빈출 문제   p.279

Leo Henderson [오전 10시 48분]
제 샌디에이고발 비행기가 다섯 시간 동안 지연되었어요. 저는 오후 6시 30분이 되어서야 시카고에 도착할 거예요. **그래서 저는 오늘 오후 4시에 예정된 지역 관리자들의 회의에 참석하지 못할 거예요.**

Shelly Summers [오전 10시 50분]
그렇다니 유감입니다. 제가 도울 수 있는 일이 있을까요?

Leo Henderson [오전 10시 52분]
이사님께 알려주실 수 있나요?

Shelly Summers [오전 10시 53분]
제가 지금 바로 이사님께 전화하겠습니다. 그는 일정을 변경하는 것을 원하실 수도 있습니다. 제가 확인해 보겠습니다.

Shelly Summers [오전 10시 59분]
네, 그는 내일 아침 8시 30분으로 일정을 변경하고 싶어 합니다. 그는 모든 지역 관리자가 참석하기를 원하십니다. 그것이 당신에게 괜찮으실까요?

Leo Henderson [오전 11시 2분]
괜찮습니다.

Shelly Summers [오전 11시 4분]
좋습니다! 즐거운 비행 되십시오!

miss v. (~에) 참석하지 못하다, 놓치다   scheduled adj. 예정된
inform v. 알리다, 통지하다   reschedule v. 일정을 변경하다
in attendance 참석한

HACKERS PRACTICE   p.281

01 (C)   02 (D)

01번은 다음 문자 메시지 대화문에 관한 문제입니다.

Jerry Mills [오전 10시 48분]
Ms. Daniels, 제가 내일 오후에 일찍 퇴근해도 될까요? 공항에 부모님을 모시러 가야 해요.

Pearl Daniels [오전 10시 50분]
괜찮아요. 01재무 보고서는 마무리했나요?

Jerry Mills [오전 10시 53분]
아직이요. 01오늘 오후에 작업할 계획이에요.

Pearl Daniels [오전 10시 54분]
오늘 근무 시간이 끝날 때까지 완료해 주실 수 있나요? 곧 있을 이사회 발표에서 그걸 사용할 거예요.

Jerry Mills [오전 10시 55분]
문제 없어요.

financial adj. 재무의   shift n. 근무 시간   upcoming adj. 곧 있을, 다가오는

01 의도 파악 문제

해석 오전 10시 53분에, Mr. Mills가 "Not yet"이라고 썼을 때, 그가 의도한 것은?
(A) 휴가 요청서를 제출하지 않았다.
(B) 발표 일정을 변경할 생각이다.
(C) 업무를 완료하지 않았다.
(D) 내일 추가 근무를 할 계획이다.

해설 지문의 'Have you finished the financial report?'에서 Ms. Daniels가 재무 보고서를 마무리했는지 묻자, Mr. Mills가 'Not yet'(아직이요)이라고 한 후, 'I'm planning to work on it this afternoon.'에서 오늘 오후에 작업할 계획이라고 한 것을 통해, Mr. Mills가 업무를 완료하지 않았다는 것을 알 수 있다. 따라서 (C)가 정답이다.

어휘 submit v. 제출하다   leave n. 휴가   extra adj. 추가의

[Paraphrasing]
finished the financial report 재무 보고서를 마무리했다 → completed an assignment 업무를 완료했다

02번은 다음 온라인 채팅 대화문에 관한 문제입니다.

Bastian Guthrie [오후 4시 35분]
저는 JEPN 제조사와 계속 함께 일하는 것이 우리에게 득이 된다고 생각하지 않아요. 많은 부품들이 결함이 있었기 때문에 지난주에 받은 긴급 주문품이 반품되어야 했어요.

Marie Holcomb [오후 4시 44분]
대체 공급업체를 찾는 것은 어때요?

Bastian Guthrie [오후 4시 48분]
02저는 제 컴퓨터에 제조업체들의 목록을 가지고 있어요. 그들은 아마 JEPN사보다 비용을 더 많이 청구하겠지만, 바꾸는 것이 결국에는 우리가 비용을 절감하게 할 거예요.

Marie Holcomb [오후 4시 49분]
말이 되네요.

in one's best interest ~에게 득이 되는   rush order 긴급 주문품
component n. 부품, 요소   faulty adj. 결함 있는, 불완전한
replacement n. 대체, 교체   supplier n. 공급업체, 공급자
manufacturer n. 제조업체   switch v. 바꾸다, 전환하다
in the long run 결국에는, 장기적으로 보면

02 의도 파악 문제

해석 오후 4시 49분에, Ms. Holcomb이 "Makes sense"라고 썼을 때, 그녀가 의도한 것은?
(A) 공급업체가 신뢰할 만하다고 생각한다.
(B) JEPN사가 더 나은 서비스를 제공하기를 바란다.
(C) 업데이트된 목록을 제공할 것이다.
(D) 비용이 절감될 것이라고 생각한다.

해설 지문의 'I have a list of manufacturers on my computer. They will probably charge more than JEPN, but switching will save us money in the long run.'에서 Mr. Guthrie가 컴퓨터에 제조업체들의 목록을 가지고 있다고 하며, 그들은 아마 JEPN사보다 비용을 더 많이 청구하겠지만, 바꾸는 것이 결국에는 비용을 절감하게 할 것이라고 하자, Ms. Holcomb이 'Makes sense'(말이 되네요)라고 한 것을 통해, Ms. Holcomb은 비용이 절감될 것이라고 생각한다는 것을 알 수 있다. 따라서 (D)가 정답이다.

어휘 reliable adj. 신뢰할 만한

HACKERS TEST   p.282

01 (A)	02 (D)	03 (B)	04 (B)	05 (A)
06 (D)	07 (A)	08 (B)	09 (B)	10 (A)
11 (B)	12 (D)	13 (D)		

01-03번은 다음 이메일에 관한 문제입니다.

수신: Adriana Cole <ad.cole@scribeofficesupplies.com>
발신: Owen Fender <owenfender@jesterenterprises.com>
제목: 구매 주문
날짜: 4월 9일

Ms. Cole께,

저희 회사에 의해 내려진 최근의 결정에 관해 귀하께 이메일을 씁니다. ㅡ [1] ㅡ. 더욱 환경친화적으로 되기 위해, 저희는 복사기 및 프린터의 종이 사용에 대해 변화를 줄 계획입니다. 03저희는 5월 1일에 저희 문서들의 대부분을 컴퓨터에 저장하기 시작할 것입니다. ㅡ [2] ㅡ. 따라서, 01저희의 월간 주문을 네 상자에서 두 상자로 줄이고자 합니다. ㅡ [3] ㅡ. 게다가, 저희는 이제부터 재생 용지만 구매하고자 합니다. 이것이 비용이 얼마나 들지 제게 알려주십시오. 02-(D)저는 귀사가 장기 고객들에게 제공하는 할인을 저희가 계속 받을 수 있기를 바랍니다. ㅡ [4] ㅡ. 감사합니다.

Owen Fender 드림
구매 담당자, Jester사

photocopier n. 복사기   store v. 저장하다, 보관하다
document n. 문서, 서류   electronically adv. 컴퓨터에, 전자적으로
recycled paper 재생 용지   long-term adj. 장기의, 장기적인

01 글을 쓴 이유 문제

해석 이메일은 왜 쓰였는가?
(A) 정기적인 주문을 조정하기 위해
(B) 신상품에 대해 문의하기 위해
(C) 정책에 대한 불만 사항을 제출하기 위해
(D) 더 높은 할인을 요구하기 위해

해설 지문의 'we would like to reduce our monthly order'에서 월간 주문을 줄이고자 한다고 하며, 정기적인 주문에 대한 조정을 요청하고 있으므로 (A)가 정답이다.

어휘 adjustment n. 조정 complaint n. 불만 사항, 불평

02 Not/True 문제

해석 Jester사에 대해 언급된 것은?
(A) 관리자가 경영 비용을 줄이기로 결정했다.
(B) 현재의 복사기와 프린터를 유지하지 않을 것이다.
(C) 환경과 관련된 노력이 긍정적인 주목을 받았다.
(D) 용지에 대해 정가를 지불하지 않아 왔다.

해설 지문의 'I hope we will continue to receive the discount that you offer to long-term customers.'에서 귀사, 즉 Jester사가 장기 고객들에게 제공하는 할인을 계속 받을 수 있기를 바란다고 했으므로 (D)가 정답이다. (A), (B), (C)는 지문에 언급되지 않은 내용이다.

어휘 operating expense 경영 비용 publicity n. (언론의) 주목, 평판

03 문장 위치 찾기 문제

해석 [1], [2], [3], [4]로 표시된 위치 중, 다음 문장이 들어갈 곳으로 가장 적절한 것은?
"하지만, 저희는 다양한 목적들을 위해 용지 공급이 여전히 필요할 것입니다."
(A) [1]
(B) [2]
(C) [3]
(D) [4]

해설 주어진 문장은 용지 공급의 필요성과 관련된 내용 주변에 들어가야 함을 알 수 있다. [2]의 앞 문장인 'We will begin storing most of our documents electronically on May 1.'에서 5월 1일에 문서들의 대부분을 컴퓨터에 저장하기 시작할 것이라고 했으므로, [2]에 주어진 문장이 들어가면 문서들의 대부분을 컴퓨터에 저장하기 시작할 것이지만 다양한 목적들을 위해 용지 공급이 여전히 필요할 것이라는 자연스러운 문맥이 된다는 것을 알 수 있다. 따라서 (B)가 정답이다.

어휘 supply n. 공급 various adj. 다양한

04-05번은 다음 문자 메시지 대화문에 관한 문제입니다.

Daniel Miller [오후 3시 40분]
안녕하세요, **04**당신은 Ms. Downing의 승진 파티에 가나요? 듣자 하니, 사무실 전체가 오늘 밤 퇴근 후에 Finlay's Grill에서 만나도록 초대된 것 같아요.

Elaine Larue [오후 3시 43분]
모르겠네요. **04**저는 오늘 꽤 피곤해요. 게다가, 여기서 일을 시작한 후로 당신이 제가 알게 된 유일한 사람이에요. **04/05**저는 혼자 파티에 가면 불편할 거예요.

Daniel Miller [오후 3시 44분]
05우리 같이 가는 게 어때요? 그것은 당신이 사람들을 만날 수 있는 좋은 기회가 될 거예요. 저는 끝내야 할 몇 가지 일들이 있지만, 오후 7시까지는 갈 준비가 될 거예요.

Elaine Larue [오후 3시 45분]
좋아요. 오후 7시 10분에 로비에서 만나요.

promotion n. 승진, 진급 apparently adv. 듣자 하니, 분명히
opportunity n. 기회

04 의도 파악 문제

해석 오후 3시 43분에, Ms. Larue가 "I don't know"라고 썼을 때, 그녀가 의도한 것은?
(A) 초대장을 받지 않았다.
(B) 파티에 가지 않을 계획이다.
(C) 직원 모임을 일찍 떠날 것이다.
(D) 장소의 주소를 필요로 한다.

해설 지문의 'are you going to Ms. Downing's promotion party?'에서 Mr. Miller가 Ms. Downing의 승진 파티에 갈 것인지 묻자, Ms. Larue가 'I don't know'(모르겠네요)라고 한 후 'I'm feeling pretty tired today.'와 'I'd feel uncomfortable going to the party alone.'에서 자신은 오늘 꽤 피곤하며 혼자 파티에 가면 불편할 것이라고 한 것을 통해 Ms. Larue가 파티에 가지 않을 계획이라는 것을 알 수 있다. 따라서 (B)가 정답이다.

어휘 gathering n. 모임 venue n. 장소

05 육하원칙 문제

해석 Mr. Miller는 무엇을 제안하는가?
(A) 함께 행사에 참석하는 것
(B) 일정보다 빨리 업무를 끝내는 것
(C) 근처 식당에서 만나는 것
(D) 다른 직원을 초대하는 것

해설 지문의 'I'd feel uncomfortable going to the party alone.'에서 Ms. Larue가 혼자 파티에 가면 불편할 것이라고 하자, 'Why don't we go together?'에서 Mr. Miller가 같이 가는 게 어떤지 물었으므로 (A)가 정답이다.

어휘 task n. 업무 ahead of ~보다 빨리

06-09번은 다음 편지에 관한 문제입니다.

3월 12일
Nelly Garrison
493번지 22번가
포틀랜드, 오리건주 97246

06Ms. Garrison께,

06지난 금요일에 여기 Weston 고고학 연구소의 부 큐레이터 직책을 위한 면접에 와 주셔서 감사합니다. 저희는 당신의 경력에 깊은 인상을 받았고 그 자리를 당신에게 제안하고자 합니다.

07저는 고용 계약서를 동봉했습니다. 그것은 면접에서 논의된 임금과 제가 언급했던 복지 혜택을 명시합니다. 저희의 제안이 받아들일 만하다면, 계약서에 서명해 주시고 그것을 저희 인사부로 발송해 주십시오.

08당신의 시작일은 4월 15일일 것입니다. 당신은 또 다른 큐레이터인 Arnold Hazelton과 함께 오리엔테이션을 거칠 것입니다. 교육 기간은 일주일 동안 계속될 것이고, 그 기간 동안 **08/09**Mr. Hazelton이 당신에게 다양한 업무들을 안내할 것입니다. 그다음 주에 당신은 당신의 정규 직무를 시작할 것입니다. Mr. Hazelton이 당신의 출근 첫날에 더 많은 세부 사항을 알려줄 것입니다.

3월 20일까지 답변을 받을 수 있다면 감사하겠습니다. 당신은 제게 555-3029로 전화 주실 수 있습니다.

Marsha Kent 드림
WAI 인사부장

associate adj. 부, 준 impressed adj. 깊은 인상을 받은
background n. 경력, 배경 employment n. 고용, 구직 contract n. 계약서
specify v. 명시하다 benefits package 복지 혜택
acceptable adj. 받아들일 수 있는, 만족스러운 forward v. 발송하다, 부치다
duty n. 직무

06 육하원칙 문제

해석 Ms. Garrison은 지난주에 무엇을 했는가?
(A) 교육 시설을 견학했다.
(B) 일자리에 대해 문의하기 위해 번호로 전화했다.
(C) 오리엔테이션 세션에 참여했다.
(D) 연구소에서 구직 면접에 참석했다.

해설 지문의 'Dear Ms. Garrison,', 'Thank you for coming in last Friday to interview for the associate curator position here at the Weston Archeological Institute.'에서 Ms. Garrison에게 지난 금요일에 여기 Weston 고고학 연구소의 부 큐레이터 직책을 위한 면접에 와 주어서 감사하다고 했으므로 (D)가 정답이다.

어휘 facility n. 시설 inquire v. 문의하다

Paraphrasing
coming ~ to interview for the ~ position 직책을 위한 면접에 오는 것
→ Attended a job interview 구직 면접에 참석했다

07 육하원칙 문제

해석 편지에 무엇이 첨부되었는가?
(A) 법적 계약서
(B) 교육 안내서
(C) 업무 일정
(D) 신청서

해설 지문의 'I have enclosed the employment contract.'에서 고용 계약서를 동봉했다고 했으므로 (A)가 정답이다.

어휘 legal adj. 법적인 manual n. 안내서, 설명서 application form 신청서

Paraphrasing
employment contract 고용 계약서 → legal agreement 법적 계약서

08 육하원칙 문제

해석 Mr. Hazelton은 4월 15일에 무엇을 할 것인가?
(A) 몇몇 구직자들을 면접 본다.
(B) 직원을 교육하는 것을 시작한다.
(C) 연구소에서의 그의 직무에서 사임한다.
(D) 인사부에 의해 주최되는 워크숍에 참여한다.

해설 지문의 'Your starting day will be April 15. You will go through an orientation with ~, Arnold Hazelton.'에서 당신, 즉 Ms. Garrison의 시작일은 4월 15일일 것이며 Mr. Hazelton과 함께 오리엔테이션을 거칠 것이라고 한 후, 'Mr. Hazelton will direct you through various tasks'에서 Mr. Hazelton이 다양한 업무들을 안내할 것이라고 했으므로 (B)가 정답이다.

어휘 job applicant 구직자 resign v. 사임하다, 그만두다

09 동의어 문제

해설 3문단 두 번째 줄의 단어 "direct"는 의미상 -와 가장 가깝다.
(A) 적용하다
(B) 안내하다
(C) 운영하다
(D) 설명하다

해설 direct를 포함한 구절 'Mr. Hazelton will direct you through various tasks'에서 direct는 '안내하다'라는 뜻으로 사용되었다. 따라서 (B)가 정답이다.

10-13번은 다음 온라인 채팅 대화문에 관한 문제입니다.

Mimi Pearson [오후 3시 40분]
11새로운 문서 작성 소프트웨어로 문제를 겪고 있는 다른 분이 계신가요?

Donald Platt [오후 3시 42분]
저요. 저는 IT 부서의 사람을 기다리고 있었어요.

Grace Helmsley [오후 3시 43분]
10-(A)저는 그들이 그 문제에 착수하고 있다는 것을 한 IT 부서 직원에게 확인했어요. 10-(B)그들은 여기 2층 작업을 방금 끝냈어요. Louis와 몇몇 다른 사람들도 문제들을 겪고 있었어요.

Louis Jones [오후 3시 46분]
제 소프트웨어는 이제 잘 작동하고 있어요. 11설치된 것이 작동하게 하려면 당신은 그저 운영 체제를 업데이트하기만 하면 돼요.

Mimi Pearson [오후 3시 47분]
그게 문제가 아니에요. 11저는 그것을 잘 설치할 수 있었어요. 저는 그 소프트웨어를 사용하는 방법을 알아내는 데 어려움을 겪고 있어요.

Donald Platt [오후 3시 48분]
Mimi, 회사 인트라넷에 사용자 설명서가 있어요.

Grace Helmsley [오후 3시 49분]
당신은 또한 도구 모음에서 도움말 버튼을 클릭하셔도 돼요.

Mimi Pearson [오후 3시 50분]
저는 설명서가 있는지 몰랐어요. 12제가 나중에 그것들을 볼게요. 제가 파일 하나를 당장 인쇄해야 해서 Grace의 제안을 먼저 시도해 볼게요.

Louis Jones [오후 3시 52분]
13회사는 정말 교육을 제공해야 해요. 하지만 먼저 누가 그것이 필요하다고 생각하는지 확인하기 위해 주변에 물어볼게요.

word processing 문서 작성 confirm v. 확인하다
work on 착수하다, ~에 노력을 들이다 installation n. 설치(된 것)
figure out 알아내다 instruction n. 설명서
ask around 주변에 물어보다, 수소문하다

10 Not/True 문제

해석 Ms. Helmsley에 대해 언급된 것은?
(A) IT 부서의 한 직원과 이야기했다.
(B) 건물의 3층에서 일한다.
(C) 운영 체제 업데이트가 필요했다.
(D) 소프트웨어가 복잡하다고 생각한다.

해설 지문의 'I confirmed with an IT employee'에서 Ms. Helmsley가 한 IT 부서 직원에게 확인했다고 했으므로 (A)는 지문의 내용과 일치한다. 따라서 (A)가 정답이다. (B)는 'They just finished here on the second floor.'에서 Ms. Helmsley가 그들, 즉 IT 부서 직원들이 여기 2층 작업을 방금 끝냈다고 했으므로 지문의 내용과 일치하지 않는다. (C)와 (D)는 지문에 언급되지 않은 내용이다.

어휘 complicated adj. 복잡한

Paraphrasing
confirmed with an IT employee 한 IT 부서 직원에게 확인했다 → spoke to a member of the IT department IT 부서의 한 직원과 이야기했다

11 의도 파악 문제

해석 오후 3시 47분에, Ms. Pearson이 "That's not the problem"이라고 썼을 때, 그녀가 의도한 것은?
(A) 설명을 이해하지 못했다.
(B) 새로운 소프트웨어를 설치했다.
(C) 문제가 해결되었다고 생각했다.
(D) IT 부서의 직원에게 연락할 수 없었다.

해설 지문의 'Is anyone else having trouble with the new word processing software?'에서 Ms. Pearson이 새로운 문서 작성 소프트웨어로 문제를 겪고 있는 사람이 있는지 물은 후, Mr. Jones가 'You just have to update your operating system for the installation to work.'에서 설치된 것이 작동하게 하려면 그저 운영 체제를 업데이트하기만 하면 된다고 하자, Ms. Pearson이 'That's not the problem'(그게 문제가 아니에요.)이라고 한 후, 'I was able to install it just fine.'에서 자신은 그것을 잘 설치할 수 있었다고 한 것을 통해, Ms. Pearson은 새로운 소프트웨어를 설치했다는 것을 알 수 있다. 따라서 (B)가 정답이다.

어휘 explanation n. 설명 issue n. 문제 resolve v. 해결하다

12 육하원칙 문제

해석 Ms. Pearson은 왜 소프트웨어 설명서를 바로 보지 않기로 하는가?
(A) 그녀의 컴퓨터를 켤 수 없다.
(B) 그것들을 찾을 수 없다.
(C) Mr. Platt으로부터 멀리서 일한다.
(D) 시간이 많지 않아서 바쁘다.

해설 지문의 'I'll look at them later. I'll try Grace's suggestion first as I need to print a file right away.'에서 Ms. Pearson이 나중에 그것들, 즉 설명서를 보겠다고 하며 파일 하나를 당장 인쇄해야 해서 Grace의 제안을 먼저 시도해 보겠다고 했다. 따라서 (D)가 정답이다.

어휘 in a hurry (시간이 많지 않아서) 바쁜, 서둘러

13 추론 문제

해석 Mr. Jones는 다음에 무엇을 할 것 같은가?
(A) 동료를 위해 문서를 인쇄한다.
(B) 몇몇 2층 직원들에 관해 문의한다.
(C) 교육 세션의 일정을 확인한다.
(D) 몇몇 다른 직원들과 이야기를 나눈다.

해설 지문의 'The company should really provide training. But first I'll ask around to see who feels they need it.'에서 Mr. Jones가 회사는 정말 교육을 제공해야 하지만 먼저 누가 그것, 즉 소프트웨어 사용에 대한 교육이 필요하다고 생각하는지 확인하기 위해 주변에 물어보겠다고 했으므로 Mr. Jones는 몇몇 다른 직원들과 이야기를 나눌 것이라는 사실을 추론할 수 있다. 따라서 (D)가 정답이다.

어휘 coworker n. 동료

Paraphrasing
ask around 주변에 물어보다 → Speak with ~와 이야기를 나누다

DAY 17 양식 및 광고

1. 양식

지문 흐름과 빈출 문제
p.286

Blue Bay 발매 파티

귀하를 색소폰 연주자 Jay Delong의 재즈 앨범 *Blue Bay*의 발매 파티에 초대합니다.

행사는 6월 9일 오후 6시부터 10시까지 로스앤젤레스, Santa Monica 대로 994번지 Starry Hills 행사 센터에서 열릴 것입니다.

이 행사는 초청 음악가인 Joelle Baker, Paul Massa, 그리고 The Pinstripes의 라이브 공연을 특별히 포함할 것입니다. 참석자들에게 음식과 칵테일이 저녁 내내 제공될 것입니다. 공간이 제한되어 있으므로, 추가로 한 명의 손님만이 초대받은 분을 동반할 수 있습니다. 참석하실 계획이라면 5월 30일까지 Cole Anderson에게 cander@marinproductions.com으로 연락하셔서 저희에게 알려주십시오.

release n. 발매, 출시, 발표 feature v. 특별히 포함하다 serve v. 제공하다
attendee n. 참석자 accompany v. 동반하다, 동행하다

HACKERS PRACTICE
p.288

01 (B) **02** (D)

01번은 다음 영수증에 관한 문제입니다.

Ronson 가정용품사
167번지 Caldwell대로, Twin Lakes, 뉴멕시코주 86515
555-8863
날짜: 8월 8일 시각: 오후 5시 26분

이 영수증을 제시할 경우에만 환불이나 교환이 될 것입니다.

93432-B	선풍기	34.99달러
88822-F	HDMI 케이블	18.50달러
	소계	53.49달러
	5퍼센트 판매세	2.67달러
	총액	56.16달러
	현금	60.00달러
	거스름돈	3.84달러

Ronson 가정용품사를 방문해 주셔서 감사합니다.
www.ronsonhome.com에서 저희의 온라인 설문조사를 완료하시거나 고객센터에 555-9933으로 전화하셔서 ⁰¹오늘 귀하의 쇼핑 경험에 대해 **귀하께서 어떻게 생각하셨는지 저희에게 알려주십시오.**

refund n. 환불 exchange n. 교환 presentation n. 제시
complete v. 완료하다

01 육하원칙 문제

해석 고객들은 무엇을 하도록 요청받는가?
(A) 웹사이트에 회원으로 가입한다.
(B) 상점에 대해 의견을 제공한다.
(C) 쿠폰을 얻기 위해 서비스 센터에 전화한다.
(D) 무료 기기를 얻기 위해 추첨식 복권을 구매한다.

해설 지문의 'Please tell us what you thought of your shopping experience today'에서 오늘 쇼핑 경험에 대해 어떻게 생각했는지 알려달라고 했으므로 (B)가 정답이다.

어휘 sign up ~에 가입하다 raffle ticket 추첨식 복권 device n. 기기, 장치

Paraphrasing
tell ~ what you thought 어떻게 생각했는지 알려주다 → Provide feedback 의견을 제공하다

02번은 다음 일정표에 관한 문제입니다.

Dianne Brennan
일정표 – 7월 8일

오전 9시 30분 – 오전 10시 30분
디자인 팀과 만나 회사 로고 변경 사항에 대해 논의한다.

오전 11시 – 오후 12시 30분
마케팅 보조 직원 자리 지원서를 검토하고, 인터뷰할 후보자 목록을 작성한다.

오후 1시 30분 – 오후 2시 30분
⁰²⁻⁽ᴰ⁾Stanford 센터에서 열리는 전국 가전제품 상품 전시회 부스를 예약한다 (금요일부터 일요일까지).

오후 3시 – 오후 4시
새로운 식기세척기 모델 출시 동안 발표자가 강조할 기능을 확정한다.

application n. 지원서, 신청서 assistant n. 보조 직원, 조수
candidate n. 후보자 trade show 상품 전시회
finalize v. 확정하다, 마무리하다 feature n. 기능 emphasize v. 강조하다

02 Not/True 문제

해석 Stanford 센터에서의 행사에 대해 사실인 것은?
(A) 몇 년 동안 매년 개최되어 왔다.
(B) 천 명이 넘는 방문객을 유치할 것으로 예상된다.
(C) 구직자를 위한 활동을 포함할 것이다.

(D) 3일 동안 진행될 것이다.

해설 (D)는 'Reserve a booth for the National Appliance Trade Show at the Stanford Center (from Friday to Sunday).'에서 금요일부터 일요일까지 Stanford 센터에서 열리는 전국 가전제품 상품 전시회 부스를 예약한다고 했으므로 지문의 내용과 일치한다. 따라서 (D)가 정답이다. (A), (B), (C)는 지문에 언급되지 않은 내용이다.

어휘 annually adv. 매년 attract v. 유치하다 job seeker 구직자

2. 광고

지문 흐름과 빈출 문제
p.289

SheerYou—Dewdrop 스킨케어의 최신 제품

피부를 촉촉하게 유지할 순하고 효과적인 방법을 찾고 계신가요? 저희는 저희의 최신 보습제 SheerYou를 공개하게 되어 자랑스럽습니다.

이것은 피부의 천연 수분을 회복시켜, 피부가 더 밝고 건강하게 보이도록 한다고 과학적으로 증명되었습니다. 천연 재료만을 사용해 피부과 전문의들에 의해 만들어진 SheerYou는 저희의 가장 순하면서도 가장 강력한 보습제입니다.

이것의 출시를 기념하기 위해, 저희는 6월 동안 특가 상품을 제공합니다. SheerYou를 구매하는 사람은 누구든지 무료 Floria 3온스 한 병을 받을 것입니다. 이것은 인기 TV 드라마 *Broken Hearts*의 주연 Jenna Harvel의 대표적인 향수입니다.

Dewdrop사의 상품을 판매하는 상점들의 목록을 위해서는, www.dewdropskin.com/vendors를 방문하십시오.

---

gentle adj. 순한 unveil v. 공개하다, 발표하다 moisturizer n. 보습제 restore v. 회복시키다, 복원하다 dermatologist n. 피부과 전문의 ingredient n. 재료 special deal 특가 상품 complimentary adj. 무료의 signature adj. 대표적인, 전형적인

HACKERS PRACTICE
p.291

01 (A) **02** (B)

01번은 다음 광고에 관한 문제입니다.

오늘 Phoenix 체육관에서 건강해지세요!

늘어난 운동 시설과 새롭게 보수된 라커룸 및 로비를 확인하기 위해 Pita Wraps와 Gilbert's Cycles 사이의 Elmwood, Ballard가에 있는 저희 체육관을 방문하세요! 개조 공사 완공을 축하하기 위하여, **01이 광고지를 제시하시면 1년 회원권을 50퍼센트 할인 받으실 수 있습니다!** 게다가, 모든 신규 회원분들은 저희 전문 트레이너 중 한 명과 함께하는 체험 수업을 받으실 수 있습니다.

이 할인 행사는 오직 Elmwood 지점에서만 2월 15일까지 유효합니다.

Phoenix 체육관
18번지 Ballard가, Elmwood
전화번호 555-3243

---

get in shape 건강해지다, 체력을 단련하다 enlarged adj. 늘어난 trial n. 체험, 시험 valid adj. 유효한 exclusively adv. 오직

01 육하원칙 문제

해석 Phoenix 체육관에 의해 무엇이 제공되고 있는가?
(A) 회원권 할인
(B) 시설 투어
(C) 무료 상담
(D) 무료 물품

해설 지문의 'present this flyer to get a 50 percent discount on a one-year membership'에서 이 광고지를 제시하면 1년 회원권을 50퍼센트 할인받을 수 있다고 했으므로 (A)가 정답이다.

어휘 facility n. 시설, 기관 consultation n. 상담 complimentary adj. 무료의

02번은 다음 구인 광고에 관한 문제입니다.

수의사 공석

Haven for Animals는 반려동물들에게 양질의 건강 관리를 제공하는 데 전념하는 동물 병원입니다. **02-(A)/(B)15년 전 샌디에이고에 시설을 연 이후**, 로스앤젤레스와 샌프란시스코로 확장해 왔습니다. 저희는 저희 팀에 합류할 다섯 명의 숙련된 수의사를 찾고 있습니다. 저희는 높은 초봉과 종합적인 복지 혜택을 제공합니다.

자격요건:
· 수의학 학위
· 수의과 진료를 할 수 있는 자격증

지원서는 12월 16일까지 www.haven.com/hr로 보내주셔야 합니다.

---

veterinarian n. 수의사 veterinary clinic 동물 병원 establishment n. 시설 expand v. 확장하다 comprehensive adj. 종합적인, 포괄적인 benefits package 복지 혜택 qualification n. 자격요건 medicine n. 진료, 치료

02 Not/True 문제

해석 Haven for Animals에 대해 언급된 것은?
(A) 로스앤젤레스에 처음 개업했다.
(B) 10년 이상 전에 설립되었다.
(C) 수의사 보조 직원을 고용하려고 한다.
(D) 시설을 개조할 계획이다.

해설 (B)는 'Since opening our establishment in San Diego 15 years ago'에서 15년 전에 샌디에이고에 시설을 열었다고 했으므로 지문의 내용과 일치한다. 따라서 (B)가 정답이다. (A)는 'Since opening our establishment in San Diego 15 years ago'에서 15년 전에 샌디에이고에 시설을 열었다고 했으므로 지문의 내용과 일치하지 않는다. (C)와 (D)는 지문에 언급되지 않은 내용이다.

어휘 renovate v. 개조하다

HACKERS TEST
p.292

01 (C)	02 (D)	03 (C)	04 (B)	05 (A)
06 (B)	07 (D)	08 (B)	09 (C)	10 (B)
11 (B)	12 (A)	13 (D)		

01-02번은 다음 광고에 관한 문제입니다.

01-(B)제35회 연례 캐나다 서부 빈티지 자동차 쇼
금요일과 토요일, **01-(A)7월 7일-8일**, 오전 10시-오후 9시

400대가 넘는 차량이 전시된 올해의 빈티지 자동차 쇼를 보기 위해 Vernon 시내를 방문하세요!

01-(D)무료로 입장하실 수 있으며, 기념품은 수많은 판매자들로부터 구입할 수 있을 것입니다. 핫도그, 햄버거, 감자튀김, 청량음료, 그리고 더 많은 것들을 사기 위해 많은 음식 부스를 이용해 보세요!

그리고 빈티지 스포츠카를 얻을 수 있는 저희의 추첨에 참여하는 것을 잊지 마세요! **02두 날 모두 박람회 안내 데스크에서 추첨을 위한 표를 구매하세요**. 더 많은 정보를 위해서는, www.wcvintageautoshow.com을 방문하세요.

---

vehicle n. 자동차, 탈것 on display 전시된 admission n. 입장 souvenir n. 기념품 vendor n. 판매자 raffle n. 추첨 draw n. 추첨

01 Not/True 문제
해석 자동차 쇼에 대해 언급되지 않은 것은?
(A) 이틀의 기간 동안 진행될 것이다.
(B) 매년 개최된다.
(C) 교외에 있는 장소에서 개최된다.
(D) 참석에 요금을 부과하지 않는다.

해설 (C)는 지문에 언급되지 않은 내용이다. 따라서 (C)가 정답이다. (A)는 'July 7-8'에서 자동차 쇼가 7월 7일과 7월 8일 이틀에 걸쳐 진행된다는 것을 알 수 있으므로 지문의 내용과 일치한다. (B)는 'The 35th Annual ~ Auto Show'에서 제35회 연례 자동차 쇼라고 했으므로 지문의 내용과 일치한다. (D)는 'You can gain admission at no cost'에서 무료로 입장할 수 있다고 했으므로 지문의 내용과 일치한다.

어휘 venue n. 장소 suburb n. 교외(도심지를 벗어난 주택 지역)
attendance n. 참석

[Paraphrasing]
can gain admission at no cost 무료로 입장할 수 있다 → does not charge a fee for attendance 참석에 요금을 부과하지 않다

02 육하원칙 문제
해설 광고에 따르면, 방문객들은 안내 데스크에서 무엇을 할 수 있는가?
(A) 차량 시승에 등록한다.
(B) 간행물 사본을 요청한다.
(C) 판매자 정보를 요청한다.
(D) 경품 추첨에 참여한다.

해설 지문의 'Purchase tickets for the draw at the fair's help desk on both days.'에서 두 날 모두 박람회 안내 데스크에서 추첨을 위한 표를 구매하라고 했으므로 (D)가 정답이다.

어휘 register v. 등록하다 publication n. 간행물, 출판물

03-05번은 다음 양식에 관한 문제입니다.

Frontward Car Rental사를 선택해 주셔서 감사합니다, Nadia Abdulhak. 저희는 5월 7일부터 13일까지 Gallapot Mini를 대여한 03귀하의 경험이 만족스러웠는지 알고 싶습니다. 이 양식을 작성한 후, 제출을 클릭하십시오.

	동의	비동의
1) 여러 가지 이용 가능한 대여 선택지들이 적절했다.	●	○
2) 예약 시스템이 편리했다.	○	●
3) 차량을 찾아갈 때 서비스의 품질이 만족스러웠다.	●	○
4) 차량이 확실하게 작동했다.	○	●
5) 차량을 반납할 때 서비스의 품질이 만족스러웠다.	○	●

추가적인 의견
04/05-(A)귀사의 Fairfield 지점에서 차량을 찾아갈 때, 04직원은 매우 도움이 되었습니다. 하지만, 이틀 뒤 차량이 99번 고속도로에서 고장 났을 때, 귀사는 상황을 해결하는 데에 약 세 시간이 걸렸습니다. 05-(A)저는 또한 귀사의 Danbury 지점에서 차량을 반납할 때 환불이 제공되지 않은 것에 실망했습니다.

[제출]

rental n. 대여, 대여료 suitable adj. 적절한 reservation n. 예약
convenient adj. 편리한 satisfactory adj. 만족스러운
reliably adv. 확실하게 resolve v. 해결하다 disappointed adj. 실망한
refund n. 환불; v. 환불하다

03 목적 문제
해석 양식의 목적은 무엇인가?
(A) 제품에 대한 관심도를 알아내기 위해
(B) 지불금에 대한 환불을 승인하기 위해
(C) 서비스에 대한 의견을 요청하기 위해
(D) 행사에 대한 예약을 확인하기 위해

해설 지문의 'We want to know whether you were satisfied with your experience'에서 귀하의 경험이 만족스러웠는지 알고 싶다고 한 후, 차량 대여 서비스에 대한 의견을 물어보고 있으므로 (C)가 정답이다.

어휘 determine v. 알아내다, 결정하다 grant v. 승인하다 confirm v. 확인하다

04 육하원칙 문제
해석 Ms. Abdulhak은 회사의 어떤 측면에 만족했는가?
(A) 예약 과정의 간단함
(B) 한 직원의 고객 서비스 기술
(C) Gallapot Mini의 연비
(D) 계약의 조건

해설 지문의 'When I picked up the car from your Fairfield location, the staff member was very helpful.'에서 Fairfield 지점에서 차량을 찾아갈 때 직원이 매우 도움이 되었다고 했으므로 (B)가 정답이다.

어휘 aspect n. 측면, 양상 fuel efficiency 연비

05 Not/True 문제
해석 Frontward Car Rental사에 대해 언급된 것은?
(A) 고객들이 다른 지점에서 차량을 찾아가고 반납하는 것을 허용한다.
(B) Danbury에 자동차 정비공들의 팀을 만들었다.
(C) Fairfield 지점을 닫기로 결정했다.
(D) 사고 발생 시 고객들이 보고서를 제출하도록 요구한다.

해설 (A)는 지문의 'When I picked up the car from your Fairfield location'과 'at your Danbury location when I returned the automobile'에서 Fairfield 지점에서 차량을 찾아갔고, Danbury 지점에서 차량을 반납했다고 했으므로 지문의 내용과 일치한다. 따라서 (A)가 정답이다. (B), (C), (D)는 지문에 언급되지 않은 내용이다.

어휘 branch n. 지점 mechanic n. 정비공 accident n. 사고

06-09번은 다음 구인 광고에 관한 문제입니다.

MediTek사
흥미로운 경력 기회를 찾고 계신가요?

30년 넘게, MediTek사는 전국의 병원과 의원에 최고급 의료 장비를 공급해 왔습니다. 06저희는 현재 인쇄물, 텔레비전, 온라인 광고를 포함한 홍보 자료 개발에 도움을 줄 수 있는 사람을 찾고 있습니다.

07-(B)합격자는 오클랜드, 시카고 또는 디트로이트 지점에서 근무할 수 있는 선택권을 가질 것입니다. 08저희는 8월 첫째 주에 모든 면접을 진행할 계획입니다. 지원 절차의 이 단계에 오는 데 성공하신 분들에게는 필요한 화상 채팅 소프트웨어 설치 방법에 대한 설명뿐만 아니라 날짜와 시간이 적힌 이메일이 발송될 것입니다.

일자리에 대한 자세한 정보를 위해 www.meditek.com/applications에 방문하세요. 09지원하려면, 온라인 지원서를 작성하여 제출하세요. 이전 고용주로부터의 추천서를 최소 두 개는 제출해야 한다는 점을 유념하세요. 모든 지원자는 7월 25일까지 서류를 제출해야 합니다.

career n. 경력, 직업 advanced adj. 고급의, 진보의
development n. 개발 promotional adj. 홍보의 material n. 자료
successful candidate 합격자 choice n. 선택권 make it 성공하다
process n. 절차, 과정 instruction n. 설명 recommendation n. 추천

06 추론 문제
해석 광고는 누구를 대상으로 하는 것 같은가?
(A) 기술자들
(B) 마케팅 보조 직원들
(C) 부동산 중개인들
(D) 회계사들

해설 지문의 'We are currently looking for someone to help with the development of promotional materials, including print, television, and online advertisements.'에서 현재 인쇄물, 텔레비전, 온라인 광고를 포함한 홍보 자료 개발에 도움을 줄 수 있는 사람을 찾고 있다고 한 것을 통해, 이 광고가 마케팅 보조 직원들을 대상으로 한다는 것을 추론할 수 있다. 따라서 (B)가 정답이다.

어휘 real estate agent 부동산 중개인 accountant n. 회계사

07 Not/True 문제

해설 MediTek사에 대해 사실인 것은?
(A) 병원과 의원을 모두 운영한다.
(B) 다른 나라로 확장했다.
(C) 소매점을 통해 제품을 유통한다.
(D) 여러 도시에 지점을 열었다.

해설 (D)는 'The successful candidate will have the choice of working out of our Oakland, Chicago, or Detroit branch.'에서 합격자는 오클랜드, 시카고 또는 디트로이트 지점에서 근무할 수 있는 선택권을 가질 것이라고 했으므로 지문의 내용과 일치한다. 따라서 (D)가 정답이다. (A), (B), (C)는 지문에 언급되지 않은 내용이다.

어휘 operate v. 운영하다 distribute v. (상품을) 유통시키다 retailer n. 소매점

08 추론 문제

해설 면접에 대해 암시되는 것은?
(A) 전화로 일정이 잡힐 것이다.
(B) 대면으로 진행되지 않을 것이다.
(C) 일부 일자리에는 요구되지 않을 것이다.
(D) 8월 말에 시작할 것이다.

해설 지문의 'We plan to conduct all interviews in the first week of August.'에서 8월 첫째 주에 모든 면접을 진행할 계획이라고 했고, 'Those who make it to this stage of the application process will be sent an e-mail with ~ instructions on how to set up the necessary video-chat software.'에서 지원 절차의 이 단계에 오는 데 성공한 사람들에게는 필요한 화상 채팅 소프트웨어 설치 방법에 대한 설명이 적힌 이메일이 발송될 것이라고 했으므로, 면접이 대면으로 진행되지 않을 것이라는 사실을 추론할 수 있다. 따라서 (B)가 정답이다.

어휘 in person 대면으로, 직접

09 육하원칙 문제

해설 광고에 따르면, 지원서와 함께 무엇이 포함되어야 하는가?
(A) 작업 견본
(B) 교육 증서
(C) 직업상의 추천서
(D) 이력서

해설 지문의 'To apply, complete and submit the online application form. Please note that at least two letters of recommendation from former employers must be provided.'에서 지원하려면 온라인 지원서를 작성하여 제출해야 하고, 이전 고용주로부터의 추천서를 최소 두 개는 제출해야 하는 점을 유의하라고 했으므로 (C)가 정답이다.

어휘 certificate n. 증서, 증명서 professional adj. 직업상의, 직업적인

Paraphrasing
recommendation from former employers 이전 고용주로부터의 추천서 → Professional references 직업상의 추천서

10-13번은 다음 웹페이지에 관한 문제입니다.

www.refurnish.com				
홈	소개	의견	연락처	

ReFurnish사에서, ¹⁰저희는 새집에 적합하도록 중고 가구를 수집하고, 청소하며, 수리합니다. 다른 중고 가구점들과 달리, ¹¹⁻⁽ᴮ⁾저희는 매우 까다로워서, 품질로 명성 있는 유명 브랜드만 제공합니다.

판매하기를 원하는 가구가 있다면, 그 가구에 대한 간단한 설명과 사진이

포함된 이메일을 purchases@refurnish.com으로 보내주세요. ¹²그다음에 저희의 담당자 중 한 명이 저희가 지불할 금액을 협상하기 위해 귀하의 집을 방문할 것입니다. 결제가 이루어진 후에, 저희는 가구를 저희 매장으로 배송할 수 있도록 준비할 것입니다.

가구를 구매하려는 분은 샌프란시스코 시내 Walker가 3746번지에 있는 저희 전시실에 들르시면 됩니다. 저희는 매우 다양한 품목을 재고로 보유하고 있으며, 매일 새로운 가구가 도착하고 있습니다. ¹³이전 고객들의 의견을 확인하려면 여기를 클릭하세요. 그들의 말에 깊은 인상을 받으실 거라고 확신합니다!

pre-owned adj. 중고의 secondhand adj. 중고의
selective adj. 까다로운, 선별적인 prestigious adj. 유명한
reputation n. 명성, 평판 brief adj. 간단한 description n. 설명
negotiate v. 협상하다 showroom n. 전시실
a wide variety of 매우 다양한 stock n. 재고(품)
impress v. 깊은 인상을 주다

10 동의어 문제

해설 1문단 첫 번째 줄의 단어 "collect"는 의미상 -와 가장 가깝다.
(A) 맡기다
(B) 수집하다
(C) 연결하다
(D) 제시하다

해설 collect를 포함한 구절 'we collect, clean, and repair pre-owned furniture'에서 collect는 '수집하다'라는 뜻으로 사용되었다. 따라서 (B)가 정답이다.

11 Not/True 문제

해설 ReFurnish사에 대해 사실인 것은?
(A) 고객들을 위한 주문 제작 가구를 생산한다.
(B) 물품 목록이 특정 브랜드로 한정되어 있다.
(C) 새 상품과 중고 상품을 모두 제공한다.
(D) 상품이 전국적인 주목을 받았다.

해설 (B)는 'we are highly selective, only offering prestigious brands with a reputation for quality'에서 ReFurnish사가 매우 까다로워서 품질로 명성 있는 유명 브랜드만 제공한다고 했으므로 지문의 내용과 일치한다. 따라서 (B)가 정답이다. (A), (C), (D)는 지문에 언급되지 않은 내용이다.

어휘 custom adj. 주문 제작한 inventory n. 물품 목록 attention n. 주목, 관심

Paraphrasing
prestigious brands 유명 브랜드 → specific brands 특정 브랜드

12 육하원칙 문제

해설 웹페이지에 따르면, ReFurnish사 직원들은 집 방문 시 무엇을 하는가?
(A) 판매자와 가격을 논의한다.
(B) 물건의 사진을 몇 장 찍는다.
(C) 배송의 도착을 확인한다.
(D) 잠재적 구매자들에게 가구를 보여준다.

해설 지문의 'One of our representatives will then visit your home to negotiate the amount we will pay.'에서 담당자 중 한 명이 지불할 금액을 협상하기 위해 집을 방문할 것이라고 했으므로 (A)가 정답이다.

어휘 confirm v. 확인하다 arrival n. 도착 potential adj. 잠재적인

Paraphrasing
negotiate the amount ~ will pay 지불할 금액을 협상하다 → discuss a price 가격을 논의하다

13 육하원칙 문제

해설 고객들은 온라인에서 무엇을 하도록 권고되는가?
(A) 서비스에 대한 질문을 게시한다.
(B) 가게의 위치를 찾는다.

(C) 주문 상태를 확인한다.
(D) 업체의 후기를 읽는다.

해설 지문의 'You should click here to check out the feedback from our previous clients.'에서 이전 고객들의 의견을 확인하려면 여기를 클릭하라고 했으므로 (D)가 정답이다.

어휘 post v. 게시하다 status n. 상태

Paraphrasing
check out the feedback from ~ clients 고객들의 의견을 확인하다 → Read reviews 후기를 읽다

DAY 18 기사 및 안내문

1. 기사

지문 흐름과 빈출 문제   p.296

과거의 공장이 새로운 삶을 찾다
Gregory McKenna 작성 (4월 3일)—어제, Grand Prairie 예술 위원회 의장 Belinda Blair는 광범위한 보수 공사 후에, 이전에 XLT사에 의해 운영되었던 폐공장이 3,000제곱미터의 복합문화공간으로 개조되었다고 발표했다.

새로운 Grand Prairie 문화 센터는 1,500명을 위한 좌석을 가진 공연 예술 시설을 특별히 포함한다.

"이 프로젝트는 Wilma Brown 시장과 Keystone 은행 같은 지역 기업들의 지원이 없었다면 불가능했을 것입니다."라고 Belinda Blair가 말했다.

이 센터는 8월 5일에 대중에게 개방한다.

chairperson n. 의장 extensive adj. 광범위한
renovation n. 보수 공사, 개조 abandoned factory 폐공장
convert v. 개조하다 cultural complex 복합문화공간
support n. 지원, 지지 public n. 대중

HACKERS PRACTICE   p.298

01 (B)   **02** (B)

01번은 다음 기사에 관한 문제입니다.

Business Buzz 주간지
지속 가능성과 당신의 사업
Jonathan Demarco 작성
11월 14일

환경 지속 가능성의 중요성에 대한 인식이 증가하면서, 사업체들이 친환경적인 생산 방법을 채택하기 위한 조치를 취하고 있다. 그럼에도 불구하고, 01Sustainable 경제학 센터의 선임 연구원인 Evelyn Harris는 "비용이 고려해야 할 주요 요인입니다."라고 지적했다. 예를 들어, 공장 설비를 친환경적인 장치로 교체하는 것은 비용이 매우 많이 드는 작업일 수 있다. 그 후에, 회사가 제품의 가격을 올림으로써 이 비용을 상쇄하려고 노력할지도 모른다. 그리고 궁극적으로, 소비자들은 어떻게 만들어졌는지가 아닌, 가격에 근거하여 상품을 구입할 가능성이 더 높다.

sustainability n. 지속 가능성, 지속성 aware adj. 인식하는, 깨닫는
step n. 조치, 단계 adopt v. 채택하다, 고르다
green adj. 친환경적인, 환경 보호의 senior researcher 선임 연구원
factor n. 요인, 요소 subsequently adv. 그 후에, 나중에

01 추론 문제

해석 Ms. Harris의 직업이 무엇일 것 같은가?
(A) 환경 자문 위원
(B) 경제 연구원
(C) 공장 관리자
(D) 마케팅 전문가

해설 지문의 'Evelyn Harris, a senior researcher at the Center for Sustainable Economics'에서 Evelyn Harris가 Sustainable 경제학 센터의 선임 연구원이라고 했으므로, Ms. Harris가 경제 연구원이라는 사실을 추론할 수 있다. 따라서 (B)가 정답이다.

어휘 consultant n. 자문 위원, 상담가 expert n. 전문가

02번은 다음 보도 자료에 관한 문제입니다.

시장 보고서

9월 8일—02Beale 의류회사는 새로운 운동복 라인을 출시할 것이라고 발표했다. 이 움직임은 성장하고 있는 스포츠 의류 시장에서 점유율을 차지하려는 분명한 시도이다. 새로운 라인은 내년 6월부터 그 회사의 소매판매점에서 판매될 것이다.

마케팅 이사 Rita Murphy는 출시 시기가 의도적으로 정해진 것이라고 말한다. 그것은 그달에 그리스 아테네에서 열리는 제43회 세계 하계 스포츠 대회와 시기가 맞물릴 것이다. 수백만 명의 세계 시청자들은 미국 선수들이 착용한 그 회사의 제품들을 보게 될 것이다.

launch v. 출시하다, 시작하다 apparent adj. 분명한, 명백한
capture v. 차지하다, 사로잡다 share n. 점유율, 몫
deliberate adj. 의도적으로 정해진, 신중한
coincide v. 시기가 맞물리다, 동시에 일어나다

02 목적 문제

해석 보도 자료의 목적은 무엇인가?
(A) 다가오는 행사의 위치를 공개하기 위해
(B) 새로운 운동복 제품 라인을 소개하기 위해
(C) 특별 할인을 홍보하기 위해
(D) 스포츠 행사 후원을 발표하기 위해

해설 지문의 'Beale Apparel has announced that it will be launching a new line of sportswear'에서 Beale 의류회사가 새로운 운동복 라인을 출시할 것이라고 발표했다고 한 후, 새로운 운동복 라인에 대한 정보를 제공하고 있으므로 (B)가 정답이다.

어휘 reveal v. 공개하다, 밝히다 promote v. 홍보하다
sponsorship n. 후원, 협찬

2. 안내문

지문 흐름과 빈출 문제   p.299

중요: 조립 전에 읽으십시오

저희 Outdoor Adventure 텐트를 구매해 주셔서 감사합니다.

처음 설치하기 전에, 모든 부품의 포장을 조심스럽게 풀고 빠진 것이 없는지 확인하세요. 최적의 조립을 위해, 부품들을 잔디처럼 부드러운 지면에 펼치세요. 아래 그림에 명시된 대로, 가장 큰 뼈대를 측면에 배치하는 것부터 시작하세요. 억지로 연결하거나 기둥을 과도하게 조이면 텐트의 구조적 온전함을 손상시킬 수 있으므로 그렇게 하지 않도록 주의하세요.

자세한 유지 관리 팁을 보기 위해서, 공식 웹사이트 www.wildgeartrek.com에 방문해주세요.

assembly n. 조립 unpack v. 포장을 풀다 component n. 부품
optimal adj. 최적의 spread v. 펼치다 surface n. 지면, 표면
frame n. 뼈대 specify v. 명시하다 illustration n. 그림, 삽화
connection n. 연결 excessively adv. 과도하게 tighten v. 조이다
compromise v. 손상시키다 integrity n. 온전함, 완전한 상태

HACKERS PRACTICE   p.301

01 (D)   **02** (B)

01번은 다음 안내문에 관한 문제입니다.

> 베스트셀러 저서 Working Together의 저자 Judith Weber가 7월 17일 오후 1시부터 5시까지 Bridgeport 비즈니스 연구소에서 워크숍을 진행할 것입니다. 초점은 의사소통 기술 향상이 될 것이며, 그녀는 동료들과 효과적으로 소통하는 방법에 대한 팁을 제공할 것입니다. Ms. Weber는 또한 참가자들이 배운 내용을 실행에 옮겨볼 수 있도록 실습 활동도 진행할 것입니다.
>
> 이것은 Ms. Weber에 의해 진행되는 워크숍 시리즈 중 첫 번째임을 참조해 주십시오. ⁰¹향후 세션의 날짜와 시간을 알아보기 위해서, 저희 웹사이트 www.bridgeportbusiness.com을 방문해 주세요.

author n. 저자, 작가   interact v. 소통하다, 상호작용하다   coworker n. 동료
put ~ into action ~을 실행에 옮기다   session n. 세션, 특정한 활동을 위한 시간

01 육하원칙 문제
해석 웹사이트에서 무엇을 확인할 수 있는가?
(A) 의견 양식
(B) 장소 지도
(C) 연설자 약력
(D) 세션 일정

해설 지문의 'To find out the dates and times of future sessions, please visit our Web site at ~.'에서 향후 세션의 날짜와 시간을 알아보기 위해서 웹사이트를 방문하라고 했으므로 (D)가 정답이다.

어휘 venue n. 장소   biography n. 약력, 전기

02번은 다음 설명에 관한 문제입니다.

> **제품 조립**
>
> Wellington Furniture사의 컴퓨터 책상 조립을 시작하기 전에, 다음 사항에 주의하십시오. 제공된 금속 나사를 올바른 구멍과 맞추는 것이 중요합니다. 제품에는 다양한 크기의 나사들이 딸려 있습니다. 각 종류의 나사는 책상의 다른 부품을 위해 설계되었습니다. 나무가 갈라지거나 손상될 위험이 있으므로, ⁰²잘못된 구멍에 나사를 끼우려고 시도하지 마십시오. 이를 방지하기 위해, 이 조립 설명서의 8페이지에 있는 그림을 참조하십시오. 그것은 각각 다른 구멍에 어떤 나사가 사용되어야 하는지 명확하게 명시합니다.

assemble v. 조립하다   take note of ~에 주의하다
metal adj. 금속의; n. 금속   screw n. 나사   come with ~이 딸려 있다
risk v. ~의 위험이 있다, ~을 위태롭게 하다   crack v. 금 가게 하다, 부수다
damage v. 손상시키다   avoid v. 막다, 피하다   refer to ~을 참조하다
indicate v. 명시하다

02 육하원칙 문제
해석 안내문에 따르면, 책상을 조립할 때 무엇을 피해야 하는가?
(A) 나무에 너무 많은 압력을 가하는 것
(B) 잘못된 위치에 나사를 사용하는 것
(C) 다른 제품의 부품을 부착하는 것
(D) 잘못된 순서로 부품을 조립하는 것

해설 지문의 'Do not attempt to put a screw in the wrong hole'에서 잘못된 구멍에 나사를 끼우려고 시도하지 말라고 했으므로 (B)가 정답이다.

어휘 pressure n. 압력   attach v. 부착하다, 붙이다

HACKERS TEST   p.302

01 (D)   **02** (A)   **03** (D)   **04** (C)   **05** (B)
06 (B)   **07** (B)   **08** (C)   **09** (C)   **10** (B)
11 (D)   **12** (B)   **13** (C)

01-02번은 다음 설명에 관한 문제입니다.

> **Maxwell사의 냉동 아침 샌드위치**
> [^{01-(A)/(B)}빵, 소시지, 계란, 치즈 포함 | 1회 제공량: 250그램]
>
> ^{01-(D)}조리할 준비가 될 때까지 제품을 냉동 보관하세요.
>
> ^{01-(C)}전자레인지 가열 방법
> 1. 비닐 포장지에서 꺼내어, 전자레인지에 사용할 수 있는 용기에 넣습니다.
> 2. 약한 열에서 2분간 가열합니다.
> 3. 제품을 뒤집고, 센 열에서 3분간 가열합니다.
>
> ^{01-(C)}오븐 가열 방법
> 1. 비닐 포장지에서 꺼내어, 호일로 감쌉니다.
> 2. 구이판 위에 놓고, 350도에서 20분간 굽습니다.
>
> 주의: ⁰²샌드위치의 먹지 않은 부분은 다시 얼리지 마세요. 그렇게 하는 것은 건강상의 위험을 초래할 수 있습니다.

microwave-safe adj. 전자레인지에 사용할 수 있는   wrapper n. 포장지
container n. 용기, 그릇   refreeze v. 다시 얼리다   portion n. 부분
risk n. 위험

01 Not/True 문제
해석 제품에 대해 명시된 것은?
(A) 다섯 가지 재료를 포함한다.
(B) 채식주의 식단에 적합하다.
(C) 하나의 방법을 사용해서만 가열될 수 있다.
(D) 여전히 냉동된 상태에서도 조리할 수 있다.

해설 (D)는 'Keep the item frozen until you are ready to heat it.'에서 조리할 준비가 될 때까지 제품을 냉동 보관하라고 했으므로 지문의 내용과 일치한다. 따라서 (D)가 정답이다. (A)와 (B)는 'Contains bread, sausage, egg, cheese'에서 제품에 빵, 소시지, 계란, 치즈가 포함된다고 했으므로 지문의 내용과 일치하지 않는다. (C)는 'Microwave Heating Instructions'와 'Oven Heating Instructions'에서 전자레인지와 오븐으로 가열할 수 있다고 했으므로 지문의 내용과 일치하지 않는다.

어휘 suitable adj. 적합한   method n. 방법

02 육하원칙 문제
해석 설명은 고객들에게 무엇을 하라고 조언하는가?
(A) 남은 음식을 냉동실에 넣지 않는다.
(B) 유효 기간을 주의한다.
(C) 먹기 전에 20분을 기다린다.
(D) 섭취를 1인분으로 제한한다.

해설 지문의 'Do not refreeze any uneaten portions of the sandwich.'에서 샌드위치의 먹지 않은 부분은 다시 얼리지 말라고 했으므로 (A)가 정답이다.

어휘 leftover n. 남은 음식   take note of ~에 주의하다
expiration date 유효 기간   consumption n. 섭취

03-05번은 다음 기사에 관한 문제입니다.

> **Casa Bella사가 인도에 진출할 계획을 발표하다**
> Reena Singh 작성
>
> ⁰³이탈리아 주요 가구 소매업체인 Casa Bella사가 인도에 첫 지점을 열 계획을 발표했다. 회사는 뭄바이에 매장을 세울 계획이며, 개점은 3월로 예정되어 있다. — [1] —. 그 매장은 다른 전 세계 지점들과 같은 제품과

서비스들을 제공할 것이다.
뭄바이 소매점에 더하여, 다른 인도 도시들의 매장들도 계획되어 있다. 회사 대표 Daniella Fieri에 따르면, [05]인도 경제의 성장이 이 나라를 매력적인 대상으로 만들었다. — [2] —. Ms. Fieri는 또한 [04-(B)]회사가 이미 생산 공장을 인도에서 운영하고 있기 때문에, 매장으로의 배송 비용이 낮을 것이라고 말했다. 가구 산업 전문가들은 높은 기대를 가지고 있으며, [04-(D)]회사 주식의 가치가 거의 10퍼센트 상승했다. — [3] —.
만약 인도의 소매판매점이 성공하면, Casa Bella사는 동남아시아로 확장할 가능성이 높다. [04-(A)]이 소매업체는 이미 유럽과 북아메리카에서 시장 주도 기업이다. — [4] —.

launch v. 진출하다; n. 진출 retailer n. 소매업체 branch n. 지점, 지사
outlet n. 소매점 attractive adj. 매력적인 target n. 대상, 목표
expert n. 전문가 expectation n. 기대, 예상 stock n. 주식

03 주제 문제
해석 기사는 주로 무엇에 대한 것인가?
(A) 한 사업체에 대한 투자 기회
(B) 한 소매업체의 확장 계획
(C) 인도에 있는 두 회사 간의 합병
(D) 제품 라인의 생산을 중단하려는 결정

해설 지문의 'Casa Bella, the ~ retailer, has announced plans to open its first branch in India.'에서 소매업체인 Casa Bella사가 인도에 첫 지점을 열 계획을 발표했다고 한 후, Casa Bella사의 지점 확장 계획에 대해 설명하고 있으므로 (B)가 정답이다.

어휘 expansion n. 확장, 확대 discontinue v. (생산을) 중단하다, 그만두다

04 Not/True 문제
해석 Casa Bella사에 대해 언급되지 않은 것은?
(A) 두 대륙에서 강력한 시장 지위를 가지고 있다.
(B) 인도에서 몇몇 물품들을 생산한다.
(C) 고객들에게 무료 배송을 제공한다.
(D) 주식 가치의 상승을 보고했다.

해설 (C)는 지문에 언급되지 않은 내용이다. 따라서 (C)가 정답이다. (A)는 'The retailer is already a market leader in Europe and North America.'에서 이 소매업체가 이미 유럽과 북아메리카에서 시장 주도 기업이라고 했으므로 지문의 내용과 일치한다. (B)는 'the company already operates a production plant in India'에서 회사가 이미 생산 공장을 인도에서 운영하고 있다고 했으므로 지문의 내용과 일치한다. (D)는 'the company's stock value has increased by nearly 10 percent'에서 회사 주식의 가치가 거의 10퍼센트 상승했다고 했으므로 지문의 내용과 일치한다.

어휘 position n. 지위 manufacture v. 생산하다

[Paraphrasing]
is ~ a market leader 시장 주도 기업이다 → has a strong market position 강력한 시장 지위를 가지고 있다
operates a production plant 생산 공장을 운영한다 → manufactures some goods 몇몇 물품들을 생산한다

05 문장 위치 찾기 문제
해설 [1], [2], [3], [4]로 표시된 위치 중, 다음 문장이 들어갈 곳으로 가장 적절한 것은?
"이는 인도의 소비자들이 이제 집을 위한 물품들에 더 많이 지출하기 때문이다."
(A) [1]
(B) [2]
(C) [3]
(D) [4]

해설 주어진 문장은 인도 소비자들의 더 많은 지출과 관련된 부분에 들어가야 함을 알 수 있다. [2]의 앞 문장인 'the growth of the Indian economy has made the country an attractive target'에서 인도 경제의 성장이 이 나라를 매력적인 대상으로 만들었다고 했으므로, [2]에 제시된 문장이 들어가면 인도의 경제 성장이 이 나라를 매력적인 대상으로 만들었으며 이는 인도의 소비자들이 이제 집을 위한 물품들에 더 많이 지출하기 때문이라는 자연스러운 문맥이 된다는 것을 알 수 있다. 따라서 (B)가 정답이다.

06-09번은 다음 안내문에 관한 문제입니다.

Sonnenville 공공 수영장
여러분이 여기 Sonnenville 공용 수영장에서 즐거운 시간을 보내길 바랍니다. [06]모든 사람이 즐겁고 안전한 시간을 보내도록 확실히 하기 위해, 다음에 주의하세요:
1. [07-(A)]매점 외에는 이 시설에서 음식과 음료가 허용되지 않습니다.
2. [07-(B)]10살 미만의 어린이들은 반드시 어른이 동반해야 합니다.
3. [07-(C)]다이빙과 수영장 속으로 뛰어드는 것은 허용되지 않습니다.

[07-(D)]수영장이 개장하면 두 명의 안전 구조원들이 그들의 위치에서 근무할 것입니다. 지침을 따르지 않는 사람은 누구든 시설에서 퇴장 요청을 받을 수 있습니다.

[08]Sonnenville 공공 수영장은 월요일부터 금요일까지는 오전 7시부터 오후 9시까지, 토요일에는 오전 6시부터 오후 9시까지, 일요일에는 오전 8시부터 오후 9시까지 개장합니다. 이 시설은 또한 모든 연령과 수준의 사람들을 위한 매우 다양한 수영 강좌를 제공합니다. 시간, 비용, 그리고 강사에 대한 정보를 얻거나 [09]강좌에 등록하기 위해서는, 안내 데스크에 있는 저희 직원 중 한 명에게 문의하세요.

ensure v. 확실하게 하다, 안전하게 하다 accompany v. 동반하다, 동행하다
lifeguard n. 안전 구조원 on duty 근무하는, 근무 중인
enroll v. 등록하다, 입학시키다

06 목적 문제
해석 안내문의 목적은 무엇인가?
(A) 회원들에게 정책 변경에 대해 최신 정보를 주기 위해
(B) 방문객들에게 지침을 알리기 위해
(C) 새로운 운영 시간을 공지하기 위해
(D) 수영 대회를 홍보하기 위해

해설 지문의 'To ensure that everyone has a pleasant and safe time, please take note of the following:'에서 모든 사람이 즐겁고 안전한 시간을 보내도록 확실히 하기 위해 다음에 주의하라고 한 후, 수영장에서 지켜야 할 지침을 나열하고 있으므로 (B)가 정답이다.

어휘 operation hours 운영 시간

07 Not/True 문제
해석 Sonnenville 공공 수영장에 대해 언급되지 않은 것은?
(A) 방문객들에게 간식을 판다.
(B) 부모가 모든 아이들을 동반할 것을 요구한다.
(C) 방문객들이 다이빙하는 것을 허용하지 않는다.
(D) 몇 명의 안전 구조원을 고용하고 있다.

해설 (B)는 'Children under 10 years of age must be accompanied by an adult.'에서 10살 미만의 어린이들은 반드시 어른이 동반해야 한다고 했지, 부모가 모든 아이들을 동반해야 하는 것은 아니므로 지문의 내용과 일치하지 않는다. 따라서 (B)가 정답이다. (A)는 'Food and beverages are not permitted in the facility except at the snack bar.'에서 매점 외에는 이 시설에서 음식과 음료가 허용되지 않는다고 했으므로 지문의 내용과 일치한다. (C)는 'Diving and jumping into the pool are not allowed.'에서 다이빙이 허용되지 않는다고 했으므로 지문의 내용과 일치한다. (D)는 'Two lifeguards will be on duty ~ when the pool is open.'에서 수영장이 개장하면 두 명의 안전 구조원들이 근무한다고 했으므로 지문의 내용과 일치한다.

어휘 employ v. 고용하다

Paraphrasing
Food and beverages 음식과 음료 → snack items 간식
Two 두 명의 → a couple of 몇 명의

08 육하원칙 문제
해석 수영장은 어느 요일에 가장 일찍 개장하는가?
(A) 월요일
(B) 금요일
(C) 토요일
(D) 일요일

해설 지문의 'The Sonnenville Public Swimming Pool is open from 7 A.M. to 9 P.M. from Monday through Friday, from 6 A.M. to 9 P.M. on Saturday, and from 8 A.M. to 9 P.M. on Sunday.'에서 Sonnenville 공공 수영장은 월요일부터 금요일까지는 오전 7시부터 오후 9시까지, 토요일에는 오전 6시부터 오후 9시까지, 일요일에는 오전 8시부터 오후 9시까지 개장한다고 했으므로 (C)가 정답이다.

09 육하원칙 문제
해석 방문객들은 어떻게 수업에 등록할 수 있는가?
(A) 강사에게 연락함으로써
(B) 신청서를 작성함으로써
(C) 안내 데스크로 감으로써
(D) 이메일을 보냄으로써

해설 지문의 'to enroll in a course, speak to one of our staff members at the front desk'에서 강좌에 등록하기 위해서 안내 데스크에 있는 직원 중 한 명에게 문의하라고 했으므로 (C)가 정답이다.

어휘 fill out ~을 작성하다, 기입하다 application n. 신청서

Paraphrasing
enroll in a course 강좌에 등록하다 → register for a class 수업에 등록하다
front desk 안내 데스크 → service desk 안내 데스크

10-13번은 다음 기사에 관한 문제입니다.

LiteraLegends가 새로운 작가들에게 출판 기회를 제공하다

자신의 작품이 출판되도록 노력하는 작가들에게 희망이 있다! ¹⁰불과 5년 전에 설립된 LiteraLegends는 작가들에게 그들의 소설, 단편 소설, 시, 그리고 비소설 작품들을 출판할 기회를 제공하는 웹사이트이다. 작가들은 그들의 작품을 사이트에 업로드하기만 하면, 회원들은 그들의 읽는 즐거움을 위해 그것들을 다운로드할 수 있다.

LiteraLegends의 최고경영자 Sam Ashoka는 "글을 처음 써본 작가들은 대개 자신의 작품을 무료로 제공합니다. ¹¹⁻⁽ᴰ⁾회원들은 그들이 읽은 것이 마음에 든다면, 그들은 긍정적인 후기를 남깁니다."라고 설명했다. 만약 한 작품이 인기를 얻게 되면, 그 작가는 그때 회원들에게 다운로드에 대한 요금을 부과할 수 있는 선택권을 갖게 된다. 그 가격은 2.99달러만큼 낮을 수도 있고 35.99달러만큼 높을 수도 있다. ¹²LiteraLegends는 20퍼센트의 수수료를 부과하며 또한 작가들이 전통적인 출판사들에 알려질 수 있도록 돕는다.

¹³The Believers의 유명한 작가 Meridiana Chase는 LiteraLegends에서 그녀의 작품에 대한 상당한 독자층을 키운 후 출판사와 계약을 맺었다. "일부 작품들은 100만 회가 넘게 다운로드되었습니다"라고 Ashoka는 또한 말했다. "LiteraLegends가 새로운 작가들에게 높은 수준의 성공을 가져다주기를 희망합니다."

author n. 작가, 저자 publication n. 출판 novel n. 소설
nonfiction n. 비소설 charge v. 요금을 부과하다 commission fee n. 수수료
publishing house 출판사 readership n. 독자(층)
remark v. 말하다, 언급하다

10 동의어 문제
해석 1문단 첫 번째 줄의 단어 "Founded"는 의미상 -와 가장 가깝다.
(A) 발견된
(B) 설립된
(C) 찾아진
(D) 밝혀진

해설 Founded를 포함한 구절 'Founded just five years ago'에서 Founded는 '설립된'이라는 뜻으로 사용되었다. 따라서 (B)가 정답이다.

11 Not/True 문제
해석 LiteraLegends에 대해 언급된 것은?
(A) 다른 웹사이트들에서 서비스를 제공한다.
(B) 고객들이 미리 비용을 지불할 것을 요구한다.
(C) 다른 회사들과 제휴를 맺고 있다.
(D) 사용자들이 의견을 제공하도록 허용한다.

해설 (D)는 'If members like what they read, they leave a positive review.'에서 회원들은 그들이 읽은 것이 마음에 든다면 긍정적인 후기를 남긴다고 했으므로 지문의 내용과 일치한다. 따라서 (D)가 정답이다. (A), (B), (C)는 지문에 언급되지 않은 내용이다.

어휘 in advance 미리 form v. 맺다, 형성하다 partnership n. 제휴, 협력

Paraphrasing
leave a ~ review 후기를 남기다 → provide feedback 의견을 제공하다

12 육하원칙 문제
해석 LiteraLegends는 어떻게 수익을 만들어내는가?
(A) 회원권에 대해 요금을 부과함으로써
(B) 판매 수수료를 가져감으로써
(C) 구독료를 받음으로써
(D) 광고를 냄으로써

해설 지문의 'LiteraLegends charges a 20 percent commission fee'에서 LiteraLegends가 20퍼센트의 수수료를 부과한다고 했으므로 (B)가 정답이다.

어휘 collect v. (급료 따위를) 받다 subscription fee 구독료

Paraphrasing
charges ~ commission fee 수수료를 부과하다 → taking sales commissions 판매 수수료를 가져가는 것

13 육하원칙 문제
해석 Meridiana Chase는 누구인가?
(A) 회사 대변인
(B) 문학 평론가
(C) 책 저자
(D) 마케팅 전문가

해설 지문의 'Well-known author of The Believers, Meridiana Chase'에서 Meridiana Chase가 The Believers의 유명한 작가라고 했으므로 (C)가 정답이다.

어휘 spokesperson n. 대변인 literary adj. 문학의 critic n. 평론가, 비평가
expert n. 전문가

DAY 19 공고 및 회람

1. 공고

지문 흐름과 빈출 문제   p.306

저희 이전합니다!

같은 장소에서의 25년 후에, Nickel Books는 Polson가 3408번지로 이전하기로 결정했습니다.

그 이유는 현재 건물의 창고에 저희의 증가하는 재고를 위한 충분한 공간이 없다는 것입니다. 새로운 장소는 4월 30일에 문을 열 것입니다. 축하하기

위해, 저희는 5월 1일부터 15일까지 모든 책과 잡지에 15퍼센트 할인을 제공할 것입니다. 게다가, 25달러 이상 구매하시는 모든 분은 저희의 로고가 있는 무료 손가방을 받을 것입니다.

*Panhurst역의 5번 출구에서부터, 두 블록 정도 직진하세요. 저희는 Color Kitchen이라는 식당 위에 위치할 것이며 그 건물의 2층과 3층을 사용할 것입니다.

지도를 보려면 저희의 웹사이트 www.nickelbooks.com을 반드시 확인해 주십시오.

storeroom n. 창고, 저장실 growing adj. 증가하는, 커지는
inventory n. 재고 celebrate v. 축하하다, 기념하다 tote bag 손가방
occupy v. (공간을) 사용하다, 차지하다

HACKERS PRACTICE p.308

01 (D)   **02** (C)

01번은 다음 공고에 관한 문제입니다.

고객 공지

01저희는 다음의 인터넷 뱅킹 서비스들이 7월 8일 일요일 오전 12시부터 오전 8시까지 중단될 것임을 고객들에게 알리고자 합니다.

- 현금 자동 입출금기(ATM기)
- 온라인 자금 송금 및 청구서 납부
- 신용 및 직불카드의 온라인 사용

이 기간 동안, 고객들은 온라인으로 그들의 계좌 잔액을 계속해서 확인할 수 있습니다. 저희는 이번 중단이 야기할 수 있는 모든 불편에 대해 유감스럽게 생각하지만, 이것은 전자 뱅킹 시스템의 보안을 보장하는 소프트웨어 업데이트의 설치를 위해 필요합니다.

advisory n. 공지, 보고 suspend v. 중단하다
automated teller machine 현금 자동 입출금기 fund n. 자금, 돈
transfer n. 송금; v. 송금하다, 옮기다 bill n. 청구서 debit card 직불카드
account balance 계좌 잔액 regret v. 유감스럽게 생각하다
inconvenience n. 불편 installation n. 설치 ensure v. 보장하다, 확보하다

01 목적 문제

해석 공고의 목적은 무엇인가?
(A) 최근의 정책 변화를 설명하기 위해
(B) 주말 영업시간에 관한 세부 사항을 제공하기 위해
(C) 개인 정보의 업데이트를 요청하기 위해
(D) 일시적인 서비스 중단을 알리기 위해

해설 지문의 'We would like to advise ~ services will be suspended on Sunday, July 8, from 12 A.M. to 8 A.M.'에서 서비스들이 7월 8일 일요일 오전 12시부터 오전 8시까지 중단될 것임을 알리고자 한다고 한 후, 서비스 중단에 대한 세부 정보를 설명하고 있으므로 (D)가 정답이다.

어휘 request v. 요청하다; n. 요청

[Paraphrasing]
advise ~ services will be suspended 서비스들이 중단될 것임을 알리다
→ announce a ~ service interruption 서비스 중단을 알리다

02번은 다음 공고에 관한 문제입니다.

연례 시상식

1월 18일에, 업무를 뛰어나게 잘한 직원들에게 감사를 표하기 위한 연례 시상식을 개최할 것입니다. 우수한 성과를 거둔 직원들에게는 증서와 상품권이 배부될 예정입니다.

02프로젝트 관리자들은 인정받을 자격이 있다고 생각되는 팀원을 추천해 주시기 바랍니다. 추천서 양식 사본과 작성 방법에 관한 자세한 설명이 다음 주 초까지 이메일로 발송될 것입니다. **02**작성된 양식을 반드시 12월

30일까지 인사부 사무실에 제출해 주십시오. 이 날짜 이후에 접수된 추천서는 고려되지 않을 것입니다.

awards ceremony 시상식 acknowledge v. 감사를 표하다
excel v. 뛰어나게 잘하다 duty n. 업무 certificate n. 증서
gift card 상품권 distribute v. 배부하다 recommend v. 추천하다
recognition n. 인정, 표창 nomination n. 추천서, 지명
detailed adj. 자세한 instruction n. 설명

02 육하원칙 문제

해석 관리자들이 팀원을 수상 후보로 추천하려면 무엇을 해야 하는가?
(A) 관리자에게 이메일을 보낸다.
(B) 자세한 평가 내용을 검토한다.
(C) 마감일까지 양식을 제출한다.
(D) 직원 의견을 수집한다.

해설 지문의 'Project managers are encouraged to recommend any team member they feel deserves recognition.'에서 프로젝트 관리자들에게 인정받을 자격이 있다고 생각되는 팀원을 추천해 달라고 한 후, 'Please make sure to drop off the completed form at the human resources office by December 30.'에서 작성된 양식을 반드시 12월 30일까지 인사부 사무실에 제출하라고 했으므로 (C)가 정답이다.

어휘 evaluation n. 평가 내용, 평가 gather v. 수집하다, 모으다
opinion n. 의견, 견해

2. 회람

지문 흐름과 빈출 문제 p.309

회람

수신: 전 직원들
발신: Spencer Buffone, 건물 서비스 관리자
날짜: 3월 6일
제목: 공지

사무실 건물의 연례 외부 창문 청소를 알리고자 합니다.

3월 12일에, 오전 10시와 오후 5시 사이에 11층부터 20층까지 창문 청소를 할 것입니다.

우리는 직원들이 그날 모든 창문을 완전히 닫아 주기를 요청드립니다. 궁금한 점이 있으면, 내선 2966번으로 건물 서비스 팀에 연락해 주세요.

exterior adj. 외부의 fully adv. 완전히 extension n. 내선, 구내전화

HACKERS PRACTICE p.311

01 (A)   **02** (D)

01번은 다음 회람에 관한 문제입니다.

회람

수신: 전 직원들
발신: 인사부
날짜: 9월 16일
제목: 복장 규정

Farnham-Price사는 직원들이 사무실에서 일상적인 업무를 위해 편하게 옷을 입는 것을 허용하는 것은 사실이지만, **01**여러분은 고객들과의 회의에 참석할 때는 비즈니스 환경에서 용인되는 옷을 입어야 합니다. 여러분이 입는 옷은 잠재적인 고객들과 기존 고객들이 회사에 대해 갖는 인상에 직접적으로 영향을 줍니다. 이 규정에 대해 질문이 있으면 언제든지 저에게 해 주십시오.

personnel n. 직원들 dress casually 편하게 옷을 입다
acceptable adj. 용인되는, 받아들일 수 있는 setting n. 환경

attend v. 참석하다 directly adv. 직접적으로 potential adj. 잠재적인

01 육하원칙 문제
해석 직원들은 무엇을 하도록 지시 받았는가?
(A) 고객들과의 상호작용을 위해 전문가답게 옷을 입는다.
(B) 복장 규정에 관한 설문지를 작성한다.
(C) 고객들과의 회의에 늦지 않게 도착한다.
(D) 회사 정책의 최근 변경 사항을 검토한다.

해설 지문의 'you should wear acceptable clothing for a business setting when attending meetings with clients'에서 고객들과의 회의에 참석할 때는 비즈니스 환경에서 용인되는 옷을 입어야 한다고 했으므로 (A)가 정답이다.

어휘 interaction n. 상호작용 questionnaire n. 설문지
punctually adv. 늦지 않게, 시간대로 corporate adj. 회사의, 기업의

[Paraphrasing]
wear acceptable clothing for a business setting 비즈니스 환경에서 용인되는 옷을 입다 → Dress professionally 전문가답게 옷을 입다

02번은 다음 회람에 관한 문제입니다.

수신: 전 직원들
발신: Michael Lewis
날짜: 12월 10일
제목: 송년회

알려드립니다. 저희 법률 사무소의 연례 송년회가 12월 17일에 열립니다. 02그것은 원래 계획되었던 Pullman 회의장이 아닌 Harborview 호텔에서 개최될 예정임을 알리고자 합니다. 회의장에 화재가 발생하여 이 조정을 할 수 밖에 없었으며, 손상을 복구하는 데 몇 주가 소요될 것입니다.
궁금한 점이 있으시면, 제게 연락해 주세요. 감사합니다.

year-end party 송년회 law firm 법률 사무소 adjustment n. 조정
damage n. 손상, 피해

02 목적 문제
해석 회람의 목적은 무엇인가?
(A) 일정의 오류를 수정하기 위해
(B) 행사에 초대하기 위해
(C) 사교 모임의 이유를 설명하기 위해
(D) 장소 변경을 알리기 위해

해설 지문의 'I'd like to inform you that it will be held at the Harborview Hotel rather than the Pullman Conference Center as originally planned.'에서 그것, 즉 송년회가 원래 계획되었던 Pullman 회의장이 아닌 Harborview 호텔에서 개최될 예정임을 알린다고 한 후, 장소 변경 이유에 대해 설명하고 있으므로 (D)가 정답이다.

어휘 extend an invitation 초대하다 social gathering 사교 모임

HACKERS TEST   p.312

01 (A)	02 (B)	03 (B)	04 (D)	05 (B)
06 (D)	07 (D)	08 (A)	09 (D)	10 (A)
11 (C)	12 (D)	13 (A)		

01-02번은 다음 회람에 관한 문제입니다.

회람
수신: 전 직원
발신: Michael Reni, 사무실 관리자
날짜: 5월 15일
제목: 주의 사항

01-(A)최근 야근을 한 직원들이 건물 밖으로 나설 때 알람을 설정하지 않은 경우가 몇 번 있었습니다. 이는 우리 회사에 상당한 보안 위험을 초래합니다. 따라서, 마지막으로 사무실을 나서는 사람은 보안 알람을 반드시 작동시켜야 합니다.

또한, 가기 전에 모든 조명, 에어컨 장치, 사무기기를 꺼야 한다는 점을 유의하시기 바랍니다. 이것들을 밤새 켜두는 것은 월간 전기 요금을 증가시키는데, 02-(B)우리 회사는 불필요한 비용을 줄이기 위해 노력하고 있습니다.
우리는 직원들이 이 정책들을 따르기 위해 노력할 것을 권장합니다. 협조해 주셔서 감사드립니다.

instance n. 경우, 사례 overtime n. 야근, 초과 근무
activate v. 작동시키다, 활성화시키다 equipment n. 기기, 설비
overnight adv. 밤새 electricity bill 전기 요금 cut back on ~을 줄이다
make an effort 노력하다, 애쓰다 cooperation n. 협조, 협력

01 Not/True 문제
해석 직원들에 대해 언급된 것은?
(A) 일부는 예정보다 더 오래 일했다.
(B) 여러 명이 최근에 채용되었다.
(C) 모두 보안 배지를 받았다.
(D) 많은 사람들이 새 사무실로 옮겼다.

해설 (A)는 'There have been several recent instances in which staff members working overtime failed to set the alarm when they left the building.'에서 최근 야근을 한 직원들이 건물 밖으로 나설 때 알람을 설정하지 않은 경우가 몇 번 있었다고 했으므로 지문의 내용과 일치한다. 따라서 (A)가 정답이다. (B), (C), (D)는 지문에 언급되지 않은 내용이다.

어휘 scheduled adj. 예정된 hire v. 채용하다

02 Not/True 문제
해석 회사에 대해 사실인 것은?
(A) 고위 관리자를 교체했다.
(B) 비용을 줄이려고 노력하고 있다.
(C) 보안 알람을 설치할 계획이다.
(D) 최근에 장비를 구입했다.

해설 (B)는 'our company is trying to cut back on unnecessary expenses'에서 회사가 불필요한 비용을 줄이기 위해 노력하고 있다고 했으므로 지문의 내용과 일치한다. 따라서 (B)가 정답이다. (A), (C), (D)는 지문에 언급되지 않은 내용이다.

어휘 senior adj. 고위의, 상위의 expense n. 비용 install v. 설치하다

[Paraphrasing]
cut back on ~ expenses 비용을 줄이다 → reduce expenses 비용을 줄이다

03-05번은 다음 공고에 관한 문제입니다.

아이슬란드 문화유산 미술관에 입장하기 전에, 저희의 지침들을 살펴봐 주십시오. 이것들은 모든 표 소지자들에게 적용됩니다. 이것들을 따르는 것은 모든 방문객들이 즐거운 경험을 할 수 있도록 보장할 것입니다.

- 03-(A)/04전시된 작품의 사진 촬영이 허용되지 않는다는 점을 유념하세요.
- 큰 가방들은 로비 너머로 가져가실 수 없습니다. 03-(B)가방과 다른 소지품들을 기념품 가게 주변에 있는 저희의 사물함들 중 하나에 보관할 수 있습니다.
- 정원을 방문하는 사람들은 지정된 쓰레기통을 사용하여 쓰레기를 처리하도록 요청받습니다.
- 05마감 15분 전에 미술관 출구로 이동하기 시작해 주시기를 요청드립니다. 이때 안내 방송이 있을 것입니다.

저희 시설과 다가오는 전시회에 대한 자세한 정보를 얻기 위해서는 www.icelandheritage.com을 방문해 주세요.

guideline n. 지침 follow v. 따르다 piece n. 작품

permit v. 허용하다, 허락하다   belongings n. 소지품, 물건
designated adj. 지정된   dispose of ~을 처리하다
proceed v. 이동하다, 진행하다

03 Not/True 문제
해석 미술관에 대해 사실인 것은?
(A) 방문객들이 전시된 예술 작품의 사진을 찍는 것을 허용한다.
(B) 개인 소지품을 위한 보관 공간을 포함한다.
(C) 여러 나라의 예술가들과 협력한다.
(D) 야외 정원의 규모를 늘릴 계획이다.

해설 (B)는 'You may store baggage and other belongings in one of our lockers near the gift shop.'에서 가방과 다른 소지품들을 기념품 가게 주변에 있는 사물함들 중 하나에 보관할 수 있다고 했으므로 지문의 내용과 일치한다. 따라서 (B)가 정답이다. (A)는 'Please note that taking photographs of the pieces on display is not permitted.'에서 전시된 작품의 사진 촬영이 허용되지 않는다는 점을 유념하라고 했으므로 지문의 내용과 일치하지 않는다. (C)와 (D)는 지문에 언급되지 않은 내용이다.

어휘 artwork n. 예술 작품   partner with ~와 협력하다

[Paraphrasing]
lockers 사물함들 → a storage area 보관 공간

04 동의어 문제
해석 2문단 첫 번째 줄의 표현 "Please note"는 의미상 ~와 가장 가깝다.
(A) 다시 시도하다
(B) 설명하다
(C) 인수하다
(D) 유의하다

해설 Please note를 포함한 구절 'Please note that taking photographs ~ is not permitted.'에서 Please note는 '유념하다'라는 뜻으로 사용되었다. 따라서 (D)가 정답이다.

05 육하원칙 문제
해석 공고에 따르면, 안내 방송이 왜 있을 것인가?
(A) 상호작인 경험에 대한 세부 사항을 제공하기 위해
(B) 방문객들에게 시설이 곧 닫힐 것임을 알리기 위해
(C) 표 소지자들에게 특별 혜택에 대해 상기시키기 위해
(D) 다가오는 행사에 대한 정보를 제공하기 위해

해설 지문의 'We ask that you begin proceeding to the gallery's exit 15 minutes before closing. An announcement will be made at this time.'에서 마감 15분 전에 미술관 출구로 이동하기 시작하기를 요청하며, 이때 안내 방송이 있을 것이라고 했으므로 (B)가 정답이다.

어휘 interactive adj. 상호작인   facility n. 시설, 기관

06-09번은 다음 회람에 관한 문제입니다.

회람
수신: 전 직원
발신: Nina Summers, 관리자
날짜: 10월 3일
제목: 로비

지난달 직원회의에서 논의된 바와 같이, **06로비 보수공사 작업은 예정대로 10월 10일에 시작될 것입니다. — [1] —.** 이 기간 동안, 직원들과 방문객들은 뒷문을 통해 건물에 들어가야 할 것입니다.

10월 17일부터 24일까지 일주일 동안, 건물 서쪽에 있는 엘리베이터만 가동될 것입니다. 이 기간 동안 엘리베이터 이용이 제한될 것이므로, 이동에 문제가 있는 분들만 그것을 이용하도록 권고합니다. — [2] —. **07계단을 이용할 수 있다면, 그렇게 해 주시기 바랍니다.**

08전체 엘리베이터 이용은 10월 25일에 재개될 것으로 예상되지만, 로비의 리모델링 작업은 11월 4일까지 계속될 것입니다. — [3] —. 09모든 고객들과 방문객들에게 로비가 보수공사 중이며 폐쇄될 것임을 상기시켜 주시기 바랍니다. — [4] —. 작업이 진행되는 동안 경비원이 그 구역에 배치될 것입니다.

로비에서 작업하는 동안 인내심을 가져주셔서 감사드립니다!

renovation n. 보수공사   back entrance 뒷문   in operation 가동 중인
access n. 이용, 접근   mobility n. 이동성, 기동성
resume v. 재개하다, 다시 시작하다   blocked off 폐쇄된, 막힌
work on 작업하다, 수리하다

06 글을 쓴 이유 문제
해석 Ms. Summers는 왜 회람을 보냈는가?
(A) 문제에 대한 해결책을 제안하기 위해
(B) 시설의 개장을 알리기 위해
(C) 기한 연장을 확인하기 위해
(D) 계획에 대한 정보를 제공하기 위해

해설 지문의 'the lobby renovation project will begin as scheduled on October 10'에서 로비 보수공사 작업이 예정대로 10월 10일에 시작될 것이라고 한 후, 보수공사 계획에 대한 세부 정보와 유의 사항을 안내하고 있으므로 (D)가 정답이다.

어휘 solution n. 해결책   extension n. 연장

07 육하원칙 문제
해석 일부 직원들에게 무엇이 권고되는가?
(A) 건물 평면도를 확인하는 것
(B) 로비에서 기다리는 것
(C) 방문객들을 돕는 것
(D) 계단을 이용하는 것

해설 지문의 'If you are able to take the stairs, please do so.'에서 계단을 이용할 수 있다면 그렇게 해 주기 바란다고 했으므로 (D)가 정답이다.

어휘 floor plan 평면도   assist v. 돕다

08 육하원칙 문제
해석 10월 25일에 무슨 일이 일어날 것인가?
(A) 일부 기계가 작동될 것이다.
(B) 회사 행사가 열릴 것이다.
(C) 일부 가구가 다시 배치될 것이다.
(D) 건물 점검이 실시될 것이다.

해설 지문의 'Full elevator access is expected to resume on October 25'에서 전체 엘리베이터 이용은 10월 25일에 재개될 것으로 예상된다고 했으므로 (A)가 정답이다.

어휘 relocate v. 다시 배치하다, 이동하다   inspection n. 점검
conduct v. 실시하다

[Paraphrasing]
elevator 엘리베이터 → machinery 기계

09 문장 위치 찾기 문제
해석 [1], [2], [3], [4]로 표시된 위치 중, 다음 문장이 들어갈 곳으로 가장 적절한 것은?

"이것은 허가 없이 아무도 이 구역에 접근하지 못하게 할 것입니다."
(A) [1]
(B) [2]
(C) [3]
(D) [4]

해설 주어진 문장은 특정 구역에 대한 접근과 관련된 내용 주변에 나와야 함을 예상할 수 있다. [4]의 앞 문장인 'Please remind all clients and visitors that the lobby is being renovated and will be blocked off.'

에서 모든 고객들과 방문객들에게 로비가 보수공사 중이며 폐쇄될 것임을 상기시켜 주기 바란다고 했으므로, [4]에 주어진 문장이 들어가면 이것, 즉 고객들과 방문객들에게 상기시켜주는 것은 허가 없이 아무도 이 구역, 즉 로비에 접근하지 못하게 할 것이라는 자연스러운 문맥이 된다는 것을 알 수 있다. 따라서 (D)가 정답이다.

어휘 permission n. 허가, 허락

10-13번은 다음 공고에 관한 문제입니다.

회사는 8월 17일 오후 2시 30분부터 3시 30분까지 웨비나를 개최할 것입니다. ¹⁰각 지점의 관리자는 모든 정규직 직원이 참여할 수 있도록 준비해야 합니다. 휴가나 다른 사유로 참여할 수 없는 직원이 있는 경우, 본사에 있는 인사부에 알려주시기 바랍니다.

¹¹웨비나는 우리 회사의 건강 보험 정책에 곧 있을 변경에 대한 자세한 정보를 제공하기 위해 준비되었습니다. 처방약 비용 전액 보장을 포함하여, 직원들을 기쁘게 할 몇 가지 개선 사항이 있습니다. ¹²웨비나는 Kyle Polanski에 의해 진행될 것인데, 그는 지난 5월 이후로 건강 보험 프로젝트를 담당해 오고 있습니다. 이것은 그가 이곳에서 일하기 시작했을 때 그의 첫 업무였고, 그는 인상적인 결과를 달성했습니다.

¹³여러분은 8월 15일까지 모든 직원이 업무용 컴퓨터에 최신 버전의 Team Chat을 제대로 설치했는지 꼭 확인해야 합니다. 이것은 우리가 웨비나에 사용할 프로그램입니다. 감사합니다.

make arrangements for ~을 준비하다 take part 참여하다, 참가하다
leave n. 휴가 notify v. 알리다, 통지하다 headquarters n. 본사
organize v. 준비하다 modification n. 변경 insurance n. 보험
coverage n. 보장 범위 prescription n. 처방약, 처방
be in charge of ~을 담당하다 impressive adj. 인상적인
properly adv. 제대로, 적절히 workstation n. 업무용 컴퓨터, 작업장

10 추론 문제

해석 공고는 누구를 대상으로 하는 것 같은가?
(A) 지점 관리자들
(B) 사업주들
(C) 시간제 근로자들
(D) 기업 교육 강사

해설 지문의 'The manager of each branch must make arrangements for all full-time employees to participate.'에서 각 지점의 관리자는 모든 정규직 직원이 참여할 수 있도록 준비해야 한다고 한 것을 통해, 이 공고가 지점 관리자들을 대상으로 한다는 것을 추론할 수 있다. 따라서 (A)가 정답이다.

어휘 part-time adj. 시간제의

11 육하원칙 문제

해석 웨비나에서 무엇이 논의될 것인가?
(A) 사무기기의 업그레이드
(B) 회사 시설의 개선 사항
(C) 직원 혜택에 대한 변경
(D) 근로 효율을 높이는 방법

해설 지문의 'The webinar has been organized to provide details about the upcoming modifications to our firm's health insurance policy.'에서 웨비나는 회사의 건강 보험 정책에 곧 있을 변경에 대한 자세한 정보를 제공하기 위해 준비되었다고 했으므로 (C)가 정답이다.

어휘 benefit n. 혜택 efficiency n. 효율(성), 능률

Paraphrasing
modifications to ~ firm's health insurance policy 회사의 건강 보험 정책에 대한 변경 → Changes to an employee benefit 직원 혜택에 대한 변경

12 추론 문제

해석 Mr. Polanski에 대해 암시되는 것은?
(A) 인사팀을 관리한다.
(B) 전직 보험 회사 직원이다.
(C) 여러 주요 프로젝트를 감독해 왔다.
(D) 몇 달 전에 고용되었다.

해설 지문의 'The webinar will be led by Kyle Polanski, who has been in charge of the health insurance project since May. This was his first assignment when he started working here'에서 웨비나는 Kyle Polanski에 의해 진행될 것인데 그는 지난 5월 이후로 건강 보험 프로젝트를 담당해 오고 있으며, 이것은 그가 이곳에서 일하기 시작했을 때 그의 첫 업무였다고 했으므로 Mr. Polanski가 몇 달 전에 고용되었다는 사실을 추론할 수 있다. 따라서 (D)가 정답이다.

어휘 oversee v. 감독하다 multiple adj. 여러

13 육하원칙 문제

해석 직원들은 8월 15일까지 무엇을 해야 하는가?
(A) 소프트웨어 애플리케이션을 설치한다.
(B) 온라인 세션에 등록한다.
(C) 건강 검진을 신청한다.
(D) 교육 안내서를 검토한다.

해설 지문의 'You must ensure that all employees have properly installed the latest version of Team Chat on their workstations by August 15.'에서 8월 15일까지 모든 직원이 업무용 컴퓨터에 최신 버전의 Team Chat을 제대로 설치했는지 꼭 확인해야 한다고 했으므로 (A)가 정답이다.

어휘 register v. 등록하다 health checkup 건강 검진

DAY 20 다중 지문

HACKERS PRACTICE p.318

01 (C) **02** (B)

01번은 다음 기사와 편지에 관한 문제입니다.

그린필드시가 시민회관의 새로운 운영 시간을 도입하다

8월 10일—8월 4일에 발표된 보도 자료에서, 그린필드시 의회는 지방 정부에 의해 운영되는 시민회관의 운영 시간을 연장하려는 계획을 발표했다. 이 결정은 시의 서비스에 대한 주민들의 의견을 요청하기 위해 5월에 배포된 설문지의 답변을 기반으로 한다. 보도 자료는 Oakwood 및 Selma 시민회관들이 오후 8시 30분까지 계속 열려있을 것인 반면, ⁰¹Belleville 및 Blanchard 시민회관들은 각각 오후 8시와 9시에 닫을 것임을 명시했다. 이 새로운 일정은 8월 15일에 적용될 것이다.

press release 보도 자료, 공식 발표 extend v. 연장하다, 확장하다
municipal government 지방 정부 questionnaire n. 설문지
distribute v. 배포하다 solicit v. 요청하다 specify v. 명시하다
respectively adv. 각각, 각자 take effect 적용되다, 시행되다

8월 12일
Wilma Gomez
공공서비스부
387번지 Paterson가
그린필드시, 매사추세츠주 02125

Ms. Gomez께,

저는 최근 발표된 우리 도시의 시민회관들의 운영 시간 변경과 관련하여 당신께 연락을 드립니다. 대체로, 제가 작년에 은퇴한 후로 다수의 프로그램에 등록했기 때문에 저는 이 계획을 찬성합니다. 하지만, 저는 ⁰¹제 아파트 건물에서 가장 가까운 시민회관은 오후 8시까지 추가로 30분 동안만 열려 있을 것을 알게 되어 실망했습니다. 저는 당신의 부서가 이 결정을

재고하고 모든 시민회관의 운영 시간이 동일한 시간만큼 연장되도록 보장해 주실 것을 요청하고 싶습니다. 감사합니다.

Adam Ferris 드림

in favor of ~을 찬성하여, 지지하여 disappoint v. 실망시키다
reconsider v. 재고하다 ensure v. 보장하다, 보증하다

01 육하원칙 문제 연계

해석 Mr. Ferris의 거주지에서 어느 시민회관이 가장 가까운가?
(A) Oakwood 시민회관
(B) Selma 시민회관
(C) Belleville 시민회관
(D) Blanchard 시민회관

해설 Mr. Ferris가 작성한 편지를 먼저 확인한다.

단서 1 편지의 'the community center nearest to my apartment building would only be staying open ~ until 8:00 P.M.'에서 저, 즉 Mr. Ferris의 아파트 건물에서 가장 가까운 시민회관은 오후 8시까지 열려 있을 것이라고 했다. 그런데 오후 8시까지 열려 있는 시민회관이 어떤 시민회관인지 제시되지 않았으므로 기사에서 관련 내용을 확인한다.

단서 2 기사의 'the Belleville ~ centers will close at 8:00 P.M.'에서 Belleville 시민회관이 오후 8시에 닫을 것이라는 사실을 확인할 수 있다. 두 단서를 종합할 때, Mr. Ferris의 거주지에서 가장 가까운 시민회관은 오후 8시까지 열려 있을 Belleville 시민회관이라는 것을 알 수 있다. 따라서 (C)가 정답이다.

어휘 residence n. 거주지

Paraphrasing
nearest to ~ apartment building 아파트 건물에서 가장 가까운 → closest to ~ residence 거주지에서 가장 가까운

02번은 다음 안내문, 양식, 이메일에 관한 문제입니다.

Buzzchain은 어떻게 운영되나요?

Buzzchain은 제품에 대해 후기를 작성하고 온라인 마케팅에 대한 도움을 제공하는 소비자들의 네트워크입니다. 02-(B)가입하기 위해서는, 회원 가입을 하고 당신이 어떤 종류의 제품들에 관심이 있는지 저희에게 알려주세요. 저희는 후기를 위해 제품이 이용 가능할 때 당신에게 알려줄 것입니다. 당신은 무료 샘플 또는 가까운 상점에서 교환될 수 있는 상품권을 받게 될 것입니다.

회원으로서, 당신은 당신이 작성하는 모든 후기에 대해 포인트를 얻을 것입니다. 저희의 파트너사의 웹사이트 www.linkchange.com에서 포인트를 제품 또는 서비스로 교환하세요.

review v. 후기를 작성하다, 검토하다; n. 후기 assistance n. 도움, 지원
notify v. (공식적으로) 알리다 voucher n. 상품권, 할인권
exchange v. 교환하다; n. 교환, 환전 earn v. 얻다, 벌다
redeem v. (쿠폰 등을 상품으로) 교환하다

02-(B)Buzzchain 후기 작성자: Sean Morgan
Buzzchain 후기 작성자 ID: M90746
제품명: Limba Air
02-(B)카테고리: 가정 제품
첨부: 제품_사진.jpg

이 제품을 처음 사용하나요?
네.

제품에 대한 당신의 전반적인 의견은 무엇인가요?
저는 Berry Fresh와 Crisp Sheets인 두 가지 향으로 구성된 세트 상품을 받았습니다. 저는 첫 번째 것은 좋아하지 않았지만, 두 번째 것은 구입할 수도 있을 것 같습니다.

household n. 가정, 가구 overall adj. 전반적인, 종합적인 scent n. 향, 향기

수신: Buzzchain 고객 서비스 <service@buzzchain.com>
발신: Sean Morgan <s.morgan@mynetmail.com>
제목: 문의
날짜: 5월 14일

관계자분께,

저는 최근에 제 첫 후기를 작성했습니다. 하지만, 제가 Linkchange 웹사이트를 방문했을 때, 저는 제가 원했던 비치 샌들을 위한 충분한 포인트가 없다는 것을 깨달았습니다. 후기를 작성할 더 많은 제품들을 가능한 빨리 저에게 보내 줄 수 있나요?

감사합니다.

Sean Morgan 드림

recently adv. 최근에 realize v. 깨닫다, 알아차리다

02 Not/True 문제 연계

해석 Mr. Morgan에 대해 사실인 것은?
(A) 방향제의 단골 이용자이다.
(B) 가정 용품에 관심을 표했다.
(C) 후기를 작성할 자격이 없다.
(D) 제품 포장을 디자인한다.

해설 Mr. Morgan이 작성한 양식을 먼저 확인한다.

단서 1 양식의 'Buzzchain Reviewer: Sean Morgan'과 'Category: Household products'에서 Sean Morgan이 가정 제품 카테고리의 제품에 대해 Buzzchain 후기를 작성했음을 알 수 있다. 그런데 Mr. Morgan이 어떻게 가정 제품 카테고리 제품에 대해 후기를 작성하게 되었는지 제시되지 않았으므로 안내문에서 관련 내용을 확인한다.

단서 2 안내문의 'To join, sign up and let us know what kinds of products you are interested in.'에서 Buzzchain에 가입하기 위해서는, 회원 가입을 하고 어떤 종류의 제품들에 관심이 있는지 알려달라고 한 사실을 확인할 수 있다.

두 단서를 종합할 때, Mr. Morgan이 Buzzchain에 가입한 후 가정 제품 카테고리의 제품에 대해 후기를 작성하기 위해 가정 용품에 관심을 표했다는 것을 알 수 있다. 따라서 (B)가 정답이다.

어휘 frequent adj. 단골의, 잦은 household item 가정 용품
unqualified adj. 자격이 없는

HACKERS TEST   p.320

01 (D)	02 (D)	03 (C)	04 (B)	05 (B)
06 (B)	07 (C)	08 (A)	09 (C)	10 (B)
11 (A)	12 (A)	13 (A)	14 (C)	15 (B)
16 (B)	17 (C)	18 (B)	19 (D)	20 (D)

01-05번은 다음 광고와 양식에 관한 문제입니다.

Glisten 요금제 가격 책정

공공 사용이 허가된 각 곡이 포함된 01높은 품질의 배경 음악을 몇 시간에 걸쳐 다수의 소매점에서 스트리밍하세요! 편리한 월간 결제 또는 더 많은 절약을 위해 일시불의 연회비를 선택하세요.

02-(B)/(C)/04-(B)Glisten 비트	02-(B)/(C)Glisten 리듬	02-(B)/(C)/(D)/03Glisten 하모니
장소당 한 달에 9.99달러 또는 일 년에 100달러	장소당 한 달에 15.99달러 또는 일 년에 150달러	장소당 03한 달에 24.99달러 또는 일 년에 250달러
02-(A)5일 무료 체험 포함	02-(A)15일 무료 체험 포함	02-(A)30일 무료 체험 포함

- 02-(B)/(C)여러 맞춤 라디오 방송국들 중에서 선택하거나 당신만의 재생 목록을 만드세요
- 당신의 모바일 기기에서 청취 경험을 관리하세요

- 02-(B)/(C)Glisten 비트 패키지의 모든 특징들
- 당신의 마케팅 활동을 지원하기 위한 오디오 광고를 제작할 수 있음
- 각 지역 또는 상점마다 음악을 맞춤 설정하세요

- 02-(B)/(C)Glisten 리듬 패키지의 모든 특징들
- 03당신의 브랜드를 홍보하는 재생 목록을 제작하는 음악 전문가 이용
- 02-(D)당신의 손님들이 저희의 스마트폰 애플리케이션을 사용해 음악을 신청하게 할 수 있도록 하세요

01/04-(B)위의 요금제는 다섯 군데 미만의 지점을 가진 사업체들만 이용할 수 있습니다. 다섯 군데 이상을 운영하신다면, 당신에게 적합한 패키지를 만들기 위해 555-3092로 저희에게 연락하세요.

plan n. 요금제 pricing n. 가격 책정 license v. 허가하다
public adj. 공공의 saving n. 절약 trial n. 체험, 시험 custom adj. 맞춤의
customize v. 맞춤 설정하다 access n. 이용, 접근
in support of ~을 홍보하는, 지지하여 operate v. 운영하다, 작동하다

GLISTEN
www.glisten.com

04-(B)회사: Coax 의류사
주소: 1228번지 Willow Wood로
       허바드, 오하이오주 44325
05연락 담당자: Andy Lewis
이메일: a_lewis@mailbot.com

웹사이트 (선택):
www.coaxclothing.com
직책: 마케팅부장
전화: 555-9946

04-(B)선호하는 요금제:
04-(B)☒ Glisten 비트   ☐ Glisten 리듬   ☐ Glisten 하모니

05당신의 체험 기간은 신청 절차 완료 시 시작됩니다.

지불 계획:
☐ 일시불   ☒ 매월

제출을 클릭하면 결제 화면으로 이동합니다. 당신의 신용카드를 준비하십시오.

05당신의 이메일에서 확정 메시지를 확인하세요. 저희의 환불 정책이나 다른 약관을 보시려면, 여기를 클릭하세요.

[재설정] [제출]

completion n. 완료, 성취 scheme n. 계획, 책략
confirmation n. 확정, 확인 terms and conditions 약관, 조건

01 추론 문제
해석 광고는 누구를 대상으로 하는가?
(A) 전문 음악가들
(B) 소프트웨어 프로그래머들
(C) 녹음 기술자들
(D) 상점 소유주들

해설 광고의 'Stream hours of high-quality background music at multiple retail locations'에서 높은 품질의 배경 음악을 몇 시간에 걸쳐 다수의 소매점에서 스트리밍하라고 했고, 'The plans above are only available to businesses with fewer than five locations.'에서 위의 요금제는 다섯 군데 미만의 지점을 가진 사업체들만 이용할 수 있다고 했으므로 상점 소유주들을 대상으로 하는 광고임을 추론할 수 있다. 따라서 (D)가 정답이다.

어휘 technician n. 기술자 owner n. 소유주

02 Not/True 문제
해석 모든 요금제에 포함되지 않은 것은?
(A) 무료 체험
(B) 라디오 방송국
(C) 맞춤형 재생 목록
(D) 손님 접속

해설 (D)는 광고의 'Glisten Harmony', 'Allow your guests to request music using our smartphone application'에서 Glisten 하모니 요금제만 손님들이 스마트폰 애플리케이션을 사용해서 음악을 신청하게 할 수 있다고 했으므로 지문의 내용과 일치하지 않는다. 따라서 (D)가 정답이다. (A)는 'Includes a 5-day free trial', 'Includes a 15-day free trial', 'Includes a 30-day free trial'에서 모든 요금제에 무료 체험이 포함된다는 것을 알 수 있으므로 지문의 내용과 일치한다. (B)와 (C)는 'Glisten Beat', 'Choose from several custom radio stations or create your own playlists'에서 Glisten 비트 요금제에 여러 맞춤 라디오 방송국들 중에서 선택하거나 재생 목록을 만드는 것이 포함되어 있다고 했고, 'Glisten Rhythm', 'All features of the Glisten Beat package', 'Glisten Harmony', 'All features of the Glisten Rhythm package'에서 Glisten 리듬과 Glisten 하모니 요금제가 Glisten 비트 패키지의 모든 특징들을 포함한다고 했으므로 지문의 내용과 일치한다.

[Paraphrasing]
your own playlists 당신만의 재생 목록 → Custom playlists 맞춤형 재생 목록

03 육하원칙 문제
해석 가장 비싼 요금제의 사용자들은 무엇을 할 수 있는가?
(A) 영상 광고를 방송한다.
(B) 소셜 미디어를 통해 메시지를 보낸다.
(C) 음악 선정에 전문가의 도움을 받는다.
(D) 추가적인 할인을 이용한다.

해설 광고의 'Glisten Harmony', '$24.99 a month or $250 a year', 'Access to music experts who create playlists in support of your brand'에서 Glisten 하모니가 한 달에 24.99달러 혹은 일 년에 250달러를 지불하는 가장 비싼 지불 요금제이며 브랜드를 홍보하는 재생 목록을 제작하는 음악 전문가를 이용할 수 있다고 했으므로 (C)가 정답이다.

어휘 broadcast v. 방송하다, 광고하다
take advantage of ~을 이용하다, 활용하다

04 Not/True 문제 연계
해석 Coax 의류사에 대해 언급된 것은?
(A) 일 년에 100달러를 지불할 것이다.
(B) 다섯 개보다 적은 지점을 가지고 있다.
(C) 그것의 체험 기간은 한 달간 지속된다.
(D) 그것의 최초 지불은 15일 이내로 해야 한다.

해설 질문의 핵심 어구인 Coax 의류사에서 작성한 양식을 먼저 확인한다.
[단서 1] 양식의 'Company: Coax Clothing', 'Preferred Plan: Glisten Beat'에서 Coax 의류사가 선호하는 요금제는 Glisten 비트임을 알 수 있다. 그런데 Glisten 비트 요금제를 선택할 수 있는 매장에 대해 제시되지 않았으므로 광고에서 관련 내용을 확인한다.
[단서 2] 광고의 'Glisten Beat', 'The plans above are only available to businesses with fewer than five locations.'에서 위의 요금제, 즉 Glisten 비트를 포함한 요금제는 다섯 군데 미만의 지점을 가진 사업체들만 이용할 수 있다는 사실을 확인할 수 있다.
두 단서를 종합할 때, Glisten 비트를 선택한 Coax 의류사는 다섯 개보다 적은 지점을 가지고 있음을 알 수 있다. 따라서 (B)가 정답이다.

어휘 last v. 지속되다 due adj. (돈을) 지불해야 하는, ~하기로 예정된

05 육하원칙 문제
해석 Mr. Lewis는 왜 그의 이메일을 확인해야 하는가?
(A) 약관을 읽기 위해

(B) 그의 신청을 확인하기 위해
(C) 그의 월간 청구서를 받기 위해
(D) 임시 비밀번호를 받기 위해

해설 양식의 'Contact: Andy Lewis', 'Your trial period begins upon completion of the application process.', 'Please check your e-mail for a confirmation message.'에서 Mr. Lewis에게 당신의 체험 기간은 신청 절차 완료 시 시작되며 이메일에서 확정 메시지를 확인하라고 했으므로 (B)가 정답이다.

어휘 verify v. 확인하다, 증명하다 registration n. 신청(서), 등록
invoice n. 청구서, 송장 temporary adj. 임시의, 일시적인

06-10번은 다음 편지와 일정표에 관한 문제입니다.

Dawn Taylor
42번지 Coote로
블러프힐, 네이피어 4110
뉴질랜드

Ms. Taylor께,

뉴질랜드 요트 타기 협회(NZSS)의 100주년을 기념하는 2월에 있을 ⁰⁶행사에서 연설해달라는 당신의 요청에 대해 영광스럽게 생각합니다. NZSS의 전 회장으로서, 저는 이 동호회의 역사에 대해 잘 알고 있습니다. 그리고 제가 지도자직에서 물러난 이후 몇 년 동안 그것이 발전해 나가는 것을 지켜보는 것은 기쁨이었습니다.

유감스럽게도, 제가 같은 날에 요트 타기 경주에 참가할 것이기 때문에 ⁰⁶저는 참여할 수 없습니다. 저 대신에, 저는 요트 타기에 열성적인 사람이자 뛰어난 대중 연설가인 Brenda Wilson을 추천하고 싶습니다. ⁰⁸또 다른 좋은 대안은 Ling Zhang일 것인데, 그녀는 단독 요트 타기에서 세계 기록을 경신했습니다. Alison Scott 또한 머릿속에 떠오릅니다. ⁰⁷그녀의 할아버지가 NZSS의 초기의 구성원이었기 때문에, 그녀는 협회의 초창기에 관한 흥미로운 이야기들을 알고 있습니다. ⁰⁸이 사람들 중 한 명이 행사에서 연설하기에 적합해 보이는지 제게 알려주시면, 제가 그 사람의 이메일 주소를 당신에게 드리겠습니다.

Patrick Patel 드림

mark v. 기념하다, 나타내다 familiar with ~을 잘 아는, ~에 익숙한
pleasure n. 기쁨, 즐거움 step down 물러나다 take part in ~에 참가하다
enthusiast n. 열성적인 사람 accomplished adj. 뛰어난, 성취된
suitable adj. 적합한

순조로운 요트 타기의 100주년 행사에 대한 일정:
뉴질랜드 요트 타기 협회의 기념일 축하

장소: Walter Donahue 클럽 회관
날짜: 2월 28일

시간	행사	⁰⁸연설자
오후 5시-5시 20분	^{10-(D)}개회사: 동료 요트 조종자들을 환영합니다	Dominika Gladstone
오후 5시 20분-5시 50분	주요 연설: 왜 요트 타기가 중요한가	⁰⁸Ling Zhang
오후 6시-7시 30분	Ketch 실에서의 저녁 연회	
오후 7시 30분-8시	^{10-(C)}슬라이드쇼: 수년 동안의 NZSS	Winny Baxter
⁰⁹오후 8시-8시 30분	⁰⁹우승자들을 위한 상품이 있는 NZSS 퀴즈	David Young
오후 8시 40분-9시	^{10-(A)}Breakwater 항구 위로의 불꽃놀이	

anniversary n. 기념일 fellow adj. 동료의; n. 동지, 동료
sailor n. 요트 조종자 address n. 연설 banquet n. 연회, 만찬
fireworks display 불꽃놀이

06 목적 문제

해석 편지의 주된 목적은 무엇인가?
(A) 행사를 여는 것을 제안하기 위해
(B) 초대를 거절하기 위해
(C) 몇몇 자격 요건을 검토하기 위해
(D) 날짜 변경을 요청하기 위해

해설 편지의 'I am honored by your request that I speak at the event'에서 행사에서 연설해달라는 요청에 대해 영광스럽게 생각한다고 했고, 'I am unable to participate'에서 자신은 참여할 수 없다고 한 후, 다른 연설자들을 추천하고 있으므로 (B)가 정답이다.

어휘 hold v. 열다, 개최하다 turn down ~을 거절하다 invitation n. 초대(장)
qualification n. 자격 요건

07 동의어 문제

해석 편지에서, 2문단 다섯 번째 줄의 단어 "original"은 의미상 -와 가장 가깝다.
(A) 독특한
(B) 새로운
(C) 최초의
(D) 진정한

해설 편지의 original을 포함한 구절 'Her grandfather was an original member of the NZSS'에서 original은 '초기의'라는 뜻으로 사용되었다. 따라서 (C)가 정답이다.

08 추론 문제 연계

해석 Mr. Patel은 무엇을 했을 것 같은가?
(A) Ms. Zhang의 연락처를 행사 주최자에게 보냈다.
(B) Ms. Taylor에게 강의에 적합한 주제를 제공했다.
(C) Ms. Scott의 경력에 대해 연설했다.
(D) Ms. Wilson에게 요트 타는 방법을 가르쳤다.

해설 질문의 핵심 어구인 Mr. Patel이 작성한 편지를 먼저 확인한다.
단서 1 편지의 'Another good choice would be Ling Zhang'에서 또 다른 좋은 대안, 즉 Mr. Patel 대신에 연설을 할 사람으로 Ms. Zhang이 있다고 했고, 'Let me know if one of these people seems suitable to speak at the event, and I will provide you with that person's e-mail address.'에서 이 사람들, 즉 Mr. Patel이 추천한 사람들 중 한 명이 행사에서 연설하기에 적합해 보이는지 알려주면 그 사람의 이메일 주소를 주겠다고 했다. 그런데 누가 연설자로 결정되었는지 제시되지 않았으므로 일정표에서 관련 내용을 확인한다.
단서 2 일정표의 'Speaker', 'Ling Zhang'에서 Ms. Zhang이 연설자가 되었음을 확인할 수 있다.
두 단서를 종합할 때, Mr. Patel이 Ms. Zhang의 연락처를 행사 주최자에게 보냈다는 사실을 추론할 수 있다. 따라서 (A)가 정답이다.

어휘 contact details 연락처 organizer n. 주최자 background n. 경력, 배경

09 육하원칙 문제

해석 일정표에 따르면, 참석자들은 언제 게임을 하기 시작할 것인가?
(A) 오후 5시에
(B) 오후 6시에
(C) 오후 8시에
(D) 오후 8시 40분에

해설 일정표의 '8:00-8:30 P.M.', 'NZSS quiz with prizes for the winners'에서 오후 8시부터 8시 30분까지 우승자들을 위한 상품이 있는 NZSS 퀴즈가 진행된다고 했으므로 (C)가 정답이다.

어휘 attendee n. 참석자

Paraphrasing
quiz 퀴즈 → game 게임

10 Not/True 문제
해석 순조로운 요트 타기의 100주년에 무슨 일이 일어나지 않을 것인가?
(A) 야외 쇼
(B) 제품 시연
(C) 시청각 발표
(D) 개회사

해설 (B)는 지문에 언급되지 않은 내용이다. 따라서 (B)가 정답이다. (A)는 일정표의 'Fireworks display over Breakwater Harbor'에서 Breakwater 항구 위로의 불꽃놀이가 있으므로 지문의 내용과 일치한다. (C)는 'Slideshow'에서 슬라이드쇼가 있으므로 지문의 내용과 일치한다. (D)는 'Opening speech'에서 개회사가 있으므로 지문의 내용과 일치한다.

어휘 outdoor adj. 야외의   demonstration n. 시연, 설명   visual adj. 시청각의

Paraphrasing
Slideshow 슬라이드쇼 → visual presentation 시청각 발표
Opening speech 개회사 → opening talk 개회사

11-15번은 다음 이메일, 송장, 그리고 편지에 관한 문제입니다.

발신: Claude Symonds <cs100@edgeattire.com>
수신: Sheila Bryant <bryant@edgeattire.com>
날짜: 8월 6일
제목: Fredericton 스타일 박람회

안녕하세요 Sheila,

논의한 바와 같이, Fredericton 스타일 박람회는 잠재 고객들에게 우리의 의류를 홍보할 수 있는 완벽한 기회입니다. **11**박람회 준비를 위해, 다음과 같이 해 주시길 바랍니다. 먼저, **12**행사의 전체 기간 동안 부스를 대여해 주세요. 우리의 의류와 액세서리를 보관할 수 있는 수납공간의 이용 여부를 꼭 문의해 주세요. 또한, 부스에 모델 한두 명이 우리의 의상을 입고 있어야 한다고 생각합니다. 적합한 후보자를 찾기 위해 이전에 함께 일했던 모델 에이전시에 연락해 주세요. 감사합니다.

Claude 드림

promote v. 홍보하다   potential adj. 잠재적인   duration n. 기간
outfit n. 의상   previously adv. 이전에   candidate n. 후보자

Fredericton 스타일 박람회
대여자: Edge 의류사
연락처: Sheila Bryant, 555-4096

부스 크기: 4×4 (제곱미터)
12대여 비용: 320달러 (일일 대여료 80달러 × 4일)
보증금: 45달러

이용약관: **13-(A)**부스 대여는 행사 티켓 4장, 테이블 1개, 의자 2개, 콘센트 1개, 조명 1세트, 일반 표지판 1개를 포함합니다. 다음은 추가 요금으로 이용 가능합니다:
추가 콘센트, 테이블, 의자: 하루 20달러
14맞춤 표지판: 50달러의 설치 비용
보관소 대여: 하루 15달러

renter n. 대여자   deposit n. 보증금   electrical outlet 콘센트
installation n. 설치

9월 27일
Fredericton 스타일 박람회
5번지 Bulkley가
셸번, 노바스코샤 B0T 1W0

Fredericton 스타일 박람회 관계자분께,

저희 회사는 최근 행사에 출품 회사로서 참여했습니다. 저희는 일반 부스와 저희의 전시에 사용되는 물품들을 위한 보관 사물함을 요청했습니다. 하지만, 제가 저희의 최종 청구서를 확인했을 때, **14**저는 저희에게 맞춤 표지판에 대한 비용 또한 청구되었다는 것을 알아차렸습니다. **14/15**저희에게 잘못 청구된 금액을 가능한 한 빨리 환불해 주십시오. **15**저는 또한 이것이 완료되었을 때 통지받기를 원합니다. 귀하께서는 555-3938로 제게 연락하실 수 있습니다. 감사합니다.

Claude Symonds 드림
Edge 의류사

exhibitor n. 출품 회사, 출품자   bill n. 청구서   notice v. 알아차리다
charge v. (비용을) 청구하다   mistakenly adv. 잘못하여

11 목적 문제
해석 이메일의 목적은 무엇인가?
(A) 몇몇 업무를 맡기기 위해
(B) 일정을 조정하기 위해
(C) 몇몇 항의를 해결하기 위해
(D) 비용을 확인하기 위해

해설 이메일의 'To get us ready for the expo, I'd like you to do the following.'에서 박람회 준비를 위해, 다음과 같이 해 주실 바란다고 한 후, 박람회 준비와 관련한 여러 업무들을 요청하고 있으므로 (A)가 정답이다.

어휘 assign v. 맡기다, 배정하다   adjust v. 조정하다, 조절하다
address v. 해결하다   confirm v. 확인하다

12 추론 문제 연계
해석 Fredericton 스타일 박람회에 대해 결론지을 수 있는 것은?
(A) 4일 동안 지속되었다.
(B) 늦게 문을 연 출품 회사들에 요금을 부과했다.
(C) 모델 에이전시와 협력했다.
(D) 그것의 웹사이트에서 출품 회사들의 상품을 홍보했다.

해설 Fredericton 스타일 박람회가 언급된 이메일을 먼저 확인한다.
단서 1 이메일의 'please rent us a booth for the entire duration of the event'에서 행사, 즉 Fredericton 스타일 박람회의 전체 기간동안 부스를 대여해 달라고 했다. 그런데 박람회의 전체 기간이 며칠인지에 대해 제시되지 않았으므로 송장에서 관련 내용을 확인한다.
단서 2 송장의 'Rental charge: $320 ($80 daily rental fee × 4 days)'에서 부스 대여 비용이 총 320달러로 일일 대여료 80달러를 총 4일간 지불했음을 확인할 수 있다.
두 단서를 종합할 때, Fredericton 스타일 박람회가 4일 동안 지속되었다는 사실을 추론할 수 있다. 따라서 (A)가 정답이다.

어휘 partner with ~과 협력하다

13 Not/True 문제
해설 송장에서 Edge 의류사에 대해 언급된 것은?
(A) 박람회에 참가하도록 여러 사람을 보낼 수 있다.
(B) 사전에 지불한 보증금을 포기해야 한다.
(C) 부스 위치를 선택하려면 추가 요금을 지불해야 한다.
(D) 더 큰 옵션으로 무료 업그레이드를 할 수 있다.

해설 (A)는 송장의 'Booth rentals include four event tickets'에서 부스 대여가 행사 티켓 4장을 포함한다고 했으므로 지문의 내용과 일치한다. 따라서 (A)가 정답이다. (B), (C), (D)는 지문에 언급되지 않은 내용이다.

어휘 in advance 사전에, 미리   free of charge 무료로

14 육하원칙 문제 연계
해석 Mr. Symonds에게 얼마가 과잉 청구되었는가?
(A) 15달러
(B) 45달러

(C) 50달러
(D) 320달러

해설 Mr. Symonds가 작성한 편지를 먼저 확인한다.
단서 1 편지의 'I noticed that we were also charged for a custom sign. Please refund me the amount ~ mistakenly charged ~.'에서 편지의 발신자인 Mr. Symonds가 자신들에게 맞춤 표지판에 대한 비용 또한 청구되었다는 것을 알아차렸으며, 잘못 청구된 금액을 환불해달라고 했다. 그런데 맞춤 표지판에 대한 비용이 얼마인지 제시되지 않았으므로 송장에서 관련 내용을 확인한다.
단서 2 송장의 'Custom sign: $50 installation fee'에서 맞춤 표지판의 설치 비용이 50달러임을 확인할 수 있다.
두 단서를 종합할 때, Mr. Symonds에게 맞춤 표지판의 설치 비용, 즉 50달러가 과잉 청구되었다는 사실을 알 수 있다. 따라서 (C)가 정답이다.

어휘 **overcharge** v. 과잉 청구하다

15 육하원칙 문제

해설 Mr. Symonds는 왜 Fredericton 스타일 박람회의 직원이 그에게 연락할 것을 요청하는가?
(A) 청구서가 부정확했던 이유를 설명하기 위해
(B) 환불이 완료되었음을 그에게 알리기 위해
(C) 할인을 요청하는 방법을 명확하게 하기 위해
(D) 어디서 대금이 지불될 수 있는지 그에게 알려주기 위해

해설 편지의 'Please refund me the amount ~ mistakenly charged ~. I would also like to be notified when this has been done.'에서 잘못 청구된 금액을 환불해 달라고 하며, 저, 즉 Mr. Symonds는 이것이 완료되었을 때 통지받기를 원한다고 했으므로 (B)가 정답이다.

어휘 **inaccurate** adj. 부정확한 **clarify** v. 명확하게 하다

16-20번은 다음 웹페이지, 이메일, 후기에 관한 문제입니다.

La Mesa		
소개	예약	연락처

30년이 넘게, La Mesa는 정통 스페인 요리를 즐기는 시애틀 주민들이 즐겨 찾는 식당이었습니다. 주인인 **16-(B)**Jose Garcia 셰프는 스페인의 안달루시아 지역의 요리 방식을 전문으로 하는데, 이곳은 그가 태어나고 자란 곳입니다. 사람들은 **20**그의 네 가지 대표 요리를 맛보기 위해 먼 지역 들에서 옵니다:

가스파초: 식초와 다양한 채소를 포함하는 상쾌한 차가운 수프
푸체로: 쇠고기, 감자, 그리고 제철 채소로 만든 스튜
토르티아 데 파타타스: 계란, 양파, 감자, 그리고 매운 소시지로 만든 오믈렛
20페스카이토 프리토: 시장에서 갓 들어와서 완벽하게 튀겨진 생선

resident n. 주민 **authentic** adj. 정통의 **cuisine** n. 요리
specialize in ~을 전문으로 하다 **signature dish** 대표 요리
refreshing adj. 상쾌한 **vinegar** n. 식초 **seasonal** adj. 제철의, 계절의

발신: Sally Mendez <s.mendez@lamesa.com>
수신: Kyle Graves <k.graves@aceair.com>
제목: 서비스 요청
날짜: 8월 2일

Mr. Graves께,

저희 식당의 에어컨 중 하나가 제대로 작동하지 않고 있습니다. **17**귀사의 직원이 지난달에 수리한 부엌에 있는 에어컨은 괜찮으나, 프라이빗 다이닝룸에 있는 것은 이제 완전히 작동을 멈췄습니다. **18**이 문제를 해결하기 위해 다른 기술자를 식당으로 보내주실 수 있나요? 저희는 매일 오전 11시 30분에 문을 열기 때문에, 귀사의 기술자가 아침 일찍 올 수 있으면 좋겠습니다.

저는 가능한 한 빨리 이것이 해결되길 원합니다. **19**메인 다이닝룸의 테이블 중 어느 것도 충분히 크지 않기 때문에, 이 프라이빗 다이닝룸은 저희가 15명 이상의 단체를 수용할 수 있는 유일한 선택입니다. 감사합니다.

Sally Mendez 드림
총지배인, La Mesa

properly adv. 제대로 **completely** adv. 완전히 **technician** n. 기술자
accommodate v. 수용하다

식당: La Mesa
후기 작성자: David Porter
날짜: 8월 5일
점수: 4/5

저는 저희 회사 최고경영자의 퇴직 기념 파티를 8월 4일에 La Mesa에서 열도록 준비했습니다. 전반적으로, 특히 **19**일행의 18명이 함께 앉아 있었다는 것을 고려하면 서비스는 훌륭했습니다. 저희에게 배정된 종업원은 친절하고 유능했습니다. 음식에 관해서는, 대부분이 주문했던 요리에 매우 만족했습니다. 저는 셰프가 확실히 정통 스페인 요리법과 양념들을 사용하려고 했다는 것이 특히 마음에 들었습니다. 하지만, **20**저는 셰프의 대표 요리 중 하나인 해산물 요리를 먹었는데, 그것은 약간 과하게 익어 있었습니다.

retirement n. 퇴직, 은퇴 **party** n. 파티, 일행 **assign** v. 배정하다
friendly adj. 친절한, 우호적인 **efficient** adj. 유능한 **obviously** adv. 확실히
seasoning n. 양념 **overcooked** adj. 과하게 익은

16 Not/True 문제

해설 Mr. Garcia에 대해 언급된 것은?
(A) 몇몇 식당들을 운영한다.
(B) 스페인에서 태어났다.
(C) 최근에 시애틀로 이사했다.
(D) 요리학교에 다닌 적이 있다.

해설 (B)는 웹페이지의 'Chef Jose Garcia, specializes in the cooking style of the Andalusia region of Spain, which is where he was born and raised'에서 Jose Garcia 셰프는 스페인의 안달루시아 지역의 요리 방식을 전문으로 하는데, 이곳은 그가 태어나고 자란 곳이라고 했으므로 지문의 내용과 일치한다. 따라서 (B)가 정답이다. (A), (C), (D)는 지문에 언급되지 않은 내용이다.

어휘 **operate** v. 운영하다 **relocate** v. 이사하다, 이동하다 **culinary** adj. 요리의

17 육하원칙 문제

해설 이메일에 따르면, 지난달에 무슨 일이 있었는가?
(A) 부엌이 개조되었다.
(B) 직원이 승진되었다.
(C) 기기가 수리되었다.
(D) 메뉴가 업데이트되었다.

해설 이메일의 'The air conditioner in the kitchen ~ fixed last month'에서 지난달에 부엌에 있는 에어컨을 수리했다고 했으므로 (C)가 정답이다.

어휘 **remodel** v. 개조하다 **promote** v. 승진시키다
appliance n. 기기, 가전제품 **repair** v. 수리하다

Paraphrasing
air conditioner 에어컨 → appliance 기기

18 육하원칙 문제

해설 Ms. Mendez는 Mr. Graves에게 무엇을 해달라고 요청하는가?
(A) 몇몇 장비를 주문한다.
(B) 작업자를 보낸다.
(C) 몇몇 가구를 수리한다.
(D) 예약을 확정한다.

해설 이메일의 'Would you be able to send another technician to the restaurant to deal with this problem?'에서 이메일 작성자인 Ms. Mendez가 이메일 수신자인 Mr. Graves에게 이 문제를 해결하기 위해

다른 기술자를 식당으로 보내줄 수 있는지 물었으므로 (B)가 정답이다.

어휘 **equipment** n. 장비, 기구 **confirm** v. 확정하다, 확인하다

[Paraphrasing]
send ~ technician 기술자를 보내다 → Send a worker 작업자를 보내다

19 추론 문제 연계

해석 Mr. Porter에 대해 암시되는 것은?
(A) 그의 동료들과 함께 다른 행사를 준비하고 있다.
(B) La Mesa에서 다시는 식사를 하지 않기로 결심했다.
(C) 머지않아 그의 회사에서 은퇴할 것이다.
(D) 식당의 메인 구역 자리에 안내받지 못했다.

해설 Mr. Porter가 작성한 후기를 먼저 확인한다.

단서 1 후기의 'there were 18 people in our party sitting together'에서 Mr. Porter가 속한 일행의 18명이 함께 앉아 있었다고 했다. 그런데 Mr. Porter가 속한 일행이 앉은 곳이 어디인지 제시되지 않았으므로 이메일에서 관련 내용을 확인한다.

단서 2 이메일의 'The private dining room is the only option we have to accommodate groups of 15 or more, as none of the tables in the main dining room are large enough.'에서 메인 다이닝룸의 테이블 중 어느 것도 충분히 크지 않기 때문에, 이 프라이빗 다이닝룸이 저희, 즉 식당이 15명 이상의 단체를 수용할 수 있는 유일한 선택지라고 한 사실을 확인할 수 있다.

두 단서를 종합할 때, Mr. Porter가 속한 일행은 18명이었으므로 메인 다이닝룸이 아닌 15명 이상의 단체를 수용할 수 있는 프라이빗 다이닝룸에서 식사를 했다는 것을 추론할 수 있다. 따라서 (D)가 정답이다.

어휘 **coworker** n. 동료 **retire** v. 은퇴하다, 퇴직하다

[Paraphrasing]
main dining room 메인 다이닝룸 → main area of the restaurant 식당의 메인 구역

20 추론 문제 연계

해석 Mr. Porter가 어느 요리를 주문했을 것 같은가?
(A) 가스파초
(B) 푸체로
(C) 토르티야 데 파타타스
(D) 페스카이토 프리토

해설 Mr. Porter가 작성한 후기를 먼저 확인한다.

단서 1 후기의 'I had the seafood dish, one of the chef's signature dishes'에서 저, 즉 Mr. Porter가 셰프의 대표 요리 중 하나인 해산물 요리를 먹었다고 했다. 그런데 해산물 요리의 이름이 무엇인지 제시되지 않았으므로 웹페이지에서 관련 내용을 확인한다.

단서 2 웹페이지의 'his four signature dishes', '*Pescaito Frito*: Fish ~ fried to perfection.'에서 그, 즉 Mr. Garcia의 네 가지 대표 요리 중 완벽하게 튀겨진 생선인 페스카이토 프리토가 있음을 확인할 수 있다.

두 단서를 종합할 때, Mr. Porter가 대표 요리 중 유일한 해산물 요리인 페스카이토 프리토를 주문했다는 것을 추론할 수 있다. 따라서 (D)가 정답이다.

MEMO

MEMO

* 토익 온라인 모의고사 추가 1회분은 해커스토익 사이트(Hackers.co.kr)에서 제공됩니다.

한 권으로 끝내는
해커스 토익 600+plus
LC + RC + VOCA

실전모의고사

해커스 어학연구소

저작권자 ⓒ 2025, 해커스 어학연구소 이 책 및 음성파일의 모든 내용, 이미지, 디자인, 편집 형태에 대한 저작권은 저자에게 있습니다.
서면에 의한 저자와 출판사의 허락 없이 내용의 일부 혹은 전부를 인용, 발췌하거나 복제, 배포할 수 없습니다.

🎧 실전모의고사

LISTENING TEST

In this section, you must demonstrate your ability to understand spoken English. This section is divided into four parts and will take approximately 45 minutes to complete. Do not mark the answers in your test book. Use the answer sheet that is provided separately.

PART 1

Directions: For each question, you will listen to four short statements about a picture in your test book. These statements will not be printed and will only be spoken one time. Select the statement that best describes what is happening in the picture and mark the corresponding letter (A), (B), (C), or (D) on the answer sheet.

Sample Answer

The statement that best describes the picture is (B), "The man is sitting at the desk." So, you should mark letter (B) on the answer sheet.

1.

2.

GO ON TO THE NEXT PAGE

3.

4.

5.

6.

PART 2

Directions: For each question, you will listen to a statement or question followed by three possible responses spoken in English. They will not be printed and will only be spoken one time. Select the best response and mark the corresponding letter (A), (B), or (C) on your answer sheet.

7. Mark your answer on the answer sheet.
8. Mark your answer on the answer sheet.
9. Mark your answer on the answer sheet.
10. Mark your answer on the answer sheet.
11. Mark your answer on the answer sheet.
12. Mark your answer on the answer sheet.
13. Mark your answer on the answer sheet.
14. Mark your answer on the answer sheet.
15. Mark your answer on the answer sheet.
16. Mark your answer on the answer sheet.
17. Mark your answer on the answer sheet.
18. Mark your answer on the answer sheet.
19. Mark your answer on the answer sheet.
20. Mark your answer on the answer sheet.
21. Mark your answer on the answer sheet.
22. Mark your answer on the answer sheet.
23. Mark your answer on the answer sheet.
24. Mark your answer on the answer sheet.
25. Mark your answer on the answer sheet.
26. Mark your answer on the answer sheet.
27. Mark your answer on the answer sheet.
28. Mark your answer on the answer sheet.
29. Mark your answer on the answer sheet.
30. Mark your answer on the answer sheet.
31. Mark your answer on the answer sheet.

PART 3

Directions: In this part, you will listen to several conversations between two or more speakers. These conversations will not be printed and will only be spoken one time. For each conversation, you will be asked to answer three questions. Select the best response and mark the corresponding letter (A), (B), (C), or (D) on your answer sheet.

32. Where most likely are the speakers?
    (A) At a clothing store
    (B) At a flower shop
    (C) At a bakery
    (D) At a cosmetics store

33. What does the woman recommend?
    (A) Asking for a refund
    (B) Repairing an item
    (C) Talking to an employee
    (D) Keeping a receipt

34. What will the woman probably do next?
    (A) Call a manager
    (B) Check a schedule
    (C) Look for a document
    (D) Write a message

35. Why is the woman calling?
    (A) To request an update
    (B) To cancel a service
    (C) To make an appointment
    (D) To open an account

36. Who is Dan Orlin?
    (A) An actor
    (B) A photographer
    (C) An instructor
    (D) A model

37. What does the woman ask for?
    (A) A full refund
    (B) A price discount
    (C) A printed receipt
    (D) A sample product

38. According to the woman, what is scheduled to take place at 10 A.M.?
    (A) An office tour
    (B) A training session
    (C) A meeting
    (D) An interview

39. What does the woman offer to do?
    (A) Notify some employees
    (B) Arrange a ride
    (C) Postpone an event
    (D) Print a program

40. What will the man most likely do next?
    (A) Drive to a park
    (B) Head to a parking lot
    (C) Make a reservation
    (D) Go to a branch office

41. Where do the speakers most likely work?
    (A) At an accommodation facility
    (B) At a travel agency
    (C) At a law firm
    (D) At a convention center

42. What does the woman offer to do?
    (A) Assist with some travel arrangements
    (B) Ask about a schedule
    (C) Explain some policies
    (D) Cancel a meeting

43. What does the man mean when he says, "I don't have any client meetings that week"?
    (A) He should start on a project.
    (B) He might give a presentation.
    (C) He will contact a customer.
    (D) He can participate in an event.

GO ON TO THE NEXT PAGE

44. Who is the woman?

(A) A musical artist
(B) A talk show host
(C) A radio producer
(D) A talent agent

45. What will probably happen in August?

(A) A tour will begin.
(B) A special program will be aired.
(C) A recording will be released.
(D) An award will be given out.

46. What did the woman do this afternoon?

(A) She listened to a song.
(B) She performed with a group.
(C) She took pictures with fans.
(D) She signed some autographs.

47. Who most likely are the speakers?

(A) Fashion designers
(B) Sales representatives
(C) Brand managers
(D) Product testers

48. What problem does the man mention?

(A) A model has been discontinued.
(B) A customer has made a complaint.
(C) A manager has changed a schedule.
(D) A promotion has been ineffective.

49. What will the manager talk about in the meeting tomorrow?

(A) Company policies
(B) Upcoming products
(C) A new branch
(D) A marketing plan

50. What does the woman ask the man about?

(A) Why a project budget has increased
(B) What a dinner menu will include
(C) Where an event venue is located
(D) Whether an activity schedule was made

51. Why does the woman say, "It's supposed to rain all weekend"?

(A) To explain a delay
(B) To suggest an alternative
(C) To approve a proposal
(D) To reject an idea

52. What will the man do next?

(A) Make a call
(B) Decorate a venue
(C) Check a forecast
(D) Visit a facility

53. What is the woman impressed by?

(A) A customer comment
(B) A Web site
(C) A slideshow presentation
(D) A business report

54. What does the woman ask the man to do?

(A) Arrange a meeting
(B) Provide feedback
(C) Conduct a survey
(D) Collect data

55. What does the man suggest the woman do?

(A) Go to a coworker's office
(B) Sign in to a Web site
(C) Take part in an interview
(D) Check a document

56. Where most likely are the speakers?

(A) At a retail outlet
(B) At a hair salon
(C) At a dental clinic
(D) At a fitness center

57. What does the man say about a product?

(A) It was recommended by an expert.
(B) It includes an accessory.
(C) It was recently released.
(D) It is available for a limited time.

58. What will the woman probably do next?

(A) Meet with a client
(B) Browse a brochure
(C) Complete a customer survey
(D) Go to a reception area

59. Where do the speakers most likely work?

(A) At a department store
(B) At a supermarket
(C) At an electronics shop
(D) At a pharmacy

60. What does Beth say about Brighton Wholesale?

(A) Its facilities are old.
(B) Its employees are hard to contact.
(C) Its deliveries are late.
(D) Its products are expensive.

61. What will the man most likely do today?

(A) Write a report
(B) Update a schedule
(C) Attend a meeting
(D) Request a discount

Preston Gallery
Featured Works

Title	Artist
Peaceful Lands	Denise Brown
Forgotten Forest	Clarissa Reed
Midnight Blue	Sandra Martinez
Mountain Song	Sunhee Kang

62. What does the woman want to do?

(A) Hold a fundraiser
(B) View an exhibit
(C) Make a purchase
(D) Recommend a product

63. Look at the graphic. Which artist does the man say he will contact?

(A) Denise Brown
(B) Clarissa Reed
(C) Sandra Martinez
(D) Sunhee Kang

64. What does the woman agree to do?

(A) Write down a mailing address
(B) Fill out an order form
(C) Provide a phone number
(D) Change an appointment time

GO ON TO THE NEXT PAGE

Gessner Corp. Sprinkler System: Summer Schedule

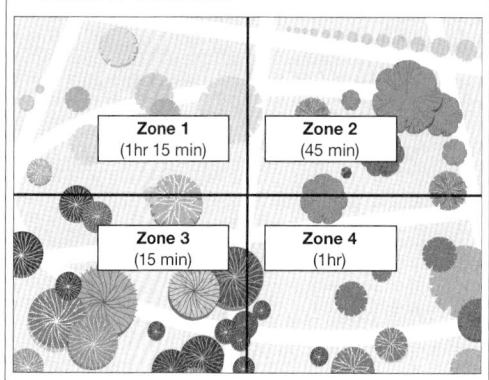

Zone 1 (1hr 15 min)	Zone 2 (45 min)
Zone 3 (15 min)	Zone 4 (1hr)

65. What did the woman do this morning?
(A) She listened to a radio show.
(B) She visited a Web site.
(C) She read a newspaper.
(D) She watched a TV program.

66. Why will the woman contact the maintenance manager?
(A) To ask that new equipment be installed
(B) To check on the health of some plants
(C) To inquire about some recent repairs
(D) To request that settings be changed

67. Look at the graphic. Where is the cactus garden located?
(A) In Zone 1
(B) In Zone 2
(C) In Zone 3
(D) In Zone 4

Spring Peony Chinese Diner
Present this coupon for our menu

Noodle Set (10% off)   * serves two
Dumpling Set (10% off)   * serves three
Phoenix Set (20% off)   * serves four
Dragon Set (25% off)   * serves five

Expires September 30

68. What must the speakers do today?
(A) Work overtime
(B) Review marketing materials
(C) Meet with team members
(D) Arrange transportation

69. Look at the graphic. Which set will be most suitable?
(A) Noodle Set
(B) Dumpling Set
(C) Phoenix Set
(D) Dragon Set

70. What does the man ask the woman to do?
(A) Download a coupon
(B) Place an order
(C) Make a reservation
(D) Call a coworker

PART 4

Directions: In this part, you will listen to several short talks by a single speaker. These talks will not be printed and will only be spoken one time. For each talk, you will be asked to answer three questions. Select the best response and mark the corresponding letter (A), (B), (C), or (D) on your answer sheet.

71. Who most likely are the listeners?

    (A) Auto mechanics
    (B) Warehouse workers
    (C) Company executives
    (D) Delivery people

72. What will be given to the listeners?

    (A) Route maps
    (B) Evaluation forms
    (C) Employee manuals
    (D) Identification cards

73. What does the speaker recommend?

    (A) Printing a document
    (B) Sending an e-mail
    (C) Visiting an office
    (D) Completing a survey

74. What is the message mainly about?

    (A) A renovation project
    (B) A government inspection
    (C) A payment method
    (D) A device installation

75. What does the speaker mean when she says, "I don't think we made the right choice"?

    (A) A customer will make a complaint.
    (B) A task needs to be redone.
    (C) A company should provide a refund.
    (D) A service has to be canceled.

76. What does the speaker want to discuss tomorrow?

    (A) An equipment upgrade
    (B) A construction schedule
    (C) A worker's availability
    (D) An additional expense

77. Where do the listeners most likely work?

    (A) At a bus station
    (B) At a head office
    (C) At an airport
    (D) At a sports facility

78. Why have some people made complaints?

    (A) Belongings did not reach the right destination.
    (B) Passengers were assigned to the same seat.
    (C) Lines have been too long.
    (D) Employees are not familiar with a policy.

79. What does the speaker say about Mr. Davidson?

    (A) He will distribute some forms.
    (B) He has met with a client.
    (C) He was recently promoted.
    (D) He is late for a meeting.

80. Who is Carla Gomez?

    (A) An editing manager
    (B) A computer technician
    (C) A news reporter
    (D) A Web site designer

81. What does the speaker mean when he says, "this feature will be added"?

    (A) A Web site's design is outdated.
    (B) A manager's expertise is important.
    (C) A magazine's popularity has declined.
    (D) A worker's assignment has changed.

82. What will happen at the meeting?

    (A) A team will show a video.
    (B) A company president will speak.
    (C) An announcement will be made.
    (D) A hiring process will be explained.

GO ON TO THE NEXT PAGE

83. What does the speaker say was discontinued?
(A) A personal computer
(B) A smartphone model
(C) A fitness tracker
(D) A waterproof watch

84. According to the speaker, what is included in *Gadgets*?
(A) Price comparisons
(B) Company profiles
(C) Application forms
(D) Product reviews

85. Why was a press release delayed?
(A) An executive is out of town.
(B) A product is not ready to be launched.
(C) A date needs to be finalized.
(D) A statement has to be approved.

---

86. Where do the listeners work?
(A) At an airline corporation
(B) At a party-planning company
(C) At a restaurant
(D) At a staffing agency

87. What did the business recently do?
(A) It moved to a new building.
(B) It hired an advisor.
(C) It offered discounts to customers.
(D) It opened an outdoor area.

88. Why does the speaker say, "This will keep things running smoothly"?
(A) To emphasize the importance of a policy
(B) To explain a benefit of a product
(C) To introduce a change to a procedure
(D) To suggest an improvement to a plan

---

89. According to the speaker, what is located in the center of the hall?
(A) A monitor
(B) A picture
(C) A sign
(D) A statue

90. What is mentioned about *Lioness*?
(A) It is not very well known.
(B) It was partially destroyed.
(C) It was improperly labeled.
(D) It is thousands of years old.

91. What does the speaker say the listeners should do?
(A) Reserve some passes
(B) Get a brochure
(C) Take some photos
(D) Attend a lecture

---

92. Which field does the speaker most likely work in?
(A) Sales
(B) Human Resources
(C) Accounting
(D) Marketing

93. What will the company offer some employees?
(A) Additional leave
(B) Financial incentives
(C) Product discounts
(D) Free parking

94. What will probably happen in May?
(A) Technicians will be replaced.
(B) A program will be developed.
(C) Employees will receive some training.
(D) A company will reduce operations.

Edgestone Apartment Building	
Floor	Facilities
Fourth Floor	Units, Vending Machines
Third Floor	Units, Lounge
Second Floor	Units, Gym
First Floor	Management Office
Basement	Units, Maintenance room

Blaze Telecom
Cable & Internet Packages

Bronze Package	**20** channels
Silver Package	**50** channels
Gold Package	**70** channels
Platinum Package	**100** channels

All packages come with a high-speed Internet connection.

95. According to the speaker, what will happen tomorrow morning?

(A) A closet will be cleaned.
(B) A utility bill will arrive.
(C) A unit will be shown.
(D) An inspection will occur.

96. What problem does the speaker mention?

(A) A door is not locked.
(B) An alarm is not working.
(C) Some noises might be heard.
(D) Some rooms might be crowded.

97. Look at the graphic. Where is the listener encouraged to stay?

(A) On the fourth floor
(B) On the third floor
(C) On the second floor
(D) On the first floor

98. What did Blaze Telecom recently do?

(A) It opened a new branch.
(B) It stopped offering a service.
(C) It acquired one of its competitors.
(D) It relocated its company headquarters.

99. Look at the graphic. What package is discounted?

(A) Bronze
(B) Silver
(C) Gold
(D) Platinum

100. What can all customers receive?

(A) A free installation
(B) A membership card
(C) A follow-up consultation
(D) A gift certificate

This is the end of the Listening test. Turn to PART 5 in your test book.

GO ON TO THE NEXT PAGE

READING TEST

In this section, you must demonstrate your ability to read and comprehend English. You will be given a variety of texts and asked to answer questions about these texts. This section is divided into three parts and will take 75 minutes to complete.

Do not mark the answers in your test book. Use the answer sheet that is separately provided.

PART 5

Directions: In each question, you will be asked to review a statement that is missing a word or phrase. Four answer choices will be provided for each statement. Select the best answer and mark the corresponding letter (A), (B), (C), or (D) on the answer sheet.

101. If it rains, ------- outdoor events will be substituted with indoor activities.

(A) every
(B) these
(C) others
(D) another

102. Monthly meetings are attended by each team's -------.

(A) supervised
(B) supervision
(C) supervise
(D) supervisor

103. The job market became ------- as many recent graduates started looking for work.

(A) competes
(B) competitively
(C) compete
(D) competitive

104. The residents must ------- for three hours while technicians restore power.

(A) wait
(B) practice
(C) grant
(D) agree

105. During his reelection campaign, Mayor Roberts promised to focus on job ------- and economic growth.

(A) create
(B) creative
(C) creation
(D) creator

106. The Tuscaloosa Airport provides wheelchair assistance to passengers who ------- it.

(A) touch
(B) request
(C) begin
(D) leave

107. The White Sands Resort considers the ------- changes in demand when pricing its rooms.

(A) seasons
(B) seasonally
(C) seasonal
(D) seasoned

108. The factory equipment will operate ------- for a period of several weeks.

(A) continuation
(B) continued
(C) continuously
(D) continuous

109. ------- requiring staff to submit daily status reports, Mr. Yang hopes to increase their productivity.
    (A) By
    (B) To
    (C) At
    (D) Within

110. The CEO spoke frankly ------- the company's problems to make sure there was no misunderstanding.
    (A) about
    (B) with
    (C) for
    (D) in

111. Following government health guidelines can ------- reduce the risk of food poisoning.
    (A) optionally
    (B) carefully
    (C) unexpectedly
    (D) substantially

112. Nelson Sportswear's marketing department was criticized for spending too much on last year's -------.
    (A) promotion
    (B) promote
    (C) promotional
    (D) promoted

113. Laurent Software's new mobile application earned a ------- review score than the developers anticipated.
    (A) high
    (B) highly
    (C) higher
    (D) highest

114. The one-month ------- period is designed to equip new employees with the necessary skills.
    (A) training
    (B) enrollment
    (C) innovation
    (D) manufacturing

115. Westgate Subway Station has only been open for a month, but it is ------- one of the city's busiest subway stops.
    (A) though
    (B) instead
    (C) therefore
    (D) nonetheless

116. Ms. Sharma found the courses at Spectrum Language Academy ------- for her career as an interpreter.
    (A) ambitious
    (B) conservative
    (C) subtle
    (D) helpful

117. Sandy's Burger Barn ------- dominates the country's fast food industry these days.
    (A) complete
    (B) more complete
    (C) completely
    (D) completing

118. The research assistant ------- the customer survey data next week.
    (A) reviewer
    (B) will review
    (C) reviewing
    (D) reviewed

119. Mr. Abrams hired a consulting firm ------- he could get some advice on dealing with suppliers.
    (A) so that
    (B) unless
    (C) even if
    (D) regarding

120. Organizers are still searching for a venue ------- they can hold an event for 200 guests.
    (A) who
    (B) what
    (C) when
    (D) where

GO ON TO THE NEXT PAGE

121. The visa application must be submitted ------- to avoid delays.

(A) punctual
(B) punctuating
(C) punctuation
(D) punctually

122. Investing in new machinery is expensive, but it is ------- in the long run.

(A) fortunate
(B) memorable
(C) beneficial
(D) sudden

123. ------- who are traveling on Flight 293 should now proceed to Gate 7.

(A) Them
(B) This
(C) Those
(D) Either

124. Two weeks -------, Prendit Corp. will hold a press conference to announce its business expansion.

(A) next
(B) later
(C) usually
(D) still

125. As a personnel manager, Ms. Goldfinch is in charge of ------- staff.

(A) indicating
(B) compiling
(C) manipulating
(D) recruiting

126. The quarterly bonus is divided -------, with all members of the sales team getting a share.

(A) equally
(B) equal
(C) equality
(D) more equal

127. The software expo in San Jose encouraged the sharing of ideas ------- developers.

(A) above
(B) among
(C) into
(D) plus

128. Parkview Tower's central location makes it extremely -------, and its high rental prices reflect this.

(A) attractive
(B) actual
(C) attentive
(D) complimentary

129. Mr. Calderon had a business partner but now runs the company by -------.

(A) himself
(B) his
(C) him
(D) he

130. Mr. Parker decided to remove the old brown sofa and place it in -------.

(A) storage
(B) usage
(C) absence
(D) procedure

PART 6

Directions: In this part, you will be asked to read four English texts. Each text is missing a word, phrase, or sentence. Select the answer choice that correctly completes the text and mark the corresponding letter (A), (B), (C), or (D) on the answer sheet.

PART 6 권장 풀이 시간   8분

Questions 131-134 refer to the following e-mail.

To: Derrian Enterprises <info@derrianenterprises.com>
From: Carlos Juarez <cjuar@jadeair.com>
Date: May 9
Subject: Inquiry

To Whom It May Concern:

I am writing on the recommendation of a colleague who has used your services before. I work in the marketing department for Jade Air, and we are running a promotional campaign ------- our 20th anniversary. As part of the campaign, we will be giving away complimentary pins to all passengers.
                131.

I am hoping you can give me a price -------. I want to know how much it will cost to get
                                     132.
4,000 pins with our logo on them. -------, could you send me a sample of this item?
                                   133.
-------. If it is satisfactory, we will proceed with an order.
134.

Thank you,

Carlos Juarez
Jade Air

---

131. (A) to celebrate
(B) celebrated
(C) celebrations
(D) celebrate

132. (A) benefit
(B) reduction
(C) analysis
(D) estimate

133. (A) Furthermore
(B) For instance
(C) Otherwise
(D) After all

134. (A) It was popular with our customers.
(B) It wasn't exactly what I requested.
(C) I will notify you when it will be sent.
(D) I will check that it matches what we need.

GO ON TO THE NEXT PAGE

Questions 135-138 refer to the following letter.

January 18
Lucinda Botello
Owner, Condesa Textiles
920 Cuevas Avenue
Mexico City, Mexico 03100

Dear Ms. Botello,

We would like to invite you to be a judge in our community's annual entrepreneurship contest. Every year, local residents present their business ideas to a panel of experienced -------. As one of these experts, you would evaluate the ideas based on selected criteria.
135.
-------. Each ------- gets only 15 minutes to share their proposal.
136.   **137.**

If you are willing to accept, please return the enclosed form by mail. The contest will be held at our community center on Friday, March 6, from 10:00 A.M. to 11:30 A.M. It -------
138.
by a casual lunch.

Further details may be found on our Web site.

Sincerely,

Rafael Pedragon
Chair, Community Entrepreneurship Program

---

135. (A) specially
(B) specialize
(C) specialists
(D) special

136. (A) We have a wide selection to offer.
(B) The presentations will be brief.
(C) Suggestions for topics are welcome.
(D) All contestants will receive a prize.

137. (A) partner
(B) representative
(C) spectator
(D) participant

138. (A) follows
(B) following
(C) followed
(D) will be followed

Questions 139-142 refer to the following information.

As of September 1, the *Canberra Post* will stop publishing the Saturday edition of its newspaper. This decision was made in response ------- a decline in the number of weekend readers. These numbers ------- from about 500,000 to 100,000 over the past three years. By discontinuing our Saturday edition, we will be able to focus on our weekday one. We will also be adding several new -------. These will include Travel, Health, Gardening, and more. -------.

139. (A) to
 (B) of
 (C) by
 (D) on

140. (A) are decreasing
 (B) have decreased
 (C) were decreased
 (D) decrease

141. (A) methods
 (B) machines
 (C) sections
 (D) positions

142. (A) They will begin appearing in our Friday issues.
 (B) There were many inquiries about refunds.
 (C) We wish our editor the best of luck in the future.
 (D) It can only be delivered within the city limits, though.

GO ON TO THE NEXT PAGE

Questions 143-146 refer to the following memo.

To: All call center workers
From: John Dooley, customer support specialist
Subject: Collecting information
Date: June 22

In the last six months, the amount of time that callers spent waiting to speak to one of our representatives has almost doubled. ------- time was 7 minutes in May, and now it is 13 minutes.
143.

-------. Thus, I will add a new page to our Web site. It will be labeled "Frequently Asked Questions" and will contain ------- answers. I would like each of you to send me a list of the 10 most common questions you ------- each day about our software programs.
144.
145.
146.

143. (A) This
(B) Its
(C) These
(D) Theirs

144. (A) We need a better way to address inquires.
(B) The new overtime policy will be effective.
(C) The product launch has been delayed.
(D) We must suspend that service temporarily.

145. (A) comprehensive
(B) comprehending
(C) comprehensively
(D) comprehension

146. (A) receiving
(B) will receive
(C) receive
(D) are received

PART 7

Directions: In this part, you will be asked to read several texts, such as advertisements, articles, instant messages, or examples of business correspondence. Each text is followed by several questions. Select the best answer and mark the corresponding letter (A), (B), (C), or (D) on your answer sheet.

 PART 7 권장 풀이 시간   54분

Questions 147-148 refer to the following notice.

City Hall Snow Removal Services Needed

Brannethville is seeking bids for the removal of snow and ice on paved areas surrounding City Hall. Before submitting a proposal, please take note of the requirements:

1. All snow and ice must be removed by 7:00 A.M. every day.
2. The contractor must be available from 7:00 A.M. to 5:00 P.M. on days when snowfall is moderate to heavy.
3. The contractor must supply all equipment.
4. The contract will last for five months from December 3 to May 3, regardless of whether snow removal services are needed.

If interested, please mail your proposal to Brannethville City Hall. Bids must be received by December 1 to qualify.

147. What is the purpose of the notice?
(A) To announce a new regulation
(B) To request applications for a seasonal job
(C) To provide helpful snow removal advice
(D) To remind residents to prepare for winter

148. What are contractors required to do?
(A) Register on a Web site
(B) Provide their own equipment
(C) Work only at night
(D) Complete a job by December

GO ON TO THE NEXT PAGE

Questions 149-150 refer to the following e-mail.

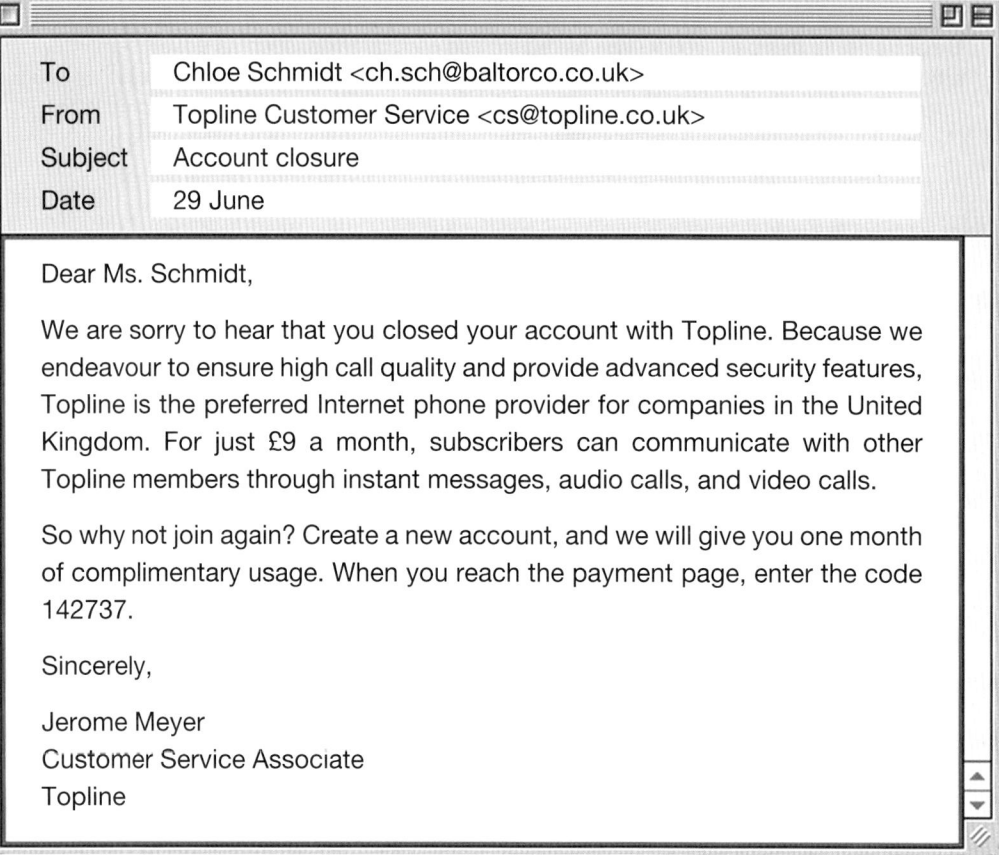

To: Chloe Schmidt <ch.sch@baltorco.co.uk>
From: Topline Customer Service <cs@topline.co.uk>
Subject: Account closure
Date: 29 June

Dear Ms. Schmidt,

We are sorry to hear that you closed your account with Topline. Because we endeavour to ensure high call quality and provide advanced security features, Topline is the preferred Internet phone provider for companies in the United Kingdom. For just £9 a month, subscribers can communicate with other Topline members through instant messages, audio calls, and video calls.

So why not join again? Create a new account, and we will give you one month of complimentary usage. When you reach the payment page, enter the code 142737.

Sincerely,

Jerome Meyer
Customer Service Associate
Topline

149. Why was the e-mail written?

(A) To apologize for a service problem
(B) To request payment of a bill
(C) To advertise a new product
(D) To persuade a customer to return

150. How can Ms. Schmidt obtain a free service?

(A) By upgrading a subscription
(B) By redeeming points
(C) By entering certain numbers
(D) By referring a friend

Questions 151-152 refer to the following online chat discussion.

Robert Patton 1:03 P.M.	Hi. I moved two months ago, but I haven't received any bank statements at my new address.
RMF Bank 1:05 P.M.	I see, Mr. Patton. You probably need to update your contact information using our online banking service. After you do this, a code will be sent to your phone to confirm your identity. You'll have to type it in within three minutes for the changes to take effect.
Robert Patton 1:06 P.M.	Actually, I already did that.
RMF Bank 1:07 P.M.	We recently made the default option for bank statements e-mail rather than regular mail. If you haven't changed this, your statements would have been e-mailed to you. You need to select the Paper option on our Web site to get hard copies sent to you.
Robert Patton 1:10 P.M.	I must have missed that. Hold on . . . OK, done. Thank you for your help.

151. What is indicated about the code?

(A) It will be selected by Mr. Patton.
(B) It must be entered within a short period.
(C) It must be given to an employee.
(D) It will be based on a customer's name.

152. At 1:10 P.M., what does Mr. Patton most likely mean when he writes, "OK, done"?

(A) He updated his contact information.
(B) He changed an online setting.
(C) He completed a bank transaction.
(D) He printed a financial document.

Questions 153-154 refer to the following article.

Ascott Foods to Say Goodbye to Plastic Bags
By Nicole Chase

March 20—Supermarket chain Ascott Foods has announced that it will no longer be providing single-use plastic shopping bags, which are bad for the environment. It will become the second chain to do so after Golden Supermarket. However, Ascott's ban will not come into effect immediately. According to a company representative, each store will keep using plastic bags for as long as supplies last.

All 166 Ascott Foods locations across the country will begin offering reusable canvas bags. They will come at no cost for three months to encourage customers to use them. The company is also looking for ways to avoid using plastic in its produce packaging.

153. The word "keep" in paragraph 1, line 10, is closest in meaning to
(A) secure
(B) continue
(C) withhold
(D) reserve

154. What is NOT true about Ascott Foods?
(A) It will be providing free shopping bags for three months.
(B) It may extend a policy to include fruit and vegetable products.
(C) It will be the first supermarket to stop using single-use bags.
(D) It has multiple store locations throughout the country.

Questions 155-157 refer to the following form.

Cadigan Industries Expense Report

Employee Name: Cole Bradley
Department: Sales
Purpose of Expense: Trip to visit client
Today's Date: March 28

Date of Expense	Description	Expense Category	Total
March 4	Gateway Air — Toronto to Fort Lauderdale, economy class, one-way	Travel	$126.25
March 4-6	Julbee Car Rental, compact car, $50/day	Travel	$150.00
March 4-5	Bonneville Hotel, single room, $90/night	Accommodation	$180.00
March 5	Cowbell Grill, 4 people	Business meal	$270.00
March 6	Natura Air — Fort Lauderdale to Toronto, business class, one-way	Travel	$316.10
		Total	**$1,042.35**

General Guidelines:
- Original receipts for all business-related expenses must be attached or reimbursement to the employee will be denied.
- Employees who purchase economy-class airline tickets will be fully reimbursed. However, those who booked business-class seats will only receive full reimbursement if they can show that there were no seats available in economy class.

155. Why did Mr. Bradley fill out the form?

(A) To reveal sales figures
(B) To provide an estimate
(C) To suggest an itinerary
(D) To request compensation

156. What can be concluded about Mr. Bradley?

(A) He used a corporate credit card on a trip.
(B) He may not be fully repaid for a flight.
(C) He did not meet the deadline to submit a report.
(D) He exceeded the acceptable limit on meal expenses.

157. According to the form, what will result in a claim for reimbursement being rejected?

(A) Waiting too long to submit a request
(B) Spending more than the amount allowed
(C) Failing to include all records of payment
(D) Booking flights with a personal credit card

GO ON TO THE NEXT PAGE

Questions 158-160 refer to the following e-mail.

To: All Trainers <instructors@silvergym.com>
From: Francesca Martinez <f.martinez@silvergym.com>
Subject: Updates for you all
Date: February 1

Hi Everyone,

Starting today, gym members can download our newly available Silver Gym smartphone app and log in with their membership ID. The app will help users to keep track of how much weight they have lost. As the personal trainers at Silver Gym, you need to encourage members to use this service.

Plus, we're holding a special promotion this month. Any member who loses at least 10 pounds by following the routines noted on the app can receive a voucher for one free class of their choice. Please let those interested in this offer know that details about our classes are posted on the bulletin board.

Regards,

Francesca Martinez, Owner, Silver Gym

158. What is one purpose of the e-mail?

(A) To notify gym members of a price change
(B) To remind customers about a policy
(C) To inform employees about a program
(D) To encourage users to join a class

159. What is NOT indicated about gym members?

(A) They can qualify for a complimentary session.
(B) They can monitor weight loss using an application.
(C) They must lose weight to win a reward.
(D) They will receive a notice about benefits in the mail.

160. Where can information about classes be found?

(A) On a notice board
(B) On a Web site
(C) In an e-mail
(D) In the locker room

Questions 161-163 refer to the following information.

Gleason's Grill Server Training Guide

Step 1

Approach customers as soon as they have been seated. If you are busy serving a table when new customers walk in, greet them loudly. — [1] —.

Step 2

Give customers a moment to go over the menu. — [2] —. Inform them of our daily special and answer any questions they have. In the event that a customer inquires about whether a dish has a specific ingredient because they are allergic to it, excuse yourself to find out from the kitchen staff. — [3] —. When the customers are ready to order, make sure to write everything down. Next, repeat their orders back to them to be certain that no mistakes have been made.

Step 3

Check back with customers several minutes after bringing the food out to see whether everything is satisfactory. Once they have finished eating, suggest dessert or coffee before bringing the bill. — [4] —.

---

161. According to the information, why do servers need to speak with kitchen staff?

(A) To complain about how slow the food is being prepared
(B) To request smaller meal portions for children
(C) To learn about newly added menu items
(D) To inquire about the contents of a dish

162. What should servers do immediately after taking customers' orders?

(A) Bring a notepad to a counter
(B) Recommend additional items
(C) Confirm some selections
(D) Add each item to the bill

163. In which of the positions marked [1], [2], [3], and [4] does the following sentence best belong?

"This will alert other staff members that they have entered the restaurant."

(A) [1]
(B) [2]
(C) [3]
(D) [4]

Questions 164-167 refer to the following text-message chain.

Riku Sato   1:35 P.M.
Last week we discussed leadership training for team managers here at BYR Incorporated. I've found a company called Rework Pro that offers corporate training.

Julianne Nash   1:37 P.M.
Great. Our monthly employee survey shows that our workers want more effective guidance.

Mallory Smithers   1:38 P.M.
What sort of services does Rework Pro offer?

Riku Sato   1:41 P.M.
They will design custom workshops for us.

Julianne Nash   1:42 P.M.
Will that be sufficient? We regularly hold workshops ourselves, but we still have this issue.

Riku Sato   1:45 P.M.
Workshops organized by qualified professionals will likely be more effective.

Mallory Smithers   1:46 P.M.
But I'm concerned about scheduling. We have several project deadlines in June.

Riku Sato   1:46 P.M.
I already checked that. The workshops could be done in July.

Julianne Nash   1:48 P.M.
Then the only issue remaining is cost.

Riku Sato   1:49 P.M.
Rework Pro is sending me an estimate in three days. Let's meet on Wednesday to determine whether these workshops will fit our budget.

164. What is suggested about BYR Incorporated?

(A) It partnered with Rework Pro previously.
(B) It provides benefits to supervisors.
(C) It requests periodic feedback from staff members.
(D) It lost workers to other companies last year.

165. At 1:42 P.M., what does Ms. Nash most likely mean when she writes, "Will that be sufficient"?

(A) A workshop might be poorly attended.
(B) A staffing issue will remain unresolved.
(C) Managers require a longer training period.
(D) An instructional method may be ineffective.

166. What does Mr. Sato say he has already done?

(A) Checked dates of staff vacations
(B) Requested schedule information
(C) Provided names of workshop attendees
(D) Confirmed venue availability

167. Why will the writers meet on Wednesday?

(A) To select the topic of a workshop
(B) To discuss the price of a service
(C) To review the deadline of a project
(D) To check the qualifications of an instructor

Questions 168-171 refer to the following letter.

GALAXIS MAGAZINE

January 7
Dr. Frederick Simons
492 Lerner Drive, Apt. 901
Bloomfield Township, MI 48401

Dear Dr. Simons,

We found your proposal for a story on the mountains of Pluto to be quite promising. We feel that it would appeal to our readers and would like you to write an article of 2,500 to 3,000 words. — [1] —.

We can offer you $2,500 for the article. — [2] —. However, take note that unlike in the past, we will not be able to compensate you fully if we decide not to use your work for any reason. — [3] —. That said, we will pay you $500 for your time. We intend to publish the article in our May issue, so we'd like you to submit your first draft by March 5. I have enclosed two contracts with this letter stating these terms. — [4] —. If you agree to them, please sign and return one of the contracts to us using the magazine's postal address. Please keep the other one for your records.

If you have any questions or concerns, don't hesitate to contact me by e-mail. We look forward to working with you again.

Molly Hamilton
Senior Editor, *Galaxis Magazine*

168. What information about the article does Ms. Hamilton NOT mention?

(A) The word length
(B) The due date
(C) The publication issue
(D) The revision process

169. What has Dr. Simons been asked to do?

(A) Mail back an agreement
(B) Negotiate some terms
(C) Save some e-mail messages
(D) Rewrite an article

170. What is suggested about *Galaxis Magazine*?

(A) Subscribers can choose to receive online content.
(B) It is available for purchase in several countries.
(C) Dr. Simons has contributed an article to it before.
(D) It pays its freelance writers less than regular staff.

171. In which of the following positions marked [1], [2], [3], and [4] does the following sentence best belong?

"Please note that if it exceeds this, we will not be able to publish it."

(A) [1]
(B) [2]
(C) [3]
(D) [4]

Questions 172-175 refer to the following advertisement.

Visit the Vallarta-Nayarit Region of Mexico with Galenus Travel

The Vallarta-Nayarit region has so much to offer, and when you book a trip using Galenus Travel, you'll have full support for the duration of your trip. Not only will representatives from our local branch be there to greet you when you land, but they'll also help arrange any activities you might be interested in. Some areas not to be missed include:

Downtown Puerto Vallarta
With the downtown area closed to vehicles, it is the perfect place to take in the sights as you shop, dine, and visit local contemporary art galleries. It's a must if you're traveling with children as the main square is always full of street performers and artists.

Mismaloya
Within walking distance of downtown, this area is full of affordable accommodations. The relaxed atmosphere of Mismaloya is ideal for travelers who want to be closer to the beach without spending too much money.

Riviera Nayarit
Famous for its spectacular beaches, Riviera Nayarit is the place to go for golf courses, amusement parks, and five-star luxury resorts. Beach restaurants serving up fish tacos and other authentic delicacies can be found throughout this 200-mile stretch of land.

172. What can be inferred about Galenus Travel?

(A) It offers discounts on trips to Mexico.
(B) It has an office in Vallarta-Nayarit.
(C) It specializes in tours for families.
(D) It provides travel insurance to clients.

173. According to the advertisement, why is Downtown Puerto Vallarta a good place to bring children?

(A) Vehicles speed limits are strictly monitored.
(B) It includes many inexpensive restaurants.
(C) Public entertainment can be found there.
(D) It is within walking distance of a beach.

174. Which group would Mismaloya probably appeal to the most?

(A) Museum lovers
(B) Budget travelers
(C) Landscape photographers
(D) Professional artists

175. What is suggested about Riviera Nayarit?

(A) It has costly accommodation facilities.
(B) It is famous for its contemporary art scene.
(C) It is a popular with newly married couples.
(D) It has several property developments planned.

GO ON TO THE NEXT PAGE

Questions 176-180 refer to the following memo and e-mail.

MEMO

To: All branch managers
From: Lori Morrison
Subject: Inventory
Date: January 5

Be reminded that we have scheduled one-day closures at all Super Parties branches to undertake our yearly inventory. During this time, all products must be counted by hand and verified against our computer records. Details are below.

Branch	Date
Chicago, Illinois	Tuesday, February 12
Fort Wayne, Indiana	Wednesday, February 13
Milwaukee, Wisconsin	Wednesday, February 20
St. Louis, Missouri	Friday, February 22

Advise your customers that orders scheduled for delivery on any of the above dates will not be affected. Also, they can still purchase products through our Web site during this period.

To: Adele Welch <a.welch@superparties.com>
From: Brian Ledford <b.ledford@superparties.com>
Subject: Follow-up request
Date: January 6

Hi Adele,

I'm contacting you because Amy Turner from the head office wants you to confirm that I am eligible for an employee discount. She told me any orders over $500 need to have a branch manager's approval. As I mentioned before, I was hoping to order costumes, party games, and balloons for my young cousin's birthday party next month, and the total amount comes to $600. Please let me know when I can stop by with the form.

I'd also like to remind you that the party is taking place in Indiana on February 23, and that last November you accepted my request for leave from February 21 to 23. I'm so sorry that I will be unavailable to take part in our branch's inventory. I've asked Lisa to cover for me while I'm away.

Thank you!

Brian

176. Why is Super Parties closing its branches?

(A) To reduce financial losses
(B) To count merchandise
(C) To address market changes
(D) To undertake renovations

177. What is NOT indicated about Super Parties?

(A) Its items may be rented.
(B) It has stores in four locations.
(C) Its merchandise is available online.
(D) It ships products to customers.

178. Who most likely is Ms. Welch?

(A) A chief executive
(B) A travel agent
(C) A branch supervisor
(D) A head accountant

179. What is Mr. Ledford planning to do?

(A) Move to a new city
(B) Join a company seminar
(C) Attend a training workshop
(D) Visit family members

180. Where most likely does Mr. Ledford work?

(A) In Chicago
(B) In Fort Wayne
(C) In Milwaukee
(D) In St. Louis

GO ON TO THE NEXT PAGE

Questions 181-185 refer to the following Web page and e-mail.

www.expressmovers.com

Express Movers

| About | Reservations | Locations |

Express Movers is the number-one business for transporting your belongings. Having specialized in long-distance moving services for over 30 years, our crew members will ensure that your goods arrive at your final destination on schedule and in the same shape as they were upon being packed up. We even tow vehicles, such as cars, trucks, and boats.* Check out our affordable prices below and click **here** to arrange times for pickup and drop-off.

Distance	Price
less than 50 miles	$300
50-200 miles	$500
201-500 miles	$750
more than 500 miles	$1,000

*There is an additional fee of $500 per vehicle, regardless of distance.

To	Customer Service <service@expressmovers.com>
From	Jacqueline Gerard <jackieger39@tellmail.net>
Subject	Moving Assistance
Date	May 23
Attachment	Apartment_Info.document

Hello,

I'm writing because I need some help moving the furniture and appliances from my current apartment in Raleigh. I've recently accepted an offer for a job in Tampa and need to relocate there before my start date of July 1. Ideally, I'd like to have my belongings picked up on June 29 and delivered the following day.

The attached document contains information about the locations of the Raleigh and Tampa apartments, as well as a list of the items I'll need to move. The approximate distance of the move will be 650 miles. I will need a receipt as my new company said they would reimburse me for my relocation expenses.

Please contact me for any further information.

Regards,

Jacqueline Gerard

181. According to the Web page, what will crew members do?

(A) Clean items at the destination
(B) Ensure delivery of items in good condition
(C) Use a navigation system to locate a residence
(D) Collect payment in advance

182. What is stated about Express Movers?

(A) It will transport automobiles for an extra charge.
(B) It has recently opened a new drop-off center.
(C) It offers an online chat service for customers.
(D) It was established a decade ago.

183. Why is Ms. Gerard relocating?

(A) To live close to some relatives
(B) To enroll in a university program
(C) To take up a new project
(D) To begin work in a new location

184. What can be inferred about Ms. Gerard?

(A) She is moving into a small apartment.
(B) She will be promoted soon.
(C) She is leaving some furniture in storage.
(D) She will pay at least $1,000 for a service.

185. What did Ms. Gerard request?

(A) A delivery schedule
(B) A transaction record
(C) A feedback form
(D) A contract copy

GO ON TO THE NEXT PAGE

Questions 186-190 refer to the following e-mail, form, and agenda.

To	Jake Walker <j.walker@renewable.com>
From	Luanne Wilkins <l.wilkins@urbanenergy.net>
Subject	9th URBAN ENERGY FORUM
Date	February 16

Dear Mr. Walker,

Thank you for your inquiry about the 9th Urban Energy Forum. This event will be held in Bern, Switzerland from April 26 to 28. Experts from various sectors will be gathering to discuss how cities around the world can effectively shift to renewable energy.

With urban populations projected to continue growing in the future, the need to develop sufficient, clean, and sustainable energy sources for the world's cities has become urgent. The Urban Energy Forum provides an opportunity for participants to generate ideas and discuss practical solutions.

In answer to your question, general admission tickets, including all presentations and discussions in the main hall, are €150 before February 1 and €185 after. Workshops are offered at an additional cost of €35 per session. Note that for members of sponsor organizations, general admission is free. For more information or to download the program in digital format, visit www.urbanenergy.net/forum.

Sincerely,

Luanne Wilkins
Urban Energy Forum

9th URBAN ENERGY FORUM
Bern, Switzerland · April 26-28

Thank you! Your payment has been received. Please retain a copy of this form for your records. If you require any changes, contact us at forum@urbanenergy.net.

ORDER DETAILS

Name: Irwin Patel
Company (optional): Solar India
Address: 75 Murti Lane, New Delhi, India 110011
Telephone: 555-2390
E-mail: i.patel@solarindia.com
Number of tickets: One(1)
Total amount paid: €35.00
　- Admission fees: €0.00
　- Workshop fees: €35.00

To obtain a full refund, please contact us at least three days before the start of the event.

9th URBAN ENERGY FORUM
Bern, Switzerland · April 26-28

Agenda for Day 2

10:00-11:00 A.M.   Opening presentation
Main hall: Urban Energy Forum president Kurt Bollinger will talk about accelerating the transition to renewable energy.

11:00 A.M.-12:00 P.M.   Morning workshops
Hall B: "Financing Green Energy"
presented by Eloisa Davide, CEO, Global Energy Investment Bank

Hall C: "How Governments Can Lead the Way"
presented by Alan Holm, Chair, UK Energy Initiative

12:00-2:00 P.M.   Lunch break

2:00-3:30 P.M.   Afternoon workshops
Hall B: "Using the Power of the Sun"
presented by Lester Agarwal, Founder, South Asian Energy Consortium (CEO, Solar India)

Hall C: "Advancements in Battery Technology"
presented by Richard Liu, Professor of Engineering, Queensland University

3:30-4:30 P.M.   Roundtable discussion
Main hall: Urban Energy Forum member Stephanie Bernard will lead a discussion on promoting renewable energy in the media.

---

186. According to the e-mail, what is true about cities?
 (A) They will each host future forums.
 (B) They need better transportation systems.
 (C) They will become more crowded.
 (D) They could suffer more frequent power outages.

187. What is available on the Urban Energy Forum's Web site?
 (A) Sponsorship applications
 (B) Copies of a program
 (C) Refund request forms
 (D) Transcripts of lectures

188. What is true about Mr. Patel?
 (A) He purchased a ticket before February 1.
 (B) His ticket grants him entry only to the main hall.
 (C) He will be participating in more than one workshop.
 (D) His firm is a sponsor of the 9th Urban Energy Forum.

189. Which workshop leader does Mr. Patel have a professional relationship with?
 (A) Alan Holm
 (B) Richard Liu
 (C) Eloisa Davide
 (D) Lester Agarwal

190. What is indicated about Day 2 of the forum?
 (A) Some speakers will give a presentation more than one time.
 (B) All participants will be provided with one hour for lunch.
 (C) A televised debate on renewable energy will take place.
 (D) A presentation on battery technology will be given.

GO ON TO THE NEXT PAGE

Questions 191-195 refer to the following form, announcement, and e-mail.

Gumbo Grocers Rewards Program
APPLICATION FORM

Drop off the completed form at your local Gumbo's customer service counter, or mail it to Gumbo Grocers Rewards Program, 104 Jefferson St., Richmond, VA 23284. If you have an online account, you may also sign up at www.shopgumbo.com.

Name: _____
Address: _____
Phone: _____
E-mail: _____

Check ☐ here to receive our weekly newsletter and get discount coupons sent to your e-mail inbox.

Program details:
- Earn 1 point for every dollar you spend in our store or online. Earn points on groceries, medical prescriptions, magazines, and more!
- Every 200 points you earn can be used toward bigger discounts on your grocery bill.
- Instantly earn 100 points by referring a friend who signs up.

Good News for Our Customers!

Customers who earn rewards points by shopping at their local Gumbo Grocers and Tiptop Appliance stores will now be able to use their rewards points when filling up at Fullerton gas stations. Every 100 points can be redeemed for $1 in savings on your fuel purchase.

This expansion of rewards promises to deliver greater value and savings to Fullerton's customers, as well as both Gumbo and Tiptop shoppers.

Fullerton's Gas Rewards Program is available at over 25 retail firms across the country and may be used at thousands of gas stations nationwide. Learn more at www.fullertongas.com, or ask about registering for gas rewards at your local Gumbo or Tiptop.

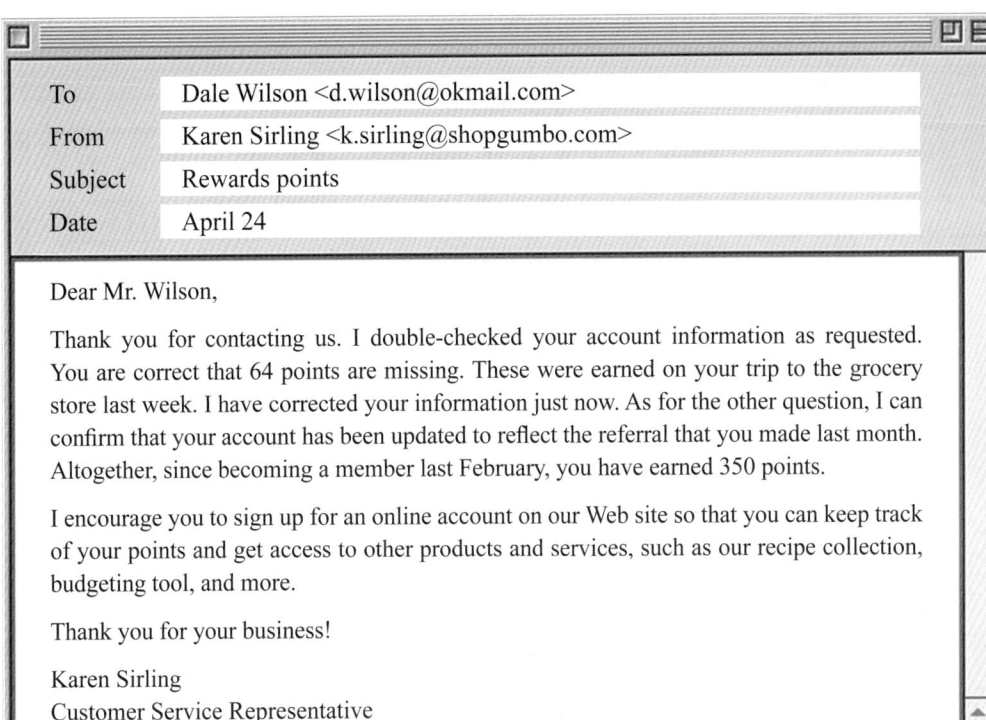

To: Dale Wilson <d.wilson@okmail.com>
From: Karen Sirling <k.sirling@shopgumbo.com>
Subject: Rewards points
Date: April 24

Dear Mr. Wilson,

Thank you for contacting us. I double-checked your account information as requested. You are correct that 64 points are missing. These were earned on your trip to the grocery store last week. I have corrected your information just now. As for the other question, I can confirm that your account has been updated to reflect the referral that you made last month. Altogether, since becoming a member last February, you have earned 350 points.

I encourage you to sign up for an online account on our Web site so that you can keep track of your points and get access to other products and services, such as our recipe collection, budgeting tool, and more.

Thank you for your business!

Karen Sirling
Customer Service Representative
Gumbo Grocers

191. According to the form, what will people who sign up for a newsletter receive?

(A) Discount vouchers
(B) Bonus points
(C) Sample products
(D) Account upgrades

192. What is true about the Gumbo Grocers' Rewards Program?

(A) A referral earns enough points for a discount on gas.
(B) Online purchases qualify for the largest number of points.
(C) A coupon will be provided for each 200 points earned.
(D) Prescriptions are worth fewer points than groceries.

193. What is suggested about Fullerton Gas Company?

(A) It will supply automotive services at stores.
(B) It partnered with over 25 companies.
(C) It is increasing its number of gas stations.
(D) It shares a building with Gumbo Grocers.

194. Why did Ms. Sirling write the e-mail?

(A) To verify a recent order
(B) To extend a special offer
(C) To request payment of a bill
(D) To address a couple of inquiries

195. What does Ms. Sirling indicate about Mr. Wilson?

(A) He redeemed his points for a fuel purchase.
(B) His membership is expiring very soon.
(C) He earned at least 100 points last month.
(D) His online password was recently changed.

GO ON TO THE NEXT PAGE

Questions 196-200 refer to the following Web page, e-mail, and employee timesheet.

Plumtree Nutritional Advice

| HOME | BLOG | Q&A | LOG IN |

Tips for Healthy Living
Posted by: Brad Shear, Head Nutritionist

Staying fit can be challenging, but I have compiled the lists below to help my clients keep on track:

Be sure to
- Drink at least three glasses of water per day
- Exercise for 20 to 30 minutes, three times per week
- Get seven hours of sleep every night

Be careful not to
- Eat dinner within one hour of going to bed
- Sit down for more than three hours at a time

To learn more, click on one of the diet and exercise plans below and e-mail me to set up an initial consultation.

Plan	Prices
FreshStart	$30
FreshUp	$35
FreshPlus	$40
FreshPremium	$45

To: Brad Shear <bshear@plumtreenutrition.com>
From: Madison Costa <maddiecosta77@rentmail.net>
Date: April 28
Subject: Consultation

Dear Mr. Shear,

I'm writing because I'd like to set up an initial appointment with you to discuss the plans on your Web site. One of my coworkers, Kerry Franklin, highly recommended you. She follows your FreshPlus plan and says that it has greatly improved her health. I'm excited to join your program, but I don't want to pay as much as she does and I also don't want the cheapest plan.

My main problem is that I have recently switched to working a later shift than I previously had at my office, and I've been having trouble adjusting my sleep and meal schedule. I'm hoping to meet with you either in the morning on May 2 or in the afternoon of May 3, since I have to travel for a training activity with my company on May 4.

Madison Costa

Plumtree Nutritional Advice Employee Timesheet

Please enter the number of hours that you have worked for each day of the week.

Employee name: <u>Brad Shear</u>

	May 1	May 2	May 3	May 4	May 5
Client consultation	4h	6h	0h	6h	4h
Administration	0h	1h	0h	1h	2h
Training	0h	0h	6h	0h	0h
TOTAL HOURS	4h	7h	6h	7h	6h

196. What advice does Mr. Shear give to his clients?

(A) Consume at least three meals a day
(B) Protect the skin from sunlight
(C) Participate in athletic competitions
(D) Engage in regular physical activities

197. What is mentioned about the FreshPlus plan?

(A) It will be updated on Plumtree's Web site.
(B) It will be discussed at an upcoming conference.
(C) It has been used by Ms. Costa's colleague.
(D) It has been discounted for a limited time.

198. How much is Ms. Costa willing to pay for a plan?

(A) $30
(B) $35
(C) $40
(D) $45

199. What will Ms. Costa do in May?

(A) Attend a corporate event
(B) Apply for health insurance
(C) Change the time of an appointment
(D) Take a day off for vacation

200. When did Ms. Costa most likely meet with Mr. Shear?

(A) On May 2
(B) On May 3
(C) On May 4
(D) On May 5

This is the end of the test. You may review Parts 5, 6, and 7 if you finish the test early.

실전모의고사 정답·해석·해설

PART 1
1. (D) 2. (B) 3. (B) 4. (B) 5. (A) 6. (C)

PART 2
7. (A) 8. (A) 9. (C) 10. (B) 11. (A) 12. (B) 13. (A) 14. (B) 15. (C) 16. (A)
17. (C) 18. (A) 19. (B) 20. (A) 21. (C) 22. (C) 23. (A) 24. (B) 25. (A) 26. (C)
27. (C) 28. (B) 29. (C) 30. (A) 31. (B)

PART 3
32. (A) 33. (C) 34. (D) 35. (C) 36. (B) 37. (B) 38. (C) 39. (A) 40. (B) 41. (C)
42. (A) 43. (D) 44. (B) 45. (C) 46. (A) 47. (B) 48. (D) 49. (B) 50. (D) 51. (D)
52. (A) 53. (D) 54. (D) 55. (A) 56. (C) 57. (C) 58. (D) 59. (B) 60. (D) 61. (A)
62. (C) 63. (B) 64. (C) 65. (B) 66. (D) 67. (C) 68. (A) 69. (D) 70. (B)

PART 4
71. (D) 72. (A) 73. (C) 74. (A) 75. (B) 76. (D) 77. (C) 78. (A) 79. (D) 80. (A)
81. (B) 82. (C) 83. (D) 84. (D) 85. (C) 86. (C) 87. (D) 88. (A) 89. (D) 90. (D)
91. (B) 92. (B) 93. (B) 94. (C) 95. (D) 96. (C) 97. (B) 98. (A) 99. (B) 100. (A)

PART 5
101. (B) 102. (D) 103. (D) 104. (A) 105. (C) 106. (B) 107. (C) 108. (C) 109. (A) 110. (A)
111. (D) 112. (A) 113. (C) 114. (A) 115. (D) 116. (D) 117. (C) 118. (B) 119. (A) 120. (D)
121. (D) 122. (C) 123. (C) 124. (B) 125. (D) 126. (A) 127. (B) 128. (A) 129. (A) 130. (A)

PART 6
131. (A) 132. (D) 133. (A) 134. (D) 135. (C) 136. (B) 137. (D) 138. (B) 139. (A) 140. (B)
141. (C) 142. (A) 143. (A) 144. (A) 145. (A) 146. (C)

PART 7
147. (B) 148. (B) 149. (D) 150. (C) 151. (B) 152. (B) 153. (B) 154. (C) 155. (D) 156. (B)
157. (C) 158. (C) 159. (D) 160. (A) 161. (D) 162. (C) 163. (A) 164. (C) 165. (D) 166. (B)
167. (B) 168. (D) 169. (A) 170. (C) 171. (A) 172. (B) 173. (C) 174. (C) 175. (A) 176. (B)
177. (A) 178. (C) 179. (D) 180. (D) 181. (B) 182. (A) 183. (D) 184. (C) 185. (B) 186. (C)
187. (B) 188. (D) 189. (D) 190. (D) 191. (A) 192. (A) 193. (B) 194. (D) 195. (C) 196. (D)
197. (C) 198. (B) 199. (A) 200. (A)

PART 1

1. 1인 사진　　　　　　　　　　　　영국

(A) She is writing with a pen.
(B) She is holding a document.
(C) She is facing a window.
(D) **She is typing on a laptop.**

hold v. 들다, 잡다　document n. 문서　face v. 마주 보다
type v. 타자를 치다, 입력하다

해석　(A) 그녀는 펜으로 쓰고 있다.
　　　(B) 그녀는 문서를 들고 있다.
　　　(C) 그녀는 창문을 마주 보고 있다.
　　　(D) 그녀는 노트북 컴퓨터에 타자를 치고 있다.

해설　(A) [×] writing with a pen(펜으로 쓰고 있다)은 여자의 동작과 무관하므로 오답이다.
　　　(B) [×] holding a document(문서를 들고 있다)는 여자의 동작과 무관하므로 오답이다.
　　　(C) [×] 여자가 창문(window)을 마주 보고 있는 것이 아니라, 등지고 있으므로 오답이다.
　　　(D) [○] 여자가 노트북 컴퓨터에 타자를 치고 있는 모습을 가장 잘 묘사한 정답이다.

2. 2인 이상 사진　　　　　　　　미국

(A) A wall is lined with mirrors.
(B) **A worker is holding a clipboard.**
(C) A sign is hanging next to a doorway.
(D) Workers are painting a building.

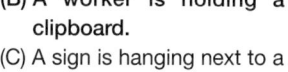

doorway n. 출입구

해석　(A) 거울들이 벽에 늘어서 있다.
　　　(B) 한 작업자가 클립보드를 들고 있다.
　　　(C) 표지판이 출입구 옆에 걸려 있다.
　　　(D) 작업자들이 건물을 페인트칠하고 있다.

해설　(A) [×] 사진에 거울들(mirrors)이 없으므로 오답이다.
　　　(B) [○] 한 작업자가 클립보드를 들고 있는 모습을 가장 잘 묘사한 정답이다.
　　　(C) [×] 사진에서 표지판(sign)을 확인할 수 없으므로 오답이다.
　　　(D) [×] painting(페인트칠하고 있다)은 작업자들의 동작과 무관하므로 오답이다.

3. 2인 이상 사진　　　　　　　　캐나다

(A) One of the people is reaching toward the floor.
(B) **One of the people is receiving a book.**
(C) Some people are entering a store.
(D) Some people are removing items from a shelf.

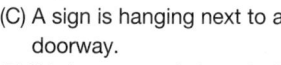

reach v. (손을) 뻗다　enter v. 들어가다
remove v. 치우다, 제거하다　shelf n. 선반, 책꽂이

해석　(A) 사람들 중 한 명이 바닥을 향해 손을 뻗고 있다.
　　　(B) 사람들 중 한 명이 책을 받고 있다.
　　　(C) 몇몇 사람들이 가게로 들어가고 있다.
　　　(D) 몇몇 사람들이 선반에서 물품들을 치우고 있다.

해설　(A) [×] 사진에 바닥을 향해 손을 뻗고 있는(reaching toward the floor) 사람이 없으므로 오답이다.
　　　(B) [○] 사람들 중 한 명이 책을 받고 있는 모습을 가장 잘 묘사한 정답이다.
　　　(C) [×] entering(들어가고 있다)은 사람들의 동작과 무관하므로 오답이다.
　　　(D) [×] removing(치우고 있다)은 사람들의 동작과 무관하므로 오답이다.

4. 1인 사진　　　　　　　　　　　호주

(A) He is changing a tire in a garage.
(B) **He is examining the bottom of a car.**
(C) He is opening a hood.
(D) He is getting into a vehicle.

examine v. 살펴보다　bottom n. 밑바닥, 하부
hood n. (자동차 엔진 등의) 보닛, 덮개
get into ~에 타다, 들어가다

해석　(A) 그는 차고에서 타이어를 바꾸고 있다.
　　　(B) 그는 차의 밑바닥을 살펴보고 있다.
　　　(C) 그는 보닛을 열고 있다.
　　　(D) 그는 차량에 타고 있다.

해설　(A) [×] changing(바꾸고 있다)은 남자의 동작과 무관하므로 오답이다. 사진에 있는 타이어(tire)를 사용하여 혼동을 주었다.
　　　(B) [○] 남자가 차의 밑바닥을 살펴보고 있는 모습을 가장 잘 묘사한 정답이다.
　　　(C) [×] opening(열고 있다)은 남자의 동작과 무관하므로 오답이다.
　　　(D) [×] getting into(타고 있다)는 남자의 동작과 무관하므로 오답이다.

5. 실내 사진　　　　　　　　　　미국

(A) **Some monitors have been placed on a counter.**
(B) Some signs have been posted outside.
(C) A light is being installed in a ceiling.
(D) A television is being taken down from a wall.

place v. 놓다　counter n. 카운터, 계산대　post v. 게시하다
install v. 설치하다　ceiling n. 천장　take down 내리다, 떼다

해석　(A) 몇몇 모니터들이 카운터에 놓여 있다.
　　　(B) 몇몇 표지판들이 야외에 게시되어 있다.
　　　(C) 전등이 천장에 설치되고 있다.
　　　(D) 텔레비전이 벽에서 내려지고 있다.

해설 (A) [○] 모니터들이 카운터에 놓여 있는 모습을 가장 잘 묘사한 정답이다.
(B) [×] 사진에 표지판들(signs)이 없으므로 오답이다.
(C) [×] 사진에서 전등(light)은 보이지만 설치되고 있는(is being installed) 모습은 아니므로 오답이다.
(D) [×] 사진에서 텔레비전(television)은 보이지만 내려지고 있는(is being taken down) 모습은 아니므로 오답이다.

6. 2인 이상 사진   미국

(A) They are walking on a sidewalk.
(B) They are trimming a tree.
(C) There are some bushes in the distance.
(D) A bicycle is being repaired.

sidewalk n. 보도 trim v. 손질하다 bush n. 관목, 덤불
in the distance 멀리, 먼 곳에 repair v. 수리하다

해석 (A) 그들은 보도를 걷고 있다.
(B) 그들은 나무를 손질하고 있다.
(C) 멀리 관목들이 있다.
(D) 자전거가 수리되고 있다.

해설 (A) [×] walking(걷고 있다)은 사람들의 동작과 무관하므로 오답이다.
(B) [×] trimming(손질하고 있다)은 사람들의 동작과 무관하므로 오답이다. 사진에 있는 나무(tree)를 사용하여 혼동을 주었다.
(C) [○] 멀리 관목들이 보이는 모습을 가장 잘 묘사한 정답이다.
(D) [×] 사진에서 자전거는 보이지만 수리되고 있는(being repaired) 모습은 아니므로 오답이다.

PART 2

7. How 의문문   미국 → 캐나다

How many people will be attending the seminar?
(A) About a hundred.
(B) The topic is communications.
(C) It was very interesting.

attend v. 참석하다 seminar n. 세미나 topic n. 주제
communications n. 정보 통신
interesting adj. 재미있는, 흥미로운

해석 몇 명의 사람들이 세미나에 참석할까요?
(A) 대략 백 명 정도요.
(B) 주제는 정보 통신이에요.
(C) 그것은 매우 재미있었어요.

해설 (A) [○] 대략 백 명이라는 말로, 세미나에 참석하는 사람의 수를 언급했으므로 정답이다.
(B) [×] seminar(세미나)와 관련 있는 topic(주제)을 사용하여 혼동을 준 오답이다.
(C) [×] 몇 명의 사람들이 세미나에 참석할지를 물었는데, 이와 관련이 없는 그것은 매주 재미있었다고 응답했으므로 오답이다. 질문의 seminar(세미나)를 나타낼 수 있는 It을 사용하여 혼동을 주었다.

8. 조동사 의문문   호주 → 캐나다

Do you have any make-up samples I can try?
(A) Yes. They are over here.
(B) She bought them online.
(C) Let me give you an example.

make-up n. 화장품 try v. 써보다, 시도해 보다

해석 제가 써볼 수 있는 화장품 견본들이 있나요?
(A) 네. 그것들은 여기 있어요.
(B) 그녀는 그것들을 온라인으로 구매했어요.
(C) 예시를 들어 볼게요.

해설 (A) [○] Yes로 화장품 견본이 있음을 전달한 후, 여기 있다는 부연 설명을 했으므로 정답이다.
(B) [×] 써볼 수 있는 화장품 견본들이 있는지를 물었는데, 이와 관련이 없는 그녀는 그것들을 온라인에서 구매했다고 응답했으므로 오답이다.
(C) [×] samples - example의 유사 발음 어휘를 사용하여 혼동을 준 오답이다.

9. What 의문문   호주 → 미국

What time does the meeting start?
(A) In the main conference room.
(B) I'll do it next time.
(C) Fairly soon, I think.

meeting n. 회의

해석 회의는 몇 시에 시작하나요?
(A) 주 회의실에서요.
(B) 그건 다음에 할게요.
(C) 제 생각엔, 꽤 금방요.

해설 (A) [×] 회의가 시작하는 시간을 물었는데, 장소로 응답했으므로 오답이다.
(B) [×] 질문의 time을 반복 사용하여 혼동을 준 오답이다.
(C) [○] 꽤 금방이라는 말로, 곧 회의가 시작될 것이라는 간접적인 응답을 했으므로 정답이다.

10. 평서문   영국 → 캐나다

This phone is currently on sale.
(A) Call them before noon.
(B) It's a great time to buy it, then.
(C) Our current project.

currently adv. 현재 on sale 할인 중인 noon n. 정오
current adj. 현재의

해석 이 휴대폰은 현재 할인 중이에요.
(A) 그들에게 정오 전에 전화하세요.
(B) 그럼, 지금이 구매하기 좋을 때네요.
(C) 우리의 현재 프로젝트요.

해설 (A) [×] phone(휴대폰)과 관련 있는 Call(전화하다)을 사용하여 혼동을 준 오답이다.
(B) [○] 지금이 구매하기 좋을 때라는 말로, 휴대폰이 현재 할인 중이라는 것에 대한 의견을 전달했으므로 정답이다.
(C) [×] currently - current의 유사 발음 어휘를 사용하여 혼동을 준 오답이다.

11. When 의문문
미국 → 영국

When will we receive the utility bill?
(A) Early next month.
(B) At Wilkins Department Store.
(C) Give it to the secretary.

receive v. 받다 utility bill 공과금 청구서

해석 우리는 언제 공과금 청구서를 받을까요?
(A) 다음 달 초에요.
(B) Wilkins 백화점에서요.
(C) 비서에게 주세요.

해설 (A) [ㅇ] Early next month(다음 달 초)라는 말로, 청구서를 받을 시점을 언급했으므로 정답이다.
(B) [×] 언제 공과금 청구서를 받을지를 물었는데, 장소로 응답했으므로 오답이다.
(C) [×] 질문의 utility bill(공과금 청구서)을 나타낼 수 있는 it을 사용하여 혼동을 준 오답이다.

12. 제안 의문문
미국 → 호주

Would you like to share an appetizer?
(A) I paid with a credit card.
(B) Sure. That's a good idea.
(C) Please pass me a napkin.

appetizer n. 애피타이저, 전채 credit card 신용카드

해석 애피타이저를 나눠 드시겠어요?
(A) 저는 신용카드로 계산했어요.
(B) 그럼요. 좋은 생각이에요.
(C) 냅킨 좀 건네주세요.

해설 (A) [×] 애피타이저를 나눠 먹을지를 물었는데, 이와 관련이 없는 신용카드로 계산했다는 말로 응답했으므로 오답이다.
(B) [ㅇ] Sure로 제안을 수락한 후, 좋은 생각이라는 부연 설명을 했으므로 정답이다.
(C) [×] appetizer(애피타이저)와 관련 있는 napkin(냅킨)을 사용하여 혼동을 준 오답이다.

13. Who 의문문
영국 → 캐나다

Who set up the meeting room?
(A) The interns, Bob and Riley.
(B) There are few employees.
(C) It begins after lunch.

set up 준비하다 intern n. 인턴

해석 누가 회의실을 준비했나요?
(A) 인턴인 Bob과 Riley요.
(B) 직원들이 거의 없어요.
(C) 그건 점심 후에 시작해요.

해설 (A) [ㅇ] 인턴인 Bob과 Riley라는 말로, 회의실을 준비한 인물들을 언급했으므로 정답이다.
(B) [×] meeting(회의)과 관련 있는 employees(직원들)를 사용하여 혼동을 준 오답이다.
(C) [×] 누가 회의실을 준비했는지를 물었는데, 시점으로 응답했으므로 오답이다.

14. 조동사 의문문
호주 → 미국

Will someone from the IT department be here soon?
(A) Thank you for arranging that.
(B) He's coming at 1 P.M.
(C) Please call if you need more help.

department n. 부서 arrange v. 준비하다, 배열하다

해석 IT 부서의 직원이 곧 여기에 올 것인가요?
(A) 그것을 준비해 주셔서 감사합니다.
(B) 그는 오후 1시에 올 거예요.
(C) 도움이 더 필요하시면 전화 주세요.

해설 (A) [×] IT 부서의 직원이 곧 여기에 올 것인지를 물었는데, 이와 관련이 없는 그것을 준비해 줘서 감사하다고 응답했으므로 오답이다.
(B) [ㅇ] 그가 오후 1시에 올 것이라는 말로, IT 부서의 직원이 오후에 올 것임을 간접적으로 전달했으므로 정답이다.
(C) [×] IT 부서의 직원이 곧 여기에 올 것인지를 물었는데, 이와 관련이 없는 도움이 더 필요하면 전화 달라고 응답했으므로 오답이다.

15. Where 의문문
캐나다 → 영국

Where do you plan to take the client for dinner?
(A) The cafeteria served fish for lunch.
(B) To discuss the marketing project.
(C) To a new French restaurant.

plan v. 계획하다 client n. 고객 cafeteria n. 구내식당 serve v. 제공하다

해석 저녁 식사를 위해 어디로 고객을 모시고 갈 계획인가요?
(A) 구내식당에서 점심으로 생선을 제공했어요.
(B) 마케팅 프로젝트를 논의하기 위해서요.
(C) 새로 생긴 프랑스 음식점으로요.

해설 (A) [×] dinner(저녁 식사)와 관련 있는 cafeteria(구내식당)를 사용하여 혼동을 준 오답이다.
(B) [×] 어디로 고객을 데려갈 계획인지를 물었는데, 이유로 응답했으므로 오답이다.
(C) [ㅇ] 새로 생긴 프랑스 음식점이라는 말로, 저녁 식사를 할 장소를 언급했으므로 정답이다.

16. Why 의문문
호주 → 영국

Why do we need to order pens with the company logo?
(A) We'll be giving them out at the job fair.
(B) Yes, I can do that now.
(C) By May 15 at the latest.

order v. 주문하다 job fair 채용 박람회 at the latest 늦어도

해설 우리는 왜 회사 로고가 있는 펜을 주문해야 하나요?
(A) 우리는 채용 박람회에서 그것들을 나눠줄 거예요.
(B) 네, 지금 그것을 할 수 있어요.
(C) 늦어도 5월 15일까지요.

해설 (A) [ㅇ] 채용 박람회에서 그것들을 나눠줄 거라는 말로, 로고가 있는 펜을 주문해야 하는 이유를 언급했으므로 정답이다.

(B) [×] 왜 회사 로고가 있는 펜을 주문해야 하는지를 물었는데, 이와 관련이 없는 지금 그것을 할 수 있다고 응답했으므로 오답이다.
(C) [×] 왜 회사 로고가 있는 펜을 주문해야 하는지를 물었는데, 시점으로 응답했으므로 오답이다.

17. 조동사 의문문　　🎧 미국 → 호주

Did you read the article I wrote?
(A) I wrote down the address.
(B) There are more articles of clothing.
(C) The one about local schools?

article n. 기사, 품목　clothing n. 의류

해석　제가 쓴 기사를 읽어 보셨나요?
(A) 저는 주소를 적어 두었어요.
(B) 의류 몇 품목이 더 있어요.
(C) 지역 학교들에 관한 것이요?

해설　(A) [×] 질문의 wrote를 반복 사용하여 혼동을 준 오답이다.
(B) [×] 질문의 article을 '품목'이라는 의미의 명사 articles로 반복 사용하여 혼동을 준 오답이다.
(C) [○] 지역 학교들에 관한 것인지를 되물어 기사에 대한 추가 정보를 요청했으므로 정답이다.

18. Who 의문문　　🎧 미국 → 캐나다

Who informed the media about the company's plans?
(A) Ms. Johnson, I believe.
(B) I know all about them.
(C) That firm recently expanded.

inform v. 알리다　media n. 언론, 매체　recently adv. 최근에

해석　누가 회사의 계획들에 대해 언론에 알렸나요?
(A) 제가 알기로는, Ms. Johnson이요.
(B) 저는 그것에 대해 모두 알고 있어요.
(C) 그 회사는 최근에 확장했어요.

해설　(A) [○] Ms. Johnson이라며 회사의 계획을 언론에 알린 인물을 언급했으므로 정답이다.
(B) [×] 질문의 plans(계획들)를 나타낼 수 있는 them을 사용하여 혼동을 준 오답이다.
(C) [×] company(회사)와 같은 의미인 firm을 사용하여 혼동을 준 오답이다.

19. 부가 의문문　　🎧 호주 → 영국

The refrigerator comes with a water filter, doesn't it?
(A) It seems cold enough.
(B) No, it doesn't have that feature.
(C) I'll have a glass.

refrigerator n. 냉장고　come with ~이 딸려 있다
feature n. 기능

해석　그 냉장고에는 정수 필터가 딸려 있죠, 그렇지 않나요?
(A) 충분히 차가운 것 같아요.
(B) 아니요, 이것은 그 기능이 없어요.
(C) 한 잔 마실게요.

해설　(A) [×] refrigerator(냉장고)와 관련 있는 cold(차가운)를 사용하여 혼동을 준 오답이다.
(B) [○] No로 정수 필터가 딸려 있지 않음을 전달한 후, 그 기능이 없다는 부연 설명을 했으므로 정답이다.
(C) [×] water(물)와 관련 있는 glass(잔)를 사용하여 혼동을 준 오답이다.

20. How 의문문　　🎧 캐나다 → 호주

How often does the regional manager visit?
(A) Actually, we talk to her through video-conferencing.
(B) She's from New York.
(C) Across from Mr. Jackson's office.

regional adj. 지역의　manager n. 관리자
video-conferencing n. 화상 회의
across from ~의 바로 맞은편에

해석　지역 관리자가 얼마나 자주 방문하나요?
(A) 사실, 우리는 화상 회의를 통해 그녀와 대화해요.
(B) 그녀는 뉴욕 출신이에요.
(C) Mr. Jackson의 사무실 바로 맞은편에요.

해설　(A) [○] 사실 화상 회의를 통해 그녀와 대화한다는 말로 지역 관리자가 방문하지 않음을 간접적으로 전달했으므로 정답이다.
(B) [×] 질문의 regional manager(지역 관리자)에서 연상할 수 있는 New York(뉴욕)을 사용하여 혼동을 준 오답이다.
(C) [×] 지역 관리자가 얼마나 자주 방문하는지를 물었는데, Mr. Jackson의 사무실 바로 맞은편이라며 관련이 없는 내용으로 응답했으므로 오답이다.

21. 제안 의문문　　🎧 영국 → 캐나다

Why don't we sell a wider selection of soft drinks?
(A) Tell the supervisor you have to go.
(B) These seem bigger than the other shoes.
(C) Our store doesn't have enough space.

a selection of 다양한　soft drinks 청량음료　space n. 공간

해석　좀 더 다양한 청량음료를 파는 것은 어떨까요?
(A) 관리자에게 당신이 가야 한다고 말하세요.
(B) 이것들은 다른 신발보다 커 보여요.
(C) 우리 매장에는 충분한 공간이 없어요.

해설　(A) [×] 좀 더 다양한 청량음료를 파는 것은 어떤지를 물었는데, 이와 관련이 없는 관리자에게 가야 한다고 말하라고 응답했으므로 오답이다.
(B) [×] 좀 더 다양한 청량음료를 파는 것은 어떤지를 물었는데, 이와 관련이 없는 이것들은 다른 신발보다 커 보인다고 응답했으므로 오답이다.
(C) [○] 우리 매장에는 충분한 공간이 없다는 말로 다양한 청량음료를 팔 수 없는 이유를 간접적으로 전달했으므로 정답이다.

22. Which 의문문　　🎧 영국 → 미국

Which cell phone repair shop has the best reputation?

(A) About 25 miles.
(B) I bought the latest model.
(C) **That would be Phone World.**

repair shop 수리점 reputation n. 평판, 명성
latest adj. 최신의

해석 어느 휴대폰 수리점이 가장 평판이 좋나요?
(A) 25마일 정도요.
(B) 최신 모델을 구입했어요.
(C) Phone World일 거예요.

해설 (A) [x] 어느 휴대폰 수리점이 가장 평판이 좋은지를 물었는데, 이와 관련이 없는 25마일 정도라는 말로 응답했으므로 오답이다.
(B) [x] cell phone(휴대폰)과 관련 있는 the latest model(최신 모델)을 사용하여 혼동을 준 오답이다.
(C) [o] Phone World일 것이라는 말로, 어느 휴대폰 수리점이 가장 평판이 좋은지를 언급했으므로 정답이다.

23. 평서문 〔캐나다 → 영국〕

If you want, we can walk to the restaurant.
(A) **Yes, it's a perfect evening for that.**
(B) The talk took longer than expected.
(C) The menu was changed.

perfect adj. 더할 나위 없는 expect v. 예상하다

해석 원하신다면, 우리는 식당으로 걸어갈 수 있어요.
(A) 네, 그러기에 더할 나위 없는 저녁이네요.
(B) 강연이 예상보다 오래 걸렸어요.
(C) 메뉴가 변경되었어요.

해설 (A) [o] Yes로 의견에 동의한 후, 그러기에 더할 나위 없는 저녁이라는 의견을 추가했으므로 정답이다.
(B) [x] walk - talk의 유사 발음 어휘를 사용하여 혼동을 준 오답이다.
(C) [x] restaurant(식당)과 관련 있는 menu(메뉴)를 사용하여 혼동을 준 오답이다.

24. Why 의문문 〔미국 → 캐나다〕

Why did you go to Miami last month?
(A) Only for a day or so.
(B) **To meet with investors.**
(C) Yes, my flight leaves in an hour.

or so ~ 정도 investor n. 투자자

해석 당신은 왜 지난달에 마이애미에 갔나요?
(A) 하루 정도만요.
(B) 투자자들을 만나기 위해서요.
(C) 네, 제 비행기는 한 시간 후에 출발해요.

해설 (A) [x] 왜 지난달에 마이애미에 갔는지를 물었는데, 이와 관련이 없는 하루 정도만이라는 말로 응답했으므로 오답이다.
(B) [o] 투자자들을 만나기 위해서라는 말로, 지난달에 마이애미에 간 이유를 언급했으므로 정답이다.
(C) [x] Miami(마이애미)에서 연상할 수 있는 flight(비행기)를 사용하여 혼동을 준 오답이다.

25. 부정 의문문 〔영국 → 호주〕

Didn't Mr. Davis approve the budget?
(A) **It's still being reviewed.**
(B) He lives in a different building.
(C) Let's increase production.

approve v. 승인하다 budget n. 예산 production n. 생산량

해석 Mr. Davis가 예산을 승인하지 않았나요?
(A) 그건 아직 검토되고 있어요.
(B) 그는 다른 건물에 살아요.
(C) 생산량을 늘립시다.

해설 (A) [o] 아직 검토되고 있다는 말로, Mr. Davis가 예산을 승인하지 않았음을 간접적으로 전달했으므로 정답이다.
(B) [x] 질문의 Mr. Davis를 나타낼 수 있는 He를 사용하여 혼동을 준 오답이다.
(C) [x] Mr. Davis가 예산을 승인하지 않았는지를 물었는데, 이와 관련이 없는 생산량을 늘리자는 말로 응답했으므로 오답이다.

26. When 의문문 〔캐나다 → 영국〕

When will the factory inspection start?
(A) That's a good choice.
(B) In the garden.
(C) **As soon as the CEO gets here.**

inspection n. 점검, 시찰 as soon as ~하자마자

해석 공장 점검은 언제 시작할까요?
(A) 그것은 좋은 선택이에요.
(B) 정원에서요.
(C) 최고 경영자가 이곳에 도착하자마자요.

해설 (A) [x] 질문의 factory inspection(공장 점검)을 나타낼 수 있는 That을 사용하여 혼동을 준 오답이다.
(B) [x] 공장 점검을 언제 시작할지를 물었는데, 위치로 응답했으므로 오답이다.
(C) [o] 최고 경영자가 이곳에 도착하자마자라는 말로, 공장 점검이 시작하는 시점을 언급했으므로 정답이다.

27. 부정 의문문 〔미국 → 호주〕

Won't Freeway 79 be shut down next week?
(A) You're going the right way.
(B) A month-long absence.
(C) **The road work has been finished.**

shut down 폐쇄하다 month-long adj. 한 달간의
absence n. 결근, 결석 road work 도로 공사

해석 79번 고속도로가 다음 주에 폐쇄되지 않나요?
(A) 당신은 맞는 길로 가고 있어요.
(B) 한 달간의 결근이요.
(C) 도로 공사는 끝났어요.

해설 (A) [x] Freeway - way의 유사 발음 어휘를 사용하여 혼동을 준 오답이다.
(B) [x] 79번 고속도로가 다음 주에 폐쇄되는지를 물었는데, 이와 관련이 없는 한 달간의 결근이라는 말로 응답했으므로 오답이다.

(C) [o] 도로 공사는 끝났다는 말로 고속도로가 폐쇄되지 않을 것임을 간접적으로 전달했으므로 정답이다.

28. 조동사 의문문
[캐나다 → 미국]

Have customers provided feedback about the laptop?
(A) Yes, on top of the shelf.
(B) A survey was sent out just last week.
(C) Place the devices over there.

provide v. 제공하다 feedback n. 의견, 피드백 shelf n. 선반
survey n. 설문 조사 device n. 장치

해석 고객들이 노트북 컴퓨터에 대해 의견을 제공했나요?
(A) 네, 선반 위에요.
(B) 설문 조사는 겨우 지난주에 발송되었어요.
(C) 그 장치들을 저기에 놓으세요.

해설 (A) [×] 고객이 노트북 컴퓨터에 대해 의견을 제공했는지를 물었는데, 이와 관련이 없는 선반 위에라는 말로 응답했으므로 오답이다.
(B) [o] 설문 조사가 겨우 지난주에 발송되었다는 말로, 고객들이 의견을 제공했는지 모른다는 간접적인 응답을 했으므로 정답이다.
(C) [×] laptop(노트북 컴퓨터)과 관련 있는 devices(장치들)를 사용하여 혼동을 준 오답이다.

29. 선택 의문문
[영국 → 호주]

Will the story be published this month or next month?
(A) One of my favorite authors.
(B) From a news magazine.
(C) I need time to check it.

publish v. 출판하다 author n. 작가
news magazine 시사 잡지

해석 그 소설은 이번 달에 출판되나요, 아니면 다음 달에 출판되나요?
(A) 제가 가장 좋아하는 작가들 중 한 명이에요.
(B) 시사 잡지에서요.
(C) 그것을 확인할 시간이 필요해요.

해설 (A) [×] story(소설)와 관련 있는 authors(작가들)를 사용하여 혼동을 준 오답이다.
(B) [×] published(출판되다)와 관련 있는 magazine(잡지)을 사용하여 혼동을 주었다.
(C) [o] 그것, 즉 소설을 확인할 시간이 필요하다는 말로, 아직 출판될 준비가 되지 않았음을 간접적으로 전달했으므로 정답이다.

30. be동사 의문문
[호주 → 미국]

Are you transferring departments once the new year begins?
(A) Yes. I'll be moving to international sales.
(B) Isn't that the fourth time this year?
(C) The money is in their account.

transfer v. 옮기다 department n. 부서 account n. 계좌

해석 새해가 시작되면 부서를 옮기시나요?
(A) 네. 저는 해외 영업으로 이동할 거예요.
(B) 올해에 네 번째 아닌가요?
(C) 그 돈은 그들의 계좌에 있어요.

해설 (A) [o] Yes로 부서를 옮길 것임을 전달한 후, 해외 영업으로 이동할 거라는 추가 정보를 제공했으므로 정답이다.
(B) [×] 질문의 year를 반복 사용하여 혼동을 준 오답이다.
(C) [×] 질문의 transferring(옮기다)에서 연상할 수 있는 money(돈)를 사용하여 혼동을 준 오답이다.

31. 요청 의문문
[미국 → 영국]

Could you enlarge the user manual font?
(A) No, I think the venue is too small.
(B) Yes, but that will affect the layout.
(C) Only online users.

enlarge v. 확대하다 manual n. 설명서 font n. 글씨체, 폰트
venue n. 장소 affect v. 영향을 미치다 layout n. 배치, 레이아웃

해석 사용자 설명서의 글씨체를 확대할 수 있나요?
(A) 아니요, 제 생각에는 장소가 너무 작아요.
(B) 네, 하지만 그건 배치에 영향을 미칠 거예요.
(C) 온라인 사용자만요.

해설 (A) [×] enlarge(확대하다)에서 연상할 수 있는 small(작은)을 사용하여 혼동을 준 오답이다.
(B) [o] Yes로 글씨체를 확대할 수 있다고 전달한 후, 배치에 영향을 미칠 거라는 부연 설명을 했으므로 정답이다.
(C) [×] 질문의 user를 반복 사용하여 혼동을 준 오답이다.

PART 3

32-34
[캐나다 → 영국]

Questions 32-34 refer to the following conversation.

M: Hi. ³²I received this sweater as a birthday gift, but it's too small. Could I exchange it for a larger one? I have the receipt right here.
W: OK. Those are located in the menswear section. ³³If you need help finding them, just talk to one of our staff members.
M: Thanks. Should I leave this item here while I look around?
W: Yes. ³⁴I'll put a note on it now so that the other cashiers know why it's here.

exchange v. 교환하다 receipt n. 영수증
staff member 직원 leave v. 놓아두다
look around 둘러보다 cashier n. 점원

해석
32-34번은 다음 대화에 관한 문제입니다.

남: 안녕하세요. ³²저는 이 스웨터를 생일 선물로 받았는데, 너무 작아요. 더 큰 것으로 교환해도 될까요? 영수증은 바로 여기 있어요.
여: 그럼요. 그것들은 남성복 코너에 위치해 있어요. ³³그것들을 찾는 데 도움이 필요하시다면, 저희 직원 중 한 명에게 말씀하세요.
남: 고마워요. 제가 둘러보는 동안에 이 물건을 여기에 놓아두어야

할까요?
여: 네. 다른 점원들이 그것이 왜 여기에 있는지 알 수 있도록 ³⁴지금 그것에 메모해 놓을게요.

32. 장소 문제

해석 화자들은 어디에 있는 것 같은가?
(A) 옷 가게에
(B) 꽃 가게에
(C) 제과점에
(D) 화장품 가게에

해설 대화에서 장소와 관련된 표현을 놓치지 않고 듣는다. 남자가 "I received this sweater as a birthday gift, but it's too small. Could I exchange it for a larger one?"이라며 스웨터를 생일 선물로 받았는데 너무 작으니 더 큰 것으로 교환해도 될지 물은 것을 통해, 대화가 이루어지고 있는 장소가 옷 가게임을 알 수 있다. 따라서 (A)가 정답이다.

어휘 bakery n. 제과점 cosmetics n. 화장품

33. 제안 문제

해석 여자는 무엇을 제안하는가?
(A) 환불을 요청하기
(B) 제품을 수리하기
(C) 직원에게 이야기하기
(D) 영수증을 보관하기

해설 여자의 말에서 제안과 관련된 표현이 언급된 다음을 주의 깊게 듣는다. 여자가 "If you need help finding them, just talk to one of our staff members."라며 그것들을 찾는 데 도움이 필요하다면, 직원 중 한 명에게 이야기하라고 제안하였다. 따라서 (C)가 정답이다.

어휘 ask for 요청하다 refund n. 환불 employee n. 직원

34. 다음에 할 일 문제

해석 여자는 다음에 무엇을 할 것 같은가?
(A) 관리자에게 전화한다.
(B) 일정을 확인한다.
(C) 문서를 찾는다.
(D) 메시지를 적는다.

해설 대화의 마지막 부분을 주의 깊게 듣는다. 여자가 "I'll put a note on it now"라며 지금 그것에 메모해 놓겠다고 하였다. 이를 통해, 여자가 메시지를 적을 것임을 알 수 있다. 따라서 (D)가 정답이다.

어휘 manager n. 관리자 look for 찾다

[Paraphrasing]
put a note 메모하다 → Write a message 메시지를 적다

35-37 〔호주 → 영국〕

Questions 35-37 refer to the following conversation.

M: Thank you for contacting Belmont Images. How can I help you today?
W: Hello. ³⁵I'd like to set up an appointment for Saturday afternoon. I plan on applying for modeling jobs this summer, so I need some professional headshots.
M: ³⁶Dan Orlin, our photographer, is available at 1 P.M. on Saturday. Is that convenient for you?

W: That works. One more thing . . . I'm a university student. Um, ³⁷can I get a discount?
M: Sure. If you present a valid student ID, you'll get 10 percent off.

contact v. 연락하다 set up an appointment 예약을 하다
apply v. 지원하다 professional adj. 전문적인
headshot n. 얼굴 사진 available adj. 시간이 있는
convenient adj. 편리한 present v. 제시하다
valid adj. 유효한

해석
35-37번은 다음 대화에 관한 문제입니다.

남: Belmont Images사에 연락해 주셔서 감사합니다. 오늘 무엇을 도와드릴까요?
여: 안녕하세요. ³⁵토요일 오후에 예약을 하고 싶어요. 저는 이번 여름에 모델 일을 지원할 계획이어서, 전문적인 얼굴 사진이 필요해요.
남: ³⁶우리 사진작가인 Dan Orlin은 토요일 오후 1시에 시간이 있어요. 이 시간이 편리하신가요?
여: 좋아요. 하나 더요... 저는 대학생이에요. 음, ³⁷할인을 받을 수 있나요?
남: 그럼요. 유효한 학생 신분증을 제시하시면, 10퍼센트 할인을 받으실 거예요.

35. 목적 문제

해석 여자는 왜 전화를 하고 있는가?
(A) 업데이트를 요청하기 위해
(B) 서비스를 취소하기 위해
(C) 약속을 정하기 위해
(D) 계좌를 개설하기 위해

해설 전화의 목적을 묻는 문제이므로, 대화의 초반을 반드시 듣는다. 여자가 "I'd like to set up an appointment for Saturday afternoon."이라며 토요일 오후로 예약을 하고 싶다고 하였다. 따라서 (C)가 정답이다.

어휘 request v. 요청하다 appointment n. 약속
open an account 계좌를 개설하다

[Paraphrasing]
set up an appointment 예약을 하다 → make an appointment 약속을 정하다

36. 특정 세부 사항 문제

해석 Dan Orlin은 누구인가?
(A) 배우
(B) 사진작가
(C) 강사
(D) 모델

해설 질문의 핵심 어구(Dan Orlin)가 언급된 주변을 주의 깊게 듣는다. 남자가 "Dan Orlin, our photographer, is available"이라며 사진작가인 Dan Orlin이 시간이 있다고 하였다. 따라서 (B)가 정답이다.

어휘 actor n. 배우 instructor n. 강사

37. 요청 문제

해석 여자는 무엇을 요청하는가?
(A) 전액 환불
(B) 가격 할인
(C) 인쇄된 영수증

(D) 제품 견본

해설 여자의 말에서 요청과 관련된 표현이 언급된 다음을 주의 깊게 듣는다. 여자가 "can I get a discount?"라며 할인을 받을 수 있는지 물었다. 따라서 (B)가 정답이다.

어휘 refund n. 환불 receipt n. 영수증

38-40 영국 → 캐나다

Questions 38-40 refer to the following conversation.

W: Mr. Rowland, I thought you already left the office. It's 9:45 A.M., and ³⁸you're supposed to have a meeting with our Swiss clients at 10 o'clock.
M: Oh, I completely forgot about that! I have a conference call with some staff members at our Newport branch in a few minutes.
W: ³⁹I'll inform those taking part in the call that you had to leave on short notice.
M: Thanks. ⁴⁰Do you know if my driver is waiting for me?
W: ⁴⁰He should be waiting for you in the parking lot. But I suggest you hurry. The hotel is over a mile away.

be supposed to ~하기로 되어 있다 completely adv. 완전히
conference call 전화 회의 inform v. 알리다
take part in ~에 참여(참가)하다
on short notice 예고 없이, 촉박하게

해석
38-40번은 다음 대화에 관한 문제입니다.
여: Mr. Rowland, 당신이 이미 사무실을 떠났다고 생각했어요. 지금은 오전 9시 45분이고, ³⁸당신은 10시에 스위스 고객들과 회의하기로 되어 있잖아요.
남: 아, 그것을 완전히 잊어버렸어요! 몇 분 후에 뉴포트 지점의 일부 직원들과 전화 회의가 있어요.
여: ³⁹제가 그 전화에 참여하는 사람들에게 당신이 예고 없이 떠나야 했다고 알려줄게요.
남: 고마워요. ⁴⁰혹시 운전기사가 저를 기다리고 있는지 알고 있나요?
여: ⁴⁰그는 주차장에서 당신을 기다리고 있을 거예요. 하지만 서두르기를 제안해요. 그 호텔은 1마일 이상 떨어져 있어요.

38. 특정 세부 사항 문제
해설 여자에 따르면, 오전 10시에 무엇이 일어나기로 예정되어 있는가?
(A) 사무실 견학
(B) 교육 세션
(C) 회의
(D) 면접

해설 질문의 핵심 어구(10 A.M.)와 관련된 내용을 주의 깊게 듣는다. 여자가 "you're supposed to have a meeting ~ at 10 o'clock"이라며 남자가 10시에 회의하기로 되어 있다고 하였다. 따라서 (C)가 정답이다.

Paraphrasing
is scheduled to ~하기로 예정되어 있다 → 're(are) supposed to ~하기로 되어 있다

39. 제안 문제
해석 여자는 무엇을 해주겠다고 제안하는가?
(A) 몇몇 직원에게 알린다.
(B) 교통편을 준비한다.
(C) 행사를 연기한다.
(D) 프로그램을 인쇄한다.

해설 여자의 말에서 제안과 관련된 표현이 언급된 다음을 주의 깊게 듣는다. 여자가 "I'll inform those taking part in the call"이라며 자신이 그 전화에 참여하는 사람들에게 알리겠다고 하였다. 따라서 (A)가 정답이다.

어휘 notify v. 알리다 employee n. 직원 postpone v. 연기하다

Paraphrasing
inform 알리다 → Notify 알리다

40. 다음에 할 일 문제
해석 남자는 다음에 무엇을 할 것 같은가?
(A) 공원으로 운전한다.
(B) 주차장으로 향한다.
(C) 예약을 한다.
(D) 지점에 간다.

해설 대화의 마지막 부분을 주의 깊게 듣는다. 남자가 "Do you know if my driver is waiting for me?"라며 혹시 운전기사가 자신을 기다리고 있는지 알고 있는지 묻자, 여자가 "He[driver] should be waiting for you in the parking lot."이라며 운전기사가 주차장에서 남자를 기다리고 있을 것이라고 한 것을 통해, 남자가 주차장으로 향할 것임을 알 수 있다. 따라서 (B)가 정답이다.

어휘 reservation n. 예약 branch office 지점

41-43 미국 → 호주

Questions 41-43 refer to the following conversation.

W: Stanley, ⁴¹can you attend a law conference in Boston later this month? Mr. Thompson wants someone from our company to go.
M: ⁴¹Are none of the other lawyers available?
W: No. They're all busy. If you're free, ⁴²I can make your hotel and flight reservations.
M: Hmm . . . How long is the conference?
W: Three days. ⁴³It runs from May 26 to 28.
M: Well, I don't have any client meetings that week.
W: Great. I'll tell Mr. Thompson.

attend v. 참석하다 law n. 법률 conference n. 회의
reservation n. 예약 run v. 진행되다, 계속되다 client n. 고객

해석
41-43번은 다음 대화에 관한 문제입니다.
여: Stanley, ⁴¹이번 달 말에 보스턴에서 있는 법률 회의에 참석할 수 있을까요? Mr. Thompson은 우리 회사에서 누군가가 가기를 원해요.
남: ⁴¹다른 변호사들 중에 참석 가능한 사람이 없나요?
여: 없어요. 그들 모두가 바빠요. 시간이 되시면, ⁴²호텔 및 항공편 예약을 해드릴 수 있어요.
남: 흠... 회의 기간은 얼마나 되나요?
여: 3일간이요. ⁴³5월 26일부터 28일까지 진행돼요.
남: 음, 그 주에는 고객 회의가 없네요.

여: 좋아요. Mr. Thompson에게 말할게요.

41. 화자 문제
해설 화자들은 어디에서 일하는 것 같은가?
(A) 숙박 시설에서
(B) 여행사에서
(C) 법률 사무소에서
(D) 컨벤션 센터에서

해설 대화에서 신분 및 직업과 관련된 표현을 놓치지 않고 듣는다. 여자가 "can you attend a law conference ~ later this month? Mr. Thompson wants someone from our company to go."라며 이번 달 말에 법률 회의에 참석할 수 있는지 물으며 Mr. Thompson이 화자의 회사에서 누군가가 가기를 원한다고 하자, 남자가 "Are none of the other lawyers available?"이라며 회사의 다른 변호사들은 법률 회의에 참석 가능한 사람이 없는지 물었다. 이를 통해 화자들이 법률 사무소에서 일하고 있음을 알 수 있다. 따라서 (C)가 정답이다.

어휘 accommodation n. 숙박

42. 제안 문제
해설 여자는 무엇을 해주겠다고 제안하는가?
(A) 출장 준비를 돕는다.
(B) 일정에 대해 문의한다.
(C) 몇몇 정책을 설명한다.
(D) 회의를 취소한다.

해설 여자의 말에서 제안과 관련된 표현이 언급된 다음을 주의 깊게 듣는다. 여자가 "I can make your hotel and flight reservations"라며 호텔 및 항공편 예약을 해줄 수 있다고 하였다. 따라서 (A)가 정답이다.

어휘 assist v. 돕다 policy n. 정책

Paraphrasing
hotel and flight reservations 호텔 및 항공편 예약 → travel arrangements 출장 준비

43. 의도 파악 문제
해설 남자는 "그 주에는 고객 회의가 없네요"라고 말할 때 무엇을 의도하는가?
(A) 프로젝트를 시작해야 한다.
(B) 발표를 할 수도 있다.
(C) 고객에게 연락할 것이다.
(D) 행사에 참여할 수 있다.

해설 질문의 인용어구(I don't have any client meetings that week)가 언급된 주변을 주의 깊게 듣는다. 여자가 "It[conference] runs from May 26 to 28."라며 회의가 5월 26일부터 28일까지 진행된다고 하였다. 남자가 이에 대해 그 주에는 고객 회의가 없다고 한 것은 행사에 참여할 수 있다는 것임을 알 수 있다. 따라서 (D)가 정답이다.

44-46 영국 → 캐나다 → 호주

Questions 44-46 refer to the following conversation with three speakers.

W: ⁴⁴I'm very excited for today's program because I'm speaking with two of Australia's most popular music stars. Ryan and Blake Holdsen, ⁴⁴welcome to *Culture Wind*.

M1: Thanks, Clara. It's a pleasure to be here with you.
M2: Yeah, we're both big fans of the program.
W: So ⁴⁵you're releasing your second album in August, right?
M2: ⁴⁵Yeah. It comes out on August 5. It is titled *Now is Good*.
W: I'm sure you're excited.
M1: We are. We've worked very hard over the past two years on the album.
W: Well, ⁴⁶after hearing the track you played for me this afternoon, I'm confident your fans will be pleased!

excited adj. 기대하는 pleasure n. 기쁨, 즐거움
release v. 발매하다 be titled 제목이 ~이다 track n. 곡
confident adj. 확신하는

해석
44-46번은 다음 세 명의 대화에 관한 문제입니다.

여: ⁴⁴호주에서 가장 인기 있는 음악 스타 중 두 분과 이야기하게 되어 오늘의 프로그램이 매우 기대되네요. Ryan과 Blake Holdsen, ⁴⁴*Culture Wind*에 오신 것을 환영해요.
남1: 감사해요, Clara. 함께하게 되어 기뻐요.
남2: 네, 저희 둘 다 이 프로그램의 큰 팬이에요.
여: 자 ⁴⁵여러분은 8월에 두 번째 앨범을 발매할 예정이죠, 맞나요?
남2: ⁴⁵네, 그건 8월 5일에 나와요. 제목은 *Now is Good*이에요.
여: 정말 기쁘시겠네요.
남1: 그렇죠. 저희는 지난 2년 동안 앨범을 위해 매우 열심히 일했어요.
여: 음, ⁴⁶오늘 오후에 저를 위해 연주해 주신 곡을 듣고 나니, 여러분의 팬들이 기뻐하실 것이라고 확신해요.

44. 화자 문제
해설 여자는 누구인가?
(A) 음악가
(B) 토크 쇼 진행자
(C) 라디오 제작자
(D) 연예인 대리인

해설 대화에서 신분 및 직업과 관련된 표현을 놓치지 않고 듣는다. 여자가 "I'm very excited for today's program because I'm speaking with ~ music stars."라며 음악 스타와 이야기하게 되어 오늘의 프로그램이 매우 기대된다고 한 후, "welcome to *Culture Wind*"라며 *Culture Wind*에 온 것을 환영한다고 한 것을 통해, 여자가 토크 쇼 진행자임을 알 수 있다. 따라서 (B)가 정답이다.

어휘 host n. 진행자 producer n. 제작자

Paraphrasing
program 프로그램 → talk show 토크 쇼

45. 다음에 할 일 문제
해설 8월에 무슨 일이 일어날 것 같은가?
(A) 투어가 시작될 것이다.
(B) 특별 프로그램이 방송될 것이다.
(C) 음반이 공개될 것이다.
(D) 상이 수여될 것이다.

해설 질문의 핵심 어구(in August)가 언급된 주변을 주의 깊게 듣는다. 여자가 "you're releasing your second album in August"라며 8월에 두 번째 앨범을 발매할 예정인지 묻자, 남

자2가 "Yeah. It[second album] comes out on August 5."라며 두 번째 앨범이 8월 5일에 나온다고 하였다. 따라서 (C)가 정답이다.

어휘 air v. 방송하다 recording n. 음반 award n. 상

Paraphrasing
album 앨범 → recording 음반

46. 특정 세부 사항 문제

해석 여자는 오늘 오후에 무엇을 했는가?
(A) 노래를 들었다.
(B) 그룹과 함께 공연했다.
(C) 팬들과 사진을 찍었다.
(D) 사인을 했다.

해설 질문의 핵심 어구(this afternoon)와 관련된 내용을 주의 깊게 듣는다. 여자가 "after hearing the track you played for me this afternoon, I'm confident your fans will be pleased"라며 오늘 오후에 자신을 위해 연주해 준 곡을 듣고 나니 팬들이 기뻐할 것이라고 확신한다고 하였다. 따라서 (A)가 정답이다.

어휘 perform v. 공연하다 autograph n. 사인

Paraphrasing
hearing the track 곡을 듣다 → listened to a song 노래를 들었다

47-49 [3m] 호주 → 미국

Questions 47-49 refer to the following conversation.

M: Sarah, ⁴⁷have you sold many products lately? My sales haven't been great.
W: ⁴⁷Not really. This month has been particularly slow. Shoppers just don't seem interested in our current collection of watches.
M: ⁴⁸Even our year-end sale isn't attracting customers. I hope things get better soon.
W: Fortunately, ⁴⁹the most popular watch brand is launching a new line early next week. Our branch manager has scheduled a meeting for tomorrow to discuss the features of these products.

lately adv. 요즘 particularly adv. 특히 slow adj. 부진한, 더딘 attract v. 끌어들이다 get better 나아지다, 좋아지다 line n. (상품의) 종류 feature n. 특징

해석
47-49번은 다음 대화에 관한 문제입니다.

남: Sarah, ⁴⁷요즘 많은 제품들을 팔았나요? 제 매출은 좋지 않았어요.
여: ⁴⁷별로였어요. 이번 달은 특히 부진했어요. 쇼핑객들이 정말 우리의 현재 시계 컬렉션에 관심이 없는 것 같아요.
남: ⁴⁸심지어 우리의 연말 할인도 고객들을 끌어들이지 못하고 있어요. 상황이 빨리 나아지면 좋겠네요.
여: 다행히도, ⁴⁹가장 인기 있는 시계 브랜드가 다음 주 초에 새로운 종류를 출시해요. 우리 지점 관리자가 이 제품들의 특징을 논의하기 위해 내일 회의 일정을 잡았어요.

47. 화자 문제

해석 화자들은 누구인 것 같은가?
(A) 패션 디자이너
(B) 판매 직원
(C) 브랜드 관리자
(D) 제품 검사자

해설 대화에서 신분 및 직업과 관련된 표현을 놓치지 않고 듣는다. 남자가 "have you sold many products lately?"라며 요즘 많은 제품들을 팔았는지 묻자, 여자가 "Not really."라며 자신도 별로였다고 한 것을 통해, 화자들이 판매 직원임을 알 수 있다. 따라서 (B)가 정답이다.

어휘 sales representative 판매 직원 tester n. 검사자

48. 문제점 문제

해석 남자는 무슨 문제를 언급하는가?
(A) 모델의 생산이 중단되었다.
(B) 고객이 불만을 제기했다.
(C) 관리자가 일정을 변경했다.
(D) 홍보가 효과가 없었다.

해설 남자의 말에서 부정적인 표현이 언급된 주변을 주의 깊게 듣는다. 남자가 "Even our year-end sale isn't attracting customers."라며 심지어 연말 할인도 고객들을 끌어들이지 못하고 있다고 하였다. 따라서 (D)가 정답이다.

어휘 discontinue v. (생산을) 중단하다 complaint n. 불만 promotion n. 홍보 ineffective adj. 효과가 없는

49. 특정 세부 사항 문제

해석 관리자는 내일 회의에서 무엇에 관해 이야기할 것인가?
(A) 회사 정책
(B) 곧 공개될 제품
(C) 새로운 지점
(D) 마케팅 계획

해설 질문의 핵심 어구(meeting tomorrow)가 언급된 주변 내용을 주의 깊게 듣는다. 여자가 "the most popular watch brand is launching a new line ~ next week. Our branch manager has scheduled a meeting for tomorrow to discuss the features of these products."라며 가장 인기 있는 시계 브랜드가 다음 주 초에 새로운 종류를 출시한다며, 지점 관리자가 이 제품들의 특징을 논의하기 위해 내일 회의 일정을 잡았다고 하였다. 따라서 (B)가 정답이다.

어휘 upcoming adj. 곧 공개될, 다가오는

50-52 [3m] 영국 → 캐나다

Questions 50-52 refer to the following conversation.

W: Hi, Evan. ⁵⁰Have you finished creating the schedule of activities for the company retreat?
M: Not yet. I still have to confirm that the dining hall is large enough for all of our attendees. Otherwise, ⁵¹we'll need to arrange for outdoor dining facilities.
W: It's supposed to rain all weekend. ⁵²Please call the event coordinator right away.
M: ⁵²OK. I'll do that.

company retreat 회사 야유회 confirm v. 확인하다 dining hall 식당 attendee n. 참석자 otherwise adv. 그렇지 않으면 outdoor adj. 야외의 facility n. 시설 coordinator n. 책임자

해석
50-52번은 다음 대화에 관한 문제입니다.
여: 안녕하세요, Evan. ⁵⁰회사 야유회를 위한 활동 일정을 만드는 것을 끝냈나요?
남: 아직이요. 저는 여전히 식당이 우리의 참석자들을 모두 수용할 수 있을 만큼 충분히 큰지 확인해야 해요. 그렇지 않으면, ⁵¹야외 식당 시설을 준비해야 할 거예요.
여: 주말 내내 비가 올 예정이에요. ⁵²행사 책임자에게 바로 전화를 해 보세요.
남: ⁵²알겠어요. 그렇게 할게요.

50. 특정 세부 사항 문제
해석 여자는 남자에게 무엇에 대해 묻는가?
(A) 왜 프로젝트 예산이 증가했는지
(B) 저녁 메뉴에 무엇이 포함될 것인지
(C) 행사 장소가 어디에 위치해 있는지
(D) 활동 일정이 만들어졌는지

해설 질문의 핵심 어구(ask ~ about)와 관련된 내용을 주의 깊게 듣는다. 여자는 "Have you finished creating the schedule of activities for the company retreat?"이라며 회사 야유회를 위한 활동 일정을 만드는 것을 끝냈는지 물었다. 따라서 (D)가 정답이다.

어휘 budget n. 예산 venue n. 장소 locate v. 위치하다

51. 의도 파악 문제
해석 여자는 왜 "주말 내내 비가 올 거예요"라고 말하는가?
(A) 지연을 설명하기 위해
(B) 대안을 제안하기 위해
(C) 제안을 승인하기 위해
(D) 방안을 거절하기 위해

해설 질문의 인용어구(It's supposed to rain all weekend)가 언급된 주변을 주의 깊게 듣는다. 남자가 "we'll need to arrange for outdoor dining facilities"라며 야외 식당 시설을 준비해야 할 것이라고 하자, 여자가 "It's supposed to rain all weekend."라며 주말 내내 비가 올 예정이라고 하였다. 이는 야외 식당 시설을 준비할 수 없다는 것으로, 남자의 방안을 거절하기 위함임을 알 수 있다. 따라서 (D)가 정답이다.

어휘 delay n. 지연 alternative n. 대안 approve v. 승인하다
reject v. 거절하다 idea n. 방안, 아이디어

52. 다음에 할 일 문제
해석 남자는 다음에 무엇을 할 것인가?
(A) 전화를 한다.
(B) 장소를 장식한다.
(C) 일기예보를 확인한다.
(D) 시설을 방문한다.

해설 대화의 마지막 부분을 주의 깊게 듣는다. 여자가 "Please call the event coordinator right away."라며 행사 책임자에게 바로 전화를 해 보라고 하자, 남자가 "OK. I'll do that."이라며 그렇게 하겠다고 하였다. 따라서 (A)가 정답이다

53-55 🎧 미국 → 호주

Questions 53-55 refer to the following conversation.

W: Allan, ⁵³did you create this report about our social media page? It's very impressive.
M: Thanks, Whitney. I'll be giving a presentation on my findings in Friday's staff meeting.

W: Oh, really? I have a favor to ask, then. ⁵⁴Would you also be able to gather data about our FAQ page? I mean how often customers click on certain questions.
M: Actually, I don't have access to that information. ⁵⁵Why don't you stop by Greg Adams's office on the third floor? He manages our main Web site, so he would probably be able to help you.
W: OK. Thanks.

finding n. 연구 결과 favor n. 부탁 certain adj. 특정한
access n. 접근 권한 stop by 들르다

해석
53-55번은 다음 대화에 관한 문제입니다.
여: Allan, ⁵³당신이 소셜 미디어 페이지에 대한 이 보고서를 작성했나요? 매우 인상적이에요.
남: 감사해요, Whitney. 금요일 직원회의에서 제 연구 결과에 대해 발표할 거예요.
여: 아, 정말요? 그렇다면, 부탁이 있어요. ⁵⁴FAQ 페이지에 대한 데이터도 수집할 수 있나요? 다시 말해 고객이 특정한 질문을 얼마나 자주 클릭하는지 말이에요.
남: 사실, 저는 그 정보에 접근 권한이 없어요. ⁵⁵3층에 있는 Greg Adams의 사무실에 들르는 것이 어떨까요? 그가 우리의 주요 웹사이트들을 관리해서, 아마도 당신을 도울 수 있을 거예요.
여: 네, 감사해요.

53. 특정 세부 사항 문제
해석 여자는 무엇에 감명받았는가?
(A) 고객 의견
(B) 웹사이트
(C) 슬라이드 쇼 발표
(D) 사업 보고서

해설 질문의 핵심 어구(impressed)와 관련된 내용을 주의 깊게 듣는다. 여자가 "did you create this report about our social media page? It's very impressive."라며 남자에게 소셜 미디어 페이지에 대한 보고서를 작성했는지 물으며 매우 인상적이라고 하였다. 따라서 (D)가 정답이다.

어휘 impressed adj. 감명받은

54. 요청 문제
해석 여자는 남자에게 무엇을 하라고 요청하는가?
(A) 회의를 준비한다.
(B) 피드백을 제공한다.
(C) 설문조사를 진행한다.
(D) 데이터를 수집한다.

해설 여자의 말에서 요청과 관련된 표현이 언급된 다음을 주의 깊게 듣는다. 여자가 "Would you also be able to gather data about our FAQ page?"라며 FAQ 페이지에 대한 데이터를 수집해 달라고 요청하였다. 따라서 (D)가 정답이다.

어휘 conduct v. 진행하다

[Paraphrasing]
gather 수집하다 → Collect 수집하다

55. 제안 문제
해석 남자는 여자에게 무엇을 하라고 제안하는가?
(A) 동료의 사무실에 간다.

(B) 웹사이트에 가입한다.
(C) 인터뷰에 참여한다.
(D) 문서를 확인한다.

해설 남자의 말에서 제안과 관련된 표현이 언급된 다음을 주의 깊게 듣는다. 남자가 "Why don't you stop by Greg Adams's office on the third floor?"라며 3층에 있는 Greg Adams의 사무실에 들르는 것을 제안하였다. 따라서 (A)가 정답이다.

어휘 coworker n. 동료 sign in 가입하다

56-58 [3인] 캐나다 → 영국

Questions 56-58 refer to the following conversation.

> M: ⁵⁶We're all done with your dental work today. Before you go, I want to remind you to use mouthwash every day. ⁵⁷I have some samples here of a new mouthwash product that just came on the market. Please feel free to take one.
> W: Thanks, I'll do that. Um, when should I come in for my next appointment, by the way?
> M: I suggest returning in 12 months for another checkup. ⁵⁸You can set up an appointment at our reception desk.
>
> be done with (~을) 마치다 remind v. 상기시키다
> mouthwash n. 구강 청결제 checkup n. (건강) 검진

해석
56-58번은 다음 대화에 관한 문제입니다.
남: ⁵⁶오늘의 모든 치과 치료를 마쳤어요. 가시기 전에, 매일 구강 청결제를 사용하시는 것을 상기시켜 드리고 싶네요. ⁵⁷여기 시장에 막 나온 새로운 구강 청결제 제품의 견본들이 몇 개 있어요. 부담 없이 하나 가져가세요.
여: 감사해요, 그렇게 할게요. 음, 그런데 다음 예약을 위해 제가 언제 다시 와야 하나요?
남: 다른 검진을 위해 12개월 후에 다시 오시는 것을 권해요. ⁵⁸저희 접수처에서 예약하실 수 있어요.

56. 장소 문제
해석 화자들은 어디에 있는 것 같은가?
(A) 소매점에
(B) 미용실에
(C) 치과에
(D) 체육관에

해설 장소와 관련된 표현을 놓치지 않고 듣는다. 남자가 "We're all done with your dental work today."라며 오늘의 모든 치과 치료를 마쳤다고 한 것을 통해, 화자들이 치과에 있음을 알 수 있다. 따라서 (C)가 정답이다.

어휘 retail outlet 소매점 fitness center 체육관

57. 언급 문제
해설 남자는 제품에 대해 무엇을 말하는가?
(A) 전문가가 추천했다.
(B) 부대용품을 포함한다.
(C) 최근에 출시되었다.
(D) 제한된 시간 동안만 구할 수 있다.

해설 질문의 핵심 어구(product)가 언급된 주변을 주의 깊게 듣는다. 남자가 "I have some samples here of a new mouthwash product that just came on the market."에서 시장에 막 나온 새로운 구강 청결제 제품의 견본들이 몇 개 있다고 하였다. 따라서 (C)가 정답이다.

어휘 accessory n. 부대용품 limited adj. 제한된

> **Paraphrasing**
> just came on the market 시장에 막 나오다 → recently released 최근에 출시되었다

58. 다음에 할 일 문제
해석 여자는 다음에 무엇을 할 것 같은가?
(A) 고객을 만난다.
(B) 안내 책자를 훑어본다.
(C) 고객 설문조사를 완료한다.
(D) 접수처 구역으로 간다.

해설 대화의 마지막 부분을 주의 깊게 듣는다. 남자가 "You can set up an appointment at our reception desk."라며 접수처에서 예약할 수 있다고 한 것을 통해, 여자가 접수처 구역으로 갈 것임을 알 수 있다. 따라서 (D)가 정답이다.

어휘 browse v. 훑어보다, 열람하다

59-61 [3인] 캐나다 → 미국 → 영국

Questions 59-61 refer to the following conversation with three speakers.

> M: I'm a little worried... ⁵⁹Several customers at our grocery store have complained about spoiled produce.
> W1: That's concerning. Maybe we should switch to a new fruit and vegetable supplier.
> M: I'm not sure. We've had a relationship with Brighton Wholesale for nearly 10 years now. What do you think, Beth?
> W2: I'm in favor of making a change. In addition to the quality issue, ⁶⁰their prices are now higher than the market average.
> M: That's a good point. OK... ⁶¹I'll research alternative suppliers and write a report on costs and delivery schedules today.
>
> complain v. 불평하다 spoil v. 상하다 produce n. 농산물
> supplier n. 공급 업체 nearly adv. 거의
> in favor of ~에 찬성하는 average n. 평균
> alternative adj. 대체의

해석
59-61번은 다음 세 명의 대화에 관한 문제입니다.
남: 약간 걱정스러워요... ⁵⁹우리 식료품점의 여러 고객들이 상한 농산물에 대해 불평했어요.
여1: 걱정스럽네요. 아마 새로운 청과물 공급 업체로 바꿔야 할 것 같아요.
남: 잘 모르겠어요. 우리는 지금 거의 10년 동안 Brighton 도매점과 관계를 유지해 왔어요. 어떻게 생각하나요, Beth?
여2: 저는 변경하는 것에 찬성해요. 품질 문제뿐만 아니라, ⁶⁰그들의 가격이 이제 시장 평균보다 높아요.
남: 좋은 지적이네요. 알겠어요... ⁶¹제가 오늘 대체 공급 업체들을 조사하고 가격 및 배송 일정에 대한 보고서를 작성할게요.

59. 화자 문제

해석 화자들은 어디에서 일하는 것 같은가?
(A) 백화점에서
(B) 슈퍼마켓에서
(C) 전자제품 가게에서
(D) 약국에서

해설 대화에서 신분 및 직업과 관련된 표현을 놓치지 않고 듣는다. 남자가 "Several customers at our grocery store have complained about spoiled produce."라며 우리 식료품점의 여러 고객들이 상한 농산물에 대해 불평했다고 한 것을 통해 화자들이 슈퍼마켓에서 일하고 있음을 알 수 있다. 따라서 (B)가 정답이다.

어휘 electronics n. 전자제품   pharmacy n. 약국

60. 언급 문제

해석 Beth는 Brighton 도매점에 대해 무엇을 말하는가?
(A) 시설이 오래되었다.
(B) 직원들이 연락하기 힘들다.
(C) 배송이 늦다.
(D) 제품이 비싸다.

해설 질문의 핵심 어구(Brighton Wholesale)와 관련된 내용을 주의 깊게 듣는다. 여자2[Beth]가 "their[Brighton Wholesale] prices are now higher than the market average"라며 Brighton 도매점의 가격이 이제 시장 평균보다 높다고 하였다. 따라서 (D)가 정답이다.

61. 다음에 할 일 문제

해석 남자는 오늘 무엇을 할 것 같은가?
(A) 보고서를 작성한다.
(B) 일정을 업데이트한다.
(C) 회의에 참석한다.
(D) 할인을 요청한다.

해설 대화의 마지막 부분을 주의 깊게 듣는다. 남자가 "I'll ~ write a report on costs and delivery schedules today."라며 오늘 가격 및 배송 일정에 대한 보고서를 작성하겠다고 하였다. 따라서 (A)가 정답이다.

62-64 영국 → 호주

Questions 62-64 refer to the following conversation and list.

W: Excuse me. ⁶²**I'm considering purchasing one of the paintings on display.** I'm just wondering if the prices are negotiable.
M: Well, that depends . . . ⁶³**Which one are you interested in?**
W: Um, ⁶³***Forgotten Forest**. It's really beautiful.*
M: ⁶³**I'll contact the artist** to find out if she would consider reducing the price. Then, I'll call you when I get an answer. ⁶⁴**Could you provide me with your phone number?**
W: ⁶⁴**Sure.** Let me write it down for you. And if the artist wants to discuss this matter in person, I'm happy to meet with her.

on display 전시된   **negotiable** adj. 협상 가능한
reduce v. 낮추다   **matter** n. 문제   **in person** 직접

해석
62-64번은 다음 대화와 목록에 대한 문제입니다.

여: 실례합니다. ⁶²전시된 그림 중 하나를 구매하려고 생각 중이에요. 그저 가격이 협상 가능한지 궁금해서요.
남: 음, 무엇인지에 따라서요... ⁶³어떤 것에 관심이 있으신가요?
여: 음, ⁶³*Forgotten Forest*요. 그건 정말 아름다워요.
남: ⁶³그 화가분께 연락해서 가격을 낮추는 것을 고려할 것인지 알아볼게요. 그러고 나서, 답변을 받으면 전화드릴게요. ⁶⁴전화번호를 주시겠어요?
여: ⁶⁴물론이죠. 제가 적어드릴게요. 그리고 만약 작가가 이 문제를 직접 논의하고 싶어 한다면, 그녀를 만나고 싶어요.

Preston 화랑 주요 작품	
제목	화가
Peaceful Lands	Denise Brown
Forgotten Forest	⁶³Clarissa Reed
Midnight Blue	Sandra Martinez
Mountain Song	Sunhee Kang

62. 특정 세부 사항 문제

해석 여자는 무엇을 하고 싶어 하는가?
(A) 모금 행사를 연다.
(B) 전시회를 본다.
(C) 구매를 한다.
(D) 제품을 추천한다.

해설 질문의 핵심 어구(want to do)와 관련된 내용을 주의 깊게 듣는다. 여자가 "I'm considering purchasing one of the paintings on display."라며 전시된 그림 중 하나를 구매하려고 생각 중이라고 하였다. 따라서 (C)가 정답이다.

어휘 view v. 보다   exhibit n. 전시회

63. 시각 자료 문제

해석 시각 자료를 보아라. 남자는 어느 화가에게 연락할 것이라고 말하는가?
(A) Denise Brown
(B) Clarissa Reed
(C) Sandra Martinez
(D) Sunhee Kang

해설 제시된 목록의 정보를 확인한 후 질문의 핵심 어구(artist ~ contact)와 관련된 내용을 주의 깊게 듣는다. 남자가 "Which one are you interested in?"이라며 어떤 것에 관심이 있는지 묻자, 여자가 "*Forgotten Forest*. It's really beautiful."이라며 *Forgotten Forest*가 정말 아름답다고 하자, 남자가 "I'll contact the artist"라며 그 화가에게 연락하겠다고 하였다. 목록에서 *Forgotten Forest*의 화가는 Clarissa Reed임을 알 수 있다. 따라서 (B)가 정답이다.

64. 특정 세부 사항 문제

해석 여자는 무엇을 하기로 동의하는가?
(A) 우편 주소를 적는다.
(B) 주문 양식을 작성한다.
(C) 전화번호를 제공한다.
(D) 약속 시간을 변경한다.

해설 질문의 핵심 어구(woman agree to do)와 관련된 내용을 주

의 깊게 듣는다. 남자가 "Could you provide me with your phone number?"라며 전화번호를 주겠냐고 묻자, 여자가 "Sure."라며 물론이라고 하였다. 따라서 (C)가 정답이다.

어휘 mailing address 우편 주소 order n. 주문

65-67 [3m] 미국 → 캐나다

Questions 65-67 refer to the following conversation and schedule.

W: Hi, David. ⁶⁵I checked the National Weather Agency's Web site this morning. It looks like the temperature might get as high as 95 degrees Fahrenheit next week.

M: Yeah, summer has come early this year. It's probably time to change our sprinkler system schedule so that the plants can stay healthy.

W: ⁶⁶I'll call the maintenance manager today to adjust the system settings. I'll ask him to give each of the landscaping zones a half hour more of watering.

M: Um . . . That may be fine for our lawns and bushes, but ⁶⁷I don't think our cactus garden needs any extra water—15 minutes is enough.

W: Good point.

maintenance n. 정비, 유지·보수 adjust v. 조정하다
setting n. 설정 landscaping n. 조경 lawn n. 잔디밭
cactus n. 선인장

해석
65-67번은 다음 대화와 일정표에 관한 문제입니다.

여: 안녕하세요, David. ⁶⁵오늘 아침에 국립 기상청의 웹사이트를 확인했어요. 다음 주에 기온이 화씨 95도까지 올라갈 것 같아요.
남: 네, 올해는 여름이 일찍 왔네요. 식물들이 건강하게 유지될 수 있도록 우리 스프링클러 시스템 일정을 변경해야 할 때인 것 같아요.
여: ⁶⁶오늘 정비 관리자에게 전화해서 시스템 설정을 조정하도록 할게요. 그에게 각각의 조경 구역에 30분씩 더 물을 주라고 부탁할게요.
남: 음... 잔디밭과 관목에는 괜찮을지 모르겠지만, ⁶⁷선인장 정원은 물이 더 필요하지 않을 것 같고, 15분이면 충분해요.
여: 좋은 지적이에요.

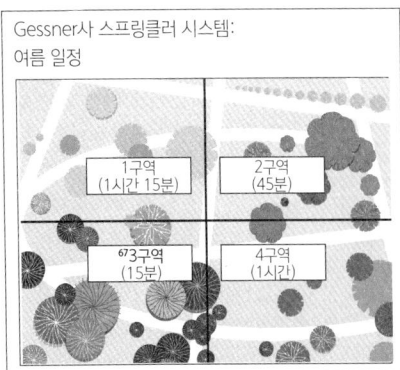

65. 특정 세부 사항 문제

해석 여자는 오늘 아침에 무엇을 했는가?
(A) 라디오 쇼를 들었다.
(B) 웹사이트에 방문했다.
(C) 신문을 읽었다.
(D) TV 프로그램을 보았다.

해설 질문의 핵심 어구(this morning)가 언급된 주변을 주의 깊게 듣는다. 여자가 "I checked the National Weather Agency's Web site this morning."이라며 오늘 아침에 국립 기상청의 웹사이트를 확인했다고 하였다. 따라서 (B)가 정답이다.

66. 이유 문제

해석 여자는 왜 정비 관리자에게 연락할 것인가?
(A) 새로운 장비를 설치하는 것을 요청하기 위해
(B) 몇몇 식물들의 건강 상태를 점검하기 위해
(C) 최근 수리에 관해 문의하기 위해
(D) 설정을 변경하는 것을 요청하기 위해

해설 질문의 핵심 어구(contact ~ maintenance manager)와 관련된 내용을 주의 깊게 듣는다. 여자가 "I'll call the maintenance manager today to adjust the system settings."라며 오늘 정비 관리자에게 전화해서 시스템 설정을 조정하도록 하겠다고 하였다. 따라서 (D)가 정답이다.

어휘 equipment n. 장비 install v. 설치하다 inquire v. 문의하다

67. 시각 자료 문제

해석 시각 자료를 보아라. 선인장 정원은 어디에 위치해 있는가?
(A) 1구역에
(B) 2구역에
(C) 3구역에
(D) 4구역에

해설 제시된 일정표의 정보를 확인한 후 질문의 핵심 어구(cactus garden)와 관련된 내용을 주의 깊게 듣는다. 남자가 "I don't think our cactus garden needs any extra water—15 minutes is enough."라며 선인장 정원은 물이 더 필요하지 않을 것 같고, 15분이면 충분하다고 하였다. 일정표에서 물을 15분 주는 곳은 3구역임을 알 수 있다. 따라서 (C)가 정답이다.

68-70 [3m] 미국 → 호주

Questions 68-70 refer to the following conversation and coupon.

W: How's your part of the budget report coming along, Oliver?

M: I'm making steady progress, but ⁶⁸I'll be staying late to finish it. Do you think your section will be done before 6 o'clock?

W: Unfortunately not. ⁶⁸I'm also going to have to work overtime tonight. Should we get some food delivered?

M: That's a good idea. Some other marketing team members will be working late as well. ⁶⁹So there will be five people, including us.

W: Got it. And I just remembered that I have a coupon for Spring Peony.

M: Great. ⁷⁰Why don't you call the restaurant now and ask for a meal set to be delivered?

steady adj. 꾸준한   progress n. 진행, 진전
unfortunately adv. 유감스럽게도
work overtime 초과 근무를 하다

해석

68-70번은 다음 대화와 쿠폰에 관한 문제입니다.

여: 예산 보고서의 당신 부분은 어떻게 되어 가나요, Oliver?
남: 꾸준히 진행하고 있지만, ⁶⁸그것을 끝내기 위해서 늦게까지 있을 거예요. 6시 전에 당신의 부분이 완성될 것이라고 생각하시나요?
여: 유감스럽게도 아니에요. ⁶⁸저도 오늘 밤 초과 근무를 해야 할 거예요. 우리 음식을 배달시킬까요?
남: 좋은 생각이에요. 다른 마케팅 팀원들도 늦게까지 일할 거예요. ⁶⁹그래서 우리를 포함해서, 다섯 사람이 되겠네요.
여: 알겠어요. 그리고 방금 제게 Spring Peony의 쿠폰이 있다는 것이 기억났어요.
남: 좋아요. ⁷⁰지금 그 식당에 전화해서 식사 세트를 배달해 달라고 요청해 보는 건 어떨까요?

```
Spring Peony 중국 음식점
저희 메뉴를 위해 이 쿠폰을 제시하세요.

Noodle 세트(10% 할인)       *2인분
Dumpling 세트(10% 할인)     *3인분
Phoenix 세트(20% 할인)      *4인분
⁶⁹Dragon 세트(25% 할인)     *5인분
                              9월 30일 만료
```

68. 특정 세부 사항 문제

해석 화자들은 오늘 무엇을 해야 하는가?
(A) 초과 근무를 한다.
(B) 마케팅 자료를 재검토한다.
(C) 팀원들과 만난다.
(D) 차편을 준비한다.

해설 질문의 핵심 어구(must ~ do today)와 관련된 내용을 주의 깊게 듣는다. 남자가 "I'll be staying late to finish it[budget report]"이라며 예산 보고서를 끝내기 위해서 늦게까지 있을 것이라고 하자, 여자가 "I'm also going to have to work overtime tonight."이라며 자신도 오늘 밤 초과 근무를 해야 할 것이라고 하였다. 따라서 (A)가 정답이다.

어휘 review v. 재검토하다   transportation n. 차편, 교통수단

69. 시각 자료 문제

해석 시각 자료를 보아라. 어떤 세트가 가장 적합할 것인가?
(A) Noodle 세트
(B) Dumpling 세트
(C) Phoenix 세트
(D) Dragon 세트

해설 제시된 쿠폰의 정보를 확인한 후 질문의 핵심 어구(set ~ suitable)와 관련된 내용을 주의 깊게 듣는다. 남자가 "So there will be five people, including us."라며 그들을 포함해서 다섯 사람이 되겠다고 하였다. 쿠폰에서 5인분은 Dragon 세트이므로, Dragon 세트가 가장 적합할 것임을 알 수 있다. 따라서 (D)가 정답이다.

70. 요청 문제

해석 남자는 여자에게 무엇을 하라고 요청하는가?
(A) 쿠폰을 다운로드한다.
(B) 주문을 한다.
(C) 예약을 한다.
(D) 동료에게 전화한다.

해설 남자의 말에서 요청과 관련된 표현이 언급된 다음을 주의 깊게 듣는다. 남자가 여자에게 "Why don't you call the restaurant now and ask for a meal set to be delivered?"라며 지금 식당에 전화해서 식사를 배달해 달라고 요청해 보는 건 어떤지 물었다. 따라서 (B)가 정답이다.

어휘 coworker n. 동료

PART 4

71-73 캐나다

Questions 71-73 refer to the following announcement.

Before you start today's shift, I have an announcement. As most of you know, Dennis Lyon left the company. ⁷¹Until we find a replacement delivery truck driver, you will all have a heavier workload than usual. In a few moments, ⁷²I'll give everyone an updated route map with the additional areas you will need to cover. If anything about your new route is unclear, ⁷³I encourage you to stop by my office and discuss it with me.

shift n. 교대 근무   announcement n. 공지, 발표
replacement n. 대체, 교체   workload n. 업무량
updated adj. 최신의   route map 노선도

해석

71-73번은 다음 공지에 관한 문제입니다.

오늘의 교대 근무를 시작하기 전에, 공지가 있습니다. 여러분 대부분이 아시다시피, Dennis Lyon이 회사를 떠났습니다. ⁷¹대체할 수 있는 배달 트럭 운전자를 찾기 전까지, 여러분 모두가 평소보다 많은 업무량을 갖게 될 것입니다. 곧, ⁷²여러분 모두에게 담당해야 할 추가적인 지역들이 있는 최신 노선도를 드리겠습니다. 여러분의 새로운 노선에 대해 분명하지 않은 게 있다면, ⁷³제 사무실에 들러서 저와 상의하시기를 권장합니다.

71. 청자 문제

해석 청자들은 누구일 것 같은가?
(A) 자동차 정비공
(B) 창고 작업자
(C) 회사 임원
(D) 배달원

해설 지문에서 신분 및 직업과 관련된 표현을 놓치지 않고 듣는다. "Until we find a replacement delivery truck driver, you will all have a heavier workload than usual."이라며 대체할 수 있는 배달 트럭 운전자를 찾기 전까지 모두가 평소보다 많은 업무량을 갖게 될 것이라고 한 것을 통해, 청자들이 배달원임을 알 수 있다. 따라서 (D)가 정답이다.

어휘 auto mechanic 자동차 정비공

PART 4   57

72. 특정 세부 사항 문제

해석 무엇이 청자들에게 주어질 것인가?
(A) 노선도
(B) 평가서
(C) 직원 수칙
(D) 신분증

해설 질문의 핵심 어구(be given)와 관련된 내용을 주의 깊게 듣는다. "I'll give everyone an updated route map"이라며 여러분 모두에게 최신 노선도를 주겠다고 하였다. 따라서 (A)가 정답이다.

어휘 identification card 신분증

73. 제안 문제

해석 화자는 무엇을 제안하는가?
(A) 문서를 출력하기
(B) 이메일을 보내기
(C) 사무실을 방문하기
(D) 설문조사를 완료하기

해설 지문에서 제안과 관련된 표현이 포함된 문장을 주의 깊게 듣는다. "I encourage you to stop by my office and discuss it with me."라며 자신의 사무실에 들러서 자신과 상의하기를 권장한다고 하였다. 따라서 (C)가 정답이다.

Paraphrasing
stop by 들르다 → Visiting 방문하기

74-76 🎧 미국

Questions 74-76 refer to the following telephone message.

> Hello, Mr. Preston. This is Annie Chow. ⁷⁴I'm calling regarding the remodeling work your company recently did over at my new house. I stopped by the property this morning, and ⁷⁵I'm very pleased with how the living room turned out. As for the kitchen, though, I don't think we made the right choice. ⁷⁵The light tan color we originally considered would work better. ⁷⁶Let's meet tomorrow morning to discuss how much more I will need to pay to have your crew do it over.
>
> regarding prep. ~에 관하여 property n. 건물
> turn out (~ 결과로) 되다, 나타나다 choice n. 선택
> crew n. 직원

해석
74-76번은 전화 메시지에 관한 문제입니다.
안녕하세요, Mr. Preston. 저는 Annie Chow에요. ⁷⁴저는 당신의 회사가 최근에 제 새로운 집에서 했던 리모델링 작업에 관해 전화드립니다. 저는 오늘 아침에 그 건물에 들렀고, ⁷⁵거실이 작업된 상태에 대해 매우 만족스럽습니다. 하지만, 주방에 대해서는, 우리가 올바른 선택을 한 것 같지 않아요. ⁷⁵우리가 원래 고려했던 밝은 황갈색 색상이 더 잘 어울릴 것 같습니다. ⁷⁶내일 아침에 만나서 당신의 직원들이 이 일을 다시 하는 데 제가 얼마나 더 지불해야 할지 논의하도록 합시다.

74. 주제 문제

해석 메시지는 주로 무엇에 관한 것인가?
(A) 개조 계획
(B) 정부 감사
(C) 지불 방법
(D) 장치 설치

해설 메시지의 주제를 묻는 문제이므로, 지문의 초반을 반드시 듣는다. "I'm calling regarding the remodeling work your company recently did"라며 청자의 회사가 최근에 했던 리모델링 작업에 관해 전화한다고 한 후, 개조 계획에 대한 내용으로 지문이 이어지고 있다. 따라서 (A)가 정답이다.

어휘 renovation n. 개조, 보수 inspection n. 감사, 점검

Paraphrasing
remodeling work 리모델링 작업 → renovation project 개조 계획

75. 의도 파악 문제

해석 화자는 "우리가 올바른 선택을 한 것 같지 않아요"라고 말할 때 무엇을 의도하는가?
(A) 고객이 불만을 제기할 것이다.
(B) 작업이 다시 되어야 한다.
(C) 회사는 환불을 제공해야 한다.
(D) 서비스가 취소되어야 한다.

해설 질문의 인용어구(I don't think we made the right choice)가 언급된 주변을 주의 깊게 듣는다. "I'm very pleased with how the living room turned out"이라며 거실이 작업된 상태에 대해 매우 만족스럽다고 한 후, "As for the kitchen, though, I don't think we made the right choice. The light tan color we originally considered would work better."라며 하지만 주방에 대해서는 올바른 선택을 한 것 같지 않으며 원래 고려했던 밝은 황갈색 색상이 더 잘 어울릴 것 같다고 하였다. 이를 통해, 거실 작업이 다시 되어야 한다는 것을 알 수 있다. 따라서 (B)가 정답이다.

어휘 complaint n. 불만 task n. 작업 redo v. 다시 하다

76. 특정 세부 사항 문제

해석 화자는 내일 무엇을 논의하고 싶어 하는가?
(A) 장비 업그레이드
(B) 공사 일정
(C) 작업자의 가능 여부
(D) 추가 비용

해설 질문의 핵심 어구(discuss tomorrow)와 관련된 내용을 주의 깊게 듣는다. "Let's meet tomorrow morning to discuss how much more I will need to pay"라며 내일 아침에 만나서 자신이 얼마나 더 지불해야 할지 논의하자고 하였다. 따라서 (D)가 정답이다.

어휘 construction n. 공사 availability n. 이용 가능성 additional adj. 추가의

Paraphrasing
how much more ~ will need to pay 얼마나 더 지불해야 할지 → additional expense 추가 비용

77-79 🎧 영국

Questions 77-79 refer to the following excerpt from a meeting.

> ⁷⁷I've called this meeting to discuss an issue we've had here at our airport. Over the last two months, ⁷⁸many passengers have complained because their suitcases were sent to the wrong city. As baggage personnel, we've

got to correct the situation. Donald Davidson, a representative from our carrier's corporate headquarters, has come up with a solution. ⁷⁹I've invited Mr. Davidson to go over the strategy, but he's running behind schedule because of traffic. Hopefully, he'll get here shortly and explain what he wants us to do.

baggage n. 수하물 personnel n. 직원
carrier n. 항공사, 수송회사 headquarters n. 본사
come up with 제시하다 go over 검토하다
behind schedule 일정이 늦은 shortly adv. 곧

해석
77-79번은 다음 회의 발췌에 관한 문제입니다.
⁷⁷저는 이곳 공항에서 우리가 겪어 왔던 문제에 대해 논의하기 위해 이 회의를 소집했습니다. 지난 2개월 동안, ⁷⁸많은 승객들이 그들의 여행 가방이 잘못된 도시로 보내져 불만을 제기했습니다. 수하물 담당 직원으로서, 우리는 이 상황을 바로잡아야 합니다. 우리 항공사의 본사 대표인 Donald Davidson이 해결책을 제시했습니다. ⁷⁹저는 그 전략을 검토하기 위해 Mr. Davidson을 초대했지만, 그는 교통 때문에 일정이 늦어지고 있습니다. 바라건대, 그가 곧 여기에 도착해서 우리가 어떻게 하기를 원하는지를 설명할 것입니다.

77. 청자 문제
해석 청자들은 어디에서 일하는 것 같은가?
(A) 버스 정류장에서
(B) 본사에서
(C) 공항에서
(D) 운동 시설에서

해설 지문에서 신분 및 직업과 관련된 표현을 놓치지 않고 듣는다. "I've called this meeting to discuss an issue we've had here at our airport."라며 이곳 공항에서 우리가 겪어 왔던 문제에 대해 논의하기 위해 이 회의를 소집했다고 한 것을 통해, 청자들이 공항에서 일하고 있음을 알 수 있다. 따라서 (C)가 정답이다.

어휘 sports facility 운동 시설

78. 이유 문제
해석 왜 몇몇 사람들이 불만을 제기했는가?
(A) 소지품이 올바른 목적지에 도착하지 못했다.
(B) 승객들이 같은 좌석에 배정되었다.
(C) 줄이 너무 길었다.
(D) 직원들이 정책에 익숙하지 않다.

해설 질문의 핵심 어구(complaints)와 관련된 내용을 주의 깊게 듣는다. "many passengers have complained because their suitcases were sent to the wrong city"라며 많은 승객들이 그들의 여행 가방이 잘못된 도시로 보내져 불만을 제기했다고 하였다. 따라서 (A)가 정답이다.

어휘 belongings n. 소지품 assign v. 배정하다
be familiar with ~에 익숙하다

Paraphrasing
suitcases were sent to the wrong city 여행 가방이 잘못된 도시로 보내졌다 → Belongings did not reach the right destination 소지품이 올바른 목적지에 도착하지 못했다

79. 언급 문제
해석 화자는 Mr. Davidson에 대해 무엇을 말하는가?
(A) 양식을 배포할 것이다.

(B) 고객과 만났다.
(C) 최근에 승진했다.
(D) 회의에 늦었다.

해설 질문의 핵심 어구(Mr. Davidson)가 언급된 주변을 주의 깊게 듣는다. "I've invited Mr. Davidson to go over the strategy, but he's running behind schedule because of traffic."이라며 그 전략을 검토하기 위해 Mr. Davidson을 초대했지만, 그가 교통 때문에 일정이 늦어지고 있다고 하였다. 따라서 (D)가 정답이다.

Paraphrasing
running behind schedule 일정이 늦어지다 → late 늦은

80-82 🎧 호주
Questions 80-82 refer to the following introduction.

Everyone, I'd like your attention for a moment. ⁸⁰I'm pleased to introduce you to the new head of our magazine's editing department, Carla Gomez. ⁸¹Ms. Gomez has never worked with fashion content, but she has experience managing online news feeds. We do not currently have one on our Web site, but this feature will be added. Also, the teams in the editing department will be reorganized. ⁸²Ms. Gomez will announce more details about that at Tuesday's staff meeting. But, for now, please welcome Ms. Gomez to our company.

attention n. 집중 editing n. 편집 department n. 부서
manage v. 관리하다 reorganize v. 재구성하다

해석
80-82번은 다음 소개에 관한 문제입니다.
여러분, 잠깐 집중해 주세요. ⁸⁰우리 잡지 편집부의 새로운 책임자인 Carla Gomez를 소개하게 되어 기쁩니다. ⁸¹Ms. Gomez는 패션 콘텐츠를 작업한 적은 없지만, 온라인 뉴스 피드를 관리한 경험이 있습니다. 우리 웹사이트는 현재 이것을 포함하지 않지만, 이 기능이 추가될 것입니다. 또한, 편집부의 팀이 재구성될 것입니다. ⁸²Ms. Gomez가 화요일 직원회의에서 더 자세한 내용을 공지할 것입니다. 하지만, 지금은 우리 회사로 오신 Ms. Gomez를 환영해 주시길 바랍니다.

80. 특정 세부 사항 문제
해석 Carla Gomez는 누구인가?
(A) 편집 관리자
(B) 컴퓨터 기술자
(C) 뉴스 기자
(D) 웹사이트 디자이너

해설 질문 대상(Carla Gomez)의 신분 및 직업과 관련된 표현을 놓치지 않고 듣는다. "I'm pleased to introduce you to the new head of our magazine's editing department, Carla Gomez."라며 Carla Gomez가 잡지 편집부의 새로운 책임자라고 하였다. 따라서 (A)가 정답이다.

어휘 technician n. 기술자 reporter n. 기자

81. 의도 파악 문제
해설 화자는 "이 기능이 추가될 것입니다"라고 말할 때 무엇을 의도하는가?
(A) 웹사이트의 디자인이 구식이다.
(B) 관리자의 전문 지식이 중요하다.

(C) 잡지의 인기도가 하락했다.
(D) 직원의 할당 업무가 변경되었다.

해설 질문의 인용어구(this feature will be added)가 언급된 주변을 주의 깊게 듣는다. "Ms. Gomez ~ has experience managing online news feeds."라며 Ms. Gomez가 온라인 뉴스 피드를 관리한 경험이 있다고 한 후, "We do not currently have one on our Web site, but this feature will be added."라며 그들의 웹사이트는 현재 온라인 뉴스 피드를 포함하지 않지만 이 기능이 추가될 것이라고 한 것을 통해, 온라인 뉴스 피드에 대한 관리자의 전문 지식이 중요하다는 것을 알 수 있다. 따라서 (B)가 정답이다.

어휘 outdated adj. 구식인 expertise n. 전문 지식
popularity n. 인기 decline v. 하락하다

82. 다음에 할 일 문제

해석 회의에서 무슨 일이 일어날 것인가?
(A) 팀에서 비디오를 보여줄 것이다.
(B) 회사 회장이 이야기할 것이다.
(C) 공지가 있을 것이다.
(D) 채용 과정이 설명될 것이다.

해설 질문의 핵심 어구(meeting)가 언급된 주변을 주의 깊게 듣는다. "Ms. Gomez will announce more details about that at Tuesday's staff meeting."이라며 Ms. Gomez가 화요일 직원회의에서 더 자세한 내용을 공지할 것임을 알 수 있다. 따라서 (C)가 정답이다.

어휘 hire v. 채용하다 process n. 과정

83-85 [미국]

Questions 83-85 refer to the following excerpt from a meeting.

I'd like to begin today by announcing that [83]we're going to discontinue one of our products, the Crest digital watch. Although [83]we hoped that the watch would be popular among swimmers because it can be used in water, its sales have failed to meet expectations. [84]This is likely because the product received negative reviews in several technology publications, including the very popular magazine *Gadgets*. [85]We were planning to issue a press release regarding the decision tomorrow. However, [85]we've had to put that off until Friday. We need more time to determine the precise date that production will end.

discontinue v. ~의 생산을 중단하다 sales n. 판매량
expectation n. 기대 publication n. 간행물
press release 언론 공식 발표 put ~ off (시간·날짜를) 미루다
precise adj. 정확한 production n. 생산

해석
83-85번은 다음 회의 발췌에 관한 문제입니다.

[83]우리 제품 중 하나인 Crest 디지털시계의 생산을 중단하겠다는 것을 발표함으로써 오늘 회의를 시작하고 싶습니다. [83]우리는 이 시계가 수중에서 사용될 수 있기 때문에 수영하는 사람들에게 인기가 있기를 희망했지만, 판매량이 기대에 미치지 못했어요. [84]이는 아마 제품이 매우 인기 있는 잡지 *Gadgets*지를 포함한 여러 기술 관련 간행물에서 부정적인 평가를 받았기 때문일 것입니다. [85]내일 이 결정에 관한 [85]언론 공식 발표를 할 계획이었습니다. 하지만, [85]우리는 금요일까지 그것을 미뤄야 했습니다. 생산이 끝나는 정확한 날짜를 결정하는 데 더 많은 시간이 필요합니다.

83. 특정 세부 사항 문제

해석 화자는 무엇의 생산이 중단되었다고 말하는가?
(A) 개인용 컴퓨터
(B) 스마트폰 모델
(C) 건강 추적 장치
(D) 방수 시계

해설 질문의 핵심 어구(discontinued)와 관련된 내용을 주의 깊게 듣는다. "we're going to discontinue one of our products, the Crest digital watch"라며 제품 중 하나인 Crest 디지털시계의 생산을 중단하겠다고 한 후, "we hoped that the watch would be popular ~ because it can be used in water"라며 이 시계가 수중에서 사용될 수 있기 때문에 인기가 있기를 희망했다고 하였다. 따라서 (D)가 정답이다.

어휘 waterproof adj. 방수의

84. 특정 세부 사항 문제

해석 화자에 따르면, *Gadgets*지에는 무엇이 포함되어 있는가?
(A) 가격 비교
(B) 회사 개요
(C) 신청서
(D) 제품 평가

해설 질문의 핵심 어구(*Gadgets*)가 언급된 주변을 주의 깊게 듣는다. "This is likely because the product received negative reviews in ~ the very popular magazine *Gadgets*."라며 이는 아마 제품이 매우 인기 있는 잡지 *Gadgets*지에서 부정적인 평가를 받았기 때문일 것이라고 하였다. 따라서 (D)가 정답이다.

어휘 comparison n. 비교 profile n. 개요

85. 이유 문제

해석 왜 언론 공식 발표가 지연되었는가?
(A) 임원이 출장 중이다.
(B) 제품이 출시될 준비가 되지 않았다.
(C) 날짜가 확정되어야 한다.
(D) 성명서가 승인되어야 한다.

해설 질문의 핵심 어구(press release delayed)와 관련된 내용을 주의 깊게 듣는다. "We were planning to issue a press release"라며 언론 공식 발표를 할 계획이었다고 한 후, "we've had to put that off until Friday. We need more time to determine the precise date that production will end."라며 금요일까지 그것을 미뤄야 했으며 생산이 끝나는 정확한 날짜를 결정하는 데 더 많은 시간이 필요하다고 하였다. 따라서 (C)가 정답이다.

어휘 executive n. 임원 finalize v. 확정하다
statement n. 성명서

[Paraphrasing]
determine the precise date 정확한 날짜를 결정하다 →
A date needs to be finalized 날짜가 확정되어야 한다

86-88 [캐나다]

Questions 86-88 refer to the following talk.

OK, everyone. The summer holiday season has just started, and [86]more couples and families are coming to our restaurant. In response,

87we opened a new outdoor seating area. The new area will certainly make more space for the additional customers. I also want to remind you about the rule for trading shifts. **88If you want to change shifts, you must inform me two days in advance.** This will keep things running smoothly.

holiday n. 휴가 in response 이에 대응하여
certainly adv. 분명히 additional adj. 추가의
trade v. 맞바꾸다, 거래하다 shift n. 교대 근무 시간
inform v. 알리다 in advance 미리, 사전에

해석
86-88번은 다음 담화에 관한 문제입니다.
좋습니다, 여러분. 여름휴가 시즌이 이제 막 시작해서, 86더 많은 연인들과 가족들이 우리 레스토랑에 올 것입니다. 이에 대응하여, 87우리는 새로운 야외 좌석 구역을 개방했습니다. 새 구역은 분명히 추가 고객들을 위한 공간을 더 만들 것입니다. 저는 또한 교대 근무 시간을 맞바꾸는 규칙에 대해 상기시켜 드리고 싶습니다. 88만약 교대 근무 시간을 바꾸고 싶으시다면, 이틀 전에 미리 제게 알려주셔야 합니다. 이는 일이 원활하게 진행되도록 해줄 것입니다.

86. 청자 문제
해설 청자들은 어디에서 일하는가?
(A) 항공사에서
(B) 파티 기획 회사에서
(C) 식당에서
(D) 채용 대행사에서

해설 지문에서 신분 및 직업과 관련된 표현을 놓치지 않고 듣는다. "more couples and families are coming to our restaurant"이라며 더 많은 연인들과 가족들이 우리 레스토랑에 올 것이라고 한 것을 통해 청자들이 식당에서 일한다는 것을 알 수 있다. 따라서 (C)가 정답이다.

어휘 corporation n. 회사, 업체 staffing agency 채용 대행사

87. 특정 세부 사항 문제
해설 업체는 최근에 무엇을 했는가?
(A) 새로운 건물로 이전했다.
(B) 고문을 고용했다.
(C) 고객들에게 할인을 제공했다.
(D) 야외 공간을 열었다.

해설 질문의 핵심 어구(business recently do)와 관련된 내용을 주의 깊게 듣는다. "we[restaurant] opened a new outdoor seating area"라며 식당이 새로운 야외 좌석 구역을 개방했다고 하였다. 따라서 (D)가 정답이다.

88. 의도 파악 문제
해설 화자는 왜 "이는 일이 원활하게 진행되도록 해줄 것입니다"라고 말하는가?
(A) 정책의 중요성을 강조하기 위해
(B) 제품의 이점을 설명하기 위해
(C) 절차에 변경 사항을 도입하기 위해
(D) 계획에 대해 개선을 제안하기 위해

해설 질문의 인용어구(This will keep things running smoothly)가 언급된 주변을 주의 깊게 듣는다. "If you want to change shifts, you must inform me two days in advance."라며 교대 근무 시간을 바꾸고 싶다면, 이틀 전에 미리 알려달라고 한 것을 통해, 근무 시간 관련 정책의 중요성을 강조하기 위함

임을 알 수 있다. 따라서 (A)가 정답이다.

어휘 emphasize v. 강조하다 importance n. 중요성
benefit n. 이점 procedure n. 절차 improvement n. 개선

89-91 3m 호주
Questions 89-91 refer to the following talk.

Now, **89if you look in the center of the hall, you'll see our final statue.** It is called *Lioness*. It stands almost six feet tall and features a female lion jumping into the air. **90Made by a famous Greek artist nearly 2,000 years ago, *Lioness* is the most famous artifact in our museum.** Images of it have been printed in history books around the world. All right, that concludes your tour. **91I want to thank you all for coming and suggest that you pick up a brochure before you leave.** It contains information about upcoming exhibits.

feature v. ~을 특징으로 삼다 artifact n. 공예품
conclude v. 마치다, 끝내다 contain v. 포함하다

해석
89-91번은 다음 담화에 관한 문제입니다.
이제, 89복도 중앙을 살펴보시면, 마지막 동상을 보실 것입니다. 그것은 *Lioness*라고 불리죠. 높이는 약 6피트이며 공중으로 뛰어오르는 암사자의 모습을 특징으로 삼고 있습니다. 90거의 2,000년 전에 유명한 그리스 예술가에 의해 만들어진 *Lioness*는 우리 박물관에서 가장 유명한 공예품입니다. 그것의 이미지는 전 세계의 역사책에 인쇄되어 있죠. 좋아요, 그것으로 우리 투어를 마칩니다. 91와주신 모든 분들께 감사드리며 떠나시기 전에 안내서를 가져가실 것을 제안드립니다. 그것은 앞으로의 전시회들에 대한 정보를 포함하고 있습니다.

89. 특정 세부 사항 문제
해설 화자에 따르면, 복도 중앙에 무엇이 위치해 있는가?
(A) 모니터
(B) 사진
(C) 표지판
(D) 동상

해설 질문의 핵심 어구(center of the hall)가 언급된 주변을 주의 깊게 듣는다. "if you look in the center of the hall, you'll see our final statue"라며 복도 중앙을 살펴보면, 마지막 동상을 볼 것이라고 하였다. 따라서 (D)가 정답이다.

어휘 sign n. 표지판, 간판

90. 언급 문제
해설 *Lioness*에 대해 무엇이 언급되는가?
(A) 잘 알려져 있지 않다.
(B) 부분적으로 훼손되었다.
(C) 부적절하게 명칭이 붙었다.
(D) 수천 년이 되었다.

해설 질문의 핵심 어구(*Lioness*)가 언급된 주변을 주의 깊게 듣는다. "Made ~ nearly 2,000 years ago, *Lioness* is the most famous artifact in our museum."이라며 거의 2,000년 전에 만들어진 *Lioness*는 박물관에서 가장 유명한 공예품이라고 하였다. 따라서 (D)가 정답이다.

어휘 partially adv. 부분적으로 improperly adv. 부적절하게
label v. 명칭을 붙이다, 라벨을 붙이다

91. 특정 세부 사항 문제

해석 화자는 청자들이 무엇을 해야 한다고 하는가?
(A) 입장권을 예약한다.
(B) 안내서를 가져간다.
(C) 사진을 찍는다.
(D) 강의에 참석한다.

해설 지문에서 제안과 관련된 표현이 포함된 문장을 주의 깊게 듣는다. "I ~ suggest that you pick up a brochure before you leave."라며 떠나기 전에 안내서를 가져갈 것을 제안한다고 하였다. 따라서 (B)가 정답이다.

어휘 lecture n. 강의

Paraphrasing
pick up 가져가다 → get 가져가다

92-94 ③ 미국

Questions 92-94 refer to the following excerpt from a meeting.

OK . . . ⁹²I'd like to take a few minutes to go over our human resources plan. We hope to hire eleven additional programmers. It's important that they all have relevant experience. Therefore, we've decided to set up an incentive program. ⁹³A $500 bonus will be given to any current employee who recommends a suitable programmer who accepts a position with our company. An announcement about this will be made tomorrow. Assuming we can meet our hiring goal, ⁹⁴the new staff members will take part in a series of workshops in May.

relevant adj. 관련 있는 incentive n. 인센티브, 혜택
current adj. 현재의 suitable adj. 적절한, 알맞은
position n. 직책 a series of 일련의

해석
92-94번은 다음 회의 발췌에 관한 문제입니다.

좋아요... ⁹²저는 우리의 인사 계획을 검토하는 데 몇 분을 보내고자 합니다. 우리는 추가로 열 명의 프로그래머를 고용하기를 희망합니다. 그들 모두가 관련 있는 경험이 있는 것이 중요합니다. 그러므로, 우리는 인센티브 프로그램을 마련하기로 했습니다. 우리 회사의 직책을 받아들이는 ⁹³적절한 프로그래머를 추천하는 현 직원 누구에게나 500달러의 보너스가 주어질 것입니다. 이것에 대한 안내는 내일 이루어질 것입니다. 우리의 채용 목표를 충족시킨다는 것을 가정하여, ⁹⁴새로운 직원들은 5월에 일련의 워크숍에 참여할 것입니다.

92. 화자 문제

해석 화자는 어느 분야에서 일하는 것 같은가?
(A) 영업
(B) 인사
(C) 회계
(D) 마케팅

해설 지문에서 신분 및 직업과 관련된 표현을 놓치지 않고 듣는다. "I'd like to take a few minutes to go over our human resources plan."이라며 인사 계획을 검토하는 데 몇 분을 보내고자 한다고 하였다. 이를 통해, 화자가 인사 부서에서 일하고 있음을 알 수 있다. 따라서 (B)가 정답이다.

어휘 accounting n. 회계

93. 특정 세부 사항 문제

해석 회사는 몇몇 직원들에게 무엇을 제공할 것인가?
(A) 추가 휴가
(B) 장려금
(C) 제품 할인
(D) 무료 주차

해설 질문의 핵심 어구(company offer)와 관련된 내용을 주의 깊게 듣는다. "A $500 bonus will be given to any current employee who recommends a suitable programmer"라며 적절한 프로그래머를 추천하는 현 직원 누구에게나 500달러의 보너스가 주어질 것이라고 하였다. 따라서 (B)가 정답이다.

어휘 leave n. 휴가 financial incentive 장려금

Paraphrasing
A $500 bonus 500달러의 보너스 → Financial incentives 장려금

94. 다음에 할 일 문제

해석 5월에 무슨 일이 일어날 것 같은가?
(A) 기술자들이 대체될 것이다.
(B) 프로그램이 개발될 것이다.
(C) 직원들이 교육을 받을 것이다.
(D) 회사가 사업을 줄일 것이다.

해설 질문의 핵심 어구(in May)가 언급된 주변을 주의 깊게 듣는다. "the new staff members will take part in a series of workshops in May"라며 새로운 직원들은 5월에 일련의 워크숍에 참여할 것이라고 한 것을 통해, 5월에 직원들이 교육을 받을 것임을 알 수 있다. 따라서 (C)가 정답이다.

어휘 technician n. 기술자 operation n. 사업, 영업

Paraphrasing
a series of workshops 일련의 워크숍 → some training 교육

95-97 ③ 캐나다

Questions 95-97 refer to the following telephone message and building directory.

Good morning. This is Frank calling from your apartment complex's management office. ⁹⁵Gas company workers will inspect the pipes in the maintenance room of our building's basement tomorrow between 9 A.M. and 11 A.M. As your unit is in the basement, ⁹⁶I want to let you know that there may be loud noises. This is because the gas company employees will need to disconnect some of the pipes to check the seals. ⁹⁷You're welcome to stay in the lounge while the inspection is being conducted. Thanks, and please call me with any questions or concerns.

management office 관리 사무소 basement n. 지하
disconnect v. 분리하다 seal n. 밀봉재; v. 밀봉하다

해석
95-97번은 다음 전화 메시지와 건물 안내판에 관한 문제입니다.

좋은 아침입니다. 아파트 단지 관리 사무소에서 전화드리는 Frank입니다. ⁹⁵가스 회사 작업자들이 내일 오전 9시에서 11시 사이에 건물

지하의 관리실에 있는 파이프를 점검할 것입니다. 귀하의 세대가 지하에 있기 때문에, ⁹⁶큰 소음이 있을 수 있음을 알려드리고자 합니다. 이는 가스 회사 직원들이 밀봉재를 점검하기 위해 일부 파이프를 분리해야 할 것이기 때문입니다. 점검이 진행되는 동안 ⁹⁷라운지에 자유롭게 머무실 수 있습니다. 감사드리며, 질문이나 우려가 있으시면 언제든지 전화 주세요.

Edgestone 아파트 건물	
층	시설
4층	세대, 자판기
⁹⁷3층	세대, 라운지
2층	세대, 체육관
1층	관리 사무소
지하	세대, 관리실

95. 다음에 할 일 문제

해석 화자에 따르면, 내일 아침에 무슨 일이 일어날 것인가?
(A) 벽장이 청소될 것이다.
(B) 공공요금 청구서가 도착할 것이다.
(C) 방 하나가 공개될 것이다.
(D) 점검이 일어날 것이다.

해설 질문의 핵심 어구(tomorrow morning)와 관련된 내용을 주의 깊게 듣는다. "Gas company workers will inspect the pipes in the maintenance room of our building's basement tomorrow between 9 A.M. and 11 A.M."이라며 가스 회사 작업자들이 내일 오전 9시에서 11시 사이에 건물 지하의 관리실에 있는 파이프를 점검할 것이라고 하였다. 따라서 (D)가 정답이다.

어휘 closet n. 벽장 occur v. 일어나다, 발생하다

96. 문제점 문제

해석 화자는 무슨 문제를 언급하는가?
(A) 문이 잠겨 있지 않다.
(B) 경보가 작동하지 않는다.
(C) 일부 소음이 들릴 수 있다.
(D) 일부 방이 혼잡할 수 있다.

해설 질문의 핵심 어구(problem)와 관련된 내용을 주의 깊게 듣는다. "I want to let you know that there may be loud noises."라며 큰 소음이 있을 수 있음을 알리고자 한다고 하였다. 따라서 (C)가 정답이다.

어휘 crowded adj. 혼잡한

97. 시각 자료 문제

해석 시각 자료를 보아라. 청자는 어디에 머무르도록 권장되는가?
(A) 4층에
(B) 3층에
(C) 2층에
(D) 1층에

해설 제시된 건물 안내판의 정보를 확인한 후 질문의 핵심 어구(encouraged to stay)와 관련된 내용을 주의 깊게 듣는다. "You're welcome to stay in the lounge"라며 라운지에 자유롭게 머물 수 있다고 하였다. 건물 안내판에서 라운지가 있는 곳은 3층임을 알 수 있다. 따라서 (B)가 정답이다.

98-100 호주

Questions 98-100 refer to the following advertisement and flyer.

Do you want a fast Internet connection and access to a wide selection of TV channels? If so, switch to Blaze Telecom today! ⁹⁸We have just opened another office in California and are offering residents of this state a special offer. ⁹⁹Our most popular package, which includes high-speed Internet and access to 50 channels, is available at a 15 percent discount. The offer will be valid until July 20. Moreover, ¹⁰⁰we will set up the cable box and router at no charge regardless of the package you choose.

connection n. 연결 access n. 이용 switch v. 바꾸다
resident n. 주민

해석
98-100번은 다음 광고와 전단지에 관한 문제입니다.

빠른 인터넷 연결과 다양한 TV 채널 이용을 원하십니까? 그렇다면, 오늘 Blaze Telecom으로 바꾸세요! ⁹⁸저희는 이제 막 캘리포니아에 또 하나의 사무실을 열었고 이 주의 주민들에게 특별 할인을 제공하고 있습니다. ⁹⁹고속 인터넷 및 50개 채널 이용을 포함하는 저희의 가장 인기 있는 패키지를 15퍼센트 할인가로 이용하실 수 있습니다. 이 할인은 7월 20일까지 유효할 것입니다. 게다가, ¹⁰⁰선택하시는 패키지와 관계없이 케이블 박스와 라우터를 무료로 설치해 드릴 것입니다.

Blaze Telecom 케이블 & 인터넷 패키지	
Bronze 패키지	20개 채널
⁹⁹Silver 패키지	⁹⁹50개 채널
Gold 패키지	70개 채널
Platinum 패키지	100개 채널
모든 패키지는 고속 인터넷 연결을 포함합니다.	

98. 특정 세부 사항 문제

해석 Blaze Telecom은 최근에 무엇을 했는가?
(A) 새로운 지점을 열었다.
(B) 서비스 제공을 중단했다.
(C) 경쟁사 중 하나를 인수했다.
(D) 회사 본사를 이전했다.

해설 질문의 핵심 어구(Blaze Telecom recently do)와 관련된 내용을 주의 깊게 듣는다. "We[Blaze Telecom] have just opened another office in California"라며 Blaze Telecom이 이제 막 캘리포니아에 또 하나의 사무실을 열었다고 하였다. 따라서 (A)가 정답이다.

99. 시각 자료 문제

해석 시각 자료를 보아라. 어떤 패키지가 할인되는가?
(A) Bronze
(B) Silver
(C) Gold
(D) Platinum

해설 제시된 전단지의 정보를 확인한 후 질문의 핵심 어구(package ~ discounted)와 관련된 내용을 주의 깊게 듣는다. "Our most popular package, which includes high-speed Internet and access to 50 channels, is available at a 15 percent discount."라며 고속 인터넷 및 50개 채널 이용을 포함한 가장 인기 있는 패키지를 15퍼센트 할인가로 이용할 수 있다고 하였다. 전단지에서 50개 채널 이용을 포함한 패키지는 Silver임을 알 수 있다. 따라서 (B)가 정답이다.

100. 특정 세부 사항 문제
해석 모든 고객들은 무엇을 받을 수 있는가?
(A) 무료 설치
(B) 회원증
(C) 후속 상담
(D) 상품권

해설 질문의 핵심 어구(all customers receive)와 관련된 내용을 주의 깊게 듣는다. "we will set up the cable box and router at no charge regardless of the package you choose"라며 선택하는 패키지와 관계없이 케이블 박스와 라우터를 무료로 설치해 줄 것이라고 하였다. 따라서 (A)가 정답이다.

어휘 follow-up adj. 후속의   consultation n. 상담

PART 5

101. 지시형용사 these 채우기
해석 만약 비가 온다면, 이 야외 행사들은 실내 활동들로 대체될 것이다.

해설 빈칸 뒤의 명사(events)를 꾸밀 수 있는 것은 형용사이므로 부정형용사 (A)와 (D), 지시형용사 (B)가 정답의 후보이다. 빈칸 뒤에 복수 명사(events)가 왔고, '이 야외 행사들은 실내 활동들로 대체될 것이다'라는 의미가 되어야 하므로 지시형용사 (B) these(이)가 정답이다. 부정형용사 (A)와 (D)는 단수 명사와 쓰여야 한다. 부정대명사 (C)는 형용사 자리에 올 수 없다.

어휘 outdoor adj. 야외의   substitute A with B A를 B로 대체하다
indoor adj. 실내의   every adj. 모든
others n. 다른 사람들, 다른 것들   another adj. 또 다른

102. 사람명사와 사물/추상명사 구별하여 채우기
해석 월간 회의들은 각 팀의 관리자에 의해 참석된다.

해설 전치사(by)의 목적어 자리에 오면서 소유격(each team's)의 꾸밈을 받을 수 있는 것은 명사이므로 명사 (B)와 (D)가 정답의 후보이다. '월간 회의들은 각 팀의 관리자에 의해 참석된다'라는 의미가 되어야 자연스러우므로 사람명사 (D) supervisor(관리자)가 정답이다. 추상명사 (B) supervision(관리)을 쓸 경우 '월간 회의들은 각 팀의 관리에 의해 참석된다'라는 어색한 문맥이 된다. 동사 또는 과거분사 (A)와 동사 (C)는 명사 자리에 올 수 없다.

어휘 attend v. 참석하다   supervise v. 관리하다, 감독하다

103. 형용사 자리 채우기
해석 구직 시장은 많은 최근의 졸업생들이 일자리를 찾기 시작하면서 경쟁적이게 되었다.

해설 2형식 동사 become의 보어 자리에 올 수 있는 것은 형용사이므로 형용사 (D) competitive(경쟁적인)가 정답이다. 동사 (A)와 (C), 부사 (B)는 보어 자리에 올 수 없다.

어휘 graduate n. 졸업생   look for ~을 찾다

compete v. 경쟁하다   competitively adv. 경쟁적으로

104. 동사 어휘 고르기
해석 기술자들이 전력을 복구시키는 동안 주민들은 세 시간을 기다려야 한다.

해설 빈칸은 조동사 must(~해야 한다) 뒤에 오는 동사원형 자리이다. '전력을 복구시키는 동안 주민들은 세 시간을 기다려야 한다'라는 문맥이므로 (A) wait(기다리다)가 정답이다.

어휘 resident n. 주민   technician n. 기술자
restore v. 복구시키다   practice v. 연습하다, 실행하다
grant v. 승인하다, 인정하다   agree v. 동의하다

105. 사람명사와 사물/추상명사 구별하여 채우기
해석 재선 캠페인 동안, Roberts 시장은 일자리 창출과 경제 성장에 집중하겠다고 약속했다.

해설 빈칸은 전치사(on)의 목적어 자리이므로 빈칸 앞 명사 job과 함께 복합 명사를 이루는 (C)와 (D)가 정답의 후보이다. 'Roberts 시장은 일자리 창출과 경제 성장에 집중하겠다고 약속했다'라는 의미가 되어야 자연스러우므로 추상명사 (C) creation(창출)이 정답이다. 사람명사 (D) creator(창조자)를 쓸 경우 'Roberts 시장은 일자리 창조자와 경제 성장에 집중하겠다고 약속했다'라는 어색한 문맥이 된다. 동사 (A)와 형용사 (B)는 명사 자리에 올 수 없다.

어휘 reelection n. 재선   economic adj. 경제의   growth n. 성장
creation n. 창출, 창조

106. 동사 어휘 고르기
해석 Tuscaloosa 공항은 휠체어 지원을 요청하는 승객들에게 그것을 제공한다.

해설 빈칸은 주격 관계대명사(who) 뒤에 오면서 목적어(it)를 취하는 동사 자리이다. '휠체어 지원을 요청하는 승객들'이라는 문맥이므로 (B) request(요청하다)가 정답이다.

어휘 provide v. 제공하다   assistance n. 지원, 보조
passenger n. 승객   touch v. 만지다   begin v. 시작하다
leave v. 남겨두다, 떠나다

107. 형용사 자리 채우기
해석 White Sands 리조트는 객실들의 가격을 정할 때 수요의 계절적 변화를 고려한다.

해설 빈칸 뒤의 명사(changes)를 꾸밀 수 있는 것은 형용사이므로 형용사 (C)와 형용사 역할을 하는 과거분사 (D)가 정답의 후보이다. '가격을 정할 때 수요의 계절적 변화를 고려하다'라는 의미가 되어야 하므로 형용사 (C) seasonal(계절적인)이 정답이다. 과거분사 (D)를 쓸 경우 '가격을 정할 때 수요의 길든 변화를 고려하다'라는 어색한 의미가 된다. 명사 또는 동사 (A)와 부사 (B)는 형용사 자리에 올 수 없다. 참고로, 동사 consider가 that이 생략된 명사절(the ___ ~ rooms)을 목적어로 취하는 것으로 보아, 명사로 쓰인 (A) seasons(계절들)를 명사절의 주어로 보고, changes를 '변화하다'라는 의미의 3인칭 단수 동사로 본다 해도, 복수 명사(seasons)와 단수 동사(changes)가 함께 쓰일 수 없고, '수요에 따라 계절이 변한다'라는 어색한 의미를 만든다.

어휘 consider v. 고려하다   price v. 가격을 정하다; n. 가격
season n. 계절; v. 양념하다
seasonally adv. 계절적으로, 정기적으로
seasoned adj. 길든, 노련한

108. 부사 자리 채우기
해석 공장 기계는 몇 주의 기간 동안 계속해서 작동할 것이다.

해설 동사(will operate)를 꾸밀 수 있는 것은 부사이므로 부사 (C) continuously(계속해서)가 정답이다. 동사 operate를 '(기계를) 가동하다'라는 의미의 타동사로 보고, 명사 (A) continuation(지속, 계속)을 목적어로 본다 해도, '공장 기계가 지속을 가동하다'라는 어색한 의미를 만든다. 참고로, 동사 operate는 자동사와 타동사로 모두 쓰임을 알아둔다. 동사 또는 과거분사 (B)와 형용사 (D)는 부사 자리에 올 수 없다.

어휘 factory n. 공장 equipment n. 기계, 장비
continue v. 계속하다, 계속되다
continuous adj. 계속되는, 지속되는

109. 전치사 채우기
해석 직원에게 일일 현황 보고서를 제출하도록 요구함으로써, Mr. Yang은 그들의 생산성을 높이기를 바란다.

해설 빈칸은 동명사구(requiring ~ reports)를 목적어로 취하는 전치사 자리이다. '직원에게 일일 현황 보고서를 제출하도록 요구함으로써, 그들의 생산성을 높이기를 바란다'라는 문맥이므로 방법이나 수단을 나타내는 전치사 (A) By(~함으로써)가 정답이다. 참고로, 전치사 by는 '~까지'라는 의미로 시점을, '~ 옆에'라는 의미로 위치를 나타내는 전치사로도 쓰일 수 있음을 알아둔다.

어휘 require v. 요구하다 status report 현황 보고서
productivity n. 생산성

110. 전치사 채우기
해석 최고경영자는 오해가 없다는 것을 확실히 하기 위해 회사의 문제들에 대해 솔직하게 말했다.

해설 빈칸은 명사구(the company's problems)를 목적어로 취하는 전치사 자리이다. '최고경영자는 회사의 문제에 대해 솔직하게 말했다'라는 의미가 되어야 하므로 (A) about(~에 대해)이 정답이다. 동사(speak)와 함께 '~을 대변하다, 대신 말하다'라는 의미의 어구 speak for를 만드는 (C) for(~의, ~ 위한)도 해석상 그럴듯해 보이지만, 전치사 for 뒤에 대변하는 대상인 사람명사가 와야 한다.

어휘 frankly adv. 솔직하게 misunderstanding n. 오해, 착오

111. 부사 어휘 고르기
해석 정부 건강 지침을 따르는 것은 식중독의 위험을 상당히 줄일 수 있다.

해설 빈칸은 동사(can reduce)를 꾸미는 부사 자리이다. '건강 지침을 따르는 것은 위험을 상당히 줄일 수 있다'라는 문맥이므로 (D) substantially(상당히)가 정답이다.

어휘 guideline n. 지침 reduce v. 줄이다
food poisoning 식중독 optionally adv. 선택적으로
carefully adv. 조심스럽게 unexpectedly adv. 예상외로

112. 명사 자리 채우기
해석 Nelson Sportswear사의 마케팅 부서는 지난해의 홍보 활동에 돈을 너무 많이 지출한 것으로 비난받았다.

해설 전치사(on)의 목적어 자리에 오면서 소유격(last year's)의 꾸밈을 받을 수 있는 것은 명사이므로 명사 (A) promotion(홍보 활동)이 정답이다. 동사 (B), 형용사 (C), 동사 또는 과거분사 (D)는 명사 자리에 올 수 없다.

어휘 criticize v. 비난하다 promote v. 홍보하다, 승진시키다
promotional adj. 홍보의, 판촉의

113. 비교급 표현 채우기
해석 Laurent Software사의 새로운 모바일 애플리케이션은 개발자들이 예상했던 것보다 더 높은 후기 평점을 얻었다.

해설 명사구(review score)를 꾸밀 수 있는 것은 형용사이므로 형용사 (A), (C), (D)가 정답의 후보이다. 빈칸 뒤에 than(~보다)이 왔으므로 함께 비교급 표현을 만드는 형용사 high(높은)의 비교급 (C) higher가 정답이다. 원급 (A)와 최상급 (D)는 비교급 표현 than과 함께 쓰일 수 없다. 부사 (B)는 형용사 자리에 올 수 없다.

어휘 earn v. 얻다 developer n. 개발자 anticipate v. 예상하다
highly adv. 매우

114. 명사 관련 어구 채우기
해석 한 달간의 교육 기간은 신입 직원들이 필수적인 기술들을 익히도록 의도되었다.

해설 빈칸은 빈칸 뒤의 명사(period)와 함께 복합 명사를 만들어 동사(is designed)의 주어 역할을 하는 명사 자리이다. '교육 기간은 필수적인 기술들을 익히도록 의도되었다'라는 의미이므로 빈칸 뒤의 명사 period(기간)와 함께 쓰여 '교육 기간'이라는 의미의 복합 명사 training period를 만드는 명사 (A) training(교육)이 정답이다.

어휘 design v. 의도하다, 설계하다 equip v. 익히게 하다, 갖추다
necessary adj. 필수적인 enrollment n. 등록
innovation n. 혁신 manufacturing n. 생산, 제조

115. 접속부사 채우기
해석 Westgate 지하철역은 연 지 한 달밖에 되지 않았지만, 그럼에도 불구하고 그것은 도시의 가장 붐비는 지하철역들 중 하나이다.

해설 첫 번째 절(Westgate Subway Station ~ month)과 등위접속사(but)로 연결된 두 번째 절(it ~ stops)이 주어와 동사를 갖춘 완전한 절이므로, 절과 절의 의미를 연결할 수 있는 접속부사 (B), (C), (D)가 정답의 후보이다. '연 지 한 달밖에 되지 않았지만, 그럼에도 불구하고 도시의 가장 붐비는 지하철역들 중 하나이다'라는 의미가 되어야 하므로 앞뒤 절의 의미를 연결해 주는 접속부사이면서 양보를 나타내는 (D) nonetheless(그럼에도 불구하고)가 정답이다. 접속사 (A) though(비록 ~이지만)는 이미 절 앞에 등위접속사 but이 있으므로 또 쓰일 수 없다. 참고로, 절과 절 사이에는 하나의 접속사만 올 수 있다.

어휘 instead adv. 대신에 therefore adv. 따라서, 그러므로

116. 형용사 어휘 고르기
해석 Ms. Sharma는 Spectrum 어학원의 강의들이 통역사로서 그녀의 경력에 도움이 된다고 생각했다.

해설 빈칸은 5형식 동사 find의 목적격 보어 역할을 하는 형용사 자리이다. '강의들이 통역사로서 그녀의 경력에 도움이 된다고 생각했다'라는 문맥이므로 (D) helpful(도움이 되는)이 정답이다.

어휘 course n. 강의 career n. 경력 interpreter n. 통역사
ambitious adj. 야망 있는 conservative adj. 보수적인
subtle adj. 미묘한

117. 부사 자리 채우기
해석 Sandy's Burger Barn은 오늘날 국내 패스트푸드 업계를 완전히 장악한다.

해설 동사(dominates)를 꾸밀 수 있는 것은 부사이므로 부사 (C) completely(완전히, 충분히)가 정답이다. 형용사 또는 동사 (A), 형용사의 비교급 (B), 동명사 또는 현재분사 (D)는 부사 자리에 올 수 없다.

어휘 dominate v. 장악하다, 지배하다 these days 오늘날, 요즘
complete adj. 완료된, 완전한; v. 완료하다

118. 올바른 시제의 동사 채우기
해석 그 연구 보조원은 다음 주에 소비자 조사 자료를 검토할 것이다.

해설 문장에 주어(The research assistant)만 있고 동사가 없으므로 동사 (B)와 (D)가 정답의 후보이다. 미래를 나타내는 시간 표현(next week)이 있으므로 미래 시제 (B) will review가 정답이다. 과거 시제 (D)는 미래를 나타내는 시간 표현과 함께 쓰일 수 없다. 명사 (A)와 동명사 또는 현재분사 (C)는 동사 자리에 올 수 없다. 현재분사 (C)를 빈칸 앞의 명사구(The research assistant)를 꾸미는 것으로 보고, survey를 '살피다, 점검하다'라는 의미의 동사로 본다 해도, 주어(The research assistant)가 3인칭 단수이므로 복수 동사(survey)와 함께 쓰일 수 없다.

어휘 assistant n. 보조원, 조수 reviewer n. 검토자, 논평가
review v. 검토하다; n. 검토

119. 부사절 접속사 채우기
해석 Mr. Abrams는 그가 공급업체들과 거래하는 것에 대한 몇 가지 조언을 얻을 수 있도록 컨설팅 회사를 고용했다.

해설 이 문장은 주어(Mr. Abrams), 동사(hired), 목적어(a ~ firm)를 갖춘 완전한 절이므로, ___ ~ suppliers는 수식어 거품으로 보아야 한다. 이 수식어 거품은 동사(could get)가 있는 거품절이므로, 거품절을 이끌 수 있는 부사절 접속사 (A), (B), (C)가 정답의 후보이다. 'Mr. Abrams는 거래하는 것에 대한 조언을 얻을 수 있도록 컨설팅 회사를 고용했다'라는 의미가 되어야 하므로 목적을 나타내는 부사절 접속사 (A) so that(~할 수 있도록)이 정답이다. 전치사 (D)는 거품절을 이끌 수 없다.

어휘 advice n. 조언 deal with ~와 거래하다
even if 비록 ~이지만 regarding prep. ~에 관하여

120. 관계부사 채우기
해석 주최자들은 그들이 200명의 손님들을 위한 행사를 열 수 있는 장소를 아직도 찾고 있다.

해설 문장은 주어(Organizers), 동사(are searching)를 갖춘 완전한 절이므로, ___ ~ guests는 수식어 거품으로 보아야 한다. 이 수식어 거품은 주어(they), 동사(can hold), 목적어(an event)를 갖춘 완전한 절이고, a venue를 선행사로 갖는 관계절이므로 장소를 나타내는 선행사와 함께 쓰일 수 있는 관계부사 (D) where가 정답이다. 관계대명사 (A)는 뒤에 주어나 목적어가 없는 불완전한 절이 와야 하며 앞에 사람 선행사가 와야 한다. 의문사 또는 관계대명사 (B)는 선행사를 가질 수 없다. 관계부사 (C)는 장소가 아닌 시간을 나타내는 관계부사이고, '~할 때'라는 의미의 부사절 접속사로 보더라도 '행사를 열 수 있는 장소를 찾을 때 아직 찾고 있다'라는 어색한 문맥이 된다.

어휘 organizer n. 주최자 venue n. 장소 hold v. 열다, 개최하다

121. 부사 자리 채우기
해석 비자 신청서는 지연을 방지하기 위해 기한을 엄수하여 제출되어야 한다.

해설 동사(must be submitted)를 꾸밀 수 있는 것은 부사이므로 부사 (D) punctually(기한을 엄수하여, 제시간에)가 정답이다. 형용사 (A), 동명사 또는 현재분사 (B), 명사 (C)는 동사를 꾸밀 수 없다.

어휘 application n. 신청(서) submit v. 제출하다

avoid v. 방지하다, 막다 delay n. 지연, 지체
punctual adj. 시간을 지키는
punctuate v. 간간이 끼어들다, 중단시키다
punctuation n. 구두점, 중단

122. 형용사 어휘 고르기
해석 새로운 기계에 투자하는 것은 돈이 많이 들지만, 장기적으로 그것은 이익이 된다.

해설 빈칸은 be동사(is)의 보어 역할을 하는 형용사 자리이다. '새로운 기계에 투자하는 것은 돈이 많이 들지만, 장기적으로 그것은 이익이 된다'라는 문맥이므로 (C) beneficial(이익이 되는, 이로운)이 정답이다.

어휘 machinery n. 기계 expensive adj. 돈이 많이 드는, 비싼
in the long run 장기적으로 fortunate adj. 운 좋은
memorable adj. 기억에 남는 sudden adj. 갑작스러운

123. 부정대명사 채우기
해석 293 항공편을 이용하는 사람들은 이제 7번 게이트로 이동해야 한다.

해설 문장에 동사(should proceed)만 있고 주어가 없으므로 주어 역할을 할 수 있는 (B), (C), (D)가 정답의 후보이다. 관계대명사절(who ~ 293)의 꾸밈을 받아 '293 항공편을 이용하는 사람들은 게이트로 이동해야 한다'라는 문맥을 만드는 부정대명사 (C) Those(~한 사람들)가 정답이다. 참고로, those는 이 문장에서 앞에 오는 명사를 대신하는 지시대명사가 아니라 막연히 '~한 사람들'이라는 의미의 부정대명사로 쓰였으며, those 뒤에는 반드시 관계절, 분사, 전치사구의 수식어가 온다는 것을 알아둔다. 지시대명사 (B) This는 '293 항공편을 이용하는 이 사람은 이제 게이트로 이동해야 한다'라는 의미로 해석상 그럴듯해 보이지만, this는 앞에 나온 단수 명사 또는 문장 전체를 대신하는 데 쓰이므로 답이 될 수 없다. 대명사 또는 형용사 (D) Either는 '둘 중 하나'라는 의미로 가리키는 대상이 두 개일 때 쓰인다. 목적격 인칭대명사 (A)는 주어 자리에 올 수 없다.

어휘 flight n. 항공편 proceed v. 이동하다, 나아가다

124. 부사 어휘 고르기
해석 2주 후에, Prendit사는 사업 확장을 발표하기 위해 기자회견을 열 것이다.

해설 빈칸은 문장 전체(Prendit Corp. ~ expansion)를 꾸미는 부사 자리이다. 빈칸 앞의 시간 표현(Two weeks)과 함께 쓰여, '2주 후에 기자회견을 열 것이다'라는 의미가 되어야 하므로 시간 표현 바로 다음에 와서 '그 시간 이후에'라는 의미를 나타내는 시간 부사 (B) later(~ 후에, 나중에)가 정답이다. 부사 (A) next(다음에)도 해석상 그럴듯해 보이지만, 시간 표현과 함께 쓰일 수 없다. 참고로, (A)를 형용사로 볼 경우 시간 표현(Two weeks)과 함께 쓸 수 있지만, 시간 표현 앞에 와야 하며 전치사 for나 in 등과 함께 쓰여, for/in next two weeks(다음 2주 동안/다음 2주 후에)의 형태가 되어야 한다.

어휘 hold v. 열다, 개최하다 press conference 기자회견
announce v. 발표하다 usually adv. 주로 still adv. 여전히

125. 동사 어휘 고르기
해석 인사부장으로서, Ms. Goldfinch는 직원들을 모집하는 것을 담당한다.

해설 빈칸은 전치사(of) 뒤에서 목적어(staff)를 갖는 동명사 자리이다. '인사부장으로서 직원들을 모집하는 것을 담당한다'라는 문맥이므로 동사 recruit(모집하다)의 동명사 (D) recruiting이 정답이다. (C)의 manipulate(다루다, 조종하다)도 해석상

그럴듯해 보이지만, '다루다'라는 의미를 지닐 때는 사물 목적어가 와야 하며, 사람 목적어가 올 경우, 부정적인 의미로 사람을 조종한다는 의미가 되므로 답이 될 수 없다.

어휘 in charge of ~을 담당하는   indicate v. 나타내다
compile v. 엮다, 편집하다

126. 부사 자리 채우기
해석 분기별 보너스는 영업팀의 모든 구성원들이 몫을 받으며, 균등하게 분배된다.
해설 동사(is divided)를 꾸밀 수 있는 것은 부사이므로 부사 (A) equally(균등하게)가 정답이다. 형용사, 명사 또는 동사 (B), 명사 (C), 형용사의 비교급 (D)는 동사를 꾸밀 수 없다.
어휘 quarterly adj. 분기별의   divide v. 분배하다, 나누다
equal adj. 평등한; n. 동등한 것; v. ~과 같다
equality n. 평등, 균등

127. 전치사 채우기
해석 산호세에서 열린 소프트웨어 박람회는 개발자들 사이에 아이디어 나누는 것을 장려했다.
해설 빈칸은 명사(developers)를 목적어로 취하는 전치사 자리이다. '개발자들 사이에 아이디어 나누는 것'이라는 의미가 되어야 하므로 (B) among(~ 사이에)이 정답이다. (D) plus(~뿐만 아니라)도 해석상 그럴듯해 보이지만, 앞의 명사에 부가를 나타내는 전치사이므로 '아이디어뿐만 아니라 개발자들을 나누는 것'이라는 어색한 문맥을 만든다.
어휘 encourage v. 장려하다, 촉진하다   above prep. ~보다 위로

128. 형용사 어휘 고르기
해석 Parkview 타워의 중심적인 위치는 그것을 몹시 매력적으로 만들며, 그것의 높은 임대료가 이것을 나타낸다.
해설 빈칸은 5형식 동사 make의 목적격 보어 역할을 하는 형용사 자리이다. '타워의 중심적인 위치는 그것을 몹시 매력적으로 만들며, 그것의 높은 임대료가 이것을 나타낸다'라는 의미가 되어야 하므로 (A) attractive(매력적인)가 정답이다.
어휘 central adj. 중심적인, 중앙의   extremely adv. 몹시, 극도로
rental price 임대료   reflect v. 나타내다, 반영하다
actual adj. 실제의   attentive adj. 주의를 기울이는
complimentary adj. 무료의

129. 재귀대명사 채우기
해석 Mr. Calderon은 동업자가 있었지만 이제는 그 혼자서 회사를 운영한다.
해설 전치사(by)의 목적어 자리에 올 수 있는 재귀대명사 (A), 소유대명사 (B), 목적격 인칭대명사 (C)가 정답의 후보이다. 'Mr. Calderon은 동업자가 있었지만, 이제는 그 혼자서 회사를 운영한다'라는 의미가 되어야 하므로 전치사 by와 함께 쓰여 '혼자, 혼자 힘으로'라는 의미의 어구 by oneself를 만드는 재귀대명사 (A) himself가 정답이다. 소유대명사 (B)는 'Mr. Calderon은 동업자가 있었지만, 이제는 그의 것에 의해 회사를 운영한다'라는 어색한 문맥을 만든다. 목적격 인칭대명사 (C)는 'Mr. Calderon은 동업자가 있었지만, 이제는 그 (Mr. Calderon이 아닌 다른 남성)에 의해 회사를 운영한다'라는 어색한 문맥이 되며, 목적격 인칭대명사 him을 쓰기 위해서는 him이 의미하는 남성이 빈칸 앞에 등장해야 하는데, Mr. Calderon 외에 언급된 남성이 없으므로 답이 될 수 없다. 주격 인칭대명사 (D)는 전치사의 목적어 자리에 올 수 없다.
어휘 business partner 동업자   run v. 운영하다

130. 명사 어휘 고르기
해석 Mr. Parker는 낡은 갈색 소파를 치우고 그것을 창고에 두기로 결정했다.
해설 빈칸은 전치사(in)의 목적어 역할을 하는 명사 자리이다. '소파를 창고에 두다'라는 문맥이므로 (A) storage(창고)가 정답이다.
어휘 remove v. 치우다, 없애다   place v. 두다
usage n. 사용(법), 관습   absence n. 부재, 결석
procedure n. 절차, 방법

PART 6

131-134번은 다음 이메일에 관한 문제입니다.

수신: Derrian Enterprises사 <info@derrianenterprises.com>
발신: Carlos Juarez <cjuar@jadeair.com>
날짜: 5월 9일
제목: 문의 사항

관계자분께:

저는 이전에 귀사의 서비스를 이용해 본 한 동료의 추천으로 글을 씁니다. ¹³¹저는 Jade 항공사 마케팅 부서에서 일하고 있으며, 저희는 저희의 20주년을 기념하기 위해 홍보 캠페인을 진행할 것입니다. 캠페인의 일환으로, 저희는 모든 승객들에게 무료 핀을 나누어 줄 것입니다.

¹³²저는 당신이 제게 가격 견적서를 줄 수 있기를 바랍니다. 저는 저희 로고가 새겨진 핀 4,000개를 받는 데 비용이 얼마나 들지 알고 싶습니다. ¹³³뿐만 아니라, 이 품목의 샘플 한 개를 제게 보내주실 수 있을까요? ¹³⁴저는 그것이 저희가 필요한 것과 일치하는지 확인할 것입니다. 그것이 만족스럽다면, 저희는 주문을 진행할 것입니다.

감사합니다,

Carlos Juarez 드림
Jade 항공사

recommendation n. 추천   colleague n. 동료
anniversary n. ~주년, 기념일   satisfactory adj. 만족스러운
proceed with ~을 진행하다

131. to 부정사 채우기
해설 첫 번째 절(I ~ Jade Air)과 등위접속사(and)로 연결된 두 번째 절(we ~ anniversary)이 주어(we), 동사(are running), 목적어(a ~ campaign)를 갖춘 완전한 절이므로, ___ ~ anniversary는 수식어 거품으로 보아야 한다. 이 수식어 거품은 동사가 없는 거품구이므로, 거품구를 이끌 수 있는 to 부정사 (A)와 과거분사 (B)가 정답의 후보이다. 빈칸 뒤에 목적어(our 20th anniversary)가 있고 '20주년을 기념하기 위해 홍보 캠페인을 진행한다'라는 목적의 의미가 되어야 하므로, 목적어를 가질 수 있으면서 목적을 나타내는 to 부정사 (A) to celebrate가 정답이다. 과거분사 (B)는 빈칸 뒤에 목적어가 있으므로 답이 될 수 없다. 명사 (C)와 동사 (D)는 수식어 거품을 이끌 수 없다.
어휘 celebration n. 기념, 축하

132. 명사 어휘 고르기 주변 문맥 파악
해설 빈칸은 빈칸 앞의 명사(price)와 함께 복합 명사를 이루어 동사(give)의 직접 목적어 자리에 올 수 있는 명사 자리이다. '당

신이 가격 ____을 줄 수 있기를 바란다'라는 문맥이므로 (B) 와 (D)가 정답의 후보이다. 뒤 문장에서 핀 4,000개를 받는 데 비용이 얼마나 들지 알고 싶다고 했으므로 가격 견적서를 받기 희망한다는 것을 알 수 있다. 따라서 (D) estimate(견적서)가 정답이다.

어휘 benefit n. 혜택   reduction n. 할인, 인하   analysis n. 분석

133. 접속부사 채우기 _주변 문맥 파악_
해설 앞 문장에서 로고가 새겨진 핀 4,000개를 받는 데 비용이 얼마나 들지 알고 싶다고 했고, 빈칸이 있는 문장에서는 이 품목의 샘플 한 개를 보내줄 수 있는지 물었으므로, 앞 문장에서 언급된 내용, 즉 요청 사항에 추가로 덧붙일 때 사용되는 접속부사 (A) Furthermore(뿐만 아니라)가 정답이다.

어휘 for instance 예를 들어   otherwise adv. 그렇지 않으면
after all 결국에

134. 알맞은 문장 고르기
해석 (A) 그것은 저희 고객들에게 인기 있었습니다.
(B) 그것은 정확히 제가 요청했던 것이 아니었습니다.
(C) 저는 그것이 언제 배송될 것인지 당신에게 알려 드릴 것입니다.
(D) 저는 그것이 저희가 필요한 것과 일치하는 확인할 것입니다.

해설 앞 문장 '(Furthermore), could you send me a sample of this item?'에서 이 품목의 샘플 한 개를 보내 달라고 한 후, 뒤 문장 'If it is satisfactory, we will proceed with an order.'에서 그것이 만족스럽다면 주문을 진행할 것이라고 했으므로 빈칸에는 샘플을 보내주면 주문을 진행할 건지 확인하겠다는 내용이 들어가야 함을 알 수 있다. 따라서 (D)가 정답이다.

어휘 request v. 요청하다   notify v. 알리다   match v. 일치하다

135-138번은 다음 편지에 관한 문제입니다.

1월 18일
Lucinda Botello
소유주, Condesa 섬유 회사
920번지 Cuevas가
멕시코시티, 멕시코 03100

Ms. Botello께,

저희는 당신을 우리 지역사회의 연례 기업가 정신 경연대회의 심사위원으로 초청하고 싶습니다. ¹³⁵매년, 지역 주민들은 그들의 사업 아이디어를 경험이 풍부한 전문가 심사원단에 제시합니다. 이러한 전문가들 중 한 명으로서, 당신은 선정된 기준에 근거하여 아이디어들을 평가할 것입니다. ¹³⁶그 발표들은 짧을 것입니다. ¹³⁷각 참가자는 그들의 제안을 공유하기 위해 오직 15분을 얻습니다.

만약 당신이 기꺼이 수락한다면, 동봉된 양식을 우편으로 돌려보내 주십시오. 이 대회는 3월 6일 금요일 오전 10시부터 오전 11시 30분까지 저희의 시민 문화 회관에서 열릴 것입니다. ¹³⁸간단한 점심 식사가 이어질 것입니다.

더 자세한 내용은 저희 웹사이트에서 찾을 수 있습니다.

Rafael Pedragon 드림
의장, 지역사회 기업가 정신 프로그램

judge n. 심사위원, 판사   entrepreneurship n. 기업가 정신
present v. 제시하다, 제출하다   panel n. 심사원단
expert n. 전문가   evaluate v. 평가하다   criteria n. 기준
proposal n. 제안, 제의   be willing to 기꺼이 ~하다

enclosed adj. 동봉된   casual adj. 간단한, 우연한
chair n. 의장, 의자

135. 명사 자리 채우기
해설 전치사(of)의 목적어 자리에 오면서 빈칸 앞의 형용사 (experienced)의 꾸밈을 받을 수 있는 것은 명사이므로 명사 (C) specialists(전문가들)가 정답이다. 부사 (A), 동사 (B), 형용사 (D)는 명사 자리에 올 수 없다. (D) special을 '특별한 것, 특별한 사람'을 의미하는 명사로 본다 해도, 가산 명사이므로 복수형으로 쓰이거나 관사와 함께 쓰여야 한다.

어휘 specially adv. 특별하게
specialize v. 전문적으로 다루다, 전공하다
special adj. 특별한; n. 특별한 것, 특별한 사람

136. 알맞은 문장 고르기
해석 (A) 저희는 폭넓은 선택을 제공합니다.
(B) 그 발표들은 짧을 것입니다.
(C) 주제에 대한 제안들은 환영받습니다.
(D) 모든 참가자들은 상을 받을 것입니다.

해설 앞부분에서 지역 주민들이 사업 아이디어를 전문가 심사원단에 제시한다고 했고, 뒤 문장 'Each (participant) gets only 15 minutes to share their proposal.'에서 각 참가자는 그들의 제안을 공유하기 위해 오직 15분을 얻는다고 했으므로 빈칸에는 발표 시간과 관련된 내용이 들어가야 함을 알 수 있다. 따라서 (B)가 정답이다.

어휘 selection n. 선택   brief adj. 짧은, 간단한
suggestion n. 제안   welcome adj. 환영받는, 좋은; v. 환영하다
contestant n. 참가자   prize n. 상

137. 명사 어휘 고르기 _전체 문맥 파악_
해설 빈칸은 동사(gets)의 주어 역할을 하는 명사 자리이다. '각 ____은 그들의 제안을 공유하기 위해 오직 15분을 얻는다'라는 문맥이므로 모든 보기가 정답의 후보이다. 앞부분에서 지역사회의 연례 기업가 정신 경연대회에 대해 언급하며, 지역 주민들은 그들의 사업 아이디어를 경험이 풍부한 전문가 심사원단에 제시할 수 있다고 했으므로, 각 참가자는 그들의 제안을 공유하기 위해 오직 15분을 얻는다는 것을 알 수 있다. 따라서 (D) participant(참가자)가 정답이다.

어휘 partner n. 동업자, 파트너   representative n. 대표, 대리인
spectator n. 관중

138. 태에 맞는 동사 채우기
해설 문장에 동사가 없으므로 동사 (A), (C), (D)가 정답의 후보이다. 빈칸 뒤에 수동태와 함께 쓰이는 by(~에 의해)가 있고 '그것(대회)이 간단한 점심 식사에 의해 뒤따라지다', 즉 대회 뒤에 간단한 점심 식사가 이어질 것이라는 수동의 의미이므로 수동태 (D) will be followed가 정답이다. 능동태 (A)와 (C)를 쓸 경우 각각 '그것(대회)이 간단한 점심 식사에 의해 다음에 오다/왔다'라는 어색한 문맥이 된다. 동명사 혹은 현재분사 (B)는 동사 자리에 올 수 없다.

139-142번은 다음 안내문에 관한 문제입니다.

9월 1일부터, *Canberra Post*지는 신문의 토요일 호를 발행하는 것을 중단할 것입니다. ¹³⁹이 결정은 주말 독자 수의 감소에 대응하여 이루어졌습니다. ¹⁴⁰이 인원수는 지난 3년간 약 50만 명에서 10만 명으로 감소했습니다. 토요일 호를 중단함으로써, 저희는 평일 호에 집중할 수 있을 것입니다. ¹⁴¹저희는 또한 몇몇 새로운 부문들을 추가할 것입니다. 이것들은

여행, 건강, 정원 가꾸기, 그리고 더 많은 것들을 포함할 것입니다. ¹⁴²그것들은 저희의 금요일 호에 나오기 시작할 것입니다.

publish v. 발행하다 edition n. 호, 판
decline n. 감소; v. 감소하다 discontinue v. 중단하다
focus on ~에 집중하다

139. 전치사 표현 채우기
해설 빈칸은 명사구(a decline ~ readers)를 목적어로 취하는 전치사 자리이다. '주말 독자 수의 감소에 대응하여'라는 의미가 되어야 하므로 빈칸 앞의 전치사구 in response와 함께 '~에 대응하여'라는 의미의 어구인 in response to를 만드는 전치사 (A) to가 정답이다.

140. 올바른 시제의 동사 채우기
해설 현재완료 시제와 함께 쓰이는 시간 표현(over the past three years)이 있으므로 과거에 발생한 일이 현재까지 계속되거나, 과거에 발생한 일이 현재까지 영향을 미치는 것을 표현할 때 사용되는 현재완료 시제 (B) have decreased가 정답이다. 현재진행 시제 (A), 과거 시제 (C), 현재 시제 (D)는 현재완료를 나타내는 시간 표현과 함께 쓰일 수 없다.

어휘 decrease v. 감소하다, 감소시키다

141. 명사 어휘 고르기 주변 문맥 파악
해설 빈칸은 동사(will be adding)의 목적어 역할을 하는 명사 자리이다. '몇몇 새로운 _____을 추가할 것이다'라는 문맥이므로 모든 보기가 정답의 후보이다. 뒤 문장에서 이것들은 여행, 건강, 정원 가꾸기, 그리고 더 많은 것들을 포함할 것이라고 했으므로 몇몇 새로운 부문들을 추가할 것임을 알 수 있다. 따라서 (C) sections(부문들)가 정답이다.

어휘 method n. 방법 machine n. 기계 position n. 위치, 자리

142. 알맞은 문장 고르기
해설 (A) 그것들은 저희의 금요일 호에 나오기 시작할 것입니다.
(B) 환불에 관한 많은 문의들이 있었습니다.
(C) 저희는 저희 편집자의 미래에 행운을 빕니다.
(D) 하지만, 그것은 시 경계 내에서만 배달될 수 있습니다.
해설 앞 문장 'These will include Travel, Health, Gardening, and more.'에서 이것들, 즉 새로운 부문들은 여행, 건강, 정원 가꾸기, 그리고 더 많은 것들을 포함할 것이라고 했으므로, 빈칸에는 신문에 새롭게 포함되는 부문과 관련된 내용이 들어가야 함을 알 수 있다. 따라서 (A)가 정답이다.

어휘 appear v. 나오다, 발간되다 inquiry n. 문의 editor n. 편집자

143-146번은 다음 회람에 관한 문제입니다.

수신: 모든 콜센터 직원들
발신: John Dooley, 고객 지원 전문가
제목: 정보 수집
날짜: 6월 22일

지난 6개월 동안, 전화를 건 사람들이 우리 직원들 중 한 명과 이야기하기 위해 대기하는 데 걸린 시간의 양이 거의 두 배가 되었습니다. ¹⁴³이 시간은 5월에 7분이었으며, 현재 그것은 13분입니다.

¹⁴⁴우리는 문의들을 더 잘 해결할 수 있는 방법이 필요합니다. 따라서, 저는 우리 웹사이트에 새로운 페이지를 추가할 것입니다. ¹⁴⁵그것은 "자주 묻는 질문들"이라고 분류될 것이며, 포괄적인 답변을 포함할 것입니다. ¹⁴⁶저는 여러분 각자가 우리 소프트웨어 프로그램들에 관해 여러분이 매일 받는 가장 흔한

10가지 질문들의 목록을 제게 보내주시기를 바랍니다.

amount n. 양, 액수 representative n. 직원, 대표자
double v. 두 배가 되다, ~의 두 배이다
label v. ~을 분류하다, ~에 라벨을 붙이다
frequently adv. 자주, 빈번하게 contain v. 포함하다, 담다
common adj. 흔한, 보통의

143. 지시형용사 this 채우기 주변 문맥 파악
해설 명사(time)를 꾸밀 수 있는 것은 형용사이므로 지시형용사 (A)와 (C), 소유격 인칭대명사 (B)가 정답의 후보이다. 앞 문장에서 '전화를 건 사람들이 대기하는 데 걸린 시간의 양이 거의 두 배가 되었다'라고 했고, 빈칸 뒤의 단수 명사(time)가 앞에서 언급한 시간을 가리키고 있으므로 '이 시간은 5월에 7분이었다'라는 문맥을 만드는 지시형용사 (A) This(이)가 정답이다. 소유격 인칭대명사 (B)는 '그것의 시간은 5월에 7분이었다'라는 어색한 문맥이 된다. 참고로, 지시형용사 (C)는 복수 명사와 함께 쓰이며, 지시대명사로 쓰이는 경우 앞에 언급된 복수 명사를 대신할 때 쓰임을 알아둔다. 소유대명사 (D)는 형용사 자리에 올 수 없다.

144. 알맞은 문장 고르기
해석 (A) 우리는 문의들을 더 잘 해결할 수 있는 방법이 필요합니다.
(B) 새로운 초과 근무 정책이 시행될 것입니다.
(C) 제품 출시가 지연되었습니다.
(D) 우리는 그 서비스를 일시적으로 중단해야 합니다.
해설 앞부분에서 지난 6개월 동안, 전화를 건 사람들이 직원과 이야기하기 위해 대기하는 데 걸린 시간의 양이 거의 두 배가 되었다고 했고, 뒤 문장 'Thus, I will add a new page to our Web site.'에서 따라서 웹사이트에 새로운 페이지를 추가할 것이라고 했으므로, 빈칸에는 문의들을 더 잘 해결할 수 있는 방법이 필요하다는 것과 관련된 내용이 들어가야 함을 알 수 있다. 따라서 (A)가 정답이다.

어휘 address v. 해결하다 overtime n. 초과 근무
effective adj. 시행되는 launch n. 출시
suspend v. 중단하다 temporarily adv. 일시적으로

145. 형용사 자리 채우기
해설 명사(answers)를 꾸밀 수 있는 것은 형용사이므로 형용사 (A)와 현재분사 (B)가 정답의 후보이다. '포괄적인 답변'이라는 의미가 되어야 하므로 형용사 (A) comprehensive(포괄적인, 종합적인)가 정답이다. 현재분사 (B)를 쓸 경우 '그것은 "자주 묻는 질문들"이라고 분류될 것이며, 이해하는 답변을 포함할 것이다'라는 어색한 의미가 된다. (B) comprehending을 동명사로 보고 명사 answers를 동명사의 목적어로 본다 해도, '그것은 "자주 묻는 질문들"이라고 분류될 것이며, 답변을 이해하는 것을 포함할 것이다'라는 어색한 의미가 된다. 부사 (C)와 명사 (D)는 형용사 자리에 올 수 없다.

어휘 comprehend v. 이해하다
comprehensively adv. 완전히, 철저히
comprehension n. 이해력

146. 태, 시제에 맞는 동사 채우기
해설 명사(questions) 다음에 나오는 목적격 관계대명사 that/which가 생략된 절(you ~ programs)에 주어(you)만 있고 동사가 없으므로 동사인 (B), (C), (D)가 정답의 후보이다. 참고로, 선행사(questions)와 주어 사이에 목적격 관계대명사 that 또는 which가 생략되었음을 알아둔다. 동사 receive가 '~을 받다'라는 의미의 타동사로 쓰여 '여러분이 질문들을 받다'라는 능동의 의미가 되어야 하고, 반복되는 동작을 나타내는

현재 시간 표현(each day)이 있으므로 현재 시제 능동태 (C) receive가 정답이다. 참고로, 현재 시제는 현재의 상태나 반복되는 동작, 일반적인 사실을 나타낼 수 있음을 알아둔다. 미래 시제 (B)는 미래 상황에 대한 추측이나 의지를 나타낸다. 현재 시제 수동태 (D)는 생략된 목적격 관계대명사를 목적어로 취할 수 없으므로 답이 될 수 없다. 동명사 또는 현재분사 (A)는 동사 자리에 올 수 없다.

PART 7

147-148번은 다음 공고에 관한 문제입니다.

시청에서 제설 서비스를 필요로 함

¹⁴⁷Brannethville은 시청 주변의 포장된 구역들에 있는 눈과 얼음의 제거에 대한 입찰을 구하고 있습니다. 제안서를 제출하기 전, 요구 조항들에 주의해 주십시오:

1. 모든 눈과 얼음이 매일 아침 7시까지 제거되어야 합니다.
2. 강설량이 보통에서 많은 날에는 계약자가 오전 7시부터 오후 5시까지 시간이 있어야 합니다.
3. ¹⁴⁸계약자는 모든 장비를 제공해야 합니다.
4. 계약은 제설 작업의 필요 여부와는 관계없이, 12월 3일부터 5월 3일까지 5개월 동안 지속될 것입니다.

관심이 있으시다면, 당신의 제안서를 Brannethville 시청으로 보내주십시오. 자격을 얻으려면 입찰이 12월 1일까지 접수되어야 합니다.

removal n. 제거 **seek** v. 구하다, 찾다 **bid** n. 입찰
pave v. (도로를) 포장하다 **proposal** n. 제안(서)
contractor n. 계약자 **snowfall** n. 강설량
supply v. 제공하다 **qualify** v. 자격을 얻다

147. 목적 문제

해석 공고의 목적은 무엇인가?
(A) 새로운 규정을 발표하기 위해
(B) 계절성 작업에 대한 지원을 요청하기 위해
(C) 유용한 제설 관련 조언을 제공하기 위해
(D) 주민들에게 겨울에 대비할 것을 상기시키기 위해

해설 지문의 'Brannethville is seeking bids for the removal of snow and ice on paved areas'에서 Brannethville이 포장된 구역들에 있는 눈과 얼음의 제거에 대한 입찰을 구하고 있다고 했으므로 (B)가 정답이다.

어휘 **regulation** n. 규정, 규제 **application** n. 지원(서)
helpful adj. 유용한 **remind** v. 상기시키다

[Paraphrasing]
removal of snow and ice 눈과 얼음의 제거 → seasonal job 계절성 작업

148. 육하원칙 문제

해석 계약자들은 무엇을 하도록 요구되는가?
(A) 웹사이트에 등록한다.
(B) 그들 소유의 장비를 제공한다.
(C) 오직 밤에만 작업한다.
(D) 12월까지 작업을 완료한다.

해설 지문의 'The contractor must supply all equipment.'에서 계약자는 모든 장비를 제공해야 한다고 했으므로 (B)가 정답이다.

어휘 **register** v. 등록하다 **complete** v. 완료하다

[Paraphrasing]
supply ~ equipment 장비를 제공하다 → Provide ~ equipment 장비를 제공하다

149-150번은 다음 이메일에 관한 문제입니다.

수신: Chloe Schmidt <ch.sch@baltorco.co.uk>
발신: Topline사 고객 서비스 <cs@topline.co.uk>
제목: 거래 종료
날짜: 6월 29일

Ms. Schmidt께,

¹⁴⁹귀하께서 Topline사와 거래를 끊었다는 소식을 듣게 되어 유감입니다. 저희는 높은 통화 품질을 보장하고 고급 보안 기능들을 제공하기 위해 노력하기 때문에, Topline사는 영국에서 선호되는 인터넷 전화 제공업체입니다. 한 달에 단 9파운드로, 가입자들은 다른 Topline사 회원들과 인스턴트 메시지, 음성 통화, 그리고 화상 통화를 통해 의사소통을 할 수 있습니다.

¹⁴⁹그러니 다시 가입하시는 것은 어떠십니까? ¹⁵⁰새로운 계정을 개설하시면, 저희는 귀하께 한 달의 무료 이용을 제공해드릴 것입니다. 귀하께서 결제 페이지에 도달하시면, 코드 142737을 입력하십시오.

Jerome Meyer 드림
고객 서비스 직원
Topline사

close an account with ~와 거래를 끊다
advanced adj. 고급의 **security** n. 보안 **prefer** v. 선호하다
communicate v. 의사소통을 하다 **usage** n. 이용, 사용

149. 목적 문제

해석 이메일은 왜 쓰였는가?
(A) 서비스 문제에 대해 사과하기 위해
(B) 청구서의 납입을 요청하기 위해
(C) 새로운 제품을 광고하기 위해
(D) 고객에게 돌아오라고 설득하기 위해

해설 지문의 'We are sorry to hear that you closed your account with Topline.'에서 Topline사와 거래를 끊었다는 소식을 듣게 되어 유감이라고 한 후, 'So why not join again?'에서 그러니 다시 가입하는 건 어떤지 물으며 다시 가입할 때 제공될 혜택에 대해 설명하고 있으므로 (D)가 정답이다.

어휘 **apologize** v. 사과하다 **payment** n. 납입, 지불 **bill** n. 청구서
persuade v. 설득하다

[Paraphrasing]
join again 다시 가입하다 → return 돌아오다

150. 육하원칙 문제

해석 Ms. Schmidt는 어떻게 무료 서비스를 받을 수 있는가?
(A) 구독을 업그레이드함으로써
(B) 포인트를 현금으로 바꿈으로써
(C) 특정 숫자들을 입력함으로써
(D) 친구를 추천함으로써

해설 지문의 'Create a new account, and we will give you one month of complimentary usage. When you reach the payment page, enter the code 142737.'에서 새로운 계정을 개설하면 한 달의 무료 이용을 제공할 것이라고 했고, 결제 페이지에 도달하면 코드 142737을 입력하라고 했으므로 (C)가 정답이다.

어휘 redeem v. (현금으로) 바꾸다 refer v. 추천하다, 주목하게 하다

[Paraphrasing]
free service 무료 서비스 → complimentary usage 무료 이용

151-152번은 다음 온라인 채팅 대화문에 관한 문제입니다.

> Robert Patton   오후 1시 3분
> 안녕하세요. 제가 두 달 전에 이사했는데도, 저는 제 새 주소로 은행 명세서를 하나도 받지 못했어요.
>
> RMF 은행   오후 1시 5분
> 그렇군요, Mr. Patton. 귀하께서는 아마도 저희 온라인 은행 서비스를 이용하여 귀하의 연락처를 업데이트해야 할 것 같습니다. 귀하께서 이렇게 한 후에, 귀하의 신원을 확인하기 위해 귀하의 전화기로 ¹⁵¹⁻⁽ᴮ⁾암호가 전송될 것입니다. 변경 사항들이 적용되려면 ¹⁵¹⁻⁽ᴮ⁾귀하께서는 3분 이내에 그것을 입력해야 할 것입니다.
>
> Robert Patton   오후 1시 6분
> 사실, 저는 이미 그것을 했어요.
>
> RMF 은행   오후 1시 7분
> ¹⁵²저희는 최근에 은행 명세서의 기본 옵션을 일반 우편이 아닌 이메일로 지정했습니다. 귀하께서 이를 변경하지 않으셨다면, 명세서가 이메일로 발송되었을 것입니다. 인쇄본을 받으시려면 저희 웹사이트에서 종이 옵션을 선택하셔야 합니다.
>
> Robert Patton   오후 1시 10분
> 제가 그것을 놓쳤던 게 틀림없어요. 잠시만요... 네, 했어요. 도움 주셔서 감사해요.

statement n. 명세서 contact information 연락처
confirm v. 확인하다 identity n. 신원 take effect 적용되다
default option 기본 옵션 hard copy 인쇄본, 출력된 자료

151. Not/True 문제

해석 암호에 대해 언급된 것은?
(A) Mr. Patton에 의해 선정될 것이다.
(B) 짧은 시간 내에 입력되어야 한다.
(C) 직원에게 제시되어야 한다.
(D) 고객의 이름을 바탕으로 할 것이다.

해설 지문의 'a code will be sent'와 'You'll have to type it in within three minutes'에서 암호가 전송될 것이며 당신, 즉 Mr. Patton이 3분 이내에 암호를 입력해야 한다고 했으므로 (B)는 지문의 내용과 일치한다. 따라서 (B)가 정답이다. (A), (C), (D)는 지문에 언급되지 않은 내용이다.

어휘 select v. 선정하다 enter v. 입력하다, 들어가다
period n. 시간, 기간

[Paraphrasing]
within three minutes 3분 이내에 → within a short period 짧은 시간 내에

152. 의도 파악 문제

해설 오후 1시 10분에, Mr. Patton이 "OK, done"이라고 썼을 때, 그가 의도한 것 같은 것은?
(A) 그의 연락처를 업데이트했다.
(B) 온라인 설정을 변경했다.
(C) 은행 거래를 완료했다.
(D) 금융 관련 서류를 인쇄했다.

해설 지문의 'We recently made the default option for bank statements e-mail rather than regular mail. If you haven't changed this, your statements would have been e-mailed to you.'에서 RMF 은행이 최근에 은행 명세서의 기본 옵션을 일반 우편이 아닌 이메일로 지정했고, 이를 변경하지 않았다면 명세서가 이메일로 발송되었을 것이라고 한 후, 'You[Mr. Patton] need to select the Paper option on our Web site to get hard copies sent to you.'에서 인쇄본을 받으려면 웹사이트에서 종이 옵션을 선택해야 한다고 하자, Mr. Patton이 'OK, done.'(네, 했어요)이라고 한 것을 통해, Mr. Patton이 온라인 설정을 변경했음을 알 수 있다. 따라서 (B)가 정답이다.

어휘 transaction n. 거래 financial adj. 금융의

153-154번은 다음 기사에 관한 문제입니다.

> **Ascott Foods사가 비닐봉지들에 작별을 고하다**
> Nicole Chase 작성
>
> 3월 20일—슈퍼마켓 체인인 ¹⁵⁴⁻⁽ᶜ⁾Ascott Foods사는 환경에 좋지 않은 일회용 비닐 쇼핑백을 더 이상 제공하지 않을 것이라고 발표했다. 그것은 Golden 슈퍼마켓 이후로 그렇게 하는 두 번째 체인이 될 것이다. 하지만, Ascott사의 금지가 바로 시행되지는 않을 것이다. 회사 대표에 따르면, ¹⁵³재고품이 지속되는 동안은 각 상점이 비닐봉지 사용을 계속할 것이다.
>
> ¹⁵⁴⁻⁽ᴰ⁾전국의 모든 166개의 Ascott Foods사 지점들이 재사용 가능한 캔버스 가방들을 제공하기 시작할 것이다. 고객들이 그것들을 사용하도록 장려하기 위해 ¹⁵⁴⁻⁽ᴬ⁾그것들은 3개월 동안 무료로 제공될 것이다. ¹⁵⁴⁻⁽ᴮ⁾그 회사는 자사의 농산물 포장에 플라스틱 사용을 막을 수 있는 방법들도 찾고 있다.

plastic bag 비닐봉지 announce v. 발표하다
single-use adj. 일회용의 come into effect 시행되다
supply n. 재고품 reusable adj. 재사용 가능한
avoid v. 막다, 방지하다 produce n. 농산물; v. 생산하다

153. 동의어 문제

해설 1문단 열 번째 줄의 단어 "keep"은 의미상 -와 가장 가깝다.
(A) 확보하다
(B) 계속하다
(C) 보류하다
(D) 보존하다

해설 keep을 포함한 구절 'each store will keep using plastic bags for as long as supplies last'에서 재고품이 지속되는 동안은 각 상점이 비닐봉지 사용을 계속할 것이라고 했으므로 keep은 '계속하다'라는 뜻으로 사용되었다. 따라서 '계속하다'라는 뜻을 지닌 (B) continue가 정답이다.

154. Not/True 문제

해석 Ascott Foods사에 대해 사실이 아닌 것은?
(A) 3개월 동안 무료 쇼핑백들을 제공할 것이다.
(B) 과일 및 채소 상품들을 포함하도록 방침을 확장할 수도 있다.
(C) 일회용 봉지 사용을 중단하는 최초의 슈퍼마켓이 될 것이다.
(D) 전국에 많은 매장 지점들을 가지고 있다.

해설 지문의 'Ascott Foods ~ will no longer be providing single-use plastic shopping bags'와 'It will become the second chain to do so'에서 Ascott Foods사는 일회용 비닐 쇼핑백을 더 이상 제공하지 않을 것이며, 그렇게 하는 두 번째 체인이 될 것이라고 했으므로 (C)는 지문의 내용과 일치하지 않는다. 따라서 (C)가 정답이다. (A)는 'They will come at no cost for three months'에서 그것들, 즉 재사용 가능

한 캔버스 가방들이 3개월 동안 무료로 제공될 것이라고 했으므로 지문의 내용과 일치한다. (B)는 'The company is also looking for ways to avoid using plastic in its produce packaging.'에서 그 회사, 즉 Ascott Foods사는 자사의 농산물 포장에 플라스틱 사용을 막을 수 있는 방법들도 찾고 있다고 했으므로 지문의 내용과 일치한다. (D)는 'All 166 Ascott Foods locations across the country'에서 전국의 모든 166개의 Ascott Foods사 지점들이라고 했으므로 지문의 내용과 일치한다.

어휘 extend v. 확장하다, 연장하다 policy n. 방침, 정책
multiple adj. 많은, 다수의

[Paraphrasing]
at no cost 무료로 → free 무료의
produce 농산물 → fruit and vegetable products 과일 및 채소 상품
166 ~ locations 166개의 지점들 → multiple store locations 많은 매장 지점들

155-157번은 다음 양식에 관한 문제입니다.

Cadigan사 경비 보고서
직원명: Cole Bradley
부서: 판매부
경비 목적: 고객 방문을 위한 출장
오늘의 날짜: 3월 28일

지출 날짜	설명	지출 분류	총액
3월 4일	Gateway 항공 — 토론토에서 포트로더데일로, 이코노미 좌석, 편도	이동	126.25달러
3월 4-6일	Julbee 자동차 대여점, 소형차, 하루당 50달러	이동	150.00달러
3월 4-5일	Bonneville 호텔, 1인용 객실, 1박당 90달러	숙박	180.00달러
3월 5일	Cowbell Grill, 4명	비즈니스 식사	270.00달러
¹⁵⁶3월 6일	Natura 항공 — 포트로더데일에서 토론토로, ¹⁵⁶비즈니스 좌석, 편도	이동	316.10달러
		총액	1,042.35달러

일반 지침:
• ¹⁵⁵/¹⁵⁷모든 업무 관련 지출들에 대한 원본 영수증이 첨부되어야 하며 그렇지 않을 경우 직원에 대한 환급이 거절될 것이다.
• 이코노미 좌석 항공권을 구매하는 직원들은 전액 상환될 것이다. 그러나, ¹⁵⁶비즈니스 좌석을 예약한 직원들은 이코노미 좌석에 이용 가능한 좌석이 없다는 것을 증명할 수 있는 경우에만 전액 상환을 받을 것이다.

expense n. 경비, 지출 trip n. 출장, 여행
compact car 소형차 original adj. 원본의 attach v. 첨부하다 reimbursement n. 환급, 상환 deny v. 거절하다, 거부하다

155. 목적 문제
해석 Mr. Bradley는 왜 양식을 작성했는가?
(A) 매출액을 밝히기 위해
(B) 견적서를 제공하기 위해
(C) 여행 일정을 제안하기 위해
(D) 보상을 요청하기 위해

해설 지문의 'Original receipts ~ must be attached or reimbursement to the employee will be denied.'에서 원본 영수증이 첨부되어야 하며 그렇지 않을 경우 직원에 대한 환급이 거절될 것이라고 한 후, 환급 관련 지침에 대해 설명하고 있으므로 (D)가 정답이다.

어휘 reveal v. 밝히다, 드러내다 sales figure 매출액
estimate n. 견적(서) itinerary n. 여행 일정
compensation n. 보상(금), 배상

[Paraphrasing]
reimbursement 환급 → compensation 보상

156. 추론 문제
해석 Mr. Bradley에 대해 결론지을 수 있는 것은?
(A) 출장에서 법인 카드를 사용했다.
(B) 항공편에 대해 전액 상환을 받지 못할 수도 있다.
(C) 보고서를 제출하는 기한을 지키지 않았다.
(D) 식사 비용에 허용되는 한도를 초과했다.

해설 지문의 'March 6', 'business class'에서 Mr. Bradley가 3월 6일에 비즈니스 좌석을 이용했다는 것을 알 수 있고, 'those who booked business-class seats will only receive full reimbursement if they can show that there were no seats available in economy class'에서 비즈니스 좌석을 예약한 직원들은 이코노미 좌석에 이용 가능한 좌석이 없다는 것을 증명할 수 있는 경우에만 전액 상환을 받을 것이라고 했으므로 Mr. Bradley가 항공편에 대해 전액 상환을 받지 못할 수도 있음을 추론할 수 있다. 따라서 (B)가 정답이다.

어휘 corporate adj. 법인의, 기업의 repay v. 상환하다
exceed v. 초과하다 acceptable adj. 허용되는, 용인되는

[Paraphrasing]
receive full reimbursement 전액 상환을 받다 → be fully repaid 전액 상환을 받다

157. 육하원칙 문제
해석 양식에 따르면, 무엇이 상환 청구가 거부되는 결과로 이어질 것인가?
(A) 요청서를 너무 늦게 제출하는 것
(B) 허용된 금액보다 더 많이 지출하는 것
(C) 모든 지불 기록을 포함하지 못하는 것
(D) 개인 신용카드로 항공편을 예약하는 것

해설 지문의 'Original receipts for all business-related expenses must be attached or reimbursement to the employee will be denied.'에서 모든 업무 관련 지출들에 대한 원본 영수증이 첨부되어야 하며 그렇지 않을 경우 직원에 대한 환급이 거절될 것이라고 하였다. 따라서 (C)가 정답이다.

어휘 claim n. 청구, 신청 request n. 요청서, 청원서
allow v. 허용하다 personal adj. 개인의

[Paraphrasing]
receipts 영수증 → records of payment 지불 기록

158-160번은 다음 이메일에 관한 문제입니다.

수신: 모든 트레이너들 <instructors@silvergym.com>
발신: Francesca Martinez <f.martinez@silvergym.com>
제목: 여러분 모두를 위한 최신 정보
날짜: 2월 1일

안녕하세요 여러분,

오늘부터, 헬스장 회원들은 우리의 새롭게 이용 가능한 Silver 헬스장 스마트폰 애플리케이션을 다운로드하여 그들의 회원 ID 로 로그인할 수 있습니다. ¹⁵⁹⁻⁽ᴮ⁾이 애플리케이션은 사용자들이 그들이 체중을 얼마나 감량했는지에 대해 계속 파악하도록 도울 것입니다. ¹⁵⁸Silver 헬스장의 개인 트레이너로서, 여러분은 회원들이 이 서비스를 이용하도록 권장해야 합니다.

또한, 이번 달에 우리는 특별 판촉 행사를 할 것입니다. ¹⁵⁹⁻⁽ᴬ⁾⁄⁽ᶜ⁾애 플리케이션에 기록된 정해진 동작들을 따라 함으로써 최소 10파운드를 감량하는 모든 회원은 그들이 선택하는 한 번의 무료 수업에 대한 쿠폰을 받을 수 있습니다. 이 제안에 관심 있는 사람들에게 ¹⁶⁰우리 수업들에 대한 세부 사항들이 게시판에 게시되어 있다는 것을 알려주시기 바랍니다.

Francesca Martinez 드림, 소유주, Silver 헬스장

keep track of ~에 대해 계속 파악하다
encourage v. 권장하다, 격려하다
promotion n. 판촉 (행사), 홍보   routine n. 정해진 동작, 일상
bulletin board 게시판

158. 목적 문제
해설 이메일의 하나의 목적은 무엇인가?
(A) 헬스장 회원들에게 요금 변경에 대해 알리기 위해
(B) 고객들에게 규정에 대해 상기시키기 위해
(C) 직원들에게 프로그램에 대해 알리기 위해
(D) 사용자들에게 수업에 참여하도록 장려하기 위해

해설 지문의 'As the personal trainers at Silver Gym, you need to encourage members to use this service.'에서 Silver 헬스장의 개인 트레이너로서, 회원들이 이 서비스, 즉 스마트폰 애플리케이션을 이용하도록 권장해야 한다고 했으므로 (C)가 정답이다.

어휘 notify v. 알리다, 공지하다   policy n. 규정, 정책

159. Not/True 문제
해설 헬스장 회원들에 대해 언급되지 않은 것은?
(A) 무료 수업의 자격을 얻을 수 있다.
(B) 애플리케이션을 사용하여 체중 감량을 관찰할 수 있다.
(C) 보상을 받기 위해 체중을 감량해야 한다.
(D) 우편으로 혜택들에 대한 공지를 받을 것이다.

해설 (D)는 지문에 언급되지 않은 내용이다. 따라서 (D)가 정답이다. (A)와 (C)는 'Any member who loses at least 10 pounds ~ can receive a voucher for one free class of their choice.'에서 최소 10파운드를 감량하는 모든 회원은 그들이 선택하는 한 번의 무료 수업에 대한 쿠폰을 받을 수 있다고 했으므로 지문의 내용과 일치한다. (B)는 'The app will help users to keep track of how much weight they have lost.'에서 이 애플리케이션은 사용자들이 그들이 체중을 얼마나 감량했는지에 대해 계속 파악하도록 도울 것이라고 했으므로 지문의 내용과 일치한다.

어휘 qualify for ~의 자격을 얻다   monitor v. 관찰하다
notice n. 공지, 알림

[Paraphrasing]
free class 무료 수업 → complimentary session 무료 수업
keep track of how much weight ~ lost 체중을 얼마나 감량했는지에 대해 계속 파악하다 → monitor weight loss 체중 감량을 관찰하다

160. 육하원칙 문제
해설 수업들에 대한 정보는 어디에서 찾을 수 있는가?
(A) 게시판에서

(B) 웹사이트에서
(C) 이메일에서
(D) 탈의실에서

해설 지문의 'details about our classes are posted on the bulletin board'에서 수업들에 대한 세부 사항들이 게시판에 게시되어 있다고 했으므로 (A)가 정답이다.

어휘 notice board 게시판   locker room 탈의실

[Paraphrasing]
information about classes 수업들에 대한 정보 → details about ~ classes 수업들에 대한 세부 사항들
bulletin board 게시판 → notice board 게시판

161-163번은 다음 안내문에 관한 문제입니다.

Gleason's Grill 종업원 교육 안내서

1단계
손님들이 자리에 앉자마자 그들에게 다가가세요. ¹⁶³만약 당신이 새로운 손님들이 들어올 때 테이블을 응대하느라 바쁘다면, 큰 소리로 그들에게 인사하세요. — [1] —.

2단계
손님들에게 메뉴를 살펴볼 시간을 주세요. — [2] —. 그들에게 우리의 일일 특선요리를 알려주고 그들이 가지고 있는 모든 질문들에 답해주세요. ¹⁶¹손님이 특정 재료에 알레르기가 있어서 그것이 요리에 그것이 있는지에 관해 묻는 경우, 자리를 뜨는 것에 양해를 구하고 주방 직원으로부터 알아내세요. — [3] —. ¹⁶²손님들이 주문할 준비가 되면, 반드시 모든 것을 기록하세요. 그다음, 실수가 없었는지 확실히 하기 위해 그들에게 그들의 주문 내역을 한 번 더 말하세요.

3단계
모든 것이 만족스러운지 알기 위해 음식을 가져다주고 몇 분 뒤에 손님들을 다시 확인해 보세요. 그들이 식사를 마치고 나면, 계산서를 가져 오기 전에 디저트나 커피를 제안하세요. — [4] —.

---

seat v. 앉히다   loudly adv. 큰 소리로   go over 살펴보다
inform v. 알리다   inquire v. 묻다   ingredient n. 재료
excuse v. (자리를 뜨는 것에 대해) 양해를 구하다
repeat v. 한 번 더 말하다, 반복하다
satisfactory adj. 만족스러운   bill n. 계산서, 고지서

161. 육하원칙 문제
해설 안내문에 따르면, 종업원들은 왜 주방 직원과 이야기해야 하는가?
(A) 음식이 얼마나 느리게 준비되고 있는지에 대해 불평하기 위해
(B) 아이들을 위한 더 작은 식사량을 요청하기 위해
(C) 새롭게 추가된 메뉴 항목들에 대해 알아보기 위해
(D) 요리의 내용물에 대해 묻기 위해

해설 지문의 'In the event that a customer inquires about whether a dish has a specific ingredient ~, ~ find out from the kitchen staff.'에서 손님이 요리에 특정 재료가 있는지에 관해 묻는 경우, 주방 직원으로부터 알아내라고 했으므로 (D)가 정답이다.

어휘 portion n. 양, 부분   added adj. 추가된

[Paraphrasing]
ingredient 재료 → contents of a dish 요리의 내용물

162. 육하원칙 문제
해설 고객들의 주문을 받은 직후 종업원들은 무엇을 해야 하는가?

(A) 계산대에 메모지를 가져간다.
(B) 추가적인 품목들을 추천한다.
(C) 몇몇 선택된 것들을 확인한다.
(D) 계산서에 각 항목을 추가한다.

해설 지문의 'When the customers are ready to order, make sure to write everything down. Next, repeat their orders back to them to be certain that no mistakes have been made.'에서 손님들이 주문할 준비가 되면 반드시 모든 것을 기록하고, 그다음 실수가 없었는지 확실히 하기 위해 그들에게 그들의 주문 내역들을 한 번 더 말하라고 했으므로 (C)가 정답이다.

어휘 notepad n. 메모지 additional adj. 추가적인
confirm v. 확인하다, 확정하다 selection n. 선택된 것

163. 문장 위치 찾기 문제

해설 [1], [2], [3], [4]로 표시된 위치 중, 다음 문장이 들어갈 곳으로 가장 적절한 것은?

"이것은 다른 직원들에게 그들이 식당에 들어왔다는 것을 알릴 것입니다."

(A) [1]
(B) [2]
(C) [3]
(D) [4]

해설 주어진 문장은 사람들이 식당에 들어왔다는 것을 다른 직원들에게 알려줄 수 있는 행동과 관련된 내용 주변에 나올 것임을 알 수 있다. [1]의 앞 문장인 'If you are busy serving a table when new customers walk in, greet them loudly.'에서 만약 새로운 손님들이 들어올 때 테이블을 응대하느라 바쁘다면, 큰 소리로 그들에게 인사하라고 했으므로, [1]에 주어진 문장이 들어가면 새로운 손님들이 들어올 때 큰 소리로 그들에게 인사하면 이것이 다른 직원들에게 손님들이 식당에 들어왔다는 것을 알릴 것이라는 자연스러운 문맥이 된다는 것을 알 수 있다. 따라서 (A)가 정답이다.

어휘 alert v. 알리다, 의식하게 하다

164-167번은 다음 문자 메시지 대화문에 관한 문제입니다.

Riku Sato   오후 1시 35분
지난주에 우리는 이곳 BYR사 팀장들을 위한 리더십 교육에 대해 논의했었죠. 저는 기업 교육을 제공하는 Rework Pro라는 회사를 발견했어요.

Julianne Nash   오후 1시 37분
좋아요. 164우리의 월별 직원 설문조사는 우리 직원들이 더 효과적인 지도를 원한다는 것을 보여줘요.

Mallory Smithers   오후 1시 38분
Rework Pro사는 어떤 종류의 서비스를 제공하죠?

Riku Sato   오후 1시 41분
165그들은 우리를 위한 맞춤 워크숍을 기획해 줄 거예요.

Julianne Nash   오후 1시 42분
그것으로 충분할까요? 165우리가 정기적으로 워크숍을 직접 열고 있지만, 우리는 여전히 이 문제를 가지고 있어요.

Riku Sato   오후 1시 45분
자격을 갖춘 전문가들에 의해 조직된 워크숍은 더 효과적일 거예요.

Mallory Smithers   오후 1시 46분
하지만 166저는 일정 계획에 대해 걱정스러워요. 우리는 6월에 몇몇 프로젝트 마감일이 있어요.

Riku Sato   오후 1시 46분
166제가 이미 그것을 확인했어요. 워크숍은 7월에 진행될 수 있어요.

Julianne Nash   오후 1시 48분
그렇다면 남아 있는 단 한 가지 문제는 비용이네요.

Riku Sato   오후 1시 49분
Rework Pro사가 3일 후에 제게 견적서를 보낼 거예요. 167수요일에 만나서 이 워크숍이 우리 예산에 맞을지 확인해 봐요.

corporate adj. 기업의 effective adj. 효과적인
guidance n. 지도, 지침 custom adj. 맞춤의
sufficient adj. 충분한 concerned adj. 걱정스러운
remaining adj. 남아 있는 estimate n. 견적서
budget n. 예산

164. 추론 문제

해설 BYR사에 대해 암시되는 것은?
(A) 이전에 Rework Pro사와 협력했다.
(B) 관리자들에게 혜택을 제공한다.
(C) 직원들로부터 주기적인 의견을 요청한다.
(D) 작년에 다른 회사에 직원들을 빼앗겼다.

해설 지문의 'Our[BYR Incorporated's] monthly employee survey'에서 BYR사의 월별 직원 설문조사에 대해 언급했으므로 BYR사가 매월 직원들에게 설문조사를 실시한다는 것을 추론할 수 있다. 따라서 (C)가 정답이다.

어휘 partner with ~과 협력하다 periodic adj. 주기적인
feedback n. 의견, 피드백

Paraphrasing
monthly 월별 → periodic 주기적인

165. 의도 파악 문제

해설 오후 1시 42분에, Ms. Nash가 "Will that be sufficient"라고 썼을 때, 그녀가 의도한 것 같은 것은?
(A) 워크숍의 참석이 저조할 수 있다.
(B) 직원 채용 문제가 계속 해결되지 않을 것이다.
(C) 관리자들이 더 긴 교육 기간을 필요로 한다.
(D) 교육 방식이 효과적이지 않을 수 있다.

해설 지문의 'They[Rework Pro] will design custom workshops for us[BYR Incorporated].'에서 Mr. Sato가 Rework Pro사가 BYR사를 위한 맞춤 워크숍을 기획해 줄 것이라고 하자, Ms. Nash가 'Will that be sufficient?'(그것으로 충분할까요?)라고 한 후, 'We regularly hold workshops ourselves, but we still have this issue.'에서 정기적으로 워크숍을 직접 열고 있지만, 여전히 이 문제를 가지고 있다고 한 것을 통해, Ms. Nash는 워크숍이 문제를 해결하는 데 효과적이지 않을 수 있다고 생각하고 있음을 알 수 있다. 따라서 (D)가 정답이다.

어휘 unresolved adj. 해결되지 않은 instructional adj. 교육의
ineffective adj. 효과적이지 않은

Paraphrasing
workshops 워크숍 → instructional method 교육 방식

166. 육하원칙 문제

해설 Mr. Sato는 그가 이미 무엇을 했다고 말하는가?
(A) 직원 휴가 날짜를 확인했다.
(B) 일정 관련 정보를 요청했다.
(C) 워크숍 참석자들의 이름을 제공했다.
(D) 장소의 이용 가능 여부를 확인했다.

해설 지문의 'I'm concerned about scheduling'에서 Ms. Smithers가 일정 계획이 걱정스럽다고 하자, 'I already checked that[scheduling]. The workshops could be done in July.'에서 Mr. Sato가 자신이 이미 일정 계획을 확인했으며 워크숍이 7월에 진행될 수 있다고 했으므로 (B)가 정답이다.

어휘 request v. 요청하다   attendee n. 참석자
confirm v. 확인하다   venue n. 장소
availability n. 이용 가능 여부, 유용성

167. 육하원칙 문제
해설 작성자들은 왜 수요일에 만날 것인가?
(A) 워크숍의 주제를 고르기 위해
(B) 서비스 가격에 대해 논의하기 위해
(C) 프로젝트 마감일을 검토하기 위해
(D) 강사의 자격을 확인하기 위해

해설 지문의 'Let's meet on Wednesday to determine whether these workshops will fit our budget.'에서 수요일에 만나서 이 워크숍들이 예산에 맞을지 확인해 보자고 했으므로 (B)가 정답이다.

어휘 qualification n. 자격

168-171번은 다음 편지에 관한 문제입니다.

GALAXIS지

1월 7일
Dr. Frederick Simons
492번지 Lerner로, 901호
블룸필드 타운십, 마이애미주 48401

Dr. Simons께,

저희는 명왕성의 산들의 이야기에 대한 당신의 제안이 꽤 전도유망하다고 생각했습니다. 171저희는 그것이 저희 독자들의 관심을 끌 것이라고 생각하며 당신이 168-(A)/1712,500에서 3,000단어의 기사를 작성해 171주면 좋겠습니다. — [1] —.

저희는 당신에게 그 기사에 대해 2,500달러를 제공할 수 있습니다. — [2] —. 하지만, 170과거와 달리, 저희가 어떠한 이유로 당신의 작업물을 사용하지 않기로 결정할 경우, 저희가 당신에게 전액을 보상할 수 없을 것이라는 점을 유의하십시오. — [3] —. 그렇긴 하지만, 저희는 당신의 시간에 대해 당신에게 500달러를 지불할 것입니다. 168-(C)저희는 그 기사를 저희의 5월호에 실을 예정이므로, 168-(B)3월 5일까지 당신의 초고를 제출해 주시길 바랍니다. 저는 이 편지에 이 계약 조건들을 명시한 두 장의 계약서들을 함께 동봉했습니다. — [4] —. 만약 그것들에 동의한다면, 169그 계약서들 중 하나에 서명을 하고 잡지사의 우편 주소를 사용하여 저희에게 돌려보내 주십시오. 나머지 하나는 당신의 기록을 위해 보관해 두십시오.

질문이나 우려 사항이 있다면, 주저하지 말고 제게 이메일로 연락하십시오. 170저희는 당신과 다시 함께 일하기를 기대합니다.

Molly Hamilton 드림
수석 편집자, Galaxis지

proposal n. 제안   promising adj. 전도유망한, 조짐이 좋은
appeal v. 관심을 끌다, 호소하다   compensate v. 보상하다
intend to ~할 예정이다, ~하려고 생각하다   enclose v. 동봉하다
state v. 명시하다, 기재하다   term n. (계약) 조건
hesitate v. 주저하다, 망설이다

168. Not/True 문제
해석 Ms. Hamilton이 기사에 대한 정보로 언급하지 않은 것은?
(A) 단어 길이
(B) 마감일
(C) 발행 호
(D) 수정 과정

해설 (D)는 지문에 언급되지 않은 내용이다. 따라서 (D)가 정답이다. (A)는 'write an article of 2,500 to 3,000 words'에서 2,500에서 3,000단어의 기사를 작성해 달라고 했으므로 지문의 내용과 일치한다. (B)는 'submit your first draft by March 5'에서 3월 5일까지 초고를 제출해 달라고 했으므로 지문의 내용과 일치한다. (C)는 'We intend to publish the article in our May issue'에서 그 기사를 5월호에 실을 예정이라고 했으므로 지문의 내용과 일치한다.

어휘 due date 마감일, 만기일   revision n. 수정
process n. 과정

169. 육하원칙 문제
해석 Dr. Simons는 무엇을 하도록 요청받았는가?
(A) 계약서를 다시 우편으로 보낸다.
(B) 몇몇 계약 조건들을 협상한다.
(C) 몇몇 이메일 메시지들을 저장한다.
(D) 기사를 다시 쓴다.

해설 지문의 'please ~ return one of the contracts to us using the magazine's postal address'에서 그 계약서들 중 하나를 잡지사의 우편 주소를 사용하여 돌려보내 달라고 했으므로 (A)가 정답이다.

어휘 agreement n. 계약서   negotiate v. 협상하다

[Paraphrasing]
return ~ contracts ~ using the ~ postal address 우편 주소를 사용하여 계약서를 돌려보내다 → Mail back an agreement 계약서를 다시 우편으로 보내다

170. 추론 문제
해석 Galaxis지에 대해 암시되는 것은?
(A) 구독자들은 온라인 콘텐츠를 수신하도록 선택할 수 있다.
(B) 몇몇 국가들에서 구매하는 것이 가능하다.
(C) Dr. Simons는 이전에 그것에 기사를 기고한 적이 있다.
(D) 그것의 프리랜서 작가들에게는 정규 직원보다 더 적은 급여를 지급한다.

해설 지문의 'unlike in the past, we will not be able to compensate you fully if we decide not to use your work for any reason'에서 과거와 달리, 자신들, 즉 Galaxis지가 어떠한 이유로 당신, 즉 Dr. Simons의 작업물을 사용하지 않기로 결정할 경우, 그에게 전액을 보상할 수 없을 것이라고 했고, 'We look forward to working with you again.'에서 당신, 즉 Dr. Simons와 다시 함께 일하기를 기대한다고 했으므로 Dr. Simons가 Galaxis지에 이전에 기사를 기고한 적이 있다는 것을 추론할 수 있다. 따라서 (C)가 정답이다.

어휘 contribute v. 기고하다, 공헌하다

171. 문장 위치 찾기 문제
해설 [1], [2], [3], [4]로 표시된 위치 중 다음 문장이 들어갈 곳으로 가장 적절한 것은?

"만약 그것이 이것을 초과한다면, 저희는 그것을 실을 수 없을 것이라는 점을 유의해 주십시오."

(A) [1]
(B) [2]

    (C) [3]
    (D) [4]

해설 주어진 문장은 실을 수 있는 범위와 관련된 내용 주변에 나올 것임을 예상할 수 있다. [1]의 앞 문장인 'We ~ would like you to write an article of 2,500 to 3,000 words.'에서 2,500에서 3,000단어의 기사를 작성해 주면 좋겠다고 했으므로, [1]에 주어진 문장이 들어가면 2,500에서 3,000단어의 기사를 작성하길 원하며, 이것을 초과할 경우 그것을 실을 수 없을 것이라는 자연스러운 문맥이 된다는 것을 알 수 있다. 따라서 (A)가 정답이다.

어휘 exceed v. 초과하다   publish v. 싣다, 게재하다

172-175번은 다음 광고에 관한 문제입니다.

Galenus 여행사와 함께
멕시코의 Vallarta-Nayarit 지역을 방문하세요

[172]Vallarta-Nayarit 지역은 제공할 것이 정말 많으며, 당신이 Galenus 여행사를 이용하여 여행을 예약하면, 여행 기간 동안 최대한의 지원을 받을 것입니다. 도착할 때 [172]당신을 맞이하기 위해 저희의 현지 지사의 직원들이 그곳에 가 있을 뿐만 아니라, 그들은 또한 당신이 관심을 가질 만한 어떠한 활동들이든 계획하는 데 도움을 줄 것입니다. 놓쳐서는 안 될 몇몇 지역들은 다음을 포함합니다:

Puerto Vallarta 시내
차량 통행이 금지된 도심 지역이 있는 이곳은 당신이 쇼핑하고, 식사하고, 그리고 현지의 현대 미술관들을 방문하면서 관광할 수 있는 완벽한 장소입니다. [173]주 광장은 길거리 공연자들과 예술가들로 항상 가득 차 있으므로 만약 당신이 아이들과 함께 여행한다면 이곳은 필수입니다.

Mismaloya
시내의 도보 거리 내에 있는 [174]이 지역은 가격이 적당한 숙박 시설들로 가득합니다. Mismaloya의 편안한 분위기는 돈을 너무 많이 쓰지 않고 해변에 더 가까이 있길 원하는 여행자들에게 이상적입니다.

Riviera Nayarit
그것의 화려한 해변들로 유명한 [175]Riviera Nayarit은 골프장, 놀이공원, 그리고 5성급 호화 리조트들을 위해 가는 장소입니다. 생선 타코들과 다른 정통 별미들을 제공하는 해변 식당들은 이 지역의 200마일 구간의 도처에서 찾을 수 있습니다.

---

duration n. 기간   greet v. 맞이하다   land v. 도착하다
arrange v. (미리) 계획하다, 주선하다   miss v. 놓치다
dine v. 식사하다   contemporary adj. 현대의
must n. 필수, 꼭 보아야 하는 것   square n. 광장
affordable adj. (가격이) 적당한, 저렴한
accommodation n. 숙박 시설   authentic adj. 정통의, 진정한
delicacy n. 별미, 진미

172. 추론 문제

해설 Galenus 여행사에 대해 추론될 수 있는 것은?
(A) 멕시코 여행 시 할인을 제공한다.
(B) Vallarta-Nayarit에 사무실이 있다.
(C) 가족을 위한 투어를 전문으로 한다.
(D) 고객들에게 여행 보험을 제공한다.

해설 지문의 'The Vallarta-Nayarit region has so much to offer'에서 Vallarta-Nayarit 지역은 제공할 것이 정말 많다고 했고, 'representatives from our[Galenus Travel's] local branch be there to greet you'에서 당신을 맞이하기 위해 Galenus 여행사의 현지 지사의 직원들이 그곳, 즉 Vallarta-Nayarit 지사에 가 있을 것이라고 했으므로 Galenus 여행사가 Vallarta-Nayarit에 사무실을 가지고 있다는 사실을 추론할 수 있다. 따라서 (B)가 정답이다.

어휘 specialize in ~을 전문으로 하다   insurance n. 보험

173. 육하원칙 문제

해설 광고에 따르면, Puerto Vallarta 시내는 왜 아이들을 데려오기 좋은 장소인가?
(A) 차량 속도 제한이 엄격하게 감시된다.
(B) 많은 저렴한 식당들이 있다.
(C) 공개된 오락거리를 그곳에서 볼 수 있다.
(D) 해변에서 도보 거리 내에 있다.

해설 지문의 'It[Downtown Puerto Vallarta]'s a must if you're traveling with children as the main square is always full of street performers and artists.'에서 주 광장은 길거리 공연자들과 예술가들로 항상 가득 차 있으므로 만약 아이들과 함께 여행한다면 Puerto Vallarta 시내는 필수라고 했으므로 (C)가 정답이다.

어휘 strictly adv. 엄격하게   inexpensive adj. 저렴한, 비싸지 않은
public adj. 공개된, 공공의   entertainment n. 오락거리

Paraphrasing
a good place to bring children 아이들을 데려오기 좋은 장소 → a must if ~ traveling with children 아이들과 함께 여행한다면 필수

174. 추론 문제

해설 Mismaloya는 어느 집단의 흥미를 가장 많이 끌 것 같은가?
(A) 박물관 애호가들
(B) 알뜰한 여행자들
(C) 풍경 사진작가들
(D) 전문적인 예술가들

해설 지문의 'this area is full of affordable accommodations. ~ Mismaloya is ideal for travelers who want to be closer to the beach without spending too much money.'에서 이 지역, 즉 Mismaloya는 가격이 적당한 숙박 시설들로 가득하며, 돈을 너무 많이 쓰지 않고 해변에 더 가까이 있길 원하는 여행자들에게 이상적이라고 했으므로 Mismaloya는 알뜰한 여행자들의 흥미를 가장 많이 끌 것이라는 사실을 추론할 수 있다. 따라서 (B)가 정답이다.

어휘 lover n. 애호가   budget adj. 알뜰한, 검소한; n. 예산

175. 추론 문제

해설 Riviera Nayarit에 대해 암시되는 것은?
(A) 비싼 숙박 시설들을 갖추고 있다.
(B) 현대 미술 장소로 유명하다.
(C) 신혼부부에게 인기가 있다.
(D) 여러 부동산 개발이 계획되어 있다.

해설 지문의 'Riviera Nayarit is the place to go for ~ five-star luxury resorts'에서 Riviera Nayarit은 5성급 호화 리조트들을 위해 가는 장소라고 했으므로, Riviera Nayarit가 비싼 숙박 시설들을 갖추고 있다는 것을 추론할 수 있다. 따라서 (A)가 정답이다.

어휘 costly adj. 비싼   scene n. 장소, 분야   property n. 부동산

Paraphrasing
luxury resorts 호화 리조트들 → costly accommodation facilities 비싼 숙박 시설들

176-180번은 다음 회람과 이메일에 관한 문제입니다.

회람

수신: 모든 지점 관리자들
발신: Lori Morrison
제목: 재고 조사
날짜: 1월 5일

우리의 연간 재고 조사에 착수하기 위해 176/177-(B)우리는 모든 Super Parties사 지점들에서 하루 동안의 휴업 일정을 잡아두었다는 것을 기억해 주십시오. 176이 기간 동안, 모든 제품들은 손으로 세어져야 하며 우리의 컴퓨터 기록과 비교하여 대조되어야 합니다. 상세 내용은 아래에 있습니다.

지점	날짜
177-(B)시카고, 일리노이	화요일, 2월 12일
177-(B)포트웨인, 인디애나	수요일, 2월 13일
177-(B)밀워키, 위스콘신	수요일, 2월 20일
177-(B)/180세인트루이스, 177-(B)미주리	금요일, 180 2월 22일

177-(D)여러분의 고객들에게 위의 어떠한 날짜에든지 배송이 예정된 주문들은 영향을 받지 않을 것임을 알리십시오. 또한, 이 기간 동안 177-(C)그들은 우리 웹사이트를 통해 제품들을 계속 구매할 수 있습니다.

inventory n. 재고 조사, 물품 목록   schedule v. 일정을 잡다
closure n. 휴업   undertake v. 착수하다
count v. (수를) 세다   verify v. 대조하다, 확인하다
against prep. ~과 비교하여, ~에 반대하여
advise v. 알리다, 조언하다   affect v. 영향을 미치다

178수신: Adele Welch <a.welch@superparties.com>
발신: Brian Ledford <b.ledford@superparties.com>
제목: 추가 요청
날짜: 1월 6일

안녕하세요 Adele,

178본사의 Amy Turner가 제가 직원 할인 혜택의 수혜 대상이라는 것에 대해 당신이 확인을 해주기를 원해서 당신께 연락을 드립니다. 그녀는 제게 178500달러가 넘는 모든 주문은 지점 관리자의 승인을 받아야 한다고 말했습니다. 이전에 제가 말씀드렸듯이, 179저는 다음 달에 있을 제 어린 사촌의 생일 파티를 위해 의상들, 파티 게임들, 그리고 풍선들을 주문하길 원하며, 그 총액은 600달러가 됩니다. 제가 양식을 가지고 언제 들르면 될지 제게 알려 주십시오.

저는 또한 179파티가 2월 23일에 인디애나에서 열릴 것이라는 점과, 지난 11월에 179/180당신이 2월 21일부터 23일까지의 제 휴가 요청을 수락해 주셨다는 점을 상기시켜 드리고자 합니다. 180저는 제가 저희 지점의 재고 조사에 참여할 수 없어서 매우 유감스럽습니다. 제가 없는 동안 Lisa에게 저를 대신해 달라고 요청하였습니다.

감사합니다!

Brian 드림

follow-up adj. 추가의; n. 후속 조치
eligible for ~의 수혜 대상이 되는   approval n. 승인
stop by 들르다   take place 열리다   accept v. 수락하다
take part in ~에 참여하다   cover v. ~를 대신하다, 덮다

---

176. 육하원칙 문제
해석 Super Parties사는 왜 그것의 지점들의 문을 닫을 것인가?
(A) 재정적 손실을 줄이기 위해
(B) 상품 수를 세기 위해
(C) 시장 변화에 대처하기 위해
(D) 수리에 착수하기 위해

해설 회람의 'we have scheduled one-day closures at all Super Parties branches'와 'During this time, all products must be counted by hand'에서 모든 Super Parties사 지점들에서 하루 동안의 휴업 일정을 잡아두었으며 이 기간 동안, 모든 제품들이 손으로 세어져야 한다고 했으므로 (B)가 정답이다.

어휘 financial loss 재정적 손실   address v. ~에 대처하다, 해결하다

Paraphrasing
closing ~ branches 지점들의 문을 닫는 것 → closures at ~ branches 지점들에서 휴업
products 제품들 → merchandise 상품

177. Not/True 문제
해석 Super Parties사에 대해 언급되지 않은 것은?
(A) 물건들은 대여될 수 있다.
(B) 네 곳에 가게를 가지고 있다.
(C) 상품은 온라인에서 구할 수 있다.
(D) 고객들에게 제품들을 배송한다.

해설 질문의 Super Parties사와 관련된 내용이 언급된 회람에서 (A)는 언급되지 않은 내용이다. 따라서 (A)가 정답이다. (B)는 'we have scheduled ~ closures at all Super Parties branches'에서 모든 Super Parties사 지점들에서 휴업 일정을 잡아두었다고 했고, 'Chicago, Illinois', 'Fort Wayne, Indiana', 'Milwaukee, Wisconsin', 'St. Louis, Missouri'에서 총 네 개의 지점에서 휴업한다는 것을 알 수 있으므로 지문의 내용과 일치한다. (C)는 'they[customers] can still purchase products through our[Super Parties'] Web site'에서 고객들은 Super Parties사의 웹사이트를 통해 제품들을 계속 구매할 수 있다고 했으므로 지문의 내용과 일치한다. (D)는 'Advise your[Super Parties'] customers that orders scheduled for delivery ~ will not be affected.'에서 Super Parties사의 고객들에게 배송이 예정된 주문들은 영향을 받지 않을 것임을 알리라고 했으므로 지문의 내용과 일치한다.

어휘 rent v. 대여하다; n. 임대료   ship v. 배송하다

Paraphrasing
can ~ purchase products through ~ Web site 웹사이트를 통해 제품들을 구매할 수 있다 → merchandise is available online 상품은 온라인에서 구할 수 있다

178. 추론 문제
해석 Ms. Welch는 누구일 것 같은가?
(A) 최고 경영자
(B) 여행사 직원
(C) 지점장
(D) 수석 회계사

해설 이메일의 'To: Adele Welch'에서 이메일이 Ms. Welch에게 보내졌다는 것을 알 수 있고, 'Amy Turner ~ wants you [Ms. Welch] to confirm'과 'any orders over $500 need to have a branch manager's approval'에서 Amy Turner는 Ms. Welch가 확인을 해주기를 원하며, 500달러가 넘는 모든 주문은 지점 관리자의 승인을 받아야 한다고 했으므로 Ms. Welch가 지점장이라는 사실을 추론할 수 있다. 따라서 (C)가 정답이다.

어휘 travel agent 여행사 직원 accountant n. 회계사

Paraphrasing
branch manager 지점 관리자 → branch supervisor 지점장

179. 육하원칙 문제

해석 Mr. Ledford는 무엇을 할 계획인가?
(A) 새로운 도시로 이사한다.
(B) 회사 세미나에 참석한다.
(C) 교육 워크숍에 참석한다.
(D) 가족들을 방문한다.

해설 이메일의 'I[Mr. Ledford] was hoping to order costumes, party games, and balloons for my young cousin's birthday party next month'에서 Mr. Ledford가 다음 달에 있을 자신의 어린 사촌의 생일 파티를 위해 의상들, 파티 게임들, 그리고 풍선들을 주문하길 원했다고 했고, 'the party is taking place ~ on February 23, and ~ you accepted my request for leave from February 21 to 23'에서 파티는 2월 23일에 열릴 것이며 2월 21일부터 23일까지의 Mr. Ledford의 휴가 요청이 수락되었다고 했으므로 (D)가 정답이다.

Paraphrasing
cousin 사촌 → family members 가족들

180. 추론 문제 연계

해석 Mr. Ledford는 어디에서 일하는 것 같은가?
(A) 시카고에서
(B) 포트웨인에서
(C) 밀워키에서
(D) 세인트루이스에서

해설 Mr. Ledford가 작성한 이메일을 먼저 확인한다.

단서 1 이메일의 'you accepted my[Mr. Ledford's] request for leave from February 21 to 23. I'm so sorry that I will be unavailable to take part in our branch's inventory.'에서 2월 21일부터 23일까지에 대한 Mr. Ledford의 휴가 요청이 수락되었으며 이에 따라 자신의 지점의 재고 조사에 참여할 수 없어서 매우 유감스럽다고 했다. 그런데 2월 21일부터 23일 사이에 재고 조사가 진행되는 지점이 어디인지 제시되지 않았으므로 회람에서 관련 내용을 확인한다.

단서 2 회람의 'St. Louis', 'February 22'에서 세인트루이스 지점의 재고 조사가 2월 22일에 열린다는 사실을 확인할 수 있다.

두 단서를 종합할 때, Mr. Ledford는 자신의 휴가 기간인 2월 21일부터 23일 사이에 재고 조사가 진행되는 세인트루이스 지점에서 일하고 있음을 추론할 수 있다. 따라서 (D)가 정답이다.

181-185번은 다음 웹페이지와 이메일에 관한 문제입니다.

www.expressmovers.com

Express Movers사

| 소개 | 예약 | 위치 |

Express Movers사는 당신의 소지품을 운반하기 위한 최고의 회사입니다. ¹⁸²⁻⁽ᴰ⁾30년 넘게 장거리 이사 서비스를 전문으로 해온 저희 ¹⁸¹직원들은 당신의 물건이 포장된 직후와 똑같은 상태로 예정된 시간에 최종 목적지에 도착하도록 보장할 것입니다. ¹⁸²⁻⁽ᴬ⁾저희는 자동차, 트럭, 그리고 보트와 같은 탈것을 견인하기도 합니다.* 아래에 있는 저희의 저렴한 가격들을 확인하시고 수거 및 반환 시간을 정하시려면 여기를 클릭하십시오.

거리	가격
50마일 미만	300달러
50-200마일	500달러
201-500마일	750달러
¹⁸⁴500마일 초과	¹⁸⁴1,000달러

*거리에 상관없이, ¹⁸²⁻⁽ᴬ⁾차량당 500달러의 추가 요금이 있습니다.

transport v. 운반하다 belongings n. 소지품, 소유물
specialize v. 전문으로 하다 goods n. 물건, 소유물
destination n. 목적지 shape n. 상태 tow v. 견인하다
affordable adj. 저렴한 pickup n. 수거, 픽업
drop-off n. 반환 regardless of ~에 상관없이

수신: 고객 서비스 <service@expressmovers.com>
발신: Jacqueline Gerard <jackieger39@tellmail.net>
제목: 이사 지원
날짜: 5월 23일
첨부: 아파트_정보.문서

안녕하세요,

저는 ¹⁸³롤리에 있는 저의 현재 아파트에서 가구와 가전제품들을 옮기는 것에 도움이 필요하여 이메일을 씁니다. ¹⁸³저는 최근 탬파에 있는 일자리 제의를 받아들였으며 7월 1일인 제 시작일 전에 그곳으로 이사를 해야 합니다. 이상적으로는, 저는 제 소지품이 6월 29일에 수거되어 그 다음 날에 배송되면 좋겠습니다.

첨부된 문서는 제가 옮겨야 할 물품들의 목록뿐만 아니라, 롤리 및 탬파의 아파트들의 위치에 관한 정보를 포함합니다. ¹⁸⁴대략적인 이동 거리는 650마일이 될 것입니다. ¹⁸⁵저의 새로운 회사가 그들이 제게 저의 이사 비용을 상환해 줄 것이라고 했으므로 저는 영수증이 필요할 것입니다.

더 자세한 정보를 위해서는 제게 연락해 주십시오.

Jacqueline Gerard 드림

appliance n. 가전제품 accept v. 받아들이다, 수락하다
relocate v. 이사하다 approximate adj. 대략적인
reimburse v. 상환하다 expense n. 비용

181. 육하원칙 문제

해석 웹페이지에 따르면, 직원들은 무엇을 할 것인가?
(A) 도착지에서 물품들을 닦는다.
(B) 물품들이 좋은 상태로 배송되도록 보장한다.
(C) 거주지의 위치를 찾기 위해 내비게이션 시스템을 사용한다.
(D) 미리 대금을 회수한다.

해설 웹페이지의 'crew members will ensure that your goods arrive ~ in the same shape as they were upon being packed up'에서 직원들은 물건이 포장된 직후와 똑같은 상태로 도착하도록 보장할 것이라고 했으므로 (B)가 정답이다.

어휘 in good condition 좋은 상태인 locate v. (위치를) 찾다
residence n. 거주지 in advance 미리

Paraphrasing
shape 상태 → condition 상태

182. Not/True 문제

해석 Express Movers사에 대해 언급된 것은?
(A) 추가 요금을 받고 자동차를 운반할 것이다.
(B) 최근 새로운 반환 센터를 열었다.

(C) 고객들을 위한 온라인 채팅 서비스를 제공한다.
(D) 10년 전에 설립되었다.

해설 웹페이지의 'We even tow vehicles, such as cars'에서 저희, 즉 Express Movers사가 자동차와 같은 탈것도 견인한다고 했고, 'There is an additional fee of $500 per vehicle'에서 이 서비스에는 차량당 500달러의 추가 요금이 있다고 했으므로 (A)는 지문의 내용과 일치한다. 따라서 (A)가 정답이다. (B)와 (C)는 지문에 언급되지 않은 내용이다. (D)는 'Having specialized in long-distance moving services for over 30 years'에서 30년 넘게 장거리 이사 서비스를 전문으로 해왔다고 했으므로 지문의 내용과 일치하지 않는다.

어휘 automobile n. 자동차 establish v. 설립하다
decade n. 10년

[Paraphrasing]
tow ~ cars 자동차를 견인하다 → transport automobiles 자동차를 운반하다
additional fee 추가 요금 → extra charge 추가 요금

183. 육하원칙 문제

해석 Ms. Gerard는 왜 이사를 가는가?
(A) 몇몇 친척들 가까이에 살기 위해
(B) 대학 프로그램에 등록하기 위해
(C) 신규 프로젝트를 시작하기 위해
(D) 새로운 장소에서 일을 시작하기 위해

해설 이메일의 'my current apartment in Raleigh'에서 저, 즉 Ms. Gerard의 아파트가 현재 롤리에 있다고 했고, 'I've ~ accepted an offer for a job in Tampa and need to relocate there'에서 저, 즉 Ms. Gerard가 탬파에 있는 일자리 제의를 받아들였으며 그곳으로 이사를 해야 한다고 했으므로 (D)가 정답이다.

어휘 relative n. 친척 enroll v. 등록하다
take up (일 등을) 시작하다

184. 추론 문제 연계

해석 Ms. Gerard에 대해 추론될 수 있는 것은?
(A) 작은 아파트로 이사할 것이다.
(B) 곧 승진될 것이다.
(C) 창고에 몇몇 가구를 놓아둘 것이다.
(D) 서비스에 대해 최소 1,000달러를 지불할 것이다.

해설 Ms. Gerard가 작성한 이메일을 먼저 확인한다.
단서 1 이메일의 'The approximate distance of the move will be 650 miles.'에서 대략적인 이동 거리가 650마일이 될 것이라고 했다. 그런데 이동 거리가 650마일일 경우 얼마의 요금이 부과되는지에 대해 제시되지 않았으므로 웹페이지에서 관련 내용을 확인한다.
단서 2 웹페이지의 'more than 500 miles', '$1,000'에서 이동 거리가 500마일을 초과할 경우 1,000달러의 요금이 부과된다는 것을 알 수 있다.
두 단서를 종합할 때, Ms. Gerard의 이동 거리가 500마일을 초과하므로 이사 비용으로 최소 1,000달러를 지불할 것임을 추론할 수 있다. 따라서 (D)가 정답이다.

어휘 promote v. 승진시키다, 홍보하다 storage n. 창고
at least 최소한

185. 육하원칙 문제

해석 Ms. Gerard는 무엇을 요청했는가?
(A) 배송 일정
(B) 거래 기록
(C) 피드백 양식
(D) 계약서 사본

해설 이메일의 'I will need a receipt as my new company ~ would reimburse me for my relocation expenses.'에서 저, 즉 Ms. Gerard의 새로운 회사에서 자신의 이사 비용을 상환해 줄 것이기 때문에 영수증이 필요할 것이라고 했으므로 (B)가 정답이다.

어휘 transaction n. 거래 copy n. 사본

186-190번은 다음 이메일, 양식, 예정표에 관한 문제입니다.

수신: Jake Walker <j.walker@renewable.com>
발신: Luanne Wilkins <l.wilkins@urbanenergy.net>
제목: 제9회 도시 에너지 포럼
날짜: 2월 16일

Mr. Walker께,

제9회 도시 에너지 포럼에 대한 귀하의 문의에 감사드립니다. 이 행사는 스위스 베른에서 4월 26일부터 28일까지 개최될 것입니다. 전 세계의 도시들이 어떻게 효과적으로 재생 가능 에너지로 바꿀 수 있을지 논의하기 위해 다양한 분야의 전문가들이 모일 것입니다.

186-(C)앞으로 계속 증가할 것으로 예상되는 도시 인구로 인해, 세계의 도시들이 충분하고, 깨끗하고, 그리고 지속 가능한 에너지 자원들을 개발해야 할 필요성이 시급해졌습니다. 도시 에너지 포럼은 참가자들에게 아이디어들을 만들어 내고 실질적인 해결책을 논의할 기회를 제공합니다.

귀하의 질문에 대해 답변드리자면, 중앙 홀에서의 모든 발표들 및 토론들을 포함하는 일반 입장권은 2월 1일 이전에는 150유로이고 이후에는 185유로입니다. 워크숍들은 회기당 35유로의 추가 비용으로 제공됩니다. 188-(D)후원 업체들의 구성원들에게는, 일반 입장료가 무료라는 것을 알아두시길 바랍니다. 더 자세한 정보를 위해 혹은 187디지털 서식으로 된 일정을 다운로드 하시려면, www.urbanenergy.net/forum을 방문하십시오.

Luanne Wilkins 드림
도시 에너지 포럼

urban adj. 도시의 inquiry n. 문의 sector n. 분야
gather v. 모이다 discuss v. 논의하다, 토론하다
shift v. 바꾸다, 전환하다
renewable energy 재생 가능 에너지 population n. 인구
project v. 예상하다, 추측하다 sufficient adj. 충분한
sustainable adj. 지속 가능한 urgent adj. 시급한, 다급한
generate v. 만들어 내다 practical adj. 실질적인
solution n. 해결책 general adj. 일반의 admission n. 입장
sponsor n. 후원 program n. 일정, 프로그램

제9회 도시 에너지 포럼
베른, 스위스 · 4월 26-28일

감사합니다! 귀하의 대금이 지불되었습니다. 귀하의 기록을 위해 이 양식의 사본을 보관해주십시오. 어떠한 변경이라도 필요하시면, forum@urbanenergy.net으로 저희에게 연락해 주십시오.

주문 세부 사항

188-(D)/189이름: Irwin Patel
189회사(선택): Solar India사
주소: 75번지 Murti로, 뉴델리, 인도 110011
전화: 555-2390
이메일: i.patel@solarindia.com
티켓 수: 한 장(1)

지급 총액: 35.00유로
- 188-(D)입장료: 0.00유로
- 워크숍 비용: 35.00유로

전액 환불을 받으시려면, 행사 시작 최소 3일 전에 저희에게 연락해 주십시오.

---

retain v. 보관하다   optional n. 선택(사항); adj. 선택적인

제9회 도시 에너지 포럼
베른, 스위스 · 4월 26-28일

190-(D)둘째 날 예정표

오전 10시-11시   개회 발표
중앙 홀: 도시 에너지 포럼 의장 Kurt Bollinger가 재생 가능 에너지로의 전환을 가속화하는 것에 대해 이야기할 것입니다.

오전 11시-오후 12시   오전 워크숍
B홀: "친환경 에너지에 자금 조달하기"
세계 에너지 투자 은행 최고 경영자 Eloisa Davide에 의해 발표됨

C홀: "정부가 어떻게 앞장설 수 있는가"
영국 에너지 계획 의장 Alan Holm에 의해 발표됨

190-(B)오후 12시-2시   190-(B)점심 휴식

오후 2시-3시 30분   오후 워크숍
B홀: "태양 에너지 사용하기"
남아시아 에너지 협회 창립자 189Lester Agarwal에 의해 발표됨(189Solar India사 최고경영자)

C홀: "190-(D)배터리 기술의 발전"
Queensland 대학교 공학 교수 Richard Liu에 의해 발표됨

오후 3시 30분-4시 30분   원탁 토론
중앙 홀: 도시 에너지 포럼의 일원인 Stephanie Bernard가 대중 매체에서 재생 가능 에너지를 홍보하는 것에 대한 토론을 진행할 것입니다.

agenda n. 예정표, 안건   accelerate v. 가속화하다
transition n. 전환   finance v. 자금을 조달하다; n. 자금
initiative n. (특정한 문제 해결·목적 달성을 위한 새로운) 계획
founder n. 창립자   advancement n. 발전
promote v. 홍보하다

186. Not/True 문제

해석 이메일에 따르면, 도시들에 대해 사실인 것은?
(A) 각각 미래 포럼들을 주최할 것이다.
(B) 더 나은 교통 시스템들이 필요하다.
(C) 더 붐벼질 것이다.
(D) 더 자주 정전을 겪을 수 있다.

해설 이메일의 'urban populations projected to continue growing in the future'에서 앞으로 계속 증가할 것으로 예상되는 도시 인구라고 했으므로 (C)는 지문의 내용과 일치한다. 따라서 (C)가 정답이다. (A), (B), (D)는 지문에 언급되지 않은 내용이다.

어휘 host v. 주최하다   crowded adj. 붐비는
suffer v. 겪다, 고통을 받다   power outage 정전

Paraphrasing
populations ~ continue growing 인구가 계속 증가하다
→ become more crowded 더 붐벼지다

187. 육하원칙 문제

해석 도시 에너지 포럼의 웹사이트에서 무엇이 이용 가능한가?
(A) 후원 신청서
(B) 일정 사본
(C) 환불 요청서
(D) 강연 필기록

해설 이메일의 'to download the program in digital format, visit www.urbanenergy.net/forum'에서 디지털 서식으로 된 일정을 다운로드하려면 웹사이트를 방문하라고 했으므로 (B)가 정답이다.

어휘 application n. 신청서   transcript n. 필기록   lecture n. 강연

188. Not/True 문제 연계

해석 Mr. Patel에 대해 사실인 것은?
(A) 2월 1일 이전에 표를 구매했다.
(B) 그의 표는 그에게 중앙 홀에만 입장을 허가한다.
(C) 하나보다 많은 워크숍에 참가할 것이다.
(D) 그의 회사는 제9회 도시 에너지 포럼의 후원 업체이다.

해설 Mr. Patel이 언급된 양식을 먼저 확인한다.
단서 1 양식의 'Name: Irwin Patel', 'Admission fees: €0.00'에서 Irwin Patel의 입장료가 0.00유로라고 했다. 그런데 어떤 경우에 입장료가 무료인지에 대해 제시되지 않았으므로 이메일에서 관련 내용을 확인한다.
단서 2 이메일의 'for members of sponsor organizations, general admission is free'에서 후원 업체들의 구성원들에게는 일반 입장료가 무료라는 것을 확인할 수 있다.
두 단서를 종합할 때, Mr. Patel의 회사가 제9회 도시 에너지 포럼의 후원 업체임을 알 수 있다. 따라서 (D)가 정답이다.

어휘 grant v. 허가하다, 인정하다; n. 보조금   entry n. 입장

189. 육하원칙 문제 연계

해석 Mr. Patel은 어느 워크숍 진행자와 직업적인 관계를 맺고 있는가?
(A) Alan Holm
(B) Richard Liu
(C) Eloisa Davide
(D) Lester Agarwal

해설 Mr. Patel이 언급된 양식을 먼저 확인한다.
단서 1 양식의 'Name: Irwin Patel', 'Company (optional): Solar India'에서 Mr. Patel이 다니는 회사가 Solar India사임을 알 수 있다. 그런데 Solar India사의 워크숍 진행자에 대해 제시되지 않았으므로 예정표에서 관련 내용을 확인한다.
단서 2 예정표의 'Lester Agarwal', 'CEO, Solar India'에서 Lester Agarwal이 Solar India사의 최고경영자라는 것을 확인할 수 있다.
두 단서를 종합할 때, Solar India사에 다니는 Mr. Patel이 Solar India사 최고경영자인 Lester Agarwal과 직업적인 관계를 맺고 있음을 알 수 있다. 따라서 (D)가 정답이다.

어휘 leader n. 진행자, 지도자

190. Not/True 문제

해석 포럼의 둘째 날에 대해 언급된 것은?
(A) 몇몇 발표자들은 발표를 한 번보다 많이 할 것이다.
(B) 모든 참가자들에게는 한 시간의 점심시간이 제공될 것이다.
(C) 텔레비전으로 방송되는 재생 가능 에너지에 대한 토론이 열릴 것이다.

(D) 배터리 기술에 대한 발표가 있을 것이다.

해설 예정표의 'Agenda for Day 2', 'Advancements in Battery Technology'에서 둘째 날 예정표에 배터리 기술의 발전에 대한 발표가 있다고 했으므로 (D)는 지문의 내용과 일치한다. 따라서 (D)가 정답이다. (A)와 (C)는 지문에 언급되지 않은 내용이다. (B)는 '12:00-2:00 P.M.', 'Lunch break'에서 점심 휴식이 두 시간임을 알 수 있으므로 지문의 내용과 일치하지 않는다.

어휘 televise v. 텔레비전으로 방송하다

191-195번은 다음 양식, 공고, 이메일에 관한 문제입니다.

Gumbo 식료품 회사 보상 프로그램
신청 양식

귀하의 지역 Gumbo사의 고객 서비스 카운터에 작성된 양식을 가져다주시거나, 그것을 104번지 Jefferson가, 리치몬드, 버지니아주 23284에 있는 Gumbo 식료품 회사 보상 프로그램으로 우편을 보내주십시오. 귀하가 온라인 계정을 갖고 있다면, 귀하는 또한 www.shopgumbo.com에서 가입할 수 있습니다.

이름: _____
주소: _____
전화: _____
이메일: _____

¹⁹¹저희의 주간 소식지를 받고 할인 쿠폰이 귀하의 이메일 수신함에 발송되도록 하려면 □ 여기에 표시하세요.

프로그램 세부 사항:
• 저희 매장 또는 온라인에서 귀하가 사용하는 1달러마다 1포인트를 받으세요. 식료품, 처방전, 잡지, 그리고 더 많은 것들에 대해 포인트를 받으세요!
• 귀하가 받은 200포인트마다 귀하의 식료품 계산서에 더 큰 할인을 위해 사용될 수 있습니다.
• 가입할 ¹⁹²⁻⁽ᴬ⁾/¹⁹⁵⁻⁽ᶜ⁾친구를 추천하여 즉시 100포인트를 받으세요.

reward n. 보상   drop off 가져다주다   sign up 가입하다
earn v. 받다, 얻다   grocery n. 식료품
medical prescription 처방전   instantly adv. 즉시
refer v. 추천하다

저희 고객분들께 좋은 소식이 있습니다!

지역 Gumbo 식료품 회사와 Tiptop 가전제품 매장들에서 쇼핑함으로써 보상 포인트를 받은 고객들은 이제 그들의 보상 포인트를 Fullerton사 주유소에서 기름을 채울 때 사용할 수 있게 될 것입니다. ¹⁹²⁻⁽ᴬ⁾100포인트마다 여러분의 연료 구매에 대해 1달러의 절약으로 교환될 수 있습니다.

¹⁹³이 보상의 확대는 Gumbo사와 Tiptop사 쇼핑객들뿐만 아니라, Fullerton사의 고객들에게도 더 큰 가치와 절약을 전달할 것을 약속합니다.

¹⁹²Fullerton사의 가스 보상 프로그램은 전국의 25개가 넘는 소매 회사들에서 이용 가능하며 전국적으로 수천 개의 주유소에서 사용될 수 있습니다. www.fullertongas.com에서 더 많이 알아보시거나, 귀하의 지역의 Gumbo사 또는 Tiptop사에서 가스 보상을 위해 등록하는 것에 대해 문의하십시오.

fill up 기름을 채우다   redeem v. 교환하다, 상환하다
fuel n. 연료   expansion n. 확대   promise v. 약속하다
saving n. 절약   nationwide adv. 전국적으로; adj. 전국의
register v. 등록하다

수신: Dale Wilson <d.wilson@okmail.com>
발신: Karen Sirling <k.sirling@shopgumbo.com>
제목: 보상 포인트
날짜: 4월 24일

Mr. Wilson께,

저희에게 연락해 주셔서 감사합니다. ¹⁹⁴요청하신 대로 저는 귀하의 계좌 정보를 재확인했습니다. 귀하의 말씀대로 64포인트가 누락된 것이 맞습니다. 이것들은 지난주 귀하의 식료품점 방문에서 지급되었습니다. 방금 전에 제가 귀하의 정보를 수정하였습니다. ¹⁹⁴다른 질문에 대해서는, ¹⁹⁵⁻⁽ᶜ⁾지난달에 귀하께서 해주셨던 추천을 반영하도록 귀하의 계정이 업데이트되었다 ¹⁹⁴는 것을 제가 확인해 드릴 수 있습니다. 모두 합쳐, 지난 2월에 회원이 되신 이후, 귀하께서는 350포인트를 받으셨습니다.

저는 귀하께서 귀하의 포인트를 파악하고 저희 레시피 모음, 예산 편성 도구 등과 같은, 다른 제품들과 서비스들에 접근할 수 있도록 저희 웹사이트에 온라인 계정을 등록하시길 권장합니다.

거래해 주셔서 감사합니다!

Karen Sirling 드림
고객 서비스 직원
Gumbo 식료품 회사

double-check v. 재확인하다   trip n. 방문, 여행
correct v. 수정하다; 정확한   reflect v. 반영하다
referral n. 추천, 소개   altogether adv. 모두 합쳐, 총
keep track of ~을 파악하다, 추적하다

191. 육하원칙 문제

해석 양식에 따르면, 소식지에 가입한 사람들은 무엇을 받을 것인가?
(A) 할인권
(B) 보너스 포인트
(C) 샘플 제품
(D) 계정 업그레이드

해설 양식의 'receive our weekly newsletter and get discount coupons sent to your e-mail inbox'에서 주간 소식지를 받고 할인 쿠폰이 이메일 수신함에 발송되도록 하라고 했으므로 (A)가 정답이다.

어휘 discount voucher 할인권

192. Not/True 문제 연계

해석 Gumbo 식료품 회사의 보상 프로그램에 대해 사실인 것은?
(A) 추천은 가스 할인을 위한 충분한 포인트를 받게 한다.
(B) 온라인 구매가 가장 많은 포인트를 받을 자격을 얻는다.
(C) 각 200포인트를 받을 때마다 쿠폰이 제공될 것이다.
(D) 처방전은 식료품보다 적은 포인트의 가치가 있다.

해설 Gumbo 식료품 회사의 보상 프로그램이 언급된 양식을 먼저 확인한다.
단서 1 양식의 'Instantly earn 100 points by referring a friend'에서 친구를 추천하여 즉시 100포인트를 받으라고 했다. 그런데 포인트로 어떤 보상을 받을 수 있는지 제시되지 않았으므로 공고에서 관련 내용을 확인한다.
단서 2 공고의 'Every 100 points can be redeemed for $1 in savings on ~ fuel purchase.'에서는 100포인트마다 연료 구매에 대해 1달러의 절약으로 교환될 수 있다는 것을 확인할 수 있다.
두 단서를 종합할 때, 추천을 통해 100포인트를 받을 수 있으

며 이는 연료 할인 1달러로 교환될 수 있다는 것을 알 수 있다. 따라서 (A)가 정답이다.

어휘 qualify for ~할 자격을 얻다

[Paraphrasing]
savings on ~ fuel purchase 연료 구매에 대한 절약 →
a discount on gas 가스 할인

193. 추론 문제

해석 Fullerton 가스 회사에 대해 암시되는 것은?
(A) 매장에서 자동차 서비스를 제공할 것이다.
(B) 25개가 넘는 회사들과 제휴를 맺었다.
(C) 주유소의 수를 늘리고 있다.
(D) Gumbo 식료품 회사와 건물을 공유한다.

해설 공고의 'Fullerton's Gas Rewards Program is available at over 25 retail firms across the country'에서 Fullerton사의 가스 보상 프로그램은 전국의 25개가 넘는 소매 회사들에서 이용 가능하다고 했으므로 Fullerton 가스 회사가 25개가 넘는 회사들과 제휴를 맺었다는 사실을 추론할 수 있다. 따라서 (B)가 정답이다.

어휘 automotive adj. 자동차의   partner v. 제휴하다

194. 목적 문제

해석 Ms. Sirling은 왜 이메일을 썼는가?
(A) 최근의 주문을 확인하기 위해
(B) 특별 할인을 제공하기 위해
(C) 청구서 납부를 요청하기 위해
(D) 몇 가지의 문의 사항들을 다루기 위해

해설 이메일의 'I double-checked your account information as requested.'에서 요청한 대로 자신, 즉 Ms. Sirling은 귀하, 즉 고객의 계좌 정보를 재확인했다고 했고, 'As for the other question, I can confirm that your account has been updated'에서 다른 질문에 대해서는, 고객의 계정이 업데이트되었다는 것을 확인해 줄 수 있다고 했으므로 (D)가 정답이다.

어휘 verify v. 확인하다, 입증하다   offer n. 할인
a couple of 몇 가지의, 둘의

195. Not/True 문제 연계

해석 Ms. Sirling이 Mr. Wilson에 대해 언급한 것은?
(A) 포인트를 연료 구매를 위해 교환했다.
(B) 그의 회원 자격은 곧 만료될 것이다.
(C) 지난달에 최소 100포인트를 받았다.
(D) 그의 온라인 비밀번호가 최근에 바뀌었다.

해설 Ms. Sirling이 작성한 이메일을 먼저 확인한다.
단서 1 이메일의 'your[Mr. Wilson's] account has been updated to reflect the referral that you made last month'에서 지난달에 Mr. Wilson이 했던 추천을 반영하기 위해 그의 계정이 업데이트되었다고 했다. 그런데 추천을 하면 계정에 어떤 업데이트가 생기는지 제시되지 않았으므로 양식에서 관련 내용을 확인한다.
단서 2 양식의 'Instantly earn 100 points by referring a friend'에서 친구를 추천하면 즉시 100포인트를 받을 수 있는 것을 확인할 수 있다.
두 단서를 종합할 때, Mr. Wilson은 지난달에 친구 추천을 통해 최소 100포인트를 받았다는 것을 알 수 있다. 따라서 (C)가 정답이다.

어휘 expire v. 만료되다

196-200번은 다음 웹페이지, 이메일, 직원 근무 시간 기록표에 관한 문제입니다.

Plumtree Nutritional Advice사
홈	블로그	질문과 답변	로그인

건강한 삶을 위한 조언들
[196]게시자: Brad Shear, 수석 영양사

건강한 상태를 유지하는 것은 어려울 수 있지만, 저는 제 고객들이 계속해서 바르게 유지할 수 있도록 돕기 위해 아래의 목록을 종합했습니다:

반드시 하세요
· 하루에 최소 세 잔의 물을 마신다
· [196]주 3회, 20분에서 30분 동안 운동을 한다
· 매일 밤 일곱 시간의 수면을 취한다

하지 않도록 유의하세요
· 취침하기 한 시간 이내에 저녁을 먹는다
· 한 번에 세 시간 넘게 앉아 있는다

더 알고 싶다면, 아래의 식단 및 운동 플랜 중 하나를 클릭하고 첫 상담을 잡으려면 제게 이메일을 보내십시오.

플랜	가격
[198]FreshStart	[198]30달러
[198]FreshUp	[198]35달러
[198]FreshPlus	[198]40달러
FreshPremium	45달러

tip n. 조언, 팁   nutritionist n. 영양사   fit adj. 건강한, 날씬한
challenging adj. 어려운   compile v. 종합하다, 모으다
on track 바르게, 순조롭게 나아가는
set up (약속을) 잡다   initial adj. 처음의
consultation n. 상담

수신: Brad Shear <bshear@plumtreenutrition.com>
[197-(C)]발신: Madison Costa <maddiecosta77@rentmail.net>
날짜: 4월 28일
제목: 상담

Mr. Shear께,

저는 당신의 웹사이트에 있는 플랜들에 대해 상의하기 위해 당신과의 첫 예약을 잡고 싶어서 이메일을 씁니다. [197-(C)]제 동료들 중 한 명인 Kerry Franklin이 당신을 적극적으로 추천했습니다. [197-(C)/198]그녀는 당신의 FreshPlus 플랜을 따르고 있으며 그것이 그녀의 건강을 크게 향상시켰다고 말합니다. 저는 당신의 프로그램에 참여하게 되어 즐겁지만, [198]저는 그녀만큼 돈을 많이 지불하고 싶지는 않고 또한 가장 저렴한 플랜도 원하지 않습니다.

제 주된 문제는 제가 이전에 제 사무실에서 그랬던 것보다 더 늦은 근무 시간에 일하는 것으로 최근에 바뀌었다는 것이고, 저는 저의 수면과 식사 일정을 조절하는 것에 어려움을 겪고 있습니다. [199]제가 5월 4일에 제 회사와의 교육 활동을 위해 출장을 가야 하기 때문에, [200]저는 5월 2일 오전이나 5월 3일 오후 중에 한 번 당신을 만나기를 희망하고 있습니다.

Madison Costa 드림

appointment n. 예약, 약속   coworker n. 동료
improve v. 향상시키다   switch v. 바뀌다, 전환하다
shift n. (교대제의) 근무 시간   previously adv. 이전에

adjust v. 조절하다, 조정하다

Plumtree Nutritional Advice사 직원 근무 시간 기록표
200요일별로 당신이 일한 시간을 기록하세요.
200직원명: Brad Shear

	5월 1일	200 5월 2일	200 5월 3일	5월 4일	5월 5일
200고객 상담 업무	4시간	200 6시간	200 0시간	6시간	4시간
행정 업무	0시간	1시간	0시간	1시간	2시간
교육 업무	0시간	0시간	6시간	0시간	0시간
총 시간	4시간	7시간	6시간	7시간	6시간

client n. 고객 administration n. 행정

196. 육하원칙 문제

해석 Mr. Shear는 그의 고객들에게 어떤 조언을 하는가?
(A) 하루에 최소 세 끼 식사를 섭취한다.
(B) 햇빛으로부터 피부를 보호한다.
(C) 운동 경기들에 참가한다.
(D) 규칙적인 신체 활동들에 참여한다.

해설 웹페이지의 'Posted by: Brad Shear', 'Exercise ~ three times per week'에서 Mr. Shear가 게시한 글에서 주 3회 운동을 하라고 했으므로 (D)가 정답이다.

어휘 protect v. 보호하다 athletic competition 운동 경기 engage in ~에 참여하다 regular adj. 규칙적인

Paraphrasing
Exercise ~ three times per week 주 3회 운동하다 → Engage in regular physical activities 규칙적인 신체 활동들에 참여하다

197. Not/True 문제

해석 FreshPlus 플랜에 대해 언급된 것은?
(A) Plumtree사의 웹사이트에 업데이트될 것이다.
(B) 곧 있을 회의에서 논의될 것이다.
(C) Ms. Costa의 동료에 의해 이용되어 왔다.
(D) 한정된 기간 동안 할인되었다.

해설 이메일의 'From: Madison Costa'에서 이메일이 Ms. Costa에 의해 작성된 것임을 알 수 있고 'One of my[Ms. Costa's] coworkers, Kerry Franklin, highly recommended you[Mr. Shear]. She follows your FreshPlus plan'에서 Ms. Costa의 동료들 중 한 명인 Kerry Franklin이 Mr. Shear를 적극적으로 추천했으며 동료가 FreshPlus 플랜을 따르고 있다고 했으므로 (C)는 지문의 내용과 일치한다. 따라서 (C)가 정답이다. (A), (B), (D)는 지문에 언급되지 않은 내용이다.

어휘 upcoming adj. 곧 있을 colleague n. 동료

Paraphrasing
One of ~ coworkers 동료들 중 한 명 → colleague 동료

198. 육하원칙 문제 연계

해석 Ms. Costa는 플랜에 대해 얼마를 지불할 의향이 있는가?
(A) 30달러
(B) 35달러
(C) 40달러
(D) 45달러

해설 Ms. Costa가 작성한 이메일을 먼저 확인한다.

단서 1 이메일의 'She[Ms. Franklin] follows your FreshPlus plan'에서 Ms. Franklin이 FreshPlus 플랜을 따르고 있다고 했고, 'I[Ms. Costa] don't want to pay as much as she[Ms. Franklin] does and I also don't want the cheapest plan'에서 Ms. Costa는 Ms. Franklin만큼 돈을 많이 지불하고 싶지는 않으며 가장 저렴한 플랜도 원하지 않는다고 했다. 그런데 가격이 FreshPlus 플랜보다 낮으면서도 가장 저렴하지는 않은 플랜이 무엇인지 제시되지 않았으므로 웹페이지에서 관련 내용을 확인한다.

단서 2 웹페이지의 'FreshStart', '$30', 'FreshUp', '$35', 'FreshPlus', '$40'에서 가격이 FreshPlus 플랜보다 낮으면서도 가장 저렴하지는 않은 플랜이 35달러의 FreshUp 플랜이라는 것을 확인할 수 있다.

두 단서를 종합할 때, Ms. Costa는 FreshUp 플랜을 선택하여 35달러를 지불할 의향이 있음을 알 수 있다. 따라서 (B)가 정답이다.

199. 육하원칙 문제

해석 Ms. Costa는 5월에 무엇을 할 것인가?
(A) 회사 행사에 참석한다.
(B) 건강 보험을 신청한다.
(C) 예약 시간을 변경한다.
(D) 휴가로 하루를 쉰다.

해설 이메일의 'I have to travel for a training activity with my company on May 4'에서 자신, 즉 Ms. Costa가 5월 4일에 회사와의 교육 활동을 위해 출장을 가야 한다고 했으므로 (A)가 정답이다.

어휘 attend v. 참석하다 corporate adj. 회사의, 기업의 take a day off 하루를 쉬다

Paraphrasing
training activity with ~ company 회사와의 교육 활동 → corporate event 회사 행사

200. 추론 문제 연계

해석 Ms. Costa는 언제 Mr. Shear를 만났을 것 같은가?
(A) 5월 2일에
(B) 5월 3일에
(C) 5월 4일에
(D) 5월 5일에

해설 Ms. Costa가 작성한 이메일을 먼저 확인한다.

단서 1 이메일의 'I[Ms. Costa]'m hoping to meet with you[Mr. Shear] either in the morning on May 2 or in the afternoon of May 3'에서 Ms. Costa가 5월 2일 오전이나 5월 3일 오후 중에 한 번 Mr. Shear를 만나기를 희망하고 있다고 했다. 그런데 Mr. Shear가 5월 2일 오전이나 5월 3일 오후 중 가능한 시간이 언제인지 제시되지 않았으므로 직원 근무 시간 기록표에서 관련 내용을 확인한다.

단서 2 직원 근무 시간 기록표의 'Please enter the number of hours that you have worked for each day of the week.'에서 요일별로 일한 시간을 기록하라고 했고, 'Employee name: Brad Shear', 'Client consultation', 'May 2', '6h', 'May 3', '0h'에서 Mr. Shear가 고객 상담 업무로 5월 2일에는 6시간, 5월 3일에는 0시간을 일했다는 것을 확인할 수 있다.

두 단서를 종합할 때, Ms. Costa와 Mr. Shear는 Mr. Shear가 고객 상담 업무로 6시간 일한 5월 2일에 만났을 것임을 추론할 수 있다. 따라서 (A)가 정답이다.

점수 환산표

아래는 실전모의고사를 위한 점수 환산표입니다. 문제 풀이 후, 정답 개수를 세어 자신의 토익 리스닝/리딩 점수를 예상해봅니다.

정답 수	리스닝 점수	리딩 점수	정답 수	리스닝 점수	리딩 점수	정답 수	리스닝 점수	리딩 점수
100	495	495	66	305	305	32	135	125
99	495	495	65	300	300	31	130	120
98	495	495	64	295	295	30	125	115
97	495	485	63	290	290	29	120	110
96	490	480	62	285	280	28	115	105
95	485	475	61	280	275	27	110	100
94	480	470	60	275	270	26	105	95
93	475	465	59	270	265	25	100	90
92	470	460	58	265	260	24	95	85
91	465	450	57	260	255	23	90	80
90	460	445	56	255	250	22	85	75
89	455	440	55	250	245	21	80	70
88	450	435	54	245	240	20	75	70
87	445	430	53	240	235	19	70	65
86	435	420	52	235	230	18	65	60
85	430	415	51	230	220	17	60	60
84	425	410	50	225	215	16	55	55
83	415	405	49	220	210	15	50	50
82	410	400	48	215	205	14	45	45
81	400	390	47	210	200	13	40	40
80	395	385	46	205	195	12	35	35
79	390	380	45	200	190	11	30	30
78	385	375	44	195	185	10	25	30
77	375	370	43	190	180	9	20	25
76	370	360	42	185	175	8	15	20
75	365	355	41	180	170	7	10	20
74	355	350	40	175	165	6	5	15
73	350	345	39	170	160	5	5	15
72	340	340	38	165	155	4	5	10
71	335	335	37	160	150	3	5	5
70	330	330	36	155	145	2	5	5
69	325	320	35	150	140	1	5	5
68	315	315	34	145	135	0	5	5
67	310	310	33	140	130			

※ 점수 환산표는 해커스토익 사이트 유저 데이터를 근거로 제작되었으며, 주기적으로 업데이트되고 있습니다. 해커스토익 사이트 (Hackers.co.kr)에서 최신 경향을 반영하여 업데이트된 점수환산기를 이용하실 수 있습니다. (토익 > 토익게시판 > 토익점수환산기)

Answer Sheet

LISTENING (PART I–IV)

READING (PART V–VII)

*시험시간: 120분 (LC 45분, RC 75분)

* 답안지 마킹은 연필을 사용하시기 바랍니다.
* 문제풀이 후 p.84에 있는 점수 환산표를 확인해보세요.

맞은 문제 개수: _____ / 200

실시간 토익시험 정답확인&해설강의
Hackers.co.kr

한 권으로 끝내는
해커스 토익 600+ *plus*

LC + RC + VOCA

시험장에도 들고 가는 토익 기출 VOCA 학습법

1. 매일 하루 분량의 단어를 암기합니다.
  본인이 선택한 학습 플랜(본책 p.20~21)에 따라 20일 또는 10일 완성을 목표로 합니다.

2. 무료 단어암기 MP3와 함께 이동할 때나 자투리 시간을 활용하여 단어를 암기합니다.
  단어암기 MP3는 www.HackersIngang.com에서 무료로 다운 받거나, DAY별 QR코드를 활용하세요.

목차		
DAY 01 PART 1 기출 어휘	**DAY 11** PART 5&6 기출 어휘
DAY 02 PART 1 기출 어휘	**DAY 12** PART 5&6 기출 어휘
DAY 03 PART 2 기출 어휘	**DAY 13** PART 5&6 기출 어휘
DAY 04 PART 2 기출 어휘	**DAY 14** PART 5&6 기출 어휘
DAY 05 PART 3 기출 어휘	**DAY 15** PART 5&6 기출 어휘
DAY 06 PART 3 기출 어휘	**DAY 16** PART 5&6 기출 어휘
DAY 07 PART 3 기출 어휘	**DAY 17** PART 5&6 기출 어휘
DAY 08 PART 4 기출 어휘	**DAY 18** PART 7 기출 어휘
DAY 09 PART 4 기출 어휘	**DAY 19** PART 7 기출 어휘
DAY 10 PART 4 기출 어휘	**DAY 20** PART 7 기출 어휘

저작권자 ⓒ 2025, 해커스 어학연구소 이 책 및 음성파일의 모든 내용, 이미지, 디자인, 편집 형태에 대한 저작권은 저자에게 있습니다.
서면에 의한 저자와 출판사의 허락 없이 내용의 일부 혹은 전부를 인용, 발췌하거나 복제, 배포할 수 없습니다.

DAY 01 PART 1 기출 어휘

☑ PART 1에 반드시 나오는 최신 기출 어휘들이므로, 확실히 암기해 둡니다.   🎧 VOCA_D01.mp3

0001	hold	v 들다, 쥐다
0002	stack	v 쌓다
0003	display	v 전시하다 n 전시
0004	examine	v 검사하다, 조사하다
0005	vehicle	n 차량
0006	counter	n 계산대, 조리대
0007	rack	n 선반
0008	shelf	n 선반
0009	board	n 판자 v 탑승하다
0010	container	n 용기
0011	clothing	n 의류
0012	walkway	n 산책로
0013	assemble	v 조립하다, 모이다
0014	remove	v 제거하다
0015	umbrella	n 우산
0016	face	v ~을 향하다
0017	tool	n 도구
0018	lift	v 들어올리다
0019	mount	v 오르다, 증가하다
0020	basket	n 바구니
0021	pole	n 기둥, 막대기
0022	merchandise	n 상품
0023	tray	n 쟁반
0024	pillow	n 베개
0025	outdoor	adj 야외의

0026	place	ⓥ 놓다, 배치하다
0027	shovel	ⓝ 삽 ⓥ 삽으로 퍼 담다
0028	trim	ⓥ 다듬다
0029	wipe	ⓥ 닦다
0030	lean	ⓥ 기대다
0031	file	ⓝ 파일 ⓥ 제출하다
0032	pedestrian	ⓝ 보행자
0033	measure	ⓥ 측정하다
0034	pot	ⓝ 냄비, 화분
0035	carton	ⓝ 상자, 판지 상자
0036	pour	ⓥ 붓다, 따르다
0037	stove	ⓝ 난로, 스토브
0038	frame	ⓝ 액자 ⓥ 틀을 만들다
0039	inspect	ⓥ 점검하다
0040	suitcase	ⓝ 여행 가방
0041	label	ⓝ 라벨 ⓥ 라벨을 붙이다
0042	flyer	ⓝ 전단지
0043	canopy	ⓝ 차양, 덮개
0044	relax	ⓥ 쉬다, 긴장을 풀다
0045	backpack	ⓝ 배낭
0046	reach for	손을 뻗다
0047	cash register	금전 등록기
0048	put on	착용하다
0049	in front of	~의 앞에
0050	in a row	줄지어

DAY 02 PART 1 기출 어휘

☑ PART 1에 반드시 나오는 최신 기출 어휘들이므로, 확실히 암기해 둡니다.　🎧 VOCA_D02.mp3

0051	**park**	v 주차하다
0052	**vacuum**	v 진공청소기로 청소하다
0053	**coast**	n 해안
0054	**bush**	n 덤불
0055	**metal**	n 금속
0056	**intersection**	n 교차로
0057	**roof**	n 지붕
0058	**patio**	n 테라스
0059	**landscape**	n 풍경
0060	**lamppost**	n 가로등
0061	**dock**	n 선착장
0062	**garage**	n 차고
0063	**outlet**	n 콘센트
0064	**suspend**	v 매달다
0065	**ramp**	n 경사로
0066	**hose**	n 호스
0067	**distance**	n 거리
0068	**occupied**	adj 사용 중인
0069	**pin**	n 핀
0070	**wooden**	adj 나무로 된
0071	**overhead**	adj 머리 위의
0072	**ceiling**	n 천장
0073	**shore**	n 해안
0074	**podium**	n 연단, 강단
0075	**field**	n 들판

0076	insert	ⓥ 삽입하다
0077	scatter	ⓥ 흩뿌리다
0078	water	ⓝ 물 ⓥ 물을 주다
0079	crate	ⓝ 나무 상자
0080	climb	ⓥ 오르다
0081	empty	ⓥ 비우다
0082	ladder	ⓝ 사다리
0083	pile	ⓥ 쌓다
0084	fence	ⓝ 울타리
0085	strap	ⓝ 끈, 줄
0086	wallet	ⓝ 지갑
0087	fuel	ⓝ 연료
0088	binder	ⓝ 바인더
0089	armchair	ⓝ 안락의자
0090	lie	ⓥ 놓여 있다
0091	sail	ⓥ 항해하다
0092	stroll	ⓥ 거닐다
0093	grab	ⓥ 움켜잡다
0094	lead to	~으로 이어지다
0095	dining area	식당 구역
0096	office supplies	사무용품
0097	bend over	몸을 앞으로 숙이다
0098	construction site	공사 현장
0099	serving utensil	서빙용 도구
0100	in the distance	멀리, 먼 곳에

PART 2 기출 어휘

☑ PART 2에 반드시 나오는 최신 기출 어휘들이므로, 확실히 암기해 둡니다.   🎧 VOCA_D03.mp3

0101	schedule	n 일정 v 일정을 잡다
0102	assign	v 할당하다, 배정하다
0103	book	v 예약하다 n 책
0104	reception	n 접수처, 환영회
0105	flight	n 항공편, 비행
0106	director	n 이사, 책임자
0107	mechanic	n 정비공, 수리공
0108	technician	n 기술자, 전문 기술자
0109	upload	v 업로드하다
0110	database	n 데이터베이스
0111	trip	n 여행 v 발을 헛디디다
0112	edit	v 편집하다
0113	generate	v 발생시키다, 만들어내다
0114	caterer	n 출장 음식 제공자
0115	agenda	n 의제, 안건
0116	produce	v 생산하다 n 농산물
0117	learn	v 배우다, 익히다
0118	restaurant	n 식당
0119	documentary	n 다큐멘터리
0120	already	adv 이미
0121	usually	adv 보통, 일반적으로
0122	consulting	n 자문, 컨설팅
0123	closet	n 옷장
0124	version	n 버전, 판
0125	luckily	adv 운 좋게도

#		
0126	**undergoing**	[adj] 겪고 있는, 진행 중인
0127	**brochure**	[n] 소책자, 안내 책자
0128	**briefcase**	[n] 서류 가방
0129	**quarter**	[n] 4분의 1, 4분기
0130	**leftover**	[n] 남은 음식 [adj] 남은
0131	**movie**	[n] 영화
0132	**sell**	[v] 팔다
0133	**pilot**	[n] 조종사 [adj] 시험적인
0134	**business trip**	출장
0135	**drop off**	내려주다, 갖다 주다
0136	**conference call**	전화 회의
0137	**human resource department**	인사부
0138	**repair person**	수리기사
0139	**fill out**	작성하다
0140	**come out**	나오다, 발행되다
0141	**review process**	검토 절차
0142	**be sold out**	매진되다
0143	**in charge of**	책임이 있는, 담당의
0144	**processing fee**	처리 수수료
0145	**name card**	명함
0146	**print out**	출력하다
0147	**watch face**	시계 문자판
0148	**fundraising event**	모금 행사
0149	**community center**	주민 센터
0150	**air conditioner**	에어컨

DAY 04 PART 2 기출 어휘

MP3 바로 듣기 ▶

☑ PART 2에 반드시 나오는 최신 기출 어휘들이므로, 확실히 암기해 둡니다. 🎧 VOCA_D04.mp3

0151	**catalogue**	n 목록 v 목록을 작성하다
0152	**stand**	v 서다 n 가판대
0153	**hallway**	n 복도
0154	**cafeteria**	n 구내식당
0155	**engrave**	v 새기다, 조각하다
0156	**cut**	v 자르다 n 삭감, 절단
0157	**stripe**	n 줄무늬
0158	**course**	n 과정, 강의, 방향
0159	**brainstorming**	n 아이디어 회의, 브레인스토밍
0160	**highway**	n 고속도로
0161	**province**	n 지방, 도
0162	**paperless**	adj 종이를 사용하지 않는
0163	**exposition**	n 박람회, 전시회
0164	**carpenter**	n 목수
0165	**stiff**	adj 뻣뻣한, 경직된
0166	**halt**	v 중단하다 n 중단
0167	**second**	adj 두 번째의 n (시간 단위의) 초
0168	**trouble**	n 문제, 어려움
0169	**prefer**	v 선호하다
0170	**projection**	n 예상, 추정, 투사, 영사
0171	**destination**	n 목적지
0172	**decide**	v 결정하다
0173	**inbox**	n 받은 편지함
0174	**several**	adj 몇몇의
0175	**headquarters**	n 본사

0176	**inspector**	n 조사관, 감독관
0177	**bulk**	n 대량 adj 대량의
0178	**leather**	n 가죽
0179	**acquisition**	n 인수, 획득
0180	**shut**	v 닫다, 닫히다
0181	**perfectly**	adv 완벽하게
0182	**launching**	n 시작, 출시
0183	**breakroom**	n 휴게실
0184	**enough**	adv 충분히 adj 충분한
0185	**waiting room**	대기실
0186	**company newsletter**	사내 소식지
0187	**be late for**	~에 늦다
0188	**salt water**	소금물
0189	**spread sheet**	계산표, 스프레드시트
0190	**starting pay**	초봉
0191	**work from home**	재택근무하다
0192	**in time**	제시간에, 늦지 않게
0193	**break down**	고장 나다, 무너지다
0194	**national holiday**	공휴일
0195	**florist shop**	꽃집
0196	**shipping fee**	배송료
0197	**in place**	제자리에, 시행 중인
0198	**for a while**	잠깐
0199	**ceramic tile**	도자기 타일, 세라믹 타일
0200	**taxi stand**	택시 승강장

PART 3 기출 어휘

☑ PART 3에 반드시 나오는 최신 기출 어휘들이므로, 확실히 암기해 둡니다.

0201	**conference**	n 회의, 학회
0202	**attend**	v 참석하다
0203	**review**	v 검토하다 n 검토
0204	**document**	n 문서
0205	**shipment**	n 배송, 선적
0206	**budget**	n 예산
0207	**contract**	n 계약 v 계약하다
0208	**client**	n 고객
0209	**consultant**	n 상담가, 컨설턴트
0210	**supplier**	n 공급업체
0211	**survey**	n 설문 조사 v 조사하다
0212	**recommendation**	n 추천
0213	**negotiate**	v 협상하다
0214	**concern**	n 우려 v 걱정시키다
0215	**adjust**	v 조정하다
0216	**staff**	n 직원
0217	**maintenance**	n 유지, 보수
0218	**reimburse**	v 환급하다, 변제하다
0219	**facility**	n 시설
0220	**delivery**	n 배달
0221	**equipment**	n 장비, 설비
0222	**discount**	n 할인
0223	**salary**	n 급여, 봉급
0224	**funding**	n 자금 지원
0225	**timeline**	n 일정표

0226	repair	v 수리하다 n 수리
0227	overtime	n 초과 근무, 잔업
0228	contact	v 연락하다 n 연락처
0229	organizer	n 주최자, 조직자
0230	journalist	n 기자
0231	workload	n 업무량
0232	accountant	n 회계사
0233	export	v 수출하다 n 수출
0234	accuracy	n 정확성
0235	complaint	n 불만, 항의
0236	dimension	n 치수, 크기
0237	availability	n 이용 가능성
0238	contractor	n 도급업자, 계약자
0239	raffle	n 추첨 행사
0240	revision	n 수정, 개정
0241	construction	n 건설, 공사
0242	colleague	n 동료
0243	promote	v 홍보하다, 촉진하다
0244	conduct	v 수행하다, 실시하다
0245	furniture	n 가구
0246	automotive	adj 자동차의
0247	set up	설치하다, 마련하다
0248	focus group	포커스 그룹
0249	test drive	시운전
0250	local business	지역 상점

DAY 06 · PART 3 기출 어휘

PART 3에 반드시 나오는 최신 기출 어휘들이므로, 확실히 암기해 둡니다.

VOCA_D06.mp3

0251	retirement	n 은퇴
0252	celebrate	v 축하하다
0253	permit	v 허락하다 n 허가증
0254	outdated	adj 구식의
0255	identification	n 신분증, 신원 확인
0256	measurement	n 측정, 치수
0257	applicant	n 지원자
0258	indicate	v 나타내다, 가리키다
0259	commitment	n 약속, 헌신
0260	ingredient	n 재료, 성분
0261	architect	n 건축가
0262	malfunction	n 오작동 v 오작동하다
0263	convention	n 대회, 협의회
0264	discuss	v 논의하다
0265	reject	v 거절하다
0266	sustainable	adj 지속 가능한
0267	plumber	n 배관공
0268	prescription	n 처방전
0269	practical	adj 실용적인
0270	useful	adj 유용한
0271	patient	n 환자
0272	rental	n 임대, 대여
0273	pharmacy	n 약국
0274	tourism	n 관광, 관광 사업
0275	factory	n 공장

0276	decorate	v 장식하다
0277	example	n 예, 본보기
0278	retrieve	v 되찾다, 회수하다
0279	urgent	adj 긴급한
0280	botanical	adj 식물의
0281	sightseeing	n 관광
0282	librarian	n 사서
0283	harbor	n 항구
0284	cabin	n 오두막, 선실
0285	laundry	n 세탁물 v 세탁하다
0286	automobile	n 자동차
0287	lodging	n 숙박
0288	handout	n 유인물
0289	advertising	n 광고 활동
0290	drawing	n 도면, 그림
0291	pond	n 연못
0292	rebate	n 환급, 할인
0293	doubt	n 의심
0294	mural	n 벽화
0295	cost estimate	비용 견적
0296	trade show	무역 박람회
0297	grocery store	식료품점
0298	solar panel	태양광 패널
0299	environmentally friendly	친환경적인
0300	hair salon	미용실

DAY 07 PART 3 기출 어휘

☑ PART 3에 반드시 나오는 최신 기출 어휘들이므로, 확실히 암기해 둡니다. 🎧 VOCA_D07.mp3

0301	**assess**	v 평가하다
0302	**port**	n 항구
0303	**allocate**	v 할당하다
0304	**directory**	n 주소록, 안내 책자
0305	**culinary**	adj 요리의
0306	**transport**	v 운송하다 n 수송
0307	**environment**	n 환경
0308	**magazine**	n 잡지
0309	**poll**	n 여론 조사
0310	**thermostat**	n 온도 조절 장치
0311	**inadequate**	adj 부적절한
0312	**flour**	n 밀가루
0313	**relieved**	adj 안도한
0314	**lifetime**	n 평생, 수명
0315	**setting**	n 환경, 설정
0316	**archeologist**	n 고고학자
0317	**usage**	n 사용량, 사용법
0318	**consistent**	adj 일관된
0319	**pottery**	n 도자기
0320	**excursion**	n 소풍, 짧은 여행
0321	**theater**	n 극장
0322	**impress**	v 깊은 인상을 주다
0323	**photocopy**	n 복사본 v 복사하다
0324	**duration**	n 지속 기간
0325	**excuse**	v 변명하다, 용서하다

0326	steel	n 강철
0327	densely	adv 밀집하여
0328	time-consuming	adj (많은) 시간이 걸리는
0329	firm	n 회사 adj 확고한
0330	housekeeper	n 호텔 객실 정리 직원
0331	layover	n 경유, 도중하차
0332	apprentice	n 견습생, 수습 직원
0333	dealership	n 대리점
0334	wrap	v 포장하다
0335	particular	adj 특정한
0336	roofing	n 지붕 재료, 지붕 공사
0337	follow-up	n 후속 조치
0338	pavilion	n 정자, 가설 건물
0339	absent	adj 부재한, 결석한
0340	border	n 경계, 국경
0341	judgment	n 판단, 평가
0342	automatic	adj 자동의
0343	appraisal	n 평가, 감정
0344	relative	n 친척 adj 상대적인
0345	turn in	제출하다
0346	utility line	(전기, 수도 등의) 공공설비선
0347	put together	조립하다
0348	drop by	잠깐 들르다
0349	park ranger	공원 관리인
0350	look over	검토하다

DAY 08 PART 4 기출 어휘

☑ PART 4에 반드시 나오는 최신 기출 어휘들이므로, 확실히 암기해 둡니다. 🎧 VOCA_D08.mp3

0351	**contest**	[n] 대회
0352	**keynote**	[n] 기조연설
0353	**cancellation**	[n] 취소
0354	**post**	[v] 게시하다 [n] 게시물
0355	**transportation**	[n] 교통편, 수송
0356	**rail**	[n] 철도, 기찻길
0357	**donation**	[n] 기부, 기증
0358	**fundraising**	[n] 모금 활동
0359	**warehouse**	[n] 창고
0360	**exhibition**	[n] 전시회
0361	**demonstration**	[n] 시연, 설명
0362	**inspection**	[n] 검사, 점검
0363	**vendor**	[n] 판매업자
0364	**software**	[n] 소프트웨어
0365	**finance**	[n] 재정, 금융
0366	**evaluation**	[n] 평가
0367	**insurance**	[n] 보험
0368	**reduction**	[n] 감소
0369	**impact**	[n] 영향
0370	**effect**	[n] 효과
0371	**temperature**	[n] 온도, 기온
0372	**safety**	[n] 안전
0373	**manual**	[n] 설명서 [adj] 수동의
0374	**task**	[n] 과제, 일
0375	**dialogue**	[n] 대화

0376	snowstorm	n 눈보라
0377	thundershower	n 번개가 따르는 소나기, 뇌우
0378	cloudy	adj 흐린
0379	itinerary	n 여행 일정표
0380	real-time	adj 실시간의
0381	museum	n 박물관
0382	trail	n 오솔길, 산책로
0383	warning	n 경고
0384	caution	n 주의, 경고
0385	sunscreen	n 자외선 차단제
0386	broadcast	v 방송하다 n 방송
0387	renovation	n 수리, 개조
0388	justify	v 정당화하다
0389	landscaping	n 조경 작업
0390	emphasize	v 강조하다
0391	prototype	n 원형, 시제품
0392	certification	n 인증서
0393	accounting	n 회계, 경리
0394	camera operator	카메라 기사
0395	public relation	홍보
0396	chance of rain	강수 확률
0397	air-conditioning system	냉방 시스템
0398	power outage	정전
0399	rent out	임대하다
0400	sales agent	영업 사원

PART 4 기출 어휘

☑ PART 4에 반드시 나오는 최신 기출 어휘들이므로, 확실히 암기해 둡니다. 🎧 VOCA_D09.mp3

0401	compliment	[n] 칭찬 [v] 칭찬하다
0402	familiar	[adj] 익숙한, 친숙한
0403	publish	[v] 출판하다
0404	vegetarian	[n] 채식주의자
0405	aviation	[n] 항공, 비행
0406	trial	[n] 시험, 재판
0407	complain	[v] 불평하다
0408	reassure	[v] 안심시키다
0409	contain	[v] 포함하다
0410	mayor	[n] 시장
0411	referral	[n] 추천, 소개
0412	traffic	[n] 교통, 교통량
0413	photograph	[n] 사진
0414	shortage	[n] 부족, 결핍
0415	extra	[adj] 추가의, 여분의
0416	track	[n] 경로 [v] 추적하다
0417	belongings	[n] 소지품
0418	van	[n] 승합차, 밴
0419	specialty	[n] 전문, 특산물
0420	opinion	[n] 의견
0421	uniform	[n] 제복
0422	stress	[n] 스트레스 [v] 강조하다
0423	bookstore	[n] 서점
0424	deny	[v] 부인하다
0425	engineer	[n] 기술자, 엔지니어

0426	attention	n 주의, 관심
0427	technique	n 기술, 기법
0428	illustrator	n 삽화가
0429	memorize	v 암기하다
0430	success	n 성공
0431	booth	n 칸막이, 부스
0432	critic	n 비평가
0433	importance	n 중요성
0434	angle	n 각도
0435	cosmetic	adj 화장품의
0436	ease	v 완화하다 n 완화
0437	definitely	adv 확실히
0438	stadium	n 경기장, 스타디움
0439	failure	n 실패
0440	restore	v 복구하다
0441	wallpaper	n 벽지
0442	unwanted	adj 원치 않는
0443	spice	n 향신료
0444	underwater	adj 수중의
0445	take place	개최되다, 일어나다
0446	city council	시의회
0447	kitchen appliance	주방 가전제품
0448	fitness center	피트니스 센터
0449	wind farm	풍력 발전 단지
0450	training session	교육 세션

PART 4 기출 어휘

PART 4에 반드시 나오는 최신 기출 어휘들이므로, 확실히 암기해 둡니다. VOCA_D10.mp3

0451	surge	[n] 급증, 급상승
0452	wrinkle	[n] 주름
0453	storyteller	[n] 이야기꾼
0454	estimates	[n] 견적서, 추정치
0455	strict	[adj] 엄격한
0456	railroad	[n] 철도
0457	confidentiality	[n] 기밀성
0458	hybrid	[adj] 혼합의
0459	browsing	[n] 둘러보기
0460	fingerprint	[n] 지문
0461	entrée	[n] 주요리
0462	path	[n] 길, 경로
0463	kiosk	[n] 매점, 키오스크
0464	fasten	[v] 고정시키다
0465	burst	[v] 터지다
0466	convenient	[adj] 편리한
0467	parade	[n] 행진, 퍼레이드
0468	east	[n] 동쪽
0469	west	[n] 서쪽
0470	injure	[v] 부상을 입히다
0471	screenwriter	[n] 시나리오 작가
0472	unpopular	[adj] 인기 없는
0473	solar	[adj] 태양의
0474	large-scale	[adj] 대규모의
0475	orient	[v] 방향을 맞추다

0476	thrilled	[adj] 매우 기쁜
0477	dairy	[n] 유제품 [adj] 유제품의
0478	spare	[adj] 여분의
0479	cookware	[n] 조리 기구
0480	work station	작업대
0481	health care	건강 관리
0482	the far end	맨 끝
0483	medical facility	의료 시설
0484	take responsibility	책임을 지다
0485	cash prize	상금
0486	convention center	컨벤션 센터
0487	community college	지역 전문 대학
0488	take out	꺼내다, 테이크아웃하다
0489	office paper	사무용 종이
0490	electronic car	전기차
0491	cabin crew	승무원
0492	sign-up sheet	등록 명단
0493	passenger seat	조수석
0494	capsule hotel	캡슐 호텔
0495	day off	휴일
0496	in a while	잠시 후에
0497	real estate agency	부동산 중개업소
0498	job duty	직무
0499	award winner	수상자
0500	cleaning crew	청소 인력

DAY 11 PART 5&6 기출 어휘

☑ PART 5&6에 반드시 나오는 최신 기출 어휘들이므로, 확실히 암기해 둡니다. 🎧 VOCA_D11.mp3

0501	**provide**	v 제공하다
0502	**business**	n 사업, 업무
0503	**offer**	v 제공하다
0504	**work**	v 일하다 n 일, 작업
0505	**ensure**	v 보장하다
0506	**payment**	n 지불
0507	**available**	adj 이용 가능한, 구할 수 있는
0508	**opportunity**	n 기회
0509	**responsibility**	n 책임, 책무
0510	**receive**	v 받다
0511	**policy**	n 정책, 방침
0512	**apply**	v 신청하다, 적용하다
0513	**product**	n 제품
0514	**proposal**	n 제안(서), 제의
0515	**submit**	v 제출하다
0516	**return**	v 반환하다 n 반환
0517	**confirm**	v 확인하다
0518	**improve**	v 향상시키다
0519	**organization**	n 단체, 조직
0520	**create**	v 창조하다, 만들다
0521	**problem**	n 문제
0522	**supply**	v 공급하다
0523	**now**	adv 지금
0524	**official**	adj 공식적인
0525	**immediately**	adv 즉시, 바로 가까이에

0526	deadline	[n] 마감 기한
0527	goal	[n] 목표
0528	legal	[adj] 법적인
0529	department	[n] 부서
0530	cancel	[v] 취소하다
0531	consider	[v] 고려하다
0532	currently	[adv] 현재, 지금
0533	confidential	[adj] 기밀의
0534	close	[v] 닫다 [adj] 가까운
0535	control	[n] 통제, 제어 [v] 통제하다
0536	regulation	[n] 규정, 규칙
0537	secure	[v] 확보하다, 보증하다
0538	continue	[v] 계속하다
0539	address	[v] 연설하다, 다루다
0540	a variety of	다양한, 여러 종류의
0541	a range of	다양한
0542	in response to	~에 대응하여
0543	be responsible for	~을 담당하다, ~에 책임이 있다
0544	comply with	준수하다, 따르다
0545	sales figures	매출액, 판매 수치
0546	host an event	행사를 주최하다
0547	look forward to	고대하다, 기대하다
0548	follow the instructions	지시를 따르다
0549	a series of	일련의
0550	safety protocol	안전 규약

DAY 12 — PART 5&6 기출 어휘

PART 5&6에 반드시 나오는 최신 기출 어휘들이므로, 확실히 암기해 둡니다.

0551	location	n 위치, 장소
0552	general	adj 일반적인, 전반적인
0553	system	n 체계, 시스템
0554	expand	v 확장하다
0555	performance	n 수행, 공연, 성과
0556	feedback	n 의견, 피드백
0557	competitive	adj 경쟁력 있는, 경쟁의
0558	position	n 직책, 일자리
0559	promotion	n 홍보, 승진
0560	free	adj 무료의, 자유로운
0561	protect	v 보호하다
0562	item	n 항목, 품목
0563	collaboration	n 협업, 협력
0564	store	n 가게 v 저장하다
0565	cooperation	n 협력, 협동
0566	presentation	n 발표, 제시
0567	directly	adv 직접, 곧장
0568	operation	n 작동, 운영
0569	promptly	adv 신속히
0570	registration	n 등록, 신청
0571	question	n 질문 v 의문을 제기하다
0572	reduce	v 줄이다
0573	open	v 열다 adj 열린
0574	mandatory	adj 의무적인, 필수적인
0575	program	n 계획, 프로그램

0576	inventory	[n] 재고, 목록
0577	fully	[adv] 완전히
0578	permission	[n] 허락, 승인
0579	effectively	[adv] 효과적으로
0580	arrange	[v] 준비하다, 주선하다
0581	partnership	[n] 제휴, 협력
0582	determine	[v] 알아내다, 결정하다
0583	role	[n] 역할
0584	status	[n] 상태, 지위
0585	design	[v] 설계하다 [n] 설계, 디자인
0586	initiative	[n] 계획, 주도권
0587	reservation	[n] 예약, 보류
0588	expense	[n] 비용, 경비
0589	consumer	[n] 소비자
0590	revenue	[n] 수입, 매출
0591	statement	[n] 성명, 명세서
0592	accurate	[adj] 정확한
0593	limited	[adj] 제한된
0594	acquire	[v] 취득하다, 얻다
0595	daily	[adj] 매일의 [adv] 매일
0596	description	[n] 설명, 묘사
0597	be eligible for	~을 받을 자격이 있다
0598	conduct a survey	설문조사를 실시하다
0599	until further notice	추후 공지가 있을 때까지
0600	be willing to	~할 의향이 있다

PART 5&6 기출 어휘

MP3 바로 듣기 ▶

☑ PART 5&6에 반드시 나오는 최신 기출 어휘들이므로, 확실히 암기해 둡니다. 🎧 VOCA_D13.mp3

0601	encourage	v 격려하다
0602	avoid	v 피하다
0603	significantly	adv 상당히, 현저하게
0604	access	v 접근하다
0605	positive	adj 긍정적인
0606	condition	n 상태, 조건
0607	especially	adv 특별히, 특히
0608	estimate	v 추정하다
0609	challenge	n 도전 v 도전하다
0610	approve	v 승인하다
0611	search	n 검색, 탐색 v 찾다, 검색하다
0612	priority	n 우선순위
0613	specifically	adv 구체적으로
0614	demonstrate	v 보여주다
0615	sign	v 서명하다 n 신호
0616	evaluate	v 평가하다
0617	material	n 재료, 자료
0618	guarantee	n 보장, 보증 v 보장하다
0619	potential	adj 잠재적인
0620	valuable	adj 가치 있는, 귀중한
0621	completely	adv 완전히
0622	successfully	adv 성공적으로
0623	announce	v 발표하다
0624	name	n 이름 v 이름을 짓다
0625	leading	adj 선도적인

0626	similar	adj 비슷한
0627	basis	n 단위, 기초
0628	capacity	n (생산) 능력, 수용력
0629	express	v 표현하다 adj 신속한
0630	analyze	v 분석하다
0631	consideration	n 고려, 배려
0632	initially	adv 처음에
0633	innovative	adj 혁신적인
0634	ship	v 배송하다 n 배
0635	frequently	adv 자주, 빈번히
0636	selection	n 선별된 것, 선정
0637	engage	v 관여하다, 참여하다
0638	commercial	adj 영리적인, 상업의
0639	level	n 수준 v 평평하게 하다
0640	balance	v 균형을 맞추다
0641	agent	n 대리인, 중개인
0642	maximize	v 최대화하다
0643	previously	adv 이전에
0644	addition	n 추가, 덧붙임
0645	increasingly	adv 점점
0646	notify	v 통지하다
0647	medical	adj 의학의, 의료의
0648	overview	n 개요, 개관
0649	collect	v 모으다
0650	replace A with B	A를 B로 교체하다

DAY 14 PART 5&6 기출 어휘

PART 5&6에 반드시 나오는 최신 기출 어휘들이므로, 확실히 암기해 둡니다. VOCA_D14.mp3

0651	precisely	adv 정확히
0652	fund	n 자금 v 자금을 대다
0653	advanced	adj 선진의, 고급의
0654	temporarily	adv 일시적으로
0655	see	v 보다, 이해하다
0656	ongoing	adj 지속적인, 진행 중인
0657	distribution	n 유통, 배포
0658	model	n 모델, 본보기
0659	popular	adj 인기 있는, 대중적인
0660	appear	v 나타나다, ~처럼 보이다
0661	assignment	n 배정, 과제
0662	closely	adv 면밀히, 긴밀히
0663	correctly	adv 정확하게, 올바르게
0664	membership	n 회원 자격, 회원(권)
0665	appreciate	v 감사하다, 인식하다
0666	expertise	n 전문 지식, 전문 기술
0667	permanent	adj 상설의, 영구적인
0668	association	n 제휴, 협회
0669	consistently	adv 일관되게
0670	observe	v 지켜보다, 관찰하다
0671	certainly	adv 확실히, 분명히
0672	rapidly	adv 빠르게
0673	feature	v 특징으로 삼다, 특별히 포함하다
0674	exact	adj 정확한
0675	qualify	v 자격을 갖추다

#		
0676	**recruit**	v 모집하다
0677	**source**	n 원천, 출처
0678	**outstanding**	adj 뛰어난, 두드러진, 미결제의
0679	**advertise**	v 광고하다
0680	**branch**	n 지점, 지사
0681	**gather**	v 모으다
0682	**outline**	v 개요를 말하다
0683	**eventually**	adv 결국, 마침내
0684	**restriction**	n 제한, 규제
0685	**extensive**	adj 폭넓은, 광범위한
0686	**together**	adv 함께
0687	**adjustment**	n 조정, 적응
0688	**briefly**	adv 간단히
0689	**decline**	n 감소, 하락
0690	**space**	n 공간
0691	**finalize**	v 마무리하다
0692	**motivated**	adj 의욕적인, 동기가 부여된
0693	**complicated**	adj 복잡한
0694	**incorporate**	v 포함하다, 통합하다
0695	**attract**	v 끌어들이다
0696	**definition**	n 정의, 설명
0697	**former**	adj 이전의
0698	**urgently**	adv 긴급히
0699	**after all**	결국, 어쨌든
0700	**be pleased to**	~하게 되어 기쁘다

PART 5&6 기출 어휘

PART 5&6에 반드시 나오는 최신 기출 어휘들이므로, 확실히 암기해 둡니다.   🎧 VOCA_D15.mp3

0701	**direction**	n 지시, 방향
0702	**extremely**	adv 극히, 극도로
0703	**lack**	n 부족, 결핍
0704	**explanation**	n 설명, 해명
0705	**strictly**	adv 엄격히
0706	**thoroughly**	adv 철저히
0707	**original**	adj 원래의, 독창적인
0708	**exceptional**	adj 뛰어난, 예외적인
0709	**adequate**	adj 충분한, 적절한
0710	**consequently**	adv 결과적으로, 그 결과로
0711	**specification**	n 명세서, 사양
0712	**provision**	n 조항, 규정
0713	**expire**	v 만료되다
0714	**impressive**	adj 인상적인
0715	**package**	n 소포, 포장 v 포장하다
0716	**enrollment**	n 등록, 가입
0717	**favorable**	adj 호의적인, 유리한
0718	**accordingly**	adv 그에 알맞게, 적절히
0719	**warranty**	n 보증(서)
0720	**exclusive**	adj 전용의, 독점적인
0721	**committee**	n 위원회
0722	**shortly**	adv 곧, 머지않아
0723	**majority**	n 과반수, 대다수
0724	**damage**	n 손상 v 손상시키다
0725	**replacement**	n 대체품, 교체

0726	reminder	n 알림, 상기시키는 것
0727	combine	v 결합하다
0728	entirely	adv 전적으로, 완전히
0729	boost	v 높이다, 북돋우다
0730	posting	n 게시물, 배치
0731	equally	adv 동등하게
0732	installation	n 설치, 시설
0733	capability	n 역량, 능력
0734	decrease	v 줄다, 감소하다 n 감소
0735	creation	n 창작(물)
0736	greatly	adv 매우
0737	mission	n 사명, 임무
0738	distinct	adj 독특한, 별개의
0739	copy	n 사본 v 복사하다
0740	phase	n 단계, 국면
0741	lease	v 임대하다
0742	unfortunately	adv 불행히도
0743	extended	adj 연장된
0744	financing	n 자금 조달
0745	considerably	adv 상당히
0746	politely	adv 정중하게
0747	adaptable	adj 적응성 있는, 적응할 수 있는
0748	preserve	v 보존하다
0749	be famous for	~으로 유명하다
0750	be attributed to	~의 덕분이다, ~에 기인하다

DAY 16 PART 5&6 기출 어휘

PART 5&6에 반드시 나오는 최신 기출 어휘들이므로, 확실히 암기해 둡니다. VOCA_D16.mp3

0751	depart	v 출발하다, 떠나다
0752	consultation	n 상담, 협의
0753	line	n 줄, 선
0754	occupy	v 차지하다, 채우다
0755	predict	v 예측하다
0756	exercise	n 운동 v 운동하다
0757	treatment	n 대우, 치료
0758	postpone	v 연기하다
0759	wait	v 기다리다
0760	authorization	n 승인, 허가
0761	workshop	n 연수회, 워크숍
0762	circumstance	n 상황, 환경
0763	relocate	v 이전하다
0764	conflicting	adj 상충하는
0765	comfortable	adj 편안한
0766	compensate	v 보상하다
0767	continuously	adv 지속적으로
0768	knowledgeable	adj 지식이 풍부한
0769	rank	v 순위를 매기다
0770	alternatively	adv 그 대신에, 대안으로
0771	transform	v 변화시키다, 변형시키다
0772	modification	n 수정, 변경
0773	profitability	n 수익성
0774	possess	v 갖추다, 소유하다
0775	absolute	adj 완전한, 절대적인

0776	exclusively	adv 오로지, 독점적으로
0777	ambitious	adj 야심 찬
0778	persuasive	adj 설득력 있는
0779	presence	n 참석, 존재(감)
0780	heavily	adv 많이, 심하게
0781	popularity	n 인기
0782	conveniently	adv 편리하게
0783	occasion	n 경우, 행사
0784	conservation	n 보호, 보존
0785	stimulate	v 활발하게 하다, 자극하다
0786	authentic	adj 진품의, 진짜의
0787	assembly	n 조립, 집회
0788	routine	n 일상, 일과 adj 일상의
0789	supplemental	adj 보충하는, 추가의
0790	excessive	adj 과도한
0791	opposition	n 반대, 대립
0792	renewable	adj 재생 가능한
0793	independently	adv 독립적으로
0794	showcase	v 선보이다
0795	lesson	n 수업, 교훈
0796	undergo	v 받다, 겪다
0797	compelling	adj 설득력 있는
0798	certainty	n 확신, 확실성
0799	reschedule	v 일정을 변경하다
0800	familiarize oneself with	~에 익숙해지다

DAY 17 PART 5&6 기출 어휘

☑ PART 5&6에 반드시 나오는 최신 기출 어휘들이므로, 확실히 암기해 둡니다. 🎧 VOCA_D17.mp3

0801	party	n 당사자, 파티
0802	seat	n 좌석
0803	formula	n 제조법, 공식
0804	credential	n 자격 증명서, 신임장
0805	signal	v 신호를 보내다 n 신호
0806	meal	n 식사
0807	merger	n 합병, 통합
0808	vacation	n 휴가
0809	dedication	n 헌신, 전념
0810	closure	n 폐쇄
0811	airline	n 항공사
0812	diligently	adv 부지런히
0813	rigorous	adj 엄격한, 철저한
0814	cargo	n 화물, 적재물
0815	honor	v 경의를 표하다, 존경하다
0816	patiently	adv 인내심 있게
0817	commence	v 시작하다
0818	tourist	n 관광객
0819	accomplishment	n 성과, 업적
0820	punctually	adv 정시에
0821	delightful	adj 매우 기쁜, 즐거운
0822	divide	v 나누다
0823	practitioner	n 전문가, 개업의
0824	abundant	adj 풍부한
0825	elsewhere	adv 다른 곳에

0826	enthusiastically	adv 열정적으로
0827	scan	v 정밀 검사하다, 스캔하다
0828	studio	n 작업실, 방송국
0829	neglect	v 소홀히 하다, 무시하다
0830	full	adj 가득 찬
0831	pledge	v 약속하다
0832	lively	adj 활기찬, 생기 있는
0833	impartial	adj 공정한
0834	donate	v 기부하다
0835	excitement	n 흥분, 신남
0836	unexpectedly	adv 뜻밖에, 예상치 않게
0837	durability	n 내구성, 지속성
0838	revolutionize	v 혁신을 일으키다
0839	waive	v 면제하다
0840	seamlessly	adv 매끄럽게
0841	evenly	adv 고르게, 균등하게
0842	absorb	v 흡수하다
0843	longevity	n 수명, 장수
0844	unusually	adv 보통과는 달리, 대단히
0845	lamp	n 전등, 램프
0846	shade	n 그늘 v 그늘지게 하다
0847	soar	v (가치·물가 등이) 급증하다, 치솟다
0848	sew	v 바느질하다
0849	reentry	n 재입장, 복귀
0850	be urged to	~하도록 촉구받다

DAY 18 PART 7 기출 어휘

☑ PART 7에 반드시 나오는 최신 기출 어휘들이므로, 확실히 암기해 둡니다. 🎧 VOCA_D18.mp3

0851	résumé	n 이력서
0852	application	n 신청서, 지원서
0853	requirement	n 요구사항, 필요조건
0854	earn	v 벌다, 얻다
0855	monthly	adj 매달의 adv 매달
0856	career	n 경력, 직업
0857	professional	adj 전문적인 n 전문가
0858	instructor	n 강사
0859	graduate	v 졸업하다 n 졸업생
0860	recommend	v 추천하다
0861	replace	v 교체하다
0862	appointment	n 약속, 예약
0863	invoice	n 송장, 청구서
0864	venue	n 장소, 개최지
0865	detail	n 세부 사항 v 자세히 설명하다
0866	inform	v 알리다
0867	plan	n 계획 v 계획하다
0868	retail	n 소매 v 소매하다
0869	license	n 면허, 허가증 v 허가하다
0870	site	n 장소, 현장 v 위치시키다
0871	public	adj 공공의, 대중의 n 대중
0872	cover	v 덮다, 포함하다 n 덮개
0873	comment	n 논평, 의견 v 논평하다
0874	eliminate	v 제거하다
0875	change	n 변화, 거스름돈 v 바꾸다

#		
0876	support	v 지지하다 n 지원
0877	extend	v 연장하다, 확장하다
0878	guide	n 안내자 v 안내하다
0879	mailroom	n 우편물 취급실
0880	envelope	n 봉투
0881	subscriber	n 구독자, 가입자
0882	reverse	v 뒤집다, 번복하다 n 반대, 역
0883	retailer	n 소매업자
0884	shipping	n 배송
0885	recycle	v 재활용하다
0886	audience	n 청중, 관객
0887	rating	n 등급, 평가
0888	additional	adj 추가의
0889	supervisor	n 감독관, 관리자
0890	lead	v 이끌다 n 선두
0891	property	n 재산, 부동산
0892	volunteer	n 자원봉사자 v 자원하다
0893	participant	n 참가자
0894	charge	v 청구하다 n 요금
0895	affordable	adj 감당할 수 있는
0896	alternative	n 대안 adj 대체의
0897	executive	n 임원 adj 실행의
0898	existence	n 존재, 생존
0899	pricing	n 가격 책정
0900	job opening	일자리

DAY 19 PART 7 기출 어휘

PART 7에 반드시 나오는 최신 기출 어휘들이므로, 확실히 암기해 둡니다.

0901	**representative**	n 대표자 adj 대표하는
0902	**direct**	v 지시하다 adj 직접적인
0903	**handle**	v 처리하다
0904	**perform**	v 수행하다, 공연하다
0905	**expert**	n 전문가
0906	**renovate**	v 개조하다, 수리하다
0907	**storage**	n 저장, 보관
0908	**multiple**	adj 다양한, 복수의
0909	**annual**	adj 연간의
0910	**refreshment**	n 다과, 간단한 음식
0911	**temporary**	adj 일시적인
0912	**invitation**	n 초대, 초대장
0913	**assistant**	n 조수, 보조자
0914	**resident**	n 거주자
0915	**fulfill**	v 이행하다, 충족시키다
0916	**valid**	adj 유효한
0917	**entrance**	n 입구
0918	**solution**	n 해결책
0919	**recipe**	n 요리법
0920	**manufacturing**	n 제조업
0921	**plant**	n 식물, 공장
0922	**paperwork**	n 서류 작업
0923	**artwork**	n 예술 작품
0924	**run**	v 운영하다, 달리다
0925	**cause**	n 원인 v 야기하다

0926	**record**	n 기록 v 기록하다
0927	**author**	n 작가, 저자
0928	**discover**	v 발견하다
0929	**realize**	v 깨닫다
0930	**view**	n 전망 v 보다
0931	**completion**	n 완료
0932	**length**	n 길이
0933	**route**	n 경로, 노선
0934	**indoors**	adv 실내에서
0935	**unique**	adj 독특한
0936	**communicate**	v 의사소통하다
0937	**individual**	n 개인 adj 개인의
0938	**regular**	adj 규칙적인, 정기적인
0939	**instructions**	n 지침, 설명서
0940	**employ**	v 고용하다
0941	**list**	n 목록 v 목록을 작성하다
0942	**explain**	v 설명하다
0943	**point**	v 가리키다 n 요점
0944	**traditional**	adj 전통적인
0945	**possibility**	n 가능성
0946	**owner**	n 소유자
0947	**greet**	v 인사하다
0948	**fair**	n 박람회 adj 공정한
0949	**social media**	소셜 미디어
0950	**conference room**	회의실

DAY 20 PART 7 기출 어휘

PART 7에 반드시 나오는 최신 기출 어휘들이므로, 확실히 암기해 둡니다.

0951	ceremony	n 행사, 의식
0952	interior	n 내부, 실내 adj 내부의, 실내의
0953	rent	v 임대하다 n 임대료
0954	pass	v 통과하다
0955	microphone	n 마이크
0956	photographer	n 사진작가
0957	manage	v 관리하다, 경영하다
0958	electronics	n 전자 제품
0959	gathering	n 모임, 집회
0960	refrigerator	n 냉장고
0961	save	v 저장하다, 절약하다
0962	missing	adj 없어진, 실종된
0963	inexpensive	adj 저렴한
0964	craft	n 공예, 기술
0965	reopen	v 다시 열다
0966	maximum	n 최대 adj 최대의
0967	occur	v 발생하다
0968	oversee	v 감독하다
0969	landscaper	n 조경사
0970	familiarize	v 익숙하게 하다
0971	private	adj 사적인, 개인적인
0972	demanding	adj 요구가 많은, 힘든
0973	drive	n 추진력, 캠페인 v 추진하다, 운전하다
0974	skill	n 기술, 능력
0975	gain	v 얻다 n 증가, 이득

0976	**footwear**	[n] 신발류
0977	**criticism**	[n] 비판
0978	**overall**	[adj] 전반적인 [adv] 전반적으로
0979	**amount**	[n] 양, 금액 [v] (총계가) ~에 달하다
0980	**drone**	[n] 무인 항공기, 드론 [v] 윙윙거리다
0981	**surface**	[n] 표면 [v] 표면화되다, 드러나다
0982	**minimum**	[n] 최소 [adj] 최소의
0983	**familiarity**	[n] 익숙함, 친숙함
0984	**common**	[adj] 일반적인, 흔한
0985	**film**	[n] 영화, 필름 [v] 촬영하다
0986	**primarily**	[adv] 주로
0987	**prospective**	[adj] 장래의, 유망한
0988	**enter**	[v] 들어가다, 입력하다
0989	**type**	[n] 유형, 종류 [v] 타자를 치다
0990	**specialized**	[adj] 전문적인, 특수한
0991	**separately**	[adv] 따로, 별도로
0992	**remodel**	[v] 개조하다
0993	**internal**	[adj] 내부의
0994	**discard**	[v] 버리다, 폐기하다
0995	**typical**	[adj] 전형적인
0996	**industrial**	[adj] 산업의
0997	**needs**	[n] 필요, 요구사항
0998	**customer service**	고객 서비스
0999	**specialize in**	~을 전문으로 하다
1000	**for free**	무료로

MEMO

MEMO

MEMO

MEMO

MEMO